DATE DUE

PRINTED IN U.S.A.

Bieber's Dictionary of Legal Abbreviations

Reference Guide for Attorneys, Legal Secretaries, Paralegals and Law Students

Prince's Fourth Edition
by

Mary Miles Prince

William S. Hein & Co., Inc.
Buffalo, New York
1993

Library of Congress Cataloging-in-Publication Data

Prince, Mary Miles.
  Bieber's dictionary of legal abbreviations : reference guide for
attorneys, legal secretaries, paralegals, and law students. --
4th ed. / by Mary Miles Prince.
      p.   cm.
  ISBN 0-89941-847-3 (acid-free paper)
  1. Law--United States--Abbreviations. 2. Citation of legal
authorities--United States. I. Bieber, Doris M. Dictionary of
legal abbreviations used in American law books. II. Title.
KF246.B46 1993
349. 73'0148--dc20   93-13817
  [347.300148]   CIP

Printed in the United States of America.

∞

This volume is printed on acid-free paper by
William S. Hein & Co., Inc.

Preface

Bieber's Dictionary of Legal Abbreviations facilitates the search for the precise meaning of the abbreviations and acronyms used in American legal literature. It includes an extensive range of acronyms and symbols found in reporters, legal treatises, law reviews, selected documents, loose-leaf services, legal encyclopedias, law dictionaries, legal reference books, and citators.

This dictionary is not intended to be used as a guide to sample legal citation forms. For determining proper citation form, one should consult *The Bluebook: A Uniform System of Citation* (15th or latest edition), *Bieber's Dictionary of Legal Citations,* 1992, or some other authoritative source.

The fourth edition reflects approximately 3,000 new or expanded entries. Foreign language entries found in the third edition have been deleted. (Foreign language abbreviations may be found in Kavass and Prince's *World Dictionary of Legal Abbreviations,* or other sources). However, Bieber's Dictionary does include abbreviations for many foreign agencies, organizations, periodicals, and other publications cited in American legal literature.

The entries in this edition are alphabetized as if each entry were one word. The ampersand "&" is treated just as the word "and" in this method of alphabetization.

I wish to thank Doris M. Bieber for the opportunity of updating this work, Professor Igor I. Kavass, Director of the Vanderbilt School of Law Alyne Queener Massey Law Library, for his support in this endeavor, William S. Hein & Co. for their assistance, Stephen Jackson for his proficiency in typing and the production of this edition, and Tiffany Villager and Jimmy Zhiyu Hu for their invaluable assistance in gathering new information.

Mary M. Prince

A

A
- Abbott
- Acquiescence
- Affirmed
- Alabama
- Alberta
- Amended
- American
- Annual
- Anonymous
- Arabic
- Arkansas
- Association(s)
- Atlantic Reporter
- Indian Reports, Allahabad Series
- Louisiana Annuals

A.
- Accountancy
- Atlantic Reporter

A.2d Atlantic Reporter, Second Series

AA
- Able and Available
- Antitrust Adviser, Third Edition
- Ars Aequi, Juridisch Studentenblad (Holland)

AAA
- Agricultural Adjustment Act
- American Arbitration Association
- Association of Attenders and Alumni of the Hague Academy of International Law.

AABA Atwood & Brewster, Antitrust and American Business Abroad

A.A.B.D. Aid to the Aged, Blind, or Disabled

A.A.C. Anno ante Christum, the year before Christ

A.A.C.E. Arrets et avis du Conseil d'Etat (Belg.) (Judgments and opinions of the Council of State) (Belg.)

A.A.C.N. Anno ante Christum natum, the year before the birth of Christ

A. & E. Appeal and Error

AAJE American Academy of Judicial Education

A.A.L.D. Australian Army Legal Department

AALL American Association of Law Libraries

A.A.L.R. Anglo American Law Review

AALS Association of American Law Schools

AALS Proc. Association of American Law Schools Proceedings

A. & A. Amendments & Additions

A. & A. Corp. Angell & Ames on Corporations

A. & C. Addenda & Corrigenda

A. & C. Cir. Accounts and Collection Unit Circulars

A. & D. High.   Angell & Durfree on Highways

A. & E.
- Admiralty and Ecclesiastical
- Adolphus & Ellis Queen's Bench Reports (1834-40) (Eng.)
- Appeal and Error

A. & E.A.C.   American and English Annotated Cases

A. & E. Ann Cas.   American & English Annotated Cases

A. & E. Anno.   American & English Annotated Cases

A. & E. Cas.   American & English Annotated Cases

A. & E.C.C.   American and English Corporation Cases (U.S.)

A. & E. Cor. Cases   American and English Corporation Cases (U.S.)

A. & E. Corp. Cas.   American & English Corporation Cases

A. & E. Corp. Cas. N.S.   American and English Corporation Cases, New Series

A. & E. Enc.   American & English Encyclopedia of Law and Practice

A. & E. Enc. L.   American & English Encyclopedia of Law

A. & E. Enc. L. & Pr.   American & English Encyclopedia of Law & Practice

A. & E. Ency.   American & English Encyclopedia of Law

A. & E. Ency. Law   American & English Encyclopedia of Law and Practice

A. & E.(n.s.)   Adolphus and Ellis's of Queen's Bench, New Series (1841-52)

A. & E.N.S.   Adolphus & Ellis, English Queen's Bench Reports.New Series

A. & E.P. & P.   American & English Pleading and Practice

A. & E.P. & Pr.   American & English Pleading and Practice

A. & E.Pat.Cas.   American & English Patent Cases

A. & E.R.C.   American & English Railway Cases

A. & E.R.Cas.   American & English Railroad Cases

A. & E.R.Cas., N.S.   American & English Railroad Cases, New Series

A. & E.R.R.C.   American & English Railroad Cases

A. & E.R.R.Cas.   American & English Railroad Cases

A. & E.R.R.Cas.(N.S.)   American & English Railroad Cases, New Series

A. & F.Fix.   Amos & Ferard on Fixtures

A. & H.   Arnold & Hodges' English Queen's Bench Reports (1840-41)

A. & H. Bank.   Avery & Hobbs' Bankruptcy Law of United States

A. & N.   Alcock & Napier's Irish King's Bench Reports. (1831-33)

A. & W. Gai.   Abdy & Walker's Gaius & Ulpian

A. & W. Just.   Abdy & Walker's Justinian

AAPSO   Afro-Asian People's Solidarity Organization

AASM   Associated African States and Madagascar

A.A.U.P. American Association of University Professors

AB Alberta

A.B.
- Able Seaman
- Aid to the Blind
- Anonymous Reports at end of Benloe or Bendloe (1661) (Eng.)
- Assembly Bill (state legislatures)

Ab.
- Abbott (see Abb.)
- Abridgment
- Abstracts
- Abstracts of Treasury Decisions (U.S.)

ABA American Bar Association

A.B.A.
- American Bankers' Association
- American Bar Association

ABA Antitrust L.J. American Bar Association Antitrust Law Journal

A.B.A. Comp. L. Bull American Bar Association Comparative Law Bulletin

ABACPD American Bar Association Center for Professional Discipline

A.B.A. J. American Bar Association Journal

A.B.A. Jo. American Bar Association Journal

A.B.A. Jour. American Bar Association Journal

Aband.Prop.
- Abandoned Property
- Abandoned, lost, and unclaimed property

ABA Rep
- American Bar Association Reporter
- American Bar Association Reports

A.B.A. Rep. American Bar Association Reports

A.B.A. Rep. Int'l. & Comp. L. Sec. American Bar Association, International and Comparative Law Section, Reports

ABA Sec. Lab. Rel. L. American Bar Association Section of Labor Relations Law

ABA Sect. Ins. N & CL American Bar Association Section of Insurance, Negligence & Compensation Law

A.B.A. Sect. Ins. N. & C.L. Proc. American Bar Association Section of Insurance, Negligence and Compensation Law Proceedings

Abat. & R. Abatement, Survival, and Revival

Abb.
- Abbott, United States Circuit and District Court Reports
- Abbott (U.S.)

Abb. Ad. Abbott's Admiralty Reports (U.S.)

Abb. Adm. Abbott, Admiralty Reports (U.S.)

Abb. Ad.R. Abbott's Admiralty Reports (U.S.)

Abb. Ap.Dec. Abbott Court of Appeals Decisions (N.Y.)

Abb. App.Dec. Abbott's Appeals Decisions, N.Y.

Abb. Beech. Tr. Abbott's Reports of the Beecher Trial

Abb. C.C.   Abbott U.S. Rep.

Abb. C.C. Abbott's Circuit Court Reports (U.S.)

Abb. Cl. Ass. Abbott's Clerks and Conveyancers' Assistant

Abb. Ct. App. Abbott Court of Appeals Decisions

Abb. Ct. of App.Dec. Abbott Court of Appeals Decisions (N. Y.)

Abb. Dec. Abbott's Decisions (N.Y.)

Abb. Dict. Abbott's Dictionary

Abb. Dig. Abbott's New York Digest

Abb. Dig. Corp Abbott's Digest of the Law of Corporations

Abb. F. Abbott's Forms of Pleading

Abb. F. Sup. Abbott's Forms of Pleading, Supplement

Abb. Ind. Dig. Abbott's Indiana Digest

Abb. Int. Abbott's Introduction to Practice under the Codes

Abb. Law Dict. Abbott's Law Dictionary (1879)

Abb. L. Dic. Abbott's Law Dictionary

Abb. Leg. Rem. Abbott, Legal Remembrancer

Abb. Mo. Ind. Abbott's Monthly Index

Abb. Nat. Dig. Abbott's National Digest

Abb. N.C. Abbott's New Cases, New York

Abb. N.Cas. Abbott's New Cases (N.Y.)

Abb. New Cas. Abbott's New Cases (N.Y.)

Abb. N.S. Abbott's Practice Reports, New Series

Abb. N.Y. App. Abbott Court of Appeals Decisions (N.Y.)

Abb. N.Y. Dig. Abbott's New York Digest

Abb. N.Y. Dig.2d Abbott's New York Digest, Second Series

Abbott
- Abbott's Dictionary
- Abbott on Merchant Ships and Seaman (1802-1901)

Abbott, Civ. Jury Trials Abbott on Civil Jury Trials

Abbott, Crim. Tr. Pr. Abbot on Crimi- nal Trial Practice

Abbott P.R. Abbott's Practice Reports (N.Y.)

Abbott Pract. Cas. Abbott's Practice Reports (N.Y.)

Abbott Pr. Rep. Abbott's Practice Reports (N.Y.)

Abbot's Adm. Abbott's Admiralty Reports (U.S.)

Abbot's Prac. Rep. Abbott's Practice Reports (N.Y.)

Abbott's Ad.Rep. Abbott's Admiralty Reports (U.S.)

Abbott's Adm. Abbott's Admiralty Reports (U.S.)

Abbott's N.C. Abbott's New Cases (N.Y.)

Abbott's Pr.Rep. Abbott's Practice Reports (N.Y.)

Abbott U.S.R. Abbott's Reports, U.S. Circuit & District Courts

Abbott U.S. Rep. Abbott's Reports, U.S. Circuit & District Courts

Abb. Pl. Abbott's Pleadings under the Code

Abb. Pr. Abbott's New York Practice Reports (1854-1875)

Abb. P.R. Abbott's Practice Reports (N.Y.)

Abb. Pr. Abbott's Practice Reports (N.Y.)

Abb. Prac. Abbott's Practice Reports (N.Y.)

Abb. Prac. N.S. Abbott's Practice (N.Y.) New Series

Abb. Pr. N.S. Abbott's Practice Reports, New Series (N.Y.)

Abb. Pr. Rep. Abbott's Practice Reports (N.Y.)

Abbr. Abbreviations

Abbrev. Plac. Placitorum Abbreviatis, Record Commissioner (Eng.)

Abb. R.P.S. Abbott's Real Property Statutes (Wn.)

Abb. Sh. Abbott on Shipping

Abb. Ship. Abbot (Lord Tenterden) on Shipping

Abb. Tr. Ev. Abbott's Trial Evidence

Abb. U.S. Abbott, Circuit Ct. Reports (U.S.)

Abb. U.S.C.C. Abbott's U.S.Circuit & District Courts Reports

Abb. U.S. Pr. Abbott's Practice in the United States Courts

Abb. Y.Bk. Abbott's Year Book of Jurisprudence

A.B.C. Australian Bankruptcy Cases

A.B.C. Newsl. International Association of Accident Boards and Commissions Newsletter

Ab.Ca. Crawford & Dix's Abridged Cases (1837-38) (Ir.)

A.B.C.C. Association of British Chambers of Commerce

A.B.C.N.Y. Association of the Bar of the City of New York

Abduct.
- Abduction
- Abduction and kidnapping

Abdy & W. Gai. Adby & Walker's Gaius & Ulpian

Abdy & W. Just. Abdy & Walker's Justinian

Abdy R. Pr. Abdy's Roman Civil Procedure

A'Beckett Judgments of the Supreme Court of New South Wales for the District of Port Philip (1846-51)

A'Beck. Judg.Vict. A'Beckett, Reserved Judgments (Victoria)

A'Beck. Res. Judg. A'Beckett's Reserved Judgments, Victoria

A'Beck. Res. Judgm. A'Beckett's Reserved Judgments (Victoria)

A'Beck. R.J.N.S.W. A'Becketts Reserved (Equity) Judgments (New South Wales)

A'Beck. R.J.P.P. A'Beckett's Reserved Judgments. (Port Phillip)

Ab. Eq. Cas. Equity Cases Abridged

ABF American Bar Foundation

A.B.F. American Bar Foundation

A.B.F. Research J. American Bar Foundation Research Journal

A.B.F. Research Reptr. American Bar Foundation Research Reporter

A.B.F. Research Reptr. J. American Bar Foundation Research Journal

A.B.F.Res. J. American Bar Foundation Research Journal.

ABF Res. Newsl. ABF Research Newsletter

ab init. ab initio (from the beginning) (Lat.)

A.B.L. Business Law Cases for Australia (CCH)

A.B.L.A. American Business Law Association

A.B.L.R. Australian Business Law Review

ABM Anti-ballistic missiles

Ab.N. Abstracts, Treasury Decisions, New Series

Ab.(NS) Abstracts, Treasury Decisions, New Series

Abort. Abortion

Abortion L. Rep. Abortion Law Reporter

A.B.R. American Bankruptcy Reports

Abr.
- Abridge(d)
- Abridgement

Abr. Ca. Eq. Abridgement of Cases in Equity. (1667-1744)

Abr. Cas. Crawford & Dix, Abridged Cases (1937-38) (Ir.)

Abr. Cas. Eq. Equity Cases Abridged (1667-1744) (Eng.)

A.B. Rep. American Bankruptcy Reports

Abr. Eq. Cas. (English) Equity Cases Abridged

A.B. Rev. American Bankruptcy Review

A'B.R.J.N.S.W. A'Beckett Reserved Judgments (Eq.), New South Wales (Aus.)

A'B.R.J.P.P. A'Beckett Reserved Judgments, Port Philip, New South Wales (Aus.)

A.B.R.N.S. American Bankruptcy Reports, New Series

Ab. Rom. Proc. Abdy's Civil Procedure among the Romans

Abs.
- Absent or Abstain
- Absolute
- Abstracts, Treasury Decisions
- Ohio Law Abstract

Abs. Crim. Pen. Abstracts on Criminology and Penology

Absent. Absentees

Abs(NS) Abstracts, New Series Treasury Decisions

abstr. abstract

Abstr.Crim. & Pen. Abstracts on Criminology and Penology

Abstr.T. Abstracts of Title

Abuse P. Abuse of Process

A. Bus. L. Rev. Australian Business Law Review (Law Book Co.) (Aus.)

abv. above

A.C.
- Advance California Reports
- anno Christi in the year of Christ (Lat.)
- Annotated Cases
- ante Christum before Christ (Lat.)

- Appeal Cases
- Appeal Cases (Can.)
- Appeal Cases (Ceylon)
- Appellate Court
- Buchanan, Cape Colony Court of Appeal Rep.
- Canadian Reports, Appeal Cases (1828-1913)
- Case on Appeal
- Law Reports Appeal Cases (Eng.)
- Law Reports Appeal Cases (Eng.) Third Series

1917, A.C. 1917, Appeal Cases, Canada

1918, A.C. Law Reports, 1918, Appeal Cases, English

A/C Account

ACA
- Administrator of Civil Aeronautics
- Advance California Appellate Reports
- Americans for Constitutional Action

A.C.A.
- Advance California Appellate Reports
- Australian Corporate Affairs Reporter (CCH) (Aus.)

ACAA Agricultural Conservation & Adjustment Administration

ACABQ Advisory Committee on Administrative and Budgetary Questions

Acad.
- Academic
- Academy

Acad. L. Rev. The Academy Law Review (India, Kerala)

Acad. Pol. Sci. Proc. Academy of Political Science Proceedings (U.S.)

ACC
- Agricultural Credit Corporation
- Administrative Committee on Coordination

A.C.C.
- Allahabad Criminal Cases, India
- American Corporation Cases, by Withrow (1868-87)

Acc. Accord

Access. Accession

Accountany L. Rep (CCH) Accountancy Law Reports Accountancy Law Reporter

acct.
- account
- accountancy
- accountant(s)
- accounting

Acctants. Accountants

Acct. for L. Firms Accounting for Law Firms

Acctg. Accounting

Acct. L. Rep. Accountant Law Reports (Eng.)

Accy Accountancy Board

ACDA Arms Control and Disarmament Agency

A.C.D.D. Advisory Committee on Drug Dependence

ACE
- Adjusted Current Earnings
- Active Corps of Executives

A.C.J.A. American Criminal Justice Association

A.C.J. (Mad.Pr.) Accident Compensation Journal, Madhva,

Pradesh (India)

Acknowl. Acknowledgements

A.C.L. Australian Current Law (Butterworths) (Aus.)

A.C.L.C. Australian Company Law Cases

A.C.L.D. Australian Current Law Digest (Butterworths) (Aus.)

A.C.L.J. American Civil Law Journal, New York

A.C.L.R.
- Australian Company Law Reports (Butterworths) (Aus.)
- Australian Current Law Review

A.C. L. Rev. Australian Current Law Review (Butterworths) (Aus.)

A.C.L.U. American Civil Liberties Union

ACLUF American Civil Liberties Union Foundation

A.C.L.U. Leg. Action Bull. American Civil Liberties Union Legislative Action Bulletin

ACM Arab Common Market

A.C.M. Court-Martial Reports, Air Force Cases

A.C.M.S. Special Court-Martial, U.S. Air Force

A.C.N. ante Christum natum before the birth of Christ (Lat.)

ACP African, Caribbean, and Pacific States

A.C.P. Agriculture Conservation Program

A.C.P.O. Association of Chief Police Officers

A.C.P.S. Advisory Council on the Penal System

Acq. Acquiescence by Commissioner in Tax Court of Board of Tax Appeals Decisions, U.S.

acq.
- Acquittal
- Acquitted

acq. in result Acquitted in result

A.C.R.
- American Criminal Reports, edit. by Hawley
- Appeal Court Reports, Ceylon

A. Cr. C. Allahabad Criminal Cases (India)

A. Crim. R. Australian Criminal Reports

A.Cr.R. Allahabad Criminal Reports (India)

ACRS Accelerated Cost Recovery System

A.C.T. Australian Capital Territory (Aus.)

Act.
- Acton
- Acton Prize Cases (1809-10) Privy Council (Eng.)

Acta
- Acta Academiae Universalis Jurisprudentiae Comparativae, Berlin, Germany
- Cancelariae English Chancery Reports, English

Acta Cancelariae English Chancery Reports

Acta Crim. Acta Criminologica

Acta Jur. Acta Juridica

Acta Jur. Acad.Sci. Hung. Acta Juridica Academiae Scientiarum Hungaricae. Budapest, Hungary

Acta Jur. (Cape Town) Acta Juridica. Cape Town, South Africa

Acta Juridica
- Acta Juridica Academiae Scientiarum Hungaricae
- Acta Juridica, Cape Town, South Africa

Acta Juridica Acad. Sci. Hungaricae Acta Juridica Academiae Scientiarum Hungaricae, Budapest, Hungary

Acta Oeconomica Acta Oeconomica Academiae Scientiarum Hungaricae

Act. Ass. Acts of the General Assembly, Church of Scotland (1638-1842)

Act. Can. Acta Cancellariae, by Monroe (Eng.)

Act. Cur. Ad. Sc. Acta Curiae Admiralatus Scotiae (Wade)

Act. Lawt. Ct. Acts of Lawting Court (Sc.)

Act. Ld. Aud. C. Acts of Lords Auditors of Causes (Sc.)

Act. Ld. Co. C.C. Acts of Lords of Council in Civil Causes (1478-1501) (Sc.)

Act. Ld. Co. Pub. Aff. Acts of the Lords of Council in Public Affairs (Sc.)

ACTLRC Australian Capital Territory Law Reform Commission

Act of Sed. Act of Sederunt

Acton Acton Prize Cases Privy Council (12 ER) (Eng.)

ACTP Australian Accounts Preparation Manual (CCH)

Act. P.C. Acts of the Privy Council (Dasent)(Eng.)

Act. P.C.N.S. Same as above, New Series (Eng.)

Act. Pr. C. Acton's reports, Prize Cases (Eng.)

Act. Pr. C. Col.S. Acts of the Privy Council, Colonial Series (Eng.)

A.C.T.R. Australian Capital Territory Reports (Butterworths) (Aus.)

Act. Reg. Acta Regia, an Abstract of Rymer's Foedera

Acts & Ords. Interregnum. Acts and Ordinances of the Interregnum (1642-1660) (United Kingdom)

Acts S. Austl. Acts of South Australia

Acts Austl. P. Acts of the Australian Parliament

Act. Sed. Act of Sederunt (Sc.)

Acts Tasm. Acts of Tasmania (Aus.)

Acts Van Diem. L. Acts of Van Dieman's Land (Aus.)

Acts. Vict. Acts of the Parliament of Victoria (Aus.)

A.C.U.S. Amendment to the United States Constitution

A.C.V. Australian & New Zealand Conveyancing Report (CCH) (Aus.)

A.D.
- Agriculture Decisions
- American Decisions
- Anno Domini in the year of Our Lord (Lat.)
- Annual Digest and Reports of Public International Law Cases

- Australian Digest
- New York Supreme Court Appellate Division Reports
- A. African Law Reports, Appelate Division
- South African Supreme Court Appellate Division Reports

Ad.
- Addams' Ecclesiastical Reports (1822-26) (Eng.)
- Addendum
- Administration
- Administrative
- Administrator

AD2d   Appellate Decisions 2d Series, New York

A.D.2d   New York Supreme Court Appellate Division Reports, 2d Series (N.Y.)

ADA
- Age Discrimination Act of 1975
- Americans for Democratic Action

Adair Lib.   Adair on Law Libels

Adam.   Justiciary Reports (1893 1916) (Sc.)

ADAMHA   Alcohol, Drug Abuse, and Mental Health Administration

Adam Jur. Tr.   Adam on Trial by Jury

Adams
- Adams County Legal Journal (Pa.)
- Adam's Reports (41, 42 Maine)
- Adams' Reports (1 New Hampshire)

Adams, Eq.   Adams' Equity

Adam Sl.   Adam on the Law of Slavery in British India

Adams Leg. J. (Pa)   Adams Legal Journal

Adams L.J.   Adams County Legal Journal (Pa.)

Adams, Rom. Ant.   Adams' Roman Antiquities

Ad. & Dur. R.P.   Adams & Durham on Real Property

Ad. & E.   Adolphus & Ellis' English King's Bench Reports (1834-40)

Ad. & El.
- Adolphus & Ellis. English King's Bench Reports
- Adolphus & Ellis Queen's Bench (English)

Ad. & El.(Eng)   Adolphus & Ellis (King's Bench) Reports (110-113 Eng. Reprint)

Ad. & El. N.S.
- Adolphus & Ellis' Reports, New Series
- Adolphus & Ellis Queen's Bench (English) New Series
- English Queen's Bench (commonly cited Q.B.)

Ad & El (NS)   Adolphus & Ellis, King's Bench Reports, English, New Series

Ad. Ang. Sax. L.   Adams' Essay on Anglo-Saxon Law

ADB-INK Newsletter   Anti-Discrimination Board Newsletter (NSW)

ADC Acta Dominorum Concilii 3 vols. (1839-1943) (Sc.)

A.D.C.   Appeal Cases, District of Columbia Reports

Ad. Con.   Addison's Contracts

Ad. Ct. Dig.   Administrative Court

Digest

Add.
- Addams' Ecclesiastical Reports (Eng.)
- Addison's Reports (Pa. Supreme Court)
- Additional

Add. Abr. Addington's Abridgment of Penal Statutes

Add. Agr. Act Addison on the Agricultural Holdings Act

Addams Addams' Ecclesiastical Reports (162 Eng. Reprint)

Addams Ecc.(Eng.) Addams, Ecclesiastical (162 ER)

Add. C. Addison on Contracts

Add. Ch. Addison Charges (see Addison's Pennsylvania Reports p.49)

Add. Con. Addison on Contracts

Add. Cont. Addison on Contracts

Add Ecc. Addams' Ecclesiastical Reports

Add. Eccl. Addams' Ecclesiastical Reports

Add. Eccl. Rep. Addams' Ecclesiastical Reports (Eng.)

Add. E.R. Addams' Ecclesiastical Reports, (1822-26)

Addis Addison's County Court Reports (Pa.)

Addison (Pa.) Addison's County Court Reports (Pa.)

addit. additional

Add.Pa. Addison's County Court Reports

Add. Penn. Addison (Pa.)

Add. Rep. Addison's County Court Reports (Pa.)

Add. T. Addison on Torts

Add. Tor. Addison on Torts

Add. Torts. Addison on Torts

Add. Torts. Abr. Addison on Torts, Abridged

Add. Torts (Banks)(or D. & B.) Addison on Torts, Dudley & Baylies' Edition

Add. Torts (Wood) Addison on Torts, Wood's Edition

Ad. Ed. Act Adams on the Education Act

Ad. Ej. Adams on Ejectment

Adel. Adelaide

Adel. L.R. Adelaide Law Review

Adelaide L. Rev. Adelaide Law Review

Adelphia L.J. Adelphia Law Journal

Adel. L. Rev. Adelaide Law Review

Ad. Eq. Adam's Equity

Ad.fin. Ad finem - near the end

A.D.I.L. Annual Digest of International Law

A.D.I.L.R. Annual Digest and Reports of Public International Law Cases

ad init. ad initium (at, or to, the beginning) (Lat.)

ad int. ad interim (in the mean time) (Lat.)

Adj.
- adjudg[ed, ing, ment]
- Adjust
- Adjustment

Adj.L. Adjoining Landowners

Adjournal, Books of   The Records of the Court of Justiciary. (Sc.)

Adj. Sess.   Adjourned Session

Ad. Jus.   Adam's Justiciary Reports (Sc.)

Adk. Town   Adkinson on Township and Town Law in Indiana

Ad. L.   Administrative Law

Ad. L.2D   Pike and Fischer. Administrative Law Reporter, Second Series

Ad. Law Rev.   Administrative Law Review, Administrative Law Section, American Bar Association

Ad. L.B.   Administrative Law Bulletin

Ad. L. Bull.   Administrative Law Bulletin

Ad. Lib.   Adair on Libels

Ad. L. News   Administrative Law News

Ad. L. Newsl.   Administrative Law Newsletter

ad loc.   ad locum (at the place) (Lat.)

Ad. L. Rep.2d (P & F)   Administrative Law Reporter Second (Pike and Fischer)

Ad. L. Rev.   Administrative Law Review

Adm.
- Administrative
- Administrator
- Admiralty
- Admitted
- High Court of Admiralty (Eng.)

Adm. & Ecc.   English Law Reports, Admiralty and Ecclesiastical

Adm. & Eccl.   English Law Reports, Admiralty and Ecclesiastical

Admin.
- Administration
- Administrative
- Administrator

Admin. Cd.   Administrative Code

Admin. Dec.   Administrative Decisions

administrn.   administration

Admin. L.   Administrative Law

Admin. L.2d (P & F)   Administrative Law Second

Admin. L.J.   Administrative Law Journal

Admin. L.J. Am. U.   Administrative Law Journal of the American University

Admin. L.R.   Administrative Law Review

Admin. L. Rev.   Administrative Law Review

adminstr.   administrator

Adminstrv.   administrative

Adm. Interp.   Administrative Interpretations

Admir.
- Admiralty Division
- Admiralty

Admis.   Admission

Adm. L. Rev.   Administrative Law Review

Admr. (also Adm.)   Administrator

Admty.   Admiralty

Admx.   Administratix

Adol. & El.   Adolphus and Ellis' English King's Bench Reports

Adol. & El.N.S. Adolphus & Ellis' Reports, New Series, English Queen's Bench

Adolph & E. Adolphus & Ellis' English King's Bench Reports

Adopt. Adoption

ADP Automatic Data Processing

ADPSO Association of Data Processess Service Organizations

A.D.R. Appellate Division Reports (Mass.)

ADR
- Asset Depreciation Range System
- European Agreement concerning the International Carriage of Dangerous Goods by Road

Ad. Rom. Ant. Adam's Roman Antiquities

Ads. Ad sectum - at suit of

Ad. Sh. Advance Sheets

ADTC American District Telegraph Company

Ad. Torts Addison on Torts

Ad. Tr.M. Adams on Trade Marks

ADTS Automated Data and Telecommunications Service

Adult. Adultery

ad us. ad usum (according to custom) (Lat.)

adv.
- advisory
- advocate

Adv Advertising

ad val. ad valorem (Lat.) in proportion to the value of goods/according to the value

Advancem. Advancements

Adv. Chron. The Advocates' Chronicle (India)

Advert. advertising

Advertis. advertising

Adv.O. Advance Opinions in Lawyers' Edition of United States Reports

Advo Givens, Advocacy

Advo(3) Givens, Advocacy, Third Edition

Advoc.
- Advocacy
- Advocate

Advocate The Advocate (Vancouver Bar Association)

Advocates' Q. Advocates' Quarterly.

Advocate (Toronto) The Advocate (Students' Law Society, University of Toronto)

Adv. Ops. Advance Opinions

Adv. Poss. Adverse Possession

Adv. Rep. N.J. New Jersey Advance Reports & Weekly Review

Adv. Sh. Advance Sheet

advt. advertising

Adye C.M. Adye on Courts-Martial

A.E. Atomic Energy

A/E Registration Board of Architects and Professional Engineers

AE(2) Acret, Architects and Engineers

AE(2s) Acret, Architects and Engineers, Second Edition, Supplement

AEA Atomic Energy Agency

AEC Atomic Energy Commission (U.S.)

13

A.E.C.
- American Electrical Cases
- Atomic Energy Commission U.S.
- Atomic Energy Commission Reports

AECPR   Atomic Energy Commission Procurement Regulations

A.E.G.   Australian Estate and Gift Duty Reporter (CCH) (Aus.)

A.E.G.R.   Australian Estate and Gift Duty Cases (CCH) (Aus.)

A/E Legal Newsl.   A/E Legal Newsletter

AELE Legal Liab. Rep.   AELE Legal Liability Reporter

A.E.L.J.   Atomic Energy Law Journal

AelLC.   Canons of Aelfric

A.E.L.R.   All England Law Reports

AEn   Buck, Alternative energy

A.E.R.   All England Law Reports

Aer   State Aeronautics Commission

A.E.R. Rep.   All England Law Reports Reprint (1558-1935)

A.E.R. Rep. Ext.   All England Law Reports Reprint Extension Volumes, Australia (1861-1935)

A.F.   Air Force

Af   Afghan

a.f.   anno futuro (next year) (Lat.)

AFB   Air Force Base

AFDA   Association francaise de droit aerien

A.F.D.C.   Aid to Families with Dependent Children

AFDC   Aid to Families with Dependent Children

Aff.
- Affairs
- affidavit
- affirmed in, or affirming

Aff. Action Compl. Man. (BNA)   Affirmative Action Compliance Manual for Federal Contractors

Aff'd   Affirmed

Aff'g   Affirming

Affi.   Affidavits

aff reh   affirmed on rehearing, or affirming on rehearing

afft.   affidavit

Afgh., Afg.   Afghanistan

AFIA   American Foreign Insurance Association

A.F. JAG L. Rev.   Air Force JAG Law Review

A.F.L.
- American Federation of Labor
- Australian Family Law and Practice (CCH) (Aus.)

A.F.L.A.   Association of Fire Loss Adjusters

A.F.L.-C.I.O.   American Federation of Labor and Congress of Industrial Organizations

A.F.L.R.   Air Force Law Review

A.F. L. Rev.   Air Force Law Review

Af. L. Studies   African Law Studies

A.F.O.   Admiralty Fleet Order

AFPI   Air Force Procurement Instruments

Afr.
- Africa
- African
- Afrikaans

Afr. Aff. African Affairs

A.F.Rep. Alaska Federal Reports

African L.R. Comm. African Law Reports, Commercial Series

African L.R. Mal. African Law Reports, Malawi Series

African L.R. S.L. African Law Reports, Sierra Leone Series

African L.S. African Law Studies

Afr. J. Int'l L. African Journal of International Law

Afr. L. Dig. African Law Digest

Afr. L. Digest African Law Digest

Afr. L.R. African Law Reports

Afr. L.R., Mal.Ser. African Law Reports, Malawi Series

Afr. L.R., Sierre L.Ser. African Law Reports, Sierre Leone Series

Afr. L. Stud. African Law Studies

afsd. aforesaid

A.F.T. Australian Federal Tax Reporter (CCH) (Aus.)

AFTR American Federal Tax Reports (P-H)

AFTR2d, A.F.T.R.2d (P-H) American Federal Tax Reports 2d Series (P-H)

AFW Newberg, Attorney Fee Awards

A.G. Attorney-General

AG Attorney General's Opinions

Ag.
- State Department of Agriculture
- Agency
- Agrees
- Agreement
- Against

Agcy. Agency

AgD Eglit, Age Discrimination

A.G. Dec. Attorney General's Decisions

Ag Dec Agriculture Decisions

(The) Age The Age (newspaper) (David Syme & Co. Ltd., Melbourne)

AGI Adjusted Gross Income

A.G.I.S. Attorney General's Information Service

AgL Davidson, Agricultural Law

Agn. Fr. Agnew on the Statute of Frauds

Agn. Pat. Agnew on Patents

AGO Adjutant General's Office, U.S.

A.G.O. Attorney General, Opinions

AGPR Department of Agriculture Procurement Regulations

Agr.
- Agreement
- Agree(s)
- Agriculture

Agra H.C. Agra High Court Reports (India)

Agr. C. Agreed Case

Agri. Agriculture

Agric.
- Agricultural
- Agriculture

Agric. & Mkts. Agriculture & Markets

Agric. C. Agricultural Code

Agric. Conserv. & Adj. Agricultural Conservation and Adjustment

Agri. Dec. Agriculture Decisions

15

Agr. L.J. Agricultural Law Journal

AGSS Laritz, Attorney Guide to Social Security Disability Claims

agt. agent

agy. agency

AHA American Hospital Association

AHERA Asbestos Hazard Emergency Response Act of 1986 (Title II of TSCA)

A.H.F. Australian High Court and Federal Court Practice (CCH) (Aus.)

a.h.l. ad hunc locum (at this place) (Lat.)

A.H.R. Academy of Human Rights

a.h.v. ad hunc vocem (at this word) (Lat.)

A .I.
- Admiralty Instruction
- Amnesty International
- Artificial Insemination

A.I. Arb. Associate of the Institute-of-Arbitrators

AIB American Institute of Banking

A.I.B. Accident Investigation Branch

A.I.C. Australian Institute of Criminology

A.I.D. Accident/Injury/Damages

AICLE Alabama Institute for Continuing Legal Education

AICPA-Prof. Stand. (CCH) American Institute for Certified Public Accountants Professional Standards (Commerce Clearing House)

A.I.Cr.D. All India Criminal De-

cisions.

AID
- Accident/Injury/ Damages
- Agency for International Development

A.I.D. Artificial insemination by donor

AIDPR Agency for International Development Procurement Regulations

AIDS Acquired Immune Deficiency Syndrome

AIDS L. & Litig. Rep. (Univ. Pub. Group) AIDS Law & Litigation Reporter

AIDS L. Rep. AIDS Law.Rep.

AIDS Litigation Rep. AIDS Litigation Reporter

A.I.I.A. Australian Institute of International Affairs

Aik.
- Aikens' Vermont Supreme Court Reports (1825-1828)
- Aikens' Report (Vt.)

Aik. Dig. Aiken's Digest of Alabama Statutes

Aikens's Rep. Aikens' Reports (Vt.)

Aikens (Vt.) Aikens Reports (Vt.)

Aik. Rep. Aikens' Reports (Vt.)

Aik. Stat. Aiken's Digest of Alabama Statutes

Aik.(Vt.)Rep. Aikens' Reports (Vt.)

A.I.L. Australian Industrial Review (CCH) (Aus.)

A.I.L.C. American International Law Cases 1783-1968

A.I.L.R. Australian Industrial Review (CCH) (Aus.)

AIM
- American Indian Movement
- American Institute of Management

A. Ins. R. American Insolvency Reports

Ainsw. Ainsworth's Lexicon

Ainsworth, Lex. Ainsworth's Latin-English Dictionary (1837)

AIOEC Association of Iron Ore Exporting Countries

AIP American Independent Party

AIPLA American Intellectual Property Law Association

AIPLA Q.J. AIPLA Quarterly Journal

A.I.R. All India Law Reporter (Usually followed by a province abbreviation, (as A.I.R. All., for Allaha- bad , Bom. for Bombay, Dacca for Dacca, H.P. for Himachal Pradesh, Hyd. for Hyderabad, etc.)

Air & Space Law. Air & Space Lawyer

Aird Civ. Law. Aird's Civil Laws of France

Air Force L.R. Air Force Law Review

Air L. Air Law

Air L.R. Air Law Review

Air L. Rev. Air Law Review

Air U. Rev. Air University Review

Aiyar Aiyar's Company Cases (India)

Aiyar C.C. Aiyar's Company Cases (India)

Aiyar L.P.C. Aiyar's Leading Privy Council Cases (India)

Aiyar Unrep. D. Aiyar's Unreported Decisions (India)

A.J.
- American Jurist
- Associate Judge
- British Guiana Supreme Court, Appellate Jurisdiction

A.J.C.L. American Journal of Comparative Law

A.J.I.L. American Journal of International Law

Ajmer-Merwara L.J. Ajmer-Merwara Law Journal (India)

A.J.R. Australian Jurist Reports

A.J.R.(N.C.) Australian Jurist Reports (Notes of Cases) (1870-74).

AJS American Judicature Society

A. Jur. Rep. Australian Jurist Reports

Ak
- Alaska
- Arkansas Reports

a.k.a. also known as

A.K. Marsh.
- A.K. Marshall's Kentucky Supreme Court Reports (1817-21)
- A.K. Marshall (Ky.)

Akron L. Rev. Akron Law Review

Akron Tax J. Akron Tax Journal

Al.
- Alabama
- Albanian
- Aleyn. King's Bench Reports (1846-49) (Eng.)
- Aleyn's Select Cases, Kings Bench
- Allen

AL   Turley, Aviation Litigation

AL5   American Law Reports, Fifth Series

ALA
- Alliance for Labor Action
- American Library Association

Ala.
- Alabama
- Alabama Reports
- Alabama Supreme Court
- Alabama Supreme Court Reports
- Minor's Alabama Reports

Ala.A.   Alabama Appellate Court

A.L.A.A.   American Labor Arbitration Awards (P-H)

Ala. Acts.   Acts of Alabama

Ala. App.
- Alabama Appellate Court Reports
- Alabama Court of Appeals

Alabama L. Rev.   Alabama Law Re-view

Alabama Rep.   Alabama Reports (Ala.)

Ala. Bar Bull.   Alabama Bar Bulletin

Alab.(N.S.)   Alabama Reports, New Series (Ala.) Ala.St.B.Found.Bull.

Alab. Rep.   Alabama Reports (Ala.)

Ala. Civ. App.   Alabama Civil Appeals

Ala. Code   Code of Alabama

Ala. Const.   Alabama Constitution

Ala. Law   Alabama Lawyer

Ala. Cr. App.   Alabama Criminal Appeals

Ala. Law.   Alabama Lawyer

Ala. L.J.   Alabama Law Journal

Ala. L. Rev.   Alabama Law Review

Al. & N.   Alcock & Napier. Irish King's Bench Reports (1831-33)

Al. & Nap.   Alcock & Napier's Irish King's Bench Reports

Ala. N.S.   Alabama Reports. New Series

Ala. P.S.C.   Alabama Public Service Commission

Ala.R.   Alabama Reports (Ala.)

Ala. R.C.   Alabama Railroad Commission

Ala. Rep.:   Alabama Reports (Ala.)

Ala. Rep. N.S.:   Alabam Reports (Ala.)

Ala. Reps.:   Alabama Reports (Ala.)

Ala. R. N.S.:   Alabama Reports, New Series (Ala.)

Alas.   Alaska

Ala. S.B.A.   Alabama State Bar Association

Alaska
- Alaska Reporter
- Alaska Reports

Ala. Sel. Cas.   Alabama Select Cases (Sup. Ct) by Shepherd. vols. 37, 38 & 39

Alas F   Alaska Federal Reports

Alaska Admin. Code   Alaska Administrative Code

Alaska B.B.   Alaska Bar Brief

Alaska B.J.   Alaska Bar Journal

Alaska B. Brief   Alaska Bar Brief

Alaska Co.   Alaska Codes, Carter

Alaska Const.   Alaska Constitu-

Alaska Const. Alaska Constitution

Alaska Fed. Alaska Federal Reports

Alaska Fed. Rep. Alaska Federal Reports

Alaska L.J. Alaska Law Journal

Alaska L. Rev. Alaska Law Review

Alaska Sess. Laws Alaska Session Laws

Alaska Stat. Alaska Statutes

Ala. St. B.A. Alabama State Bar Association

Ala. St. Bar Assn. Alabama State Bar Association

Ala. St. B. Found. Bull. Alabama State Bar Foundation Bulletin

Alb.
- Albania, Albanian
- Albany

Albany L. Rev. Albany Law Review

Alb. Arb. Albert Arbitration (Lord Cairns' Decisions)

Alberta L.(Can) Alberta Law Reports

Alberta L.Q. Alberta Law Quarterly

Alberta L. Rev. Alberta Law Review

Alb. Law J. Albany Law Journal

Alb. L.J. Albany Law Journal

Alb. L.J. Sci. & Tech. Albany Law Journal of Science & Technology

Alb. L.Q. Alberta Law Quarterly

Alb. L.R. Alberta Law Reports

Alb. L. Rev. Albany Law Review

Alb. L.S. Jour. Albany Law School Journal

Albuquerque B.J. Albuquerque Bar Journal

Alc. Alcock's Irish Registry Cases

Alcohol Treat. Q. Alcoholism Treatment Quarterly

A.L.C. American Leading Cases

A.L.C. (or ALC) American Labor Cases (P-H)

Alc. & N. Alcock & Napier King's Bench (Irish)

Alc. & Nap. Alcock & Napier's Irish King's Bench Reports

Alco. Bev. Alcoholic Beverage

Alco. Bev. Cont. Alcoholic Beverage Control

Alcock & N Alcock & Napier King's Bench (Ir.) 1 vol

Alc. Per. Prop. Alcock on Personal Property

Alc. Reg. C. Alcock's Registry Cases (1832-41) (Ir.)

Alc. Reg. Cas.
- Alcock's Registry Cases (English)
- Alcock Registry Cases (Irish)

A.L.D.
- African Law Digest
- Administrative Law Decisions (Butterworths) (Aus.)

Ald. Alden's Condensed Reports (Pa.)

Ald. Abr. Alden's Abridgment of Law

Ald. & V.H. Alden & Van Hoesen's Digest of Mississippi Laws

19

Ald. Ans. Cont. Aldrich's Edition of Ansen on Contracts

Ald. Hist. Aldridge's History of the Courts of Law

Ald. Ind. Alden's Index of United States Reports

Ald. Ques. Aldred's Questions on the Law of Property

Aldridge History and Jurisdiction of the Courts of Law (1835)

Ale. & N. Alcock & Napier, Irish King's Bench Reports and Exchequer

ALEHU Advanced Legal Education, Hamline University School of Law

Alexander. Alexander's Reports, vols. 66-72 Mississippi

Alex. Br.S tat. Alexander's British Statutes in Force in Maryland

Alex. Cas. Report of the "Alexandra" Case by Dudley

Alex. Ch. Pr. Alexander's Chancery Practice in Maryland

Alex. Com. Pr. Alexander's Practice of the Commissary Courts, Scotland

Alex. Dig. Alexander's Texas Digest

Alex. Ins. Alexander on Life Insurance in New York

Aleyn Aleyn's Select Cases, English King's Bench, (82 ER)

Aleyn (Eng.) Aleyn, Select Cases (82 Eng. Reprint)

Alg. Algeria, Algerian

Alger's Law Promoters & Prom. Corp. Alger's Law in Relation to Promoters and Promotion of Corporations

Alg. Med. Algemene Mededelingen (Netherlands)

A.L.I. American Law Institute

ALIABA American Law Institute-American Bar Association Committee on Continuing Professional Educa-tion

ALI-ABA CLE Rev. ALI-ABA CLE Review

ALI-ABA Course Materials J. ALI-ABA Course Materials Journal

ALI-ABA Course Mat. J. ALI-ABA Course Materials Journal

ALI-ABA Course M. J. American Law Institute-American Bar Association Course Materials Journal

ALI Fed. Income Tax Project ALI Federal Income Tax Project

A.L.I. Proc. American Law Institute Proceedings

Alison Pr. Alison's Practice (Sc.)

Alis. Princ. Scotch Law. Alison's Principles of the Criminal Law of Scotland

Alive Australian Leave & Holidays Practice Manual (CCH)

A.L.J.
- Administrative Law Judge
- Albany Law Journal
- Allahabad Law Journal (India)
- American Law Journal (1884 85)
- Australian Law Journal
- The Australian Law Journal, Sydney, Australia

A.L.J. N.S. American Law Journal, New Series, Philadelphia

A.L.J.R. The Australian Law Journal Reports (Aus.)

Alk
- Alaska
- Alaska Reports

Al.Kada Native Tribunals' Reports (Egypt)

All.
- All Courts
- Allen's Massachusetts Reports
- Allen's New Brunswick Reports (1848-66) (Can.)
- Indian Law Reports, Allahabad Series (India)

Allahabad L.J. AllahabadLaw Journal

Alla. L.J. Allahabad Law Journal, (India)

All. & Mor. Tr. Allen & Morris' Trial

All. Cr. Cas. Allahabad Criminal Cases

Allen
- Allen's Massachusetts Supreme Judicial Court Reports (1861-67)
- Allen's Reports, New Brunswick (Can.)
- Allen's Reports (Washington Territory, 1854-85)
- Aleyn's English King's Bench Reports

All Eng All England Law Reports

Allen N.B. Allen, New Brunswick

Allen's Rep. Allen (Charles) Reports (V. 1-14 Mass.)

Allen Tel. Cas. Allen's Telegraph Cases

All.E.R. All England Law Reports (formerly All England Law Reports Annotated)

All E.R. Rep. All England Law Reports Reprint (1558-1935)

All E.R. Rep. Ext. All England Law Reports Reprint, Australian Extension Volumes (1865-1935)

All E.R. Repr. The All England Law Reports Reprint

All I.C.R. All Indian Criminal Reports

Allin. Allinson's Pennsylvania Superior and Dist. Court Reports

All Ind. Cr. R. All Indian Criminal Reports

All Ind. Cr. T. All India Criminal Times

All India Crim. Dec. All India Criminal Decisions

All India Rep. All India Reporter, Nagpur, India

All India Rptr. All India Reporter

All Ind. Rep. All India Reporter

All Ind. Rep. N.S. All India Reporter, New Series

Allinson Allinson, Pennsylvania Superior and District Court Reports

All.I.R. All India Reports

Allison's Am. Dict. Allison's American Dictionary

All.L.D. of Mar. Alleyne,Legal decrees of marriage (1810)

All.L.J. & Rep. Allahabad Law Journal and Reports. (India)

All.L.R. Allahabad Law Review (India)

All.L.T. Allahabad Law Times (India)

All.N.B. Allen's New Brunswick

Reports (1948-66) (Can.)

All Nig. L.R. All Nigeria Law Reports

All N.L.R. All Nigeria Law Reports (1961-62)

Alln. Part. Allnat, Law of Partition (1820)

Alln. Wills Allnutt on Wills

allowing app. allowing appeal

allowing reh. allowing rehearing

All Pak. Legal. Dec. The All Pakistan Legal Decisions

All Pak. Leg. Dec. All Pakistan Legal Decisions

All.Ser. Allahabad Series, Indian Law Reports

All.Sher. Allen on Sheriffs

All-St. Sales Tax Rep. (CCH) All-State Sales Tax Reporter

All States Tax Guide (P-H) All States Tax Guide (Prentice-Hall)

All.Tel.Cas. Allen, Telegraph Cases (American and English)

All.W.N. Allahabad Weekly Notes (and Supplement) (India)

Allwood Allwood's Appeal Cases under the Weights & Measures Act (Eng.)

All.W.R. Allahabad Weekly Reporter (India)

A.L.M. American Law Magazine, Philadelphia

A.L.M.D. Australian Legal Monthly Digest

Al.Pr. Alison on the Principles of the Scottish Criminal Law

A.L.R.
- Adelaide Law Review

- Alden Law Reports
- Alberta Law Reports (Canada)
- American Labor Cases (P-H)
- American Law Register (1852-1907)
- American Law Reports
- American Law Reports, Annotated
- Argus Law Reports (Victoria)
- Australian Law Reports

A.L.R.2d American Law Reports Annotated, Second Series

A.L.R.3d American Law Reports Annotated, Third Series

A.L.R.4th American Law Reports Annotated, Fourth Series

A.L.R.5th American Law Reports Annotated, Fifth Series

A.L.R.A. Abortion Law Reform Association

A.L.R.A.C. Australian Law Reform Agencies Conference

A.L.R.A.N.L. Abortion Law Reform Association News Letter

A.L.R.C. Australian Law Reform Commission

A.L.R.(C.N.) Argus Law Reports Current Notes

A.L.R.Com. African Law Reports. Commercial Law Series

A.L.R.Comm. Africa Law Reports, Commercial Series

A.L.Rec. American Law Record, Cincinnati

A.L.Reg. American Law Register, Philadelphia

A.L.Reg.(N.S.) American Law Register, New Series

A.L.Reg.(O.S.) American Law Register, Old Series

A.L.Rep. American Law Reporter, Davenport, Iowa

Al.Rep. Alabama Reports (Ala.)

A.L.Rev. American Law Review, Boston

A.L.R. Fed. American Law Reports, Federal
- American Law Reports Annotated, Federal

A.L.R.L.C.S. American Law Reports Later Case Service

A.L.R.Mal. African Law Reports, Malawi Series

A.L.R. (Malawi ser.) African Law Reports (Malawi series)

A.L.R. (Sierra L. ser.) African Law Reports (Sierra Leone series)

A.L.R. S.L. African Law Reports, Sierra Leone Series

Alsager. Alsager's Dictionary of Business Terms

Al. Sc. Cr. L. Alison on Scottish Criminal Law

A.L.T.
- American Law Times
- Australian Law Times

Alt. Alternative

Alta.
- Alberta
- Alberta Law Reports (1907-1932) (Can.)

Alta. Gaz. Alberta Gazette

Alta. L. Alberta Law

Alta. L.Q. Alberta Law Quarterly (1908-32) (Can.)

Alta. L.R. Alberta Law Reports. (Can.)

Alta. L.R.(2d) Alberta Law Reports, Second Series

Alta. L. Rev. Alberta Law Review

Alta. Rev. Stat. Alberta Revised Statutes (Can.)

Alta. Stat. Alberta Statutes (Can.)

A.L.T. Bankr. American Law Times, Bankruptcy Reports

A.L.T.B.R. Law Times Bankruptcy Reports (U.S.)

Alt. County Gov't. Alternative County Government

Alt. Disp. Res. Alternative Dispute Resolution

Al. Tel. Ca. Allen's Telegraph Cases

Alt. Inst. Alteration of Instruments

A.L.T.R. American Law Times Reports

A.L.T.R.N.S. American Law Times Reports, New Series

Alves Dampier & Maxwell's British Guiana Reports

Am.
- Amended
- Amendment
- American(s)
- Amharic

AMA American Management Association

A.M.A. American Medical Association

Am. Acad. Matri. Law. J. American Academy of Matrimonial Lawyers Journal

Am. Acad. Pol. & Soc. Sci. American Academy of Political and Social Science

Am. & E. Corp. Cas. American & English Corporation Cases

Am. & E. Corp. Cas. N.S. American & English Corporation Cases New Series

Am. & E. Eq. D. American & English Decisions in Equity

Am. & Eng. Ann. Cas. American & English Annotated Cases

Am. & Eng.Corp.Cas. American & English Corporation Cases

Am. & Eng.Corp.Cas.N.S. American & English Corporation cases, New Series

Am. & Eng.Dec.Eq. American and English Decisions in Equity

Am. & Eng. Dec. in Eq. American and English Decisions in Equity

Am. & Eng. Enc. Law American and English Encyclopedia of Law

Am. & Eng. Enc. Law & Pr. American & English Encyclopedia of Law & Practice

Am. & Eng. Enc. Law Sup. American and English Encyclopedia of Law, Supplement

Am. & Eng. Ency. Law American and English Encyclopedia of Law

Am. & Eng. Eq. D. American & English Decisions in Equity

Am. & Engl. R.C. American and English Railway Cases

Am.& Eng.Pat.Cas. American and English Patent Cases

Am. & Eng. R. Cas. American and English Railroad Cases

Am. & Eng. R. Cas. N.S. American and English Railroad Cases, New Series

Am.& Eng.R.R.Ca. American and English Railroad Cases

Am. & Eng. R.R.Cas. American and English Railroad Cases

Am. & Eng. R.R.Cases American and English Railroad Cases (U.S.)

Am. & Eng.Ry.Cas. American and English Railway Cases

Am. & Eng.Ry.Cas.N.S. American & English Railroad Cases, New Series

Am. & E.R. Cas. American & English Railroad Cases

Am. & E.R. Cas. N.S. American & English Railroad Cases New Series

Am. & Fer. Amos & Ferard on Fixtures

A.M. & O. Armstrong, Macartney & Ogle's Nisi Prius (1840-42) (Ir.)

Am. Ann. Cas. American Annotated Cases (1904-12)

Am. A. Psych. L. Bull. American Academy of Psychiatry and the Law Bulletin

AMAS African and Malagasy Associated States

Am. Assoc. Univ. Prof. Bull. American Association of University Professors Bulletin

Amb. Ambler's Reports, Chancery. (27 ER) (Eng.)

Am. B.A. American Bar Association

Am. Banker. American Bankruptcy (U.S.)

Am. Bank. R. American Bankruptcy Reports

Am. Bankr. American Bankruptcy

Am. Bankr. L.J. American Bankruptcy Law Journal

Am. Bankr. N.S. American Bankruptcy, New Series

Am. Bank. Rev. American Bankruptcy Review

Am. Bankr. J. American Bank-
rupt-cy Journal

Am. Bankr. L.J. American Bank-
rupt- cy Law Journal

Am. Bankr. N.S. American Bank-
rupt- cy, New Series

Am. Bankr. R. American Bank-
rupt-cy Reports

Am. Bankr. Reg. American Bank-
rupt-cy Register (U. S.)

Am. Bankr. Rep. American Bankruptcy Reports

Am. Bankr. Rep. N.S. American
Bankruptcy Reports, New Series

Am. Bankr. Rev. American Bankruptcy Review

Am. Bankr. R.(N.S.) American
Bankruptcy Reports, New Series

Am. Bankruptcy Reps. American
Bankruptcy Reports

Am. Bar Ass. J. American Bar
Assn. Journal

Am. Bar Asso. Jour. American
Bar Association Journal

Am Bar Asso Rep American Bar
Association Reports

Am. Bar Found. Res. J. America
Bar Foundation Research Journal

Am. Bar N. American Bar News

Ambass. Ambassadors

Am. B. Found. Res. J. American
Bar Foundation Research Journal

Am. B'Kc'y. Rep. American Bankruptcy Reports

Ambl. Ambler's Reports, Chancery. (27 ER) (Eng.)

Am. B. News American Bar News

Am. B.(N.S.) American Bankruptcy New Series

Am. B.R. American Bankruptcy
Reports

Am. B.R.(N.S.) American Bankruptcy Reports, New Series

Am. Bus. L.J. American Business
Law Journal

A.M.C. American Maritime Cases

Am Cent Dig American Digest
(Century Edition)

Am. Ch. Dig. American Chancery
Digest

Am. Civ. L.J. American Civil Law
Journal

Am. C. L.J. American Civil Law
Journal, New York

Am. Consul. Bul. American Con-
sular Bulletin

Am. Corp. Cas. American Corporation Cases (Withrow)

Am. Cr. American Criminal Reports

Am. Crim. L.Q. American Criminal Law Quarterly

Am. Crim. L. Rev. American
Criminal Law Review

Am. Cr. R. American Criminal Reports

Am. Cr. Rep. American Criminal
Reports, edited by Hawley

Am. Cr. R.(Hawley) American
Criminal Reports, edit. by Hawley

Am. Cr. Tr. American Criminal Trials, Chandler's

am.cur. amicus curiae (friend of the court) (Lat.)

Amd. Amended

Am.D. American Decisions

Am. Dec. American Decisions (Select Cases), San Francisco

Am. Dec's. American Decisions (U.S.)

Am. Dig. American Digest

Am. Dig. Cent. Ed. American Digest (Century Edition)

Am. Dig. Dec. Ed. (or Decen.Ed.) American Digest (Decennial Edition) (West)

Am. Dig. Eighth Dec. Ed. American Digest (Eighth Decennial Edition) (West)

Am. Dig. Fifth Dec. Ed. American Digest (Fifth Decennial Edition) (West)

Am. Dig. Fourth Dec. Ed. American Digest (Fourth Decennial Edition) (West)

Am. Dig. Key No. Ser. American Digest (Key Number Series) (West)

Am. Dig. Secd. Dec. Ed. American Digest (Second Decennial Edition) (West)

Am.Dig. Seventh Dec.Ed. American Digest (Seventh Decennial Edition) (West)

Am.Dig. Sixth Dec.Ed. American Digest (Sixth Decennial Edition) (West)

Am.Dig. Third Dec.Ed. American Digest (Third Decennial Edition)

(West)

Am. Econ. Rev. American Economic Review

Am. Ed. American Edition

Am. Elect. Cas. American Electrical Cases

Am. Electr. Cas. American Electrical Cases.

Am. Enc. Dict. American Encyclopedic Dictionary

Amend. Amendment

amend. amended;amending; amendment; amendments

amend'g amending

amends. amendments

Am. Eng. Ann. Cases American and English Annotated Cases (U.S.)

Am. Eng. Corp. Cas. N.S. American and English Corporation Cases, New Series (U.S.)

Am. Ent. The American Enterprise

Amer.
- America; American
- Amerman's Reports (Vols. 111-115 Pennsylvania Reports)

Amer. & Eng. Enc. Law American & English Encyclopedia of Law

Amer. Anthrop. American Anthropologist

Amer. Corp. Cas. American Corporation Cases

Amer. Dec. American Decisions

Amer. Econ. Rev. American Economic Review

Amer. Elec. Ca. American Electrical Cases

Amer. Fed. Tax Rep. American Federal Tax Rep. (P-H)

American Repts. American Reports

American State Rep. American State Reports

Amer. J. Comp. L. American Journal of Comparative Law

Amer. J. Econ. & Soc. American Journal of Economics and Sociology

Amer. J. Int'l. L. American Journal of International Law

Amer. Jur. American Jurist

Amer. Law. American Lawyer, New York

Amer. Law Reg. (N. S.) American Law Register, New Series

Amer. Law Reg. (O. S.) American Law Register, Old Series

Amer. Law Rev. American Law Review

Amer. Lawy. American Lawyer

Amer. Lea. Cas. American Leading Cases

Amer. Rep. American Reports

Amer. Reports American Reports

Amer. Reps. American Reports

Amer. Rev. E. -W. Tr. American Review of East-West Trade

Amer. R'y. Rep. American Railway Reports

Amer. State Reps. American State Reports

Amer. St. Rep. American State Reports

Amer. Univ. L. Rev. The American University Law Review

Amer. with Disab. Act Americans With Disability Act

Ames
- Ames' Reports (1 Minnesota)
- Ames' Reports (4-7 Rhode Island)

Ames Cas. B. & N. Ames' Cases on Bills and Notes

Ames Cas. Par. Ames' Cases on Partnership

Ames Cas. Pl. Ames' Cases on Pleading

Ames Cas. Sur. Ames' Cases on Suretyship

Ames Cas. Trusts. Ames' Cases on Trusts

Ames, K. & B. Ames, Knowles & Bradley's Reports (8 Rhode Island)

Am. Fed. Tax R. American Federal Tax Reports (P-H)

Am. Fed. Tax R.2d American Federal Tax Reports, Second Series (P-H)

Am. For. L. Ass'n Newsl. American Foreign Law Association Newsletter

Am. Hist. Rev. American Historical Review

Amicus
- Amicus (South Bend, Ind.)
- Amicus (Thousand Oaks, CA)

Am. Indian J. American Indian Journal

Am. Indian L. Rev. American Indian Law Review

Am. Ind. J. American Indian Journal

Am. Ind. L. Newsl. American Indian Law Newsletter

Am. Ind. L.R. American Indian Law Review

Am. Ind. L. Rev. American Indian Law Review

Am. Ins. Arnold on Marine Insurance

Am. Insolv. Rep. American Insolvency Reports

Am. Ins. Rep. American Insolvency Reports

Am. J.2d American Jurisprudence (Second Series)

Am. J. Comp. L. American Journal of Comparative Law

Am. J. Comp. Law American Journal of Comparative Law

Am. J. Crim. L. American Journal of Criminal Law

Am. J. Fam. L. American Journal of Family Law

Am. J. For. Psych. American Journal of Forensic Psychiatry

Am. J. Int'l Arb. American Journal of International Arbitration

Am. J. Int. L., Am J Intl L American Journal of International Law

Am. J. Int. Law Proc. American Journal of International Law, Proceedings

Am. J. Int'l. L. American Journal of International Law

Am. J. Juris. American Journal of Jurisprudence

Am. J. Jurispr. American Journal of Jurisprudence

Am. J. Jurisprud. American Journal of Jurisprudence

Am. J. L. & Med. American Journal of Law & Medicine

Am. J. Law & Med. American Journal of Law & Medicine

Am. J. Legal Hist. American Journal of Legal History

Am. J. Leg. Forms Anno. American Jurisprudence Legal Forms Annotated

Am. J. Leg. Hist. American Journal of Legal History

Am. J. L.Rev. American Journal Law Review

Am. J. of Law & Med. American Journal of Law and Medicine

Am. Jour. Pol. American Journal of Politics

Am. Jour. Soc. American Journal of Sociology

Am. J. Philol. American Journal of Philology

Am. J. Pl. & Pr. Forms Anno. American Jurisprudence Pleading & Practice Forms Annotated

Am. J. Police Sci. American Journal of Police Science

Am. J. Pol. Sc. American Journal of Political Science

Am. J. Proof of Facts American Jurisprudence Proof of Facts

Am. Jr. American Jurisprudence/American Jurist

Am. J. Soc. Sci. American Journal of Social Sciences

Am. J. Tax Pol'y American Journal of Tax Policy

Am. J. Trial Advoc. American Jour-nal of Trial Advocacy

Am. J. Trials American Jurisprudence Trials

Am. Jud. Soc. American Judicature Society (Bulletins or Journal)

Am. Jud. Soc'y. Journal of American Judicature Society

Am. Jur.
- American Jurisprudence
- American Jurist

Am. Jur. 2d American Jurisprudence, Second Series

Am. Jurist American Jurist

Am. Jur. Legal Forms American Jurisprudence Legal Forms

Am. Jur. Legal Forms 2d. American Jurisprudence Legal Forms, Second Series

Am. Jur. Leg. Forms Anno. American Jurisprudence Legal Forms Annotated

Am. Jur. Pl. & Pr. Forms American Jurisprudence Pleading and Practice Forms Annotated

Am. Jur. Pl. & Pr. Forms (Rev. ed.) American Jurisprudence Pleading and Practice Forms, Revised Editions

Am. Jur. POF2d American Jurisprudence Proof of Facts, Second Series

Am. Jur. Proof of Facts American Jurisprudence Proof of Facts

Am. Jur. Proof of Facts Anno. American Jurisprudence Proof of Facts Annotated

Am. Jur. Trials American Jurisprudence Trials

Am. Lab. Arb. Awards (P-H) American Labor Arbitration Awards (P-H)

Am. Lab. Arb. Cas. American Labor Arbitration Cases (P-H)

Am. Lab. Arb. Serv. American Labor Arbitration Services

Am. Lab. Cas. American Labor Cases (P-H)

Am. Lab. Cas. (P-H) American Labor Cases (P-H)

Am. Lab. Leg. Rev. American Labor Leg-islation Review

Am. Labor Legis. Rev. American Labor Legislation Review

Am. Law. American Lawyer

Am. Law Inst. American Law Institute, Restatement of the Law

Am. Law J. American Law Journal

Am. Law J. N. S. American Law Jour-nal, New Series

Am. Law Mag. American Law Maga-zine

Am. Law Rec.
- American Law Record (Cincinnati)
- American Law Record (Reprint) (Ohio)

Am. Law Record American Law Record (Reprint) (Ohio)

Am. Law Reg. American Law Register

Am. Law Reg. N. S. American Law Register, New Series

Am. Law Reg. (old ser.) American Law Register (Reprint) (Ohio)

Am. Law Reg. O. S. American Law Register, Old Series

Am. Law Rev. American Law Review

Am. Law S. Rev. American Law School Review

Am. Law T. Rep. American Law Times Reports

Am. Lawy. American Lawyer

Am. L. C. American Leading Cases (U. S.)

Am. L. Cas. American Leading Cases

Am. L. C. R. P. Sharswood and Budd's Leading Cases on Real Property

Am. Lead. Ca. (ed. of 1871) American Leading Cases

Am. Lead. Cas. American Leading Cases (Hare & Wallace's)

Am. Lead. Cas. (H & W) American Leading Cases (Hare & Wallace)

Am. Lead. Cases American Leading Cases

Am. Leading Cas. American Leading Cases

Am. Leading Cases, notes by Hare and Wallace American Leading Cases

Am. Leg. American Legislator

Am. Leg. N. American Legal News

Am. L. Elec. American Law of Elections, by McCrary

Am. L. Ins.
- American Law Institute
- American Law Institute, Restatement of the Law

Am. L. Inst. American Law Institute, Restatement of the Law

A. M. L. J. Ajmer-Merwara Law Journal (India)

Am. L. J.
- American Law Journal (Hall's) (Philadelphia)

- American Law Journal (Ohio)

Am. L. J. N. S. American Law Journal, New Series, Philadelphia

Am. L. J. (O) American Law Journal (Ohio)

Am. L. J. (O. S.) America Law Jour- nal (Hall's)

Am. L. M. American Law Magazine, Philadelphia

Am. L. Mag. American Law Magazine

Am. L. Rec. American Law Record (Ohio)

Am. L. Rec. (Ohio) American Law Record (Reprint) (Ohio)

Am. L. Reg. American Law Register, Philadelphia

Am. L. Reg. & Rev. American Law Register and Review

Am. L. Reg. (N. S.) American Law Register, New Series

Am. L. Reg., (O. S.) American Law Register, Old Series

Am. L. Rep. American Law Reporter, Davenport (Iowa)

Am. L. Rev. American Law Review

Am. L. School Rev. American Law School Review

Am. L. Sch. Rev. American Law School Review

Am. L. S. Rev. American Law School Review

Am. L. T. American Law Times, Washington, D. C. and New York

Am. L. T. Bankr. American Law Times Bankruptcy Reports

Am. L. T. Bankr. Rep. American Law Times Bankruptcy Reports

Am. L. T. R. American Law Times Reports

Am. L. T. Rep. American Law Times Reports

Am. L. T. R. N. S. American Law Times Reports, New Series

Am. Mar. Cas. American Maritime Cases

Am Marit Cases American Maritime Cases

Am.Mo.Rev. American Monthly Review

Am. Neg. Ca. American Negligence Cases

Am. Neg. Cas. American Negligence Cases

Am. Neg. Cases American Negligence Cases

Am. Neg. Dig. American Negligence Digest

Am. Negl. Cas. American Negligence Cases

Am. Negl. R. American Negligence Reports

Am. Negl. Rep. American Negligence Reports

Am. Neg. Rep. American Negligence Reports

Am. Notary American Notary

A. Moor. A. Moor's Reports, in 1 Bosanquet & Puller (Eng.)

Am. Oriental Soc'y American Oriental Soceity Journal

Amos & F. Amos and Ferard on Fixtures

Amos & F. Fixt. Amos & Ferrard on Fixtures

Amos Eng. Code Amos on an Eng-lish Code

Amos Engl. Const. Amos' Primer of the English Constitution

Amos Fifty Years Amos' Fifty Years of the English Constitution

Amos Int. Law Amos on International Law

Amos Jur. Amos' Science of Jurisprudence

Amos Reg. Vice Amos on Laws for Regulation of Vice

AMP Bauernfeind, Income Taxation: Accounting Methods and Periods

Am. Pat. L. A. Bull. American Patent Law Association Bulletin

Am. Pat. L. Assoc. Bull. American Patent Law Association Bulletin

Am. Pat. L. Q. J. American Patent Law Quarterly Journal

Am. Phil. Q. American Philosophical Quarterly

Am. Pl. Ass. American Pleader's Assistant

A. M. P. L. J. Australian Mining and Petroleum Law Journal (Aus.)

Am. Pol. Q. American Politics Quarterly

Am. Pol. Science Rev. American Political Science Review

Am. Pol. Sci. J. American Political Science Journal

Am. Pol. Sci. Rev. American Political Science Review

Am. Pol. Sc. Rev. American Political Science Review

Am. Pr. American Practice

Am. Prob. American Probate Reports

Am. Prob. N. S. American Probate, New Series

Am. Prob. Rep. American Probate Reports

Am. Property American Law of Property

Am. Pro. Rep. American Probate Reports

Am. Pr. Rep. American Practice Reports (D. C.)

Am. Pr. Rep. NS American Practice Reports, New Series

Am. Q. Reg. American Quarterly Register

Am. Q. Rev. American Quarterly Review

AMR Advanced Management Research

Am. R. American Reports

Am. Rail. Cas. American Railway Cases

Am. Rail. R. American Railway Reports

Am. Railw. Cas. American Railway Cases (Smith & Bates)

Am. R. & Corp. American Railroad Corporation

Am. R. & C. Rep. American Railroad and Corporation Reporter

Am. R. Ca. American Railway Cases

Am. Rep. American Reports

Am. Reports American Reports

Am. Rev. Int'l Arb. American Review of International Arbitration, The

Am. Rev. of Hist. & Politics American Review of History and Politics

Am. Rev. on the Soviet Union American Review on the Soviet Union

Am. R. R. & C. Rep. American Railroad & Corporation Reports

Am. R. R. Ca. American Railway Cases

Am. R. R. Cas. American Railway Cases (Smith & Bates)

Am. R. Rep. American Railway Reports

Am. R. R. Rep. American Railway Reports (U. S.)

Am. Ry. Ca. American Railway Cases

Am. Ry. Cases American Railway Cases

Am. Ry. Rep. American Railway Reports

AMS Agricultural Marketing Services

Am. Sam. American Samoa

Am. Samoa American Samoa

Am. Samoa Code Ann. American Samoa Code Annotated

Am. Slav. & East Europ. Rev. American Slavic and East European Review

Am. Soc. Int. L. American Society of International Law

Am. Soc. Int'l. L. Proc. American Society of International Law Proceedings

Am. Soc. Int. L. Proc. American Society of International Law Proceedings

Am. Sociolog. Rev. American Sociological Review

Am. Soc. Rev. American Sociological Review

Am. Soc'y Int'l L. Proc. American Society of International Law Proceedings

A. M. S. , P. & S. Agricultural Marketing Service, P. & S. Docket (U. S.)

Am. S. R. American State Reports

Am. Sta. Rep. American State Reports

Am. State Papers American State Papers

Am. State Rep. American State Reports

Am. Stock Exch. Rules Rules of the American Stock Exchange

Am. Stock Ex. Guide American Stock Exchange Guide (CCH)

Am. St. P. American State Papers

Am. St. Papers American State Papers

Am. St. R. American State Reports (1886-1911)

Am. St. R. D. American Street Railway Decisions

Am. St. Rep. American State Reports

Am. St. Reports American State Reports

Am. St. Ry. Dec. American Street Railway Decisions

Am. St. Ry. Rep. American Street Railway Reports

AMT alternative minimum tax

Am. Taxp. Q. American Taxpayers' Quarterly

Am. Tax Q. American Taxpayer's Quarterly

Am. Them. American Themis

AMTI Alternative Minimum Taxable Income

Am. T.-M. Cas. American Trade Mark Cases (Cox's)

Am. Trade Mark Cas. American Trade Mark Cases (Cox)

Amtrak National Railroad Passenger Corporation

Am. Trial Law. J. American Trial Lawyers Journal

Am. Trial Law. L. J. American Trial Lawyers Law Journal

Am. Tr. M. Cas. Cox's American Trade Mark Cases

Am. U. Int. L. Rev. American University, Intramural Law Review

Am. U. Intra. L. Rev. American University Intramural Law Review

Am. U. J. Int'l L. & Pol'y American University Journal of International Law & Policy

Am. U.L. American University Law Review

Am. U. L. Rev. American University Law Review

Am. Univ. L. Rev. American University Law Review

Amuse. Amusements and Exhibitions

Am. Vets. American Law of Veterans

A. N.
- Abbott's New Cases (N. Y.)
- Appeals Notes

An. Anonymous, at end of Benloe Reports 1661

Anal. Analysis

An. B. Anonymous Reports at end of Benloe, or Bendloe (1661) (Eng.)

ANB Australian National Bibliography (National Library of Australia)

A.N.C.
- Abbott's New Cases N. Y.
- American Negligence Cases

anc. Ancient

A. N. C. A. B. Alaska Native Claims Appeals Board (in U. S. Interior Decisions)

Anc. Charters Ancient Charters, 1692

Anc. Dial. Exch. Ancient Dialogue upon the Exchequer

& and

And.
- All India Reporter, Andhra Series (1954-56)
- Anderson's Agriculture Cases (Eng.)
- Anderson's English Common Pleas Reports (1534-1605)
- Andrew's English King's Bench Reports (1737-38)
- Andrews' Reports (63-73 Conn.)
- Indian Law Reports, Andhra Series

And. Agr. Dec. Anderson's Agricultural Decisions (Sc.)

And. & Ston. J. A. Andrews & Stoney's Supreme Court of Judicature Acts

And. Ch. W. Anderson on Church Wardens

And. Com. Anderson's History of Commerce

And. Cr. Law. Andrews on Criminal Law

And. Dig. Andrews, Digest of the Opinions of the Attorneys-General

Ander. (Eng.) Anderson's Reports, English Court of Common Pleas

Anders. Anderson's Reports, English Court of Common Pleas

Anderson Anderson's Reports, English Court of Common Pleas

Anderson UCC Anderson's Uniform Commercial Code

Andh. All India Reporter, Andhra Series

Andh. Pra. All India Reporter, Andhra Pradesh Series

Andhra W. R. Andhr Weekly Reporter (India)

Andh. W. R. Andhra Weekly Reporter (India)

And. Ind. Andhra, India

And. L. & Cts. Andrews on United States Laws and Courts

And. Law Dict. Anderson's Law Dictionary

And. Man. Const. Andrews' Manual of the United States Constitution

And. Pr. Lea. Andrews' Precedents of Leases

And. Pr. Mort. Andrews' Precedents of Mortgages

And. Q. & A. Anderson's Examination Questions and Answers

Andr. Andrews, English King's

Bench Reports (95 ER)

And. Rev. Law Andrews on the Revenue Law

Andrews (Eng.) Andrews, English King's Bench Reports. (95 ER)

And. W. R. Andhra Weekly Reporter (India)

ANF Agriculture, Nutrition, and Forestry

Ang.
  • Angell & Durfee Reports (1 Rhode Island)
  • Angell's Rhode Island Reports

Ang. Adv. Enj. Angell on Adverse Enjoyment

Ang. & A. Corp. Angell & Ames on Corporations

Ang. & A. L. Rev. Anglo and American Law Review

Ang. & D. High Angell and Durfree on Highways

Ang. & Dur. Angell & Durfee's Reports (1 Rhode Island)

Ang. Ass. Angell on Assignment

Ang. B.T. Angell on Bank Tax

Ang. Car. Angell on Carriers

Ang. Corp. Angell & Ames on Corporations

Ang. High. Angell & Durfree on Highways

Ang. Highw. Angell & Durfee on Highways

Ang. Ins. Angell on Insurance

Ang. Lim. Angell on Limitation of Actions

Anglo-Soviet J. Anglo-Soviet Journal, London, England

Ang. T.W. Angell on Tide Waters

Ang. Wat. Angell on Watercourses

Anglo-Am. L.R. Anglo-American Law Review

Anglo-Am. L. Rev. Anglo-American Law Review

Ang. Tide Water Angell on Tide Waters

Ang. Water Courses Angell on Water Courses

Ani. Animals

Animal Rights L.Rep. Animal Rights Law Reporter

Ann.
  • Annaly's Hardwicke, 7-10 Geo. II, King's Bench, tempore (1733-38)
  • annotated
  • Announcements by the IRS
  • Annual
  • Cases in King's Bench, 7-10 Geo. II. tempore
  • Cunningham's Reports, King's Bench, 7-10 Geo. II. tempore
  • Queen Anne, as 8 Ann. c. 19

Annals Annals of the American Academy of Political and Social Science

Annals Air & Space Annals of Air and Space Law

Annals Air & Space L. Annals of Air and Space Law

Annals Am. Acad. Pol. & Soc. Sci. Annals of the American Academy of Political and Social Science

Annals of Air L. & Space Annals of Air Law and Space, Montreal, Canada

35

Annaly Lee's K. B. Report temp. Hardwicke. Annaly edition (1733-38) (Eng.)

Ann. Am. Acad. Annals of the American Academy of Political and Social Science

Ann.C. Annals of Congress

Ann. Cal. Codes West's Annotated California Codes

Ann. Cas.
- American & English Annotated Cases
- American Annotated Cases
- New York Annotated Cases

Ann. Cas. 1912A American Annotates Cases 1912A, Et. seq.

Ann. Code Annotated Code

Ann. Codes & St. Bellinger and Cotton's Annotated Codes and Statutes, Or.

Ann. Conf. on Intell. Prop. Annual Conference on Intellectual Property

Ann. Cong. Annals of Congress

Ann. Dig. Annual Digest and Reports of International Law Cases

Ann. Dig. I. L. C. Annual Digest and Reports of Public International Law Cases

Anne. Queen Anne (thus "I Anne," denotes the first year of the reign of Queen Anne)

Ann. Hitotsubashi Acad. The Annals of the Hitotsubashi Academy

Ann. Ind. Prop. L. Annual of Industrial Property Law

Ann. Indus. Prop. L. Annual of Industrial Property Law

Ann.Ins. Annesley on Insurance

Ann. Law Reg. Annual Law Register of the U. S.

Ann. Leg. Bibliog. Annual Legal Bibliography

Ann. Leg. Forms Mag. Annotated Legal Forms Magazine

Ann.L.Reg.U.S. Annual Law Register of the United States

Ann. L. Rep. Annotated Law Reporter (1932-35) (India)

Ann. Notre Dame Est. Plan. Inst. Annual Notre Dame Estate Planning Institute

Anno. Annotated

Anno. Cases American Annotated Cases

Annot. Code of Professional Responsibility American Bar Foundation Annotated Code of Professional Responsibility.

Ann. Pr. Annual Practice

Ann. Proc. Nat. Asso. R. Coms. Annual Proceedings of the National Association of Railway Commissions

Ann. Reg. Annual Register, London

Ann. Reg. N. S. Annual Register, New Series

Ann. Rep. Annual Report

Ann. Rep. & Op. Ind. Att'y. Gen. Annual Report and Official Opinions of the Attorney General of Indiana

Ann. Rep. & Op. Md. Att'y. Gen. Annual Report and Official Opinions of the Attorney General of Maryland

Ann. Rep. Fla. Att'y. Gen. Annual Report of the Attorney General, State of Florida

Ann. Rep. S. C. Att'y. Gen. Annual Report of the Attorney General for the State of South Carolina to the General Assembly

Ann. Rev. Banking L. Annual Review of Banking Law

Ann. Rev. Banking Law Annual Review of Banking Law

Ann.Rev. Int'l Aff. Annual Review of International Affairs

Ann. St. Annotated Statutes

Ann. St. Ind. T. Annotated Statutes of Indian Territory

Ann. Surv. Afr. L. Annual Survey of African Law

Ann. Surv. Am. Annual Survey of American Law

Ann. Surv. Am. L. Annual Survey of American Law

Ann. Surv. Austl. L. Annual Survey of Australian Law

Ann. Surv. Banking L. Annual Survey of Banking Law

Ann. Surv. Colo. L. Annual Survey of Colorado Law

Ann. Surv. Comm. L. Annual Survey of Commonwealth Law

Ann. Surv. Commonw. L.
- Annual Survey of Commonwealth Law
- Annual Survey of Commonwealth Law (Ceased pub. 1977)

Ann. Survey Annual Survey of Massachusetts Law

Ann. Survey Am. L. Annual Survey of American Law

Ann. Surv. Ind. L. Annual Survey of Indian Law

Ann. Surv. Mass. L. Annual Survey of Massachusetts Law

Ann. Surv. S. Afr. L. Annual Survey of South African Law

Ann. Surv. S. A. L. Annual Survey of South African Law

Ann. Tax Cas. Annotated Tax Cases (English)

Annual L. Rev. Western Australian Annual Law Review, Nedlands, Australia

Annual R. Louisiana Annual Reports (La.)

Annui. Annuities

Annul. Annulment of Marriage

Ann. Unidroit L'Unification du droit Annuaire/ Unification of Law Yearbook

Annu. Surv. of Afr. L. Annual Survey of African Law

Annu. Surv. of Amer. L. Annual Survey of American Law

Annu. Surv. of Indian L. Annual Survey of Indian Law. New Delhi, India

Annu. Surv. of South Afr. L. Annual Survey of South African Law. Cape Town, South Africa

anon. anonymous

A. N. R.
- American Negligence Reports, Current Series
- The National Economic and Legislative Report (CCH)

anr. another

ANRPC Association of Natural Rubber Producing Countries

Ans. Con. Anson on Contracts

ANSI　American National Standards Institute

Anson, Cont.　Anson on Contracts

Anst.　Anstruther's English Exchequer Reports (145 ER)

Anst. Eng. Law.　Anstey's Guide to the English Law and Constitution

Anst. Pl. Gui.　Anstey's Pleader's Guide

Anstr.　Anstruther's English Exchequer Reports (145 ER)

Anstr. (Eng)　Anstruther's English Exchequer Reports (145 ER)

Ant. & Barb.　Antigua and Barboda

Anth.　Anthon's New York Nisi Prius Reports

Anth. Black.　Anthon's Abridgment of Blackstone

Anth. L.S.　Anthon's Law Student

Anth. N. P.　Anthon's Nisi Prius (N. Y.)

Anth. N. P. R.　Anthon's Nisi Prius Reports (N. Y.)

Anthon NP (N. Y.)　Anthon's New York Nisi Prius Reports

Anthon Rep.　Anthon's Nisi Prius Reports (N. Y.)

Anthon's N. P.　Anthon's Nisi Prius Reports (N. Y.)

Anthon's N. P. (2d ed.)　Anthon's Nisi Prius Reports

Anthon's Rep.　Anthon's Nisi Prius Reports (First Edition) (N. Y.)

Anth. Prec.　Anthon's New Precedents of Declarations

Anth. R.R. Cons.　Anthony on Consolidation of Railroad Companies

Anth. Shep.　Anthony's edition of Shephard's Touchstone

Anth. St.　Anthon's Study of Law

Antitrust & Trade Reg. Rep. (BNA)　Antitrust & Trade Regulation Report (BNA)

Antitrust Bull.
- Antitrust Bulletin
- The Antitrust Bulletin

Antitrust L. & Econ. Rev.　Antitrust Law and Economics Review

Antitrust L. J.　Antitrust Law Journal

Antitrust L. Sym.　Antitrust Law Symposium

Antitrust Newsl.　Antitrust Newsletter

A. N. V.　Australian and New Zealand Environmental Report (CCH) (Aus.)

An. W. R.　Andhra Weekly Reporter (India)

A.N.Z.I.T.R.　Australian and New Zealand Income Tax Reports

ANZUS　ANZUS Council; treaty signed by Australia, New Zealand, and the United States.

A. O.
- Administrative orders or directives
- Administrative order
- Army Order

AOA　Administration of Aging

A. O. A.　Accident Offices' Association

A. O. C. Newsl.　Administrative Office of the Courts Newsletter

AOD   action on decision

AOR   Asset depreciation range

AOS   Asset depreciation system

A. P.
- Annual Practice (Eng.)

Ap.   New York Supreme Court Appellate Division Reports

Ap. 2d   New York Appellate Division Reports, Second Series

ap.   apud; in the works of (an author) (Lat.)

APA   Administrative Procedure Act   Assistance Payments Administration

A. P. A.   Additional personal allowance

APAIS   Australian Public Affairs Information Service (National Library of Austrlia)

Apart   Apartment

A. P. B.   Ashurst's Paper Books, in Lincoln's Inn Library

A. P. B. Op.   Accounting Principles Board Opinions

Ap. Bre.   Appendix to Breese's Reports (Illinois)

APC
- African Peanut (Groundnut) Council
- Alien Property Custodian (U. S.)

A. P. C. N.   Anno post Christum natum, the year after the birth of Christ

A. P. D.   Alien Property Division (Justice Dept.) (U. S.)

APEX   Association of Professional, Executive, Clerical and Computer Staff

APHIS   Animal and Plant Health

Inspection Service

Ap. Just.   Apud Justinianum (or Justinian's Institutes)

Ap. Justin.   Apud Justinianum; In Justinian's Institutes

APLA   American Patent Law Association

APLA Bull.   Bulletin of the American Patent Law Association

APLA Q.   American Patent Law Association Quarterly

APLA Q. J.
- American Patent Law Association Quarterly Journal
- APLA Quarterly Journal

A. P. L. Cas.   Archbold's Poor Law Cases 1842-58

APM   Australian Personnel Management (CCH)

App.
- Appeal Cases
- appellant
- appendix
- Appleton's Reports (19, 20 Maine) Ohio Appellate Reports
- Cour d'Appel, Hof van Beroep (District Court of Appeal)
- Illinois Appellate Court Reports (Ill.)
- Ohio Appellate Reports (Ohio)
- Texas Court of Appeals Reports (Tex.)

APP   Army Procurement Procedures

app. allowed   appeal allowed

App. Bd. O. C. S.   Office of Contract Settlement, Appeal Board Decisions

App. Ca.   Buchanan, Reports of

39

Courts of Appeal, Cape Colony (S. Africa)

App. Cas.
- Appeal cases, District of Columbia
- Appeal Cases, District of Columbia V. 1-74 (D. C.)
- Appeal Cases, English Law Reports (1875-90)
- Appeal cases in the United States
- Appeal cases of the different states
- Law Reports, Appeal Cases (Eng.)

App. Cas.2d Law Reports Appeal Cases (Eng.) Second Series

App. Cas. Beng. Sevestre & Marshall's Bengal Reports

App. Cas. (D. C.) Appeal Cases, District of Columbia V. 1-74 (D. C.)

App. C. C. Texas Civil Cases (Tex.)

App. C. C. (White & W.) Texas Civil Cases (Tex.)

App. C. C. (Willson) Texas Civil Cases (Tex.)

App. Civ. Cases Texas Civil Cases (Tex.)

App. Court Ad. Rev. Appellate Court Administration Review

App Ct Appellate Court

App. Ct. Admin. Rev. Appellate Court Administrative Review

App. Ct. Rep.
- Appeal Court Reports, New Zealand
- Bradwell's Illinois Appeal Court Reports

App. D. South Africa Law Reports, Appellate Division

Appd. Approved

App. D. C. Appeals Cases, District of Columbia

app. den. appeal denied

App. Dep't. Appellate Department

app. dism. appeal dismissed

App. Div.
- Appellate Division
- New York Supreme Court, Appellate Division
- New York Supreme Court, Appellate Division Reports

App. Div. 2d New York Supreme Court, Appellate Division Reports, Second Series

App. Div. (NY) New York Supreme Court, Appellate Division Reports

App. Div. N. Y. Sup. Ct. New York Supreme Court Appellate Division Reports (N. Y.)

App. Div. R. New York Supreme Court Appellate Division Reports (N. Y.)

App. Div. Rep. Massachusetts Appellate Division Reports

Appear. Appearance

Append. Appendix

App.Ev. Appleton's Rules of Evidence

App. Exam. Appeal(s) Examiner

App. Fish. Com. Appeals from Fisheries Commission (1861-93) (Ir.)

App. Jur. Act 1876 Appellate Jurisdiction Act, 1876, 39 & 40 Vict., C. 59

Appl. Applicable

appl. applied

Appleton. Appleton's Reports (vols. 19, 20 Maine)

App. N.Z. Appeal Reports, New Zealand

App. N.Z.2d Appeal Reports, New Zealand, Second Series

appr. approved in, or approving

App. Ref. Appeal(s) Referee

App. Rep. Ontario Appeal Reports (1876-1900) (Can.)

App. Rep. Ont. Ontario Appeal Reports

App. R. N.Z. Appeal Reports, New Zealand

Approp. Appropriation(s)

apps. appendixes

App. T. Supreme Court Appellate Term

App. Tax Serv. Appeals Relating to Tax on Servants 1781 (Eng.)

apptd. appointed

App. Term Supreme Court Appellate Term

App. Trib. (also AT) Appeal Tribunal

Appx. appendix

Appx. Bre. Appendix to Breese's Reports, Illinois

A. P. R.
- Atlantic Provinces Reports (Can.)
- Atlantic Provinces Reports, 1977-

Apr. April

A. P. R. C. Anno post Roman conditam, year after the foundation of

Rome

A. P. S. The Acts of the Parliaments of Scotland (1124-1707, 1814-75)

A. P. S. C. Alabama Public Service Commission Decisions

A. P. S. R. American Political Science Review

A. P. T. D. Aid to the Permanently and Totally Disabled

A. P. X. Australian Tax Planning Report (CCH) (Aus.)

AQ Australian Quarterly (Australian Institute of Political Science)

Ar. Arrête

AR Additional requirements

A. R.
- Alberta Reports (Can.)
- Alberta Reports, 1977-
- American Reports
- Anno Regni. In the Year of the reign
- Annual Register
- Annual Return
- Appeal Reports, Upper Canada (1846-66)
- Argus Reports (Aus.)
- Army Regulations
- Atlantic Reporter
- Industrial Arbitration Reports (New South Wales)
- Ontario Appeal Reports

ARA
- Agricultural Research Aministration (U. S.)
- Area Redevelopment Administration

A. R. A. American Railway Association

41

Arabin. Decision of Sergeant Arabin

A. R. A. M. C. O. Arabian American Oil Company

ARAP Analytical Review: A Guide to Analytical Procedures

A. R. (Austrl.) Industrial Arbitration Reports (New South Wales)

A. R. B.
- Accounting Research Board Opinion
- Air Registration Board
- Labor Arbitration Awards (CCH)

Arb.
- Arbitration
- Arbitrator(s)
- Labor Arbitration Awards (CCH)

Arb. Nat'l Arbitration Materials

ARBA
- American Revolution Bicentennial Administration
- Arkansas Bar Association

Arb. & A. Arbitration and Award

Arbitr. Arbitration

Arbitration Arbitration Journal of the Institute of Arbitrators, England

Arbitration J. The Arbitration Journal

Arb. J. Arbitration Journal

Arb. J. (N. S.) Arbitration Journal, New Series

Arb. J. of the Inst. of Arbitrators Arbitration Journal of the Institute of Arbitrators

Arb. J. (O. S.) Arbitration Journal, Old Series

Arb. L. Dig. Arbitration Law; A Digest of Court Decisions

Arb. Mat'l Arbitration Materials

Arb. Schools Arbitration in the Schools

Arbuth. Arbuthnot's Select Criminal Cases, (Madras)

A. R. C.
- American Railway Cases
- American Red Cross
- American Ruling Cases

Arch.
- Court of Arches (Eng.)
- Architects

Arch. Arb. Archbold's Law of Arbitration and Award

Arch. Baines' Acts Archbold on Baines' Acts on Criminal Justice

Arch. Bank. Archbold on Bankruptcy (1825-56)

Archb. Civil Pl. Archbold's Civil Pleading

Archb. Crim. Pl. Archbold's Criminal Pleading

Archb. Cr. Law Archbold's Pleading and Evidence in Criminal Cases

Archb. Cr. Prac. & Pl. Archbold's Pleading and Evidence in Criminal Cases

Arch B.L. Archbold's Bankrupt Law

Arch. Black. Archbold's Edition of Blackstone's Commentaries

Archb. Landl. & Ten. Archbold's Landlord and Tenant

Archb. New Pr. Archbold's New Practice

Archb. N. P. Archbold's Nisi Prius

Law

Archb. N. Prac. Archbold's New Practice

Archb. Pr. Archbold's Practice

Archb. Pr. K. B. Archbold's Practice King's Bench

Arch. Civ. Pl. Archbold's Civil Pleading and Evidence

Arch. C. L. Pr. Archbold's New Common Law Practice

Arch. C. P. Archbold's Practice in the Common Pleas

Arch. Cr. Archbold's Pleading and Evidence in Criminal Cases (1822-959)

Arch. Cr. L. Archbold's Criminal Law

Arch. Cr. Pl. Archbold's Criminal Pleading

Arch. Cr. Pl. (or Archb. Crim. Pl.) Archbold's Criminal Pleading

Arch. Cr. Prac. Archbold's Criminal Practice

Arch. Cr. Proc. Archbold's Criminal Procedure

Arch. C. S. Pr. Archibald, Country Solicitor's Practice in the Queen's Bench (1881)

Archer Archer's Reports (2 Florida)

Archer & H. Archer & Hogue Reports (vol. 2 Florida)

Archer & Hogue Archer & Hogue's Reports (vol. 2 Florida)

Arch. Forms Archbold, Indictments, with Forms (1916)

Arch. Forms Ind. Archbold's Forms of Indictment

Architects' L. R. Architects' Law Reports, 4 vols. 1904-09

Arch. J. C. Pr. Archibald on Practice of Judges' Chambers

Arch. J. P. Archbold, Justice of the Peace. 7ed. (1859)

Arch. K. B. Forms Archbold's Forms in King's Bench and Common Pleas

Arch. K. B. Pr. Archbold's King's Bench Practice

Arch. L. & T. Archbold, Law of Landlord and Tenant. 3ed (1864)

Arch. L. R. Architects Law Reports (1904-09) (Eng.)

Arch. Lun. Archbold, Lunacy Laws. 5ed. (1915)

Arch. Mun. Corp. Archbold, Municipal Corporations Act (1836)

Arch. N. P. Archbold's Law of Nisi Prius

Arch. Part. Archbold's Law of Partnership

Arch. P. C. Archbold's Pleas of the Crown

Arch. P. Ch. Archbold's Practice by Chitty

Arch. P. C. P. Archbold, Practice of the Court of Common Pleas (1829)

Arch. P. K. B. Archbold's Practice in the King's Bench

Arch. P. L. Archbold's Poor Law (1840-1930)

Arch. P. L. C. Archbold, Poor Law Cases (1842-58)

Arch. P. L. Cas. Archbold's Abridgment of Poor Law Cases (1842-58)

Arch. Pl. Cas. Archbold's Abridgment of Poor Law Cases

Arch.P.L. Archbold's New Practice in Poor Law Removals and Appeals

Arch. Pr. Ch. Archbold's Practice by Cholty

Arch. Pr. C.P. Archbold's Practice, Common Pleas

Arch. Pr. J.C. Archbold's Practice in Judges Chambers

Arch. Pr. Q. S. Archbold's Practice in Quarter Sessions

Arch. Q.B. Archbold's Practice in the Queen's Bench

Arch. Sum. Archbold's Summary of Laws of England

ARD Application for Review Decisions

A. Rep.
- American Reports
- Atlantic Reporter (Commonly cited Atl. or A.)

Arg.
- Argentina
- Arguendo in arguing (Lat.)

Arg. Bilis Ex. Argles' French Law of Bills of Exchange

Argen. Argentina

Arg. Fr. Merc. Law. Argles (Napoleon), Treatise Upon French Mercantile Law, etc.

Arg. L. R. Argus Law Reports (Aus.)

Arg. Mo. Moore's King's Bench Reports (Arguments of Moore) (Eng.)

Arg. Rep. Reports printed in Melbourne Argus, Australia

Argus L.R. Argus Law Reports

Argus L. Rep. Argus Law Reports

Argus (Newspr)(Vic.) Argus Reports (Newspaper) (Aus.)

Arist. Aristotle

Ariz.
- Arizona
- Arizona Reports
- Arizona Supreme Court Reports

Ariz. Admin. Comp. Arizona Official Compilation of Administrative Rules and Regulations

Ariz. Admin. Comp. R. Arizona Official Compilation of Administrative Rules and Regulations

Ariz. Admin. Dig. Arizona Administrative Digest

Ariz. App. Arizona Appeals Reports

Ariz. Att'y Arizona Attorney

Ariz. B. J. Arizona Bar Journal

Ariz. C. C. Arizona Corporation Commission

Ariz. Const. Arizona Constitution

Ariz. J. Int'l & Comp. L. Arizona Journal of International and Comparative Law

Ariz. Law Arizona Lawyer

Ariz. Legis. Serv. Arizona Legislative Service (West)

Ariz. L. Rev. Arizona Law Review

Arizona J. Int'l & Comp. L. Arizona Journal of International and Comparative Law

Arizona L. Rev. Arizona Law Review

Arizona State L. J. Arizona State Law Journal

Ariz. R. C. Arizona Railway Commission

Ariz. Rev. Stat. Arizona Revised Statutes

Ariz. Rev. Stat. Ann. Arizona Revised Statutes Annotated

Ariz. Rev. State Arizona Revised Statutes

Ariz. Sess. Laws Arizona Session Laws

Ariz. State L.J. Arizona State Law Journal

Ariz. St. L. F. Arizona State Law Forum

Ariz. St. L. J. Arizona State Law Journal

Ar. J. Arbitration Journal

Ark.
- Arkansas
- Arkansas Reports
- Arkansas Supreme Court Reports
- Arkley's Justiciary Reports (1846-48) (Sc.)

Ark. Acts General Acts of Arkansas

Ark. Admin. Reg. Arkansas Register

Arkansas L. Rev. Arkansas Law Review

Ark. App. Arkansas Appeals Reports

Ark. App. Rep. Arkansas Appellate Reports

Ark. B. A.
- Arkansas Bar Association
- Arkansas Bar Association, Proceedings

Ark. C. C. Arkansas Corporation Commission Report

ARKCLE Arkansas Institute for Continuing Legal Education

Ark. Const. Arkansas Constitution

Ark. Just. Arkley's Justiciary Reports (Sc.)

Arkl. Arkley's Justiciary Reports, (Sc.)

Ark. L. Notes Arkansas Law Notes

Ark. Law. Arkansas Lawyer

Ark. Law. Q. Arkansas Lawyer Quarterly

Arkley Arkley's Justiciary Reports (Sc.)

Ark. L.J. Arkansas Law Journal

Ark. L. Rev. Arkansas Law Review

Ark. P. U. Arkansas Department of Public Utilities Report

Ark. R. Arkansas Reports (Ark.)

Ark. R. C. Arkansas Railroad Commission

Ark. Reg. Arkansas Register

Ark. Rep. Arkansas Reports (Ark.)

Ark's Arkansas Reports (Ark.)

Ark. Stat. Ann. Arkansas Statutes Annotated

Ark. Stats. Arkansas Statutes

ARm O'Reilly, Administrative Rulemaking

A. R. M.
- Internal Revenue Bureau Committee on Appeals & Review, Memorandum (U. S.)
- Appeals & Review Memorandum Committee (I.R.Bull.)

Arm. & O. Armstrong, Macartney and Ogle's Nisi Prius Reports

(1840-42) (Ir.)

Arm. Mac. & Og. Armstrong, Macartney and Ogle's Nisi Prius Reports (1840-42) (Ir.)

Arm. M. & O. Armstrong, Macartney and Ogle's Reports

Armour Manitoba Queen's Bench tempore Wood, by Armour

Arms. Br. P. Cas. Armstrong's Breach of Privilege Cases, New York

Arms. Con. El. Armstrong Contested Election Cases (N. Y.)

Arms. Con. Elec. Armstrong's New York Contested Elections

Arms. Elect. Cas. Armstrong's Cases of Contested Elections, New York

Arms. Mac. & Og. Armstrong, Macartney, & Ogle's Irish Nisi Prius Reports

Arms. M. & O. Armstrong, Macartney & Ogle's Irish Nisi Prius Reports

Arms. Tr. Armstrong's Limerick Trials, (Ir.)

Armstrong M & O (Ir) Armstrong, Macartney, & Ogle's Irish Nisi Prius Reports

Army Law. Army Lawyer

Army Lawy. Army Lawyer

Arn.
- Arnold's English Common Pleas Reports (1838-39)
- Arnot's Criminal Trials (1536-1784) (Sc.)
- Arnould on Marine Insurance

Arn. & H. Arnold & Hodges Queen's Bench Reports (1840-41)

(Eng.)

Arn. & H. B. C. Arnold & Hodges' Bail Court Reports (Eng.)

Arn. & Hod. Arnold and Hodges' English Queen's Bench Reports

Arn. & Hod. B. C. Arnold & Hodges' English Bail Court Reports

Arn. & Hod. P. C. Arnold & Hodges' Practice Cases (Eng.)

Arn. & Hod. Pr. Cas. Arnold & Hodges' Practice Cases, English

Arn. El. Cas. Arnold's Election Cases (Eng.)

Arn. ins. Arnould on Marine Insurance

Arn. Mun. Cor. Arnold's Municipal Corporations

Arnold Arnold's Common Pleas Reports (Eng.)

Arnold & H Arnold & Hodges Queen's Report (Eng.)

Arnot Cr. C. Arnot's Criminal Cases, Scotland. (1536-1784)

Arn. Pub. M. Arnold, Public Meetings and Political Societies. (1833)

Arn. Pub. Meet. Arnold on the Law of Public Meetings

A.R.(N.S.W.) Industrial Arbitration Reports (New South Wales)

A.R.O. Army Routine Order

A.R.(Ont.) Ontario Appeal Reports

A.R.R.
- American Railway Reports
- Appeals & Review Recommendation (I.R.Bull.)
- Internal Revenue Bureau Committee on Appeals & Review, Recommendation (U.S.)

Arrang. Arrangement

Ar. Rep. Argus Reports, Victoria

A.R.R.R. American Railway Reports

A.R.S.
- Advanced Record System
- Agricultural Research Service
- Anno Regni Regis/ Reginae (in the year of the King's/Queen's reign) (Lat.)
- Anno Reparatae Salutis (Lat.) in the year of redemption
- Arizona Revised Statutes

Art. Article

Art & L. Art and the Law

Art & Law Art and the Law

Artic. Cl. Articled Clerk (1867-68)

Artic. Cl. Deb. Articled Clerk and Debater (1866)

Artic. Cleri Articuli Cleri (Articles of the Clergy)

Artic. Cl. J. Exam. Articled Clerks' Journal and Examiner (1879-81)

Artic. sup. Chart. Articuli super Chartas (Articles upon the charters)

arts. articles

Arun. Mines Arundell on the law of Mines

A.R.V.R.22. Anno Regni Victoriae Regina Vicesimo Secundo

AS or A/S or A/s. Account sales; also after sight, at sight

AS Massachusetts Appellate Court Advance Sheets

A.S.
- Act of Sederunt, Scotland
- American Samoa
- Anglo Saxon
- Armed Services

ASA
- American Standards Association
- Massachusetts Appellate Court Advance Sheets

ASAC American Samoa Administrative Code

ASAL Annual Survey of American Law

A.S.A.L. Annual Survey of African Law.

A.S.A. Newsl. Association for the Study of Abortion Newsletter

A.S.A.R. All South Africa Law Reports

ASB Air Safety Board (U.S.)

ASBCA U.S. Armed Services Board of Contract Appeals Decisions A.S.C. Australian Consumer Sales and Credit Law Reporter (or Cases) (CCH) (Aus.)

A.S.C.A.P. Cop.L.Symp. Copyright Law Symposium (American Society of Composers, Authors and Publishers)

A.S.C.A.P. Copyright L.Symp. Copyright Law Symposium (American Society of Composers, Authors and Publishers)

Ascap Sympos. Copyright Law symposium

A.S.C.L. Annual Survey of Commonwealth Law

A. S. Code American Samoa Code

ASCS Agricultural Stabilization and Conservation Service

ASEAN Association of Southeast

Asian Nations

A.S.E.L. Annual Survey of English Law

Ash. Ashmead Pennsylvania Reports, 1808-1841

ASHA American Society of Hospital Attorneys

Ashb. Ashburner, Principles of Equity. 2ed. (1933)

Ashe Ashe's Tables to the Year Books, Coke's Reports, or Dyer's Reports

Ashm. Ashmead Pennsylvania Reports (1808-41)

Ashmead Ashmead's Reports (Pa.)

Ashmead (Pa.) Ashmead's Reports (Pa.)

Ashmead's Penn. Rep. Ashmead's Reports (Pa.)

Ashm. (Pa.) Ashmead Pennsylvania Reports, 1808-1841

Ashton. Ashton's Reports, vols. 9-12 Opinions of the United States Attorneys General

Ashurst
- Ashurst's manuscript Reports, printed in vol. 2, Chitty
- Ashurst's Paper Books, Lincoln's Inn Library

Ashurst MS.
- Ashurst's Manuscript Reports, printed in vol. 2, Chitty
- Ashurst's Paper Books, Lincoln's Inn Library

Asian & Afr. Stud. Asian and African Studies

Asian Comp. L. Rev. Asian Compara-tive Law Review

Asian Pac. Comm. Law. Asian Pacific Commercial Lawyer

Asian Surv. Asian Survey

Asia Q. Asia Quarterly

Asiatic Soc. of Japan Asiatic Society of Japan, Transactions, Tokyo

ASIL
- American Society of International Law
- Annual Survey of Indian Law

ASIL Proc. Proceedings of the American Society of International Law

ASILS Association of Student International Law Societies

ASILS Intl. L.J., ASILS Int'l L.J. ASILS International Law Journal

A.S.L. Advanced Student in Law

A.S.L.C. Australian Securities Law Cases

ASLH American Society for Legal History

A.S.L.I.B. Association of Special Libraries and Information Bureaux

A.S.L.O. Associated Scottish Life Offices

Asm. All India Reporter, Assam Series.

Aso. See Asso.

Asp. aspects

A.S.P. Australian Superannuation Practice (CCH) (Aus.)

Asp. Aspinall's Maritime Cases (1871-1940) (Eng.)

ASPAC Asian and Pacific Council

Asp. Cas. Aspinall's Maritime Cases (1871-1940) (Eng.)

Aspin. Aspinall's Maritime Cases (1871-1940) (Eng.)

Asp. Mar. Law Cas. Aspinall's Maritime Law Cases (1871-1940) (Eng.)

Asp. Mar. L. Cas.(Eng.) Aspinall's Maritime Law Cases (1871-1940) (Eng.)

Asp. M.C. Aspinall's Maritime Cases (1871-1940) (Eng.)

Asp. M.C.L. Aspinall's Maritime Cases (1870-1940)

Asp. M.L.C. Aspinall's Maritime Law Cases (1871-1940) (Eng.)

ASPR Armed Services Procurement Regulation

Asp. Rep. Aspinall's Maritime Cases (1870-1940)

A.S.R.
- American State Reports
- Australian Securities Law Reporter (CCH) (Aus.)

ASRB Armed Services Renegotiation Board (U.S.)

Ass. Liber Assissarum or Pleas of the Crown (Book of Assizes), Pt. 5 of Year Books (1327-77)

A.S.S.A.L. Annual Survey of South African Law.

Assam All India Reporter, Assam Series

Assd. Assigned

Assem. Assembly, State Legislature

Assign. Assignments

Assign. for Crs. Assignments for Benefits of Creditors

Assist. Assistance, Writ of

Ass. Jerus. Assizes of Jerusalem

Asslt. & B. Assault and Battery

Assn. Association

Ass'n Trial Law. Am. Newsl. Association of Trial Lawyers of America Newsletter

Asso.
- Association
- Associations and Clubs

Asso & Man. Asso & Manuel's Institutes of Spanish Civil Law

assoc.
- associate
- association
- associations and clubs

Ass. Reg. Da. Assia Regis David

asst. assistant

Ass. Tax. Assessed Taxes (Decisions of Judges)

Ast. Ent. Aston's Entries, 1673

A.S.T.M.S. Association of Scientific, Technical and Managerial Staffs

ASV Eck, Asset Valuation

AT Appeal Tribunal

A.T.
- Alcohol & Tobacco Tax. Div., Internal Revenue Bureau (U.S.)
- Alcohol Tax Unit (I.R. Bulletin)

At. Atlantic Reporter

AT & T American Telephone and Telegraph Co.

A.T. & T. Co. Com. L. American Telephone and Telegraph Co. Commission Leaflets

A.T. & T. Co. T.C. American Telephone and Telegraph Co. Commission Telephone Cases

A.T.C.
- Annotated Tax Cases (Eng.)
- Assessed Tax Case
- Australian Tax Cases (CCH) (Aus.)

Atch. Atchison, English Navigation and Trade Reports

Atch. E.C. Atcheson's Election Cases. (Eng.)

A.T.D.
- Accession Treaty and Decision concerning the ECSC
- Australian Tax Decisions

Ateneo L.J. Ateneo Law Journal

A.T.F.C.B. Alcohol Tobacco & Firearms Cumulative Bulletin

A.T.G. Australian Income Tax Guide (CCH)

Ath. State Athletic Commission

Ath. Mar. Set. Atherley on Marriage Settlements

Atk.
- Atkinson's Quarter Sessions Records, Yorkshire (Eng.)
- Atkyns' English Chancery Reports (1736-55)

Atk. Ch. Pr. Atkinson's Chancery Practice

Atk. Con. Atkinson on Conveyancing

Atkinson Atkinson's Law of Solicitors' Liens. 1905

Atk. P.T. Atkyn's Parliamentary Tracts

Atk Sher. Atkinson on Sheriffs

Atk. Titles Atkinson on Marketable Titles

Atl.
- Atlantic

- Atlantic Reporter

Atl.2d Atlantic Reporter, Second Series (West)

ATLA Association of Trial Lawyers of America

A.T.L.A.J. American Trial Lawyers Association Journal

ATLA L.J. Journal of the Association of Trial Lawyers of America

Atlan. Atlantic Monthly

Atl. Comm. Q. Atlantic Community Quarterly

A.T.L.J. American Trial Lawyers Association Journal

Atl. Mo. Atlantic Monthly

Atl.P.R. Atlantic Province Reports

Atl.Prov. Atlantic Provinces Reports (Canada)

Atl. R. Atlantic Reporter

Atl. Rep. Atlantic Reporter

Atl. Repr. Atlantic Reporter

Atom. Atomic

Atom Ener L J Atomic Energy Law Journal

Atom. Energy L.J. Atomic Energy Law Journal

Atom. En. L. Rep. CCH. Atomic Energy Law Reporter (CCH)

Atomic E. Atomic Energy

Atomic Energy L.J. Atomic Energy Law Journal

Atomic Eng. L.J. Atomic Energy Law Journal

A.T.P.R. Australian Trade Practices Reports (CCH) (Aus.)

A.T.R. Australian Tax Reports (Butterworths) (Aus.)

At.Rep. Atlantic Reporter

A.T. Rev. Australian Tax Review (Law Book Co.)

A. Trial Law. Am. L.J. Association of Trial Lawyers of America Law Journal

A.T.R.R. Antitrust & Trade Regulation Reporter (BNA)

Ats. At suit of

ATSDR Agency for Toxic Substances and Disease Registry

AtSN Attorney Sanctions Newsletters

Att. Attorney

Attach. Attachment

Att. Gen., A.G. Attorney-General

atty.
- attorney[s]
- att'y[s]

Atty. Gen. Attorney General

Att'y Gen. Attorney General

Att'y Gen. Ann. Rep. Attorney General's Annual Report

Att'y Gen. L.J. Attorney General's Law Journal

Atty. Gen. Op. Attorney General's Opinions

Atty. Gen. Op. N.Y. Attorney-General's Opinions, New York

Att'y. Gen. Rep. United States Attorneys General's Reports

Attys. Attorneys

Atw. Atwater's Reports (vol. 1 Minnesota)

Atwater. Atwater's Reports, vol. 1 Minnesota

A.T.X. Australian Sales Tax Guide (CCH)

Auch. Auchinleck's Manuscript Cases, Scotch Court of Session

Auckland U. L. Rev. Auckland University Law Review (N.Z.)

Auckland Univ. L. Rev. Auckland University Law Review, Dunedin, New Zealand

Auck. U. L. Rev. Auckland University Law Review

Auct. Auction

Auct. Reg. & L. Chron. Auction Register & Law Chronicle

Aud. Audit; Auditor

Aud.-Gen. Auditor-General

Aud. Q. Audita Querela

Aug. August

Aul. Gell. Noct. Att. Auli Gellii Noctes Atticae

AULR American University Review

A.U.L.R. American University Law Review

Ault. Court Rolls of Ramsey Abbey (1928) (Eng.)

Aus. Austria(n)

Aus. Quart. Australian Quarterly

Aust.
- Austin's English County Court Cases (1867-69)
- Australia
- Austria

Aust. & N.Z. J. Criminol.

Aust Acc, Aust Acctnt Australian Accountant (Journal of the Australian Society of Accountants)

Aust Accountant Australian Accountant

51

Aust. & N.Z. J. Crim. Australian and New Zealand Journal of Criminology, Melbourne, Australia

Aust. Argus L. Rep. Australian Argus Law Reports

Aust Banker The Australian Banker

Aust. Bankr. Cas. Australian Bankruptcy Cases

Aust. Bar Gaz. Australian Bar Gazette (1963-70)

Aust. Bus. L. Rev. Australian Business Law Review, Sydney, Australia

Aust. C. L. Rev. Australian Current Law Review

Aust. Conv. Sol. J. Australian Conveyancer and Solicitors' Journal (1948-59)

Aust. Curr. L. Rev. Australian Current Law Review

Aust. Digest Australian Digest (LBC)

Aust Director Australian Director (Institute of Directors in Australia)

Austin Austin's Reports (Ceylon)

Austin C.C. Austin's English County Court Reports

Austin (Ceylon). Austin's Ceylon Reports

Aust. Ind. L.R. Australian Industrial Law Review

Aust. J. Pub. Admin. Australian Journal of Public Administration

Aust. Jr.
- Austin's Lectures on Jurisprudence
- Australian Jurist

Aust. Jur.
- Austins Lectures on Jurisprudence
- Australian Jurist
- Austin's Jurisprudence

Aust. Jur. Abr. Austin's Lectures on Jurisprudence, abridged

Aust. Jr. R. Australian Jurist Reports (1870-74)

Aust. Jur. Rep. Australian Jurist Reports (1870-74)

Aust. K.A. Austin's Kandran Appeals (Ceylon)

Austl. Australia(n)

Austl. Acts Acts of the Parliaments of the Commonwealth of Australia

Austl. Acts P. Acts of the Australian Parliament

Austl. A.D. Australian Annual Digest

Austl. & N.Z. J. Crim. Australian and New Zealand Journal of Criminology

Austl. & N.Z. J. Criminology Australian and New Zealand Journal of Criminology

Austl. Argus L.R. Australian Argus Law Reports

Aust.Law. Australian Lawyer

Aust. Law News Australian Law News

Aust. Lawyer Australian Lawyer (Butterworths) (Aus.)

Austl. B. Rev. Australian Bar Review

Austl. Bankr. Cas. Australian Bankruptcy Cases

Austl. Bus. L. Rev. Australian Business Law Review

Austl. C. Acts Commonwealth Acts (Aus-tralia)

Austl.Cap.Terr. Laws Laws of the Australian Capital Territory

Austl. Cap. Terr. Ord. Ordi-nances of the Australian Capital Territory

Austl. Cap. Terr. Subs. Leg. Sub-sidiary Legislation of the Austra-lian Capital Territory

Austl. Com. J. Australian Com-mercial Journal

Austl. Convey. & Sol. J. Austra-lian Conveyancer and Solicitors Journal

Austl. Current L. Rev. Austra-lian Current Law Review

Austl. D. The Australian Digest

Austl. D.2d The Australian Di-gest, Second Edition

Aust. L.J. Australian Law Journal

Austl. J. Comp. L. Australian Journal of Corporate Law

Austl. J. Fam. L. Australian Jour-nal of Family Law

Austl. J. For. Sci. Australian Journal of Forensic Sciences

Austl. J. L. Soc'y Australian Jour-nal of Law and Society

Austl. J. Lab. L. Australian Jour-nal of Labour Law

Austl. Jr. Australian Jurist

Aust. L.J. Rep. Australian Law Journal Reports

Austl. Jur. R. Australian Jurist Reports (1870-1874)

Austl. Law. Australian Lawyer

Austl. L.J.
- Australian Law Journal
- Australian Law Journal, Sydney

Austl. L.J. Rep. Australian Law Journal Reports

Austl. L.M.D. Australia Legal Monthly Digest

Austl. L.R. Australian Law Re-ports

Austl. L. Times Australian Law Times

Aust. L.N. Australian Law News

Aust. L. Rep. Australian Law Re-ports

Austl. Stat. R. Official Common-wealth Statutory Rules

Austl. Stat. R. Consol. Statutory Rules, Consolidation, Australian Parliament

Aust. L.T. Australian Law Times, Melbourne

Austl. Tax Australian Tax Deci-sions

Austl. Tax Rev. Australian Tax Review

Austl.Y.B. Intl L., Austl. Y.B. Int'l L. Australian Yearbook of Inter-national Law

Aust. Quart. Australian Quarterly

Austral. Australia

Austr. B.C. Australian Bankrupts' Cases

Austr. C.L.R. Australia, Common-wealth Law Rep.

Austr. Jur. Australian Jurist

Austr. L.J. Australian Law Jour-nal

Austr. L.T. Australian Law Times

Austr. Tax Australian Tax Decisions

Aust. Tax Rev. Australian Tax Review

Aust. Yb. Int'l L. Australian Yearbook of International Law, Sydney, Australia

Aust. Yearbook Int.L. Australian Yearbook of International Law

Aust. Y. Int.L. Australian Yearbook of International Law

Aust. Yr. Bk. I.L. Australian Yearbook of International Law

Auth.
- Authentica
- Authorised
- Authorities; Authority

Auto Automobiles and highway traffic

Auto. C. Automobile Cases (CCH)

Auto. Cas. Automobile Cases (CCH)

Auto. Cas.2d Automobile Cases, Second Series (CCH)

Auto. Ins. Automobile insurance

Auto. Ins. Cas. Automobile Insurance Cases (CCH)

Auto. Ins. Rep.(CCH) Automobile Insurance Reporter

Auto. L. Rep. (CCH)
- Automobile Law Reports
- Automobile Law Reporter (CCH)

A/V Adult and Vocational Education

Av.
- Average
- Aviation

Av. Adj. Assoc. Dig. Digest of Reports of the Average Adjusters Association (1895)

Av. & H.B.L. Avery & Hobb's Bankrupt Law

Av. Cas. Aviation Cases (CCH)

A.V.Ch. Assistant Vice-Chancellor

Ave. Avenue

Averbach Acci.Cas. Averbach on Handling Accident Cases

Avi. Aviation

Aviation Q. United States Aviation Quarterly

Av. L. Rep. (CCH)
- Aviation Law Reports
- Aviation Law Reporter (CCH)

A.V.T. Added Value Tax

A.W. Articles of War

A.W.N. Allahabad Weekly Notes (India)

A.W.O.L. Absent Without Leave (military term)

A.W.R. Allahabad Weekly Reporter (India)

AWT Advanced Wastewater Treatment

A.Y.B.I.L. Australian Yearbook of International Law

Ayck. Ch. F. Ayckbourn's Chancery Forms

Ayck. Ch. Pr. Ayckbourn's Chancery Practice

Ayck. Jur. Auckbourn's Jurisdiction of the Supreme Court of Judicature

Ayi. Char. Ayliffe, Calendar of Ancient Charters (1774)

Ayliffe. Ayliffe's Pandects; Ayliffe's Parergon Juris Canonici Angelicani

Ayl.Int.   Ayliffe's Introduction to the Calendar of Ancient Charters

Ayl. Pan.   Ayliffe's Pandect of the Roman Civil Law

Ayl. Pand.   Ayliffe's Pandect of the Roman Civil Law

Ayl. Par.   Ayliffe's Parergon Juris Canonici Anglicani (1726-1734)

Ayr   Ayr's Registration Cases (Sc.)

Ayr & Wig.   Ayr & Wigton's Registration Cases (Sc.)

Ayr. Land Tr.   Ayrton's Land

Transfer Act

Az.
- Arizona
- Arizona Reports

Az. A.   Arizona Court of Appeals Reports

Az. L.   Arizona Law Review

Az. L.R.   Arizona Law Review

Az. Mar. Law.   Azuni's Maritime Law

Azo.   See Asso.

Azuni Mar.Law   Azuni on Maritime Law

B

B
- All India Reporter, Bombay Series
- Bar
- Barber's Gold Law (S. Africa)
- Barbour's N.Y. Reports
- Baron (judge), Court of Exchequer, England and Wales
- Beavan's Rolls Court Reports (1838-66) (Eng.)
- Boston
- Buchanan's Supreme Court Reports, Cape (1868-79) (S. Africa)
- Budget
- Bulgarian
- Burgerlijk Wetboek (Neth.) civil code
- Common Bench
- Indian Law Reports, Bombay Series Weekly Law Bulletin (Ohio)

B. Weekly Law Bulletin

B.A. Bachelor of Arts

Ba. & Be. Ball & Beatty's Irish Chancery Reports

Bab. Auc. Babington's Law of Auctions

Bab. Set-off. Babington's Law of Set-off

B.A. Bull. L.A. Bar Assn. Bulletin, Los Angeles

B.A.C. Buchanan's Appeal Court Reports, Cape (1880-1909) (S. Afr.)

Bac. Ab. Bacon's Abridgment (1736-1832)

Bac. Abr. Bacon's Abridgment (1736-1832) (Eng.)

Bac. Aph. Bacon's (Sir Francis) Aphorisms

Bac. Aphorisms Aphorisms Bacon's (Sir Francis)

Bac. Ben. Soc. Bacon on Benefit Societies and Life Insurance

Bac. Ca. Bacon's Case of Treason, 1641

Bac. Chanc. Bacon's Chancery Cases (Eng.)

Bac. Comp. Arb. Bacon's Complete Arbitration

Bac. Dec. Bacon's Dec.(Ritchie), Eng.

Bac. Dig. Bacon's Georgia Digest

Bac. El. Bacon's Elements of the Common Law

Bac. Gov. Bacon on Government

Bach. Bach's Reports (v. 19-21 Montana Reports)

Bache Pa. Just. Bache's Pennsylvania Justice's Manual

Bac. Ins. Bacon on Benefit Societies and Life Insurance

Back. Sher. Backus on Sheriffs

Bac. Law Tr. Bacon's Law Tracts

Bac. Law Tracts Bacon's Law Tracts

Bac. Lease. Bacon on Leases and

Terms of Years

Bac. Lib. Reg. (or T.E.) Bacon's Liber Regis, vel Thesaurus Rerum Ecclesiasticarum

Bac. Max. Bacon's Maxims of the Law

Bacon
- Bacon, Arguments in Law
- Bacon, Liber Regis
- Bacon on Government
- Bacon on Leases and Terms of Years
- Bacon on Uses
- Bacon's Abridgment
- Bacon's Aphorisms
- Bacon's Complete Arbitrator
- Bacon's Elements of the Common Law
- Bacon's Law Tracts
- Bacon's Maxims

Bacon Max. Reg. Bacon's (Sir Francis) Maxims

Bac. Read. Uses. Bacon (Sir Francis), Reading upon the Statute of Uses

Bac. Rep. Bacon's Decisions (Ritchie) (Eng.)

Bac. St. Uses. Bacon (Sir Francis), Reading upon the Statute of Uses

Bac.Tr. Bacon's (Sir Francis) Law Tracts

Bac. Uses. Bacon's Essay on Uses

Bac. Works. Bacon's (Sir Francis), Works

BAE Bureau of Agricultural Economics

Bag. & Har. Bagley & Harman (Cal.)

Bag. Ch. Pr. Bagley, Practice: at Chambers (1834)

Bag. Eng. Const. Bagehot, English Constitution, 8ed. (1904)

Bag. Engl. Const. Bagehot's English Constitution

Bagl.
- Bagley's Reports (16 California)
- Bagley (Cal.)

Bagl. & H. Bagley & Harman's Reports (Vols. 17-19 California)

Bagl. & Har. Bagley & Harman's Reports (Vols. 17-19 California)

Bagl. & Har. (Cal.) Bagley & Harman's Reports (Vols. 17-19 California)

Bagl. (Cal.) Bagley's Reports (Vols. 16-19 California)

Bah. Bahamas

Bahamas L.R.C. Law Revision Committee, Bahamas

Bah. L.R. Bahamas Law Reports (1900-06)

Bahr. Bahrain

B.A.I. Bureau of Animal Industry Docket

Bai. Bailey's Law Reports, South Carolina

Bai. Eq. Bailey's. Equity Reports, South Carolina

Bail. Bailey's Law Reports, South Carolina (1828-1832)

Bail C.C. Lowndes & Maxwell, English Bail Court Cases (1852-54)

Bail & R. Bail & Recognizance

Bail Cr. Rep. Lowndes & Maxwell, English Bail Court Cases

Bail Ct. Bail Court

Bail Ct. Cas. Lowndes & Maxwell, English Bail Court Cases (1852-54)

Bail Ct. R. Bail Court Reports, Saunders and Cole (1846-48)

Bail Ct. Rep.
- Lowndes & Maxwell, English Bail Court Cases (1852-54)
- Saunders & Cole, English Bail Court Reports (1846-48)

Baild. Baildon's Select Cases in Chancery (Selden Society Publication, Vol. 10)

Bail. Dig. Bailey's North Carolina Digest

Bail. Eq. Bailey's Equity Reports (South Carolina 1830-31)

Bail. Eq. (S.C.) Bailey's Equity Reports, South Carolina (1830-31)

Bailey Bailey's Equity or Law Reports, South Carolina

Bailey, Ch. Bailey's Chancery Reports South Carolina

Bailey, Dict. Nathan Bailey's English Dictionary

Bailey Eq. Bailey's Equity Reports, South Carolina Court of Appeals

Bailey, Mast. Liab. Bailey's Law of Master's Liability for Injuries to Servant

Baill. Inher. Baillie's Mohammedan Law of Inheritance

Bail. L. Bailey's Law Reports, South Carolina

Baill. Dig. Baillie's Digest of Mohammedan Law

Bail. L.(S.C.) Bailey's Law Reports, South Carolina

Bailm. Bailment

B.A.I.M.R. U.S. Bureau of Animal Industry. Monthly Record

Bainb. M. & M. Bainbridge on the Law of Mines and Minerals

Bainb. Mines Bainbridge on Mines and Minerals

Bak. Bur. Baker on the Law relating to Burials

Bak. Corp. Baker's New York Corporation Laws

Baker, Quar. Baker's Law of Quarantine

Bak. Health L. Baker's Health Laws

Bak. Highw. Baker's Law of Highways

Bak. Quar. Baker's Law of Quarantine

Bal.
- Balance
- Balasingham's Reports, Ceylon

Balance of Payments Rep.(CCH) Balance of Payments Report

Bal. Ann. Codes Ballinger's Annotated Codes & Statutes (Wash.)

Balas. Balasingham's Supreme Court Reports (Ceylon)

Balas. N.C. Balasingham's Notes of Cases (Ceylon)

Balas. R.C. Balasingham's Reports of Cases (Sri Lanka) 1904-09

Bald.
- Baldasseroni (on Maritime Law)
- Baldus (Commentator on the Code)
- Baldwin's United States Circuit

Court Reports

Bald. App. Appendix to 11 Peters, U.S. Reports

Bald. App. 11 Pet. Baldwin, Appendix to 11 Peters

Bald. Bank. Baldwin, Law of Bankruptcy. 11ed. 1915

Bald. C.C.
- Baldasseroni (on Maritime Law)
- Baldus (Commentator on the Code)
- Baldwin's United States Circuit Court Reports

Bald. Cir. C. Baldwin's U.S. Circuit Court Reports

Bald. Conn. Dig. Baldwin's Connecticut Digest

Bald. Const. (or Op.) Baldwin, View of the United States Constitution with Opinions

Baldev. P.C. Baldeva Ram Dave, Privy Council Judgment (India)

Bald. Pat. Cas. Baldwin's Patent, Copyright, Trade-Mark Cases (U.S.)

Bald. Pat. Etc. Cas. Baldwin Patent, Copyright, Trade-mark Cases (1930) 10 vols.

Bald. Rep. Baldwin's U.S. Circuit Court Reports

Bald. U.S. Sup.Ct.Rep. United States Supreme Court Reports, Photo reproduction set by Baldwin

Baldw.
- Baldasseroni (on Maritime Law)
- Baldus (Commentator on the Code)
- Baldwin's United States Circuit Court Reports

- Baldwin

Baldw. Dig. Baldwin's Connecticut Digest

Baldwin Baldwin on Bankruptcy

Baldwin's C.C. U.S.Rep. Baldwin's U.S. Circuit Court Reports

Baldwin's Rep. Baldwin's U.S. Circuit Court Reports

Balf. Balfour's Practice, Laws of Scotland (1754)

Balf. Pr. Balfour's Practice, Laws of Scotland

Ball. Ballard's Somerton Court Rolls (Oxford Arch. Soc. No. 50) (Eng.)

Ball & B. Ball & Beatty's Irish Chancery Reports (1807-14)

Ball & Beatty Ball & Beatty's Irish Chancery Reports (1807-14)

Ball & B. (Ir.) Ball & Beatty's Irish Chancery Reports (108-14)

Ball Banks Ball on National Banks

Ball Conv. Ball's Popular Conveyancer

Ball Dig. Ball's Digest of the Common Law

Ballentine Ballentine's Law Dictionary

Ballentine's Law Dict.
- Balletine's Law Dictionary
- Ballentine's Self Pronouncing Law Dictionary

Bal. Lim. Ballantine on Limitations

Ball. Ind. Ball's Index to Irish Statutes

Ballinger's Ann. Codes & St. Ballinger's Annotated Codes and

Statutes, Washington

Ball. Lim.
- Ballantine on Limitations
- Ballantine, Statute of Limitations (1810)

Ball St. Guide Ball's Student Guide to the Bar

Bal. Pay't Rep. Balance of Payments Reports (CCH)

Ba. L.R. University of Baltimore Law Review

Bal. R.D. Baldeva Ram Dave, Privy Council Judgment (India)

Balt. C. Rep. Baltimore City Reports

Balt. L.T. Baltimore Law Transcript

Balt. L. Tr. Baltimore Law Transcript

Bamber. Report of mining cases decided by the Railway and Canal Commission

BAMSL Bar Association of Metropolitan St. Louis Bankruptcy Reporter

Ban. & A. Banning & Arden's Patent Cases, U.S.

Banaras L.J. Banaras Law Journal, India

Ban.Br. Sir Orlando Bridgman's Common Pleas Reports, ed. by Bannister (1660-67) (124 ER)

Banc. Sup. Upper Bench

B. & A.
- Banning & Arden's Patent Reports (U.S.)
- Barnewell & Adolphus' English King's Bench Reports
- Barnewell & Alderson's English

King's Bench Reports (1817-22)
- Barron & Arnold's English Election Cases (1843-46)
- Barron & Austin's English Election Cases (1842)

B. & Ad. Barnewall & Adolphus' English King's Bench Reports (1830-34)

B. & Ald. Barnewall & Alderson's English King's Bench Reports

B. & Arn. Barron & Arnold's English Election Cases (1843-46)

B. & Aust. Barron & Austin's English Election Cases (1842)

B. & Aust. Cases (Eng.) Barron & Austin Election

B. & B.
- Ball & Beatty Chancery Reports (1807-14) (Ir.)
- Bench & Bar (periodical)
- Bowler & Bowers, vols. 2, 3 U.S. Comptroller's Decisions
- Broderip & Bingham's Common Pleas Reports (1819-22) (Eng.)

B. & Bar Bench & Bar

B. & C. Barnewall & Cresswell's English King's Bench Reports (1822-30)

B. & C. Comp. Bellinger and Cotton's Annotated Codes and Statutes (Or.)

B. & C. Pr. Cas. British & Colonial Prize Cases (1914-22) (Eng.)

B. & C. R. Reports of Bankruptcy & Companies Winding up Cases (1918-41) (Eng.)

B. & D. Benloe & Dalison Common Pleas Reports (Eng.)

B. & F. Brodrick & Fremantle, English Ecclesiastical Reports

(1840-64)

B. & G. Brownlow and Goldesborough (N.P. Reports) (1569-1624) (Eng.)

B. & H. Blatchford & Howland's United States District Court Reports

B. & H. Black. Broom & Hadley's Blackstone

B. & H. Cr. Cas. Bennett & Heard Leading Criminal Cases (Eng.)

B. & H. Crim. Cas. Bennet & Heard's Criminal Cases (Eng.)

B. & H. Dig. Bennett & Heard's Massachusetts Digest

B. & H. Lead. Ca. Bennett & Heard's Leading Criminal Cases (Eng.)

B. & H. Lead. Cas. Bennett & Heard Leading Criminal Cases (Eng.)

B. & I. Bankruptcy and Insolvency Cases (1853-55) (Eng.)

B. & L. Browning & Lushington's Admiralty Reports (1864-65) (Eng.)

B. & L. Assoc. Building and Loan Associations

B. & L. Pr. Bullen & Leake's Precedents of Pleading

B. & M. Browne & Macnamara Railway Cases (Eng.)

B. & Mac. Browne and Macnamara Railway Cases (Eng.)

B. & Macn. Browne & Macnamara, Eng. Brown & Macnamara Railway Cases (Eng.)

B. & N. Bills and Notes

B. & O. Bd. of Rev. Selected Decisions of the Board of Revenue, Bihar and Orissa

B. & P. Bosanquet & Puller, English Common Pleas, Exchequer and House of Lords Reports (1796-1804)

B. & P.N.R. Bosanquet & Puller's New Reports (1804-07) (Eng.)

B. & S.
- Best & Smith, English Queen's Bench Reports (1861-70)
- Beven and Siebel's Reports (Ceylon)

B. & T. Bank and Trust

B. & V. Beling & Vanderstraaten's Reports, Ceylon

Bangl. Bangladesh

Bang.L.R. Bangala Law Reporter (India)

Bank.
- Bankruptcy
- Bankruptcy Court
- International Bank for Reconstruction and Development

Bank. & Ins. Bankruptcy and Insolvency Reports (1853-55) (Eng.)

Bank. & Insol. Rep. Bankruptcy and Insolvency Reports (1853-55) (Eng.)

Bank. & Ins. R. Bankruptcy and Insolvency Reports (1853-55) (Eng.)

Bank. C. Banking Code

Bank. Cas. Banking Cases

Bank. Ct. Rep.
- Bankrupt Court Reporter (New York)
- The American Law Times Bankruptcy Reports

62

Bank Eng. Q.B. Bank of England Quarterly Bulletin

Banker's L.J. Banker's Law Journal

Bank. Gaz. Bankruptcy Gazette

Bank. I. Bankter's Institutes of Scottish Law

Banking L.J. Banking Law Journal

Banking L. Rev. Banking Law Review

Bank. Insol. Rep. Bankruptcy and Insolvency Cases (1853-55) (Eng.)

Bank. Inst. Bankter's Institutes of Scottish Law

Bank. L.J. Banking Law Journal

Bank. Mag. Banker's Magazine

Bankr. Bankruptcy

Bankr. Act. Bankruptcy Act

Bankr. B. Bull. Bankruptcy Bar Bulletin

Bankr. Ct. Dec. (CRR) Bankruptcy Court Decisions

Bankr. Dev. J. Bankruptcy Developments Journal

Bank. Reg. Bankruptcy Register

Bank. Rep. American Law Times Bankruptcy Report

Bankr. Form Bankruptcy Forms

Bankr. Ins. R. Bankrupty and Insolvency Reports (1853-55) (Eng.)

Bankr. L. Rep. (CCH)
- Bankruptcy Law Reports
- Bankruptcy Law Reporter (CCH)

Bankr. L. Rptr. Bankruptcy Law Reporter

Bankr. R. Rules of Bankruptcy and Official Forms

Bankr. Reg. National Bankruptcy Register (N.Y.)

Bankr. Rule Bankruptcy Rules

Banks. Banks' Reports (vols. 1-5 Kansas)

Banks. & Ins. Bankruptcy and Insolvency Reports (1853-55) (Eng.)

Bankt. MacDouall's (Lord Bankton) Institutes of Laws of Scotland. 3 vols. (1751-53)

Bankt. I. Bankton's Institutes of the Laws of Scotland

Ban. L.J. Banares Law Journal (1965) (India)

Bann. Bannister's Reports, English Common Pleas

Bann. & A. Banning & Arden's Patent Cases (U.S.)

Bann. & A. Pat. Cas. Banning & Arden's Patent Cases (U.S.)

Bann. & Ard. Banning & Arden, Patent Cases (U.S.)

Bann. Br. Bannister's edition of O. Bridgman's English Common Pleas Reports

Bann. Lim. Banning, Limitations of Actions. 3ed. (1906)

B.A.O. Bankruptcy Annulment Order

Bar.
- Barber's Reports (vols. 14-42 Arkansas)
- Barnardiston's Chancery
- Barnardiston's English King's Bench Reports
- Bar Reports in all the Courts (Eng.)

- Barrister
- Barrow's Reports (vol. 18 Rhode Island)

Bar. Anc. Stat. Barrington, Observations upon the Statutes. 5ed. 1796

Bar. & Ad. Barnewall & Adolphus' King's Bench Reports (1830-34) (109-110 ER)

Bar. & Al. Barnewall & Alderson's English King's Bench Reports

Bar. & Arn. Barron & Arnold, Election Cases (1843-46) (Eng.)

Bar. & Au. Barron & Austin's English Election Cases (1842)

Bar. & Aust. Barron & Austin's English Election Cases (1842)

Bar. & Cr. Barnewall & Cresswell's English King's Bench Reports

Bar & Leg. W. Bar & Legal World (Eng.)

Barb.
- Barbados
- Barber's Gold Law (S. Africa)
- Barber's Reports (vols. 14-42 Arkansas)
- Barbour's Supreme Court Reports (N.Y.)

Barb. Abs. Barbour's Abstracts of Chancellor's Decisions (N.Y.)

Barb. & C. Ky. St. Barbour and Carroll's Kentucky Statutes

Barb. App. Dig. Barber's Digest (N.Y.)

Barb. Ark. Barber's Reports (vols. 14-24 Arkansas)

Barb. Ch. Barbour's Chancery Reports (N.Y.)

Barb. Chancery Rep. Barbour's Chancery Reports (N.Y.)

Barb. Ch.(N.Y.) Barbour's Chancery Reports (N.Y.)

Barb. Ch. Pr. Barbour's Chancery Practice (N.Y.)

Barb. Ch. Rep. Barbour's Chancery Reports (N.Y.)

Barb. Cr. L. Barbour's Criminal Law

Barb. Cr. Law Barbour's Criminal Law

Barb. Cr. P.
- Barbour's Criminal Pleadings
- Barbour's Criminal Practice

Barb. Dig. Barber's Digest of Kentucky

Barbe. Barber's Reports, Arkansas

Barber
- Barber (N.Y.)
- Barber's Gold Law (Africa)
- Barber's Reports (vols. 14-42 Arkansas)

Barb. Gro. Barbeyrac's Edition of Grotius on War and Peace

Barb. Ins. Barber on Insurance

Barb. L.R. Barbados Law Reports

Barb. (N.Y.)S.C.R. Barbour's Supreme Court Reports (N.Y.)

Barbour Barbour's Supreme Court Reports (N.Y.)

Barbour (N.Y.) Barbour's Supreme Court Reports (N.Y.)

Barbour's Ch.Pr. Barbour's Chancery Reports (N.Y.)

Barbour's Ch.R. Barbour's Chancery Reports (N.Y.)

Barbour's Sup. Court Rep. Barbour's Supreme Court Reports (N. Y.)

Barb. Par. Barbour on Parties in Law and Equity

Barb. Puf. Barbeyrac's Edition of Puffendorf's Law of Nature and Nations

Barb. R. Barbour's Supreme Court Reports (N.Y.)

Barb. S.C. Barbour's Supreme Court Reports (N.Y.)

Barb. S.C.R. Barbour's Supreme Court Reports (N.Y.)

Barb. Set-Off Barbour on the Law of Set-Off

Barb. Sup. Ct. Barbour's Supreme Court Reports (N.Y.)

Barb. Sup. Ct. Reports Barbour's Supreme Court Reports (N.Y.)

Bar Bull. (N.Y. County L.A.) Bar Bulletin, New York County Lawyers'

Barc. Dig. Barclay's Missouri Digest

Barc. Dig. Law Sc. Barclay's Digest of the Law of Scotland

Barc. Dig. (or Leg.Man.) Barclay's Digest, or Legislative Manual of Congress

Bar. Ch. Barnardiston's English Chancery Reports

Barc. High. Barclay's Law of Highways

Bar. Chy. Barnardiston's English Chancery Reports

Barc. Mo.Dig. Barclay's Missouri Digest

Bar. Dig. Barclay, Digest of the Law of Scotland. 1894

Bar. Eq. Barton's Suit in Equity

Bar Exam. Bar Examiner

Bar. Ex. Ann. Bar Examination Annual (1893-94)

Bar Ex. Guide Bar Examination Guide (1895-99)

Bar Ex. J. Bar Examination Journal (1871-92)

Bar Ex. Jour. Bar Examination Journal (London)

Bar Gaz. Bar Gazette (1961-63) (N.S.W., Aus.)

Barh. Pre. Ex. Barham's Student's Guide to the Preliminary Examinations

Bar Lead. Bar Leader

Barl. Just. Barlow, Justice of Peace. 1745

Bar. Mag. Barrington's Magna Charta

Bar. N. Barnes' Notes, English Common Pleas Reports

Barn.
- Barnardiston's English King's Bench Reports
- Barnes' English Common Pleas Reports
- Barnfield's Reports (vols. 19-20 Rhode Island)

Barn. & A.
- Barnewall & Adolphus K.B. Rep., Eng.
- Barnewall & Alderson K.B. Rep., Eng.

Barn. & Ad. Barnewall & Adolphus, King's Bench (vols. 109-110 ER)

Barn & Ad. (Eng.) Barnewall & Adolphus, King's Bench (vols.

109-110 ER)

Barn. & Adol. Barnewall and Adolphus' English King's Bench Reports (1830-34)

Barn. & Ald. Barnewall & Alderson, English King's Bench Reports (vol. 106 ER)

Barn. & Ald.(Eng.) Barnewall & Alderson, English King's Bench Reports (vol. 106 ER)

Barn. & C. Barnewall & Cresswell's English King's Bench Reports (vols. 107-109 ER)

Barn. & C.(Eng.) Barnewall & Cresswell's English King's Bench Reports (vols. 107-109 ER)

Barn. & Cr. Barnewall & Cresswell's English King's Bench Reports (vols. 107-109 ER)

Barn. & Cress. Barnewall & Cresswell's English King's Bench Reports (vols. 107-109 ER)

Barnard.
- Barnardiston, King's Bench Reports (1726-34) (Eng.)
- Barnardiston, temp. Hardwicke Reports, Chancery (1740-41) (Eng.)

Barnard. Ch. Barnardiston's English Chancery Reports (27 ER)

Barnard.Ch. (Eng.) Barnardiston's English Chancery Reports (27 ER)

Barnard. Ch. Rep. Barnardiston's Reports, Chancery (1740-41)

Barnardiston C.C. Barnardiston's Chancery Cases (1740-41)

Barnard. K.B. Barnardiston's King's Bench Reports (94 ER)

Barn. C. Barnardiston's Reports, Chancery (1740-41)

Barn. Ch. Barnardiston's English Chancery Reports (1740-41)

Barn. Eq. Pr. Barnes' Equity Practice

Barnes Barnes' Notes of Cases of Practice in Common Pleas (94 ER)

Barnes, N.C. Barnes' Notes of Cases of Practice in Common Pleas (94 ER)

Barnes Notes Barnes' Notes of Cases of Practice in Common Pleas (94 ER)

Barnes Notes (Eng.) Barnes' Notes of Cases of Practice in Common Pleas (94 ER)

Barnes's Fed. Code Barnes's Federal Code

Barnet. Barnet, English Central Criminal Courts Reports (vols. 27-92)

Barnf. & S. Barnfield and Stiness' Reports (vol. 20 Rhode Island)

Barn. K.B. Barnardiston, King's Bench Reports (1726-34) (Eng.)

Barn. No. Barnes' Note of Cases, English Common Pleas

Barn. Pr.M. Barnstaple, Printed Minutes and Proceedings

Barn. Sh. Barnes, Exposition of the Law respecting Sheriff. 1816

Barnw. Dig. Barnwall's Digest of the Year Books

Bar. Obs. St. Barrington's Observations upon the Statutes from Magna Charta to 21 James I

Bar. Ob. Stat. Barrington's Observations on the Statutes

Baroda L.R. Baroda Law Reports

(India)

Baron. Barony of Urie Court Records (1604-1747) (Sc.)

Baron Ch. Mort. Baron on Chattel Mortgages

Bar. Prec. Conv. Barton's Precedents in Conveyancing

Barr.
- Barrows' Reports (vol. 18, Rhode Island)
- Barr's Reports (vols. 1-10, Pennsylvania)
- The Barrister

Barr. & Arn. Barron & Arnold's English Election Cases

Barr. & Aus. Barron & Austin's English Election Cases

Barr. Ch. Pr. Barroll Chancery Practice (Md.)

Bar Re. Bar Reports in all Courts (1865-71) (Eng.)

Bar Rep. Bar Reports (see Law Times Reports, v. 1-12) (1865-71)

Barring. Obs. St. Barrington's Observations upon the Statutes from Magna Charta to 21 James I

Barring. St. Barrington's Observations upon the Statutes from Magna Charta to 21 James I

Barrister
- Barrister (Chicago)
- Barrister (Coral Gables, Fla.)
- Barrister (Davis, Cal.)
- Barrister (Fort Lauderdale, Fla.)
- Barrister (Toronto)

Barr.M. Barradall, Manuscript Reports (Virginia)

Barr.MSS. Barradall Manuscript Reports (Va.)

Barr Ob. (or Stat.) Barrington's Observations on the Statutes

Barr. Obs. St. Barrington's Observations on the Statutes

Barron Barony of Urie Court Records (1604-1747) (Sc.)

Barron & H. Fed. Pr. & Proc. Barron & Holtzoff's Federal Practice & Procedure

Barron Mir. Barron's Mirror of Parliament

Barrows Barrows' Reports (vol. 18, Rhode Island)

Barrows (R.I.) Barrows' Reports (vol. 18 Rhode Island)

Barr. (Pa.) Barr's Reports (vols. 1-10, Pennsylvania)

Barr. St. Barrington's Observations upon the Statutes from Magna Charta to 21 James I

Barr. Ten. Barry on Tenures

Barry Build. Soc. Barry on Building Societies

Barry Ch. Jur. Barry's Chancery Jurisdiction

Barry Ch. Pr. Barry, Statutory Jurisdiction of Chancery. 1861

Barry Conv. Barry, Practice of Conveyancing. 1865

Barry Forms Conv. Barry on Forms and Precedents in Conveyancing

Barry Ten. Barry on Tenures

Bar. S.C. Rep. Barbour's Supreme Court Reports (N.Y.)

Bart.Cong. Election Cases Bartlett, Congressional Election Cases

Bart. Conv. Barton, Science of

Conveyancing. 2ed. (1810-22)

Bart. El. Cas. Bartlett's Congressional Election Cases

Bart. Elec. Cas. Bartlett's Election Cases

Bart. Eq. Barton's Suit in Equity

Bartholoman Bartholoman's Reports, Yorkshire Lent Assize, March 9, 1911 (Eng.)

Bart. Ind. Bartlett's Index of the Laws of Rhode Island

Bart. L. Pr. Barton's Law Practice

Bart. Max. Barton's Maxims in Conveyancing

Bart. Mines Bartlett, Law of Mining. 1850

Bart. Prec. Conv. Barton, Modern Precedents in Conveyancing. 3ed. 1826

BASF The Bar Association of San Francisco

Bass. Crim. Pl. Bassett's Illinois Criminal Pleading and Practice

Bast. Bastards

B.A.S.W. British Association of Social Workers

Batch. Mfg. Cor. Batchelder's Law of Massachusetts Manufacturing Corporations

Bat. Dig. Battle's Digest, North Carolina

Bate. Ag. Bateman on Agency

Bate. Auct. Bateman, Law of Auctions. 11ed. 1953

Bate. Com. L. Bateman's Commercial Law

Bate. Const. Bateman's United States Constitutional Law

Bate. Exc. Bateman, General Laws of Excise. 2ed. 1840

Bates Bates' Delaware Chancery Reports

Bates Ch. Bates Chancery (Del.)

Bates' Ann. St. Bates' Annotated Revised Statutes, Ohio

Bates' Dig. Bates' Digest, Ohio

Bateson Leicester Records (Municipal Courts 1103-1603) (Eng.)

Bates, Part. Bates' Law of Partnership

Bat. Rev. St. Battle's Revisal of Public Statutes of North Carolina

Bat. Sp. Perf. Batten, Specific Performance on Contracts, 1849

Bat. Stan. Batten on the Stannaries Act

Bat. Stat. Battle's Revised Statutes of North Carolina, 1873

Batt. Batty's Irish King's Bench Reports (1825-26)

Battle's Revisal Battle's Revisal of the Public Statutes of North Carolina

Batts' Ann. St. Batts' Annotated Revised Civil Statutes, Texas

Batts' Rev. St. Batts' Annotated Revised Civil Statutes, Texas

Batty (Ir.) Batty's Irish King's Bench Reports

Bax. Baxter's Reports (vols. 60-68 Tennessee)

Bax. Jud. Acts Baxter on Judicature Acts and Rules

Baxt. Baxter's Reports (Tenn.)

Baxter Baxter's Reports (vols. 60-68 Tennessee)

Baxt. (Tenn.) Baxter's Reports (vols. 60-68 Tennessee)

Bay Bay's Reports (1-3, 5-8 Missouri) Bay's South Carolina Reports (1783-1804)

Bay. Bills Bayley on Bills and Notes

Bay. Cons. Bayard on the Constitution of the United States

Bay. Dig. Ind. Baylies' Digested Index of English and American Reports

Bay. Dom. Serv. Baylies on Domestic Servants

Bay. Ev. Bayard on Evidence

Bayl. B. Bayley on Bills

Bayl. Ch. Pr. Bayley's Chancery Practice

Bayl. Com. Bayley's Commentaries on the Laws of England

Bayley, Bills Bayley on Bills

Bayl. F. & R. Bayley on Fines and Recoveries

Baylles, Sur. Baylles on Sureties and Guarantors

Baylor L. Rev. Baylor Law Review

Bayl. Q. & A. Bayley's Questions and Answers for Students

B.B.
- Bailey on Bills
- Ball on National Banks
- Bail Bond

B. Bar Bench & Bar

B.B.J. Boston Bar Journal

B. Bull. Bar Bulletin

BC U.S. Bankruptcy Court

B.C.
- Bail Court
- Bankruptcy Cases
- Before Christ
- Bell, Commentaries on the Laws of Scotland (1870)
- Board of Control
- British Columbia
- British Columbia Law Reports (Canada)
- New South Wales Bankruptcy Cases (Aus.)

B.C.A. (CCH) Board of Contract Appeals Decisions (CCH)

B.C. Branch Lec. Canadian Bar Association, British Columbia Branch Meeting Program Reports

B.C. Branch Lectures British Columbia Branch Lectures

B.C.C.
- Bail Court Cases Lowndes & Maxwell (1852-54) (Eng.)
- Bail Court Reports, Sanders & Cole (Eng.)
- British Columbia Reports
- Brown's Chancery Cases (Eng.)

B.C.D. Bankruptcy Court Decisions (a loose-leaf published by the Corporate Reorganizations Reporter, Inc.)

B.C. Envtl. Aff. L. Rev. Boston College Environmental Affairs Law Review

B.C. Gaz. British Columbia Gazette

B.Ch. Barbour's Chancery Reports, New York

B.C. Ind. & Com. L.R. Boston College Industrial & Commercial Law Review

B.C. Ind. & Com. L. Rev. Boston College Industrial and Commercial Law Review

B.C. Ind. Com'l. L. Rev. Boston College Industrial and Commercial Law Review

B.C. Indus. & Com. L. Rev. Boston College Industrial and Commercial Law Review

B.C. Int'l. & Comp. L.J. Boston College International and Comparative Law Journal

B.C. Int'l. & Comp. L. Rev. Boston College International and Comparative Law Review

B.C.L.
- Bachelor of Cannon Law
- Bachelor of Civil Law

BCA Board of Contract Appeals

BCLB Bituminous Coal Labor Board

B.C.L. Lectures British Columbia Annual Law Lectures (Can.)

B.C.L. Notes British Columbia Law Notes

B.C.L.R. British Columbia Reports

B.C.L.R.C. British Columbia Law Reform Commission

B.C. L. Rev. Boston College Law Review

B.C. (N.S.W.) New South Wales Bankruptcy Cases (1890-99)

B. Co. Leg. J'nal. Beaver County Legal Journal (Pa.)

B.C.R.
- Bail Court Cases, Lowndes & Maxwell (1852-54) (Eng.)
- Bail Court Reports, Sanders & Cole (1846-47) (Eng.)
- British Columbia Reports
- Brown's Chancery Cases (1778-

94) (Eng.)

B.C. Rep.
- Bail Court Cases, Lowndes & Maxwell (Eng.)
- Bail Court Reports, Sanders & Cole (Eng.)
- British Columbia Reports
- Brown's Chancery Cases (Eng.)

B.C. Rev. Stat. British Columbia Revised Statutes (Canada)

B.C. Stat. British Columbia Statutes (Canada)

B.C.T. Bell on Completing Titles, Scotland

B.C. Tax Rep. (CCH) British Columbia Tax Reporter

B.C. Third World L.J. Boston College Third World Law Journal

B. Current L. Butterworth's Current Law

Bcy. Bankruptcy

Bd. Board

B.D. & O. Blackham, Dundas, & Osborne's Nisi Prius Reports (1846-48) (Ir.)

BDC Bureau of Domestic Commerce

Bd. Cont. App. Dec. Board of Contract Appeals Decisions (CCH)

Bd of Dirs Board of Directors

Bd. of Rev. Board of Review

BDSA Business and Defense Services Administration

B.E. "Baron of the Court of Exchequer"

b.e. bill of exchange

B.E.A.
- British East Africa

- British European Airways

Bea.   Beavan (1838-66)

Bea. Bank.   Beame's Commitments in Bankruptcy

Bea C.E.   Beames' Costs in Equity

Beach, Contrib. Neg.   Beach on Contributory Negligence

Beach, Eq. Prac.   Beach's Modern Practice in Equity

Beach, Inj.   Beach on Injunctions

Beach, Mod. Eq. Jur.   Beach's Commentaries on Modern Equity Jurisprudence

Beach, Priv. Corp.   Beach on Private Corporations

Beach, Pub. Corp.   Beach on Public Corporations

Beach, Rec.   Beach on the Law of Receivers

Bea. Costs (or C.E.)   Beames' Costs in Equity

Bea. Eq. Pl.   Beames' Equity Pleading

Beam.   Beames (see Bea)

Beames, Glanv.   Beames' Glanville

Bea. Ne Ex.   Beames on the Writ of Ne Exeat Regno

Bea. Ord.   Beames' Orders in Chancery (Eng.)

Bea. Pl. Eq.   Beames' Pleas in Equity

Bear. Tithes   Bearblock, Treatise upon Tithes. 6ed. 1832

Beas.
- Beasley's New Jersey Chancery Reports
- Beasley's New Jersey Equity Reports (vols. 12-13)

Beasl.   Beasley, New Jersey Equity Reports

Beat.   Beatty's Irish Chancery Reports (1814-36)

Beatt.   Beatty's Irish Chancery Reports (1814-36)

Beatty   Beatty's Irish Chancery Reports (1814-36)

Beatty Ir. Ch.   Beatty's Irish Chancery Reports (1814-36)

Beau. Bills   Beaumont, Bills of Sale. 1855

Beau. Ins.   Beaumont, Life and Fire Insurance. 2ed. 1846

Beav.   Beavan's English Rolls Court Reports (vols. 48-55 ER)

Beavan, Ch.   Beavan's English Rolls Court Reports

Beav. & W.   Beavan and Walford's Railway Cases (1846)

Beav. & Wal.   Beavan & Walford's Railway and Canal Parliamentary Cases. 1846

Beav. & Wal. Ry. Cas.   Beavan & Walford's Railway and Canal Cases (Eng.)

Beav. & W. Ry. Cas.   Beavan & Walford's Railway & Canal Cases (Eng.)

Beav. (Eng.)   Beavan's English Rolls Court Reports (vols. 48-55 ER)

Beaver   Beaver County Legal Journal (Pa.)

Beaver County L.J.   Beaver County Legal Journal (Pa.)

Beaver Co. L.J. (Pa.)   Beaver County Legal Journal (Pennsylvania)

Beav. O.C. Beavan's Ordines Cancellariae

Beav. R. & C. Beavan, Railway & Canal Cases (Eng.)

Beav. R. & C. Cas. English Railway and Canal Cases, by Beavan and others

Beaw. Beawes' Lex Mercatoria (Eng.)

Beawes' Lex Merc. Meawes' Lex Mercatoria (Eng.)

Beaw. Lex Mer. Beawes Lex Mercatoria (Eng.)

BEC Bureau of Employees' Compensation

B. Ecc. L. Burn's Ecclesiastical Law

Bec. Cr. Beccaria on Crimes and Punishments

Be. (Ceylon) Beven's Ceylon Reports

Beck Beck's Colorado Reports: vols. 12-16 Colorado, and vol. 1 Colorado Court of Appeals

Beck (Colo.) Beck's Colorado Reports: vols. 12-16 Colorado, and vol. 1 Colorado Court of Appeals

Beck, Med. Jur. Beck's Medical Jurisprudence

Bedell Bedell's Reports (163-191 N. Y.)

Bee Bee's United States District Court Reports

Bee Adm. Bee's Admiralty. An Appendix to Bee's District Court Reports

Bee Alm. Bee's Dist.Ct.Rep.,U.S.

Bee. Anal. Beebee, Analysis of Common Law Practice

Beebe Cit. Beebe's Ohio Citations

Bee C.C.R. Bee's Crown Cases Reserved (Eng.)

Beeler Beeler's Reports (Tenn.)

bef. before

Begg Code Begg, Conveyancing Code (Sc.)

Begg L. Ag. Begg, Law Agents (Sc.)

Behari Revenue Reports of Upper Provinces (India)

Behav. behavior

Behav. Sci. & L. Behavior Sciences and the Law

Bel.
- Belasis' Bombay Reports
- Beling's Ceylon Reports
- Bellewe's English King's Bench Reports (1378-1400)
- Bellinger's Reports (vols. 4-8 Oregon)

Bel. Ca.t.H.VIII Bellewe's Cases tempore. Henry VIII, Brooke's New Cases (Eng.)

Belg.
- Belgian
- Belgium

Belg. Rev. Int'l L. Belgian Review of International Law

Beling Beling's Ceylon Reports

Beling & Van. Beling & Vanderstraaten's Ceylon Reports

Bell.
- Bellasis Bombay Reports
- Bell, Calcutta Reports
- Bell, English Crown Cases Reserved
- Bellewe, English King's Bench Reports

- Bellinger, Reports (vols. 4-8 Oregon)
- Bell, Scotch Appeal Cases (1842-50)
- Bell, Scotch Session Cases
- Brooke, New Cases, by Bellewe

Bell Ap.Ca. Bell's Scotch Appeals

Bell App. Bell's House of Lords Appeal Cases (1842-50) (Sc.)

Bell App. Bell (Sc.) House of Lords (1842-50)

Bell App. Cas. Bell's House of Lords Appeal Cases (Sc.)

Bell Arb. Bell's Law of Arbitration in Scotland

Bellas. Bellasis Criminal (or Civil) cases (Bombay)

Bellasis Bombay Sudder Dewanny Adawlut Reports

Bell Aw. Bell's Law of Awards

Bell, C. Bell Reports, Court of Session (1790-92) (Sc.)

Bell Cas. Bell's Cases, Scotch Court of Session

Bell. Cas.t.H.VIII Brooke's New Cases (collected by Beliewe)

Bell. Cas.t.Hen.VIII Brooke's New Cases (1515-58)

Bell. Cas.t.R.II Bellewe's King's Bench Reports (1378-1400)

Bell. Cas.t.Rich.II Bellewe's English King's Bench Reports (time of Richard II)

Bell C. Bell (Sc.) Court of Session (1790-95) (Sc.)

Bell C.C.
- Bellasis, Civil Cases (Bombay)
- Bellasis, Criminal Cases (Bombay)

- Bell, English Crown Cases Reserved (vol. 169 ER)

Bell C. C.(Eng.)
- Bellasis, Civil Cases (Bombay)
- Bellasis, Criminal Cases (Bombay)
- Bell, English Crown Cases Reserved (vol. 169 ER)

Bell C.H.C. Bell's Reports, Calcutta High Court (India)

Bell Comm. Bell's Commentaries on the Law of Scotland

Bell Convev. Bell, Lecture on Conveyancing (Sc.)

Bell Cr. C.
- Beller's Criminal Cases (Bombay)
- Bell's English Crown Cases

Bell Cr. Ca.
- Beller's Criminal Cases (Bombay)
- Bell's English Crown Cases

Bell Cr. Cas.
- Beller's Criminal Cases (Bombay)
- Bell's English Crown Cases

Bell C.T. Bell, Completing Titles (Sc.)

Bell Ct. of Sess. R. Bell's Decisions, Court of Session (Sc.)

Bell Ct. of Sess. fol. R. Bell's Decisions, Session Cases (1794-95) (Sc.)

Bell Deeds Bell, System of Forms of Deeds (Sc.)

Bell. Del. Beller's Delineations of Universal Law

Bell Dict. Bell's Dictionary and Digest of the Laws of Scotland

73

Bell Dict. Dec Bell, Dictionary of Decisions, Court of Session (Scotland)

Bell Elec. Bell, Election Law of Scotland

Bellewe Bellewe's English King's Bench Reports

Bellewe (Eng.) Bellewe's English King's Bench Reports

Bellewe's Ca. temp.Hen.VIII Brooke's New Cases (1515-58)

Bellewe's Ca. Temp.R.II Bellewe's Richard II (1378-1400)

Bellewe t.H.VIII Brooke's New Cases (collected by Bellewe)

Bell Ex. Bell on Excise

Bell Exp. Test. Bell on Expert Testimony

Bell fol. Bell's folio Reports, Scotch Court of Session (1794-95)

Bell folio R. Bell's Decisions, Session Cases (1794-95) (Scotland)

Bell H.C. Bell's Reports, High Court of Calcutta (India)

Bell H.L. Bell's House of Lords Cases, Scotch Appeal (1842-50) (Eng.)

Bell H.L. Sc. Bell's House of Lords Cases, Scotch Appeals

Bell H.W. Bell, Property as arising from the Relation of Husband and Wife, 1849

Bell Illust. Bell's Illustrations of Principles

Bell (In.)
- Bell's Reports, High Court of Calcutta (1858-1906) (India)
- Bell's Reports (India)

Bellinger. Bellinger's Reports

(vols. 4-8 Oregon)

Bellingh. Tr. Report of Bellingham's Trial

Belli's Mod. Trials Belli's Modern Trials

Bell L. & T. Bell on Landlord and Tenant (Bengal)

Bell Leas. Bell on Leases, Scotland

Bell Med. L.J. Bell's Medico Legal Journal

Bell No. Bell's Supplemented Notes to Hume on Crimes

Bell Oct. Bell's octavo Reports Scotch Court of Sessions (1790-92)

Bell. (Or.) Bellinger's Reports (Oregon)

Bell P.C. Bell's Cases in Parliament: Scotch Appeals

Bell Prin. Bell's Principles of the Law of Scotland. 10 editions (1829-99)

Bell Put. Mar. Bell's Putative Marriage Case (Scotland)

Bell S. Bell on Sales

Bell Sale Bell, Sale of Food and Drugs. 14 ed. (1968)

Bell's App. Bell's House of Lords Appeal Cases (1842-50) (Scotland)

Bell Sc. App. Bell's Appeals to House of Lords from Scotland

Bell Sc. App.Cas. (Scotland) Bell, Scotch Appeal Cases

Bell Sc. Cas. Bell's Scotch Court of Sessions Cases

Bell Sc.Dig. Bell's Scottish Digest

Bell's Comm. Bell's Commentaries on Laws of Scotland. 7 editions (1800-70)

Bell Scot. Dig. Bell's Scottish Digest

Bell's Dict. Bell's Dictionary of Decisions (Scotland), Court of Session (1808-32)

Bell Ses. Cas. Bell's Cases in the Scotch Court of Session

Bell Sty. Bell, System of the Forms of Deeds (Styles) (Scotland)

Bell Sty. (or Syst.) Bell's System of the Forms of Deeds (Styles) of Scotland

Bell T.D. Bell, Testing of Deeds (Scotland)

Bell. U.L. Beller's Delineation of Universal Law

Bel. Prob. Belknap's Probate Law of California

Belt Bro. Belt's edition of Brown's Chancery Reports (1778-94)

Belt's Supp. (Eng.) Belt's Supplement to Vesey Senior's English Chancery Reports (1746-56)

Belt. Sup. Belt's Supplement to Vesey Senior's English Chancery Reports (1746-56)

Belt Supp. Belt's Supplement to Vesey, Sen. (1746-56)

Belt. Sup.Ves. Belt's Supplement to Vesey Senior's English Chancery Reports (1746-56)

Belt Ves. Sen. Belt's edition of Vesey Senior's English Chancery Reports

Ben.
- Benedict United States District Reports

- Bengal Law Reports
- Benloe's English Reports, King's Bench and Common Pleas

Ben. Adm. Benedict's American Admiralty Practice

Ben. Adm. Prac. Benedict's Admiralty Practice

Ben. & D. Benloe and Dalison (1486-1580)

Ben. & Dal. Benloe & Dalison's English Common Pleas Reports

Ben. & H.L.C. Bennett & Heard Leading Criminal Cases (Eng.)

Ben. & S.Dig. Benjamin & Slidell's Louisiana Digest

Ben. Av. (Stephens &) Benecke on Average

Bench. Benchmark

Bench & B. Bench and Bar (periodical)

Bench & Bar Bench and Bar

Bench & B. Minn. Bench & Bar of Minnesota

Bender Matthew Bender and Company Incorporated

Bendl. Bendloe's English Common Pleas (1531-1628)

Bendloe Bendloe's or New Benloe's Reports, English Common Pleas, Edition of 1661

Bene. Benedict's U.S. District Court Reports

Bened. Benedict, United States District Court Reports

Benedict Benedict's United States District Court Reports

Benedict, Admiralty Benedict on Admiralty

Benef. Beneficiary

Benefit Series, U.C.I.S. U.S.Social Security Board Unemployment Compensation Interpretation Service. Benefit Series

Benefits L.J. Benefits Law Journal

BENELUX Belgium, Netherlands, Luxembourg Economic Union

Benet Ct.-M Benet on Military Law and Courts-Martial

Ben. F.B. Full Bench Rulings, High Court, Fort William (Bengal)

Ben. F.I. Cas. Bennett's Fire Insurance Cases

Beng.
- Bengal, India
- Bengal Law Reports (1868-75) (India)

Beng. L.R. Bengal Law Reports (India)

Beng. L.R. App. Cas. Bengal Law Reports, Appeal Cases (India)

Beng. L.R.P.C. Bengal Law Reports, Privy Council (India)

Beng. L.R. Supp. Bengal Law Reports, Supp. (India)

Beng. S.D.A. Bengal Sadr Diwani Adalat Cases (India)

Beng. Zillah Decisions of the Zillah Courts, Lower Provinces (India)

Ben. in Keil. Benloe's King's Bench Reports (1531-1628) (73 ER)

Ben. Ins. Benecke on Marine Insurance

Ben. Ins. Cas. Bennett's Insurance Cases

Benj.
- Benjamin. New York Annotated Cases
- Benjamin on Sales of Personal Property (1868-1955)

Benj. Chalm. Bills & N. Benjamin's Chalmer's Bills and Notes

Benj. Sa. Benjamin on Sales (1868-1955)

Benj. Sales Benjamin on Sales (1868-1955)

Ben.Just. (or J.P.) Benedict's New York Civil and Criminal Justice

Benl.
- Benloe & Dalison Reports, Common Pleas (1486-1580) (Eng.)
- Benloe's or Bendloe's English King's Bench Reports (73 ER)

Benl. & D. Benloe & Dalison Common Pleas (123 ER)

Benl. & Dal. Benloe & Dallison's English Common Pleas Reports (123 ER)

Benl. & D.(Eng.) Benlow & Dalison Common Pleas (123 ER)

Benl. (Eng.) Benloe's or Bendloe's English King's Bench Reports (73 ER)

Benl. in Ashe. Benlie at the end of Ashe's Tables

Benl. in Keil. Benloe or Bendloe in Keilway's Reports

Benl. K.B. Benloe's King's Bench (1531-1628) (Eng.)

Benl. New. Benloe, Reports, English King's Bench, Common Pleas, Ed. of 1661

Benloe Benloe's or New Benloe's Reports. English King's Bench. Edition of 1661

Benl. Old. Benloe & Dalison, English Common Pleas Reports, Edition of 1689

Ben. Monroe Ben Monroe's Kentucky Reports, vols. 40-57

Benn. Bennett's Reports (1 California) Bennett's Reports (1 Dakota) Bennett's Reports (16-21 Missouri)

Benn. & H. Cr. Cas. Bennett & Heard's Leading Criminal Cases

Benn. & H. Dig. Bennett & Herard Massachusetts Digest

Benn. & H.Lead.Crim.Cas. Bennett Leading Cases in Criminal Law

Benn. Cal. Bennett's Reports, vol. 1 California

Benn.(Dak.) Bennett's Dakota Cases

Benne. Reporter of vol. 7, Modern Reports (Eng.)

Bennett
- Bennett, Reports (1 California)
- Bennett, Reports, (1 Dakota)
- Bennett, Reports (16-21 Missouri)

Benn. Farm. Bennett's Rights and Liabilities of Farmers

Benn. F.I. Cas. Bennett's Fire Insurance Cases

Benn. (Mo.) Bennett's Missouri Cases

Benn. Pr. M.C. Bennett's Dissertation on Practice of Masters in Chancery

Benn. Rec. Bennett on Receivers

Ben. Ord. Benevolent Orders

Ben. Rev. Bd. Serv.(MB) Benefits Review Board Service

Benefits L.J. Benefits Law Journal

Bent. Bentley's Reports, Irish Chancery

Bent. Abr. Benton's Abridgment of the Debates of Congress

Bent. Cod. Bentham's Codification

Bent. Const. Code Bentham's Constitutional Code for all Nations

Bent. Ev.(or Jud.Ev.) Bentham's Judicial Evidence

Benth. Ev. Bentham on Rationale of Judicial Evidence

Benth. Jud. Ev.
- Bentham on Rationale of Judicial Evidence
- Bentham's Judicial Evidence (1825)

Bentl. Atty.-Gen. Bentley's Reports, vols. 13-19 Attorneys-General's Opinions

Bent. Mor. & Leg. Bentham's Principles of Morals and Legislation

Bent. Mor. Leg. Bentham's Principles of Morals and Legislation. 3ed. 1876

Bent. Pack. Jur. Bentham. Act of Packing as applied to Special Juries. 1821

Bent. Pun. Bentham's Rationale of Punishment

Bent. The. Leg. Bentham's Theory of Legislation

Beor. Queensland Law Reports (1876-78) (Aus.)

B.E.Q.B. Bank of England Quarterly Bulletin

beqd. bequeathed

beqt. bequest

Ber. Berton. New Brunswick Reports (2 New Brunswick Reports) (1835-39)

Berar Berar Law Journal (India)

Berk Co. L.J. Berk's County Law Journal (Pa.)

Berkeley Women's L.J. Berkeley Women's Law Journal

Berks Berks County Law Journal (Pa.)

Berks Co.: Berks County Law Journal (Pa.)

Berks Co LJ (Pa) Berk's County Law Journal (Pa.)

Berm. Bermuda

Bermuda L.R.C. Law Reform Committee, Bermuda

Bern. Bernard's Church Cases (Ir.)

Bern. Ch. Cas. Bernard's Church Cases (1870-75) (Ir.)

Berry Berry's Reports (1-28 Missouri Appeals)

Bert. Berton's New Brunswick Reports, vol. 2

BES Bureau of Employment Security

Bess. Prec. Besson's New Jersey Precedents

Best & S. Best and Smith's English Queen's Bench Reports (1861-69)

Best & S. (Eng.) Best and Smith's English Queen's Bench Reports (1861-69)

Best & Sm. Best and Smith's English Queen's Bench Reports (121, 122 ER)

Best Beg. & Rep. Best on the Right to Begin and Reply

Best Ev. Best on Evidence

Best Jur. Tr. Best on Trial by Jury

Best Law Dic. Best's Law Dictionary

Best, Pres. Best on Presumptions of Law and Fact

Best, Presumptions Best on Presumptions of Law and Fact

Betts' Adm. Pr. Betts' Admiralty Practice

Betts' Dec.
- Blatchford & Howland's United States District Court Reports
- Olcott's United States District Court Reports

B.E.U. Benelux Economic Union

Bev Beverage

Bev. & M. Bevin & Mill's Reports (Ceylon)

Bev. & Sieb. Beven & Sievel's Reports (Ceylon)

Bevans Treaties and Other International Agreements of the United States of America 1776-1949, compiled under direction of Charles I. Bevans

Bev. Emp. L. Bevin on Employer's Liability for Negligence of Servants

Beven
- Beven on Negligence in Law

(1889-1928)

- Beven's Ceylon Reports

Beverly Hills B. Ass'n J. Beverly Hills Bar Association Journal

Bev. Hills B.A.J. Beverly Hills Bar Association Journal

Bev. Hom. Bevil on Homicide

Bev. Pat. Bevill's Patent Cases (Eng.)

BEW Board of Economic Welfare

Bew. & N. Pr. Bewley & Naish on Common Law Procedure

BEWT Bureau of East-West Trade

B.Exam. Bar Examiner

B.Exam.J. Bar Examination Journal

B.F. bonum factum, a good or proper act, deed, or decree; signifies "approved"

b.f.
- bankruptcy fee
- brought forward

BFOQ Bona Fide Occupational Qualification

b.f.p. bona fide purchaser

B.F.S.P. British and Foreign State Papers

B.F.U.A. Banking, Finance and Urban Affairs

B.G. British Guiana Law Reports

b/g bonded goods

B.G.L. Bachelor of General Laws

B.G.L.R. British Guiana Law Reports (Old and New Series)

B.H.C. Bombay High Court Reports (India)

B.H.C.P.J. Bombay High Court Printed Judgments (1869-1900)

(India)

B.H.C.R. Bombay High Court Reports (1862-75) (India)

Bhd. Brotherhood

Bhop. All India Reporter, Bhopal

BHUA Banking, Housing and Urban Affairs

BIA Bureau of Indian Affairs

B.I.A.
- Administrative Decisions Under Immigration and Nationality Laws of the United States
- Board of Immigration Appeals
- British Insurance Association

B.I.A.L.L. British and Irish Association of Law Librarians

BIB Board of International Broadcasting

B.I.B.A. British Insurance Brokers' Association

Bibb. Bibb's Kentucky Reports (1808-17) (vol. 4-7 Kentucky)

Bibb. (Ky.) Bibb's Kentucky Reports (1808-17) (vol. 4-7 Kentucky)

Bibl. Cott. Cotton MSS.

BIC Bureau of International Commerce

Bich. Crim. Proc. Bishop on Criminal Procedure

Bick. Bicknell & Hawley's Reports (vols. 10-20 Nevada)

Bick. & H. Bicknell & Hawley's Reports (vols. 10-20 Nevada)

Bick. & Hawl. Bicknell & Hawley's Reports (vols. 10-20 Nevada)

Bick. Civ. Pr. Bicknell's Indiana

Civil Practice

Bick. Cr. Pr. Bicknell's Indiana Criminal Practice

Bick. (In.) Bicknell's Reports (India)

Bid.
- Bidder's Court of Referees Reports (Eng.)
- Bidder's Locus Standi Reports (Eng.)

Bidd. Bidder's Locus Standi Reports, I. (1820-36)

Bid. Ins. Biddle on Insurance

Bid. Retr. Leg. Biddle on Retrospective Legislation

Bid. Tab. Stat. Biddle's Table of Statutes

Bid. War. Sale Chat. Biddle on Warranties in Sale of Chattels

Biennial Rep. & Op. W.Va. Atty's Gen. Biennial Report and Official Opinions of the Attorney General of the State of West Virginia

Biennial Rep. Iowa Att'y Gen. Biennial Report of the Attorney General, State of Iowa

Biennial Rep. S.D. Att'y Gen. Biennial Report of the Attorney General of the State of South Dakota

Biennial Rep.Vt. Att'y Gen. Biennial Report of the Attorney General of the State of Vermont

BIEPR Bureau of International Economic Policy and Research

B.I.F.D. Bulletin for International Fiscal Documentation

Big. Bignell Reports, India

Big. B. & B. Bigelow's Bench and

Bar of New York

Big. B. & N. Bigelow's Cases on Bills & Notes

Big. Cas. Bigelow, Cases, William I. to Richard I

Big. Cas. B. & N. Bigelow's Cases on Bills & Notes

Big. Cas. Torts Bigelow's Leading Cases in Torts

Bigelow, Estop. Bigelow on Estoppel

Bigelow, Lead. Cas. Bigelow's Leading Cases on Bills and Notes, Torts, or Wills

Big. Eng. Proc. Bigelow's English Procedure

Big. Eq. Bigelow on Equity

Big. Est. Bigelow on Estoppel

Big. Fr. Bigelow on Frauds

Bigg Cr. L. Bigg's Criminal Law

Bigg. L.I.Cas. Bigelow's Life and Accident Insurance Cases

Bigg R.R. Acts Bigg on Acts Relating to Railways

Big. Jarm. Wills Bigelow's edition of Jarman on Wills

Big. L. & A. Ins. Cas. Bigelow's Life and Accident Insurance Cases

Big. L. & A. Ins. Rep. Bigelow, Life & Accident Insurance Reports

Big. Lead. Cas. Bigelow's Leading Cases in Bills and Notes, Torts; or Wills

Big. L.I. Cas. Bigelow's Life and Accident Insurance Cases

Bign. Bignell's Reports (Bengal)

India

Big. Ov. Cas. Bigelow's Overruled Cases (U.S., Eng., Ir.)

Big. Plac. Bigelow's Placita Anglo-Normanica (1066-1195) (Eng.)

Big. Proc. Bigelow's English Procedure

Big. Torts Bigelow on Torts

Bih. L.J. Rep. Bihar Law Journal Reports (India)

B.I.H.R. British Institute of Human Rights

Bih. Rep. Bihar Reports (India)

B.I.H.R. British Institute of Human Rights

Bih. Rep. Bihar Reports (India)

B.I.I.C.L. British Institute of International and Comparative Law

B.I.I.C.L. Newsl. British Institute of International and Comparative Law Newsletter

B.I.L.A. British Insurance Law Association

B.I.L.A. Bull. British Insurance Law Association Bulletin

Bil & Pr. Pat. Billing & Prince's Law and Practice of Patents

Bilas. All India Reporter. Bilaspur

Bil. Aw. Billing, Law of Awards and Arbitration. 1845

Bilb. Ord. Ordinances of Bilboa

B.I.L.C. British International Law Cases

Bill. Billing

Bill of Rights J. Bill of Rights Journal

Bill Rights J. Bill of Rights Journal

Bill Rights Rev. Bill of Rights Review

Bill Rts. J. Bill of Rights Journal

Bil. Pews Billing, Law relating to Pews. 1845

B.I.L.S. British International Law Society

Bi-Mo. L. Rev. Bi-Monthly Law Review, University of Detroit

Bin. Binney's Reports (Pa. 1799-1814)

Bin. Dig. Binmore's Digest, Michigan

Bing. Bingham's English Common Pleas Reports (vols. 130, 131 ER)

Bing. Act. & Def. Bingham's Actions and Defences in Real Property

Bing & Colv. Rents Bingham & Colvin on Rents

Bing. Des. Bingham on the Laws of Descent

Bing. (Eng.) Bingham's English Common Pleas Reports (vols. 130, 131 ER)

Bing. Ex. Bingham, Judgments and Executions. 1815

Bing. Ex. Cont. Bingham's Executory Contracts, & c.

Bing. Inf. Bingham, Infancy and Coveture 1826

Bing. Judg. Bingham, Judgments and Executions. 1815

Bing. L. & T. Bingham, Landlord and Tenant. 1820

Bing. N.C. Bingham, New Cases, English Common Pleas (131-133 ER)

Bing. N. Cas. Bingham, New

Cases, English Common Pleas (131-133 ER)

Bing. N.C. (Eng.) Bingham, New Cases, English Common Pleas (131-133 ER)

Bing. R.P. Bingham on the Law of Real Property

Binm. Ind. Binmore's Index-Digest of Michigan Reports

Binn. Binney's Pennsylvania Supreme Court Reports (1799-1814)

Binn Jus. Binn's Pennsylvania Justice

Binn. (Pa.) Binney's Pennsylvania Reports (1799-1814)

Binns' Just. Binns' Justice (Pa.)

Biog.
- Biographical
- Biography

Bior. & D. Laws Bioren & Duane's United States Laws (see n.1, p.15)

B.I.R. Board of Inland Revenue

Bird Conv. Bird, New Pocket Conveyancer, 5ed. 1830

Bird L. & T. Bird, Laws respecting Landlords, Tenants & Lodgers, 11 ed. 1833

Bird Sol. Pr. Bird, Solution of Precedents of Settlements 1800

Birds. St. Birdseye's Statutes (N.Y.)

Bird. Supp. Bird's Supplement to Barton's Conveyancing

Birdw. Birdwood's Printed Judgments (India)

Birk. J. Birkenhead's Judgments, House of Lords (1919-22) (Eng.)

Birmingham I.J.A. Institute of Judicial Administration, Birmingham

Birth Con. Birth Control

BIS Bank for International Settlements

Bis. Bissell's United States Circuit Court Reports

Bish. Burr. Bishop's edition of Burrill on Assignments

Bish. Con. Bishop on Contracts

Bish. Cont. Bishop on Contracts

Bish. Cr.L. Bishop on Criminal Law

Bish. Cr. Law Bishop on Criminal Law

Bish. Cr. Proc. Bishop on Criminal Procedure

Bish. First Bk. Bishop, First Book of the Law

Bish. Ins. Bishop on Insolvent Debtors

Bish. Mar. & Div. Bishop on Marriage and Divorce

Bish. Mar., Div. & Sep. Bishop on Marriage, Divorce, and Separation

Bish. Mar. Wom. Bishop on Married Women

Bish. New Cr. Law Bishop's New Criminal Law

Bish. New Cr. Proc. Bishop's New Criminal Procedure

Bish. Noll. Pros. Bishop's Law of Nolle Prosequi

Bish. Non-Cont. Law Bishop on Non-Contract Law, Rights and Torts

Bishop Dig. Bishop's Digest,

Montana

Bish. Stat. Cr. Bishop on Statutory Crimes

Bish. St. Crimes Bishop on Statutory Crimes

Bish. Wr. L. Bishop on Written Law

Bisp. Eq. Bispham's Principles of Equity

Bisph. Eq. Bispham's Principles of Equity

Biss. Bissell's United States Circuit Court Reports

Biss. & Sm. Bissett & Smith's Digest (S. Africa)

Bissell Bissell's U.S. Circuit Court Reports, Seventh Circuit

Biss. Est. Bisset's Estates for Life. 1842

Bissett, Est. Bissett on Estates for Life

Biss. Part. Bisset's Partnership and Joint Stock Companies. 1847

Biss. Stat. Bissell's Minnesota Statutes

Biss. (U.S.) Bissell's U.S. Circuit Court Reports (7th Cir.)

BIT Business insurance trust

Bit. & Wise Bittleston and Wise, New Magistrate Cases (Eng.)

Bit. Prac. Cas. Bittleston's Practice Cases, under Judicature Act (Eng.)

Bitt. Bittleston's Reports in Chambers, Queen's Bench Division (Eng.)

Bitt. Ch. Bittleston's Reports in Chambers, Queen's Bench Division (Eng.)

Bitt. Cha. Cas. Bittleston's Chambers Cases (1883-84)

Bitt. Chamb. Rep. Bittleston's Reports in Chambers, Queen's Bench Division (Eng.)

Bitt. Ch. Cas. Bittleston's Reports in Chambers, Queen's Bench Division (1875-76) (1883-84)

Bitt. P.C. Bittleston's Practice Cases under Judicature Acts (Eng.)

Bitt. Pr. Cas. Bittleston's Practice Cases under Judicature Acts (Eng.)

Bitt. Pr. Case Bittleston's Practice Cases under Judicature Act (Eng.)

Bitt. Rep. in Ch. Bittleston's Reports in Chambers, Queen's Bench Division (Eng.)

Bitt. W. & P. Bittleston, Wise & Parnell's Reports (2, 3 New Practice Cases) (Eng.)

B.J.A.L. British Journal of Administrative Law

B.J. Crim. British Journal of Criminology

B.J. Delinq. British Journal of Delinquency

B.J. Ind. Rel. British Journal of Industrial Relations

B.J.I.R. British Journal of Industrial Relations

B.J. Lea Lea's Reports (Tenn.)

B.J.L.S. British Journal of Law and Society

B.Jur. Baccalaureus Juris

B.Jur. & Soc.S. Bachelor of Juridical and Social Sciences

B.Just. Burn's Justice of the Peace

Bk Bank

Bk.
- Black. United States Supreme Court Reports, vols. 66-67
- book

Bk. Judg. Book of Judgments by Townsend

Bk. L.J. Banking Law Journal

Bk. Reg. National Bankruptcy Register Reports

bks. Books

Bky. Bankruptcy

BL Business Lawyer

B.L.
- Bachelor of Law
- Bachelor of Letters
- Barrister-at-Law
- Bill of Lading
- Black Letter
- British Library

B.L. Bell on Leases

Bl.
- Blackford's Indiana Reports (1817-47)
- Blackstone's Commentaries
- Black's United States Supreme Court Reports
- Blatchford's United States Circuit Court Reports
- Blount's Law Dictionary
- Henry Blackstone's English Common Pleas Reports
- William Blackstone's English King's Bench Reports

b/l bill of lading

B.L.A. British Legal Association

Bla. Blackstone, W. 1746-80

Bla. Ch. Bland's Maryland Chancery Reports

Black
- Blackerby's Magistrates Reports (1327-1716) (Eng.)
- Blackford's Reports (Indiana 1817-1847, vols. 30-53)
- Black's Reports (vols. 30-53 Indiana)
- Black's Supreme Court Reports (vols. 66, 67 U.S. Reports)
- Blackstone's Reports, King's Bench, tempore George II & III; Common Pleas, George III (Eng.)
- H. Blackstone's Common Pleas Reports (1788-96) (Eng.)
- W. Blackstone's King's Bench Reports (1746-80) (Eng.)

Black. Abr. Blackstone's Commentaries, Abridged

Black. Anal. Blackstone's Analysis of the Laws of England

Blackb. Blackburn on Sales 3 editions (1845-1910)

Black Bk. Adm. Twiss' Black Book of the Admiralty

Blackb. Sales Blackburn on Sales

Black. Com. Blackstone's on the Laws of England

Black. Cond. Blackwell's Condensed Illinois Reports

Black. Cond. Rep. Blackwell's Condensed Illinois Reports

Black, Const. Law Black on Constitutional Law

Black, Const. Prohib. Black's Constitutional Prohibitions

Black. D. & O. Blackham, Dundas, & Osborne's Irish Nisi Prius

Reports

Black. Dict. Black's Law Dictionary

Black Emp. Li. Black on Employer's Liability

Blackf. Blackford's Reports (Indiana 1817-47)

Blackf.(Ind.) Blackford's Reports (Indiana 1817-47)

Blackford's Ia. R. Blackford's Indiana Reports (Ind.)

Black. H. Henry Blackstone's English Common Pleas Reports (1788-96)

Black, Interp. Laws Black on the Construction and Interpretation of Laws

Black, Intox. Liq. Black on the Laws Regulating the Manufacture and Sale of Intoxicating Liquors

Black, Judg. Black on Judgments

Black, Judgm. Black on Judgments

Black. Jus. Blackerby's Justices' Cases (Eng.)

Black. Just. Blackerby's Justice of the Peace

Black, Law Dict. Black's Law Dictionary

Black L.D. Black's Law Dictionary

Black L.J. Black Law Journal

Black L.Tr. Blackstone's Law Tracts

Black. Mag. Ch. Blackstone on Magna Charta

Black R.
- Black's United States Supreme Court Reports

- W. Blackstone's English King's Bench Reports (1746-80)

Black.R. Blackford's Indiana Reports (Ind.)

Black Rep. Black, United States Supreme Court Reports

Black. Sal. Blackburn on Sale. 3ed. 1910

Black Ship. Ca. Black's Decisions in Shipping Cases

Black's Law Dict. Black's Law Dictionary

Blackst. Blackstone's Reports in King's Bench.temp.George II & III; and Common Pleas,George III (1746-80)

Black St. Const. Black on Construction and Interpretation of Laws

Blackstone's Commen. Blackstone's Commentaries on the Laws of England

Blackst.R. William Blackstone's King's Bench (1746-80) (Eng.)

Black. Tax Tit. Blackwell's Tax Titles

Black Tax Titles Black on Tax Titles

Black.W. William Blackstone's English King's Bench Reports (1746-80)

Blackw. Cond. Blackwell's Condensed Reports (Ill.)

Blackw. Sc. Acts Blackwell's Scotch Acts

Blackw. Sc. Atc. Blackwell's Scotch Acts

Blackw. Tax Titles Blackwell's Tax Titles

Blackw. T.T. Blackwell on Tax Titles

Bla. Com. Blackstone's on the Law of England

Bldg. Building

Bldg. & Constr. C. Building and Construction Law

Bla.H. Henry Blackstone's English Common Pleas Reports

Blair Blair, Manual for Scotch Justices of the Peace

Blair Co. Blair County Law Reports, Pennsylvania

Blair Co. L.R. Blair County Law Reports, Pennsylvania

Blair Co. L.R.(Pa.) Blair County Law Reports, Pennsylvania

Blake Blake's Reports (1-3 Montana)

Blake & H. Blake and Hedges' Reports (2-3 Montana)

Blake Ch. Pr. Blake's Chancery Practice, New York

Bla. Life Ass. Blayney, Life Assurance. 1837

Blan. & W. Lead. Cas. Blanchard & Weeks' Leading Cases, Mines

Blanc. & W.L.C. Blanchard & Weeks' Leading Cases on Mines, etc.

Bland Bland's Maryland Chancery Reports (1811-32)

Bland Ch.(Md.) Bland's Maryland Chancery Reports

Bland.Ch.R. Bland's Chancery Reports (Md.)

Bl. & H.
- Blake & Hedges' Reports (2-3 Montana)

- Blatchford & Howland's United States District Court Reports

Bl. & How. Blatchford & Howland's United States District Court Reports

Bland's Ch.
- Bland's Chancery Reports (Md.)
- Bland's Maryland Chancery Reports (Md.)

Bland's Ch. R. Bland's Chancery Reports (Md.)

Bland's Chy. Rep. Bland's Chancery Reports (Md.)

Bl. & W. Mines Blanchard & Weeks' Leading Cases on Mines

Blan. Lim. Blanshard on Statute of Limitations

Blansh. Lim. Blanshard, Statutes of Limitations. 1826

Blas.
- Blasphemy
- Blasphemy and Profanity

Blash. Juries. Blashfield, Instructions to Juries

Blat. C.C.R. Blatchford's U.S. Circuit Court Reports

Blatch. Blatchford's U.S. Circuit Court Reports

Blatch. & H. Blatchford & Howard's Dist.Ct.Rep.(34,35 Ga.)

Blatchf. Blatchford's United States Circuit Court Reports

Blatchf. & H. Blatchford & Howland's United States District Court Reports

Blatchf. C.C. Blatchford's United States Circuit Court Reports

Blatchf. C.C. Rep. Blatchford's U.S. Circuit Court Reports

Blatchford & H. Blatchford and Howland's Reports (U.S.)

Blatchf. Pr. Cas. Blatchford's Prize Cases (U.S.)

Blatch.Pr.Cas. Blatchford's Prize Cas.,U.S.

Blatchf.Prize Cas. Blatchford's Prize Cases (U.S.)

Blatchf. (U.S.Circ.Ct.) Blatchford's U.S. Circuit Court Reports

Blatch. (U.S.Cir.Ct.) Blatchford's U.S. Circuit Court Reports

Bldg. Contr. Building and Construction Contracts

Bldgs. Buildings

Bla.W. Sir William Blackstone's Reports English King's Bench

Blax. Eng. Co. Blaxland's Codex Legum Angelicanum

Blay. Ann. Blayney, Life Annuities. 1817

Blay. Life Ins. Blayney, Life Assurance 1837

Bl.B. Adm. Twiss, Black Book of the Admiralty

Bl.C.C.R. Blatchford's U.S. Circuit Court Reports

Bl.C.C. Blatchford's United States Circuit Court Reports

Bl. Chr. R. Bland's Chancery Reports

Bl. Chy. Pr. Blake, Chancery Practice

Bl. Com. Blackstone's Commentaries

Bl. Comm. Blackstone's Commentaries on the Law of England

Bl.D. Blount, Law Dictionary

Bl.D. & O. Blackham, Dundas & Osborne's Irish Nisi Prius Reports (1846-48)

Bl.D. & Osb. Blackham, Dundas and Osborne's Reports, N.P. Ireland (1846-48)

Bldg. Contr. Building and Construction Contracts

Bldgs. Buildings

Bl. Dict. Black's Law Dictionary

B. Leader Bar Leader

Bleck. Bleckley's Reports (34, 35 Georgia)

Bleckley Bleckley's Reports (34, 35 Georgia)

Bl. Emp. L. Black, Employer's Liability

BLEU Belgium-Luxembourg Economic Union

Bl.H. Henry Blackstone's English Common Pleas Reports (1788-96)

Bli. Bligh's English House of Lords Reports

Blick. Rev. Blickenaderfer, Law Student's Review

Bligh Bligh's English House of Lords Reports (1819-21)

Bligh N.S. (Eng.) Bligh's English House of Lords Reports, New Series (1827-37) (4-6)

B.L.I.J. Burma Law Institute Journal

Bli.N.S. Bligh's English House of Lords Reports, New Series (1827-37)

Bli. (O.S.) Bligh's English House of Lords Reports, Old Series (1819-21)

Bliss Delaware County Reports,

Pennsylvania

Bliss Co. Pl. Bliss on Code Pleading

Bliss Ins. Bliss on Life Insurance

Bliss N.Y. Co. Bliss's New York Code

B.L.J.
- Bihar Law Journal Reports
- Burma Law Journal

Bliss N.Y. Code Bliss' Annotated New York Code

Bl. Judgm. Black on Judgments

B.L.L. Bachelor of Laws

Bl. Law Tracts Blackstone's Law Tracts

Bl.L.D.
- Black's Law Dictionary
- Blount's Law Dictionary

Bl.L.J. Black Law Journal

Bl.L.T. Blackstone's Law Tracts

BLM Bureau of Land Management

Blm. Neg. Bloomfield's Negro Cas., N.J.

BLMR Bureau of Labor-Management Reports

Bl.N.S. Bligh, House of Lords Reports, New Series

Bloom. Man. Bloomfield' Manumission (or Negro) Cases, New Jersey

Bloom. Man. Neg. Cas. Bloomfield's Manumission (or Negro) Cases, New Jersey

Blount Blount's Law Dictionary

Blount Frag.Ant. Blount, Fragmenta Antiquitatis

Blount L.D. Blount's Law Dictionary

Blount Ten. Blount on Tenures

Blount Tr. Blount's Impeachment Trial

B.L.P.L. & M.Cas. Brainard's Legal Precedents in Land and Mining Cases, Washington

Bl. Pr. Cas. Blatchford. Prize Cases, United States

Bl. Prize Blatchford's Prize Cases

B.L.R.
- Bahamas Law Reports
- Barbados Law Reports
- Baylor Law Review
- Bengal Law Reports, High Courts (India)
- Bermuda Law Reports
- Bombay Law Reporter (India)
- Business Law Reports (Annotated) (Can.)
- Business Law Review

Bl.R. Sir William Blackstone's English King's Bench Reports (1746-80)

B.L.R.A.C. Bengal Law Reports, Appeal Cases

B.L.R.P.C. Bengal Law Rep. Privy Council

B.L.R. Suppl. Vol. Bengal Law Reports, Supplemental Volume, Full Bench Rulings

BLS
- Bureau of Labor Statistics
- Business Lawyer, Special Issue

B.L.S.A. British Legal Services Agency

B.L.S. Bull. US Bureau of Labor Statistics Bulletin

B.L.T.
- Baltimore Law Transcript

- Burma Law Times

Bl.Ti.   Block on Tithes

Bl.T.T.   Blackwell on Tax Titles

Blu.   Bluett's Advocate's Note Book (Isle of Man) (1720-1846)

Blue Sky L. Rep. (CCH)
- Blue Sky Law Reports
- Blue Sky Law Reporter (CCH)

Bluett   Bluett's Isle of Man Cases

Blum. B'k'cy.   Blumenstiel, Bankruptcy

Bl.W.   Blackstone W. Reports, King's Bench (1746-80) (Eng.)

B.L.W.A.   Black Legal Workers' Association

Bly.Us.   Blydenburgh, Law of Usury. 1844

B.M.
- Ben Monroe's Reports, Kentucky
- British Museum
- Burrow's Reports tempore Mansfield (1756-72) (Eng.)
- Moore's Reports (Eng.)

B.M.L.A.   British Maritime Law Association

B.Mon.   Ben Monroe's Kentucky Supreme Court Reports (1840-1857)

B.Mon. (Ky.)   Ben Monroe's Reports, Kentucky (40-57)

B.Monr.
- Ben Monroe's Reports, Kentucky
- Burrow's Reports tempore Mansfield (Eng.)
- Moore's Reports (Eng.)

B.Moore.   Bayly Moore, English Common Pleas Reports

Bn.   Baron

BNA   Bureau of National Affairs

B.N.A.   Bureau of National Affairs, Inc. Washington, D.C.

B.N.A. Act.   British North America Act

BNA Banking Rep.   BNA Banking Report

BNA Sec. Reg.   Securities Regulation & Law Report (BNA)

B.N.B.   Bracton's Note Book (Temp. Henry III)

B.N.C.
- Bingham, New Cases, English Common Pleas (1834-40)
- Brooke, New Cases, English King's Bench (1515-58)
- Busbee, North Carolina Law Reports (44, 45 North Carolina)

BNDD   Bureau of Narcotics and Dangerous Drugs

B.N.P.   Buller's Nisi Prius

Board of Review Decisions   Decisions of the Income Tax Board of Review (1936-50) (Aus.)

BOB   Bureau of the Budget

Bogert, Trusts   Bogert on Trusts & Trustees

Boh. Att.   Bohun, Practising Attorney

Boh. Curs. Can.   Bohun's Cursus Cancellariae

Boh. Dec.   Bohun's Declarations and Pleadings

Boh. Eccl. Jur.   Bohun, Ecclesiastical Jurisdiction

Boh. Eng. L.   Bohun, English Lawyer

Boh Ti.   Bohun, Titles

Bohun Bohun's Election Cases (Eng.)

Bohun. Curs. Canc. Bohun's Cursus Cancellariae

Bol. Bolivia

Bolland Select Bills in Eyre (Selden Society Pub. 30) (Eng.)

BOM Bureau of Mines

Bom. Bombay High Court Reports (India)

Bom. A.C. Bombay Reports, Appellate Juris (India)

Bomb. Indian Law Reports, Bombay Series (India)

Bombay L.J. Bombay Law Journal

Bomb. Cr. Rul. Bombay High Ct., Criminal Rulings (India)

Bomb. H.C. Bombay High Ct. Reports (India)

Bomb. H.Ct. Bombay High Court Reports

Bomb. Hg.Ct. Bombay High Court Reports (India) (1862-75)

Bomb. L.R. Bombay Law Reporter

Bomb. Sel. Cas. Bombay Select Cases, Sadr Diwani Adalat (India)

Bomb. Ser. Indian Law Reports, Bombay Series (India)

Bomb. Cr. Cas. Bombay Reports, Crown Cases (India)

Bom. H.C.R. Bombay High Court Reports (1862-75) (India)

Bom. L.J. Bombay Law Journal (India)

Bom. L.R. Bombay Law Reporter (India)

Bom. L. Rep. Bombay Law Reports, Bombay, India

Bom. L.R.J. Bombay Law Reporter (India)

Bom. O.C.
- Bombay Reports, Civil Jurisdiction (India)
- Bombay Reports, Oudh Cases (India)

Bom. Unrep. Cr. C. Bombay Unreported Criminal Cases (India) (1862- 98)

Bond Bond's United States Circuit Reports

Bond L. Rev. Bond Law Review

Bond Md. App. Proceedings of Court of Appeal of Maryland (in American Legal Records, 1)

Bone Prec. Bone Precedents in Conveyancing (1838-40)

Bon. Ins. Bonney, Insurance

Bonn.Car. Bonney on Railway Carriers

Bonnetti, Ital. Dict. Bonnetti's Italian Dictionary

Bonn. Ins. Bonney on Insurance

Bon. R.R. Car. Bonney, Railway Carriers

Book of Judg. Book of Judgments (Eng.)

Books S. Books of Sederunt

Books Sed. Books of Sederunt

Boone Corp. Boone on Corporations

Boor. Booraem's Reports (vols. 6-8 California)

Boo. R. Act. Booth, Real Actions

Booraem Booraem's Reports (vols. 6-8 California)

Boote Boote's Suit at Law

Boote Act. Boote's Action at Law

Boote Ch. Pr. Boote, Chancery Practice

Boote S.L. Boote's Suit at Law

Boote, Suit at Law Boote's Suit at Law

Booth Chester Palatine Courts 1811 (Eng.)

Booth Ind. Of. Booth's Indictable Offenses

Booth In. Of. Booth, Indictable Offences

Booth R. Act. Booth on Real Actions

Booth, Real Act. Booth on Real Action

Booth Wills Booth's Law of Wills

Bor. Ct. Borough Court

Borr. Borradaile's Civil Cases, Bombay (1800-24) (India)

Borth. Borthwick, Modes of Prosecuting for Libel. 1830

Bos. Bostworth's Superior Court Reports (N.Y.)

Bos. & D. Lim. Bosanquet & Darby's Limitations

Bos. & P. Bosanquet and Puller's English Common Pleas Reports

Bos. & Paul. Bosanquet & Puller's Reports, Common Pleas (1796-1804) (Eng.)

Bos. & P. (Eng.) Bosanquet & Puller's English Common Pleas Reports (vols. 126, 127 ER)

Bos. & P.N.R. Bosanquet & Puller's New Reports, English Common Pleas (127 ER)

Bos. & P.N.R. (Eng.) Bosanquet & Puller's New Reports, English Common Pleas (127 ER)

Bos. & Pu. Bosanquet and Puller's English Common Pleas Reports (126, 127 ER)

Bos. & Pul. Bosanquet & Puller's English Common Pleas Reports (vols. 126, 127 ER)

Bos. & Pul. N.R. Bosanquet & Puller's New Reports, English Common Pleas

Bosc. Con. Boscawen on Convictions

Bos. C. Third World L. J. Boston College Third World Law Journal

Bos. Pl. Bosanquet's Rules of Pleading

Bos. Pol. Rep. Boston Police Reports

Bost. Coll. Ind. L. Rev. Boston College Industrial and Commercial Law Review

Bost. Law Rep. Boston Law Reporter

Bost. L.R. Boston Law Reporter

Boston B.J. Boston Bar Journal

Boston Col. Ind. Com. L. Rev. Boston College Industrial and Commercial Law Review

Boston Col. Int.Comp. L. Rev. Boston College International and Comparative Law Review

Boston Col. Int'l. & Comp. L.J. Boston College International and Comparative Law Journal

Boston College L. Rev. Boston College Law Review

Boston U. L. Rev. Boston University Law Review

Bost. Pol. Rep. Boston Police Court Reports

Bost.U. L.Rev. Boston University Law Review

Bos. U. Int. L.J. Boston University International Law Journal

Bosw.
- Boswell's Reports (Scotch Court of Sessions)
- Bosworth, New York Superior Court Reports, vols. 14-23

B.o.T. Board of Trade

B.O.T.Jo. Board of Trade Journal

Bots. Botswana

Botswana L.R.C. Botswana Law Reform Committee

Bott. Bott's Poor Law Settlement Cases (1761-1827)

Bott P.L. Bott's Poor Laws

Bott P.L. Cas. Bott's Poor Law Cases (1560-1833) (Eng.)

Bott P.L. Const. Const's Edition of Bott's Poor Law Cases

Bott Poor Law Cas. Bott's Poor Laws Settlement Cases (Eng.)

Bott Set. Cas. Bott's Poor Law (Settlement) Cass

Bott's P.L. Bott's Poor Law Cases (1560-1833)

Bou. Dic. Bouvier, Law Dictionary

Bou. Inst. Bouvier's Institutes of American Law

Bould. Bouldin's Reports (vol. 119 Alabama)

Bouln. Boulnois' Reports, Bengal

Boulnois Boulnois' Reports, Bengal

Bound. Boundaries

Bount. Bounties

Bourd. L.T. Bourdin on the Land Tax

Bourke Bourke's Reports, Calcutta High Court (India)

Bourke Lim. Bourke on the Indian Law of Limitations

Bourke P.P. Bourke's Parliamentary Precedents (1842-56) (Eng.)

Bout. Man. Boutwell's Manual of the United States Tax System

Bouv. Bouvier Law Dictionary

Bouvier Bouvier's Law Dictionary

Bouv. Inst. Bouvier's Institutes of American Law

Bouv. Law Dict. Bouvier's Law Dictionary

Bouv. L. Dict. Bouvier's Law Dictionary

Bov. Pat. Cas. Bovill's Patent Cases

Bow.
- Bowler & Bowers (U.S. Comptroller's Dec., v. 2, 3)
- Bowler's London Session Records (1605-85)

Bow. Civ. Law Bowyer, Modern Civil Law. 1848

Bow. Com. Bowyer, Commentaries on Universal Public Law. 1854

Bow. Cons. Law Bowyer, Commentaries on the Constitutional Law of England. 2ed. 1846

Bowen, Pol. Econ. Bowen's Political Economy

Bow. Int. Bowyer, Introduction to the Study and Use of the Civil Law. 1874

Bowler's First Comp. Dec. Decisions of the First Comptroller of the U.S. Treasury

Bowl. Lib.   Bowles on Libel

Bow. Pub. Law   Bowyer, Commentaries on Universal Public Law. 1854

Bowstead   Bowstead on Agency (1896-1951)

Bowy.   Bowyer (see Bow.)

Bowyer, Mod.Civil Law   Bowyer's Modern Civil Law

Box. & Pul. N.R.   Bosanquet & Puller's New Reports, English Common Pleas

Boyce   Boyce's Delaware Supreme Court Reports (1909-19)

Boyce U.S. Pr.   Boyce's Practice in the United States Courts

Boy. Char.   Boyle, Charities. 1837

Boyd. Adm.   Boyd's Admiralty Law, Ireland

Boyd Jus.   Boyd, Justice of the Peace

Boyd Sh.   Boyd, Merchant Shipping Laws. 1876

Boyle Act.   Boyle's Precis of an Action at Common Law

Boyle Char.   Boyle's Law of Charities

Boys Cor.   Boys on Coroners

BP
- Benefit Principles
- Drake & Mullins, Bankruptcy Practice

BP2   Drake & Homer, Bankruptcy Practice, Second Edition

B.P.B.   Buller's Paper Book, Lincoln's Inn Library

B.P.C.   Brown's Cases in Parliament (1701-1800)

B.P.L.   Bott's Poor Law Cases (1560-1833) (Eng.)

B.P.L. Cas.   Bott's Poor Law Cases (1560-1833)

B.P.L. Cases   Bott's Poor Law Cases

B.P.N.R.   Bosanquet & Puller's New Reports, English Common Pleas (1804-07)

B.P.R.   Brown's Parliamentary Reports (Eng.)

B.Proc.   Baccalaureus Procurationis

BPS   Bureau of Product Safety

BR   Board of Review

B.R.
- Baltimore City Reports
- Bancus Reginae, or Queen's Bench
- Bancus Regis, or King's Bench
- Bankruptcy Register
- Bankruptcy Reports
- Board of Review, U.S. Army (1929-1949)
- Brooklyn Law Review
- United States Bankruptcy Court
- West's Bankruptcy Reporter

Br.
- Bracton
- Bradford
- Bradwell
- Brayton
- Breese
- Brevard
- Brewster
- Bridgman
- Brief

- Brightly
- British
- Britton
- Brockenbrough
- Brooke
- Broom
- Brown
- Browne
- Brownlow
- Bruce, Reports, Court of Session (1714-15) (Sc.)
- Qubec Official Reports, Queen's Bench (1892-1900) (Can.)

b.r. bills receivable

B.R.A. Butterworth's Rating Appeals (1913-31) (Eng.)

Bra.
- Bracton de Legibus Angliae
- Brady's English History (1648)

Br. Abr. Brooke's Abridgment (Eng.)

Brac.
- Bracton de Legibus et Consuetudinibus Angliae (Eng.)
- Bracton's Note Book, King's Bench (1217-40)

Bra. Cit. Brady's Historical Treatise on Cities

Brack. Misc. Brackenridge's Miscellanies

Brack. Tr. Brackenridge on the Law of Trusts

Brac. L.J. Bracton Law Journal

B.R.Act. Booth's Real Action

Bract.
- Bracton de Legibus et Consuetudinibus Angliae (Eng.)
- A digest of Maxims by James S. Bracton

Bracton Bracton de Legibus et Consuetudinibus Angliae (Eng.)

Bracton L.J. Bracton Law Journal

Brad.
- Bradford's Kentucky Statutes
- Bradford's New York Surrogate Reports
- Bradford's Reports (Iowa 1838-41)
- Bradford's Somerset Star Chamber
- Bradwell's Reports (1-20 Ill. App.) Cases (Somerset Record Society No. 27) (Eng.)
- Brady's History of the Succession of the Crown of England

Bradb. Bradbury's Pleading and Practice Reports (N.Y.)

Brad. Dis. Bradby on Distresses

Bradf.
- Bradford's New York Surrogate Reports
- Bradford's Proceedings in the Court of Star Chamber (Somerset Record Society Publications, vol. 27)
- Bradford's Reports (Iowa)

Bradford Bradford's Iowa Supreme Court Reports (1839-41)

Bradford's R. Bradford's New York Surrogate's Court Reports

Bradford's Sur. R. Bradford's New York Surrogate's Court Reports (N.Y.)

Bradf. Rep. Bradford's New York Surrogate's Court Reports

Bradf. Sur. Bradford's New York Surrogate Court Reports

Bradf. Sur. R. Bradford's New York Surrogate's Court Reports

94

Bradf. Surr. Bradford's New York Surrogate Court Reports

Bradl. Bradley's Rhode Island Reports

Bradl. P.B. Bradley's Point Book

Bradl.(R.I.) Bradley's Rhode Island Reports

Brad. R. Bradford's New York Surrogate's Court Reports

Brad. Sur. Bradford's New York Surrogate's Court Reports

Bradw. Bradwell's Appellate Reports (Illinois)

Brady Ind. Brady's Index, Arkansas Reports

Brady's Tr. Brady's Treatise upon Cities and Boroughs

Bra. Ind. Soc. Brabrook, Industrial and Provident Societies. 1869

Brain. L.P. Brainard's Legal Precedents in Land & Mining Cases (U.S.)

Braith. Jamaica Law Reports (Braithwaite)

Braith. Chy. Braithwaite, Times of Procedure in Chancery. 1864

Braith. Oaths
- Braithwaite, Oaths in Chancery, 2ed. 1864
- Braithwaite Oaths in the Supreme Court. 4ed. 1881

Braith. Pr. Braithwaite, Record and Writ Practice of the Court of Chancery. 1858

Brame. Brame's Reports (vols. 66-72 Mississippi)

Branch. Branch's Reports (vol. 1 Florida)

Branch, Max. Branch's Maxims

Branch Pr. Branch's Principia Legis et Equitatis (Maxims)

Branch, Princ. Branch's Principia Legis et Equitatis

Brand. Brandenburg's Reports, vol. 21, Opinions Attorneys-General

Br. & B. Broderip & Bingham, Common Pleas (Eng.)

Br. & Col. British & Colonial Prize Cases

Br. & Col. Pr. Cas. British and Colonial Prize Cases (1914-19)

Brande. Brande's Dictionary of Science, etc.

Brandenburg Bankr. Brandenburg's Bankruptcy

Brandenburg Dig. Brandenburg's Bankruptcy Digest

Brand.F. Attachm. (Or Brand.For. Attachm.) Brandon on Foreign Attachment

Br. & F. Ecc. Broderick & Fremantle's Ecclesiastical Cases (1840-64) (Eng.)

Brand. For. Att. Brandon on Foreign Attachment

Br. & Fr. Broderick & Fremantle's Ecclesiastical Cases (1840-64) (Eng.)

Br. & G. Brownlow and Goldesborough's Reports, Common Pleas (1569-1624)

Br. & Gold. Brownlow & Goldesborough, English Common Pleas Reports

Br. & Had. Broom & Hadley, Commentaries on the Laws of England, 2ed. 1875

B.R. & J.C.(Army) Board of Review and Judicial Council of the Army

Br. & L. Browning & Lushington, English Admiralty Reports (1863-65)

Br. & Lush Browning & Lushington, English Admiralty Reports (1863-65)

Brand. May. Ct. Brandon, Practice of the Mayor's Court. 1864

Br. & R. Brown & Rader's Reports (vol. 137 Missouri)

Brandt, Sur. Brandt on Suretyship and Guaranty

Brans. Dig. Branson's Digest (Bombay)

Brant. Brantly's Reports, (vols. 80-90 Maryland)

Brantly Brantly's Reports (vols. 80-90 Maryland)

B.R. (Army) Board of Review (Army)

Bra. Tr. Un. Brabrook's Law of Trade Unions

Bray. Brayton's Vermont Reports

Bray. R. Brayton's Reports (Vt.)

Brayt. Brayton (Vt.)

Brayton's Rep. Brayton's Reports (Vt.)

Brayton (Vt.) Brayton's Reports (Vermont)

Brayt. Rep. Brayton's Reports (Vt.)

Braz. Brazil

Br. Brev. Jud. Brownlow's Brevia Judicialia, etc. (1662)

Br. Brev. Jud. & Ent. Brownlow's Brevia Judicialia, etc. 1662

B.R.B.S. Benefits Review Board Service (Matthew Bender)

Br. Bur. British Burman

B.R.C. British Ruling Cases

Br.C.C.
- British (or English) Crown Cases (American reprint)
- Brown's Chancery Cases, (Eng.)

Br. Col. British Columbia

Br. Com. Broom, Common Law. 9ed. 1896

Br. Cons. Law Broom, Constitutional Law. 3ed. 1885

Br. Cr. Ca. British (or English) Crown Cases (American Reprint)

Br. Cr. Cas. British Crown Cases

Brd. Board

Breach P. Breach of Peace and Disorderly Conduct

Breach Prom. Breach of Promise

b.rec. bill(s) receivable

Br. Eccl. Brown's Ecclesiastical (Eng.)

Breese Breese's Reports (vol. 1 Illinois)

B. Reg. Bankrupt Register

Br. Ent. Brownlow, Entries

Bresse Bresse's Illinois Supreme Court Reports (1819-1831) (1 Ill.)

Brett Ca. Eq. Brett's Cases in Modern Equity

Brev. Brevard's South Carolina Reports (1793-1816)

Brev. Dig. Brevard's Digest of the Public Statute Law, South Carolina

Brev. Ju. Brevia Judicialia (Judicial Writs)

Brev. Sel. Brevia Selecta, or Choice Writs

Brew. Brewer's Reports (vols. 19-26 Maryland)

Brewer Brewer, Reports (19-26 Maryland)

Brew. (Md.) Brewer's Reports (vols. 19-26 Maryland)

Brews. Brewster's Reports (Pa.)

Brews. (Pa.) Brewster's Reports (Pa.)

Brewst. Brewster (Pennsylvania Reports, 4 vols.)

Brewster Brewster's Reports (Pa.)

Brewst. Pa. Dig. Brewster's Pennsylvania Digest

Br. Fed. Dig. Brightly's Federal Digest

B.R.H. Cases in King's Bench tempore Hardwicke (1733-38) (Eng.)

Brib. Bribery

Brice Ult.V. Brice's Ultra Vires

Brick. Ala. Dig. Brickell's Alabama Digest

Brick. Dig. Brickell's Digest (Alabama)

Bridg. J. Bridgman's Reports, Common Pleas (1614-21)

Bridg. Conv. Bridgman on Conveyancing

Bridg. Dig. Ind. Bridgman's Digested Index

Bridg. Eq. Ind. Bridgman. Index to Equity Cases

Bridg. J. Sir J. Bridgman, English Common Pleas Reports

Bridg. Leg. Bib. Bridgman, Legal Bibliography. 1801

Bridg. O. Sir Orlando Bridgman, English Common Pleas Reports (1660-67)

Bridg. Ref. Bridgman, Reflections on the Study of the Law. 1804

Bridg. Thes. Bridgman's Thesaurus Juridicus

Bridgeport L. Rev. Bridgeport Law Review

Brief
- Brief of the Phi Delta Phi (Menasha, Wisconsin)
- Law Society of Western Australia Brief

Brief Case Brief Case, National Legal Aid Association

Briggs Ry. Acts Briggs' General Railway Acts

Brigham Young U. L. Rev. Brigham Young University Law Review

Brigham Young Univ. L. Rev. Brigham Young University Law Review

Brigham Y.U.L.R. Brigham Young University Law Review

Bright. Brightly, Pennsylvania Nisi Prius Reports

Bright. Bank. Law Brightly's Annotated Bankrupt Law

Bright. Costs Brightly on the Law of Costs in Pennsylvania

Bright. Dig.
- Brightly's Analytical Digest of the Laws of the United States
- Brightly's Digest (New York)
- Brightly's Digest (Pennsylvania)

Bright. E.C. Brightly's Leading Election Cases (Pa.)

Bright. Elec. Cas. Brightly's Leading Election Cases (Pa.)

Bright. Eq. Jur. Brightly's Equitable Jurisdiction (Pennsylvania)

Bright. Fed. Dig. Brightly's Federal Digest

Bright H. & W. Bright, Husband and Wife. 3ed. 1849

Brightly Brightly, Pennsylvania Nisi Prius Reports

Brightly Dig.
- Brightly's Analytical Digest of the Laws of the United States
- Brightly's Digest (New York)
- Brightly's Digest (Pennsylvania)

Brightly El. Brightly's Leading Election Cas., Pa.

Brightly El. Cas. Brightly's Election Cases (Pa.)

Brightly, Elect. Cas. Brightly's Leading Election Cases (Pa.)

Brightly Election Cas. (Pa.) Brightly's Leading Election Cases (Pa.)

Brightly, N.P. Brightly's Nisi Prius Reports (Pa.)

Brightly's Elec. Cas Brightly, Leading Cases on Elections (Pa.)

Brightly's Rep. Brightly Pennsylvania Nisi Prius Reports

Bright. N.P. Brightly's Pennsylvania Nisi Prius Reports

Bright. N.Y. Dig. Brightly's New York Digest

Bright. (Pa.) Brightly Pennsylvania Nisi Prius Reports

Bright. Pa. Dig. Brightly's Pennsylvania Digest

Bright. Purd. Brightly's Edition of Purdon's Digest of Pennsylvania Laws

Bright. Pur. Dig. Brightly's Edition of Purdon's Digest of Pennsylvania Laws

Bright. Tr. & H. Pr. Brightly's Edition of Troubat & Haly's Practice

Bright. U.S. Dig. Brightly's Digest of United States Laws

Brig. Yo. U. L.R. Brigham Young University Law Review

Bri. Pub. Wor. Brice, Law relating to Public Worship. 1875

Brisb. Brisbin (Minn.)

Brisbin Brisbin's Reports (vol. 1 Minnesota)

Brisb. Minn. Brisbin's Reports (vol. 1 Minnesota)

Brit.
- Britain
- Britannia
- Britannica
- British
- Britton's Ancient Pleas of the Crown

Brit. & Col. Pr. Cas. British & Colonial Prize Cases

Brit. Burm. British Burman

Brit. Col. British Columbia

Brit. Cr. Cas. British (or English) Crown Cases

Brit. Gui. British Guiana

Brit. Hond. British Honduras

Brit. J. Ad. L. British Journal of Administrative Law

Brit. J. Admin. Law British Journal of Administrative Law

Brit. J. Adm. L. British Journal of Administrative Law

Brit. J. Criminol. British Journal of Criminology

Brit. J. Criminology British Journal of Criminology

Brit. J. Delinq. British Journal of Delinquency

Brit. J. Ind. Rel. British Journal of Industrial Relations

Brit. J. Int'l. L. British Journal of International Law, England

Brit. J.L. & Soc'y. British Journal of Law and Society

Brit. J. Law & Soc. British Journal of Law and Society

Brit. J. of Crimin. British Journal of Criminology, London, England

Brit. J. of Delinquency British Journal of Delinquency, London, England

Brit. Prac. Int'l L. British Practice in International Law

Brit. Quar. Rev. British Quarterly Review

Brit. Rul. Cas. British Ruling Cases

Brit. Ship. L. British Shipping Laws (Stevens)

Britt. Britton's Ancient Pleas of the Crown

Brit. Tax Rev.
- British Tax Review
- British Tax Review, London, England

Brit. T.S. British Treaty Series

Brit. Y.B. Int'l. British Yearbook of International Law

Brit. Y.B. Int'l.L. British Yearbook of International Law

Bri. Ult. V. Brice's Ultra Vires

B.R.J. Bill of Rights Journal

B.R.-J.C. (Army) Board of Review and Judicial Council of the Army

Br. Leg. Max. Broom's Legal Maxims

Br. L.R. Brooklyn Law Review

Br. Max. Broom's Legal Maxims. 10 ed. 1939

Brn. Brownlow and Goldesborough (1569-1625)

Br. N.B. Braeton's Note Book (1217-40)

Br. N.C. Brooke's New Cases, English King's Bench (1515-58)

Br. N.Cas. Brooks New Cases, King's Bench (Eng.)

Br. Not. Brooke's Office of a Notary

Bro.
- Brother
- Browne's Reports (1872-1902) (Ceylon)
- Browne's Reports (Pa. 1801-14)
- Brown's English Chancery Reports
- Brown's Michigan Nisi Prius Reports
- Brown's Parliamentary Cases (Eng.)
- Brown's Reports (53-65 Missouri)
- Brown's Reports (80-136 Missouri)
- W.G. Brooke's Ecclesiastical Re-

ports (1850-72)

Bro. A. & C.L. Browne's Admiralty and Civil Law

Bro. A. & R. Brown, United States District Court Reports (Admiralty and Revenue Cases)

Bro. Ab. Brooke's Abridgment (1573, 1576, 1586 Editions) (Eng.)

Bro. Abr. Brooke's Abridgment (1573, 1576, 1586 Editions) (Eng.)

Bro. Abr. In Eq. Browne's New Abridgment of Cases in Equity

Bro. Ac. Browne, Actions at Law. 1843

Bro. (A.) C.L. Arthur Brown's Compendious View of the Civil Law

Bro. Act. Browne's Actions at Law

Bro. Adm. Brown's United States Admiralty Reports

Bro. Adm. & C.L. Browne's Admiralty and Civil Law

Bro. Ag. Brown on Agency and Trust

Bro. & F. Broderick & Freemantle's Ecclesiastical Cases (Eng.)

Bro. & Fr. Broderick & Freemantle's Ecclesiastical Cases (Eng.)

Bro. & G. Brownlow & Goldesborough's English Common Pleas Reports

Bro. & H. Brown & Hemingway's Reports (53-65 Mississippi)

Bro. & L. Browning & Lushington's English Admiralty Reports (1863-65)

Bro. & Lush. Browning & Lushington's English Admiralty Reports (1863-65)

Bro. & Lush. M. & D. Browning & Lushington on Marriage and Divorce

Bro. & M.
- Brown & Macnamara, Railway Cases (1855)
- Brown & McCall's Yorkshire Star Chamber (Yorkshire Arch. Society Record, Series 44, 45, 51, 70)

Bro. & Mac. Browne and Macnamara's Railway Cases (1855)

Bro. C. & A.L. Browne's Civil and Admiralty Law

Bro. Car. Browne, Law of Carriers. 1873

Bro. C.C. Brown's English Chancery Cases, or Reports (1778-94)

Bro.C.C. (or C.R.) Brown's English Chancery Cases, or Reports

Bro. Ch. Brown's English Chancery Reports (28, 29 ER)

Bro. Ch. Cas. Brown's English Chancery Reports (28, 29 ER)

Bro. Ch. Pr, Browne's Practice of the High Court of Chancery

Bro. Ch. R. Brown's English Chancery Reports (28, 29 ER)

Bro. Civ. Law Browne's Civil and Admiralty Law

Bro. Civ. Proc. Broughton's Civil Procedure, India

Brock. Brockenbrough's Marshall's Decisions, United States Circuit Court

Brock. & H. Brockenbrough & Holmes (Va.)

Brock. & Ho. Brockenbrough & Holmes, Virginia Cases, v. 1

Brock. & Hol. Brockenbrough & Holmes' "Virginia Cases"

Brock. & Hol. Cas. Brockenbrough & Holmes Cases (Va.)

Brock. Cas. Brockenbrough, Virginia Cases

Brock. C.C. Brockenbrough's Marshall's Decisions, United States Circuit Court

Brock. Marsh. Brockenbrough's Marshall's Decisions, United States Circuit Court

Bro. Co. Act. Browne on the Companies' Acts

Bro. Com. Broom's Commentaries on the Common Law

Brod. Brodrick & Freemantle Ecclesiastical Cases

Brod. & B. Broderip & Bingham's English Common Pleas Reports (129 ER)

Brod. & Bing. Broderip & Bingham's English Common Pleas Reports (129 ER)

Brod. & F. Ecc. Cas. Broderick & Freemantle's Ecclesiastical Cases (Eng.)

Brod. & F. Broderick & Freemantle's Ecclesiastical Cases (1840-64)

Brod. & F. (Eng.) Broderick & Freemantle's Ecclesiastical Cases (1840-64)

Brod. & Fr. Broderick & Freemantle's Ecclesiastical Cases (1840-64)

Brod. & Fr. Ecc. Cas. Broderick & Freemantle's Ecclesiastical Cases (Eng.)

Brod. & Frem. Brodrick and Free-mantle's Ecclesiastical Cases (1840-64)

Bro. Dig. Div. Browne's Digest of Decisions on Divorce and Alimony

Bro. Div. Pr. Browne's Divorce Court Practice

Brodix Am. & El. Pat. Cas. Brodix American and English Patent Cases

Brodix Am. & Eng. Pat. Cas. Brodix's American and English Patent Cases

Brodix Am. & E. Pat. Cas. Brodix's American & English Patent Cases

Brod. Stair. Brodie's Notes to Stair's Institutes (Sc.)

Bro. Ecc. Brooke, Six Judgments in Ecclesiastical Cases (1850-72) (Eng.)

Bro. Eccl. Brown's Ecclesiastical, Eng.

Bro. Ent.
- Brown's Entries
- Brownlow's Latine Redivivus; or Entries

Bro. Fix. Brown on Fixtures

Bro. For.
- Brown's The Forum
- Brown on Forestalling, Regrating and Monopolizing, with Cases

Bro. Form. Brown's Formulae Bene Placitandi

Bro. Fr. Browne on the Statute of Frauds

Bro. Hered. Browne, Law of Rating of Hereditaments, 2ed. 1886

Bro. Humor. Browne's Humorous

101

Phrases of the Law

Bro. Ins. Browne's Medical Jurisprudence of Insanity

Bro. Just. Broun's Justiciary, Scotland

Bro. Law Dic. Brown, Law Dictionary, 2ed. 1880

Bro. Leg. Max. Brooms' Legal Maxims

Bro. Lim. Brown, Limitations as to Real Property. 1869

Bro. M. & D. Browning on Marriage and Divorce

Bro. Max. Brooms' Legal Maxims

Bro. N.B. Cas. Browne, National Bank Cases

Bro. N.C. Brooke, New Cases, English King's Bench (1515-58)

Bro. Not. Brooke on the Office of a Notary in England

Bro. NP.
- Brown's Michigan Nisi Prius Reports
- Brown's Nisi Prius Cases (Eng.)

Brook Abr. Brook's Abridgments (Eng.)

Brook L. Rev. Brooklyn Law Review

Brooke
- Brooke's Ecclesiastical Cases (1850-72) (Eng.)
- Brooke's New Cases, King's Bench (Eng.)

Brooke, Abr. Brooke's Abridgment (73 ER)

Brooke Bib. Leg. Brooke's Bibliotheca Legum Angliae

Brooke Ch. W. Brooke's Churchwarden's Guide

Brooke Eccl. Brooke's Six Ecclesiastical Judgments

Brooke Eccl. Judg. Brooke's Ecclesiastical Judgments

Brooke Lim. Brooke's Reading on the Statute of Limitations

Brooke N.C. Brooke, New Cases, English King's Bench Reports

Brooke Not. Brooke on the Office and Practice of a Notary

Brooke (Petit). Brooke, New Cases

Brooke Six Judg. Brooke's Six Ecclesiastical Judgments (or Reports)

Brook. J. Int'l L. Brooklyn Journal of International Law

Brookl. Bar. Brooklyn Bar Association

Brookl. J. Int. L. Brooklyn Journal of International Law

Brookl. L. Rev. Brooklyn Law Review

Brookl. Rec. Brooklyn Daily Record, Brooklyn, New York

Brooklyn Bar. Brooklyn Barrister

Brooklyn Daily Rec. Brooklyn Daily Record

Brooklyn J. Int. L. Brooklyn Journal of International Law

Brooklyn J. Int'l. L. Brooklyn Journal of International Law

Brooklyn L. Rev. Brooklyn Law Review

Brook N. Cas. Brook's New Cases, King's Bench (Eng.)

Brooks. Brooks' Reports (vols. 106-119 Michigan)

Broom A Selection of Legal Maxims, by Herbert Broom

Broom & H. Com. Broom & Hadley's Commentaries on the Laws of England

Broom & H. Comm. Broom & Hadley's Commentaries on the Law of England

Broom C.L. Broom's Commentaries on the Common Law

Broom, Com. Law. Broom's Commentaries on the Common Law

Broom Const. L. Broom's Constitutional Law

Broom, Leg. Max. (or Broom, Max.) Broom's Legal Maxims

Broom Part. Broom on Parties to Actions

Broom Ph. Law Broom's Philosophy of the Law

Bro. Pa. Browne's Pennsylvania Reports (1801-14)

Bro. Parl. Cas. Brown's Cases in Parliament

Bro. Pat. Pr. Browne's Patent Office Practice

Bro. P.C. Brown, English Parliamentary Cases (1-3 ER)

Bro. Prac. Brown's Practice (Praxis), or Precedents in Chancery

Bro. Prac. (or Prax.) Brown's Practice (Praxis), or Precedents in Chancery

Bro. Prob. Pr. Browne's Probate Practice

Bro. Read. Brooke's Reading on the Statute of Limitations

Bro. Reg. Act Browne's Parliamentary and Municipal Registration Act

Bro. R.P.L. Brown on Limitations as to Real Property

Bros. Brothers

Bro. Sal. Brown, Treatise on Law of Sale (Sc.)

Bro. Sp. David Paul Brown's Speeches

Bro. St. Brodie, Notes and Supplement to Stair's Institutions (Sc.)

Bro. Stair Brodie's Notes and Supplement to Stair's Institutions (Sc.)

Bro. St. Fr. Browne on the Statute of Frauds

Bro. Supp. Brown, Supplement to Morrison's Dictionary, Court of Session (1622-1750, 5 vols.) (Sc.)

Bro. Sup. to Mor. Brown's Supplement to Morrison's Dictionary of Decisions (1622-1780) (Sc.)

Bro. Syn. Brown's Synopsis of Decisions, Scotch Court of Sessions (1540-1827)

Bro. Synop. Brown's Synopsis of Decisions, Scotch Court of Sessions (1540-1827)

Bro. Tr. M. A Treatise on the Law of Trade-Marks

Brough. Civ. Pro. Broughton's Indian Civil Procedure

Brough Elec. Brough's Law of Elections

Broun. Broun's Justiciary Reports, Scotland (1842-45)

Broun. Just. Broun's Reports, Scotch Justiciary Court (1842-45)

Bro. Us. & Cus. Browne's Law of

Usages and Customs

Bro. V.M. Brown's Vade Mecum

Brow. Brev. Brownlow's Brevia Judicialia

Brown
- Brownlow (& Goldesborough's English Common Pleas Reports)
- Brown's English Chancery Reports
- Brown's English Parliamentary Cases
- Brown's Law Dictionary
- Brown's Law Dictionary and Institute (1874)
- Brown's Michigan Nisi Prius Reports
- Brown's Reports (vols. 53-65 Mississippi)
- Brown's Reports (vols. 80-137 Missouri)
- Brown's Reports (vols. 4-25 Nebraska)
- Brown's Scotch Reports
- Brown's United States Admiralty Reports
- Brown's United States District Court Reports

Brown A. & R. Brown's United States District Court Reports (Admiralty and Revenue Cases)

Brown Adm. Brown's Admiralty (U.S.)

Brown. & G. (Eng.) Brownlow & Goldesborough. English Common Pleas Reports, 2 Parts, tempore Eliz. & Jac, 1675. (123 ER)

Brown. & Gold. Brownlow & Godes-borough English Common Pleas Reports

Browne & H. Browne & Hemingway's Reports (53-58 Mississippi)

Browne & Hemingway. Browne & Hemingway's Reports (53-58 Mississippi)

Brown. & L. Browning & Lushington's English Admiralty Reports (167 ER)

Brown. & L. (Eng.) Browning & Lushington's English Admiralty Reports (167 ER)

Brown. & Lush. Browning & Lushington's English Admiralty Reports (167 ER)

Brown & Lush. M. & D. Browning & Lushington on Marriage and Divorce

Brown & Mac.N. Brown & Mac-Namara, Railway Cases (Eng.)

Brown & R. Brown & Rader (Mo.)

Brown C. Brown's English Chancery Cases or Reports (Eng.)

Brown, C.C. Brown's English Chancery Cases or Reports

Brown Ch. Brown's Chancery Cases (Eng.), tempore Lord Thurlow

Brown Ch. C. Brown's Chancery Cases (Eng.), tempore Lord Thurlow

Brown, Civ. & Adm. Law. Brown's Civil and Admiralty Law

Brown Dict. Brown's Law Dictionary

Brown. Div. Pr. Browning's Divorce Court Practice

Browne
- Browne's Civil Procedure Reports (N.Y.)
- Browne's Reports (Ceylon)

- Browne's Reports (97-109 Massachusetts)
- Browne's Reports (Pennsylvania 1801-14)

Browne Act. Browne, Actions at Law. 1843

Browne Adm. & C.L. Browne's Admiralty and Civil Law

Browne & G. Browne & Gray's Reports (vols. 110-111 Massachusetts)

Browne & Gray. Browne & Gray's Reports (110-114 Massachusetts)

Browne & H. Browne & Hemingway Reports (Miss.)

Browne & Macn. Browne & MacNamara's English Railway and Canal Cases

Browne & Th. Railw. Browne & Theobald, Railways. 4ed. 1911

Browne Bank. Cas. Browne's National Bank Case

Browne Car. Browne on Carriers

Brown Ecc. Brown's Ecclesiastical Cases (Eng.)

Browne Civ. L. Browne on Civil and Admiralty Law

Browne, Civ. Law Browne's Civil and Admiralty Law

Browne, Div. Browne's Divorce Court Practice

Browne Div. Pr. Browne, Practice in Divorce and Matrimonial Causes. 11ed. 1931

Browne Fr. Browne on the Statute of Frauds

Browne, Jud. Interp. Browne's Judicial Interpretation of Common Words and Phrases

Browne N.B.C. Browne's National Bank Cases

Brown. Ent. Brownlow's Entries

Browne (Pa.) Browne's Reports (Pa.)

Browne Pa. R. Browne's Reports (Pa.)

Browne, Prob. Pr. Browne's Probate Practice

Browne's Rep. Browne's Reports (Pa.)

Browne, St. Frauds Browne on Statute of Frauds

Browne Tr.M. A Treatise on the Law of Trade-Marks

Browne Us. Browne on Usages and Customs

Brown, Ga.Pl. & Pr.Anno. Browne, Georgia Pleading & Practice & Legal Forms Annotated

Brownl. Brownlow & Goldesborough. English Common Pleas Reports. 2 Parts, tempore Eliz. & Jac, 1675 (123 ER)

Brownl. & G. Brownlow & Goldesborough. English Common Pleas Reports. 2 Parts, tempore Eliz. & Jac, 1675 (123 ER)

Brownl. & Gold. Brownlow & Goldesborough. English Common Pleas Reports, 2 Parts, tempore Eliz. & Jac, 1675. (123 ER)

Brownl. Brev. Brownlow's Brevia Judicialia

Brownl. Ent. Brownlow's Entries

Brownl. Redv. Brownlow's Latine Redivivus

Brown. M. & D. Browning on Marriage and Divorce

Brown N.P. Brown's Michigan Nisi Prius Reports

Brown N.P.Cas. Brown's Nisi Prius Cases (Eng.)

Brown N.P.(Mich.) Brown. Michigan Nisi Prius Reports (Mich.)

Brown Parl. Brown's House of Lords Cases (Eng.)

Brown Parl.Cas. Brown's House of Lords Cases (Eng.)

Brown P.C. Brown's House of Lords Cases (Eng.)

Brown's Adm. App. Brown's Admiralty Reports (Appendix) (U.S.)

Brown's (Penn.) Browne's Reports (Pa.)

Brown's Penn. Rep. Browne's Reports (Pa.)

Brown's Roman Law Brown's Epitome and Analysis of Savigny's Treatise on Obligations in Roman Law

Brown Sup. or Brown Sup. Dec. Brown's Supplement to Morrison's Dictionary, Session Cases (Sc.)

Brown Syn. Brown's Synopsis of Decisions of the Scotch Court of Session

Br. Par. Brown's Parties to Actions

Br. P.C. Brown's Chancery Cases (Eng.)

Br. Phil. Law. Broom, Philosophy of Law, 3ed. 1883

Br. R. Browne's Reports (Ceylon)

Br. Reg. Braithwaite's Register

Br. Rul. Cas. British Ruling Cases

Bru. M.L. Bruce's Military Law, Scotland

Br. Sup. Brown's Supplement to Morrison's Dictionary, Sessions Cases (1622-1780) (Sc.)

Br. Syn. Brown, Synopsis of Decisions, Scotch Court of Session (1540-1827)

BRTA Bureau of Resources and Trade Assistance

Bru. Bruce's Scotch Court of Session Reports (1714-15)

Bru. & Wil. Adm. Bruce & Williams, Admiralty Jurisdiction

Bruce Bruce's Scotch Court of Session Reports (1714-15)

Brun. Col. Cas. Brunner's Collected Cases

Brunk. Ir. Dig. Brunker's Irish Common Law Digest

Brunn. Coll. Cas. Brunner's Collected Cases (U.S.)

Brunn Col. Cas. (F) Brunner's Collected Cases (U.S.)

Brunner, Col. Cas. Brunner's Collected Cases (U.S.)

Brunner Sel. Cas. Brunner's Selected Cases United States Circuit Courts

Brunn. Sel. Cas. Brunner's Selected Cases

Brun. Sel. Cas. Brunner's Selected Cases

Brunskill Brunskill's Land Cases (1891-95) (Ir.)

Bruns. L.C. Brunskill's Land Cases (Ir.)

Bru. Princip. Bruce, Principia Juris Feudalis

Brux. Bruxelles (Brussels)

Bruzard Mauritius Reports by Bruzard. (1842-45)

B.R.V. Bill of Rights of Virginia

BRW Bankruptcy Reporter

Bry. & Str.Com.L. Bryant & Stratton, Commercial Law

Bryce Civ. L. Bryce's Study of the Civil Law

Bryce Tr. M. Bryce, Registration of Trade Marks

B.S.
- Bancus Superior (upper bench)
- British Standard
- Brown's Suppt. to Morison's Dictionary of Decisions, Court of Sessions (1622- 1780) (Sc.)

B/S Bill of sale

b.s. balance sheet

BSI British Standards Institute

Bs.L. Bills of Lading

Bs/L Bills of Lading

BSSUI Benefit Series Service, Unemployment Insurance (U.S. Dept. of Labor)

Bt. Benedict's United States District Court Reports

B.T.A. United States Board of Tax Appeals Reports

B.T.A.C.C.H. Board of Tax Appeals Decisions (CCH)

B.T.A.M. (P-H) Board of Tax Appeals Memorandum Decisions (Prentice-Hall)

B.T.A.P.H. Board of Tax Appeals Decisions (P-H)

BTCL Givens, Business Torts and Competitor Litigation

B.T.D. Bell on the Testing of Deeds, Scotland

B.T.R.
- Brewing Trade Review Licensing Law Reports (Eng.)
- British Tax Review

B.Tr. Bishop's Trial

B.T.R. L.R. Brewing Trade Review Law Reports

Buch.
- Buchanan (Eben J. or James) Reports (Cape of Good Hope)
- Buchanan (Sc.), Court of Session (1800-13)
- Buchanan's New Jersey Equity Reports (vols. 71-85)
- Buchanan, Supreme Court Reports (Cape Colony)

Buch. A.C. Buchanan's Reports of Appeal Court (Cape of Good Hope)

Buchan. Buchanan's Rep. (71-85 N.J.)

Buchanan. Buchanan's Reports, Court of Session and Justiciary (Sc.)

Buch. App. Cas. Buchanan's Appeal Court Reports, Cape of Good Hope (1880-1910) (S. Afr.)

Buch. Cas. (or Tr.) Buchanan's Remarkable Criminal Cases (Sc.)

Buch. Ct. Ap. Cape G.H. Buchanan's Court of Appeals Reports (Cape of Good Hope)

Buch. E.Cape G.H. E. Buchanan's Reports (Cape of Good Hope)

Buch. E.D. Cape G.H. Buchanan's Eastern District Reports (Cape of Good Hope)

Buch. Eq. (N.J.) Buchanan's New Jersey Equity Reports

Buch. J. Cape G.H. J. Buchanan's Reports (Cape of Good Hope)

Buch. Lien Law Buchan's California Lien Laws

Buch. Pr. Pl. Buchanan's Precedents of Pleading

Buch. Rep. Buchanan's (Eben J. or James) Reports (Cape of Good Hope)

Buch. S.C. Rep. Buchanan's Reports, Supreme Court of Good Hope (1868-79) (S. Afr.)

Buck
- Buck, English Cases in Bankruptcy (1816-20)
- Buck's Reports (vols. 7-8 Montana)

Buck. Bucknill's Cooke's Cases of Practice Common Pleas (Eng.)

Buck Bankr. (Eng.) Buck, English Cases in Bankruptcy (1816-20)

Buck Cas. Buck's Bankruptcy Cases (Eng.)

Buck. Comp. Act Buckley's Law and Practice under the Companies' Act

Buck. Cooke Bucknill's Cooke's Cases of Practice, Common Pleas (Eng.)

Buck. Eccl. Law Buck's Massachusetts Ecclesiastical Law

Buck. Dec. Buckner's Decisions (in Freeman's Mississippi Chancery Reports 1839-43)

Buck. Ins. Bucknill, Care of the Insane. 1880

Buckl. Buckley on the Companies Acts (1873-1949)

Buck Lun. Bucknill on Lunacy

Bucks Bucks County Law Reporter, Pa.

Bucks Co. L. Rep. Bucks County Law Reporter (Pa.)

Bucks Co. L.R. (Pa) Bucks County Law Reporter (Pa.)

Buffalo L. Rev. Buffalo Law Review

Buff. L. Rev. Buffalo Law Review

Buffalo L. Rev. Bull. Buffalo Law Review Weekly Law Bulletin

Buff. Super. Ct. Sheldon's Superior Court Reports (Buffalo, New York)

Buff. Super. Ct. (N.Y.) Sheldon's Superior Court Reports (Buffalo, New York)

B.U.Int'l L.J. Boston University International Law Journal

B. U. J. Tax L. Boston University Journal of Tax Law

B.U.L. Boston University Law Review

Bul. Bulletin

Bulg.
- Bulgaria
- Bulgarian

Bull.
- Bulletin
- Bulletin Weekly Law Bulletin (Ohio)

Bull. Am. Acad. Psych. & L. Bulletin of the American Academy of Psychiatry and the Law

Bull & B. Bank. Buller and Bund's Manual of Bankruptcy

Bull. & C. Dig. Bullard & Curry's Louisiana Digest

Bull. & Cur. Dig. Bullard and Curry's Louisiana Digest

Bull. & L. Bullen and Leake's Pleadings on Actions in King's Bench Decisions, 11 editions (1860-1959)

Bull. & L. Pr. Bullen & Leake's Precedents of Pleading

Bull. Anglo-Sov.L.A. Bulletin of the Anglo-Soviet Law Association

Bull. Can.Welfare L. Bulletin of Canadian Welfare Law

Bull. Can. Welfare Law Bulletin of Cana-dian Welfare Law

Bull. Coll. Wm. & Mary William & Mary College Bulletin

Bull. Comp. L. American Bar Association Comparative Law Bureau. Bulletin

Bull. Comp. Lab. Rel. Bulletin of Comparative Labour Relations

Bull. Cop. Soc. Bulletin of the Copyright Society of the U.S.A.

Bull. Copyright Soc'y. Bulletin of the Copyright Society of the U.S.A.

Bull. C'right Soc'y. Bulletin of the Copyright Society of the U.S.A.

Bull. Cr. Soc. Bulletin of the Copyright Society of the U.S.A.

Bull. Czech. L. Bulletin of Czechoslovak Law

Bull. Dis. Buller's Law of Distress for Rent

Bull. Eccl. Bullingbroke's Ecclesiastical Law

Buller MSS. J. Buller's Paper Books, Lincoln's Inn Library

Buller N.P. Buller's Nisi Prius (Eng.)

Bulletin Comp. L. Bulletin, Comparative Law Bureau

Bull. Eur. Communities Bulletin of the European Communities

Bull. for Internat. Fiscal Docum. Bulletin for International Fiscal Documentation. Amsterdam, Netherlands

Bull. for Int'l. Fisc. Doc. Bulletin for International Fiscal Documentation, Amsterdam, Netherlands

Bull. I.B.A. Bulletin of the International Bar Association

Bull. I.C.J. Bulletin of the International Commission of Jurists

Bull. Int. Fisc. Doc. Bulletin for International Fiscal Documentation (Amsterdam)

Bull. JAG Bulletin of Judge Advocate General of Army (U.S.)

Bull. Legal Devel. Bulletin of Legal Developments

Bull. Leg. Dev. Bulletin of Legal Developments

Bull. L.Sci. & Tech. Bulletin of Law, Science & Technology

Bull. L. Science & Tech Bulletin of Law, Science and Technology

Bull. Mediev. Canon L. Bulletin of Medieval Canon Law

Bull. Nat. Tax Assoc. Bulletin of the Na-tional Tax Association

Bull. N.P. Buller's Law of Nisi Prius (Eng.)

Bull. NP (Eng.) Buller's Law of

Nisi Prius (Eng.)

Bull. N.T.A. Bulletin of the National Tax Association

Bull. O Weekly Law Bulletin (Ohio)

Bull. (Ohio) Weekly Law Bulletin (Ohio)

Bull. Que. Soc. Crim. Bulletin of the Quebec Society of Criminology

Bull. Waseda U. Inst. Comp. L. Bulletin, Waseda University Institute of Comparative Law

Bull. Waseda Univ. Inst. of Comp.Law Waseda University, Institute of Comparative Law, Bulletin, Tokyo, Japan

Bu. L.R. Buffalo Law Review

B.U.L.Rev.; BU L Rev Boston University Law Review

Buls Bulstrode's English King's Bench Reports (1610-25)

Bulst. Bulstrode's English King's Bench Reports (1610-25)

Bulstr. Bulstrode (London), English King's Bench Reports (80, 81 ER)

Bump B'k'cy Bump on Bankruptcy

Bump Comp. Bump on Composition in Bankruptcy

Bump Const. Dec. Bump, Notes of Constitutional Decisions

Bump Fed. Pr. Bump, Federal Procedure

Bump. Fraud. Conv. Bump on Fraudulent Conveyances

Bump Fr. Conv. Bump on Fraudulent Conveyances

Bump Int. Rev. Bump's Internal Revenue Laws

Bump N.C. Bump's Notes on Constitutional Decisions

Bump Pat. Bump's Law of Patents, Trade-Marks, & c.

Bump's Int. Rev. Law Bump's Internal Revenue Laws

Bump St. L. Bump, United States Stamp Laws

Bunb. Bunbury, English Exchequer Reports (145 ER)

Banbury (Eng.) Banbury, English Exchequer Reports (145 ER)

Buny. Dom. L. Bunyon, Domestic Law. 1875

Buny. Fire Ins. Bunyon, Fire Insurance, 7ed. 1923

Buny. Life Ass. Bunyon on Life Assurance

Buny. Life Ins. Bunyon, Life Insurance. 5ed. 1914

B. U. Pub. Int. L.J. Boston University Public Interest Law Journal

Bur.
- Bureau
- Burnett's Wisconsin Supreme Court Reports (1841-43)
- Burrow, English King's Bench Reports

Bur. & Gres. Eq. Pl. Burroughs & Gresson's Irish Equity Pleader

Bur. Ass. Burrill on Voluntary Assignment

Bur. Chy. Burrough's History of the Chancery

Bur. Circ. Ev. Burrill on Circumstantial Evidence

Burdick, Crime Burdick's Law of

Crime

Burdick, Roman Law Burdick's Principles of Roman Law

Burf. Burford's Reports (6-18 Oklahoma)

Bur. Forms Burrill's Forms

Burg, Col. & For. Law Burge on Colonial and Foreign Law

Burg. Dig. Burgwyn's Digest Maryland Reports

Burge App. Burge, Appellate Jurisdiction. 1841

Burge Col. Law Burge, Colonial and Foreign Law. 2ed. 1907-08

Burge, Confl. Law. Burge on the Conflict of Laws

Burge Mar. Int. L. Burge on Maritime International Law

Burgen Burgess' Reports (vols. 16-49 Ohio State)

Burge, Sur. Burge on Suretyship

Burgess Burgess (Ohio)

Burgl. Burglary

Burgw. Md. Dig. Burgwyn's Maryland Digest

Burk Burk (Va.)

Burke Cel. Tr. Burke's Celebrated Trials

Burke Cop. Burke, Copyright, 1842

Burke Cr. L. Burke, Criminal Law. 2ed. 1845

Burke Int. Cop. Burke, International Copyright. 1852

Burke Pub. Sch. Burke on the Law of Public Schools

Burke Tr. Burke's Celebrated Trials

Burk, Faso Burkina Faso

Burks Burks' Reports (91-98 Virginia)

Burlamaqui. Burlamaqui's Natural and Political Law

Bur. Law Dic. Burrill's Law Dictionary

Burlesque Reps. Skillman's New York Police Reports

Bur. L.J. Burma Law Journal

Burl. Nat. Burlamaqui's Principles of Natural and Politic Law

Burl. Natural & Pol. Law Burlamaqui's Natural and Politic Law

Bur. L.R. Burma Law Reports (India)

Bur. L.T. Burma Law Times (India)

Bur. M. Burrow's Reports tempore Mansfield (Eng.)

Burma Law Inst. J. Burma Law Institute Journal. 1958-60

Burma L. Inst. J. The Burma Law Institute Journal, Rangoon, Burma

Burma L.R. Burma Law Reports (1948)

Burm. L.J. Burma Law Journal

Burm. L.R. Burma Law Reports (India)

Burm. L.T. Burma Law Times (India)

Burn.
- Burnett's Reports (Wisconsin)
- High Commission Court 1865 (Eng.)
- Star Chamber Proceedings (Eng.)

Burn Att. Pr. Burn's Attorney's Practice

Burn. Cr. L. Burnet, Criminal Law of Scotland

Burn, Dict. Burn's Law Dictionary

Burn Eccl. Burn's Ecclesiastical Law

Burn, Ecc. Law Burn's Ecclesiastical Law

Burnet Burnet, Manuscript Decisions, Scotch Court of Session

Burnett
- Burnett's Reports (vols. 20-22 Oregon)
- Burnett's Wisconsin Reports

Burnett's Rep. Burnett's Wisconsin Reports (1842-1843) (Wis.)

Burnett (Wis.) Burnett's Wisconsin Reports

Burn, J.P. Burn's Justice of the Peace

Burn J.P. (or Jus.) Burn's Justice of the Peace

Burn Law Dict. Burn's Law Dictionary

Burn Mar. Ins. Burn's Marine Insurance

Burns' Ann. St. Burns' Annotated Statutes (Ind.)

Burns-Begg Southern Rhodesia Reports

Burns' Ecc. Law Burns' Ecclesiastical Law

Burn's JP (Eng.) Burn's Justice of Peace

Burns Pract. Burns, Conveyancing Practice (Sc.)

Burns' Rev. St. Burns' Annotated Statutes (Ind.)

Burn St. Job. Burn on Stock Jobbing

Bur. Pr. Burrill's New York Practice

BURPs business unreported profits

Burr. Burrow, English King's Bench Reports tempore Lord Mansfield (97, 98 ER)

Burr. Adm. Burrell's Admiralty Cases. (1584-1839)

Burr. & Gr. Eq. Pl. Burroughs & Gresson, Irish Equity Pleader

Burr. Ass. Burrill on Assignments

Burr. Ch. Burrough's History of the Chancery

Burr. Circ. Ev. Burrill on Circumstantial Evidence

Burr. Dict. Burrill's Law Dictionary

Burrell Burrell's Reports, Admiralty, ed. by Marsden. (167 ER)

Burrell (Eng.) Burrell's Reports, Admiralty, ed. by Marsden. (167 ER)

Burr. (Eng.) Burrow, English King's Bench Reports tempore Lord Mansfield (97, 98 ER)

Burr. Forms Burrill's Forms

Burrill Burrill's Law Dictionary

Burrill Ass. Burrill, Voluntary Assignments

Burrill, Assignm. Burrill on Assignments

Burrill, Circ. Ev. Burrill on Circumstantial Evidence

Burrill, Pr. Burrill's Practice

Burr. Law Dict. Burrill's Law Dictionary

Burrnett. Burrnett's Oregon Reports (vols. 20-22)

Burrow. Burrow's Reports, English King's Bench

Burrow, Sett. Cas. Burrow's English Settlement Cases

Burr. Pr. Burrill's New York Practice

Burr. Pub. Sec. Burroughs on Public Securities

Burr. S.C. Burrows' English Settlement Cases (1732-76)

Burr. S.Cas. Burrows' English Settlement Cases (1732-76)

Burr. S. Cases Burrow's Settlement Cases (Eng.)

Burr. Sett. Cas. Burrows' English Settlement Cases (1732-76)

Burr. Sett. Cas. (Eng.) Burrows' English Settlement Cases (1732-76)

Burr. Tax. Burroughs on Taxation

Burr.t.M. Burrow's Reports, tempore Mansfield (Eng.)

Burr. Tr. Burr's Trial, reported by Robertson

Burr. Tr. Rob. Burr's Trial, reported by Robertson

Bur. S.C. Burrow's Settlement Cases

Bur. Tax. Burroughs on Taxation

Burt. Bank. Burton on Bankruptcy

Burt.Cas. Burton's Collection of Cases and Opinions (Eng.)

Burt. Man. Burton, Manual of the Laws of Scotland

Burt. Parl. Burton's Parliamentary Diary

Burt. Real Prop. Burton on Real Property

Burt. R.P. Burton, Real Property. 8ed. 1856

Burt. Sc. Tr. Burton's Scotch Trials

Bus. Business

Bus. Am. Business America

Bus. & Com. Business and Commerce

Bus. & L. Business and Law

Bus. & Prof. Business and Professions

Bus. & Prof. C. Business and Professions Code

Bus. & Soc'y. Rev. Business and Society Review

Busb. Busbee's Law Reports (vol. 44 North Carolina) (1852-53)

Busb. Cr. Dig. Busbee's Criminal Digest (North Carolina)

Busbee Eq. (N.C.) Busbee, Equity Reports (North Carolina, vol. 44)

Busb. Eq. Busbee, Equity Reports (1852-53) (vol. 44, North Carolina)

Busb. L. Busbee Law (N.C.)

Bus. Corp. Business Corporation

Bus. Eq. Busbee's Equity Rep.(45 N.C.)

Bus. Franchise Guide (CCH) Business Franchise Guide

Bush Bush's Kentucky Reports (vols. 64-77 Kentucky)

Bush Dig. Bush's Digest of Florida Laws

Bush. Elec.   Bushby, Parliamentary Elections. 5ed. 1880

Bush (Ky.)   Bush's Kentucky Report, (vols. 64-77 Kentucky)

Business L.J.   Business Law Journal

Business L.R.   Business Law Review

Business Q.   Business Quarterly

Busk. Pr.   Buskirk, Indiana Practice

BUSL   Boston University School of Law

Bus. L.   Business Lawyer

Bus. Law.   Business Lawyer

Bus. Lawyer   Business Lawyer

Bus. L.J.   Business Law Journal

Bus. L.R.   Business Law Review
- Business Law Review
- Business Law Review (1980)

Bus. L. Rep.   Business Law Reports

Bus. L. Rev.   The Business Law Review

Bus. L. Rev. (Butterworths)   Business Law Review (Butterworths)

Bus. Reg.   Business Regulation

Bus. Reg. L. Rep.   Business Regulation Law Report

Bus. Trust   Business Trust

Busw. & Wol. Pr.   Buswell & Wolcott, Massachusetts Practice

Bus. Wk.   Business Week

But. Law. & Cl.   Butler's Lawyer and Client

Butl. Co. Litt.   Butler's Notes to Coke on Littleton

Butler   Butler County Legal Journal (Pa.)

Butler, Co. Litt.   Butler's Notes to Coke on Littleton

Butler, Hor. Jur.   Butler's Horae Juridicae

Butl. Hor. Jur.   Butler's Horae Juridicae Subsecivae

Butterworth's S.A. Law Review   Butterworth's South African Law Review

Butterworth's South Afr. L. Rev.   Butterworth's South African Law Review, Durban, South Africa

Butt. R.A.   Butterworth's Rating Appeals. (1913-31)

Butt. Rat. App.   Butterworth's Rating Appeals (Eng.)

Butt. S.A. Law Rev.   Butterworth's South African Law Review

Butts Sh.   Butts' Edition of Shower's English King's Bench Reports

Butt. W.C.C.   Butterworth's Workmen's Compensation Cases (1908-47)

Butt. Work. Comp. Cas.   Butterworth's Workmen's Compensation Cases (1908-47)

Buxton   Buxton's Reports (vols. 123-129 North Carolina)

Buxton (N.C.)   Buxton's Reports (Vols. 123-129 North Carolina)

B/V   Book value

B.W.C.C.   Butterworth's Workmen's Compensation Cases (1908-49) (Eng.)

B.W.C.C. (Eng.)   Butterworth's

Workmen's Compensation Cases (1908-49)

B.W.I. British West Indies

B.Y.I.L. British Yearbook of International Law

Byl. Bills. Byles on Bills of Exchange

Byles Byles on Bills of Exchange. 20 editions (1829-1939)

Byles, Bills Byles on Bills

Byl. Exch. Byles' Law of Exchange

By. L.R. Baylor Law Review

Byl. Us. L. Byles on the Usury Laws

Bynk. Bynkershoek's Quaestionum Juris Publici

Bynks. Obs. Jur. Rom. Bynkershoeks Observationum Juris Roman Libri

Byn. War Bynkershoek's Law of War

Byrne B.S. Bryne, Bills of Sale. 2ed. 1870

Byrne Pat. Byrne on Patents

Byth. Conv. Bythewood, Precedents in Conveyancing. 4ed. 1884-90

Byth. Prec. Bythewood, Precedents in Conveyancing, 4ed. 1884-90

B.Y.U. J. Pub. L. BYU Journal of Public Law

B.Y.U. L.R. Brigham Young University Law Review

B.Y.U. L. Rev. Brigham Young University Law Review

C

C
- All India Reporter, Calcutta Series
- Calcutta
- California
- California Reports
- Canada (Province)
- Cape Provincial Division Reports (1910-46) (S. Afr.)
- Catholic
- Century
- Chancellor
- Chancery
- Chapter
- Chinese
- Circuit
- College
- Colorado
- Congress
- Connecticut
- Conservative Party
- Court
- Cowen (New York)
- Indian Law Reports, Calcutta Series

c.
- cases
- chapter
- circa (about) (Lat.)
- civil
- condemnation
- contre (against, versus) (Fr.)
- criticised; soundness of decision or reasoning in cited case criticised for reasons given. (Used in

Shephard's Citations)

C. California Supreme Court Reports

C.
- cited
- code
- codex
- Lord Chancellor
- Corpus
- Centum

C. 2d California Supreme Court Reports, Second Series

C. 3d California Supreme Court Reports, Third Series

Ca.
- Case or Placitum
- cases (see cas.)

C.A.
- California Appellate Reports
- Chartered Accountant
- Chief Accountant
- Commercial Agent
- Consumers' Association
- Court of Appeal (English)
- Court of Appeals
- Court of Appeals Reports (New Zealand)
- Court of Customs and Patent Appeals Reports (Customs)
- Court of Customs Appeals Reports
- Crown Agent
- United States Court of Appeals

C.A.
- Court of Arches
- Chancery Appeals

C.A. 2d California Appellate Reports, Second Series

C.A. 2d Supp. California Appellate Reports, Second Series Supplement

C.A. 3d California Appellate Reports, Third Series

C.A. 3d. Supp. California Appellate Department of the Superior Court, Third Series

CAA Clean Air Act

C.A.A.
- Civil Aeronautics Administration
- Civil Aeronautics Authority
- Civil Aeronautics Authority Reports

Ca. A. California Appellate Reports

Ca. A. 2d California Appellate Reports, Second Series

Ca. A. 3d California Appellate Reports, Third Series

C.A.J. Civil Aeronautics Journal

C.A.A. Op. Civil Aeronautics Authority Opinions

CAB Contract Adjustment Board

C.A.B.
- Civil Aeronautics Board
- Civil Aeronautics Board Reports

Cab. & E. Cababe and Ellis' Queen's Bench Reports (1882-85) (Eng.)

Cab. & El. Cababe and Ellis' Queen's Bench Reports (1882-85) (Eng.)

Cab. & El. (Eng.) Cababe and Ellis' Queen's Bench Reports (1882-85) (Eng.)

Cab. & Ell. Cababe and Ellis' Queen's Bench Reports (1882-85)

Cab. Int. Cababe on Interpleader and Attachment of Debts

Cab. Lawy. Cabinet Lawyer by John Wade (Eng.)

Ca. Celeb. Causes Celebres (Quebec Provincial Reports)

CACM Central American Common Market

C.A.D.
- Canadian Annual Digest
- Customs Appeals Decisions

C.A.D.C. District of Columbia Circuit Court or District of Columbia Court of Appeals

Cadwalader. Cadwalader's Cases, U.S. District Court, Eastern District of Pennsylvania

Cadw. Dig. Cadwalader's Digest of Attorney-General's Opinions

Cadw. Gr. R. Cadwalader on Ground Rents (Pennsylvania)

C.A.F. cost and freight

CA FC U.S. Court of Appeals for the Federal Circuit

Ca. G.C.L. California General Corporation Law

CAH Acret, Construction Arbitration Handbook

Cahill's Ill. St. Cahill's Illiniois Statutes

CAH(s) Acret, Construction Arbitration Handbook, Supplement

Cai.
- Caines' New York Cases in Er-

ror (1796-1805)
- Caines' Reports, New York Supreme Court
- Caines' Term Reports, New York Supreme Court

Cai. Ca. Caines' Cases (N.Y.)

Cai. Cas.
- Caines' Cases
- Caines' New York Cases in Error
- Caines' Reports, New York Supreme Court (1803-1805)
- Caines' Term Reports, New York Supreme Court

Cai. Cas. Err. Caines' New York Cases in Error

Cai.Cas. (or Cas.Err.) Caines' New York Cases in Error

Cai. Forms Caines' Practical (New York) Forms

Caii Caii or Gaii Institutiones

Cai. Lex Mer. Caines' Lex Mercatoria Americana

Cain
- Caines' New York Cases in Error
- Caines' Reports, New York Supreme Court
- Caines' Term Reports, New York Supreme Court

Cain. Cas. in Error Caines' Cases (N.Y.)

Cain. C.E. Caines' Cases (N.Y.)

Cain. E. Caines' Cases (N.Y.)

Caine. R. Caines' Reports (N.Y.)

Caines
- Caines' New York Cases in Error
- Caines' Reports, New York Su-

preme Court
- Caines' Term Reports, New York Supreme Court

Caines Ca. in E. Caines' Cases (N.Y.)

Caines' Ca. in Er. Caines' Cases (N.Y.)

Caines Cas.
- Caines' New York Cases in Error
- Caines' Reports, New York Supreme Court
- Caines' Term Reports, New York Supreme Court

Caines' Cas. in Er. Caines' Cases (N.Y.)

Caines (N.Y.)
- Caines' New York Cases in Error
- Caines' Reports, New York Supreme Court
- Caines' Term Reports, New York Supreme Court

Caines' R. Caines' Reports (N.Y.)

Caines Rep. Caines' Reports (N.Y.)

Caines Term. Rep. (N.Y.) Caines' Term Reports, New York Supreme Court

Cains. C. Caines' Cases (N.Y.)

Cain's. R. Caines' Reports (N.Y.)

Cai. (N.Y.) Caines' Reports (N.Y.)

Cai. Pr. Caines' Practice

Cai. R.
- Caines' New York Cases in Error
- Caines' Reports, New York Supreme Court
- Caines' Term Reports, New

York Supreme Court

Cairns Dec. Cairns, Decisions in the Albert Arbitration (Reilly) (1871-75) (Eng.)

Cai. T.R. Caines' Term Reports, New York Supreme Court

CAJC California Jury Instructions, Criminal

CAJI California Jury Instructions, Civil

CAJR New York State Commission on Administration of Justice, Report

Cal California Supreme Court Reports

Cal.
- All India Reporter, Calcutta Series
- Calcutta
- Calendae
- California
- California Reports
- Calcutta (Indian Law Reports, Calcutta Series)
- Calthrop English King's Bench Reports (1609-18)
- Caldecott, English Settlement Cases (1776-85)
- Calendars of the Proceedings in Chancery, Record Commission

Cal. 2d California Reports, Second Series

Cal. 3d California Reports, Third Series

Cal. 4th Reports of Cases Determined in the Supreme Court of the State of California

cal. calendar

C.A.L.A. Civil Aviation Licensing Act

Cal. Adm. Code. California Administrative Code

Cal. Admin. Code California Administrative Code

Cal. Admin. Reg. California Administrative Register

Cal. Adv. Legis. Serv. California Advance Legislative Service (Deering)

Cal. Agric. Code California Agriculture Code

Cal. App. California Appellate Reports

Cal. App. 2d California Appellate Reports, Second Series

Cal. App. 3d California Appellate Reports, Third Series

Cal. App. 3d (Adv.) California Appellate Reports, 3d Series (Advance Parts)

Cal. App. Dec. California Appellate Decisions

Cal. App. Supp. California Appellate Reports Supplement

Cal. App. 2d Supp. California Appellate Reports, Second Series Supplement

Cal. App. 3d Supp. California Appellate Reports, Third Series, Supplement

Cal. Bankr. J. California Bankruptcy Journal

Cal. Bd. R. Co. California Board of Railroad Commissioners

C.A.L. Bull. Association of the Bar, City of New York, Committee on Amendment of the Law, Bulletin

Calc. Indian Law Reports, Calcutta Series

Cal. Ch. Calendar of Proceedings in Chancery, tempore Elizabeth (1827-32)

Calc. L.J. Calcutta Law Journal (India)

Cal. Code Deerings Annotated California Code

Cal. Comp. Cases California Compensation Cases

Cal. Const. California Constitution

Calc. Ser. Calcutta Series, Indian Law Reports

Calcutta L.J. Calcutta Law Journal

Calcutta W.N. Calcutta Weekly Notes

Calc. W.N. Calcutta Weekly Notes, (India)

Cald.
- Caldecott's Magistrates' and Settlement Case (1776-85) (Eng.)
- Caldwell's Reports (vols. 25-36 West Virginia)

Cald. Arb.
- Caldwell, Arbitration. 2ed. 1825
- Caldwell on Arbitration

Cal. Dec. California Decisions

Cald. (Eng.) Caldecott's Magistrates' and Settlement Cases (Eng.)

Cald. J.P. Caldecott's Magistrates' and Settlement Cases (Eng.)

Cald. Mag. Cas. Caldecott's Magistrates' and Settlement Cases (Eng.)

Cald. M. Cas. Caldecott's Magistrates' and Settlement Cases (Eng.) .

Cald. S.C.
- Caldecott's Settlement Cas.,Eng.
- Caldecott's Magistrate's and Settlement Cases (Eng)

Cald. Set. Cas. Caldecott's Magistrates' and Settlement Cases (Eng.)

Cald. Sett. Cas. Caldecott's Settlement Cas.,Eng.

CALE Conference of American Legal Executives

Cal. Gen. Laws Ann. (Deering) Deering's California General Laws Annotated

Cal. I.A.C. C.C. California Industrial Accident Commission, Compensation Cases

Cal. I.A.C. Dec. California Industrial Accident Decisions

Calif. California Reports (Cal.)

Calif. Ind. Accdt. Com. Dec. Decisions of the Industrial Accident Commission of California

Calif. L.R.C. California Law Revision Commission

Calif. L. Rev. California Law Review

Calif. Management Rev. California Management Review

California West. L. Rev. California Western Law Review

Calif. S.B.J. California State Bar Journal

Calif. Western Int. L.J. California Western International Law Journal

Calif. Western L. Rev. California Western Law Review

Calif. West. Int'l. L.J. California Western International Law Journal

Calif. West. L. Rev. California Western Law Review

Calif. W. Int. L.J. California Western International Law Journal

Calif. W. Int'l. L.J. California Western International Law Journal

Calif. W. L. Rev. California Western Law Review

Cal. I.A.C. Decisions of the Industrial Accident Commission of California

Cal. Ind. Acc. Com. Decisions of the Industrial Accident Commission of California

Cal. Ind. Acc. Com. Dec. Decisions of the Industrial Accident Commission of California

Cal. Ind. Acci. Dec. California Industrial Accidents Decisions

Cal. Ind. Acct. Dec. California Industrial Accidents Dec.

Cal. Ind. Com. Decisions of the Industrial Accident Commission of California

Cal. Int'l Prac. California International Practitioner

Cal. J.I.C. California Jury Instructions, Criminal

Cal. Jur. California Jurisprudence

Cal. Jur. 2d California Jurisprudence, Second Edition

Call Call's Virginia Reports (1797-1825) (vols. 5-10 Virginia)

Callaghan Callaghan & Co.

Cal. Law. California Lawyer

Cal. Leg. Adv. Calcutta Legal Adviser (India)

Cal. Legis. Serv. California Legislative Service (West)

Cal. Leg. Obs. Calcutta Legal Observer

Cal. Leg. Rec. California Legal Record, San Francisco

Callis The Reading of Robert Callis on the Statute of Sewers. 23 Hen. 8. c. 5. delivered by him at Gray's Inn August 1622

Callis, Sew. Callis on Sewers

Cal. L.J.
- Calcutta Law Journal Reports (India)
- California Law Journal

Cal. Real Prop. J. California Real Property Journal

Callman, Unfair Comp. Callman on Unfair Competition & Trade Marks

Call. Mil. L. Callan's United States Military Laws

Cal. Mil. Laws Callan's Military Laws of the United States

Cal LR California Law Review

Cal. L.R. Calcutta Law Reporter (India)

Cal. L. Rev. California Law Review

Call.Sew. Callis on Sewers

Call. (Va.) Call, Virginia Reports (1797-1825) (vols. 5-10 Virginia)

Cal. P. Ch. Calendar of Proceedings in Chancery, tempore Elizabeth (1827-32)

Cal. Penal Code California Penal Code

Cal. Prac. California Practice

Cal. P.U.C. Decisions of the California Public Utilities Commission

CALR Computer-assisted legal research

Ca. L.R. California Law Review

Cal. R.C. Dec. California Railroad Commission Decisions

Cal. R.C. Dec. Dig. California Railroad Commission Digest of Decisions

Cal. R. Com. Opinions and Orders of the Railroad Commission of California

Cal. Reg. L. Rep. California Regulatory Law Reporter

Cal. Rep.
• California Reports
• Calthrop, English King's Bench Reports

Cal. Rptr. California Reporter (West)

Cal. S.B.J. California State Bar Journal

Cal. S.D.A. Calcutta Sadr Diwani Adalat Reports (India)

Cal. Ser. Calcutta Series, Indian Law Reports

Cal. Sew. Callis on Sewers. 4ed. 1810

Cal. Stat. Statutes and Amendments to the Code of California

Cal. Stats. Statutes of California

Cal. St. B.J. California State Bar Journal

Cal. [subject] Code (Deering) Deerings Annotated California Code

Cal. [subject] Code (West) West's Annotated California Code

Cal. Sup.
• California Superior Court, Reports of Cases in Appellate Departments
• California Supplement

Cal. Sup. (Cal.) California Superior Court, Reports of Cases in Appellate Departments

Cal. Supp. California Superior Court, Reports of Cases in Appellate Departments

CALT Center for Advanced Legal Training

Calth.
• Calthrop's City of London Cases, King's Bench (Eng.)
• Calthrop's King's Bench Reports (80 ER)

Calth. Copyh. Calthorpe on Copyholds

Calth. (Eng.)
• Calthrop's City of London Cases, King's Bench (Eng.)
• Calthrop's King's Bench Reports (80 ER)

Calthr.
• Calthrop's City of London Cases, King's Bench (Eng.)
• Calthrop's King's Bench Reports (80 ER)

Cal. Unrep. California Unreported Cases (1855-1910)

Cal. Unrep. Cas. California Unreported Cases (1855-1910)

Calvin. Calvinus Lexicon Juridicum

Calvin Lex. Calvininus Lexicon Juridicum

Calvin. Lex. Jurid. Calvinus Lexicon Juridicum

Calv. Lex. Calvini Lexicon Juridicum

Calv. Par. Calvert's Parties to Suits in Equity

Calv. Parties Calvert's Parties to Suits in Equity

Cal. W. Int'l. L.J. California Western International Law Journal

Cal. W. L. Rev. California Western Law Review

Cal. W.N. Calcutta Weekly Notes (India)

Cal. W.R. Calcutta Weekly Reporter (India)

CAM
- Cameron's Privy Council Decisions (1832-1929) (Canada)
- Cameron's Supreme Court Cases (1880-1905) (Canada)
- Church Assembly Measure
- Civil Aeronautics Manual

Cam. Cameron, Reports, Upper Canada, Queen's Bench

Cam. & N. Cameron & Norwood's North Carolina Conference Reports

Cam. & Nor. Cameron & Norwood's North Carolina Conference Reports (1800-04)

Camb. Co. L.J. Cambria County Reports (Pa.)

Camb. L.J. Cambridge Law Journal

Cambria Cambria County Legal

Journal (Pa.)

Cambria Co. L.J. Cambria County Legal Journal (Pa.)

Cambria Co. (Pa.) Cambria County Legal Journal (Pa.)

Cambrian L.R. Cambrian Law Review

Cambrian L. Rev. Cambrian Law Review

Cambridge L.J. Cambridge Law Journal

Cam. Brit. Camden's Britannia

Cam. Cas. Cameron's Supreme Court Cases, Canada

Camd. Brit. Camden's Britannia

Camden Camden's Britannia

Camd. Soc. Camden Society

Cam. Duc. Camera Ducata (Duchy Chamber)

Cameron Cameron's Supreme Court Cases

Cameron (Can.) Cameron's Supreme Court Cases (Canada)

Cameron Cas. (Can.) Cameron's Supreme Court Cases (Canada)

Cameron Pr. Cameron's Practice (Canada)

Cameron Pr. (Can.) Cameron's Practice (Canada)

Cameron S.C. Cameron's Supreme Court Cases (1880-1905) (Can.)

Cam. Int. Suc. Cameron, Intestate Succession in Scotland

Cam. J.S. Comp. Cameron on Joint Stock Companies, Scotland

Cam. Op. Cameron's Legal Opinions, Toronto

Camp.
- Campbell's Compendium of Roman Law
- Campbell's English Nisi Prius Reports
- Campbell's Legal Gazette Reports (Pa.)
- Campbell's Reports (vols. 27-58 Nebraska)
- Campbell's Reports of Taney's United States Circuit Court Decisions
- Camp's Reports (vol. 1 North Dakota)

Campaign L. Rep. Campaign Law Reporter

Campb.
- Campbell's Compendium of Roman Law
- Campbell's English Nisi Prius Reports
- Campbell's Legal Gazette Reports Pennsylvania
- Campbell's Reports (vols. 27-58 Nebraska)
- Campbell's Reports of Taney's United States Circuit Court Decisions

Campb. Dec. Campbell's Reports of Taney's Decisions, U.S. Circuit Court

Campbell
- Campbell's Compendium of Roman Law
- Campbell's English Nisi Prius Reports
- Campbell's Legal Gazette Reports (Pa.)
- Campbell's Lives of the Chief Justice
- Campbell's Lives of the Lord

Chancellors
- Campbell's Reports (vols. 27-58 Nebraska)
- Campbell's Reports of Taney's United States Circuit Court Decisions

Campbell L. Rev. Campbell Law Review

Campb. (Eng.) Campbell's English Nisi Prius Reports (170, 171 ER)

Campb. L.G. Campbell's Legal Gazette (Pa.)

Campb. (Pa.) Campbell's Legal Gazette Reports (Pa.)

Camp. Ch. Jus. Campbell's Lives of the Chief Justices

Camp. Cit. Campbell on Citation and Diligence

Camp. Dec. Campbell's Reports of Taney's Decisions, U.S. Circuit Court

Camp. Ex. Campbell on Executors and Administrators in Pennsylvania

Camp. Ld. Ch. Campbell's Lives of the Lord Chancellors

Camp. L.G. Campbell's Legal Gazette, Pa.

Camp. Lives Ld.Ch. Campbell's Lives of the Lord Chancellors

Camp L Rev Campbell Law Review

Camp. Merc. L. Campbell, Mercantile Law. 3ed. 1904

Camp. Neg. Campbell, Negligence. 2ed. 1878

Camp. N.P. Campbell's English Nisi Prius Reports (1807-16)

Cam. Prac. Cameron's Supreme Ct. Practice (Canada)

Camp. Rom. L. Campbell's Compendium of Roman Law

Camp. Rom. L. Comp. Campbell's Compendium of Roman Law

Camp. Rom. L. (or Comp.) Campbell's Compendium of Roman Law

Camp. Sale Campbell, Sale of Goods and Commercial Agency. 2ed. 1891

Camp. Sale (or Com. Ag.) Campbell on Sale of Goods and Commercial Agency

Cam. S.C. Cameron's Supreme Court Cases (Canada)

Cam.Scac. Camera Scaccaria (Exchequer Chamber)

Cam. Scacc. Camera Scaccarii (Exchequer Chamber) (Eng.)

Cam. Stell. Camera Stellate (Star Chamber) (Eng.)

Can.
- Canada
- Canon

Can. Abr. Canadian Abridgment

Can.Abr. (2d) The Canadian Abridgment (Second Edition)

Canada Commerce. Canadian Department of Industry, Trade and Commerce

Canada L.T. Canadian Law Times

Canal Z. Canal Zone

Canal Zone Canal Zone Supreme Court

Canal Zone Sup. Ct. Canal Zone Supreme Court Reports

Can.-Am. L.J. Canadian American Law Journal

Can. App. Canadian Reports, Appellate Cases

Can. App. Cas. Canadian Appeal Cases

Can. B.A. Canadian Bar Association, Proceedings

Can. B.A. J. Canadian Bar Association Journal

Can. Bank. Canadian Banker

Can. Bank. R. Canadian Bankruptcy Reports

Can. Bankr. Canadian Bankruptcy Reports

Can. Bankr. Ann. Canadian Bankruptcy Reports Annotated

Can. Bankr. Ann. (N.S.) Canadian Bankruptcy Reports Annotated, New Series

Can. Bankr. Rep. Canadian Bankruptcy Reports

Can. Bar. A.J. Journal: the Canadian Bar Association

Can. Bar J. Canadian Bar Journal

Can. Bar J. (N.S.) The Canadian Bar Journal, New Series

Can. Bar. Rev. Canadian Bar Review

Can. Bar Year Book Year Book, Canadian Bar Association

Can. B. Ass'n Y.B. Canadian Bar Association:Year Book

Can. B.J. Canadian Bar Journal

Can. B.R. Canadian Bar Review

Can. B. Rev. Canadian Bar Review

Can. Bus. L.J. Canadian Business Law Journal

Can. B. Year Book. Canadian Bar

Association Year Book

Can. Cases L. Torts Canadian Cases on the Law of Torts

Can. C.C. Canada Criminal Cases Annotated

Can. Chart. Acc. Canadian Chartered Accountant

Canc. Instr. Cancellation of Instruments

Can. Com. Cas. Canadian Commercial Law Reports (1901-05)

Can. Com. L. Guide (CCH) Canadian Commercial Law Guide

Can. Com. L.J. Canadian Community Law Journal

Can. Com. L.R. Canadian Commercial Law Reports (1901-05)

Can. Com. L. Rev. Canadian Communications Law Review

Can. Community L.J. Canadian Community Law Journal

Can. Com. R. Canadian Commercial Law Reports (1901-05)

Can. Cr. Acts. Canada Criminal Acts, Taschereau's edition

Can. Cr. Cas. Canadian Criminal Cases

Can. Crim. Criminal Reports (Canada)

Can. Crim. Cas. Canadian Criminal Cases Annotated

Can. Crim. Cas. Ann. Canadian Criminal Cases Annotated

Can. Crim. Cas. (N.S.) Canadian Criminal Cases, New Series

Can. Cr. R. Canadian Criminal Reports

C. & A. Cook & Alcock's Irish

King's Bench Reports (1833-34)

C. & C.
- Case and Comment
- Coleman's & Caines' Cases (N.Y.)

C. & D.
- Corbett and Daniell's English Election Cases (1819)
- Crawford & Dix's Irish Circuit Cases

C. & D.A.C. Crawford & Dix's Irish Abridged Cases (1839-46)

C. & D.C.C. Crawford & Dix's Irish Circuit Cases (1841-42)

C. & E. Cababe & Ellis Queen's Bench (1882-85) (Eng.)

C. & F.
- Clark & Finnelley's English House of Lords Reports
- Cost and freight (1831-46)

C. & H. Char. Tr. Cooke & Harwood, Charitable Trusts. 2ed. 1867

C. & H. Dig. Coventry & Hughes' Digest

C. & H. Elec. Cas. Clarke & Hall, Cases of Contested Elections in Congress (1789-1834) (U.S.)

C. & J. Crompton & Jervis' English Exchequer Reports (1830-32)

C. & K. Carrington & Kirwan's English Nisi Prius Reports (1843-50)

C. & L. Conner & Lawson's Irish Chancery Reports (1841-43)

C. & L. C.C. Caines & Leigh Crown Cases (Eng.)

C. & L. Dig. Cohen & Lee's Maryland Digest

C. & M.
- Carrington & Marshman's English Nisi Prius Reports (1840-42)
- Crompton & Meeson's English Exchequer Reports (1832-34)

C. & Mar. Carrington and Marshman's Reports, Nisi Prius (1840-42)

C. & Marsh. Carrington & Marshman's English Nisi Prius Reports

C. & M. Bills Collier & Miller on Bills of Sale

C. & N. Cameron & Norwood's North Carolina Conference Reports

C. & O. R. Cas. Carrow & Oliver's English Railway & Canal Cases

C. & P.
- Carrington & Payne's English Nisi Prius Reports (1823-41)
- Craig & Phillips' Chancery Reports (1840-41).

C. & R.
- Clifford and Richards, Locus Standi (1873-84) (Eng.)
- Cockburn and Rowe's Election Cases. (1833) (Eng.)

C. & S.
- Clarke & Scully's Drainage Cases (Ontario)
- Clifford & Stephen, English Locus Standi Reports (1867-72)

C. & S. Dig. Connor & Simonton's South Carolina Digest

Candy. Printed Judgments of Sind by Candy and Birdwood (India)

Candy M.C. Candy, Mayor's Court Practice. 1879

Cane & L. Cane & Leigh Crown Cases Reserved (Eng.)

Can. Environ. L. N. Canadian Environmental Law News

Can. Env. L. News Canadian Environmental Law News

Can. Ex. Exchequer Court (Canada)

Can. Exch.
- Canada Exchequer Court Reports
- Canada Law Reports, Exchequer

Can. Ex. C.R. Canada Exchequer Court Reports (1875-1922)

Can. Ex. R. Canadian Exchequer Reports

Can. F.C. Federal Court of Canada

Can. Gaz. Canada Gazette (regulations)

Can. Green Bag Canadian Green Bag

Can. Human Rights Rep. Canadian Human Rights Reporter

Can. Hum. Rts. Advocate Canadian Human Rights Advocate

Can. in Wld. Aff. Canada in World Affairs. Toronto, Ontario

Can. J. Admin. L. & Prac. Canadian Journal of Administrative Law & Practice

Can. J. Corr. Canadian Journal of Crimi-nology and Corrections

Can. J. Correction Canadian Journal of Correction

Can. J. Crim. & Corr. Canadian Journal of Criminology and Corrections

Can. J. Crim. & Correct. Canadian Journal of Criminology and

Corrections

Can. J. Criminol. Canadian Journal of Criminology

Can. J. Criminology Canadian Journal of Criminology

Can. J. Criminology & Corr. Canadian Journal of Criminology and Corrections

Can. J. Fam. L. Canadian Journal of Family Law

Can. J.L. & Juris. Canadian Journal of Law and Jurisprudence

Can. J. Pol. Sc. Canadian Journal of Political Science

Can. J. Women & L. Canadian Journal of Women and the Law

Can. Lab. Canadian Labour

Can. Law. Canadian Lawyer

Can. Lawyer Canadian Lawyer

Can. Legal Aid Bul. Canadian Legal Aid Bulletin

Can. Legal Stud. Canadian Legal Studies

Can. Leg. N. Canada Legal News

Can. Leg. Stud. Canadian Legal Studies

Can. Leg. Studies Canadian Legal Studies

Can. L.J.
- Canada Law Journal, Montreal
- Canada Law Journal, Toronto

Can. L.J. N.S. Canada Law Journal, New Series

Can. L.R. Canada Law Reports, Exchequer & Supreme Court, in two series

Can. L.R.B.R. Canadian Labour Relations Board Reports, 1974-

Can. L. Rev. Canadian Law Review

Can. L.T. Canadian Law Times

Can. L. Times Canadian Law Times

Can. L.T. Occ. N. Canadian Law Times, Occasional Notes

Can. L.T. Occ. Notes Canadian Law Times Occasional Notes

Can. Mun. J. Canadian Municipal Journal

Can. Native L. Rep. Canadian Native Law Reporter

Can. Oil & Gas Canadian Oil & Gas (Butterworth's)

Can. Pat. Off. Rec. Canadian Patent Office Record

Can. Pat. Rep. Canadian Patent Reporter

Can. Persp. Canadian Perspectives on International Law and Organization

Can. P.R. Canadian Patent Reporter

Can. Pub. Ad. Canadian Public Administration

Can. Pub. Admin. Canadian Public Administration

Can. R. A.C. Canadian Reports, Appeal Cases

Can. R. App. Cas. Canadian Reports, Appeal Cases

Can. R.C. Railway Commission of Canada

Can. R. Cas. Canadian Railway Cases

Can. Rev. Stat. Revised Statutes of Canada

Can. Ry. & T. Cas. Canadian Railway and Transport Cases

Can. Ry. Cas. Canada Railway Cases

Can. Sales Tax Rep. (CCH) Canadian Sales Tax Reporter

Can. S.C.
- Canada Supreme Court
- Canada Supreme Court Reports

Can. S.C. R. Canada Supreme Court Reports (1876-1922)

Can. S.C. Rep. Canada Supreme Court Reports

Can. S.Ct.
- Canada Law Reports, Supreme Court
- Canada Supreme Court Reports

Can. Stat. Statutes of Canada

Can. Stat. O. & Regs. Statutory Orders & Regulations

Can. Sup.Ct. Canada Supreme Court Reports

Can. Tax App. Bd. Canada Tax Appeal Board Cases

Can. Tax Cas. Canada Tax Cases

Can. Tax Cas. Ann. Canada Tax Cases Annotated

Can. Tax Found. Canadian Tax Foundation (Conference Report)

Can. Tax Found. Rep. Proc. Tax Conf. Canadian Tax Foundation Report of Proceedings of the Tax Conference

Can. Tax J. Canadian Tax Journal

Can. Tax L.J. Canadian Tax Law Journal

Can. Tax News Canadian Tax News

Can. Tax Rep. (CHH)
- Canadian Tax Reports
- Canadian Tax Reporter

Canterbury L. Rev. Canterbury Law Review

Can. Terr. Territories Law Reports (1885-1907) (Canada)

Cantor, Med. & Surg. Cantor's Traumatic Medicine & Surgery for the Attorney

Can. T.S. Canada Treaty Series

Cantwell Cantwell's Cases on Tolls & Customers (Ir.)

Can.-U.S. Bus. L. Rev. Canada-U.S. Business Law Review

Can. U.S. L.J. Canada-United States Law Journal

Can. Wel. Canadian Welfare

Can. Y.B. I.L. Canadian Yearbook of International Law

Can. Y.B. Int. Law Canadian Yearbook of International Law

Can. Y.B. Int'l. L. Canadian Yearbook of International Law

Can. Yb. of Internat. The Canadian Yearbook of International Law. Vancouver, British Columbia, Canada

Can. Yearbook Int. L. Canadian Yearbook of International Law

CAP Civil Air Patrol

Ca.P. Cases in Parliament (Eng.)

Cap.
- Capital
- Capitulo
- Chapter

Ca. Parl. Cases in Parliament (Shower) (1694-99)

CAPDA California Public Defenders Association

Cap. Def. Dig. Capital Defense Digest

Cape Law J. Cape Law Journal (S. Africa)

Cape L.J. Cape Law Journal (S. Africa)

Cape P. Div. Cape Provincial Division Reports (S. Africa)

Cape S.C. R. Supreme Court Reports, Cape Colony (1880-1910) (S. Afr.)

Cape T. Div. Cape Provincial Division Reports (S. Africa)

Cape T.R. Cape Times Reports, Supreme Court, Cape of Good Hope (S. Africa)

Capital U. L.R. Capital University Law Review

Capital U. L. Rev. Capital University Law Review

Capital Univ. L. Rev. Capital University Law Review

C. App. R. Criminal Appeal Reports (Eng.)

Cap. U. L. Rev. Capital University Law Review

C.A.R.
- Civil Air Regulations ("Safety Regulations") (U.S.)
- Commonwealth Arbitration Reports (Australia)
- Criminal Appeal Reports (Eng.)

CaR California Reporter

Ca.R. California Reporter

Car.
- Carolus (as 4 Car. II)
- Carolina

CaR 2d California Reporter, Second Series

Car. & K. Carrington & Kirwan's English Nisi Prius Reports (174, 175 ER)

Car. & K.(Eng.) Carrington & Kirwan's English Nisi Prius Reports (174, 175 ER)

Car. & Kir Carrington & Kirwan's English Nisi Prius Reports (174, 175 ER)

Car. & M. Carrington & Marshman's English Nisi Prius Reports (1840-42)

Car. & Mar. Carrington & Marshman's English Nisi Prius Reports (1840-42)

Car. & M. (Eng.) Carrington & Marshman's English Nisi Prius Reports (1840-42)

Car. & O. English Railway & Canal Cases, by Carrow, Oliver et al (1835-55)

Car. & Ol. English Railway & Canal Cases, by Carrow, Oliver et al (1835-55)

Car. & P. Carrington's & Payne's English Nisi Prius Reports (1823-41)

Car. & P. (Eng.) Carrington's & Payne's English Nisi Prius Reports (1823-41)

Car. Cr. L. Carrington, Criminal Law. 3ed 1828

Cardozo Arts & Entertainment L.J. Cardozo Arts & Entertainment Law Journal

Cardozo L. Rev. Cardozo Law Review

Cardozo Stud. L. & Lit. Cardozo

Studies in Law and Literature

Ca. resp. Capias ad responden-
dum a judicial writ (Lat.)

Carey. M.R. Manitoba Reports
(1875)

Car. H. & A. Carrow, Hamerton &
Allen's New Sessions Cases (1844-
51) (Eng.)

Caribbean L. Libr. Caribbean
Law Liberation

Carib. L.J. Caribbean Law Journal (Ja-maica)

CARICOM Caribbean Common
Market

CARIFTA Caribbean Free Trade
Association

Carl. Carleton, New Brunswick
Reports

Car. Law Repos. Carolina Law
Repository (N.C.)

Car. Laws. Caruther's History of
a Lawsuit. Cases in Chancery

Car. L.J. Carolina Law Journal

Car. L.R. Carolina Law Repository (N.C.)

Car. L. Rep. Carolina Law Repository, North Carolina Reports, vol.
4 (1813-16)

Car. L. Repos. Carolina Law Repository (N.C.)

Carmody-Wait, N.Y. Prac. Car-
mody-Witt Cyclopedia of New
York Practice

Car. O. & B. English Railway &
Canal Cases, by Carrow, Oliver,
Bevan et al (1835-55)

Carolina L.J. Carolina Law Journal

Carolina L.Repos. Carolina Law

Repository (N.C.)

Carp.
- Carpenter's Reports (vols. 52-53
California)
- Carpmael's Patent Cases (1602-
1842)

Carp. Pat. Cas. Carpmael's Patent Cases (1602-1842)

Carpenter Carpenter's Reports
(vols. 52-53 California)

Carp. P.C. Carpmael's Patent
Cases (1602-1842) (Eng.)

Carr.
- Carriers
- Carrington (see Car.)

Carr. & K. Carrington & Kirwan

Carr. & M. Carrington and
Marshman's English Nisi Prius
Reports

Carrau. Carrau's edition of "Summary Cases," Bengai

Carr. Cas. Carran's Summary
Cases, India

Carribean L.J. Carribean Law
Journal

Carr., Ham. & Al. Carrow, Hamerton & Allen's New Sessions Cases
(Eng.)

Carsh. Carshaltown's Court Rolls
(Eng.)

Carswell's Prac. Carswell's Practice Cases

Cart.
- Carter's English Common Pleas
Reports, 1664-76
- Carter's Reports (1, 2 Indiana)
- Carthew's English King's Bench
Reports (1686-1701)
- Cartwright's Cases on British

North America Act (Canada)

Cart. B.N.A. Cartwright's Constitutional Cases (1868-96) (Can.)

Cart. Cas. (Can.) Cartwright's Cases

Cartel Cartel, Review of Monopoly, Developments and Consumer Protection, London, England

Carter
- Carter's English Common Pleas Reports, same as Orlando Bridgman
- Carter's Reports (vols. 1, 2 Indiana)

Carter (Eng.) Carter (124 ER)

Carth. Carthew's English King's Bench Reports (1686-1701)

Carth. (Eng.) Carthew (King's Bench) (90 ER)

Cartm. Cartmell's Trade Mark Cases (1876-92) (Eng.)

Cartw. C.C. Cartwright's Constitutional Cases (Canada)

Cartwr. Cas. Cartwright's Cases (Canada)

Carv. Carr. Carver's Treatise on the Law Relating to the Carriage of Goods by Sea

Carver. Carver on Carriage of Goods by Sea (1885-1957)

Cary. Cary's English Chancery Reports (1537-1604)

Cary (Eng.) Cary (21 ER)

Cary Jur. Cary on Juries

Cary Lit. Cary's Commentary on Littleton's Tenures

Cary Part. Cary on Partnership

C.A.S. Codifying Act of Sederunt

C.A. 3S. California Appellate Reports, Third Series Supplement

Cas.
- Casey's Reports (vols. 25-36 Pennsylvania State)
- Casualty

Ca. sa. Capias ad satisfaciendum (writ of execution)

Cas. & Op. Cases with Opinions, by Eminent Counsel (1700-75) (Eng.)

Cas. App. Cases of Appeal to the House of Lords

Cas. Arg. & Dec. Cases Argued and Decreed in Chancery, English

Cas. B.R. Cases Banco Regis tempore William III (12 Modern Reports)

Cas. B.R. (T.W. III) 12 Modern Reports (1690-1702) (Eng.)

Cas. Ch.
- Cases in Chancery (Eng.)
- Cases in Chancery (vol. 9 Modern Reports)
- Select Cases in Chancery (1724-33) (Eng.)

Cas. Ch. 1, 2, 3 Cases in Chancery tempore Car. II

Cas. C.L. Cases in Crown Law (Eng.)

Cas. C.R. Cases tempore Wm. III (vol. 12 Modern Reports) (Eng.)

Case & Com. Case and Comment

Case & Comm Case and Comment

Cas.Eq.
- Cases and Opinions in Law Equity, and Conveyancing
- Cases in Equity, Gilbert's Reports

Cas. Eq. Abr. Cases in Equity Abridged (1667-1744) (Eng.)

Cases in Ch. Select Cases in Chancery (Eng.)

Ca. Sett. Cases of Settlements and Removals. (1710-42) (Eng.)

Case West.Reserve L. Rev. Case Western Reserve Law Review

Case West. Res. J. Int'l L. Case Western Reserve Journal of International Law

Case West. Res. L. Rev. Case Western Reserve Law Review

Case W. Res. J. Int.L. Case Western Reserve Journal of International Law

Case W. Res. J. Intl L. Case Western Reserve Journal of International Law

Case W. Res. L. Rev. Case Western Reserve Law Review

Casey. Casey's Reports (25-36 Pennsylvania State)

Cas. F.T. Cases tempore Talbot, by Forrester, English Chancery

Cas. H.L. Cases in the House of Lords (Eng.)

Cas. in C.
- Cases in Chancery (Eng.)
- Select Cases in Chancery (Eng.)

Cas. in. Ch. Cases in Chancery, 3 Parts. (1660-88) (Eng.)

Cas. K.B. Cases in King's Bench (8 Modern Reports) (Eng.)

Cas. K.B.t.H. Cases tempore Hardwicke (W. Kelynge, English King's Bench Reports) (1730-35)

Cas. K.B.t.Hard. Cases tempore Hardwicke (W. Kelynge's King's Bench Reports) (1730-35)

Cas. L. & Eq.
- Cases in Law and Equity (vol. 10 Modern Reports) (Eng.)
- (Gilbert's) Cases in Law and Equity (Eng.)

Cas. L. Eq. Cases in Law and Equity (10 Mod.) (1720-73)

Cas. Op. Burton. Cases and Opinions

Casp. For. Med. Casper's Forensic Medicine

Cas. P. Cases in Parliament

Cas. Parl. Cases in Parliament

Cas. Pr. Cases of Practice, English King's Bench (1603-1774)

Cas. Prac. C.P. Cases of Practice, Common Pleas (1702-27) (Eng.)

Cas. Prac. K.B. Cases of Practice in King's Bench (1603-1774)

Cas. Pra. C.P. Cases of Practice, Common Pleas (1702-27) (Eng.)

Cas. Pra. K.B. Cases of Practice in King's Bench (1603-1774) (Eng.)

Cas. Pr. C.P. Cases of Practice. English Common Pleas (Cooke's Reports)

Cas. Pr. K.B. Cases of Practice in the King's Bench (1603-1774) (Eng.)

Cas. Proc. Cassell, Procedure in the Courts of Canada

Cas. R. Casey's Reports (25-36, Pennsylvania State)

Cass. Cour de Cassation, Corte di Cassazione (Supreme Court of Appeal)

Cas. S.C. (Cape G.H.) Cases in

the Supreme Court, Cape of Good
Hope

Cass. Dig. Cassel's Digest (Canada)

Cas. Self Def. Horrigan &
Thompson's Cases on Self-Defense

Cas. Sett. Cases of Settlement
and Removals (1710-42) (Eng.)

Cassiod. Var. Cassiodori Variarum

Cas. Six Cir. Cases on the Six Circuits, (1841-43) (Ir.)

Cass. L.G.B. Casson's Local Government Board Decisions (1902-16) (Eng.)

Cas. S.M. Cases of Settlement,
King's Bench (1713-15) (Eng.)

Cass. Prac. Cassels' Practice
Cases (Can.)

Cass. Prac. Cas. Cassel's Practice
Cases (Can.)

Cass. Proc. Cassell's Procedure,
Canada

Cass. S.C. Cassels' Supreme Court
Decisions

Cass. Sup. C. Prac. Cassel's Supreme court Practice, 2d edition
by Masters

Cas. Tak. & Adj. Cases Taken
and Adjudged (Report in Chancery, First Edition) (Eng.)

Cas. Tak. & Adj. Cases Taken
and Adjudged (Report in Chancery, First Edition) (Eng.)

Cas. Tax Canada Tax Cases Annotated

Cas.t.ch.II. Cases tempore Charles II., in vol. 3 of Reports in

Chancery (Eng.)

Cast. Com. Castle's Law of Commerce in Time of War

Cas. temp.F. Cases tempore
Finch, Chancery (1673-81) (23
ER)

Cas. temp.H. Cases tempore Hardwicke, King's Bench (1733-8) (95
ER)

Cas. temp. Hardw. Cases tempore Hardwicke

Cas. temp. Lee. Cases tempore
Lee (Eng. Ecc.)

Cas. temp. Talb. Cases tempore
Talbot

Cas. t.F. Cases tempore Finch,
English Chancery (23 ER)

Cas. t. Finch (Eng.) Cases tempore Finch, English Chancery (23
ER)

Cas. t. Geo.I. Cases tempore
George I., English Chancery (8, 9
Modern Reports)

Cas. t. H.
- Cases tempore Hardwicke, English King's Bench (Ridgway,
  Lee, or Annaly) (1733- 38)
- Cases tempore Holt, English
  King's Bench (Holt's Reports)
- West, Chancery Reports, tempore Hardwicke

Cas. t. Hard. Cases tempore Hardwicke by Lee and Hardwicke

Cas. t. Hard. (by Lee) Cases tempore Hardwicke, Lee's English
King's Bench Reports (1733-38)

Cas. t. Hardw.
- Cases tempore Hardwicke, English King's Bench (Ridgway, Lee
  or Annaly) (1733- 38)

- West, Chancery Reports, tempore Hardwicke (Eng.)

Cas. t. Holt. Cases tempore Holt, English King's Bench (Holt's Reports)

Cas.t.K.
- Moseley, Chancery Reports, tempore King
- Select Cases tempore King, English Chancery (edited by Mac-Naghten) (1724-33)

Cas. t. King
- Moseley, Chancery Reports, tempore King (Eng.)
- Select Cases tempore King, English Chancery (edited by Mac-Naghten) (1724-33)

Cas. t. Lee. (Phillimore) Cases tempore Lee, English Ecclesiastical

Cas. t. Mac. Cases tempore Macelessfield (10 Modern Reports) (1710-25) (Eng.)

Cas. t. Maccl. Cases tempore Macelesfield (10 Modern Reports) (1710-25) (Eng.)

Cas. t. Nap. Drury's Irish Chancery Reports tempore Napier (1858-59)

Cas. t. North. Eden's Chancery Reports tempore Northington (1757-66) (28 ER)

Cas. t. Northington Cases tempore. Northington, Chancery Reports (Eng.)

Cas. t. Plunk. Lloyd & Goold's Chancery Reports tempore Plunkett (1834-39) (Ir.)

Cas. t. Q.A. Cases tempore Queen Anne (11 Modern Reports) (1702-30) (Eng.)

Cas. t. Q. Anne Cases tempore Queen Anne (11 Modern Reports) (1702-30) (Eng.)

Cast. Rat. Castle, Rating. 4ed. 1903

Cas. t. Sugd. Cases tempore Sugden, Irish Chancery

Cas. t. Tal. Cases tempore Talbot, English Chancery (1734-38)

Cas. t. Talb. Cases tempore Talbot (1734-38) (Eng.)

Cas. t. Wm. III. Cases tempore William III. (12 Modern Reports)

C.A. Supp. California Appellate Reports Supplement

Casw. Cop. Caswall, Copyholds. 3ed. 1841

Cas. w. Op. Cases with opinions, by Eminent Counsel (1700-75)

Cas. Wm. I. Bigelow, Cases, William I. to Richard I.

cat.
- catalogue
- catalogues
- cataloguer
- cataloguing

Ca. t. Ch.2 Cases tempore Charles 2 (1681-98)

Ca. temp. F. Cases tempore Finch, Chancery (1673-81)

Ca. temp. H. Cases tempore, Hardwicke, King's Bench (1733-38)

Ca. temp. Hard. Cases tempore Hardwicke, King's Bench (1733-38)

Ca. temp. Holt Cases tempore Holt, King's Bench

Ca. temp. K. Cases in Chancery tempore King, King's Bench (1724-33) (Eng.)

Ca. temp. King Cases in Chancery tempore King (1724-33) (25 ER)

Ca. temp. Talb. Cases in Chancery tempore Talbot, King's Bench (1734-38) (Eng.)

Ca. temp. Talbot Cases tempore Talbot (1734-38)

Cates Cates' Reports (vols. 109-127 Tennessee Reports)

Ca. t. F. Finch's Chancery Reports (1673-81) (23 ER)

Ca. t. Geo.I 8 & 9 Modern Reports (1721-26)

Ca. t. H.
- Cases tempore Hardwicke, King's Bench (1733-38) (95 ER)
- Cases tempore Holt, 11 Modern Reports (1702-10) (88 ER)

Cath. Catholic

Ca. t. Hard. Cases tempore Hardwicke, King's Bench. (1733-38) (Eng.)

Cath. Law. Catholic Lawyer

Cath. Lawyer Catholic Lawyer

Catholic Law. Catholic Lawyer

Catholic U. A. L.R. Catholic University of America Law Review

Catholic U. L.R. Catholic University Law Review

Catholic U. L.Rev. Catholic University Law Review

Catholic Univ. L. Rev. Catholic University Law Review

Ca. t. Holt. Cases tempore Holt, 11 Modern Reports (1702-10) (88 ER)

Cath. U. A. L.R. Catholic University of America Law Review

Cath. U. L.R. Catholic University Law Review

Cath. U. L. Rev.
- Catholic University of America Law Review
- Catholic University Law Review

Ca. t. K. Cases tempore King, Chancery (1724-33)

Ca. t. King Cases tempore King, Chancery. (1724-33)

Ca. t. Lee Cases tempore Lee. (1752-58)

Ca. t. Mac. Cases in Law and Equity, 10 Modern Reports (1710-24) (88 ER)

Ca. t. N. Eden's Chancery Reports tempore Northington (1757-66) (28 ER)

Ca. t. Nap. Drury's Chancery Reports tempore Napier (1858-59) (Ir.)

Ca. t. North. Eden's Chancery Reports tempore Northington (1757-66) (28 ER)

Ca. t. Plunk. Cases in Chancery tempore Plunkett (1834-39) (Ir.)

Ca. t. Q.A. Cases tempore Holt, 11 Modern Reports (1702-10) (88 ER)

Ca. t. Sugd. Drury's Chancery Reports tempore Sugden (1841-44) (Ir.)

Ca. t. Talb. Cases tempore Talbot, Chancery (1734-38)

C. Atty. The Complete Attorney

Ca. t. Wm.3 Cases tempore William 3, 12 Modern Reports (1690-

1732) (88 ER)

CATx. Civil Appeals Texas

Ca. U. California Unreported Cases

C.A.V. Curia advisari vult (court will be advised)

Cav. Deb. Cavendish's Debates, House of Commons

Cav. Deb. Can. Cavender's Debates on Canada

Cav. Mon. Sec. Cavanagh's Law of Money Securities

Ca. W. I. L.J. California Western International Law Journal

Ca. W. L.R. California Western Law Review

Cawl. Cawley's Laws concerning Jesuits, etc. 1680

Cay Abr. Cay's Abridgment of the English Statutes

CB Chief Baron, Court of Exchequer, England and Wales; also Court of Common Bench (Common Pleas)

C.B.
- Chief Baron
- Common Bench
- Common Bench (Manning, Granger & Scott) (Eng.)
- Cumulative Bulletin, Internal Revenue Bureau (U.S.)
- Customs Bulletin
- English Common Bench Reports (1840-56)

CBA
- Collective Bargaining Agreement
- Connecticut Bar Association

CBA Rec. CBA Record

C.B.C. Collier's Bankruptcy Cases

C.B. Dig. U.S. Customs Bureau, Digest of Customs and Related Laws

C.B. (Eng.) English Common Bench Reports, Manning, Granger, & Scott (135-139 ER)

C. B.J. Connecticut Bar Journal

Cb.L.R. Columbia Law Review

C.B. (N.S.) English Common Bench Reports, Manning, Granger, & Scott, New Series (140-144 ER)

C.B.N.S. (Eng.) English Common Bench Reports, Manning, Granger, & Scott, New Series (140-144 ER)

CBO Congressional Budget Office

C.B.R. Canadian Bankruptcy Reports (Anno.)

C.B.R. (N.S.) Canadian Bankruptcy Reports (Annotated) (New Series)

C.C.
- California Compensation Cases
- Cases in Chancery (Eng.)
- Causes Celebres
- Cepi Corpus
- Chamber of Commerce
- Chancery Cases
- Circuit Court
- City Court
- Civil Code
- Civil Court
- Code Civil Francais
- Code Napoleon
- Coleman's New York Cases
- County Council
- County Court
- Crown Cases

- Current Cases (Ghana) (1965-71)
- Federal Carriers Reporter, Federal Carriers Cases (CCH)
- Ohio Circuit Court Reports

cc Connected case: different case from case cited but arising out of same subject matter or intimately connected therewith (used in Shepard's Citations)

C.C.A.
- Circuit Cours of Appeals, prior to Sept. 1, 1948 (U.S.)
- County Court Appeals
- Court of Criminal Appeal (Eng.)

CCALI Center for Computer Assisted Legal Instruction

C.C. & B.B. Cepi Corpus and Bail Bond

C.C. & C. Cepi Corpus and Committitur

C.C.A. (U.S.) Circuit Court of Appeals (United States)

C.C.C.
- Canadian Criminal Cases
- Central Criminal Court (Old Bailey)
- Choyce Cases in Chancery (1557-1606)
- Civilian Conservation Corps (U.S.)
- Commodity Credit Corporation (U.S.)
- Cox's English Criminal Cases (1844-1941)

C.C.C.Bull. Bulletin, Committee on Criminal Courts' Law & Procedure, Assn. of the Bar, City of New York

C.C.C. Cas. Central Criminal Court Session Papers (1834-1913)

C.C. Chr. Chancery Cases Chronicle (Ontario)

C.C. Chron.
- Chancery Cases Chronicle (Ontario)
- County Courts Chronicle (1848-59) (Eng.)

CC Com. Proc. Code of Civil and Commercial Procedure

C.C.C. Sess. Pap. Central Criminal Court Session Paper (1834-1913) (Eng.)

C.C. Ct. Cas. Central Criminal Court Cases (1834-1913) (Eng.)

CCE Center for Continuing Education

C.C.E.
- Caines' Cases in Error, New York
- Cases of Contested Elections

CCEB Continuing Legal Education of the Bar, University of California Extension

C.C.F. Contract Cases Federal (CCH)

CCH Commerce Clearing House, Inc.

CCH Atom. En. L. Rep. Atomic Energy Law Reporter (CCH)

CCH BCA Dec. Board of Contract Appeals Decision (Commerce Clearing House)

CCH Comm. Mkt. Rep. Common Market Reporter (CCH)

CCH EEOC Dec. Decisions of the Equal Employment Opportunity Commission (Commerce Clearing House)

CCH Fed. Banking L. Rep, Federal Banking Law Reporter (CCH)

CCH Fed. Sec. L. Rep. Federal Securities Law Reporter (CCH)

CCH Inh. Est. & Gift Tax Rep. Inheritance, Estate, and Gift Tax Reporter (CCH)

CCH Lab. Arb. Awards Labor Arbitration Awards (CCH)

CCH Lab.Cas. Labor Cases (CCH)

CCH Lab. L. Rep. Labor Law Reporter (CCH)

CCH L.L.R. Labor Law Reporter (CCH)

CCH NLRB National Labor Relations Board Decisions (Commerce Clearing House)

CCH Stand. Fed. Tax Rep. Standard Federal Tax Reporter (CCH)

CCH State Tax Cas.Rep. State Tax Cases Reporter (CCH)

CCH State Tax Rev. State Tax Review (CCH)

CCH Tax Ct. Mem. Tax Court Memorandum Decisions (CCH)

CCH Tax Ct. Rep. Tax Court Reporter (CCH)

C.C.J. County Court Judge

C.Cl. Court of Claims Reports (U.S.)

CCLE Continuing Legal Education in Colorado, Inc.

C.C.L.J. Centre County Legal Journal (Pa.)

CCLM(3) Acret, California Construction Law Manual, Third Edition

CCLM(3s) Acret, California Construction Law Manual, Third Edition, Supplement

CCLM(4) Acret, California Construction Law Manual, Fourth Edition

C.C.L.T. Canadian Cases on the Law of Torts. 1976-

CCns Ohio Circuit Court Reports, New Series

C.C.N.S. Ohio Circuit Court Reports, New Series

C.C. (N.S.) Ohio Circuit Court Reports, New Series

CCom.C Civil and Commercial Code

CComm.C Civil and Commercial Code

C.C.P.
- Code of Civil Procedure
- Court of Common Pleas

C.C.P.A. Court of Customs & Patent Appeals Reports (U.S.)

CCProc. Code of Civil Procedure

C.C.R.
- Circuit Court Reports
- City Courts Reports
- County Courts Reports
- Court of Crown Cases Reserved (Eng.)
- Crown Cases Reserved (1865-75)

CCRC County Court Rules Committee

C.C. Rep. County Courts Reporter (in Law Journal, London)

C. Crim. Proc. Code of Criminal Procedure

C. Cr. Pr. Code of Criminal Procedure

C.C. Supp. City Court Reports,

Supplement (N. Y.)

C.C.T. Common Customs Tariff

C. Cts. Chr. County Courts Chronicle (1847-1920)

C.C. U.S. Circuit Court of the United States

CD
- Central District
- Commission Decision

C.D.
- Application for certiorari denied
- Century Digest, in American Digest System
- Chancery Division, English Law Reports
- Circuit Decisions
- Commissioner's Decisions, U.S. Patent Office
- Complaint Docket
- Customs Court Decisions
- Customs Decisions (U.S. Treasury Dept.)
- Ohio Circuit Decisions

C/D Certificate of deposit

Cd. Command Papers

CDC
- Center for Disease Control
- Civil Defense Committee
- Civil District Court

C.D. Cal. United States District Court for the Central District of California

C. de D. (Les) Cahiers de Droit

C. D. Fisc. Int'l Cahiers de Droit Fiscal International (International Fiscal Association)

C.D. (N.S.) Ohio Circuit Court Decisions New Series

CDO Commissioner Delegation Order

CE Council of Europe

c.e. caveat emptor (let the buyer beware) (Lat.)

CEA
- Commodity Exchange Authority
- Council of Economic Advisers

CEAO West African Economic Community

CEB California Continuing Education of the Bar

Ce.C. Cepi Corpus

CEC
- European Community Cases
- European Community Cases (CCH)

C.E.D. Canadian Encyclopedic Digest

C.E.Gr. C.E. Greene, New Jersey Equity Reports, (vols. 16-27)

C.E. Greene C.E. Greene, New Jersey Equity Reports (vols. 16-27)

C.E.L.A. Newsletter Canadian Evironmental Law Association Newsletter

C.E.L.R. Canadian Environmental Law Reports

Cel.Tr. Burke's Celebrated Trials

Cem. Cemeteries

CEMA Council for Economic Mutual Assistance

Census Bureau of the Census

Cent.
- Central
- Central Reporter (Pa.)

Cent. Afr. Rep. Central African Republic

Cent. Crim. C. Cas. Central Criminal Court Cases, Sessions Papers (Eng.)

Cent. Crim. C.R. Central Criminal Court Reports (Eng.)

Cent. Dict. Century Dictionary

Cent. Dict. and Cyc. Century Dictionary and Cyclopedia

Cent. Dict. & Ency. Century Dictionary and Encyclopedia

Cent. Dig. Century Edition of the American Digest System (West)

Cent. Law J. Central Law Journal (St. Louis, Mo.)

Cent. L.J. Central Law Journal (St. Louis, Mo.)

Cent. L.Mo. Central Law Monthly

CENTO
- Central Treaty Organization
- Colombo Plan
- Council of Europe

Cent. Prov. L.R. Central Provinces Law Reports (India)

Central L.J. The Central Law Journal (St. Louis)

Centr. Cr. Ct. R. Central Criminal Court, Sessions Papers, London

Cent. Rep. Central Reporter

Centr. L.J. Central Law Journal

Cent. R.(Pa.) Central Reporter (Pa.)

C. Environ. L. N. Canadian Environmental Law News

CEO Chief Executive Officer

CEP Concentrated Employment Program

C.E.P. Community Enterprise Programme

CEQ Council on Environmental Quality

CER Anderson, Chapter 11 Reorganizations

cert.
- certificate
- certified from
- certified to
- certify
- certiorari

cert. den. Certiorari denied

Cert. denied Certiorari denied

cert. dis. Certiorari dismissed

cert. dismissed Certiorari dismissed

Cert. Gr. Certiorari granted

Cert. granted Petition to U.S. Supreme Court for writ of certiorari granted

C.E.S. Court of Exchequer (Sc.)

CET Common External Tariff

CETA Comprehensive Employment and Training Act

CEW Aron, Duffy & Rosner, Cross Examination of Witnesses

Ceyl. Cr. App. R. Ceylon Criminal Appeal Reports

Ceyl. Lab. L.J. Ceylon Labour Law Journal

Ceyl. Leg. Misc. Ceylon Legal Miscellany

Ceyl. L.J. Ceylon Law Journal

Ceyl. L.R. Ceylon Law Recorder

Ceyl. L. Rec. Ceylon Law Recorder

Ceyl. L. Rev. Ceylon Law Review

Ceyl. L.W. Ceylon Law Weekly

Ceylon Law Rec.   Ceylon Law Recorder

Ceylon L.R.   Ceylon Law Review and Reports

Ceylon L. Rev.   Ceylon Law Review

Ceylon L. Soc. J.   The Ceylon Law Society Journal

cf.
- conferre (compare)
- refer to

CF   Sheneman, California Foreclosure: Law and Practice

CFA   Consumer Federation of America

c.f. & i.   cost, freight and insurance

c.f.i.   cost, freight and insurance

C.F.R.   Code of Federal Regulations (U.S.)

CFTC   Commodity Futures Trading Commission

CG   Coast Guard

CGA   Riley, Federal Contracts Grants & Assistance

C. Gaz.   Canada Gazette

CGCM   Court Martial Reports, Coast Guard Cases (N.Y.)

CGCMM   Coast Guard Court Martial Manual (U.S.)

CGCMR   Coast Guard Court of Military Review

CGCMS   Special Court-Martial, Coast Guard (U.S.)

C.G.H.   Cape of Good Hope (S. Afr.)

C.G. L. Bull.   Coast Guard Law Bulletin

C.G.O.   Comptroller General's Opinion (U.S. Treasury Department)

C.G.P.M.   General Conference on Weights and Measures

CGPR   Coast Guard Procurement Regulations

CGR   Coast Guard Regulations (U.S.)

C.G.S.A.   Connecticut General Statutes Annotated

CGSMCM   Coast Guard Supplement to Manual for Courts-Martial (U.S.)

C.G.T.   Capital Gains Tax

Ch.
- Chalmers' Colonial Opinions
- Chancellor's Court (Eng.)
- Chancery Court or Division
- Chapter
- China
- Church
- Court of Chancery, New Jersey
- English Law Reports, (1891 onwards) Chancery Appeals
- English Law Reports, Chancery Division

1891 Ch.   Law Reports, 1891, Chancery, Eng.

Cha.   Charles

Cha. Add.   Chapman's Addenda

Cha. App.   Chancery Appeal Cases English Law Reports

Cha. Dig.   Chaney's Michigan Digest

Chaffee & Admin. Law   Chaffe & Nathanson's Administrative Law, Cases & Materials

Cha. L. & T.   Chambers, Landlord and Tenant. 1823

Challis   Challis on Real Property

(1885-1911)

Chalmers Chalmers on Bills of Exchange (1878-1952)

Chal. Op. Chalmers' Opinions, Constitutional Law (1669-1809) (Eng.)

Cham. Chambers' Upper Canada Reports

Cham. & P.R.R. Chambers & Parsons' Railroad Laws

Chamb. Chambers' Upper Canada Reports

Chamb. Dig. P.H.C. Chambers' Digest of Public Health Cases

Chamber. Chamber Reports, Upper Canada

Chambers' Cyclopedia. Ephraim Chambers English Cyclopedia

Chamb. R. Upper Canada Chancery Chambers Reports (1857-72) (Ont.)

Chamb. Rep.
- Chancery Chambers' Reports, Ontario
- Upper Canada Chambers Reports (1846-52) (Ont.)

Cham. Chy. Jur. Chambers' Chancery Jurisdiction as to Infants

Cham. Com. Chambers, Commons and Open Spaces. 1877

Cham. Com. Law. Chamberlin's American Commercial Law

Cham. Est. Chambers on Estates and Tenures

Cham. L & T. Chambers on Landlord and Tenant

Cham. Leas. Chambers, Leases. 1819

Champ.
- Champerty and Maintenance
- Champion's Cases, Wine & Beer-Houses Act (Eng.)

Cham. Pr. Chambers Practice

CHAMPUS Civilian Health and Medical Program of Uniformed Services

Cham. Rat. Chambers, Rates and Rating. 2ed. 1889

Cham. Rep. Chambers Reports, Upper Canada (1849-82)

Chan.
- Chancellor
- Chancery
- Chaney's Reports (vols. 37-58 Michigan)

Chanc.
- Chancellor
- Chancery

Chan. Cas. Cases in Chancery (1660-97)

Chance Pow. Chance on Powers

Chanc. Ex. Chancellor of the Exchequer

Chan. Chamb. Chancery Chambers Reports, Upper Canada (1857-72)

Chanc. Pow. Chance on Powers. 1831 supplement 1841

Chan. Ct. Chancery Court

Chand.
- Chandler's Reports (vols. 20, 38-44 New Hampshire)
- Chandler's Reports (Wisconsin) (1849-52)

C.H. & A. Carro, Hamerton & Allen's New Session Cases (1844-51) (Eng.)

Ch. & Cl. Cas. Cripp's Church and Clergy Cases

Chand. Crim. Tr. Chandler's American Criminal Trials

Chand. Cr. T. Chandler's American Criminal Trials

Chand. Cr. Tr. Chandler's American Criminal Trials

Chandl.
- Chandler's Reports (vols. 20, 38-44 New Hampshire)
- Chandler's Reports (Wisconsin) (1849-52)

Chandler Chandler's Wisconsin Reports (Wis.)

Chandler Wis. Chandler's Wisconsin Reports (Wis.)

Chand. (NH) Chandler's Reports (vols. 20, 38-44 New Hampshire)

Ch. & P. Chambers and Pretty, Cases on Finance Act (1909-10) (Eng.)

Chand. R. Chandler's Wisconsin Reports (Wis.)

Chand. (Wis.) Chandler's Reports (Wisconsin 1849-52)

Chaney Chaney's Reports (vols. 37-58 Michigan)

Chaney (Mich.) Chaney's Reports (vols. 37-58 Michigan)

Chan. Rep. C. Reports in Chancery (21 ER) (1615-1710)

Chan. Rev. Virginia Acts, published by the Chancery Judges of Va., 1785

Chan. Sentinel Chancery Sentinel, N.Y.

Chan Toon. Leading Cases on Buddhist Law

Chap.
- Chaplain
- Chapter

Chap. & Sh. Chappell & Shoard, Copyright. 1863

Ch.App.Cas. Chancery Appeal Cases, English Law Reports
- Court of Appeal in Chancery (Eng.)
- Law Reports, Chancery Appeals (1885-75) (Eng.)

Cha. Pr. Chapman, Practice of the Court of King's Bench. 2ed. 1831

Char. Charities

Char.Cham.Cas. Charley's Chamber Cases (1875-76) (Eng.)

Charl. Cha. Cas. Charley's Chamber Cases (1875-76) (Eng.)

Charl. Chas.Ca. Charley's Chamber Cases (1875-76) (Eng.)

Charlet. (Ga.) R.M. Charlton's Georgia Reports

Charley Ch. Cas. Charley's Chamber Cases (1875-76) (Eng.)

Charley Pr. Cas. Charley's Practice Cases (1875-81) (Eng.)

Charl. Pl. Charley's Pleading under the Judicature Acts

Charl. Pr. Cas. Charley's Practice Cases (1875-81) (Eng.)

Charl. R. R.M. Charlton Reports (Ga.)

Charl. R.M. R.M. Charlton's Georgia Reports

Charl. R.P. Stat. Charley's Real Property Statutes

Charlt.
- R.M. Charlton's Georgia Reports
- T.U.P. Charlton's Georgia Re-

ports

Charlton's R. R.M. Charlton Reports (Ga.)

Charlton's (Rob't. M.) Rep. R.M. Charlton Reports (Ga.)

Charlt. R.M. R.M. Charlton's Georgia Reports

Charlt. T.U.P. Charlton's Georgia Reports

Charl. T.U.P. T.U.P. Charlton's Georgia Reports

Char. Merc. Charta Mercatoria

Char. Pr. Cas. Charley's Practice Cases (1875-81) (Eng.)

Chart. Rotulus Chartarum (The Charter Roll)

Chart. Antiq. Chartae Antiquae

Chart. (or Rot. Chart) Rotulus Chartarum (The Charter Roll)

Chas. Charles

Chase. Chase's United States Circuit Court Decisions

Chase Dec. Chase, U.S. Circuit Court Decisions

Chase's Bl. Chase's Edition of Blackstone

Chase's St. Chase's Statutes at Large, Ohio

Chase, Steph. Dig. Ev. Chase on Stephens' Digest of Evidence

Chase Tr. Chase's Trial (Impeachment) by the United States Senate

Ch. B. Ex. Chief Baron of the Exchequer

Ch. Bills. Chitty on Bills

Ch. Black.
- Chitty's Blackstone

- Chase's Blackstone

Ch. Burn's J. Chitty's Burn's Justice

C.H.C. Clerk to the House of Commons

Ch. Ca. Cases in Chancery (1660-97) (22 ER)

Ch. Ca. Ch. Choyce Cases in Chancery (1557-1606) (Eng.)

Ch. Cal. Calendar of Proceedings in Chancery (Eng.)

Ch. Cas. Cases in Chancery (1660-97) (Eng.)

Ch. Cas. Ch. Choyce Cases in Chancery (1557-1606) (21 ER)

Ch. Cas. (Eng.) Cases in Chancery (1660-97) (Eng.)

Ch. Cas. in Ch. Choyce Cases in Chancery (1557-1606) (Eng.)

Ch. Ch. Upper Canada Chancery Chambers Reports

Ch. Cham. Upper Canada Chancery Chambers Reports

Ch. Chamb. Chancery Chambers (Upper Canada)

Ch. Chamb. (Can.) Chancery Chambers (Upper Canada)

Ch. Col. Op. Chalmers' Colonial Opinions (Eng.)

Ch. C.P. Chief Justice, Court of Common Pleas

Ch. Cr. L. Chitty's Criminal Law

Ch. ct. Chancery Court

Ch.D. English Law Reports, Chancery Division

Ch.D. 2d English Law Reports, Chancery Division, Second Series

Ch. Dig. Chaney's Digest, Michigan Reports

Ch. Div. English Law Reports, Chancery Division

Ch. Div. (Eng.) English Law Reports, Chancery Division

Ch. Div'l.Ct. Chancery Divisional Court (Eng.)

Cheev. Med. Jur. Cheever's Medical Jurisprudence for India

Chem. Chemical

Chem. Reg. Rep. (BNA) Chemical Regulation Reporter

Ch. (Eng.)
- Chalmers' Colonial Opinions
- English Law Reports, Chancery Appeals
- English Law Reports, Chancery Division

Cher. Ca. Cherokee Case

Ches. Ca. Report of the Chesapeake Case, New Brunswick

Ches. Co. Chester County Reports (Pa.)

Ches. Co Rep. Chester County Reports (Pa.)

Cheshire Smith's New Hampshire Reports (N. H.)

Chest. Chester County (Pa.)

Chest. Ca. Case of the City of Chester, on Quo Warranto

Chest. Co. Chester County Reports (Pa.)

Chest. Co. (Pa.) Chester County Reports (Pennsylvania)

Chest. Co. Rep. Chester County Reports (Pa.)

Chester Chester County Reports

(Pa.)

Chester Co. (Pa.) Chester County Reports (Pa.)

Chester Co. Rep. Chester County Reports (Pa.)

Chetty Sudder Dewanny Adawlut Cases, Madras (India)

Chev. Cheves' South Carolina Law Reports (1839-1940)

Chev. Ch. Cheves' South Carolina Equity Reports (1839-1940)

Chev. Eq. Cheves' South Carolina Equity Reports (1839-1940)

Cheves. Cheves' South Carolina Law Reports (1839-1940)

Cheves Eq. (SC) Cheves' South Carolina Equity Reports

Cheves L. (SC) Cheves' South Carolina Equity Reports (1839-1940)

Chi. Chicago

Chi. B.A. Rec. Chicago Bar Association Record

Chi. Black. Chitty's Blackstone

Chi. B. Rec. Chicago Bar Record

Chi. B. Record Chicago Bar Record

Chicago Bar Rec. Chicago Bar Record

Chicago Bd. Options Ex. Guide (CCH) Chicago Board Options Exchange Guide

Chicago B. Rec. Chicago Bar Record

Chicago-Kent L. Rev. Chicago Kent Law Review

Chicago L.B. Chicago Law Bulletin, Ill.

Chicago Leg. News (Ill.) Chicago Legal News

Chicago L.J. Chicago Law Journal

Chicago L. Rec. Chicago Law Record

Chicago L. Record (Ill.) Chicago Law Record

Chicago L.T. Chicago Law Times

Chicano-Latino L. Rev. Chicano-Latino Law Review

Chicano L. Rev. Chicano Law Review

Chic. L.B. Chicago Law Bulletin

Chic. Leg. N. Chicago Legal News, Illinois

Chic. L.J. Chicago Law Journal

Chic.L.R.
- Chicago Law Record

Chic. L.T. Chicago Law Times

Chi.-Kent Chicago-Kent

Chi-Kent L. Rev. Chicago-Kent Law Review

Chi-Kent Rev. Chicago-Kent Law Review

Chi. L.B. Chicago Law Bulletin

Child. Ct. Children's Court

Child. Legal Rights J. Children's Legal Rights Journal

Child. Legal Rts. J. Children's Legal Rights Journal

Chi. Leg. N. Chicago Legal News (Ill.)

Chi. L.J. Chicago Law Journal

Chi. L.R. Chicago Law Record

Chil. Rts. Rep. Children's Rights Rep.

Chi. L.T. Chicago Law Times

China Law Rev. China Law Review, Shanghai, China

China L. Rep. China Law Reporter

China L. Rev. China Law Review

China (PR) People's Republic of China

China (Rep.) Republic of China

Chinese L. & Govt. Chinese Law and Government

Chinese L. J. Chinese Law Journal

Chinese Soc'y. Int'l. L. Annals The Annals of the Chinese Society of International Law. Taipei, Taiwan

Chin. L. and Gov. Chinese Law and Government

Chin. Law & Gov. Chinese Law and Government

Chip.
- Chipman's Reports, New Brunswick (1825-35)
- Chipman's Reports (Vermont 1789-1824)

Chip. Cont. Chipman on the Law of Contracts

Chip. D. D. Chipman, Vermont Reports, 2 vols.

Chip. Gov. Chipman's Principles of Government

Chip. Ms. Chipman's Manuscript Reports, New Brunswick

Chip. N. N. Chipman's Vermont Reports

Chip (Vt.) Chipman's Reports (Vermont 1789-1824)

Chip. W. Chipman's New Brunswick Reports

Chir. Wisconsin Board of Examiners in Chiropractic

Ch. Is. Rolls. Rolls of the Assizes in Channel Islands

Chit.
- Chitty's English Bail Court Reports
- Chitty's English King's Bench Practice Reports (1819-20)

Chit. & H. Bills. Chitty & Hulme on Bills of Exchange

Chit. & M. Dig. Chitty's Mew's Supplement to Fisher's English Digest

Chit. & T. Car. Chitty & Temple on Carriers

Chit. Ap. Chitty's Law of Apprentices

Chit. Archb. Pr. Chitty's Edition of Archbold's Practice

Chit. Arch. Pr. Chitty's Edition of Archbold's Practice

Chit. B.C. Chitty's English Bail Court Reports (1770-1822) (Eng.)

Chit. Bills Chitty on Bills

Chit. Bills (or B. & N.) Chitty on Bills

Chit. Bl. Chitty's edition of Blackstone's Commentaries

Chit. Bl. Comm. Chitty's Edition of Blackstone's Commentaries

Chit. Burn's J. Chitty's edition of Burn's Justice

Chit. Car. Chitty's Treatise on Carriers

Chit. Com. Law. Chitty on Commercial Law

Chit. Con. Chitty on Contracts

Chit. Const. Chitty on Constables

Chit. Cont. Chitty on Contracts

Chit. Crim. Law Chitty's Criminal Law

Chit. Cr. L. Chitty's Criminal Law

Chit. Cr. Law Chitty's Criminal Law

Chit. Des. Chitty on the Law of Descents

Chit. Eq. Dig. Chitty's Equity Digest (or Index)

Chit. Eq. Ind. Chitty's Equity Index

Chit. F. Chitty's King's Bench Forms (Eng.)

Chit. Gen. Pr. Chitty's General Practice

Chit. G.L. Chitty on the Game Laws

Chit. Jun. B. Chitty (Junior) on Bills

Chit. Lawy. Chitty's Commercial and General Lawyer

Chit. L.of N. Chitty's Law of Nations

Chit. Med. Jur. Chitty on Medical Jurisprudence

Chit. Nat. Chitty, Law of Nations. 1812

Chit. Pl. Chitty on Pleading

Chit. Pr. Chitty's General Practice

Chit. Prec. Chitty's Precedents in Pleading.

Chit. Prer. Chitty's Prerogatives of the Crown

Chit. R. Chitty's English Bail Court Reports

Chi. Trib. Chicago Tribune

Chit. St. Chitty's Statutes of Practical Utility (1235-1948) (Eng.)

Chit. St. A. Chitty's Stamp Act

Chit. Stat. Chitty's Statutes of Practical Utility (1235-1948) (Eng.)

Chit. Sum. P. Chitty's Summary of the Practice of the Superior Courts

Chitt. Chitty's English Bail Court Reports

Chitt. & Pat. Chitty & Patell's Supreme Court Appeals (India)

Chitt. L.J. Chitty's Law Journal

Chitty. Chitty on Bills

Chitty B.C. Chitty's Bail Court Reports (1770-1822)

Chitty BC (Eng.) Chitty Bail Court Reports

Chitty, Bl. Comm. Chitty's Edition of Blackstone's Commentaries

Chitty, Com. Law. Chitty on Commercial Law

Chitty, Contracts Chitty on Contracts

Chitty Eq. Ind. Chitty's Equity Index

Chitty L.J. Chitty Law Journal

Chitty's L.J. Chitty's Law Journal

Ch. J.
- Chief Judge
- Chief Justice

Ch. K. Charter K, Home Loan Bank Board (U.S.)

Ch. L. University of Chicago Law Review

Ch. L.R. University of Chicago Law Review

chmn. chairman

CHOA Hyatt, Condominiums and Home Owners Associations

CHOB Cannon House Office Building

Cho. Ca. Ch. Choyce's Cases in Chancery (1557-1606) (21 ER)

Cho. Ca. Ch. Choyce Cases in Chancery (1557-1606) (Eng.)

C. Home Clerk Home Court of Session. (1735-44) (Sc.)

Choyce Cas. Ch. Choyce's Cases in Chancery (Eng.)

Choyce Cas. (Eng.) Choyce's Cases in Chancery (Eng.)

Ch. Pl. Chitty on Pleading

Ch. Pr. Chancery Practice

Ch. Pre. Precedents in Chancery (1689-1723) (Eng.)

Ch. Prec. Precedents in Chancery

Ch. Q.B. Chief Justice, Court of Queen's Bench

Ch. R.
- Chitty's King's Bench Reports (Eng.)
- Irish Chancery Reports
- Reports in Chancery (1615-1712) (Eng.)
- Upper Canada Chancery Chambers Reports

Chr. Ch. Christian's Charges to Grand Juries

C.H. Rec. City Hall Recorder (Rogers), New York City

C.H. Rep. City Hall Reporter (Lomas), New York City

Ch. Rep.
- Irish Chancery Reports
- Reports in Chancery

Ch. Rep. Ir.   Irish Chancery Reports

Ch. Repts.
- Reports in Chancery
- Irish Chancery Reports

Chris. B.L.   Christian's Bankrupt Law

Ch. R.M.   Charlton's Reports (Georgia Reports, 1811-37)

Ch. Rob.   Robinson's Admiralty Reports (1799-1808) (Eng.)

chron.
- chronicle
- chronological

Chron. Div. Cts.   Chronicles of the Divorce Courts

Chron. Jur.   Chronica Juridicalia

Chr. Pr. W.   Christie's Precedents of Wills

Chr. Rep.   Chamber Reports (Upper Canada)

Chr. Rob.   Christopher Robinson's English Admiralty Reports

chs.   chapters

Ch. Sent.   Chancery Sentinel, Saratoga, New York

Ch. Sent. (NY)   Chancery Sentinel, Saratoga, New York

Chtd   Chartered

Ch. T.U.P.   T.U.P. Charlton's Georgia Reports

Church. & Br. Sh.   Churchill & Bruce, Office and Duties of Sheriff. 2ed. 1882

Chute, Eq.   Chute's Equity under the Judicature Act

Chy. App. Rep.   Wright, Tennessee Chancery Appeals Reports

Chy. Ch.   Upper Canada Chancery Chambers Reports

Chy. Chrs.   Upper Canada Chancery Chambers Reports

C.I.
- Channel Islands
- Committee of Inspection
- Constitutional Instrument (Ghana)
- Cumulative Index

CIA
- Central Intelligence Agency (U.S.)
- Coopers' International Union of North America

C.I.B.   Commercial and Industrial Bulletin (Ghana)

C.I.C.   Current Indian Cases, Old Series (India)

CICT   Commission on International Commodity Trade

C.I.D.   Criminal Investigation Department

C.I.E.C.   Centre international d'etudes criminologiques (International Centre of Criminological Studies)

CIEP   Council on International Economic Policy

CIF   Cushman, Simon & Stokes, Construction Industry Formbook

C.I.F.   Cost, insurance, and freight

c.i.f. & c.   cost, insurance, freight and commission

c.i.f.c.i.   cost, insurance, freight, commission and interest

c.i.f.e.   cost, insurance, freight and exchange

c.i.f.i.   cost, insurance, freight and

interest

C.I.I. Chartered Insurance Institute

C.I.L.C. Commonwealth International Law Cases

C.I. L.J. S.A. Comparative and International Law Journal of Southern Africa

Ci. L.R. Cincinnati Law Review

CILS Center for International Legal Studies

CIM International Convention for the Carriage of Goods by Rail

Cin. Cincinnati

Cin. B.A. J. Cincinnati Bar Association Journal

Cin. B. Ass'n J. Cincinnati Bar Association Journal

Cinc. (Ohio) Cincinnati Superior Court Reports (Ohio)

Cinc. Cincinnati

Cincinnati Law Bull. Weekly Law Bulletin (Ohio)

Cinc. L. Bul.
- Cincinnati Law Bulletin
- Weekly Law Bulletin (Ohio)

Cinc. Sup. Ct. Rep. Cincinnati Superior Court Reporter

Cinc. Super. Cincinnati Superior Court Reporter (Oh.)

Cin. Law Bul. Cincinnati Law Bulletin

Cin. Law Bull.
- Weekly Cincinnati Law Bulletin (Ohio)
- Weekly Law Bulletin (Ohio)

Cin. Law Rev. University of Cincinnati Law Review

Cin. L. Bull. Cincinnati Law Bulletin

Cin. L. Rev. University of Cincinnati Law Review

Cin. Mun. Dec. Cincinnati Municipal Decisions

Cin. R. Cincinnati Superior Court Reports (Ohio)

Cin. Rep. Cincinnati Superior Court Reports (Ohio)

Cin. S.C. R. Cincinnati Superior Court Reports (Ohio)

Cin. S.C. Rep. Cincinnati Superior Court Reports (Ohio)

Cin. Sup. Ct. Cincinnati Superior Ct. Rep.

Cin. Sup. Ct. R. Cincinnati Superior Court Reporter (Ohio)

Cin. Sup. Ct. Rep. Cincinnati Superior Court Reports (Ohio)

Cin. Super. Ct. Cincinnati Superior Court Reporter (Ohio)

Cin. Super. Ct. Rep'r. Cincinnati Superior Court Reports (Ohio)

Cin. Super. (Ohio) Cincinnati Superior Court Reports (Ohio)

CIO
- Committee for Industrial Organization
- Congress of Industrial Organizations

C.I.P.A. Chartered Institute of Patent Agents

CIPEC Intergovernmental Council of Copper Exporting Countries

C.I.R. Commissioner of Internal Revenue

Cir.
- Circuit

- Circuit Court
- Circuit Court of Appeals (federal)
- Connecticut Circuit Court Reports

Circ.
- Circuit
- Treasury Department Circular

Circ. Dec. Ohio Circuit Decisions (Ohio)

Cir. Ct. Circuit Court (state)

Cir. Ct. App. Circuit Court of Appeal[s] (state)

Cir. Ct. Dec. Circuit Court Decisions

Cir.Ct.Dec. (Ohio) Circuit Court Decisions (Ohio)

Cir. Ct. Ohio Ohio Circuit Court Reports (Ohio)

Cir. Ct. R. Circuit Court Reports (Ohio)

Cir. Ct. Rule Circuit Court Rule

Cir. Ord. N.W.P. Circular Orders, Northwestern Provinces (India)

C.I.T. Court of International Trade Reports

Cit. Citator and Indian Law Journal (1908-14) (India)

cit.
- citation
- cited in
- citing
- The Citator

CITEJA International Technical Committee of Aerial Legal Experts

C.I.T.R. Court of International Trade Rules

City Civ. Ct. Act. New York City

Civil Court Act

City Crim. Ct. Act. New York City Criminal Court Act

City Ct. City Court

City Ct. R. City Court Reports (N.Y.)

City Ct. Rep. City Court Reports (N.Y.)

City Ct. Rep. Supp. City Court Reports, Supplement (N.Y.)

City Ct. R. Supp. City Court Reports, Supplement, N.Y.

City Ct. Supp. (NY) City Court Reports, Supplement (N.Y.)

City Hall Rec. (NY) City Hall Recorder (N.Y.)

City Hall Rep. City Hall Reporter, Lomans (N.Y.)

City Hall Rep. (NY) City Hall Reporter, Lomas (N.Y.)

City H. Rec. New York, City Hall Recorder

City H. Rep. City Hall Reporter (Lomas, N.Y.)

City Rec. New York, City Record

City Rec. (NY) New York, City Record

Civ.
- Civil
- Civil Appeals
- civilian
- Texas Civil Appeals Reports

Civ. & Cr. L.S. Civil & Criminal Law Series (India)

Civ. & Military L.J. Civil and Military Law Journal, New Delhi, India

Civ. and Mil. L.J. Civil and Military Law Journal, New Delhi, India

Civ. App.   Court of Civil Appeals

Civ. Code   Civil Code

Civ. Code Prac.   Civil Code of Practice

Civ. Code Practice   Civil Code of Practice

Civ. Ct.   Civil Court

Civ. Ct. Rec.   Civil Court of Record

Civ. D. Ct.   Civil District Court

Civil Lib.Dock.   Civil Liberties Docket

Civil Liberties Rev.   The Civil Liberties Review

Civil Pro. R.   Civil Procedure Reports (N.Y.)

Civ. Just. Q.   Civil Justice Quarterly

Civ. Lib.   Civil Liberty

Civ. Lib. Dock.   Civil Liberties Docket

Civ. Lib. Rev.   Civil Liberties Review

Civ. Lib. Rptr.   Civil Liberties Reporter

Civ. Litigation Rep.   Civil Litigation Reporter (CEB)

Civ. Pr.   Civil Procedure Reports, New York

Civ. Prac.   Civil Practice Law and Rules

Civ. Prac. Act   Civil Practice Act

Civ. Prac. (NY)   New York Civil Practice

Civ. Pro.   Civil Procedure Reports (New York)

Civ. Proc.   Civil Procedure

Civ. Proc. (N.S.)   Civil Procedure Reports, New Series (N.Y.)

Civ. Proc. (NY)   New York Civil Procedure

Civ. Proc. R.   Civil Procedure Reports (New York)

Civ. Proc. Rep.   Civil Procedure Reports (New York)

Civ. Proc. Rep. N.S.   Civil Procedure Reports, New Series (New York) (1908-13)

Civ. Proc.R. (N.S.)   Civil Procedure Reports, New Series (New York) (1908-13)

Civ. Pro. R.   Civil Procedure Reports (New York)

Civ. Pro. Reports   Civil Procedure Reports (N.Y.)

Civ. Pro. R. (N.S.)   Civil Procedure Reports, New Series (New York) (1908-13)

Civ. Pr. Rep.   Civil Procedure Reports, New York

Civ. R.   Civil Rights

Civ. Rights   Civil Rights

Civ.Rts.Dig.   Civil Rights Digest

Civ. S.   Civil Service

Civ. Serv.   Civil Service

C.J.
- Chief Justice
- Circuit Judge
- Corpus Juris
- Journal of the House of Commons
- Lord Chief Justice (Eng.)

C.J. Ann.   Corpus Juris Annotations

C.J.B.   Chief Judge in Bankruptcy

C.J.C.
- Corpus Juris Civilis
- Couper's Judiciary Cases (1868-85) (Sc.)

C.J. Can. Corpus Juris Canonici

C.J. Civ. Corpus Juris Civilis

C.J.C.P. Chief Justice of the Common Pleas

C.J.D. Campaign for Justice in Divorce

C.J.E.C. Court of Justice of the European Communities

C.J.F. Chief Justice of the Federation (Nigeria)

C.J.K.B. Chief Justice of the King's Bench

CJL Columbia Journal of Law and Social Problems

C.J.N. Chief Justice of Nigeria

C.J.Q.B. Chief Justice of the Queen's Bench

C.J.S. Corpus Juris Secundum

C.J.U.B. Chief Justice of the Common (Upper) Bench

C. Jud. Proc. Code of Judicial Procedure

C.K. Chicago-Kent Law Review (Ill.)

C.K. L.R. Chicago-Kent Law Review

C.L.
- Civil Law
- Commission Leaflets, American Telephone and Telegraph Cases
- Common Law
- Common Law Reports (1853-85)
- Compiled Laws
- Current Law Yearbooks (1947)
- English Common Law Reports, American Reprint
- Irish Common Law Reports, (17 vols.)

Cl.
- Clark
- Clarke
- clause
- Rotulus Clausarum (Close Roll) (Eng.)

CLA Computer Law Association

C.L.A. University of California at Los Angeles Law Review

C.L.A. Bulletin Commercial Law Association Bulletin

C.L.A.I.T. Constitutions and Laws of the American Indian Tribes (Scholarly Resources)

Clancy, Husb. & W. Clancy's Treatise of the Rights, Duties and Liabilities of Husband and Wife

Clancy Rights Clancy's Treatise of the Rights, Duties and Liabilities of Husband and Wife

Cl. & F. Clark & Finnelly's House of Lords Cases (1831-46) (Eng.)

Cl. & Fin. Clark & Finnelly's House of Lords Cases (1831-46) (Eng.)

Cl. & Fin. (N.S.) Clark & Finnelly's H.L. Cas., Eng., New Series

Cl. & Fin.N.S. House of Lords Cases, by Clark

Cl. & H. Clarke's & Hall's Contested Elections in Congress

Cl. & Sc. Dr. Cas. Clarke & Scully's Drainage Cases (Canada)

Cl. App. Clark's Appeal Cases,

House of Lords (Eng.)

Clark
- Clark's Reports (vol. 58 Alabama)
- English House of Lords Cases, by Clark
- Pennsylvania Law Journal Reports, edited by Clark
- Supreme Court Judgments by Clark (1917-32) (Jamaica)

Clark (Ala). Clark's Reports (vol. 58 Alabama)

Clark & F. Clark and Finnelly's House of Lords Reports (6-8 ER)

Clark & F. (Eng.) Clark and Finnelly's House of Lords Reports (6-8 ER)

Clark & Fin. Clark and Finnelly's House of Lords Cases (Eng.)

Clark & Fin. (N.S.) Clark and Finnelly's House of Lords Reports, New Series (1847-66) (9-11 ER)

Clark & F. (N.S.) Clark and Finnelly's House of Lords Reports (New Series)

Clark & F. (N.S.), Eng. Clark and Finnelly's House of Lords Cases New Series (Eng.)

Clark App. Clark Appeal Cases House of Lords (Eng.)

Clark Col. Law Clark Colonial Law

Clark Dig. Clark's Digest, House of Lords Reports

Clarke
- Clarke, edition of 1-8 Iowa
- Clarke, New York Chancery Reports
- Clarke, Notes of Cases, Bengal
- Clarke's Pennsylvania Reports,

5 vols.
- Clarke, Reports (19-22 Michigan)

Clarke Adm. Pr. Clarke's Admiralty Practice

Clarke & H. Elec. Cas. Clarke & Hall's Contested Elections in Congress (U.S.)

Clarke & S. Dr. Cas. Clarke & Scully's Drainage Cases (Canada)

Clarke B. Clarke on Bills and Notes, Canada

Clarke Bib. Leg. Clarke's Bibliotheca Legum

Clarke Ch. Clarke's New York Chancery Reports

Clarke Ch. (NY) Clarke's New York Chancery Reports

Clarke Const. Clarke's Constable's Manual, Canada

Clarke C.R. Clarke's Chancery Reports (N.Y.)

Clarke Cr. L. Clarke's Criminal Law, Canada

Clarke Extr. Clarke on Extradition

Clarke (Ia.) Clarke, edition of 1-8 Iowa

Clarke Insol. Clarke's Insolvent Acts, Canada

Clarke Insur. Clarke's Insurance Law, Canada

Clarke (Mich.) Clarke, Reports (19-22 Michigan)

Clarke Not. Clarke's Notes of Cases, in his "Rules and Orders," Bengal

Clarke (Pa.) Clarke's Pennsylvania, 5 vols.

Clarke Pr. Clarke's (or Clerke's) Praxis Admiralitatis

Clarke R. & O. Clarke's Notes of Cases, in his "Rules and Orders," Bengal

Clarke Rom. L. Clarke's Early Roman Law

Clarke's Chy. (N.Y.) Clarke's Chancery Reports (N.Y.)

Clark (Jam.) Judgments, Jamaica Supreme Court of Judicature

Clark (Pa.) Clark's Pennsylvania Law Journal Reports

Clark, Receivers Clark on Receivers

Clark's Code. Clark's Annotated Code of Civil Procedure (N.C.)

Clark's Summary Clark's Summary of American Law

Clar. Parl. Chr. Clarendon's Parliamentary Chronicle

C.L.A.S. Criminal Law Audio Series

Cl. Ass. Clerk's Assistant

Class Act. Rep. Class Action Reports

Clay. Clayton's Reports & Pleas of Assizes at York (1631-50) (Eng.)

Clay. Conv. Clayton on Conveyancing

Clay. L. & T. Claydon on Landlord and Tenant

Clay's Dig. Clay's Digest of Laws of Alabama

Clayt. Clayton's English Reports, York Assizes

Clayton Clayton's English Reports, York Assizes

Clayton (Eng.) Clayton's English Reports, York Assizes

C.L.B. Commonwealth Law Bulletin

Cl. Bills Clarke on Bills and Notes

ClC Claims Court Reporter

C.L.C. Current Law Consolidation (Eng.)

Cl. Can. Ins. Clarke's Canada Insolvent Acts

C.L. Ch. Common Law Chamber Reports (Ontario)

Cl. Ch. Clarke's New York Chancery Reports (1839-41)

C.L. Chamb.
- Chamber's Common Law, (Upper Canada)
- Common Law Chamber Reports, Ontario

C.L. Chambers Chambers' Common Law (Upper Can.)

C.L. Chamb. Rep. Common Law Chamber Reports, Ontario

Cl. Col. Clark's Colonial Laws

CLCP McNamara, Constitutional Limitations on Criminal Procedure

Cl Ct Claims Court

Cl. Ct. R. United States Claims Court Rules (Rules of the United States Claims Court)

CLD Acret, Construction Law Digests

CLE Continuing Legal Education

C.L.E. Council of Legal Education

Clearinghouse Rev. Clearinghouse Review

Cleary R.C. Cleary's Registration

Cases (Eng.)

Cleary Reg. Cas. Cleary's Registration Cases (Ir.)

Cleav.Bank. L. Cleaveland's Banking Laws of New York

C. Leg. Rec. California Legal Record

CLE J. & Reg. CLE Journal and Register

Cl. Elec. Clark's Treatise on Elections

CLEM Continuing Legal Education, University of Montana

Clem. Clemens Reports (57-59 Kansas)

Clem. Corp. Sec. Clemens on Corporate Securities

Clerke Am. L. Clerke's American Law and Practice

Clerke & Br. Conv. Clerke & Brett on Conveyancing

Clerke Dig. Clerke's Digest, New York

Clerke Pr. Clerke's (or Clarke's) Praxis Admiralitatis

Clerke Prax. Clerke's Praxis Curiae Admiralitatis

Clerke Rud. Clerke's Rudiments of American Law and Practice

Clerk Home. Clerk Home's Decisions, Scotch Court of Session (1735-44)

Clev. Cleveland

Clev. B.A. J. Cleveland Bar Association Journal

Clev. Bar Ass'n. J. Cleveland Bar Association Journal

Clev. B. Assn. J. The Cleveland

Bar Association Journal

Clev. B.J. Journal of the Cleveland Bar Association

Cleve. Bank. Cleaveland on the Banking System

Cleveland S. L.J. Cleveland State Law Journal

Cleve. Law R. Cleveland Law Reporter (Ohio)

Cleve. Law Rec. Cleveland Law Record (Ohio)

Cleve. Law Reg. Cleveland Law Register (Ohio)

Cleve. Law Rep. Cleveland Law Reporter (Ohio)

Cleve. L.R. (Ohio) Cleveland Law Reporter (Ohio)

Cleve. L. Rec. Cleveland Law Record (Ohio)

Cleve. L. Rec. (Ohio) Cleveland Law Record (Ohio)

Cleve. L. Reg. Cleveland Law Register (Ohio)

Cleve. L. Reg. (Ohio) Cleveland Law Register (Ohio)

Cleve. L. Rep. Cleveland Law Reporter (Ohio)

Cleve. Mar. L. Rev. Cleveland-Marshall Law Review

Cleve. Rep. Cleveland Law Reporter (Reprint) (Ohio)

Clev. Insan. Clevenger's Medical Jurisprudence of Insanity

Clev. Law Rep. Cleveland Law Reporter (Reprint) (Ohio)

Clev. L. Rec. Cleveland Law Record (Ohio)

Clev. L. Reg. Cleveland Law Register (Ohio)

Clev. L. Rep. Cleveland Law Reporter (Ohio)

Clev.-Mar. Cleveland-Marshall

Clev.-Mar. L. Rev. Cleveland Marshall Law Review

Clev. R. Cleveland Law Reporter (Reprint) (Ohio)

Clev. St. L.R. Cleveland State Law Review

Clev. St. L. Rev. Cleveland State Law Review

CLEW Continuing Legal Education for Wisconsin

Cl. Extr. Clarke on Extradition

C.L.F. Current Legal Forms with Tax Analysis

CLH Acret, Construction Litigation Handbook

Cl. Home. Clerk Home, Scotch Session Cases

CLH(s) Acret, Construction Litigation Handbook, Supplement

Clif. Clifford, United States Circuit Court Reports, 1st Circuit

Clif & R. Clifford & Richard's English Locus Standi Reports

Clif. & Rich. Clifford & Richard's Locus Standi Reports (1873-84)

Clif & Rick. Clifford & Richard's English Locus Standi Reports (1873-84)

Clif. & St. Clifford & Stephens' English Locus Standi Reports (1867-72)

Clif. & Steph. Clifford and Stephen's Locus Standi Reports (1867-72)

Clif. El. Clifford's English Southwick Election Cases (1796-97)

Clif. El. Cas. Clifford's English Southwick Election Cases (1796-97)

Cliff.
- Clifford's Southwark Election Cases (1796) (Eng.)
- Clifford, United States Circuit Court Reports, 1st Circuit

Cliff. & Rich. Clifford & Richard's Locus Standi Reports (1873-84)

Cliff. & Rick. Clifford & Richard's Locus Standi Reports (1873-84)

Cliff. & Steph. Clifford and Stephens, Locus Standi Reports (1867-72)

Cliff. (C.C.) Clifford's U.S. Circuit Court Reports (1st Cir.)

Cliff. El. Cas. Clifford's Southwick Election Cases (Eng.)

Clif. Prob. Clifford's Probate Guide

Clif. South. El. Clifford's English Southwick Election Cases (1796-97)

Clif. South. El. Cas. Clifford, Southwick Election Cases

Clift Clift's Entries (1719) (Eng.)

clin. clinical

Clin. Dig. Clinton's Digest, New York

Cl. Ins. Clarke on Law of Insurance, Canada

C.L.J.
- Calcutta Law Journal
- California Law Journal
- Cambridge Law Journal
- Canada Law Journal

- Cape Law Journal
- Central Law Journal
- Ceylon Law Journal (Sri L.)
- Chicago Law Journal
- Colonial Law Journal Reports
- Criminal Law Journal (Aus.)
- Criminal Law Journal (India)

C.L.J. & Lit. Rev. California Law Journal and Literary Review

C. L.J. N.S. Canada Law Journal, New Series

C. L.J. O.S. Canada Law Journal, Old Series

Clk. Clerk

Clk. Ct. Clerks of Court

Clk. Mag.
- The Clerk's Magazine, London
- The Rhode Island Clerk's Magazine
- Clerk's Magazine, London

Clk's. Mag.
- Clerk's Magazine (London)
- Clerk's Magazine (R.I.)
- Clerk's Magazine (Upper Canada)

C.L.L.C. Canadian Labour Law Cases

C.L.L.R. Crown Lands Law Reports (Queensland)

C.L.M. Current Law Monthly

Clms. Claims

C.L.N. Chicago Legal News

Clode M.L. Clode's Martial Law

Clow L.C. on Torts. Clow's Leading Cases on Torts

C.L.P.
- Common law procedure (Eng.)
- Current Legal Problems

C.L.P.A. Common Law Procedure Acts

C.L.P.Act. English Common Law Procedure Act

C.L.Q.
- Cornell Law Quarterly (New York)
- Crown Land Reports, Queensland

C.L.R.
- Calcutta Law Reporter
- Canada Law Reports
- Canadian Law Review and Corporation Legal Journal
- Cape Law Reports (S. Africa)
- Ceylon Law Reports
- Cleveland Law Record
- Columbia Law Review
- Common Law Reports (1853-55) (Eng.)
- Commonwealth Law Reports (Aus.)
- Crown Lands Reports, Queensland
- Current Law Reports (Palestine)
- Cyprus Law Reports (1883)

Cl.R. Clarke's New York Chancery Reports

C.L.R. Aust. Commonwealth Law Reports (Aus.)

C.L.R.C.
- Canada Law Reform Commission
- Criminal Law Revision Committee

C.L.R. (Can.)
- Canada Law Reports, Exchequer Court and Supreme Court: series began 1923 and is properly cited by year as 1923 Ex.C.R. and 1923 S.C.R. etc.

- Common Law Reports (Can.) (1835-55)

C. L. Rec. Cleveland Law Record

C. L. Reg. Cleveland Law Register

C. L. Rep. Cleveland Law Reporter

C. L. Rev. California Law Review

Cl. R. L. Clarke's Early Roman Law

CLS Cornell Law School

Cls.
- Claims
- clauses

Cls. Ct. The former U.S. Court of Claims

C.L.S.R. Computer Law Service Reporter

C.L. Stats. Current Law Statutes Annotated

C.L.T. Canadian Law Times (1881 -1922)

C.L.T. Occ. N. Canadian Law Times Occasional Notes

C. L. U. Chartered Life Underwriter

CLU J.
- Chartered Life Underwriter Journal
- CLU Journal

CLUP Ramos, California Land Use Procedure

Clusk. Pol. T.B. Cluskey's Political Text Book

CLUU The College of Law, University of Utah

C.L.W. Commercial Laws of the World (Oceana)

C.L. Y.B. Current Law Year Book (Eng.)

C.M.
- Cleveland-Marshall Law Review (Ohio)
- Cleveland State Law Review
- Court Martial Report Army Cases (U.S.)

C/M Chattel mortgage

c.m. causa mortis (by reason of death) (Lat.)

C.M.A.
- Court of Military Appeals
- Court of Military Appeals Reports

C.-M.A.C. Courts-Martial Appeal Court

C.M. & H. Cox, Macrae and Hertslet, County Courts (1847-58) (Eng.)

C.M. & R. Compton, Meeson, & Roscoe's English Exchequer Reports (1834-36)

C.M.A.R. Canadian Court Martial Appeal Reports, 1957-

CMC Collective Measures Commission (UN)

Cmd. Command Papers

C.-M.E.T.O. Court-Martial, European Theater of Operations (U.S.)

C.M. J. Canadian Municipal Journal

cml. commercial

C.M. L.R.
- Cleveland-Marshall Law Review
- Common Market Law Reports (Eng.)
- Common Market Law Review

C.M. L. Rev. Common Market Law Review

Cmnd. Command Papers

C.M.O. U.S. Judge-Advocate General (Navy) Compilation of Court-Martial Orders

CMP Reg. Controlled Materials Plan Regulation (National Production)

CMR Convention on the Contract for the International Carriage of Goods by Road (Geneva, 19 May 1956)

C.M.R.
- Common Market Reporter (CCH)
- Court-Martial Reports, judge Advocates General of the Armed Forces and the United States Court of Military Appeals
- Court of Military Review

CMR (AF) Court-Martial Reports of the Judge Advocate General of the U.S. Air Force

C.M.R. (Air Force) Court-Martial Reports of the Judge Advocate General of the Air Force

CMR, Cit. & Ind. Court Martial Reports, Citators & Indexes

CMR JAG AF. Court Martial Reports of the Judge Advocate General of the Air Force

CMR JAG & US Ct. of Mil. App. Court Martial Reports of the Judge Advocate General of the Armed Forces and the U.S. Court of Military Appeals

C.N. Code Napoleon (or Civil Code)

C.N. Conf. Cameron & Norwood's North Carolina Conference Reports

C.N.J.F.D.C. Food and Drug Administration. Notices of Judg-

ment: Cosmetics

CNO Chief of Naval Operations

C.N.P. Cases at Nisi Prius

C.N.P.C. Campbell's Nisi Prius Cases (Eng.)

C.N.R. Canadian National Railways

C.O.
- Colonial Office
- Common Orders
- Criminal Office
- Crown Office

Co.
- Coke's English King's Bench Reports (1572-1616)
- Coke's Institutes
- Colorado
- Colorado Reports
- Company
- County

c/o
- Care of
- carried over

Co. A.
- Cook's Lower Canada Admiralty, Court Cases
- Colorado Court of Appeals Reports Co.

COA Causes of Action

Co. & Al. Cooke & Alcocke's Great Britain Reports (Ir.)

Cobb.
- Cobb's New Digest, Laws of Georgia (1851)
- Cobb's Reports (vol. 121 Alabama)
- Cobb's Reports (vols. 4-20 Georgia)

Cobb, Dig. Cobb's Digest of Statute Laws (Ga.)

Cobbey, Repl. Cobbey's Practical Treatise on the Law of Replevin

Cobbey's Ann. St. Cobbey's Annotated Statutes (Neb.)

Cobb. P. & Pl. Cobbett on Pawns and Pledges

Cobb. Parl. Hist. Cobbett's Parliamentary History

Cobb. Pol. Reg. Cobbett's Political Register

Cobb. Slav. Cobb on Slavery

Cobb.St.Tr. Cobbett's (afterwards Howell's) State Trials

Co. B.L. Coke's Bankrupt Law

COBRA Consolidated Omnibus Budget Reconciliation Act

Cob. St. Tr. Cobbett's (Howell's) State Trials (1163-1820) (Eng.)

COC Certificate of Competency

Coch. Cochran's Nova Scotia Reports (1859)

Coch. Ch. Ct. Chief Court of Cochin, Select Decisions

Cochin Cochin Law Reports

Cochin L.J. Cochin Law Journal

Cochin L.R. Cochin Law Reports (1909-48) (India)

Coch. N.Sc. Cochran's Nova Scotia Reports (1859) (Can.)

Cochr.
- Cochran's Nova Scotia Reports
- Cochran's Reports (3-10 North Dakota)

Cochran. Cochran's Reports (vols. 3-10 North Dakota Reports)

Cochr. Hind. L. Cochrane's Hindu Law

Cock. & R. Cockburn and Rowe's English Election Cases (1833)

Cock. & Rowe Cockburn & Rowe's English Election Cases (1833)

Cockb. & R. Cockburn & Rowe's Election Cases (Eng.) (1833)

Cockb. & Rowe Cockburn & Rowe's Election Cases. 1833

Cocke
- Cocke, Reports (vols. 16-18 Alabama)
- Cocke, Reports (vols. 14, 15 Florida)

Cocke Const. Hist. Cocke's Constitutional History of the United States

Cocke U.S. Pr. Cocke's Common and Civil Law Practice of the U.S.Courts

Cock. Nat. Cockburn on Nationality

Cock. Tich. Ca. Cockburn's Charge in the Tichborne Case

Co. Cop. Coke's Compleat Copyholder 5 editions (1630-73) (Eng.)

Co. C.R. Pennsylvania County Court Reports (Pa.)

Co. Ct. County Court

Co. Ct. Cas. County Court Cases (Eng.)

Co.Ct.Ch. County Court Chronicle (Eng.)

Co. Ct. Chr. County Courts Chronicles (1847-1920) (Eng.)

Co. Ct. I.L.T. Irish Law Times, County Courts

Co. Ct. R. County Courts Reports (1860-1920)

Co. Ct. Rep.
- County Courts Reports (1860-1920) (Eng.)
- Pennsylvania County Court Reports

Co. Ct. Rep. (Pa.) County Court Reports (Pa.)

Co. Cts. Coke's Courts (4th Institute) (Eng.)

C.O.D.
- Cash on delivery
- Collect on delivery

Cod.
- Codex Justinianus
- Gibson's Codex Ecclesiastia, (1715)
- Gibson's Codex Juris Civilis

CODAs Cash or deferred arrangements

Codd. Tr. M. Coddington's Digest of the Law of Trade Marks

Code.
- Code of Justinian (Roman Law)
- Codex Justiniani
- Internal Revenue Code of 1986

Code Am. Code Amendments

Code Civ. Proc. Code of Civil Procedure

Code Civ. Pro. Code of Civil Procedure

Code Crim. Proc. Code of Criminal Procedure

Code Cr. Proc. Code of Criminal Procedure

Code Cr. Pro. Code of Criminal Procedure

Code La. Civil Code of Louisiana

Code M. Code Municipal, Quebec

Code N. Code Napoleon (or Code Civil)

Code Nap. Code Napoleon (or Code Civil)

Code N.Y. Rep. Code Reporter (N.Y.)

Code of Civ. Proc. Code of Civil Procedure

Code P. Code Penal

Code P.C. Code de Procedure Civile

Code Prac. Code of Practice

Code Pro. Code of Procedure

Code Proc. Code of Procedure

Code Pub. Gen. Laws Code of Public General Laws

Code Pub. Loc. Laws Code of Public Local Laws

Code R. Code Reporter (N.Y.)

Code Rep. Code Reporter (N.Y.)

Code Rep. N.S. New York Code Reports, New Series

Code R.N.S. Code Reports, New Series, New York

Code R.N.S. (NY) Code Reports, New Series, New York

Code R. (NY) Code Reports, New York

Code Supp. Supplement to the Code

Code Theod. Code of Theodosius (Roman Law)

Code Theodos. Codex Theodosianus

Cod. Jur. Gibson's Codex Ecclesiastia (1715)

Cod. Jur. Civ.
- Codex Juris Civilis
- Justinian's Code

Cod. St. Codified Statutes

Cod. Theodos. Codex Theodorianus

Coe Ch. Pr. Coe, Practice of the Judges' Chambers. 1876

Co. Ent. Coke's Book of Entries (1614) (Eng.)

Cof. Coffey's California Probate Decisions

C. of C.E. Cases of Contested Elections (U.S.)

C of. Dig. Cofer's Kentucky Digest

C. of E.
- Church of England
- Council of Europe

C. of E. Agr. P.I. General Agreement on Privileges and Immunities of the Council of Europe

Coffey Coffey's Probate Decisions (Cal.)

Coffey Probate Dec. Coffey's Probate Decisions (Cal.)

Coffey Prob.Dec. Coffey's Probate Decisions (Cal.)

Coffey's Prob. Dec.
- Coffey's California Decisions
- Coffey's Probate Decisions (Cal.)

Coff. Prob. Coffey's California Probate Decisions

Cof. Pro. Coffey's Probate Decisions (Cal.)

Cof. Prob. Coffey's Probate Decisions (Cal.)

Cof. Prob. Dec. (Cal.) Coffey's California Probate Decisions

C. of S. Ca. Court of Session Cases (Sc.)

C. of S. Ca. 1st Series Court of Session Cases, First Series. By Shaw, Dunlop, & Bell (Sc.)

C. of S. Ca. 2d Series. Court of Session Cases, Second Series. By Dunlop, Bell & Murray (Sc.)

C. of S. Ca. 3rd Series. Court of Session Cases, Third Series. By Maepherson, Lee & Bell (Sc.)

C. of S. Ca. 4th Series. Court of Session Cases, Fourth Series. By Rettie, Crawford & Melville (Sc.)

C. of S. Ca. 5th Series. Court of Session Cases, Fifth Series (Sc.)

Co.G. Reports and Cases of Practice in Common Pleas tempore Anne, Geo. I., and Geo II., by Sir G. Coke. (Same as Cooke's Practice Reports) (1706-47) (Eng.)

Cogh. Epit. Coghlan's Epitome of, Hindu Law Cases

Cohen, Adm. Law Cohen's Admiralty Jurisdiction, Law, and Practice

C.O.I. Central Office of Information

Co. Inst. Coke's Institutes (Eng.)

Co. inst. (Eng.) Coke's Institutes (Eng.)

Co. Jurid. Collectanea Juridica

Coke Coke, English King's Bench Reports (76, 77 ER)

Coke (Eng.) Coke, English King's Bench Reports (76, 77 ER)

Coke Ent. Coke's Book of Entries

Coke Inst. Coke's Institutes

Coke Lit. Coke on Littleton

Col.
- Coldwell's Reports (vols. 41-47 Tennessee)

- Coleman's Reports, (vols. 99, 101, 106, 110-129 Alabama)
- Colonial
- Colorado Reports
- Columbia
- column

Col. & Cai. Coleman and Caines' Cases, New York

Col. & Cai. Cas. Coleman and Caines, New York Cases

Col. & Caines Cas. (N.Y.) Coleman & Caines' Cases (Common Law)

Col. & C. Cas. Coleman & Caines' Cases (N.Y.)

Col. App. Colorado Appeals Reports

Colb. Pr. Colby's Practice

Col. Cas. Coleman, Cases of Practice (N.Y.)

Col. Cas. (NY) Coleman Cases (of Practice) (New York)

Col. C.C. Collyer's English Chancery Cases (1845-47)

Col. Crim. Law Colby's Criminal Law and Practice, New York

Cold. Coldwell's Tennessee Supreme Court Reports (1860-70)

Colds. Pr. Coldstream's Scotch Court of Session Procedure

Cold. (Tenn.) Coldwell's Reports (Tenn.)

Coldw. Coldwell's Reports (vols. 41-47 Tennessee)

Coldwell Coldwell's Reports (Tenn.)

Coldw. (Tenn.) Coldwell's Reports (vols. 41-47 Tennessee)

Cole.
- Coleman's Reports (vols. 99, 101-106, 110-129 Alabama)
- Cole's edition of Iowa Reports

Cole. & Cai. Cas. Coleman & Caines' Cases (New York 1794-1805)

Cole. Cas. Coleman's Cases, New York (1791-1800)

Cole. Cases Coleman's Cases(N.Y.)

Cole. Cas. Pr. Coleman's Cases, New York

Cole Cond. Cole, Particulars and Conditions of Sale. 1879

Cole Cr. Inf. Cole, Criminal Informations. 1843

Cole. Dig. Colebrooke's Digest of Hindu Law

Cole Ejec. Cole, Ejectment, 1857

Cole Eject. Cole's Law and Practice of Ejectment

Colem. Coleman's Cases (N.Y.)

Coleman Coleman's Cases (N.Y.)

Colem. & C. Cas. Coleman & Caines, New York Cases

Colem. Cas. Coleman, New York Cases

Col. Fr. Suc. Colin on French Interstate Successions

Col. Hum. R. L. Rev. Columbia Human Rights Law Review

Co. Lit. Coke on Littleton (1 lnst.)

Co. Litt.
- Commentaries upon Littleton, by Sir Edward Coke
- Coke on Littleton (Eng.)

Co. Litt. (Eng.) Coke on Littleton

(Eng.)

Co. L.J. Cochin Law Journal Colonial Law Journal (New Zealand)

Col. J. Environ. L. Columbia Journal of Environmental Law

Col. J. L. & Soc. Probl. Columbia Journal of Law and Social Problems

Col. J. Transnat'l L. Columbia Journal of Transnational Law

Col. J. World Bus. Columbia Journal of World Business

Coll.
- Collector
- Colles, Parliamentary Cases (1697- 1714)
- Collyer, English Chancery Cases (1845-47)

Coll. & Cr. A. Collection and Credit Agency

Coll. & E. Bank. Collier's & Eaton's American Bankruptcy Reports

Coll. & Mil.B.S. Collier & Miller on Bills of Sale

Coll. & U. Colleges and Universities

Col. Law Rep. Colorado Law Reporter

Col. Law Review Columbia Law Review

Coll.Bank. Collier's Law of Bankruptcy

Coll.Caus.Cel. Collection des Causes Celebres, Paris

Coll.C.C. Collyer's Chancery Cases tempore Bruce, V.-C. (63 ER) (1844-45)

Coll.Contr. Collier, Law of Contri-

bution. 1875

Coll.C.R. Collyer's Chancery Reports (Eng.)

Collective Bargaining Negot. & Cont. (BNA) Collective Bargaining Negotiations & Contracts

College L. Dig. (Nat'l Ass'n College & Univ. Att'ys) College Law Digest

Collier Bankr. Cas. 2d (MB) Collier Bankruptcy Cases, Second Series

Colles Colles Cases in Parliament (1697-1714) (Eng.)

Colles (Eng.) Colles Cases in Parliament (1697-1714) (Eng.)

Colles, P.C. Colles's Cases in Parliament (1697-1714) (Eng.)

Coll. Id. (or Lun.) Collinson on the Law of Idiots and Lunatics

Collier & E. Am. Bankr. Collier & Eaton's American Bankruptcy

Collier Bank. Collier & Eaton's Bankruptcy Reports

Collier, Bankr. Collier's Bankruptcy

Collier Bankr. Cas. Collier Bankruptcy Cases

Collin. Ind. (or Lun.) Collinson on the Law of Idiots and Lunatics

Col. L.J. Colonial Law Journal (New Zealand)

Col. L.J. N.Z. Colonial Law Journal (1865-75) (N.Z.)

Coll. Jurid. Collectanea Juridica (Eng.)

Coll. L. Bull. College Law Bulletin

Coll. L. Dig. College Law Digest

Coll. Min. Collier on Mines

Coll.N.C. Collyer's Chancery Cases tempore Bruce, V.-C. (63 ER) (1844-45)

Coll. Part. Collyer on the Law of Partnership

Coll. Pat. Colliers on Patents

Coll. P.C. Colles' English Parliamentary (House of Lords) Cases (1697-1714)

Col. L. Rep. Colorado Law Reporter

Col. L. Rev. Columbia Law Review

Coll. St. L. Collinson on the Stamp Laws

Coll. Tor. Collet on Torts and Measure of Damages

Coll. Tr. Collateral trust

Colly. Collyer's English vice Chancellors' Reports (1845-47)

Colly Ch. Cas. (Eng.) Collyer, Chancery Cases (63 Eng. Reprint)

Colly. Part. Collyer on Partnership

Collyl. Partn. Collyer on Partnership

Col. Mass. Pr. Colby's Massachusetts Practice

Col. Mines Collier's Law of Mines

Col. Mort. Colby on Mortgage Foreclosures

Col. Mun. B. Coler's Law of Municipal Bonds

Col. N.P. Colorado Nisi Prius Decisions

Colo.
- Colorado
- Colorado Reports

Colo. Admin. Code. Code of Colorado Regulations

Colo. Admin. Reg Colorado Register

Colo. App. Colorado Court of Appeals Reports

Colo. B.A. Colorado Bar Association

Colo. Const. Colorado Constitution

Colo. Dec. Colorado Decisions

Colo. Dec. Fed. Colorado Decisions, Federal

Colo. Dec. Supp. Colorado Decisions Supplement

Colo. I.C. Colorado Industrial Commission Report

Colo. L.R. Colorado Law Reporter

Colo. J. Int'l Envtr. L. & Pol'y Colorado Journal of International Environmental Law and Policy

Colo. Law. Colorado Lawyer

Colo. L. Rep., Colo. Law Rep. Colorado Law Reporter (Colo.)

Colom. Columbia

Colombo L.J. Colombo Law Journal

Colombo L. Rev. Colombo Law Review (Ceylon)

Colonial Law. Colonial Lawyer

Colo N.P. Dec. Colorado Nisi Prius Decisions (1900-02)

Colo. P.U.C. Colorado Public Utilities Commission Decisions

Colo. P.U.C. Rep. Colorado Public Utilities Commission Report

Colo. Sess. Laws. Session Laws of Colorado

Colo. S.R.C. Colorado State Railroad Commission

Colo. St. B.A. Colorado State Bar Association. Report

Col. Part. Collyer, Law of Partnership, 2ed. 1840

Colq.
- Colquit
- Colquit's Reports (1 Modern) (Eng.)

Colq. Civ. Law. Colquhoun on Roman Civil Law

Colq. C.L. Colquhoun's Civil Law

Colq. Jud. A. Colquhoun on the Judicature Acts

Colq. Rom. Civ. Law Colquhoun's Roman Civil Law

Colq. Rom. Law Colquhoun's Roman Civil Law

Colquit. Colquit's Reports (1 Modern) (Eng.)

Co LR Construction Litigation Reporter

Col.Rep. Colorado Reports (Colo.)

Col. Rev. Stat. Colorado Revised Statutes

cols. columns

Coltm. Coltman Registration Appeal Cases (1879-85) (Eng.)

Colt. (Reg.Ca.) Coltman's Registration Appeal Cases (1879-85)

Colt. Reg. Cas. Coltman Registration Appeal Cases (1879-85) (Eng.)

Colum. Columbia

Columbia J. of L. and Soc.Probl. Columbia Journal of Law and Social Problems

Columbia J. of Transnat. L. Columbia Journal of Transnational Law

Colum. Bus. L. Rev. Columbia Business Law Review

Colum. Human Rights L. Rev. Columbia Human Rights Law Review

Colum. Hum. Rts. L. Rev. Columbia Human Rights Law Review

Colum. J.Environ. L. Columbia Journal of Environment Law

Colum. J. Env. L. Columbia Journal of Environmental Law

Colum. J.Envt'l L. Columbia Journal of Environmental Law

Colum. J. Gender & L. Columbia Journal of Gender and Law

Colum. J.Int'l Aff. Columbia Journal of International Affairs

Colum J L & Arts Columbia Journal of Law and the Arts

Colum. J.L. & Soc.Prob. Columbia Journal of Law & Social Problems

Colum. J.L. & Soc.Probs. Columbia Journal of Law and Social Problems

Colum. J.Law & Soc.Prob. Columbia Journal of Law and Social Problems

Colum. Jr. Columbia Jurist (1855-57)

Colum. J. Transnat. L. Columbia Journal of Transnational Law

Colum. J.Transnat'l. Law Columbia Journal of Transnational Law

Colum. Jur. Columbia Jurist

Colum. J.World Bus. Columbia

Journal of World Business

Colum. L. Rev. Columbia Law Review

Colum. L.T. Columbia Law Times

Colum. Soc. Int. L. Bull. Columbia Society of International Law Bulletin

Colum. Soc'y. Int'l. L. Bull. Columbia Society of International Law Bulletin

Colum. Survey Human Rights L. Columbia Survey of Human Rights Law

Colum. Surv. Hum. Rts. L. Columbia Survey of Human Rights Law

Colum.-VLA J.L. & Arts Columbia - VLA Journal of Law & the Arts

Colvil. Colvil's Manuscript Decisions, Scotch Court of Session

Coly.Guar. (De) Colyar on Guarantees

COM
- Council of Ministers document
- Council of Ministers (E.E.C.)

Com.
- Blackstone's Commentaries
- Comberbach, English King's Bench Reports (1685-99)
- Comment
- Commerce(ial)
- Commission
- Commissioner
- committee
- Common
- Commonwealth
- Communication(s)
- Comstock, Reports (vols. 1-4 New York Court of Appeals)

- Comyn, Reports, English King's Bench, 2 vols. (1695-1741)
- U.S. Commerce Court Opinions

Com. Act Commonwealth Act

Com. Affrs. Community Affairs

Com. & L. Communications and the Law

Com. & Law. Communications and the Law

Com. & Leg. Rep. Commercial & Legal Reporter

Com. & Mun. L. Rep. Commercial & Mu-nicipal Law Reporter

Com. App. Commissioner of Appeals

Co. Mass. Pr. Colby Mass. Practice

Com. Att. Complete Attorney

Com.B. Common Bench Reports (Manning, Granger, and Scott) (1846-65) (Eng.)

Comb. Comberbach English King's Bench Reports (1685-99)

Com. Black. A'Beckett's Comic Blackstone

Comb. B. (N.S.) Common Bench (Manning, Granger & Scott) (Eng.)

Com.B. N.S. English Common Bench Reports, New Series

Co.M.C. Coke's Magna Charta (2d Institute)

Com. C. Commercial Code

Com. Cas.
- Commercial Cases (1896-1941) (Eng.)
- Company Cases (India)

Com. Cas. S.C.C. Commercial Cases, Small Cause Court, Bengal (1851-60) (India)

Com. Con. Comyn, Law of Contracts. 2ed. 1824

comd. commanded

Com. Dec. Commissioners' Decisions (Patent)

Com. Dig. Comyn, Digest of the Laws of England (1762-1882)

Com. Dow. Comstock's Digest of the Law of Dower

Com. Forms Comer's Forms of Writs

Com. G. & W. Comstock on Guardian and Ward

Com. G.S. Commissioners of the Great Seal

Com. Jour. Journals of the House of Commons

Com. L. Commercial Law (Canada)

com'l. commercial

Com. L.A. Commercial Law Annual

Com. L. & T. Comyn on Landlord and Tenant

Com. Law
- Commercial Law
- Common Law

Com. Law Ann. Commercial Law Annual

Com. Law R.
- Common Law Reports, published by Spottiswoode
- English Common Law Reports (1853-55)

Com. Law Rep.
- Common Law Reports, published by Spottiswoode
- English Common Law Reports

Com. L.J. Commercial Law Journal

Com. L. L. A. Commercial Law League of America

Com. L. League J. Commercial Law League Journal

Com. L.R.
- Common Law Reports, published by Spottiswoode
- English Common Law Reports (1853-55)

Com. L.Rep. Common Law Reports 1853-55, Eng.

Comm.
- Blackstone's Commentaries
- Commentaries
- commerce
- commercial
- Commission(er)
- Committee
- Communication(s)

Comm. A.R. Commonwealth Arbitration Reports (Aus.)

Comm. B. Common Bench (Manning, Granger & Scott) (Eng.)

Comm. C. Commercial Code

Comm. Cause Common Cause

Comm. Code Commercial Code

Comm. Ct. Commerce Court

commd. commissioned

Comm. Del. Order Commissioner's Delegation Order

Comm. Fut. L. Rep. (CCH)
- Commodity Futures Law Reports
- Commodity Futures Law Reporter (CCH)

Commiss. Commission

Comm. Journ. House of Commons Journal (Eng.)

Comm. Jud. J. Commonwealth Judicial Journal

comml. commercial

Comm. & L. Communications and the Law

Comm. L.B. Commonwealth Law Bulletin

Comm. L. Law. Common Law Lawyer

Comm. L.R.
- Commercial Law Reports (Canada)
- Commonwealth Law Reports (Aus.)

Comm. Market L. Rev. Common Market Law Review, Leiden, Netherlands

Comm. Mkt. Common Market

Comm. Mkt. L.R. Common Market Law Reports

Comm. Mkt. L. Rep. Common Market Law Reports

Comm. Mkt. L. Rev. Common Market Law Review

Comm. Mkt. Rep. Common Market Reporter (CCH)

Commn. Commission

Commodity Futures L. Rep. Commodity Futures Law Reporter (CCH)

Common Mkt. L. Rev. Common Market Law Review

Common Mkt. Rep. (CCH) Common Market Reports

Commonw. Commonwealth

Commonw. Act Commonwealth Act

Commonw. L. Rep. Commonwealth Law Reports

Commonw. L. Rev. Commonwealth Law Review, Melbourne, Australia

Comm. Print Congressional Committee Prints

Comm. Prop. J. Community Property Journal

commr. commissioner

Commrs. Commissioners

Comm. Sec. Commonwealth Secretariat

Comm. Tel. Cas. Commission Telephone Cases Leaflets (New York)

Commun. & Law Communications and the Law

Community Prop. Community Property

Community Prop. J. Community Property Journal

Commw. Commonwealth

Commw. Arb. Commonwealth Arbitration Reports (Aus.)

Commw. Art. Commonwealth Arbitration Reports (Aus.)

Commw. Ct. Commonwealth Court

Commw. Jud. J. Commonwealth Judicial Journal

Commw. L.B. Commonwealth Law Bulletin

Commw. L.R. Commonwealth Law Reports (Aus.)

Commw. Sec. Commonwealth Secretariat

Com. on Con. Comyn's Law of

Contracts

Comp.
- Comparative
- compare
- Compensation
- compilation
- compile
- Compiled
- compiler
- composer
- computer

Comp. Admin. Sci. Q. Comparative Administrative Science Quarterly

Comp. & Int. L.J. S. Afr. Comparative and International Law Journal of South Africa

Comp. & Int. L.J. South Africa Comparative and International Law Journal of South Africa

Comp. & Int. L.J. South Africa Comparative and International Law Journal of South Africa

Comp. & Int'l. L.J. S.Afr. Comparative and International Law Journal of South Africa

Comp. & Law Computers and Law

Company Law The Company Lawyer

Company & Sec. L.J. Company & Securities Law Journal

Comparisons in L. & Monet. Com. Comparisons in Law and Monetary Comments

Comp. Armed Forces Compendium of Laws of Armed Forces (U.S.)

Com. Pat. Commissioner of Patents

Comp. Cas. Company Cases (India)

Comp. Cred. Composition with Creditors

Comp. Crimes Compounding Crimes

Comp. Dec. Decisions of the Comptroller of the Treasury (U.S.)

Com. P.Div. Common Pleas Division, English Law Reports

Comp. Ex. Comstock on Executors

Comp. Gen.
- Comptroller General
- Decisions of the Comptroller General

Comp. Gen. Op. Comptroller General Opinion

Comp. Jurid. Rev. Comparative Juridical Review

Comp. Jur. Rev. Comparative Juridical Review

Com. Pl. Common Pleas, English Law Reports

Compl. Compliant

Comp. Lab. L. Comparative Labor Law

Comp. Lab. L.J. Comparative Labor Law Journal

Comp Labor L Comparative Labor Law

Comp. Laws Compiled Laws

Comp. Lawy. Company Lawyer

Compleat Law. Compleat Lawyer

Comp. L.J. Company Law Journal

Com. Pl. Div. Common Pleas Division, English Law Reports

Com. Pl. Reptr. Common Pleas

Reporter, Scranton, Pennsylvania

Comp. L. Rev. Comparative Law Review (Tokyo)

Comp. L. Rev. (Japan Inst.) Comparative Law Review. The Japan Institute of Comparative Law, Tokyo, Japan

Com. Pl. R. (Pa.) Common Pleas Reporter, Scranton, Pennsylvania

Comp. L.S. Comparative Law Series

Comp. L. Ser. Comparative Law Series, U.S. Bureau of Foreign and Domestic Commerce General Legal Bulletin

Comp. L. Yb. Comparative Law Yearbook, Alphen aan den Rijn, Netherlands

COMPR Department of Commerce Procurement Regulations

Com. P. Reptr. Common Pleas Reporter (Scranton)

Comp. Rev. Compensation Review (India)

Comp. Sol. Complete Solicitor

Comp. St. Compiled Statutes

Comp. Stat. Compiled Statutes

Comptr. Treas. Dec. Comptroller Treasury Decisions

Comput. & Law Computers and Law

Computer L. & Prac. Computer Law & Practice

Computer L. & Tax Computer Law & Tax Report

Computer L. & T. Rep. Computer Law & Tax Report

Computer Law. Computer Lawyer

Computer L. J. Computer Law Journal

Computer L. Serv. Rep. (Callaghan) Computer Law Service Reporter

Computers & L. Computers and Law

Com'r. Commissioner

Com. Rep. Comyns, English King's Bench Reports (1695-1741)

Comr. of Bkg. and Ins. Commissioner of Banking and Insurance

Com'r Pat. Commissioner of Patents and Trademarks

Com.S. Common Scold

C.O.M.S.A.T. Communications Satellite Corporation

Coms. Comstock's Reports (1-4 New York Court of Appeals)

Comst. Comstock's Reports (1-4 New York Court of Appeals)

Com. Us. Comyn on the Law of Usury

Com'w'th. Commonwealth

Comyn. Comyn's King's Bench Reports (1695-1741) (92 ER)

Comyns. Comyns' English King's Bench Reports

Comyns' Dig. Comyns' Digest (Eng.)

Comyn, Usury Comyn on Usury

Con.
- Connoly, New York Reports
- Conover's Reports (Wisconsin)
- Continuation of Rolle's Reports (2 Rolle)

Con. & L. Connor & Lawson's Irish Chancery Reports (1841-43)

Con. & Law. Connor & Lawson's Irish Chancery Reports (1841-43)

Con. & Sim. Connor and Simonton's South Carolina Equity Digest

Con. B.J. Connecticut Bar Journal

concl. conclusion

Con. Cus. Conroy's Custodian Reports (Eng.,Ir.)

Cond. Ch. R. Condensed English Chancery Reports

Cond. Eccl. Condensed Ecclesiastical Reports

Cond. Ecc. R. Condensed Ecclesiastical Reports

Condem. Condemnation

Cond. Eng. Ch. Condensed English Chan-cery Reports

Condensed Rep.
- Louisiana Supreme Court Condensed Reports (La.)
- Peters' Condensed U.S. Reports

Cond. Exch. R. Condensed Exchequer Reports

Cond. Ex. R. Condensed Exchequer Reports

Cond. Gen. Conductor Generalis

Cond H.C. Conders Highway Cases

Con. Dig. Connor's Irish Digest

Con. Dig. Ind. Conover's Digested Index (Ohio, Ind., & Ill.)

Condit. Sale — Chat. Mort. Rep. Conditional Sale Chattel Mortgage Reporter (CCH)

Cond. Lou'a. Reps. Louisiana Supreme Court Condensed Reports (La.)

Cond. Marsh. Condy's Edition of Marshall on Insurance

Condomin. Condominiums and Cooperative Apartments

Cond. R. Peters' Condensed U.S. Reports

Cond. Rep. Peters' Condensed U.S. Reports

Cond. Rep. U.S. Peters, Condensed United States Reports

Conf.
- Conference
- Conference Reports by Cameron and Norwood (North Carolina)
- Confirmation
- Confirming

Conf. Chart. Confirmatio Chartarum

Conf. Comm. Uniformity Legis. Conference of Commissioners on Uniformity of Legislation in Canada

Conference (NC) Conference Reports (N.C.)

Conf. L. Conflict of Laws

Conf. on Char. Found. N.Y.U. Proc. Conference on Charitable Foundations, New York University Proceedings

Conf. Pers. Fin. L.Q.R. Conference on Personal Finance Law, Quarterly Report

Conf. Proc. Inter-Amer. Bar Assoc. Conference Proceedings. Inter-American Bar Association

Conf. R. Conference Reports, N.C.

Conf. Rept. Conference Report

Conf. Teach. Int'l L. Conference of Teachers of International Law

175

Cong.
- Congress
- Congressional

Cong. Deb. Congressional Debates (U.S.)

Cong. Dig.
- Congdon's Digest (Canada)
- Congressional Digest

Cong. El. Cas. Congressional Election Cases (U.S.)

Cong. Gl. Congressional Globe

Cong. Globe Congressional Globe

Cong. Index (CCH) Congressional Index

Congl.
- Congregational
- Congressional

Cong. Min. L. Congdon's Mining Laws of California

Cong. Q. W. Repts. Congressional Quarterly Weekly Reports

Cong. Rec. Congressional Record (U.S.)

Conk. Adm. Conkling's Admiralty

Conk. Ex. Pow. Conkling's Executive Po-wers

Conk. J.P. Conkling's Iowa Justice of the Peace

Conk. Treat. (or U.S.Pr.) Conkling's Treatise on Jurisdiction and Practice of the United States Courts

Con. L.R. Connecticut Law Review

Con. L. Rev. Connecticut Law Review

Conn.
- Connecticut
- Connecticut Reports

- Connoly's Surrogate Reports (New York)

Conn. Acts Connecticut Public and Special Acts

Conn. Agencies Reg. Regulations of Connecticut State Agencies

Conn. App. Proc. Maltbie's Appellate Procedure

Conn. Bar J. Connecticut Bar Journal

Conn. B.J. Connecticut Bar Journal

Conn.Cir. Connecticut Circuit Court Reports

Conn. Cir. Ct. Connecticut Circuit Court Reports

Conn. Comp. Com. Connecticut Compensation Commissioners, Compendium of Awards

Conn. Comp. Dec. Connecticut Workmen's Compensation Decisions

Conn. Const. Connecticut Constitution

Conn. Dec. Connecticut Decisions

Connecticut L. Rev. Connecticut Law Review

Connecticut R. Connecticut Reports (Conn.)

Connecticut Rep. Connecticut Reports (Conn.)

Connect.Rep. Connecticut Reports (Conn.)

Conn. Gen. Stat. General Statutes of Connecticut

Conn. Gen. Stat. Ann. Connecticut General Statutes Annotated

Conn. J. Int'l L. Connecticut Journal of International Law

Conn. Legis. Serv. Connecticut Legislative Service (West)

Conn. L.J. Connecticut Law Journal (Conn.)

Conn. L. Rev. Connecticut Law Review

Connoly. Connoly's New York Surrogate Reports

Connoly Sur. Rep. Connoly's Surrogate Reports (N.Y.)

Connoly Surr. Rep. Connoly's Surrogate Reports (N.Y.)

Connor. & L. Connor and Lawson Chancery Reports (Ir.)

Conn. Prob. L.J. The Connecticut Probate Law Journal

Conn. Pub. Acts Connecticut Public Acts

Conn. P.U.C. Connecticut Public Utilities Commission

Conn. R. Connecticut Reports (Conn.)

Conn. R.C. Connecticut Railroad Commissioners

Conn. Rep. Connecticut Reports (Conn.)

Conn. Reports Connecticut Reports

Conn. S. Connecticut Supplement

Conn. Spec. Acts Connecticut Special Acts

Conn. Sup.
- Connecticut Law Journal (Conn.)
- Connecticut Supplement

Conn. Supp. Connecticut Supplement

Conn. Surr. Connoly's New York Surrogate Reports

Conn. Surr. Rep. Connoly's Surrogate Reports (N.Y.)

Conov. Conover (Wis.)

Conover Conover Reports (16-153 Wisconsin Reports)

Con. Par. Connell on Parishes

Conr. Conroy, Custodian Reports (1652-1788) (Ir.)

Cons.
- Conservator
- Consolidated
- Constable
- Constitution
- Constitutional
- Consul
- Consulting, consultant

Cons. & Bor. Pro. Consumer and Borrower Protection

Cons. & Com. Cred. (P-H) Consumer and Commercial Credit (Prentice-Hall)

Cons. Cred. Guide. Consumer Credit Guide (CCH)

Cons. del M. Consolato del Marc

Consist. English Consistorial Reports, by Haggard (1788-1821)

Consist. Rep. English Consistorial Reports, by Haggard

Cons. L. Today Consumer Law Today

consol. consolidated

Consol. T.S. Parry's Consolidated Treaty Series

Consolid. Ord. Consolidated General Orders in Chancery

Cons. Ord. in Ch. Consolidated General Orders in Chancery

Consort. Newsl. Consortium

Newsletter

Conn. Spec. Acts Connecticut Special Acts

Consp. Conspiracy

Cons. Prod. Warr. Consumer Product Warranty Acts

Con. St. Consolidated Statutes

Const.
- Bott's Poor Laws, by Const. (1560-1833)
- Constitution(al)
- Constitutional Reports, Vol. 1 South Carolina, by Harper
- Constitutional Reports, South Carolina, by Mills
- Constitutional Reports, South Carolina, by Treadway
- Construction

Const. Afr. States Constitutions of African States (Oceana)

Const. Amend. Amendment to Constitution

Const. & Parliam. Inf. Constitutional and Parliamentary Information

Con. Stat. Consolidated Statutes

Const Bott Const's Edition of Bott's Poor Laws

Const. Commentary Constitutional Commentary

Const Conn Constitutional Commentary

Const. Dep. & Sp. Sov. Constitutions of Dependencies and Special Sovereignties

Const. Hist. Hallam's Constitutional History of England

Const. L. Constitutional Law

constl. constitutional

Const. L.J. Constitutional Law Journal (Seton Hall Law School)

constn. constitution

Const. Nations Constitutions of Nations (Nijhoff)

Const. N.S. Constitutional Reports, (Mill), South Carolina, New Series

Const. Oth. Constitutiones Othoni (found at the end of Lyndewood's Provinciale)

Constr. Construction

Const. Rep. Constitutional Reports (S.C.)

Const. Rev. Constitutional Review

Const. R.S.C. Constitutional Reports, South Carolina, printed by Treadway

Construction Law Construction Lawyer

Const. S.C. Constitutional Reports (South Carolina, printed by Treadway)

Const. S.C.N.S. Constitutional Reports, New Series, Printed by mills

Const. U.S. Constitution of the United States

Const. U.S. Amend. Amendment to the Constitution of the United States

Const. World Constitutions of the Countries of the World (Oceana)

Consuet. Feud. Consuetudiness Feudorum; or, the Book of Feuds

Consumer Cred. Guide (CCH) Consumer Credit Guide (Commerce Clearing House)

Consumer Fin. L.Q. Rep. Consumer Finance Law Quarterly Report

Consumerism Consumerism (CCH)

Consumer Prod. Safety Guide (CCH), Consumer Prod. Saf'y Guide Consumer Product Safety Guide (Commerce Clearing House)

Con.Sur. Connoly's Surrogate Reports (N.Y.)

Consv. Conservatorship

Cont.
- containing
- contents
- continent
- continental
- continue
- continued
- contra
- Contracts
- Control(s)

Cont. App.Dec. (CCH) Contract Appeals Decisions

Cont. Bond Contractors' Bond

Cont. Cas. Fed. Contract Cases, Federal

Cont. El. Controverted Elections Judges (Eng.)

Cont. Elect. Case. Contested Election Cases (U.S.)

Contemp. Contemporary

Contemp. Drug Prob. Contemporary Drug Problems

Contin. Continuance

Cont. L. Rev. Contemporary Law Review (India)

Cont. of Banking (P-H) Control of Banking (Prentice-Hall)

Contrib. Contribution

CONUS Continental United States

Conv. The Conveyancer

conv.
- convention
- conversion
- convertible
- Conveyancer & Property Lawyer
- conveyancing

Conv. & Prop. Law. (N.S.) Conveyancer and Property Lawyer

Conv. Asst. Conveyancer's Assistant

Conv. Est. Convention of the Estates of Scotland

Convey Conveyancer

Convey. N.S. Conveyancer & Property Lawyer, New Series

Conv. F.J. European Community Convention on the Jurisdiction of the Courts and Enforcement of Judgments in Civil and Commercial Matters, 27 Sept. 1968

Conv. (N.S.) Conveyancer and Property Lawyer (New 1936, current Series)

Conv. Rev. Conveyancing Review (1957-63) (Sc.)

Conv. Y.B. Conveyancers' Year Book (1940--51)

Coo. Agr.T. Cooke, Agricultural Tenancies, 3ed. 1882

Coo. & Al. Cooke & Alcock, Irish King's Bench Reports (1833-34)

Coo. & H.Tr. Cooke & Harwood's Charitable Trusts Acts

Coo. Bankr. Cooke, Bankrupt Law. 8ed. 1823

Coo. Cop. Cooke, Enfranchisement of Copyholds. 2ed. 1853

Coo. Def. Cooke's Law of Defamation

Coode Leg. Exp. Coode's Legislative Expression

Coode Wr.L. Coode on the Written Law

Coo. I.A. Cooke's Inclosure Acts

Cook Adm.
- Cooke's Admiralty Cases (Quebec)
- Cook's Vice Admiralty Reports (1873-84) (Can.)

Cook, Corp. Cook on Corporations

Cooke
- Cases under Sugden's Act (1838) (Eng.)
- Cooke, Act Book of the Ecclesiastical Court of Whalley
- Cooke's Cases of Practice, English Common Pleas
- Cooke's Reports (3, Tennessee) (1811-14)

Cooke Agr. Hold. Cooke on the Agricultural Holdings Act

Cooke Agr. T. Cooke on Agricultural Tenancies

Cooke & A. Cooke & Alcock's Reports (Ir.)

Cooke & Al. Cooke & Alcock's Reports (Ir.)

Cooke & Alc. Cooke & Alcock's Reports (Ir.)

Cooke & Al.(Ir.) Cooke & Alcock Reports, Irish Kings Bench

Cooke & H.Ch.Tr. Cooke & Harwood's Charitable Trust Acts

Cooke B.L. Cooke's Bankrupt Laws

Cooke Com. Cooke on Rights of Common

Cooke Cop. Cooke's Law of Copyhold Enfranchisement

Cooke C.P. Cooke's Common Pleas Reports (1706-47)(Eng.)

Cooke Def. Cooke on the Law of Defamation

Cooke (Eng.) Cooke, Cases of Practice (125 ER)

Cooke High. Cooke's New York Highway Laws

Cooke I.A. Cooke's Inclosure Act

Cooke. Incl. Acts Cooke's Inclosure Acts

Cooke, Ins. Cooke on Life Insurance

Cooke Pr. Cas. Cooke's Practice Reports, English Common Pleas

Cooke Pr. Reg. Cooke's Practical Register of the Common Pleas

Cooke's Rep. Cooke's Reports (Tenn.)

Cooke (Tenn.) Cooke's Tennessee Reports (Tennessee)

Cook's Pen. Code. Cook's Penal Code (N.Y.)

Cook, Stock, Stockh. & Corp.Law. Cook on Stock, Stockholders, and General Corporation Law

Cook V. Adm. Cook's Vice-Admiralty Reports (Nova Scotia)

Cook Vice-Adm. Cook's Vice-Admiralty Reports (Nova Scotia)

Cool. Black. Cooley's edition of Blackstone

Cool. Con. Law. Cooley's Constitutional Law

Cool. Con. Lim. Cooley's Constitutional Limitations

Cooley. Cooley's Reports (5-12 Michigan)

Cooley, Bl. Comm. Cooley's Edition of Blackstone's Commentaries

Cooley, Const.Law. Cooley's Constitutional Law

Cooley, Const.Lim. Cooley on Constitutional Limitations

Cooley, Const.Limit. Cooley on Constitutional Limitations

Cooley L. Rev. Cooley Law Review

Cooley, Tax Cooley on Taxation

Cooley, Tax'n. Cooley on Taxation

Cooley, Torts. Cooley on Torts

Cool. Mich. Dig. Cooley's Michigan Digest

Cool. Tax. Cooley on Taxation

Cool. Torts Cooley on Torts

Coo. Mort. Coote on Mortgages

Co. on Courts Coke's 4th Institute (Eng.)

Coop.
- Cooper, Tennessee Chancery Reports
- Cooper, English Chancery Reports tempore Eldon
- Cooper, English Chancery tempore Cottenham
- Cooper, English Chancery Reports tempore Brougham
- Cooper, English Practice Cases, Chancery
- Cooperative
- Cooper's Reports, Florida Reports (21-24)

Co-op. Co-operative

Coop. Asso. Cooperative Association

Coop. C. & P.R. Cooper's Chancery & Practice Reporter, Upper Canada

Coop.C.C. Cooper's Chancery Cases tempore Cottenham (Eng.)

Coop. C. Cas. Cooper's Chancery Cases tempore Cottenham (Eng.)

Coop. Ch Cooper's Tennessee Chancery, Reports

Coop. Ch. (Eng.) Cooper's Chancery (35 ER)

Coop. Ch. Pr. Cooper's Chancery Practice Reports (Eng.)

Coop. Chy. Tennessee Chancery Reports Cooper (Tenn.)

Coop. Corp. Cooperative Corporations

Coop. C.P. C.P. Cooper's Cases tempore Cottenham (1846-48) (47 ER)

Co-op. Dig. Co-operative Digest, United States Reports

Coop. Eq. Dig. Cooper's Equity Digest

Coop. Eq. Pl. Cooper's Equity Pleading

Cooper
- Cooper's Chancery Practice Cases (1837-38) (47 ER)
- Cooper's Chancery Reports tempore Brougham (1833-34) (47 ER)
- Cooper's Chancery Reports tempore Cottenham (1846-48) (47 ER)
- Cooper's Chancery Reports tempore Eldon (1815) (35 ER)
- Cooper's Florida Reports (21-24 Florida)

- Cooper's Tennessee Chancery Reports (1837-39)
- Upper Canada Chancery Chamber Reports (1857-72)

Cooper Ch. Cooper, Tennessee Chancery Reports (Tenn.)

Cooper, C.P. Cooper, Charles Purton (1837-38)

Cooper, G. Cooper, George (1815, with a few earlier cases in and from 1792)

Cooper, Just. Inst. Cooper's Justinian's Institutes

Cooper Pr. Cas (Eng.) Cooper's Practice Cases (47 ER)

Cooper t. Brougham Cooper, Charles Purton, tempore Brougham (1833-34)

Cooper t. Cott. Cooper, Charles Purton, tempore Cottenham (1846-48)

Cooper t. Eldon Cooper's Chancery Reports tempore Eldon (1815) (35 ER)

Cooper Tenn. Ch. Cooper's Tennessee Chancery Reports

Coop. For. Ct. Coopers's Effect of a Sentence of a Foreign Court of Admiralty

Coop. G. G.Cooper's Chancery Reports (Eng.)

Coop. Inst. Cooper's Institutes of Justinian

Coop. Inst. Just. Cooper's Institutes of Justinian

Coop. Judg. Cooper's Judgment

Coop. Lib. Cooper's Law of Libel

Coop. Med. Jur. Cooper's Medical Jurisprudence

Coop. P.C. Cooper's Practice Cases (1837-38) (47 ER)

Coop. Pr. C. Cooper's Practice Cases (1837-89)

Coop. Pr. Cas. Cooper's Practice Cases, English Chancery

Coop. Rec. Cooper's Public Records of Great Britain

Coop. Sel. Ca. Cooper's Select Cases tempore Eldon, English Chancery

Coop. Sel. E.C. Cooper's Select Early Cases (Sc.)

Coop. t. Br. Cooper's Cases tempore Brougham, English Chancery

Coop. t. Brough. Cooper's Cases tempore Brougham Chancery (47 ER) (1833-34) (Eng.)

Coop.t. Brougham Cooper's Cases tempore Brougham, English Chancery (47 ER) (1833-34) (Eng.)

Coop.t. Brougham (Eng.) Cooper, Cases tempore Brougham (47 ER) (Eng.)

Coop. t. Cott. Cooper's Reports tempore Cottenham (1846-48)

Coop.t.Cott. (Eng.) Cooper, Cases tempore Cottenham (47 ER)

Coop. t. Eld. Cooper's Reports tempore Eldon (1815) (Eng.)

Coop. t. Eld. (Eng.) Cooper Reports tempore Eldon (1815) (Eng.)

Coop.t. Eldon Cooper's Reports tempore Eldon Chancery (Eng.)

Coop. temp. Cooper, Cases tempore

Coop. temp. Brougham Cooper

C.P. tempore Brougham (1832-34)

Coop. temp. Cottenham Cooper C.P. tempore Cottenham (1846-48)

Coop. temp. Eldon Cooper's Chancery Reports tempore Eldon (1815) (35 ER)

Coop. Ten.Chy. Cooper's Tennessee Chancery Reports

Coop. Tenn. Ch. Cooper's Tennessee Chancery Reports

Coord. Coordinator

Coote Coote on Mortgages

Coote Adm. Coote's Admiralty Practice

Coote & Tr. Pr. Pr. Coote's Probate Court Practice, Edited by Tristram

Coote Ecc. Pr. Coote's Ecclesiastical Court Practice

Coote L. & T. Coote's Law of Landlord and Tenant

Coote Mor. Coote on Mortgages

Coote Pro. Pr. Coote, Practice of the Court of Probate. 9ed. 1883

Co. Pal. Counties Palatine

Co. P.C. Coke's Pleas of the Crown (3d Institute)

Cop. Cop. Copinger, Copyright 11ed. 1971

COPE Committee on Political Education

Cope. Cope's Reports (63-72 California Reports)

Cop. Ind. Pr. Copinger's Index to Precedents

Co. Pl. Coke's Pleadings (sometimes published separately)

Copp. Ct. Mar. Coppe's Manual for Courts-Martial

Copp Land. Copp's Land Office Decisions

Copp. L.L. Copp's Public Land Laws

Copp. Min. Dec. Copp's United States Mining Decision

Copp Pub. Land Laws Copp's United States Public Land Laws

Copp Pub. L.L. Copp's United States Public Land Laws

Cop. Tit. D. Copinger on Title Deeds

Copy. Copyright

Copy. & Lit. P. Copyright and Literary Property

Copy. Bull Copyright Bulletin

Copy. Dec. Copyright Decisions

Copyright Copyright; Monthly Review of the United International Bureau for the Protection of Intellectual Property (BIRPI), Geneva, Switzerland

Copyright Bull. UNESCO Copyright Bulletin

Copyright L. Dec. (CCH) Copyright Law Decisions

Copyright L. Rep. (CCH) Copyright Law Reporter (Commerce Clearing House)

Copyright L.Sym. (ASCAP) Copyright Law Symposium (ASCAP)

Copyright L. Symp. (ASCAP) Copyright Law Symposium

Copyright World Copyright World

Copy. Soc. Bull. Bulletin of the

Copyright Society of the U.S.A.

C.O.R. Crown Office Rules

Co.R. Code Reporter (New York)

Cor.
- Cornell Law Review
- Corvton's Reports (Bengal)

cor.
- corpus
- correction
- corrective

Coran N. Coran Nobis and Allied Statutory Remedies

Corb. & D Corbett & Daniell's Election Cases (1819) (Eng.)

Corb. & Dan. Corbett & Daniell's Election Cases (1819) (Eng.)

Cor. Cas. American & English Corporation Cases

Cord Mar. Wom. Cord on Legal and Equitable Rights of Married Women

Cord. Sol. Cordery, Solicitors. 6ed. 1968

Co. Rep.
- Code Reporter (New York)
- Coke, Reports, King's Bench (1572-1616) (Eng.)

COREPER European Communities Committee of Permanent Representatives

Cor. Jud. Correspondances Judiciaires (Canada)

Cor. L.Q. Cornell Law Quarterly

Corn. Deeds. Cornish on Purchase Deeds

Corn. Dig. Cornwell's Digest

Cornell Internat. L.J. Cornell International Law Journal

Cornell Int'l L.Forum Cornell Intenational Law Forum

Cornell Int'l. L.J. Cornell International Law Journal

Cornell L.F. Cornell Law Forum

Cornell L.J. Cornell Law Journal

Cornell L.Q. Cornell Law Quarterly

Cornell L. Rev. Cornell Law Review

Cornish, Purch. Deeds Cornish on Purchase Deeds

Corn L Q Cornell Law Quarterly

Corn. Pr. Corner's Queen's Bench Practice

Corn. Pur. D. Cornish on Purchase Deeds

Corn. Rem. Cornish on Remainders

Co. R.N.S. Code Reporter, New Series (New York)

Corn. Us. Cornish on Uses

Corn. Wr. Corner's Forms of Writs on the Crown Side

Cornw. Tab. Cornwall's Table of Precedents

Co. R. (N.Y.) Code Reporter (New York)

Coron. Coroners

Corp.
- Corporate
- Corporation
- Pennsylvania Corporation Reporter

Corp. & Ass'ns. Corporations and Associations

Cor. Pat. Coryton on Patents

Corp. & Bus. L.J. Corporate &

Business Law Journal

Corp. C Corporations Code

Corp. Counsel Rev. Corporate Counsel Review

Corp. Counsel Rev. J. Corp. Counsel Section, St. B. Tex. Corporate Counsel Review Journal of the Corporate Counsel Section, State Bar of Texas

Corp. Couns. Rep. Corporate Counsel Reporter

Corp. Couns. Wkly. (BNA) Corporate Counsel Weekly (Bureau of National Affairs)

Corp. Dep. Corporate depositary

Corp. Forms (P-H) Corporation Forms (Prentice-Hall)

Corp. Guide (P-H) Corporation Guide (P-H)

Corp. J. Corporation Journal

Corp. Jur. Corpus Juris

Corp. Jur. Can. Corpus Juris Canonici

Corp. Jur. Civ. Corpus Juris Civilis

Corp. Jur. Germ. Corpus Juris Germaniel

Corp. Jus. Canon. Corpus Juris Canonique

Corp. L. Guide Corporation Law Guide

Corp. L. Rev. Corporation Law Review

Corp. Mgmt.Ed. (P-H) Corporation-Management Edition (Prentice-Hall)

Corp. Mgt. Tax Conf. Corporate Management Tax Conference

Corp. Prac. Com. Corporate Practice Commentator

Corp. Prac. Comm. Corporate Practice Commentator

Corp. Prac. Comment. Corporate Practice Commentator

Corp. Prac. Rev. Corporate Practice Review

Corp. Prac. Ser. (BNA) Corporate Practice Series (Bureau of National Affairs)

Corp. Pract. Comment. Corporate Practice Commentator

Corp. Pract. Rev. Corporate Practice Review

Corp. Reorg. Corporate Reorganizations

Corp. Reorg. & Am. Bank. Rev. Corporate Reorganization & American Bankruptcy Review

Corp. Rep. Pennsylvania Corporation Reporter (Pa.)

Corp. Rep. (Pa.) Pennsylvania Corporation Reporter

Corp. Tr. Corporate trustee

corr.
- correspond
- correspondence
- correspondent
- corresponding

Correc. Correction

Cor. Soc. Cas. Coroner's Society Cases (Eng.)

Corvin. El. Corvinus' Elementa Juris Civilis

Corvin. Et. Corvinus Elementa Juris Civilis

Corv. Jus. Corvinus' Jus Feodale

Cory. Coryton's Reports (Calcutta)

Cory Acc. Cory on Accounts

Cory. Cop. Coryton on Copyrights

Cory. Pat. Coryton on Patents

Cory. St. R. Coryton on Stage Rights

Coryton Coryton's Reports, Calcutta High Court

Cos. Consul

Cosm. Cosmetic

Coss. Consules

Cost Acc'g. Stand. Guide Cost Accounting Standards Guide (CCH)

Cost Accounting Stand. Guide (CCH) Cost Accounting Standards Guide

Costa R. Costa Rica

C.O.T. Council on Tribunals

Cot. Court

Cot. Abr. Cotton's Abridgment of the Records

Co-T/Agt. Co-transfer agent

Coten. & Jt. O. Cotenancy and Joint Ownership

Coth. Stat. Cothran's Annotated Statutes of Illinois

Co-Tr. Co-trustee

Cott. Cottenham Reports, Chancery (1846-48) (Eng.)

Cott. Mss. Cottonian Manuscripts (British Museum)

Cou. Couper's Justiciary Reports (Sc.)

Coul. & F. Wat. Coulston & Forbes on Waters. 6ed. 1952

Coun. Council

Council Legal Educ. Prof. Resp. Newsl. Council on Legal Education for Professional Responsibility. Newsletter

couns. counsel

Counsellor. The Counsellor (New York City)

Couns. Mag. Counsellors' Magazine (1796-98)

Countcl. Counterclaim

Count. Cts. Ch. County Courts Chronicle (1847-1920) (London)

Count. Cts. Chron. County Courts Chronicle (1847-1920) (London)

Counterf. Counterfeiting

County Co. Cas. County Council Cases (Sc.)

County Court Pennsylvania County Court Reports (Pa.)

County Court R. Pennsylvania County Court Reports (Pa.)

County Court Rep. Pennsylvania County Court Reports (Pa.)

County Ct. County Court

County Cts. & Bankr. Cas. County Courts & Bankruptcy Cases

County Cts. Chron. County Courts Chronicle (1847-1920)

County Cts. Rep. County Courts Reports (1860-1919)

County J.Ct. County Judge's Court

County R. County Reports

Coup. Couper's Justiciary Reports (1868-85) (Sc.)

Couper Couper's Justiciary Reports (Sc.)

Coup. Just. Couper's Justiciary Reports (Sc.)

Cour. & Macl. Courtenay & Maclean's Scotch Appeals (6 & 7 Wilson & Shaw)

Court Bott's Poor Laws by Court

Court. & Macl. Courtnay & Maclean's Scotch Appeals (6 and 7 Wilson and Shaw)

Court Appeals Texas Court of Appeals Reports (Tex.)

Court Cl. United States Court of Claims Reports

Court J. & Dist. Ct. Rec. Court Journal and District Court Record

Court Mgt. J. Court Management Journal

Court R. Court Review

Court Sess. Ca. Court of Sessions Cases (Sc.)

Cout. Coutlee's Unreported Cases (Canada)

Cout. de N. Coutumes de Normandie

Cout. de P. Coutumes de Paris

Cout. Dig. Coutlee's Digest, Canada Supreme Court

Coutlea Coutlea's Supreme Court Cases

Coutlee Coutlee's Unreported Cases (1875-1907) (Can.)

Coutlee Unrep. (Can.) Coutlee's Unreported Cases

Cout. S.C. Notes of Unreported Cases, Supreme Court of Canada (Coutlee)

Cov. & H. Dig. Coventry Hughes,

Digest of the Common Law Reports

Cov. Conv. Ev. Coventry, Conveyancers' Evidence. 1832

Coven. Covenants

Cov. Mort. Conventry, Mortgage Precedents. 1827

Cov. Rec. Coventry, Common Recoveries. 1820.

Cow.
- Cowen's New York Reports
- Cowper's English King's Bench Reports

Cow. Att. Cowan on Warrants of Attachment

Cow. Cr. Cowen's Criminal Reports, New York

Cow. Cr. Dig. Cowen's Criminal Digest

Cow. Crim. (NY) Cowen's Criminal Reports

Cow. Cr. L. Cowen's New York Criminal Law

Cow. Cr. R. Cowen's Criminal Reports, New York

Cow. Cr. Rep. Cowen's Criminal Reports, New York

Cow. Dic. Cowell's Law Dictionary

Cow. Dict.
Cowell's Law Dictionary

Cow. Dig.
- Cowell's East India Digest
- Digest to Cowen's New York Reports

Cowd. L. Enc. Cowdery's Law Encyclopaedia (California)

Cowell.
- Cowell's Interpreter

- Cowell's Law Dictionary

Cow. Inst. Cowell's Institutiones Juris Anglicani

Cow. Int. Cowell's Interpreter

Cow. J.P. Cowen's New York Justice of the Peace

Cow. Just. Cowen's New York Justice of the Peace

Cow. L.R. Cowan's Land Rights in Scotland

Cow. N.Y. Cowen's New York Reports

Cowp. Cowper's English King's Bench Reports (1774-78)

Cowp. Cas. Cowper's Cases (in the third volume of Reports in Chancery)

Cowp. (Eng.) Cowper's English King's Bench Reports (1774-78)

Cowp. Ins. Cowperthwaite on Insanity in its Medico-Legal Relations

Cow. R. Cowen's Reports (N.Y.)

Cow. Tr. Cowen's New York Treatise on Justices of the Peace

Cox Cox's English Chancery Reports (1783-96)
- Cox's English Criminal Cases
- Cox's Reports (vols. 25-27 Arkansas)

Cox Adv. Cox, Advocate. 1852

Cox Am. T. Cas. Cox's American Trademark Cases

Cox Am. T.M. Cas. Cox's American Trade-Mark Cases

Cox Anc. L. Cox on the Law and Science of Ancient Lights

Cox & Atk. Cox & Atkinson's Registration Appeal Cases (1843-46)

(Eng.)

Cox & M'C. Cox, Macrae & Hertslet's County Court Cases (1847-57)

Cox & S.Cr. L. Cox & Saunders, Criminal Law Consolidation Acts. 3ed. 1870

Cox C.C.
- Cox's County Court Cases
- Cox's Crown Cases
- Cox's English Criminal Cases (1843-1948)

Cox Ch. Cox's English Chancery Cases

Cox Ch.Cas. (Eng.) Cox, Chancery Cases (29, 30 ER)

Cox, Ch. Pr. Cox, Chancey Practice

Cox C.L. Pr. Cox, Common Law Practice

Cox, Cr. Ca. Cox, English Criminal Cases

Cox Cr. Cas. Cox's English Criminal Cases

Cox Cr. Dig. Cox's Criminal Law Digest

Cox Crim. Cas. Cox's Criminal Cases

Cox Cty. Ct. Ca. Cox's County Court Cases (1860-1919) (Eng.)

Cox Cty. Ct. Cas. Cox's County Court Cases. (1860-1919)

Coxe
- Coxe (N.J.)
- Coxe's Reports (1 New Jersey Law)

Coxe Bract. Coxe's translation of Guterbach's Bracton

Cox Elect. Cox, Registration and

Elections. 14ed. 1885

Cox Eq. Cox's Equity Cases (Eng.)

Cox Eq. Cas. Cox's Equity Cases (Eng.)

Cox Gov. Cox's Institutions of the English Government

Cox Inst. Cox's Institutions of the English Government

Cox J.S. Cas. Cox's Joint Stock Cases

Cox J.S. Comp. Cox on Joint Stock Companies

Cox Jt. Stk. Cox's Joint Stock Co. Cases (1864-72) (Eng.)

Cox Mag. Ca. Cox's Magistrate Cases

Cox, M. & H. Cox, McCrae & Hertslet's English County Court Reports

Cox Man. Tr. M. Cox's Manual of Trade-Mark Cases

Cox M.C. Cox's Magistrates' Cases (1859-1919) (Eng.)

Cox, Mc. & H. Cox, McCrae & Hertslet's English County Court Reports (1847-58)

Cox, McC. & H. Cox, McCrae & Hertslet's English County Court Reports

Cox Pun. Cox, Principles of Punishment. 1877

Cox P.W. Cox's ed. of Peere Williams' Reports (Eng.)

Cox. Ques. Cox's Questions for the Use of Students

Cox Reg. Cox's Practice of Registration and Elections

Cox Tr. M. Cox's Manual of Trade Mark Cases

Cox Tr. M. Ca. Cox's American Trade Mark Cases

Cox Tr. M. Cas. Cox's American Trade-Mark Cases

CP Charging Party

C.P.
- Cape Province (S. Afr.)
- Central Provinces (Madhya Pradesh, India)
- Charter Party
- Civil Power
- Civil Procedure
- Civil Procedure Reports (New York)
- Clerk of the Peace
- Code of Practice
- Code of Procedure
- Common Pleas
- Convicted Poacher
- Court of Common Pleas
- Court of Probate
- Crown Pleas
- Law Reports, Common Pleas (Eng.)
- Upper Canada Common Pleas

Cp. Compare

C.P.A.
- Certified Public Accountant
- Civil Practice Act, New York

C.P.A.C. Consumer Protection Advisory Committee

CPAG Child Poverty Action Group

CPC Committee for Programme and Co-ordination

C.P.C.
- Carswell's Practice Cases 1976-
- Clerk of the Privy Council
- C. P. Cooper's English Chancery Practice Cases (1837-38)

C.P.Coop. C.P. Cooper's Chancery Practice Cases (1837-38) (47 ER)

C.P. Cooper Cooper's English Chancery Practice Cases (1837-38) (47 ER)

C.P.C. t. Br. C.P. Cooper's English Chancery Reports tempore Brougham

C.P.C. t. Cott. C.P. Cooper's English Chan-cery Reports tempore Cottenham

C.P.C.U. Chartered Property and Casualty Underwriter

C.P.D.
- Cape Provincial Division Report (S. Africa)
- Commissioner of the Public Debt
- Law Reports, Common Pleas Division (1875-80) (Eng.)
- South African Law Reports, Cape Provincial Division (S. Africa)

C.P. Div. Common Pleas Division, English Law Reports (1875-80)

C.P.Div. (Eng.) Common Pleas Division, English Law Reports (1875-80)

C.P.E. Common Professional Examination

C.P. (Eng.) Common Pleas Division, English Law Reports (1875-80)

CPEPBA Committee on Professional Education of The Philadelphia Bar Association

CPFF Cost-Plus-Fixed-Fee

CPI
- Consumer Price Index
- Court Practice Institute

CPIF Cost-Plus-Incentive-Fee

C.P. Ind. Central Provinces, India

C.P.L.
- Conveyancer and Property Lawyer (New Series) (Eng.)
- Current Property Lawyer (1852-53) (Eng.)

C.P.L.R.
- Central Provinces Law Reports (India)
- Civil Practice Law and Rules

CPM Critical Path Method

CPPC Cost-Plus-a-Percentage-of-Cost

C.P.Q. Code of Civil Procedure, Quebec (1897)

C.P.R.
- Canadian Pacific Railway Company
- Canadian Patent Reporter
- Ceiling Price Regulation

C. Pr. Code of Procedure

C.P.R. (2d) Canadian Patent Reports, Second Series

C.P.R.C. (N.S.) Civil Procedure Reports, New Series (N.Y.)

C.P. Rep. Common Pleas Reporter, Scranton, Pennsylvania

C.P. Rept. Common Pleas Reporter, Scranton, Pa.

C. Priv. Committee for Privileges, House of Commons Lords

C.P.R. (N.S.) Civil Procedure Reports, New Series (N.Y.)

CPS Act Consumer Product Safety Act

C.P.S.A.R. Commonwealth Public Service Arbitration Reports (Aus.)

CPSC Consumer Product Safety Commission

CPS Commission Consumer Product Safety Commission

C.P.U.C. Common Pleas Reports, Upper Canada

C.R.
- Canadian Reports, Appeal Cases
- Carolina Regina (Queen Caroline)
- Carolus Rex (King Charles)
- Central Reporter
- Chancery Reports tempore Car. I to Queen Anne
- Code Reporter
- Columbia Law Review
- Conveyancing Review (Sc.)
- Criminal Reports (Canada)
- Curia regis (King's Court)
- Custos Rotulorum (Keeper of the Rolls)

C.R. (3d) Criminal Reports (Canada), Third Series (Annotated)

Cr.
- Craig (Sir T.), Jus Feudale. 5 editions (1655-1934)
- Cranch's Reports, United States Supreme Court
- Cranch's United States Circuit Court Reports
- Credit
- Creditor
- Criminal
- Crown
- Texas Court of Appeals Reports
- Texas Criminal Reports

Cra. Cranch's United States Circuit Court Reports

Crab. Crabbe's United States District Court Reports

Crabb C.L. Crabb on the Common Law

Crabb, Com. Law Crabb on the Common Law

Crabb Conv. Crabb's Treatise on Conveyancing

Crabb Dig. Stat. Crabb's Digest of Statutes

Crabbe Crabbe's United States District Court Reports

Crabb, Eng. Crabb's English Synonyms

Crabb Eng. L. Crabb's History of the English Law

Crabb, Hist. Eng. Law Crabb's History of the English Law

Crabb Prec. Crabb's Precedents in Conveyancing

Crabb, Real Prop. Crabb on the Law of Real Property

Crabb R.P. Crabb on Real Property

Crabb, Technol. Dict. Crabb's Technological Dictionary

C.R.A.C. Canadian Reports, Appeal Cases (1828-1913)

C.R. [date] A.C. Canadian Appeal Cases

Cra.C.C. Cranch's United States Circuit Court Reports

Cr. Act. Criminal Act

Craig & P. Craig and Phillips' English Chancery Reports

Craig & Ph. Craig & Phillips Chancery (1840-41) (Eng.)

Craig & Ph. (Eng.) Craig & Phillips, Chancery

Craig. & St. Craigie, Stewart & Paton's Appeal Cases (1726-1821) (Sc.)

Craig, Dict. Craig's Etymological, Technological, and Pronouncing Dictionary

Craigius, Jus Feud. Craigius Jus Feudale 5th ed. 1934

Craig Jus. Feud. Craigius' Jus Feudale

Craig Pr. Craig's Practice

Craig. S. & P. Craigie, Stewart & Paton's Appeal Cases (Sc.)

Craig. St. & Pat.
- Craigie, Stewart, and Paton, Scotch Appeals Cases
- Craigie, Stewart & Paton's Appeal Cases (1726-1821) (Sc.)

Craig Tr. & W. Craig on Trees and Woods

Craik C.C. Craik's English Causes Celebres

Cran. Cranch (William) U.S. Supreme Court Reports

Cran.C.C.R. Cranch (William) Circuit Court Reports (D.C.)

Cranch
- Cranch's District of Columbia Reports (1-5 D.C.) (1801-40)
- Cranch's United States Supreme Court Reports (vols. 5-13 United States) (1801-40)

Cranch C.C.
- Cranch's Circuit Court Reports, United States
- District of Columbia Appeals Cases (vols. 1-5 United States Reports)
- District of Columbia Supreme Court Reports (1-5 D.C.) (1801-40)

Cranch C.C.Rep. Cranch (William) Circuit Court Reports (D.C.)

Cranch (C.Ct.) Cranch (William) Circuit Court Reports (D.C.)

Cranch D.C. Cranch's United States Circuit Court Reports, District of Columbia

Cranch Pat. Dec. Cranch's Patent Decisions (U.S.)

Cranch R. Cranch (William) Supreme Court Reports (U.S.)

Cranch Rep. Cranch (William) U.S. Supreme Court Reports

Cranch (US) Cranch's United States Supreme Court Reports (vols. 5-13 United States Reports)

Cr. & Dix. Crawford & Dix's Irish Circuit Court Cases (1839-46)

Cr. & Dix Ab.Ca. Crawford and Dix's Abridged Cases (1837-38)

Cr. & Dix Ab.Cas. Crawford and Dix's Irish Abridged Cases (1837-38)

Cr. & Dix C.C. Crawford and Dix's Irish Circuit Court Cases

Cr. & J. Crompton & Jervis (1830-32)

Cr. & M. Crompton & Meeson's English Exchequer Reports (1832-34)

Cr. & Ph. Craig & Phillips' English Chancery, Reports (1840-41)

Cr. & St. Craigie, Stewart, & Paton's Scotch Appeal Cases

Crane Crane's Reports (vols. 22-29 Montana)

Crane. C.C. Cranenburgh's Criminal Cases (India)

Cran. Rep. Cranch (William) U.S. Supreme Court Reports

Cra. N.Y. Pr. Crary's New York

Practice, Special Pleading

Cr. App. Criminal Appeals

Cr. App. R. Criminal Appeal Reports

Cr. App. Rep. Criminal Appeal Reports

Cr. App. R. (S.) The Criminal Appeal Reports (Sentencing)

Crar. Pr. Crary's New York Practice (Special Pleading)

Craw. Crawford's Reports (vols. 53-69, 72-101 Arkansas Reports)

Craw. & D. Crawford & Dix, Circuit Court Cases (Ir.)

Craw. & D. Ab. Cas. Crawford & Dix's Abridged Cases (Ir.)

Craw. & D. Abr. Cas. Crawford & Dix's Abridged Cases (Ir.)

Craw. & D.C.C. (Ir.) Crawford & Dix Circuit Cases (Ir.)

Craw. & D. (Ir.) Crawford & Dix (Abridged Cases) (Ir.)

Craw. & Dix Crawford & Dix's Circuit Cases (Ir.)

Craw (Ark) Crawford's Reports (vols. 53-69, 72-101 Arkansas Reports)

Craw Co.Leg.J. (Pa.) Crawford County Legal Journal (Pa.)

Crawf. & D. Crawford & Dix's Circuit Court Cases (Ir.)

Crawf. & D. Abr. Cas. Crawford & Dix's Abridged Cases (Ir.)

Crawf. & Dix
- Crawford & Dix Circuit Cases (Ir.)
- Crawford & Dix Criminal Cases (Ir.)

Crawford Co. Leg. Jour. Crawford County Legal Journal (Pa.)

CRB Murphy, Creditors' Rights in Bankruptcy

C.R.C.
- California Railroad Commission Decisions
- Canadian Railway Cases

Cr. C.A. Crown Circuit Assistant

Cr. Cas. Res. Crown Cases Reserved

Cr. C.C. Cranch's United States Circuit Court Cases (Reports)

Cr. C.C. Rep. Cranch (William) Circuit Court Reports (D.C.)

Cr. Cir. Comp. Crown Circuit Companion, Irish

C.R.-C.L. Civil Rights-Civil Liberties

CRCL Nahmod, Civil rights and Civil Liberties Litigation

CRCL(3) Nahmod, Civil Rights and Civil Liberties Litigation, Third Series

Cr. Code. Criminal Code

Cr. Code Prac. Criminal Code of Practice

CRD Customs Rules Decisions

C.R.E. Commission for Racial Equality

Creas. Col. Const. Creasy's Colonial Constitutions

Creas. Eng. Cons. Creasy's Rise and Progress of the English Constitution

Creas. Int. L. Creasy on International Law

Creasy. Creasy's Ceylon Reports

Cred. B. Creditors' Bill

CREF Saft, Commercial Real Estate Forms

Creighton L. Rev. Creighton Law Review

CREL Saft, Commercial Real Estate Leasing

Cress. Cresswell's Insolvency Cases (1827-29) (Eng.)

Cress. Ins. Ca. Cresswell's English Insolvency Cases

Cress. Ins. Cas. Cresswell's Insolvency Cases (1827-29) (Eng.)

Cress. Insolv. Cas. Cresswell's Insolvency Cases (1827-29) (Eng.)

CRET Saft, Commercial Real Estate Transactions

CREW Saft, Commercial Real Estate Workouts

Crim. Criminal

Crim. & Delin. Crime and Delinquency

Crim. & Soc. Just. Crime and Social Justice

Crim. App.
- Court of Criminal Appeals
- Criminal Appeal Reports (Eng.)

Crim. App. (Eng.) Criminal Appeal Reports (Eng.)

Crim. App. R. Criminal Appeal Reports

Crim. App. Rep. Cohen's Criminal Appeals Reports (Eng.)

Crim. Case & Com. Criminal Case and Comment

Crim. Code Criminal Code

crim. con.
- criminal conspiracy
- criminal conversation

- criminal conversion

Crim. Def. Criminal Defense

Crime & Del. Crime and Delinquency

Crime & Delin. Crime & Delinquency

Crime & Delin'cy Crime & Delinquency

Crime & Delin'cy Abst. Crime and Delinquency Abstracts

Crime & Delin'cy Lit. Crime and Delinquency Literature

Crime & Delinq. Crime and Delinquency

Crime & Just. Crime and Justice

Crime & Soc. Just. Crime and Social Justice

Criminal L. Mag. & Rep. Criminal Law Magazine and Reporter

Criminal L.Q. Criminal Law Quarterly

Crim. Inj. Comp. Bd. Criminal Injuries Compensation Board

Criminol.
- Criminologist
- Criminology

Crim. J.J. Criminal Justice Journal

Crim. Just. Criminal Justice

Crim. Just. & Behavior Criminal Justice and Behavior

Crim. Just. Ethics Criminal Justice Ethics

Crim. Just. J. Criminal Justice Journal

Crim. Just. Newsl. Criminal Justice Newsletter

Crim. Just. Q. Criminal Justice

Quarterly

Crim. Just. Rev. Criminal Justice Review

Crim. Law Criminal Law

Crim. Law Reps. (Green) Criminal Law Reports (U.S.)

Crim. Law Rev.Cttee. Criminal Law Revision Committee

Crim. L. Bull. Criminal Law Bulletin

Crim. L.F. Criminal Law Forum

Crim. L.J. Criminal Law Journal

Crim. L.J. I. Criminal Law Journal of India

Crim. L.J. Ind. Criminal Law Journal of India

Crim. L.J. (Sydney) Criminal Law Journal, Sydney, Australia

Crim. L. Mag. Criminal Law Magazine (Jersey City, N.J.)

Crim. L. Mag. & Rep. Criminal Law Magazine and Reporter

Crim. L.Q. Criminal Law Quarterly

Crim. L.R. Criminal Law Review

Crim. L.R.C. Criminal Law Revision Committee

Crim. L. Rec. Criminal Law Recorder (1804-09, 1815)

Crim. L. Rep.
- Criminal Law Reporter (BNA)
- Criminal Law Reporter (CCH)

Crim. L. Rev. Criminal Law Review

Crim.L.Rev. (England) Criminal Law Review, London, England

Crim. L. Rptr.
- Criminal Law Reporter

- Criminal Law Reporter (1911-23) (India)

Crim. Prac. L. Rev. Criminal Practice Law Review

Crim. Pro. Criminal Procedure

Crim. Proc. Criminal Procedure

Crim. R. (Can.) Criminal Reports

Crim. Rec.
- Criminal Recorder, London (1804-09) (1815)
- Criminal Recorder, Philadelphia
- Criminal Recorder (1 Wheeler's New Criminal Reports)

Crim. Rep. Criminal Reports

Crim. Rep. (N.S.) Criminal Reports, New Series

Cripp Ch. Cas. Cripp's Church and Clergy Cases

Cripp Ch.L. (or Ecc.L.)
- Cripp's Church Law
- Cripps, Law Relating to Church and Clergy. 8ed. 1937

Cripp Comp. Cripps, Compulsory Acquisition of Land. 11ed. 1962

Cripps Cripps' Church & Clergy Cases (1847-50) (Eng.)

Cripps Cas. Cripps' Church and Clergy Cases (1847-50)

Cripp's Ch. Cas. Cripp's Church and Clergy Cases (1847-50)

Cripps Church Cas. Cripps' Church and Clergy Cases (1847-50)

Crit. criticized in or criticizing

Critch. Critchfield's Reports (vols. 5-21 Ohio State)

Critch (Ohio St.) Critchfield's Reports (vols. 5-21 Ohio State)

Cr. Just. Criminal Justice

Cr.L. The Criminal Lawyer (India)

Cr. Law Mag. Criminal Law Magazine (N.J.)

Cr. Law Rec. Criminal Law Recorder

Cr. Law Rep. Criminal Law Reporter

Cr. L.J. Criminal Law Journal (India)

Cr. L. Mag. Criminal Law Magazine

Cr.L.R. Criminal Law Reporter (India)

Cr. M. & R. Crompton. Meeson & Roscoe's English Exchequer Reports (1834-36)

C.R.N.S.
- Code Reports, New Series, New York
- Criminal Reports (Canada) New Series

Cro.
- Croke, English King's Bench Reports (1582-1641)
- Keilway, English King's Bench Reports (1496-1531)

C.Rob. Christopher Robinson's English Admiralty Reports (165 ER)

C.Rob. Adm. Christopher Robinson's English Admiralty Reports

C.Rob. (Eng.) Christopher Robinson's English Admiralty Reports (165 ER)

Cro. Car. Croke's English King's Bench Reports tempore Charles I, 3 Cro. (79 ER)

Cro. Car. (Eng.) Croke's English King's Bench Reports tempore Charles I, 3 Cro. (79 ER)

Cro. Cas. Croke's English King's Bench Reports tempore Charles I, 3 Cro. (79 ER)

Crock. Cor. Crocker on the Duties of Coroners in New York

Crockford. English Maritime Law Reports, published by Crockford (1860-71)

Crock. Forms Crocker's Notes on Common Forms (Massachusetts)

Crock. Notes Crocker's Notes on the Public Statutes of Massachusetts

Crock. Sh. Crocker on Sheriffs and Constables

Cro. Eliz. Croke's English King's Bench Reports tempore Elizabeth, I Cro. (78 ER)

Cro. Eliz. (Eng.) Croke's English King's Bench Reports tempore Elizabeth, 1 Cro. (78 Er)

Cro. Jac. Croke's Reports tempore James (Jacobus), English (79 ER)

Cro. Jac. (Eng.) Croke's Reports tempore James (Jacobus), English (79 ER)

Croke
- Croke's King's Bench Reports (1582-1641) (Eng.)
- Keilway's King's Bench Reports (1496-1531) (72 ER)

Crom. Crompton's Office of a Justice of the Peace (1637)

Cromp. Star Chamber Cases by Crompton

Cromp. & F. Fitzherbert's Justice, enlarged by Crompton

Cromp. & J. Crompton & Jervis English Exchequer Reports (148, 149 ER)

Cromp. & J. (Eng.) Crompton & Jervis English Exchequer Reports (148, 149 ER)

Cromp. & Jer. Crompton and Jervis's Exchequer Reports (1830-32)

Cromp. & Jerv. Crompton & Jervis, English Exchequer Reports (1830-32)

Cromp. & M. Crompton & Meeson's English Exchequer Reports (149 ER)

Cromp. & Mees. Crompton & Meeson's English Exchequer Reports (1832-34) (149 ER)

Cromp. & M. (Eng.) Crompton & Meeson's English Exchequer Reports (149 ER)

Cromp. Cts. Crompton's jurisdiction of Courts

Cromp. Exch. R. Crompton's Exchequer Reports (Eng.)

Cromp. Ex. R. Crompton's Exchequer Reports, Eng.

Cromp. J.C. Crompton's Jurisdiction of Courts

Cromp. Jur. Crompton's Jurisdiction of Courts

Cromp. Just. Crompton's Office of Justice of the Peace

Cromp. M. & R. Crompton, Meeson & Roscoe, Exchequer, (149, 150 ER)

Cromp. M. & R. (Eng.) Crompton, Meeson & Roscoe, Exchequer, England (149, 150 ER)

Cromp. R. & C.Pr. Crompton's Rules and Cases of Practice

Crompt. Star Chamber Cases by Cromn

Cross-cl. Cross-claim

Cross Lien Cross, Lien and Stoppage in Transitu. 1840

Cros. Wills Crosley, Wills. 1828

Crosw. Pat. Ca. Croswell's Collection of Patent Cases, United States

Crosw. Pat. Cas. Croswell's Collection of Patent Cases, United States

Crounse. Crounse's Reports (vol. 3 Nebraska Reports)

Crow. Crowther's Reports (Ceylon)

Crown C.C. Crown Circuit Companion

Crown L.C. Crown Land Cases (Aus.)

Crowth. Crowther's Ceylon Reports

Crowther. Crowther's Ceylon Reports

C.R.P. Calendarium Rotulorum Patentium

Cr.P. Criminal Procedure

Cr. Pat. Dec. Cranch's Decisions on Patent Appeals

Cr. Prac. Criminal Practice

Cr. Prac. Act. Criminal Practice Act

Cr. Proc. Criminal Procedure

Cr. Proc. Act. Criminal Procedure Act

CRR Corporate Reorganization Reporter, Inc.

C.R.R. Chief Registrar's Reports (Fr. Soc.) (Eng.)

Cr.R.
- The Criminal Reports (India)
- Curia Regis Roll

Cr. Rep. Criminal Reports (Can.)

Cr. Rg. Criminal Rulings, Bombay (India)

C.R.S.
- Community Relations Service
- Congressional Research Service

Cr.S. & P. Craigie, Stewart and Paton's Scottish Appeal Cases (1726-1821)

Cr. St. Criminal Statutes

C.R.T.C. Canadian Railway & Transport Cases

Cru. Cruise's Digest (1804-35) (Eng.)

Cru. Dig. Cruise, Digest of Law of Real Property

Cru. Dign. Cruise on Dignities

Cru.Fin. Cruise's Fines and Recoveries

Cruise Dig. Cruise's Digest of the Law of Real Property

Cruise's Dig. Cruise's Digest of the Law of Real Property

Crump Ins. Crump on Marine Insurance

Crump Jud. Pr. Crump, Practice under the Judicature Acts

Crump Mar. Ins. Crump on Marine Insurance

Crump S. & Pl. Crump, Sale and Pledge.

Crumrine
- Crumrine's Reports (vols. 116-146 Pennsylvania)
- Pittsburgh Reports, edited by Crumrine

Cru. Titl. Cruise on Titles of Honor

Cru. Us. Cruise on Uses

C.S.
- Camden Society
- Civil Servant
- Civil Service
- Clerk of Session
- Clerk to the Signet (Scot.)
- Common Serjeant
- Compiled Statutes
- Connecticut Supplement
- Consolidated Statutes
- Court of Session, Scotland
- Custos Sigilli (Keeper of the Seal)
- Quebec Reports, Supreme Court

CSA Community Services Administration

C.S.A.A. Civil Service Arbitration Awards

C.S.A.B.
- Civil Service Arbitration Awards
- Contract Settlement Appeal Board (U.S.)

C.S. & J. Cushing, Storey & Joselyn's Election Cases (Mass.)

C.S. & P. Craigie, Stewart & Paton's Scotch Appeal Cases (1726-1821)

C.S.B.C. Consolidated Statutes, British Columbia

C.S.C.
- Canada Supreme Court
- Civil Service Commission (United States)
- Consolidated Statutes of Canada
- Court of Sessions Cases (Scotland)

C.S.C.R. Cincinnati Superior

Court Reporter

C.S.D.   Civil Service Department

C.Sess.   Court of Session (Sc.)

C.S.I.   Decisions of the Commissioners under the National Insurance (Industrial Injuries) Acts, relating to Scotland

CSJAG   Opinion of Judge Advocate General, U.S. Army

CSJAGA   Military Affairs Division, Judge Advocate of U.S. Army

CSJAGE   Assistant Judge Advocate General for Procurement (Army); Contract Division Office of Judge Advocate General of Army

C.S.L.C.   Consolidated Statutes of Lower Canada

C.S.L.R.   Cleveland State Law Review

C.S.M.   Consolidated Statutes of Manitoba

C.S.N.B.   Consolidated Statutes of New Brunswick

C.S.O.   Central Statistical Office

C. Sol   Complete Solicitor

C.S.P.R.U.   Civil Service Pay Research Unit

CSRS   Cooperative State Research Service

CSS   Commodity Stabilization Service

C.S. Supp.   Supplement to the Compiled Statutes

C.S.T.
- Capital Stock Tax Ruling, Internal Revenue Bureau (U.S.)
- Commerce, Science, and Transportation

C.S.U.C.   Consolidated Statutes, Upper Canada

CSULA   California State University, Los Angeles

C.S.V.S.   Chartered Surveyors Voluntary Service

C.T.
- Cape Times
- Carrier's Tax
- Carriers Taxing Ruling (I.R. Bull)
- Constitutiones Tiberii
- Corporation Tax
- Council on Tribunals
- Court Trust (includes executor, administrator, guardian)

Ct.
- Connecticut
- Connecticut Reports
- Court

CT   O'Hara, Durst, Griffith & Shurtz, Corporate Taxation

C.T.A.   Cum testamento annexo (with will annexed)

Ct. App.   Court of Appeal[s] (state)

Ct. App.C.C.
- Texas Civil Cases (Tex.)
- Texas Court of Appeals Reports (Tex.)

Ct. App. N.Z.   Court of Appeals Reports (New Zealand)

Ct. Apps.   Texas Court of Appeals Reports (Tex.)

C. Tax C.   Canadian Tax Cases

C.T.B.R. (N.S.)   Taxation Board of Review Decisions, New Series (Aus.)

CTC   Canadian Transport Commission

C.T.C. Canada Tax Cases

Ct. Cl. United States Court of Claims Reports

Ct. Cl. Act. Court of Claims Act

Ct. Cl. N.Y. Court of Claims Reports (N.Y.)

Ct. Cl. R. Court of Claims Rules

C.T.C.L.R. Cape Times Common Law Reports (S. Africa)

Ct. Cls. U.S. Court of Claims

Ct Cl Tr Div Court of Claims Trial Division

Ct. Com. Pl. Court of Common Pleas

Ct. Com. Pleas Court of Common Pleas

Ct. Crim. App. Court of Criminal Appeal (Eng.)

Ct. Cust. & Pat. App. Court of Customs & Patent Appeals

Ct. Cust. App.
• Court of Customs Appeals

Court of Customs Appeals Reports (1919-29)

Ct. D. Court Decisions the National Labor Relations Act

Ct. Dec. N.L.R.A. Court Decisions Relating to the National Labor Relations Act

Ct. Err. Court of Error

Ct. Err. & App. Court of Errors and Appeals

Ct. Errors and App. Court of Errors and Appeals (New Jersey)

Ctf. Certificate

Ct. Gen. Ses. Court of General Sessions

Ct. Gen. Sess. Court of General Sessions

Ct. [Gen., Spec.] Sess. Court of [General, Special] Sessions

CTHF Stein, Cable Television: Handbook and Forms

C.Theod. Codex Theodosiani

Ct. Int'l Trade Court of International Trade

Ct. Just. Court of Justiciary

C. t. K. Cases tempore King (Macnaghten's Select English Chancery Cases)

CTL Soma, Computer Technology and the Law

C.T. L.J. California Trial Lawyers Journal

Ct. Mgmt. J. Court Management Journal

Ct Mil App United States Court of Military Appeals

Ct Mil App Rule Revised Rules of the United States Court of Military Appeals

C. t. N. Cases tempore Northington (Eden's English Chancery Reports).

Ct/O. Court Order

Ct. of App. Court of Appeals

Ct. of Cls. U.S. Court of Claims

Ct. of Com. Pleas Court of Common Pleas

Ct. of Er. and Appeals Court of Errors and Appeals, New Jersey

Ct. of Sess.
• Court of Session
• Session Cases

Ct. of Sp.App. Court of Special

Appeals

Ctr. Center

C.T.R. Cape Times Supreme Court Reports, Cape of Good Hope (S. Africa)

C.Tr. Corporate trust

Ct. Rep. N.Z. Court of Appeals Reports (New Zealand)

Ct. Rev. Court Review

C.T.S. Consolidated Treaty Series

Cts. & Jud. Proc. Courts and Judicial Proceedings

Ct. Sess. Court of Sessions, Scotch

Ct. Sess. Cas. Court of Session Cases (Sc.)

Ct. Sess. 1st Ser. Scotch Court of Sessions Cases, 1st Series

Ct. Spec. Sess. Court of Special Sessions

C.T.T. Capital Transfer Tax

C.t.T. Cases tempore Talbot, English Chancery.

Cty.
- Counties
- County

Cty. Ct. County Court

Cty. Ct. Chron. County Courts Chronicle (1847-1920)

Cty. Ct. R. County Courts Reports (1860-1920)

C.U. California Unreported Cases

C.U.A. L.R. Catholic University of America Law Review

CUALS Catholic University of America Law School

Cu.Ct. Customs Court Reports

Cudd. Copyh. Cudden on the

Copyhold Acts

Cujacius Cujacius, Opera, quae de Jure feeit, etc.

C.U.L. Cambridge University Library

Cul. Culpabilis (guilty)

Cull. B.L. Cullen's Bankrupt Law

Culp Kulp, Luzerne Legal Register Reports (Pa.)

C.U. L.R. Catholic University Law Review

Cum.
- Cumberland
- Cumulative

Cum. & Dun. Rem. Tr. Cummins & Dunphy's Remarkable Trials

Cumb. Cumberland Law Journal (Pa.)

Cumberland L.J. (Pa.) Cumberland Law Journal

Cumberland L. Rev. Cumberland Law Review

Cumberland-Samford Cumberland-Samford Law Review

Cumberland-Samford L.Rev. Cumberland-Samford Law Review

Cumb. Law Jrnl. Cumberland Law Journal (Pa.)

Cumb. L. Rev. Cumberland Law Review

Cumb. Nat. Cumberland's Law of Nature

Cumb.-Sam. L. Rev. Cumberland-Samford Law Review

Cum. Bull. Cumulative Bulletin, Internal Revenue Bureau, Treasury Department

Cum. Civ. L. Cummuns' Manual

of Civil Law

Cum. L. Rev. Cumberland Law Review

Cummins Cummins' Reports (Idaho 1866-67)

Cum. P.P. Cumulative Pocket Parts

Cum.-Sam. Cumberland-Samford Law Review

Cum. Sam. L. Rev. Cumberland-Samford Law Review

Cum. Supp. Cumulative Supplement

Cun. Cunningham's English King's Bench Reports

Cun. Bill. Exch. Cunningham's Law of Notes and Bills of Exchange

Cun. Bills Cuningham's Bills, Notes, and Insurances

Cun. Dict. Cunningham's Dictionary

Cun. Hind. L. Cunningham on Hindu Law

Cun. L.D. Cunningham's Law Dictionary

Cunn. Cunningham King's Bench (1734-36) (Eng.)

Cunningham Cunningham's Reports, English King's Bench

Cunningham (Eng.) Cunningham's Reports, English King's Bench

Cun. Pl. Cunningham's Maxims and Rules of Pleading

Cun. Sim. Cunningham on Simony

CUR Curia (court)

C.U.R. University of Colorado Law Review

Cur.
- Curia
- Curtis' United States Circuit Court Reports

Cur. Ab. Tit. Curwen's Abstract of Titles

Cur. adv. vult Curia advisare vult

Cur. Bl. Curry's Abridgment of Blackstone

Cur. Com. Current Comment & Legal Miscellany

Cur. Cr. Proc. Indian Code of Criminal Procedure, Curries' Edition

Cur. Dec. Curtis' Decisions, United States Supreme Court

Cur. I.C. Current Indian Cases (1912-15)

Cur. Ind. Cas. Current Indian Cases (1912-15)

Cur. Leg. Bibliog. Current Legal Bibliography

Cur. Leg. Prob. Current Legal Problems

Cur. Leg. Thought Current Legal Thought

Cur. L.R. Current Law Reports (Ceylon)

Cur. Mun. Prob. Current Municipal Problems

Cur. Ov. Ca. Curwen, Overruled Cases (Ohio)

Cur. Phil. Curia Phillippica

Cur. Prop. L. Current Property Law

Cur. Reg. R. Curia Regis Rolls (Eng.)

Current Com. & Leg. Mis. Current Comment and Legal Miscellany

Current Ct. Dec. Current Court Decisions

Current L. Current Law

Current L. & Soc. Prob. Current Law and Social Problems. Toronto, Canada

Current Legal Prob. Current Legal Problems

Current Leg. Bibliog. Current Legal Bibliography

Current Leg. Prob. Current Legal Problems

Current L.Y. Current Law Yearbook

Current L. Y.B. Current Law Yearbook

Current Med. Current Medicine for Attorneys

Current Med. for Att'ys Current Medicine for Attorneys

Current Prop. L. Current Property Law

Curr. Indian. Stat. Current Indian Statutes

Curr. Legal Prob. Current Legal Problems

Curr. Leg. Probl. Current Legal Problems. London

Curr. L. Y.B. Current Law Year Book

Curry. Curry's Reports (6-19 Louisiana)

Cur. Scacc. Cursus Scaccarii

Curs. Can. Cursus Cancellariae

Cur. Stat. Curwen's Ohio Statutes

Curt.
- Curteis' Ecclesiastical Reports (1834-44) (Eng.)
- Curtis' Circuit Court Reports, United States
- Curtis' Edition, U.S. Supreme Court Reports

Curt. Adm. Dig. Curtis' Admiralty Digest

Curt. C.C. Curtis' United States Circuit Court Decisions

Curt. Cond.
- Curtis' (Condensed) Decisions, United States Supreme Court
- Curtis' Edition, U.S. Supreme Court Reports

Curt. Cond. Rep. Curtis, Decisions of the U.S. Supreme Court

Curt. Conv. Curtis' American Conveyancer

Curt. Cop. Curtis, Copyright. 1847

Curt. Dec. Curtis' United States Supreme Court Decisions

Curt. Dig. Curtis' Digest, United States

Curt. Ecc. Curteis' English Ecclesiastical Reports (163 ER)

Curt. Eccl. Curteis' English Ecclesiastical Reports (163 ER)

Curt. Eccl. (Eng.) Curteis' English Ecclesiastical Reports (163 ER)

Curt. Eq. Pr. Curtis' Equity Precedents

Curtis
- Curtis' Circuit Court Reports (U.S.)
- Curtis' Edition, U.S. Supreme Court Reports

Curtis C.C. Curtis' U.S. Circuit Court Reports

Curtis S.C. Reports Curtis, Decisions of the U.S. Supreme Court

Curtis' U.S. Sup. Ct. R. Curtis, Decisions of the U.S. Supreme Court

Curt. Jur. Curtis on the Jurisdiction of United States Courts

Curt. Mer. Sea. Curtis' Rights and Duties of Merchant Seaman

Curt. Pat. Curtis on Patents

Curt. U.S. Const. Curtis' History of the Constitution of the United States Courts

Curt. U.S. Courts Curtis' Commentaries on the United States Courts

Curw.
- Curwen's Overruled Cases
- Curwen's Statutes of Ohio

Curw. Abs. Tit. Curwen on Abstracts of Title

Curw. L.O Curwen's Laws of Ohio 1854, 1 vol.

Curw. Ov. Cas. Curwen's Overruled Ohio Cases

Curw. R.S. Curwen's Revised Statutes of Ohio

Cus. & Us. Customs and Usages

Cush.
- Cushing's Massachusetts Supreme Judicial Court Reports (1848-53) (vols. 55-66 Massachusetts Reports)
- Cushman, Mississippi Reports (vols. 23-29 Mississippi)

Cush. Elec. Cas. Cushing's Election Cases in Massachusetts

Cushing. Cushing's Reports (55-66 Massachusetts)

Cush. Law & Prac. Leg. Assem. Cushing's Law and Practice of Legislative Assemblies

Cush. Leg. Ass. Cushing's Law and Practice of Legislative Assemblies

Cushm. Cushman's Reports (vols. 23-29 Mississippi)

Cush. Man. Cushing's Manual of Parliamentary Law

Cushman
- Cushman's Mississippi Reports
- Cushman's Rep. (23-29 Miss)

Cush. (Mass.) Cushing's Reports (vols. 55-66 Massachusetts)

Cush. Parl. Law. Cushing's Law and Practice of Legislative Assemblies

Cush. Rom. Law Cushing's Study of the Roman Law

Cush. Trust. Pr. Cushing on Trustee Process

Cust. Custody

Cust. A. United States Customs Appeals

Cust & Pat App Rule Rules of the United States Court of Dustoms and Patent Appeals

Cust. & Pat. App. (Cust.)(F) Customs And Patent Appeals Reports (Customs)

Cust. & Pat. App. (Pat.XF) Customs and Patent Appeals Reports (Patents)

Cust. App. United States Customs Appeals

Cust. B. & Dec. Customs Bulletin

and Decisions

Cust. Bull. Customs Bulletin

Cust. Ct. Custom Court Reports (U.S.)

Cust. Ct. R. Customs Court Rules (Rules of the United States Customs Court)

Cust. D. Customs Duties and Import Regulations

Customs United States Customs Service

Cust. Per. Dec. Customs Penalty Decisions

Cust. Rep. Custer's Ecclesiastical Reports

Cut. Indian Law Reports. Orissa

Cut. Ins. L. Cutler's Insolvent Laws of Massachusetts

Cut. Leg. Sys. Cutler's Legal System of the English, the Hindoos, & c.

Cutler Reports of Patent Cases (1884)

Cut. L.T. Cuttack Law Times (Orissa, India)

Cut. Nat. Cutler on Naturalization Laws

Cut. Pat. Cas. Cutler's Trademark & Patent Cases

Cut. Sett. Cutler on Settlements

Cutt. L.T. Cuttack Law Times (India)

C.V. Constitution of Virginia

C.Vict. Dominion of Canada Statutes in the Reign of Victoria

CWA
- Clean Water Act
- Communications Workers of America

C.W.Dud. C.W. Dudley's Law or Equity Reports, South Carolina

C.W.Dud. Eq. C.W. Dudley's Equity Reports, South Carolina

C.W.Dudl. Eq. C.W. Dudley's Equity (S.C.)

C.W.H. Committee of the Whole House, House of Lords

C.W.I. Decisions of the Commissioners under the National Insurance (Industrial Injuries) Acts relating to Wales (Eng.)

C.W.L. Case Western Reserve Law Review (Ohio)

C.W. L.R. California Western Law Review

Cwlth. Record Commonwealth Record (Aus.)

C.W.N. Calcutta Weekly Notes (India)

CWU Congress of World Unity

Cy. Connoly's Surrogate's Court Reports (N.Y)

C.Y.C. Cyclopedia of Law and Procedure, New York

Cyc. Cyclopedia of Law & Procedure

Cyc. Ann. Cyclopedia of Law & Procedure Annotations

Cyc. Corp. Fletcher's Cyclopedia of Corporations

Cyc. Dict. Cyclopedia Law Dictionary

Cyc. Law & Proc. Cyclopedia of Law and Procedure

Cyclop. Dict. Shumaker & Longsdorf's Cyclopedic Dictionary

Cyprus L.R.   Cyprus Law Reports

C.Z.   Canal Zone

C.Z.C.   Canal Zone Code

C.Z. Code   Canal Zone Code

Czech.   Czechoslovakia

Czech. J. Int'l L.   Czechoslovak Journal of International Law

Czech. Y.B. Int'l L.   Czechoslovak Yearbook of International Law

CZO   Canal Zone Order

C.Z. Rep.   Canal Zone Reports, Supreme and District Courts

D

D.
- Application for writ of error dismissed for want of jurisdiction
- Court of Divorce and Matrimonial Causes (Eng.)
- Dallas' Pa. Reports 1754-1806
- Dallas' United States Supreme Court Reports (1-4 US) (1790-1800)
- Dallas' U.S. & Pennsylvania Reports
- Davis
- Decree
- Delaware Reports
- Democrat
- Denied
- Denio' Reports (New York)
- Denison's Crown Cases (1844-52) (Eng.)
- Dicta
- Dictionary (particularly Morison's Dictionary of Scotch Session Cases)
- Dictum
- Digest (Justinian's)
- Dismissed: appeal from the same case dismissed
- Disney's Ohio Superior Court Reports
- District Court (federal)
- Dixbury
- Doctor
- Dowling. See Dow
- Duke
- Dunlop, Bell, & Murray, Reports Scotch Session Cases, Second Series (1838-62)
- Dutch
- Duxbury's Reports of the High Court of the South African Republic
- Dyer, ed.Valiant. King's Bench Reports (1513-82) (Eng.)

d
- deceased
- decree
- degree
- delete
- distinguished: case at bar different either in law or fact from case cited for reasons given (used in Shepard's Citations)

D.A.
- Defence Act
- Deputy Advocate
- District Attorney

D/A Documents against acceptance

Da.
- Dakota
- Dakota Territory Reports
- Danish

d/a
- days after acceptance
- documents against acceptance

Da. & Bos. Darby & Bosanquet, Statutes of Limitation. 2ed. 1893

D.Abr.
- D'Anvers' Abridgment
- D'Anvers' General Abridgment of the Common Law. 2ed. 1725-37

DAC Development Assistance Committee (OECD)

D.A.C. Defense Acquisition Circular

Dacca
- All India Reporter, Dacca Series (1949-50)
- Pakistan Law Reports, Dacca Series.

D.A.D. Deputy Assistant Director

Dady. Dadyburjar, Small Court Appeals (India)

Dag. Cr. L. Dagge's Criminal Law

Dag. Ct. M. D'Aguilar on Courts-Martial

Dahl. Mar. Int. L. Dahlgren's Maritime International Law

Daily Leg. News (Pa.) Daily Legal News

Daily Leg. (Pa.) Daily Legal Record (Pennsylvania)

Daily L.N. Daily Legal News (Pa.)

Daily L.R. Daily Legal Record (Pa.)

Daily Trans. New York Daily Transcript, Old and New Series

Daily Transc. New York Daily Transcript (N.Y.)

Dai. Reg. New York Daily Register

D.A. J.A.G. Deputy Assistant Judge Advocate General

Dak.
- Dakota
- Dakota Territory Reports

Dak. Law Rev. Dakota Law Review

Dak. L. Rev. Dakota Law Review

Dakota Dakota Reports (Dak.)

Dal.
- Benloe and Dalison's Common Pleas Reports (1486-1580) (Eng.)
- Dalison's Common Pleas Reports (Eng.)
- Dallas' Pennsylvania Reports (1754-1806)
- Dallas' United States Reports (1-4 U.S.)
- Dalrymple's Session Cases (Sc.)
- Daly's Reports (New York)

D. Alaska United States District Court for the District of Alaska

DALBA Dallas Bar Association

D.A.L.C. Danquah, Akan Laws and Customs (Ghana)

Dal. Coop. Dallas' Report of Cooper's Opinion on the Sentence of a Foreign Court of Admiralty

Dal. C.P. Dalison's Common Pleas (Eng.)

Dale
- Dale's Judgments (1868-71) (Eng.)
- Dale's Reports (2-4 Oklahoma)

Dale Cl. H.B. Dale's Clergyman's Legal Handbook

Dale Ecc. Dale's Ecclesiastical Reports (Eng.)

Dale Eccl. Dale's Ecclesiastical Reports (Eng.)

Dale Leg.Rit. Dale's Legal Ritual (Ecclesiastical Reports (1868-71) (Eng.)

Dale Par. Ch. Dale, Law of the Parish Church. 5ed. 1975

Dalhousie L.J. Dalhousie Law Journal

Dal. in Keil. Dalison's Reports in Keilway (1533-64) (Eng.)

Dalison Dalison's English Common Pleas Reports, bound with Benloe (123 ER)

Dalison (Eng.) Dalison's English Common Pleas Reports, bound with Benloe (123 ER)

Dall Dallas' Reports

Dall.
- Dallam's Texas Supreme Court Decisions
- Dallas, Laws of Pennsylvania
- Dallas' Pennsylvania and United States Reports (1754-1809)
- Dallas' Styles, Scotland

Dallam Dig. (Tex.) Dallam's Digest

Dallas Dallas' Pennsylvania and United States Reports

Dall. Coop. Dallas, Report of Cooper's Opinion on the Sentence of a Foreign Court of Admiralty

Dall. Dec. Dallam's Texas Decisions, from Dallam's Digest

Dall. Dig. Dallam's Digest and Opinions (Tex.)

Dall. in Keil Dallison's Reports in Keilway's King's Bench Report, Eng.

Dall. L. Dallas' Laws of Pennsylvania

Dall. Laws Dallas' Laws (Pa.)

Dall. (Pa.) Dallas' Pennsylvania Reports (4)

Dall. S.C. Dallas' United States Supreme Court Reports

Dall. Stv. Dallas, Styles of Writs (Sc.)

Dall. Sty. Dallas' Styles, Scotland

Dall. (Tex.) Dallam's Texas Supreme Court Decisions

Dalr.
- (Dalrymple of) Stair's Decisions, Scotch Court of Session
- Dalrymple's Decisions, Scotch Court of Session (1698-1718)

Dalr. Dec. Dalrymple's Decisions (Sc.)

Dalr. Ent. Dalrymple on the Polity of Entails

Dalr. Feud. Prop. Dalrymple on Feudal Property

Dalr. Feu. Pr. Dalrymple's Feudal Property in Great Britain

Dalr. Ten. Dalrymple on Tenures

Dalrymple
- (Sir David Dalrymple of) Hailes' Scotch Session Cases
- (Sir Hew) Dalrymple's Scotch Session Cases
- (Sir James Dalrymple of) Stair's Scotch Session Cases

Dal. Sh. Dalton on Sheriffs

Dalt. Dalton's Justices of the Peace. Many editions (1618-1746)

Dalt. Just. Dalton's County Justice

Dalt. Sh. Dalton's Sheriff

Daly Daly's New York Common Pleas Reports

Daly May. Ct. Daly's Hand-Book on Practice in the Lord Mayor's Court

Daly (NY) Daly's New York Common Pleas Reports

Daly's R. Daly's New York Common Pleas Reports (N.Y.)

Daly Sur. Daly's Nature, & C., of

Surrogate's Courts, New York

Damg. Damages

Dampier MSS. Dampier's Paper Book, Lincoln's Inn Library

D'An. d'Anvers' Abridgment of Common Law. 2 editions (1705-37, 1725-37)

Dan
- Dana's Reports (31-39 Ky.)
- Daniell's Exchequer in Equity Reports (1817-23) (159 ER)
- Daniels' Compendium Compensation Cases (Eng.)
- Danish
- Danner's Reports (42 Alabama)

Dana Dana's Kentucky Supreme Court Reports (1833-40)

Dana (Ky.) Dana's Reports (31-39 Kentucky)

Dan. Abr. Dane's Abridgement of American Law

Dan. & L. Danson and Lloyd's Mercantile Cases

Dan. & Ll. Danson and Lloyd's Mercantile Cases (Eng.)

Dan. & Lld. Danson & Lloyd's English Mercantile Cases

Dan. Att. Daniel's Law of Attachment

Dana Wh. Dana's edition of Wheaton's International Law

Dan. Ch. Daniell's Chancery Practice, 8 editions (1837-1914)

Dan. Ch. Pr. Daniell's Chancery Practice, 8 editions (1837-1914)

D. & A. Deas and Anderson, Session Cases (1829-32) (Sc.)

D. & B.
- Dearsly & Bell, English Crown Cases (1856-58)
- Devereux & Battle, North Carolina Law Reports (18-20)
- Devereux & Battle's North Carolina Equity Reports (21-2 NC) (1834-39)

D. & B. C.C. Dearsley & Bell, English Crown Cases

D. & B. Pr. Pr. Dodd & Brook's Probate Practice

D. & C.
- Deacon & Chitty's English Bankruptcy Reports
- District and County Reports, Pennsylvania
- Dow & Clark, English House of Lords (Parliamentary) Cases (1827-32)

D. & C.2d District and County, Second Series, Pa.

D. & C.C. Pennsylvania District and County Reports (Pa.)

D. & Ch. Deacon & Chitty's English Bankruptcy Reports (1832-35)

D. & Chit. Deacon & Chitty's English Bankruptcy Reports (1832-35)

D. & Cl. Dow and Clark's Reports

D. & D. Drunk and Disorderly

D. & E. Durnford & East (Term) Reports, English King's Bench (1785-1800)

D. & F. Judgments of Divisional and Full Courts, Gold Coast

D. & F'11-16 Divisional and Full Court Judgments (1911-16) (Ghana)

D. & G. Diprose & Gammon's Reports of Law Affecting Friendly

Societies (1801-97) (Eng.)

D & J. De Gex & Jones' English Chancery Reports (1857-60)

D. & J.B. De Gex & Jones' English Bankruptcy Reports (1857-59)

D & K Int. Rev. Davidge & Kimball's Compendium of Internal Revenue

D. & L. Dowling & Lowndes' English Bail Court Reports (1843-49)

D. & M. Davison & Merivale's English Queen's Bench Reports

D. & Mer. Davison and Merivale's Queen's Bench Reports (1843-44) (Eng.)

D. & P. Denison & Pearce's Crown Cases (Eng.)

D. & R. Dowling & Ryland's English King's Bench Reports (1821-27)

D. & R. Mag. Cas. Dowling & Ryland's Magistrate Cases (Eng.)

D. & R. M.C. Dowling & Ryland's English Magistrate Cases (1822-27)

D. & R. N.P. Dowling & Ryland's English Nisi Prius Cases (1822-23)

D. & R. N. P. C. Dowling & Ryland's English Nisi Prius Cases

D. & S.
- Deane & Swabey, English Ecclesiastical Reports
- De Gex & Smale's Chancery Reports (1846-52) (63-4 ER)
- Doctor and Student
- Drewry & Smale's Chancery Reports (1860-65) (Eng.)

D. & Sm.
- De Gex & Smale, temp. Knight-

Bruce & Parker Reports, Vice-Chancellor's Court (1846-52) (Eng.)
- Drewry & Smale's Chancery (Eng.)

D. & Sw. Deane & Swabey Ecclesiastical (Eng.)

D. & W.
- Drury & Walsh's Irish Chancery Reports (1837-40)
- Drury & Warren's Irish Chancery Reports (1841-43)

D. & Wal. Drury & Walsh's Chancery Reports (1837-40) (Ir.)

D. & War. Drewry & Warren's Chancery (Ir.)

Dane Abr. Dane's Abridgment of American Law

Dane's Abr. Dane's Abridgment of American Law

Dan. Exch. (Eng.) Daniell's Exchequer & Equity (159 ER)

Dan. Forms Daniell, Forms and Precedents in Chancery. 7ed. 1932

Daniell, Ch. Pl & Prac. Daniell's Chancery Pleading and Practice

Daniell, Ch. Pr. Daniell's Chancery Pleading and Practice

Daniell, Ch. Prac. Daniell's Chancery Pleading and Practice

Daniel, Neg. Inst. Daniel's Negotiable Instruments

Dann
- Danner's Reports (42 Alabama)
- Dann's Reports (1 Arizona)
- Dann's Reports (in 22 California) 2d ed. 1871

Dann. Danner (Ala.)

Dan. Neg. Ins. Daniel's Negotiable Instruments

Danner Danner's Reports (42 Alabama)

Dan. Ord. Danish Ordinances

Danquah Cases in Gold Coast Law

Dans. & L. Danson & Lloyd's English Mercantile Cases

Dans. & LL., Dans. & Lld. Danson & Lloyd's Mercantile Cases (Eng.)

Dan. T. M. Daniel, Trade Marks. 1876

Danv. Danvers' Abridgment of Law (Eng.)

D'Anv. Abr. D'Anver's Abridgment, (Eng.)

Danv. Abr. Danvers' Abridgment of Law

DAP Application for writ of error dismissed by agreement of parties

d. a. p. documents against payment

D. A. P. M. Deputy Assistant Provost Marshall

D.A.R. Defense Acquisition Regulation

Darb. & B. Lim. Darby & Bosanquet on Limitations

D. Ariz. United States District Court for the District of Arizona

Darl. Pr. Ct. Sess. Darling, Practice of the Court of Session (Sc.)

DARPA Defense Advanced Research Projects Agency

Dart Dart on Vendors and Purchasers 8 editions (1851-1929)

Dart. Col. Ca. Dartmouth College Case

Dart, Vend. Dart on Vendors and Purchasers

Darw. Cr. L. Darwin's Criminal Law

Das.
- Common Law Reports, 3 (Eng.)
- Dasent's Bankruptcy & Insolvency Reports (1853-55) (Eng.)

d.a.s. delivered alongside ship

Dasent
- Acts of Privy Council, ed. Dasent (Eng.)
- Dasent's Bankruptcy & Insolvency Rep. (Eng.)

Dass. Dig. Dassler's Kansas Digest

Dass. Ed. Dassler's Edition, Kansas Reports

Dass. Ed. (Kan.) Dassler's Edition, Kansas Reports

Dass. Stat. Dassler's Kansas Statutes

DATA Defense Air Transportation Administration (U. S.)

Dau. Co. Rep.: Dauphin County Reports (Pa.)

Dauph. Dauphin County Reporter (Pa.)

Dauph. Co. Dauphin County (Pa.)

Dauph. Co. (Pa.) Dauphin County (Pa.)

Dauph. Co. Rep. Dauphin County Reporter (Pa.)

Dauphin Dauphin County Reports (Pa.)

Dauphin Co. Reps. Dauphin County Reports (Pa.)

Dav.

- Davies' English Patent Cases
- Davies' King's Bench & Exchequer Reports (1604-12) (Ir.)
- Davies' United States District Court Reports (now republished as 2 Ware)
- Davis' Reports (Abridgment of Sir Edward Coke's Reports)
- Davis' Reports (2 Hawaii)
- Davis' United States Supreme Court Reports
- Reports of Irish Cases, 1604-1611, by Sir John Davis

Dav. & Dic. Pr. Davidson & Dicey's Concise Precedents in Conveyancing

Dav. & Kim. I.R.L. Davidge & Kimball's Internal Revenue Laws

Dav. & M. Davison & Merivale Queen's Bench (Eng.)

Dav. & M. (Eng.) Davison & Merivale Queen's Bench (Eng.)

Dav. & Mer. Davison & Merivale Queen's Bench (1843-44) (Eng.)

Dav.Ann. Davies on Annuities

Dav. B. & B. Davidson on Banks and Banking, Canada

Dav. Bdg. Soc. David on Building Societies

Dav. Can. Davis' English Church Canons

Dav. Coke. Davis' Abridgment of Coke's Reports

Dav. Conv. Davidson's Conveyancing

Dav. Cr. Cons. Davis' Criminal Law Consolidation Acts

Dav. Cr. Law Davis' Criminal Law

Dav. Dig. Davis' Indiana Digest

Daveis Daveis District Court Reports (v.2 of Ware), U.S.

Dav. Elec. Davis' Law of Registration and Election

Dav. Eng. Ch. Can. Davis' English Church Canon

Dav. Fr. Merc. Law Davies on French Mercantile Law

Dav. Fr. Soc. Davis on Friendly Societies and Trade Unions

Davidson Davidson's Reports (92-111 North Carolina)

Davies

- Davies (or Davis, or Davys), Irish King's Bench Reports
- Davies' Patent Cases (1785-1816)
- Davies, United States District Court Reports (Ware, 2)

Davies (Eng.) Davies' English Patent Cases

Davies (Ir.) Davies' King's Bench Reports

Davies (U. S.) Davies' District Court Reports, 2 of Ware (U. S.)

Dav. Ind. Dig. Davis' Indiana Digest

Dav. Ind. Soc. Davis on Industrial and Provident Societies

Dav. Ir. Davys' or Davies' Reports, Irish King's Bench

Dav. Ir. K. B. Davys' or Davies' Reports, Irish King's Bench

Davis

- Davies' (or Davys') Irish King's Bench Reports
- Davis' Hawaiian Reports
- Davis' Reports, 108-176, United

States Supreme Court

Davis, Admin. Law Davis' Administrative Law Treatise

Davis Bdg. Davis' Law of Building Societies

Davis, Bldg. Soc. Davis' Law of Building Societies

Davis Cr. Law Davis Criminal Law

Davis (J. C. B.) Davis' United States Supreme Court Reports

Davis L. Ct. Cas.
- Davis Land Court Decisions (1898-1908)
- Massachusetts Land Court Decisions (Mass.)

Davis, Mass. Convey. Hdbk. Davis' Massachusetts Conveyancer's Handbook

Davis Rep. Davis' Hawaiian Reports (Sandwich Islands)

Dav. Jus. Davis' Justice of the Peace

Dav. Lab. L. Davis on the Labor Laws

Dav. Land. Ct. Cas. Davis' Land Court Decisions. 1898-1908

Dav. M. & S. Davis' Law of Master and Servant

Dav. Pat. Cas. Davies' English Patent Cases (1785-1816)

Dav. P. C. Davies' English Patent Cases (1785-1816)

Dav. Prec. Conv. Davidson's Precedents in Conveyancing

Dav. Prec. Ind. Davis' Precedents of Indictment

Dav. Reg. Davison on Registration and Elections

Dav. Rep. Davies' (Sir John) Reports, King's Bench (Ir.)

Dav. Tr. Un. Davis' Trade Unions

Dav. (U. S.) Davies District Court Reports (2 of Ware) (U. S.)

Davy Davies' Irish King's Bench Reports (1604-12) (80 ER)

Davys Davys King's Bench Reports (Eng.)

Davys (Eng.) Davys King's Bench Reports (Eng.)

Daw. Ar. Dawe on Arrest in Civil Cases

Daw. Att. Dawson's Attorney's

Daw. Cr. & Pun. Dawes on Crimes and Punishments

Daw. Land. Pr. Dawe's Epitome of the Law of Landed Property

Daw. Or. Leg. Dawson's Origo Legum

Daw. Real Pr. Dawe's Real Estate Law

Dawson's Code Dawson's Code of Civil Procedure, Colo.

Dax Exch.Pr. Dax's Exchequer Precedents

Dax Mast.Pr. Dax's Practice in the Offices of the Masters

Day
- Day's Connecticut Reports (1802- 13)
- Day's Election Cases (1892-93) (Eng.)

Day (Conn.) Connecticut Reports, by Day (1802-13)

Day Elect. Cas. Day's Election Cases (1892-93)

Day's Ca. Day's Reports (Conn.)

Day's Ca. Er. Day's Reports (Conn.)

Day's Cases Day's Reports (Conn.)

Day's Conn. Rep. Day's Reports (Conn.)

Day. (or Dayt.) Sur. Dayton's Law of Surrogates

Dayton
- Dayton (Laning) Reports (Ohio)
- Dayton Superior & Common Pleas Reports (Ohio)
- Univ. of Dayton Intramural Law Review

Dayton (Ohio) Dayton Ohio Reports

Dayton Rep. Dayton Reports (Ohio)

Dayton Term Rep. Idding's Term Reports, Ohio

Dayt. Term Rep. Dayton Term Reports (Dayton, Ohio)

Dayton T.R. Idding's Term Reports, Ohio

DB Der Betrieb (Ger.)

D. B.
- Day Book
- Dock Brief
- Domesday Book

d. b. a. de bonis asportatis (trespass to personalty)

d/b/a doing business as

D. B. & M. Dunlop, Bell & Murray's Court of Session Cases (Sc.) (1838-62)

D. B. E. De bene esse, (q. v.) (conditionally)

D. B. J. Duke Bar Journal

D. B. N. De bonis non (of the goods not administered)

D. C.
- Death Certificate
- Deputy Chief
- Deputy Commissioner
- Deputy Counsel
- Deviation Clause
- Diplomatic Corps
- Disarmament Commission (UN)
- District Commissioner
- District Court
- District of Columbia
- District of Columbia Reports
- Divisional Court
- Pennsylvania District and County Reports
- Treasury Department Circular (U. S.)
- United States District Court

D. C. 2d Pennsylvania District and County Reports, Second Series

DC3d Pennsylvania District and County Reports, Third Series

DC4th Pennsylvania District and County Reports, Fourth Series

D/C Deviation Clause

D. C. A. Dorion's Queen's Bench Reports (Canada)

DCAA Defense Contract Audit Agency

D. C. A. L. Danquah, Cases in Akan Law (Ghana)

D.C. App. District of Columbia Appeals Reports

D. C. B. Decimal Currency Board

DCBA The Bar Association of the District of Columbia

D.C. B. J. District of Columbia Bar Journal

D. C. C. Diocesan Consistory Court

DCCA District of Columbia Compensation Act

D.C. C. E. District of Columbia Code Encyclopedia

D.C. Cir. District of Columbia Court of Appeals Cases

D.C. Cir. R. D. C. Circuit Court Rules

D.C. Code District of Columbia Code

D.C. Code Ann. District of Columbia Code Annotated

D.C. Code Encycl. (West) District of Columbia Code Encyclopedia

D.C. Code Legis & Admin. Serv. District of Columbia Code Legislative and Administrative Service (West)

DC Ct App District of Columbia Court of Appeals

D.C.D. Comyn's Digest, by Day

DC DC U.S. District Court for the District of Columbia

D.C. Dist. Col. United States District Court for the District of Columbia

DCFR Defense Contract Finance Regulations

DCh Delaware Court of Chancery

D. C. H. Reports of the United States District Court of Hawaii

D. Ch. Delaware Chancery Reports

D. Chip. D. Chipman's Vermont Supreme Court Reports (1789-1824)

D. Chipm. D. Chipman's Reports (1789-1824) (Vermont)

D. Chip. (Vt.) D. Chipman's Reports (1789-1824) (Vermont)

D. C. L.
- Doctor of Civil Law
- Doctor of Comparative Law

D. C. Lab. S. Dominion of Canada Labour Service (CCH)

D. C. L. R. (Can.) Dominion Companies Law Reports (Can.)

DCMA District of Columbia Manpower Administration

D.C. Mun. App. Municipal Court of Appeals, D. C.

D. Cn. L. Doctor of Canon Law

D. C. O. Duchy of Cornwall Office

D. Colo. United States District Court for the District of Colorado

D. Com. L. Doctor of Commerical Law

D. Conn. United States District Court for the District of Connecticut

D. C. P. Daniell, Chancery Practice. 8ed. 1914

DCPA Defense Civil Preparedness Agency

DCR Myers, Debtor Creditor Relations

D. C. R. District Court Reports (N. S. W. , Aus.)

D. C. R. (NSW) District Court Reports (New South Wales) (Butterworths)

D.C.R. & Regs. D.C. Rules & Regulations

D. C. S. Deputy Clerk of Session

D. Ct.
- District Court (usually U. S.)

- Selected Judgments of the Divisional Courts (Ghana)

dct. document

DD Department of Defense (Forms)

D.D.
- Dono dedit
- Doctor of Divinity

d. d.
- days after date (Bills of Exchange)
- delivered at dock
- dono dedit (Lat.) gave as a gift

DDA Dividend Disbursing Agent

D. D. A. Dangerous Drugs Act

D. D. & Shpg. Dock Dues and Shipping

D. D. C.
- Dewey Decimal Classification
- District Court, District of Columbia

D.D.D.D. Dignum Deo donum dedit

D. Dec. Dix, School Law Decisions, New York

D. Del. United States District Court for the District of Delaware

D. D. G. Deputy Director-General

D. D. NJ., F. D. C. Food and Drug Administration, Notices of Judgment

DDPA Collins, Lombard, Moses & Spitler, Drafting the Durable Power of Attorney

D. E.
- Department of Employment
- Division of Employment

De. Delaware

DEA Drug Enforcement Administration

Dea. Deady, United States Circuit and District Court Reports

Dea. & Ch. Deacon & Chitty, Bankruptcy Reports

Dea. & Chit. Deacon & Chitty's English Bankruptcy Reports

Dea. & Sw. Deane & Swabey, English Ecclesiastical Reports (1855-57)

Deac. Deacon, English Bankruptcy Reports (1835-40)

Deac. & C. Deacon & Chitty's English Bankruptcy Reports

Deac. & Ch. Deacon & Chitty's Bankruptcy Reports (1832-35)

Deac. & Chit. Deacon and Chitty's Bankruptcy Reports (1832-35)

Deac. Bank. Pr. Deacon, Bankruptcy Law and Practice. 3ed. 1864

Deac. Cr. Law Deacon on Criminal Law of England

Deac. Dig. Deacon's Digest of the Criminal Law

Deacon & C. Deacon & Chitty, Bankruptcy (Eng.)

Deacon & C. Bankr. Cas. Deacon & Chitty's Bankruptcy Records (1832-35)

Deacon & C. Bankr. Cas. (Eng.) Deacon & Chitty, Bankruptcy Cases (Eng.)

Deacon, Bankr. Cas, Deacon, Bankruptcy (Eng.)

Deacon Bankr. (Eng.) Deacon, Bankruptcy (Eng.)

Dead B.   Dead bodies

Dead. Or. Laws   Deady & Lane's Oregon General Laws

Deady   Deady's Circuit & District Court Reports (U. S.)

Deane
- Deane & Swabey's Ecc. Reports (Eng.)
- Deane & Swabey's Probate & Divorce Reports (Eng.)
- Deane's Blockade Cases (Eng.)
- Deane's Reports (24-26 Vermont)

Deane & S. Eccl.   Deane & Swabey's Ecclesiastical Reports (1855-57) (164 ER)

Deane & S. Eccl. (Eng.)   Deane & Swabey, Ecclesiastical (164 ER)

Deane & S. Eccl. Rep.   Deane & Swabey's Ecclesiastical Reports (Eng.)

Deane & Sw.   Deane & Swabey's Ecclesiastical Reports (Eng.)

Deane Bl.   Deane's Law of Blockade

Deane Ecc.   Deane & Swabey's Ecclesiastical (Eng.)

Deane Ecc. Rep.   Deane & Swabey's Ecclesiastical Reports (Eng.)

Deane Ecc. Rep. B.   Deane and Swabey's Ecclesiastical Reports (1855-57)

Deane Neut.   Deane on the Effect of War as to Neutrals

Dean Med. Jur.   Dean's Medical Jurisprudence

Dears   Dearsley's Crown Cases Reserved (1852-56) (169 ER)

Dears. & B.   Dearsley and Bell's English Crown Cases (1856-58)

Dears. & B. C. C.   Dearsley and Bell's English Crown Cases (1856-58)

Dears. & B. Crown Cas.   Dearsley and Bell's English Crown Cases (1856-58)

Dears. C. C.   Dearsly's Crown Cases (1852-56) (Eng.)

Dears. Cr. Pr.   Dearsley, Criminal Process. 1853

Dearsl. Cr. Pr.   Dearsly on Criminal Process

Deas & A.   Deas & Anderson's Decisions (1829-33)

Deas & And.   Deas & Anderson's Decisions (1829-33) (Sc.)

Deas Ry.   Deas on the Law of Railways in Scotland

Death Pen. Rep.   Death Penalty Reporter

Deb.
- debate(s)
- Debenture
- debit

Deb. Jud.   Debates on the Judiciary

DeB. Mar. Int. L.   De Burgh's Maritime International Laws

Debt. & Cred.   Debtor and Creditor

Dec.
- December
- Decision

dec.
- deceased
- decimal
- declaration
- declination

- decoration

Decalogue Decalogue Journal

Decalogue J. Decalogue Journal

De. C. Ann. Delaware Code Annotated

Dec. Ch. Decisions from the Chair (Parliamentary) (Eng.)

Dec. Col. Coleccion de los Decretos

De Coly. De Colyar's County Court Cases (1867-82)

Dec. Comm'r Pat. Patents, Decisions of the Commissioner and of U. S. Courts

Dec. Com. Pat. Decisions of the Commissioner of Patents

Dec'd. deceased

Dec. Dig. American Digest System, Decennial Digests

Decen. Dig. American Digest, Decennial Edition

Dec. Fed. Mar. Comm'n. Decisions of the Federal Maritime Commission

De. CH. Delaware Chancery Reports

Dec. Jt. Com. Decisions of Joint Commission

Decl. declaration

Decl. J. Declaratory Judgements

Dec. O. Ohio Decisions

Dec. of Ind. Acc. Com. Decisions of the Industrial Accident Commission of California (Cal.)

De Col. De Colyar's English County Court Cases (1867-82)

De Col. Guar. De Colyar's Law of Guaranty

Dec. R. Ohio Decisions Reprint

(Ohio)

Dec. Re. Ohio Decisions Reprint (Ohio)

Dec. Rep. Ohio Decisions, Reprint (Ohio)

Dec. Repr. Ohio Decisions Reprint (Ohio)

Decretal. The Decretalia of the Canon Law

Decret. Childeb. ad L. Salic. Decreta Childeberti ad Legem Salicam

Decs. Decisions

Dec. S. D. A. Bengal Sadr Diwani Adalat Decisions

Dec. t. H. & M. Admiralty Decisions tempore Hay & Marriott (Eng.)

Dec. U. S. Comp. Gen. Decisions of the Comptroller General of the United States

Dec. U. S. Compt. Gen. Decisions of U. S. Comptroller General

Dec. U. S. Mar. Comm'n. Decisions of the United States Maritime Commission

Ded.
- Dedicated
- Dedication

Dedic. Dedication

DEEC Diedrich & Gaus, Defense of Equal Employment Claims

Deering's Cal. Adv. Legis. Serv. Deering's California Advance Legislative Service

Deering's Cal. Code Ann. Deering's Annotated California Code

Deering's Cal. Gen. Laws. Ann. Deering's California General

Laws Annotated

Dees Ins. Dees on the Law of Insolvent Debtors

Def.[s]
- Defendant[s]
- Defense
- Defined
- Definition
- Defunctus (Lat.) deceased

Def. Couns. J. Defense Counsel Journal

Defense L.J. Defense Law Journal

Def. L.J. Defense Law Journal

DeF. Min. De Fooz on Mines

Defs.['] Defendants[']

De G. De Gex's Bankruptcy Reports (1844-48)

Deg. (or Degge) Degge's Parson's Counsellor and Law of Tithes

deg. degree .

De G. & J. De Gex & Jones' Chancery Reports, Eng.

De G. & J. B. De Gex & Jones' Bankruptcy Appeals (1857-59)

De G. & J.By. De Gex & Jones' English Bankruptcy Appeals

De G. & S. De Gex & Smale's Chancery Reports (1846-52) (63-64 ER)

De G. & Sm. De Gex & Smales' Chancery Reports, Eng.

De G. Bankr. De Gex's Bankruptcy Reports (1844-48)

De G. Bankr. (Eng.) De Gex, Bankruptcy Reports

De Gex De Gex's English Bankruptcy Reports (1844-50)

De Gex, F. & J. De Gex, Fisher &

Jones' English Chancery Reports

De Gex, J. & S. De Gex, Jones, and Smith's English Chancery Reports

De Gex, M. & G. De Gex, Macnaghten & Gordon's Reports (Eng.)

De Gex, M. & G. B. De Gex, Macnaghten & Gordon's Bankruptcy Reports (1851-57)

De G. F. & J. De Gex, Fisher, & Jones' English Chancery Reports (45 ER)

De G. J. & J. By. DeGex, Fisher & Jones Bankruptcy Appeals (1860) (Eng.)

De G. J. & S. De Gex, Jones & Smith Chancery Reports, England (46 ER)

De G. J. & S. By. De Gex, Jones & Smith's English Bankruptcy Appeals (1862-65)

De G. J. & S. (Eng.) De Gex, Jones & Smith Chancery Reports, England (46 ER)

De. G. J. & Sm. De Gex, Jones & Smith's Chancery Reports (46 ER)

De G. M. & G.
- De Gex, Macnaghten, & Gordon's English Bankruptcy Reports
- De Gex, Macnaghten, & Gordon's English Chancery Reports (42-44 ER)

DeG. M. & G. By. DeGex, Macnaghten, & Gordon Bankruptcy Appeals (1837-55) (Eng.)

DeHart, Mil. Law DeHart on Military Law

De H.M.L. De Hart's Military Law

and Courts-Martial

De Jure Mar. Hale's De Jure Maris, Appendix to Hall on the Sea Shore

De Krets. DeKretser's Matara Appeals (Ceylon)

DEL Baker/Seck, Determining Economic Loss

Del.
- Delane's English Revision Cases (1832-35)
- Delaware
- Delaware County Reports, Pennsylvania
- Delaware Reports

Delane Delane's Revision Courts Decisions (Eng.)

Delaware Co. Reps. Delaware County Reports (Pa.)

Delaware J. Corp. L. The Delaware Journal of Corporate Law

Del. Cas. Delaware Cases (1792-1830)

Del. Ch. Delaware Chancery Reports

Del. Ch. Supp. Delaware Chancery Reports, Supplement

Del. Civ. Dec. Delaware Chancery Reports

Del. Civ. Dec. Delhi Civil Decisions (India)

Del. Co. Delaware County (Pa.)

Del. Code Delaware Code

Del. Code Ann. Delaware Code Annotated

Del. Co. L.J. (Pa.) Delaware County Law Journal (Pa.)

De L. Const. De Lolme on the English Constitution

Del. Const. Delaware Constitution

Del. Co. (Pa.) Delaware County Reports (Pa.)

Del. Co. R. Delaware County Reports (Pa.)

Del. Co. Reps. Delaware County Reports (Pa.)

Del. County Delaware County Reports

Del. County Rep.
- Delaware County Reports (Pa.)
- Delaware Supreme Court Reports
- Delegate
- Delhi

Del. Cr. Cas. Delaware Criminal Cases

Del. Ct. M. Delafon on Naval Courts Martial

dele. Deleatur (Lat.) omit

Deleg. Court of Delegates

Delehanty New York Miscellaneous Reports

Del. El. Cas. Delane's Election Revision Cases (Eng.)

Del. G. C. L. Delaware General Corporation Law

Delhi L.R. Delhi Law Review

Delhi L. Rev. Delhi Law Review, Delhi, India

Delhi L. Times The Delhi Law Times, Delhi, India

Delinq. delinquent

Del. J. Corp. L. Delaware Journal of Corporate Law

Dell. Dellam's Texas Opinions (1840-44)

Del. Law. Delaware Lawyer

Del. Laws Laws of Delaware

Del. L.R. Delhi Law Review

De Lolme, Eng. Const. De Lolme on the English Constitution

Del. Order Delegation Order

Del. P.M. Ex. Delafield on Post Mortem Examinations

Del. Reg. of Regs. Delaware Register of Regulations

Del. Sup. Delaware Supreme Court Decisions

Del. Term R. Delaware Term Reports

delv. delivered

De M. De Mello's Extradition Cases (1877-1913) (Malaya)

Dem.
- Demarest's Surrogate's Court Reports (New York)
- Demurrer

Demarest Demarest, New York Surrogate's Court Reports

Dem. Cond. Etran. Demangeat's Condition Civile, Etrangers en France

Dem. (NY) Demarest's Surrogate's Court Reports (New York)

Demol. Demolombe's Code Napoleon

Demol. C. N. Demolombe's Code Napoleon

Dem. Sur. Demarest's Surrogate (New York)

Dem. Surr. Demarest's Surrogate (New York)

Den.
- Denied
- Denio's New York Reports

- Denison & Pearce's Crown Cases Reserved (1844-52) (169 ER)
- Denis' Reports (vols. 32-46 Louisiana)
- Denmark
- Denver
- Deny[ing]

Denning L.J. Denning Law Journal

Den. & P. Denison & Pearce's Crown Cases (1844-52) (Eng.)

Den. & P. C. C. Denison and Pearce's Crown Cases (1844-52) (Eng.)

Den. & Sc. Pr. Denison & Scott's House of Lords Appeal Practice

den. app. denying appeal

Den. B. A. Rec. Denver Bar Association Record

Den. C. C. Denison's Crown Cases (1844-52) (Eng.)

den'g denying

Denio Denio's New York Supreme Court Reports (1845-48)

Denio (N. S.) Denio's Reports (N. Y.)

Denio R. Denio's Reports (N. Y.)

Denis Denis' Reports (vols. 32-46 Louisiana)

Denison, Cr. Cas. Denison's English Crown Cases

Den. J. I. L. P. Denver Journal of International Law and Policy

Den. J. Int'l. L. & Pol'y. Denver Journal of International Law and Policy

Den. L. C. J. Denver Law Center Journal. 1963-65

Den. L.J. Denver Law Journal

Den. L. N. Denver Legal News

Denning L Rev Denning Law Review

Denom. Denomination

den. rearg. denying reargument

den. reh. denying rehearing

Dens. Denslow's Notes to second edition (vols. 1-3 Michigan Reports)

Den. U. L. Rev. Denver University Law Review

Denver J. Int'l. L. Denver Journal of International Law

Denver J. Int. L. & Policy Denver Journal of International Law and Policy

Denver L. J. Denver Law Journal

Denver L. N. Denver Legal News

Denv. U. L. Rev. Denver University Law Review

den. writ of error denying writ of error

De Orat. Cicero, De Oratore

D. E. P. Department of Employment and Productivity

DeP. DePaul Law Review (Ill.)

Dep.
- Department
- Deposit
- Deposition
- Depositary
- Deputy

DEPA Defense Electric Power Administration

DePaul Bus. L.J. DePaul Business Law Journal

DePaul L. Rev. DePaul Law Review

view

Dep. in Ct. Deposits in Court

Depos. & D. Depositions and Discovery

Dept. Department

Dept. Dec. Departmental Decisions (Eng.)

Dept. of State Bull. U. S. Department of State, Bulletin

Dep't. St. Bull. Department of State Bulletin (U. S.)

Dept. R. Department Reports, State Dept. (N. Y.)

Dept. R. Un. New York State Department Reports, Unofficial

Dept. State Bull. Department of State Bulletin

Dept. St. Bull. The Department of State Bulletin

D. E. R. I. C. De ea re ita censuere (concerning that matter have so decreed)

DES
- Department of Economic Security
- Department of Employment Security
- Division of Employment Security

Des. Desaussure, South Carolina Equity Reports (1784-1816)

Desai. Handbook of Criminal Cases (India)

Desaus Desaussure, South Carolina Equity Reports

Desaus. Eq. Desaussure, South Carolina Equity Reports

Desc. & D. Descent and Distribution

Descr. Description

Desert. & N. Desertion and Non-support

Dess. Dessaussure's Equity (S.C.)

Dessaus. Dessaussure's Equity (S.C.)

D. es S. L.J. Dar es Salaam Law Journal

D. es S. U. L. J. Dar es Salaam University Law Journal

Dest. Cal. Cit. Desty's California Citations

Dest. Cal. Dig. Desty's California Digest

Dest. Com. & Nav. Desty on Commerce and Navigation

Dest. Cr. L. Desty's Criminal Law

Dest. Fed. Cit. Desty's Federal Citations

Dest. Fed. Cons. Desty on the Federal Constitution

Dest. Fed. Proc. Desty's Federal Procedure

Dest. Sh. & Adm. Desty on Shipping and Admiralty

Desty, Tax'n. Desty on Taxation

Det.
- Detachable
- Detached
- Detective
- Detroit

Det. B.J. Detroit Bar Journal

Det. C. L.R. Detroit College of Law Review

Det. C. L. Rev. Detroit College of Law Review

Det. Coll. L.R. Detroit College of Law Review

Det. Coll. L. Rev. Detroit College Law Review

Det. Law Detroit Lawyer (Detroit Bar Association)

Det. Leg. N. Detroit Legal News

Det. L. J. Detroit Law Journal

Det. L. Rev. Detroit Law Review

Detroit B.Q. Detroit Bar Quarterly

Detroit Coll. L. Detroit College of Law

Detroit Coll L Rev Detroit College of Law Review

Detroit L. Detroit Lawyer

Detroit Leg. N. Detroit Legal News, Mich.

Detroit L.J. Detroit Law Journal

Detroit L. Rev. Detroit Law Review

Dev.
- Development
- Devereux's North Carolina Law Reports (1826-34)
- Devereux's Reports, United States Court of Claims

Dev. & B.
- Devereux & Battle's North Carolina Law Reports (1834-39) (18-20NC)
- Devereux & Battle's Reports (vols. 21, 22 North Carolina Equity)

Dev. & Bat. Devereux & Battle's Reports (vols. 17-20 North Carolina Law Reports)

Dev. & Bat. Eq. Devereux & Battle's Reports (vols. 21, 22 North Carolina Equity) (1834-39)

Dev. & B. Eq. Devereux & Battle's

Reports (vols. 21, 22 North Carolina Equity) (1834-39)

Dev. & BL. (NC) Devereux & Battle's Reports (vols. 17-20 North Carolina Law Reports)

Dev. C. C. Devereux's Reports, United States Court of Claims

Dev. Ct. Cl. Devereux's Reports, United States Court of Claims

Dev. Deeds. Devlin, Deeds and Real Estate

Devel Development

Dev. Eq. Devereux's North Carolina Equity (1826-34)

DEVI Givens, Demonstrative Evidence

DeVilliers Reports Orange Free State (S. Afr.)

Dev. Kin. Bl. Devereux's Kinne's Blackstone

Dev. Kin. Kent Devereux's Kinne's Kent

Dev. L. Devereux's North Carolina Law Reports

Dev. L. (or Dev.N.B.) Devereux's North Carolina Law Reports

Devl. Deeds Devlin on Deeds

Dew.
- Dewey's Kansas Court of Appeals Reports
- Dewey's Reports (60-70 Kansas)

Dew. Div. Dewey on Divorce Law

D'Ewes J. D'Ewes' Journal and Parliamentary Collection

DeWitt DeWitt's Reports (24-42 Ohio State)

Dew. St. Dewey's Compiled Statutes of Michigan

d. f. dead freight

DFA Defense Fisheries Administration (U. S.)

D. F. & J. DeGex, Fisher & Jones' Chancery Reports (1860-62) (Eng.)

D. F. & J. B. De Gex, Fisher & Jones, English Bankruptcy Reports (1860)

DFL Democrat-Farmer-Labor party

DFO Defense Food Order (Production & Marketing Adm.) (U. S.)

DFO, SO Defense Food Order, Sub-Order (U. S.)

dft.
- defendant
- draft

D. G. De Gex, English Bankruptcy Reports (1845-50)

D. G. & J. De Gex & Jones' Chancery Reports (1857-59) (44-5 ER)

D. G. & J. B. De Gex & Jones' Bankruptcy Reports (1857-59)

D. G. F. & J. De Gex, Fisher, & Jones' English Chancery Reports

D. G. F. & J. B. De Gex, Fisher, & Jones' English Bankruptcy Reports

D. G. J. & S. De Gex, Jones, & Smith's English Chancery Reports

D. G. J. & S. B. De Gex, Jones, & Smith's English Bankruptcy Reports

D. G. M. & G. De Gex, Macnaghten, & Gordon's English Chancery Reports

D. G. M. & G. B. De Gex, Macnaghten, & Gordon's English

Bankruptcy Reports

D. Guam United States District Court for the District of Guam

DH Balsam & Zabin, Disability Handbook

D.Haw. United States District Court for the District of Hawaii

D. Hawaii United States District Court for the District of Hawaii

D. H. L. House of Lords Appeals, in Dunlop's Court of Session Cases from vol. 13 (1851- 62)

D. H. S. S. Department of Health & Social Security

Di. Dyer's Reports, King's Bench (73 ER)

DIA Defense Intelligence Agency

Dial. de Scacc. Dialogus de Scaccario

DIALOG On-Line Search Service (Lockheed)

DIBA Domestic and International Business Administration

Dibb F. Dibb's Forms of Memorials

Dic. Dicta

Dic. Dom. Dicey on Domicil

Dice Dice's Reports (vols. 79-91 Indiana)

Dicey & Morris Dicey, Conflict of Laws. 10ed. 1980

Dicey, Confl. Laws Dicey on Conflict of Laws

Dicey, Const. Dicey, Lectures Introductory to the Study of the Law of the English Constitution

Dicey, Dom. Dicey's Law of Domicil

Dicey, Domicil Dicey's Law of

Domicil

Dick.
- Dickens' English Chancery Reports (1559-1798)
- Dickenson's Reports (vols. 46-58 New Jersey Equity)
- Dickens, Scotland
- Dickinson, New Jersey

Dick. Black. Dickson's Analysis of Blackstone's Commentaries

Dick. Ch. Dickens' Chancery Reports (1599-1798) (21 ER)

Dick. Ch. (Eng.) Dicken's Chancery Reports (21 ER)

Dickens Dickens' English Chancery Reports

Dick. Eq. Pr. Dickinson's Equity Precedents (New Jersey)

Dick. Ev. Dickson, Law of Evidence in Scotland

Dickinson. L. Rev. Dickinson Law Review

Dick. Int'l L. Ann. Dickinson's International Law Annual

Dick. J. Int'l L. Dickinson Journal of International Law

Dick. Just. Dickinson's Justice

Dick. Kent. Dickson's Analysis of Kent's Commentaries

Dick. Law. Dickinson Lawyers

Dick. L.R. Dickinson Law Review

Dick. L. Rev. Dickinson Law Review

Dick. (NJ) Dickinson's New Jersey Equity

Dick. Quar. Ses. Dickinson's Practical Guide to the Quarter Sessions

Dic. Par. Dicey on Parties to Actions

Dict. Dictionary

Dicta Dicta of Denver Bar Association

D. Idaho United States District Court for the District of Idaho

Dig.
- Digest
- Digest of Justinian
- Digesta
- Digesta of Justiniaus
- Digest (Lahore, India) (1901-06)
- Digest of Writs
- Digestum

Digby, R. P. Digby's History of the Law of Real Property

Dig. C.L.W. Digest of Commercial Law of the World (Oceana)

Dig. Crim. Proc. Stephen, Digest of Criminal Procedure. 9ed. 1950

Digest Digest of Justinina (Roman Law)

Dig. Fla. Thompson's Digest of Laws (Fla.)

Dig. L.L. Digest Law of Libels

Dig. Ops. J. A. G. Digest of Opinions of Judge Advocate General, United States

Dig. Proem. Digest of Justinian, Proem

Dig. R. Pr. Digby's Introduction to the History of Real Property

Dig. Shares Digby's Sales and Transfer of Shares

Dig. St. English's Digest of the Statutes (Ark.)

Dil. Dillon's United States Circuit Court Reports

D.I.L. (Hack.) Digest of International Law (Hackworth)

Dil. Cir. Court Rep. Dillon's U. S. Circuit Court Reports

Dill. Dillon's United States Circuit Court Reports

Dill. Ir. Jud. A. Dillon on the Irish Judicature Act

Dill. Laws Eng. & Am. Dillon's Laws and Jurisprudence of England and America

Dill. Mun. Bonds Dillon on Municipal Bonds

Dill. Mun. Cor. Dillon on Municipal Corporations

Dill. Mun. Corp. Dillon on Municipal Corporations

Dillon Dillon's United States Circuit Court Reports

Dillon Cir. Court Rep. Dillon's U. S. Circuit Court Reports

Dillon C. C. Dillon's U. S. Circuit Court Reports

Dillon, Mun. Corp. Dillon on Municipal Corporation

Dill. Rep. Dillon's U. S. Circuit Court Reports

Dill. Rem. Caus. Dillon on the Removal of Causes

D.I.L. (Moore) Digest of International Law (Moore)

D.I.L. (White.) Digest of International Law (Whiteman)

Dip. Cor. Diplomatic Correspondence of the United States, edited by Sparks

Dipl. diplomacy

DIPR Department of the Interior Procurement Regulations

DIR Department of Industrial Relations

Dir. Director

Dirl. Dirleton's Decisions, Court of Sessions (1665-77) (Sc.)

Dirl. D. Dirleton's Doubts and Questions in the Law

Dirl. Dec. Dirleton's Decisions, Court of Sessions (Sc.)

DIS Defense Investigative Service

Dis. Disney's Ohio Superior Court Reports

disappr. disapproved in or disapproving

DISC Domestic International Sales Corporation

Disc.
- Discount
- Discovered
- Discovery

DISC Domestic International Sales Corporation

Disc. L. & Proc. Adv. Sheets Disciplinary Law & Procedure Advance Sheets

dism. app. dismissing appeal

Dism'd. Dismissed

Dism'g. Dismissing

Disn. Disney's Superior Court of Cincinnati Reports (Ohio)

Disney (Ohio) Disney, Superior Court of Cincinnati Reports (Ohio)

Disn. Gam. Disney, Gaming. 1806

Disn. (Ohio) Disney's Ohio Superior Court Reports

dis. op. dissenting opinion

Disord. H. Disorderly Houses

Dispute Res. N. Dispute Resolution Notes

Dis. R. Disney, Superior Court of Cincinnati Reports (Ohio)

diss. dissertation

Diss. ad Flet. Selden's Dissertatio ad Fletam

Dist.
- distinguished
- distinguishing
- district

Dist. & Co. Rep. Pennsylvania District and County Reports (Pa.)

Dist. C. District Court

Dist. Col. District of Columbia

Dist. Col. App. District of Columbia Court of Appeals

Dist. Col. P. U. District of Columbia Public Utilities Commission

Dist. Ct. District Court (state)

Dist. Ct. App. District Court of Appeal

Dist. R. Pennsylvania District Reports (Pa.)

Distr. Distribution; Distributive

Distr. Col. B. A. J. District of Columbia Bar Association Journal

Dist. Rep. District Reports

Dist. Reports Pennsylvania District Reports (Pa.)

Dist. Reps. Pennsylvania District Reports (Pa.)

Distrib.
- Distribute or Distributing
- Distributor

District Pennsylvania District Reports (Pa.)

District Court L.R. District

228

Court Law Reports (Hong Kong)

District Law   District Lawyer

District Law. (D.C.)   District Lawyer

District Reps.   Pennsylvania District Reports (Pa.)

Disturb. M.   Disturbing Meetings

Div.
- divide
- Dividend
- divinity
- division
- divorce proceedings

Div. & Mat. Ct.   Divorce and Matrimonial Causes Court

Div. & S.   Divorce and Separation

Div. C.   Division Court (Can.)

Div. Ct.   Divisional Court Selected Judgments, Divisional Courts of the Gold Coast Colony

Dix. Av.   Dixon on General Average

Dix. Dec.   Dix's School Decisions, New York

Dix. Dec. (NY)   Dix's School Decisions (New York)

Dix. Farm   Dixon, Law of the Farm. 6ed. 1904

Dix. Mar. Ins.   Dixon's Marine Insurance and Average

Dix. Mar. Law   Dixon's Abridgment of the Maritime Law

Dix. Part.   Dixon, Partnership. 1866

Dix. Pr.   Dixon, Probate and Administration Law and Practice. 3ed. 1912

Dix. Ship.   Dixon's Law of Shipping

Dix. Subr.   Dixon's Law of Subrogation

Dix. Tit. D.   Dixon on Title Deeds

D. J.
- Denver Law Journal (Colo.)
- District Judge

D. J. A. G.   Deputy Judge Advocate General

D. J. & S.   De Gex, Jones & Smith, English Chancery Reports (1862-66)

D. J. & S. B.   De Gex, Jones & Smith English Bankruptcy Reports (1862-65)

DJC   Application for writ of error dismissed, judgment correct

Djib   Djibouti

D. Kan.   United States District Court for the District of Kansas

Dk. L.R.   Dickinson Law Review

D. K. S.   Deputy Keeper of the Signet

Dkt.
- Docket
- West Publishing Co.'s Docket (1909-41)

D. L.
- Doctor of Law

DLC
- Disaster Loan Corporation (U. S.)
- Donation Land Claim

DLI   Department of Labor and Industry

D. L.J.   University of Detroit Law Journal (Mich.)

D. L. N.   Daily Legal News

D. L. R.
- Dickinson Law Review (Pennsylvania)

- Dominion Law Reporter (India), usually with a Province abbreviation, as D. L. M. (A. M.), Ajmer-Merwara
- Dominion Law Reports (Can.)

D. L. R. 2d. Dominion Law Reports, 2d Series (Can.)

D. L. R. 3d. Dominion Law Reports, 3d Series (Can.)

D. L. R. (Can.) Dominion Law Reports (Canada)

D. L. R. 2d. (Can.) Dominion Law Reports, Second Series (Can.)

D. M. Davison & Merivale's King's Bench Reports (1843-44) (64 RR)

DMA Defense Manpower Administration (U. S.)

D. M. & G. De Gex, Macnaghten & Gordon, English Chancery Reports (1851-57)

D. M. & G. B. De Gex, Macnaghten & Gordon, English Bankruptcy Reports

D. Mass. United States District Court for the District of Massachusetts

DMB Defense Mobilization Board (U. S.)

D. Md. United States District Court for the District of Maryland

D. Me. United States District Court for the District of Maine

DMEA Defense Materials Exploration Agency (U. S.)

D. Minn. United States District Court for the District of Minnesota

DMO Defense Mobilization Order (U. S.)

D. Mont. United States District Court for the District of Montana

DMP Defense Materials Procurement Agency (U. S.)

DMS Defense Materials System

DNA Defense Nuclear Agency

D. N.D. United States District Court for the District of North Dakota

D. Nev. United States District Court for the District of Nevada

D. N.H. United States District Court for the District of New Hampshire

D. N.J. United States District Court for the District of New Jersey

Dn. L.J. Denver Law Journal

D. N.M. United States District Court for the District of New Mexico

D. N. S.
- Dowling's Reports, New Series, English Bail Court
- Dow, New Series (Dow & Clark, English House of Lords Cases)

DO Delegation Order

DOA Dead on arrival at hospital

DOB Date of Birth

DOC Department of Commerce

Doc.
- Doctor
- Document

Docket
- Docket (and the barrister) (Can.) (1889-98)
- The Docket (Tennessee Bar Association Newsletter)
- West Publishing Co's Docket.

(1909-41)

Doct. & St. Doctor & Student (Eng.)

Doct. & Stud. Doctor and Student

Doct. and Stud. Doctor and Student

Doct.Dem. Doctrine of Demurrers

Doct. Pl. Doctrina Placitandi

Doct. Plac. Doctrina Placitandi

DOD Department of Defense

Dod.
- Dodson's English Admiralty
- Dod's Parliamentary Companion. Annual.
- Dodson's English Admiralty Reports (165 ER)

Dod. Adm. Dodson's Reports, English Admiralty Courts

Dod. Ant. Parl. Doderidge on the Antiquity and Power of Parliaments

Dodd & Br. Pr. Pr. Dodd & Brook's Probate Court Practice

Dodd Bur. Fees Dodd on Burial and other Church Fees

Dod. Eng. Law Doderidge's English Lawyer

DODISS Department of Defense Index of Specifications and Standards

Dod. Law L. Doderidge's The Lawyer's Light

Dod. Nobility Doderidge's Nobility

Dods. Dodson's English Admiralty Reports (165 ER)

Dodson Adm. (Eng.) Dodson's English Admiralty Reports (165 ER)

DOE Department of Energy

DOI Department of the Interior

DOJ Department of Justice

DOL Department of Labor

DOM Green, Dissolution of Marriage

Dom.
- Domat
- Dominus
- Dominion

dom. domestic

Domat, Civ. Law Domat's Civil Law

Domat, Dr. Pub. Domat's Droit Publique

Domat, Liv. Prel. Domat's Lives du Droit Public

Dom. Boc. Domesday Book

Dom. Book Domesday Book

Dom. Civ. Law Domat's Civil Law

Domes. Domesday Book

Domesday Domesday Book

Dominion Tax Cas. (CCH) Dominion Tax Cases

Dom. L.R. Dominion Law Reports (Can.)

Dom. Proc. Domus Procerum; In the House of Lords

Dom. Rel. Domestic Relations

Dom. Rel. Ct. Domestic Relations Court

Dom. Rep. Dominican Republic

Dona.
- Donnelly's Chancery (Eng.)
- Donnelly's Irish Land Cases

Donaker Donaker's Reports (165 Indiana)

Donn.
- Donnell's Irish Land Cases (1871 -76)
- Donnelly's Reports, English Chancery (1836-37)

Donnelly Donnelly's Chancery Reports (47 ER)

Donnelly (Eng.) Donnelly's Chancery Reports (47 ER)

Donn. Eq. Donnelly's Chancery Reports (1836-37) (47 ER)

Donn. Ir. Land Cas. Donnell's Irish Land Cases (1871-76)

Don. Tr. Donovan, Modern Jury Trials

D. Or. United States District Court for the District of Oregon

Dor. Dorion's Reports (Quebec)

D. O. R. A. Defense of the Realm Act

Dor. Bank Doria, Law and Practice in Bankruptcy. 2ed, 1873

Dor. Ins. Dorsay's Law of Insolvency

Dorion Dorion's Quebec Queen's Bench Reports

Dorion (Can.) Dorion's Quebec Queen's Bench Reports

Dorion Q. B. Dorion's Quebec Queen's Bench Reports

Dor. Md. Laws Dorsey's Maryland Laws

Dor. Q. B. Dorion's Quebec Queen's Bench Reports

Doshisha L.J. Doshisha Law Journal, Int'l. Edition, Kyoto, Japan

Doshisha L. Rev. Doshisha Law Review

Dos Passos, Stock-Brok. Dos Passos on Stock-Brokers and Stock Exchanges

DOSPR Department of State Procurement Regulations

DOT Department of Transportation

Doug.
- Douglas' English Election Cases (1774-76)
- Douglas' English King's Bench Reports (1778-85)
- Douglas' Michigan Supreme Court Reports
- Douglass' Reports

Doug. El. Ca. Douglas' English Election Cases

Doug. El. Cas. Douglas' Election Cases (1774-76)

Doug. K. B. Douglas' English King's Bench Reports (1778-85)

Dougl. Douglas (Mich.)

Dougl. El. Cas. Douglas English Election Cases (1774-76)

Dougl. K. B. Douglas, King's Bench Reports (99 ER)

Dougl. K. B. (Eng.) Douglas, King's Bench Reports (99 ER)

Dougl. (Mich.) Douglas' Michigan Supreme Court Reports

Doug. (Mich.) Douglas Michigan Supreme Court Reports

Dow
- Dowling's English Practice Cases (1812-18)
- Dow's House of Lords (Parliamentary) Cases, same as Dow's Reports (3 ER)

Dow & C. Dow & Clark's English House of Lords Cases (6 ER)

Dow & C. (Eng.) Dow & Clark's English House of Lords Cases (6 ER)

Dow & Cl. Dow & Clark's English House of Lords Cases (6 ER)

Dow. & L. Dowling & Lowndes' English Bail Court Reports (1841-49)

Dow. & Lownd. Dowling & Lowndes' Practice Cases, Eng.

Dow. & Ry.
- Dowling & Ryland's English King's Bench Reports (1821-27)
- Dowling & Ryland's English Nisi Prius Cases

Dow. & Ry. K. B.
- Dowling & Ryland's English King's Bench Reports
- Dowling & Ryland's English Nisi Prius Cases

Dow. & Ry. M. C. Dowling & Ryland's English Magistrates' Cases (1822-27)

Dow. & Ry. N. P. Dowling & Ryland's English Nisi Prius Cases

Dowd. Ins. Dowdeswell on Life and Fire Insurance

Dow. Inc. Dowell, Income Tax Acts. 9ed. 1934

Dowl. Dowling's English Bail Court (Practice) Cases (1830-41)

Dowl. & L. Dowling & Lowndes' English Bail Court Reports

Dowl. & Lownd. Dowling & Lowndes' English Bail Court Reports

Dowl. & R.
- Dowling and Ryland's English King's Bench Reports
- Dowling & Ryland's Queen's Bench & Magistrates' Cases (Eng.)

Dowl. & R. (Eng.) Dowling and Ryland's English King's Bench Reports

Dowl. & R. Mag. Cas. (Eng.) Dowling & Ryland's Magistrates' Cases

Dowl. & R. N. P. Dowling & Ryland's Nisi Prius Cases (1822-23) (171 ER)

Dowl. & R. NP (Eng.) Dowling & Ryland's Nisi Prius Cases (171 ER)

Dowl. & Ryl. Dowling and Ryland's English King's Bench Reports

Dowl. & Ryl. M. C. Dowling & Ryland's English Mastriates' Cases

Dowl. & Ryl. N. P. Dowling & Ryland's English Nisi Prius Cases

Dowl. (Eng.) Dowling's English Bail Court (Practice) Cases

Dowl. N. S. Dowling's English Bail Court Reports, New Series (1841-43)

Dowl. NS (Eng.) Dowling's English Bail Court Reports, New Series (1841-43)

Dowl. P. C. Dowling's English Bail Court (Practice) Cases

Dowl. PC (Eng.) Dowling's English Bail Court (Practice) Cases

Dowl. P. C. N. S. Dowling's Practice Cases, New Series (Eng.)

Dowl. P. R. Dowling Practice Reports

Dowl. Pr. Dowling's Common Law Practice

Dowl. Pr. Cas. Dowling Practice

Cases (Eng.)

Dowl. Pr. C. N. S. Dowling's Reports, New Series, English Practice Cases

Down. & Lud. Downton & Luder's English Election Cases

Dow N. S.
- Dow & Clark's English House of Lords Cases (1827-32) (1841-42)
- Dowling's New Series Reports, Bail Court (1814-43) (Eng.)

Dow P. C.
- Dowling's English Practice Cases (1812-18) (1830-41)
- Dow's House of Lords (Parliamentary) Cases, same as Dow's Reports (3 ER)

Dow. PC (Eng.)
- Dowling's English Practice Cases (1812-18) (1830-40)
- Dow's House of Lords (Parliamentary) cases, same as Dow's Reports (3 ER)

Dow. P. R. Dowling's Practice Cases (1830-41)

Dow. St. Dowell, Stamp Duties. 1873

D. P.
- Data processing
- Discussion Paper
- Domus Procerum (the House of Lords)

DPA Defense Production Adm. (U. S.)

D. P. B. Dampier Paper Book, in Lincoln's Inn Library

D. P. C. Dowling, English Practice Cases (1830-40)

D.P.L. Dunlop's Parochial Law

D. P. L.R. De Paul Law Review

D. P. P. Director of Public Prosecutions

D. P. R.
- Porto Rico Reports (Spanish ed.)
- United States District Court for the District of Puerto Rico

D.Pr. Darling's Practice, Scotch Court of Sessions

D. P. U. C. Division on Placement and Unemployment Compensation

D. P. U. I. Division on Placement and Unemployment Insurance

DR
- Dacca Reports (India)
- De-rating and Rating Appeals, England and Scotland
- Distribution Regulation (Office of Price Stabilization, U. S.)
- Drake Law Review (Iowa)

D. R.
- Deputy Remembrancer
- District Registry

Dr.
- Drewry's English Vice Chancellor's Reports (1852-59)
- Drury's Irish Chancery Reports tempore Napier (1858-59)
- Drury's Irish Chancery Reports tempore Sugden (1843-44)

Dr.
- Debtor
- Doctor
- Drawer

DRA Dependent relative allowance

D. R. A. De-rating Appeals (Eng.)

Dra. Draper's Upper Canada King's Bench Reports

Dra. Dow. Draper on Dower

Drake Att. Drake on Attachment

Drake Attachm. Drake on Attachment

Drake L. Rev. Drake Law Review

Dr. & Nap. Drury's Irish Chancery Reports tempore Napier (1858-59)

Dr. & Sm. Drewry & Smale's English Vice Chancellor's Reports (1860-65)

Dr. & Sug. Drury's Irish Chancery Reports tempore Sugden (1843-44)

Dr. & Wal. Drury & Walsh, Irish Chancery Reports (1837-40)

Dr. & War. Drury & Warren's Irish Chancery Reports (1841-43)

Draper Draper's Upper Canada King's Bench Reports (1828-31)

Draper (Can.) Draper's Upper Canada King's Bench Reports

Draper (Ont.) Draper's Upper Canada King's Bench Reports

Dr. Att. Drake on Attachment

DRC Defense Relocation Corporation (U. S.)

DRE Kushner, Fair Housing; Discrimination in Real Estate, Community Development and Revitalization

D. Rep. Ohio Decisions Reprint

D. Repr. Ohio Decisions Reprint

Dres. Int. Rev. Dresse on Internal Revenue Laws

Drew.
- Drewry's English Vice Chancellors' Reports (61, 62 ER)
- Drew's Reports (13 Florida)

Drew. & S. Drewry & Smale's Chancery (Eng.)

Drew. & S. (Eng.) Drewry & Smale's Chancery Reports (Eng.)

Drew. & Sm. Drewry & Smale's Chancery Reports (Eng.)

Drew. Ch. F. Drewry, Chancery Forms. 1876

Drew. (Eng.) Drewry's English Chancery Reports (Eng.)

Drew. Eq. Pl. Drewry's Equity Pleading

Drew. Inj. Drewry, Injunctions. 1841

Drew. Pat. Drewry, Patent Law Amendment Act. 1838

Drew. Tr. M. Drewry, Trade Marks. 1878

DRI Defense Research Institute

D. R. I. United States District Court for the District of Rhode Island

Drink. Drinkwater's English Common Pleas Reports (1840-41)

Drinkw. Drinkwater Common Pleas (Eng.)

Drinkwater Drinkwater's Common Pleas Reports (60 RR) (1840-41)

Drinkw. (Eng.) Drinkwater Common Pleas

Dr. L.R. Drake Law Review

Drone Cop. Drone on Copyrights

Dr. R. t. Nap. Drury's Irish Chancery Reports tempore Napier

Dr. R. t. Sug. Drury's Irish Chancery Reports tempore Sugden

D. R. S. Dominion Report Service (Canada)

Dr. t. Nap. Drury's Irish Chancery Report tempore Napier

Dr. t. Sug. Drury's Irish Chancery Reports tempore Sugden (1843-44)

Dru. Drury's Irish Chancery Reports tempore Sugden

Dru. & Nap. Drury's Irish Chancery Reports tempore Napier (1858-59)

Dru. & Sug. Drury's Irish Chancery Reports tempore Sugden (1843-44)

Dru. & Wal. Drury & Walsh's Irish Chancery Reports (1837-40)

Dru. & War. Drury & Warren's Irish Chancery Reports (1841-43)

Drug Abuse L.R. Drug Abuse Law Review

Drug Abuse L. Rev. Drug Abuse Law Review

Drug Enforce. Drug Enforcement

Drug L.J. Drug Law Journal

Drury Drury's Chancery Irish Reports

Drury & Wal. Drury & Walsh's Irish Chancery Reports (1837-40)

Drury & Wal. (Ir.) Drury & Walsh's Irish Chancery Reports

Drury & War. Drury & Warren's Irish Chancery Reports (1841-43)

Drury & War. (Ir.) Drury & Warren's Irish Chancery Reports

Drury (Ir.) Drury's Chancery Irish Reports

Drury t. Nap. Drury's Irish Chancery Reports tempore Napier (1858-59)

Drury t. Sug. Drury's Irish Chancery Reports tempore Sugden

Dru. t. Nap. Drury's Irish Chancery Reports tempore Napier

Dru. t. Sug. Drury's Reports tempore Sugden Chancery (Ir.)

Dru. t. Sugden Drury's Irish Chancery Reports tempore Sugden (1843-44)

DS Deputy Sheriff

D. S.
- Dalton on Sheriffs
- Doctor and Student
- Dalloz-Sirey

DSA Defense Supply Agency

DSAA Defense Security Assistance Agency

DSARC Defense Systems Acquisition Review Council

DSB Drug Supervisory Body (UN)

D. S. B. Debitum sine brevi, debit sans breve (debt without writ)

D. S. C. United States District Court for the District of South Carolina

D. S. D. United States District Court for the District of South Dakota

DSFA Defense Solid Fuels Administration (U. S.)

DSM Designation of Scarce Materials (U. S.)

DSOB Dirksen Senate Office Building (also known as NSOB)

d. s. p. decessit sine prole (died without issue) (Lat.)

d. s. p. l. decessit sine prole legitima (died without legitimate issue) (Lat.)

d. s. p. m. decessit sine prole mascula (died without male issue) (Lat.)

d. s. p. m. s. decessit sine prole mascula superstite (died without surviving male issue) (Lat.)

DSPR Defense Supply Procurement Regulations

d. s. p. s. decessit sine prole superstite (died without surviving issue) (Lat.)

d. s. p. v. decessit sine prole virile (died without male issue) (Lat.)

DTA Defense Transport Administration (U. S.)

D. Tax Dominion Tax Cases (Canada)

D. T. C. Dominion Tax Cases

DTFV Karp, Domestic Torts: Family Violence and Sexual Abuse

D. T. I. Department of Trade and Industry

D. T. (Newspr) (Tas.) Daily Telegraph Reports (Newspaper)

DTPS Brown, Divorce Tax Planning Strategies

Duane Nat. Duane on the Law of Nations

Duane Road L. Duane's Road Laws of Pennsylvania

Dub.
- Dubitatur
- Dubitante

Dublin U. L.J. Dublin University Law Journal

Dublin U. L. Rev. Dublin University Law Review

DUC Division of Unemployment Compensation

Du Cange. Du Cange's Glossarium

Duc.Gl. Ducange's Glossarium

Dud.
- Dudley's Georgia Reports
- Dudley's South Carolina Law Reports (1837-38)

Dud. Ch. Dudley's South Carolina Equity Reports (13 SCEq.) (1837-38)

Dud. Eq. Dudley's South Carolina Equity Reports (1837-38)

Dud. Eq. (S. C.) Dudley's Equity Reports (South Carolina)

Dud. (Ga.) Dudley's Georgia Reports (1830-35)

Dud. (Geo.) Dudley's Georgia Reports

Dud. L. Dudley's South Carolina Law Reports (1837-38)

Dudl.
- Dudley's Georgia Reports (1830-35)
- Dudley's South Carolina Equity Reports
- Dudley's South Carolina Law Reports (1837-38)

Dud. Law. Dudley's South Carolina Law Reports (1837-38)

Dudley (Ga.) Dudley's Georgia Reports (1830-35)

Dud. L. S. C. Dudley's South Carolina Law Reports (1837-38)

Dud. R. Dudley's Reports (Ga.)

Dud. S. C. Dudley's South Carolina Law Reports (1837-38)

Duer. Duer's New York Superior Court Reports

Duer Const. Jur. Duer's Constitutional Jurisprudence

Duer, Ins. Duer on Insurance

Duer Mar. Ins. Duer on Marine Insurance

Duer (NY) Duer's New York Superior Court Reports

Duer Rep. Duer on Representation

Duff. Duff, Feudal Conveyancing (Sc.)

Duff Conv. Duff on Conveyancing, Scotland

Dufresne Dufresne's Glossary

Dug. Mon. Dugdale's Monasticon

Dug. Sum. Dugdale on Summons

Duke Duke's Law of Charitable Uses

Duke B. A. J. Duke Bar Association Journal

Duke B. A. Jo. Duke University Bar Association Journal

Duke Bar J. Duke Bar Journal

Duke B. Ass'n J. Duke Bar Association Journal

Duke B.J. Duke University Bar Association Journal

Duke Ch. Us. Duke on Charitable Uses (1676)

Duke J. Comp. & Int'l L. Duke Journal of Comparative & International Law

Duke L.J. Duke Law Journal

Dulck. Dulcken's Eastern District Reports, Cape Colony (S. Africa)

D.U.L.J. Dublin University Law Journal

Du. L.J. Duke Law Journal

D. U. L.R.
- Dublin University Law Review
- Duquesne University Law Review

Dun.
- Duncan
- Dunlap
- Dunlop

Dun. & Cum. Dunphy's & Cummins' Remarkable Trials

Dunc. Eccl. L. Duncan's Scotch Parochial Ecclesiastical Law

Dunc. Ent. Cas. Duncan's Scotch Entail Cases

Dunc. Ev. Duncombe on the Law of Evidence

Dunc. Man. Duncan's Manual of Summary Procedure

Dunc. Mer. Cas. Duncan's Mercantile Cases (1885-86) (Sc.)

Dunc. Merc. Cas. Duncan's Mercantile Cases (1885-86) (Sc.)

Dunc. N. P. Duncombe's Nisi Prius

Dund. L. C. Dundee Law Chronicle (1853-58)

Dungl. Med. Dict. Dunglison, Dictionary of Medical Science and Literature

Dunl. Dunlop, Bell & Murray's Reports, Second Series, Scotch Session Cases (1838-62)

Dunl. Abr. Dunlap's Abridgment of Coke's Reports

Dunl. Adm. Pr. Dunlop's Admiralty Practice

Dun L. & T. Dun's Landlord and Tenant in Ireland

Dunl. B & M. Dunlop, Bell & Murray's Reports, Second Series, Scotch Session Cases

Dunl. F. Dunlap's Forms

Dunl. L. Pa. Dunlop's Laws of Pennsylvania

Dunl. L. U.S. Dunlop's Laws of the United States

Dunlop Dunlop, Bell & Murray's Reports, Second Series, Scotch Session Cases (1838-62)

Dunl. Paley Ag. Dunlap's Paley on Agency

Dunl. Par. Dunlop on Parochial Law, Scotland

Dunl. Pr. Dunlap's Admiralty Practice

Dunn. Dunning's English King's Bench Reports (1753-54)

Dunning Dunning's Reports (King's Bench) (1753-54)

Dup. Const. Duponceau on the Constitution

Dup. Jur. Duponceau on Jurisiction of United States Courts

Duponceau, U.S. Cts. Duponceau on Jurisdiction of United States Courts

Duq. Duquesne Law Review (Pa.)

Duq. L. Rev. Duquesne Law Review

Duquesne L. Rev. Duquesne University Law Review

Duquesne U. L. Rev. Duquesne University Law Review

Duq.U. L. Rev. Duquesne University Law Review

Durand. Spec. Jur. Durandi Speculum Juris

Durf Durfee's Reports (2 Rhode Island)

Durfee Durfee's Reports (2 Rhode Island)

Durie Durie's Court of Session Decisions (1621-42) (Sc.)

Durn. & E. Durnford & East's (Term) Reports (1785-1800) (Eng.)

D. Utah, D.Utah United States District Court for the District of Utah

Dut. & Cowd. Rev. Dutton & Cowdrey's Revision of Swift's Digest of Conn. Laws

Dutch. Dutcher's Reports (25-29 N. J. Law Reports)

Duv.
- Duvall's Reports (62, 63 Kentucky)
- Duvall's Supreme Court Reports (Canada)

Duvall Duvall's Reports, Canada Supreme Court

Duvall Duvall's Supreme Court Reports (Can.)

Duv. (Can.) Duvall's Reports, Canada Supreme Court

Dux. Duxbury's High Court Reports, South African Republic. 1895

D. V. I. United States District Court for the District of the Virgin Islands

d. v. n. devisavit vel non (issue of fact as to whether a will in question was made by the testator) (Lat.)

d. v. p. decessit vita patris (died during his father's life) (Lat.)

D. Vt. United States District Court for the District of Vermont

Dwar. Dwarris on Statutes (1830-48)

Dwar. St. Dwarris on Statutes

DWB Dismissed for want of bond

D. W. I.
- Descriptive Word Index
- Died without issue
- Driving while intoxicated

Dwight Dwight's Charity Cases (Eng.)

Dw. Mil. Dwyer on the Militia Laws

DWP Dismissed for want of prosecution

Dw. Stat. Dwarris on Statutes

DWTA Wilkins, Drafting Wills and Trust Agreements

D. Wyo. United States District Court for the District of Wyoming

Dy. Dyer's English King's Bench Reports (73 ER)

Dyche & P. Dict. Dyche and Pardon's Dictionary

Dyer Dyer's English King's Bench Reports (73 ER)

Dyer (Eng.) Dyer's English King's Bench Reports (73 ER)

Dym. Death Dut. Dymond, Death Duties, 15ed. 1973

Dy. Sum. Proc. Dyett's Summary Proceedings

E

E.
- Cases in the Eastern District's Local Division of the Supreme Court (1910-46) (S. Afr.)
- Earl
- Easter Term
- East
- Eastern
- East's Term Reports, King's Bench (1800-12) (102-4 ER)
- Eminence
- England
- Eodem (in the same place or under the same title)
- Equity
- Exchequer; English; Edward; Equity; East; Eastern; Easter; Ecclesiastical; East's English King's Bench Reports (1801-12)
- Explained
- Explained; Statement of import of decision in cited case. Not merely a restatement of the facts.

E.A.
- Eastern Africa Law Reports
- Europe Archiv

Ea.
- East's English King's Bench Reports (1801-12)
- East's Notes of Cases (Bengal, India) (1785-1821)

E.A.B. Export Administration Bulletin

EAC East African Community

E.A.C.A. Law Reports of the Court of Appeals of Eastern Africa

E.A.E.C. Treaty setting up the European Atomic Energy Community

E. African L.J. East Africian Law Journal

E. Afr. Ct. App. Law Reports of the Court of Appeal for Eastern Africa

E. Afr. Ct. App. Dig. Court of Appeal for East Africa Digest of Decisions of the Court

E. Afr. L.J. East African Law Journal

E. Afr. L.R. East Africa Law Reports

E. Afr. L. Rep. East Africa Law Reports

E. Afr. L. Rev. Eastern Africa Law Review

Eag. & Y. Eagle & Younge's English Tithe Cases

Eag. & Yo. Eagle & Younge's English Tithe Cases

EAGGF European Agricultural Guidance and Guarantee Fund

Eag. Mag. Com. Eagle's Magistrate's Pocket Companion

Eag. T. Eagle, Law of Tithes. 2ed. 1836

E.A.H.C. East African High Commission

EAJA Equal Access to Justice Act

E.A.J. Criminol. East African
Journal of Criminology

E.A.L.J. East African Law Journal

E.A.L.R. East Africa Law Reports

E.A.L. Rev. Eastern Africa Law
Review

EAMA African States associated
with the EEC

E. & A.
- Ecclesiastical and Admiralty Report (1853-55)
- Error and Appeal
- Spink's Ecclesiastical and Admiralty Reports
- Upper Canada Error and Appeal Reports

E. & A.R. Error and Appeal Reports, Ontario (1846-66)

E. & A.U.C. Grant's Error and Appeal Reports Ontario (Can.)
(1846-66)

E. & A.W.C. Grant's Error and Appeal Reports (Ontario)

E. & B Ellis & Blackburn's English Queen's Bench Reports (1852-58)

E. & E. Ellis & Ellis' English
Queen's Bench Reports (1858-61)

E. & E.D. English and Empire Digest

E. & E. Dig. English and Empire
Digest

E. & I. English and Irish Appeals,
House of Lords

E. & I. App. Law Reports, House
of Lords, English and Irish Appeals

E. & O.E. Errors and omissions excepted

E. & W. England and Wales

E. & Y. Eagle & Younge, English
Tithe Cases (1204-1825)

E.A.P.L.R. East Africa Protectorate Law Reports (1897-1921)

E.A. Prot. L.R. East Africa Protectorate Law Reports

Earn. Earnshaw's Gold Coast
Judgments (1909-10) (Ghana)

Earnshaw Gold Coast Judgments,
by Earnshaw (1909-10) (Ghana)

Earth Law J. Earth Law Journal.
Leyden, Netherlands

Earth L.J. Earth Law Journal,
Leyden, Netherlands

Earw. Earwalker's Manchester.
Court Leet Records (Eng.)

EAS Executive Agreement Series

E.A.S. Executive Agreement Series. United States

Ease. Easements and Licenses

E. Asian Executive Rep. East
Asian Executive Reports

East
- East's King's Bench Reports
(102-104 ER)
- East's Notes of Cases in Morley's East Indian Digest

East. Eastern Law Reporter, Can.

East Af East Africa Court of Appeals Reports

East Afr. J. Criminol. East African Journal of Criminology

East Afr. L.J. East African Law
Journal

East. Afr. L.R. Eastern Africa
Law Review

East Afr. L. Rep.
- East Africa Law Reports (London)
- Eastern Africa Law Reports (Durban)

East. Afr. L. Rev. Eastern Africa Law Review (Dar es Salaam)

East. D.C. Eastern District Court Reports (S. Africa)

East. D.L. Eastern Districts, Local Division, South African Law Reports

East (Eng.)
- East's King's Bench Reports (102-104 ER)
- East's Notes of Cases in Morley's East Indian Digest

Eastern J. Int'l. L. Eastern Journal of International Law

Eastern J. of Internat. L. The Eastern Journal of International Law. Madras, India

East Europe International Market Letter: East Europe

East. J. Int. L. Eastern Journal of International Law (India)

East. L.R. Eastern Law Reporter (Canada)

East. L.R. (Can.) Eastern Law Reporter (Canada)

East N. of C. East's Notes of Cases (in Morley's East Indian Digest)

East Pak. East Pakistan

East P.C. East's Pleas of the Crown (1803)

East PC (Eng.) East's Pleas of the Crown

East Pl. Cr. East's Pleas of the Crown

East Punjab All India Reporter, East Punjab (1948-50)

East. Rep.
- Eastern Law Reporter, Can.

Eastern Reporter

East. T. Eastern Term (Eng.)

East. U.S. Bus.L.Rev. Eastern United States Business Law Review

E.A.T. Employment Appeals Tribunal

Eat. Cont. Eaton's Supplement to Chipman on Contracts

Eaves. Eavesdropping

E.A.W.R. Employment-At-Will Reporter

E.B. Ecclesiastical Compensations (or "Bots")

E.B. & E. Ellis, Blackburn & Ellis' English Queen's Bench Reports (1858)

E.B. & S. (Ellis) Best & Smith's English Queen's Bench Reports

EBC Employee Benefits Cases

Ebersole Ebersole's Reports (59-80 Iowa)

Ebersole (Ia.) Ebersole's Reports (59-80 Iowa)

Ebs. Inf. Ebsworth on the Law of Infants

E.C.
- Ecclesiastical Commissioner
- Election Cases
- Employment Commission
- English Chancery
- English Chancery Reports (American Reprint)

- Established Church
- European Communities
- Ontario Election Cases (1884-1900) (Can.)

Ec. Ecclesiastical

ECA
- Economic Commission for Africa
- Economic Corporation Administration (U. S.)
- Exceptional circumstances allowance
- United States Economic Commission for Africa

ECAB Decisions of the Employee's Compensation Appeals Board (U. S.)

ECAFE Economic Commission for Asia & the Far East (UN)

Ec. & Mar. Notes of Cases, Ecclesiastical & Maritime Courts (1844-50) (Eng.)

Ecc. Ecclesiastical

Ecc. & Ad. Spink's Ecclesiastical and Admiralty Reports (1853-55)

E.C.C.J. European Communities Court of Justice

Eccl. Ecclesiastical

Eccl. & Ad.
- Ecclesiastical and Admiralty
- Spink's Ecclesiastical and Admiralty Reports

Eccl. & Adm. Spink's Ecclesiastical & Admiralty (Upper Can.)

Eccl. Ct. Ecclesiastical Court

Ecc. L.J. Ecclesiastical Law Journal

Eccl. R. English Ecclesiastical Reports

Eccl. Rep. Ecclesiastical Reports (Eng.)

Eccl. Stat. Ecclesiastical Statutes

E.C.C.P. European Committee on Crime Problems

ECE Economic Commission for Europe (UN)

ECG Export Credit Guarantees

E.C.G.D. Export Credits Guarantee Department

EC Human Rights European Commission of Human Rights

ECI Engineer Contract Instructions

ECITO European Inland Transport Organization

E.C.J. Court of Justice of the European Communities

ECLA Economic Commission for Latin America (UN)

E.C.L. (Eng.) English Common Law Reports, American Reprint

E.C.L.R. European Competition Law Review

E.C.M. European Common Market

ECMT European Conference of Ministers of Transport

E.C.O. Entry Clearance Officer (Immigration)

Ecol L Q Ecology Law Quarterly

Ecol. L. Quart. Ecology Law Quarterly

Ecology L.Q. Ecology Law Quarterly

Econ. Economic(s); Economy

Econ. Bull. Eur. Economic Bulletin for Europe

Econ. Bull. for Europe Economic Bulletin for Europe

Econ. Contr. Economic Controls (CCH)

Econ. Stand. (CCH) Economic Standards

ECOSOC United Nations Economic and Social Council

ECOWAS Economic Community of West African States

ECPA Energy Conservation and Production Act

E.C.R.
- Canada Exchequer Court Reports (1875-1922)
- European Court Reports (European Communities)

ECS European Company Statute

ECSC European Coal and Steel Community

ECWA Economic Commission for Western Asia (UN)

E.D.
- Eastern District Court Reports, Cape of Good Hope (S. Afr.) (1880--1909)
- Entertainment Duty
- Estate Duty(-ies)
- Exchequer Division, Law Reports (Eng.)

ed.
- edition
- editor

ED Edition

Ed.
- Eden's English Chancery Reports (1757-66)
- Edgar's Decisions. Court of Session (1724--25) (Sc.)

- Edinburgh

Edited
- Edition
- Editor
- Edward

EDA Economic Development Administration

E.D. Ark. United States District Court for the Eastern and Western Districts of Arkansas

Ed. Ass. Eddis, Administration of Assets. 1880

Ed. Bills Eddis on Bills of Exchange

Ed. B.L. Eden's Bankrupt Law

Ed. Bro. Eden's Edition of English Chancery Reports (1757-66)

E.D.C.
- Eastern District Court Reports, Cape of Good Hope (S. Africa)
- European Defence Community
- European Documentation Centre

E.D. Cal. United States District Court for the Eastern District of California

Ed. Ch. Edward's New York Chancery Reports

Ed. Ch (N. Y.) Edwards' Chancery Reports (N. Y.)

Ed. Ch. R. Edwards' Chancery Reports (N. Y.)

Ed. Comment Editorial Comment

Ed. C.R. Edwards' New York Chancery Reports

Ed. Cr. Edwards' Chancery Reports (N. Y.)

Ed. Dept. Rep. Education Department Reports (N. Y.)

EDE European Defense Community

Eden. Eden, English Chancery Reports (28 ER)

Eden. Bankr. Eden's Bankrupt Law

Eden (Eng.) Eden, English Chancery Reports (28 ER)

Eden, Pen. Law Eden's Principles of Penal Law

Eden's Prin. P.L. Eden's Principles of Penal Law

EDF European Development Fund

Edg. Edgar's Reports. Court of Session, Scotland (1724-25)

Edgar Edgar Reports, Court of Session (1724-25) (Sc.)

Edg. C. Cannons enacted under King Edgar

Edg. Leas. Edges' Forms of Leases

Ed. H.L.R Education for the Handicapped Law Report

Edict Edicts of Justinian

Edicta Edicts of Justinian

E.D. Ill. United States District Court for the Eastern District of Illinois

Edinb. L.J. Edinburgh Law Journal

Ed. Inj. Eden, Injunctions. 1821

E.D.I.T. Estate Duties Investment Trust

Edit.
- Edited
- Edition
- Editor

E.D. Ky. United States District Court for the Eastern District of Kentucky

E.D.L. South African Law Reports, Eastern Districts Local Division (S. Africa)

E.D. La. United States District Court for the Eastern District of Louisiana

Ed. L.J. Edinburgh Law Journal (1831-37)

Edm. Addr. Edmands' Address to his Law Students

Edm. Exch. Pr. Edmund's Exchequer Practice

E.D. Mich. United States District Court for the Eastern District of Michigan

E.D. Mo. United States District Court for the Eastern District of Missouri

Edmonds' St. at Large Edmonds' Statutes at Large (N. Y.)

Edm. Sel. Ca. Edmonds' New York Select Cases

Edm. Sel. Cas. Edmonds' New York Select Cases

Edm. Sel. Cas. (NY) Edmonds' New York Select Cases

Edm. Stat. Edmonds' Edition of the New York Statutes

E.D.N.C. United States District Court for the Eastern District of North Carolina

E.D.N.Y. United States District Court for the Eastern District of New York

Ed. O. Education Order

E.D. Okla. United States District Court for the Eastern District of Oklahoma

EDP
- Electronic data processing
- Golden, Equitable Distribution of Property

E.D. Pa. United States District Court for the Eastern District of Pennsylvania

Ed. P.L. Eden's Principles of Penal Law

E.D.R. Roscoe, Eastern District Reports (Cape of Good Hope)

E.D.S. E. D. Smith's New York Common Pleas Reports

Eds.
- Editions
- editors

E.D. Smith E. D. Smith's New York Common Pleas Reports

E.D. Smith (N. Y.) E.D. Smith's New York Common Pleas Reports

E.D. Smith R. E. D. Smith's New York Common Pleas Reports (N. Y.)

E.D. Smith's C. P. R. E. D. Smith's New York Common Pleas Reports (N. Y.)

E.D. Smith's R. E. D. Smith New York Common Pleas Reports (N. Y.)

E.D. Tenn. United States District Court for the Eastern District of Tennessee

E.D. Tex. United States District Court for the Eastern District of Texas

E.D. Va. United States District Court for the Eastern District of Virginia

Educ. Education; Educational

Educ. L. Rep. (West) Education Law Reporter

Edw.
- Edward
- Edwards' Chester Palatine Courts (Eng.)
- Edwards' English Admiralty Reports
- Edwards' New York Chancery Reports
- Edwards' Reports (2,3 Missouri)

Edw. Abr.
- Edward's Abridgment Prerogative Court Cases (1846)
- Edward's Abridgment Privy Council

Edw. Adm. Edward's Admiralty (Eng.) (165 ER)

Edw. Adm. (Eng.) Edward's Admiralty (Eng.) (165 ER)

Edw. Adm. Jur. Edwards, Admiralty Jurisdiction. 1847

Edwards' Chr. R. Edwards' Chancery Reports (N. Y.)

Edwards' Rep. Edwards' Chancery Reports (N. Y.)

E.D. Wash. United States District Court for the Eastern District of Washington

Edw. Bail. Edwards on the Law of Bailments

Edw. Bailm. Edwards on the Law of Bailments

Edw. Bills Edwards on Bills and Notes

Edw. Bills & N. Edwards on Bills and Notes

Edw. Brok. & F. Edwards on Factors and Brokers

Edw. Ch. Edwards' New York Chancery Reports (1831-50)

Edw. Chan. Edwards' Chancery Reports (N. Y.)

Edw. Ch. (NY) Edwards' New York Chancery Reports (N. Y.)

Edw. Conf. Edward the Confessor

Edw. Eccl. Jur. Edwards on Ecclesiastical Jurisdiction

Edw. Fac. Edwards, Factors and Brokers

Edw. Gam. Edwards' Law of Gaming

E.D. Wis. United States District Court for the Eastern District of Wisconsin

Edw. Jur. Edwards' Juryman's Guide

Edw. Lead. Dec. Edwards' Leading Decisions in Admiralty (Edwards' Admiralty Reports)

Edw. Mo. Edward's Reports (2-3 Missouri)

Edw. (N.Y.) Edwards' Chancery Reports (N. Y.)

Edw. Part. Edwards on Parties in Chancery

Edw. P.C. Edwards' Prize Cases (Eng.)

Edw. Pleas. Edwards' Pleasantries of the Courts of New York

Edw. Pr. Cas. Edwards' Prize Cases (English Admiralty Reports)

Edw. Pr. Ct. Cas. Edwards' Abridgement of Prerogative Court Cases

Edw. Rec. Edwards on Receivers in Equity

Edw. Ref. Edwards on the Law of Referees

Edw. Rep. Edwards'Chancery Reports (N. Y.)

Edw. St. Act Edwards on the Stamp Act

Edw. (Tho.) Edwards' English Admiralty Reports

Edw. Treat. Edwards' Justices' Treatise

EE Schwartz, Engineering Evidence

E.E.
- English Exchequer Reports (American Reprint) Equity Exchequer
- Equity Exchequer
- errors excepted

E.E. & M.P. Envoy Extraordinary and Minister Plenipotentiary

EEC European Economic Community (Common Market)

E.E.C.J.O. Official Journal of the European Communities

E.E.C.L. Encyclopedia of European Community Law

E.E.C. Prot. P.I. Protocol on Privileges and Immunities of the European Economic Community

EEI Executive Enterprises, Inc.

EEO Equal Employment Opportunity

EEOC
- Equal Employment Opportunity Commission
- Compl. Man.
- Equal Employment Opportunity Commission Compliance Manual (CCH)

E.E.O.C. Compliance Manual
Equal Employment Opportunity Commission Compliance Manual (CCH)

EEOC Comp. Man.
- EEOC Compliance Manual (Bureau of National Affairs)
- EEOC Compliance Manual (Commerce Clearing House)

E.E.R.
- English Ecclesiastical Reports (American Reprint)
- European Economic Review

E.E.T.S.   Early English Text Society

Eff.   Effective

Efird   Efird's Reports (45-56 South Carolina)

EFT   Electronic Fund Transfers

EFTA   European Free Trade Association

E.G.   Estate Gazette

e.g.   for example

Egan Bills   Egan, Bills of Sale. 4ed. 1882

E.G.D.   Estates Gazette Digest of Cases

E.G.D.C.   Estates Gazette Digest of Cases

Eg. Ext.   Egan, Extradition. 1846

Egg.Dam.   Eggleston on Damages

E.G.L.   Encyclopedia of Georgia Law

Egr. High.   Egremont on the Law of Highways

EHLR   Education for the Handicapped Law Report

E.H.R.R.   European Human Rights Reports

EHS   Environmental Health Services

E.I.
- East India
- East Indian
- East Indies
- Ecclesiastical Institutes
- Executive Instruments (Ghana)

EIA   Energy Information Administration

EIB   European Investment Bank

EIC   Energy Information Council

E.I.C.   East India Company

Eif. Jud. Act   Eiffe on the Irish Judicature Act

Eil. Wom.   Eiloart, Laws relating to Women. 1878

E. India Co.   East India Company

Eir.   Lambards Eirenarcha

E.I.R.R.   European Industrial Relations Review

E.I.S.   Environmental Impact Statement

Eject.   Ejectment

EL   Selz & Simensky, Entertainment Law

E.L.   Education and Labor

El.
- Elchies' Decisions, Scotch Court of Session

- Queen Elizabeth

El. & B. Ellis & Blackburn's English Queen's Bench Reports (118-120 ER)

El. & Bl. Ellis & Blackburn's English Queen's Bench Reports (118-120 ER)

El. & Bl. (Eng.) Ellis & Blackburn's English Queen's Bench Reports (118-120 ER)

El. & El. Ellis & Ellis' English Queen's Bench Reports (120, 121 ER)

El. & El. (Eng.) Ellis & Ellis' English Queen's Bench Reports (120, 121 ER)

E.L. & Eq. English Law and Equity, American Reprint

El. B. & E. Ellis, Blackburn, & Ellis' English Queen's Bench Reports

El. B. & El. Ellis, Blackburn & Ellis' English Queen's Bench Reports

El. B. & S. Ellis, Best & Smith's Queen's Bench Reports (1861-69) (121-22 ER)

El. B. & S. (Eng.) Ellis, Best, & Smith, English Queen's Bench Reports

El., Bl. & El. Ellis, Blackburn, and Ellis' English Queen's Bench Reports (120 ER)

El. Bl. & El. (Eng.) Ellis, Blackburn, and Ellis' English Queen's Bench Reports (120 ER)

E.L.C. Acts Expiring Law Continuance Acts

El. Cas.
- Election Cases (Ontario)
- New York Election Cases (Armstrong's)

El. Cas. (NY) New York Election Cases (Armstrong's)

Elch. Elchies, Court of Session Cases (Sc.)

Elchies Elchies' Court of Session Cases (Sc.)

Elchies' Dict. Elchies' (Dictionary of) Decisions, Scotch Court of Session

eld.
- elder
- eldest

El. Dict. Elchies' Dictionary of Decisions, Court of Session (Sc.)

El. Dig. Eller's Minnesota Digest

ELDO European Space Vehicle Launcher Development Organization

Elec.
- Election
- Electric(ity)
- Electrical
- Electronic

Elec. C. Elections Code

Elec. L.R. Election Law Reports (India)

Elect. Cas. Election Cases Armstrong, N.Y.

Elect. Cas. N. Y. New York Election Cases (Armstrong's)

Elect. Rem. Election of Remedies

Elect. Rep. Election Reports (Ontario)

Elev. Elevators

ELI Environmental Law Institute

Eliz. Queen Elizabeth, as 13 Eliz.

Ell. & Bl. Ellis & Blackburn's English Queen's Bench Reports

Ell. & Ell. Ellis & Ellis' English Queen's Bench Reports

Ell. Ann. Ellison Law of Annuities

Ell. B. & S. Ellis, Best and Smith Queen's Bench Reports

Ell. Bl. & Ell. Ellis, Blackburn, & Ellis' English Queen's Bench Reports

Ell. D. & Cr. Ellis, Debtor and Creditor. 1822

Ell. Deb. Elliot's Debates on the Federal Constitution

Ell. Dip. Code Elliot's American Diplomatic Code

Ellesm. Post N. Ellesmere's Post Nati

Ellesm. Postn. Ellesmere's Post Nati

Ell. Ins. Ellis on Fire and Life Insurance and Annuities

Elliot, Deb. Fed. Const. Elliot's Debates on the Federal Constitution

Elliott, App. Proc. Elliott's Appellate Procedure

Elliott, Roads & S. Elliott on Roads and Streets

Elliott, Supp. Elliott Supplement to the Indiana Revised Statutes

Ellis Ellis on Insurance

Ellis & Bl. Ellis and Blackburn's Queen's Bench Reports (118-120 ER) (1851-58)

Ellis & Vl. Ellis and Blackburn's English Queen's Bench Reports

Ellis Dr. & Cr. Ellis on the Law of Debtor and Creditor

Ell. Trade Ellet on the Laws of Trade

Ells. Cop. Man. Ellsworth's Copyright Manual

Elm. Arch. Jur. Elmes on Architectural Jurisprudence

Elm. Dig. Elmer's Digest of Laws (N. J.)

Elm. Dilap. Elmes on Ecclesiastical Civil Dilapidation

Elmer, Lun. Elmer's Practice in Lunacy

Elm. Exec. Dep. Elmes' Executive Departments of the United States

Elm. Lun. Elmer's Practice in Lunacy

Elm. N.J. Laws Elmer's New Jersey Laws

El Paso Trial Law. Rev. El Paso Trial Lawyers Reviews

Elph. Elphinstone, Norton and Clark, Interpretation of Deeds (1885)

Elph. Conv. Elphinstone's Introduction to Conveyancing

Elph. Interp. Deeds Elphinstone's Rules for Interpretation of Deeds

E.L.R.
- Eastern Law Reporter (Canada)
- Election Law Reports (India)
- European Law Review

E.L. Rev. European Law Review

El. Sal. El Salvador

Els. W. Bl. Elsley's edition of Wm. Blackstone's English King's Bench Reports

Elsyn. Parl. Elsynge on Parliaments

E.L.T. Eagle on the Law of Tithes

Elt. Com. Elton on Commons and Waste Lands

Elt. Copyh. Elton on Copyholds

Elton, Com. Elton on Commons and Waste Lands

Elton, Copyh. Elton on Copyholds

Elt. Ten. of Kent Elton's Tenures of Kent

Elw. Mal. Elwell on Malpractice and Medical Jurisprudence

Elw. Med. Jur. Elwell on Malpractice and Medical Jurisprudence

EMA European Monetary Agreement

Em. App. Emergency Court of Appeals (U. S.)

Embez. Embezzlement

Embrac. Embracery

EMCF European Monetary and Cooperation Fund

Em. Ct. App. Emergency Court of Appeals (U. S.)

Em. Dom. Eminent Domain

Emer. Ct. App. Emergency Court of Appeals (U. S.)

Emerig. Ins. Emerigon on Insurance

Emerig. Mar. Loans Emerigon on Maritime Loans

Emer. Ins. Emerigon on Insurance

Emer. Mar. Lo. Emerigon on Maritime Loans

Emerson & Haber, Pol. & Civ. Rits. Emerson & Haber's Political & Civil Rights in the United States

E. Min. L. Inst. Eastern Mineral Law Institute

Em. J. Int. Disp. Resol. Emory Journal of International Dispute Resolution

Em. L.J. Emory Law Journal

Emory Int'l L. Rev. Emory International Law Review

Emory L.J. Emory Law Journal

Emp.
- Emperor
- Empire
- Empress

Empl. & Training Rep. (BNA) Employment and Training Reporter

Empl. Com. Employment Commission

Empl. Comp. App. Bd. Decisions of the Employees' Compensation Appeals Board

Empl. Coordinator (R.I.A.) Employment Coordinator

Employ. Ag. Employment Agency

Employee Benefits Cas. (BNA) Employee Benefits Cases

Employee Rel. L.J. Employee Relations Law Journal

Empl. Prac. Dec. (CCH) Employment Practices Decisions (CCH)

Empl. Prac. Guide (CCH) Employment Practices Guide (CCH)

Empl. Rel. L.J. Employee Relations Law Journal

Empl'rs. Liab. Employers' Liability

Empl. Safety & Health Guide (CCH) Employment Safety and Health Guide (Commerce Clearing House)

Empl. Saf'y & Health Guide (CCH) Employment Safety and Health Guide (CCH)

EMS Export Marketing Service

Em. T.
- Employment Taxes, Social Security Act rulings (U. S. Internal Revenue Service)
- Employment Tax Ruling (U. S.)

EMU Economic and Monetary Union

Enc. Amer. Encyclopedia Americana

Enc. Arch. Gwilt's Encyclopedia of Architecture

Enc. Brit. Encyclopedia Britannica

Enc. Dict. Encyclopedia Dictionary, Edited by Robert Hunter (1879-88)

Enc. Forms Encyclopedia of Forms

Enc. Law American and English Encyclopedia of Law

Enc. Pl. & Pr. Encyclopedia of Pleading and Practice

Enc. Pl. & Prac. Encyclopedia of Pleading and Practice

Enc. U.S. Sup. Ct. Rep. Encyclopedia of United States Supreme Court Reports

Encyc. Encyclopedia of the Laws of England, 2 editions (1897-1919)

Ency. L. & P. American & English Encyclopedia of Law & Practice

Ency. Law American and English Encyclopedia of Law

Ency. of Ev. Encyclopedia of Evidence

Ency. of Forms Encyclopedia of Forms & Precedents

Ency. of L. & Pr. Encyclopedia of Law and Practice

Ency. of Pl. & Pr. Encyclopedia of Pleading and Practice

Ency. P. & P. Encyclopedia of Pleading & Practice

Ency. U.S. Sup. Ct. Encyclopedia of United States Supreme Court Reports

Ency. U.S. Sup. Ct. Rep. Encyclopedia of Pleading and Practice Supplement

End. Bdg. Ass. Endlich on Building Associations

ENDC Eighteen-Nation Disarmament Committee

End. Interp. St. Endlich's Commentaries on the Interpretation of Statutes

Endl. Bidg. Ass'ns. Endlich on Building Associations

E.N.E.A. European Nuclear Energy Agency

Energy Cont. (P-H) Energy Controls (Prentice-Hall)

Energy L.J. Energy Law Journal

Energy L. Serv. (Callaghan) Energy Law Service

Energy Mgmt. (CCH) Energy Management

Energy Users Rep. (BNA) Energy Users Report (Bureau of National Affairs)

Enf. enforced, enforcement, enforcing

Enfd. Enforced

enf'. den. enforcement denied

enf'g enforced; enforcing; enforcement

Eng.
- England
- English
- English Reports by N. C. Moak
- English's Reports (6-13 Arkansas)

Eng. Ad.
- English Admiralty
- English Admiralty Reports

Eng. Adm. English Admiralty

Eng. Adm. R. English Admiralty Reports

Eng. & Ir. App. Law Reports, English & Irish Appeal Cases

Eng. C.C. English Crown Cases (American Reprint)

Eng. Ch.
- English Chancery
- English Chancery Reports (American Reprint)

Eng. C.L. English Common Law Reports (American Reprint)

Eng. Com. L.R. English Common Law Reports

Eng. Cr. Cas. English Crown Cases (American Reprint)

Eng. Eccl. English Ecclesiastical Reports

Eng. Ecc. R. English Ecclesiastical Reports

Eng. Exch. English Exchequer Reports

Eng'g. engineering

Eng. Hist. Rev. English Historical Review

Eng. Ir. App. Law Reports, English and Irish Appeal Cases

Eng. Judg. Scotch Court of Session Cases, decided by the English Judges (1655-61)

Engl. England

Eng. L. & Eq. English Law and Equity Reports (American Reprint)

Eng. L. & Eq. R. English Law and Equity Reports (American Reprint)

Eng. Law & Eq. English Law and Equity Reports (American Reprint)

English English's Reports (6-13 Arkansas)

Eng. Pews English on Church Pews

Eng. Pl. The English Pleader

Eng. Pr. Cas. Roscoe's English Prize Cases

Eng'r. Engineer; Engineering

Eng. R. & C. Cas. English Railway and Canal Cases

Eng. Re. English Reports (Full Reprint)

Eng. Rep.
- English Reports, Full Reprint (1220-1865)
- English Reports (Moaks Amer. Reprint)
- English's Reports (6-13 Arkansas)

Eng. Rep. Anno. English Reports Annotated

Eng. Rep. R. English Reports (Full Reprint)

Eng. Rep. Re. English Reports (Full Reprint)

Eng. Reprint English Reprint

Eng. R.R. Ca. English Railway & Canal Cases

Eng. Ru. Ca. English Ruling Cases

Eng. Ru.Cas. English Ruling Cases

Eng. Rul. Cas. English Ruling Cases

Eng. Ry. & C. Cas. English Railway and Canal Cases

Eng. Sc. Ecc. English & Scotch Ecclesiastical Reports

enjoin enjoined; enjoining

E.N.L.N. Eastern Nigeria Legal Notice

E.N.L.R.
- Eastern Nigeria Law Reports (1956-60)
- Eastern Region of Nigeria Law Reports

ENP Exceptional needs payment

ENR Energy and Natural Resources

Ent.
- entertainment
- Coke's Entries
- Rastell's Entries

Ent. & Sports Law. Entertainment & Sports Lawyer

ENTENTE Political-Economic Association of Ivory Coast, Dahomey, Niger, Upper Volta, and Togo

enter
- entered
- entering

Enter. enterprise

Entertainment & Med. L. Entertainment & Media Law

Entertainment L.J. Entertainment Law Journal

Entertainment L.R. Entertainment Law Reporter

Entries, Antient. Rastell's Entries (so cited in Rolle Abr.)

Entries, New Book of Rastell's Entries, to distinguish from Liber Intrationum; - Coke's Entries, to distinguish from Rastell's Entries

Entries, Old Book of Liber Intrationum

En. Users Rep. Energy Users Report (CCH)

Env. Aff. Environmental Affairs

Env. Extr. Envoy Extraordinary

Envir. Conserv. Environmental Conservation

Envir. L. Rep. Environmental Law Reporter

Environ. L. Environmental Law

Environ. L. Rev. Environment Law Review

Environmental Law Environmental Law

Environm. L. Environmental Law

Environm. Policy & L. Environmental Policy and Law

Envir. Rep. Environment Reporter (BNA)

Env. L. Environmental Law

Env. L. Rev. Environmental Law Review

Env. L. Rptr. Environmental Law Reporter

Env't Environment

Envt'l. Environmental

Envtl. Affairs Environmental Affairs

Envtl. Claims J. Environmental Claims Journal

Envtl.F. Environmental Forum

Envt'l. L. Environmental Law

Envtl. L.J. Environmental Law Journal

Envt'l. L.Q. Newsl. Environmental Law Quarterly Newsletter

Envt'l. L. Rep. (Envtl. L. Inst.) Environmental Law Reporter

Envtl. L. Rev. Environmental Law Review

Envtl. L. Rptr. Environmental Law Reporter

Envtl. & Plan. L.J. Environmental and Planning Law Journal

Envtl. Pol'y & L. Environmental Policy and Law

Env't Reg. Handbook (Env't Information Center) Environment Regulation Handbook

Env't. Rep. (BNA) Environment Reporter (Bureau of National Affairs)

Env't Rep. Cas. (BNA) Environment Reporter Cases

E.O. Presidential Executive Order (U. S.)

E.O.C. Equal Opportunities Commission

Eod. Eodem

E. of Cov. Trial of the Earl of Coventry

EP Skillern, Environmental Protection: The Legal Framework

E.P. Estate Planning

EPA Equal Pay Act of 1963

E.P.A.
- Emergency Powers Act. 1940
- Environmental Protection Agency

E.P.C.
- East's Pleas of the Crown (Eng.)
- Excess Profits Tax Council Ruling or Memorandum, Internal Revenue Bureau (U. S.)
- Roscoe's Prize Cases (Eng.)

E.P.C.A. Energy Policy and Conservation Act

EP(C)A Employment Protection (Consolidation) Act

E.P.D.
- Employment Practice Decisions (CCH)
- Excess Profit Duty

E.P.D.A. Emergency Powers (Defence) Act

EPFR Kelley & Ludtke, Estate Planning for Farmers and Ranchers

EPGA Emergency Petroleum and Gas Administration

E.P.T. Excess Profits Tax

EPTL New York Estate Power and Trust Law

EPU European Payments Union

EPW Environment and Public Works

Eq.
- Equitable

- Equity
- Equity Court or Division
- Equity Reports (1835-55)

Eq. Ab. Abridgment of Cases in Equity

Eq. Ca. Abr. Abridgment of Cases in Equity (1667-1744) (21-2 ER)

Eq. Cas.
- Equity Cases, Modern Reports (vols. 9, 10)
- Gilbert, Equity Cases

Eq. Cas. Abr. Equity Cases Abridged (English), 2 vols. (21, 22 ER)

Eq. Cas. Abr. (Eng.) Equity Cases abridged (English), 2 vols. (21, 22 ER)

Eq. Cas. Mod. Equity Cases, 9 Modern Reports (1722-55) (88 ER)

Eq. Conv. Equitable Conversion

Eq. Draft. Equity Draftsman (Van Heythuysen's, edited by Hughes)

Eq. Empl. Compl. Man. (Callaghan) Equal Employment Compliance Manual

Eq. Guinea Equatorial Guinea

Eq. Judg. Equity Judgments (by A'Beckett) New South Wales

Eq. R.
- Common Law and Equity Reports. (1853-55)
- Gilbert's Equity Reports (1705-27)
- Harper's South Carolina Equity Reports. 1824

Eq. R. (Eng.) Equity Reports

Eq. Rep.
- Equity Reports (1853-55)

- Equity Reports, published by Spottiswoode
- Gilbert's Equity Reports (1705-27)
- Harper's South Carolina Equity Reports

Equi. Dist. Rep. Equitable Distribution Reporter

Equip. Equipment

Equity Rep.
- Common Law and Equity Reports (1853-55)
- English Chancery Appeals
- Equity Reports (Gilbert) (Eng.)
- Harper's Equity (S. C.)

E.R.
- Eastern Region
- East's King's Bench Reports (Eng.)
- Economic Regulations (CAB)
- Edwardus Rex (King Edward)
- Election Reports (Ontario)
- Elizabeth Regina (Queen Elizabeth)
- English Reports, Full Reprint (1220-1865)

E.R.A. English Reports Annotated

ERB Employment Relations Board

ERC Energy Resources Council

E.R.C.
- English Ruling Cases
- Environmental Reporter Cases (BNA)

E.R.C. (Eng.) English Ruling Cases

Erck Erck's Ecclesiastical Register (1608-1825) (Eng.)

ERDA Energy Research and Development Administration

Erg. Erganzung (Ger.) Amendment, supplement

Erie Erie County Legal Journal (Pa.)

Erie Co. Leg. J. Erie County Legal Journal

Erie Co. L.J. (Pa.) Erie County Law Journal (Pa.)

Erie L.J. Erie County Legal Journal (Pa.)

ERISA Employment Relations Income Security Act

Erle Tr. Un. Erle on the Law of Trade-Unions

E.R.L.R. Eastern Region of Nigeria Law Reports

E.R.N.L.R. Eastern Region of Nigeria Law Reports

E.R.O. European Regional Organisation of the International Confederation of Free Trade Unions

EROS Earth Resources Observation Systems

ERP European Recovery Program

E.R.P.N. Eastern Region Public Notice (Nigeria)

Err. & App. Error and Appeals Reports (Upper Canada)

erron.
- erroneous
- erroneously

ERS Economic Research Service

Ersk.
- Erskine's Institutes of the Law of Scotland
- Erskine's Principles of the Law of Scotland

Ersk. Dec. Erskine's United States Circuit Court, etc. , Decisions (vol. 35 Georgia)

Erskine I. Erskine's Institutes of the Law of Scotland 8 editions (1773-1871)

Erskine, Inst. Erskine's Institutes of the Law of Scotland. 8 editions (1773-1871)

Ersk. Inst. Erskine's Institutes of the Law of Scotland

Ersk. Prin. Erskine's Principles of the Law of Scotland

Ersk. Speech Erskine's Speeches

Ersk. Speeches Erskine's Speeches

ERTA Economic Recovery Tax Act of 1981

e. s. eldest son

ESA
- Economic Stabilization Agency
- Employment Security Agency
- Employment Standards Administration
- European Space Agency

ESARS Employment Service Automated Reporting System

ESB
- Employment Security Board
- Employment Services Bureau

ESC
- Economic and Social Committee
- Employment Security Commission
- Employment Stabilization Commission

Esc. Escrow

ESCAP Economic and Social Commission for Asia and the Pacific (UN)

E. School L. Rev. Eastern School Law Review

ESCOR Economic and Social Council

Escriche, Dict. Escriche's Dictionary of Jurisprudence

ESD
- Employment Security Department
- Employment Security Division
- Employment Service Division

ESOP Employee Stock Ownership Plan

Esp. Espinasse's English Nisi Prius Reports (1793-1810)

Esp. Act. Espinasse's Actions on Statutes

Esp. Bank Espinasse, Law of Bankrupts. 1825

Esp. Dig. Espinasse's Digest of the Law of Actions and Trials

Esp. Ev. Espinasse, Evidence, 2ed. 1825

Esp. N.P. Espinasse's English Nisi Prius Reports (1793-1810)

Esp. Pen. Ev. Espinasse on Penal Evidence

Esp.P. St. Espinasse on Penal Statutes

Esq. Esquire

Esq. Ins. Esquirol on Insanity

ESRO European Space Research Organization

Ess. Ang. Sax. Law Essays on Anglo-Saxon Law

Est. Estate(s)

est. established

Estab. Establishment

Est. & Tr. J. Estates & Trusts Journal

Est. & Tr. Q. Estate and Trusts Quarterly

Est. & Tr. Rep. Estates and Trusts Reports

Est. & Trusts Estates and Trusts

Estates Gaz. Estates Gazette

Estates Q. Estates and Trusts Quarterly

Estee Estee's District Court of Hawaii

Estee (Hawaii) Estee's District Court of Hawaii

Est. Gaz. Estates Gazette

Est. Gaz. Dig. Estates Gazette Digest of Land and Property Cases

Est. Gifts & Tr. J. Estates, Gifts & Trusts Journal

Estm. Estimated

Estop. & W. Estoppel and Waiver

Est. Plan. Estate Planning

Est. Plan. Inst. Estate Planning Institute

Est. Plan. Rev. Estate Planning Review (CCH)

Est. Powers & Trusts Estates, Powers and Trusts

Est. Prac. Estee's Code Pleading, Practice and Forms

Est. Prac. Pl. Estee's Code Pleading Practice and Forms

ESV Experimental Safety Vehicle

ET Arnolds, Carroll, Lewis & Seng. Eyewitness Testimony, Strategies and Tactics

E.T.
- Easter Term
- Entertainment Tax
- Estate and gift tax ruling
- Estate Tax Division (I.R.Bull.)
- Estate Tax ruling

ETA Employment and Training Administration

et al.
- et alia, and other things
- et alibi, and elsewhere
- et alii, and others

etc. et cetera (and the others, and so forth)

Eth. Ethiopia

Eth. Nic. Aristotle, Nicomachean Ethics

E.T.R. Estate and Trusts Reports. 1977-

E.T.S. European Treaty Series of Agreements and Conventions of the Council of Europe

et seq.
- et sequens (and the following)
- et sequitur (and as follows)

Ett. Ad. Etting's American Admiralty Jurisdiction

et ux. et uxor (and wife)

et vir. And husband

Euer Euer Doctrina Placitandi (Eng.)

Eun. Wynne's Eunomus

Eur.
- Europe
- European

Eur. Arb. European Arbitration

Eur. Ass. Arb. European Assurance Arbitration (1872-75)

EURATOM European Atomic Energy Community

Euratom European Atomic Energy Community

Eur. C.J. European Court of Justice

Eur. Comm'n H.R. Dec. & Rep. Collections of Decisions of the European Commission of Human Rights

Eur. Comm. on Human Rights European Community on Human Rights

Eur. Conslt. Ass. Deb. Council of Europe, Debates of the Consultative Assembly

Eur.Consult. Ass. Deb. Council of Europe, Debates of the Consultative Assembly

Eur. Ct. H.R. European Court of Human Rights

Eur. H.R. Rep. Europen Human Rights Reports

Eur. Intell. Prop. R. European Intellectual Property Review

Eur. L. Dig. European Law Digest

Eur. L. Newsl. European Law Newsletter

Eur. L. Rev. European Law Review

Eurolaw Com. Intel. Eurolaw Commercial Intelligence

European L. Rev. European Law Review

Europ. Intell. Prop. Rev. European Intellectual Property Review

Europ. T.S. European Treaty Series

Europ. Y.B. European Yearbook, The Hague, Netherlands

Eur. Parl. Deb. European Parliamentary Assembly Debates

Eur. Parl. Doc. European Parliament Working Documents

Eur. Parl. Docs. European Parliament Working Documents

Eur. Tax. European Taxation

Eur. Taxation European Taxation. Netherlands

Eur. T.L. European Transport Law (Belgium)

Eur. Trans. L. European Transport Law

Eur. Transp. L. European Transport Law. Journal of Law and Economics. Antwerp, Belgium

Eur. Y.B. European Yearbook

Ev. Evidence

Ev. Ag. Evans on Agency

Eval. Q. Evaluation Quarterly

Eval. Rev. Evaluation Review

Evans
- Evans' King's Bench Reports (1756-88)
- Evans' Reports, Washington Territory (announced, but never published)
- Lord Mansfield's Decisions (1799-1814) (Eng.)

Everybody's L.M. Everybody's Law Magazine

Ev. Harr. Evans' Edition of Harris' Modern Entries

Evid. Evidence

Ev. Jud. Pr. Evans' Practice of the Supreme Court of Judicature

Ev. Md. Pr. Evans' Maryland Practice

Ev. Pl. Evans on Pleading

Ev. Poth. Evans' Translation of Pothier on Obligations

Ev. Pr. & Ag. Evans on the Law of Principal and Agent

Ev. R.L. Evans' Road Laws of South Carolina

Ev. Stat. Evans' Collection of Statutes

Ev. Tr. Evans' Trial

E.W.C. European Works Council (of the Societaas Europea)

Ewell Bl. Ewell's edition of Blackstone

Ewell Cas. Inf. (or L. C.) Ewell's Leading Cases on Infancy, etc.

Ewell Ess. Ewell's Essentials of the Law

Ewell Evans Ag. Ewell's Edition of Evans on Agency

Ewell Fix. Ewell on the Law of Fixtures

Ewell L.C. Ewell's Leading Cases on Infancy, etc.

Ewing Just. Ewing's Justice

E.W.T. Eastern War Time

Ex.
- Citation in Examiner's decision
- Court of Exchequer (Eng.)
- English Exchequer Reports (1848-56)
- Examiner's decision
- Exchequer

ex.
- example
- exchange
- executive
- executor
- extract

Exam. The Examiner

Ex. & Ad. Executors and Administrators

Exch.
- Court of Exchequer; also Exchequer Division, High Court (1875-80)
- English Exchequer Reports
- English Law Reports, Exchequer
- Exchange
- Exchequer
- Exchequer Reports (Welsby, Hurlstone, & Gordon)

Exch. C. Canada Law Reports, Exchequer Court

Exch. Can. Exchequer Reports (Canada)

Exch. Cas. Exchequer Cases (Legacy Duties, etc. (Sc.)

Exch. Cham. Exchequer Chamber

Exch. C.R. Exchequer Court Reports (Canada)

Exch. Ct. (Can.) Canada Law Reports, Exchequer Court

Exch. Div. Exchequer Division, English Law Reports

Exch. Div. (Eng.) Exchequer Division, English Law Reports

Exch. P. Exchange of Property

Exch. Rep.
- English Exchequer Reports (American Reprint)

- Exchequer Reports (Welsby, Hurlstone & Gordon), 11 vols.

Exch. Rep. W.H. & G. Exchequer Reports (Welsby, Hurlstone & Gordon) (1847-56) (154-6 ER)

Ex. Com. Extravagantes Communes

Ex. C.R.
- Canada Exchequer Court Reports
- Canada Law Reports (Ex. Court)

Ex. D. Law Reports Exchequer Division (1875-80) (Eng.)

Ex. Div. Law Reports Exchequer Division (Eng.) (To 1880)

Exec.
- Execution
- Executive
- Executor

Exec. Disclosure Guide (CCH) Executive Disclosure Guide

Exec. Doc. Executive Document

Exec. Order Presidential Executive Order (U. S.)

execx. executrix

Exemp. Exemptions

Exempt. Org. Rep. (CCH) Exempt Organizations Guide

ExER Expert Evidence Reporter

EXIMBANK Export-Import Bank of the United States

Eximbank Export-Import Bank

Ex. Or. Executive Orders

exor. executor

exor/s. executor/s

exp.
- ex parte (Lat.)
- expenses

- Expired
- Explained
- expression
- expropriation

expld.   explained

Explos.   Explosions and explosives

exr.   executor

ex rel.   ex relatione (on the relation of)

Ex'r[x].   Executor[trix]

Ex. Sess.   Extra Session

Ext.
- Extended; extension
- external

Extd.   Extended

Exter. Ca.   Lobingier's Extraterritorial Cases, U. S. Court for China

extl.   external

Extn.   Extension

extn.   extension

Exton Mar. Dic.   Exton's Maritime Dicaeologie

Extort.
- Extortion
- Extortion, blackmail and threats

Extra. Ca.   Lobingier's Extraterritorial Cases, U. S. Court for China

Extrad.   Extradition

Extra. Sess.   Extraordinary Session

exx.   executrix

Eyre   Eyre's King's Bench Reports tempore William III (Eng.)

Eyre, MS   Eyre, Manuscript Notes of Cases, King's Bench (in Library of the New York Law Institute)

F

F
- Consuetudines Feudorum
- Faculty Collection, Court of Sessions Decisions, Scotland
- Federal Reporter (US)
- Finance
- Finalis
- Fitzherbert's Abridgment, octavo edition
- Followed
- Foord's Cape of Good Hope Reports (S. Africa)
- Foord, Supreme Court Reports, Cape Colony
- Forum
- French
- Fraser, Scotch Sessions Cases, 5th Series (1898-1905)
- Cited as controlling (used in Shepard's Citations)
- followed
- footnote

F.2d
- Federal Reporter, Second Series
- Federal Reporter, 2d Series

FAA Federal Aviation Administration

F.A.A. Free of all average

F.A.A. Order Federal Aviation Administration Orders

F. Abr. Fitzherbert's Abridgment

Fac.
- Faculty
- Faculty of Advocate, Collection of Decisions

Fac. Coll. Faculty Collection of Decisions, Court of Sessions (Sc.) First and SecondSeries, 38 vols.

Fac. Coll. N.S. Faculty of Advocates Collection of Decisions, Court of Session (Sc.)

Fac. Dec. Faculty Collection of Decisions, Court of Sessions (Sc.) First and SecondSeries, 38 vols.

Fac. L. Rev. Faculty of Law Review (Toronto)

Fac. of L.R. Faculty of Law Review, Toronto University (Can.)

Fac. of L. Rev. (Toronto) Faculty of Law Review

Facs. Facsimile

F.A.D. Federal Anti-Trust Decisions

FAIR Fair Access to Insurance Requirements

Fairchild
- Fairchild's Reports (10-12 Maine)
- Fairfield (John) (Me.)

Fair Empl. Prac. Cas. (BNA) Fair Employment Practices Cases

Fairf. Fairfield's Reports (10-12 Maine)

Fairfield Fairfield's Reports (10-12 Maine)

Fairf. (Me.) Fairfield's Reports (10-12 Maine)

Fair. M. & D. Fairbanks' Marriage and Divorce Laws of Massachusetts

Fair Tr. Fair Trade Laws

Falc. Falconer's Scotch Court of Session Cases (1744-51)

Falc. & F. Falconer & Fitzherbert's Election Cases (Eng.)

Falc. & Fitz. Falconer & Fitzherbert's Election Cases (1835-39) (Eng.)

Falc. Co. Cts. Falconer, County Court Cases (Eng.)

Falc. Marine Dict. Falconer's Marine Dictionary

Falk. Is. Falkland Islands

False Imp. False Imprisonment

False Pers. False Personation

False Pret. False Pretenses

Fam.
- Family
- Family Division, High Court, England and Wales

Fam. Adv. Family Advocate

Fam. Advocate Family Advocate

Fam. Cas. Cir. Ev. Famous Cases of Circumstantial Evidence, by Phillips

Fam. Ct. Family Court

Fam. Ct. Act. Family Court Act

Fam. Div. Family Division

Fam. Div'l Ct. Family Divisional Court (UK)

Family Adv. Family Advocate

Family L.Q. Family Law Quarterly

Fam. Law Family Law

Fam. L. Commtr. Family Law Commentator

Fam. L.N. Family Law Notes (Butterworths) (Aus.)

Fam. L. Newsl. Family Law Newsletter

Fam. L.Q. Family Law Quarterly

Fam. L.R. Family Law Reports (Butterworths) (Aus.)

Fam. L. Rep. (BNA) Family Law Reporter (BNA)

Fam L. Rev. Family Law Review

Fam. L. Tax Guide (CCH) Family Law Tax Guide

F. & C.C. Fire & Casualty Cases (CCH)

F. & F. Foster & Finlason's English Nisi Prius Reports (1856-67)

F. & Fitz. Falconer & Fitzherbert's English Election Cases (1835-39)

F. & J. Bank. De Gex, Fisher & Jones' Bankruptcy Reports (1859-61)

F. & J. Bank. De Gex Fisher & Jones' English Bankruptcy Reports

F. & S.
- Fox and Smith's Irish King's Bench Reports (1822-24)
- Fox and Smith's Registration Cases (1886-95)

F. & W. Pr. Frend & Ware, Precedents of Instruments Transfer of Land to Railway Companies.2ed. 1866

Fan. Rom. Law Fanton's Tables of Roman Law

FAO Food and Agriculture Organization of the United Nations

FAP Tigar, Federal Appeals: Jurisdiction & Practice

FAPR Federal Aviation Administrative Procurement Regulations

FaR Anderson/Morris, Chapter 12 Farm Reorganizations

F.A.R.
- Federal Acquisition Regulation
- Federal Aviation Regulations

Far.
- Farresley's Cases in Holt's King's Bench Reports
- Farresley's Reports, vol. 7 Modern Reports

Far Eastern Econ. Rev. Far Eastern Economic Review

Far East L.R. Far Eastern Law Review (Philippines)

Far East. L. Rev. Far Eastern Law Review

Farq. Chy. Farquharson's Court of Chancery

Farr. Farresley's Reports (7 Modern Reports) (1733-45) (87 ER)

Farrant Digest of Manx Cases (1925-47)

Farr. Bill Farren's Bill in Chancery

Farr. Const. Farrar's Manual of the United States Constitution

Farresley Farresley's Reports (7 Modern Reports) (1733-45) (87 ER)

Farr. Life Ass. Farren on Life Assurance

Farr. Mas. Farren's Masters in Chancery

Farr Med. Jur. Farr's Medical Jurisprudence

Farwell Farwell on Powers 3 editions (1874-1916)

Farw. Pow. Farwell on Powers

F.A.S.
- Foreign Agricultural Service
- Free alongside ship

FASB Financial Accounting Standards Board

fasc. fascicule (installment)

Faust Faust's Compiled Laws, (S. C.)

Fawc. Fawcett's on Landlord and Tenant 3 editions (1870-1905)

Fawc. L & T. Fawcett on Landlord and Tenant

Fawc. Ref. Fawcett, Court of Referees (1866)

Fayette Leg. J. (Pa.)
- Fayette Law Journal (Pa.)
- Fayette Legal Journal (Pa.)

Fay. L.J. Fayette Legal Journal, Pa.

FBA Federal Bar Association

F.B.C. Fonblanque, Bankruptcy Cases

f.b.c. fallen building clause

f.b.c.w. fallen building clause waiver

FBI Federal Bureau of Investigation

F.B.I. Full Bench Decisions (India)

F.B.I.S. Foreign Broadcast Information Service

FBILEB FBI Law Enforcement Bulletin

FBO Kelley & Ludtke, Family Business Organization

F/B/O For benefit of

F.B.R. Full Bench Rulings Bengal (India)

F.B.R.N.W.P. Full Bench Rulings, Northwest Provinces (India)

F.C.
- All India Reporter, Federal Court (1947-50)
- British Guiana Full Court Reports (Official Gazette)
- Canada Law Reports, Federal Court
- Faculty Collection of Decisions, Scotch Court of Session (1738-1841)
- Federal Cases, (United States), 31 vols.
- Full Court Judgments (1919-29) (Ghana)
- Selected Judgments of the Full Court, Accra and Gold Coast

f.c. fidei commissum (Lat.) bequeathed in trust

F.C. '20-I Full Court Judgments (1920-1) (Ghana)

F.C. '22 Full Court Judgments (1922) (Ghana)

F.C. '23-25 Selected Judgments of the Full Court (1923-25) (Ghana)

F.C. '26-29 Selected Judgments of the Full Court (1926-29) (Ghana)

FCA Farm Credit Administration

F.C.A. Federal Code Annotated

f.c. & s. free from capture and seizure

F. Carr. Cas. Federal Carriers Cases (CCH)

F. Carrier Cas. Federal Carrier Cases (CCH)

F. Cas. Federal Cases (1789-1880)

F. Cas. No. Federal Cases Number

FCC Federal Communications Commission

F.C.C. Federal Communications Commission Reports

FCC 2d Federal Communications Commission Reports, 2d Series (U. S.)

FCC Rulemaking Rep. (CCH) Federal Communications Commission Rulemaking Reports (Commerce Clearing House)

FCDA Federal Civil Defense Administration

FCIA Foreign Credit Insurance Association

FCIC Federal Crop Insurance Corporation

F.C.J. Federal Chief Justice (Nigeria)

F.C.L.
- Femme Couleur Libre
- Sarbah, Fanti Customary Law (Ghana)

FCLI Fordham University School of Law, Corporate Law Institute

FCLM(2) Leiby, Florida Construction Law Manual, Second Edition

FCLM(2s) Leiby, Florida Construction Law Manual, Second Edition

F.C.R.
- Fearne on Contingent Remainders
- Federal Court Reports (India)

FCS Farmer Cooperative Service

F.C.S.C. Ann. Rep. Foreign Claims Settlement Commission of the US, Annual Report

F.C.S.C. Dec. & Ann. Foreign Claims Settlement Commission of the US; Decisions & Annotations

FC (Scott) Faculty Collection of Decisions

F.C.T. Federal Capital Territory

F. Ct. Sess. Fraser's Court of Sessions Cases (Sc.)

FCU Federal Credit Union (U. S.)

F.D.
- Family Division
- Finance Decisions

FDA Food and Drug Administration

FDAA Federal Disaster Assistance Administration

F.D.A. Cons. FDA Consumer

FDC Food, Drug and Cosmetic Docket

F.D.C. Act Federal Food, Drug, and Cosmetic Act

F.D. Cosm. L. Rep. Food, Drug, Cosmetic Law Reporter (CCH)

FDIC Federal Deposit Insurance Corporation

F. Dict. Kames & Woodhouselee, (folio) Dictionary, Scotch Court of Session Cases

Fdn. Foundation

FDPC Federal Data Processing Centers

FEA
- Federal Energy Administration
- Foreign Economic Administration

Fea. Posth. Fearne's Posthumous Works

Fear. Rem. Fearne on Contingent Remainders (1722-1844)

FEB Fair Employment Board

FEBs Federal Executive Boards

FEC
- Far Eastern Commission
- Federal Election Commission

F.E.C.B. Foreign Exchange Control Board

Fed.
- Federal
- Federal Reporter (US)
- The Federalist, by Hamilton

Fed.2d Federal Reporter, 2nd Series

Fed. Alc. Adm. Federal Alcohol Administration

Fed. Anti-Tr. Cas. Federal Anti-Trust Cases, Decrees & Judgments (1890-1918)

Fed. Anti-Tr. Dec. Federal Anti-Trust Decisions

Fed. Audit Guide (CCH) Federal Audit Guide

Fed. B.A.J. Federal Bar Association Journal

Fed. B.A. Jo. Federal Bar Association Journal

Fed. Banking L. Rep. (CCH)
- Federal Banking Law Reports
- Federal Banking Law Reporter (CCH)

Fed. B.J. Federal Bar Journal

Fed. B.N. Federal Bar News

Fed. B. News Federal Bar News

Fed. B. News & J. Federal Bar News and Journal

Fed. Ca. Federal Cases

Fed. Carr. Cas. (CCH) Federal Carrier Cases (CCH)

Fed. Carr. Rep. (CCH) Federal Carriers Reporter (CCH)

Fed. Cas. Federal Cases (U. S.)

Fed. Case. Federal Cases (U. S.)

Fed. Cas. No. Federal Case Number

Fed. Com. B.J. Federal Communications Bar Journal

Fed. Com. L.J. Federal Communications Law Journal

Fed. Comm. B.J. Federal Communications Bar Journal

Fed. Comm. L.J. Federal Communications Law Journal

Fed. Cont. Rep. (BNA) Federal Contracts Report (Bureau of National Affairs)

Fed. Crim. L. Rep. Federal Criminal Law Report

Fed. Ct. Indian Rulings, Federal Court (1938-47)

Fed. Ctr. B.J. Federal Circuit Bar Journal

Fed. Ct. Rep. Federal Court Reports (Aust.)

Fed. Election Camp. Fin. Guide (CCH) Federal Election Campaign Financing Guide

Fed. Energy Reg. Comm'n Rep. (CCH) Federal Energy Regulatory Commission Reports

Fed. Est. & Gift Tax Rep. (CCH)
- Federal Estate and Gift Tax Reports

- Federal Estate and Gift Tax Reporter (CCH)

Federal L. Rev. Federal Law Review. Canberra, Australia

Fed. Evid. R. Federal Rules of Evidence

Fed. Ex. Tax Rep.
- Federal Excise Tax Reports
- Federal Excise Tax Reporter (CCH)

Fed. Home Loan Bank Board J. Federal Home Loan Bank Board Journal

Fed. Immigr. L. Rep. Federal Immigration Law Reporter

Fed. Inc. Gift & Est. Tax'n (MB) Federal Income Gift and Estate Taxation

Fed. Ins. Counsel Q. Federal Insurance Counsel Quarterly

Fed. Juror Federal Juror

Fed. L.J.
- Federal Law Journal (India) (1944-49)
- Federal Law Journal

Fed. L.J. Ind. Federal Law Journal of India

Fed. L.Q. Federal Law Quarterly

Fed. L. Rep. Federal Law Reports

Fed. L. Rev. Federal Law Review

Fed'n. Federation

Fed. Nigeria Federation of Nigeria

Fed'n. Ins. & Corp. Couns. Q. Federation of Insurance & Corporate Counsel Quarterly

Fed'n. Ins. Counsel Q. Federation of Insurance Counsel Quarterly

Fed. Power Sev. (MB) Federal Power Service

Fed. Prac. Federal Practice and Procedure

Fed. Prob. Federal Probate, Washington, D. C.

Fed. Probation Federal Probation

Fed. Prob. N.L. Federal Probation Newsletter

Fed. R.
- Federal Court Reporter, Can.
- Federal Reporter

Fed. R. App. P. Federal Rules of Appellate Procedure

Fed. R. Civ. P. Federal Rules of Civil Procedure

Fed. R. Civil P. Federal Rules of Civil Procedure

Fed. R. Crim. P. Federal Rules of Criminal Procedure

Fed. R.D. Federal Rules Decisions

Fed. Reg. Federation Register

Fed. Reg. Empl. Serv. (Law. Co-op) Federal Regulation of Employment Service

Fed. Rep. Federal Reporter

Fed. Res. Bull. Federal Reserve Bulletin

Fed. R. Evid. Federal Rules of Evidence

Fed. R. Evid. Serv. (Callaghan) Federal Rules of Evidence Service

Fed. R. Serv. 2d (Callaghan) Federal Rules Service 2d

Fed. Revenue Forms (P-H) Federal Revenue Forms (Prentice-Hall)

Fed. R. Evid. Federal Rules of Evidence

Fed. R. Evid. Serv. Federal Rules of Evidence Service

Fed. Rules Civ. Proc. Federal Rules of Civil Procedure

Fed. Rules Cr. Proc. Federal Rules of Criminal Procedure

Fed. Rules Dec. Federal Rules Decisions

Fed. Rules Serv. Federal Rules Service

Fed. Rules Serv. 2d Federal Rules Service, Second Series

Fed. Sec. L. Rep. (CCH)
- Federal Securities Law Reports
- Federal Securities Law Reporter (CCH)

Fed. Stat. Ann. Federal Statutes Annotated

Fed. Sup. Federal Supplement

Fed. Supp. Federal Supplement

Fed. Tax. Federal taxation

Fed. Tax Articles (CCH)

Fed. Tax Coordinator 2d (Res. Inst. Am.) Federal Tax Coordinator

Fed. Tax Coordinator 2d (RIA) Federal Tax Coordinator Second (Tax Research Institute of America)

Fed. Tax. Enf. Federal Tax Enforcement

Fed. Tax Guide Rep. (CCH) Federal Tax Guide Reports

Fed. Tax Manual (CCH) Federal Tax Manual (Commerce Clearing House)

Fed. Taxes (P-H) Federal Taxes (P-H)

Fed. Taxes Est. & Gift Federal Taxes; Estate and Gift Taxes (P-H)

Fed. Taxes Excise Federal Taxes: Excise Taxes (P-H)

Fed. Taxes (P-H) Federal Taxes (Prentice-Hall)

Fed. Taxes Tax Ideas (P-H) Federal Taxes: Tax Ideas (Prentice-Hall)

Fed. Taxes Treaties (P-H) Federal Taxes: Tax Treaties (Prentice-Hall)

Fed. Tax Forms (CCH) Federal Tax Forms (Commerce Clearing House)

Fed. Tort Federal Tort Claims Act

Fed. Tr. Rep. Federal Trade Reporter

F.E.L.A. Federal Employers' Liability and Compensation Acts

Fell Guar. Fell on Guaranty and Suretyship

F.E.L.R. Far Eastern Law Review (Philippines)

FEMA Federal Emergency Management Agency

Fent.
- Fenton's Important Judgments (New Zealand)
- Fenton's Reports (New Zealand)

Fent. Imp. Judg. Fenton's Important Judgments (New Zealand)

Fent. (New Zealand) Fenton's New Zealand Reports

Fent. N. Z. Fenton 's New Zealand Reports

Fenton Fenton's Important Judgments (New Zealand) (1866-79)

FEP Fair Employment Practice Cases, (BNA)

FEPC Fair Employment Practices Commission

F.E.P. Cas. Fair Employment Practice Cases

FERA Federal Emergency Relief Administration

Ferard, Fixt. Amos & Ferard on Fixtures

F.E.R.C. Federal Energy Regulatory Commission

Fer. Fixt. Ferard on Fixtures

Ferg.
- Consistorial Decisions, Scotland, by George Ferguson, Lord Hermand
- James Fergusson's Consistorial Decisions, Scotland

Ferg. Cons. Fergusson's (Sc.) Consistorial Reports

Ferg. M. & D. Fergusson, Divorce Decisions by Consistorial Courts (Sc.)

Ferg. Proc. Ferguson's Common Law Procedure Act, Ireland

Ferg. Ry. Cas. Fergusson's Five Years' Railway Cases

Fergusson
- Fergusson's Consistorial Decisions (Scotland)
- Fergusson's Scotch Session Cases (1738-52)

Fernald, Eng. Synonyms Fernald's English Synonyms

FES Final Environmental Statement

Fessen. Pat. Fessenden on Patents

Fess. Pat. Fessenden on Patents

FET Federal estate tax

Fett. Carr. Fetter's Treatise on Carriers of Passengers

Feud. Feudal

Feud. Lib. The Book of Feuds.

F.E.U.L. Rev. Far Eastern Law Review (Philippines)

Ff. Pandects of Justinian

FFC Fiscal and Financial Committee

FFMC Federal Farm Mortgage Corp.

FFP Firm Fixed-Price

F.G.A. Free from general average; foreign general average

F.G.C.M. Field General Court Martial

F.G.I.S. Federal Grain Inspection Service

FGT Federal gift tax

FHA Federal Housing Administration

F.H.L. Fraser, House of Lords Reports (Sc.)

F.H.L.B. Federal Home Loan Bank

FHLBB Federal Home Loan Bank Board

FHLMC Federal Home Loan Mortgage Corporation

FHWA Federal Highway Administration

Fi.
- Fidell's Precedents
- Finnish

FIA Federal Insurance Administration

FIC Federal Information Centers

FICA Federal Insurance Contribution Act

FICB Federal Intermediate Credit Banks

FICC Q. Federation of Insurance and Corporate Counsel Quarterly

FICEI Federal Inter-Agency Council on Energy Information

FID O'Reilly, Federal Information

FID(2) O'Reilly, Federal Information Disclosure, Second Edition

Fid. Bonds Fidelity Bonds and Insurance

Fid. L. Chron. Fiduciary Law Chronicle

Fiduciary Fiduciary Reporter (Pa.)

Fiduciary R. (Pa.) Fiduciary Reporter (Pa.)

Fiduciary Rptr. Fiduciary Reporter (Pa.)

Fiduc. Rep. Fiduciary Reporter (Pa.)

Field Anal. Field's Analysis of Blackstone's Commentaries

Field & D. Ch. Pr. Field & Dunn's Chancery Practice

Field Com. Law Field on the Common Law of England

Field Corp. Field on Corporations

Field Cur. Field on Protestant Curates and Incumbents

Field Dam. Field on the Law of Damages

273

Field Ev. Field's Law of Evidence in British India

Field Int. Code Field's International Code

Field on Inh. Field on the Hindu and Mohammedan Laws of Inheritance

Field Pen. L. Field's Penal Law

Field Pr. Cor. Field on Private Corporations

fi. fa. fieri facias (Writ of execution of property)

FIFO First-in, first-out inventory method

Fiji L.R. Fiji Law Reports

F.I.L.E. Fellow of the Institute of Legal Executives

Fin.
- Finance
- Financial
- Finch's English Chancery Reports (1673-81)
- Finland
- Finlay's Irish Digest

Fin. & Dul. Finnemore & Dulcken's Natal Law Reports

Fin. C. Financial Code

Finch.
- English Chancery Reports tempore Finch
- Finch's Precedents in Chancery (Eng.)

Finch Cas. Cont. Finch's Cases on Contract. 1886

Finch Cas. Contr. Finch's Cases on Contract. 1886

Finch (Eng.)
- English Chancery Reports tempore Finch

- Finch's Precedents in Chancery (Eng.)

Finch Ins. Dig. Finch's Insurance Digest

Finch, Law Finch, Sir Henry; a Discourse of Law (1759)

Finch L. C. Finch's Land Cases

Finch Nomot. Finch's Nomotechnia

Finch Prec. Precedents in Chancery, edited by Finch

Finch Sum. C.L. Finch's Summary of the Common Law

Fin. Dig. Finlay's Irish Digest, 1769-1771

FIN. E.F.T.A. Finland-European Free Trade Association Treaty

Fin. H. H. Finch's Chancery Reports (1673-81) (Eng.)

Fink Ev. Fink's Indian Evidence Act

Finkel, Medical Cyc. Finkel, et al. , Lawyers' Medical Cyclopedia

Finl. Ch. Tr. Finlason on Charitable Trusts

Finl. Com. Finlason on Commons

Finl. Dig. Finlay's Irish Digest

Finl. Jud. Sys. Finlason's Judicial System

Finl. L.C. Finlason's Leading Cases on Pleading

Finl. Ld. Ten. Finlason on Land Tenures

Finl. Mar. L. Finlason's Commentaries on Martial Law

Finl. Rep. Finlason's Report of the Gurney Case

Finl. Riot   Finlay on Repression of Riot or Rebellion

Finl. Ten.   Finlason, History of Law of Tenures of Land. 1870

Fin. Plan. Today   Financial Planning Today

Fin. Pr.   T. Finch's Precedents in Chancery (1689-1722) (Eng.)

Fin. Prec.   Finch's Precedents in Chancery (1689-1722) (24 ER)

Fin. Ren.   Finlay on Renewals

Fin. T.   T. Finch's Precedents in Chancery (1689-1722) (Eng.)

Fin. Tax. & Comp. L.   Finance Taxation and Company Law (Pakistan)

FIP   Forestry Incentive Program

Fire & Cas. Cas.   Fire and Casualty Cases

Fire & Casualty Cas. (CCH)   Fire and Casualty Cases (CCH)

First Bk. Judg.   First Book of Judgments (1655) (Eng.)

First Book Judg.   First Book of Judgments. 1655

First pt. Edw. III.   Part II. of the Year Books

First Pt. H. VI.   Pan VII. of the Year Books

FIS   Family income supplement

Fish.
- Fisher's U. S. Patent Cases
- Fisher's U. S. Prize Cases

Fish & G.   Fish and game

Fish & G.C.   Fish and Game Code

Fish. & L. Mort.   Fisher & Lightwood, Mortgages. 9ed. 1977

Fish. Cas.   Fisher's Cases, United States District Courts

Fish. C.L. Dig.   Fisher's Digest of English Common Law Reports

Fish. Const.   Fisher on the United States Constitution

Fish. Cop.   Fisher on Copyrights

Fish. Crim. Dig.   Fisher's Digest of English Criminal Law

Fish. Dig.   Fisher's English Common Law Digest

Fisher
- Fisher on Mortgages 7 editions (1856-1947)
- Fisher's Prize Cases, U. S.

Fisher & Lightwood   Fisher & Lightwood on Mortgages. 9ed. 1977

Fisher Pat. Cas. (F.)   Fisher, US Patent Cases

Fisher Pr. Cas. (F.)   Fisher, US Prize Cases

Fisher Pr. Cas. (Pa.)   Fisher Pennsylvania Prize Cases

Fisher's Pat. Cas.   Fisher's Patent Cases (U. S.)

Fish. Mort.   Fisher on Mortgages

Fish. Mortg.   Fisher on Mortgages

Fish. Pat.   Fisher's United States Patent Cases

Fish. Pat. Cas.   Fisher's United States Patent Cases

Fish. Pat. Dig.   Fisher's Digest of Patent Law

Fish. Pat. R.   Fisher's Patent Reports (U. S.)

Fish. Pat. Rep.   Fisher's United States Patent Reports

Fish. Pr. Cas. Fisher's United States Prize Cases

Fish. Prize Fisher's United States Prize Cases

Fish. Prize Cas. Fisher's Prize Cases, U. S.

Fish. W.A. Fisher on the Will Act

Fisk Anal. Fisk, Analysis of Coke on Littleton. 1824

FIT Federal insurance tax

f.i.t. free of income tax

Fitch R.E. Ag. Fitch on Real Estate Agency

Fits. Nat. Brev. Fitzherbert's Natura Brevium

Fitz. Fitzgibbon's K.B.Rep., Eng.

Fitz. Abridg. Fitzherbert's Abridgment (1516)

Fitzad. Jud. Act Fitzadams on the Judicature Act

Fitz. -G. Fitzgibbon's King's Bench Reports (1727-31) (94 ER)

Fitzg.
- Fitzgibbon's King's Bench Reports (1728-33) (Eng.)
- Fitzgibbon's Land Reports (Ir.)
- Fitzgibbon's Registration Appeals (Ir.)

Fitzg. Land R. Fitzgibbon's Irish Land Reports

Fitzg. L.G. Dec. Fitzgibbon's Irish Local Government Decisions

Fitzg. Pub. H. Fitzgerald on the Public Health

Fitzg. Reg. Ca. Fitzgibbon's Irish Registration Appeals (1894)

Fitzh. Fitzherbert's Abridgment (Eng.)

Fitzh. Abr. Fitzherbert's Abridgment (1516)

Fitzh. Nat. Brev. Fitzherbert's Natura Brevium

Fitzh. N.B. Fitzherbert, New Natura Brevium (1534)

Fitzh. N.Br. Fitzherbert's Natura Brevium (Eng.)

Fitz. L.G. Dec. Fitzgibbon, Irish Local Government Decisions

Fitz. Nat. Brev. Fitzherbert's Natura Brevium. 1534

FIU Florida International University

Fixt. Fixtures

F.J.
- Federal Justice (Nigeria)
- First Judge

F.J.C.
- Fraser, Reports, Justiciary Court (Sc.)
- The Federal Judicial Center

F. JJ. Federal Justices (Nigeria)

F.J.R. Factories Journal Reports (India)

Fl.
- Flanders
- Fleta, seu Commentarius Juris Anglici (1647) (Eng.)
- Florida

FL Turley/Rooks, Firearms Litigation: Law, Science & Practice

F.L.A. Fellow of the Library Association

Fla.
- Florida
- Florida Reports

Fla. Admin. Code Florida Administrative Code

Fla. Admin. Weekly Florida Administrative Weekly

Fla. & K. Flanagan & Kelly, Rolls (I r.)

Fla. App. Florida Appellate Reports

Fla. B.J. Florida Bar Journal

Fla. Const. Florida Constitution

Fla. Dig. Thompson's Digest of Laws (Florida)

Fla. Int'l L.J. Florida International Law Journal

Fla. J. Int'l. L. Florida Journal of International Law

Fla. Jur. Florida Jurisprudence

Fla. Laws Laws of Florida

Fla. L.J. Florida Law Journal

Fla. L. Rev. Florida Law Review

Flan. & K. Flanagan & Kelly's Irish Rolls Court Reports (1840-42)

Flan. & Ke. Flanagan & Kelly's Irish Rolls Court Reports (1840-42)

Flan. & Kel. Flanagan & Kelly, Rolls (Ir.)

Fla. N.B.A. Flather's New Bankrupt Act

Fland. Ch. J. Flanders' Lives of the Chief Justices of the United States

Fland. Const. Flanders on the United States Constitution

Fland. Fire Ins. Flanders on Fire Insurance

Fl. & K. Flanagan & Kelly's Rolls Court Reports (Ireland) (1840-42)

Fland. Mar. L. Flanders' Maritime Law

Fland. Sh. Flanders on Shipping

Fla. R. Florida Reports (Fla.)

Fla. R.C. Railroad Commission for the State of Florida

Fla. Rep. Florida Reports (Fla.)

Fla. S.B.A. Jo. Florida State Bar Association Journal

Fla. S.B.A.L.J. Florida State Bar Association Law Journal

Fla. Sess. Law Serv. Florida Session Law Service (West)

Fla. Stat. Florida Statutes

Fla. Stat. Ann. Florida Statutes Annotated

Fla. Stat. Anno. Annotations to Official Florida Statutes

Fla. State L.J. Florida State Law Journal

Fla. State L. Rev. Florida State University Law Review

Fla. St. U. L. Rev. Florida State University Law Review

Fla. St. Univ. Slavic Papers Florida State University Slavic Papers

Fla. Supp. Florida Supplement

Flax. Reg. Flaxman, Registration of Births and Deaths. 1875

FLB The Florida Bar

F.L.C. Australian Family Law Cases (CCH)

Fleta Fleta, seu Commentarius Juris Anglici

FLETC Federal Law Enforcement Training Center

Fletcher, Corporations
Fletcher's Cyclopedia Corporations

Fletcher Cyc. Corp. Fletcher, Cyclopedia Corporations

Fletcher F. Fletcher Forum

Fletcher F. World Aff. Fletcher Forum of World Affairs

Fletch. Tr. Fletch on Trustees of Estates

Fleury, Hist. Fleury's History of the Origin of French Laws (1724)

Flint. Conv. Flintoff's Introduction to Conveyancing

Flint. R. & P. Flintoff's Rise and Progress of the Laws of England and Wales

Flint. R. Pr. Flintoff, Real Property (1839-40)

Flip. Flippin's Circuit Court Reports (U. S.)

Flipp. (F.) Flippin's Circuit Court Reports (U. S.)

F.L.J.
- Canada Fortnightly Law Journal
- Federal Law Journal (India)
- Forum Law Journal (U. of Baltimore)
- Federal Law Journal (1939)

Fl. L.R. University of Florida Law Review

F.L.M.C. Federal Labor-Management Consultant

Flood El. Eq. Flood, Equitable Doctrine of Election. 1880

Flood Lib. Flood, Slander and Libel. 1880

Flood Wills Flood on Wills of Personal Property

Flo. R. Florida Reports (Fla.)

Flor.
- Florida
- Florida Reports

Florida Florida Reports

Florida B.J. Florida Bar Journal

Florida R. Florida Reports (Fla.)

Florida Rep. Florida Reports (Fla.)

Floy. Proct. Pr. Floyer's Proctors' Practice

F.L.P. Florida Law and Practice

F.L.R.
- Family Law Reporter (BNA)
- Federal Law Reports (Aus.)
- Federal Law Reports (India)
- Federal Law Review (Aus.)
- Fiji Law Reports
- University of Florida Law Review

F.L.R.C. U.S. Federal Labor Relations Council Decisions and Interpretations

F.L. Rev. Federal Law Review

Fl. S. Florida Supplement

FLSA Fair Labor Standards Act U. S.

FLT Barton, Florida Taxation

FM Field Manual, U. S. Army

F. Mac. N. MacNaghten, Hindu Law (India)

F.M.B.
- Federal Maritime Board Reports, U. S. Maritime Administration, Department ofCommerce

278

- U. S. Federal Maritime Board

F.M.C. Decisions of the Federal Maritime Commission (U. S.) (1947-date)

FMCS Federal Mediation and Conciliation Service

Fm. H.A. Farmers Home Administration

F. Moore English King's Bench Reports (72 ER)

F.M.S.H.R.D. Federal Mine Safety & Health Review Decisions

F.M.S.L.R. Federated Malay States Reports

F.M.S.R. Federated Malay States Reports

F.N.B. Fitzherbert's Natura Brevium (Eng.)

F.N.D. Finnemore's Notes and Digest of Natal Cases

F.N.J. , F.D.C. U. S. Food and Drug Administration. Notices of Judgment: Foods

FNMA Federal National Mortgage Association

FNS Food and Nutrition Service

fo. folio

Foard Mer.Sh. Foard on Merchant Shipping

f.o.b. free on board

f.o.c. free of charge

f.o.d. free of damage

F. of M. Federation of Malaya

Fogg Fogg's Reports (32-35 New Hampshire)

FOIA Freedom of Information Act

F.O.I.C.R. Freedom of Information Center Reports

F.O.I. Dig. F.O.I. Digest

Fol.
- Foley's Poor Law Cases (Eng.)
- folio

Fol. Dic. Kames & Woodhouselee's Folio Dictionary, Court of Session (1540-1796) (Sc.)

Fol. Dict. Kames & Woodhouselee's Dictionary, Court of Session (Sc.)

Folk. Pl. Folkard, Loands and Pledges, 2ed. 1876

Folk. St. Sl. Folkard's Edition of Starkie on Slander and Libel

foll. followed in, or following

Fol. P.L.C. Foley's Poor Law Cases (1556-1730)

Fol. P.L. Cas. Foley's English Poor Law Cases (1556-1730)

Fo. L.R. Fordham Law Review

fols. folios

Fon. B.C. Fonblanque, Bankruptcy Cases (1849-1852)

Fonb. Eq. Fonblanque's Equity (Eng.)

Fonbl.
- Fonblanque on Medical Jurisprudence
- Fonblanque's Equity
- Fonblanque's New Reports, English Bankruptcy

Fonbl. Eq. Fonblanque's Equity (Eng.)

Fonbl. Eq. (Eng.) Fonblanque's Equity (Eng.)

Fonbl. Med. Jur. Fonblanque, Medical Jurisprudence

Fonbl. N.R.
- Fonblanque on Medical Jurisprudence
- Fonblanque's Cases in Chancery (Eng.)
- Fonblanque's Equity
- Fonblanque's New Reports, English Bankruptcy (1849-52)

Fonbl. R. Fonblanque's English Cases (or New Reports) in Bankruptcy (1849-52)

Fonbl. R. & Wr. Fonblanque, Rights and Wrongs. 1860

Food & Agric. Food and Agricultural

Food Drug Cos. L. Rep. Food Drug Cosmetic Law Reporter (CCH)

Food Drug Cosm. L.J. Food Drug Cosmetic Law Journal

Food Drug Cosm. L.Q. Food, Drug, Cosmetic Law Quarterly

Food Drug Cosm. L. Rep.(CCH) Food, Drug, Cosmetic Law Reporter

Food Drug Cosm. & Med. Device L. Dig. Food, Drug, Cosmetic & Medical Device Law Digest Food Drug Cosmetic Law Reporter

Food Drug L.J. Food and Drug Law Journal

Foord Foord, Supreme Court Reports, Cape Colony (S. Africa)

Foote & E. Incorp. Co. Foote and Everett's Law of Incorporated Companies Operating under MunicipalFranchises

Foote B. & B. Foote's Bench and Bar of the South and Southwest

Foote Highw. Foote's Law of Highways

Foote Int. Jur. Foote on Private International Jurisprudence

For.
- Foreign
- Forensic
- Forrester's Chancery Reports (cases tempore Talbot)
- Forrest's Exchequer Reports
- Fortescue de Laudibus Legum Angliae

For. Aff. Foreign Affairs

Forb.
- Forbes' Cases in St. Andrews Bishop's Court
- Forbes' Court of Session Dec. (Sc.)
- Forbes' Journal of the Session (1705-13) (Sc.)

Forb. Bills Forbes on Bills of Exchange

Forbes. Forbes' Journal of the Session (1705-13) (Sc.)

Forb. Inst. Forbes' Institutes of the Law of Scotland

Forb. Tr. Forbes on Trustees and Post Office Savings Banks

For. Cas. & Op. Forsyth's Cases and Opinions on Constitutional Law

Forc. Ent. Forcible Entry and Detainer

For. Comp. Forsyth on Composition with Creditors

For. Cons. Law. Forsyth's Cases and Opinions on Constitutional Law

For. Corp. Foreign Corporations

For Def. For the Defense

For. de Laud. Fortescue de Laudibus Legum Angliae

Fordham Corp. Inst. Proceedings of the Fordham Corporate Law Institute

Fordham Ent. Media & Intell. Prop. L.F. Fordham Entertainment, Media & Intellectual Property Law Forum

Fordham Int'l. L.F. Fordham International Law Forum

Fordham Int'l. L.J. Fordham International Law Journal

Fordham L. Rev. Fordham Law Review

Fordham Urban L.J. The Fordham Urban Law Journal

Fordham Urb. L.J. Fordham Urban Law Journal

Fordh. L. Rev. Fordham Law Review

Ford. L. Rev. Fordham Law Review

Ford Oa. Ford, Oaths. 8ed. 1903

Ford. Urban L.J. Fordham Urban Law Journal

Forester Chancery Cases tempore Talbot (Eng.)

For. Exch. Bull. Foreign Exchange Bulletin (Association of American Law)

Forf. & P. Forfeiture and Penalties

For. Hort. Forsyth's Hortensius

For. Inf. Forsyth's Custody of Infants

For. Jury Tr. Forsyth's Trial by Jury

Form. Forman's Reports (1 Scammon, 2 Illinois)

Forman Forman's Reports (1 Scammon, 2 Illinois)

Forman (Ill.) Forman's Reports (1 Scammon, 2 Illinois)

For. Pla. Brown's Formulae bene Placitandi

For. Pr. Foran, Code of Civil Procedure of Quebec

Forr.
- Forrester's English Chancery Cases (commonly cited, Cases tempore Talbot)(1734-38)
- Forrest's English Exchequer Reports

Forrest Forrest's Reports, English Exchequer (1800-01)

Forrester Forrester's Chancery Cases tempore Talbot (Eng.)

Fors. Cas. & Op. Forsyth's Cases and Opinions on Constitutional Law (1869)

For. Sci. Forensic Science

Fors. Comp. Forsyth's Composition with Creditors

Fors. Hor. Forsyth's Hortensius, or, the Duties of an Advocate

Fors. Inf. Forsyth's Custody of Infants

Forst. Cust. Forster's Digest of the Laws of Customs

Fors. Tr. Forsyth on Trusts and Trustees in Scotland

Fors. Tr. Jur. Forsyth's History of Trial by Jury

Fort.
- Fortescue's King's Bench Reports (1695-1738) (Eng.)

- Fortnightly

For. Tax Bull. Foreign Tax Law Bi-Weekly Bulletin

For. Tax L. S.-W. Bull. Foreign Tax Law Semi-Weekly Bulletin

For. Tax L.W. Bull. Foreign Tax Law Weekly Bulletin

For. Tax L.S. Weekly Bull. Foreign Tax Law Semi-Weekly Bulletin

Fort. de Laud. Fortescue de Laudibus Legum Angliae (1616)

Fortes. Fortescue's Reports, English courts

Fortesc. Fortescue's English King's Bench Reports (92 ER)

Fortesc. de L. L. Angl. Fortescue de Laudibus Legum Angliae

Fortescue Fortescue's King's Bench Reports (1695-1738) (92 ER)

Fortescue (Eng.) Fortescue's English King's Bench Reports (92 ER)

Fortes. de Laud. Fortescue, De Laudibus Legum Angliae

Fortes. Rep. Fortescue's King's Bench Reports (Eng.)

Fort. L.J. Fortnightly Law Journal

Fortnightly L.J. Fortnightly Law Journal

Fortn. L.J. Fortnightly Law Journal

Fort. Tell. Fortune telling

Forum
- Forum: Bench & Bar Review
- Forum, Dickinson School of Law
- Forum Law Review
- The Forum

Forum L.R. Forum Law Review (1874)

Fos. Foster

Foss
- E. Foss, The Judges of England, 9 vols. 1848-64

Foss Judg. Foss' Judges of England 9 vols, 1848-64

Fost.
- Foster's English Crown Law or Crown Cases (1743-61)
- Foster's Legal Chronicle Reports, Pennsylvania
- Foster's New Hampshire Reports
- Foster's Reports (vols. 5, 6, and 8 Hawaii)

Fost. & F. Foster and Finlason's English Nisi Prius Reports (175, 176 ER)

Fost. & F. (Eng.) Foster and Finlason's English Nisi Prius Reports (175, 176 ER)

Fost. & Fin. Foster and Finlason's English Nisi Prius Reports (175, 176 ER)

Fost. C.L. Foster's Crown Law or Crown Cases (1743-61) (168 ER)

Fost. C.L. (Eng.) Foster's English Crown or Crown Cases (168 ER)

Fost. Cr. Law Foster's English Crown Law or Crown Cases (168 ER)

Fost. Crown Law Foster's English Crown Law or Crown Cases (168 ER)

Fost. Doct. Com. Foster on Doctors' Commons

Fost. El. Jur. Foster, Elements of Jurisprudence. 1853

Foster
- Foster's English Crown Law
- Foster's New Hampshire Reports
- Legal Chronicle Reports (Pennsylvania), edited by Foster

Foster Fed. Pr. Foster on Federal Practice

Foster (Pa.) Foster Legal Chronicle Reports

Fost. Fed. Prac. Foster's Treatise on Pleading and Practice in Equity in Courts of UnitedStates

Fost. (Haw.) Foster's Hawaiian Reports (5, 6 and 8)

Fost. Jt. Own. Foster on Joint Ownership and Partition

Fost. (N. H.) Foster's Reports (New Hampshire, 21-31)

Fost. on Sci. Fa. Foster on the Writ of Scire Facias

Fost. Sc. Fa. Foster on Writ of Scire Facias

Fost. Sci. Fa. Foster on the Writ of Scire Facias. 1851

Fost. Tr. Reb. Trial of the Rebels, & c. (Foster's Crown Cases)

Foulk. Act. Foulke's Action at Law

Found. foundation(s)

Found. L. Rev. Foundation Law Review

Fount. Fountainhall's Decisions, Scotch Court of Session (1678-1712)

Fount. Dec. Fountainhall's Decisions (Sc.)

Fowl. Col. Fowler, Collieries and Colliers. 4ed. 1884

Fowl. L. Cas. Fowler's Leading Cases on Collieries

Fowl. Pews Fowler on Church Pews

Fowl. Pr. Fowler's Exchequer Practice

Fox
- Fox's Circuit & District Court Decisions (U. S.)
- Fox's Patent, Trade Mark, Design & Copyright Cases (Canada)
- Fox's Registration Cases (Eng.)

Fox & S. Fox & Smith's Irish King's Bench Reports

Fox & S. Ir. Fox & Smith's Irish King's Bench Reports

Fox & S. (Ir.) Fox & Smith's Irish King's Bench Reports

Fox & Sm.
- Fox & Smith Irish King's Bench Reports (1822-24)
- Fox & Smith, Registration Cases (1886-95)

Fox & Sm. R.C. Fox & Smith's Registration Cases (1886-95)

Fox & S. Reg. Fox and Smith's Registration Cases (Eng.)

Fox Dig. Part. Fox's Digest of the Law of Partnership

Fox Pat. C. Fox's Patent, Trade Mark, Design & Copyright Cases (Canada)

Fox Pat. Cas. Fox's Patent, Trade Mark, Design & Copyright Cases (Canada)

Fox P.C. Fox's Patent, Trade Mark, Design and Copyright Cases (Can.) (1940)

Fox. Reg. Ca. Fox's Registration Cases

F.P. Federal Parliament

F.P.A.
- Federal Preparedness Agency
- Free from particular average

FPC
- Federal Power Commission
- Federal Power Commission Reports

F.P.C. U. S. Federal Power Commission Opinions and Decisions

FPHA Federal Public Housing Agency

FPI Federal Publications Inc.

FPIC Fixed-Price Incentive Contract

F.P.M. Federal Personnel Manual

F. P. R. Federal Procurement Regulations

F. R.
- Federal Register
- Federal Reporter
- Federal Republic
- Fordham Law Review (N. Y.)
- Foreign Relations

Fr.
- Fragment or Excerpt, or Laws in titles of Pandects
- France
- Freeman, English King's Bench and Chancery Reports
- French

FRA
- Federal Railroad Administration
- Federal Reports Act

Fra. Francis' Maxims of Equity; 4 editions (1722-1746)

FRA Keating, Franchising Adviser

Frac. Fractional

France France's Reports (3-11 Colorado)

France (Colo.) France's Reports (3-11 Colorado)

Franch. Franchises

Fran. Char. Francis, Law of Charities. 2ed. 1855

Franchise L.J. Franchise Law Journal

Franchise L. Rev. Franchise Law Review

Francis, Max. Francis' Maxims

Franc. Judg. Francillon's County Court Judgments (Eng.)

Fran. Coll. L.J. Franciso College Law Journal

F. R. & N. Federation of Rhodesia & Nyasaland

Fr. & W. Prec. Frend & Ware, Precedents of Instruments relating to the Transfer of Land toRailway Companies, 2ed. 1866

Fran. Eng. Law Francillon, Lectures on English Law (1860-61)

Fran. Max. Francis' Maxims of Equity

Fran. Prec. Francis' Common Law Precedents

FRAP Federal Rules of Appellate Procedure

Fras. Fraser's Election Cases (Eng.)

Fras. Div. Fraser's Conflict of Laws in Cases of Divorce

Fras. Dom. Rel. Fraser on Personal and Domestic Relations (Sc.)

Fras. Elec. Cas.   Fraser's English Election Cases

Fraser
- Fraser, English Cases of Controverted Elections (1776-77)
- Fraser's Court of Session Cases, 5th Series (1989-1906)
- Fraser's Husband and Wife (1876-1878) (Sc.)

Fraser (Scot.)
- Fraser, English Cases of Controverted Elections (1776-77)
- Scotch Court of Session Cases, 5th Series, by Fraser

Fras. M. & S.   Fraser on Master and Servant in Scotland

Fras. Par. & Ch.   Fraser, Parent and Child (Sc.)

Frat.   Fraternal orders and benefit societies

Fraud. Conv.   Fraudulent Conveyances

Fraz.   Frazer's Admiralty Cases, etc. (Sc.)

Fraz. Adm.   Frazer's Admiralty Cases, etc. (Sc.)

FRB   Fedral Reserve Board, Board of Governors of the Federal Reserve System

F.R.B.   Federal Reserve Bulletin

Fr. Bank.   Frank on the United States Bankrupt Act of 1867

FRC   Federal Radio Commission

Fr. Ch.
- Freeman's English Chancery Reports (1660-1706)
- Freeman's Mississippi Chancery Reports

Fr. Chy.
- Freeman, English Chancery Reports (1660-1706)
- Freeman, Mississippi Chancery Reports

FRCI   O'Reilly, Federal Regulation of the Chemical Industry

FRCP   Federal Rules of Civil Procedure

F.R.C.P.   . Federal Rules of Civil Procedure

FR Crim P   Federal Rules of Criminal Procedure

FRCs   Federal Regional Councils

F.R.D.   Federal Rules Decisions

FRE
- Federal Rules of Evidence
- Fox, Federal Regulation of Energy

Fr. E. C.   Fraser's Election Cases (1776-1777)

Fred. Code   Frederician Code, Prussia

Free.
- Freeman's Chancery Reports (1600-1706) (Eng.)
- Freeman's King's Bench Reports (1670-1704) (Eng.)
- Freeman's Reports (31-96 Illinois)

Free. Ch.
- Freeman's English Chancery Reports (1660-1706)
- Freeman's Mississippi Chancery Reports (1839-43)

Free. K.B.   Freeman's King Bench Reports (89 ER) (1670-1704)

Freem.
- Freeman's Chancery (Eng.)
- Freeman's Chancery (Miss.)

Freeman Ch. R. Freeman's Chancery Reports (Miss.)

Freeman's (Miss.) Rep. Freeman's Chancery Reports (Miss.)

Freem. C.C. Freeman's English Chancery Cases

Freem. Ch. Freeman's English Chancery Reports (22 ER)

Freem. Chan. Freeman's Chancery Reports (Miss.)

Freem. Ch. (Eng.) Freeman's English Chancery Reports (22 ER)

Freem. Ch. (Miss.) Freeman's Mississippi Chancery Reports

Freem. Ch. R. Freeman's Chancery Reports (Miss.)

Freem. Compar. Politics Freeman, Comparative Politics

Freem. Cot. Freeman on Cotenancy and Partition

Freem. Eng. Const. Freeman, Growth of the English Constitution. 3ed. 1876

Freem. Ex. Freeman on Executors

Freem. (Ill.) Freeman's Reports (31-96 Illinois)

Freem. Judgm. Freeman on Judgments

Freem. K.B. Freeman's English King's Bench & Common Pleas Reports (89 ER)

Freem. (Miss.) Freeman's Chancery Reports (Mississippi)

Freem. Pr. Freeman's Practice, Illinois

Free Speech Y.B. Free Speech Yearbook

French French's Reports (6 New Hampshire)

French (N.H.) French's Reports (6 New Hampshire)

Frend & W. Prec. Frend & Ware's Precedents of Railway Conveyancing

FRES Federal Regulation of Employment Service (Lawyers Co-op Pub. Co.)

FRG Family Rights Group

F.R.G. Germany, Federal Republic of

Fries Tr. Trial of John Fries (Treason)

Frith. United States Opinions Attorneys-General (pt. 2, vol. 21)

Fr. M. (or Fra.M.) Francis' Maxims of Equity

Fr. Ord. French Ordinances

F.R.S. Federal Reserve System (U.S.)

FRU Free Representation Unit

Fry Fry on Specific Performance of Contracts

Fry Lun. Fry on Lunacy

Fry Sp. Per. Fry on Specific Performance of Contracts

Fry Vac. Fry on the Vaccination Acts

F.S. Federal Supplement

FSA
- Farm Security Administration
- Federal Security Agency (U.S.)

F.S.A.
- Federal Statutes Annotated
- Florida Statutes Annotated

FSC Foreign Sales Corporation

F.S.C.   Selected Judgments, Federal Supreme Court (1956-61) (Nigeria)

F.S.C. (Nig.)   Judgments of the Federal Supreme Court (1956-61) (Nigeria)

FSG   Federal Sentencing Guidelines Handbook: Text, Analysis, Case Digests

FSIP   Federal Service Impasses Panel

F.S.L.I.C.   Federal Savings and Loan Insurance Corp.

F.S.O.   Foreign Service Officer

FSQS   Food Safety and Quality Service

F.S.R.   Fleet Street Reports of Patent Cases (Eng.)

FSS   Federal Supply Service

F. Supp.   Federal Supplement

F.T.   Financial Times

FTAB or TAB   McQueen & Crestol, Federal Tax Aspects of Bankruptcy

FTAC   Schneider/Hoelschen, Federal Tax Aspects of Corporate Reorganizations

FTC   Federal Trade Commission

F.T.C.   Federal Trade Commission Decisions

F.T.C.A.   Federal Tort Claims Act

FTCR   Kanwit, Federal Trade Commission: Regulatory Manual

FTLR   Financial Times Law Report

FTP(2)   Westin, Federal Tax Planning, Second Edition

F.T.R.   Federal Travel Regulations

FTS   Federal Telecommunications System

Fulb. Par.   Fulbeck's Parallel

Fulb. St. Law   Fulbecke's Study of the Law

Full B.R.   Bengal Full Bench Rulings (North-Western Provinces) (India)

Full. Ch. Hist.   Fuller's Church History

Fuller   Fuller's Reports (59-105 Mich.)

Fuller (Mich.)   Fuller's Reports (59-105 Mich.)

Fult.   Fulton's Supreme Court Reports, Bengal (1842-44) (India)

Fulton   Fulton, Supreme Court Reports Bengal (India)

Fund   International Monetary Fund

Funeral D.   Funeral directors and embalmers

FURA   Federal Utility Regulation Annotated

Furl. L. & T.   Furlong on the Irish Law of Landlord and Tenant

FUTA   Federal Unemployment Tax Act

FWPCA   Federal Water Pollution Control Act

FWS   Fish and Wildlife Service

FY   Fiscal Year

G

G.
- Application for writ of error granted
- Gale, English Exchequer Reports
- Georgia
- German
- Gift tax
- Gregorowski's Reports of the High Court of the Orange Free State, South Africa
- King George, as 15 Geo. II
- Reports of the High Court of Griqualand (1882-1910) (S.Afr.)

GA
- Decisions of General Appraisers (U.S.)
- General Assembly (UN)

G.A.
- Decisions of General Appraisers (U.S.)
- General Assembly (United Nations)
- Governmental Affairs

Ga.
- General Appraisers' Decisions (U.S.)
- Georgia
- Georgia Reports
- Georgia Supreme Court Reports

Ga. A. Georgia Appeals Reports (Ga.)

Ga. Admin.Comp. Official Compilation of the Rules and Regulations of the State of Georgia.

Ga. App. Georgia Appeals Reports (1807-date)

Ga. App. (N.S.) Georgia Appeals Reports (Ga.)

Ga. B.A. Georgia Bar Association

Gabb. Cr. Law. Gabbett's Criminal Law

Gabb. Stat. L. Gabbett's Digest of the Statute Law

Ga. B.J. Georgia Bar Journal

Ga. Bus. Law. Georgia Business Lawyer

Ga. Code Code of Georgia

Ga. Code Ann. Code of Georgia Annotated

Ga. Const. Georgia Constitution

Ga. Dec. Georgia Decisions

Ga. Dec. (Dudley) Dudley's Reports (Ga.)

Gaii. Gaius' Institutes (Gaii Institutionum Commentarii)

Gaius Gaius' Institutes (Gaii Institutionum Commentarii)

Gaius, Inst. Gaius' Institutes

Ga. J. Int. & Comp. L. Georgia Journal of International & Comparative Law

Ga. J. Int'l. & Comp. L. Georgia Journal of International & Comparative Law

Ga. J.S. Legal Hist. Georgia Journal of Southern Legal History, The

Ga. L.
- Georgia Law Review
- Georgia Lawyer
- Georgia Sessions Laws

Gal. Gallison's Reports, United States Circuit Courts

Gal. & Dav. Gale & Davison's Queen's Bench Reports (Eng.)

Ga. Law Reporter The Georgia Law Reporter (Ga.)

Ga. Laws Georgia Laws

Ga. Lawyer Georgia Lawyer

Galb. Galbraith's Reports (9-11 Florida)

Galb. & M. Galbraith & Meek's Reports (9-12 Florida)

Galb. & M. (Fla.) Galbraith & Meek's Reports (9-12 Florida)

Galbraith Galbraiths' Reports (9-12 Florida)

Gale
- Gale on Easements, 12 editions (1839-1950)
- Gale's Exchequer Reports (1835-36) (Eng.) Gale's New Forest Decisions (Eng.)

Gale & D. Gale & Davison's Queen's Bench Reports (1841-43) (Eng.)

Gale & Dav. Gale & Davison' Queens Bench Reports (1841-43) (Eng.)

Gale & D. (Eng.) Gale & Davison's Queen's Bench Reports (1841-43) (Eng.)

Gale & Whatley Easem. Gale and Whatley, afterwards Gale, on Easements

Gale & Wh. Eas. Gale & Whatley (afterwards Gale) on Easements

Gale Eas. Gale on Easements

Gale's St. Gale's Statutes (Ill.)

Gale Stat. Gale's Statutes of Illinois

Ga. L.J. Georgia Law Journal

Gall. Gallison's Reports, United States Circuit Courts

Gall. C.C.R. Gallison, Reports, United States Circuit Courts

Gall. Cr. Cas. Gallick's Reports (French Criminal Cases)

Gall. Int. L. Gallaudet on International Law

Gallison Gallison's United States Circuit Court Reports

Gallison's Rep. Gallison, Reports, United States Circuit Courts

Ga. L. Rep. Georgia Law Reporter

Ga. L. Rev. Georgia Law Review

Gam. Gambia

Gamb. & Bar. Dig. Gamble & Barlow's Irish Equity Digest

Gamb. & Barl Gamble & Barlow's Digest (Ir.)

Gambl. Gambling

Gamboa Gamboa's Introduction to Philippine Law

Gamboa, Philippine Law Gamboa's Introduction to Philippine Law

Ganatra Ganatra's Criminal Cases (India)

G. & D. Gale & Davidson's English Queen's Bench Reports (1841-43)

G. & G. Goldsmith & Guthrie's Reports (36-67 Missouri Appeals)

G. & G. (Mo.) Goldsmith & Guthrie's Reports (36-67 Missouri Appeals)

G. & H. Gavin & Hord's Indiana Statutes

G. & J.
- Gill and Johnson's Maryland Court of Appeals Reports (1829-42)
- Glyn & Jameson's English Bankruptcy Reports (1821-28)

G. & J. (Md.) Gill & Johnson, Maryland Reports (Md.)

G. & Jo. Gill & Johnson Maryland Reports (Md.)

G & John. Gill & Johnson, Maryland Reports (Md.)

G. & P.R.R. Laws Gregg & Pond's Railroad Laws of the New England States

G. & R. Geldert & Russell's Nova Scotia Reports

G. & Sh. R.R. Godefroi & Shortt's Law of Railway Companies

G. & T. Gould & Tucker's Notes on Revised Statutes of United States

G. & Wh. Eas. Gale & Whatley (afterwards Gale) on Easements

G. & W. New Tr. Graham & Waterman on New Trials

Gane Eastern District Court Reports, Cape Colony (S. Africa)

Gantt Dig. Gantt's Digest Statutes, Arkansas

Gantts Dig. Gantt's Digest of Arkansas Statutes

GAO General Accounting Office

G.A.O. Let. Rep. General Accounting Office Letter Report

GAOR General Assembly Official Record (United Nations)

G.A.O. Rep. General Accounting Office, Reports to

G.A.O. Rev. General Accounting Office Review

Ga. Prac. Stand, Georgia Practice

Ga. P.S.C. Georgia Public Service Commission Reports

Ga.R. Georgia Reports (Ga.)

Ga. R.C. Georgia Railroad Commission

Garden. Gardenhire (Mo.)

Gardenhire. Gardenhire's Reports (vols. 14, 15 Missouri)

Gard. Ev. Garde, Evidence. 1830

Gard. Int. Law Gardner's Institute of American International Law

Gardn. P.C. Gardner Peerage Case, reported by Le Marchant

Gard. N.Y. Rep. Gardenier's New York Reporter

Gard. N.Y. Rept. Gardenier, New York Reporter

Gard. N.Y. Rptr. Gardenier's New York Reporter

Gard. Pl. Garde's First Principles of Pleading

Ga. Rep. Georgia Reports (Ga.)

Ga. Rep. Ann. Georgia Reports Annotated (Ga.)

G.A. Res. General Assembly Resolution

Gas & O. Gas and oil

Ga.S.B.J. Georgia State Bar Journal

Gaspar. Gaspar's Small Cause Court Reports (Bengal)

Ga. St. B.J. Georgia State Bar Journal

Ga. St. U.L. Rev. Georgia State University Law Review

Ga.Sup. Georgia Reports Supplement (Ga.)

Ga. Supp. Georgia Reports Supplement (Ga.)

Ga. Supplement Georgia Reports Supplement (Ga.)

GATT General Agreement on Tariffs and Trade

GATT/CP General Agreement Tariffs & Trade, Contracting Parties (U.S.)

Gav. & H. Rev. St. Gavin and Hord's Revised Statutes (Ind.)

Gavel
- The Gavel (The State Bar Association of North Dakota)
- Milwaukee Bar Ass'n Gavel

G.A.W Guaranteed Annual Wage

Gayaree Gayaree's Reports (25-28 Louisiana Annual)

Gay. (La.) Gayarre's Reports (25-28 Louisiana Annual)

Gaz. Weekly Law Gazette, Cincinnati

Gaz. & B.C. Rep. Gazette & Bankrupt Court Reporter, New York

Gaz. Bank. Gazette of Bankruptcy, London (1862-63)

Gaz. Bank. Dig. Gazzam, Digest of Bankruptcy Decisions

Gaz. Bankr. Gazette of Bankruptcy

Gazette The Law Society Gazette

Gaz. L.R. Gazette Law Reports

Gaz. L.R. (N.Z.) New Zealand Gazette Law Reports

Gaz. L. Soc. of Upper Can. Gazette. The Law Society of Upper Canada

G.B. Great Britain

G.B.J. Georgia Bar Journal

GC General Counsel

G.C. General Code

G.C.D.C. Gold Coast Divisional Court Reports

G.C. Div. C. Selected Judgments of the Divisional Courts (Ghana)

G.C. Div. Ct. Gold Coast Selected Judgments of the Divisional Courts

G.C.F.C. Gold Coast Full Court Selected Judgments

G.C. Full. Ct. Gold Coast Full Court Selected Judgments (Ghana)

GCM, G.C.M. General Counsel's, Assistant General Counsel's, or Chief Counsel's memorandum (U.S. Internal Revenue Service)

G. Coop. G. Cooper's English Chancery (35 ER)

G. Cooper G. Cooper's Chancery Reports 1815 (35 ER)

G. Cooper (Eng.) G. Cooper's English Chancery (35 ER)

GCP Government Contracts Program, George Washington University Law Center

G.C.P.R. General Ceiling Price Regulation

GDN. Guardian

G.D.R. Germany, Democratic Republic of

Gear, Landl. & T. Gear on Landlord and Tenant

GEBL Pollard/Burton, Guide to Effective Bankruptcy Litigation

Geld. & M. Geldart & Maddock's English Chancery Reports, vol. 6 Maddock's Reports

Geld. & O. Nova Scotia Decisions by Geldert & Oxley

Geld. & Ox. Nova Scotia Decisions by Geldert & Oxley

Geld. & R. Geldert & Russel Reports (28-39, 41-60 Nova Scotia Reports)

Geldart. Geldart & Maddock's English Chancery Reports (vol. 6 Maddock's Reports)

Gen. General

Gen. Abr. Cas. Eq. General Abridgment of Cases in Equity (Equity Cases Abridged (1677-1744))

Gen. Arb. Geneva Arbitration

Gen. Assem. General Assembly

Gen. Ass'ns. General Associations

Gen. Bus. General Business

Gen. City General City

Gen. Constr. General Construction

Gen. Dig. General Digest

Gen. Dig. N.S. General Digest, New Series

Gen. Dig. U.S. General Digest of the United States

Genl General

Gen. Laws General Laws

Gen. Mtg. General mortgage

Gen. Mun. General Municipal

Gen. Oblig. General Obligations

Gen. Ord. General Orders, Ontario Court of Chancery

Gen. Ord. Ch. General Orders of the English High Court of Chancery

Gen. Prov. General Provisions

Gen. R.R. Act General Railroad Act

Gen. Sess. General Sessions

Gen. St. General Statutes

Gen. Stat. Ann. General statute annotated

Gen. T. General Term

Gen. View Cr. L. Stephen, General View of the Criminal Law. 2ed. 1890

Geo.
- George
- Georgetown
- Georgetown Law Journal (D.C.)
- Georgia
- Georgia Reports
- King George, as 15 Geo. II

Geo. Coop. George Cooper's English Chancery Cases, time of Eldon

Geo. Dec. Georgia Decisions

Geo. Dig. George's Digest (Mississippi)

Geo. Immigr. L.J. Georgetown Immigration Law Journal

Geo. Int'l Envtl. L. Rev. Georgetown International Environmental Law Review

Geo J. Legal Ethics Georgetown Journal of Legal Ethics

Geo. Lib. George, Libel. 1812

Geo. L.J. Georgetown Law Journal

Geo. Mason L. Rev. George Mason Law Review

Geo. Mason U. Civ. Rts. L.J. George Mason University Civil Rights Law Journal

Geo.Mason U. L. Rev. George Mason University Law Review

Geopp. Geopposserde (Neth.) defendant

Geo. R. Georgia Reports (Ga.)

Geo. Rep. Georgia Reports (Ga.)

Geo. Rev. Georgia Law Review

George. George's Reports (30-39 Mississippi)

George. Partn. George on Partnership

Georget. L.J. Georgetown Law Journal

Georgetown Immig L J Georgetown Immigration Law Journal

Georgetown L.J. The Georgetown Law Journal

George Wash. L. Rev. The George Washington Law Review

Georgia Georgia Reports (Ga.)

Georgia B.J. Georgia Bar Journal

Georgia J. Int. Comp. L. Georgia Journal of International and Comparative Law

Georgia J. Int'l. L. & Compl. L. Georgia Journal of International Law and Comparative Law

Georgia L. Rev. Georgia Law Review

Georgia R. Georgia Reports (Ga.)

Georgia Rep. Georgia Reports (Ga.)

Georgia Reports Georgia Reports (Ga.)

Georgia Reps. Georgia Reports (Ga.)

Georgia St. B.J. Georgia State Bar Journal

Georgia (Supplement) Georgia Reports Supplement (Ga.)

Geo. Wash. J. Int'l. L. & Econ. George Washington Journal of International Law and Economics

Geo. Wash. Law Rev. George Washington Law Review

Geo. Wash. L. Rev. George Washington Law Review

Ger. Germany

German Yb. Int'l. L. German Yearbook of International Law. Berlin, Germany

Germany (FR) Federal Republic of Germany

G.E.R.R. Government Employee Relations Report (BNA)

Ger. Tit. Gerard's Titles to Real Estate (in New York)

Getz F. Getz's Forms in Conveyancing

GFP Government Furnished Property

GFR General Flight Rules (CAB) U.S.

G. Gr. G. Green's Reports (Iowa 1847-1854)

G. Greene (Iowa) G. Green's Reports (Iowa 1847-1854)

GGUALE Golden Gate University Advanced Legal Education Program

Ghana C.C. Ghana Current Cases (1965-1971)

Ghana L.R.C. Ghana Law Reform Commission

Ghose Mort. Ghose on Mortgages in India

GIA General International Agreement

Giauq. El. Giauque's Election Laws

Gib.
* Gibbon's Surrogate's Court Reports (N.Y.)
* Gibraltar

Gib. Aids Gibson's Aids to the Examinations

Gib. & Na. Eq. Jur. Gibbons & Nathans' Equitable Jurisdiction of County Courts

Gibb. Gibbons

Gibbon Gibbon on Nuisances

Gibbon, Rom. Emp. Gibbon, History of the Decline and Fall of the Roman Empire

Gibbons Gibbons' Reports, New York Surrogate Court

Gibbons (N.Y.) Gibbons' Reports, New York Surrogate Court

Gibb. Rom. Emp. Gibbon's Decline and Fall of the Roman Empire

Gibbs Gibbs' Reports (2-4 Michigan)

Gibbs F. Gibbs' Practical Forms

Gibbs' Jud. Chr. Gibbs' Judicial Chronicle

Gibb. Sur. Gibbon's Surrogate (N.Y.)

Gibb. Surr. Gibbon's Surrogate (N.Y.)

Gib. Civ. L. Gibbon on the Civil Law

Gib. Cod. Gibson's Codex Juris Ecclesiastical Angelicani

Gib. Cont. Gibbons on Contracts

Gib. Dec. Gibson's Scottish Decisions

Gib. Dil. Gibbons, Dilapidations and Nuisances. 2ed. 1849

Gib. Fix. Gibbons, Law of Fixtures. 1836

Gib. Lim. Gibbons' Lex Temporis (Limitation and Prescription)

Gib. L.N. Gibson's Law Notice (1882-84)

Gib. Lynd. Gibson's Memoir of Lord Lyndhurst

Gib. Nui. Gibbons' Law of Dilapidations and Nuisances

Gibs. Camd. Gibson's [edition of] Camden's Britannia

Gibs. Code. Gibson's Codex

Gibs. L.N. Gibson's Law Notes (1882-84)

Gibson. (Gibson od) Durie's Decisions, Scotch Court of Session (1621-42)

GICL Vishny, Guide to International Commerce Law

GICLE Institute of Continuing Legal Education in Georgia, University of Georgia School of Law

Gif. Giffard's English Vice-Chancellor's Reports (65-66 ER)

Giff. Giffard's English Vice-Chancellor's Reports (65-66 ER)

Giff. & H. Giffard and Hemming's Reports, English Chancery

Giffard Giffard (Eng.)

Giff. (Eng.) Giffard's English Vice-Chancellor's Reports (65-66 ER)

GII Government Institutes, Inc.

Gil.
- Gilbert's Cases in Law and Equity
- Gilbert's Chancery Reports (1705-1727)
- Gilfillan's Reports (1-20 Minnesota)
- Gilman's Reports (6-10 Illinois)
- Gilmer's Reports (21 Virginia)

Gil. & Fal. Gilmour & Falconer's Scotch Session Cases (1661-86)

Gilb.
- Gilbert's Cases in Law and Equity
- Gilbert's Chancery Reports (1705-27)

Gilb. Bank. Gilbart on Banking

Gilb. Cas. Gilbert's Cases, Law & Equity (1713-15) (Eng.)

Gilb. Cas. L. & Eq. Gilbert's Cases in Law & Equity (93 ER) (1713-15)

Gilb. Cas. L. & Eq. (Eng.) Gilbert's Common Pleas, (93 ER)

Gilb. Ch. Gilbert, English Chancery Reports (1705-27)

Gilb. Ch. Pr. Gilbert's History and Practice of the Exchequer

Gilb. Com. Pl. Gilbert's Common Pleas (93 ER)

Gilb. C.P. Gilbert's Common Pleas (93 ER)

Gilb. Debt Gilbert on the Action of Debt (appended to Gilbert's Cases in Law and Equity)

Gilb. Dev. Gilbert's Law of Devises

Gilb. Dis. Gilbert on Distress and Replevin

Gilb.Ej. Gilbert on Ejectments

Gilb. Eq. Gilbert's Equity or Chancery Reports (1705-27) (25 ER)

Gilb. Eq. (Eng.) Gilbert's English Equity or Chancery Reports (25 ER)

Gilb. Eq. Rep. Gilbert, English Equity or Chancery Reports

Gilbert, Ev. Gilbert's Law of Evidence

Gilbert, Tenures Gilbert on tenures

Gilbert, Uses, by Sugd. Gilbert's Uses and Trusts by Sugden

Gilb. Ev. Gilbert, Law of Evidence

Gilb. Ex. Gilbert's Executions

Gilb. Exch. Gilbert's Exchequer Reports (Eng.)

Gilb. Exch. Pr. Gilbert's History and Practice of the Exchequer

Gilb. For. Rom. Gilbert's Forum Romanum

Gilb. Forum Rom. Gilbert's Forum Romanum

Gilb. Hist. C.P. Gilbert, History of Common Pleas

Gilb. K.B. Gilbert's Cases in Law and Equity (Eng.)

Gilb. Lex Pr. Gilbert's Lex Praetoria

Gilb. P.C. Gilbert's Common Pleas (Cases in Law and Equity) (1713-14) (93 ER)

Gilb. Rem. Gilbert's Remainders

Gilb. Rents Gilbert's Treatise on Rents

Gilb. Rep. Gilbert, English Chancery Reports

Gilb.Repl. Gilbert on Replevin

Gilb. R.R. Gilbert's Railway Law of Illinois

Gilb. Ten. Gilbert on Tenure

Gilb. U.S. Gilbert's Uses and Trusts

Gilb. Uses Gilbert on Uses and Trusts

Gilchr. Gilchrist's Local Government Cases

Gild. Gildersleeve's Reports (vols. 1-8 New Mexico)

Gildersleeve Gildersleeve's Reports (1-10 New Mexico)

Gildersleeve (N.Mex.) Gildersleeve's Reports (1-10 New Mexico)

Gildr. Gildersleeve (N.Mex.)

Gilf. Gilfillan (Minn.)

Gilfillan Gilifillan's Reports (1-20 Minnesota)

Gill Gill's Maryland Court of Appeals Reports (1843-1851)

Gill & J. Gill & Johnson's Reports (Maryland)

Gill and J.(Maryland) Gill & Johnson, Maryland Reports (Md.)

Gill & J. (Md.) Gill & Johnson's Reports (Maryland)

Gill & Johns. Gill & Johnson's Reports (Maryland)

Gill & Johnston Maryland Reports--Gill & Johnson (Md.)

Gillett, Cr. Law Gillett's Treatise on Criminal Law and Procedure in Criminal Cases

Gill (Md.) Gill's Maryland Reports

Gill Pol. Rep. Gill's Police Court Reports (Boston, Mass.)

Gilm.
- Gilman's Reports (vols. 6-10 Illinois)
- Gilmer's Reports (21 Virginia)
- Gilmour's Reports, Scotch Court of Session (1661-66)

Gilman Gilman's Reports (6-10 Illinois)

Gilm. & F. Gilmour & Falconer's Decisions, Scotch Court of Session (1961-66)

Gilm. & Fal. Gilmour & Falconer's Decisions, Scotch Court of Sesssion (1961-66)

Gilm. & Falc. Gilmour & Falconer's Reports, Scotch Court of Session

Gilm. Dig. Gilman's Digest (Illinois and Indiana)

Gilmer Gilmer's Reports (1820-1821) (21 Virginia)

Gilmer (Va.) Gilmer's Reports (21 Virginia)

Gilm.(Ill.) Gilman's Reports (vols. 6-10 Illinois)

Gil. (Minn.) Gilfillan's Edition (vols. 1-20 Minnesota)

Gilp. Gilpin, United States District Court Reports

Gilp. Opin. Gilpin, Opinions of the United States Attorneys-General

Gir. W.C. Report of the Girard Will Case

G.J. Gill and Johnson's Reports (Maryland)

G.J.W. Great Jurists of the World, by Sir John Macdonnel & Edward Manson. 1913

Gl. Glossa (A Gloss or Interpretation)

G.L. General Laws

Gl. & J. Glyn & Jameson's Bankruptcy Reports (1821-28) (Eng.)

Glan. El. Cas. Glanville's Election Cases (1623-24)

Glan. llb. Glanville, De Legibus et Consuetudinibus Angliae

Glanv. Glanville, De Legibus et Consuetudinibus Angliae (1554)

Glanv. El. Cas. Glanville, English Election Cases (1624)

Glanvil. Glanville, De Legibus et Consuetudinibus Angliae

Glas. Glascock's Reports in all the Courts of Ireland (1831-32)

Glasc. Glascock's Reports in all the Courts of Ireland

Glascock Glascock's Reports in all the Courts of Ireland

Glassf. Ev. Glassford on Evidence

G.L.D. Cases in the Griqualand West Local Division of the Supreme Court (1910-46) (S. Afr.)

Glendale L.R. Glendale Law Review

Glendale L. Rev. Glendale Law Review

Glen High. Glen's Highway Laws

Glenn Glenn's Reports (16-18 La. Annual)

Glen Pub. H. Glen on the Public Health Laws

Glen Reg. Glen on Registration of Births and Deaths

GLO General Land Office (Interior Dept.) (U.S.)

Gloag & Henderson Gloag & Henderson, Introduction to the Law of Scotland, 7ed. 1968

Glov. Mun. Cor. Glover's Municipal Corporations

G.L.R.
- Gazette Law Reports (New Zealand)
- Georgia Law Review
- Ghana Law Reports
- Gujarat Law Reporter (India)

G.L.R. (N.Z.) Gazette Law Reports (N.Z.)

Glyn & J. Glyn & Jameson English Reports, English Bankruptcy

Glyn & Jam. Glyn & Jameson English Reports, English Bankruptcy (1821-28)

Glyn & J. (Eng.) Glyn & Jameson English Reports, English Bankruptcy

Glynn Wat. Pow. Glynn on Water Powers

G.M. Dud. Dudley's Reports (Georgia 1830-1833)

G.M. Dudl. Dudley's Reports (Georgia 1830-1833)

GMS Schwartz, Lee & Kelly, Guide to Multistate Litigation

GMU L. Rev. George Mason University Law Review

G.N. Gazette Notice (Ghana)

GNMA Government National Mortgage Association

GNP Gross National Product

G.O. General Orders, Court of Chancery (Ontario)

Go. Goebel's Probate Court Cases (Ohio)

Godb. (Eng.) Godbolt's English King's Bench Reports (78 ER)

Goddard Goddard on Easements, 8 editions (1871-1921)

Godd. Ease. Goddard on Easements. 8ed.

Godd. Easem. Goddard on Easements

Godef. & Sh. R.C. Godefroi & Shortt on Railway Companies

Godefroi Godefroi on Trusts and Trustees, 5 editions (1879-1927)

Godef. Trust Godefroi, Law of Trusts and Trustees. 5ed. 1927

Godo.
- Godolphin on Admiralty Jurisdiction
- Godolphin's Abridgment of Ecclesiastical Law
- Godolphin's Orphan's Legacy
- Godolphin's Repertorium Canconicum

Godol. Godolphin's Orphan's Legacy

Godolph (or Godolph.Rep.Can.) Godolphin's Repertorium Canonicum, - Abridgment of the Ecclesiastical Laws

Godolph. Adm. Jur. Godolphin Admiralty Jurisdiction. 2ed, 1685

Godolph. Ecc. Law Godolphin's Ecclesiastical Law

Godolph. Leg. Goldophin's Orphan's Legacy. 1701

Godolph. Orph. Leg. Godolphin's Orphan's Legacy

Godolph. Rep. Can. Godolphin's Repertorium Canonicum. 3ed. 1687

GODPT General Order Defense Transport Administration (U.S.)

Godson Godson's Mining Commissioner's Cases (Ontario)

Gods. Pat. Godson, Patents. 2ed. 1840

Goeb. Goebel's Probate Court Cases (Ohio)

Goebel Goebel's Probate Reports (Ohio)

Goebel (Ohio) Goebel's Probate Court Cases (Ohio)

Goebel's Rep. Goebel's Probate Reports (Ohio)

Gog. Or. Goguet's Origin of Laws

Goir. Fr. Co. Goirand's French Code of Commerce

Gold. Goldesborough's or Gouldsbourough's English King's Bench Reports (1586-1602)

Gold. & G. Goldsmith & Guthrie's Reports (36, 37 Missouri Appeals)

Goldb. Goldbolt's King's Bench, Common Pleas, and Exchequer Reports (Eng.)

Gold Coast Judgments (Full Court, Privy Council, Divisional Courts)

Golden Gate L. Rev. Golden Gate Law Review

Golden Gate L. Review Golden Gate Law Review

Golden Gate U. L. Rev. Golden Gate University Law Review

Goldes. Goldesborough's or Goulds-borough's English King's Bench Reports

Golds. Eq. Goldsmith, Doctrine and Practice of Equity. 6ed. 1871

Gonz. Gonzaga

Gonzaga L. Rev. Gonzaga Law Review

Gonz. L. Rev. Gonzaga Law Review

Gonz. Pub. Lab. L. Rep. Gonzaga Special Report:Public Sector Labor Law

Good. & Wood. Full Bench Rulings, Bengal (edited by Goodeve & Woodman)

Good. Ev. Goodeve's Law of Evidence (in India)

Goodeve Goodeve on Real Property. (1883-1906)

Good. Pat. Goodeve's Abstract of Patent Cases (1785-1883) (Eng.)

Good. Pr. Goodwin's Probate Practice

Goodrich-Amram Goodrich--Amram Procedural Rules Service

Good. Ry. C. Goodeve on Railway Companies and Passengers

Good W. Good will

GOR General Overruling Regulation (Office of Price Stabilization) (U.S.)

Gord. Dec. Gordon on the Law of Decedents in Pennsylvania

Gord. Dig. Gordon's Digest of United States Laws

Gordon Gordon's Reports (vols. 24-26 Colorado and vols. 10-13 Colorado Appeals)

Gord. Tr. Gordon's Treason Trials

Gore-B. Comp. Gore-Brown, Companies. 43ed. 1977

GORMAC Government Research Management Consultants

Gosf. Gosford's Manuscript Reports, Scotch Court of Session

Gottschall Gottschall's Dayton (Ohio) Superior Court Reports

Goud. Pand. Goudsmit's Pandects (Roman Law)

Gould. Gouldsborough's English King's Bench Reports (1586-1602)

Gould & T. Gould & Tucker's Notes on Revised Status of United States

Gould, Pl. Gould on the Principles of Pleading in Civil Actions

Gouldsb. Gouldsborough's English King's Bench Reports (75 ER)

Gouldsb. (Eng.) Gouldsborough's English King's Bench Reports (75 ER)

Gould's Dig. Gould's Digest of Laws (Ark.)

Gould Sten. Rep. Gould's Stenographic Reporter (Monographic Series Albany, N.Y.)

Gould, Wat. Gould on Waters

Gour. Gourick's Patent Digest (1889-91)

Gourl. Gen. Av. Gourlie on General Average

Gov. Governor

Gov. Cont. Rep. Government Contracts Reporter (CCH)

Govt. Government

Gov't. Cont. Rep. Government Contracts Reporter (CCH)

Gov't. Empl. Rel. Rep. (BNA) Government Employee Relations Report (BNA)

govtl. governmental

Govt. Pubns. Rev. Government Publications Review

Govt. Pub. Rev. Government Publications Review

Gov't. Union Rev. Government Union Review

Gow. Gow's English Nisi Prius Cases (171 ER)

Gow N.P. Gow's English Nisi Prius Cases (171 ER)

Gow. N.P. (Eng.) Gow's Nisi Prius Cases (171 ER)

Gow Part. Gow on Partnerships

GPO Government Printing Office

GPPS Dunkle, Guide to Pension and Profit Sharing Plans

Gr.
- Grant's Cases
- Grant's Pennsylvania Cases (1814-63)
- Grant's Reports (1774-87) (Jamaica)
- Grant's Upper Canada Chancery Reports
- Greek
- Greenleaf's Reports (1-9 Maine)

- Green's Reports (N.J. Law & Equity)

Gra.
- Graham's Reports (vols. 98-107 Georgia)
- Grant

Gra. & Wat. N.T. Graham and Waterman on New Trials

Grad. Fix. Grady on Fixtures

Grad. Hind. Inh. Grady's Hindoo Law of Inheritance

Grad. Hind. L. Grady's Manual of Hindoo Law

Grad. Ind. Co. Grady's Indian Codes

Grafton Smith's New Hampshire Reports (N.H.)

Grah. & W. New Trials Graham and Waterman on New Trials

Grand J. Grand jury

Granger Granger's Reports (vols. 22-23 Ohio State.)

Grant
- Grant of Elchies' Scotch Session Cases
- Grant's Chancery Chamber Reports (1850-65) (Upper Canada)
- Grant's Jamaica Reports
- Grant's Pennsylvania Cases (3 vols.)
- Grant's Upper Canada (Ontario) Chancery Reports (1849-82)

Grant, Bank. Grant on Banking

Grant Cas. Grant's Pennsylvania Cases

Grant Cas. (Pa.) Grant's Pennsylvania Cases

Grant Ch. Grant's Upper Canada Chancery Reports

Grant Ch. (Can.) Grant's Upper Canada Chancery Reports

Grant, Corp. Grant on Corporations

Grant E. & A. Grant's Error and Appeal Reports, (1846-66) (Ontario)

Grant Err, & App. Grant's Error & Appeal, Upper Canada

grant'g granting

Grant, Jamaica Grant's Jamaica Reports

Grant Pa. Grant's Pennsylvania Cases

Grant (Pa) Grant, Pennsylvania Cases

Gra. N. Tr. Graham on New Trials

Grant's R. Grant's Reports (1774-87) (Jamaica)

Grant U.C. Grant's Upper Canada Chancery Reports

Grant U.S. Grant's Upper Canada Chancery Reports

Grap. Just. Grapel, Translation of the Institutes of Justinian

Gra. Pr. Graham's Practice of the New York Supreme Court

Grap. Rom. Law Grapel's Sources of the Roman Civil Law

GRASR General Railroad and Airline Stabilization Regulations (U.S.)

Grat. Grattan's Virginia Reports

Gratt. Grattan's Virginia Supreme Court Reports (1844-1880)

Gratt. (Va.) Grattan's Virginia Reports

Grav. de Jur. Nat. Gent. Gravina, De Jure Naturale Gentium, etc.

Graves Proceedings in King's Council (1392-93) (Eng.)

Gravin. Gravina, Originum Juris Civilis.

Gray
- Gray's Massachusetts Supreme Judicial Court Reports (1854-1860) (67-82 Massachusetts)
- Gray's Reports (112-22 North Carolina)

Graya Graya (a periodical)

Gray Att. Pr. Gray, Country Attorney's Practice. 9ed. 1869

Gray. Forms Graydon's Forms of Conveyance

Gray (Mass.) Gray's Massachusetts Reports (vols. 67-82)

Gray, Perpetuities Gray's Rule Against Perpetuities

Gr. Brice. Green's edition of Brice on Ultra Vires

Gr. Brit. Great Britain

Gr. Brit. T.S. Great Britain Treaty Series

Gr. Ca. Grant's Cases

Greav. Cr. L. Greaves, Criminal Consolidation. 2ed. 1862

Greaves Judgments of the Windward Islands Court of Appeal (1866-1904)

Greav. Russ. Greave's Edition of Russell on Crimes

Green
- Green's Reports (1-9 Maine)

- Green's Reports (N.J. Law & Equity)
- Green's Reports (1 Oklahoma)
- Green's Reports (11-17 Rhode Island)

Green. & H. Conv. Greenwood & Horwood's Conveyancing

Green Bag Green Bag, A Legal Journal (Boston)

Green B.L. Green's Bankrupt Law

Green Bri. Green's edition of Brice's Ultra Vires

Green C.E. Green's Reports (16-27 N.J. Equity)

Green. C.E. C.E. Greene's Chancery Reports (New Jersey)

Green Ch. H.W. Green's New Jersey Chancery Reports (vols. 2-4 New Jersey Equity)

Green. Conv. Greenwood, Manual of Conveyancing. 9ed. 1897

Green Cr. Green's Criminal Law, (Eng.)

Green Cr. Cas. Green's Criminal Cases

Green Crim. Reports: Criminal Law Reports (U.S.)

Green, Cr. Law R. Green's Criminal Law Reports (N.Y.)

Green Cr. L. Rep. Green's Criminal Law Reports

Green Cr. Rep. Criminal Law Reports (U.S.)

Green. Cruise Greenleaf's Edition of Cruise's Digest of Real Property

Green. Cts. Greenwood on Courts

Greene
- Greene's Iowa Reports (1847-54)

- Greene's Reports (7 N.Y. Ann. Cases)

Greene G. (Iowa) G. Greene's Iowa Reports

Green. Ev. Greenleaf's Law of Evidence

Green. Forms Greening's Forms of Declarations, Pleadings, & c.

Greenh. Pub. Pol. Greenhood's Doctrine of Public Policy in the Law of Contracts

Greenh. Sh. Greenhow's Shipping Law Manual

Green L. J.S. Green's Law Reports (13-15 New Jersey)

Greenl. Greenleaf's Reports (1-9 Maine)

Greenl. Cr. Greenleaf's Edition of Cruise's Digest of Real Property

Greenl. Cruise Greenleaf's Edition of Cruise's Digest of Real Property

Greenl. Cruise Real Prop. Greenleaf's Edition of Cruise's Digest of Real Property

Greenl. Ev. Greenleaf on Evidence

Greenl. Ov. Cas. Greenleaf's Overrules Cases

Greenl. Test. Ev. Greenleaf's Testimony of the Evangelists

Green (NJ) Green's New Jersey Law or Equity

Green. Ov. Cas. Greenleaf's Overruled Cases

Green R.I. Green's Reports (11-17 R.I.)

Green (R.I.). Green's Reports (Rhode Island. vols. 11-17)

Green. Rom. Law Greene's Outlines of Roman Law

Green's Brice, Ultra Vires. Green's Edition of Brice's Ultra Vires

Green Sc. Cr. Cas. Green's Criminal Cases (1820) (Sc.)

Green Sc. Tr. Green's Scottish Trials for Treason

Green. Ship. Greenhow's Law of Shipowners

Green. Test. Ev. Greenleaf on the Testimony of the Evangelists

Greenw. & M. Mag. Pol. Greenwood & Martin's Magistrates' Police Guide

Greenw. Conv. Greenwood on Conveyancing

Greenw. Cts. Greenwood on Courts

Greer. Greer, Irish Land Acts. Leading Cases. (1872-1903)

Greg. Gregorowski's High Court Reports

Gregg Bank. Gregg on the Law of Bankruptcy

Gregorowski High Court Reports, Orange Free State

Greg. Turon. Gregory on Tours.

Grein. Dig. Greiner's Louisiana Digest

Grein. Pr. Greiner Louisiana Practice

Gren.
- Greiner's Ceylon Reports
- Grenada

Grenier Grenier, Ceylon Reports

Gr. Eq.
- Gresley's Equity Evidence

- H.W. Green's New Jersey Equity Reports

Gre. Rom. Law Greene's Outlines of Roman Law

Gres. Eq. Ev. Gresley's Equity Evidence

Gretton
- Oxford Quarter Sessions Records (Oxford Record Soc. 16)

Gr. Ev. Greenleaf on Evidence

Grey Deb. Grey, House of Commons Debates

Grif. Cr. Griffith on Arrangements with Creditors

Grif. Ct. Mar. (or Mil.Law) Griffith on Military Law and Courts-Martial

Griffin Pat. Cas. Griffin's Patent Cases (England) (1866-87)

Griffin P.C. Griffin's Abstract of Patent Cases (Eng.)

Griffith Griffith's Reports (vols. 1-5 Indiana Appeals and vols. 117-132 Indiana)

Griff. Pat. Cas. Griffin's Patent Cases. 1866-87

Grif. Inst. (or Eq.) Griffith's Institutes of Equity

Grif. Jud. Acts Griffith on the Judicature Acts

Grif. L. Reg. Griffith's Law Register (Burlington, New Jersey)

Grif. Mar. Wom. Griffith's Married Women's Property Act

Grif. Pat. C. Griffin's Patent Cases (1866-87)

Grif. P.C. Griffin's Patent Cases (1866-87)

Grif. P.L.C. Griffin's London Poor Law Cases (1821-31)

Grif. P.L. Cas. Griffith's London Poor Law Cases (1821-31)

Grif. Pr. Griffith's Practice

Grif. P.R.C. Griffith's Poor Rate Cases

Grif. P.R. Cas. Griffith's English Poor Rate Cases

Grif. St. Griffith's Stamp Duties

Grim. Bank. Grimsey's Proceedings in Bankruptcy

Grimke Ex. Grimke on Executors and Administrators

Grimke Jus. Grimke's Justice

Grimke P.L. Grimke's Public Laws of South Carolina

Gris., Grisw. Griswold's Reports (14-19 Ohio)

Griswold Griswold's Reports (14-19 Ohio)

Grisw. Und. Griswold's Fire Underwriter's Text-Book

G.R.O. General Register Office

Gro.
- Gross' Select Cases Concerning the Law Merchant (Selden Society)
- Grotius' Rights of War and Peace; many editions (1625-1901)

G.R.O.B.D.M. General Register Office for Births, Deaths and Marriages

Gro. B.P. Grotius, De Jure Belli ac Pacis

Gro. de J.B. Grotius, De Jure Belli ac Pacis

Gross Laws (or St.) Gross' Illinois Compiled Laws

Gross, St. Gross Illinois Compiled Laws, or Statutes

Grot. de Acquit. Grotius de Aequitate

Grot. Soc'y Transactions of the Grotius Society, England

Group Legal Rev. Group Legal Review

Gr. S. GroBer Senat (in banc)

Grt. Grant's Cases (Pa.)

G.S. General Statutes

GSA General Services Administration (U.S.)

GSAPR General Services Administration Procurement Regulations

G.S.B. Georgia State Bar Journal

GSO General Salary Order (U.S.)

G.S.R. Gongwer's State Reports (Ohio)

GSSR General Salary Stabilization Regulations (U.S.)

GT Gift Tax Ruling

Gtd. Guaranteed

Gt. L.J. Georgetown Law Journal

Gty. Guaranty

Gu. Guam

Guam Admin R. Administrative Rules and Regulations of the Government of Guam.

Guam Civ. Code Guam Civil Code

Guam Code Civ. Pro. Guam Code of Civil Procedure

Guam Gov't. Code Guam Government Code

Guam Prob. Code Guam Probate Code

Guar. Guaranty

Guar. & W. Guardian and Ward

Guat. Guatemala

Gude Pr. Gude, Practice of the Crown Side of the Court of King's Bench. 1828

Guern. Eq. Jur. Guernsey, Key to Equity Jurisprudence

Guern. Ins. Guernsey on Questions of Insanity

Guern. Mech. L. Guernsey's Mechanics' Lien Laws of New York

Guide to Computer L. (CCH) Guide to Computer Law (Commerce Clearing House)

Guild Law. Guild Lawyer, National Lawyers' Guild, N.Y. Chapter

Guild Prac. Guild Practitioner

Guild Q. National Lawyers' Guild Quarterly

Guj. L.T. Gujerat Law Times (India)

Gulzot, Rep. Govt. Guizot, History of Representative Government

Gunby Gunby's District Court Reports (La. 1885)

Gunby(La.) Gunby's District Court Reports (La. 1885)

Gunby's Dec. Gunby's District Court Reports (La.)

Gundry. Gundry Manuscripts in Lincoln's Inn Library

Gunn. Tolls Gunning on Tolls

Gut. Brac. Guterbock's Bracton

Guth. L. & T. Guthrie's Landlord & Tenant

Guth. Pr. Guthrie, Principles of the Laws of England. 1843

Guthrie
- Guthrie's Reports (33-83 Mo. Appeals)
- Guthrie's Sheriff Court Cases (Sc.)

Guth. Sh. Cas. Guthrie's Sheriff Court Cases (1861-92) (Sc.)

Guth. Sher. Cas. Guthrie's Sheriff Court Cases (1861-92) (Sc.)

Guth. Tr. Un. Guthrie on Trade Unions

Guy. Guyana

Guy For. Med. Guy, Forensic Medicine. 7ed. 1895

Guy, Med. Jur. Guy, Medical Jurisprudence

Guyot, Inst. Feod. Guyot, Institutes Feodales.

G.W.
- Cases in the Griqualand West Local Division of the Supreme Court (1910-46) (S. Afr.)
- George Washington Law Review

G.W.D. South African Law Reports, Griqualand West Local Division

Gwil. Gwillim's Tithe Cases (1224-1824)

Gwill Gwillim's Tithe Cases (Eng.)

Gwill. Bac. Abr. Gwillim's Tithe Cases (Eng.)

Gwill. T. Cas. Gwillim's Tithe Cases (Eng.)

Gwill. Ti. Cas. Gwillim's Tithe Cases (Eng.)

Gwil. Ti. Cas. Gwillim's Tithe Cases, (Eng.)

G.W.L. Reports of Cases decided in the Supreme Court of South Africa (Griqualand West Local Division) by Kitchin

G.W.L.D. South Africa Law Reports, Griqualand West Local Division

G.W.L.R. George Washington Law Review

G.W.R. Griqualand High Court Reports

Gw. Sh. Gwynne on Sheriffs

GWSR General Wage Stabilization Regulations (U.S.)

GYIL German Yearbook of International Law

H

H.
- Handy's Reports
- Hare's Chancery Reports (Eng.)
- Hawaii Reports
- Hebrew
- Hertzog's High Court Reports (S.Af.)
- Hic (here, in the same paragraph)
- Hilary Term
- Hill New York Reports (1841-44)
- House Bill
- House Bill (State Legislatures)
- Howard Supreme Court Reports (42-65 U.S.)
- King Henry

h. harmonized: apparent inconsistency explained and shown not to exist (used in Shepard's Citations)

H.A.
- Hoc anno (this year)
- House Administration

Ha.
- Haggard
- Hall
- Hare, English Vice-Chancellors' Reports (1841-53)
- Hawaii

Ha. & Tw. Hall & Twell, English Chancery Reports (1849-50)

Ha. App. Appendix to volume 10 of Hare's Vice-Chancellor's Reports (Eng.)

Hab. Corp. Habeas Corpus

Hab. fa. poss. Habere facias possessionem

Hab. fa. seis. Habere facias seisnam

Habit. Crim. Habitual criminals and subsequent offenders

Hack. Gen. Aw. Hackett on the Geneva Award Acts

Had.
- Haddington, Reports, Scotch Court of Session (1592-1624)
- Hadley's Reports (45-48 New Hampshire)

Had. Chy. Jur. Haddan's Administrative Jurisdiction of the Court of Chancery

Hadd. Haddington, Manuscript Reports, Scotch Court of Session

Haddington Haddington, Manuscript Reports, Scotch Court of Session

Hadl. Hadley's Reports (vols. 45-48 New Hampshire)

Hadley Hadley's Reports (45-48 New Hampshire)

Hadl. Rom. Law Hadley's Introduction to the Roman Law

Hag.
- Hagan's Reports (1-2 Utah)
- Hagans' Reports (1-5 West Virginia)
- Haggard's Admiralty Reports (Eng.)

Hag. Adm. Haggard, English Admiralty Reports, 3 vols. (1822-38)

Hagan Hagan's Reports (1, 2 Utah)

Hagans Hagans' Reports (1-5 West Virginia)

Hag. Con. Haggard's consistory Reports (1789-1821) (Eng.)

Hague Ct. Rep. (Scott) Hague Court Reports, First Series

Hague Ct. Rep. 2d (Scott) Hague Court Reports, Second Series

Hag. Ecc. Haggard's English Ecclesiastical Reports (1827-33)

Hagg. Adm. Haggard's English Admiralty Reports (166 ER)

Hagg. Adm. (Eng.) Haggard's English Admiralty Reports (166 ER)

Hagg. Con. Haggard's English Consistory Reports (161 ER)

Hagg. Cons. Haggard's English Consistory Reports (161 ER)

Hagg. Consist. Haggard's English Consistory Reports (161 ER)

Hagg.Consist. (Eng.) Haggard's English Consistory Reports (161 ER)

Hagg. Ecc. Haggard's English Ecclesiastical Reports (162 ER)

Hagg. Eccl. Haggard's Ecclesiastical Reports (1827-1833) (162 ER)

Hagg. Eccl. (Eng.) Haggard's Ecclesiastical Reports (162 ER)

Hagn. & M. Hagner & Miller's Reports (2 Maryland Chancery)

Hagn. & Mill. Hagner & Miller's Reports (2 Maryland Chancery)

Hague Ct. Rep. Hague Court Reports

Hague Y.B. Int'l L. Hauge Yearbook of International Law

Hailes Dalrymple (Lord Hailes) Decisions of the Court of Session (1776-91) (Sc.)

Hailes' Ann. Hailes, Annals of Scotland

Hailes Dec. Hailes' Decisions, Scotch Court of Sessions

Hain.J.P. Haine's Illinois Justice of the Peace

Hal. Anal. Hale, Analysis of the Law. 6ed. 1820

Hal. & Tw. Hall & Twell's Chancery (Eng.)

Halc. Halcomb's Mining Cases (Eng.)

Hal. Civ. Law Hallifax's Analysis of the Civil Law

Halc. Min. Cas. Halcomb's Mining Cases (London, 1826)

Hal. Const. Hist. Hallam's Constitutional History

Hale
- Hale's Common Law (Eng.)
- Hale's Reports (vols. 33-37 California)

Hale, Anal. Hale's Analysis of the Law

Hale C.L. Hale's History of the Common Law

Hale Com. Law Hale's History of the Common Law

Hale Cr. Prec. Hale's Precedents in Criminal Cases (1475-1640) (Eng.)

Hale, De Jure Mar. Hale's De Jure Maris, Appendix to Hall on the Sea Shore

Hale de Port. Mar.   Hale's De Portibus Maris

Hale Ecc.   Hale's Ecclesiastical Reports (1583-1736) (Eng.)

Hale, Hist. Eng. Law   Hale's History of the English Law

Hale Jur. H.L.   Hale, Jurisdiction of the House of Lords. 1796

Hale Parl.   Hale, History of Parliament. 2ed. 1745

Hale P.C.   Hale's Pleas of the Crown (Eng.)

Hale P.C. (Eng.)   Hale's Pleas of the Crown (Eng.)

Hale Prec.   Hale's Precedents in (Ecclesiastical) Criminal Cases

Hale's   Hale's Precedents in Ecclesiastical Criminal Cases. 1475-1640

Hale Sug. C.M.   Hale's Suggestion on Courts-Martial

Hale Sum.   Hale, Summary of the Pleas of the Crown

Hale, Torts   Hale on Torts

Hal. Ev.   Halsted's Digest of the Law of Evidence

Halh. Gent. L.   Halhed's Code of Gentoo Laws

Halifax, Anal.   Halifax' Analysis of the Roman Civil Law

Hal. Int. Law   Halleck's International Law

Halk.
- Halkerston's Compendium of Scotch Faculty Decisions
- Halkerston's Digest of the Scotch Marriage Law
- Halkerston's Latin Maxims

Halk. Comp.   Halkerston's Compendium of Scotch Faculty Decisions

Halk. Dig.   Halkerston's Digest of Scotch Marriage Law

Halk. Lat. Max.   Halkerston's Latin Maxims

Halk. Max.   Halkerston's Latin Maxims

Halk. Tech. Terms   Halkerston's Technical Terms of the Law

Hall.
- Decisions of the Water Court (S. Afr.) (1913-36)
- Hallett's Reports (1, 2 Colorado)
- Hall's New York Superior Court Reports
- Hall's Reports (56, 57 New Hampshire)

Hall Adm.   Hall's Admiralty Practice and Jurisdiction

Hall A.L.J.   Hall's American Law Journal

Hallam.   Hallam's Constitutional History of England

Hall Am. L.J.   Hall's American Law Journal

Hall & T.   Hall & Twell, Reports, English Chancery (47 ER)

Hall & Tw.   Hall & Twell, Reports, English Chancery (47 ER)

Hall & Tw. (Eng.)   Hall & Twell, Reports, English Chancery (47 ER)

Hal. Law   Halsted's Reports (6-12 N.J. Law)

Hall. Ch. Pr.   Halliday's Elementary View of Chancery Proceedings

Hall. Civ. Law Hallifax's Analysis of the Civil Law

Hall. (Col.) Hallett's Colorado Reports

Hall. Const. Hist. Hallam's Constitutional History of England

Hall Const. L. Hall's Tracts on Constitutional Law

Halleck, Int. law Halleck's International Law

Hall, Emerig. Mar. Loans Hall, Essay on Maritime Loans from the French of Emerigon

Hallet Hallett's Reports (1, 2 Colorado)

Hall. Hist. Hallan's Constitutional History of England

Hallifax, Anal. (or Civil Law) Hallifax's Analysis of the Civil Law

Hallif. C.L. Hallifax, Analysis of the Civil Law

Hall Int. Law
- Halleck's International Law
- Hall on International Law

Hall, J. Criminal Law Hall, Jerome on General Principles of Criminal Law

Hall Jour. Jur. Journal of Jurisprudence (Hall's)

Hall. Law of W. Halleck's Law of War

Hall L.J. Hall's American Law Journal

Hall, Marit. Loans Hall, Essay on Maritime Loans from the French of Emerigon

Hall, Mex. Law Hall, Laws of Mexico Relating to Real Property, etc.

Hall, Neut. Hall, Rights and Duties of Neutrals, 1874

Hall N.H. Hall's Reports (56, 57 New Hamp.)

Hall (N.Y.) Hall's New York Superior Court Reports

Hall, Profits a Prendre Hall, Treatise on the Law Relating to Profits a Prendre, etc.

Hall's Am. L.J. Hall's American Law Journal

Hall Shores Hall, Rights in the Sea Shores

Hall's J.Jur. Journal of Jurisprudence (Hall's)

Hal. Min. Law Halleck's Mining Laws of Spain and Mexico

Hals. Halsted's Reports (6-12 N.J. Law Reports)

Halsbury
- Halsbury's Laws of England
- Halsbury's Statutes of England

Halsbury L. Eng. Halsbury's Law of England

Halsbury's Laws Halsbury's Laws of England

Halsbury's S.I.s. Halsbury's Statutory Instruments

Halsbury's Statutes Halsbury's Statutes of England

Hals. Ch. Halsted's Reports (5-8 N.J. Equity Reports)

Hals. Eq. Halsted's New Jersey Equity Reports

Halst.
- Halsted's Equity (N.J.)

- Halsted's Law (N.J.)

Halst. Ch.   Halsted's Chancery (New Jersey)

Halsted (N.J.)   Halsted's Chancery (New Jersey)

Halst. Ev.   Halsted's Digest of the Law of Evidence

Ham.
- Hamilton's Court of Session Reports (Sc.)
- Hammond (Ga.)
- Hammond's India & Burma Election Cases
- Hammond's Reports (1-9 Ohio State Reports)

Ham. A. & O.   Hammerton, Allen & Otter, English Magistrates' Cases (vol. 3 New Sessions Cases)

Ham. & J.   Hammond & Jackson's Reports (45 Georgia)

Ham. Cont.   Hammon on Contracts

Ham. Cust.   Hamel's Laws of the Customs. 3ed. 1881

Hamel, Cust.   Hamel's Laws of the Customs

Ham. Fed.   Hamilton's Federalist

Hamilton
- Haddington's Manuscript Cases, Court of Session (Sc.)
- Hamilton on Company, Law, 3 editions (1891-1910)
- Hamilton's American Negligence Cases

Ham. Ins.
- Hammond on Insanity
- Hammond on Fire Insurance

Ham. Int.   Hamel's International Law

Hamlin   Hamlin's Reports (vols. 81-93 Maine)

Hamline J. Pub. L. & Pol'y   Hamline Journal of Public Law & Policy

Hamline L. Rev.   Hamline Law Review

Ham. Mar. Laws   Hammick, Marriage Laws. 2ed. 1887

Hammond
- Hammond's Reports (36-45 Georgia)
- Hammond's Reports (1-9 Ohio)

Hammond & Jackson   Hammond & Jackson's Reports (45 Georgia)

Ham. N.P.   Hammond's Nisi Prius

Ham. O.   Charles Hammond's Reports (Ohio)

Ham. O.R.   Charles Hammond's Reports (Ohio)

Ham. Part.   Hammond on Parties to Actions

Ham. Parties   Hammond on Parties to Action

Ham. Pl.   Hammond, Principles of Pleading. 1819

Hamps. Co. Cas.   Hampshire County Court Reports (Eng.)

Hamp. Tr.   Hampson, Trustees. 2ed. 1830

Han.
- Handy's Ohio Reports (12 Ohio Dec.)
- Hannay's Reports (12, 13 New Brunswick)
- Hansard's Book of Entries (1685)
- Hanson's Bankruptcy Reports (1915-17)

Hanb. Pat. Hanbury's Judicial Error in the Law of Patents

Hanb. Us. Hanbury-Jones on Uses

Hanc. Conv. Hancock's System of Conveyancing (Canada)

Hand.
- Hand's Reports (40-45 New York)
- Handy's Ohio Reports (12 Ohio Decisions)

H. & B. Hudson & Brooke's Irish King's Bench Reports (1827-31)

Handb. Mag. Handbook for Magistrates (1853-55)

H. & C. Hurlstone & Coltman, English Exchequer Reports (1862-66)

Hand Ch. P. Hand's Chancery Practice

Hand Cr. Pr. Hand's Crown Practice

H. & D. Lalor's Supplement to Hill & Denio's New York Reports

H. & D. Pr. Holmes & Disbrow's Practice

Han. Deb. Hansard, Parliamentary Debates

Handelsgericht Commercial Court (Switz.)

Hand Fines Hand on Fines and Recoveries

H. & G.
- Harris & Gill's Maryland Court of Appeals Reports (1826-29)
- Hurlstone's & Gordon's Reports (Eng.)

H. & H.
- Harrison & Hodgin's Municipal Reports (Upper Canada)

- Horn & Hurlstone's English Exchequer Reports (1838-39)

H. & J.
- Harris and Johnson's Maryland Court of Appeals Reports (1800-26)
- Hayes & Jones' Exchequer Reports (1832-34) (Ir.)

H. & J. Forms Hayes and Jarman's Concise Forms of Wills

H. & J. Ir. Hayes & Jones' Exchequer Reports (1832-34) (Ir.)

H. & John. Harris & Johnson's Maryland Reports (Md.)

H. & M.
- Hay & Marriott's Admiralty Reports (1776-1779) (165 ER)
- Hemming & Miller's Vice-Chancellor's Reports (1862-65) (Eng.)
- Hening & Munford's Reports (11-14 Virginia)

H. & M. Ch. Hemming & Miller's English Vice-Chancellors' Reports

H. & McH. Harris and McHenry's Maryland Court of Appeals Reports (1785-99)

H. & McHenry Harris & McHenry's Maryland Reports (Md.)

H. & M. (Va.) Hening & Munford's Reports (11-14 Virginia) (1806-10)

H. & N. Hurlstone & Norman's Exchequer (1856-62) (Eng.)

H. & P. Hopwood & Philbrick's English Election Cases (1863-67)

Hand. Pat. Hands on Patents

H. & R. Harrison & Rutherfurd's English Common Pleas Reports (1865-66)

H. & R. Bank. Hazlitt & Roche's Bankruptcy Reports

H. & S. Harris & Simrall's Reports (49-52 Miss.)

H. & T. Hall & Twell's Chancery Reports (1849-50) (Eng.)

H. & T. Self-Def. Harrigan & Thompson's Cases on the Law of Self-Defense

H. & Tw. Hall & Twells, English Chancery Reports (1849-50)

H. & W.
- Harrison & Wollaston's K.B. Reports (1835-36)
- Hazzard & Warburton's Prince Edward Island Reports
- Hurlstone & Walmsley's Exchequer Reports (1840-41) (Eng.)

Handy Handy's Ohio Reports (12 Ohio Decisions)

Handy (Ohio) Handy's Ohio Reports (12 Ohio Decisions)

Handy R. Handy, Cincinnati Superior Court Reports (Ohio)

Hane. Cr. Dig. Hanes' United States Digest of Criminal Cases

Han. Ent. Hansard's Entries

Hanes Hanes' English Chancery

Hanf. Hanford's Entries (1685)

Hanh. Mar. Wom. Hanhart on Married Women

Han. Hor. Hanover on the Law of Horses

Han. Mar. Wom. Hanhart on the Laws Relating to Married Women

Hanmer Lord Kenyon's Notes (English King's Bench Reports), edited by Hanmer

Hann. Hannay's Reports (12, 13 New Brunswick) (1867-71)

Han. (N.B.) Hannay's Reports (New Brunswick)

Han. Prob. Hanson on the Probate and Legacy Acts

Hans. Hansbrough (Va.)

Hans. Al. Hansard on Aliens

Hansb. Hansbrough's Reports (76-90 Virginia)

Hans. Deb. Hansbrough's Reports (76-90 Virginia)

Hans. Deb. Hansard's Parliamentary Debates (Eng.)

Hans. Ent. Hansard's Entries

Hans. Parl. Deb. Hansard, Parliamentary Debates

Hans. Pr.
- Hanson on Probate Acts, & c.

Har.
- Harrington (Delaware)
- Harrington's Chancery (Michigan)
- Harrison (Louisiana)
- Harrison's Chancery (Michigan)
- Harrison's Reports (15-17, 23-29 Indiana)
- Harris' Pennsylvania Reports

Har. & G. Harris & Gill, Maryland Reports (Md.)

Har. & Gil. Harris & Gill's Maryland Reports, 2 vols.

Har. & Gill Harris & Gill's Maryland Reports

Har. & G. Rep. Harris & Gill, Maryland Reports (Md.)

Har. & J. Harris & Johnson's Maryland Reports

Har. & J. (Md.) Harris & Johnson's Maryland Reports

Har. & John. Harris & Johnson's Maryland Appeal Reports (1800-26)

Har. & Johns. Md. Rep. Harris & Johnson, Maryland Reports (Md.)

Har. & McH. Harris & McHenry's Maryland Reports

Har. and M'Hen. Harris & McHenry, Maryland Reports (Md.)

Har. & Nav. Harbors & Navigation

Har. & Ruth. Harrison & Rutherford's English Common Pleas Reports (1865-66)

Har. & W. Harrison & Wollaston's King's Bench Reports (1835-36) (47 ER)

Har. & Woll. Harrison & Wollaston's English King's Bench Reports, 2 vols. (1835-36)

Har. App. Hare's Chancery Reports, Appendix to vol. X (Eng.)

Harb. & Nav. C. Harbors and Navigation Code

Harc. Harcarse's Decisions, Scotch Court of Session (1681-91)

Har. Ch. Harrington's Chancery Reports (Mich.)

Har. Ch. Pr. Harrison's Chancery Practice

Har. Chy. Harrington's Chancery Reports (Mich.)

Har. Col. Jur. Hargrave's Collectanea Juridica

Har. Com. Harrison's Compilation of the Laws of New Jersey

Har. Com. Proc. Harrison's Common Law Procedure Act, Canada

Har. Ct. Mar. Harwood's Practice of United States Naval Courts-Martial

Hard.
- Hardesty Team Reports (Del.)
- Hardin's Reports (3 Kentucky) (1805-08)
- Hardres' English Exchequer Reports (145 ER)
- Kelyngs (W.), Chancery Reports (Eng.)

Hard. Eccl. L. Harding on Ecclesiastical Law

Har. Del. Harrington's Reports (1-5 Delaware)

Hard. El. Pet. Hardcastle on Election Petitions

Hardes. Hardesty's Reports (Delaware Term)

Har. Dig.
- Harrison's English Common Law Digest
- Harris' Georgia Digest

Hardin Hardin's Kentucky Reports

Hardin (Ky.) Hardin's Kentucky Reports

Hardr. Hardres' Exchequer Reports (1655-69) (145 ER)

Hardr. (Eng.) Hardres' English Exchequer Reports (145 ER)

Hardres Hardres' English Exchequer Reports (145 ER)

Hard. St. L. Hardcastle on Statutory Law

Hard. Tr. M. Hardingham on Trade Marks

Hardw.
- Cases tempore Hardwicke, by Lee
- Cases tempore Hardwicke, by Ridgeway

Hardw. Cas. Temp. Cases tempore Hardwicke, by Lee and Hardwicke

Hardw. (Eng.)
- Cases tempore Hardwicke, by Lee
- Cases tempore Hardwicke, by Ridgeway

Hardw. N.B. Hardwicke, Note Books

Hare Hare's English Vice-Chancellor's Reports (1841-53) (66-68 ER)

Hare & W. Hare & Wallace's American Leading Cases

Hare & Wallace Amer. Leading Cases American Leading Cases (U.S.)

Hare & Wallace Lead. Cases (Am.) American Leading Cases, edited by Hare & Wallace

Hare & Wal. L.C. American Leading Cases, edited by Hare & Wallace

Hare App. Hare's Reports (Appendix to vol. X)

Hare, Const. Law Hare's American Constitutional Law

Hare Disc. (or Ev.) Hare on Discovery of Evidence

Hare Elec. Hare on Elections

Hare (Eng.) Hare's English Vice-Chancellors' Reports (1841-53) (66-68 ER)

Harg. Hargrave's State Trials (Eng.) Hargrove's Reports (68-75 North Carolina)

Harg. & B. Co. Litt. Hargrave & Butler's Edition of Coke upon Littleton

Harg. Co. Litt. Hargrave's Notes to Coke on Littleton

Harg. Coll. Jur. Hargrave, Collectanea Juridica (1791-92)

Harg. Exer. Hargrave's Jurisconsult Exercitations

Harg. Jur. Arg. Hargrave's Juridical Arguments and Collections

Harg. Law Tracts Hargrave's Law Tracts

Harg. L.T. Hargrave's Collection of Law Tracts

Hargrave & Butlers Notes on Co. Litt. Hargrave and Butler's Notes on Coke on Littleton

Hargr. Co. Litt. Hargrave's Notes to Coke on Littleton

Hargrove Hargrove's Reports (68-75 North Carolina)

Harg. State Tr. Hargrave's State Trials

Harg. St. Tr. Hargrave's State Trials (1407-1776)

Harg. Th. Hargrave on the Thellusson Act

Hari Rao Indian Income Tax Decisions

Har. Just. Harris' Justinian

Harland Manchester Court Leet Records

Harl. C.B.M. Harleian Collection, British Museum

Har. L.R. Harvard Law Review

Harm.
- Harmon's Reports (13-15 California)
- Harmon's Upper Canada Common Pleas Reports (1850-81)

Harman   Harman's Upper Canada Common Pleas Reports (1850-82)

Harm. Pens.   Harmon on the United States Pension Laws

Harp.
- Harper's Equity Reports (South Carolina)
- Harper's South Carolina Law Reports (1823-30)

Harp. Con. Cas.   Harper's Conspiracy Cases (Maryland)

Har. Pen. Man.   Harmon's Manual of United States Pension Laws

Harp. Eq.   Harper's Equity Reports (South Carolina)

Harp. Eq. (S.C.)   Harper's Reports (1824 South Carolina Equity)

Harper
- Harper's Conspiracy Cases (Md.)
- Harper's South Carolina Equity Reports (5 SCEq.) 1824
- Harper's South Carolina Law Reports (16 SCL) (1823-30)

Harper & James, Torts   Harper & James on Torts

Harp. L.   Harper's Reports (1823-30 South Carolina Law)

Harp. L. (S.C.)   Harper's Reports (1823-30 South Carolina Law)

Harr.
- Harrington's Chancery Rep. (Mich. 1836-42)
- Harrington's Reports (1-5 Delaware)

- Harrison's Reports (15-17, 23-29 Indiana)
- Harrison's Reports (16-19 N.J. Law Reports)
- Harris' Reports (13-24 Pa. State)

Harr. Adv.   Harris.Hints on Advocacy. 18 ed. 1943

Harr. & Cl. Conv.   Harris & Clarkson on Conveyancing, & c.

Harr. & G.   Harris & Gill's Maryland Reports

Harr. & H.   Harrison & Hodgin's Upper Canada Municipal Reports (1845-51)

Harr. & Hodg.   Harrison & Hodgin's Upper Canada Municipal Reports (1845-51)

Harr. & J.   Harris & Johnson's Maryland Reports

Harr. & J. (Md.)   Harris & Johnson's Maryland Reports

Harr. & M.   Harris & McHenry (Md.)

Harr. & McH.   Harris & McHenry's Maryland Reports

Harr. & McHen.   Harris & McHenry, Maryland Reports (Md.)

Harr. & McH. (Md.)   Harris & McHenry's Maryland Reports

Harr. & M'H.   Harris & McHenry's Maryland Reports

Harr. & R.   Harrison & Rutherford's English Common Pleas Reports

Harr. & Ruth.   Harrison & Rutherford's English Common Pleas Reports (1865-66)

Harr. & Sim. Harris & Simrall's Reports (49-52 Mississippi)

Harr. & W. Harrison & Wollaston's English King's Bench Reports

Harr. & W. (Eng.) Harrison & Wollaston's English King's Bench Reports

Harr. & Woll. Harrison & Wollaston's English King's Bench Reports (1835-36)

Harr Ch.
- Harrison's Chancery (Eng.)
- Harrington's Chancery Reports (Mich.)

Harr. Ch. (Mich.) Harrington's Chancery Reports (Mich.)

Harr. Ch. R. Harrington's Chancery Reports (Mich.)

Harr. Con. La. R. Harrison's Condensed Louisiana Reports

Harr. Cr. L. Harris, Principles of the Criminal Law. 22ed. 1973

Harr. (Del.) Harrington Reports, Delaware

Harr. Dig. Harrison's Digest (Eng.)

Harr. Ent. Harris' Modern Entries

Harr. (Ga.) Harris' Georgia Digest

Harr. Hints Harris' Hints on Advocacy

Harring.
- Harrington's Michigan Chancery
- Harrington's Reports (1-5 Delaware)

Harring. Ch. (Mich.) Harrington's Chancery Reports (Mich.)

Harrington
- Harrington's Delaware Supreme Court Reports (1832-55)
- Harrington's Michigan Chancery Reports (1836-42)

Harris Harris' Reports

Harris & G. Harris & Gill's Reports (Maryland)

Harris & Gill's Md. R. Harris & Gill, Maryland Reports (Md.)

Harris & J. Harris & Johnson, Maryland Reports (Md.)

Harris & S. Harris & Simrall's Reports (49-52 Mississippi)

Harris & Sim. Harris & Simrall's Reports (49-52 Mississippi)

Harris & Simrall Harris & Simrall's Reports (49-52 Mississippi)

Harris Dig. Harris' Digest (Georgia)

Harrison
- Harrison's Reports (15-17, 23-29 Indiana)
- Harrison's Reports (16-19 N.J. Law Reports)

Harrison, Ch. Harrison's Chancery Practice

Harrison Dig. Harrison's Digest of English Common Law Reports

Harr. Just. Harris' Translation of the Institutes of Justinian

Harr. (Mich.) Harrington's Michigan Chancery Reports

Harr. Min. Harris on Titles to Mines

Harr. Mun. Law Harrison's Municipal Law of Ontario

Harr. N.J. Harrison's Reports (1619 N.J. Law Reports)

Harr. Prin. Harris' Principiae Primae Legum

Harr. Pr. K.B. Harrison's Practice of the Courts of K.B. and C.P.

Harr. Prob. Harrison on Probate and Divorce

Harr. Proc. Harrison's Common Law Procedure Act, Canada

Harr. Rom. Law Harris' Elements of Roman Law

Hars. Pr. Harston's California Practice and Pleading

Har. St. Tr. Hargrave's State Trials

Hart.
- Hartley's Digest of Texas Laws
- Hartley's Reports (4-10 Texas)

Hart. & H. Hartley & Hartley, Reports (11-21 Texas)

Hart. Bank. Hart's Bankrupt Law and Practice

Hart. Dig. Hartley's Digest of Laws (Texas)

Hartley Hartley's Reports (4-10 Texas)

Hartley & Hartley Hartley & Hartley, Reports (11-21 Texas)

Hartley & Hartley Rep. Hartley & Hartley Reports (11-21 Texas)

Hart Min. Laws Hart's United States Mining Statutes

Harv. Harvard

Harvard Civil Rights L. Rev. Harvard Civil Rights-Civil Liberties Law Review

Harvard Int.L.J. Harvard International Law Journal

Harvard J. on Legis. Harvard Journal on Legislation

Harvard L. Rev. Harvard Law Review

Harv. Blackletter J. Harvard Blackletter Journal

Harv. Bus. Rev. Harvard Business Review

Harv. Bus. World Harvard Business World

Harv. Civ. Rights-Civ. Lib. L. Rev. Harvard Civil Rights-Civil Liberties Law Review

Harv. C.R.-C.L.L. Harvard Civil Rights-Civil Liberties Law Review

Harv. C.R.-C.L. L. Rev. Harvard Civil Rights-Civil Liberties Law Review

Harv. Ed. Rev. Harvard Ed'l Review

Harv Envir L Rev Harvard Environmental Law Review

Harv. Env. L. Rev. Harvard Environmental Law Review

Harv. Envt'l L. Rev. Harvard Environmental Law Review

Harv. Hum. Rts. J. Harvard Human Rights Journal

Harv. Int. L.J. Harvard International Law Journal

Harv. Int'l L. Club Bull. Harvard International Law Club Bulletin

Harv. Int'l. L. Club J. Harvard International Law Club Journal

Harv. Int'l. L.J. Harvard International Law Journal

Harv. J.L. & Pub. Pol'y Harvard Journal of Law and Public Policy

Harv. J.L. & Tech. Harvard Journal of Law & Technology

Harv. J. Legis. Harvard Journal on Legislation

Harv. J. on Legis. Harvard Journal on Legislation

Harv. L. Lib. Inf. Bull. Harvard Law Library Information Bulletin

Harv LR Harvard Law Review

Harv. L. Rev. Harvard Law Review

Harv. L.S. Bull. Harvard Law School Bulletin

Harv. L.S. Rec. Harvard Law School Record

Harv. Women L.J. Harvard Women's Law Journal

Harv. Women's L.J. Harvard Women's Law Journal

Harv. Women L.R. Harvard Women Law Review

Harv. W. Tax Ser. Harvard World Tax Series

HAS Hospital Advisory Service

Hasb. Hasbrouck's Reports (Idaho)

H.A.S.C. House Armed Services Committee

Hask. Haskell's Reports for U.S. Courts in Maine (Fox's Decisions)

Hasl. Med. Jur. Haslam's Medical Jurisprudence

Hast. Hastings' Reports (69, 70 Maine)

Hast. Const. L.Q. Hastings Constitutional Law Quarterly

Hastings Comm. & Ent. L.J. Hastings Communications & Entertainment Law Journal

Hastings Const. L.Q. Hastings Constitutional Law Quarterly

Hastings Intl. & Comp. L. Rev. Hastings International and Comparative Law Review

Hastings L.J. Hastings Law Journal

Hast. Int. & Comp. L. Rev. Hastings' International and Comparative Law Review

Hast. L.J. Hastings Law Journal

Hast. Tr. Trial of Warren Hastings

Hatcher's Kan. Dig. Hatcher's Kansas Digest

Hats. Hatsell's Parliamentary Precedents (1290-1818)

Hats. Pr. Hatsell's Parliamentary Precedents

Hats. Prec. Hatsell's Parliamentary Precedents (1290-1818)

Hav. Haviland's Prince Edward Island Chancery Reports, by Peters (1850-72) (Can.)

Hav. Ch. Rep. Haviland's Ch. Reports, Prince Edward Island (1850-72)

Havil. Haviland's Reports, Prince Edward Island

Hav. P.E.I. Haviland's Reports, Prince Edward Island

Haw.
- Hawaii
- Hawaii Reports
- Hawaii Supreme Court Reports
- Hawarde's Star Chamber Cases (1593-1609)
- Hawkins' Pleas of the Crown (Eng.)
- Hawkins Reports (19-24 La. Annual)
- Hawley's Reports (10-20 Nevada)

Hawaii Hawaii Reports

Hawaiian Rep. Hawaii Reports

Hawaiian Reports Hawaii Reports (Haw.)

Hawaii App. Hawaii Appeals Reports

Hawaii B.J. Hawaii Bar Journal

Hawaii B.N. Hawaii Bar News

Hawaii Const. Hawaii Constitution

Hawaii Dist. U.S. District Courts of Hawaii

Hawaii. Fed. Hawaiian Federal

Hawaii P.U.C. Dec. Hawaii Public Utilities Commission Decisions

Hawaii Rep. Hawaii Reports

Hawaii Rev. Stat. Hawaii Revised Statutes

Hawaii Rules & Reg. Hawaii Rules and Regulations

Hawaii Sess. Laws Session Laws of Hawaii

Hawarde Hawarde's Star Chamber Cases (1894) (Eng.)

Hawarde St. Ch. Hawarde, Star Chamber Cases

Haw. Ass. Hawes on Assignments

Haw. Cr. Rep. Hawley's American Criminal Reports

Hawes, Jur. Hawes on Jurisdiction of Courts

Haw. Fed. Hawaii Federal

Hawk.
- Hawkins' Louisiana Annual
- Hawkins' Pleas of the Crown (Eng.)

Hawk. Abr. Hawkins, Abridgment of Coke upon Littleton

Hawk. Coke Abr. Hawkins, Abridgment of Coke upon Littleton

Hawk. Co. Litt. Hawkins'Coke upon Littleton

Hawkins Hawkins' Reports (19-24 Louisiana Annual)

Hawk. P.C. Hawkins' Pleas of the Crown (Eng.)

Hawk. Pl. Cr. Hawkins'Pleas of the Crown (Eng.)

Hawks Hawks' North Carolina Reports (1820-26)

Hawks (N.C.) Hawks' Reports (81 North Carolina)

Hawk. Wills Hawkins' Construction of Wills

Hawl. Hawley's Reports (10-20 Nevada)

Hawl. Cr. R. Hawley's American Criminal Reports

Hawley
- Hawley's American Criminal Reports
- Hawley's Reports (10-20 Nevada)

Hawley's Crim. Rep. Hawley, American Criminal Reports (U.S.)

Hawn. Hawaii Reports (Haw.)

Haw. Rep. Hawaii Reports (Haw.)

Haw. Rev. Stat. Hawaii Revised Statutes

Hawaii Sess. Laws Session Laws of Hawaii

Haw. Sess. Laws Session Laws of Hawaii

Haw. W.C. Hawes' Will Case

Hay.
- Hayes' Irish Exchequer Reports, (1830-32)
- Hayes' Reports, Calcutta
- Hay's High Court Appeals Reports (1862-63) (Bengal, India)
- Hay's Poor Law Decisions (1711--1859) (Sc.)
- Hay's Scotch Decisions
- Haywood's North Carolina Reports
- Haywood's Tennessee Reports (Haywood's Reports are sometimes referred to as though numbered consecutively from North Carolina through Tennessee)

Hay Acc. Hay's Decisions on Accidents and Negligence (1860) (Sc.)

Hay & H. Hay & Hazelton (U.S.)

Hay. & H. Hayward & Hazelton Circuit Court Reports (D.C.)

Hay. & Haz. Hayward & Hazelton, Circuit Court, District of Columbia (1840-63)

Hay & J. Hayes & Jones' Reports (Irish Exchequer)

Hay. & Jo. Hayes & Jones' Exchequer Reports (1832-34) (Ir.)

Hay & M. Hay & Marriott's Admiralty Reports (usually cited, Marriott's Reports) (165 ER)

Hay & Mar. Hay & Marriott's Admiralty Decisions Reports (165 ER) (1776-79)

Hay & Marr. Hay & Marriott's Admiralty Reports (usually cited, Marriott's Reports) (165 ER)

Hay & M. (Eng.) Hay & Marriott's Admiralty Reports (usually cited, Marriott's Reports) (165 ER)

Hay (Calc.) Hay's Reports (Calcutta)

Hay Dec. Hay's Decisions on Accidents and Negligence (1860) (SC.)

Hay. Eq. Haynes, Outlines of Equity. 5ed. 1880

Hayes Hayes' Irish Exchequer Reports (1830-32)

Hayes & J. Hayes & Jones' Irish Exchequer Reports (1832-34)

Hayes & J.(Ir.) Hayes & Jones' Irish Exchequer Reports (1832-34)

Hayes & Jo. Hayes & Jones' Irish Exchequer Reports (1832-34)

Hayes & Jon. Hayes & Jones' Irish Exchequer Reports (1832-34)

Hayes & J. Wills Hayes & Jarman, Concise Forms of Wills. 18ed. 1952

Hayes Con. Conv. Hayes' Concise Conveyancer

Hayes, Conv. Hayes on Conveyancing

Hayes Cr. & P. Hayes on Crimes and Punishments

Hayes Exch. Hayes' Irish Exchequer Reports (1830-32)

Hayes Exch. (Ir.) Hayes' Irish Exchequer Reports

Hayes Heirs Hayes' Dispositions to Heirs in Tail, & c.

Hayes Intr. Hayes' Introduction to Conveyancing

Hayes Lim. Hayes on Limitations as to Heirs of the Body, & c.

Hayes R. Est.   Hayes' Real Estate

Hayes U.D. & T.   Hayes' Law of Uses, Devises, and Trust

Hay. Exch.   Hayes' Irish Exchequer Reports

Hay Exp.   Hay on Expatriation

Hayford   Gold Coast Native Institutions

Hayn. Ch. Pr.   Haynes' Chancery Practice. 1879

Hayn. Eq.   Haynes' Outlines of Equity. 5ed. 1880

Haynes, Eq.   Haynes' Outlines of Equity

Hayn. Lead. Cas.   Haynes' Students' Leading Cases

Hay P.L.   Hay's Poor Law Decisions (1711-1859) (Sc.)

Hayw.
- Haywood's North Carolina Reports (1789-1806)
- Haywood's Reports (4-6 Tennessee)

Hayw. & H.
- Hayward & Hazelton's District of Columbia Reports (1840-63)
- Hayward & Hazelton's United States Circuit Court Reports

Hayw. & H.D.C.   Hayward & Hazelton Circuit Court Reports (D.C.)

Hayw. L.R.   Hayward's Law Register, Boston

Hayw. Man.   Haywood's Manual of the Statute Laws of North Carolina

Hayw. N.C.   Haywood's Reports (23 North Carolina)

Haywood Tenn. Rep.   Haywood's Reports (Tenn.)

Hayw. Tenn.   Haywood's Reports (4-6 Tennessee)

Haz. & R. M. War.   Hazlitt & Roche on Maritime Warfare

Haz. Pa. Reg.   Hazard's Pennsylvania Register (16)

Haz. Pa. Reg. (Pa.)   Hazard's Pennsylvania Register (16)

Haz. Reg.   Hazard's Register (Pennsylvania)

Haz. U.S. Reg.   Hazard's United States Register

H.B.
- H. Blackstone's Common Pleas Reports (1788-96) (126 ER)
- House Bill
- House Bill (state Legislatures)

H. Bl.   H. Blackstone's Common Pleas Reports (1788-96)

H. Black.   H. Blackstone's Common Pleas Reports (1788-96) (126 ER)

H. Bl. (Eng.)   Henry Blackstone's Common Pleas (Eng.) (126 ER)

H.B.M.   His (or Her) Britannic Majesty

H.B.R.
- Hansell's Bankruptcy Reports (1915-17)
- Harvard Business Review

H.C.
- Habeas corpus
- Hague Convention
- High Commission(er)
- High Court-High Court (Eire I)
- Highway Code
- House of Commons

- Housing Centre
- Reports of the High Court of Griqualand West, South Africa

H.C. A. High Court of Australia

HCC Haralambie, Handling Child Custody Cases

H.C.F. A.R. Health Care Financing Adminitration Rulings

H.C.F.R. Health Care Financing Review

H.C.F. Rev. Health Care Financing Review

H.C.G. Griqualand High Court Reports (S. Africa)

H.C.J. High Court of Justiciary (Sc.)

H.C. Jour. House of Commons Journals (United Kingdom)

HCLIP Harvard Computer-Aided Legal Instruction Project

H.C.L.M. Health Care Labor Manual

H.C. of A. High Court of Australia

H. Con. Res. House of Representatives Concurrent Resolution

H.C.R. High Court Reports (India)

H.Cr. Houston's Criminal Reports (Del.)

H.C.Res. House of Representatives Concurrent Resolution

H.C.R.N.W.F. High Court Reports, North West Frontier

H.C.R.N.W.P. High Court Reports, Northwest Provinces (India)

H.C.S. Home Civil Service

H.C.T. High Commission Territories

HCTAA Hastings Center for Trial and Appellate Advocacy

H.C.T.R. High Commission Territories Reports (Basutoland, Bechuanaland and Swaziland)

H.C. Wkly. Inf. Bull. House of Commons Weekly Information Bulletin

hdbk. handbook

H. Dist. Ct.
- U.S. District Court, District of Hawaii (Haw.)
- U.S. District Court, District of Hawaii Reports (Haw.)

H.Doc. House of Representatives Document

Hdqrs. Headquarters

HEA Higher Education Act

Head Head's Tennessee Supreme Court Reports (1858-59)

Head (Tenn.) Head's Reports (38-40 Tennessee)

Heal. J.S. Comp. Healy on Joint Stock Companies

Heal. Pews Heale's Law of Church Pews

Health & S.C. Health and Safety Code

Health L. Can. Health Law in Canada

Heard Civ. Pl. Heard's Civil Pleading

Heard Cr. Pl. Heard's Criminal Pleading

Heard Cur. Rep. Heard's Curiosities of the Law Reporters

Heard Eq. Pl. Heard's Equity Pleading

Heard Lib. & Sl. Heard on Libel and Slander

Heard's Shortt, Extr. Rem. Heard's Edition of Shortt on Extraordinary Legal Remedies

Heard St. Pl. Heard's Edition of Stephen on Pleading

Hear. Exam. Hearing Examiner

Hearnshaw Southampton Court Leet Records

Heath Heath's Reports (36-40 Maine)

Heath, Max. Heath's Maxims

H.E.C. Hodgin's Election Cases (Ontario)

Heck. Cas. Hecker's Cases on Warranty

Hedges Hedges' Reports (2-6 Montana)

Hein. Heineccius, Elementa Juris Naturae et Gentium

Hein William S. Hein & Co., Inc.

Heinecc. Ant. Rom. Heineccius (J.G.) Antiquitatum Romanarum (Roman Antiquities)

Heinecc. de. Camb. Heineccius (J.G. Elementa Juris Cambialis)

Heinecc. Elem. Heineccius (J.G.) Elementa Juris Civilis (Elements of the Civil Law)

Heinec.Elem. Jur.Camb. Heineccii Elementa Juris Cambialis

Heinec.Elem. Jur.Civ. Heineccii Elementa Juris Civilis

Heisk. Heiskell's Tennessee Supreme Court Reports (1870-74)

Heisk. (Tenn.) Heiskell's Reports (48-59 Tennessee)

H.E.L. History of English Law edited by W. Holdsworth

Helm Helm's Reports (2-9 Nevada)

Hem. Hempstead

Hem. & M. Hemming & Miller's English Vice-Chancellors' Reports (71 ER)

Hem. & M. (Eng.) Hemming & Miller's English Vice-Chancellors' Reports (71 ER)

Hem. & Mill. Hemming & Miller's English Vice-Chancellors' Reports

Hem. Bl. H. Blackstone's Common Pleas, Reports, English

Heming. Hemingway's Reports (53-65 Mississippi)

Heming. (Miss.) Hemingway's Mississippi Reports

Hemmant Hemmant's Select Cases in Exchequer Chamber (Selden Society Publ. v. 51) (1377-1460)

Hemp.
- Hempstead's Reports (Ark.)
- Hempstead's United States Circuit Court Reports

Hempst.
- Hempstead's Reports (Ark.)
- Hempstead's United States Circuit Court Reports

Hen. King Henry, as 8 Hen. VI

Hen. Am. Pl. Hening's American Pleader

Hen. & M. Hening & Munford's Virginia Supreme Court Reports (1806-10)

Hen. & Mun. Hening & Munford's Reports (11-14 Virginia)

Hen. Bl. Henry Blackstone's English Common Pleas Reports

Hen. B.L. Henley's Bankrupt Law

Hen. For. L. Henry on Foreign Law

Hen. Forms Hennell's Forms

Heng. Hengham

Hen. J.P. Hening's Virginia Justice of the Peace

Hen. La. Dig. Hennen, Louisiana Digest

Hen. Man. Cas. Henry's Manumission Cases

Hen. Max. Hening's Maxims

Hennepin Law Hennepin Lawyer

Henning CLE Rep. Henning CLE Reporter

Henn. Law. Hennepin Lawyer (Minn.)

Henry Judg. Henry, Judgment in Ordwin v. Forbes

Hen. St. Hening's Statutes (Va.)

Hent Forms Hent's Forms and Use of Blanks in California

Hepb.
- Hepburn (Colo.)
- Hepburn's Reports (3, 4 California)
- Hepburn's Reports (13 Pennsylvania)

Her. Herne's Law of Charitable Uses (2 editions, 1660, 1663)

Herb. Ant. Herbert's Antiquities of the Inns of Court, & c.

Her. Char. U. Herne on Charitable Uses

Her. Chat. Herman on Chattel Mortgages

Her. Est. Herman's Law of Estoppel

Her. Ex. Herman's Law of Executors

Her. Jur. Heron, Jurisprudence. 1860

Herm. Hermand Consistorial Decisions (1684-1777) (Sc.)

Hermand Hermand's Consistorial Decisions (Sc.)

Herm. Chat. Mortg. Herman on Chattel Mortgages

Herm. Estop. Herman's Laws of Estoppel

Herm. Ex'ns. Herman's Law of Executions

Her. Mort. Herman on Mortgages of Real Estate

Her. Prec. Herne's Precedents

Hert. M. & Serv. Hertslet on Master and Servant

Hert. Map Eur. Hertslet's Map of Europe

Hert. Treat. Hertslet's Treaties

Hertzog Hertzog's Reports of Transvaal High Court

Het. Hetley's English Common Pleas Reports (124 ER)

Het. C.P. Hetley's Common Pleas Reports (Eng.)

Het. (Eng.) Hetley's English Common Pleas Reports (124 ER)

Hetl. Hetley's Common Pleas Reports (1627-1631) (124 ER)

HEW Department of Health, Education and Welfare

HEWPR Department of Health, Education and Welfare Procurement Regulations

Heyl Imp. D. Heyl's United States Import Duties

Heyw. Ca. Heywood's Table of Cases (Georgia)

Heyw. Co. Ct. Heywood, County Courts Practice. 4ed. 1876

Heyw. Elec. Heywood on Elections

Heywood & Massey Heywood & Massey, Court of Protection Practice. 9ed. 1971

HGB Handelsgesetzbuch (German Commercial Code)

H.H. Hayward and Hazelton's Reports

H. (Ha.) Hare tempore Wigram, etc. (1841-53)

HHb Binder, Hearsay Handbook

HHb(3) Binder, Hearsay Handbook, Third Edition

H.H.C.L. Hale, History of the Common Law. 6ed. 1820

HHFA Housing & Home Finance Agency (U.S.)

H. (Hil.) Hilary Term

H.H.L. Court of Session Cases. House of Lords (Sc.)

H.H.P.C. Hale's History of Pleas of the Crown

HHS Dep't. of Health and Human Services

Hi.
- Hawaii
- Hawaii Reports
- Hindi

H.I.A. Housing Improvement Association

Hibb.
- Hibbard's Reports (vol. 67 New Hampshire)
- Hibbard's Reports, vol. 20 Opinions Attorneys-General

Hic Here (in the same paragraph or title)

Hick. Ct. Mar. Hickman on Naval Courts-Martial

Hicks, Ethics Hicks' Organization and Ethics of Bench and Bar

Hicks, Leg. Research Hicks on Materials and Methods of Legal Research

Hicks, Men & Books Hicks on Men and Books Famous in the Law

HICOG High Commissioner for Germany (U.S.)

Higgins Higgin's Tennessee Civil Appeals Reports

High. Highway

High. Bail Highmore on Bail

High Court The High Court of Justice, England and Wales

High Ct.
- High Court
- High Court Reports (Northwest Provinces of India)

High Ex. Rem. High on Extraordinary Legal Remedies

High, Extr. Leg. Rem. High on Extraordinary Legal Remedies

High Inj. High on Injunctions

High. Lun. Highmore on Lunacy

High. Mort. Highmore on Mortmain

High Rec. High on the Law of Receivers

Hight Hight's Reports (vols. 57-58 Iowa)

High Tech. L.J. High Technology Law Journal

Hig. Pat. Dig. Higgins' Digest of Patent Cases (1890)

Hig. Waterc. Higgins, Pollution and Obstruction of Watercourses. 1877

H.I.H. His (or Her) Imperial Highness

Hil. Hilary Term (Eng.)

Hil. Abr. Hilliard's American Law

Hild. Ins. Hildyard on Insurance

Hild. Mar. Ins. Hildyard's Marine Insurance

Hil. Elem. Law Hilliard's Elements of Law

Hill
- Hill's New York Supreme Court Reports (1841-44)
- Hill's South Carolina Law Reports (1833-37)

Hill. Abr. Hillard, Abridgment of Real Property Law

Hill. Am. Jur. Hilliard, American Jurisprudence

Hill. Am. Law Hilliard's American Law

Hill & D. Lalor's Supplement to Hill & Denio's Reports, New York (1842-44)

Hill & Den. Lalor's Supplement to Hill & Denio's Reports, New York (1842-44)

Hill & Den. Supp. Lalor's Supplement to Hill & Denio's Reports, New York (1842-44)

Hill & D. Supp. Hill & Denio, Lalor's Supplement (N.Y.)

Hill & Redman Hill & Redman's Law of Landlord and Tenant. 16ed. 1976

Hill. Bank. (or B. & I.) Hilliard on Bankruptcy and Insolvency

Hill Ch. Hill's Equity South Carolina Reports (1833-37)

Hill Ch. Pr. Hill's Chancery Practice

Hill. Cont. Hilliard on Contracts

Hill. Elem. Law Hilliard's Elements of Law

Hill Eq. Hill's Equity South Carolina Reports (1833-37)

Hill Eq. (S.C.) Hill's Equity South Carolina Reports (1833-37)

Hill Fixt. Hill's Law of Fixtures

Hilliard, R.P. Hilliard on Real Property

Hill Ill. Chy. Hill's Illinois Chancery Practice

Hill Ill. Com. Law Hill's Illinois Common Law Jurisdiction and Practice

Hill. Inj. Hilliard on the Law of Injunctions

Hill, Law Hill's Law (S.C.)

Hill Lib. & Law Hill's Liberty and Law

Hill. Mor. Hilliard on the Law of Mortgages

Hill. Mortg. Hilliard's Law of Mortgages

Hill. New Trials Hilliard on New Trials

Hill. N.Tr. Hilliard on the Law of New Trials

Hill N.Y. Hill's New York Reports

Hill N.Y.R. Hill's Reports (N.Y.)

Hill Prob. Hill's Illinois Probate Jurisdiction and Practice

Hill. Real Prop. Hilliard on Real Property

Hill Rem. Hilliard on Remedies for Torts

Hill. Sales Hilliard on Sales of Personal Property

Hill's Ann. Codes & Laws Hill's Annotated Codes and General Laws (Or.)

Hill's Ann. St. & Codes Hill's Annotated General Statutes and Codes (Wash.)

Hill S.C. Hill's South Carolina Reports (Law or Equity)

Hill's Code
- Hill's Annotated Codes and General Laws (Oregon)
- Hill's Annotated General Statutes and Codes (Washington)

Hill's Reports Hill's Reports (N.Y.)

Hill. Tax. Hilliard on the Law of Taxation

Hill. Torts Hilliard on the Law of Torts

Hill Tr. Hill on Trustees

Hill. Vend. Hilliard on the Law of Vendors

Hillyer Hillyer's Reports (20-22 California)

Hil. T. Hilary Term (Eng.)

Hilt. Hilton's New York Common Pleas Reports

Hil. Term 4, Will.IV Hilary Term 4, William IV

Hilt. (NY) Hilton's New York Common Pleas Reports

Hil. Torts Hilliard on the Law of Torts

Hil. Vac. Hilary Vacation

Him. Pra. All India Reporter, Himachal Pradesh (1949)

Hincmar. Epist. Hincmari Epistolae

Hinde Ch. Pr. Hinde, Modern Practice of the High Court of Chancery

Hind. L.J. Hindu Law Journal

Hind. L.Q. Hindu Law Quarterly

Hind. Pat. Hindmarch on Patents

Hind Pr. Hind's Practice

Hine & N. Ass. Hine & Nicholas on Assignment of Life Policies

Hine & N. Dig. Hine & Nicholas Insurance Digest

Hines Hines' Reports (83-96 Kentucky)

H.I. Rep. Hawaiian Islands Reports

Hirsh Juries Hirsh on Juries

Hist.
- Historical
- History

Hitch, Pr. & Proc. Hitch's Practice & Procedure in the Probate Court of Massachusetts

Hitotsubashi J.L. & Pol. Hitotsubashi Journal of Law and Politics, Tokyo, Japan

Hitt. Cod. Hittell's California Codes

Hittell's Laws Hittell's General Laws (Cal.)

HIV Human Immunodeficiency Virus

H.J.Res. U.S. House of Representatives Joint Resolution

H.K. Hong Kong

H.K. Law Reports Hong Kong Law Reports

H.K. L.J. Hong Kong Law Journal

H.K. L.R. Hong Kong Law Reports

H.L.
- House of Lords
- House of Lords Clark's House of Lords Cases (Eng.)
- Law Reports, House of Lords, English & Irish Appeals (1866-75)

H.L. & T. Hunter on Landlord & Tenant

HLBB Home Loan Bank Board (U.S.)

H.L.C. Clark's House of Lords Cases (Eng.)

H.L. Cas. House of Lords' Cases (Clark) (1847-66)

H.L. Cas. (Eng.) House of Lords Cases (9-11 ER)

H.L.F. Hall's Legal Forms

H.L.G. Housing and Local Government

H.L.J.
- Hastings Law Journal
- Hindu Law Journal

H.L. Jour. House of Lords Journals (Eng.)

H.L.N.R. Health Lawyers News Report

H.L.R. Harvard Law Review

H.L. Rep. English House of Lords Reports

H.L.R.O. House of Lords Record Office

H.L.R.S. Homosexual Law Reform Society

H.L.S. Harvard Law School

H.L.Sc. App.Cas. English Law Reports, House of Lords, Scotch and Divorce Appeal Cases (1866-75)

H.L. Wkly. Inf. Bull. House of Lords Weekly Information Bulletin

H.M. His Majesty/Her Majesty

H.M.C. Royal Commission on Historical Manuscripts

H.M.G. His or Her Majesty's Government

H.M.S.O. Her Majesty's Stationery Office

H.O. Home Office

Hob.
- Hobart's Common Pleas & Chancery (Eng.)
- Hobart's King's Bench Reports (1603-25) (Eng.)

Hobart Hobart's English King's Bench Reports (80 ER)

Hobart (Eng.) Hobart's English King's Bench Reports (80 ER)

Hob. R.
- Hobart's Common Pleas Reports (1613-25) (80 ER)
- Hobart's King's Bench Reports (1603-25) (80 ER)

Hod. Hodges' English Common Pleas Reports (1835-37)

Hodg.
- Hodges' English Common Pleas Reports (1835-37)
- Hodgins' Election Cases, Ontario (1871-79)

Hodg. Can. Elec. Cas. Hodgin's Canada Election Cases

Hodg. El. Hodgin's Election, Upper Canada

Hodg. El. Cas. Hodgins' Election Cases (Ontario)

Hodg. El. Cas. (Ont.) Hodgins' Election Cases (Ontario)

Hodge, Presb. Law Hodge on Presbyterian Law

Hodges Hodges' English Common Pleas Reports (1835-37)

Hodges (Eng.) Hodges' English Common Pleas Reports (1835-37)

Hodg. Ont. Elect. Hodgins' Election Cases (Ontario)

Hodg. Ry. Hodges' Law of Railways

H. of C. House of Commons

Hoff.
- Hoffman's Land Cases. United States District Court
- Hoffman's New York Chancery Reports

Hoff. Ch. Hoffman's New York Chancery Reports (1838-40)

Hoff. Ch. Pr. Hoffman's New York Chancery Reports

Hoff. C.R. Hoffman's New York Chancery Reports (N.Y.)

Hoff. Dec. Hoffman's Decisions

Hoff. Ecc. mL. Hoffman's Ecclesiastical Law

Hoff. Land Hoffman's Land Cases, United States District Court

Hoff. Land Cas. Hoffman's U.S. District Court Reports

Hoff. L.C. Hoffman's Land Cases, United States District Court

Hoff. L. Cas. Hoffman's Land Cases, United States District Court

Hoff. Lead. Cas. Hoffman's Leading Cases

Hoff. Leg. St. Hoffman's Course of Legal Study

Hoffm.
- Hoffman's Chancery (N.Y.)
- Hoffman's Land Cases (U.S.)

Hoffman Ch. R. Hoffman's New York Chancery Reports (N.Y.)

Hoffman's Ch. R. Hoffman's New York Chancery Reports (N.Y.)

Hoff. Mast. Hoffman's Master in Chancery

Hoff. Mast. Ch. Hoffman's Master in Chancery

Hoffm. Ch.
- Hoffman's Chancery (N.Y.)
- Hoffman's Land Cases (U.S.)

Hoffm. Ch. (N.Y.) Hoffman's Chancery Reports (New York)

Hoffm. Dec. (F.) Hoffman's Decisions, U.S. District Court

Hoffm. Land Cas. (F.) Hoffman's Land Cases, U.S. District Court

Hoffm. Ops. (F.) Hoffman's Opinions, U.S. District Court

Hoffm. Rep. Land Cases Hoffman's U.S. District Court Reports

Hoff. N.Y. Hoffman's New York Chancery Reports

Hoff. Op. Hoffman's Opinions

Hoff. Out. Hoffman's Legal Outlines

Hoff. Pr. Rem. Hoffman's Provisional Remainders

Hoff. Pub. P. Hoffman's Public Papers, New York

Hoff. Ref. Hoffman on Referees

Hofstra Prop. L.J. Hofstra Property Law Journal

H. of K. House of Keys

H. of L. House of Lords

H. of R. House of Representatives

Hofstra Lab. L.F. Hofstra Labor Law Forum

Hofstra Lab. L.J. Hofstra Labor Law Journal

Hofstra L. Rev. Hofstra Law Review

Hofstra Prop. L.J. Hofstra Property Law Journal

Hog.
- Hogan's Irish Rolls Court Reports (1816-34)
- Hog of Harcarse, Scotch Session Cases

Hogan
- Hogan's Irish Rolls Court Reports (2 vols.)
- Hog of Harcarse, Scotch Session Cases

Hogan (Ir.) Hogan's Irish Rolls Court Reports (2 vols.)

Hog. St. Tr. Hogan's State Trials (Pennsylvania)

Hogue Hogue's Reports (1-4 Florida)

Hokp. Adm. Hopkinson's Pennsylvania Admiralty Judgments

HOLC Home Owners' Loan Corporation (U.S.)

Ho. L. Cas. Clark's House of Lords Cases (1847-66) (Eng.)

Holc. Debt. & Cr. Holcombe's Law of Debtor and Creditor

Holc. Eq. Jur. Holcombe, Equity Jurisdiction

Holc. L. Cas. Holcombe's Leading Cases of Commercial Law

Holdsw. Hist. E.L. Holdsworth History of English Law

Holdsworth Sir W.S. Holdsworth, History of English Law, 17 vols. (1922-66)

Holl.
- Holland
- Hollinshead's Reports (1 Minn.)

Holl. Comp. Deeds Holland on Composition Deeds

Holl. El. Jur. Holland's Elements of Jurisprudence

Hollinshead Hollinshead's Reports (vol. 1 Minnesota)

Holl. Jur. Holland's Elements of Jurisprudence

Holl. Just. Holland, Institutes of Justinian

Holm.
- Holmes' Reports (vols. 15-17 Oregon)
- Holmes' United States Circuit Court Reports

Holm. Com. Law   Holmes on the Common Law

Holmes
- Holmes (Ore.)
- Holmes Circuit Court Reports (U.S.)

Holm. Statesman   Holmes' Statesman

Ho. Lords C.   Clark's House of Lords Cases (1847-66) (9-11 ER)

Ho. Lords Cas.   Clark's House of Lords Cases (1847-66) (Eng.)

Holt
- Holt's English Equity Reports (1845)
- Holt's English King's Bench
- Holt's English Nisi Prius Reports

Holt Adm.   Holt's English Admiralty Cases (Rule of the Road) (1863-67)

Holt Adm. Ca.   Holt's Admiralty Cases (1863-67)

Holt Adm. Cas.   Holt's English Admiralty Cases (Rule of the Road) (1863-67)

Holt Eq.
- Holt's English Equity Reports (1845)
- Holt's Equity Vice-Chancery (Eng.)

Holthouse (or Holthouse, Law Dict.)   Holthouse's Law Dictionary

Holt K.B.   Holt's English King' Bench Reports (1688-1710)

Holt. L. Dic.   Holthouse's Law Dictionary

Holt Lib.   Holt on Libels

Holt Nav.   Holt on Navigation

Holt N.P.   Holt's English Nisi Prius Reports (1815-17)

Holt Reg.   Holt on Registration of Title

Holt R. of R.   Holt's Rule of the Road Cases

Holt Sh.   Holt on Shipping

Holt, Shipp.   Holt on Shipping

Holt's Judgments   in Ashby v. White and Re Patey et al. 1704-05

Home   Home's Manuscript Decisions, Scotch Court of Session

Home (Cl.)   Clerk Home, Decisions of Court of Session (1735-44) (Sc.)

Home (Clk.)   Home's Decisions Court of Session (1735-44) (Scot.)

Home Ct. of Sess.   Home's Manuscript Decisions, Scotch Court of Session

Home H. Dec.   Home's Manuscript Decisions, Scotch Court Session

Homi.   Homicide

Homstd.   Homestead

Hon.
- Honorary
- Honorable

Hond.   Honduras

Hong Kong L.J.   Hong Kong Law Journal

Hong Kong L.R.   Hong Kong Law Reports

Hong Kong U. L.Jo.   Hong Kong University, Law Journal

Hon. Magist.   Honorary Magistrate (Aus.)

Hood Ex.   Hood on Executors

Ho. of Dels.   House of Delegates

Ho. of Reps. House of Representatives

Hook. Hooker's Reports (25-62 Conn.)

Hooker Hooker's Reports (25-62 Connecticut)

Hoon. Hoonahan's Sind Reports (India)

Hoonahan Hoonahan's Sind Reports (India)

Hop. Hopkins

Hop. & C. Hopwood & Coltman's Registration Cases (1868-78) (Eng.)

Hop. & Ch. Hopwood & Philbrick's Registration Cases

Hop. & Colt. Hopwood & Coltman's Registration Cases (Eng.)

Hop. & Ph. Hopwood & Philbrick, English Registration Cases (1863-67)

Hop. & Phil. Hopwood & Philbrick's Registration Cases (1863-67)

Hope Hope (of Kerse) Manuscript Decisions, Scotch Court of Session

Hope Com. Law Hope's Compendium of the Commercial Law of the Pacific

Hope Dec. Hope Manuscript Decisions, Scotch Court of Sessions

Hope. Maj. Pr. Sir Thomas Hope's Major Practicks (Scotland)

Hope Min. Pr. Sir Thomas Hope's Minor Practicks (Scotland)

Hopk Hopkins' Chancery Reports (N.Y.)

Hopk. Adm. Hopkinson's Judgments in Admiralty (Pa. 1779-89)

Hopk. Adm. Dec. Admiralty Decisions of Hopkinson in Gilpin's Reports

Hopk. Av. Hopkins, Average. 4ed. 1884

Hopk. C.C. Hopkins Chancery Reports (N.Y.)

Hopk. Ch. Hopkins' New York Chancery Reports (1823-26)

Hopk. Chanc. Rep. Hopkins' Chancery Reports (N.Y.)

Hopk. Dec.
- Hopkins' Decisions, Pa.
- Hopkinson's Admiralty Decisions (Pa.)

Hopk. Judg. Hopkinson's Pennsylvania Admiralty Judgments (1779-89)

Hopk. Mar. Ins. Hopkins on Marine Insurance

Hopk. Rep. Hopkins' Chancery Reports (N.Y.)

Hopk. W. Hopkinson's (Francis Works)

Hopk. Wks. Hopkinson's Works (Pennsylvania)

Hopk. Works (Pa.) Hopkinson's Works (Pa.)

Hop. Maj. Pr. Hope (Sir T.), Major Practicks, (Sc.)

Hop. Min. Hope, Minor Practicks (Sc.)

Hop. Min. Pr. Hope (Sir T.), Major Practicks (Sc.)

Hopw. & C. Hopwood & Coltman's English Registration Appeal Cases

Hopw. & Colt. Hopwood & Coltman's English Registration Appeal Cases

Hopw. & P. Hopwood & Philbrick's English Registration Appeal Cases

Hopw. & Phil. Hopwood & Philbrick's English Registration Appeal Cases

Hor. & Th.Cas. Horrigan & Thompson's Cases on Self-Defense

Horn & H. Horn & Hurlstone's English Exchequer Reports (1838-39)

Horne Dip. Horne on Diplomacy

Horne Mir. Horne's Mirror of Justice

Horne, M.J. Horne's Mirror of Justice

Horner Horner's Reports (vols. 11-23 South Dakota)

Horner's Ann. St. Horner's Annotated Revised Statutes (Ind.)

Horner's Rev. St. Horner's Annotated Revised Statutes (Ind.)

Horr & B. Mun. Ord. Horr and Bemis' Treatise on Municipal Police Ordinances

Horr. & T. Cas. Self-Def. Horrigan and Thompson's Cases on Self-Defense

Horr. & Th. Horrigan and Thompson's Cases on Self-Defense

Horw. Y.B. Horwood's Year Books of Edward I

Hosea Hosea's Reports (Ohio)

Hosea's Rep. Cincinnati Superior Court Decisions (Ohio)

Hoskins Hoskins' Reports (2 North Dakota)

Hosp. Hospital

Hospit. Hospitals and asylums

Hotom. in Verb. Feud. Hotomannus de Verbis Feudalibus

Hou. Houston's Reports (Del.)

Hou. Ang. Sax. Law. Houard's Anglo-Saxon Laws, & c.

Houard, Ang. Sax. Laws Houard's Anglo-Saxon Laws

Houck Mech. Lien Houck on Mechanics' Lien Law

Houck Riv. Houck on the Law of Navigable Rivers

Hou. Dict. Houard's Dictionary of the Customs of Normandy

Hough Am. Cons. Hough's American Constitutions

Hough C.M. Hough's Military Law and Courts-Martial

Hough C.-M.Cas. Hough's Court-Martial Case Book (London, 1821)

Houghton Houghton's Reports (97 Alabama)

Hough V.-Adm. Reports of Cases in Vice-Admiralty of Province of New York, 1715-88 (1925 Reprint)

Hou. L.R. Houston Law Review

Hous.
- Housing
- Houston's Delaware Reports

Hous. & Dev. Rep. (BNA) Housing & Development Reporter (BNA)

House of L. House of Lords Cases

Housing & Devel. Rep. Housing and Development Reporter (BNA)

Housing L. Housing Laws and urban development

Hous. J. Int'l.L. Houston Journal of International Law

Hous. Law. Houston Lawyer

Hous. Life Ass. Houseman, Life Assurance. 9ed. 1977

Hous. L. Rev. Houston Law Review

Hous. Pr. Housman, Precedents in Conveyancing. 1861

Houst. Houston's Reports (6-14 Delaware)

Houst. Cr. Houston's Criminal Cases (Del.)

Houst. Cr. Cas. Houston's Delaware Criminal Cases (1856-79)

Houst. Crim. Cas. Delaware Criminal Cases (Del.)

Houst. Crim. Cases Delaware Criminal Cases (Del.)

Houst. Crim. (Del.) Houston's Delaware Criminal Cases (1856-79)

Houst. Crim. Rep. Delaware Criminal Cases (Del.)

Houst. Cr. Rep. Delaware Criminal Cases (Del.)

Houst. (Del.) Houston (John W.) (Del.)

Houst. L. Rev. Houston Law Review

Houston Houston's Delaware Supreme Court Reports (1855-1893)

Houston J. Int'l. L. Houston Journal of International Law

Houston Law. Houston Lawyer

Houston L. Rev. Houston Law Review

Houston, Tex. P.S.C. Houston, Texas Public Service Commission

Houst. St. Tr. Houston's Law of Stoppage in Transitu

Hov.
- Hovenden on Frauds
- Hovenden's Supplement to Vesey, Jr's English Chancery Reports

Hov. Ann. Hoveden's Annals

Hoved. Hoveden, Chronica

Hov. Fr. Hovenden on Frauds

Hov. Sup. Hovenden's Supplment to Vesey, Jr's English Chancery Reports (1789-1817)

Hov. Supp. Hovenden's Supplement to Vesey, Jr., Reports, (1789-1817)

How.
- Howard's New York Practice Reports
- Howard's Reports (2-8 Mississippi)
- Howard's Reports (42-65 U.S.)
- Howell Reports (22-26 Nevada)

How. A. Cas. Howard's Appeal Cases (New York)

How. & Beat. Howell & Beatty's Reports (vol. 22 Nevada)

How. & H. St. Howard and Hutchinson's Statutes (Mississippi)

How. & N. Howell & Norcross (Nev.)

How. & Nor. Howell & Norcross' Reports (vols. 23, 24 Nevada)

How. Ann. St. Howell's Annotated Statutes (Mich.)

How. App. Howard's Appeal Cases (N.Y.)

How. App. Cas. Howard, New York Court of Appeals Cases

How. App. Cases Howard, New York Court of Appeals Cases

How. Ct. App. Cas. Howard, New York Court of Appeals Cases

Howard Howard's Mississippi Supreme Court Reports (1834-43)

Howard Journal
- Howard Journal
- Howard Journal of Penology and Crime Prevention

Howard L.J. Howard Law Journal

Howard Pr. Howard's Practice Reports (N.Y.)

Howard Pr. Rep. Howard's Practice Reports (N.Y.)

Howard Rep. Howard, United States Supreme Court Reports

Howard S.C. United States Reports, vols. 42-65

Howard's Prac. Reports Howard's Practice Reports (N.Y.)

Howard's Practice Howard's Practice Reports (N.Y.)

Howard's Spec. Term Rep. Howard's Practice Reports (N.Y.)

How. C. Howard's Chancery Practice (1775) (Ir.)

How. Cas.
- Howard's New York Court of Appeals Cases
- Howard's Property Cases

How. Ch. Howard's Chancery Practice (1760-62) (Ir.)

How. Ch. P. Howard's Chancery Practice (1760-62) (Ir.)

How. Ch. Pr. Howard's Chancery Practice. (1775) (Ir.)

How. Cr. Tr. Howison's Criminal Trials (Virginia)

How. E.E. Howard's Equity Exchequer Reports (Ir.)

Howell N.P. Howell's Nisi Prius Reports, Michigan

Howell, St. Tr. Howell's English State Trials

Howe Pr. Howe's Practice, Massachusetts

How. Eq. Ex. Howard's Equity Exchequer Practice, Ireland

How. Eq. Exch. Howard's Equity Exchequer (Ir.)

How. J. Howard Journal

How. J. Crim. Just. Howard Journal of Criminal Justice, The

How. J. Pen. Howard Journal of Penology and Crime Prevention

How. L.J. Howard Law Journal

How. L. Rev. Howard Law Review

How. Miss. Howard (Miss.)

How.N.P. (Mich.) Howell, Nisi Prius

How. N.S. Howard's New York Practice Reports, New Series

How. (N.Y.) Howard's Practice Reports (N.Y.)

How. Pat. Howson on Patents

How. Po. Ca. Howard's Property Cases (1720-73) (Ir.)

How. Po. Cas. Howard Property Cases (1720-73) (Ir.)

How. P.R. Howard's Practice Reports (N.Y.)

How. Pr. Howard's New York Practice Reports (1844-86)

How. Prac. Howard's Practice Reports (N.Y.)

How. Prac., N.S. Howard's Practice Reports New Series (New York)

How. Prac. (N.Y.) Howard's Practice Reports (New York)

How. Prac. Rep. Howard's Practice Reports (N.Y.)

How. Pr. N.S.
- Howard's Practice, New Series (New York)
- Howard's Practice Reports, New Series (N.Y.)

How. Prob. Pr. Howell, Probate Practice (Ontario, Can.)

How. Pr. Rep. Howard's Practice Reports (N.Y.)

How. Pr. Sup. C. Howard's Practice Reports (N.Y.)

How. S.C. Howard's United States Supreme Court Reports

Hows. Pat. Howson on Patents

Hows. Reis. Pat. Howson on Reissued Patents

How. St. Howell's Annotated Statutes (Michigan)

How. State Tr. Howell's English State Trials (1163-1820)

How. St. Tr. Howell's English State Trials (1163-1820)

How. U.S. Howard's United States Supreme Court Reports

Hoyt Comp. L. Hoyt's Compiled Laws of Arizona

H.P.
- All India Reporter, Himachal Pradesh
- Hire Purchase
- Houses of Parliament

H.P.C.
- Hale's Pleas of the Crown 7 editions (1716-1824)
- Hawkins' Pleas of the Crown

H.P.R. Howard's Practice Reports (N.Y.)

H. Pr. Howard's Practice Reports, New Series (N.Y.)

HPWT Aron & Rosner, How to Prepare Witnesses for Trial

H.Q. Headquarters

H.R.
- Designates file number of a bill as introduced in the U.S. House of Representatives
- Hoge Raad (Dutch Supreme Court)
- House Roll
- Human Resources
- Human Rights Convention (Council of Europe)

HRA Health Resources Administration

H.R. Comm. Commission of Human Rights (Council of Europe)

H.R. Con. Res. House of Representatives Concurrent Resolutions

H.R. Conv. Human Rights Convention (Council of Europe)

H.R. Court Court of Human Rights (Council of Europe)

H.R. Doc. House Document

H. Rept. House of Representatives Reports

H. Res. House of Representatives Resolution

Hr'g Hearing

H.R.J. Res. House of Representatives Joint Resolutions

H.R. L.J. Human Rights Law Journal

H.R. Rep. House of Representatives Reports

H.R. Rept. House of Representatives Report

H.R. Res. House of Representatives Resolution

H.R.S. Hawaii Revised Statutes

HSA Health Services Administration

H.S.C. Health Service Commissioner

H.S.E. Health and Safety Executive

H.T. Hoc titulo (this title)

Hu.
- Hughes' Kentucky Reports
- Hughes' United States Circuit Court Reports
- Hungarian

Hub.
- Hobart's Common Pleas Reports (1613-25) (80 ER)
- Hobart's King's Bench Reports (1603-25) (80 ER)

Hubb. Hubbard's Reports (45-51 Maine)

Hubbard. Hubbard's Reports (45-51 Maine)

Hubb. Succ. Hubback's Evidence of Succession

Hub. Leg. Dir. Hubbell's Legal Directory

Hub. Leg. Direc. Hubbell's Legal Directory

Hub. Prael. J.C. Huber, Praelectiones Juris Civilis

Hub. Suc. (or Ev.) Hubback's Evidence of Succession

HUD Department of Housing and Development

Hud. & B. Hudson & Brooke's Irish King's Bench Reports (1827-31)

Hud. & Br. Hudson & Brooke's Irish King's Bench Reports (1827-31)

Hud. & Bro. Hudson & Brooke's Irish King's Bench Reports (1827-31)

Hud. Exec. Hudson's Executor's Guide

Hudson Hudson on Building Contracts

Hud. Wills Hudson on Wills

Huff. Ch. Hoffman's New York Chancery Reports (N.Y.)

Hugh.
- Hughes' Circuit Court Reports
- Hughes' Reports (1 Kentucky) (1785-1801)

Hugh. Abr. Hughes' Abridgment (1663-65) (Eng.)

Hugh. Con. Hughes' Precedents in Conveyancing

Hugh. Conv. Hughes, Precedents in Conveyancing, 2ed. (1855-57)

Hugh. Ent. Hughes' Entries (1659)

Hugh. Eq. D. Hughes' Edition of Van Heythuysen's Equity Draftsman

Hughes
- Hughes' Kentucky Supreme Court Reports (1785-1801)
- Hughes' United States Circuit Court Reports

Hughes'
- Circuit Court Reports (U.S.)
- Hughes' Reports (1 Kentucky)

Hughes Fed. Prac. Hughes Federal Practice

Hughes (U.S.) Hughes' Circuit Court Reports (U.S.)

Hugh. Ins. Hughes on Insurance

Hugh. Prec. Hughes' Precedents in Conveyancing

Hugh. Wills Hughes on Wills

Hugh.Wr. Hughes on Writs

H.U.L. Houston Law Review (Tex.)

Hull. Costs Hullock on Costs

Hult. Conv. Hulton, Convictions. 1835

Hum.
- Human
- Humphreys' Tennessee Supreme Court Reports (1839-51)

Human.
- Humanity
- Humanities

Human Reprod. & L. Rep. (Legal Medical Studies) Reporter on Human Reproduction and the Law

Human Rights Rev. Human Rights Review

Human Rts. Human Rights

Human Rts. J. Human Rights Journal

Human Rts. Rev. Human Rights Review

Hume Hume's Court of Session Decisions (1781-1822) (Sc.)

Hume Com. Hume, Commentaries on Crimes (Sc.)

Hume, Hist. Eng. Hume's History of England

Hum. Life Rev. Human Life Review, The

Humph. Humphrey's Reports (20-30 Tennessee)

Humph. Prec. Humphry, Common Precedents in Conveyancing. 2ed. 1882

Humphr. Humphrey's (Tenn.)

Hum. Rts. Human Rights

Hum. Rts. L.J. Human Rights Law Journal

Hum. Rts. Q. Human Rights Quarterly

Hum. Rts. U.S.S.R. Human Rights in U.S.S.R.

Hun
- Hun's New York Appellate Division Reports
- Hun's Supreme Court Reports
- New York Supreme Court Reports

Hung. Hungary

Hung. L. Rev. Hungarian Law Review

Hunt.
- Hunter's Torrens Cases (Canada)
- Hunts' Annuity Cases (Eng.)

Hunt Ann. Cas. Hunt's Annuity Cases (Eng.)

Hunt, Bound. Hunt's Law of Boundaries and Fences

Hunt Cas. Hunt's Annuity Cases

Hunt, Eq. Hunt's Suit in Equity

Hunter, Rom. Law. Hunter on Roman Law

Hunter, Suit Eq. Hunter's Proceeding in a Suit in Equity

Hunt Fr. Conv. Hunt, Fraudulent Conveyances. 2ed. 1897

Hunt. L. & T. Hunter, Landlord and Tenant (Sc.)

Hunt Mer. Mag. Hunt's Merchant's Magazine, New York

Hunt. Rom. L. Hunter on Roman Law

Hunt's A.C. Hunt's Annuity Cases (1776-96)

Hunt. Suit Hunter's Proceedings in a Suit in Equity

Hunt. Torrens Hunter's Torrens Cases

Hunt. Tr. Huntingdon's Trial (for Forgery)

Hur. Hurlstone

Hurd F. & B. Hurd on the Laws of Freedom and Bondage in the United States

Hurd Hab. Cor. Hurd on the Writ of Habeas Corpus

Hurd Pers. Lib. Hurd on Personal Liberty

Hurd's Rev. St. Hurd's Revised Statutes (Ill.)

Hurd St. Hurd's Illinois Statutes

Hurl. & C. Hurlstone & Coltman's English Exchequer Reports (1862-66) (158, 159 ER)

Hurl. & Colt. Hurlstone & Coltman Reports, Exchequer (1862-66) (Eng.)

Hurl. & G. Hurlstone and Gordon's Reports, 10, 11, English Exchequer Reports (1847-56)

Hurl. & Gord. Hurlstone and Gordon's Reports (10, 11 Exchequer Reports), (1847-1856)

Hurl. & N. Hurlstone & Norman's English Exchequer Reports (156, 158 ER)

Hurl. & Nor. Hurlstone & Norman's English Exchequer Reports (156, 158 ER)

Hurl. & W. Hurlstone & Walmsley's English Exchequer Reports (1840-41)

Hurl. & Walm. Hurlstone & Walmsley's English Exchequer Reports (1840-41)

Hurl. Bonds. Hurlstone on Bonds

Hurl. Colt. Hurlstone & Coltman's English Exchequer Reports (158, 159 ER)

Hurlst. & C. Hurlstone & Coltman's Exchequer Reports (1862-66) (158-159 ER)

Hurlst. & C. (Eng.) Hurlstone & Coltman's English Exchequer Reports (158, 159 ER)

Hurlst. & G. Hurlstone & Gordon's Exchequer Reports (1854-56) (156 ER)

Hurlst. & N. (Eng.) Hurlstone & Norman's English Exchequer Reports (156, 158 ER)

Hurlst. & W. Hurlstone & Walmsley's Exchequer Reports (1840-41) (58 RR)

Hurlst. & W. (Eng.) Hurlstone & Walmsley's English Exchequer Reports

Husb. & W. Husband and Wife

Husb. For. Med. Husband's Forensic Medicine

Husb. Mar. Wom. Husband on Married Women

Hust. Hustings Court (as in Virginia)

Hust. L. Tit. Huston on Land Titles in Pennsylvania

Hut. Hutton's English Common Pleas Reports (1612-39)

Hutch. Hutcheson's Reports (vols. 81-84 Alabama)

Hutch. Car. Hutchinson on Carriers

Hutch. Carr. Hutchinson on Carriers

Hutch. Code. Hutchinson's Code (Miss.)

Hutch. Dig. St. Hutchinson's Code (Miss.)

Hutch J.P. Hutcheson's Justice of the Peace

Hut. Ct. Req. Hutton's Courts of Requests, 4 editions (1787-1840)

Hutt. Hutton's English Common Pleas Reports (1612-39)

Hutt. Ct. Req. Hutton's Courts of Requests

Hutton. Hutton's Common Pleas Reports (1612-39) (123 ER)

Hutton (Eng.) Hutton's English Common Pleas Reports (123 ER)

Hux. Judg. Huxley's Second Book of Judgments (1675) (Eng.)

H.V. Hoc verbo or hac voce (this word, under this word)

H.W.Gr. H.W. Green's Reports (24 N.J. Eq.)

Hy. All India Reporter, Hyderabad

Hy. Bl. Henry Blackstone's Com. Pleas Reports (1788-96) (Eng.)

Hyd. All India Reporter, Hyderabad

Hyde Hyde's Bengal Reports (India)

Hyderabad Indian Law Reports, Hyderabad Series

I

I.
- Idaho
- Illinois
- Income tax
- Independent
- Indiana
- Institutes of Justinian
- Iowa
- Irish; Ireland
- Italian

I.A.
- Indian Affairs
- Law Reports, Privy Council, Indian Appeals (1875-1950) (India)

Ia.
- Iowa
- Iowa Reports

Ia. Bar Rev. Iowa Bar Review

IABD Inter-American Defense Board

Ia. B.Rev. Iowa Bar Review

IAC Industrial Accident Commission Decisions

I.A.C.
- Immigration Appeal Cases (Can.)
- Industrial Assurance Commissioner
- Inflation Accounting Committee

IACAC Inter-American Commercial Arbitration Commission

I.A.C. Dec. Decisions of the Industrial Accident Commission of California (Cal.)

I.A.C. of Cal. Decisions of the Industrial Accident Commission of California (Cal.)

IAD Immediate Action Directive

IADB
- Inter-American Defense Board
- Inter-American Development Bank

I.A.D.L. International Association of Democratic Lawyers

IAEA
- International Atomic Energy Agency
- International Atomic Energy Agency (U.N.)

IAIC International Association of Insurance Counsel

I.A.L.A. International African Law Association

Ia. L.Bull. Iowa Law Bulletin

IALL International Association of Law Libraries

I.A.L.L.Bull. Bulletin of International Association of Law Libraries

Ia. L. Rev. Iowa Law Review
- Institute of Advanced Law Study

I. & C.L.Q. International and Comparative Law Quarterly

I. & N. Doc. Immigration and Naturalization Service Decisions

I. & N. Immigration & Nationality Laws Administrative Decisions (Justice Dept.)

I. & N. Dec. Immigration and Nationality Decisions

I. & N.S. Immigration and Naturalization Service (U.S.)

IAPR United State Information Agency Procurement Regulation

IARA Inter-Allied Reparation Agency

I. Arb. Institute of Arbitrators

Ia. R.C. Iowa Board of Railroad Commission

I. A.Sup.Vol. English Law Reports, Indian Appeals, Supplementary Volume

Ib. Ibidem (the same)

I.B.A.
- Independent Broadcasting Authority
- International Bar Association

I.B.C. International Broadcasting Convention

I.B.C.A. Interior Board of Contract Appeals (in U.S. Interior Decisions)

IBEC International Bank for Economic Cooperation

I.B.E.W. International Brotherhood of Electrical Workers

ibid. ibidem (in the same place)

I.B.J. Illinois Bar Journal

I.B.I.A. Interior Board of Indian Affairs (in U.S. Interior Decisions)

I.B.M.A. Interior Board of Mine Operations Appeals (in U.S. Interior Decisions)

I.B.R.D. International Bank for Reconstruction and Development (World Bank)

I.B.S.M.A. Interior Board of Surface Mine Appeals (in U.S. Interior Decisions)

I.C.
- Indian Cases
- Industrial Arbitration Cases (West Australia)
- Industrial Court
- Interstate Commerce Reports

Ic. Icelandic

I.C.A.
- Iowa Code Annotated
- Indian Council of Arbitration
- Institute of Chartered Accountants

ICAC International Cotton Advisory Committee

ICAF Industrial College of the Armed Forces

ICAN International Commission for Air Navigation (UN)

ICAO International Civil Aviation Organization (UN)

ICAO Bull. Bulletin of the International Civil Aviation Organization (Can.)

I.C. Arb.Q. Indian Council Arbitration Quarterly

ICBM Intercontinental ballistic missile

ICC
- Indian Claims Commission (U.S.)
- International Chamber of Commerce
- Interstate Commerce Commission (U.S.)

ICCD Turner, Insurance Coverage of Construction Disputes

I.C.C. Prac.J. ICC Practioner's Journal

I.C.C. Pract.J. Interstate Commerce Commission Practitioners' Journal

I.C.C.R. Interstate Commerce Commission Reports (U.S.)

I.C.C. Rep. Interstate Commerce Commission Reports

ICC Valuation Rep. Interstate Commerce Commission, Valuation Reports

ICD Windt, Insurance Claims and Disputes

Ice. Iceland

ICEF International Children's Emergency Fund (UN)

ICEM Intergovernmental Committee on European Migration

ICEREPAT Paris Union Committee for International Co-operation in Information Retrieval Among Patent Offices

ICFTU International Confederation of Free Trade Unions

I.Ch.R. Irish Chancery Reports

ICITO Interim Commission for International Trade Organization (UN)

ICJ International Court of Justice Reports (UN)

ICJR Institute for Criminal Justice, University of Richmond

I.C.J. Rev. Review of the International Commission of Jurists

I.C.J. Y.B. International Court of Justice Yearbooks

ICLEF Indiana Continuing Legal Education Forum

ICLM Emalfarb, Illinois Construction Law: Manual and Forms

I.C.L.Q. International and Comparative Law Quarterly

I.C.L.R. Irish Common Law Reports (1850-66)

I.C.L.R. Can. Index to Current Legal Research in Canada

ICM Institute for Court Management

ICNAF International Commission for Northwest Atlantic Fisheries

ICO
- International Coffee Organization
- International Lead and Zinc Study Group

I.C.R.
- Industrial Court Reports
- Irish Chancery Reports
- Irish Circuit Reports (1841-43)

I.C.Rep. Interstate Commerce Commission Reports (U.S.)

I.C.R.V. Inns of Court Rifle Volunteers

ICSAB International Civil Service Advisory Board

I.C.S.I.D. International Centre for Settlement of Investment Disputes

ICT Postlewaite, International Corporate Taxation

ICTB International Customs Tariff Bureau

I.D. Interior Department Decisions (U.S.)

Id.
- Idaho
- Idaho Reports
- idem (the same)

IDA   International Development Association (IBRD Affiliate)

Ida.   Idaho Reports

Idaho   Idaho Supreme Court Reports

Idaho Code   Idaho Code

Idaho Const.   Idaho Constitution

Idaho L.J.   Idaho Law Journal

Idaho L. Rev.   Idaho Law Review

Idaho N.S.   Idaho Reports, New Series (Idaho)

Idaho   Idaho Reports

Idaho Sess. Laws   Session Laws, Idaho

Ida. I.A.B.   Idaho Industrial Accident Board Reports

Ida. P.U.C.   Idaho Public Utilities Commission

Ida. Supp.   Idaho Supplement (Idaho)

IDB   Inter-American Development Bank

Idding   Idding's Term Reports (Dayton, Ohio)

Iddings D.R.B.   Iddings Dayton Term Reports

Iddings D.R.D.   Iddings Dayton Term Reports

Iddings T.R.D.   Iddings' Dayton (Ohio) Term Reports

IDD.T.R.   Idding's Term Reports (Dayton, Ohio)

Idea
- Idea: the Journal of Law and Technology
- Patent, Trademark and Copyright Journal of Research and Education

Idea: J.L. Tech.   Idea: The Journal of Law and Technology

Idings T.R.D.   Iddings' Term Reports (Ohio)

IDLF   Idaho Law Foundation

Id. L.J.   Idaho Law Journal

Id. L.R.   Idaho Law Review

IDO   International Disarmament Organization

IDRC   International Development Research Centre

i.e.   id est (that is)

IEA   International Energy Agency

IEFC   International Emergency Food Council

IEP   Newton, International Estate Planning

I.Eq.R.   Irish Equity Reports (1838-50)

I.E.R.
- Irish Equity Reports

Individual Employment Rights

IFA   International Franchise Association

IFAD   International Fund for Agricultural Development

IFB   Invitation for Bids

IFC
- International Finance Corporation (IBRD Affiliate)
- Interstate and Foreign Commerce

I.F.C.L. International Faculty of Comparative Law

IFLA International Federation of Library Associations

I.F.L.P. Index to Foreign Legal Periodicals

IFL Rev. International Financial Law Review

I.F.L.S. International Federation of Law Students

IFR Imported Food Regulations

IFTU International Federation of Trade Unions

I.F.W.L. International Federation of Women Lawyers

IGC Inter-Governmental Committee on Refugees

I.H.A. Issuing Houses Association

IHO International Hydrographic Organization

IIA
- Interior and Insular Affairs
- International Institute of Agriculture

I.I.A.C. Industrial Injuries Advisory Committee

IIC International Review of Industrial Property and Copyright Law (Ger.)

IICLE Illinois Institute of Continuing Legal Education

I.I.L.C. International Legal Center Newsletter

I.I.L.P. Index to Indian Legal Periodicals

IILS Institute for Improved Legal Services
- International Institute of Labour Studies

I.Inf.Sc. Institute of Information Scientists

I/Ins. Inactive Insurance

I.I.P. Industrial and intellectual Property in Australia

I.I.S.L. International Institute of Space Law

IIT Collins & Postlewaite, International Individual Taxation

I.J.
- Indian Jurist, Old Series
- Irish Jurist (Dublin)

IJA Indiana Judges Association

IJC Indiana Judicial Center

I.J.C. Irvine, Justiciary Cases (Sc.)

I.J.Cas. Irvine's Justiciary Cases (Sc.)

I.J.I.L. Indian Journal of International Law

IJLL International Journal of Law Libraries

I.J.N.S. Irish Jurist, New Series

I.J.O. International Juridicial Organisation for Developing Countries

I.J.P.A. Indian Journal of Public Administration

I.L. The Irish Land Reports (Fitzgibbon)

IlA Illinois Appellate Court Reports

Il. Illinois Supreme Court Reports

Il.2d. Illinois Supreme Court Reports, Second Series

ILA International Longshoremen's Association (AFL-CIO)

Il.A. Illinois Appellate Court Reports

IlA.2d. Illinois Appellate Court Reports, Second Series

Il.A.3d. Illinois Appellate Court Reports, Third Series

I.L.A.A. International Legal Aid Association

ILC International Law Commission (UN)

IlC.Cl. Illinois Court of Claims Reports

I.L.C. Newl. International Legal Center Newsletter

I.L.E. Indiana Law Encyclopedia

Ilex. Institute of Legal Executives

ILGWU International Ladies' Garment Workers' Union (AFL-CIO)

ILIR Institute of Labor and Industrial Relations (University of Illinois)

I.L.J. Indiana Law Journal

Ill.
- Illinois
- Illinois Reports

Ill.2d. Illinois Reports, Second Series

Ill.A. Illinois Appellate Court Reports

Ill. Admin. Reg. Illinois Register

Ill. Ann. Stat. Smith-Hurd Illinois Annotated Statutes

Ill. Ap. Illinois Appellate Court Reports (Ill.)

Ill. App. Illinois Appellate Court Reports

Ill. App 2d Illinois Appellate Court Reports, 2d Series

Ill. App.3d Illinois Appellate Court Reports, 3d Series

Ill. App. Ct. Rep. Illinois Appellate Court Reports (Ill.)

Ill. Apps. Illinois Appellate Court Reports (Ill.)

Ill. B.A. Bull. Illinois State Bar Association Quarterly Bulletin

Ill. Bar J. Illinois Bar Journal

Ill. B.J. Illinois Bar Journal

Ill.C.C.
- Illinois Commerce Commission Opinions & Orders
- Matthew and Bangs, Illinois Circuit Court Reports (Ill.)

Ill. Cir. Illinois Circuit Court

Ill. Cir.Ct. Illinois Circuit Court Reports

Ill. Const. Illinois Constitution

Ill. Cont. L.Ed.
- Illinois Continuing Law Education
- Illinois Continuing Legal Education

Ill. Cont. Legal Ed. Illinois Continuing Legal Education

Ill. Ct.Cl.
- Illinois Court of Claims Reports
- Illinois Court of Claims

Ill. Dec. Illinois Decisions

Il. L.F. Illinois Law Forum

Ill. Forest. Illingsworth on Forestalling

Illinois Rep. Illinois Reports (Ill.)

Ill. Laws Laws of Illinois

Ill. L.B. Illinois Law Bulletin

Ill. Legis. Serv. Illinois Legislative Service (West)

Ill. Leg.N. Illustrated Legal News (India)

Ill. L.Q. Illinois Law Quarterly

Ill LR University of Illinois Law Review

Ill. L.Rec. Illinois Law Record

Ill. L. Rev. Illinois Law Review

Ill. Op. Att'y Gen. Illinois Attorney General's Opinion

Ill. P.U.C. Ops. Illinois Public Utilities Commission Opinions & Orders

Ill. R. Illinois Reports (Ill.)

Ill. R. & W.C. Illinois Railroad & Warehouse Commission Reports

Ill. R. & W.C.D. Illinois Railroad & Warehouse Commission Decisions

Ill. Rep. Illinois Reports (Ill.)

Ill. Rev. Stat. Illinois Revised Statutes

Ills. Illinois Reports (Ill.)

Ills.App. Illinois Appellate Court Reports (Ill.)

Ill. S.B.A. Illinois State Bar Association Reports

Ill. S.B.A. Q.B. Illinois State Bar Association Quarterly Bulletin

Ills. R. Illinois Reports (Ill.)

Ills. Rep. Illinois Reports (Ill.)

Ill. W.C.C. Illinois Workmen's Compensation Cases

I.L.M. International Legal Materials (periodical)

ILO International Labour Organisation

I.L.P.
- Illinois Law and Practice
- Index to Legal Periodicals

I.L.P.L. Index to Legal Periodical Literature (1887-1937)

I.L.Q.
- Indian Law Quarterly
- International Law Quarterly

I.L.Q.R. Indian Law Quarterly Review

I.L.R.
- Indian Law Reports
- Indian Law Review
- Insurance Law Reporter (Canada)
- International Law Reports
- Iowa Law Review
- Irish Law Reports

I.L.R. All. Indian Law Reports, Allahabad Series

I.L.R. And. Indian Law Reports, Andhra Series

I.L.R. Assam Indian Law Reports, Assam Series

I.L.R. Bom. Indian Law Reports, Bombay Series

I.L.R.C. Indian Law Reports, Calcutta Series

I.L.R. Cal. Indian Law Reports, Calcutta Series

I.L.R. Calc. Indian Law Reports, Calcutta Series

I.L.R. Cut. Indian Law Reports, Orissa Series

I.L.R. Hyderabad Indian Law Reports, Hyderabad Series

I.L.R. Kar. Indian Law Reports, Karachi Series

I.L.R. Ker. Indian Law Reports, Kerala Series

I.L.R. Lah. Indian Law Reports, Lahore Series

I.L.R. Luck. Indian Law Reports, Lucknow Series

I.L.R. Mad. Indian Law Reports, Madras Series

I.L.R. Madhya Bharat Indian Law Reports, Madhya Bharat Series

I.L.R. Mysore Indian Law Reports' Mysore Series

I.L.R. Nag. Indian Law Reports, Nagpur Series

I.L.R. Or. Indian Law Reports, Orissaa Series

I.L.R.P. Indian Law Reports, Patna Series

I.L.R. Pat. Indian Law Reports, Patna Series

I.L.R. Patiala Indian Law Reports, Patiala Series

I.L.R. Pun. Indian Law Reports, Punjab Series

I.L.R.R. Industrial and Labor Relations Review

I.L.R. Rajasthan Indian Law Reports, Rajasthan Series

I.L.R. Ran. Indian Law Reports, Rangoon Series

ILR Rev. Industrial & Labor Relations Review

I.L.R. Trav.-Cochin Indian Law Reports, Kerala Series

I.L.S. Incorporated Law Society

ILSA J. Int'l L. ILSA Journal of International Law

ILSCLE Iowa Law School Continuing Legal Education

I.L.T. Irish Law Times (Dublin)

I.L.T. & S.J. Irish Law Times and Solicitors' Journal

I.L.T. Jo. Irish Law Times Journal

I.L.T.R. Irish Law Times Reports (Eire)

I.L.W. Investment Laws of the World (Oceana)

ILWU International Longshoremen's and Warehousemen's Union

IMAW International Molders' and Allied Workers' Union of North America (AFL-CIO)

IMC International Materials Conference

IMCO Inter-Governmental Maritime Consultative Organization (UN)

IMF International Monetary Fund (UN)

IMF (FUND) International Monetary Fund

IMF Staff Papers International Monetary Fund Staff Papers

Imm. A.R. Immigration Appeal Reports

Immig. & Naturalization Serv. Mo. Rev. U.S. Immigration and Naturalization Service, Monthly Review

Immig. B. Bull. Immigration Bar Bulletin

Immig. Brief Immigration Briefings

Immig. L. & Bus. News. Immigration Law & Business News

Immig. Newsl. Immigration Newsletter

Immigr. Immigration

Immigr. J. Immigration Journal

Imm.J. Immigration Journal

IMO
- International Maritime Organization
- International Meteorological Organization (UN)

Imp. Imperial: United Kingdom Statute

imp. implement(ed)

Imp. Dict. Imperial Dictionary

Imp. Fed. Imperial Federation (London)

Imp. Man. Impey, Law and Practice of Mandamus. 1826

Imp. Pl. Impey, Modern Pleader. 2ed. 1814

Imp. Pr. C.P. Impey's Practice, Common Pleas

Imp. Pr. K.B. Impey's Practice, King's Bench

Improv. Improvements

Imp. Sh. Impey, Office of Sheriff. 6ed. 1835

Impt. Improvement

impt. important

IMU International Mailers' Union

In Indonesian

In. Indian Reports

In.A. Indiana Appellate Court Reports

Inc.
- Income
- Incorporated

inc.
- included
- includes
- including

Incl.
- Included
- Includes
- Including

Income Tax'n Nat. Resources (P-H) Income Taxation of Natural Resources (Prentice-Hall)

Incomp. P. Incompetent Persons

incorp. incorporated

Inc. Tax Cas. Reports of Cases on Income Tax

Inc. Tax L.J. Income Tax Law Journal (India)

Inc. Tax R. Income Tax Reports (India)

Ind.
- Independent
- Index
- India
- Indiana
- Indiana Reports
- Indiana Supreme Court Reports
- Industrial
- Industry

Ind. Acc. Com. Decisions of the Industrial Accident Commission of California (Cal.)

Ind. Acts Acts, Indiana

Ind. A.Dig. U.S. Indian Affairs Office, Digest of Decisions

Ind. Admin. Code Indiana Administrative Code

IND. Admin. R. Burns Indiana Administrative Rules & Regulations

Ind. Adv.
- Indian Advocate (Bombay) (1961)
- Indian Advocate (Lahore)

Ind. Advocate Indian Advocate

Ind. & Intell.Prop. Austl. Industrial and Intellectual Property in Australia

Ind. Int'l & Comp. L. Rev. Indiana International & Comparative Law Review

Ind. & Int. Prop. Aus. Industrial and Intellectual Property in Australia

Ind. and Labor Rels. Rev. Industrial and Labor Relations Review

Ind. & Lab. Rel. Rev. Industrial and Labor Relations Review

Ind. & L. Rel. Rev. Industrial & Labor Relations Review

Ind. App.
- Indiana Court of Appeals Reports
- Law Reports, Indian Appeals

Ind. App. Ct. Indiana Appellate Court Reports (Ind.)

Ind. App. Supp. Supplemental Indian Appeals, Law Reports

Ind. Awards Industrial Awards Recommendations (New Zealand)

Ind. Can. L.P. Lit. Index to Canadian Legal Periodical Literature

Ind. Cas. Indian Cases (India)

Ind. C. Aw. Industrial Court Awards

Ind. Cl. Comm. Indian Claims Commission (Ind.)

Ind. Code Indiana Code

Ind. Code Ann. Burns Indiana Statutes Annotated Code Edition

Ind. Com. Law Indermaur & Thwaites, Principles of the Common Law. 12ed. 1914

Ind. Comm. Industrial Commission

Ind. Const. Indiana Constitution

Ind. Court Aw. Industrial Court Awards (Eng.)

Ind. Ct. Awards Industrial Court Awards (Eng.)

Ind. Dec.
- Indiana Decisions (Ind.)
- Indiana Decisions and Law Reporter (Ind.)

Ind. Dig. All India Reporter, Indian Digest (1946-52)

Ind. Div. Inderwick, Divorce & Matrimonial Causes Acts. 1862

Indebt. Indebtedness

Indem. Indemnity

Indep. independent

Indep. Contr. Independent Contractors

India A.I.R. Manual A.I.R. Manual: Unrepealed Central Acts, 2d edition (India)

India Cen. Acts Central Acts (India)

India Code Civ.P. Code of Civil Procedure (India)

India Code Crim.P. Code of Criminal Procedure (India)

India Crim. L.J.R. Criminal Law Journal Reports (India)

India Gen. R. & O. General Rules and Orders (India)

India L.C. Law Commission of India

Indian Indian

Indiana Indiana Reports (Ind.)

Indiana Leg. Forum Indiana Legal Forum

Indiana L.J. Indiana Law Journal

Indiana L.Rev. Indiana Law Review

Indian App. Law Reports, Privy Council, Indian Appeals (1873-75) (India)

Indiana Sup. Ct. Rep. Indiana Reports (Ind.)

Indian Cas. Indiana Cases

Indian J. Int. Law Indian Journal of International Law

Indian J. Int'l. L. Indian Journal of International Law

Indian J. of Internat. L. Indian Journal of International Law. New Delhi, India

Indian J. of Publ. Adm. The Indian Journal of Public Administration. New Delhi, India

Indian J. Pub. Admin. Indian Journal of Public Administration

Indian L.J. Indian Law Journal

Indian L.R. Indian Law Reports

Indian L.R. Calc. Indian Law Reports, Calcutta Series

Indian L. Rep. (Am. Indian Law Training Program) Indian Law Reporter

Indian L.R. [e.g.] Allahabad Ser. Indian Law Reports [e.g.] Allahadad Series

Indian L. Rev. Indian Law Review

Indian L.R. Mad. Indian Law Reports, Madras Series

Indian Rul. Indian Rulings

Indian Terr. Indian Territory Reports

Indian Yb. of Internat. Aff. The Indian Year Book of International Affairs. Madras, India

India Pen. Code Indian Penal Code

India S.Ct. India Supreme Court Reports

India Subs. Leg. Subsidiary Legislation (India)

Indict. Indictments and informations

Ind. Ind. L.P. Index to Indian Legal Periodicals

Ind. Int'l & Comp. L. Rev. Indiana International & Comparative Law Review

Ind. J.Int.L. Indian Journal of International Law

Ind. J.Int'l.L. Indiana Journal of International Law

Ind. J. Pol. Sci. Indian Journal of Political Science, Allahabad, India

Ind. J. Pub. Admin. Indian Journal of Public Administration

Ind. Jud. Pr. Indermaur's Practice in the Supreme Court of Judicature

Ind. Jur. Indian Jurist (Calcutta or Madras)

Ind. Jur. N.S. Indian Jurist, New Series

Ind. Jur. O.S.
- Indian Jurist, Old Series (Calcutta) (1862-63)
- Indian Jurist, Old Series (Madras) (1877-83)

355

Ind. Jur. Pr. Indermaur, Practice of the Supreme Court of Judicature. 12ed. 1919

Ind. Law J. Indiana Law Journal

Ind. L.C. Com. Law Indermaur, Leading Cases in Common Law. 10ed. 1921

Ind. L.C. Eq. Indermaur's Leading Cases in Conveyancing and Equity

Ind. Legal F. Indiana Legal Forum

Ind. Leg. Forum Indiana Legal Forum

Ind. Leg. Per. Index to Legal Periodicals

Ind. L.H. Indian Law Herald

Ind. L.J. Indiana Law Journal

Ind. L. Mag.
- Indian Law Magazine (Bombay) (1878)
- Indian Law Magazine (Calcutta) (1895)

Ind. L.Q. Indian Law Quarterly. 1914-17

Ind. L.Q.Rev. Indian Law Quarterly Review

Ind. L.R.
- Indiana Law Reporter (1881)
- Indiana Law Review
- Indiana Legal Register
- Indian Law Reports (East)
- Indian Law Review

Ind. L.R. All. Indian Law Reports, Allahabad Series

Ind. L.R. Alla. Indian Law Reports, Allahabad Series

Ind. L.R. And. Indian Law Reports, Andhra Series

Ind. L.R. Assam Indian Law Reports, Assam Series

Ind. L.R. Bomb. Indian Law Reports, Bombay Series

Ind. L.R. Calc. Indian Law Reports, Calcutta Series

Ind. L. Reg. Indiana Legal Register

Ind. L.Rep.
- Indiana Law Reporter. 1881
- Indian Law Reporter

Ind. L. Rev.
- Indiana Law Review
- Indian Law Review

Ind. L.R. Hyderabad Indian Law Reports, Hyderabad Series

Ind. L.R. Kar. Indian Law Reports, Karachi Series

Ind. L.R. Ker. Indian Law Reports, Kerala Series

Ind. L.R. Lah. Indian Law Reports, Lahore Series

Ind. L.R. Luck. Indian Law Reports, Lucknow Series

Ind. L.R. Mad. Indian Law Reports, Madras Series

Ind. L.R. Madhya Bharat Indian Law Reports, Madhya Bharat Series

Ind. L.R. Mysore Indian Law Reports, Mysore Series

Ind. L.R. Nag. Indian Law, Reports, Nagpur Series

Ind. L.R. Or. Indian Law Reports, Orissa Series

Ind. L.R. Pat. Indian Law Reports, Patna Series

Ind. L.R. Patiala Indian Law Reports, Patiala Series

Ind. L.R. Pun. Indian Law Reports, Punjab Series

Ind. L.R. Rajasthan Indian Law Reports, Rajasthan Series

Ind. L.R. Ran. Indian Law Reports, Rangoon Series

Ind. L.S. Indiana Law Student

Ind. L. Stud. Indiana Law Student

Ind. L.T. Indian Law Times

Indon. Indonesia

Ind. Prop. Industrial Property

Ind. Prop. Q. Industrial Property Quarterly

Ind. P.S.C. Indiana Public Service Commission

Ind. R. Indiana Reports (Ind.)

Ind. R.C. Indiana Railroad Commission

Ind. Rel. Industrial Relations (P-H)

Ind.Relations Industrial Relations

Ind. Rel. Guide (P-H) Industrial Relations Guide (Prentice- Hall)

Ind. Rel. J. Econ. & Soc. Industrial Relations: Journal of Economy and Society

Ind. Rel. L.J. Industrial Relations Law Journal

Ind. Rep. Indiana Reports

Ind. S.B.A. Indiana State Bar Association Reports

Ind. S.C. Indiana Superior Court

Ind. Super. Wilson's Indiana Superior Court Reports

Ind. T. Indian Territory

Ind. T. Ann. St. Indian Territory Annotated Statutes

Ind. Ter. Indian Territory Reports

Ind. Terr. Indian Territory

Indty. Indemnity

Ind. U.C.D. Indiana Unemployment Compensation Division, Selected Appeal Tribunal Decisions

Indus.
- Industrial
- Industry

Indus. & Lab. Rel. F. Industrial and Labor Relations Forum

Indus. & Lab. Rel. Rev. Industrial and Labor Relations Review

Indus. Cas. R. Industrial Cases Reports

Indus. L.J. Industrial Law Journal

Indus. Rel. Guide (P-H) Industrial Relations Guide

Indus. L. Rev. Industrial Law Review

Indus. Rel. Industrial Relations

Indus. Rel. Guide (P-H) Industrial Relations Guide (Prentice-Hall)

Indus. Rel. L.J. Industrial Relations Law Journal

Indust. & L. Rel. Rev. Industrial and Labor Relations Review

Indust. Bull. Industrial Bulletin

Indust. C. Aw. Industrial Court Awards

Indust. Ct. Aw. Industrial Court Awards (Eng.)

Indust. Law Rev. Industrial Law Review

Indust. L.J. Industrial Law Journal

Indust. L. Rev. Industrial Law Review

Indust. L. Rev. Q. Industrial Law Review Quarterly

Indust. L.Soc. Industrial Law Society

Indust. L. Soc. Bull. Bulletin of the Industrial Law Society

Indust. Prop. Industrial Property

Indust. Prop. Q. Industrial Property Quarterly

Indust. Rel. L.J. Industrial Relations Law Journal

Industrial Acc. Com. Decisions of the Industrial Accident Commission of California (Cal.)

Industr. Prop'y.Q. Industrial Property Quarterly, Berne, Switzerland

Indust. Prop,y. Yb. Industrial Property Yearbook

Ind. Wilis Inderwick, Wills. 1866

Ind. Y.B.I.A. Indian Year Book of International Affairs

Ind. Y.B. Int'l Aff. Indian Yearbook of International Affairs

Inequal. Ed. Inequality in Education

Inequal. Educ. Inequality in Education

Inf.
- Infra (beneath or below)
- In fine (at the end of a paragraph or title)
- Inferior
- Infants

Inf. Law. Infant's Lawyer

Info. Information

Ing. Comp. Ingram, Compensation for Interest in Lands. 2ed. 1869

Ing. Dig. Ingersoll's Digest of the Laws of the United States

Ing. Hab. Corp. Ingersoll on Habeas Corpus

Ing. Insolv. Ingraham on Insolvency, Pennsylvania

INGO International Non-Governmental Organization

Ing. Roc. Ingersoll's Edition of Roccus' Maritime Law

Inher. Inheritance

Inher. Est. & Gift Tax Rep. Inheritance, Estate & Gift Tax Reporter

Inher. Tax. Inheritance, Estate and Gift Taxes

Init. & Ref. Initiative and Referendum

Inj.
- Injunction
- injury

InL Insurance Litigation Reporter

In. L.F. Indiana Legal Forum

In. L.J. Indiana Law Journal

In. L.R. Indiana Law Review

Inn. Eas. Innes, Easements. 8ed. 1911

Inn. Ease. Innes on Easements

Inn. Sc. Leg. Ant. Innes, Scotch Legal Antiquities

INPFC International North Pacific Fisheries Commission

In Pub. Interest In the Public Interest

In re   In the matter of; concerning (Lat.)

INS   Immigration and Naturalization Service

Ins.
- Insolvency
- Insurance

Ins.C.   Insurance Code

Insc. Counsel J.   Insurance Counsel Journal

Ins. Counsel J.   Insurance Counsel Journal

Ins. Couns. J.   Insurance Counsel Journal

Ins. Law J.   Insurance Law Journal

Ins. Liability Rep.   Insurance Liability Reporter

Ins. L.J.   Insurance Law Journal

Ins. L.R.   Insurance Law Reporter

Ins. L. Rep. (CCH)
- Insurance Law Reports
- Insurance Law Reporter (CCH)

Ins. Mon.   Insurance Monitor

Insolv.   Insolvency

Insp. L.   Inspection Laws

Ins. Rep.   Insurance Reporter

Inst.
- Coke's Institutes (Eng.)
- Institute; Institution
- Institutes of England, in two parts, or A Commentary upon Littleton by Sir Edward Coke
- Justinian's Institutes

Inst. Ad. Legal Stud. Ann.   Institute of Advanced Legal Studies Annal

Inst. Cler.   Instructor Clericalis

Inst. Com. Com.   Interstate Commerce Commission Reports (U.S.)

Inst. Epil.   Epilogue to (a designated part or volume of Coke's Institutes)

Inst. Estate Plan   Institute on Estate Planning

Inst. Est. Plan.   Institute on Estate Planning (U. of Miami)

Inst. Fed. Tax   Institute of Federal Taxation

Institutes   Institutes of Justinian (Roman Law)

Inst. Jur. Angl.   Institutions Juris Anglicani by Cowell

Inst. Lab. Rel. Bull.   Institute for Labor Relations Bulletin

Inst. Min. L.   Institute on Mineral Law

Instn.   Institution

Inst. on Est. Plan.   Institute on Estate Planning

Inst. on Fed. Tax.   Institute on Federal Taxation

Inst. on Fed. Tax'n.   Institute on Federal Taxation (New York University)

Inst. on Min. L.   Institute on Mineral Law (Louisiana State University)

Inst. on Oil & Gas L. & Tax'n.   Institute on Oil and Gas Law and Taxation (Southwestern Legal Foundation)

Inst. on Plan. Zon. & Eminent Domain Proc.   Institute on Planning, Zoning and Eminent Domain Proceedings (Southwestern Legal Foundation)

Inst. on Plan. Zoning & Eminent Domain Institute on Planning, Zoning and Eminent Domain Proceedings (Southwestern Legal Foundation)

Inst. on Priv. Inv. & Inv. Abroad Institute on Private Investments and Investors Abroad Proceedings

Inst. on Priv. Invest. & Investors Abroad Proc. Institute on Private Investments & Investors Abroad Proceedings

Inst. on Sec. Reg. Institute on Securities Regulation

Inst. Plan. & Zoning Institute on Planning and Zoning

Inst. Plan. Zoning & E.D. Institute on Planning and Zoning and Eminent Domain

Inst. Proem. Proeme (introduction) to (a designated part or volume of Coke's Institutes

instr. instruction

Instr. Cler. Instructor Clericalis

Inst. Sec. Reg. Institute on Securities Regulation (PLI)

Inst. Securities Reg. Institute on Securities Regulation (PLI)

Insur. Counsel J. Insurance Counsel Journal

Insur. L.J. Insurance Law Journal

Insur. L. Rep. Insurance Law Reporter (CCH)

Insurr. Insurrection

Int.
- Intelligence
- Interest
- International
- Introduction

Int. Aff. International Affairs

Int.-Am. L. Rev. Inter-American Law Review

Int. & Comp. International & Comparative Law Quarterly

Int. & Compl. L.Q. International & Comparative Law Quarterly

Int. Arb. J. International Arbitration Journal

Int. BarJ. International Bar Journal

Int. Bull. Indust. Prop. International Bulletin of Industrial Property

Int. Bull. Res. E. Eur. International Bulletin for Research on Law in Eastern Europe

Int. Bus. Lawy. International Business Lawyer

Int. Cas. Rowe's Interesting Cases (Eng., Ir.)

Int. Case Rowe's Interesting Cases (Eng., Ir.)

Int. Com. Com. Interstate Commerce Commission, U.S.

Int. Com. Commn. Interstate Commerce Commission

Int. Comp. L.Q. International and Comparative Law Quarterly

Int. Com. Rep. Interstate Commerce Commission Reports

Int. Concil. International Conciliation

Int. Dig. International Digest

Intell. Intellectual

Intellectual Property L. Rev. Intellectual Property Law Review

Intelligencer Legal Intelligencer (Pa.)

Intell. Prop. L. Rev. Intellectual Property Law Review

INTELSAT International Telecommunications Satellite Consortium

Int. Enc. Comp. Law International Encyclopedia of Comparative Law

Inter-Alia Inter-Alia, Journal of the Nevada State Bar

Inter.Am. Inter-American Quarterly

Inter-Am. C.H.R. Annual Report of the Inter-American Commission on Human Rights

Inter-Am. L. Rev. Inter-American Law Review

Int'l Bus. & Trade L. Rep. International Business & Trade Law Reporter

Int'l Comm. Arb. International Chamber of Commerce Arbitration

Interest & U. Interest and Usury

Interfer. Interference

Interior Dec. Decisions of the Department of the Interior

intern. international

Intern. L. International Law

Interna. L.N. International Law Notes (London)

Internat. International

Internat. Bar Assoc. International Bar Association.

Internat. Comp. L.Q. International and Comparative Law Quarterly

Internat. Dict. Webster's International Dictionary

Internat. J. of Leg. Res. The International Journal of Legal Research. An International Journal for Promotion of Legal Research. Meerut, India

Internat. Lawyer The International Lawyer. Quarterly Publication of the Section of International and Comparative Law of the American Bar Association

Internat. L.N. International Law Notes

Internat. L.Q. International Law Quarterly

Interp. Interpretation

Interpl. Interpleader

Interp. No. Interpretation Number

INTERPOL International Criminal Police Organization

Interp. Op. Interpretative Opinion

Interrog. Interrogatory

Inters. Com. Interstate Commerce

Inters. Com. Com. Interstate Commerce Commission

Inters. Com. Rep. Interstate Commerce Commission Reports (U.S.)

Interstate Com. R. Interstate Commerce Reports

Interst. Com. R. Interstate Commerce Commission Reports

Int. J. Est. & Coast. L. International Journal of Estuarine and Coastal Law

Int. J. Criminol. International Journal of Criminology and Penology

Int. J. Law Libs. International Journal of Law Libraries

Int. J. Pol. International Journal of Politics

Int. Jurid. Assn. Bull. International Juridical Association Bulletin

Intl. International

Int'l Dig. Health Legis. International Digest of Health Legislation

Int. Lab. Rev. International Labor Review

Int'l. Aff. International Affairs

Int'l. Affairs International Affairs

Int'l. Affairs (Moscow) International Affairs

Int'l & Comp. L. Bull. International and Comparative Law Bulletin

Int'l. & Comp. L.Q. International and Comparative Law Quarterly

Int'l Arb. Awards Reports of International Arbitral Awards

Int'l. Arb. J. International Arbitration Journal

Int'l. Assoc. L. Lib. Bull. International Association of Law Libraries Bulletin.

Int'l Envt. Rep. (BNA) International Environment Reporter (Bureau of National Affairs)

Int'l J. L. & Fam. International Journal of Law and the Family

Int'l J.L. & Psychiatry International Journal of Law and Psychiatry

Int'l J. World Peace International Journal on World Peace

Int'l L. & Trade Persp. International Law & Trade Perspective

Int. Law The International Lawyer

Int'l Law. International Lawyer

Int. Law Tr. International Law Tracts

Int'l. B.A. Bull. International Bar Association Bulletin

Int'l. Bar J. International Bar Journal

Int'l. B.J. International Bar Journal

Int. L. Bull. International Law Bulletin

Int'l. Bull. Research E. Eur. International Bulletin for Research on Law in Eastern Europe

Int'l. Bus. Law. International Business Lawyer

Int'l. Bus. Lawyer International Business Lawyer, London, England

Int'l Bus.Ser. International Business Series (Ernst & Ernst)

Int'l. Comm. Jurists Rev. International Commission of Jurists Review

Int'l Concil. International Conciliation

Int'l Constr. L. Rev. International Construction Law Review

Int'l Crim. Pol. Rev. International Criminal Police Review

Intl. Dig. International Digest

Int'l Dig. Health Leg. International Digest of Health Legislation

Int'l J. L. & Fam. International Journal of Law & the Family

Int'l J. Refugee L. International Journal of Refugee Law

Int. Legal Materials International Legal Materials

Int'l Encycl. Comp. L. International Encyclopedia of Comparative Law

Int'l Envtl. Rep. (BNA) International Environmental Reporter

Int'l Fin. L. Rev. International Financial Law Review

Int'l. J. International Journal

Int'l. J. Comp. & App. Crim. Just. International Journal of Comparative and Applied Criminal Justice

Int'l J. Crim. & Pen. International Journal of Criminology and Penology

Int'l. J. Crimin. & Penol. International Journal of Criminology and Penology

Int'l. J. Envir. Stud. International Journal of Environmental Studies

Int'l. J.L. & Psych. International Journal of Law and Psychiatry

Int'l. L. Comm'n. International Law Commission

Int'l Leg. Persp. International Legal Perspectives

Int'l. J. Legal Info. International Journal of Legal Information

Int'l. J. Legal Infor. International Journal of Legal Information

Int'l J. Legal Res. International Journal of Legal Research

Int'l. J. L. Lib. International Journal of Law Libraries

Int'l. J. L. Libr. International Journal of Law Libraries

Int'l. J. Offend. Ther. & Comp. Criminology International Journal of Offender Therapy & Comparative Criminology

Int'l J. Off. Ther. & Comp. Crim. International Journal of Offender Therapy and Comparative Criminology

Int'l. J. Pol. International Journal of Politics

Int'l. J. Soc. L. International Journal of the Sociology of the Law

Int'l Jurid. Ass'n Bull. International Juridicial Association Monthly Bulletin

Int'l. Lab. Off. Leg. S. International Labour Office, Legislative Series, London, England

Int'l. Lab. Reports International Labour Reports

Int'l. Lab. Rev. International Labour Review

Int'l. L. Ass'n. Reports of the International Law Association

Int'l. L. Ass'n. Bull. Bulletin of the International Law Association (1936-3 8)

Int'l. Law. The International Law

Int'l. Lawyer International Lawyer

Int'l L. Comm'n International Law Commission

Int'l L. Doc. International Law Documents

Int'l Legal Ed. Newsl. International Legal Education Newsletter

Int'l. Legal Mat. International Legal Materials

Intl. Legal Materials International Legal Materials

Int'l. L. News International Law News

Int'l L. Persp. International Law Perspective

Int'l. L.Q. International Law Quarterly

Int'l. L. Rep. International Law Reports

Int'l L. Stud. International Law Studies (Naval War College)

Int. L.N. International Law Notes

Int. L. Notes International Law Notes (Eng.)

Int'l. Org. International Organization

Int'l Prop. Inv. J. International Property Investment Journal

Int. L.Q. International Law Quarterly

Int'l Org. International Organization

Int'l Rev. Ad. Sci. International Review of Administrative Sciences

Int'l. Rev. Crim. Policy International Review of Criminal Policy

Int'l. Rev. Ind. Prop. & C'right L. International Review of Industrial Property and Copyright Law

Int'l. Rev. Ind. Prop'y. & Copyr. International Review of Industrial Property and Copyright, Munich, Germany

Int'l. Rev. L. & Econ. International Review of Law and Economics

Int'l Soc. Sec. Rev. International Social Security Review

Int'l Soc'y of Barr. Q. International Society of Barristers Quarterly

Int'l Surv. L.D. L.L. International Survey of Legal Decisions on Labour Laws

Int'l Sym. Comp.L. International Symposium on Comparative Law

Int'l. Symp. on Comp. L. International Symposium on Comparative Law

Int'l Tax & Bus. Law International Tax & Business Lawyer

Int'l. Tax J. International Tax Journal

Int'l Tax Planning Man. (CCH) International Tax Planning Manual (Commerce Clearing House)

Int'l. Trade L. & Prac. International Trade Law and Practice

Int'l. Trade L.J. International Trade Law Journal

Int'l Trade Rep. (BNA) International Trade Reporter

Int'l Woman Law. International Woman Lawyer

Int. Org. International Organization

Intox. L. Intoxicating Liquor

Int. Persp. International Perspectives

Int. Private Law Private International Law

Intra. Intramural

Intramural L.J. Intramural Law Journal

Intra. L. Rev. (N.Y.U.) Intramural Law Review, New York University

Intra. L. Rev. (St.L.U.) Intramural Law Review, St. Louis University

Intra. L. Rev. (U.C.L.A.) Intramural Law Review, University of California at Los Angeles

Intramural L. Rev. Intramural Law Review

Int. Rev. Bull. Internal Revenue Bulletin

Int. Rev. Code Internal Revenue Code

Int. Rev. Code of 1954 Internal Revenue Code of 1954

Int. Rev. Crim. Pol. International Review of Criminal Policy (U.N.)

Int. Rev. Manual Internal Revenue Manual

Int. Rev. Rec. Internal Revenue Record

Introd. Introduction

Int. Tax Jour. International Tax Journal

Int. Trade L.J. International Trade Law Journal

Int. Woman L. International Woman Lawyer

Inv.
- Investment

- investor
- Invoice

Inv. Co. Investment companies and advisers

Invol. Serv. Involuntary servitude and peonage

Inv. Reg. Cas. Notes of Decisions of Appeal Court of Registration at Inverness (1835-53) (Sc.)

I.O. Law Opinions

I.O.C.C. Bull. Interstate Oil Compact Commission Bulletin

IOOC International Olive Oil Council

Iow. Iowa Reports (Iowa)

Iowa
- Iowa Reports
- Iowa Supreme Court Reports

Iowa Acts Acts and Joint Resolutions of the State of Iowa

Iowa Admin. Code Iowa Administrative Code

Iowa Admin. Bull. Iowa Administrative Bulletin

Iowa Bar Rev. Iowa Bar Review

Iowa B. Rev. Iowa Bar Review

Iowa Code Code of Iowa

Iowa Code Ann. Iowa Code Annotated

Iowa Const. Iowa Constitution

Iowa Law. Iowa Lawyer, The

Iowa L.B. Iowa Law Bulletin

Iowa L. Bull. Iowa Law Bulletin

Iowa Legis. Serv. Iowa Legislative Service (West)

Iowa L. Rev. Iowa Law Review

Iowa R.C. Iowa Railroad Commissioners Reports

Iowa S. B.A. Iowa State Bar Association Proceedings

Iowa St. B.A. News Bull. Iowa State Bar Association News Bulletin

Iowa St. B.A. Q. Iowa State Bar Assn. Quarterly

Iowa Univ. L. Bull. Iowa University Law Bulletin

Iowa W.C. S. Iowa Workmen's Compensation Comm. Reports

I.P.A.A. International Prisoners' Aid Association

I.P.A.L. Index to Periodical Articles Related to Law

I.P.C.
- International Classification of Patents for Invention (Council of Europe Convention)
- International Publishing Corporation

I.P.L.A. Institute of Public Loss Assessors

I.P.P. In Propria Persona (in person)

IPPC International Penal & Penitentiary Commission (UN)

I.P.P.F.
- International Penal and Penitentiary Foundation
- International Planned Parenthood Federation

IPT The Institute for Paralegal Training

IPU Inter-Parliamentary Union

IR. Law Reports (IR.)

I.R.
- Indian Rulings
- Industrial Relations
- Information Release
- Internal Revenue Decisions (U.S. Treasury Department)
- International Relations
- Irish Law Reports
- South Australian Industrial Reports

Ir.
- Iredell's North Carolina Law or Equity Reports
- Ireland
- Irish

1891 Ir. Law Reports, 1891, Irish

I.R.A. Individual Retirement Account

I.R. All. Indian Rulings, Allahabad Series

Iran-U.S. Cl. Trib. Rep. Iran - United States Claims Tribunal Reports

I.R.B. Internal Revenue Bulletin (U.S.)

I.R. Bom. Indian Rulings, Bombay Series

IRC International Red Cross

I.R.C. Internal Revenue Code (U.S.)

I.R. Cal. Indian Rulings, Calcutta Series

Ir. Ch. Irish Chancery Reports (1850-66)

Ir. Ch. Rep. Irish Chancery Reports

Ir. Cir. Irish Circuit Reports (1841-43)

IR Circ. Internal Revenue Circular

Ir. Cir. Cas. Crawford and Dix's Abridged Circuit Cases (1837-38) (Ir.)

Ir. Circ. Cas. Irish Circuit Cases

Ir. Circ. Rep. Irish Circuit Reports (1841-43)

Ir. Cir. Rep. Reports of Irish Circuit Cases

I.R.C.L. Irish Reports, Common Law Series

Ir.C.L. Irish Common Law Reports (1866-78)

Ir. Com. Law Rep.
- Irish Common Law Reports (1866-78)
- Irish Common Law Reports (2nd Series) (1850-66)

Ir. Com. L. Rep. Irish Common Law Reports

I. R. Comrs. Inland Revenue Commissioners (Eng.)

Ire. Ireland

Ir. Eccl. Irish Ecclesiastical Reports, by Milward. (1819-43)

Ired. Iredell's Reports (36-43 North Carolina Equity)

Ired. Dig. Iredell, North Carolina Digest

Ired. Eq. Iredell's Reports (36-43 N.C. Equity)

Ired. Eq. (N.C.) Iredell's Reports (36-43 North Carolina Equity)

Ired. L. Iredell's Reports (36-43 North Carolina Equity)

Ired. L. (NC) Iredell's Law Reports

I.R. Eq. Irish Reports, Equity Series

Ir. Eq. Irish Equity Reports

Ir. Eq. Rep. Irish Equity Reports

I.R. Fed. Ct. Indian Rulings, Federal Court

Irish Jur. The Irish Jurist

Irish L.T. Irish Law Times

I. R. Jour. Indian Rulings, Journal Section

Ir. Jur. Irish Jurist Reports (1849-66)

Ir. Jur. N.S.
- Irish Jurist (New Series) (1856-67)
- Irish Jurist (New Series)

Ir. Jur. Rep. Irish Jurist Reports (1849-66)

Ir. Jur. (Rep.) Irish Jurist Reports

Ir.L. Irish Law Reports. (1839-52)

I. R. Lah. Indian Rulings, Lahore Series

Ir. L. & Eq. Irish Law & Equity (1838-50)

Ir. Law & Ch. Irish Common Law and Chancery Reports (New Series) (1850-53)

Ir. Law & Eq. Irish Law and Equity Reports (1838-50)

Ir. Law Rec. Irish Law Recorder (1827-38)

Ir. Law Rec. N.S. Irish Law Recorder (New Series) (1833-38)

Ir. Law Rep. Irish Law Reports (1838-50)

Ir. Law Rep. N.S. Irish Common Law Reports

Ir. Law T. Irish Law Times

IRLIB Industrial Relations Legal Information Bulletin

Ir. L.J. Irish Law Journal (1895-1902)

Ir. L.N.S. Irish Common Law Reports

Ir. L.R.
- Irish Law Reports (1838-50)
- Irish Law Reports (1st Series) (1838-50)
- Irish Law Reports (4th Series) (1878-1893)

Ir. L. Rec. Irish Law Recorder (1st Series) (1827-1831)

Ir. L. Rec. N.S. Law Recorder (New Series, 6 vols.) (Ir.)

IR. L. Rec. lst ser. Law Recorder 1st Series, 4 vols. (Ir.)

Ir. L.T.
- Irish Law Times (1867)
- Irish Law Times and Solicitors Journal

Ir. L. Times and Solicitors' J. The Irish Law Times and Solicitors' Journal. A Weekly Gazette of Legal News and Information. Dublin, Ireland

Ir. L.T. J.
- Irish Law Times and Solicitors' Journal
- Irish Law Times Journal

Ir. L.T. Jour. Irish Law Times Journal

Ir. L.T. Journal Irish Law Times and Solicitors' Journal

Ir. L.T. R. Irish Law Times Reports

Ir. L.T. Rep. Irish Law Times Reports

IRM Internal Revenue Manual

I.R. Mad. Indian Rulings, Madras Series

I.R.-M.I.M. Published Internal Revenue Mimeograph

IRM Supp. Internal Revenue Manual Supplement

I.R. Nag. Indian Rulings, Nagpur Series

IR News Release Internal Revenue News Release

IRO International Refugee Organization (UN)

Irons Pol. Law Irons on Police Law

Irons Pub. H. Irons on Public Houses

I.R. Oudh Indian Rulings, Oudh Series

I.R. Pat. Indian Rulings, Patna Series

Ir. Pat. Off. Irish Patent Office

I.R.P.C. Indian Rulings, Privy Council (1929-47)

I.R. Pesh. Indian Rulings, Peshawar Series

I.R. Peshawar Indian Rulings, Peshawar Series (1933-47)

Ir. Pet. S.J. Irish Petty Sessions Journal

I.R. Pr.C. Indian Rulings, Privy Council

I.R.R. International Revenue Record (New York City)

Ir. R. Irish Law Reports (Ir.)

Ir. R. 1894 Irish Law Reports for year 1894

IR-Mim. Internal Revenue Mimeograph

I.R. Ran. Indian Rulings, Rangoon Series

Irrig. Irrigation

I.R.R. & L. Irish Reports, Registry Appeals in Court of Exchequer Chamber, and Appeals in Court for Land Cases Reserved

Ir.R. Ch. Irish Reports, Chancery

Ir.R. C.L. Irish Reports, Common Law Series (1867-78)

irreg. irregular

I.R. Rep. Reports of Inland Revenue Commissioners

Ir. Rep. Ch. Irish Reports, Chancery

Ir. Rep. C.L. Irish Reports. Common Law

Ir. Rep. Eq. Irish Reports, Equity

Ir. Rep. N.S. Irish Common Law Reports, New Series

Ir. Rep. V.R. Irish Reports, Verbatim Reprint

Ir. R. Eq. Irish Reports, Equity Series (1866-78)

I.R.R. Newsl. Individual Rights and Responsibilities Newsletter

Ir. R. Reg. & L. Irish Reports, Registry & Land Cases (1868-76)

Ir. R. Reg. App. Irish Reports, Registration Appeals (1868-76)

IRS Internal Revenue Service

I.R. Sind. Indian Rulings, Sind Series

IRS Mem. (P-H) Internal Memoranda of the IRS

Ir. Soc'y for Lab. L.J. Irish Society for Labor Law Journal

IRS Pos. (CCH) Internal Revenue Service Positions

IRS Pub. Internal Revenue Service Publication

Ir. Stat. Irish Statutes

Ir. St. Tr. Irish State Trials (Ridgeway's)

Ir. Term Rep. Irish Term Reports (by Ridgeway, Lapp & Schoales)

Ir. T.R. Irish Term Reports (by Ridgeway, Lapp & Schoales) (1793-95)

Irv. Irvine's Scotch Justiciary Reports (1851-68)

Irv. Civ. Law Irving's Civil Law

Irvine Just.Cas. Irvine's Justiciary Cases

Irving, Civ. Law Irving's Civil Law

Irv.Just. Irvine's Justiciary Cases (Eng.)

Ir. W.C.C. Irish Workmen's Compensation Cases

Irwin's Code Clark, Cobb and Irwin's Code (Ga.)

Ir. W.L.R. Irish Weekly Law Reports (1895-1902)

Is.
- Islands
- Isles

ISBA Indiana State Bar Association

ISBD International Standard Bibliographic Description

ISE Institute for Shipboard Education

I.S.F. International Shipping Federation

I.S.L.L. International Survey of Legal Decisions on Labour Law (1925-1938)

ISL L. Rev. ISL Law Review

I.S. L.R. International Survey of Legal Decisions on Labour Law

Is. L.R. Israel Law Review. Jerusalem, Israel

I.S.M.A.C. Israel-Syrian Mixed Armistice Commission

ISO International Sugar Organization

Isr. Israel

Israel L. Rev. Israel Law Review

Israel Stud. Criminol. Israel Studies in Criminology, Jerusalem, Israel

Israel Y.B. Human Rights Israel Yearbook on Human Rights

Israel Yb. of Human Rights Israel Yearbook of Human Rights, Tel Aviv, Israel

Isr. L. Rev. Israel Law Review

Iss. Issue

Issues Crim.

Issues L. & Med. Issues in Law & Medicine　Issues in Criminology

IT
- Indian Territory Reports
- Turner, Irrevocable Trusts

IT(2) Turner, Irrevocable Trusts, Second Edition

I.T.
- Income Tax Division Ruling (U.S. Internal Revenue Bureau)
- Income Tax Unit Ruling

It.
- Italian
- Italy

Ital.
- Italian
- Italic

Italian Yb. of Int'l. L. Italian Yearbook of International Law, Napoli, Italy

IT & T International Telephone & Telegraph Co.

ITC International Tin Council

I.T.C. Spinivasan's Reports of Income Tax Cases (India)

I.T.D.A. Income Tax Decisions of Australia

ITII International Tax Institute, Inc.

I.T. Info. Income Tax Information Release (U.S.)

I.T.J. Indian Tax Journal

I.T. L.J. Income Tax Law Journal (India)

ITO International Trade Organization (UN)

ITP Hertzburg, Kaye & Plaia, International Trade Practice

I.T.R.
- Australian Income Tax Reports
- Income Tax Reports (India)
- Irish Term Reports (Ridgeway, Lapp & Schoales)

ITS International Trading Service

I.T.S. International Trade Secretaries

ITU
- Income Tax Unit Order
- International Telecommunication Union (UN)

IUE International Union of Electrical, Radio and Machine Workers

I.U.L.A. International Union of Local Authorities

IUOTA International Union of Official Travel Organizations

Iv. Ersk. Ivory's Notes on Erskine's Institutes

Ives Mil. Law Ives on Military Law

IVT Cohan & Hemmerling, Inter Vivos Trusts

IW Aron, Duffy and Rosner, Impeachment of Witnesses: The Cross-Examiner's Art

IWC
- International Whaling Commission
- International Wheat Council

IWTO International Wool Textile Organization

J

J.
- Institutes of Justinian
- Japanese
- Johnson's New York Reports
- Journal
- Judge
- Judgment
- Judiciary
- Jurisprudence
- Justice
- Justice of the U.S. Supreme Court
- Justiciary Cases (Scotland)
- Juta's South African Reports
- Lower Canada Jurist (Quebec) (1848-91)
- Scottish Jurist (1829-73)

j   dissenting opinion citation in dissenting opinion (used in- Shepard's Citations)

J.A.
- Joint Appendix
- Judge Advocate
- Justice of Appeal

Ja.   James

J.A.A.   Journal of African Administration

J.A.A.M.L.   Journal of American Academy of Matrimonial Lawyers

JAC   Jacobus (James) (Eng. statutes)

Jac.
- Jacob's English Chancery Reports (1821-22)

- Jacob's Law Dictionary
- Jacobus (King James), as 21 Jac.1

Jac. & W.   Jacob & Walker's English Chancery Reports (37 ER)

Jac. & Walk.   Jacob & Walker's English Chancery Reports (37 ER)

Jac. & W. (Eng.)   Jacob & Walker's English Chancery Reports (37 ER)

J. Account.   Journal of Accountancy

J. Accountancy   Journal of Accountancy

J. Acct.   Journal of Accountancy

Jac. Dict.   Jacob's Law Dictionary

Jac. Fish. Dig.   Jacob's American edition of Fisher's English Digest

Jac. Int.   Jacob's Introduction to the Common, Civil, and Canon Law

Jack.   Jackson (Ga.)

Jack & G. Landl. & Ten.   Jackson & Gross, Treatise on the Law of Landlord and Tenant in Pennsylvania

Jack. & L.   Jackson & Lumpkin (Ga.)

Jack. Geo. Ind.   Jackson's Index to the Georgia Reports

Jack Pl.   Jackson, Pleadings. 1933

Jackson
- Jackson's Reports (46-58 Georgia)
- Jackson's Reports (1-29 Texas Appeals)

Jackson & Lumpkin Jackson & Lumpkin's Reports (59-64 Georgia)

Jack. Tex. App. Jackson's Reports (1-29 Court of Appeals Reports)

Jac. Law Dict. Jacob's Law Dictionary

Jac. L.D. Jacob's Law Dictionary

Jac. L.Dict. Jacob's Law Dictionary

Jac. Lex Mer. Jacob's Lex Mercatoria, or the Merchants' Companion

Jac. L.G. Jacob's Law Grammar

Jacob.
- Jacob's Chancery Reports (1821-22)
- Jacob's Law Dictionary, 16 editions (1729-1835)

Jac. Sea Laws. Jacobsen's Law of the Sea

J. Admin. Overseas Journal of Administration Overseas

J. Adv. Judge Advocate

JAEC Headquarters, United States Air Force

Jaeger, Labor Law. Jaeger's Cases and Statutes on Labor Law

J.A.F. Judge Advocate of the Fleet

J. African L. Journal of African Law

J. Afr. L. Journal of African Law

JAG Judge Advocate General

JAGA Military Affairs Division, Office of Judge Advocate General, U.S.Army

JAG Bull. JAG Bulletin (USAF)

JAGC Judge Advocate General's Corps

JAG C.M.R.(A.F.) Judge Advocate General Court Martial Reports

JAG COMPC.M.O.(Navy) Judge Advocate General Compilation of Court Martial Orders(Navy)

JAG (Def.Dept.) Holdings & Decisions of Judge Advocate General Boards of Review & United States Court of Military Appeals

JAG Dig. Op. Judge Advocate General Digest of Opinions

Jagg. Torts. Jaggard on Torts

JAG J. JAG Journal

JAG J. JAG Journal

JAG L. Rev. United States Air Force Judge Advocate General Law Review

JAG Man. Manual of the Judge Advocate General (Navy)

J. Agr. Tax'n & L. Journal of Agricultural Taxation and the Law

JAGS Judge Advocate General's School

JAGT. Procurement Division, Judge Advocate General, U.S. Army

Jaipur L.J. Jaipur Law Journal (India)

J. Air. L. Journal of Air Law

J. Air L. & Com. Journal of Air Law and Commerce

J.A.J. Judge Advocate Journal

J.A.L. Journal of African Law, London, England

J.A.L.T. Journal of the Association of Law Teachers

Jam. Jamaica

JAMA Journal of the American Medical Association

J. Am. Acad. Matrimonial Law Journal of the American Academy of Matrimonial Lawyers

Jamaica L.R.C. Jamaica Law Reform Committee

J. Am. Bankers' Assn. Journal of American Bankers Association

James James' Reports (2 Nova Scotia)

James. & Mont. Jameson & Montagu's English Bankruptcy Reports (in vol. 2 Glyn& Jameson) (1821-28)

James Bk. L. James' Bankrupt Law

James. Const. Con. Jameson's Constitutional Convention

James Ct. Mar. James on Courts-Martial

James Fr. Soc. James' Guide to Friendly Societies

James J.S. James' Law of Joint Stock Companies

James (N.Sc.) James' Reports (2 Nova Scotia)

James Op. James, Opinions, Charges, etc.

James Salv. James, Salvage. 1867

James Sel. Cas. James' Select Cases, Nova Scotia

James Sel. Cases. James' Select Cases, Nova Scotia (1835-55)

James Sh. James, Merchant Shipping. 1866

J. Am. Jud. Soc. Journal of American Judicature Society

J. Am. Jud. Soc'y. Journal of the American Judicature Society

Jam. L.J. Jamaica Law Journal

J. Am. Soc. C.L.U. Journal of American Society of Chartered Life Underwriters

J. Am. Soc'y C.L.U.
- Journal of the American Society of CLU
- Journal of American Society of Chartered Life Underwriters

Jam. St. Jamaica Statutes

Jan. Angl. Jani Anglorum facies Nova (1680)

J. & C. Jones & Cary's Irish Exchequer Reports (1838-39)

J. & H. Johnson & Hemming's English Vice Chancellors' Reports

J. & H. Hind. L. Johnson & Houghton's Institutes of Hindoo Law

J.& K. All India Reporter, Jammu and Kashmir

J. & L. Jones & La Touche's Irish Chancery Reports

J. & La T. Jones & La Touche's Irish Chancery Reports

J. & Lat. Jones & La Touche's Irish Chancery Reports

J. & S.
- Jebb and Syms (1838-40) (Ir.)
- Jones & Spencer's Reports (33-61 New York Superior)
- Judah and Swan Reports, Jamaica (1839)

J. & S. Jam. Judah & Swan's Jamaica Reports

J. & V. Jones & Varick, Laws of New York

J. & W. Jacob & Walker's English Chancery Reports (1819-21)

Japan Japan

Japan Ann. L. & Pol. Japan Annual of Law and Politics

Jap. Ann. Intl. L. Japanese Annual of International Law, Tokyo, Japan

Jap. Ann. of Law & Pol. Japan Annual of Law and Politics, Tokyo, Japan

Jar. & By. Conv. Jarman & Bythewood's Conveyancing

Jar. Chy. Pr. Jarman's Chancery Practice

Jar. Cr. Tr. Jardine's Criminal Trials

Jard. Ind. Jardine's Index to Howell's State Trials

Jarm. Jarman

Jar. Pow. Dev. Jarman's Edition of Powell on Devises

Jar. Prec. Bythewood & Jarman's Precedents

J. Arts Mgt. & L. Journal of Arts Management & Law

J. Arts Mgmt. & L. Journal of Arts Management & Law

Jar. Wills. Jarman on Wills 8 editions, (1841-51)

Jas. James

J. As. Judicial Assessor (Ghana)

J. Ass'n. L. Teachers Journal of the Association of Law Teachers

J. Assoc. L. Teachers Journal of the Association of Law Teachers (The Law Teacher),London, England

JATLA Journal of American Trial Lawyers Association

JATLA L.J. Journal of American Trial Lawyers Association Law Journal

Jay W. Jaywardine's Appeal Cases (Ceylon)

J.B. Jurum Baccalaureus, Bachelor of Laws

J.B.A.D.C. Journal of Bar Assn. of the District of Columbia

J.B.A. Dist. Colum. Journal of the Bar Association of the District of Columbia

J.B.A. Kan. Journal of Bar Association of Kansas

J.B. Ass'n D.C. Journal of the Bar Association of the District of Columbia

J.B. Ass'n. St. Kan. Journal of the Bar Association of the State of Kansas

J.B.C. Journal of the State Bar of California

J. Beverly Hills B.A. Journal of the Beverly Hills Bar Association

J. Beverly Hills B. Ass'n Journal of the Beverly Hills Bar Association

J. Bev. Hills B.A. Journal of the Beverly Hills Bar Association

J.B.K. Journal of the Bar Association of the State of Kansas

J.B.L. The Journal of Business Law

J.B. Moo. J.B. Moore's Common Pleas Reports, Eng.

J.B. Moore J.B. Moore's Common Pleas Reports

J.B. Moore (Eng.) J.B. Moore's English Common Pleas Reports

J.Bridg. Sir John Bridgman's Reports, Common Pleas, English (123 ER)

J. Bridg. (Eng.) Sir John Bridgman's Reports, Common Pleas (123 ER)

J. Bridgm. Sir John Bridgman's Reports, Common Pleas, English (123 ER)

J. Broadcast. Journal of Broadcasting

J. Broadcasting Journal of Broadcasting

J. Broadcasting & Electronic Media Journal of Broadcasting & Electronic Media

J. Bus. L. Journal of Business Law

J.C.
- Johnson's Cases or Reports (N.Y.)
- Justiciary Cases (Sc.)

JCAE Joint Committee on Atomic Energy

J. Can. B.A. Journal of the Canadian Bar Association

J. Can. B. Ass'n. Journal of the Canadian Bar Association

J.C. & U.L. Journal of College and University Law

J.C.B.
- Juris Canonici Bachelor
- Kansas Judicial Council Bulletin

J.C.C. Joint Consultative Document

J.C.D.
- Juris Canonici Doctor (Doctor of Canon Law)
- Juris Civilis Doctor (Doctor of Civil Law)

J. Ceylon L. Journal of Ceylon Law

J. Ch. Johnson's New York Chancery Reports

J. Chinese L. Journal of Chinese Law

J. Chin. L. Journal of Chinese Law

J. Christ. Juris. Journal of Christian Jurisprudence

J. Church & St. Journal of Church and State

J. Church S. Journal of Church and State

J. Cin. B.A. Journal of the Cincinnati Bar Association

J.C.L.
- Journal of Criminal Law
- Juris Canonici Lector

J.C.L. & I.L. Journal of Comparative Legislation & International Law

J. CLU Journal of the American Society of CLU

J.C.N.P.S. Journal of Collective Negotiation in Public Sector

J. Coll. & U.L. Journal of College and University Law

J. Coll. & Univ. L. Journal of College and University Law

J. Collective Negot. Pub. Sector Journal of Collective Negotiations in the Public Sector

J. Commerce Journal of Commerce

J. Comm. Mt. Stud. Journal of Common Market Studies

J. Common Mkt. Stud. Journal of Common Market Studies

J. Common Market Stud. Journal of Common Market Studies

J. Common Market Studies. Journal of Common Market Studies

J. Comp. Corp. L. & Sec. Reg. Journal of Comparative Corporate Law & Securities Regulation

J. Comp. Leg. Journal of Society of Comparative Legislation (London)

J. Comp. Leg. & Int. Law Journal of Comparative Legislation & International Law

J. Comp. Leg. & Int'l. L.3d Journal of Comparative Legislation and International Law, Third Series

J. Conat. Law Journal of Conational Law

J. Confl. Res. Journal of Conflict Resolution

J. Cons. Affairs Journal of Consumer Affairs

J. Const. & Parliam. Stud. Journal of Constitutional and Parliamentary Studies, Geneva,Switzerland

J. Const. & Parl. Stud. Journal of Constitutional and Parliamentary Studies

J. Contemp. Crim. Just. Journal of Contemporary Criminal Justice

J. Contemp Health L & Policy Journal of Contemporary Health Law & Policy

J. Contemp. Health L. & Pol'y The Journal of Contemporary Health Law & Policy

J. Contemp. L. Journal of Contemporary Law

J. Contemp. Legal Issues Journal of Contemporary Legal Issues

J. Contemp.R.D.L. Journal of Contemporary Roman-Dutch Law

J. Cont. L. Journal of Contract Law

J. Copr. Soc'y Journal of the Copyright Society of the U.S.A.

J. Copyright, Ent. & Sports L. Journal of Copyright, Entertainment & Sports Law

J. Copyright Entertainment Sports L. Journal of Copyright Entertainment and Sports Law

J. Copyright Soc'y. U.S.A. Journal of the Copyright Society of the U.S.A.

J. Corp. Disclosure & Confid. Journal of Corporate Disclosure and Confidentiality

J. Corp. L. Journal of Corporation Law

J. Corpn. L. Journal of Corporation Law

J. Corp. Tax. Journal of Corporate Taxation

J. Corp. Tax'n Journal of Corporate Taxation

J.C.R.
- Johnson's Chancery (New York)
- Judicial Council Reports

J.C. Rettie Rettie, Crawford and Melville's Court of Session Cases, 4th Series (1873-98) (Sc.)

J Crim L & Criminal Journal of Criminal Law & Criminology

J.Crim. Just. Journal of Criminal Justice

J. Crim. L.
- Journal of Criminal Law
- Journal of Criminal Law & Criminology

J. Crim. L. & Crim. Journal of Criminal Law and Criminology

J. Crim. L. & Criminology Journal of Criminal Law and Criminology

J. Crim. Law.
- Journal of American Institute of Criminal Law & Criminology(Chicago)
- Journal of Criminal Law

J. Crim. L., C. & P.S. Journal of Criminal Law, Criminology and Police Science

J. Crim. L.(Eng.) Journal of Criminal Law (Eng.)

J. Crim. Sci. Journal of Criminal Science

JCS Joint Chiefs of Staff (U.S.)

Jctus Jurisconsultus

JD, J.D.
- Judicial District
- Juris Doctor
- Doctor of Jurisprudence

JDC Judicial District Court

J.Denning L.S. Journal of the Denning Law Society (Tanzania)

J.Denning L.Soc'y Journal of the Denning Law Society

J. Dev. Planning Journal of Development Planning

J. Disp. Resol. Journal of Dispute Resolution

J. Dispute Resolution Journal of Dispute Resolution

J.d'Ol. Les Jugemens d'Oleron

J.D.R. Juta's Daily Reporter, Cape Provincial Division (South Africa)

J. Drug Issues Journal of Drug Issues

Jeaf. Jeaffreson's Book about Lawyers

Jebb. Jebb's Irish Crown Cases (1822-40)

Jebb. & B. Jebb & Bourke's Irish Queen's Bench Reports (1841-42)

Jebb. & B.(Ir.) Jebb & Bourke's Irish Queen's Bench Reports (1841-42)

Jebb. & S. Jebb & Symes' Irish Queen's Bench Reports (1838-41)

Jebb & S.(Ir.) Jebb & Symes' Irish Queen's Bench Reports

Jebb & Sym. Jebb & Symes' Irish Queen's Bench Reports

Jebb. C.C. Jebb's Irish Crown Cases (1822-40)

Jebb. C.C.(Ir.) Jebb's Irish Crown Cases (1822-40)

Jebb Cr. & Pr. Cas. Jebb's Irish Crown and Presentment Cases

J. Econ. Persp. Journal of Economic Perspectives

J. Educ. Fin. Journal of Education Finance

Jeff. Jefferson's Reports (Virginia General Court)

Jeff. Man. Jefferson's Manual of Parliamentary Law

Jeff.(Va.) Jefferson's Reports (Virginia General Court)

Jenck. Bills Jencken, Bills of Exchange. 1880

Jenck. Neg. B. Jencken on Bills of Exchange, & c.

Jenck. Neg. S. Jencken, Negotiable Securities. 1880

J. Energy & Devel. Journal of Energy and Development

J. Energy & Natural Resources L. Journal of Energy & Natural Resources Law

J. Energy L. & Pol'y. Journal of Energy Law & Policy

J. Energy Nat. Resources & Envtl. L. Journal of Energy, Natural Resources & Environmental Law

Jenk. Jenkins, Eight Centuries of Reports, English Exchequer, 1220-1623(145 ER)

Jenk. & Formoy Jenkinson & Formoy's Select Cases in the Exchequer of Pleas.(Selden Society Publication, v. 48)

Jenk. Cent. Jenkins, Eight Centuries of Reports, English Exchequer, 1220-1623(145 ER)

Jenk. Cl. Ass. Jenkins' Clerk's Assistant

Jenkins (Eng.) Jenkins, Eight Centuries of Reports, English Exchequer, 1220-1623(145 ER)

Jenks Jenks' Reports (58 New Hampshire)

Jenn. Jennison's Reports (14-18 Michigan).

Jenn. Sug. A. Jennett's Sugden Acts

J. Envir L & Litig Journal of Environmental Law and Litigation

J. Envtl. L. Journal of Environmental Law

J. Envtl. L. & Litig. Journal of Environmental Law & Litigation

Jer. Car. Jeremy on Carriers

Jer. Dig. Jeremy's Digest (1817-49)

Jeremy, Eq. Jeremy's Equity Jurisdiction

Jeremy, Eq. Jur. Jeremy's Equity Jurisdiction

Jer. Eq. Jur. Jeremy's Equity Jurisdiction

Jerr. Copyr. Jerrold on Copyright

Jerv. Cor. Jervis, Coroners. 9ed. 1957

Jerv. N.R. Jervis' New Rules

Jes. Analysis and Digest of the Decisions of Sir George Jessel(England)

J. Eth. L. Journal of Ethiopian Law

Jev. Cr. Law Jevons on Criminal Law

Jew. Y.B. Int'l L. Jewish Yearbook of International Law

J. Family L. Journal of Family

J. Fam. L. Journal of Family Law

J. Fin. Journal of Finance

JFMIP Joint Financial Management Improvement Program

J. Forensic Sci. Journal of Forensic Sciences

J. For. Med. Journal of Forensic Medicine

J. For. Med. Soc'y Journal of the Forensic Medicine Society

J. For. Sci. Journal of Forensic Sciences

J. For. Sci. Soc. Journal of the Forensic Science Society

J. For. Sci. Soc'y. Journal of the Forensic Science Society

J. Glos. Juncta Glossa

J.H. Journal, House of Representatives (U.S.)

J. Health & Hosp. L. Journal of Health and Hospital Law

J. Health Pol. Journal of Health Politics, Policy and Law

J.Health Pol. Pol'y & L. Journal of Health, Politics, Policy & Law

J.I.C.J. Journal of the International Commission of Jurists

Jick. Est. Jickling, Legal and Equitable Estates. 1829

J.I.L. Japan Institute of Labour

J.I.L.I. Journal of the Indian Law Institute

J.I.L.T.A. Journal of the Indian Law Teachers Association Affairs

J. Ind. L. Inst. Journal of the Indian Law Institute

J. Int'l Aff. Journal of International Affairs

J. Int'l Arb. Journal of International Arbitration

J. Int'l & Comp. L. Journal of International & Comparative Law

J. Int. L. & Econ. Journal of International Law and Economics

J. Int. L. & Pol. Journal of International Law and Politics

J. Int. Law & Econ. Journal of International Law & Economics

J. Int'l Comm. Jur. Journal of the International Commission of Jurists

J. Int'l L. & Dipl. Journal of International Law and Diplomacy

J.Int'l.L. & Econ. Journal of International Law and Economics

J. Intl. L. & Pol. Journal of International Law and Politics

J. Int'l Money & Fin. Journal of International Money and Finance

J. Ir. Soc. Lab. L. Journal of the Irish Society for Labour Law

J. Islam & Comp. L. Journal of Islamic and Comparative Law (Nig.)

J.I.T. Job Instruction Training

J.J.
- Judges
- Junior Judge
- Justices

JJ.A. Justices of Appeal

J.J.Mar. Marshall's Reports (24-30 Kentucky)

J.J.Marsh. J.J Marshall's Kentucky Supreme Court Reports (1829-1832)

J.J.Marsh.(Ky.) Marshall's Reports (24-30 Kentucky)

JJ.S.C. Justices of the Supreme Court

J. Jur. Journal of Jurisprudence

J. Juris. Journal of Jurisprudence

J. Jur. Papyrol. Journal of Juristic Papyrology, Warsaw, Poland

J. Juv. L. Journal of Juvenile Law

J. Kan.B.A. Journal of Kansas Bar Association

J. Kan. B. Ass'n Journal of the Kansas Bar Association

J.K.B. Justice of the King 's Bench

J. Kel. Sir John Kelyng's English Crown Cases (84 ER)

J. Kelyng Sir John Kelyng's Crown Cases (1662-1707) (84 ER)

J. Kelyng (Eng.) Sir John Kelyng's English Crown Cases (84 ER)

J.L.
  • Journal of Law

J. Lab. Res. Journal of Labor Research

J. Land & Pub. Util. Econ. Journal of Land & Public Utility Economics

J L & Commerce Journal of Law and Commerce

J. Land & P.U. Econ. Journal of Land and Public Utility Economics

J.L. & Com. Journal of Law and Commerce (Hong Kong)

J.L. & Com. Soc. Journal of the Law and Commerce Society (Hong Kong)

J.L. & Econ. Journal of Law & Economics

J.L. & Econ. Dev. Journal of Law and Economic Development

J.L. & Econ. Develop. The Journal of Law & Economic Development

J.L. & Educ. Journal of Law & Education

J.L. & Health Journal of Law & Health

J.L. & Info. Sci. Journal of Law & Information Science

J.L. & Pol. Journal of Law and Politics

J.L. & Religion Journal of Law and Religion

J.L. & Soc. Pol'y Journal of Law and Social Policy

J. L. & Tech. Journal of Law and Technology

J. Land Use & Envtl. L. Journal of Land Use & Environmental Law

J.Law & Econ. Journal of Law and Economics

J. Law & Econ. Dev. Journal of Law and Economic Development

J. Law & Ed. Journal of Law and Education

J. Law & Health Journal of Law and Health

J. Law & Pol. Journal of Law and Politics

J. Law & Tech. Journal of Law & Technology

J. Law, Econ. & Org. Journal of Law, Economics and Organization

J. Law Reform Journal of Law Reform

J. Law Soc. Sc. Journal of the Law Society of Scotland

J. Law Soc'y, Scotland Law Society of Scotland, Journal, Edinburgh, Scotland

J. Legal Ed.   Journal of Legal Education

J. Legal Educ.   Journal of Legal Education

J. Legal Hist.   Journal of Legal History

J. Legal Med.   Journal of Legal Medicine

J. Legal Pluralism   Journal of Legal Pluralism

J. Legal Prof.   Journal of the Legal Profession

J. Legal Stud.   Journal of Legal Studies

J. Legal Studies   Journal of Legal Studies

J. Leg. Ed.   Journal of Legal Education

J. Leg. Hist.   Journal of Legal History

J. Legis.   Journal of Legislation

J. Leg. Med.   Journal of Legal Medicine

J. Leg. Prof.   Journal of the Legal Profession

J.L.R.
- Jamaica Law Reports (1953-55)
- Johore Law Reports (India)

J.L.S.   Journal of the Law Society of Scotland

J.L.Soc.   Journal of the Law Society of Scotland

J. L. Soc. Scotland   Journal of the Law Society of Scotland

J. L. Soc'y.   Journal of the Law Society of Scotland

J. L. Soc'y Scot.   Journal of the Law Society of Scotland

J.M.   Master of Jurisprudence

J. Mal. & Comp. L.   Journal of Malaysian and Comparative Law

J. Mar.   John Marshall

J Marit L & Comm   Journal of Maritime Law & Commerce

J. Maritime L.   Journal of Maritime Law & Commerce

J. Mar. J. Prac. & Proc.   John Marshall Journal of Practice and Procedure

J. Mar. L. & Com.   Journal of Maritime Law and Commerce

J. Mar. Law & Com.   Journal of Maritime Law and Commerce

J. Mar. L.J.   John Marshall Law Journal

J. Mar. L.R.   John Marshall Law Review

J. Mar. L.Q.   John Marshall Law Quarterly

J. Mar. L. Rev.   John Marshall Law Review

J. Marshall J.   John Marshall Journal of Practice and Procedure

J. Med. & Phil.   Journal of Medicine and Philosophy

J. Min. L. & Pol'y   Journal of Mineral Law & Policy

J.M.J.   John Marshall Journal of Practice & Procedure

JMLS   John Marshall Law School

J.O.   Official Journal of the European Communities

John Marshall L Rev   John Marshall Law Review

J. Mo. B.   Journal of the Missouri Bar

J. Mo. Bar Journal of the Missouri Bar

J.N.A. Referees Bank. Journal of the National Association of Referees in Bankruptcy

J.N.C. Referees Bank. Journal of the National Conference of Referees in Bankruptcy

Jnt. Stk. Co. Joint Stock Company

Jnt. Ven. Joint Venture

Jo. Jones' Exchequer Reports (1834-1838) (Ir.)

Jo. & Car. Jones and Carey's Reports, Exchequer, Ireland (1838-39)

Jo. & La.T. Jones & La Touche, Irish Chancery Reports, 3 vols. (1844-46)

Jo. & Lat. Jones & La Touche's Chancery Reports (1844-46) (Ir.)

Job Discrim. Job discrimination

J.O.B.S. Job Opportunities in the Business Sector

Jo. Ch. Johnson's Chancery (N.Y.)

Jo. Ex. Ir. Jones' Exchequer Reports (Ir.)

Jo. Ex. Pro.W. Jones' Exchequer Proceedings Concerning Wales (1939)

J. of Account. Journal of Accountancy

J. of Afr. L. Journal of African Law. London

J. of Air L. & Commerce Journal of Air Law and Commerce

J.of Business Journal of Business

J. of Bus. L. The Journal of Business Law. London.

J. of Ceylon L. The Journal of Ceylon Law. Colombo, Ceylon

J. of Conflict Resolution Journal of Conflict Resolution

J. of Ethiop. L. Journal of Ethiopian Law. Addis Abada, Ethiopia

J. of Ins. of Arbitrators Journal of the Institute of Arbitrators

J. of Internat. L.and Econ. The Journal of International Law and Economics.

J. of J.Bassett Moore Soc'y Intl Law Virginia Journal of International Law

J. of L. and Econ. The Journal of Law and Economics.

J. of Law & Politics Journal of Law and Politics, Nishinomiva, Japan

J. of Leg. Educ. Journal of Legal Education.

J. of Leg. Stud. The Journal of Legal Studies.

J. of Marit. L. and Commerce Journal of Maritime Law and Commerce.

J. of Publ. L. Journal of Public Law.

J. of Space L. Journal of Space Law.

J. of the B.A. of Kansas The Journal of the Bar Association of the State of Kansas

J. of the L. Soc. of Scotl. Journal of the Law Society of Scotland. Edinburgh, Scotland

J. of the Soc. of Publ.Teachers of L. The Journal of the Society of Public Teachers of Law. London

J. of Urban L. Journal of Urban Law.

Joh. Ch. Rep. Johnson's Chancery Reports (N.Y.)

John.
- Chase's Circuit Court Decisions, ed., by Johnson, U.S.
- Johnson's English Vice Chancellors' Reports (1858-60)
- Johnson's New York Reports
- Johnson's Reports (Md.Ch.)
- Johnson's Reports (N.Y.Sup. or Ch.)

John. Am. Not. John's American Notaries

John. & H. Johnson and Hemming's English Chancery Reports

John. Cas. Johnson's Cases (N.Y.)

John. Chan. Johnson's Chancery Reports (N.Y.)

John. Ch. Rep. Johnson's Chancery Reports (N.Y.)

John. Dict. Johnson's English Dictionary

John. Eng. Ch. Johnson's English ViceChancellors' Reports

John Mar. J. Prac. & Proc. John Marshall Journal of Practice and Procedure

John Marshall Jr. John Marshall Journal of Practice and Procedure

John Marshall L.J. John Marshall Law Journal

John Marshall L.Q. John Marshall Law Quarterly

John Marsh. L.J. John Marshall Law Journal

John Marsh. L.Q. John Marshall Law Quarterly

John Marsh. L. Rev. John Marshall Law Review

John[s].
- Chase's Circuit Court Decisions, edited by Johnson (U.S.)
- Johnson's Reports (Md. Chancery)
- Johnson's Reports (New York Supreme or Chancery)
- Johnson's Vice-Chancery Reports (Eng.)

Johns. & H. Johnson & Hemming's English Chancery Reports (70 ER)

Johns, & Hem. Johnson & Hemming's English Chancery Reports (70 ER)

Johns. & H.(Eng.) Johnson & Hemming's English Chancery Reports (70 ER)

Johns. Bills Johnson, Bills of Exchange. 2ed. 1839

Johns. C. Johnson's Cases (N.Y.)

Johns. Cas. Johnson's Cases (New York) (1799-1803)

Johns. Cases Johnson's Cases (N.Y.)

Johns. Cas.(N.Y.) Johnson's Cases (New York 1799-1803)

Johns. Ch.
- Johnson's Chancery Reports (N.Y. 1814-23)
- Johnson's Maryland Chancery Decisions
- Johnson's Vice-Chancery Reports (Eng.)

Johns. Ch. Cas. Johnson's Chancery Reports (New York)

Johns. Ch.(N.Y.) Johnson's Chancery Reports (New York)

Johns. Civ. L. Sp.   Johnson's Civil Law of Spain

Johns. Ct. Err.   Johnson's Reports, New York Court of Errors

Johns. Dec.   Johnson's Maryland Chancery Decisions

Johns. Eccl. L.   Johnson's Ecclesiastical Law

Johns. Eng. Ch.   Johnson's English Chancery Reports

Johns. H.R.V.   Johnson's Chancery Reports (1859) (70 ER)

Johns. Mar. R.   Johnson on Maritime Rights

Johns.(N.Y.)   Johnson's New York Reports

Johns. N.Z.   Johnson's New Zealand Reports

Johnson.
- Johnson's English Vice Chancellors' Reports
- Johnson's Maryland Chancery Decisions
- Johnson's Reports, New York

Johnson N.Y.R.   Johnson's Reports (N.Y.)

Johnson R.   Johnson's Reports (N.Y.)

Johnson's Cases in Error   Johnson's Cases (N.Y.)

Johnson's Quarto Dict.   Johnson's Quarto Dictionary

Johnson's Rep.   Johnson's Reports (N.Y.)

Johns. Pat. Man.   Johnson's Patent Manual

Johns. R.   Johnson's Reports (N.Y.)

Johns. Rep.   Johnson's Reports, New York Supreme Court

Johnst. Inst.   Johnston's Institutes of the Laws of Spain

Johnst.(N.Z.)   Johnston's Reports, New Zealand

Johns. Tr.   Johnson's Impeachment Trial

Johns. U.S.   Johnson's Reports of Chase's United States Circuit Court Decisions

Johns. V.C.   Johnson's English Vice Chancellors' Reports (70 ER)

Johns. V.C.(Eng.)   Johnson's English Vice-Chancellor's Reports (70 ER)

Jo. Jur.   Journal of Jurisprudence

Jon.
- Jones' Irish Exchequer Reports (Ir.)
- T. Jones' King's Bench & Common Pleas Reports (Eng.)
- W. Jones' King's Bench & Common Pleas Reports (Eng.)

Jon. & Car.   Jones & Cary's Irish Exchequer Reports (1838-39)

Jon. & L.   Jones & La Touche's Irish Chancery Reports

Jon. & La.T.   Jones & La Touche's Irish Chancery Reports

Jones
- Jones' Irish Exchequer Reports (1834-38)
- Jones' Reports (43-48, 52-57, 61, 62 Alabama)
- Jones' Reports (22-30 Missouri)
- Jones' Reports (N.C. Law or Equity) (1853-63)
- Jones' Reports (11, 12 Pennsylvania)
- Jones, T., King's Bench (Eng.)

- Jones' Upper Canada Common Pleas Reports (1850-82)
- Jones, W., King's Bench (Eng.)

Jones 1. Sir William Jones' English King's Bench Reports (1620-41)

Jones 2. Sir Thomas Jones English King's Bench Reports (1667-85)

Jones & C. Jones & Cary's Irish Exchequer Reports (1838-39)

Jones & H. Hind. Law Jones & Haughton's Hindoo Law

Jones & L. Jones & La Touche's Irish Chancery Reports

Jones & La T. Jones & La Touche's Irish Chancery Reports

Jones & L. (Ir.) Jones & La Touche's Irish Chancery Reports

Jones & McM. Jones & McMurtrie's Pennsylvania Supreme Court Reports

Jones & McM. (Pa.) Jones & McMurtrie's Pennsylvania Supreme Court Reports

Jones & S. Jones & Spencer's Reports (33-61 New York Superior)

Jones & Sp. Jones & Spencer's Reports (33-61 New York Superior)

Jones & Spen. Jones & Spencer's Reports (33-61 New York Superior)

Jones & V. Laws. Jones and Varick's Laws (N.Y.)

Jones B. Jones' Law of Bailments

Jones, Bailm. Jones' Law of Bailments

Jones, B. & W. (Mo.) Jones, Barclay & Whittelsey's Reports (31 Missouri)

Jones, Barclay & Whittelsey Jones, Barclay, & Whittelsey's Reports (vol. 31 Missouri)

Jones Ch. Mort. Jones on Chattel Mortgages

Jones, Easem. Jones' Treatise on Easements

Jones Eq. Jones, North Carolina Equity Reports (vols. 54-59) (1853-63)

Jones Eq.(N.C.) Jones, North Carolina Equity Reports (vols. 54-59)

Jones Exch.
- Jones Exchequer (Ir.)
- T. Jones' Irish Exchequer Reports

Jones Fr. Bar. Jones' History of the French Bar

Jones, French Bar. Jones' History of the French Bar

Jones Inst. Jones' Institutes of Hindoo Law

Jones Intr. Jones' Introduction to Legal Science

Jones Ir. Jones' Irish Exchequer Reports

Jones L. Jones, Law Reports

Jones Law. Jones' North Carolina Law Reports

Jones Lib. Jones, Libel. 1812

Jones, Liens. Jones on Liens

Jones L. Of. T. Jones on Land and Office Titles

Jones Mort. Jones on Mortgages

Jones N.C. Jones' North Carolina Law Reports (46-53 N.C. Law)

Jones Pa. Jones' Reports (11, 12 Pennsylvania State)

Jones (Pa.) Jones' Reports (11, 12 Pennsylvania State)

Jones, Pledges. Jones on Pledges and Collateral Securities

Jones Ry. Sec. Jones' Railway Securities

Jones Salv. Jones' Law of Salvage

Jones, Securities Jones on Railroad Securities

Jones T. Sir Thomas Jones' English King's Bench Reports (1667-85)

Jones U.C. Jones, Reports, Upper Canada

Jones Uses Jones' Law of Uses

Jones W. Sir William Jones, English King's Bench Reports (1620-44)

Jon. Ex. Jones' Exchequer Reports (Ir.)

Jon. Exch. Jones' Irish Exchequer Reports

Jon. Ir. Exch. Jones' Irish Exchequer Reports

Jo. Radio Law Journal of Radio Law

Jord. Jt. St. Comp. Jordan on Joint Stock Companies

Jord. P.J. Jordan's Parliamentary Journal

Jornand. de Reb. Get. Jornandes de Rebus Geticis

Jos. Joseph's Reports (21 Nevada)

Jos. & Bev. Joseph and Beven's Digest of Decisions (Ceylon)

Jo. T. T. Jones' King's Bench Reports (Eng.)

Jour. Am. Jud. Soc. Journal of the American Judicature Society

Jour. Comp. Leg. Journal of the Society of Comparative Legislation

Jour. Conat. Law. Journal of Conational Law

Jour. Crim. L. Journal of Criminal Law and Criminology

Jour. Jur. Journal of Jurisprudence (1857-91) (Sc.)

Jour. Juris. Hall's Journal of Jurisprudence

Jour. Jur. Sc. Journal of Jurisprudence & Scottish Law Magazine

Jour. Law Journal of Law

Journ. Jur. Journal of Jurisprudence

Jour. Ps. Med. Journal of Psychological Medicine & Medical Jurisprudence

Jow. Dict. Jowitt, Dictionary of English Law. 2ed. 1977

Joy Acc. Joy, Evidence of Accomplices. 1836

Joyce Joyce on Injunctions

Joyce, Ins. Joyce on Insurance

Joyce Lim. Joyce on Limitations

Joyce Prac. Inj. Joyce, Law & Practice of Injunctions. 1872

Joyce Prin. Inj. Joyce, Doctrinces and Principles of Injunctions. 1877

Joy Chal. Joy, Peremptory Challenge of Jurors. 1844

Joy Conf. Joy, Admissibility of Confessions. 1842

Joy Ev. Joy, Evidence of Accomplices. 1836

Joy Leg. Ed. Joy on Legal Education

Joyn. Lim. Joynes on Limitations

J.P.
- Journal of Politics
- Justice of the Peace & Local Government Review
- Justice of the Peace (Weekly Notes of Cases) (Eng.)

J. Pat. [& Trademark] Off. Soc'y. Journal of the Patent [and Trademark] Office Society

J. Pat. & Trademark Off. Soc'y Journal of the Patent and Trademark Office Society

J.P.C. Judge of the Prize Court

J.P. Ct. Justice of the Peace's Court

J.P.E.L. Journal of Planning and Environment Law

J.P. (Eng.)
- Justice of the Peace & Local Government Review
- Justice of the Peace (Weekly Notes of Cases) (Eng.)

J. Pension Plan. & Compliance Journal of Pension Planning & Compliance

J.P.J.
- Justice of the Peace & Local Government Review
- Justice of the Peace (Weekly Notes of Cases)

J.P. Jo. Justice of the Peace (Weekly Notes of Cases) (Eng.)

J.P.L.
- Journal of Planning Law Journal of Public Law
- Journal of Planning and Environment Law. London

J. Plan. & Environ. L. Journal of Planning and Environment Law

J. Plan. & Env. L. Journal of Planning and Environment Law

J. Plan. & Envt'l L. Journal of Planning and Environmental Law

J. Plan. & Prop. L. Journal of Planning and Property Law

J.Pl.L. Journal of Planning Law

J.P.M.D.L. Judicial Panel on MultiDistrict Litigation

J.P.M.L. Judicial Panel on Multidistrict Litigation

J.P.N.S.W. Justice of the Peace (New South Wales)

J. Pol. Econ. Journal of Political Economy

J. Police Sci. & Ad. Journal of Police Science and Administration

J. Pol. Sci. & Admin. Journal of Police Science and Administration

J.P.O.S. Journal of the Patent Office Society

J.P.P.L. Journal of Planning and Property Law

J.P.R. Justice of the Peace and Local Government Review Reports

J. Prod. L. Journal of Products Law

J. Prod. Liab. Journal of Products Liability

J. Prod.Liability Journal of Products Liability

J.P.Sm. J.P. Smith's English King's Bench Reports (1803-06)

J.P. Smith J.P. Smith's English King's Bench Reports

J.P. Smith (Eng.) J.P. Smith's English King's Bench Reports

J. Psych. & L. Journal of Psychiatry & Law

J. Psych. & Law. Journal of Psychiatry and Law

J. Psychiatry & L. Journal of Psychiatry and Law

J. Psychological Medicine Journal of Psychological Medicine & Medical Jurisprudence

J. Pub. L. Journal of Public Law

J.P.(W.A.) Justice of the Peace (Western Australia)

J.Q.B. Justice of the Queen's Bench

J. Quantitative Criminology Journal of Quantitative Criminology

J.R.
- Johnson's Reports (N.Y.)
- J.R. Jacobus Rex (King James)
- Judges' Rules
- Juridical Review (Sc.)
- Jurist Reports (1873-78) (New Zealand)

J. Radio L. Journal of Radio Law

J. Real Est. Tax. Journal of Real Estate Taxation

J.Rep.
- Johnson's Reports (N.Y.)
- Johnson's Reports, Chancery, Maryland

- Johnson's Reports of Chase's Decisions

J. Reprints Antitrust L. & Econ. Journal of Reprints for Antitrust Law and Economics

J. Res. Crime & Del. Journal of Research in Crime and Delinquency

J.R.N.S. Jurist Reports, New Series (New Zealand)

J.R.N.S.C.A. Jurist Reports, New Series, Court of Appeal (New Zealand)

J.R.N.S.M.L. Jurist Reports, New Series, Mining Law Cases (New Zealand)

J.R.N.S.S.C. Jurist Reports, New Series, Supreme Court (New Zealand)

J.S.
- Jones and Spencer's Superior Court Reports, New York
- Jury Sittings (Faculty Cases, Sc.)

J.Scott Reporter English Common Bench Reports

J.Scott, N.S. English Common Bench Reports, New Series, by John Scott

J.S.D.
- Doctor of Juridical Science
- Doctor of Juristic Science

J. St. Gov't Journal of State Government, The

J.S.Gr. J.S.Green's Reports (13-15 New Jersey Law Reports)

J.S.Gr. (N.J.) J.S. Green's Reports (13-15 New Jersey Law Reports)

J.Shaw John Shaw, Justiciary Reports, Scotland (1848-52)

J.Shaw Just. John Shaw's Justiciary Reports (1848-52) (Sc.)

J.S.M. Master of the Science of Law

J. Soc. Pub. Teach. Law Journal of the Society of Public Teachers of Law

J. Soc. Pub. Teach. Law N.S. Journal of the Society of Public Teachers of Law (New Series)

J. Soc. Pub. T. L. Journal of the Society of Public Teachers of Law

J. Soc. Welfare L. Journal of Social Welfare Law

J. Soc'y Comp. Leg. Journal of the Society of Comparative Legislation

J. Soc'y Pub. Tchrs L. Journal of the Society of Public Teachers of Law

J. Space L. Journal of Space Law

J.S.P.T.L. Journal of the Society of Public Teachers of Law.

J.S.T. Job Safety Training

J. St. Bar Calif. Journal of the State Bar of California

J. St. Tax'n Journal of State Taxation

J. Suffolk Acad. L. Journal of the Suffolk Academy of Law

J. Sup. Ct. Hist. Journal of Supreme Court History

Jt. Joint

J.Tax. Journal of Taxation

J. Taxation Journal of Taxation

J. Tax'n Journal of Taxation

J. Tax'n Invest. Journal of Taxation of Investments

J. Tax'n S Corp. Journal of Taxation of S Corporations

Jt. Com. Joint Committee

J.T.R. Joint Travel Regulations (Dep. of Defense, looseleaf)

J.T.R.S. Joint tenant with right of survivorship

J.U.B. Justice of the Upper Bench

J.U.D. Juris Utriusque Doctor: Doctor of Both (Canon and Civil) Laws

Ju.D. Doctor of Law

Jud.
- Book of Judgments
- Judicature
- judicial
- judiciary
- Sir R. Phillimore's Ecclesiastical Judgments (1867-75)

Jud. & Sw. Jodah & Swan's Reports, Jamaica (1839)

Jud. C. Judicial counsils and conferences

Jud. Chr. Judicial Chronicle

Jud. Com. P.C. Judicial Committee of the Privy Council

Jud. Conduct Rep. Judicial Conduct Reporter

Jud. Coun. N.Y. Judicial Council, New York, Annual Reports

Judd Judd's Reports (4 Hawaii)

Jud. G.C.C. Judgments, Gold Coast Colony

Judge Advo. J. The Judge Advocate Journal

Judge's J. Judge's Journal

Judgm. Judgment

Judg. U.B. Judgments of Upper Bench (Eng.)

Judicature Journal of the American Judicature Society

Judicature. J. Am. Jud. Soc'y Judicature. Journal of the American Judicature Society

Jud. Pan. Mult. Lit. Rulings of the Judicial Panel on Multidistrict Litigation

Jud. Q.R. Judicature Quarterly Review. 1896

Jud. Rep. New York Judicial Repository

Jud. Repos. Judicial Repository (N.Y.)

Jud. S. Judicial Sales

J.U.L. Journal of Urban Law (Mich.)

Jul. Frontin. Julius Frontinus

Jur.
- Juridical
- Jurisprudence
- Jurist
- Jurist (New York)
- Jurist Reports (English, 18 vols.)
- The Jurist, London (1854)
- The Jurist, or Quarterly Journal of Jurisprudence (1827)
- The Jurist (Washington, D.C.)

J. Urban Journal of Urban Law

J. Urban L. Journal of Urban Law

Jur. D. Juris Doctor (Doctor of Law)

Jur. Eccl. Jura Ecclesiatica

Jur. (Eng.) The Jurist (London)

Jur. Ex. Hargrave, FrancisJurisconsult Exercitations

Jurid. Rev. Juridical Review (Edinburgh)

Jurid. Soc'y Pap. Juridical Society Papers, England

Jurimet J Jurimetrics Journal

Jurimetrics Jurimetrics Journal

Jurimetrics J. Jurimetrics Journal

Juris. Jurisprudence

jurisd. jurisdiction

Juris Dr. juris doctor

Jurispr. Jurisprudence

Jurist
- Jurist (Wash., D.C.)
- The Jurist

Jur. Mar. Molloy's De Jure Maritimo

Jur. N.S. The Jurist, New Series Jurist Reports, New Series (Eng.)

Jur. N.S. (Eng.) Jurist (New Series) Exchequer

Jur. (N.S.)Ex. Jurist (New Series) Exchequer

Jur. N.Y. The Jurist, or Law and Equity Reporter (New York)

Jur. Rev. Juridical Review (1889) (Sc.)

Jur. Ros. Roscoe, Jurist (London)

Jur. (Sc.) The Scottish Jurist (Edinburgh)

Jur. Soc. P. Juridical Society Papers (1858-74) (Sc.)

Jur. St. Juridical Styles (Sc.)

JuS Jordan, Jury Selection

JuS(2) Jordan & Gobert, Jury Selection, Second Edition

Jus. Code
- Justices' Code (Oregon)
- Code of Justinian

Jus. Inst. Institutes of Justinian

Jus. Nav. Rhod. Jus Navale Rhodiorum

Just.
- Justice
- Justices' Law Reporter (Pennsylvania)
- Justiciary

Just. Cas. Justiciary Cases

Just. Ct. Justice Court

Just. Ct. Act Justice Court Act

Just. Dig. Digest of Justinian, 50 books (Never translated into English)

Justice British Section of the International Commission of Jurists

Justice's L.R. (Pa.) Justices' Law Reporter (Pennyvania)

Just. Inst. Justinian's Institutes

Just. Itin. Justice Itinerant or of Assize

Just. L.R. Justices' Law Reporter (Pa. 1902-18)

Just. P. Justice of the Peace and Local Government Review

Just. Peace Justice of the Peace and Local Government Review

Just.S .L. Justice's Sea Law

Just. Sys. J. The Justice System Journal

Juta.
- Juta's Daily Reporter (S. Africa)
- Juta's Prize Cases (S. Africa)
- Juta's Reports, Suprerat Court, Cape of Good Hope 1880-1910)

Juv. Juvenile

Juv. & Dom. Rel. Ct. Juvenile and Domestic Relations Court

Juv. & Fam. Courts J. Juvenile and Family Courts Journal

Juv. & Fam. Ct. J. Juvenile and Family Court Journal

Juv. Ct. Juvenile Court

Juv. Ct. J. Juvenile Court Journal

Juv. Ct. J.J. Juvenile Court Judges Journal

Juv. Ct. Judges J. Juvenile Court Judges Journal

Juv. Cts. Juvenile courts and delinquent and dependent children

Juv. Just. Juvenile Justice

Juv. Justice Juvenile Justice

JV Nachmias/Nasuti, Joint Ventures

J.Voet, Com.ad Pand. Voet (Jan), Commentarius and Pandectas

J. World Trade Journal of World Trade

J. World Trade L. Journal of World Trade Law

J. World Tr. L. Journal of World Trade Law

J.W.T.L. Journal of World Trade Law

K

K.
- Kenyon's King's Bench Reports (England)
- Keyes' Court of Appeals Reports (40-43 New York)
- King
- Korean
- Kotze's Reports, Transvaal High Court (South Africa)

Ka. A. Kansas Appeals Reports

Kam.
- Kames' Dictionary of Decisions, Court of Session (Sc.)
- Kames, Remarkable Decisions, Scotch Court of Session, 2 vols. (1716-52)

Kam. Eluc. Kames, Elucidations of the Laws of Scotland

Kam. Eq. Kames, Principles of Equity

Kames
- Kames' Dictionary of Decisions, Court of Session (Sc.)
- Kames, Remarkable Decisions, Scotch Court of Session, 2 vols.

Kames Dec. Kames, Dictionary of Decisions, Court of Session (Sc.)

Kames Dict. Dec. Kames' Dictionary of Decisions, Court of Session (Sc.)

Kames Elucid. Kames' Elucidation (Sc.)

Kames, Eq. Kames' Principles of Equity

Kames Rem. Kames' Remarkable Decisions, Sc.

Kames Rem. Dec. Kames Remarkable Decisions (Sc.)

Kam. Ess Kames' Essays

Kames Sel. Dec. Kames' Select Decisions (Sc.)

Kam. L. Tr. Kames, Historical Law Tracts (Sc.)

Kam. Rem. Kames, Remarkable Decisions, Scotch Court of Session, 2 vols. (1716-52)

Kam. Rem. Dec. Kames' Select Decisions, Scotch Court of Session

Kam. Sel. Dec. Kames' Select Decisions (1752-68) (Sc.)

Kam. Sel. Kames' Select Decisions (1752-68) (Sc.)

Kan.
- Kansas
- Kansas Reports

Kan Ap2d Kansas Appellate Court 2d Series
- Kansas Supreme Court Reports

Kan Admin. Regs. Kansas, Administration Regulations

Kan. Ann. Vernon's Kansas Statutes Annotated

Kan. App. Kansas Appeals Reports

Kan. App.2d Kansas Court of Appeals Reports

Kan. B.A.J. Kansas Association Journal

Kan. B. Ass'n. J. Kansas Bar Association Journal

Kan. City L. Rep. Kanses City Law Reporter

Kan. City L. Rev. Kansas City Law Review

Kan. Civ. Pro. Stat. Ann. Vernon's Kansas Statutes Annotated, Code of Civil Procedure

Kan. Civ. Pro. Stat. Ann. (Vernon) Vernon's Kansas Statutes Annotated, Code of Civil Procedure

Kan. C.L. & I.W.C. Kansas Commission of Labor and Industry Workmen's Compensation Dept. Reports

Kan. C.L. Rep. Kansas City Law Reporter

Kan. Const. Kansas Constitution

Kan. Crim. Code & Code of Crim. Proc. Criminal Code and Code of Criminal Procedure (Kansas)

Kan. Crim. Code & Code of Crim. Proc. (Vernon) Vernon's Kansas Statutes Annotated Criminal Code and Code of Criminal Procedure

Kan. Ct. App. Kansas Appellate Reports (Kan.)

K. & B. Kotze & Barber Transvaal Reports (Supreme or High Court) (1885-88)

K. & B. Dig. Kerford & Box, Victorian Digest

K. & E. Conv. Key & Elphinstone, Conveyancing. 15ed. 1953-54

K. & F.N.S.W. Knox & Fitzhardinge's New South Wales Reports

K. & G. Keane & Grant, English Registration Appeal Cases (1854-62)

K. & Gr. Keane & Grant, English Registration Appeal Cases

K. & G.R.C. Keane & Grant, English Registration Appeal Cases (1854-62)

Kan. Dig. Hatcher's Kansas Digest

K. & J. Kay & Johnson's English Vice-Chancellors' Reports (1854-58)

K. & O. Knapp & Ombler, English Election Cases (1834-35)

K. & R. Kent and Radcliffs Law of New York, Revision of 1801

K. & W. Kames and Woodhouselee's Dictionary (Scot.) 1540-1796

K. & W. Dic. Kames and Woodhouselee's folio Dictionary (1540-1796) (Sc.)

Kan. J.L. & Pub. Pol'y Kansas Journal of Law and Public Policy

Kan. Jud. Council Bul. Kansas Judicial Council Bulletin

Kan. Law. Kansas Lawyer

Kan. L.J. Kansas Law Journal

Kan. L. Rev. University of Kansas Law Review

Kan. P.S.C. Kansas Public Service Commission

Kan. P.U.C. Kansas Public Utilities Commission

Kan. R.C. Kansas Railroad Commission

Kans. Kansas Reports

Kans. App. Kansas Appeals Reports

Kansas City L. Rev. University of Kansas City Law Review

Kansas L.J. Kansas Law Journal

Kansas R. Kansas Reports (Kan.)

Kans. B.A. Kansas City Bar Journal

Kan. S.C.C. Kansas State Corporation Commission Reports

Kan. Sess. Laws Session Laws of Kansas

Kans. R. Kansas Reports (Kan.)

Kans. S.B.A. Kansas State Bar Association

Kan. Stat. Kansas Statutes

Kan. Stat. Ann. Kansas Statutes Annotated

Kan. St. L.J. Kansas State Law Journal

Kan. Subject Ann.Vernon's Vernon's Kansas Statutes Annotated

Kan. U.C.C. Ann. (Vernon) Vernon's Kansas Statutes Annotated, Uniform Commercial Code

Kan. U. Lawy. Kansas University Lawyer

Kan. Univ. Lawy. Kansas University Lawyer

Kar.
- Indian Law Reports, Karachi Series
- Pakistan Law Reports, Karachi Series

Karachi L.J. Karachi Law Journal (Pakistan)

Kar. L.J. Karachi Law Journal (India)

Kas. Kansas Reports (Kan.)

Kashmir L.J. Kashmir Law Journal (India)

Kas.R. Kansas Reports (Kan.)

Katch. Pr. Law Katchenovsky, Prize Law. 2ed. 1867

Kauf. Mack. Kaufmann's Edition of Mackeldey's Civil Law

Kaufm. Mackeld. Civ. Law Kaufmann's Edition of Mackeldey's Civil Law

Kay Kay's English Vice Chancellors' Reports (69 ER)

Kay & J. Kay and Johnson's English Vice-Chancellors' Reports (69, 70 ER)

Kay & J. (Eng.) Kay and Johnson's English Vice-Chancellors' Reports (69, 70 ER)

Kay & John. Kay and Johnson's English Vice-Chancellors' Reports (69, 70 ER)

Kay & Johns. Kay and Johnson's English Vice-Chancellors' Reports (69, 70 ER)

Kay (Eng.) Kay's English Vice Chancellors' Reports (69 ER)

Kay Ship. Kay, Shipmasters and Seamen. 2ed. 1894

K.B.
- English Law Reports, King's Bench (1901-52)
- King's Bench

KBA Kansas Bar Association

K.B.B. Kentucky Bench and Bar

K.B.C. King's Bench Court

K.B.D. King's Bench Division

K.B. Div'l. Ct. King's Bench Divisional court (Eng.)

397

K.B. (Eng.)　English Law Reports, King's Bench (1901-52)

K.B.J.　Kentucky State Bar Journal or Kentucky Bar Journal

KBPQ.　Kappa Beta Phi Quarterly

K.B.U.C.　Upper Canada King's Bench Reports

K.B. (U.C.)　King's Bench Reports (Upper Canada)

K.C.　King's Counsel

KCLE　Continuing Legal Education, University of Kentucky College of Law

KCMOBA　Kansas City, Missouri, Bar Association

K.C. Mo. P.U.C.　Kansas City, Missouri, Public Utilities Commission Reports

K. Counsel　King's Counsel

K.C.R.
- Kansas City Law Review.
- Reports in the time of Cancellor King
- The University of Kansas City Law Review
- The University of Missouri at Kansas City Law Review

Ke.　Keen's English Rolls Court Reports (1836-38)

Keane & Gr.　Keane & Grant's English Registration Appeal Cases (1854-62)

Keane & G.R.C.　Keane & Grant's Registration Appeal Cases (Eng.)

Keat. Fam. Sett.　Keatinge, Family Settlements, 1810

Keb.　Keble's English King's Bench Reports (83, 84 ER)

Keb. J.　Keble's Justice of the Peace

Keble　Keble's King's Bench Reports (1661-79) (83-84 ER)

Kebl.　Keble's English King's Bench Reports (83, 84 ER)

Keble (Eng.)　Keble's English King's Bench Reports (83, 84 ER)

Keb. Stat.　Keble's Statutes

Keen　Keen's English Rolls Court Reports (48 ER)

Keen Ch.　Keen's English Rolls Court Reports (48 ER)

Keen (Eng.)　Keen's English Rolls Court Reports (48 ER)

Keener, Quasi Contr.　Keener's Cases on Quasi Contracts

Keil.　Keilway, English King's Bench Reports (72 ER)

Keilw.　Keilway, English King's Bench Reports (72 ER)

Keilway　Keilway's English King's Bench Reports

Keilw. (Eng.)　Keilway, English King's Bench Reports (72 ER)

Keio L. Rev.　Keio Law Review

Keith Ch. Pa.　Registrar's Book, Keith's Court of Chancery (Pa.)

Kel.　Sir John Kelyng's English Crown Cases

Kel.1.　Sir John Kelyng's English Crown Cases (1662-69)

Kel.2.　Wm. Kelynge's English Chancery Reports (1730-36)

Kel. An.　Kelly, Life Annuities. 1835

Kel. C.C.　Sir John Kelyng's English Crown Cases

Kel. Cont.　Kelly on Contracts of Married Women

Kel. Draft Kelly's Draftsman. 14ed. 1978

Kel. Ga. Kelly's Reports (1-3 Georgia)

Kelh. Kelham's Norman French Law Dictionary

Kelham Kelham's Norman Dictionary

Kelh. Dict. Kelham's Norman French Law Dictionary

Kel. J. Sir John Kelyng's English Crown Cases (1662-69)

Kelk. Jud. Acts Kelke's Judicature Acts

Kellen Kellen's Reports (146-55 Mass.)

Kell. Ga. R. Kelly (James M.) (Ga.)

Kel. Life Ann. Kelly on Life Annuities

Kelly Kelly's Reports (1-3 Georgia)

Kelly & C. Kelly & Cobb (Ga.)

Kelly & Cobb. Kelly & Cobb's Reports (4, 5 Georgia)

Kel. Sc. Fac. Kelly, Scire Facias. 2 ed.1849

Kel. Us. Kelly, Usury. 1835

Kel. W. Wm. Kelynge's English Chancery Reports (1730-36)

Kelynge, W. Kelynge's English Chancery Reports

Kelynge, W. (Eng.) Kelynge's English Chancery Reports

Kelyng. J. Kelyng's English Crown Cases

Kelyng. J. (Eng.) Kelyng's English Crown Cases

Kemble, Sax. Kemble, The Saxons in England

Ken. Kenyon's King's Bench Reports (Eng.)

Kenan Kenan's Reports (76-91 North Carolina)

Ken. Dec. Kentucky Decisions, Sneed (2 Ky.)

Ken. L.R. Kentucky Law Reporter

Ken. L. Re. Kentucky Law Reporter

Kenn. Ch. Kennedy, Chancery Practice. 2ed. 1852-53

Kenn. C. Mar. Kennedy on Courts-Martial

Kennett
• Kennett's Glossary
• Kennett upon Impropriations

Kennett, Gloss. Kennett's Glossary

Kennett, Par. Ant. Kennett's Parochial Antiquities

Kenn. Gloss. Kennett's Glossary

Kenn. Imp. Kennett upon Impropriations

Kenn. Jur. Kennedy on Juries

Kenn. Par. Antiq. Kennett, Parochial Antiquities

Kenn. Pr. Kennedy's Chancery Practice

Ken. Opin. Kentucky Opinions (1864-86)

Kent Kent's Commentaries on American Law

Kent & R. St. Kent and Radcliffs Law of New York, Revision of 1801

Kent, Com. Kent's Commentaries on American Law

Kent, Comm. Kent's Commentaries on American Law

Kent's Commen. Kent's Commentaries

Kentucky L.J. Kentucky Law Journal

Keny.
- Kenyon's King's Bench Reports (1753-59) (Eng.)
- Kenyon's Notes of King's Bench Reports (Eng.)

Kenya L.R. Kenya Law Reports

Keny. Ch. Chancery Cases (v.2 of Notes of King's Bench Cases) (Eng.)

Keny. Chy. (3 Keny.) Chancery Reports, at end of 2 Kenyon (Eng.)

Ker. Indian Law Reports, Kerala Series

Kerala All Indian Law Reports, Kerala Series

Kerala L.J. Kerala Law Journal

Ker. Ind. Kerala, India

Ker. L.T. Kerala, Law Times (India) (1928)

Kern.
- Kernan's Reports (11-14 New York)
- Kern's Reports (100-116 Indiana)

Kerr
- Kerr's Reports (18-22 Indiana)
- Kerr's Reports (3-5 New Brunswick)
- Kerr's Reports (27-29 N.Y. Civil Procedure Reports)

Kerr. Act. Kerr, Actions at Law. 3ed. 1861

Kerr Anc. L. Kerr on Ancient Lights

Kerr Black Kerr's Blackstone. 12ed. 1895

Kerr Disc. Kerr, Discovery. 1870

Kerr Ext. Kerr on Inter-State Extradition

Kerr F. & M. Kerr, Fraud and Mistake, 7ed. 1952

Kerr Fr. Kerr's Law of Fraud and Mistake

Kerr, Inj. Kerr on Injunctions

Kerr (N.B.) Kerr's New Brunswick Reports

Kerr, Rec. Kerr on Receivers

Kerr Stu. Black Kerr's Student's Blackstone

Kerr W. & M. Cas. Kerr's Water and Mineral Cases

Kerse Kerse's Manuscript Decisions, Scotch Court of Session

Kersey, Dict. John Kersey's English Dictionary (1708)

Key. Keyes' New York Court of Appeals Reports

Key.Ch. Keyes on Future Interest in Chattels

Key & Elph. Conv. Key & Elphinstone, Conveyancing. 15ed. 1953-54

Keyes Keyes' New York Court of Appeals Reports

Keyl. Keilway's English King's Bench Reports

Key. Lands Keyes on Future Interest in Lands

Key. Rem. Keyes on Remainders

Keys. St. Ex. Keyser, Stock Exchange. 1850

K.F. Gold Coast Judgments and the Masai Cases by King-Farlow (1915-17) (Ghana)

Kh. Khmer

Khairpur, Pak. Khairpur, Pakistan

K.H.C.D. Kenya High Court Digest

Kilb. Kilburn's Magistrates' Cases (Eng.)

Kilk. Kilkerran's Scotch Court of Session Decisions (1738-52)

Kilkerran Kilkerran's Scotch Court of Session Decisions

King
- King's Reports, vols. 5, 6 Louisiana Annual
- King's Civil Practice Cases (Colo.)
- Select Cases, t. King, ed. Machaghten, Chancery (1724-33) (Eng.)

King Cas. Cases in King's Colorado Civil Practice

King Cas. temp. Select Cases tempore King, English Chancery (1724-33)

King Dig. King, Tennessee Digest

King-Farlow Gold Coast Judgments and the Masai Case by King-Farlow (1915-17) (Ghana)

King's Con. Cs. King's Conflicting Cases (Texas)

King's Conf. Ca. King's Conflicting Cases (Texas)

Kingston L.R. Kingston Law Review

Kingston L. Rev. Kingston Law Review

Kinney, Law Dict. & Glos. Kinney's Law Dictionary and Glossary

K.I.R. Knight's Industrial Reports

Kir. Kirby's Reports & Supplement (Connecticut 1785-89)

Kirb. Kirby's Reports & Supplement (Connecticut 1785-89)

Kirby Kirby's Reports & Supplement (Connecticut 1785-89)

Kirby's Conn. R. Kirby's Reports (Conn.)

Kirby's R. Kirby's Reports (Conn.)

Kirby's Rep. Kirby's Reports (Conn.)

Kirt. Sur. Pr. Kirtland on Practice in Surrogates' Courts

Kisb. Ir. Land L. Kisbey on the Irish Land Law

Kit. Kitchin's Retourna Brevium, 4 editions (1581-92)

Kitch. Kitchin on Jurisdictions of Courts-Leet, Courts-Baron, etc.

Kitch. Courts Kitchin on Jurisdictions of Courts-Leet, Courts-Baron, etc.

Kitch. Cts. Kitchin on Courts

Kitchen Griqualand West Reports, Cape Colony (S. Africa)

Kit. Ct. Kitchin on Jurisdictions of Courts-Leet, Courts-Baron, etc. 5ed 1675

Kit. Jur. Kitchin on Jurisdictions of Courts-Leet, Courts-Baron, etc. 5ed. 1675

Kit. Rd. Trans. Kitchin, Road Transport Law. 19ed. 1978

K.K.K. Ku Klux Klan

K. Law Rep. Kentucky Law Reporter (Ky.)

K.L.G.R. Knight's Local Government Reports

K.L.J. Kentucky Law Journal

K.L.R.
- Kathiawar Law Reports (India)
- Kentucky Law Reporter (Ky.)
- Kenya Law Reports

K.L.T. Kerala Law Times (India)

Kluber, Dr. des Gens. Kluber's Droit des Gens

Kn. Knapp's Privy Council Cases (1829-36) (Eng.)

Kn. A.C. Knapp's Appeal Cases (Privy Council (1829-36) (Eng.)

Kn. & Moo. 3 Knapp's Privy Council Reports (Eng.)

Kn. & O. Knapp & Ombler's English Election Reports (1834-35)

Kn. & Omb. Knapp & Ombler's Election Cases (Eng.)

Knapp. Knapp's Privy Council Reports (Eng.) (12 ER)

Knapp & O. Knapp & Ombler's Election Cases (Eng.)

Knapp P.C. (Eng.) Knapp's Privy Council Reports (Eng.) (12 ER)

Kn. Civ. Proc. Knox on Civil Procedure in India

Kn. Cr. Law Knox, Bengal Criminal Law

Knight, Mech.Dict. Knight's American Mechanical Dictionary

Knight's Ind. Knight's Industrial Reports

Kn. L.G.R. Knight's Local Government Reports (Eng.)

Kn. N.S.W. Knox's New South Wales Reports

Knowles Knowles' Reports (3 Rhode Island)

Knox Knox, New South Wales Reports (1877)

Knox & F. Knox & Fitzhardinge (N.S. Wales)

Knox & Fitz. Knox & Fitzhardinge (N. S. Wales)

Knox (N.S.W.) Knox Supreme Court Reports (N.S.W., Aus.) 1877

Kn. P.C. Knapp's Privy Council Cases (Eng.)

Kobe U.L. Rev. Kobe University Law Review

Kobe Univ. L. Rev. Kobe University Law Review. Kobe, Japan

Koch Koch's Supreme Court Decisions (Ceylon)

Kolze Transvaal Reports by Kolze

Konst. & W. Rat. App. Konstam's & Ward Rating Appeals (1909-12)

Konst. Rat. App. Konstam's Rating Appeals (1904-08)

Korea Korea, Republic of

Korea & World Aff. Korea and World Affairs: A Quarterly Review

Korea (DPR) Democratic People's Republic of Korea

Korea L.R. Korea Law Review

Korean J. Comp. L. Korean Journal of Comparative Law, Seoul, Korea

Korean J. Int'l L. Korean Journal of International Law

Korean J. of Internat. L. Korean Journal of International Law. Seoul, Korea

Korean L. Korean Law

Korea (Rep.) Republic of Korea

Kotze Kotze's Transvaal High Court Reports (1857-81)

Kotze & B. Supreme Court Reports, Transvaal (1885-88) (S. Afr.)

Kotze & Barb. Supreme Court Reports, Transvaal (1885-88) (S. Afr.)

Kotze & Barber Transvaal Court Reports

Kreider Kreider's Reports (1-23 Washington)

Kress
- Kress's Reports (166-194 Pa. State)
- Kress's Reports (2-12 Pa. Superior)

KRS Kentucky Revised Statutes

Krummeck Decisions of the Water Courts (1913-36) (S. Afr.)

K.S. King's Sergeant

Ks. Kansas Reports

K.S.A. Kansas Statutes Annotated

Ks. L.R. Kansas Law Review

Kt. Knight

Kulp Kulp's Luzerne Legal Register Reports (Pa.)

Kutch All India Reporter, Kutch (1949-56)

Kwansei Gak. L. Rev. Kwansei Gaknin Law Review

K.W.I.C. Keyword-in-context

Ky.
- Kentucky
- Kentucky Reports
- Kentucky Supreme Court Reports (1879-1951)

Ky. Acts Kentucky Acts

Ky. Admin. Reg. Kentucky Administrative Register

Ky. Admin. Regs. Kentucky Administration Regulations Services

Ky. Bench & B. Kentucky Bench & Bar

Ky.B.J. Kentucky Bar Journal

Ky. Comment'r. Kentucky Commentator

Ky. Const. Kentucky Constitution

Kyd Kyd on Bills of Exchange

Kyd Aw. Kyd on Awards

Kyd Bills Kyd on Bills of Exchange

Kyd Corp. Kyd on Corporations

Ky. Dec. Sneed's Kentucky Decisions (2 Ky.)

Ky. L. Kentucky Law Reporter

Ky. Law Rep. Kentucky Law Reporter

Ky. L.J. Kentucky Law Journal

Ky. L.R. Kentucky Law Reporter

Ky. L. Rep. Kentucky Law Reporter

Ky. L. Rev. Kentucky Law Review

Ky. L. Rptr. Kentucky Law Reporter (Ky.)

Ky. Op. Kentucky Court of Appeals Opinions

Ky. Opin. Kentucky Opinions (Ky.)

Kyoto L. Rev.   Kyoto Law Review

Ky. R.   Kentucky Reports (Ky.)

Ky. R.C.   Kentucky Railroad Commission

Ky. Rev. Stat.   Kentucky Revised Statutes

Ky. Rev. Stat. & Rules Serv.   Kentucky Revised Statutes and Rules Service (Baldwin)

Ky. Rev. Stat. Ann.   Baldwin's Kentucky Revised Statutes Annotated

Ky. S.B.A.   Kentucky State Bar Association

Ky. S.B.J.   Kentucky State Bar Journal

Kyshe   Kyshe's Reports (Mal.) 1808-90

Ky. St. B.J.   Kentucky State Bar Journal

Ky. St. Law.   Morehead and Brown Digest of Statute Laws (Ky.)

Ky. W.C. Dec.   Kentucky Workmen's Compensation Board Decisions

L

L.
- Lansing's Select Cases in Chancery (New York) 1824, 1826
- Lansing's Select Cases in Chancery (N.Y.)
- Lansing, Supreme Court Reports (New York, 7 vols. Law)
- Laotian
- Law(s)
- Lawson, Notes of Decisions, Registration
- Liber
- Limited
- Louisiana Reports
- Refusal to extend decision of cited case beyond precise issues involved (used in Shepard's Citations)

L.A.
- Labor Arbitration Reports
- Lawyers' Reports Annotated
- Legal Adviser
- Legislative Assembly
- Library Association
- Licensing Act
- Local Authority
- Lord Advocate of Scotland
- Los Angeles

L/A Letter of authority

La.
- Lane, English Exchequer Reports (1605-12)
- Louisiana
- Louisiana Reports
- Louisiana Supreme Court Reports

La. A.
- Louisiana Annual Reports (1846-1900)
- Louisiana Court of Appeals Reports (1924-32)
- Louisiana Courts of Appeal Reports (La.)

L.A.A.C. Lord Chancellor's Legal Aid Advisory Committee

La. Acts State of Louisiana: Acts of the Legislature

La. Admin. Code Louisiana Administrative Code

La. Admin. Reg. Louisiana (Administrative) Register

La. An. Lawyers' Reports, Annotated

La. Ann. Louisiana Annual Reports

La. Ann. Reps. Louisiana Annual Reports (La.)

La. An. R. Louisiana Annual Reports (La.)

La. An. Rep. Louisiana Annual Reports (La.)

La. A. (Orleans) Louisiana Court of Appeals (Parish of Orleans)

La. App. Louisiana Courts of Appeal Reports

La. App. (Orleans) Court of Appeals, Parish of Orleans

L.A.B. Los Angeles Bar Bulletin

La. B. The Louisiana Bar

Lab.
- Labatt's District Court Reports (California 1857-58)
- Labor
- laboratory[ies]
- Labour

La. B.A. Louisiana Bar Association

Lab. A.C. Labour Appeal Cases (India)

Lab. & Auto. Bull. Labor and Automation Bulletin

Lab. & Empl. L. Labor and Employment Law

Lab. Arb.
- Labor Arbitration
- Labor Arbitration Reports (BNA)

Lab. Arb. & Disp. Settl. Labor Arbitration and Dispute Settlements

Lab. Arb. Awards (CCH) Labor Arbitration Awards (CCH)

Lab. Arb. Rep. (BNA) Labor Arbitration Reports

Lab. Arb. Serv. Labor Arbitration Service

La. Bar. Louisiana Bar. Official Publication of the Louisiana State Bar Association

La. Bar J. Louisiana Bar Journal

L.A.B. Bull. Los Angeles Bar Bulletin

Lab. Cas. (CCH) Labor Cases

Lab. Gaz. Labour Gazette

L.A.B.J. Los Angeles Bar Journal

La. B.J. Louisiana Bar Journal

Lab. Law. (The) Labor Lawyer

Lab. L.J. Labor Law Journal

Lab. L. Rep. (CCH)
- Labor Law Reports
- Labor Law Reporter (CCH)

Labor C. Labor Code

Labor Law Labor Lawyer

Labor Law J. Labor Law Journal

Labor L.J. Labor Law Journal

Labour L.J. Labour Law Journal (India)

LABPR Local Advisory Board Procedural Regulation (Office of Rent Stabilization. Economic Stabilization Agency) (U.S.)

L. Abr. Lilly's Abridgment (Eng.)

Lab. Rel. & Empl. News Labor Relations & Employment News

Lab. Rel. Guide (P-H) Labor Relations Guide (Prentice-Hall)

Lab. Rel. L. Letter Labor Relations Law Letter

Lab. Rel. Rep. (BNA) Labor Relations Reporter (BNA)

Lab. Stu. J. Labor Studies Journal

L.A.C. Labour Arbitration Cases

L.A.C.C. Land Appeal Court Cases (1890-1921) (N.S.W., Aus.)

Lacey Dig. Lacey's Digest Railway Decisions

La. Civ. Code Ann. (West) West's Louisiana Civil Code Annotated

Lac. Jur. Lackawanna Jurist (Pa.)

Lacka. Leg. News Lackawanna Legal News (Pa.)

Lackawanna B. Lackawanna Bar

Lack. Bar. Lackawanna Bar (Pa.)

Lack. Bar. R. Lackawanna Bar Reporter (Pa.)

Lack. Co.(Pa.) Lackawanna County Reports

Lack. Jur. Lackawanna Jurist (Pa.)

Lack. Jurist Lackawanna Jurist (Pa.)

Lack. Leg. N. Lackawanna Legal News (Pa.)

Lack. Leg. News (Pa.) Lackawanna Legal News

Lack. Leg. R. Lackawanna Legal Record (Pa.)

Lack. Leg. Rec. Lackawanna Legal Record (Pa.)

Lack. L.N. Lackawanna Legal News (Pa.)

Lack. L.R. Lackawanna Legal Record (Pa.)

La. Code Civ. Pro. Ann. West's Louisiana Code of Civil Procedure Annotated

La. Code Crim. Pro. Ann. West's Louisiana Code of Criminal Procedure Annotated

La. Const. Louisiana Constitution

Lac. R.R. Dig. Lacey, Digest of Railroad Decisions

Ladd. Ladd's Reports (59-64 New Hampshire)

L. Adv. Lord Advocate

L. Advertiser Law Advertiser

LAFTA Latin American Free Trade Association

L.A.G. Legal Action Group

L.A.G. Bull. Legal Action Group Bulletin

Lagos H.C.R. Lagos High Court Reports

Lagos R. Judgments in the Supreme Court, Lagos (1884-92) (Nigeria)

Lah.
- Indian Law Reports, Lahore Series
- Indian Rulings, Lahore
- Pakistan Law Reports, Lahore Series

Lah. Cas. Lahore Cases (India)

Lah. L.J. Lahore Law Journal (India)

Lah. L.T. Lahore Law Times (India)

Lahore L. Times Lahore Law Times. Chandigarh, India

L.A.J.P.E.L. Latin American Journal of Politics, Economics and Law

L.A. Law Los Angeles Lawyer

L. Alem Law of the Alemanni

La. L.J.
- Louisiana Law Journal (New Orleans)
- Louisiana Law Journal (Schmidt's), (New Orleans, 1842)

L. All. Leges Allemanni

Lalor. Lalor's Supplement to Hill & Denio's New York Reports

Lalor, Pol. Econ. Lalor, Cyclopaedia of Political Science, Political Economy, etc.

Lalor's Suppl. Lalor's Supplement to Hill and Denio (N.Y.)

Lalor's Supp. (Hill & Denio) Lalor's Supplement to Hill and Denio (N.Y.)

Lalor, Supp. Lalor's Supplement to Hill & Denio's Reports (N.Y.)

La. L.R. Louisiana Law Review

La. L. Rev. Louisiana Law Review

Lal. R.P. Lalor's Law of Real Property

Lamar. Lamar's Reports (25-40 Florida)

Lamb.
- Lambard's Archainomia, 1568
- Lambard's Archeion. 1635
- Lambard's Eirenarcha; many editions (1581-1619)
- Lambard's Explication
- Lamb's Reports (103-105 Wisconsin)

Lamb. Arch. Lambard's Archaionomia

Lamb. Archaion. Lambard's Archaionomia

Lamb. Const. Lambard, Duties of Constables, etc.

Lamb. Dow. Lambert's Law of Dower

Lamb. Eir. Lambard's Eirenarcha

Lamb. Eiren. Lambard's Eirenarcha

Lamb. Explic. Lambard's Explication

L. Am. Soc. Law in American Society

L. Am. Soc'y Law in American Society

Lanc. Bar Lancaster Bar (Pa. 1869-83)

Lanc. Law Rev. Lancaster Law Review

Lanc. L. Rev. Lancaster Law Review

Lanc. Rev. Lancaster Review (Pa.)

L. & A. Leembruggen & Asirvatham's Appeal Court Reports (Ceylon)

L. & B. Bull Weekly Law Bank Bulletin (Ohio)

L. & C. Lefroy and Cassels' Practice Cases (Ont.)

L & Contemp Probs Law and Contemporary Problems

L & Human Beh Law and Human Behavior

L. & Soc. Inquiry: J. Am. B. Found. Law and Social Inquiry: Journal of the American Bar Foundation

Land & Water L.R. Land & Water Law Review

Land & Water L. Rev. Land & Water Law Review

Land App. Ct. Cas. Land Appeal Court Cases, N.S.W. (Aus.)

L. & B. Leadam & Baldwin's Select Cases before the King's Council (Eng.)

L. & Bank. Lawyer and Banker

L. & B. Bull. Daily Law & Bank Bulletin (Ohio).

L. & B. Ins. Dig. Littleton & Blatchley's Insurance Digest

L. & B. Prec. Leake & Bullen's Precedents of Pleading

L. & C. Leigh & Cave, English Crown Cases Reserved (1861-65)

L. & C.C.C. Leigh & Cave, English Crown Cases Reserved

L. & Comm. Law and Communication

Land Comp. Rep. Land Reports by Roche, Dillon & Kehoe (1881-82) (Ir.)

L. & Comp. Technol. Law and Computer Technology

L. & Computer Tech. Law and Computer Technology

Land Com. Rep. Land Reports, by Roche, Dillon & Kehoe (1881-82) (Ir.)

L. & Contemp. Prob. Law and Contemporary Problems

L. and Contemp. Probl. Law and Contemporary Problems

L & CP Law and Contemporary Problems

L. & D. Conv. Leigh & Dalzell, Conversion of Property. 1825

Land Dec. Land Decisions, U.S.

L. & E. English Law and Equity Reports

L. & Eq. Rep. The Law and Equity Reporter (U.S.)

L. & E. Rep. English Law & Equity Reports (American reprint)

Land. Est. C. Landed Estate Court (Eng.)

L. & G. temp. Plunk. Lloyd & Goold's Irish Chancery Cases tempore Plunkett

L. & G. temp. Sugd. Lloyd & Goold's Irish Chancery Reports tempore Sugden. 1835

L. & G.t.P. Lloyd & Goold's Irish Chancery Cases tempore Plunkett

L. & G.t. Plunk. Lloyd & Goold's Irish Chancery Reports tempore Plunkett (1834-39)

L. & G.t.S. Lloyd & Goold. Irish Chancery Reports tempore Sugden

L. & G.t. Sug. Lloyd & Goold's Irish Chancery Reports tempore Sugden (1835)

L. & Human Behav. Law and Human Behavior

L. & J. Tr. Mar. Ludlow & Jenkyns on the Law of Trade-Marks

L. & Just. Law and Justice

L. & Justice Law and Justice

L. & Leg. GDR Law and Legislation in the German Democratic Republic

L. & Legis. in G.D.R. Law and Legislation in the German Democratic Republic

L. & LeM. Leigh & Le Marchant, Elections. 4ed. 1885

L. & Lib. Law and Liberty

Land L. Serv. Law Book Company's Land Laws Services (NSW)

L. & M. Lowndes & Maxwell's English Practice Cases (1852-54)

L. & Order Law and Order

L. and Policy in Internat. Bus. Law and Policy in International Business

L. & Pol. Int'l. Bus. Law and Policy in International Business

L. & Psychology Rev. Law and Psychology Review

L. & Psych. Rev. Law and Psychology Review

L. & R. Loring and Russell, Election Cases in Massachusetts (Mass.)

L. & R. Election Cases Loring and Russell, Election Cases in Massachusetts (Mass.)

L. & Soc. Order Law & the Social Order

L. and Soc. Rev. Law & Society Review

L. & T.
- Landlord and Tenant
- Longfield & Townsend, Irish Exchequer Reports (1841-42)

Land U. Pl. Rep. Land Use Planning Reports

Land Use & Env. L. Rev. Land Use and Environment Law Review

Land Use & Env't L. Rev. Land Use and Environment Law Review

L. & W. Lloyd and Welsby's Commercial and Mercantile Cases (1829-30) (Eng.)

L. & Welsb. Lloyd & Welsby's Commercial and Mercantile Cases (1829-30)

Lane Lane's Exchequer Reports (Eng.) (1605-12)

Lang. Language

Lang. Ca. Cont. Langdell's Cases on the Law of Contracts

Lang. Ca. Sales. Langdell's Cases on Law of Sales

Lang. Cont.
- Langdell's Cases on Contracts
- Langdell's Summary of the Law of Contracts

Langd. Cont. Langdell's Cases on Contracts; Langdell's Summary of the Law of Contracts

Lang. Eq. Pl.
- Langdell's Cases in Equity Pleading
- Langdell's Summary of Equity Pleading

Lang. Sales Langdell's Cases on the Law of Sales

Lang. Sum. Cont. Langdell's Summary of the Law of Contracts

Lang. Tr. Langley's Trustees' Act

L. Ann. Louisiana Annual Reports (La.)

Lans. Lansing's Supreme Court Reports (N.Y. 1869-73)

Lans. Ch. Lansing's Select Cases, Chancery (N.Y. 1824, 1826)

Lansg. New York Supreme Court Reports - Lansing (N.Y.)

Lansing New York Supreme Court Reports - Lansing (N.Y.)

Lans. Sel. Cas. Lansing's Select Cases, Chancery (N.Y. 1824, 1826)

L. Ap. Louisiana Courts of Appeal Reports

Lap. Dec. Laperriere's Speaker's Decisions (Canada)

La. P.S.C. Louisiana Public Service Commission Reports

L.A.R. Labor Arbitration Reports (BNA)

La. R. Louisiana Reports

La Raza L.J. La Raza Law Journal

La. R.C. Louisiana Railroad Commission

Larc. Larceny

La. Rep. Louisiana Reports

La. Reports Louisiana Reports

La. Rev. Stat. Ann. (West) West's Louisiana Revised Statutes Annotated

LASB Zeidman, Legal Aspects of Selling and Buying

LASB(2) Zeidman, Legal Aspects of Selling and Buying, Second Edition

La. S.B.A. Louisiana State Bar Association

Lasc. H. War. Lascelles, Horse Warranty. 2ed. 1880

Lasc. Juv. Off. Lascelles on Juvenile Offenders

La. Sess. Law Serv. Louisiana Session Law Service

La. S.U.Q. Louisiana State University Quarterly

Lat. Latch's King's Bench Reports (1625-28) (Eng.)

Latch Latch's King's Bench (1625-28) (Eng.)

Lath. Lathrop's Reports (115-145 Massachusetts)

Lathrop. Lathrop's Reports (115-145 Massachusetts)

Lath. Wind. L. Latham on the Law of Window Lights

Lat. Jus. Latrobe's Justice

La. T.R. Louisiana Term Reports (3-12 Martin's Louisiana)

La. T.R. (N.S.) Louisiana Term Reports, New Series (Martin) (1823-30)

Latt. Pr. C. Pr. Lattey, Privy Council Practice. 1869

Lauder Fountainhall's Session Cases (Scotland) (1678-1712)

Laur. Reports of the High Court of Griqualand (1882-1910) (S. Afr.)

Laurence Laurence's Reports of the High Court of Griqualand (1882-1910) (S. Afr.)

Laur. H.C. Ca. Lauren's High Court Cases (S. Africa)

Laur. Prim. Laurence, Primogeniture. 1878

Lauss. Eq. Laussat's Equity Practice in Pennsylvania

Law.
- Alabama Lawyer
- Law (1st word)
- Lawyer (1955) (India)
- Lawyer(s)('s)
- The Law (1889-90)
- The Law, London (periodical)

Law Advert. Law Advertiser (1823-31)

Law Alm. Law Almanac (New York)

Law. Am. Lawyer of the Americas

Law Amdt. J. Law Amendment Journal (1855-58)

Law. Americas Lawyer of the Americas

Law Am. Jour. Law Amendment Journal (1855-58)

Law. & Bank.
- Lawyer & Banker (New Orleans)
- Lawyers'& Bankers' Quarterly (St. Louis)

Law & Banker Lawyer and Banker and Central Law Journal

Law & Bk. Bull. Weekly Law and Bank Bulletin (Ohio)

Law & Computer Tech. Law and Computer Technology

Law & Comput. Tech. Law and Computer Technology

Law & Contemp. Probs. Law & Contemporary Problems

Law & Contempt. Problems Law & Contemporary Problems (Duke)

Law & Eq. Rep. Law and Equity Reporter (New York)

Law & Hist. Rev. Law and History Review

Law & Housing J. Law and Housing Journal

Law & Human Behavior Law and Human Behavior

Law & Ineq. Law and Inequality

Law & Ineq. J. Law & Inequality Journal

Law & Int. Aff. Law and International Affairs (Bangladesh)

Law & Just. Law and Justice

Law & Legisl. in the German Dem. Rep. Law and Legislation in the German Democratic Republic, Berlin, E. Germany

Law & Lib. Law and Liberty

Law. & L.N. Lawyer & Law Notes (Eng.)

Law. & Mag. Lawyer & Magistrate Magazine, Dublin (1898-99)

Law. & Magis. Mag. Lawyer's and Magistrate's Magazine

Law. & Mag. Mag. The Lawyer's and Magistrate's Magazine (1898-99) (Eng.)

Law & Phil. Law & Philosophy

Law & Pol. Int. Bus. Law & Policy in International Business

Law & Pol'y. Int'l. Bus. Law and Policy in International Business

Law & Pol'y. Q. Law and Policy Quarterly

Law & Psychology Rev. Law and Psychology Review

Law & Psych. Rev. Law and Psychology Review

Law & Sex. Law and Sexuality

Law Sea Inst. Proc. Law of the Sea Institute Proceedings

Law & Soc. Law and Social Change

Law & Soc. Inquiry Law & Social Inquiry

Law & Soc. Ord. Law and the Social Order (Arizona State Law Journal)

Law & Soc. Probs. Law and Social Problems

Law & Soc. Rev. Law & Society Review

Law & Soc'y. Rev. Law and Society Review

Law & State Law and State, Tubingen, Germany

Lawasia Lawasia, Journal of the Law Association for Asia and the Western Pacific. Sydney, Australia

Lawasia L.J. Lawasia Law Journal, Sidney, Australia

Law Bk. Rev. Dig. Law Book Review Digest & Current Legal Bibliography

Law Bul. Law Bulletin

Law Bul. & Br. Law Bulletin &
Brief

Law Bul. Ia. Law Bulletin, State
University of Iowa

Law Bull.
- Law Bulletin (Zambia)
- Weekly Law Bulletin (Ohio)

Law Cases Law Cases, Wm.I to
Rich.I (Eng.) (Placita Anglo-Normannica)

Law Cas. Wm.I. Law Cases, William I to Richard I (Eng.)

Law Ch. Bdg. Soc. Law on
Church Building Societies

Law. Ch. P. Lawes, Charterparties. 1813

Law Chr. Law Chronicle (1811-
12) and (1854-58)

Law Chr. & Auct. Rec. Law
Chronicle & Auction Record

Law Chr. & Jour. Jur. Law
Chronicle & Journal of Jurisprudence

Law Ch.Ward. Law on Church
Wardens

Law Cl. Law Clerk (periodical)

Law Cl. Rec. Law Clerk Record
(1910-11)

Law Coach Law Coach (Cambridge) (Eng.)

Law Com.
- Law Commission
- Law Commission Report

Law. Committee News Lawyers
Committee News

Law. Con. Lawson on Contracts

Law Ct. Law Court

Law Dept. Bull. Law Department
Bulletin, Union Pacific Railroad
Co.

Law Dig. Law Digest, London (periodical)

Law Div. Law Division

Law Ecc. Law Law, Ecclesiastical
Law. 2ed. 1844

Law. Ed. Lawyer's Edition,
United States Supreme Court Reports

Law. Ed.2d United States Supreme Court Reports, Lawyers'
Edition, 2d Series

Law. Ed. Adv. Op. United States
Supreme Court Reports, Lawyers' Edition, Advance Opinions

Lawes Ch. Lawes on Charter-Par-
ties

Lawes, Pl. Lawes on Pleading

Law Ex. J. Law Examination Journal (1869-85)

Law Ex. Rep. Law Examination
Reporter

Law Forms Law's Forms of Ecclesiastical Law

Law Forum University of Illinois
Law Forum

Law Fr. Dict. Law French Dictionary

Law Gaz. Law Gazette

Law. Guild M. Lawyers' Guild
Monthly

Law. Guild Rev. Lawyers' Guild
Review

Law in Context Law in Context

Law Inst. J. Law Institute Journal

Law Int. Law Intelligencer (U.S.)

Law J.
- Law Journal (periodical)
- Law Journal Reports

Law J. Ch. Law Journal, New Series, Chancery

Law J. Exch. Law Journal, New Series, Exchequer

Law Jour.
- Law Journal (1866-1965)
- Law Journal Reports

Law Jour. (M. & W.) Morgan & Williams, Law Journal (London)

Law Jour. (Smith's) J.P. Smith, Law Journal (London)

Law J.P.D. Law Journal, Probate Division

Law J.P.D. & A. Law Journal Reports, New Series, Probate, Divorce and Admiralty (1875-1946)

Law J.Q.B. Law Journal, New Series, Queen's Bench, England

Law J. R., Q.B. Law Journal, New Series, Queen's Bench, England

Law Jur. Law's Jurisdiction of the Federal Courts

Law Lat. Dict. Law Latin Dictionary

Law Lib. Law Librarian

Law Lib. J. Law Library Journal

Law Lib. N. Law Library News

Law Libn. Law Librarian

Law Lib. N.S. Law Library, New Series (Philadelphia)

Law Libr. J. Law Library Journal

Law. L.J. Lawrence Law Journal, Pa.

Law Mag. Law Magazine (1828-1915)

Law Mag. & Law Rev. Law Magazine and Law Review (1856-61)

Law Mag. & R. Law Magazine and Review

Law Mag. & Rev. Law Magazine and Review

Law, Med. & Health Care Law, Medicine & Health Care

Law. Med. J. Lawyers Medical Journal

Law Mo. Western Law Monthly (Reprint) (Ohio)

Law N.
- Law News, St. Louis (1872-73)
- Law Notes (London or Northport, N.Y.)

Law Notes Law Notes (London or Northport, N.Y.)

Law Off. Econ. & Mgt. Law Office Economics and Management

Law Off. Information Service Law Office Information Service

Law of Trusts, Tiff. & Bul. Tiffany and Bullard on Trusts and Trustees

Law Pat. Law's United States Patent Cases

Law Pat. Dig. Law's Digest of United States Patent Cases

Law. Pl.
- Lawes, Pleading in Assumpsit. 1810
- Lawes, Pleading in Civil Actions. 1806

Law Pr. Law's Practice in United States Courts

Law Q. Rev. Law Quarterly Review

Law Quar. Rev. Law Quarterly Review (London)

Law Quart. Rev. Law Quarterly Review (London)

Lawr. Lawrence High Court Reports, Griqualand

Law Rec.
- Ceylon Law Recorder
- Law Recorder (1827-31) (Ir.)

Law Rec. (N.S.) Law Recorder, New Series (Ir.)

Law Rec. (O.S.) Law Recorder, 1st Series (Ir.)

Law Ref. Com. Law Reform Committee

Law Ref. Cttee. Law Reform Committee

Law Reg.
- American Law Register, Philadelphia
- Law Register, Chicago

Law Reg. Cas. Lawson's Registration Cases (Eng.)

Lawrence Lawrence's Reports (20 Ohio)

Lawrence Comp. Dec. Lawrence's First Comptroller's Decisions (U.S.)

Lawrence, Compt. Dec. Lawrence's First Comptroller's Decisions (U.S.)

Law Rep.
- Law Reporter (Eng.)
- Law Reporter (Ramsey & Morin), Canada
- Law Reports (Eng.)
- Louisiana Reports
- Monthly Law Reporter, Boston Mass.

- New Zealand Law Reports
- Ohio Law Reporter

Law Rep. A. & E. Law Reports, Admiralty and Eccesiastical

Law Rep. App. Cas. Law Reports, Appeal Cases

Law Rep. C.C. Law Reports, Crown Cases

Law Rep. Ch. Law Reports, Chancery Appeal cases

Law Rep. Ch. App. Law Reports, Chancery Appeal Cases (1865-75)

Law Rep. Ch. D. Law Reports, Chancery Division

Law Rep. C.P. Law Reports, Common Pleas

Law Rep. C.P.D. Law Reports, Common Pleas Division

Law Rep. Dig. Law Reports Digest

Law Rep. Eq. Law Reports, Equity Cases

Law Rep. Ex. Law Reports, Exchequer

Law Rep. Ex. D. Law Reports, Exchequer Division

Law Rep. H.L. Law Reports, House of Lords, English and Irish Appeal Cases

Law Rep. H.L. Sc. Law Reports, Scotch and Divorce Appeal Cases, House of Lords

Law Rep. Ind. App. Law Reports, Indian Appeals

Law Rep. Ir. Law Reports, Irish

Law Rep. Misc. D. Law Reports, Miscellaneous Division

Law Rep. N.S. Law Reports, New Series (N.Y.)

Law Repos. Carolina Law Repository

Law Repository Carolina Law Repository (Reprint) (N.C.)

Law Rep. P. Law Reports, Probate

Law Rep. P. & D. Law Reports, Probate and Divorce Cases

Law Rep. P.C. Law Reports, Privy Council, Appeal Cases

Law Rep. Q.B. Law Reports, Queen's Bench

Law Rep. Q.B.D. Law Reports, Queen's Bench Division

Law Repr. Law Reporter (Ramsey & Morin) (Can.)

Law Rep. (Tor.) Law Reporter (Toronto)

Law Rev. Law Review

Law Rev. & Qu. J. Law Review & Quarterly Journal

Law Rev. Com. Law Revision Committee

Law Rev. Comm. Law Revision Commission

Law Rev. Cttee. Law Revision Committee

Law Rev. J. Law Review Journal

Law Rev. Qu. Law Review Quarterly (Albany, N.Y.)

Law Rev. U. Det. Law Review University of Detroit

Lawr. Wh. Lawrence's Edition of Wheaton's International Law

Laws Austl. Cap. Teff. Laws of the Australian Capital Territory (1911-1959), in force on 1st January, 1960

Law School Rec. Law School Record (Chicago)

Law School Rev. Law School Review, Toronto University (Can.)

Laws. Cont. Lawson on Contracts

Law Ser. Mo. Bull. University of Missouri Bulletin, Law Series

Laws. Man. on Prof. Conduct (ABA/BNA) Lawyers' Manual on Professional Conduct

Law Soc. Gaz. Law Society's Gazette (London or Regina)

Law Soc. J. Law Society Journal (N.S.W., Aus.)

Law Soc. Jo. Law Society of Massachusetts, Journal

Law Soc'y. Gaz. Law Society Gazette

Law Soc'y. J. Law Society Journal (New South Wales)

Law Soc'y. Scotl. Law Society of Scotland, Journal, Edinburgh, Scotland

Lawson, Exp. Ev. Lawson on Expert and Opinion Evidence

Lawson, Pres. Ev. Lawson on Presumptive Evidence

Lawson, Rights, Rem. & Pr. Lawson on Rights, Remedies and Practice

Lawson's Reg. Cas. Lawson's Registration Cases

Lawson, Usages & Cust. Lawson on the law of Usages and customs

Laws. Reg. Cas. Lawson's Registration Cases, Irish (1885-1914)

Law Stu. Law Student

Law Stud. Law Student (American Law Book Co.)

Law Stud. H. Law Student's Helper

Law Stud. Mag. Law Students' Magazine

Law Stud. Mag. N.S. Law Students' Magazine, New Series

Law Stu. Mag. Law Students' Magazine, London

Laws Wom. Laws of Women

Law T. Law Times Reports

Law Tcher Law Teacher

Law Tchr. Law Teacher

Law-Tech. Law-Technology

Law Tenn. Rep. Tennessee Reports (Tenn.)

Law Times
• Law Times (London)
• Law Times (Pa.)

Law Times (N.S.) Law Times, New Series (Lackawanna, Pa.)

Law Times (O.S.) Law Times, Old Series, (Luzerne, Pa.)

Law. Title Guar. Funds News Lawyers Title Guaranty Funds News

Law T., N.S.
• Law Times Reports, New Series
• Law Times, New Series (Pennsylvania) (1879-85)

Law Tr. Law Tracts

Law T. Rep. N.S. Law Times Reports, New Series

Law T. Rep. O.S. Law Times Reports, Old Series

Law U.S. Cts. Law's Practice in United States Courts

Law. V. & S. Lawrence's Visitation and Search

Law W. Law Weekly

Law. Wheat. Lawrence's Edition of Wheaton on International Law

Lawy. Lawyer or Lawyers'

Lawy. & L.N. Lawyer and Law Notes

Lawyer & Banker Lawyer and Banker and Central Law Journal

Lawyers Co-op Lawyers Cooperative Publishing Co.

Lawyers' Med. J. Lawyers' Medical Journal

Lawyers' Rep. Ann. Lawyers' Reports Annotated

Lawyers' Rep. Annotated Lawyers' Reports Annotated

Lawyers' Reports Annotated Lawyers' Reports Annotated

Lawyer's Rev. The Lawyers' Review, (Seattle, Wash.)

Lawy. Mag. Lawyers' Magazine (London)

Lawy. Med. J. Lawyer's Medical Journal

Lawy. Rep. Ann. Lawyers' Reports Annotated

Lawy. Rev. The Lawyers' Review (Seattle, Wash.)

Lay Lay's Chancery Reports (Eng.)

L. Bai. Leges Baiarum

L. Baivar. Law of the Bavarians

L. Bar.
• Lancaster Bar (Pa.)
• Lancaster Law Review (Pa.)

L. Boior Law of the Bavarians

L. Book Adviser Law Book Adviser

L.B.R. Lower Burma Rulings (India)

LC
- Legal Corporation
- Library of Congress

L.C.
- Labor Cases
- Land Court.
- Law Commission
- Law Courts
- Leading Cases
- Library of Congress
- Lord Chancellor
- Lord High Chancellor of Great Britain
- Lower Canada
- Scottish Land Court Reports

L.C.A. Leading Cases Annotated

L.C. & M. Gaz. Lower Courts & Municipal Gazette (Canada)

L.C.B.
- Land and Concessions Bulletin (Ghana)
- Lord Chief Baron

L.C.C.
- Land Court Cases (New South Wales)
- Leach's Crown Cases (1730-1815)
- London County Council

L.C.C.C. Lower Canada Civil Code

L.C.C.N.S.W. Land Court Cases (New South Wales) (1890-1921)

L.C. Cont. Langdell's Cases on the Law of Contracts

L.C.C.P. Lower Canada Civil Procedure

L.C.D.
- Lord Chancellor's Department

- Ohio Lower Court Decisions

L.C.D.C. Land Conservation & Development Commission (Oregon)

L.C. Eq. White & Tudor's Leading Cases in Equity

LCF Law Centres Federation

L.C.G. Lower Courts Gazette (Ontario)

L. Chr. Law Chronicle, England

L. Chron. Law Chronicle

L. Chron. & L. Stud. Mag. Law Chronicle and Law Students' Magazine

L. Chron. & L. Stud. Mag., (N.S.) Law Chronicle and Law Student's Magazine, New Series

L.C.J.
- Lord Chief Justice
- Lower Canada Jurist, Montreal (1848-91)

L.C. Jur. Lower Canada Jurist

L.C.L.J. Lower Canada Law Journal (1865-68)

L.C.L. Jo. Lower Canada Law Journal

L.C.O. Lord Chancellor's Office

L. Coach Law Coach

L. Comment. Law Commentary

L. Comment'y Law Commentary
LCP(3) Law and Contemporary Problems

L.C.P. Law and Contemporary Problems

L.C.R. Lower Canada Reports (1850-67)

L.C. Rep. S. Qu. Lower Canada Reports Seignorial Questions

L.C. Sales Langdell's Cases on the Law of Sales

L. Ct., Div. Law Court or Division

L.C.V. League of Conservation Voters

L.C.W.P. Law Commission Working Paper

L.C.Z. Laws of the Canal Zone

L.D.
- Labor Dispute
- Land Office Decisions, United States
- Law Dictionary

Ld. Birk. Lord Birkenhead's Judgments. House of Lords (Eng.)

Ld. Br. Sp. Lord Brougham's Speeches

L. Dec. Land Office Decisions, United States

L. Dict. Law Dictionary

Ld. Ken. Lord Kenyon's King's Bench Reports (1753-59) (Eng.)

Ld. Kenyon Lord Kenyon's King's Bench Reports (1753-59) (Eng.)

Ld. Kenyon (Eng.) Lord Kenyon's King's Bench Reports, (Eng.)

L.D.L.R. Land Development Law Reporter

Ld. Ray. Lord Raymond's Reports (1694-1732)

Ld. Raym. Lord Raymond's King's Bench & Common Pleas Reports (1694-1732)

L.E. Lawyers' Edition, United States Supreme Court Reports

L.E.2d Lawyers' Edition, United States Supreme Court Reports, Second Series

Lea. Lea's Tennessee Reports

LEAA Law Enforcement Assistance Administration

L.E.A.A. Legal Op. Legal Opinions of the Office of General Counsel of the Law Enforcement Assistance Administration

Leach. Leach's English Crown Cases (1730-1815)

Leach C.C. Leach's Crown Cases, King's Bench (Eng.)

Leach C.L. Leach, Cases in Crown Law

Leach Cl. Cas. Leach's Club Cases (London)

Leach, Cr. Cas. Leach's English Crown Cases

Lead. Leader Law Reports (Ceylon)

Leadam Leadam's Select Cases before King's Council in the Star Chamber (Selden Society Publications, v. 16, 25)

Leadam Req. Select Cases in the Court of Requests. Ed. by I.S. Leadam (Selden Society Publications, vol. 12)

Lead. Cas. Am. American Leading Cases, by Hare & Wallace

Lead. Cas. Eq. Leading Cases in Equity by White and Tudor

Lead. Cas. in Eq. Leading Cases in Equity by White and Tudor

Lead Cas. In. Eq. (Eng.) Leading Cases in Equity, by White and Tudor

Lead. L.R. Leader Law Reports (1909-10) (S. Afr.)

League of Nations Off. J. League of Nations Official Journal

League of Nations O.J. League of Nations Official Journal

League of Nations O.J., Spec.Supp. League of Nations Official Journal, Special Supplement

Leake
- Leake on Contracts, 8 editions (1861-1931)
- Leake's Digest of the Law of Property in Land

Leake, Cont. Leake on Contracts

Leake Land Leake's Digest of the Law of Property in Land

Leam. & Spic. Leaming and Spicer's Laws, Grants, Concessions and Original Constitutions (N.J.)

Le. & Ca. Leigh & Cave's Crown Cases Reserved (1861-65) (Eng.)

Leap. Rom. Civ. L. Leapingwell on the Roman Civil Law

Learn. & L. Learning and the Law

Learn. & Law Learning and the Law

L. East. Eur. Law in Eastern Europe

Leb. Lebanon

Lebanon Lebanon County Legal Journal (Pa.)

Lebanon Co. L.J.(Pa.) Lebanon County Legal Journal (Pa.)

LEC Landed Estates Courts Commission (Eng.)

Lect. Lecture

Lect. L.S.U.C. Special Lectures of the Law Society of Upper Canada

Lectures L.S.U.C. Special Lectures of the Law Society of Upper Canada

L.Ed. Lawyers' Edition Supreme Court Reports (United States)

L.Ed.2d. Lawyers' Edition Supreme Court Reports, Second Series

L.Ed. (Adv.Ops.) United States Supreme Court Reports, Lawyers' Edition, Advance Opinions

L.Ed. (U.S.) Lawyers' Edition Supreme Court Reports (United States)

Lee
- Lee's English Ecclesiastical Reports (1752-58)
- Lee's Reports (9-12 California)

Lee Abs. Lee, Abstracts of Title. 1843

Lee & H. Lee's King's Bench Cases tempore Hardwicke (1733-38) (95 ER)

Lee Bank. Lee, Law and Practice of Bankruptcy. 3ed. 1887

Lee Cap. Lee on Captures

Lee, Dict. Lee's Dictionary of Practice

Lee Eccl. Lee's Ecclesiastical (Eng.)

Lee G. Sir George Lee's English Ecclesiastical Reports

Leese Leese's Reports (vol. 26 Nebraska)

Lee Ship. Lee's Laws of Shipping

Lee t. Hard. Lee's Cases tempore Hardwicke (1733-38)

Lee t. Hardw. Lee tempore Hardwicke (1733-38) (Eng.)

Lef. & Cas. Lefroy and Cassel's Practice Cases (1881-83) (Ontario)

Lef. Cr. L. Lefroy, Irish Criminal Law

Lef. Dec. Lefevre's Parliamentary Decisions, by Bourke (Eng.)

Lefroy Lefroy's Railroad & Canal Cases (Eng.)

Leg.
- Legal
- Legislation
- Legislative
- Legislature

Leg. Adv. Legal Adviser, Chicago, Ill.

Leg. Aid Rev. Legal Aid Review

Legal Ad. Legal Administrator

Legal Adv.
- Legal Advertiser (Chicago)
- Legal Adviser (Denver)

Legal Aid Rev. Legal Aid Review

Leg. Alfred. Leges Alfredi (laws of King Alfred.)

Legal Aspects Med. Prac. Legal Aspects of Medical Practice

Legal Asp. Med. Prac. Legal Aspects of Medical Practice

Legal Econ. Legal Economics

Legal Educ. Newsl. Legal Education Newsletter

Legal Educ. Rev. Legal Education Review

Legal Gazette Legal Gazette (Pa.)

Legal Gaz. (Pa.) Legal Gazette, Philadelphia

Legal Int. Legal Intelligencer (Pa.)

Legal Intel. Legal Intelligencer (Pa.)

Legal Intell. Legal Intelligencer (Pa.)

Legal Intelligencer Legal Intelligencer (Pa.)

Legal Med. Ann. Legal Medicine Annual

Legal Med. Q. Legal Medical Quarterly

Legal Obser. Legal Observer

Legal Observer New York Legal Observer (N.Y.)

Legal Reference Services Q. Legal Reference Services Quarterly

Legal Rep. Legal Reporter, New Series (Tenn.)

Legal Research J. Legal Research Journal

Legal Res. J. Legal Research Journal

Legal Resp. Child Adv. Protection Legal Response:Child Advocacy and Protection

Legal Services Bull. Legal Services Bulletin

Legal Stud. Legal Studies

Legal Stud. Forum Legal Studies Forum

Legal Times Legal Times

Legal Video Rev. Legal Video Review

Leg. & Ins. R. Legal & Insurance Reporter (Pa.)

Leg. & Ins. Rep. Legal & Insurance Reporter

Leg. & Ins. Rept. Legal and Insurance Reporter (Philadelphia)

Leg. Bib.   Legal Bibliography

Leg. Bibl.   Legal Bibliography

Leg. Canut.   Leges Canuti (laws of King Canute or Knut)

Leg. Ch. Forms   Leggo's Chancery Forms (Ontario)

Leg. Ch. Pr.   Leggo's Chancery Practice (Ontario)

Leg. Chron.   Legal Chronicle (Foster's Pa. Reports)

Leg. Chron. Rep.   Legal Chronicle Reports (Pottsville, Pa.)

Leg. Econ.   Legal Economics

Leg. Edm.   Leges Edmundi (laws of King Edmund.)

Leg. Ethel.   Leges Ethelredi

Leg. Exam.   Legal Examiner (London or N.Y.) (1831-35); (1862-68); (1869-72)

Leg. Exam. & L.C.   Legal Examiner & Law Chronicle (London)

Leg. Exam. & Med. J.   Legal Examiner Medical Jurist (London)

Leg. Exam. N.S.   Legal Examiner, New Series (Eng,)

Leg. Exam. W.R.   Legal Examiner Weekly Reporter

Leg. Exch.   Legal Exchange (Des Moines, Ia.)

Leg. Exec.   Legal Executive

Leg. Fluv.   Leges Fluviorum

Leg. G.   Legal Guide

Legg.   Leggett, Reports (India)

Leg. Gaz.   Legal Gazette

Leg. Gaz. R.   Campbell's Legal Gazette Reports (Pennsylvania 1869-71)

Leg. Gaz. Rep.   Campbell's Legal Gazette Reports (Pennsylvania 1869-71)

Legg. Bills L.   Leggett on Bills of Lading

Legge.
  • Legge's Reports (Australia)
  • Legge's Supreme Court Cases, New South Wales (1825-62)

Legg. Out.   Legge on Outlawry

Leg. H.I.   Laws of [King] Henry the First

Leg. Hist.
  • Legal Historian
  • Legal History (India)

Leg. Inf. Bul.   Legal Information Bulletin

Leg. Inq.   Legal Inquirer (London)

Leg. Int.   Legal Intelligencer (Philadelphia)

Leg. Intel.   Legal Intelligencer (Pa.)

Leg. Intell.   Legal Intelligencer (Pa.)

Leg. Inti.   Legal Intelligencer (Pa.)

Legis.
  • Legislation
  • Legislative
  • Legislature

Legis. Stud. Q.   Legislative Studies Quarter

Leg. J.   Pittsburgh Legal Journal (Pa.)

Leg. Jour.   Pittsburgh Legal Journal (Pa.)

Leg. M. Dig.   Legal Monthly Digest (Aus.)

Leg. Med.   Legal Medicine

Leg. Misc. Legal Miscellany (Ceylon)

Leg. Misc. & Rev. Legal Miscellany & Review (India)

Leg. News Legal News (Montreal Sunbury, Pa.; Toledo, Ohio)

Leg. Notes Legal Notes on Local Government (New York)

Leg. Notes & View. Q. Legal Notes & Viewpoints Quarterly

Leg. Obs.
- Legal Observer & Solicitor's Journal (London)
- Legal Observer (London)

Leg. Oler. Laws of Oleron

Leg. Op. Legal Opinion (Harrisburg, Pa.)

Leg. Ops. (Pa.) Legal Opinions

Leg. Out. Legge on Outlawry

Leg. Port. Leges Portuum

Leg. Pract. & Sol. J. Legal Practitioner and Solicitors' Journal (1846-47, 1849-51)

Leg. R. Legal Record Reports (Pa.)

Leg. Rec. Legal Record (Detroit, Mich.)

Leg. Rec. Rep. Legal Record Reports (1-2 Schuykill Co. (Pa.) Legal Record Reports)

Leg. Ref. Legal Reformer (1819-20)

Leg. Rem. Legal Remembrancer (Calcutta)

Leg. Rep.
- Legal Reporter (1840-43) (Ir.)
- Legal Reporter (Baxter)

Leg. Rep. (Ir.) Legal Reporter, Irish Courts

Leg. Res. J. Legal Research Journal

Leg. Rev. Legal Review (1812-13) (London)

Leg. Rhod. Laws of Rhodes

Leg. R. (Tenn.) Legal Reporter parallel to Shannon Cas.

Leg. Serv. Bull.
- Legal Service Bulletin (American Bankers' Assoc., New York) 1926
- Legal Service Bulletin (Monash University, Aus.)

Leg. Stud. Q. Legislative Studies Quarterly

Leg. T. Cas. Legal Tender Cases

Legul. The Leguleian (1850-65)

Leg. Ult. The Last Law

Leg. W. Legal World (India)

Leg. Wisb. Laws of Wisbury

Leg. Y.B. Legal Year Book (London)

Leh. Lehigh County Law Journal (Pa.)

Leh. Co. L.J. (Pa.) Lehigh County Law Journal

Lehigh Lehigh Valley Law Reporter (Pa.)

Lehigh Co. L.J. Lehigh County Law Journal (Pa.)

Lehigh L.J. Lehigh County Law Journal (Pa,)

Lehigh Val. Law Rep. Lehigh Valley Law Reporter (Pa.)

Lehigh Val. L.R. Lehigh Valley Law Reporter (Pa.)

Lehigh Val. L. Rep. Lehigh Valley Law Reporter (Pa.)

Leh. L.J.   Lehigh County Law Journal

Leh. V.L.R. (Pa.)   Lehigh Valley Law Reporter

LEICSC   Legal Education Institute, United States Civil Service Commission

Leiden J. Int'l L.   Leiden Journal of International Law

Leigh
- Leigh (Pa.)
- Leigh's Virginia Supreme Court Reports (1829-42)
- Ley's King's Bench Reports (1608-29)

Leigh Abr.   Leigh, Abridgment of the Law of Nisi Prius. 1838

Leigh & C.   Leigh and Cave's Crown Cases (1861-65)

Leigh & C.C.C.   Leigh & Cave's Crown Cases (Eng.)

Leigh & D. Conv.   Leigh & Dalzell, Conversion. 1825

Leigh & L.M. Elec.   Leigh & Le Marchant, Elections. 4ed. 1885

Leigh G.A.   Leigh's Game Act

Leigh N.P.   Leigh's Abridgment of the Law of Nisi Prius

Leigh (Va.)   Leigh's Virginia Supreme Court Reports (1829-42)

Leith Black.   Leith, Blackstone on Real Property. 2ed. 1880

Leith R. Pr.   Leith's Real Property Statutes, Ontario

Lely & F. Elec.   Lely & Foulkes, Elections. 3ed. 1887

Lely & F. Jud. Acts   Lely & Foulkes, Judicature Acts. 4ed. 1883

Lely & F. Lic. Acts   Lely & Foulkes, Licensing Acts. 3ed. 1887

Lely Railw.   Lely, Regulation of Railway Acts. 1873

Le Mar.   Le Marchant's Gardner Peerage Case

Lending L.F.   Lending Law Forum

Leo.   Leonard's King's Bench Reports (1540-1615) (Eng.)

Leon.   Leonard's King's Bench, Common Pleas Exchequer Reports (Eng.)

Leon. La. Dig.   Leonard, Louisiana Digest of United States Cases

Leon. Prec.   Leonard, Precedents in County Courts. 1869

Lesotho L.J.   Lesotho Law Journal

Lest. & But.   Lester & Butler's Supplement to Lester's Georgia Reports

Lester.   Lester's Reports (31-33 Georgia)

Lester & B.   Lester & Butler's Supplement (Ga.)

Lester Supp.   Lester & Butler's Supplement to Lester's Georgia Reports

Lest. P.L.   Lester's Decisions in Public Land Cases

LETS   National Law Enforcement Teletype System

Letter Cred.   Letter of credits, and credit cards

Lev.   Levinz's King's Bench & Common Pleas Reports (1660-97) (Eng.)

Lev. Ent.   Levinz's Entries (Eng.)

Levi Com. L. Levi, International Commercial Law. 2ed. 1863

Levi Merc. L. Levi, Mercantile Law. 1854

Lev. J.P. Levinge's Irish Justice of the Peace

Lew.
- Lewin's English Crown Cases Reserved (1822-38)
- Lewis, Missouri
- Lewis, Nevada

Lew. App. Lewin, Apportionment. 1869

Lew. B. & S. Lewis on Bonds and Securities

Lew. C.C. Lewin's English Crown Cases

Lew. C.L. Lewis' Criminal Law

Lew. Conv. Lewis' Principles of Conveyancing

Lew. Dig. Cr. L. Lewis' Digest of United States Criminal Law

Lew. Elec. Lewis' Election Manual

Lew. Eq. Dr. Lewis on Equity Drafting

Lewin Lewin on Trusts; 15 editions (1837-1950)

Lewin C.C. Lewin's Crown Cases Reserved (1822-38) (168 ER)

Lewin C.C. (Eng.) Lewin, Crown Cases (168 ER)

Lewin, Cr. Cas. Lewin's English Crown Cases Reserved

Lew. Ind. Pen. Lewis' East India Penal Code

Lewis
- Lewis' Kentucky Law Reporter
- Lewis' Reports (29-35 Missouri Appeals)

- Lewis' Reports (1 Nevada)

Lewis, Em. Dom. Lewis on Eminent Domain

Lewis, Perp. Lewis' Law of Perpetuity

Lew. L. Cas. Lewis Leading Cases on Public Land Law

Lew. L.T. Lewis on Land Titles in Philadelphia

Lew. Perp. Lewis, Law of Perpetuities. 1843

Lew. St. Lewis on Stocks, Bonds, & c.

Lew. Tr. Lewin, Trusts. 16ed. 1964

Lew. U.S. Cr. L. Lewis' Digest of United States Criminal Law

Lex & Sci. Lex et Scientia

Lex Cust. Lex Custumaria

Lex et Scientia Lex et Scientia. Official Organ of the International Academy of Law and Science

Lex Man. Lex Maneriorum

Lex Mer. Am. Lex Mercatoria Americana

Lex Merc. Red. Lex Mercatoria Rediviva, by Beawes

Lex Parl. Lex Parliamentaria

Ley
- Ley's Court of Star Chamber (Eng.)
- Ley's Court of Wards Reports (Eng.)
- Ley's King's Bench Reports (1608-29) (Eng.)

Ley Wards Ley on Wards and Liveries (usually appended to Ley's Reports)

L.F.
- Law French
- University of Illinois Law Forum

L. Fr.   Law French

LFTC   Burnett & Kafka, Litigation of Federal Tax Controversies

L.G.   Law Glossary

L/G   Land grant

L.G.A.T.R. (NSW)   Local Government Appeals Tribunal Reports (NSW) (Law Book Co.)

L. Gaz.   Law Gazette

L.G.B.
- Local Government Board
- Local Government Bulletin (Ghana)

L.G.C.
- Local Government Chronicle (1855)
- Lord Great unam berlain

L.G.R.
- Knight's Local Government Reports (1903)
- Local Government Reports (Eng.)
- Local Government Reports, New South Wales (Australia)

L.G.R.A.   Local Government Reports of Australia

L.G.R. (Eng.)   Local Government Reports (Eng.)

L.G. Rev.   Local Government Review

L.G.R. (N.S.W.)   Local Government Reports (New South Wales)

L. Guard.   Law Guardian

L/H   Leasehold

LHA   Lanham Housing Act (U.S.)

L.H.C.   Lord High Chancellor

L.H.C.A.   Longshoremen's & Harbor Worker's Compensation Act

L.H.O.B.   Longworth House Office Building

L.I.   Legal Intelligence (Philadelphia)

L.I.A.   International Union of Life Insurance Agents

Liab.   Liability

Lib.
- Liberal Party
- Liberties
- Librarian
- Library

Lib.   Liberia

Lib. & Sl.   Libel and Slander

Lib. Ass.   Liber Assisarum (Year Books, Part V)

Lib. Cong. Q.   Library of Congress Quarterly (title varies)

Lib. Ent.   Old Books of Entries

Liberian L.   Liberian Law

Liberian L.J.   Liberian Law Journal

Lib. Feud.   Liber Feudorum, at the end of the Corpus Juris Civilis

Lib. Int.   Liber Intrationum (Book of Entries) (1510)

Lib. Intr.   Liber Intrationum, Old Book of Entries

Lib. L. & Eq.   Library of Law and Equity

Lib. Nig.   Liber Niger, the Black Book

Lib. Nig. Scacc.   Liber Niger Scaccarii; Black Book of the Exchequer

Lib. Pl. Liber Placitandi, Book of Pleading

Lib. Plac. Lilly's Assize Reports (1688-93)

Libr.
- library
- librarian
- libraries

Lib. Rames. Liber Ramesiensis, Book of Ramsey

Lib. Reg. Register Books

Lib. Rub. Liber Rubens, the Red Book

Lib. Rub. Scacc. Liber Ruber Scaccarii; Red Book of the Exchequer

License & P. Licenses and permits

Licensing L. & Bus. Rep. Licensing Law and Business Report

LICROSS League of Red Cross Societies

Lieber Civ. Lib. Lieber on Civil Liberty and Self Government

Lieb. Herm. Lieber's Hermeneutics

Liech. Liechtenstein

L.I.E.E. Law in Eastern Europe

Life and Acc. Ins. R. Bigelow's Life and Accident Insurance Reports

Life & Acc. Ins. R. Bigelow. Life and Accident Insurance Reports

Life C. Life Cases, including Health and Accident (Insurance Case Series) (CCH)

Life Cas. Life (Health & Accident) Cases (CCH)

Life Cas.2d Life (Health & Accident) Cases (CCH), Second Series

Life Health & Accid. Ins. Cas. 2d (CCH) Life, Health & Accident Insurance Cases, 2d

Life Ten. Life tenants and remainderman

LIFO Last-in, first-out inventory method

Lig. Dig. Ligon's Digest (Alabama)

L.I.L. Lincoln's Inn Library

Lil. Lilly's English Assize Reports (1688-93)

Lil. Abr. Lilly's Abridgment

Lil. Conv. Lilly's Conveyancer

Lill. Ent. Lilly's Entries (Eng.)

Lilly Lilly's Reports and Pleadings of Cases in Assize (1688-93) (170 ER)

Lilly, Abr. Lilly's Abridgment, or Practical Register

Lilly Assize Lilly's Reports & Pleadings of Cases in Assize (1688-93) (170 ER)

Lilly Assize (Eng.) Lilly's Reports & Pleadings of Cases in Assize (1688-93) (170 ER)

Lil. Reg. Lilly's Practical Register

Lim. Act. Limitation of Action

Lincoln L. Rev.
- Lincoln Law Review (Buffalo)
- Lincoln Law Review (San Francisco)

Lind. Jur. Lindley's Study of Jurisprudence

Lindl. Co. Lindley on Companies

Lindley. Lindley's Law of Companies; 6 editions (1860-1950)

Lindley Comp.
- Lindley on Companies
- Lindley's Law of Companies. 6ed. 1902

Lindley P.   Lindley on Partnership

Lindley Part.   Lindley on Partnership. 13ed. 1971

Lindl. Partn.   Lindley on Partnerships

Lind. Part.   Lindley's Laws of Partnership

Lind. Pr.   Lindewoode's Provinciales

Lind. Prob.   Lindsay on Probates

L. in Eastern Eur.   Law in Eastern Europe. Leiden, Netherlands

L. in Japan   Law in Japan. An Annual. Tokyo, Japan

Linn Ind.   Linn's Index of Pennsylvania Reports

Linn, Laws Prov. Pa.   Linn on the Laws of the Province of Pennsylvania

L. in Soc'y   Law in Society

L. Inst. J.   Law Institute Journal (Aus.)

L. Inst. J. Vict.   Law Institute Journal of Victoria

L. Intell.   Law Intelligencer. 1843

L. In. Trans. J.   Law in Transition Journal

L. in Trans. Q.   Law in Transition Quarterly

Lip. Bib. Jur.   Lipenius' Bibliotheca Juridica

Lipp. Cr. L.   Lippitt's Massachusetts Criminal Law

Liquor Cont. L. Rep. (CCH)   Liquor Control Law Reports

Liquor Cont. L. Serv.(CCH)   Liquor Control Law Service

Liquor Liab. J.   Liquor Liability Journal

Lis Pen.   Lis Pendens (Lat.)

L.I.T.   Life Insurance Trust

Lit.
- Littell's Reports (11-15 Kentucky)
- Littleton's Common Pleas Reports (1626-32) (Eng.)
- Littleton's Tenures

Lit. & Bl. Dig.   Littleton & Blatchley's Insurance Digest

Lit. Brooke   Brooke's New Cases, King's Bench (1515-58) (Eng.)

Litig.   litigation

Lit. Sel. Ca.   Littell's Select Kentucky Cases

Litt.
- Coke on Littleton
- Littell's Kentucky Supreme Court Reports (1822-24)
- Littleton's Common Pleas Reports (Eng.)

Litt. & S. St. Law   Littell and Swigert's Digest of Statute Law (Ky.)

Litt. Comp. Laws   Littell's Statute Law (Ky.)

Littell.   Littell's Kentucky Reports

Litt. (Ky.)   Littell

Little Brooke   Brooke's New Cases (Eng.)

Littleton.   Littleton's English Common Pleas and Exchequer Reports

Litt. Rep. Littleton's English Common Pleas and Exchequer Reports

Litt. Sel. Cas. Littell's Select Cases (Ky.)

Litt. Ten. Littleton's Tenures.

Liv. Livingston, Mayor's Court Reports (New York)

Liv. Ag. Livermore, Principal and Agent

Liv. Cas. Livingston's Cases in Error (New York)

Liv. Dis. Livermore's Dissertation on the Contrariety of Laws

Liverm. Ag. Livermore on Principal and Agent

Livermore, Ag. Livermore on Principal and Agent

Liverpool L. Rev. Liverpool Law Review

Livingston's M.L. Mag. Livingston's Monthly Law Magazine

Liv. Judic. Op. Livingston's Judicial Opinions (N.Y.)

Liv. Jud. Op. (or Cas.) Livingston, Judicial Opinions (New York)

Liv. La. Cr. Code Livingston's Louisiana Criminal Code

Liv. Law Mag. Livingston's Law Magazine, N.Y.

Liv. L. Mag. Livingston's Law Magazine (New York)

Liv. L. Reg. Livingston's Law Register (New York)

Liv. U.S. Pen. Co. Livingston's System of United States Penal Laws

Lizars Lizar's Scotch Exchequer Cases (1840-50)

Liz. Sc. Exch. Lizar's Exchequer Cases (Sc.)

L.J.
- British Guiana Limited Jurisdiction (Official Gazette) (1899-1955)
- Hall's Law Journal
- House of Lords Journal
- Law Journal
- Law Judge
- Library Journal
- Lord Justice
- Lower Canada Law Journal (Quebec)
- New York Law Journal
- Ohio State Law Journal

L.J. Adm. Law Journal, New Series, Admiralty

L.J. Adm. N.S. Law Journal Reports, Admiralty, New Series (1865-75)

L.J. Adm. N.S. (Eng.) Law Journal Reports, New Series, Admiralty

L. Japan Law in Japan

L.J. App. Law Journal Reports, New Series, Appeals

L.J. Bank. Law Journal Reports, Bankruptcy

L.J. Bank. N.S. Law Journal Reports New Series, Bankruptcy

L.J. Bankr. Law Journal Reports, Bankruptcy

L.J. Bankr. N.S. (Eng.) Law Journal Reports, New Series, Bankruptcy

L.J. Bcy. Law Journal Reports, New Series, Bankruptcy

L.J. Bk. Law Journal Reports, Bankruptcy

L.J.C. Law Journal Reports, New Series, Common Pleas (Eng.)

L.J.C.C. Law Journal, County Courts Reporter

L.J.C.C.A. Law Journal Newspaper County Court Appeals

L.J.C.C.R. Law Journal Reports, New Series, Crown Cases Reserved (Eng.)

L.J.C.C.R. (N.S.) Law Journal Reports, New Series, Crown Cases Reserved, Eng., New Series

L.J. Ch. Law Journal Reports, New Series, Chancery

L.J. Ch. (Eng.) Law Journal Reports, New Series, Chancery

L.J. Ch. N.S. (Eng.) Law Journal Reports, New Series, Chancery

L.J. Ch. (O.S.) Law Journal Reports, Chancery, Old Series (1822-31) (Eng.)

L.J.C.P. Law Journal Reports, Common Pleas Decisions (Eng.)

L.J.C.P.D. Law Journal Reports, Common Pleas Decisions (Eng.)

L.J.C.P. (Eng.) Law Journal Reports, Common Pleas Decisions (Eng.)

L.J.C.P.N.S. Law Journal Reports, Common Pleas Decisions, New Series (1831-75)

L.J.C.P.N.S. (Eng.) Law Journal Reports, Common Pleas, New Series

L.J.C.P. (O.S.) Law Journal Common Pleas Old Series (Eng.)

L.J.D. & M. Law Journal Reports, New Series, Divorce & Matrimonial (Eng.)

L.J. Ecc. Law Journal Reports, New Series, Ecclesiastical Cases

L.J. Eccl. Law Journal Reports, New Series, Ecclesiastical Cases

L.J. Eq. Law Journal Reports, Chancery, New Series (1831-1946)

L.J. Ex. Law Journal Reports, New Series, Exchequer Division (Eng.)

L.J. Exch. Law Journal Reports, New Series, Exchequer Division (Eng.)

L.J. Exch. (Eng.) Law Journal Reports, New Series, Exchequer Division (Eng.)

L.J. Exch. in Eq. (Eng.) English Law Journal, Exchequer in Equity

L.J. Exch. N.S. Law Journal Reports, New Series, Exchequer (1831-75)

L.J. Exch. N.S. (Eng.) Law Journal Reports, New Series, Exchequer Division (Eng.)

L.J. Exch. (O.S.) Law Journal Reports, Exchequer, Old Series

L.J. Ex. D. Law Journal Reports, New Series, Exchequer Division (Eng.)

L.J. Ex. Eq. Law Journal, Exchequer in Equity (Eng.)

L.J.G. Lord Justice-General of Scotland

L.J.H.L. Law Journal Reports, New Series, House of Lords (Eng.)

L.J.I.F.S. Law Journal, Irish Free State (1931-32)

L.J.Ir. Law Journal, Irish (1933-34)

L.J. Lord Justices

L.J.K.B. Law Journal Reports, King's Bench

L.J.K.B. (Eng.) Law Journal Reports, King's Bench

L.J.K.B.N.S. Law Journal Reports, King's Bench, New Series

L.J.K.B. (N.S.) Law Journal Reports, King's Bench, New Series (1822-1949) (Eng.)

L.J.K.B.N.S. (Eng.) Law Journal Reports, King's Bench, New Series

L.J.K.B.O.S. Law Journal King's Bench Old Series (Eng.)

L.J.L.C. Law Journal (Lower Canada)

L.J.L.T. Law Journal (Law Tracts) (Eng.)

L.J. Mag. Law Journal New Series Common Law, Magistrates Cases (discontinued)

L.J. Mag. Cas. Law Journal Reports, Magistrates' Cases (1822-31)

L.J. Mag. Cas. (Eng.) Law Journal Reports, Magistrates' Cases

L.J. Mag. Cas. N.S. Law Journal Reports, Magistrates' Cases, New Series (1831-96)

L.J. Mag. Cas. N.S. (Eng.) Law Journal Reports, Magistrates' Cases, New Series

L.J.M. & W. Morgan & Williams' Law Journal (1803-04) (London)

L.J. Mat. Law Journal, Matrimonial

L.J. Mat. Cas. Law Journal, New Series, Divorce and Matrimonial (Eng.)

L.J. Mat. (Eng.) Law Journal, Matrimonial (Eng.)

L.J.M.C. Law Journal Reports, New Series, Magistrates' Cases (Eng.)

L.J.M. Cas. Law Journal Reports, New Series, Magistrates' Cases (Eng.)

L.J.M.C.O.S. Law Journal Reports, Old Series, Magistrates' Cases (Eng.)

L.J.M.P.A. Law Journal Reports, Matrimonial, Probate and Admiralty (Eng.)

L.J.N.C. Law Journal, Notes of Cases

L.J.N.C.C.A. Law Journal Newspaper, County Court Appeals (Eng.)

L.J.N.C.C.R. The Law Journal Newspaper County Court Reports (1934-47) (Eng.)

L.J.N.C. (Eng.) Law Journal, Notes of Cases (Eng.)

L.J. News. Law Journal Newspaper (1866-1965)

L.J. News (Eng.) Law Journal Newspaper

L.J. Newsp. Law Journal Newspaper (1866-1965)

L.J.N.S. Law Journal, New Series (1832-49) (Eng.)

L. Jo. Law Journal Newspaper (Eng.)

L.J. of the Marut Bunnag Internat. L. Off. Law Journal of the Marut Bunnag International Law Office. Bangkok, Thailand

L. Jo. N.C. Law Journal, Notes of Cases. (1866-92)

L.J.O.S. The Law Journal, Old Series (1822-31) (London)

L.J.O.S. Ch. Law Journal, Old Series, Chancer (1822-23)

L.J.O.S.C.P. Law Journal, Old Series, Common Pleas (1822-31)

L.J.O.S. Ex. Law Journal, Old Series, Exchequer (1830-31)

L.J.O.S.K.B. Law Journal, Old Series, King's Bench (1822-31)

L.J.P.
- Law Journal Reports, New Series, Privy Council (Eng.)
- Law Journal Reports, Probate, Divorce, Admiralty (Eng.)

L.J.P. & M. Law Journal Probate & Matrimonial (Eng.)

L.J.P.C. Law Journal Reports, Privy Council (Eng.)

L.J.P.C. (Eng.) Law Journal Reports, Privy Council (Eng.)

L.J.P.C.N.S.
- Law Journal Privy Council, New Series (Eng.)

L.J.P.C. (N.S.)
- Law Journal Reports, New Series, Privy Council (Eng.)

L.J.P.D. & A. Law Journal Reports, New Series, Probate, Divorce & Admiralty. (1875-1946)

L.J.P.D. & Adm. Law Journal Reports, New Series, Probate, Divorce, and Admiralty (Eng.)

L.J.P.M. & A. Law Journal Reports, New Series, Probate, Matrimonial, & Admiralty (Eng.)

L.J. Prob. Law Journal Reports, New Series. Probate & Matrimonial (1858-9, 1866-75)

L.J. Prob. & Mat. Law Journal Probate & Matrimonial (Eng.)

L.J. Prob. (Eng.) Law Journal Probate & Matrimonial (Eng.)

L.J. Prob. N.S. Law Journal Reports, New Series, Probate & Matrimonial (1858-59, 1866-75)

L.J. Prob. N.S. (Eng.) Law Journal, Probate, & Matrimonial, New Series (Eng.)

L.J.Q.B. Law Journal Reports, New Series, Queen's Bench (Eng.)

L.J.Q.B.D. Law Journal Reports, New Series, Queen's Bench Division (Eng.)

L.J.Q.B.D.N.S. Law Journal Reports, New Series, Queen's Bench Division (Eng.)

L.J.Q.B. (Eng.) Law Journal Reports, New Series, Queen's Bench (Eng.)

L.J.Q.B.N.S. Law Journal Reports, New Series, Queen's Bench (1831-1946)

L.J.Q.B.N.S. (Eng.) Law Journal Reports, Queen's Bench, New Series

L.J.R. Law Journal Reports (1823-1949)

L.J.R. (Eng.) Law Journal Reports

L.J. Rep. Law Journal Reports

L.J. Rep. N.S. Law Journal Reports, New Series

L.J. Sm. Smith's Law Journal (London)

L.J.U.C. Law Journal of Upper Canada

L.K. Lord Keeper of the Great Seal

L.L.
- Law Latin
- Law Library (Philadelphia), reprint of English treatises
- Used in citing old collections of statute law, as L.L.Hen.I.

Ll.
- Leges (Laws)
- Lloyd

Ll. Aluredi. Laws of Alfred

Ll. & G.t.P. Lloyd & Goold's Irish Chancery Reports Tempore Plunkett (1834-39)

Ll. & G.t. Pl. Lloyd & Goold's Irish Chancery Reports tempore Plunkett

Ll. & G.t.S. Lloyd & Goold's Irish Chancery Reports tempore Sugden (1835)

Ll. & W. Lloyd & Welsby's English Merchantile Cases (1829-30)

Ll. & Weis. Lloyd & Welsby. C.C.

L. Lat. Law Latin

LL. Athelst. Laws of Athelstan

LL. B Bachelor of Law

LL. Burgund Laws of Burgundians

LL. Canuti R. Laws of King Canute

Ll. C.C. Pr. Lloyd's County Courts Practice

LL. C.M. Master of Comparative Laws

Ll. Comp Lloyd, Compensation for Lands, etc. 6ed. 1895

LL. D. Doctor of law

LL. Edw. Conf. Laws of Edward the Confessor

LL. Hen. I. Laws of Henry I

L. Lib. Law Librarian, England

L. Lib. J. Law Library Journal

L. Libr. J. Law Library Journal.

L.L.J.
- Labor Law Journal
- Lahore Law Journal (India)
- Law Library Journal (U.S.)

Ll. Jud. Act Lloyd, Supreme Court of Judicature Acts. 1875

LL. L. Licentiate of Laws

Ll. List. L.R. Lloyd's List Law Reports (Eng.)

Ll. L.L.R. Lloyd's List Law Reports (1919-50)

LL. Longobard Laws of the Lombards

Ll. L. Pr. Cas. Lloyd's Prize Cas. (Eng.)

Ll. L.R. Lloyd's List Law Reports (1919-50)

Ll. L. Rep. Lloyd's List Law Reports (Eng.)

LL. M. Master of law

LL. Malcom, R. Scott. Laws of Malcolm, King of Scotland

Ll. Mar. L.N. Lloyd's Maritime Law Newsletter

LL. Neapolit. News of Naples

L.L.N.S. Law Library, New Series, Philadelphia Reprint of English Treatises

Lloyd & Goold (tempore Plunkett)

Lloyd & Goold (t.Plunkett) (Ir.) Lloyd & Goold (tempore Plunkett)

Lloyd & Goold (t.Sugden) (Ir.)
Lloyd & Goold (tempore Sugden)

Lloyd & W. Lloyd & Welsby's English Mercantile Cases

Lloyd List Lloyd's List (Eng.)

Lloyd, L.R. Lloyd's Law Reports (Eng.)

Lloyd Pr. Cas. Lloyd's List Prize Cases Reports (1914-24)

Lloyd Pr. Cas. N.S. Lloyd's List Prize Case Reports, 2nd Series (1939-53)

Lloyd's List. Lloyd's List (Daily, and weekly) (London)

Lloyd's List L.R. Lloyd's List Law Reports (Eng.)

Lloyd's L. Rep. Lloyd's Law Reports

Lloyds Mar. & Com. L.Q. Lloyds Maritime and Commercial Law Quarterly

Lloyd's Mar. L.N. Lloyd's Maritime Law Newsletter.

Lloyd's Pr. Cas. Lloyd's Prize Case Reports (Eng.)

Lloyd's Prize Cas. Lloyd's Prize Cases, (London)

Lloyd's Rep. Lloyd's List Law Reports (Eng.)

LLP Cohen & Gobert, The Law of Probation and Parole

Ll. Pr. Lloyd, Prohibition. 1849

Ll. Pr. Cas. Lloyd's List Prize Cases (1914-22; 1940)

Ll. Pr. Cas. N.S. Lloyd's List Prize Cases, New Series (1939-53)

L.L.R.
- Lancaster Law Review (Pa.)
- Leader Law Reports (S. Africa)

- Luzerne Legal Register (Pa.)

Ll. Rep. Lloyd's List Law Reports (1919)

Ll. R. Pr. Cas. Lloyd's List Prize Case Reports, 2nd Series (1939-53)

Ll. St. Lloyd's Statutes of Practical Utility

Ll. Suc. Lloyd, Succession Laws. 1877

L.L.T. Lahore Law Times (India)

Ll. Tr. M. Lloyd on Trade-Marks

LL. Wisegotho. Laws of the Visigoths

LL. Wm. Conq. Laws of William the Conqueror

LL. Wm. Noth. Laws of William the Bastard

L.M. Law Magazine, London (1828-1915)

L. Mag. Law Magazine, London (1828- 1915)

L. Mag. & L.R. Law Magazine and Law Review (London)

L. Mag. & Rev. Law Magazine & Review (London)

L.M. & L.R. Law Magazine and Law Review (London)

L.M. & P. Lowndes, Maxwell, & Pollock's Rep., Bail Court & Practice (1850-51) (Eng.)

LMCLQ Lloyds Maritime and Commercial Law Quarterly

L.M.D. Legal Monthly Digest (Aus.)

L.M.O.S.M.C. Law Journal, Old Series, Magistrates' Cases (1826-31)

L.M.Q. Legal Medical Quarterly

L.M.R.A. Labor Management Relations Act

LMRDA Labor-Management Reporting and Disclosure Act

LMSA Labor Management Services Administration

L.M.T.P.J. Legal Member of the Town Planning Institute

LN Shoenfield, Legal Negotiations

L.N.
- Law Notes, American Bar Association Section of General Practice
- Law Notes, a periodical published by Edward Thompson Company (Northport, Long Island, New York)
- Law Notes, London
- League of Nations
- Legal News (Canada)
- Legal Notification (Ghana)
- Liber Niger, or the Black Book

L. Notes Law Notes, England

L. Notes Gen. Pract. Law Notes for the General Practitioner

L. Notes (N.Y.) Law Notes, New York

Lns Lawyers Reports Annotated, New Series

L.N.T.S. League of Nations Treaty Series

L.N.Y. Laws of New York

L.O.
- Law Observer (1872) (India)
- Legal Observer (1831-56)
- Legal Opinion (1870-73)
- Solicitor's Law Opinion (U.S. Internal Revenue Bureau)

Lobin. Lobingier's Extraterritorial Cases, U.S. Court for China

Loc. Local

Loc. Acts Local Acts

Local Ct. & Mun. Gaz. Local Courts and Municipal Gazette

Local Fin. Local Finance

Local Gov. Local Government & Magisterial Reports

Local Gov. R. Aust. Local Government Reports of Australia

Local Gov't Local Government and Magisterial Reports (Eng.)

Local Govt. R. Austl. Local Government Reports of Australia

Local Govt. R. (N.S.W.) Local Government Reports, New South Wales (Aus.)

Locc. Loccenius, De Jure Maritimo et Navali

Locc. de Jur. Mar. Loccenius de Jure Maritimo

Loc. cit. Loco citato (in the place cited)

Loc. Code Local Code

Loc. Ct. Gaz. Local Courts and Municipal Gazette (Toronto, Ontario)

Loc. Gov. Local Government (Eng.)

Loc. Gov. Chron. The Local Government Chronicle, London, England

Loc. Gov. Rev. Local Government Review

Loc. Govt. Chr. & Mag. Rep. Local Government Chronicle & Magisterial Reporter (London)

Loc. Govt. Rev. Local Government Review

Lock. For. At. Locke on Foreign Attachment

Lock. G.L. Locke, Game Laws. 5ed. 1866

Lock. Rev. Ca Lockwood's Reversed Cases (N.Y.)

Lock. Rev. Cas. Lockwood's Reversed Cases (N.Y.)

Loc. Laws. Local Laws

Locus Standi Locus Standi Reports (Eng.)

L. Off. Econ. & Man. Law Office Economics & Management

L. Off. Econ. & Mgt. Law Office Economics and Management

Lofft. Lofft. English Kings Bench Reports (1772-74)

Lofft, Append. Lofft's Maxims, Appended to Lofft's Reports

Lofft Lib. Lofft on the Law of Libels

Lofft Max. Maxims, appended to Lofft's Reports

Lofft's Rep; Loft. Lofft's English King's Bench Reports (1772-74)

Lofft Un. L. Lofft's Elements of Universal Law

Log. Comp. Logan's Compendium of Ancient Law   Lois Recentes du Canada

Lo. L.R. Loyola Law Review

Lomax, Ex'rs. Lomax on Executors

Lom. C.H. Rep. Lomas's City Hall Reporter (N.Y.)

Lom. Dig. Lomax's Digest of Real Property

Lom. Ex. Lomax on the Law of Executors

Lo N League of Nations

Lond. London Encyclopedia

Lond.Gaz. London Gazette

Lond. Jur. London Jurist Reports (Eng.)

Lond. Jur. N.S. London Jurist, New Series

Lond. L.M. London Law Magazine

Lond. L. Mag. London Law Magazine

London L. Rev. City of London Law Review

Long & R. Long & Russell's Election Cases (Mass.)

Long. & T. Longfield & Townsend's Exchequer Reports (Ireland) (1841-42)

Long Beach B. Bull. Long Beach Bar Bulletin

Longf. & T.
- Longfield & Townsend (Ir.)
- Longfield & Townsend's Exchequer Reports (1841-42) (Ir.)

Longf. Dist. Longfield on Distress and Replevin

Longf. Ej. Longfield on Ejectment

Long, Irr. Long on Irrigation

Long.Q. Long Quinto (Year Books, Part X)

Long Quinto Year Books (Part X) 5 Edw. 4. 1465

Long S. Long on Sales of Personal Property

Lons. Cr. L. Lonsdale's Statute Criminal Law

LORAN Long-range navigation

Lor. & Russ. Loring & Russell's Election Cases (Mass.)

Lords Jour. Journals, House of Lords (Eng.)

Lorenz Lorenz's Ceylon Reports (1856-59)

Lorenz. App. R. Lorenz's Appeal Reports (Ceylon)

Loring & Russell. Loring & Russell's Massachusetts Election Cases

Loring & Russel El. Cases Loring and Russell, Election Cases in Massachusetts (Mass.)

Lor. Inst. Lorimer's Institutes of Law

Lor. Sc. L. Lorimer's Handbook of Scotch Law

Los Angeles B.A.B. Los Angeles Bar Association Bulletin

Los Angeles Bar Bull. Los Angeles Bar Bulletin

Los Angeles B. Bull. Los Angeles Bar Bulletin

Los Angeles Bd. P.U. Los Angeles, California, Board of Public Utilities

Los Angeles L. Rev. Los Angeles Law Review

Loss & Dam. Rev. Loss & Damage Review

Loss, Sec. Reg. Loss' Security Regulations

Lost Instr. Lost and destroyed instruments

Lou. Louisiana

Louisiana Ann. Louisiana Annual Reports (La.)

Louisiana Ann.Rep. Louisiana Annual Reports (La.)

Louisiana L. Rev. Louisiana Law Review.

Louisiana Rep. Louisiana Reports

Louis. Rep. Louisiana Reports

Louisville Law Louisville Lawyer

Lou. Leg. N. Louisiana Legal News

Lou. L.J. Louisiana Law Journal

Lou. L. Jour. Louisiana Law Journal

Lou. L. Rev. Louisiana Law Review

Lou. R. Louisiana Reports

Lou. Rep. N.S. Martin's Reports, New Series (La.)

Lou. Reps. Louisiana Reports

Love. Arb. Lovesy, Arbitration. 1867

Love. Bank. Lovesy, Bankruptcy Act, 1869. 1870

Lov. W. Lovelass on Wills

Low. Lowell's District Court Reports (U.S., Mass. District)

Low. Can. Lower Canada Reports

Low. Can. Jur. Lower Canada Jurist (1848-91)

Low. Can. Jurist Lower Canada Jurist

Low. Can. L.J. Lower Canada Law Journal

Low. Can. R. Lower Canada Reports

Low. Can. Rep. Lower Canada Reports (1850-67)

Low. Can. Rep. S.Q. Lower Canada Reports, Seignorial Questions

Low. C. Seign. Lower Canada Seignorial Rep.

Low. Dec. (F) Lowell's Decisions

Low. Dis. Lowell's U.S. District Court Reports

Lowell Lowell's District Court Reports (U.S., Mass. District)

Lower Can. Lower Canada Reports

Lower Can. Jur. Lower Canada Jurist

Lower Can. S.Q. Lower Canada Reports, Seigniorial Questions

Lower Ct. Dec. Ohio Lower Court Decisions

Lown. & M. Lowndes & Maxwell's English Bail Court Reports (1852-54)

Lownd. & M. Lowndes & Maxwell's Bail Court Reports (1852-54) (Eng.)

Lownd. Av. Lowndes, General Average. 10ed. 1975

Lownd. Col. Lowndes on Collisions at Sea

Lownd. Cop. Lowndes on Copyright

Lowndes & M. Lowndes & Maxwell's Bail Court Reports (1852-54)

Lowndes & M. (Eng.) Lowndes & Maxwell's Bail Court Reports (1852-54) (Eng.)

Lowndes, M. & P. Lowndes, Maxwell & Pollock's Bail Court Reports (1850-51) (86 RR)

Lownd. Ins. Lowndes on Insurance

Lownd. Leg. Lowndes on Legacies. 1824

Lownd. M. & P. Lowndes, Maxwell, & Pollock's Bail Court Reports (1850-51) (Eng.)

Lown. Leg, Lowndes on Legacies

Lown. M. & P. Lowndes, Maxwell, & Pollock's English Bail Court Reports (1850-51)

Low. Pr. Code Lower Provinces Code (India)

Loy. Loyola

Loy. Chi. L.J. Loyola University of Chicago Law Journal

Loy. Con. Prot. J. Loyola Consumer Protection Journal (Los Angeles)

Loy. Cons. Prot. J. Loyola Consumer Protection Journal (Los Angeles)

Loy. Consumer L. Rep. Loyola U. Consumer Law Reporter

Loy. Dig. Loyola Digest

Loy. Ent. L.J. Loyola (L.A.) entertainment Law Journal

Loy. L.A. Ent. L. J. Loyola of Los Angeles Entertainment Law Journal

Loy. L.A. Int'l & Comp. L. Ann. Loyola of Los Angeles Int'l & Comparative Law Annual

Loy. L.A. Int'l & Comp. L.J. Loyola of Los Angeles International and Comparative Law Journal

Loy. L.A. L. Rev. Loyola University of Los Angeles Law Review

Loy. Law. Loyola Lawyer

Loy. L.J. Loyola Law Journal (New Orleans) (1920-32)

Loy. L. Rev. Loyola Law Review (New Orleans)

Loyola Dig. Loyola Digest

Loyola L.J. Loyola Law Journal

Loyola Los A.L. Rev. Loyola of Los Angeles Law Review

Loyola Los. Ang. Int'l & Comp. L. Ann. Loyola of Los Angeles International and Comparative Law Annual

Loyola L. Rev. Loyola Law Review

Loyola of Los Angeles L. Rev. Loyola of Los Angeles Law Review.

Loyola U. Chi. L.J. Loyola University of Chicago Law Journal

Loyola U.L.A.L. Rev. Loyola University of Los Angeles Law Review

Loyola U.L.J. (Chicago) Loyola University Law Journal

Loyola U.L. Rev. (LA) Loyola University of Los Angeles Law Review

Loyola Univ. L. Rev. Loyola University Law Review (Chicago)

Loyola Univ. of Chicago L.J. Loyola University of Chicago Law Journal

Loy. R Loyola Law Review (La.)

Loy. U. Chi. L.J. Loyola University of Chicago Law Journal

Loy. U.L.J. Loyola University Law Journal (Chicago)

L.P.
- Limited Partnership

- Lord President of the Court of Session, Scotland

LPAA Jones, Litigating Private Antitrust Actions

L.P.B. Paper Book of Laurence, J., in Lincoln's Inn Library

L.P.C. Lords of the Privy Council Lower Provinces Code (India)

LPIB Wall, Litigation and Prevention of Insurer Bad Faith

L.P.R. Lilly's Practical Register (1745)

L.P.R.A. Laws of Puerto Rico Annotated

L. Prac. Mgmt. Law Practice Management

L.Q.
- Law Quarterly
- International & Comparative Law Quarterly

L.Q.R. Law Quarterly Review (1885)

L.Q. Rev. Law Quarterly Review

L.R.
- Alabama Law Review
- Land Registry
- Law Recorder (1827-38) (Ir.)
- Law Record (1911-12) (India)
- Law Register (1880-1909)
- Law Reporter (1821-22)
- Law Reports (Eng.)
- Law Review (1844-56)
- Louisiana Reports
- New Zealand Law Reports
- Ohio Law Reporter

L.R.A. Lawyers' Reports Annotated

L.R.A.1951A Lawyers' Reports Annotated 1915A, et seq.

L.R.A. & E. English Law Reports, Admiralty and Ecclesiastical (1865-75)

L.R.A.C. English Law Reports, Appeal Cases

L.R. Adm. & Ecc. Law Reports, Admiralty & Ecclesiastical Cases (1865-75)

L.R. Adm. & Eccl. Law Reports Admiralty & Ecclesiastical Cases (1865-75)

L.R. Adm. & Eccl. (Eng.) Law Reports, Admiralty & Ecclesiastical

L.R. Ann. Lawyers' Reports Annotated

L.R.A.N.S. Lawyers' Reports Annotated, New Series

L.R.A. (N.S.) Lawyers' Reports Annotated, (New Series)

L.R. App. English Law Reports, Appeal Cases, House of Lords

L.R. App. Cas. English Law Reports, Appeal Cases, House of Lords

L.R. App. Cas. (Eng.) English Law Reports, Appeal Cases, House of Lords

LRB Loyalty Review Board (U.S.)

L.R.B.G. Law Reports, British Guiana (1890-1955)

L.R.B urm. Law Reports (British Burma)

L.R. Burma. Law Reports (British Burma) (1948)

LRC Horowitz & Davidson, Legal Rights of Children

L.R.C.
- Law Reform Committee
- Law Revision Committee

L.R.C.A. Law Reports, Court of Appeals (New Zealand)

L.R.C.C. English Law Reports, Crown Cases Reserved (1865-75) 2vols.

L.R.C. Canada Law Reform Commission of Canada

L.R.C.C. (Eng.) English Law Reports, Crown Cases Reserved (1865-75) 2 vols.

L.R.C.C.R. Law Reports, Crown Cases Reserved (Eng.)

L.R. Ch. Law Reports, Chancery Appeal Cases (Eng.)

L.R. Ch. App. Chancery Appeal Cases (1865-75)

L.R.Ch. D. English Law Reports, Chancery Division

L.R. Ch. D. (Eng.) Law Reports, Chancery Division, English Supreme Court of Judicature

L.R. Ch. Div. (Eng.) Law Reports, Chancery Division, English Supreme Court of Judicature

L.R. Ch. (Eng.) Law Reports, Chancery Appeal Cases (Eng.)

L.R.C.P. Law Reports, Common Pleas, England (1865-75)

L.R.C.P.D. English Law Reports, Common Pleas Division (Eng.)

L.R.C.P. Div. Law Reports, Common Pleas Division

L.R.C.P. Div. (Eng.) English Law Reports, Common Pleas Division (Eng.)

L.R.C.P. (Eng.) Law Reports, Common Pleas (Eng.)

L.R. Cr. Cas. Res. Law Reports Crown Cases Reserved (Eng.)

L.R. Dig. Law Reports, Digest

L.R.E.A. Law Reports, East Africa

L.R.E. & I. App. Law Reports, House of Lords (English & Irish Appeals) (1866-75)

L. Rec. Law Recorder, Dublin, Ireland

L. Rec.N.S. Law Recorder, New Series (Ir.)

L. Record. Law Recorder

L. Rec. O.S. Law Recorder 1st Series, 4 vols. (Ir.)

L.R. Eng. & Ir. App. Law Reports, English & Irish Appeals (1866-75)

L. Rep. Carolina Law Repository (Reprint) (N.C.)

L. Rep. Mont. Law Reporter (Montreal)

L. Repos. Law Repository

L.R. Eq. English Law Reports, Equity (1866-75)

L.R. Eq. (Eng.) English Law Reports, Equity (1866-75)

L. Rev.
- The Law Review (Eng.)
- Law Review, Manila, Philippines

L. Rev. & Quart. J. Law Review and Quarterly Journal (London)

L. Rev. Dig. Law Review Digest

L. Rev. U. Detroit Law Review, University of Detroit

L.R. Ex. English Law Reports, Exchequer (1866-75)

L.R. Ex. Cas. English Law Reports, Exchequer (1866-75)

L.R. Exch. English Law Reports, Exchequer (1866-75)

L.R. Exch. D. English Law Reports, Exchequer Division

L.R. Exch. Div. Law Reports, Exchequer Division

L.R. Exch. Div. (Eng.) English Law Reports, Exchequer Division

L.R. Exch. (Eng.) English Law Reports, Exchequer (1866-75)

L.R. Ex. D. Law Reports, Exchequer Division (1865-75)

L.R. Ex. Div. English Law Reports, Exchequer Division

L.R.H.L. Law Reports, English & Irish Appeals & Peerage Claims, House of Lords (Eng.)

L.R.H.L. (Eng.) Law Reports, English & Irish Appeals & Peerage Claims, House of Lords (Eng.)

L.R.H.L. Sc. English Law Reports, House of Lords, Scotch and Divorce Appeal Cases (1866 75).

L.R.H.L. Sc. App. Cas. Law Reports, House of Lords, Scotch & Divorce Appeal Cases (1866-75)

L.R.H.L. Sc. App. Cas. (Eng.) English Law Reports, House of Lords, Scotch and Divorce Appeal Cases (1866-75)

L.R.I.A. English Law Reports, Indian Appeals

L.R. Ind. App. English Law Reports, Indian Appeals (1872-1950)

L.R. Ind. App. Supp. English Law Reports, Indian Appeals Supplement

L.R. Indian App. English Law Reports, Indian Appeals

L.R. Indian App. (Eng.) English Law Reports, Indian Appeals

L. Ripuar. Law of the Ripuarians

L.R. Ir. Law Reports, Ireland (1877-93)

L.R.K. Kenya Law Reports (1897-1956)

L.R.K.B. English Law Reports, King's Bench Division

L.R.M. Labor Relations Reference Manual

L.R. Mad. Indian Law Reports, Madras Series

L.R. Misc. D. Law Reports, Miscellaneous Division

L.R.N.S.
- Irish Law Recorder, New Series
- Nova Scotia Law Reports

L.R. (N.S.)
- Irish Law Recorder, New Series
- Nova Scotia Law Reports

L.R.N.S.W. Law Reports, New South Wales Supreme Court

L.R. (N.S.W.) B. & P. Law Reports, Bankruptcy & Probate (1880-1900) (N.S.W., Aus.)

L.R. (N.S.W.) D. Law Reports, Divorce (1880-1900) (N.S.W., Aus.)

L.R. (N.S.W.) Eq. Law Reports, Equity (1880-1900) (N.S.W., Aus.)

L.R. (N.S.W.) Vice-Adm. Law Reports, Vice-Admiralty (1880-1900) (N.S.W., Aus.)

L.R.N.Z. Law Reports (New Zealand)

L.R.P. English Law Reports, Probate Division

L.R.P. & D. Probate and Divorce Cases (1865-75) (Eng.)

L.R.P. & M. Law Reports, Probate and Matrimonial (1866-75)

L.R.P.C. English Law Reports, Privy council, Appeal Cases (1866-75)

L.R.P.C. (Eng.) English Law Reports, Privy Council, Appeal Cases (1866-75)

L.R.P.D. Law Reports, Probate Division (1875-90)

L.R.P. Div. English Law Reports, Probate, Divorce, and Admiralty Division

L.R. Prob. & Div. English Law Reports, Probate, Divorce and Admiralty Division

L.R. Prob. & M. (Eng.) English Law Reports, Probate, Divorce, and Admiralty Division

L.R. Prob. Div. English Law Reports, Probate, Divorce, and Admiralty Division

L.R. Prob. Div. (Eng.) English Law Reports, Probate, Divorce, and Admiralty Division

L.R.Q.B
- English Law Reports, Queen's Bench (1866-75)
- Quebec Reports, Queen's Bench (Canada)

L.R.Q.B.D. English Law Reports, Queen's Bench Division (1865-75)

L.R.Q.B. Div. English Law Reports, Queen's Bench Division

L.R.Q.B. Div. (Eng.) English Law Reports, Queen's Bench Division

L.R.Q.B. (Eng.) English Law Reports, Queen's Bench (1865-75)

L.R.R. Labor Relations Reporter (B.N.A.)

L.R.R.M. (BMA) Labor Relations Reference Manual (BNA)

L.R.R.P. Law Reports, Restrictive Practices Cases (1958-72)

L.R.R.P.C. Restrictive Practices Cases (Eng.) (1958-72)

L.R.S.A. Law Reports (South Australia)

L.R.S. & D. App. Law Reports, Scotch and Divorce Appeals (1866-75)

L.R.S.C. Law Reports, New Zealand Supreme Court

L.R. Sc. & D. English Law Reports, Scotch and Divorce Cases, before the House of Lords

L.R. Sc. & D. App.
- Scottish and Divorce Cases, before the House of Lords
- Scottish and Divorce Appeals (1866-75)

L.R. Sc. & Div. Scotch and Divorce Appeals (1866-75)

L.R. Sc. App. Law Reports, Scotch Appeals

L.R. Sc. Div. App. Law Reports, Scotch Appeals

L.R. Sess. Cas. English Law Reports, Sessions Cases

L.R.S.L. Law Reports, Sierra Leone Series

L.R. Stat. English Law Reports, Statutes

L.S.
- Law Student
- Locus sigilli (the place of the seal)

L.S.A.
- Louisiana Statutes Annotated.

- R.S. ... Revised Statutes
- C.C. ... Civil Code
- C.C.P. ... Code of Civil Procedure
- C.Cr.P. ... Code of Criminal Procedure

L. Sal. Salic Law

L. Salic. Salic Law

LSA.R.S. West's Louisiana Revised Statues

L.S.A.T. (U.S.) Law School Admission Test

LSB Louisiana State Bar

L. Sea Law of the Sea

L.S.G. Law Society Gazette (Eng.)

L.S. Gaz. Law Society's Gazette

L. Soc. Gaz. Law Society's Gazette

L. Soc. J. Law Society Journal

L. Soc'y Gaz. Law Society Gazette, England

L. Soc'y J. Law Society Journal

L.S.R. Locus Standi Reports (1936-60)

L. Stud. H. Law Students' Helper

L. Stud. Helper Law Student's Helper

L. Stud. J. Law Students' Journal

L. Stu. Mag. Law Student's Magazine (1844-54)

LSU Institute of Continuing Legal Education, Louisiana State University Law Center

L. Sup. H. & D. Labor's Supplement to Hill and Denio (N.Y.)

L.T.
- Law Times Journal
- Law Times Newspaper
- Law Times Reports, London

- Law Times, Scranton, Pennsylvania

L.T.B. Law Times Bankruptcy Reports (U.S.)

L.T.C. Land Transfer Committee

L.(T.C.) Tax Cases Leaflets

Ltd. Limited

L. Teach. Law Teacher

L. Teacher The Law Teacher. Journal of the Association of Law Teachers. London

L.T. (Eng.) Law Times Journal (Eng.)

L.T.G.F. Newl. Lawyers' Title Guaranty Funds Newsletter

L.T.J. Law Times Journal (a newspaper)

L.T. Jo. Law Times

L.T. Jo. (Eng.) Law Times Journal (a newspaper)

L.T. Jour. Law Times

L.T. Newsp. Law Times

L.T.N.S.
- Law Times, New Series (Pa.)
- Law Times Reports, New Series (Eng.)

L.T.N.S. (Eng.) Law Times, New Series

L.T.(N.S.) Law Times, New Series (Eng.)

L.T. (O.S.) Law Times, Old Series (Eng.)

L.T.O.S. Law Times Reports, Old Series (1843-59) (Eng.)

L.T.R. Law Times Reports (1859-1947) (Eng.)

L.T.R.A. Lands Tribunal Rating Appeals (1950)

L. Trans. Q. Law in Transition Quarterly

L.T. Rep. Law Times Reports, New Series (1859-1947)

L.T. Rep. N.S. Law Times Reports, New Series (Eng.)

L.T.R.N.S. Law Times Reports, New Series (1859-1947) (Eng.)

L.T.T. Land title trust

Lube Eq. (or Pl.) Lube on Equity Pleading

Luc. Lucas' Reports (Modern Reports, Part X) (1710-25)

Lucas. Lucas' Reports (Modern Reports, Part X)

Luck. Indian Law Reports, Lucknow Series (1926-49)

Luck. Ser. Indian Law Reports, Lucknow Series

Lud. & J. Tr. M. Ludlow & Jenkyns on Trade-Marks

Ludd. Ludden's Reports (vols. 43, 44 Maine)

Ludden. Ludden's Reports (vols. 43, 44 Maine)

Lud.E.C. Luder's Election Cases (Eng.)

Lud. El. Cas. Luder's Election Cases (1784-87)

Luder Elec. Cas. Luder's Election Cases (1784-87)

Luders Elec. Cas. (Eng) Luders Election Cases

Lum. Ann. Lumley on the Law of Annuities

Lum. Bast. Lumley on Bastardy

Lum.B.L. Lumley on Bye-Laws

Lumley P.L.C. Lumley's Poor Law Cases. (1834-42)

Lum. Parl. Pr. Lumley's Parliamentary Practice

Lumpkin
- Lumpkin
- Lumpkin's Reports (59-77 Ga.)

Lum.P.L.C. Lumley's Poor Law Cases (1834-42) (Eng.)

Lum.P.L.Cas. Lumley's Poor Law Cases (1834-42)

Lum. Pub. H. Lumley, Public Health Acts. 12ed. 1950-55 & supps.

Lum. Sett. Lumley on the Law of Settlements

Lund Pat. Lund on Patents

LUR Salsich, Land Use Regulation

L.U.S. Laws of the United States

Lush. Lushington's English Admiralty Reports (1859-62)

Lush. Adm. Lushington's English Admiralty Reports (1859-62)

Lush. Pr. Lush's Common Law Practice

Lush. Pr. L. Lushington on Prize Law

LUSL Loyola University School of Law

Lut. E. Lutwyche's Entries & Reports, Common Pleas (1682-1704) (Eng.)

Lut.E. Lutwyche's Entries & Reports, Common Pleas (1682-1704) (125 ER)

Lut. Elec. Cas. Lutwyche's Election Cases (Eng.)

Lut. Ent. Lutwyche's Entries (1704;1718)

Lut. R.C. Lutwyche's English Registration Appeal Cases (1843-45)

Lut. Reg. Cas. A.J. Lutwyche's Registration Cases (Eng.)

Lutw.

A.J. Lutwyche's Registration Cases (Eng.)
- E. Lutwyche's Entries and Reports, Common Pleas (1682-1704) (125 ER)

Lutw. E. Lutwyche's English Common Pleas Reports

Lutw. Reg. Cas. Lutwyche's Registration Cases (Eng.)

Lux. Luxembourg

Luzerne Leg. Obs. (Pa.) Luzerne Legal Observer

Luzerne Leg. Reg. (Pa) Luzerne Legal Register

Luzerne Leg. Reg. R. (Pa) Luzerne Legal Register Reports

Luzerne Leg. Reg. R. (PH) Luzerne Legal Register Reports

Luzerne L.J. (Pa) Luzerne Law Journal

Luz. Law T. Luzerne Law Times, (Pa.)

Luz. Leg. Obs. Luzerne Legal Observer (Pa.)

Luz. Leg. Reg. Luzerne Legal Register (Pa.)

Luz. Leg. Reg. Rep. Luzerne Legal Register Reports (Pa.)

Luz. L.J. Luzerne Law Journal (Pa.)

Luz. L.O. Luzerne Legal Observer (pa.)

Luz. L.R. Luzerne Legal Register (Pa.)

Luz. L. Reg. Rep. Luzerne Legal Register Reports (Continuation of Kulp) Pa.

Luz. L.T. Luzerne Law Times, Pa.

Luz. L.T. (N.S.). Luzerne Law Times, New Series (Pa.)

Luz, L.T. (O.S.) Luzerne Law Times, Old Series, (Pa.)

L.V. Laws of Virginia

LVC Decisions of the Lands Tribunal (Rating)

L.V.R. Land and Valuation Court Reports (New South Wales)

L.V. Rep. Lehigh Valley Law Reporter (Pa. 1885-87)

L.V.R. (N.S.W.) Land and Valuation Court Reports

L.W. Law Weekly, Madras (India)

L.W.L.R. Land and Water Law Review

L.W.R. Land and Water Law Review

Lw Stu. H. Law Students' Helper

LWV League of Women Voters

Lycoming Lycoming Reporter (Pa.)

Lycoming R. (Pa.) Lycoming Reporter

Lynd. Lyndwood, Provinciale (Eng.)

Lynd. Prov. Lyndwood's Provinciales

Lyndw. Prov. Lyndwood's Provinciale

Lyne Lyne's Chancery Cases (Wallis) (1766-91) (Ir.)

Lyne Lea. Lyne on Leases for Lives

Lyne on Renew. Lyne on Renewals

Lyne (Wall.) Wallis' Select Cases ed. by. Lyne (1766-91) (Ir.)

Lyon & R.B.S. Lyon & Redman on Bills of Sale

Lyon Ind. L. Lyon on the Laws of India

Lyon Just. Lyon's Institutes of Justinian

M

M.
- Indian Law Reports, Madras Series
- Macpherson's Session Cases (1862-73) (Sc.)
- Madras
- Magistrate
- Maine; Manitoba; Maryland; Massachusetts; Michigan; Minnesota; Mississippi; Missouri; Montana
- Maritime
- Marquess
- Menzie's Cape Colony Supreme Court Reports
- Michaelmas Term
- Miles' Pennsylvania Reports
- Modified
- Mongolian
- Morison's Dictionary of Sessions (1540-1808) (Sc.)
- Mortgage
- New York Miscellaneous Reports
- Ohio Miscellaneous Reports
- Queen Mary
- Session Cases, 3d Series, Scotland (Macpherson, & c.)

m.
- male
- married
- Modified; regulation or order modified (used in Shepard's Citations)

M' See Mac

M.A.
- Magistrates' Association
- Maritime Administration
- Medicaid
- Missouri Appeals Reports
- Munitions Tribunals Appeals, Great Britain High Court of Justice

MA Maritime Administration Reports

Ma.
- Malay
- March's Action for Slander and Arbitrament
- Massachusetts Reports

Ma.A. Massachusetts Appeals Court Reports

MAC Military Airlife Command

M.A.C. Magistrates Appeal Cases (Mal.)

Mac.
- Macassey's Reports, New Zealand (1861-72)
- Macnaghten's English Chancery Reports

Macal. McAllister's United States Circuit Court Reports

Macall. McAllister, United States Circuit Court Reports

Macalp.Mon.L. Macalpin on Money Lenders

Mac. & C. Macnaghten & Gordon's Chancery Reports (1849-51) (Eng.)

Mac. & H. Cox, Macrae & Hertslet Reports, Crown Cases (1847-58) (Eng.)

Mac. & I. Macrae and Hertslet's Insolvency Cases (1847-52) (Eng.)

Mac. & R. Maclean and Robinson, Appeal Cases (1839) (Sc.)

Mac. & Rob. Maclean & Robinson's Scotch Appeal Cases (1839)

Mac. A. Pat. Cas. MacArthur's Patent Cases (D.C.)

MacAr.
- MacArthur's Patent Cases
- MacArthur's Reports (8-10 District of Columbia)

MacAr. & M. MacArthur & Mackey's District of Columbia Supreme Court Reports.

MacAr. & Mackey. MacArthur & Mackey's District of Columbia Supreme Court Reports.

MacAr.Pat.Cas. MacArthur's Patent Cases (D.C.)

MacArth.
- MacArthur's Patent Cases
- MacArthur's Reports (8-10 District of Columbia) (1873-79)

MacArth. & M. MacArthur & Mackey's District of Columbia Supreme Court Reports (11 D.C.) (1879-80)

MacArth. & M. (Dist.Col.) MacArthur & Mackey's District of Columbia Supreme Court (11 D.C.)

MacArth. Ct. Mar. MacArthur on Courts-Martial

MacArth. Pat. Cas. MacArthur's Patent Cases (U.S.)

MacArthur
- MacArthur's Patent Cases

- MacArthur's Reports (8-10 District of Columbia)

MacArthur & M. MacArthur & Mackey's District of Columbia Supreme Court Reports.

MacArthur, Pat. Cas. MacArthur's Patent Cases (U.S.)

Macas. Macassey's Reports (New Zealand)

Macask. Ex. Macaskie on Executors, & c.

Macaulay, Hist. Eng. Macaulay's History of England

MacCarthy MacCarthy's Irish Land Cases (Ir.)

MacG.C. MacGillivray's Copyright Cases (1901-49)

Macc.Cas. Maccala's Breach of Promise Cases

Maccl. Maccala's Reports (Modern Reports, Part X) (1710-25)

Maccl.Tr. Macclesfield's Trial (Impeachment), London (1725)

Mac.C.M. Macomb on Courts-Martial

Macd. Macdevitt's Land Commissioner's Reports (Ir.)

Macd. Cr. L. Macdonald, Scotch Criminal

MacDermott Commission Commission on the Isle of Man Constitution. Report. 1959

MacDev.
- MacDevitt's Irish Land Cases (Ir.)
- MacDevitt's Land Cases (1882-84) (Ir.)

Macd. Jam. Macdougall's Jamaica Reports

MacF. MacFarlane's Jury Trials (Sc.)

Mac.F. Macfarlane (1838-39)

Macf. Macfarlane's Reports, Jury Courts (1838-39) (Sc.)

Macfar. Macfarlane's Reports, Jury Courts (1838-39) (Sc.)

MacFarl. Macfarlane's Jury Trials (Sc.)

Macfarlane Macfarlane's Jury Trials (Sc.)

Macf. Cop. Macfie on Copyright

Macf. Min. Macfarland's Digest of Mining Cases

Macf. Pr. MacFarlane, Practice of the Court of Sessions

Mac.G.C.C. MacGillivray's Copyright Cases (Eng. P)

MacGillivray & Parkington MacGillivray & Parkington's Insurance Law, 6ed. 1975

Mach. Machine[ry]

Mack. Mackenzie's Institutions of the Law of Scotland

Mack. & F. Jud. A. Mackeson & Forbes' Judicature Acts

Mack. B.L. Mackenzie on Bills of Lading

Mack. C.L. Mackeldey on Civil Law

Mack. Crim. MacKenzie's Treatise on Criminal Law 4 editions (1678-1758) (Sc.)

Mack. Cr. L. Sir G. Mackenzie's Criminal Law of Scotland

Mack. Ct. Sess. Mackey's Court of Session Practice

Mackeld.
- Mackeldey on Modern Civil Law
- Mackeldey on Roman Law

Mackeld. Civil Law Mackeldey on Modern Civil Law

Mackeld. Rom. Law Mackeldey on Roman Law

Mackey
- Mackey's District of Columbia Reports (1863-72, 1880-92)
- Mackey's Reports (12-20 D.C.)

Mack. Inst. Mackenzie's Institutes of the Law of Scotland 9 editions (1684-1758)

Mack. Law of Prop. Mackay, Law of Property. 1882

Mack. Nat. Mackintosh, Law of Nature and Nations. 5ed. 1835

Mack. Obs. Mackenzie's Observations on Acts of Parliament (1675, etc.) (Sc.)

Mack. Rom. Law Mackenzie's Studies in Roman Law

Macl.
- Maclaurin's Scotch Criminal Decisions
- McLean's United States Circuit Court Reports

Macl. & R. Maclean & Robinson, Scotch Appeal Cases (9 ER)

Macl. & Rob. Maclean & Robinson, Scotch Appeal Cases (9 ER)

Macl. Bank. Macleod, Theory and Practice of Banking

Maclean & R. Maclean & Robinson's Scotch Appeal Cases (1839) (9 ER)

Maclean & R. (Sc.) Maclean & Robinson, Scotch Appeal Cases (9ER)

Macl. Rem. Cas. Maclaurin's Remarkable Cases (1670-1773) (Sc.)

Macl. Sh. Maclachian on Merchant Shipping. 7ed. 1932

Macl. Shipp. Maclachian on Merchant Shipping

Macl. Wills Maclaren on Wills and Successions

Macn.
- Macnaghten's Hindu Law Cases (India)
- Macnaghten's Nizamut Adawlut Cases (1805-50) (Bengal, India)
- Macnaghten's Select Cases in Chancery tempore King
- Macnaghten's Select Cases, Sudder Dewanny Adawlut (1791-1858) (Bengal, India)
- W.H. Macnaghten's Reports, India

Macn. & G. Macnaghten & Gordon's English Chancery Reports (41, 42, ER)

Macn. & G. (Eng.) Macnaghten & Gordon's English Chancery Reports (41, 42 ER)

Macn.C. M. Macnaghten on Courts-Martial

Macn.Cr. Ev. Macnaghten's Criminal Evidence

Macn. El. Hind. L. Macnaghten's Elements of Hindu, & c., Law

Macn. Ev. Macnally's Rules of Evidence on Pleas of the Crown

Macn. Fr. Francis Macnaghten's Bengal Reports

Macn. N. A. Beng. Macnaghten's Nizamut Adawlut Reports, Bengal (India)

Macn. Nul. Macnamara, Nullities & Irregularities in Law. 1842

Macn. S.D.A. Macnaghten's Select Cases, Sudder Dewanny Adawlut (1791-1858) (Bengal, India)

Macn. S.D.A. Beng. (W.H.)Macnaghten's Sadr Diwani Adalat Reports (India)

Macn. Sel. Cas. Select Cases in Chancery tempore King, edited by Macnaghten (1724-33)

Mac. N.Z. Macassey's New Zealand Reports

Macomb C.M. Macomb on Courts-Martial

Mac. Pat.Cas. Macrory's Patent Cases (Eng.)

Mac. P.C. Macrory's Patent Cases (1847-60)

Macph.
- Macpherson, Lee & Bell's Session Cases (Sc.)
- Macpherson's Court of Session Cases (1862-73) (Sc.)

Macph. Inf. Macpherson on Infancy

Macph. Jud. Com. Macpherson, Practice of the Judicial Committee of the Privy Council

Macph. L. & B. Macpherson, Lee & Bell (Sc.)

Macph. Pr. C. Macpherson's Practice of the Judicial Committee of the Privy Council. 2ed. 1873

Macph. Priv. Counc. Macpherson's Privy Council Practice

Macph. S. & L. Macpherson, Shirreff & Lee (Sc.)

450

Macq. Macqueen's Scotch Appeal Cases, Houses of Lords (1851-65)

Macq.D. Macqueen's Debates on Life-Peerage Question

Macq. Div. Macqueen on Divorce

Macq. H. & W. Macqueen, Rights and Liabilities of Husband Wife. 4ed. 1905

Macq. H.L. Cas. Macqueen's Scotch Appeal Cases (House of Lords)

Macq. Mar. Macqueen, Marriage, Divorce and Legitimacy. 2ed. 1860

Macq. Sc. App. Cas. Macqueen Scotch Appeal Cases

Mac.R. Macdougall's Reports (Jamaica)

Macr. Macrory's Patent Cases (Eng.)

Macr. & H. Macrae & Hertslet's Insolvency Cases (1847-52) (Eng.)

Macr. Pat. Cas. Macrory's Patent Cases (Eng.)

Macr. P.Cas. Macrory's Patent Cases (1847-60)

MACRS Modified Accelerated Cost Recovery System

MacS. MacSweeney on Mines, Quarries and Minerals 5 editions (1884-1922)

Mad.
- All India Reporter, Madras
- Indian Law Reports, Madras Series (Eng.)
- Indian Rulings, Madras (1929-47)
- Maddock's Chancery Reports (1815-22) (56 ER)

- Maddock's Chancery Reports (1815-22) (Eng.)
- Maddock's Reports (9-18 Montana)
- Madras High Court Reports (India)

Madag. Madagascar

Mad. & B. Maddox & Bach's Reports (19 Montana)

Mad. & Gel. Maddock & Geldart's English Chancery Reports, 6, Maddock's Reports (1821-22)

Mad. Bar. Madox, Barona Anglia

Mad. Ch. Pr. Maddock, Chancery Practice. 3ed. 1837

Mad. Co. Madras Code (India)

Madd.
- Maddock's Chancery Reports (Eng.)
- Maddox's Reports (9-18 Montana)

Madd. & B. Maddox & Bach's Reports (19 Montana)

Madd. & G. Maddock and Geldart's Reports, Chancery, being volume 6 of Maddock's Reports (Eng.)

Madd. & Gel. Maddock & Geldart's Chancery Reports (1821-22) (56 ER)

Madd. Ch. Maddock's Chancery Reports (1815-22) (56 ER)

Madd. Ch. (Eng.) Maddock, Chancery Reports (56 ER)

Madd. Ch. Pr. Maddock's Chancery Practice (Eng.)

Made p. Made perpetual

Mad. Exch. Madox's History of the Exchequer

Mad. Fir. Burg.　Madox's Firma Burgi

Mad. Form.　Madox's Formulare Anglicarum

Mad. Form. Angl.　Madox' Formulare Anglicanum

Mad. H.C.　Madras High Court Reports (India)

Mad. Hist. Exch.　Madox'History of the Exchequer

Madh. Pra.　All India Reporter, Madhya Pradesh

Madhya Bharat　Indian Law Reports, Madhya Bharat

Mad. Jur.　Madras Jurist (India)

Mad. Law Rep.　Madras Law Reporter (India)

Mad. L.J.　Madras Law Journal (India)

Mad. L.Rep.　Madras Law Reporter (India)

Mad. L.T.　Madras Law Times (India)

Mad. L.W.　Madras Law Weekly (India)

Madox
- Madox's Formulare Anglicanum
- Madox's History of the Exchequer

Mad. Papers　James Madison's Papers

Madr.　Madras

Madras L.J.
- Madras Law Journal
- Madras Law Journal and Reports, India

Madras L.J. Crim.　Madras Law Journal Criminal

Mad. Reg.　Madden on Registration of Deeds

Mad. S.D.A.R.　Madras Sadr Diwani Adalat Reports (India)

Mad. Sel. Dec.　Madras Select Decrees

Mad. Ser.　Indian Law Reports, Madras Series

Mad. W.N.　Madras Weekly Notes

Mad.W.N.C.C.　Madras Weekly Notes, Criminal Cases (India)

MAELU　Mutual Atomic Energy Liability Underwriters (mutual liability pool)

MAERP　Mutual Atomic Energy Reinsurance Pool (mutual property damage pool)

M.A.F.F.　Ministry of Agriculture, Fisheries & Food

Mag.
- magazine
- Magistrate and Municipal and Parochial Lawyer (London, 5)
- Magruder's Reports (1, 2 Maryland)
- The Magistrate, London

Mag. & Con.　Magistrate and Constable

Mag. & Const.　Magistrate and Constable

Mag. & E. Comp.　Magnus & Estrin, Companies. 5ed. 1978

Mag. & M. & P.L.　Magistrate and Municipal & Parochial Lawyer

Mag. Cas.
- Bittleston, Wise, & Farnell's Magistrates Cases (Eng.)
- Magisterial Cases (Eng.)

- Magistrates' Cases (Reprinted from Law Journal Reports) (1892-1910)

Mag. Char. Magna Carta or Charta.

Mag. Ct. Magistrates' Court

Mag. Dig. Magrath's South Carolina Digest

Mag. Ins. Magen on Insurance

Magis. & Const. (Pa.) Magistrate & Constable (Pa.)

Magis. Ct. Magistrate's Court

Mag. (Md.) Magruder's Reports (1, 2 Maryland)

Mag. Mun. Par. Law Magistrate and Municipal and Parochial Lawyer

Magna Cart. Magna Charta (or Carta)

Magna Chart. Magna Charta (or Carta)

Mag. Rot. Magnus Rotulus (the Great Roll of the Exchequer)

Magna Rot. Pip.
- Great Roll of the Pipe
- Magnus Rotulus Pipae

Magruder Magruder's Reports (1, 2 Maryland)

Mah. & D.R.T. Mahaffy & Dodson, Road Traffic. 3ed. 1961

Maharashtra L.J. Maharashtra Law Journal (India)

Mah.L.J. Maharashtra Law Journal (India)

Mai. Maine; Maine's Reports

Mai. Anc. L. Maine's Ancient Law

Mai. Inst. Maine's History of Institutions

Maine Maine Reports

Maine Anc.Law Maine's Ancient Law

Maine Bar Maine State Bar Association Reports

Maine L. Rev. Maine Law Review

Maine P.U.R. Maine Public Utilities Commission Reports

Maine R. Maine Reports (Me.)

Maine Rep. Maine Reports (Me.)

Maine S.B.A. Maine State Bar Association

Maint. Maintenance

Mait. Maitland's Select Pleas of the Crown (1888)

Mait. Gl. Maitland's Pleas of the Crown, County of Gloucester

Maitland
- Maitland's Manuscript Session Cases (Sc.)
- Maitland's Pleas of the Crown, 1221 (Eng.)
- Maitland's Select Pleas of the Crown (Eng.)

Mai.VII.Com. Maine's Village Communities

Major Tax Plan. Major Tax Planning

Makerere L.J. Makerere Law Journal (Uganda)

Mak. L.J. Makerere Law Journal (Uganda)

M.A.L. Modern American Law

Mal.
- Malaya
- Malayan
- Malaysia

Malay. Malaysia

Malaya L.R. Malaya Law Review

Malaya L. Rev. Malaya Law Review, Singapore, Singapore

Malayan L.J. Malayan Law Journal

Malaysia R.C. Royal Commission on Non-Muslem Marriage and Divorce Laws (Malaysia)

M.A.L.C.M. Mercantile Adjuster and the Lawyer and Credit Man

Malcolm, Ethics Malcolm, Legal and Judicial Ethics

M.A.L.D. Master of Arts in Law and Diplomacy

Male El. Male's Law of Elections

Mal. Law M. Malyne's Ancient Law Merchant

Mall. Ent. Mallory's Modern Entries

Mal. Lex Merc. Malyne's Lex Mercatoria

Mal. L.J. Malayan Law Journal

Mallory Mallory's Chancery Reports (Ir.)

Mal. L. Rev. Malaya Law Review

Mal. Misch. Malicious Mischief

Malone Editor, 6, 9, and 10, Heiskell's Tennessee Reports

Mal. Pros. Malicious Prosecution

Malt. C.M. Maltby on Courts-Martial

Malynes Malynes, Lex Mercatoria. 3 editions (1622-36)

Man.
- Manhattan
- Manitoba
- Manitoba Law Reports (Canada)
- Manning Reports (1 Michigan)

- Manning Reports, Revision Court (1832-35) (Eng.)
- Manson's Bankruptcy Cases (Eng.)

Man. & G. Manning and Granger's C.P. Reports (1840-44) (Eng.)

Man. & R.
- Manning & Ryland's English Magistrates' Cases
- Manning & Ryland's King's Bench Reports (1827-30) (31-34RR)

Man. & Ry.
- Manning & Ryland's English King's Bench Reports (1827-30)
- Manning & Ryland's Magistrates' Cases (1827-30)

Man. & Ry. Mag. Manning & Ryland's Magistrates' Cases (Eng.)

Man. & Ry. Mag. Cas. Manning & Ryland's English Magistrates' Cases (1827-30)

Man. & Ry. M.C. Manning & Ryland's Magistrates' Cases (1827-30)

Man. & S. Manning & Scott, English Common Bench Reports (Old Series), IX

Man. & Sask. Tax Rep. (CCH) Manitoba & Saskatchewan Tax Reporter

Man. & Sc. Manning & Scott, English Common Bench Reports (Old Series), IX

Man. Bar News Manitoba Bar News

Manb. Coke Manby's Abridgment of Coke's Reports

Manb. Fines Manby on Fines

Man. B. News   Manitoba Bar News

Man. Cas.   Manumission Cases in New Jersey, by Bloomfield

Mand.   Mandamus

M. & A.   Montague and Ayrton's Bankruptcy Reports (1833-38) (Eng.)

M. & A.B.L.   Montagu & Ayrton on the Bankrupt Law

M. & Ayr.   Montague & Ayrton's Bankruptcy Reports (1833-38) (Eng.)

M. & B.   Montagu and Bligh's Bankruptcy Reports (1832-33) (Eng.)

M.& C.
- Montagu and Chitty's Bankruptcy Reports (1838-40)
- Mylne and Craig's Chancery Reports (1836-40) (Eng.)

M. & C. Bills   Miller & Collier on Bills of Sale

M. & Chit. Bankr.   Montagu & Chitty's Bankruptcy Reports (1838-40)

M. & Cht. Bankr.   Montagu & Chitty's English Bankruptcy Reports

M. & C. Partidas.   Moreau-Lislet and Carleton's Laws of Las Siete Partidas in force in Louisiana

Man. Dem.
- Mansel on Demurrer
- Mansel, Demurrer. 1828

M. & G.   Macnaghten & Gordons Chancery Reports (1848-52) (Eng.)
- Maddock & Geldart's Chancery Reports (1815-22) (Eng.)

- Manning & Granger's Common Pleas Reports (1840-44) (Eng.)

M. & Gel.   Maddock & Geldart's Chancery Reports (1815-22) (Eng.)

M. & Gord.   Macnaghten & Gordon's Chancery Reports (1848-52) (Eng.)

M. & H.   Murphy & Hurlstone's Ex. Reports (1836-37) (Eng.)

M. & K.   Mylne & Keen's Chancery Reports (1832-35) (Eng.)

M. & M.
- Montagu & Macarthur's Bankruptcy Reports (1828-29) (Eng.)
- Moody & Malkin's Nisi Prius Reports (1826-30) (Eng.)

M. & M'A.   Montagu & Macarthur's Bankruptcy Reports (1828-29) (Eng.)

M. & Mc.A.   Montague & McArthur's Bankruptcy (Eng.)

M. & P.   Moore & Payne's Common Pleas Reports (1827-31) (Eng.)

M. & P. Sh.   Maude & Pollock, Law of Merchant Shipping. 4ed. 1881

M. & R.
- Maclean & Robinson's Appeal Cases (1839) (Sc.)
- Manning & Ryland's King's Bench Reports (1827-30) (Eng.)
- Moody & Robinson's Nisi Prius Reports (1830-44) (Eng.)

M. & R.M.C.   Manning & Ryland's Magistrates Cases (1827-30) (Eng.)

M.& Rob.
- Maclean & Robinson's Appeal Cases (1839) (Sc.)

- Moody & Robinson's Nisi Prius Reports (1830-44) (Eng.)

M. & S.
- Manning & Scott's Reports (9 Common Bench) (Eng.)
- Master and Servant
- Maule & Selwyn's King's Bench Reports (1813-17) (Eng.)
- Moore & Scott's Common Pleas Reports (1831-34) (Eng.)

M. & Sc. Moore & Scott's Common Pleas Reports (1831-34) (34-8 RR)

M. & Scott. Moore & Scott's Common Pleas Reports (1831-34) (Eng.)

M. & W. Meeson & Welsby's Exchequer Reports (1836-47) (Eng.)

M. & W. Abr. Marshall & Wood's Abridgment

M. & W. Cas. Mining & Water Cases Annotated (U.S.)

M. & W. Law Dic. Mozley & Whitby's Law Dictionary

M. & Y. Martin & Yerger's Reports (8 Tenn.)

M. and Yerger's Rep. Martin (John H.) and Yerger (George S.) (Tenn.)

M. & Y.R. Martin & Yerger's Reports (Tenn.)

Man. El. Cas. Manning's English Election Cases (Court of Revision)

Man. Exch. Pr. Manning's Exchequer Practice (Eng.)

Man., G. & S. Manning, Granger & Scott, English Common Bench Reports, Old Series (I-VIII)

Man. Gaz. Manitoba Gazette

Man. Gr. & S. Manning, Granger & Scott, English Common Bench Reports, Old Series (I-VIII)

Man. Int. Law Manning, Commentaries on the Law of Nations

Manip. All India Reporter, Manipur

Manitoba
- Armour Queen's Bench and County Court Reports tempore Wood (Manitoba)
- Manitoba Law Reports

Manitoba L. (Can.) Manitoba Law Reports

Manitoba L.J. Manitoba Law Journal. Winnipeg, Manitoba, Canada

Man. Lim. Mansel, Limitations. 1839

Man. L.J. Manitoba Law Journal (Canada)

Man. L.R. Manitoba Law Reports

Man. L.R.C. Manitoba Law Reform Commission

Man. L.S. Chron. Manchester Law Students' Chronicle

Man. L.S.J. Manchester Law Students' Journal

Mann.
- Manning, Digest of the Nisi Prius Reports (Eng.)
- Manning, English Court of Revision Reports
- Manning's Reports (Michigan Reports, 1)

Mann. & G. (Eng.) Manning & Granger English Common Pleas Reports (133-135 ER)

Mann. & R.
- Manning & Ryland's King's Bench Reports (1827-30) (31-4 RR)
- Manning & Ryland's Magistrates' Cases. 1827-30

Mann. & R. (Eng.) Manning & Ryland's English King's Bench Reports

Mann. Bills Manning on Bills and Notes

Mann. Com. Manning's Commentaries on the Law of Nations

Mann. E.C. Manning's Revision Cases (1832-35)

Mann. Ex. Pr. Manning's Exchequer Practice

Mann. G & S. Manning, Granger & Scott's Common Bench Reports (1845-56) (135-9 ER)

Mann. G. & S. (Eng.) Manning, Granger & Scott, English Common Bench Reports, Old Series (I-VIII)

Manning
- Manning's Reports (1 Michigan)
- Manning's Unreported Cases (Louisiana)

Manning La. Manning's Unreported Cases (La.)

Manning's U.C. Manning's Unreported Cases (La.)

Manning's Unrep.Cases Manning's Unreported Cases (La.)

Mann. Nat. Manning's Law of Nations

Mann. Unrep. Cas. Manning's Unreported Cases (La.)

Man. P.U.C. Manitoba Public Utilities Commission (Canada)

Man. R. Manitoba Law Reports (Canada)

Man. Rev. Stat. Manitoba Revised Statutes (Canada)

Man. R.t. Wood Manitoba Reports, tempore Wood (Canada)

Mans.
- Mansfield's Reports (49-52 Arkansas)
- Manson's Bankruptcy and Companies' Winding-Up Cases (Eng.)

Mans. Dem. Mansel on Demurrer

Mansf. Mansfield (Ark.)

Mansf. Dig. Mansfield's Digest of Statutes (Ark.)

Mans. Lim. Mansel on Limitations

Manson Manson's Bankruptcy and Winding-Up Cases (1894-1914) (Eng.)

Manson, Bankr. Cas. Manson's Bankruptcy and Winding-Up Cases

Mans. on C. Mansel on Costs

Manson (Eng.) Manson's Bankruptcy (Eng.)

Man.Stat. Manitoba Statutes (Canada)

Man. T. Wood Manitoba Reports, tempore Wood (Canada)

Manum. Cas. Bloomfield's Manumission Cases (N.J.)

Manum. Cases Bloomfield's Manumission Cases (N.J.)

Man. Unr. Cases Manning's Unreported Cases

Man. Unrep. Cas. Manning's Unreported Cases (Louisiana)

Man.Unrep.Cas. (La.) Mannings Unreported Cases (La.)

Manw. Manwood's Forest Laws

Manw. For. Law Manwood's Forest Law (1592; 1598; 1615)

Manwood Manwood's Forest Laws (1592, 1598, 1615)

M.A.P. Military Assistance Program

M.A.R. Municipal Association Reports, New South Wales

Mar.
- March's King's Bench Reports (1639-42) (Eng.)
- Maritime
- Marshall & Sevestre's Appeals (1862-64) (Bengal, India)
- Marshall's Circuit Court Reports (U.S.)
- Marshall's Reports (Bengal)
- Marshall's Reports (Ceylon)
- Marshall's Reports (24-30 Kentucky)
- Martin Reports (Lousiana 1809-30)
- Martin's Reports (1 N.C.)
- Marvel's Reports (Del.)
- Mary

Mar. & Yer. Martin & Yerger's Reports (Tenn.)

Mar. Av. Marvin on General Average

Mar. Bills Marius on Bills of Exchange

Mar. B.J. Maryland Bar Journal

Mar Br. March's Brooke's New Cases (Eng.)

MARC Machine Readable Cataloging (cataloging format)

Mar.Cas. Maritime Cases by Crockford and Cox (1860-71)

March.
- March's King's Bench & Common Pleas Reports (Eng.)
- March's Translation of Brooke's New Cases, English King's Bench (82 ER)

March N. March's New Cases, King's Bench and C.P., Eng.

March N.C.
- March's New Cases, English King's Bench (1639-42)
- Translation of Brook's New Cases (1515-58)

March N.R. March's New Cases, King's Bench (1639-42) (82 ER)

Mar. Conv. Marcy, Epitome of Conveyancing. 1881

Mar. Conv.St. Marcy, Conveyancing Statutes. 5ed. 1893

Marijuana Rev. The Marijuana Review

Marine Ct. R. Marine Court Reporter (McAdam's) (New York)

marit. maritime

Maritimes L. Rep. (CCH) Maritimes Law Reporter

Marius Marius, Concerning Bills of Exchange. 4 editions (1651 -84)

Mark. El. Markby, Elements of Law. 6ed. 1905

Marks & Sayre Marks & Sayre's Rep. (108 Ala.)

Mark's & Sayre's Mark's & Sayre's (Ala.)

Mar. La. Martin's Louisiana Reports

Mar.Law Maritime Lawyer

Mar.L.C. Maritime Law Cases, by Crockford (1860-71)

Mar. L.Cas. (N.S.) Maritime Law Cases, New Series

Mar. L.C.N.S. Maritime Law Cases, New Series by Aspinall (1870-1940) (Eng.)

Mar. Leg. Bib. Marvin, Legal Bibliography

mar. lic. marriage license

Mar. L.J. Maryland Law Journal & Real Estate Record

Mar. L.R.
- Maritime Law Cases, New Series by Aspinall (1870-1940)
- Maritime Law Cases, 1st Series by Crockford (1860-71)

Mar. L.Rec. Maryland Law Record

Mar. L.Rev. Maryland Law Review

Mar. N. & Q.
- Maritime Notes & Queries (1873-1900)

Mar. N.C.
- March's New Cases, King's Bench (Eng.)
- Martin's Reports (1 North Carolina)

Mar. (N.C.) March's Translation of Brook's New Cases (1515-58) (73 ER)

Mar. N.R. March's New Cases (1639-42) (82 ER)

Mar. N.S. Martin's Louisiana Reports, New Series

Mar. Prov. Maritime Provinces Reports (Can.)

Marq. Marquette

Marq. L.Rev. Marquette Law Review

Marq. Sc. App. Cas. Macqueen's Scotch Appeal Cases (House of Lords)

Marq. Sports L. J. Marquette Sports Law Journal

Marquette Bus. Rev. Marquette Business Review

Marquette L. Rev. Marquette Law Review

Mar. R. Maritime Law Reports

Mark. & M. Markets and marketing

Marr.
- Hay & Marriott's Admiralty Decisions (1776-79) (Eng.)
- Marrack's European Assurance Cases (Eng.)
- Marriage

Marr. Adm. Marriott's Reports, English Admiralty

Mar. Rec. B. Martin's Recital Book

Mar. Reg. Mitchell's Maritime (1856-83) (London)

Marr. Form. Marriott, Formulare Instrumentorum (Admiralty Court) 1802

marr. settl. marriage settlement

Mars. Marsden's Select Pleas in the Court of Admiralty (Selden Society Publications, 6, 11)

Mars. Adm. Marsden's Admiralty (Eng.)

Mars. Coll. Marsden, Collisions At Sea. 11ed. 1961

Marsh.
- Marshall & Sevestre's Appeals (1862-64) (Bengal, India)

- Marshall High Court Reports (Bengal)
- Marshall's Circuit Court Decisions (U.S.)
- Marshall's Common Pleas Reports (1814-16)
- Marshall's Reports, Ceylon
- Marshall's Reports (8-10, 24-30 Ky.)
- Marshall's Reports (4 Utah)

Marsh. A. Marshaling Assets

Marsh. A.K. A.K. Marshall's Reports (8-10 Ky.)

Marshall
- Marshall's Reports (Bengal)
- Reports of Cases on Appeal (Calcutta)

Marsh. Beng. Marshall's Reports (Bengal)

Marsh. Calc. Marshall's Reports (Calcutta)

Marsh. Car. (or Ry.) Marshall on Railways as Carriers

Marsh. Ceylon Marshall's Ceylon Reports

Marsh. Costs Marshall on the Law of Costs

Marsh. C.P. Marshall's English Common Pleas Reports

Marsh. Dec.
- Marshall on the Federal Constitution
- Marshall's Circuit Court Decisions, by Brockenbrough (U.S.)

Marsh. (Eng.) Marshall (Common Pleas)

Marsh. Ins. Marshall on Marine Insurance

Marsh. J.J. J.J. Marshall's Reports (24-30 Ky.)

Marsh. (Ky.) Marshall's Reports (8-10, 24-30 Ky.)

Marsh. Op. Marshall's Constitutional Opinions

Marsh. Ry. Marshall's Duties and Obligations of Railway Companies

Mart.
- Martin (Louisiana Term Reports (1809-30)
- Martin's North Carolina Reports (1778-98)

Mart. & Y. Martin & Yerger's Tennessee Reports (8 Tennessee) (1825-28)

Mart. & Yer. Martin & Yerger's Tennessee Reports (8 Tennessee) (1825-28)

Mart. & Yerg. Martin & Yerger's Tennessee Reports (8 Tennessee) (1825-28)

Mart. & Y. (Tenn.) Martin & Yerger's Tennessee Reports (8 Tennessee) (1825-28)

Mart. Ark. Martin's Decisions in Equity (Ark.)

Mart. Cond. La. Martin's Condensed Louisiana Reports

Mart. Conv. Martin's Practice of Conveyancing

Mart. Dec. United States Decisions in Martin's North Carolina Reports

Mart. Ex. Martin on Executors

Mart. Ga. Martin's Reports (21-30 Georgia)

Marth. W.Ca. Martha Washington Cases, see United States v. Cole,

5 McLean, 513, Fed.Cas. No. 14,832

Martin
- Martin's Reports (21-30 Georgia)
- Martin's Reports (54-70 Georgia)
- Martin's Reports (Louisiana 1809-30)
- Martin's Reports (1 North Carolina)

Mart. Ind. Martin's Reports (54-70 Indiana)

MartinDict. Edward Martin's English Dictionary

Martin Index. Martin's Index to Virginia Reports

Martin (Lou.)N.S. Martin's Reports, New Series (La.)

Martin Mining
- Martin Mining Cases
- Martin's New Series (La.)

Martin's Chy. Martin's Chancery Decisions (Ark.)

Martin's La. Rep. Martin's Louisiana Reports (La.)

Martin's La. Rep. N.S. Martin's Reports, New Series (La.)

Martin's Louisiana R. Martin's Louisiana Reports (La.)

Martin's N.S. Martin's Reports, New Series (La.)

Martin's R.N.S. Martin's Reports, New Series (La.)

Mart. La. Martin's Reports (Louisiana, Old and New Series)

Mart. Law Nat. Martens' Law of Nations

Mart. M.C. Martin's Mining Cases (Canada)

Mart. N.C. Martin's Reports (1 N.C.)

Mart. N.S. Martin's Louisiana Reports, New Series (1809-30)

Mart. N.S. (La.) Martin's Louisiana Reports, New Series

Mart. O.S. (La.) Martin's Louisiana Reports, Old Series

Mart. Rep. Martin's Louisiana Reports (La.)

Mart. Rep. N.S. Martin's Reports, New Series (La.)

Mart. U.S.C.C. Martin's Circuit Court Reports, in 1 North Carolina

Marv. Marvel's Reports (15-16 Delaware)

Marv. Av. Marvin on General Average

Marv.(Del.) Marvel's Reports (15-16 Delaware)

Marvel Marvel's Reports (15-16 Delaware)

Marv. Leg. Bib. Marvin's Legal Bibliography

Marv. Wr. & S. Marvin on Wreck and Salvage

Mar. Wr. & S. Marvin on Wreck and Salvage

Mary. Maryland Reports (Md.)

Maryland Maryland Reports

Maryland Ch.Dec. Maryland Chancery Decisions (Md.)

Maryland Ch.Rep. Maryland Chancery Decisions (Md.)

Maryland L. Rev. Maryland Law Review

Mary. L. Rev. Maryland Law Review

Mas.
- Mason, United States Circuit Court Reports (5 vols.)
- Massachusetts Reports

Mascard.de Prob. Mascardus de Probationibus

Mas. N.E.Pr. Mason's New England Civil Practice

Mason Mason's U.S. Circuit Court Reports

Mason C.C.R. Mason's U.S. Circuit Court Reports

Mason Circt.Ct.R. Mason's U.S. Circuit Court Reports

Mason R. Mason's U. S. Circuit Court Reports

Mason's Code Mason's United States Code Annotated

Mason's R. Mason's U.S. Circuit Court Reports

Mason's Rep. Mason's U.S. Circuit Court Reports

Mason U.S. Mason's U.S. Circuit Court Reports

Mason U.S. Cir.Ct.Rep. Mason's U.S. Circuit Court Reports

Mason U.S.R. Mason's U.S. Circuit Court Reports

Mas. R. Massachusetts Reports (Mass.)

Mas. Rep. Massachusetts Reports (Mass.)

Mass.
- Massachusetts
- Massachusetts Reports
- Massachusetts Supreme Judicial Court Reports

Mass. Acts Acts and Resolves of Massachusetts

Mass. A.D. Massachusetts Appellate Decisions (Mass.)

Mass. Admin. Code Code of Massachusetts Regulations

Mass. Admin. Reg. Massachusetts Register.

Mass. A.D.R. Massachusetts Appellate Division Reports (Mass.)

Mass. Adv. Legis. Serv. Massachusetts Advance Legislative Service (Lawyers Coop.)

Mass. Adv. Sh. Massachusetts Advance Sheets (Mass.)

Mass. Adv. Sheets Massachusetts Advance Sheets (Mass.)

Mass. Ann. Laws Annotated Laws of Massachusetts

Mass Ap Massachusetts Appellate Reports

Mass. App. Ct. Massachusetts Appeals Court Report

Mass. App.Ct. Adv. Sh. Massachusetts Appeals Court Advance Sheets

Mass. App. Dec. Massachusetts Appellate Decisions

Mass. App. Div. Massachusetts Appellate Division Reports

Mass. App. Rep. Massachusetts Appeals Court Reports

Mass. B.C. & A. Massachusetts Board of Conciliation & Arbitration Reports

Mass. B.T.A. Massachusetts Board of Tax Appeals

Mass. Const. Massachusetts Constitution

Mass. Cont. Election, Cushing, S. & J. Massachusetts Controverted Election Cases (Mass.)

Mass. D.I.A. Massachusetts Department of Industrial Accidents Bulletin

Mass. Dr. Com. Masse, Le Droit Commercial

Mass. E.C., L. & R. Loring and Russell, Election Cases in Massachusetts (Mass.)

Mass. Elec. Ca. Massachusetts Election Cases

Mass. Elec. Cas. Massachusetts Election Cases

Mass. Election Cases
- Loring & Russell's Election Cases in Massachusetts (Mass.)
- Russell's Contested Election Cases (Mass.)

Mass.G. & E.L.C. Massachusetts Board of Gas & Electric Light Commissioners

Mass. Gen. Laws Massachusetts General Laws

Mass. Gen. Laws Ann. (West) Massachusetts General Laws Annotated

Mass. High. Com. Massachusetts Highway Commission

Mass. I.A.B. Massachusetts Industrial Accident Board Reports of Cases

Mass. L.Q. Massachusetts Law Quarterly

Mass. L.R. Massachusetts Law Review

Mass. L.R.C. Dec. Massachusetts Labor Relations Commission Decisions

Mass. L. Rev. Massachusetts Law Review

Mass. P.S.C. Massachusetts Public Service Commission

Mass. P.U.R. Massachusetts Public Utility Commission Reports

Mass. R. Massachusetts Reports (Mass.)

Mass. R.C. Massachusetts Board of Railroad Commissioners

Mass. Rep. Massachusetts Reports (Mass.)

Mass. St.B.C. & A. Massachusetts State Board of Conciliation & Arbitration Reports

Mass. U.C.C. Op. Massachusetts Unemployment Compensation Commission Opinions

Mass. U.C. Dig. Massachusetts Division of Unemployment Compensation Digest of Board of Review Decisions

Mass. U.C. Ops. Massachusetts Division of Unemployment Compensation Opinions

Mass. W.C.C. Massachusetts Workmen's Compensation Cases

Mast. Master's Reports (25-28 Canada Supreme Court)

Mast. El. Masterman, Parliamentary Elections, 1880

MAT Maritime, Aviation & Transport (Insurance)

Mat. Maturity

Math. Mathieu's Quebec Reports

Mathews Mathews (W.Va.)

Math. Pres. Ev. Mathews on Presumptive Evidence

Mat. L. & T. Mathews on Landlord and Tenant

Mat. Par. Matthew Paris, Historia Minor

Mat. Paris. Matthew Paris, Historia Minor

Mat. Part. Mathews on the Law of Partnership

Mat. Por. Mathews on the Law of Portions

Mats. Matsons' Reports (22-24 Connecticut)

Matson Matson's Reports (22-24 Connecticut)

Matth. Com. Matthews' Guide to Commissioner in Chancery

Matth. Cr.L. Matthews' Digest of Criminal Law

Matthews
- Matthews' Reports (75 Virginia)
- Matthews' Reports (6-9 West Virginia)

Matth. Exe. Matthews, Executors and Administrators. 2ed. 1839

Matth. Part. Matthews on Partnership

Matth. Pr.Ev. Matthews on Presumptive Evidence

Mau. & Pol.Sh. Maude & Pollock's Law of Shipping

Mau. & Sel. Maule & Selwyn's King's Bench Reports (1813-17) (Eng.)

Maude & P. Maude & Pollock's Law of Merchant Shipping 4 editions (1853-81)

Maude & P. Mer. Shipp. Maude & Pollock's Law of Merchant Shipping

Maude & P. Shipp. Maude & Pollock's Law of Merchant Shipping

Maud. Ment. Res. Maudsley on Mental Responsibility

Maug. Att.
- Maugham, Attorneys, Solicitors and Agents. 1825
- Maugham, Statutes relating to Attorneys, etc, 1839

Maug. Cr. L. Maugham, Outlines of Criminal Law. 2ed. 1842

Maug. Jur. Maugham, Outlines of the Jurisdiction. 1838

Maug. Law Maugham, Outlines of Law. 1837

Maugh. Lit. Pr. Maugham, Literary Property. 1828

Maugh. R.P. Maugham, Outlines of Real Property Law. 1842

Maug. R.P. Maugham's Outlines on Real Property Law

Maul. & Sel. Maule & Selwyn's English King's Bench Reports

Maule & S. Maule & Selwyn's English King's Bench Reports

Maur. Dec. Mauritius Decisions

Max. Maxim

Max. Dig. Maxwell's Nebraska Digest

Max. Int. Stat. Maxwell's Interpretation of Statutes. 12ed. 1969

Max. L. D. Maxwell's Law Dictionary

Max. Mar. L. Maxwell's Marine Law

Maxw. Adv. Gram. W.H. Maxwell's Advanced Lessons in English Grammar

Maxw. Cr. Proc. Maxwell's Treatise on Criminal Procedure

Maxwell
- Irish Land Purchase Cases (1904-11)
- Maxwell on the Interpretation of Statutes. 10 editions (1875-1953)

Maxw. Interp. St. Maxwell on the Interpretation of Statutes

May. Act. Mayhew, Action at Law. 1828

May Const. Hist. May's Constitutional History of England

May Crim. Law May's Criminal Law

May. Dam. Mayne on the Law of Damages

May Fr. Conv. May, Fraudulent Conveyances. 3ed. 1908

May, Ins. May on Insurance

May. Just. Mayo's Justice

May. L.R. Mayurbhani Law Report (India)

May. Merg. Mayhew, Merger. 1861

Mayn. Maynard's Reports, Exchequer Memoranda of Edward I, & Year Books of Edward II (Eng.)

Mayo & Moul. Mayo & Moulton's Pension Laws

Mayo Just. Mayo Justice

May, Parl. Law. May's Parliamentary Law

May, Parl. Pr. May's Parliamentary Practice

May. P.L. May's Parliamentary Practice, 19ed. 1976

M.B.
- All India Reporter, Madhya Bharat (1950-57)
- Matthew Bender
- Miscellaneous Branch, Internal Revenue Bureau (U.S.)
- Monthly Bulletin of Decisions of the High Court of Uganda
- Morrell's Bankruptcy Reports (Eng.)
- Munitions Board (U.S.)

M.B.A. Master of Business Administration

MBACLE Multnomah Bar Association Committee on Continuing Legal Education

M.B.J. Michigan State Bar Journal

M.B.L.R. Madhya Bharat Law Reports (India)

M.C.
- American Maritime Cases
- Magistrates' Cases (1892-1910) (Eng.)
- Magistrates' Court
- Malayan Cases (1908-58)
- Marriage Certificate
- Matara Cases (Ceylon)
- Mayor's Court

Mc See also Mac

M.C.A.
- Mississippi Code Annotated
- Montana Code Annotated

McAdam, Landl. & T. McAdam on Landlord and Tenant

McAl. McAllister's Circuit Court Reports (U.S.)

McA.L. & Ten. McAdam on Landlord and Tenant

McAll.
- McAllister's Circuit Court Reports (U.S.)
- McAllister's U.S. Circuit Court Reports

McAll.(Cal.) McAllister's U.C. Circuit Court Reports

McAllister U.S. Circ. Court R. McAllister's U.S. Circuit Court Reports

McA. Mar. Ct. McAdam's Marine Court Practice

McAr. McArthur's District of Columbia Reports

McArth. & M. MacArthur and Mackey's District of Columbia Reports (1879-80)

McBride McBride's Reports (1 Missouri)

M.C.C.
- Interstate Commerce Commission Reports, Motor Carrier Cases (U.S.)
- MacGillivray's Copyright Cases (1901-49)
- Martin's Mining Cases (British Columbia)
- Mining Commissioner's Cases (Canada)
- Mixed Claims Commission
- Moody's English Crown Cases Reserved (1824-44) (Eng.)
- Motor Carrier Cases
- Municipal Corporation's Chronicle (privately printed)

McCah. McCahon's Reports (Kansas 1858-68)

McCahon. McCahon's Reports (Kansas 1858-68)

McCall Pr. McCall's Precedents (Forms)

McCanless McCanless' Reports (Tenn.)

McCar. McCarter's New Jersey Equity Reports

McCart.
- McCarter's Reports (14, 15 N.J. Equity
- McCarty's New York Civil Procedure Reports

McCarter McCarter's Chancery (N.J.)

McCartney McCartney's Civil Procedure (N.Y.)

McCarty McCarty's Civil Procedure Reports (New York)

McCarty, Civ.Proc. McCarty's Civil Procedure Reports (N.Y.)

M.C.Cas. Municipal Corporation Cases Annotated. 11 vols.

McC.Cl.Ass. McCall's Clerk's Assistant

McC.F. McCall's Forms

McC.Just. McCall's New York Justice

McCl. McCleland's Exchequer Reports (1824) (Eng.)

Mccl. 10 Modern Reports, Macclesfield's Cases in Law and Equity (1710-24)

McClain, Cr. Law McClain's Criminal Law

McClain's Code. McClain's Annotated Code and Statutes (Iowa)

McCl. & Y. McCleland & Younge's Exchequer Reports (1824-25) (Eng.)

McCl. Dig. McClellan, Florida Digest

McCle. McClelland's Exchequer Reports (1824) (Eng.),

McCle. & Yo. Mccleland and Younge's Exchequer Reports (1824-25) (Eng.)

McClel. McClelland's Ex.Reports

McClel. Dig. McClellan's Digest of Laws (Fla.)

McClell. McClelland's Exchequer (Eng.)

McClell. & Y. McClelland & Younge's Exchequer Reports (1824-25) (Eng.)

McCl. Ex. McClellan's Manual for Executors

McCl. Ia. Co. McClain, Iowa Code

McCl. Mal. McClelland on Civil Malpractice

McCl. Pr. McClellan's Probate Practice

McCook McCook's Reports (1 Ohio State)

McCord McCord's Reports (S.C. Law 1821-28)

McCord Ch. McCord's Reports (S.C. Equity 1825-27)

McCord Eq. McCord's South Carolina Chancery Reports (1825-27)

McCork. McCorkle (N.C.)

McCorkle McCorkle's Reports (65 North Carolina)

McCr. McCrary's Circuit Court Reports (U.S.)

McCrary McCrary's U.S. Circuit Court Reports

McCrary, Elect. McCrary's American Law of Elections

McCrary's Rep. McCrary's U.S. Circuit Court Reports

McCr. Elect. McCrary's American Law of Elections

McCul. Dict. McCullough's Commerical Dictionary

McCul. Pol. Econ. McCulloch, Political Economy

M.C.D. Magistrates' Court Decisions (N.Z.)

McDer. Land L. McDermot, Land Laws (Ir.)

McDevitt. McDevitt's Land Commissioner's Reports (Ir.)

McDon. Jus. McDonald's Justice

McDonnell McDonnell's Sierra Leone Reports

McDow. Inst. McDowall, Institutes of the Law of Scotland

McFar. McFarlane's Jury Court Reports (Sc.)

McG. McGloin (La.)

McGill McGill's Manuscript Decisions, Court of Session (Sc.)

McGill L.J. McGill Law Journal

McGl. McGloin's Court of Appeal Reports (1881-84) (La.)

McGl. Al. McGlashan, Aliment (Sc.)

McGl. (La) McGloin's Louisiana Courts of Appeal Reports (La.)

McGloin. McGloin's Court of Appeal Reports (La.)

McGloin Rep. (La.) McGloin's Louisiana Courts of Appeal Reports (La.)

McGl. Sh. McGlashan, Sheriff Court Practice (Sc.)

McGrath McGrath's Mandamus Cases (Michigan)

Mch. Michigan Reports

McIn. & E. Jud.Pr. McIntyre & Evans' Judicature Practice

M.C.J.
- Master of Comparative Jurisprudence
- Michigan Civil Jurisprudence

McK. Consol. Laws McKinney's Consolidated Laws of New York

McKelvey, Ev. McKelvey on Evidence

McKin. Jus. McKinney's Justice

McKin. Phil. Ev. McKinnon's Philosophy of Evidence

McL Michigan Law Review

M.C.L.
- Master of Civil Law
- Master of Comparative Law

Mc.L. McLean's Circuit Court Reports (U.S.)

M'Cl. McCleland's Exchequer Reports (Eng.) (148 ER)

M.C.L.A. Michigan Compiled Laws Annotated

McL. & R. McLean & Robinson's Appeal Cases (1839) (Sc.)

M'Cl. & Y. McCleland & Younge's Ex. Reports (Eng.)

M'Cl. & Yo. M'Clelland & Younge's Ex. Reports, Eng.

McLar. Tr. McLaren, Trusts in Scotland

McLar. W. McLaren, Law of Wills (Sc.)

M'Cle. M'Cleland's Exchequer Reports (Eng.) (148 ER)

McLean McLean's U.S. Circuit Court Reports

M'Cle. & Yo. M'Cleland & Younge's Exchequer Reports (Eng.) (148 ER)

McLean's C.C.R. McLean's U.S. Circuit Court Reports

McLean's Rep. McLean's U.S. Circuit Court Reports

M'Clel. M'Cleland's Exchequer Reports (148 ER)

M'Clel. & Y. M'Cleland & Younge's Exchequer Reports (148 ER)

M'Clel. & Y. (Eng.) M'Cleland & Younge's Exchequer Reports (Eng.) (148 ER)

M'Clel. (Eng.) McCleland's Exchequer Reports (Eng.) (148 ER)

M.C.L.J. Mifflin County Legal Journal (Pa.)

MCLNEL Massachusetts Continuing Legal Education -- New England Law Institute, Inc.

M.C.M.
- Manual for Courts-Martial (U.S.)
- Municipal Court of Montreal

McMas. R.R. McMaster's New York Railroad Laws

McM. Com. Cas. McMaster's Commercial Cases (U.S.)

McM. Com. Dec. McMaster's Commercial Decisions

McMul. McMullan's Reports (S.C. Law Reports 1840-42)

McMul. Eq. McMullan's Reports
(S.C. Equity Reports, 1840-42)

McMull. Eq. (S.C.) McMullan,
South Carolina Equity Reports

McMull. L. (S.C.) McMullan,
South Carolina Law Reports

McNagh. Macnaghten's Select
Cases Chancery temp. King, Eng.
(See Macn.)

McNal. Ev. Macnally's Rules of
Evidence

M'Cord. Eq. (S.C.) M'Cord, South
Carolina Equity Reports

M'Cord. L. (S.C.) M'Cord, South
Carolina Law Reports

McPherson McPherson, Lee, &
Bell's Session Cases (Sc.)

M.C.P.Q. Municipal Code of the
Province of Quebec

McQ. MacQueen's Scotch Appeal
(House of Lords) Cases (1851-65)

McQuillin Mun.Corp. McQuillin
on Municipal Corporations

M.C.R.
- Magistrates' Courts Reports
(New Zealand)
- Matrimonial Causes Rules
- Montreal Condensed Reports

M. Cr. C. Madras Criminal Cases

McVey Dig. McVey's Ohio Digest

McWillie McWillie's Reports (73-
76 Miss.)

M.D.
- Application for writ of manda-
mus dismissed for want of juris-
diction
- Doctor of Medicine
- Master's Decisions (Patents)
- Middle District

Md., Md
- Harris & McHenry's Maryland
Reports
- Maryland
- Maryland Reports
- Maryland Supreme Court Re-
ports

Md. A. Maryland Appellate Reports

Md. Admin. Code Code of Maryland Regulations

Md. Admin. Reg. Maryland Register

M.D. Ala. United States District
Court for the Middle District of
Alabama

M.D. & D. Montagu, Deacon, De-
Gex's Bankruptcy Reports (Eng.)

M.D. & DeG. Montagu, Deacon,
DeGex's Bankruptcy Reports
(1840-44) (Eng.)

Md. Ann. Code Annotated Code
of Maryland

Md. App. Maryland Appellate Reports

Md. B.J. Maryland Bar Journal

M.D.C. Metropolitan District
Council

Md. Ch. Maryland Chancery Reports, by Johnson, 4 vols,

Md. Chan. Maryland Chancery
Decisions (Md.)

Md. Chan. Dec. Maryland Chancery Decisions (Md.)

Md. Ch. D. Maryland Chancery
Decisions (Md.)

Md. Ch. Dec. Maryland Chancery
Decisions (Md.)

Md. Code Ann. Annotated Code of Maryland

Md. Const. Maryland Constitution

M.D. Fla. United States District Court for the Middle District of Florida

M.D. Ga. United States District Court for the Middle District of Georgia

M. Dict. Morison's Dictionary of Decisions, Scotch Court of Session

Md. J. Contemp. Legal Issues Maryland Journal of Contemporary Legal Issues

Md. J.Int'l L. & Trade Maryland Journal of International Law & Trade

M.D. La. United States District Court for the Middle District of Louisiana

Md. Laws Laws of Maryland

Md. L.F. Maryland Law Forum

Md. L.R. Maryland Law Review

Md. L.Rec. Maryland Law Record (Baltimore)

Md. L.Rep. Maryland Law Reporter (Baltimore)

Md. L.Rev. Maryland Law Review

M.D.N.C. United States District Court for the Middle District of North Carolina

M.D. Pa. United States District Court for the Middle District of Pennsylvania

Md. P.S.C. Maryland Public Service Commission

Md. P.U.R. Maryland Public Utility Commission

Md. R. Maryland Reports (Md.)

Md.Rep. Maryland Reports (Md.)

Mdse. Merchandise

M.D. Tenn. United States District Court for the Middle District of Tennessee

Md.W.C.C. Maryland Workmen's Compensation Cases

Me.
- Maine
- Maine Reports
- Maine Supreme Judicial Court Reports

Me. Acts Acts, Resolves and Constitutional Resolutions of the State of Maine

Means. Mean's Kansas Reports

Mears Just. Mears' edition of Justinian & Gaius

Me. B.J. Maine Bar Journal

Mechem.
- Mechem on Agency
- Mechem on Partnership

Mechem, Ag. Mechem on Agency

Mechem, Pub. Off. Mechem on Public Offices and Officers

Mech. L. Mechanics' Liens

Me. Const. Maine Constitution

Med.
- Mediator
- Medical(cine)
- State Board of Medical Examiners

Med. & L. Medicine and Law

Medd. Meddaugh's Reports (13 Michigan)

Meddaugh. Meddaugh's Reports (13 Michigan)

470

Med. Devices Rep. (CCH) Medical Devices Reports

Media L. & P. Media Law and Practice

Media L. Notes Media Law Notes

Media L. Rep. (BNA) Media Law Reporter

Medico-Legal J. Medico-Legal Journal

Med. Jur. Medical Jurisprudence

Med. L. & P. Media Law and Practice. 1980

Med. L. & Pub.Pol Medicine, Law and Public Policy

MEDLARS Medical literature and analysis and retrieval system

Med.-Legal Crim. Rev. Medico-Legal and Criminological Review

Med.-Legal J. Medico-Legal Journal

Med.-Legal Soc'y Trans. Medico-Legal Society Transactions

Med. Leg. & Crim. Rev. Medico-Legal & Criminological Review

Med. Leg. Bul. Medico-Legal Bulletin

Med. Leg. J. Medico-Legal Journal

Med. Leg. N. Medico Legal News (New York)

Med. Leg. Pap. Medico-Legal Papers

MEDLINE Medical Literature On-Line

Med.L.J. Medico-Legal Journal (New York)

Med. L.N. Medico Legal News (New York)

Med. L.P. Medico Legal Papers (New York)

Med. Sci. & L. Medicine, Science & the Law

Med. Trial Tech. Q. Medical Trial Technique Quarterly

Med. Tr. T.Q. Medical Trial Technique Quarterly

Mees. & Ros. Meeson and Roscoe's English Exchequer Reports (1834-36)

Mees. & W. Meeson and Welsby's English Exchequer Reports (1836-47)

Mees. & Wels. Meeson and Welsby's English Exchequer Reports (1836-47)

Meg. Megone's Companies Acts Cases (1888-90) (Eng.)

Megarry Megarry. The Rent Acts

Megg. Ass. Meggison, Assets in Equity. 1832

Megone Megone's Company Acts Cases (1888-90)

Meigs Meigs' Tennessee Supreme Court Reports (1838-39)

Meigs, Dig. Meigs' Digest of Decisions of the Courts of Tennessee

Meigs'R. Meigs' Reports (Tenn.)

Me. L. University of Maine Law Review

Melanesian L.J.
- Melanesian Law Journal (Papua and New Guinea)
- Melanesian Law Journal, Sydney, Australia

Me. Laws Laws of the State of Maine

Melb. Melbourne

Melbourne U. L.R. Melbourne University Law Review

Melbourne Univ. L. Rev. Melbourne University Law Review, Melbourne, Australia

Melb.U. L. Rev. Melbourne University Law Review

Melb.Univ. L.R. Melbourne University Law Review

Melb.Univ. L. Rev. Melbourne University Law Review (Aus.)

Me. Legis. Serv. Maine Legislative Service

Mell Parl.Pr. Mell's Parliamentary Practice

MeLR Medical Liability Reporter

Me. L. Rev. Maine Law Review

Melv. Tr. Melvill's Trial (Impeachment) (London)

Mem.
- Memorandum
- Memphis

Mem.in Scacc. Memorandum or memoranda in the Exchequer

Mem. L.J. Memphis Law Journal (Tenn.)

Memo. Memorandum

Memphis L.J. Memphis Law Journal (Tenn.)

Memphis State U. L. Rev. Memphis State University Law Review

Memphis State Univ. L. Rev. Memphis State University Law Review.

Memphis St.U. L. Rev. Memphis State University Law Review

Memp. L.J. Memphis Law Journal (Tenn.)

Mem. St. U. L. Rev. Memphis State University Law Review

Men. Menie's Cape of Good Hope Reports

Mence Lib. Mence, Law of Libel. 1824

Menken. Menken's Reports, vol. 30 New York Civil Procedure Reports

Mental & Physical Disab.L.Rep. Mental and Physical Disability Law Reporter

Mental Disab. L.Rep. Mental Disability Law Reporter

Mental Hyg. Mental Hygiene

Menz. Menzie's Cape of Good Hope Reports (1828-49)

Menz. Conv. Menzies' Conveyancing

Menzies Menzies' Reports, Capes of Good Hope (1828-49) (S. Afr.)

Me. P.U.C. Maine Public Utilities Commission

Mer.
- Mercer Law Review (Ga.)
- Merivale's English Chancery Reports (1815-17)

Mer. & St.Corp. Merewether & Stephen's Municipal Corporations

Me. R.C. Maine Railroad Commissioners

MERC Mich. Employment Relations Commission

Merc. Ad. & Law. & Credit Man Mercantile Adjuster & Lawyer & Credit Man

Merc. Cas. Merchantile Cases

Mercer Mercer County Law Journal (Pa.)

Mercer, Beasley L. Rev. Mercer, Beasley Law Review

Mercer B.L. Rev. Mercer Beasley Law Review

Mercer Law Rev. Mercer Law Review

Mercer L. Rev. Mercer Law Review

Merch. Dict. Merchants' Dictionary

Merc.L.J. Mercantile Law Journal (New York or Madras)

Meredith Lect. W.C.J. Meredith Memorial Lectures

Me. Rev. Stat. Maine Revised Statutes

Me. Rev. Stat. Ann. Maine Revised Statutes Annotated

Merg. & Acq. Mergers & Acquisitions

Meriv. Merivale's English Chancery Reports (35, 35 ER)

Meriv. (Eng.) Merivale's English Chancery Reports (35, 36 ER)

Merlin, Repert. Merlin's Repertoire

Mer. L.J. Mercantile Law Journal (Madras, India)

Merr. Att. Merrifield, Attorneys. 1830

Merr. Costs Merrifield's Law of Costs

Merrimack. Smith's New Hampshire Reports (N.H.)

Mert. Merten's Law of Federal Income Taxation

MESA Mining Enforcement and Safety Administration

MESBIC Minority Enterprise Small Business Investment Companies

Met.
- Metcalfe's Reports (58-61 Kentucky) (1858-63)
- Metcalf's Reports (42-54 Massachusetts) (1840-47)
- Metcalf's Reports (3 Rhode Island)
- Metropolitan

Metc.
- Metcalfe's Reports (58-61 Kentucky)
- Metcalf's Reports (42-54 Massachusetts)
- Metcalf's Reports (3 Rhode Island)

Metc. Cont. Metcalf on the Law of Contracts

Metc. Ky. Metcalfe's Reports (58-61 Kentucky)

Metc. Mass. Metcalf's Reports (42-54 Mass.)

Metc. Yelv. Metcalf's Edition of Yelverton

Meth. Ch. Ca. Report of Methodist Church Cases

Metro. Metropolitan

Metrop.
- Metropolis
- Metropolitan

Mews
- The Reports (1893-95) (Eng.)
- Mews' Digest of English Case Law

Mews Dig. Mews' Digest of English Case Law

Mex. Mexico

Mfg. Manufacturing

MFI Marans, Williams, Griffin & Pattison, Manual of Foreign Investment in the United States

MFLA Green & Long, Marriage and Family Law Agreements

MFP Givens, Manual of Federal Practice

MFP(4) Givens, Manual of Federal Practice, Fourth Edition

M.F.P.D. Modern Federal Practice Digest

M'F.R. MacFarlane, Reports, Jury Court (Sc.)

Mfr.
- Manufacturer
- Manufacturing

M.G. & S. Manning, Granger, & Scott's English Common Pleas Reports (1845-56)

MGIC Mortgage Guaranty Insurance Corporation

M.G.L.A. Massachusetts General Laws Annotated

Mgmt. Management

M.G.P. Application for mandamus granted in part

Mgt Management

M.H.C. Madras High Court Reports (India)

M.H.C.R. Madras High Court Reports (India)

M. (H.L.) House of Lords, Appeals, 1862-73, in Macpherson's Court of Sessions Cases, 3d Series (Sc.)

Mi. Michigan; Michigan Reports

M.I. Writ of mandamus will issue

M.I.A. Moore's Indian Appeals (1836-71)

Miami L.Q. Miami Law Quarterly

Miami L. Rev. Miami Law Review (Florida)

Mich.
- Michaelmas Term
- Michigan
- Michigan Reports
- Michigan Supreme Court Reports

Mich. Admin Code Michigan Administrative Code

Mich. Adv. Michigan Reports Advanced Sheets

Mich. App. Michigan Court of Appeals Reports

Mich. Att'y Gen. Biennial Rep. Biennial Report of the Attorney General of the State of Michigan

Mich. B.J. Michigan Bar Journal

Mich. Bus. L.J. Michigan Business Law Journal

Mich. C.C.R. Michigan Circuit Court Reporter

Mich. Comp. L. Ann. Michigan Compiled Laws Annotated

Mich. Comp. Laws Michigan Compiled Laws

Mich. Comp. Laws Ann. Michigan Compiled Laws Annotated

Mich. Const. Michigan Constitution

Mich. Corp. Finance & Bus. L.J. Michigan Corporate Finance and Business Law Journal

Mich. Cr. Ct. Rep. Michigan Circuit Court Reporter

Mich. Ct. Cl. Michigan Court of Claims Reports

Michie's Ga. Repts. Ann. Georgia Reports Annotated (Ga.)

Mich. J. Int'l L. Michigan Journal of International Law

Michie's Jur. Michie's Jurisprudence of Va. and W.Va.

Mich. Jur. Michigan Jurisprudence

Mich. L. Michigan Lawyer

Mich. Lawyer Michigan Lawyer

Mich. Legis. Serv. (West) Michigan Legislative Service

Mich. Leg. News Michigan Legal News

Mich. L.J. Michigan Law Journal

Mich. LMB Michigan Labor Mediation Board

Mich. L. Rev. Michigan Law Review

Mich LR Michigan Law Review

Mich. Nisi Prius Brown's Michigan Nisi Prius Reports (Mich.)

Mich. N.P. Brown's or Howell's Michigan Nisi Prius Reports or Cases

Mich. Pol. Soc. Michigan Political Science Association

Mich. Pub. Acts Public and Local Acts of the Legislature of the State of Michigan

Mich. P.U.C. Ops. Michigan Public Utilities Commission Orders and Opinions

Mich. R. Michigan Reports (Mich.)

Mich. R.C. Dec. Michigan Railroad Comm. Dec.

Mich. S.B.A. Jo. Michigan State Bar Assn. Journal

Mich. S.B.J. Michigan State Bar Journal

Mich. Stat. Ann. Michigan Statutes Annotated

Mich. St.B.J. Michigan State Bar Journal

Mich. Supr. Ct. Rep. Michigan Reports (Mich.)

Mich. T. Michaelmas Term (Eng.)

Mich.Vac. Michaelmas Vacation

Mich. W.C.C. Michigan Industrial Accident Board, Workmen's Compensation Cases

Mich. Y.B.Int'l.Legal Stud. Michigan Yearbook of International Legal Studies

MICLE The Institute of Continuing Legal Education, University of Michigan

MICPEL The Maryland Institute for Continuing Professional Education of Lawyers, Inc.

Middle E. Executive Rep. Middle East Executive Reports

Middx.Sit. Sittings for Middlesex at Nisi Prius

Mid. East L. Rev. Middle East Law Review

Mi. L.
- Michigan Law Review
- University of Miami Law Review (Fla.)

Mil.
- Miles' Pennsylvania Reports
- Military
- Military and civil defense
- Miller's Reports (1-5 Louisiana)

- Miller's Reports (3-18 Maryland)
- Mills' South Carolina Constitutional Reports
- Mill's Surrogate's Court Reports (N.Y.)

Mil. & Vet. C. Military and Veterans Code

Milbank Q. Milbank Quarterly, The

Miles Miles' District Court Reports (Philadelphia 1825-41)

Miles (Pa.) Miles' Pennsylvania Reports

Miles R. Miles Reports (Pa.)

Miles R. & O. Miles' Rules and Orders (Common Pleas)

Miles Rep. Miles Reports (Pa.)

Milit. Military

Military L.J. Military Law Journal

Milit. L.R. Military Law Review

Mil. Jur., Cas. & Mat. Military Jurisprudence, Cases & Materials

Mill.
- Miles' Pennsylvania Reports
- Miller's Reports (1-5 Louisiana)
- Miller's Reports (3-18 Maryland)
- Mills' South Carolina Constitutional Reports (1817-18)
- Mill's Surrogate's Court Reports (N.Y.)

Mill. & C. Bills Miller & Collier on Bills of Sale

Mill. & F.Pr. Miller & Field's Federal Practice

Mill. & V.Code Milliken & Vertrees' Code (Tenn.)

Mill. Civ.L. Miller, Civil Law of England. 1825

Mill. Code Miller's Iowa Code

Mill Const. Mill's South Carolina Constitutional Reports

Mill, Const. (S.C.) Mill's South Carolina Constitutional Reports

Mill. Dec.
- Miller's Circuit Court Decisions (Woolworths) (U.S.)
- Miller's U.S. Supreme Court Decisions (condensed, continuation of Curtis)

Mill. Eq. M. Miller, Equitable Mortgages. 1844

Miller
- Miller's Reports (1-5 Louisiana)
- Miller's Reports (3-18 Maryland)

Miller, Const. Miller on the Constitution of the United States

Miller's Code. Miller's Revised and Annotated Code (Iowa)

Millin Petty Sessions Cases (1875-98) (Ir.)

Mill.Ins. (or El.) Miller's Elements of the Law of Insurances

Mill. La. Millers Reports (1-5 Louisiana)

Mill, Log. Mill's Logic

Mill. Md. Miller's Reports (3-18 Maryland)

Mill.Op. Miller's Circuit Court Decisions (Woolworth) (U.S.)

Mill. Part. Miller on Partition

Mill. Pl. & Pr. Miller's Iowa Pleading and Practice

Mill, Pos. Ec. Mill's Political Economy

Mil. L.Rep. Military Law Reporter

Mil. L. Rep.(Pub.L.Educ.Inst.) Military Law Reporter

Mil. L. Rev. Military Law Review

Mills. Mills' Reports, New York Surrogate Court

Mills Ann. St. Mills' Annotated Statutes (Colo.)

Mills Em.D. Mills on Eminent Domain

Mills, Em. Dom. Mills on Eminent Domain

Mills (N.Y.) Mills' Reports, New York Surrogate Court

Mills' Surr. Ct. Mills' Surrogate Court Reports (New York)

Mil. Rep. Militia Reporter (Boston)

MILSTAMP Military Standard Transportation and Movement Procedures

Mil. Std. Military Standards

Milw. Milward's Irish Ecclesiastical Reports (1819-43)

Milwaukee Law. Milwaukee Lawyer

Milw.B.A.G. Milwaukee Bar Assn. Gavel

Milw. Ir. Ecc. Rep. Milward's Irish Ecclesiastical Reports (1819-43)

Mim.
- Mimeographed letter
- United States Internal Revenue Bureau, Commissioner's Mimeographed Published Opinions

Min.
- Mineral
- Minister
- Ministry
- Minnesota Reports

- Minor
- Minor's Reports (Alabama 1820-26)
- Minute

Min. Dig. Minot's Digest (Massachusetts)

Mine Safety & Health Rep. (BNA) Mine Safety and Health Reporter

Min. Ev. Minutes of Evidence

Min. H.M.D. National Health Insurance (Ministry of Health Decisions)

Min. Inst. Minor's Institutes of Common and Statute Law

Minn.
- Minnesota
- Minnesota Reports
- Minnesota Supreme Court Reports

Minn. Admin. Reg. Minnesota State Register.

Minn. Code Agency Minnesota Code of Agency Rules

Minn. Code Ann. Minnesota Code Annotated

Minn. Const. Minnesota Constitution

Minn. Cont. L. Ed. Minnesota Continuing Legal Education

Minn. Cont. Legal Ed. Minnesota Continuing Legal Education

Minn. Ct. Rep. Minnesota Court Reporter

Minn. D.L. & I. Comp. Minnesota Department of Labor and Industries. Compilation of Court Decisions

Minnesota L. Rev. Minnesota Law Review.

Minn. Gen. Laws Minnesota General Laws

Minn. (Gil.) Minnesota Reports (Gilfillan Edition) (Minn.)

Minn. (Gill.) Minnesota Reports (Gilfillan Edition) (Minn.)

Minn. Law J. Minnesota Law Journal

Minn. Laws Laws of Minnesota

Minn.L.J. Minnesota Law Journal (St. Paul, Minn.)

Minn. L. Rev., Minn LR Minnesota Law Review

Minn. R. & W.C. Minnesota Railroad and Warehouse Commission

Minn. R & W.C.A.T. Div. Minnesota Railroad and Warehouse Commission. Auto Transportation Co. Division. Reports

Minn. Rep. Minnesota Reports (Minn.)

Minn. Reps. Minnesota Reports (Minn.)

Minn. S.B.A. Minnesota State Bar Association

Minn. Sess. Law Serv. (West) Minnesota Session Law Service

Minn. Stat. Minnesota Statutes

Minn. Stat. Ann. Minnesota Statutes Annotated

Minn. Stat. Ann. (West) West's Minnesota Statutes Annotated

Minn. W.C.D. Minnesota Workmen's Compensation Decisions

Minor
- Minor's Alabama Supreme Court Reports (1820-26)
- Minor's Institutes

Minor (Ala.)
- Minor's Institutes
- Minor's Reports (Alabama 1820-26)

Minor, Inst. Minor's Institutes of Common and Statute Law

Minor's Alabama Rep. Minor's Reports (Ala.)

Minor's Ala. R. Minor's Reports (Ala.)

Minor's Ala. Rep. Minor's Reports (Ala.)

Minor's R. Minor's Reports (Ala.)

Minor's Rep. Minor's Reports (Ala.)

Minor's Reports Minor's Reports (Ala.)

Min.R. Minnesota Reports (Minn.)

Min. Rep. Minnesota Reports (Minn.)

Mins. Minutes

Mir. Horne's Mirror of Justices

Mirch. D. & S. Mirchall's Doctor and Student

Mireh. Advow. Mirehouse, Advowsons. 1824

Mireh. Ti. Mirehouse, Tithes. 2ed. 1822

Mir. Just. Horne's Mirror of Justices

Mir. Parl. Mirror of Parliament, London

Mir.Pat.Off. Mirror of the Patent Office (Washington, D.C.)

Mirr. Horne's Mirror of Justices

MIRV Multiple Independently Targetable Reentry Vehicles

Mis.
- Mississippi
- Mississippi Reports

MIS Military Inspection Service (Manual-USN)

Misc. Miscellaneous Reports (New York)

Misc.2d Miscellaneous Reports, Second Series (New York)

misc. miscellaneous

Misc. Dec. Ohio Miscellaneous Decisions (Gottschall 1865-73)

Miscel. Miscellaneous Reports (New York)

Misc. Laws Miscellaneous Laws, Or.

Misc. (N.Y.) Miscellaneous Reports (New York)

Misc. Rep. Miscellaneous Reports (New York)

Misc. Reports New York Miscellaneous Reports (N.Y.)

Misc. Repts. New York Miscellaneous Reports (N.Y.)

Mis.
- Missouri Reports (Mo.)
- New York Miscellaneous Reports (N.Y.)

Mis. R. Missouri Reports (Mo.)

Mis. Rep. Missouri Reports (Mo.)

Miss.
- Mississippi
- Mississippi Reports
- Mississippi Supreme Court Reports
- Missouri

Miss. C.L. Rev. Mississippi College Law Review

Miss. Code Ann. Mississippi Code Annotated

Miss. Const. Mississippi Constitution

Miss. Dec. Mississippi Decisions

Miss. Law. Mississippi Lawyer

Miss. Law. Rev. Mississippi Law Review

Miss. Laws General Laws of Mississippi

Miss. Lawyer Mississippi Lawyer

Miss. L.J. Mississippi Law Journal

Miss. L. Rev. Mississippi Law Review

Misso. Missouri Reports (Mo.)

Misso. R. Missouri Reports (Mo.)

Misso. Rep. Missouri Reports (Mo.)

Missour. Rep. Missouri Reports (Mo.)

Missouri Missouri Reports (Mo.)

Missouri R. Missouri Reports (Mo.)

Missouri Rep. Missouri Reports (Mo.)

Missouri Reports Missouri Reports (Mo.)

Miss. R. Mississippi Reports (Miss.)

Miss. R.C. Mississippi Railroad Commission Reports

Miss. Rep. Mississippi Reports (miss.)

Miss. S.B.A. Mississippi State Bar Association

Miss. St. Ca. Morris' Mississippi State Cases (1818-72)

Miss. St. Cas. Morris' Mississippi State Cases (1818-72)

Mister
- Mister (Mo.)
- Mister's Reports (17-32 Mo.App.)

Mister Mister's Reports (17-32 Mo. Appeals)

MIT
- Massachusetts Institute of Technology
- Westin, Middle Income Tax Planning and Shelters

Mitch. B. & N. Mitchell, Bills, Notes, etc. 1829

Mitchell's Mar.Reg. Mitchell's Maritime Register

Mitch. M.R. Mitchell's Maritime Register (1856-83)

Mitch. Mod. Geog. Mitchells Modern Geography

Mit. Ch. Pl. Mitford's Equity Pleading

Mit. Drunk Mittermaier's Effect of Drunkenness on Criminal Responsibilty

Mitf. & Ty. Eq. Pl. Tyler's Edition of Mitford's Equity Pleading

Mitf. Eq. Pl. Mitford on Equity Pleading

M.J.
- Madras Jurist (1866-76) (India)
- Military Justice Reporter (West)

M.J.S. Master of Juridical Science

Mkt. Market

Mktg Marketing

Mkts. Markets

ML Military Laws of the United States (Army) annotated

M.L. Master of Laws

M.L.A.A.N.Z. Newsletter Maritime Law Association of Australia and New Zealand Newsletter

M'Laur. M'Laurin's Judiciary Cases (1774) (Sc.)

MLB Maritime Labor Board (U.S.)

M.L. Dig. & R. Monthly Law Digest & Reporter (Canada)

M.L.E. Maryland Law Encyclopedia

M'Lean's R. McLean's U.S. Circuit Court Reports

M.L.J.
- Madras Law Journal (India)
- Makere Law Journal (Uganda)
- Malayan Law Journal
- Manitoba Law Journal
- Memphis Law Journal
- Mississippi Law Journal

M.L.J. Supp. Malayan Law Journal, Supplement

M.L.P. Michigan Law and Practice

M.L.Q. Malabar Law Quarterly

M.L.R.
- Malayan Law Reports (1950-54)
- Manitoba Law Reports (Can.)
- Maryland Law Record
- Mauritius Law Reporter
- Minimum Lending Rate
- Modern Law Review
- Monthly Labor Review
- Montreal Law Reports

MLRC Mass. Labor Relations Commission

M.L.R.C. Manitoba Law Reform Commission

M.L.R., C.B.R.   Montreal Law Reports, Queen's Bench (Quebec, Can.) 1884-91

M.L.R., C.S.   Montreal Law Reports, Superior Court (1880-91) (Can.)

M.L.R.Q.B.   Montreal Law Reports (Queen's Bench)

M.L.R.S.C.   Montreal Law Reports, Superior Court (Canada)

M.L.S.
- Master of Library Science
- Multiple Listing Service

M.L.T.   Madras Law Times (India)

M.L.W.   Madras Law Weekly (India)

MMBL   McCafferty & Meyer, Medical Malpractice: Bases of Liability

M.M.C.   Martin's Reports of Mining Cases (Canada)

M.McA.   Montague & McArthur's Bankruptcy, Eng.

M.M.Cas.   Martin's Reports of Mining Cases (Canada)

MMCC   Rosenblum, Medical Malpractice: Handling Cardilogy and Cardiovascular Surgery Cases

MMD(2)   Schafler, Medical Malpractice: Handling Dental Cases, Second Edition

MMDC   Schafler, Medical Malpractice: Handling Dental Cases

MMEM   Flick, Medical Malpractice: Handling Emergency Medicine Cases

M.M.F.   Merchant Marine and Fisheries

MMGS   Shiffman, Medical Malpractice: Handling General Surgery Cases

MMO   Rabin, Medical Malpractice: Handling Ophthalmology Cases

MMOC   Harsha, Medical Malpractice: Handling Orthopedic Cases

MMON   Volk & Morgan, Medical Malpractice: Obstetrics and Neonatal Cases

MMPC   Smith, Medical Malpractice: Psychiatric Care

MMPL   Brushwood, Medical Malpractice: Pharmacy Law

MMPSC   Cucin, Medical Malpractice: Handling Plastic Surgery Cases

M.M.R.   Mitchell's Maritime Register (Eng.)

MMUC   Morton, Medical Malpractice: Handling Urology Cases

M'Mul.Ch.S.C.   M'Mullan's Equity Reports (South Carolina, 1840-42)

M'Mul.L.S.C.   M'Mullan's Law Reports (S.C. 1840-42)

Mn.   Minnesota

MNC   Aker, Beam & Walsh, Mental Capacity

MNCLE   Minnesota Continuing Legal Education

MnL   Minnesota Law Review

Mn. L.R.   Minnesota Law Review

MNR   Minister of National Revenue

M.N.S.   Martin's Reports, New Series (La.)

M.O.
- Military Orders issued by the President as Commander in Chief of the Armed Forces
- Mineral Order (Defense Minerals Exploration Administration, Department of the Interior) U.S.
- Motion for mandamus overruled

Mo., Mo
- Missouri
- Missouri Reports
- Missouri Supreme Court Reports (1821-1956)
- Modern Reports (Eng.) (1669-1732)
- Monthly
- Moore's Common Pleas Reports (Eng.) (1817-27)
- Moore's Indian Appeal Cases (1836-72)
- Moore's King's Bench Reports (Eng.) (1512-1621)
- Moore's Privy Council Reports (Eng.) (1836-62)

Mo. Admin. Code Missouri Code of State Regulations

Mo. Admin. Reg. Missouri Register

Moak Moak's English Reports

Moak & Eng. Rep. Moak's English Reports

Moak (Eng.) Moak's English Reports

Moak, Eng. R. Moak's English Reports

Moak Eng. Rep. Moak's English Reports

Moak Und. Moak's edition of Underhill on Torts

Moak, Underh.Torts. Moak's Edition of Underhill on Torts

Moak Van S.Pl. Moak's Edition of Van Santvoord's Equity Pleading

Mo. & P. Moore & Payne's English Common Pleas Reports

Mo. & R. Moody & Robinson's English Nisi Prius Reports

Mo. & S. Moore & Scott's English Common Pleas Reports (1831-34)

Mo. & Sc. Moore and Scott C.P. Reports (1831-34)

Mo. Ann. Stat. (Vernon) Vernon's Annotated Missouri Statutes

Mo. Ap. Missouri Appeal Reports (Mo.)

Mo. App. Missouri Appeal Reports

Mo. Appeals Missouri Appeal Reports (Mo.)

Mo. App.(K.C.) Missouri Appeal Reports (Mo.)

Mo. App. Rep. Missouri Appeal Reports

Mo. Apps. Missouri Appeal Reports (Mo.)

Mo. App. (St.L.) Missouri Appeal Reports (Mo.)

Mo. A.R. Missouri Appellate Reporter

MOB The Missouri Bar

Mob. Mobley, Contested Election Cases, U.S. House of Representatives (1882-89)

Mo. Bar Missouri Bar

Mo. Bar J. Missouri Bar Journal

Mobil H. Mobile homes, trailer parks and transit camps

Mo. B.J. Missouri Bar Journal

Mobl. Mobley, Contested Election Cases, U.S. House of Representatives (1882-89)

Mo.Const. Missouri Constitution

Mod.
- Modern
- Modern Reports, 1669-1755 (Eng.)
- modification
- modified
- Modified in
- Modifying
- Style's King's Bench Reports (1646-55) (Eng.)

Mod. Am. Law Modern American Law

Mod. Ca. L. & Eq. 8 & 9 Modern Reports (1721-55) (88 ER)

Mod. Ca.per Far. 6 and 7 Modern Reports (1702-45)

Mod. Cas. Modern Cases (6 Modern Reports) (1702-45)

Mod. Cas. L. & Eq. Modern Cases at Law and Equity, vols. 8, 9 Modern Reports (1721-55)

Mod. Cas. Per. Far. Modern Cases tempore Holt, by Farresley, vol. 7 Modern Reports

Mod. Cas. per Far. (t.Holt) Modern Cases, tempore Holt, by Farresby (6,7 Modern Reports)

Mod. Cas.t.Holt. Modern Cases tempore Holt, by Farresley, vol. 7 Modern Reports

Mod. Ca.t.Holt. 7 Modern Reports (1702-45)

Mo. Dec. Missouri Decisions

Model Business Corp. Act American Bar Association Model Business Corporation Act Annotated

Model Bus. Corp. Act. Anno.2d. American Bar Association Model Business Corporation Act Annotated, second series

Model Code of Professional Responsibility American Bar Association Model Code of Professional Responsibility

Model Land Dev.Code American Law Institute Model Land Development Code

Model Penal Code American Law Institute Model Penal Code

Mod. (Eng.) English King's Bench Modern Reports (86-88 ER)

Mod. Ent. Modern Entries

Modern L.R. Modern Law Review

Modern L. Rev. Modern Law Review

Mod'g Modifying

Modif. Modified; Modification

Mod.Int. Brown's Modus Intrandi

Mod.L. & Soc'y Modern Law and Society

Mod. L. Rev. Modern Law Review

Mod. Pract. Comm. Modern Practice Commentator

Mod. Rep.
- Modern Reports (1669-1755) (Eng.)
- Style's King's Bench Reports, (1646-55)

mods. modifications

Mo.(F.) Sir Francis Moore's English King's Bench Reports

Mo.I.A. Moore's Indian Appeals (1836-72)

Moir Cap. Pun. Moir on Capital Punishment

MO-JAGA Memorandum Opinions, Judge Advocate General of the Army (U.S.)

Mo.J.B. J. B. Moore's Common Pleas Reports (Eng.)

Mo. Jur. Monthly Jurist

Mo. L. Rev. Missouri Law Review

Mol.
- Molloy's Chancery Reports (1827-31) (Ir.)
- Molloy's De Jure Maritimo

Mo Labor R Monthly Labor Review

Mo. Lab.R ev. Monthly Labor Review

Mo. Law Rep. Monthly Law Reporter

Mo. Laws Laws of Missouri

Mo. Leg. Exam. Monthly Legal Examiner (New York)

Mol.de Jure Mar. Molloy, De Jure Maritimo et Navali

Mo. Legis. Serv. (Vernon) Missouri Legislative Service Moll.

Mol. J. M. Molloy de Jure Maritimo et Navali

Moll.
- Molloy's Chancery Reports (1827-31) (Ir.)
- Molloy's De Jure Maritimo

Molloy Molloy, Ir.

Mo. L. Mag. Monthly Law Magazine (1838-47) (London)

Mo. L. Rev. Missouri Law Review

Mo. Labor Rev. Monthly Labor Review

Mo. L. Rev. Missouri Law Review

Moly. Molyneaux's Reports. English Courts, tempore Car. I.

Mon.
- B. Monroe's Reports (40-57 Kentucky) (1840-57)
- Monaghan's Unreported Cases (Pennsylvania Superior Court)
- Montana
- Montana Reports
- Montana Supreme Court Reports
- Montana Territory
- Monthly
- T.B. Monroe's Reports (17-23 Kentucky)

Mona. Monaghan's Reports (147-165 Pennsylvania)

Monag.
- Monaghan's Reports (Pennsylvania 1888-90)
- Monaghan's Reports (147-165 Pennsylvania Statutes)

Monaghan. Monaghan's Reports (147-165 Pennsylvania)

Monaghan (Pa.)
- Monaghan's Reports (Pennsylvania 1888-90)
- Monaghan's Reports (147-165 Pennsylvania Statutes)

Mon. Angl. Monasticon Anglicanum

Monash U. L. Rev. Monash University Law Review

Monash Univ. L. Rev. Monash University Law Review

Mon.B. Monroe's Reports (40-57 Kentucky)

Monc. Inn. Moncrieff, Liability of Innkeepers, 1874

Monc. Rev. Moncrieff on the Liability of Innkeepers

Money Lend. Money lenders and pawn brokers

Mong. Mongolia

Mon. Law Mag. Monthly Law Magazine (1834-41)

Mon. Law Rep. Monthly Law Reporter

Mon. Leg. R. (Pa.) Monroe Legal Reporter

Mon. L. R. Monash University Law Review

Mon. L. Rev., Univ.of Detroit Monthly Law Review of University of Detroit

Mon. Meth. Monahan, Method of the Law. 1878

Momop. Monopolies, restraints of trade and unfair trade practices

Monr. Monroe

Monro. Acta Cancellariae (Eng.)

Monro. A.C. Monro's Acta Cancellariae (1545-1625)

Monroe Monroe Legal Reporter (Pa.)

Monroe L.R. Monroe Legal Reporter (Pa.)

Mont.
- Montagu, English Bankruptcy Reports (1829-32)
- Montana
- Montana Reports
- Montana Supreme Court Reports
- Montriou, Bengal Reports

Mont. Admin. R. Administrative Rules of Montana

Mont. Admin. Reg. Montana Administrative Register

Montana L. Rev. Montana Law Review

Montana Reports Montana Reports (Mont.)

Mont. & A. Montagu & Ayrton's English Bankruptcy Reports (1833-38)

Mont. & Ayr. Montagu & Ayrton's English Bankruptcy Reports (1833-38)

Mont. & Ayr. Bankr. Montagu & Ayrton's Bankruptcy Reports (1833-38)

Mont. & Ayr. Bankr. (Eng.) Montagu & Ayrton's English Bankruptcy Reports

Mont. & Ayr. B.L. Montagu & Ayrton on the Bankrupt Laws

Mont. & B. Montagu & Bligh's English Bankruptcy Reports

Mont. & B. Bankr. Montagu & Bligh's Bankruptcy Reports (1832-33)

Mont. & B. Bankr.(Eng.) Montagu & Bligh's English Bankruptcy Reports (1832-33)

Mont. & Bl. Montagu & Bligh's English Bankruptcy Reports (1832-33)

Mont. & C. Montagu & Chitty's English Bankruptcy Reports (1838-40)

Mont. & C. Bankr. Montagu & Chitty's Bankruptcy Reports (1838-40)

Mont. & C. Bankr. (Eng.) Montagu & Chitty's English Bankruptcy Reports

Mont. & Ch. Montagu & Chitty's English Bankruptcy Reports

Mont. & Chitt. Montagu & Chitty's English Bankruptcy Reports

Mont. & M. Montagu and MacArthur's English Bankrupty Reports (1826-30)

Mont. & MacA. Montagu and MacArthur's English Bankruptcy Reports (1826-30)

Mont.& M. Bankr. (Eng.) Montagu and MacArthur's English Bankruptcy Reports (1826-30)

Mon. T.B. T.B. Monroe's Reports (17-23 Ky.)

Mont. Bankr. (Eng.) Montagu's English Bankruptcy Reports

Mont. Bank. Rep. Montagu's English Bankruptcy Reports

Mont. B.C. Montagu's English Bankruptcy Reports

Mont. Bk. L. Montagu, Bankrupt Law. 4ed. 1827

Mont. Cas. Montriou's Cases in Hindoo Law

Mont. Code Ann. Montana Code Annotated

Mont. Co. L.R. Montgomery County Law Reporter (Pa.)

Mont. Co. L. Rep. Montgomery County Law Reporter (Pa.)

Mont. Comp. Montagu, Composition. 1823

Mont. Cond. Rep. Montreal Condensed Reports (1853-54)

Mont. Const. Montana Constitution

Mont. D. & DeG. Montagu, Deacon, & DeGex, Bankruptcy Reports (1840-44) (Eng.)

Mont. Dig. Montagu's Digest of Pleadings in Equity

Mont. Eq. Pl. Montagu's Digest of Pleadings in Equity

Montesq. Montesquieu, Esprit des Lois

Montesq. Esprit des Lois. Montesquieu, Esprit des Lois

Montg. Montgomery County Law Reporter (Pa.)

Montg.Co. Montgomery County Law Reporter (Pa.)

Montg. Co. Law Rep'r. Montgomery County Law Reporter (Pa.)

Montg. Co. L.R. Montgomery County Law Reporter, Pennsylvania

Mont'g. Co. L. Rep. Montgomery County Law Reporter (Pa.)

Montg. Co. L. Rep'r. Montgomery County Law Reporter (Pa.)

Montg. Co. L. R. (Pa.) Montgomery County Law Reporter (Pa.)

Mont'g. L. Rep. Montgomery County Law Reporter (Pa.)

Montg.(Pa.) Montgomery County Law Reporter (Pa.)

Month. Dig. Tax Articles Monthly Digest of Tax Articles

Month. J.L. Monthly Journal of Law

Month. Jur. Monthly Jurist (Bloomington, Ill.)

Month. Lab. Rev. Monthly Labor Review

Month. Law Bul. Monthly Law Bulletin (N.Y.)

Month. Law Rep. Law Reporter (Boston)

Month. L. Bull. (N.Y.) Monthly Law Bulletin

Month. Leg. Ex. Monthly Legal Examiner

Month. Leg. Exam. Monthly Legal Examiner (N.Y.)

Month. Leg. Exam. (N.Y.) Monthly Legal Examiner (New York)

Month. L.J. Monthly Journal of Law (Wash.)

Month. L.M. Monthly Law Magazine (London)

Month. L.Mag. Monthly Law Magazine, London

Month. L. Rep.
- Monthly Law Reporter (Boston)
- Monthly Law Reports (Canada)

Month. L. Rev. Monthly Law Review

Monthly Lab. Rev. Monthly Labor Review

Monthly L. Bul. New York Monthly Law Bulletin (N.Y.)

Month. West. J. Monthly Western Journal, Bloomington

Month. West. Jur. Monthly Western Jurist

Mont. Ind. Monthly Index to Reporters

Mont. Inst. Montriou, Institutes of Jurisprudence

Mont. Law. Montana Lawyer

Mont. Laws Laws of Montana

Mont. Leg. News Montreal Legal News

Mont. Liens Montagu on Liens

Mont. L.R.
- Montreal Law Reports, Queen's Bench
- Montreal Law Reports, Superior Court

Mont. L.Rev. Montana Law Review

Mont. L.R.Q.B. Montreal Law Reports, Queen's Bench

Mont. L.R.S.C. Montreal Law Reports, Superior Court

Mont. Merc. Law Montefiore's Synopsis of Mercantile Law

Mont. Part. Montagu's Digest of the Law of Partnership

Montr.
- Montriou's Reports, Bengal
- Montriou's Supplement to Morton's Reports

Mont. R. & P.S. Co. Railroad and Public Service Commission of Montana

Mont. R.C. Montana Railroad Commission

Montr. Cond. Rep. Montreal Condensed Reports

Montreal L.Q.B. (Can.) Montreal Law Reports, Queen's Bench

Montreal L.R.Q.B. Montreal Law Reports, Queen's Bench (Canada)

Montreal L.R.S.C. Montreal Law Reports, Superior Court (Canada)

Montreal L.S.C. (Can.) Montreal Law Reports, Superior Court (Canada)

Mont. Rep. Montriou's Reports, Supreme Court (1846) (Bengal, India)

Mont. Rev. Code Ann. Montana Revised Code Annotated

Mont. Rev. Codes Ann. Revised Codes of Montana Annotated

Montr. Leg. N. Montreal Legal News

Montr. Q.B. Montreal Law Reports Queen's Bench

Montr. Super. Montreal Law Reports, Superior Court

Mont. S.O. Montagu, Set-Off. 2ed. 1828

Mont. Sp. L. Montesquieu's Spirit of Laws

Mont. Super. Montreal Law Reports (Superior Court)

Mon. W.J. Monthly Western Jurist

Moo.
- E.F. Moore's Privy Council Cases (1836-62) (12-15 ER)
- Francis Moore's English King's Bench Reports (1512-1621)
- J.B. Moore's Common Pleas Reports 1817-27 (19-29 RR)
- J.M. Moore's English Common Pleas Reports
- Moody's English Crown Cases

Moo. A. Moore's Reports (1 Bosanquet & Puller, after page 470) (1796-97)

Moo. & M. Moody and Malkin's Nisi Prius Reports (1826-30)

Moo. & Mal. Moody & Malkin's English Nisi Prius Reports (1826-30)

Moo. & P. Moore & Payne, English Common Pleas Reports, 5 vols. (1828-31)

Moo. & Pay. Moore & Payne, English Common Pleas Reports, 5 vols. (1828-31)

Moo. & R. Moody & Robinson's English Nisi Prius Reports (1830-44)

Moo. & Rob. Moody & Robinson's English Nisi Prius Reports (1830-44)

Moo. & S. Moore & Scott's English Common Pleas Reports (1831-34)

Moo. & Sc. Moore & Scott's English Common Pleas Reports (1831-34)

Moo. C.C. Moody's English Crown Cases Reserved (1824-44)

Moo. C.P. Moore's English Common Pleas Reports

Moo. Cr. C. Moody's English Crown Cases Reserved

Mood. Moody's English Crown Cases Reserved (1824-44)

Mood. & M. Moody & Malkin's English Nisi Prius Reports

Mood. & Mack. Moody & Mackin's Nisi Prius (Eng.)

Mood & Malk. Moody & Malkin's English Nisi Prius Reports

Mood. & R. Moody & Robinson's English Nisi Prius Reports

Mood. & Rob. Moody & Robinson's English Nisi Prius Reports

Mood. C.C. Moody's Crown Cases Reserved (Eng.)

Moody. Moody's Crown Cases (168, 169 ER)

Moody & M. Moody & Mackin's English Nisi Prius Reports (173 ER)

Moody & M. Moody & Mackin's English Nisi Prius Reports (173 ER)

Moody & M. (Eng.) Moody & Mackin's English Nisi Prius Reports

Moody & R. Moody & Robinson's English Nisi Prius Reports (174 ER)

Moody & R. (Eng.) Moody & Robinson's English Nisi Prius Reports (174 ER)

Moody C.C. (Eng.) Moody's Crown Cases (168, 169 ER)

Moody Cr.C. Moody's Crown Cases (168, 169 ER)

Moody, Cr.Cas. Moody's Crown Cases; English Courts

Moo. F. Moore's King's Bench Reports (1512-1621) (Eng.)

Moo. G.C. Moore: The Gorham Case, English Privy Council

Moo. Ind. App. Moore's Reports, Privy Council, Indian Appeals (1836-72)

Moo. J.B. Moore's English Common Pleas Reports (1817-27)

Moo. K.B. Moore's English King's Bench Reports (1512-1621)

Moon. Moon's Reports (133-144 Indiana and 6-14 Indiana Appeals)

Moo. N.S. E.F. Moore's Privy Council Cases, New Series (1862-73) (15-17 ER)

Moo. P.C. Moore's Privy Council Cases, Old and New Series

Moo. P.C.C. Moore's Privy Council Cases (Eng.)

Moo. P.C.Cas.N.S. Moore's Privy Council Cases, New Series (Eng.) 9 vols.

Moo. P.C.C.N.S. Moore's Privy Council Cases, New Series (Eng.)

Moo. P.C. (N.S.) Moore's Privy Council Cases, New Series (1862-73) (15-17 ER)

Moor English King's Bench Reports by Sir Francis Moore (1512-1621)

Moore
- Moore's Common Pleas Reports (Eng.)
- Moore's King's Bench Reports (Eng.)
- Moore's Privy Council Reports (Eng.)
- Moore's Reports (67 Alabama)
- Moore's Reports (28-34 Arkansas)
- Moore's Reports (22-24 Texas)

Moore. A. Moore's Reports (1 Bosanquet & Puller, after p. 470) (Eng.)

Moore. Abs. Moore, Abstracts of Title. 6ed. 1925

Moore & P. Moore & Payne's English Common Pleas Reports

Moore & P. (Eng.) Moore & Payne's English Common Pleas Reports

Moore & S. Moore & Scott's English Common Pleas Reports

Moore & S. (Eng.) Moore & Scott's English Common Pleas Reports

Moore & W. Moore & Walker's Reports (22-24 Texas)

Moore & Walker. Moore & Walker's Reports (22-24 Texas)

Moore B.B. Moore's King's Bench (Eng.)

Moore C.P. Moore's Common Pleas Reports (Eng.)

Moore, Cr. Law. Moore's Criminal Law and Procedure

Moore E.I. Moore's East Indian Appeals

Moore, Fed. Practice Moore's Federal Practice

Moore G.C. Moore, Gorham Case (English Privy Council)

Moore Ind. App. Moore's Indian Appeals Reports

Moore Ind. App. (Eng.) Moore's Indian Appeals (18-20 ER)

Moore Indian App. Moore's Indian Appeals (Eng.)

Moore Int. L. Moore's Digest of International Law

Moore K.B. Sir F. Moore's English King's Bench Reports

Moore K.B. (Eng.) Sir F. Moore's English King's Bench Reports

Moore P.C. Moore's English Privy Council Reports

Moore P.C.C. Moore's English Privy Council Cases (12-15 ER)

Moore P.C.C. (Eng.) Moore's English Privy Council Cases (12-15 ER)

Moore P.C.C.N.S. Moore's Privy Council Cases, New Series (1862-73) (15-17 ER)

Moore P.C.C.N.S. (Eng.) Moore's English Privy Council Cases, New Series (15-17 ER)

Moore P.C.N.S. Moore's English Privy Council Reports, New Series

Moore, Presby. Dig. Moore's Presbyterian Digest

Moore Q.B. Moore's Queen's Bench Reports (Eng.)

Moo. Sep. Rep. Moore, Separate Report of Westerton v. Liddell

Moot Ct. Bull. University of Illinois Moot Court Bulletin

Moo. Tr. Moore's Divorce Trials

Mo.P.C. Moore's Privy Council Reports (Eng.)

Mo. Prec. Moile's Precedents

Mo. P.S.C. Public Service Commission Reports (Mo.)

Mo. P.S.C. (N.S.) Public Service Commission Reports, New Series (Mo.)

Mo. P.S.C.R. Missouri Public Service Commission Reports

Mo. P.U.R. Missouri Public Utility Reports

Mo. R. Missouri Reports (Mo.)

Mor. Morrison's Dictionary of Decisions in the Court of Session, Scotland (1540- 1808)

Mor. & Carl. Moreau-Lislet and Carleton's Laws of Las Siete Partidas in force in Louisiana

Mo.R. & W.C. Missouri Railroad & Warehouse Commission

Mo. R. C. Missouri Railroad Commissioners

Mor. Chy. Acts Morgan, Chancery Acts and Orders. 6ed. 1885

Mor. Comp. Morris on Compensations

Mor. Corp. Morawetz on Private Corporations

Mor. Dic. Morison, Dictionary of Decisions, Scotch Court of Session

Mor. Dict. Morrison, Dictionary of Decisions, Scotch Court of Session

Mor. Dig.
- Morley, Digest of the Indian Reports
- Morrison, New Hampshire Digest

Mor. Dil. Morris, Dilapidations. 2ed. 1871

Mor. E. & R. D. Law Morice, English & Roman Dutch Law

Mor. Eas. Morris on the Law of Easements

Moreau & Carleton's Moreau Lislet and Carleton's Laws of Las Siete Partidas in force in Louisiana

More. Lect. More, Lectures on the Law of Scotland

More St. More, Notes on Stair's Institutions of Scotland

Mo. Rep. Missouri Reports (Mo.)

Mo. Rev. Monthly Review

Mo. Rev. Stat. Missouri Revised Statutes

Morey Out. Rom. Law. Morey Outlines of Roman Law

Morg. Morgan's Chancery Acts & Orders (Eng.)

Morgan. Morgan's Digest (Ceylon)

Morg. & Ch. Jud. Acts Morgan & Chute on the Judicature Acts

Morg, & W.L.J. Morgan & Williams, Law Journal (London)

Morgan L. M. Morgan's Legal Miscellany (Ceylon)

Morg. Ch. Morgan, Chancery Acts and Orders. 6ed. 1885

Morg. Lit. Morgan on the Law of Literature

Morg. Tar. Morgan on the United States Tariff

Mor. Hors. Morrell on the Law of Horses

Mor. Ia. Morris' Reports (Iowa 1839-46)

Morl. Dig. Morley's East Indian Digest

Mor. Lit. Morgan on the Law of Literature

Mor. Min. Rep. Morrison's Mining Reports

Mor. Miss. Morris' Reports (43-48 Miss.)

Mor. Pr. Morehead's Practice

Mor. Priv. Corp. Morawetz on Private Corporations

Morr.
- Morrell's Bankruptcy Reports (1884-93) (Eng.)
- Morris' Reports, Bombay (India)

- Morris' Reports (5 California)
- Morris' Reports (Iowa 1839-46)
- Morris' Reports (Jamaica)
- Morris' Reports (23-26 Oregon)

Morr. Bankr. Cas. Morrell's Bankruptcy Cases (Eng.)

Morr. B.C. Morrell's Bankruptcy Reports (Eng.)

Morr. Bomb. Morris' Reports Bombay (India)

Morr. Cal. Morris' Reports (5 California)

Morr. Dict. (or M.Dict.) Morrison's Dictionary of Decisions, Scotch Court of Session

Morr. Dig.
- Morrison, Digest of Mining Decisions
- Morrison, New Hampshire Digest

Morrell, Bankr. Cas. Morrell's English Bankruptcy Cases

Morrell B.C. Morrell's Bankruptcy Cases (1884-93)

Morrell (Eng.) Morrell's English Bankruptcy Cases

Mor. Rep. Morris' Law of Replevin

Morris.
- Morrissett's Reports (80, 98 Alabama)
- Morris' Reports, Bombay (India)
- Morris' Reports (5 California)
- Morris Reports (Iowa 1839-46)
- Morris' Reports Jamaica
- Morris Reports (43-48 Mississippi)
- Morris' Reports (23-26 Oregon)

Morris & Har. Morris & Harrington's Reports, Bombay (India)

Morris (Ia.) Morris Iowa Reports (Iowa)

Morris (Iowa) Morris Iowa Reports (Iowa)

Morrison Min. Rep. Morrison's Mining Reports (U.S.)

Morris R. Morris's Reports (Jamaica)

Morris St. Cas. Morris' State Cases (Miss.)

Morris Repl. Morris on Replevin

Morr. Jah. Morris' Jamaica Reports

Morr. Jam. Morris' Reports (Jamaica)

Morr. Mines. Morrison, Digest of Mining Decisions

Morr. Min. R. Morrison's Mining Reports (U.S.)

Morr. Min. Rep. Morrison's Mining Reports

Morr. Miss. Morris' Reports (43-48 Miss.)

Morr. M. R. Morrison's Mining Reports (U.S.)

Morrow Morrow (Ore.)

Morr. Repl. Morris on Replevin

Morr. St. Cas. Morris' State Cases (Miss.)

Morr. Supp. Supplement to Morrison's Dictionary. Scotch Court of Session

Morr. Trans. Morrison's, Transcript, United States Supreme Court

Mor. Ry. Com. Morris on Railway Compensations

Morse Arb. Morse on the Law of Arbitration and Award

Morse, Banks. Morse on the Law of Banks and Banking

Morse Bk. Morse on the Law of Banks and Banking

Morse Exch. Rep. Morse's Exchequer Reports (Canada)

Morse Tr. Morse's Famous Trials

Mor. St. Ca. Morris' State Cases (Miss. 1818-72)

Mor. St. Cas. Morris' State Cases (Miss. 1818-72)

Mor. Supp. Morison's Dictionary, Court of Session Decisions, Supplement (1620-1768) (Sc.)

Mor. Syn. Morison's Synopsis, Scotch Session Cases (1808-16)

mort. mortgage

Morton. Morton's Reports, Calcutta Superior Court (India)

Mor. Tran. Morrison's Transcript of United States Supreme Court Decisions

Mort. Vend. Morton, Vendors and Purchasers. 1837

Mor. Wills Morrell on the Law of Wills

Mos. Mosely's English Chancery Reports (25 ER)

Mos. Cont. Moseley, Contraband of War. 1861

Moseley Moseley's Chancery Reports (1726-31) (25 ER)

Mos. El. L. Moseley, Elementary Law. 2ed. 1878

Mosely (Eng.) Moseley's English Chancery Reports (25 ER)

Mos.Man. Moses on the Law of Mandamus

Mo.St.Ann. Missouri Statutes Annotated

Mo. St.B.J. Missouri Bar Journal

Mot. Motion

Moult. Ch. Moulton's Chancery Practice (New York)

Moult. Ch. P. Moulton's Chancery Practice (New York)

Mo.W.Jur. Monthly Western Jurist

Mow. St. Mowbray, Styles of Deeds

Moyle
- Moyle's Criminal Circulars (India)
- Moyle's Entries 1658 (Eng.)

Mozam. Mozambique

Moz. & W. Mozley & Whiteley's Law Dictionary. 9ed. 1977

Mozley & W. Mozley & Whitely's Law Dictionary (Eng.)

Mozley & Whiteley. Mozley & Whiteley's Law Dictionary

M.P.
- All India Reporter, Madhya Pradesh
- Member of Parliament

M.P.C. Moore's Privy Council Cases (1836-73) (Eng.)

M.P.E.P. Manual of Patent Examining Precedure

M.P. Ex. Modern Practice of the Exchequer

MPI Midwest Practice Institute

M.P.Ind. Madhya Pradesh, India

M.P.I. Regulations Meat & Poultry Inspection Regulations

MPL Master of Public Law

M.P.L. Master of Patent Law

M.P.L.R. Municipal and Planning Law Reports (Annotated) (Can.)

M.P.P. Miscellaneous personal property

M.P.R. Maritime Provinces Reports (Canada)

M.P.S. Minimum Property Standards (HUD)

M.P.T.M.H. Major Peace Treaties of Modern History, 1648-1967

M.Q. Massachusetts Law Quarterly

M.Q.D. Milner, Questions de Droit

Mq.L. Marquette Law Review

Mq.L.R. Marquette Law Review

M.R.
- Application for writ of mandamus refused
- Manitoba Law Reports, Canada
- Master of the Rolls
- Mauritius Decisions
- Mauritius Reports
- Mining Reports (R.S. Morrison, editor; Chicago, 22)
- Montana Law Review
- Roll's Court (Eng.)

MRG Minority Rights Group

M.R.P. Application for writ of mandamus refused in part

M.R.S.A. Maine Revised Statutes Annotated

Mr.S.B.A. Maryland State Bar Association, Report

M.S. Manuscript Reports

Ms.
- Manuscript Reports or Decisions
- Mississippi

ms. manuscript

M.S.A.
- Minnesota Statutes Annotated
- Mutual Security Agency (U.S.)

MSC Military Staff Committee (UN)

Msc. New York Miscellaneous Reports

Msc2d New York Miscellaneous Reports, Second Series

MSCLE Mississippi Institute of Continuing Legal Education

Ms.D.
- Manuscript Decisions, Commissioner of Patents (U.S.)
- Manuscript Decisions, Comptroller General (U.S.)

MSB Maritime Subsidy Board

Ms.I.T. Manuscript, Inner Temple

Ms.L.I. Manuscript, Lincoln's Inn

Ms.L.J. Mississippi Law Journal

M.S.L.S.
- Master of Science in Law & Society
- Master of Science in Library Service

M.S.M. Marine Safety Manual (Coast Guard)

MS.M.T. Manuscript, Middle Temple

M.S.P.B. Decisions of US Merit System Protection Board

mss. manuscripts

MSSD Model Secondary School for the Deaf

M. St. More's Notes on Stair's Institutes

M.S.U. Business Topics Michigan State University Business Topics

MSUCLE Missouri State University Continuing Legal Education

MT Internal Revenue Bureau (U.S.) Miscellaneous Tax Ruling

Mt.
- Montana
- Montana Reports

MTB Materials Transportation Bureau

Mtg. Mortgage

mtgee. mortgagee

mtgor. mortgagor

Mthly. Monthly

Mt.L.R. Monthly

MTMTS Military Traffic Management and Terminal Service

M.U.C.C. Michigan Unemployment Compensation Commisson

Much. D. & S. Muchall's Doctor and Student

Mu. Corp. Ca. Municipal Corporation Cases (U.S.)

Mu. Corp. Cir. Municipal Corporation Circular (Eng.)

Muir. Gai. Muirhea's Institutes of Gaius

Mulford, Nation Mulford, The Nation

Mu. L.J. Municipal Law Journal

M.U.L.R. Melbourne University Law Review

Mult. Multiple

Mult. Dwell. Multiple Dwelling

Mult.Resid. Multiple Residence

Mumf. Mumford's Reports (Jamaica)

Mum. Jam. Mumford's Jamaica Reports

Mun.
- Munford's Reports (15-20 Virginia)
- Municipal
- Municipal Law Reporter
- Municipal Law Reports (Sc.)
- Municipal Law Reports (1845-51) (Can.)
- Munitions Appeal Reports (1916-20)

Mun. & El. Cas. Municipal & Election Cases (India)

Mun. App. Munitions Appeals Reports (Eng.)

Mun. App. Rep. Munitions Appeals Reports (Eng.)

Mun. App. Sc. Munitions of War Acts, Appeal Reports (1916-20) (Sc.)

Mun. Att'y. Municipal Attorney

Mun. Atty. Municipal Attorney

Mun. Code Municipal Code

Mun. Corp. Cas. Municipal Corporation Cases

Mun. Ct. Municipal Court

Mun. Ct. App. Dist. Col. Municipal Court of Appeals for the District of Columbia

Mundy Abstracts of Star Chamber Proceedings (1550-58)

Munf. Munford's Reports (15-20 Virginia) (1810-20)

Munf. (Va.) Munford's Reports (15-20 Virginia)

Mung. Pay. Munger on Application of Payments

Mun. Home Rule Municipal Home Rule

Mun. Fin. J. Municipal Finance Journal

Munic. Municipal

Munic. & P.L. Municipal & Parish Law Cases (Eng.)

Municipal Court Rule Rules for the Municipal Courts

Munic. L. R. (Pa.) Municipal Law Reporter

Munk. Emp. Liab. Munkman, Employer's Liability at Common Law. 8ed. 1975

Mun. L. Ct. Dec. Municipal Law Court Decisions

Mun. L.J. Municipal Law Journal

Mun. L.R.
- Municipal Law Reporter (Pa.)
- Municipal Law Reports (1903-13) (Sc.)

Mun. L. Rep. Chrostwaite's Pennsylvania Municipal Law Reporter (Pa.)

Mun. Ord. Rev. Municipal Ordinance Review

Mun. Plan. L. Rep. Municipal and Planning Law Reports

Mun. Rep. Municipal Reports (Canada)

Mun. Tort Lib. Municipal, School and State Tort Liability

M.U.R.
- Motor Vehicle Reports, 1978-
- Montana Utilities Reports

Mur.
- Murphey's Reports (5-7 N.C.)
- Murray's Jury Court Cases, (1815-30) (Sc.)
- Murray's Reports (Ceylon)
- Murray's Reports New South Wales (Aus.)

Mur. & H. Murphy & Hurlstone's Exchequer Reports (1836-37)

Mur. & Hurl. Murphy & Hurlstone's English Exchequer Reports (1836-37)

Murat. Antiq. Med. Aevi. Muratori's Antiquitates Medii Aevi

Murd. Epit. Murdoch's Epitome Canada

Murfree, Off. Bonds Murfree on Official Bonds

Murph. Murphey's Reports (5-7 North Carolina)

Murph. & H. Murphy & Hurlstone, English Exchequer Reports

Murph. (N.C.) Murphey's Reports (5-7 North Carolina)

Murr.
- Murray's Ceylon Reports
- Murray's Jury Court Cases, Sc. (1815-30)
- Murray's Laws and Acts of Parliament (Sc.)
- Murray's New South Wales Reports

Murray Murray's Scotch Jury Court Reports

Murray (Ceylon) Murray's Ceylon Reports

Murray (Scot.) Murray's Scotch Jury Trials

Murray's Eng. Dict. Murray's English Dictionary

Murr. Over. Cas. Murray's Overruled Cases

Murr. Us. Murray on Usury

Mur. Tab. Cas. Murray, Table of United States Cases

Mur. Us. Murray's History of Usury

Mur. U.S. Ct. Murray's Proceedings in the United States Courts

Mut. Mutual
- Mutukisna's Reports (Ceylon)

Mut. Funds Guide (CCH) Mutual Funds Guide (CCH)

Mutukisna Mutukisna's Ceylon Reports

M.V. & P. Morton, Vendors & Purchasers. 1837

M.V.D. Motor Vehicle Department

M.W.N. Madras Weekly Notes (India)

M.W.N.C.C. Madras Weekly Notes, Criminal Cases (India)

M.W.N.L.N. Mid-West Nigeria Legal Notice

My. & C. Mylne & Craig's Chancery Reports (Eng.)

My. & Cr. Mylne & Craig's Chancery Reports (Eng.)

My. & K. Mylne & Keen's English Chancery Reports (39, 40 ER)

Myer Dig. Myer's Texas Digest

Myer Fed. Dec. Myer's Federal Decisions

Myer's Fed. Dec. Myer's Federal Decisions (U.S.)

Myl. & C. Mylne & Craig's English Chancery Reports

Myl. & C. (Eng.) Mylne & Craig's English Chancery Reports (40, 41 ER)

Myl. & Cr. Mylne & Craig's English Chancery Reports (40, 41 ER)

Myl. & K. Mylne & Keen's English Chancery Reports (39, 40 ER)

Myl. & K. (Eng.) Mylne & Keen's English Chancery Reports (39, 40 ER)

My. L. J. Mysore Law Journal (India)

Mylne & K. Mylne & Keen's English Chancery Reports (39, 40 ER)

Myr. Myrick's California Probate Court Reports (California 1872-79)

Myr. Cal. Prob. Myrick's Probate Reports (Cal.)

Myrick (Cal.) Myrick's California Probate Court Reports (California 1872-79)

Myrick Prob. (Cal.) Myrick's California Probate Court Reports (California 1872-79)

Myrick's Prob. Rep. Myrick's Probate Reports (Cal.)

Myr. Prob. Myrick's California Probate Court Reports (California 1872-79)

Myr. Prob. Rep. Myrick's Probate Reports (Cal.)

Mys. All India Reporter, Mysore

Mys. Ch. Ct. Mysore Chief Court Reports (India)

Mys. H.C.R. Mysore High Court Reports (India)

Mys. Ind. Mysore, India

Mys. L.J. Mysore Law Journal (India)

Mys. L.R. Mysore Law Reports (India)

Mysore Mysore Law Reports (India)

Mysore, L.J. Mysore Law Journal, Bangalore, India

Mys.R.(R.) Mysore Reports (Reprint) (India) 1878-1923

Mys. W.N. Mysore Weekly Notes (1891-92) (India)

N

N.
- Nebraska
- Nevada
- Newfoundland
- North
- Northern
- Northeastern Reporter
- Northern Ireland Law Reports
- Northwestern Reporter
- Norwegian
- Note
- Novelloe (the Novels of Justinian), north
- South African Law Reports, Natal Province Division (1910-46)

n. footnote
- note

N.A., NA.
- Nizamut Adalut Reports (India)
- Nonacquiescence
- Non Allocatur

NAA National Academy of Arbitrators

NAACP National Association for the Advancement of Colored People

N.A. & D., C. & O. Selection of Cases decided in the Native Appeal and Divorce Court (Cape and Orange Free State)

N.A. & D.T. & N. Transvaal & Natal Native Appeal & Divorce Court Decisions

Naar Elec. Naar on Suffrage and Elections

N.A.B.
- National Alliance of Businessmen
- National Association of Businessmen

N.A.C. Native Appeal Courts (South Africa)

NACA National Advisory Committee for Aeronautics (U.S.)

N.A.C. & O. Cape & Orange Free State Native Appeal Court, Selected Decisions

N.A.C. (C.) Selected Decisions of the Native Appeal Court (Central Division) (1948-51) (S.Afr.)

NACCA National Association of Claimants' Compensation Attorneys

NACCALJ National Association of claimants' Compensation Attorneys Law Journal

Nacca L.J. Nacca Law Journal, National Association of Claimants' Compensation Attorneys

NACCA L.J. NACCA Law Journal

Nag.
- All India Reporter, Nagpur (1914-51)
- Indian Law Reports, Nagpur
- Indian Rulings, Nagpur (1929-47)

Nag. L.J. Nagpur Law Journal (India)

Nag. L.N. Nagpur Law Notes (India)

Nag. L.R. Nagpur Law Reports (India)

Nag. U.C.L. Mag. Nagpur University College of Law Magazine (1933-34) (India)

N.A.I. Netherlands Arbitration Institute

N.A.L.N. Native Authority Legal Notice (Northern Nigeria)

Nal. St. P. Nalton's Collection of State Papers

N. Am. North America

Namib. Namibia

N.A.M.L. Dig. National Association of Manufacturers Law Digest

N. Am. Rev. North American Review

N. & Dr. Nevile & Manning's King's Bench (Eng.)

N. & H.
- Nott & Hopkins' Reports (8-29 U.S. Court of Claims)
- Nott & Huntington's Reports (1-7 U.S. Court of Claims)

N. & Hop. Nott & Hopkins' Reports (8-29 U.S. Court of Claims)

N. & Hunt. Nott & Huntington's Reports (1-7 U.S. Court of Claims)

N. & M. Nevile & Manning's King's Bench Reports (1831-36) (Eng.)

N. & Macn. Nevile & Macnamara Railway & Canal Cases (Eng.)

N. & Mc. Nott & McCord's South Carolina Reports

N. & McC. Nott & McCords South Carolina Reports

N. & McN. Neville & Macnamara's Railway & Canal Cases (1855-1950)

N. & M. Mag. Nevile & Manning's English Magistrates' Cases

N. & M.M.C. Nevile and Mannings' Magistrate Cases (1832-36)

N. & P. Nevile & Perry's English King's Bench Reports (1836-38)

N. & P.E.I.R. Newfoundland and Prince Edward Island Reports

N. & P. Mag. Nevile & Perry's English Magistrates' Cases

N. & P.M.C. Nevile and Perry's Magistrate Cases (1836-37)

N. & S. Nicholls & Stops' Reports (1897-1904) (Tasmania)

Napt. Napton's Reports (4 Missouri)

Napton. Napton's Reports (4 Missouri)

NARAS J. NARAS Journal

Nar. Conv. Nares, Penal Convictions. 1815

Narcotics Control Dig. Narcotics Control Digest

Narcotics L. Bull. Narcotics Law Bulletin

Narr. Mod. Narrationes Modernae (Style's King's Bench Reports) (1646-55) (Eng.)

NARS National Archives and Records Service

NAS National Academy of Science

NASA National Aeronautics and Space Agency

NASD National Association of Securities Dealers

NASAPR National Aeronautics and Space Administration Procurement Regulations

Nash Pl. Nash's Ohio Pleading and Practice

Nas. Inst. Nasmith's Institutes of English Law

Nas. Inst. Priv. Nasmith, Institutes of English Private Law. 1873

Nas. Inst. Pub. Nasmith, Institutes of English Public Law. 1873

NAS-NRC National Academy of Sciences-National Research Council

N.A. So. Rhod. Southern Rhodesia Native Appeal Court, Reports

Nassau L. Nassau Lawyer

Nat.
- National
- Natural

Natal L.J. Natal Law Journal (S.Afr.)

Natal L.M. Natal Law Magazine (S.Afr.)

Natal L.Q. Natal Law Quarterly (S. Afr.)

Natal L.R. Natal Law Reports (S.Afr.)

Natal U.L. Rev. Natal University Law Review (S.Afr.)

N.A., T. & N. Selected Decisions of the Native Appeal Court (Transvaal and Natal)

NATB National Automobile Theft Bureau

Nat. Bank. Reg. National Bankruptcy Register Reports (U.S.)

Nat. Bankr. Law. National Bankruptcy Law

Nat. Bankr. N. & R. National Bankruptcy News and Reports

Nat. Bankr. R. National Bankruptcy Register (U.S.)

Nat. Bankr. Reg. National Bankruptcy Register (U.S.)

Nat. Bankr. Rep. National Bankruptcy Register Reports (U.S.)

Nat. Bar Bull. National Bar Bulletin

Nat. Bar. J. National Bar Journal

Nat. B.C. National Bank Cases (U.S.)

Nat. B.J. National Bar Journal

Nat. B.R. National Bankruptcy Register (U.S.)

Nat. Brev. Fitzherbert's Natura Brevium

Nat. Civic Rev. National Civic Review (formerly National Municipal Review)

Nat. Civ. Rev. National Civic Review

Nat. Corp. Rep. National Corporation Reporter

Nat. Gas Law J. The Natural Gas Lawyer's Journal

Nathan Nathan, Common Law of South Africa

Nat. Inc. Tax Mag. National Income Tax Magazine

Nat. Ins. Commiss. National Insurance Commissioner

Nat. Ins. L.R. National Insurance Law Review

Nat. J. Crim. Def. National Journal of Criminal Defense

Nat. J. Leg. Ed. National Journal of Legal Education

Natl. National

Nat'l Acad. Arb. Proc. Ann. Meeting National Academy of Arbitrators: Proceedings of the Annual Meeting

N. Atlantic Reg. Bus. L. Rev. North Atlantic Regional Business Law Review

Nat. Law Guild Q. National Lawyers' Guild Quarterly

Nat'l Black L. J. National Black Law Journal

Nat'l Civic Rev. National Civic Review

Nat. Legal Mag. National Legal Magazine

Nat. L.F. Natural Law Forum

Nat. L. Guild Q. National Lawyer's Guild Quarterly

Nat'l Income Tax Mag. National Income Tax Magazine

Nat. L.J. Natal Law Journal (S.Afr.)

Nat'l J.Crim. Def. National Journal of Criminal Defense

Nat'l Jewish L. Rev. National Jewish Law Review

Nat'l Law Guild Prac. National Lawyers' Guild Practitioner

Nat'l Legal Mag. National Legal Magazine

Nat'l L.J. National Law Journal

Nat. L.M. Natal Law Magazine (S.Afr.)

Nat'l Mun. Rev. National Municipal Review

Nat'l Pub. Empl. Rep. (Lab.Rel.Press) National Public Employment Reporter

Nat. L.Q. Natal Law Quarterly (S.Afr.)

Nat. L. Rec. National Law Record

Nat. L. Rep. National Law Reporter

Natl. Rep. Sys. National Reporter System

Nat. L. Rev. National Law Review

Nat'l School L. Rptr. National School Law Reporter

Nat'l Tax J. National Tax Journal

Nat. Munic. Rev. National Municipal Review

Nat. Mun. Rev. National Municipal Review

NATO North Atlantic Treaty Organization

Nat. Q. Rev. National Quarterly Review

Nat. Reg. National Register, edited by Mead, 1816

Nat. Rept. Syst. National Reporter System

Nat. Res. Natural Resources

Nat. Res. J. Natural Resources Journal

Nat. Res. Lawyer Natural Resources Lawyer

Nat. Resources & Env't Natural Resources & Environment

Nat. Resources J. Natural Resources Journal

Nat. Resources Law Natural Resources Lawyer

Nat. Resources L. Newsl. Natural Resources Law Newsletter

Nat. Rev. National Review (London)

Nat. School L. Rptr. National School Law Reporter

Nat. Tax. J. National Tax Journal

Nat. Tax Mag. National Tax Magazine

Nat. U.L. Rev.
- Natal University Law Review (S.Afr.)
- National University Law Review (1921-31)

Natural L.F. Natural Law Forum

Natural Resources J. Natural Resources Journal

Natural Resources Lawy. Natural Resources Lawyer

Nav. Navigation

Naval L. Rev. Naval Law Review

Nav. War C. Rev. Naval War College Review

N.B.
- Nulla bona
- Nota bene
- New Benloe or Bendloe King's Bench Reports
- New Brunswick
- New Brunswick Reports (Canada)

N.B.2d. New Brunswick Reports, 2d Series (Canada)

Nb. Nebraska

N.B. Bd. P.U.C. New Brunswick Board of Public Utilities Commission, Canada

N. Ben. New Benloe's Reports, King's Bench (1531-1628) (Eng.)

N. Benl. New Benloe's Reports, English King's Bench (1531-1628) (Eng.)

N.B. Eq. New Brunswick Equity Reports

N.B. Eq. Ca. New Brunswick Equity Cases

N.B. Eq. R. New Brunswick Equity Reports (1894-1912)

N.B. Eq. Rep. New Brunswick Equity Reports (1894-1912)

N.B.J. National Bar Journal

N. Bkpt. R. National Bankruptcy Register Reports (U.S.)

N. Bkpt. Reg. National Bankruptcy Register Reports (U.S.)

N. Bk. R. National Bankruptcy Register Reports (U.S.)

Nb. L. Nebraska Law Review

N.B.L.B. Nebraska Law Bulletin

N.B.L.R. North Borneo Law Reports

Nb. L.R. Nebraska Law Review

N.B.N.R. National Bankruptcy News and Reports

N.B.N. Rep. National Bankruptcy News and Reports

N.B.R.
- National Bankruptcy Register Reports (U.S.)
- New Brunswick Reports (1883-1929)

N.B.R.2d. New Brunswick Reports, Second Series (Can.)

N.B.R. All. Allen's New Brunswick Reports

N.B.R. Ber. Berton's New Brunswick Reports

N.R.B. Carl. Carleton's New Brunswick Reports

N.B.R. Chip. Chipman's New Brunswick Reports

N.B. Rep. New Brunswick Reports

N.B. Rev. Stat. New Brunswick Revised Statutes (Canada)

N.B.R. Han. Hannay's New Brunswick Reports

N.B.R. Kerr. Kerr's New Brunswick Reports

N.B.R.P. & B. Pugsley & Burbridge's New Brunswick Reports

N.B.R.P. & T. Pugsley & Trueman's New Brunswick Reports

N. B. R. Pug. Pugsley's New Brunswick Reports

N.B.R. Pugs. Pugsley's New Brunswick Reports (1876-93) (Can.)

N.B.R. Tru. Trueman's New Brunswick Reports

N. Bruns. New Brunswick Reports (1883-1929)

N.B.S. National Bureau of Standards (U.S.)

N.B. Stat. New Brunswick Statutes (Can.)

NBTA National Board of Trial Advocates

N.B.V. Ad. New Brunswick Vice Admiralty Reports

N.C.
- New Cases (Bingham's New Cases) in Common Pleas (1834-40)
- Non callable

- North Carolina
- North Carolina Reports
- North Carolina Supreme Court Reports
- Notes of Cases (Australian Jurist)
- Notes of Cases (Ecclesiastical & Maritime) (1841-50)
- Notes of Cases, T. Strange, Madras (India)

N.C.A.
- No coupons attached
- North Carolina Court of Appeals Reports

N.C. Admin. Code North Carolina Administrative Code

N.C. Adv. Legis. Serv. North Carolina Advance Legislative Service (Michie)

NCAJ National Center for Administrative Justice

NC App North Carolina Appellate Reports

N.C. & B. Naval Courts and Boards (U.S.)

N.C. App. North Carolina Court of Appeals Reports

N. Car.
- North Carolina
- North Carolina Reports (N.C.)

N. Car. Central L.J. North Carolina Central L.J.

N. Car. Law Rep. Carolina Law Repository (Reprint) (N.C.)

N. Carolina Cases North Carolina Reports (N.C.)

N. Car. Rep. North Carolina Reports (N.C.)

N. Car. S.B.A. North Carolina State Bar Association

N.C.B. North Carolina Bar

NCBF North Carolina Bar Foundation

N.C.C. New Chancery Cases (Younge & Collyer) (1841-43) (Eng.)

N.C.C.A. Negligence & Compensation Cases, Annotated

N.C.C.A.3d Negligence & Compensation Cases, Annotated, 3d Series

N.C.C.A.N.S. Negligence & Compensation Cases, Annotated, New Series

N.C.C.C. North Carolina Corporation Commission

NCCD National Council on Crime and Delinquency

NCCDL National College of Criminal Defense Lawyers and Public Defenders

N.C. Cent. L.J. North Carolina Central Law Journal

N.C. Conf. North Carolina Conference Reports

N.C. Conf. Rep. North Carolina Conference Reports (1800-04)

N.C. Conf. Rep. (N.C.) North Carolina Conference Reports

N.C. Const. North Carolina Constitution

N.C.D. Nemine contra dicente (no one dissenting)

NCDA National College of District Attorneys

N.C. Ecc. Notes of Cases in Ecclesiastical & Maritime Courts (Eng.)

N. Cent. School L. Rev. North Central School Law Review

N.C.F.A. National Consumers' Finance Assn. Law Bulletin

N.C. Gen. Stat. General Statutes of North Carolina

N. Chip. N. Chipman's Reports (Vermont 1789-91)

N. Chipm. N. Chipman's Reports (Vermont 1789-91)

N. Chip. (Vt.) N. Chipman's Reports (Vermont 1789-91)

N. Ch. R.
- H. Finch's Chancery Reports (1673-81) (Eng.)
- Nelson's Chancery Reports (Eng.)

NCIC National Crime Information Center

N.C.I.C. Ops. North Carolina Industrial Commission Advance Sheets

NCJCJ National Council of Juvenile Court Judges

N.C.J. Int'l L. & Com. Reg. North Carolina Journal of International Law and Commercial Regulation

NCJJ National College of Juvenile Justice

N.C.J. of L. North Carolina Journal of Law

N.C.L. North Carolina Law Review

N.C. Law Repos. North Carolina Law Repository

N.C. Law Repository   North Carolina Law Repository (Reprint) (N.C.)

NCLE   Nebraska Continuing Legal Education, Inc.

N.C.L.J.   North Carolina Law Journal

N.C.L.R.   North Carolina Law Review

N.C.L. Rep.   North Carolina Law Repository

N.C.L. Reps.   North Carolina Law Repository (Reprint) (N.C.)

N.C.L. Rev.   North Carolina Law Review

N.C.L. Review   North Carolina Law Review

N.C.M.   Court-Martial Reports, Navy Cases

N.C.P.S.   Non-contributory Pension Scheme

N. Cr.   New York Criminal Reports

N.C.R.C.   North Carolina Board of Railroad Commissioners

N.C. Rep.   North Carolina Reports (N.C.)

N.C. Rep. Appendix   North Carolina Reports, Appendix (N.C.)

N.C. Reports   North Carolina Reports (N.C.)

N.C. Sess. Laws   Session Laws of North Carolina

NCSJ   National College of the State Judiciary

NCSL   National Civil Service League

N.C. St. B. Newsl.   North Carolina State Bar Newsletter

N.C. St. B.Q.   North Carolina State Bar Quarterly

N.C. Str.   Strange's Notes of Cases, Madras (1798-1816)

N.Ct.   Native Court (Ghana)

N.C. Term R.   North Carolina Term Reports

N.C. Term Rep.   North Carolina Term Reports

N.C.T.R.   Taylor's North Carolina Term Reports (N.C.)

N.C.T. Rep.   North Carolina Term Rep. (4 N.C.)

NCUA   National Credit Union Administration

N.C.U.C.   North Carolina Utilities Commission Reports

N.D.
- No Date
- North Dakota Reports
- North Dakota
- North Dakota Supreme Court Reports (1890-1953))
- Northern District

Nd.
- Newfoundland
- Newfoundland Reports

N.D.A.   National Defense Act (U.S.)

NDAA   National District Attorneys Association

N.D. Admin. Code   North Dakota Administrative Code

N. Dak.   North Dakota Reports (N.D.)

N.D. Ala.   United States District Court for the Northern District of Alabama

N.D.B.   Navy Department Bulletin (U.S.)

N.D.B.B. North Dakota Bar Brief

N.D. Cal. United States District Court for the Northern District of California

N.D. Cent. Code North Dakota Century Code

N.D.C. of R. North Dakota Commissioners of Railroads

N.D. Const. North Dakota Constitution

N.D. Fla. United States District Court for the Northern District of Florida

N.D. Ga. United States District Court for the Northern District of Georgia

N.D. Ill. United States District Court for the Northern District of Illinois

N.D. Ind. United States District Court for the Northern District of Indiana

N.D. Iowa United States District Court for the Northern District of Iowa

N.D. J. Legis. N.D. Journal of Legislation

N.D.L. Notre Dame Lawyer

N.D.L.R. North Dakota Law Review

N.D.L. Rev. North Dakota Law Review

N.D. Miss. United States District Court for the Northern District of Mississippi

N.D.N.Y. United States District Court for the Northern District of New York

N.D. Ohio United States District Court for the Northern District of Ohio

N.D. Okla. United States District Court for the Northern District of Oklahoma

N.D.P.A. National Democratic Party of Alabama

N.D.R. North Dakota Law Review

N.D.R.C. North Dakota Board of Railroad Commissioners

N.D. Sess. Laws Laws of North Dakota

N.D. Tex. United States District Court for the Northern District of Texas

NDU National Defense University

N.E.
- New edition
- New England
- North Eastern Reporter
- North East

Ne.
- Nepal
- Nepalese

NE Nebraska

N.E.2d Northeastern Reporter, Second Series

Neb.
- Nebraska
- Nebraska Reports
- Nebraska Supreme Court Reports
- United States District Court for the District of Nebraska

Neb. Admin. R. Nebraska Administrative Rules and Regulations

Neb. Bd. R.C. Nebraska Board of Railroad Commissioners

Neb. Bd. Trans. Nebraska Board of Transportation

Neb. Const. Nebraska Constitution

Neb. Laws Nebraska Laws

Neb. L.B. Nebraska Law Bulletin

Neb. L. Bull. Nebraska Law Bulletin

Neb. Leg. N. Nebraska Legal News

Neb. L. Rev. Nebraska Law Review

Nebraska L. Rev. Nebraska Law Review

Nebr. Nebraska Reports (Neb.)

Nebr. B.A. Nebraska State Bar Journal

Neb. R.C. Nebraska Railway Commission Reports

Neb. Rev. Stat. Revised Statutes of Nebraska

Nebr. L.B. Nebraska Law Bulletin

Nebr. L. Rev. Nebraska Law Review

Neb. S.B.J. Nebraska State Bar Journal

Neb. S.R.C. Nebraska State Railway Comm.

Neb. St. B.J. Nebraska State Bar Journal

Neb. Sup. Ct.J. Nebraska Supreme Court Journal (1931-44)

Neb. (Unof.) Nebraska Unofficial Reports

Neb. Unoff. Nebraska Unofficial Reports (1901-04)

Neb. W.C.C. Nebraska Workmen's Compensation Court Bulletin

N.E.C. Notes of Ecclesiastical Cases (Eng.)

N.E.D.C. National Economic Development Council

Nederl. Yb. of Internat. L. Netherlands Yearbook of International Law. Leiden, Netherlands

Need. Needham's Annual Summary of Tax Cases (Eng.)

Ne. Ex. Ne Exeat

Neg. C. Negligence Cases (CCH)

Neg. Cas. Bloomfield's Manumission (or Negro) Cases (N.J.)

Neg. Inst. Negotiable Instrument

Neg. Inst. Law Negotiable Instrument Law

Negl. Negligence

Negl. & Comp. Cas. Ann. Negligence & Compensation Cases Annotated

Negl. & Comp. Cas. Ann.3d. Negligence & Compensation Cases Annotated, Third Series

Negl. & Comp. Cas. Ann. (N.S.) Negligence & Compensation Cases Annotated, New Series

Negl. Cas. Negligence Cases (CCH)

Negl. Cas.2d Negligence Cases (CCH), Second Series

Negligence Cases (2d) Negligence Cases (other than Automobile) 2d Series

Negotiation J. Negotiation Journal

Negro. Cas. Bloomfield's Manumission (N.J.)

N.E.I. Non est inventus (he is not found)

Nel.
- H. Finch's Chancery Reports (1673-81) (Eng.)
- Nelson's Chancery Reports (1625-93) (Eng.)

Nel. C.R. Nelson's Chancery Reports (Eng.)

Nell Nell's Reports (1845-55) (Ceylon)

Nels.
- H. Finch's Chancery Reports (Eng.)
- Nelson's Chancery Reports (Eng.)

Nels. Abr. Nelson's abridgment of the Common Law

Nels. Cler. Nelson's Rights of the Clergy

Nels. F. Finch's Chancery Reports by Nelson (1673-81) (23 ER)

Nels. Fol. Finch's Reports (ed. by Nelson), Chancery (1673-81) (Eng.)

Nels. Fol. Rep. H. Finch's Chancery Reports, by Nelson (21 ER)

Nels. Lex Man. Nelson's Lex Maneriorum

Nelson (Eng.)
- H. Finch's Chancery Reports, by Nelson (21 ER)
- Nelson's Chancery Reports (1625-93) (21 ER)

Nelson's Rep. Nelson tempore Finch (1673-81)

Nels. 8 vo. Nelson's Chancery Reports (1625-93) (21 ER)

nem. con. nemine contradicente (nobody contradicting) (Lat.)

nem. dis. nemine dissentiente nobody (dissenting) (Lat.)

N. Eng. J. Prison L. New England Journal on Prison Law

N. Eng. L. Rev. New England Law Review

N. Engl. L. Rev. New England Law Review

N. Eng. Rep. New England Reporter

N.E.P.A. National Environmental Policy Act

N.E.R.
- New England Reporter
- North Eastern Reporter (commonly cited N.E.)

N.E.R.C. National Environment Research Council

N.E. Rep.
- New England Reporter
- North Eastern Reporter (commonly cited N.E.)

N.E. Reporter. North Eastern Reporter

N.E. Repr. North Eastern Reporter

Neth. Netherlands

Netherl. Int'l L. Rev. Netherlands Yearbook of International Law, The Hague, Netherlands

Neth. Int'l L. Rev. Netherlands International Law Review

Neth. Y.B. Int'l Law Netherlands Yearbook of International Law

Nev.
- Nevada
- Nevada Reports
- Nevada Supreme Court Reports

Nevada Rep. Nevada Reports (Nev.)

Nevada Repts. Nevada Reports (Nev.)

Nevada State Reports Nevada Reports (Nev.)

Nev. Admin. Code Nevada Administrative Code

Nev. & Mac. Neville & Macnamara' s Railway Cases (1855-1950) (Eng.)

Nev. & MacN. Neville & Macnamara's Railway & Canal Cases (1855-1950)

Nev. & Macn. Neville & Macnamara's English Railway and Canal Cases

Nev. & Man. Nevile & Manning's King's Bench Reports (1831-36) (Eng.)

Nev. & Man. Mag. Cas. Nevile & Manning's Magistrates' Cases (1832-36) (Eng.)

Nev. & McN. Neville & McNamara's Railway Cases (Eng.)

Nev. & M. (Eng.) Nevile & Manning (King's Bench)

Nev. & M.K.B. Nevile & Manning's King's Bench Reports (1832-36) (Eng.)

Nev. & M.M.C. Nevile & Manning's Magistrates' Cases (Eng.)

Nev. & P.
- Nevile & Perry's King's Bench Reports (1836-38) (Eng.)
- Nevile & Perry's Magistrates' Cases (Eng.)

Nev. & P.K.B. Nevile & Perry's King's Bench Reports (1836-38)

Nev. & P. Mag. Cas. Nevile & Perry's English Magistrates' Cases (1836-37)

Nev. & P.M.C. Nevile & Perry's Magistrates' Cases (1836-37)

Nev. Const. Nevada Constitution

Nev. P.S.C. Nevada Public Service Commission

Nev. P.S.C. Op. Nevada Public Service Commission Opinions

Nev. R.C. Nevada Railroad Commission

Nev. Rev. Stat. Nevada Revised Statutes

Nev. S.B.J. Nevada State Bar Journal

Nev. Stats. Statutes of Nevada

Nev. St. Bar J. Nevada State Bar Journal

Nev. St. B.J. Nevada State Bar Journal

New. Newell, Illinois Appeal Reports

New Ann. Reg. New Annual Register (London)

Newark L. Rev. University of Newark Law Review

Newb. Newberry's United States District Court, Admiralty Reports

Newb. Adm. Newberry's United States District Court, Admiralty Reports

New Benl. New Benloe's Reports, English King's Bench (1531-1628)

New B. Eq. Ca. New Brunswick Equity Cases

New B. Eq. Rep. New Brunswick Equity Reports, vol, 1

Newberry Newberry's Admiralty Reports (U.S.)

Newberry Adm. (F.) Newberry's United States District Court, Admiralty Reports

Newberry's Ad. Rep. Newberry's Admiralty Reports (U.S.)

Newblyth Newblyth's Manuscript Decisions, Session Cases (1668-77) (Sc.)

Newbon Newbon's Private Bills Reports (1895-99) (Eng.)

New Br. New Brunswick Reports

New Br. Eq. (Can.) New Brunswick Equity Reports

New Br. Eq. Cas. (Can.) New Brunswick Equity Cases

New Br. R. New Brunswick Reports (Can.)

Newbyth Newbyth's Manuscript Decisions, Scotch Session Cases

New Cas. New Cases (Bingham's New Cases)

New Cas. Eq. New Cases in Equity, vols. 8, 9 Modern Reports (1721-55)

New Commun. New Community

Newell Newell's Reports, vols. 48-90 Illinois Appeals

Newell, Defam. Newell on Defamation, Slander and Libel

Newell, Eject. Newell's Treatise on the Action of Ejectment

Newell, Mal. Pros. Newell's Treatise on Malicious Prosecution

Newell, Sland. & L. Newell on Slander and Libel

New Eng. New England Reporter

New Eng. Hist. New England Historical and Genealogical Register

New Eng. J. Crim. & Civil Confinement New England Journal on Criminal & Civil Confinement

New Eng. J. Med. New England Journal of Medicine

New Eng. J. on Crim. & Civ. Confinement New England Journal on Criminal and Civil Confinement

New Eng. J. Prison New England Journal of Prison Law

New Eng. J. Prison L. New England Journal of Prison Law

New England L. Rev. New England Law Review

New Eng. L. Rev. New England Law Review

New Eng. R. New England Reporter

New Eng. Rep. New England Reporter

Newf. Newfoundland

Newfld. L.R. Newfoundland Law Reports

Newf. L.R. Newfoundland Law Reports (1817-1949) (Can.)

Newfoundl. Newfoundland

Newfoundl. L.R. Newfoundland Law Reports

Newfoundl. R. Newfoundland Reports

Newfoundl. Sel. Cas. Newfoundland Select Cases

Newf. S. Ct. Newfoundland Supreme Court Decisions

Newf. Sel. Cas. Newfoundland Select Cases (1817-28)

New Hamp. New Hampshire Reports (N.H.)

New Hamp. B.J. New Hampshire Bar Journal

New Hamp. R. New Hampshire Reports (N. H.)

New Hamp. Rep. New Hampshire Reports (N. H.)

New Hampshire Rep. New Hampshire Reports (N.H.)

New Ir. Jur. New Irish Jurist & Local Government Review (1900-05)

New Jersey New Jersey Law Reports (N.J.)

New Jersey Eq. New Jersey Equity Reports (N.J.)

New Jersey Equity New Jersey Equity Reports (N.J.)

New Jersey Leg. Rec. New Jersey Legal Record

New Jersey L.J. New Jersey Law Journal

New Jersey L. Rev. New Jersey Law Review

New Jersey S.B.A. Qu. New Jersey State Bar Association Quarterly

Newl. Ch. Pprac. Newland's Chancery Practice

Newl. Ch. Pr. Newland, Chancery Practice. 3ed. 1830

Newl. Cont. Newland, Contracts. 1806

New L.J. New Law Journal

New Mag. Cas. New Magistrates' Cases (Bittleston, Wise & Parnell) (1844-51)

Newm. Conv. Newman on Conveyancing

New Mex. B.A. New Mexico State Bar Association, Minutes

New Mexico L. Rev. New Mexico Law Review

New Mex. L. Rev. New Mexico Law Review

New Mex. S.B.A. New Mexico State Bar Association, Report of Proceedings

New Nat. Brev. New Natura Brevium

New Pract. Case. New Practice Cases (1844-48)

New Pr. Cases. New Practice Cases (1844-48) (Eng.)

New Rep.
- Bosanquet & Puller's New Reports (4, 5 Bosanquet & Puller) (1804-07) (Eng.)
- New Reports (1862-65) (Eng.)

New Series Martin's Reports, New Series (La.)

New Sess. Cas. New Session Cases (Carrow, Hamerton & Allen) (1844-51)

Newsl. Newsletter

Newsl. Leg. Act. Newsletter on Legislative Activities (Council of Europe)

News Media & L. News Media and the Law

New So. W.L. New South Wales Law Reports

New So. W. St. New South Wales State Reports

New So. W.W.N. New South Wales Weekly Notes

Newsp. Newspapers, periodicals and press associations

New Term Rep.
- Dowling & Ryland's King's Bench Reports
- New Term Reports

New Tr. New Trial

New York Att'y Gen. Annual Rep. New York Attorney General Reports

New York City B.A. Bul. Bulletin of Ass'n. of the Bar of the City of N.Y.

New York R. New York Court of Appeals Reports (N.Y.)

New York Rep. New York Court of Appeals Reports (N.Y.)

New York Supp. New York Supplement

New Yugo. L. New Yugoslav Law

New Zeal. New Zealand

New Zeal. Jur. R. New Zealand Jurist Reports

New Zeal L. New Zealand Law Reports

New Zeal. L.J. New Zealand Law Journal

New Zeal. L.R. New Zealand Law Reports

N.F.
- Newfoundland
- Newfoundland Reports

NFFE National Federation of Federal Employees

NFLA National Farm Loan Association (U.S.)

Nfld.
- Newfoundland

- Newfoundland: Court with jurisdiction in Newfoundland
- Newfoundland Supreme Court Decisions (Canada)

Nfld. & P.E.I.R. Newfoundland and Prince Edward Island Reports, 1971

Nfld. & P.E.I.R. Newfoundland and Prince Edward Island Reports, 1971

Nfld. L.R. Newfoundland Law Reports

Nfld. R. Newfoundland Reports

Nfld. Rev. Stat. Newfoundland Revised Statutes (Canada)

Nfld. Sel. Cas. Tucker's Select Cases (Nfld.) 1817-1828

Nfld. Stat. Newfoundland Statutes (Canada)

NFPA National Fire Protection Association

NFPCA National Fire Protection and Control Association

NFU National Farmers' Union

NGO Non-Governmental Organization

NGR National Guard Regulation

N.H.
- New Hampshire
- New Hampshire Reports
- New Hampshire Supreme Court Reports

N.H. Act National Housing Act

N.H. Admin. Code New Hampshire Code of Administrative Rules

N. Hamp. New Hampshire Reports (N.H.)

N. Hamp. R. New Hampshire Reports (N.H.)

N. Hamp. Rep. New Hampshire Reports (N.Y.)

N. Hamp. S.B.A. New Hampshire State Bar Association

N. Hampshire Rep. New Hampshire Reports (N.H.)

N.H. & C. Railway & Canal Cases (1835-55) (Eng.)

N.H.B.J. New Hampshire Bar Journal

N.H.C. Native High Court Reports (South Africa)

N.H. Const. New Hampshire Constitution

N.H.J. New Hampshire Bar Journal

N.H. Judicial Council New Hampshire Judicial Council

N.H.L. Notes from Hume's Lectures

N.H. Laws Laws of the State of New Hampshire

N.H.L. Rep. New Hampshire Law Reporter

N.H.P.S.C.R. New Hampshire Public Service Commission Reports

N.H.R. New Hampshire Reports

N.H.R.C. New Hampshire Board of Railroad Commissioners

N.H. Rep. New Hampshire Reports (N.H.)

N.H. Reports New Hampshire Reports (N.H.)

N.H. Rev. Stat. Ann. New Hampshire Revised Statutes Annotated

N.H.R.S. New Hampshire Revised Statutes

N.H. Rulemaking Reg. New Hampshire Rulemaking Register

N.H.T.S.A. National Highway Transportation Safety Administration

N.I.
- Northern Ireland
- Northern Ireland Law Reports

Nic. Adult. Bast. Nicolas, Adulterine Bastardy. 1836

Nic. & Fl. Reg. Nicoll & Flaxman on Registration

Nicar. Nicaragua

Nic. Elec. Nicolson, Elections in Scotland

Nic. Ha. C. Nicholl, Hare & Carrow's Railway & Canal Cases (1835-55)

Nich. Adult. Bast. Nicholas on Adulterine Bastardy

Nich. H. & C. Nicholl, Hare & Carrow's Railway & Canal Cases (1835-55)

Nicholl Englilsh Railway and Canal Cases, by Nicholl, & c.

Nicholl H. & C. Nicholl, Hare and Carrow (1835-55)

Nichols-Cahill Nichols-Cahill Annotated New York Civil Practice Acts

Nicholson Nicholson, Manuscript Decisions, Scotch Session Cases

Nicolas Proceedings and Ordinances of the Privy Council, edited by Sir Harry Nicolas

N.I.D.L.R. Office of the Director of Law Reform (Northern Ireland)

NIE National Institute of Education

Niebh. Hist. Rom. Niebuhr, Roman History

Nient cul. Nient culpable (not guilty)

NIER National Industrial Equipment Reserve

Nig.
- Nigeria
- Nigerian

Nig. Ann. Int'l L. Nigerian Annual of International Law

Nig. Bar. J. The Nigerian Bar Journal, Lagos, Nigeria

Nig. B.J. Nigerian Bar Journal

Nigeria Bar J. The Nigerian Bar Journal. Annual Journal of the Nigeria Bar Association. Lagos, Nigeria

Nigeria L.R. Nigeria Law Reports

Nigerian Ann. Int'l L. Nigerian Annual of International Law

Nigerian L.J. The Nigerian Law Journal. London

Nig. J. Contemp.L. Nigerian Journal of Contemporary Law

Nig. Lawy. Q. Nigeria Lawyers' Quarterly

Nig. L.J. Nigerian Law Journal

Nig. L.Q.R. Nigerian Law Quarterly Review

Nig. L.Q.R. Nigerian Law Quarterly Review

Nig. L.R. Nigeria Law Reports

NIH National Institutes of Health

N.I.J. New Irish Jurist

N.I.J.R. New Irish Jurist (1900-05)

N.I.L. Negotiable Instruments Law

NILECJ National Institute of Law Enforcement and Criminal Justice

Niles Reg. Niles' Weekly Register

N. Ill. U.L. Rev. Northern Illinois University Law Review

N.I.L.Q. Northern Ireland Legal Quarterly

NILR Netherlands International Law Review

N.I.L.R.
- Northern Ireland Law Reports
- Netherlands International Law Review. Leiden, Netherlands.

Nil. Reg. Niles' Weekly Register

N.I.L. Rev. Netherlands International Law Review

NIMH National Institute of Mental Health

N.I.M.L.O. Mun. L. Rev. N.I.M.L.O. Municipal Law Review

NIOSH National Institute for Occupational Safety and Health

N. Ir.
- North Ireland
- Northern Ireland
- Northern Ireland Law
- Northern Ireland Law Reports

N.I.R.A. National Industrial Recovery Act, U.S.

N.I.R.C. National Industrial Relations Court National Labour Tribunal (Eng.)

N. Ir. Legal Q. Northern Ireland Legal Quarterly

N. Ir. L.Q. Northern Ireland Legal Quarterly

N. Ir. L.R. Northern Ireland Law Reports

N. Ir. Pub. Gen. Acts Northern Ireland Public General Acts

N. Ir. Stat. Northern Ireland Statutes

Nisbet. Nisbet of Dirlecton's Scotch Session Cases (1665-77)

Nisi Prius & Gen. T. Rep. Nisi Prius & General Term Reports (Ohio)

Nisi Prius Rep. Ohio Nisi Prius Reports (Ohio)

NITA National Institute for Trial Advocacy

N.I.T.M. National Income Tax Magazine

Nix. Dig. Nixon's Digest of Laws (N.J.)

Nix. F. Nixon's Forms

N.J.
- New Jersey
- New Jersey Reports
- New Jersey Supreme Court Reports
- Notice of Judgment (official)

N.J. Admin. Code New Jersey Administrative Code

N.J. Admin. Reg. New Jersey Administrative Register.

N.J. Ch. New Jersey Equity Reports (N.J.)

NJCLE Institute for Continuing Legal Education (N.J.)

N.J. Const. New Jersey Constitution

N.J.E. New Jersey Equity Reports (N.J.)

N.J. Eq. New Jersey Equity Reports (N.J.)

N.J. Eq. R. New Jersey Equity Reports (N.J.)

N.J. Equity New Jersey Equity Reports (N.J.)

N. Jersey R. New Jersey Law Reports (N.J.)

N.J.F.D. Notices of Judgment, U.S. Food & Drug Administration

N.J.I.F.R. Notices of Judgment under the Federal Insecticide, Fungicide & Rodenticide Act

N.J. Jur. & Dom. Rel. Ct. New Jersey Juvenile and Domestic Relations Court

N.J.L. New Jersey Law Reports

N.J. Law.
- New Jersey Law Reports
- New Jersey Lawyer

N.J. Law J. New Jersey Law Journal

N.J. Law N. New Jersey Law News

N.J. Law Rep. New Jersey Law Reports (N.J.)

N.J. Laws Laws of New Jersey

N.J. Lawy. New Jersey Lawyer

N.J. Leg. Rec. New Jersey Legal Record

N.J.L.J. New Jersey Law Journal

N.J.L. Rep. New Jersey Law Reports (N.J.)

N.J.L. Rev. New Jersey Law Review

NJM New Jersey Miscellaneous Reports

N.J. Mis. New Jersey Miscellaneous Reports (N.J.)

N.J. Misc. New Jersey Miscellaneous Reports

N.J. Mis. R. New Jersey Miscellaenous Reports (N.J.)

N.J. Mun. Ct. New Jersey Municipal Court

N.J.P.U.C. New Jersey Public Utility Commission Reports

N.J.R. New Jersey Register, The (N.J.)

N.J.R.C. New Jersey Board of Railroad Commissioners Annual Reports

N.J. Rep. New Jersey Law Reports (N.J.)

N.J. Reports New Jersey Law Reports (N.J.)

N.J. Re. Tit. N. New Jersey Realty Title News

N.J. Rev. Stat. New Jersey Revised Statutes

N.J.S. New Jersey Superior Court Reports

N.J.S.A. New Jersey Statutes Annotated

N.J.S.B.A. New Jersey State Bar Association

N.J.S.B.A.Q. New Jersey State Bar Association Quarterly

N.J.S.B.J. New Jersey State Bar Journal

N.J.S.B.T.A. Ops. New Jersey State Board of Tax Appeals, Opinions

N.J. Sess. Law Serv. New Jersey Session Law Service

N.J. Stat. Ann. (West) New Jersey Statutes Annotated

N.J. St. B.J. New Jersey State Bar Journal

N.J. Sup. New Jersey Superior Court Reports (N.J.)

N.J. Super. New Jersey Superior Court Reports

N.J. Tax New Jersey Tax Court Reports

nka Now known as

N. Ky. L. Rev. Northern Kentucky Law Review

N. Ky. St. L.F. Northern Kentucky State Law Forum

N.L. Nelson's Lutwyche, English Common Pleas Reports

NLADA Brief. NLADA Briefcase

N.L.C.D. National Liberation Council Decree (1966-69) (Ghana)

NLCPI National Legal Center for the Public Interest

NLF National Law Foundation

N.L.F. National Liberation Front

N.L.G.Q. National Lawyers' Guild Quarterly

N.L.J. Nagpur Law Journal (India)

N.L.L.
- New Library of Law and Equity, (Eng.)
- New Library of Law, Harrisburg, Pennsylvania

NLM National Library of Medicine

N.L.Q. Nigeria Lawyers' Quarterly

N.L.Q.R. Nigeria Law Quarterly Review

N.L.R.
- Nagpur Law Reports, India

- Natal Law Reports, India
- Newfoundland Law Reports
- New Law Reports, Ceylon
- Nigeria Law Reports (1881-1955)
- Nyasaland Law Reports
- South African Law Reports, Natal Province Division (1910-46)

N.L.R.A.   National Labor Relations Act

N.L.R.B.
- National Labor Relations Board Decisions and Orders
- National Labor Relations Board (U.S.)

NLRB Advice Mem. Case No.   National Labor Relations Board Advice Memorandum Case Number

NLRB Ann. Rep.   National Labor Relations Board Annual Report

N.L.R.B. Dec.   National Labor Relations Board Decisions

NLRB Dec. (CCH)   NLRB Decisions

N.L. Rev.   Northeastern Law Review

N.L.R. (O.S.)   Natal Law Reports, Old Series (1867-72) (S. Afr.)

N.M.
- New Mexico Court of Appeals
- New Mexico
- New Mexico Reports
- New Mexico Supreme Court Reports
- New Mexico Territorial Court

N. Mag. Ca.   New Magistrates' Cases (Eng.)

N.M. App.   New Mexico Court of Appeals

NMB   National Medication Board

NMC   Naval Material Command

NMCLE   Continuing Legal Education of New Mexico, Inc.

N.M. Const.   New Mexico Constitution

N. Mex   New Mexico Territorial Courts

N. Mex. L. Rev.   New Mexico Law Review

N.M. (G.)   New Mexico Reports (Gildersleeve) (1852-89)

N.M. (J.)   New Mexico Reports (Johnson)

N.M.L.   New Mexico Law Review

N.M. Laws   Laws of New Mexico

N.M.L.R.
- New Mexico Law Review
- Nigerian Monthly Law Reports (1964-65)

N.M.L. Rev.   New Mexico Law Review

N.M.S.   New Mexico Statutes

N.M.S.B.A.   New Mexico State Bar Association

N.M.S.C.C.   New Mexico State Corporation Commission

N.M. Stat. Ann.   New Mexico Statutes Annotated

N.M. St. Bar Assn.   New Mexico State Bar Association

nn.
- footnotes
- notes

N.N.C.N.   Northern Nigeria Case Notes

N.N. (G.)   New Mexico Reports (Gildersleeve)

N.N.H.C. Natal Native High Court Reports (1899-1915) (S. Afr.)

N.N.L.N. Northern Nigeria Legal Notes

N.N.L.R.
- Northern Nigeria Law Reports
- Northern Region Law Reports (Nigeria)

N/O Registered in name of

no. number

NOAA National Oceanic and Atmospheric Administration

Noble Noble's Current Court Decisions (N.Y.)

NOCA Newberg on Class Actions

No. Ca. Ecc. & Mar. Notes of Cases (Eng.) Ecclesiastical and Maritime

No. Cas. L.J. Notes of Cases, Law Journal

No. East. Rep. Northeastern Reporter

N. of Case.
- Notes of Cases at Madras (by Strange)
- Notes of Cases, English Ecclesiastical and Maritime Courts (1841-50)

N.O.I.B.N. Not otherwise indexed by name (used under terms of tariffs, filed with Interstate Commerce Commission)

No. Ire. L.Q. Northern Ireland Legal Quarterly

Noise Reg. Rep. (BNA) Noise Regulation Reporter (BNA)

Nok. Mort. Nokes, Mortgages & Receiverships. 3ed. 1951

NOL Net operating loss

Nol.
- Nolan's Magistrates' Cases (1791-92) (Eng.)
- Nolan's Settlement Cases (Eng.)

Nolan
- Nolan on the Poor Laws. 4 editions (1805-33)
- Nolan's Magistrate's Cases (1791-92) (Eng.)

Nol. Mag. Nolan's Magistrates' Cases (1791-92) (Eng.)

Nol.(Just.) Nolan's English Magistrates' Cases

NOLPE
- National Organization on Legal Problems of Education
- NOLPE School Law Journal

NOLPE Sch. L.J. NOLPE School Law Journal

NOLPE School L.J. NOLPE School Law Journal

NOLPE School L. Rep. NOLPE School Law Reporter

Nol. P.L. Nolan, Poor Laws. 4ed. 1825

nol-pros nolle prosequi

No. Sett. Cas. Nolan's English Magistrates' Cases

Nomos Nomos, Yearbook of the American Society of Political and Legal Philosophy

No.N. Novae Narrationes, 1516

Nonacq. Nonacquiescence by Commissioner in a Tax Court or Board of Tax Appeals decision (U.S.)

Non cul. Non culpabilis (not guilty)

non pros. non prosequitur (delay or neglect in prosecuting) (Lat.)

non seq. non sequitur (it does not follow) (Lat.)

No. of Cas. Madras. Notes of Cases at Madras (by Strange)

Nor. Norway

Norc. Norcross' Reports (vols. 23-24 Nevada)

Nor. Fr. Norman French

Nor. Pat. Norman, Letters Patent. 1853

Nor. Pro. Pr. North's Probate Practice (Illinois)

Norr. Norris Reports (vols. 82-96 Pennsylvania)

Norris Norris Reports (82-96 Pennsylvania)

Norris & L, Perpetuities Norris & Leach on Rule Against Perpetuities

Norris Seamen Norris' Law of Seamen

Norr. Peake Norris' Edition of Peake's Law of Evidence

North
- Northington, Eng.
- Northampton County Reporter (Pa.)
- Reports tempore Northington (1757-67) (Eden. English Chancery Reports)

Northam. Northampton Law Reporter (Pa.)

Northam. Law Rep. Northampton County Law Reporter, Pa.

Northam. L. Rep. Northampton Law Reporter (Pa.)

Northamp. Co. Repr. Northampton County Reporter (Pa.)

Northampton Co. Rep. Northampton County Reporter (Pa.)

North & G. North Guthrie's Reports (vols. 68-80 Missouri Appeals)

North Car. J. Int'l. L. & Comm. North Carolina Journal of International Law and Commercial Regulation

North Carolina Cent. L.J. North Carolina Central Law Journal

North Carolina College L.J. North Carolina College Law Journal

North. Co. Northampton County Reporter (Pa.)

North. Co. Rep. Northampton County Reporter (Pa.)

North. Co. R. (Pa.) Northampton County Reporter

North Dakota L. Rev. North Dakota Law Review

North. Ireland L.Q. Northern Ireland Legal Quarterly, Belfast, Northern Ireland

North. Ken'y. S.L. Rev. Northern Kentucky State Law Review

North. Ky. L.R. Northern Kentucky Law Review

North Pr. North's Illinois Probate Practice

Northrop U.L.J. Aero. Energy & Envt. Northrop University Law Journal of Aerospace, Energy and the Environment

Northrop U.L.J. Aerospace Bus. & Tax'n Northrop University Law Journal of Aerospace, Business and Taxation

Northrop U.L.J. Aerospace Energy and Env. Northrop University Law Journal of Aerospace, Energy and the Environment

North St. L. North, Study of the Laws. 1824

North U.L. Rev. Northwestern University Law Review

Northum. Northumberland County Legal News (Pa.)

Northumb. Co. Northumberland County Legal News (Pa.)

Northumb. Co. Leg. News Northumberland County Legal News (Pa.)

Northumberland Co. Leg. Jour. Northumberland Legal Journal (Pa.)

Northumberland L.J. Northumberland Legal Journal (Pa.)

Northumb.Legal J. Northumberland Legal Journal

Northumb. L.J. Northumberland Legal Journal News (Pa.)

Northumb. L.N. Northumberland Legal Journal (Pa.)

Northum. Co. Leg. N. Northumberland County Legal News

Northum. Leg. J. Northumberland Legal Journal (Pa.)

Northum Leg. J. (Pa.) Northumberland Legal Journal

Northum. Leg. N. (Pa.) Northumberland County Legal News

Northw. SL of L & C Coll. Northwestern School of Law of Lewis & Clark College

Northwest. J. Int'l. L. & Bus. Northwestern Journal of International Law and Business

Northwestern U.L. Rev. Northwestern University Law Review

Northwestern Univ. L. Rev. Northwestern University Law Review

North. W. L.J. Northwestern Law Journal

Northw. L.J. Northwestern Law Journal

Northw. L. Rev. Northwestern University Law Review

Northw. Pr. Northwest Provinces. India

Northw. Rep. Northwestern Reporter

Nort. L.C. Norton's Leading Cases on Inheritance (India)

Norton Norton's Cases on Hindu Law of Inheritance (1870-71) (India)

nos. numbers

Not. Cas.
- Notes of Cases at Madras, T. Strange (India)
- Notes of Cases, Ecclesiastical & Maritime (1841-50) (Eng.)

Not. Cas. Ecc. & M. Notes of Cases in the Ecclesiastical & Maritime Courts (1841-50)

Not. Cas. Madras. Notes of Cases at Madras (Strange)

Notc. on Fac. Notcutt, Factories and Workshops. 2ed. 1879

Not. Dec. Notes of Decisions (Martin's North Carolina Reports)

Not. Dig. Boddam & Greenwood's Notanda Digest

note. footnote in cross-reference

notes. footnotes in cross-reference

Notes of Ca. Notes of Cases(Eng.)

Notes of Cas. Notes of Cases, Ecclesiastical & Maritime (Eng.)

Notes of Cases Notes of Cases, Ecclesiastical & Maritime (Eng.)

Notes on U.S. Notes on United States Reports

Not-For-Profit Corp. Not-for Profit Corporation

NOTIS Northwestern On-Line Total Integrated System

Not. J. Notaries Journal

Not. Op. Wilmot's Notes of Opinions and Judgments

Notre Dame Est. Plan. Inst. Notre Dame Estate Planning Institute Proceedings

Notre Dame Est. Plan. Inst. Proc. Notre Dame Estate Planning Institute Proceedings

Notre Dame Inst. on Char. Giving

Found. & Tr. Notre Dame Institute on Charitable Giving Foundations and Trusts

Notre Dame Inst. on Char. Giving Foundations & Tr. Notre Dame Institute on Charitable Giving Foundations and Trusts

Notre Dame J. Leg. Notre Dame Journal of Legislation

Notre Dame J.L. Ethics & Pub. Pol'y Notre Dame Journal of Laws, Ethics, & Public Policy

Notre Dame L. Notre Dame Lawyer

Notre Dame Law. Notre Dame Lawyer

Notre Dame L. Rev. Notre Dame Law Review

Nott & Hop. Nott & Hopkins' Reports (8-15 U.S. Court of Claims)

Nott & Hunt. Nott & Huntington's Reports, vols. 1-7 United States Court of Claims

Nott & McC. Nott & McCord's South Carolina Reports (1817-20)

Nott & M'C. (S.C.) Nott & M'Cord, South Carolina Law Reports

Nott Mech. L. Nott on the Mechanics' Lien Law

N.O.V. Non Obstante Veredicto (the judgment notwithstanding)

Nov.
- Novation
- Novellae, The Novels or New Constitutions
- Novels (Roman Law)

Nova L.J. Nova Law Journal

Nova L. Rev. Nova Law Review

Nova Scotia L.R.A.C. Nova Scotia Law Reform Advisory Commission

Nov. Recop. Novisima Recopilacion Nov.Sc. Nova Scotia Supreme Court Reports (Canada)

Nov. Sc. Dec. Nova Scotia Decisions Nov.Sc.L.R. Nova Scotia Law Reports

Nov. Sc. P.U.C. Nova Scotia Board of Commissioners of Public Utilities (Canada)

No.West. Rep. Northwestern Reporter

Noy Noy's King's Bench Reports (1559-1649) (Eng.)

Noy. Ch. U. Noyes on Charitable Uses

Noye The grounds and Maxims of English Law by William Noye

Noy (Eng.) Noy's King's Bench Reports (1559-1649) (Eng.)

Noye's Max. Maxims of the Laws of England by William Noye

Noy, Max. Noy's Maxims

NP Ohio Nisi Prius Reports

n.p. no place

N. P.
- New Practice
- Nisi Prius

N.P.A. National Production Authority (U.S.)

N.P. & G.T. Rep. Nisi Prius & General Term Reports (Ohio)

N.P.C.
- National People's Congress (China)
- National Petroleum Council
- New Practice Cases. Bail Court. (1844-48)
- Nisi Prius Cases, Eng.

N.P.D.
- National Democratic Party (Germany)
- South African Law Reports, Natal Provinces Division

N.P.D.E.S. National Pollutant Discharge Elimination System, Adjudicatory Hearings Proceedings

NPF Gray, Nonprivate Foundations

N.P.N.S. Ohio Nisi Prius Reports, New Series

NPns Ohio Nisi Prius Reports, New Series

NPO Hand/Smith, Neighboring Property Owners

N.P. Ohio Ohio Nisi Prius Reports

N.P.R. Nisi Prius Reports

N.R. Navy Regulations

N.R.
- Bosanquet & Pullers New Reports (1804-07) (Eng.)
- Natal Reports (S. Afr.)
- The New Reports (1862-65) (Eng.)

N.R.A. National Recovery Administration (U.S.)

N.R.A.B. National Railroad Adjustment Board Awards

N.R.A.B. (1st D.) U.S. National Railroad Adjustment Board Awards, First Division

N.R.A.B. (2d D.) U.S. National Railroad Adjustment Board Awards, Second Division

N.R.A.B. (3d D.) U.S. National Railroad Adjustment Board Awards, Division

N.R.A.B. (4th D.) U.S. National Railroad Adjustment Board Awards, Fourth Division

N.R.B.P. New Reports of Bosanquet & Puller

NRC
- National Research Council
- Nuclear Regulatory Commission

N.R.C.D. National Redemption Council Decree (Ghana)

NRCI Nuclear Regulatory Commission Issuances

NRCLS National Resource Center for Consumers of Legal Services

N.R.D.C. National Research Development Corporation

N.R.G. Northern Rhodesia Gazette

N.R.J. Natural Resources Journal

N.R.L. Revised Laws 1813, N.Y.

NRLI Natural Resources Law Institute

N.R.L.N. Northern Regional Legal Notice (1954-61) (Nigeria)

N.R.L.R. Northern Rhodesia Law Reports

N.R.N.L.R. Northern Region of Nigeria Law Reports

N.R.R. & C. Russell & Chesley's Nova Scotia Reports

N.R.S. Nevada Revised Statutes

(n.s.)
- new series
- new style
- Nova Scotia
- Nova Scotia Reports, Canada

NSA National Security Agency (U.S.)

N.S. Am. Law Register American Law Register (Reprint) (Ohio)

NSC National Security Council (U.S.) N.S.C. New Session Cases (Sc.)

N. Sc. Dec. Nova Scotia Decisions

N.S.D. Geldert & Oxley's Nova Scotia Decisions (NSR 7-9) (1866-75) (Can.)

N.S. Dec. Nova Scotia Decisions (1867-74)

NSF National Science Foundation

N.S.I. National Security Index of the American Security Council

N.S.L. News Nova Scotia Law News

N.S.L.R. Nova Scotia Law Reports (1834-52) (Can.)

N.S.M.C.M. Naval Supplement, Manual for Courts-Martial (U.S.)

NSOB New Senate Office Building

N.S.R. Nova Scotia Reports (Can.)

N.S.R.2d. Nova Scotia Reports, 2d Series (Can.)

N.S.R.B. National Security Resources Board (U.S.)

N.S.R. Coch. Cochran's Nova Scotia Reports (NSR 4) (1859)

N.S.R. Coh. Cohen's Nova Scotia Reports

N.S. Rep. Nova Scotia Reports

N.S. Rev. Stat Nova Scotia Revised Statutes (Canada)

N.S.R.G. & O. Nova Scotia Reports, Geldert & Oxley

N.S.R.G. & R. Nova Scotia Reports, Geldert & Russell

N.S.R.J. Nova Scotia Reports (James)

N.S.R. (James) Nova Scotia Reports (James) (Canada)

N.S.R. Old. Oldright's Nova Scotia Reports

N.S.R.(Old.) Nova Scotia Reports, Old rights (Canada)

N.S.R.R. & C. Russell & Chesley's Nova Scotia Reports (1875-79) (NSR 10-12)

N.S.R.R. & G. Russell & Geldert's Nova Scotia Reports

N.S.R. Thom. Thomson's Nova Scotia Reports

N.S.R. Wall. Wallace's Nova Scotia Reports (1884-1907) (NSR 6)

NSSR New School of Social Research

N.S. Stat. Nova Scotia Statutes (Can.)

N.S.V.P. National Student Volunteer Program

N.S.W.
- New South Wales
- New South Wales Reports, Old and New Series (Aus.)

N.S.W. Adm. New South Wales Reports Admiralty

N.S. Wales New South Wales

N.S. Wales L. New South Wales Law

N.S. Wales L.R. Eq. New South Wales Law Reports Equity

N.S.W.A.R. New South Wales Arbitration Reports

N.S.W.B. New South Wales Reports, Bankruptcy Cases

N.S.W. Bktcy. Cas. New South Wales Reports, Bankruptcy Cases

N.S.W.C. Eq. New South Wales Reports, Equity

N.S.W.C.R.D. New South Wales Court of Review Decisions

N.S.W.C.R.L. New South Wales Law Reports (Supreme Court)

N.S.W. Eq. New South Wales Equity Reports

N.S.W. Eq. Rep. New South Wales Law Reports Equity

N.S.W. Inc. Acts New South Wales Incorporated Acts 1944-date

N.S.W. Ind. Arbtn. New South Wales Industrial Arbitration Cases

N.S.W. Ind. Arbtn. Cas. New South Wales Industrial Arbitration Cases

N.S.W. Indus. Arb. R. New South Wales Industrial Arbitration Reports (1902-date)

N.S.W. Land App. New South Wales Land Appeal Court Cases (1890-1921)

N.S.W. Land App. Cts. New South Wales Land Appeal Courts

N.S.W. Local Gov't R. New South Wales Local Government Reports (1913-1932)

N.S.W.L.R. New South Wales Law Reports (1880-1900) (Aus.)

N.S.W.L.V.R. New South Wales Land Valuation Reports

N.S.W. Pub. Acts Public Acts of New South Wales (1824-1957)

N.S.W. Pub. Stat. New South Wales: Public Statutes (1824-1874)

N.S.W.R. New South Wales Reports (Aus.)

N.S.W. Regs., B. & Ords. New South Wales Regulations, By-Laws and Ordinances (Aus.)

N.S.W.S.C.R. New South Wales Supreme Court Reports

N.S.W.S.C.R. (Eq.) Supreme Court Reports Equity (1862-79) (New South Wales)

N.S.W.S.C.R. (L.) Supreme Court Reports, Law (1862-79) (New South Wales)

N.S.W.S.C.R.N.S. New South Wales Supreme Court Reports, New Series

N.S.W.S. Ct. Cas. New South Wales Supreme Court Cases

N.S.W.S. Ct. R. New South Wales Supreme Court Reports (Aust.)

N.S.W.S.R. New South Wales State Reports

N.S.W. Stat. Statutes of New South Wales

N.S.W. St. R. New South Wales State Reports

N.S.W.W.C.R. New South Wales Workmen's Compensation Reports

N.S.W.W.N. New South Wales Weekly, Notes (Aus.)

N.S.W. Worker's Comp. R. New South Wales Worker's Compensation Reports

N.T.A. Proceedings National Tax Association Proceedings

N.Terr. Austl. Ord. Northern Territorial Ordinances (1917-date)

NTIS National Technical Information Service

N.T.L.R.C. Northern Territory Law Review Committee (Aus,)

N. Trans. S. Dec. National Transportation Safety Board Decisions

N.T. Rep. New Term Reports, Queen's Bench (Eng.)

N.T. Repts. New Term Reports, Queen's Bench

Nts. Notes

N.T.S.B.
- National Transportation Safety Board Decisions
- National Transportation Safety Board

N.U. Nebraska Unofficial Reports

Nuclear L. Bull. Nuclear Law Bulletin

Nuclear Reg. Rep. (CCH) Nuclear Regulation Reporter (Commerce Clearing House)

Nuis Nuisances

N.U.L.R. Northwestern University Law Review

N/V No value

Nv. Nevada

N.W.
- North West
- North-Western Provinces, High Court Reports (India)
- North Western Reporter (National Reporter System)

N.W.2d. North Western Reporter, Second Series

Nw. Northwestern

NWC National War College

Nw. J. Intl. L. & Bus. Northwestern Journal of International Law & Business

N.W.L. Northwestern University Law Review

Nw.L. Northwestern University Law Review

N.W. Law Rev. Northwestern Law Review

N.W.L.B. National War Labor Board

N. WLR North Western Law Review

N.W.L. Rev. North Western Law Review (Chicago)

Nw. L.S. Northwestern University Law Review, Supplement (111.)

N.W.P. North-Western Provinces High Court Reports (India)

N.W.P.C. Northwest Provinces (India) Code

N.W.P.H.C. Northwest Provinces, High Court Reports (India)

N.W.R. Northwestern Reporter

N.W. Rep. Northwestern Reporter

N.W. Repr. North Western Reporter

N.W. Rev. Ord. Northwest Territories Revised Ordinances (Canada)

N.W.T.
- North-West Territories, Canada
- Northwest Territories Reports (1885-1907) (Can.)

N.W. Terr. Northwest Territories, Supreme Court Reports

N.W. Terr. (Can.) Northwest Territories Reports (1885-1907) (Canada)

N.W.T.L.R. North West Territories Law Reports

N.W.T. Ord. Northwest Territories Ordinances (Can.)

N.W.T.R. North West Territories Reports, Canada (1885-1907)

N.W.T. Rep. Northwest Territories Reports (Can.)

N.W.T. Rev. Ord. Northwest Territories Revised Ordinances

NWU Northwestern University School of Law

N.W.U.L. Rev. Northwestern University Law Review

Nw. U.L. Rev. Northwestern University Law Review

N.Y.
- New York
- New York Reports
- New York Court of Appeals Reports

N.Y.2d New York Court of Appeals Reports, Second Series

Ny. Nyasaland

NYA National Youth Administration

N.Y. Admin. Code Official Compilation of Codes, Rules and Regulations of the State of New York

N.Y. Ann. Ca. New York Annotated Cases

N.Y. Ann. Cas. New York Annotated Cases

N.Y. Anno. Cas. New York Annotated Cases

N.Y. Anno. Dig. New York Annotated Digest

N.Y. Annot. Dig. New York Annotated Digest

N.Y. App. Dec. New York Court of Appeals Decisions

N.Y. App. Div. New York Supreme Court Appellate Division Reports

N.Y. Bank. Law New York Banking Law NYC Neighborhood Youth Corps

NYC New York City

N.Y.C.A. New York Court of Appeals Reports (N.Y.)

N.Y. Cas. Err. Caines' New York Cases in Error

N.Y. Cas. in Error Caines' Cases (N.Y.)

N.Y.C.B.A. New York City Bar Association Bulletin

N.Y.C.B.A. Bull. Bulletin of the Association of the Bar of the City of New York

N.Y.C.C.D. New York Current Court Decisions (N.Y.)

N.Y.C.C.H. New York Advance Digest Service (Commerce Clearing House)

N.Y. Ch. The Chancery Sentinel (N.Y.)

N.Y. Ch. Sent. New York Chancery Sentinel

N.Y. City Ct. New York City Court

N.Y. City Ct. Rep. New York City Court Reports

N.Y. City Ct. Supp. New York City Court Reports Supplement

N.Y. City H. Rec. New York City Hall Recorder

N.Y. Civ. Prac. Law & R. New York Civil Practice Law and Rules

N.Y. Civ. Pro. New York Civil Procedure

N.Y. Civ. Proc. New York Civil Procedure

N.Y. Civ. Proc. (N.S.) New York Civil Procedure, New Series

N.Y. Civ. Proc. R. New York Civil Procedure Reports

N.Y. Civ. Proc. Rep. Civil Procedure Reports (N.Y.)

N.Y. Civ. Proc. R., N.S. New York Civil Procedure Reports, New Series

N.Y. Civ. Pr. Rep. New York Civil Procedure Reports

N.Y. Cn. New York University Annual Conference on Labor

N.Y. Code R. New York Code Reporter

N.Y. Code Rep. New York Code Reporter

N.Y. Code Rep. N.S. New York Code Reports, New Series

N.Y. Code Report. New York Code Reporter

N.Y. Code Report. N.S. New York Code Reporter, New Series (1850-52)

N.Y. Code Reports, N.S. New York Code Reports, New Series

N.Y. Code Reptr. New York Code Reporter

N.Y. Code Reptr. N.S. New York Code Reporter, New Series

N.Y. Code R. N.S. New York Code Reports, New Series

N.Y. Cond. New York Condensed Reports (1881-82)

N.Y. Cont. L. Ed. New York Continuing Legal Education

N.Y. Cont. Legal Ed. New York Continuing Legal Education

N.Y. Const. New York Constitution

N.Y. Co. Rem. New York Code Remedial Justice

N.Y. County B. Bull. New York County Lawyers Association Bar Bulletin

N.Y. County Law. Assn. B. Bull. New York County Lawyers Association Bar Bulletin

N.Y. County Law Ass'n. B. Bull. New York County Lawyers Association Bar Bulletin

N.Y.C.P. Civil Procedure Reports (N.Y.)

N.Y. Cr. New York Criminal Reports (1878-1924)

N.Y. Crim. New York Criminal Reports (1878-1924)

N.Y. Crim. R. New York Criminal Reports (N.Y.)

N.Y. Crim. Rep. New York Criminal Reports (N.Y.)

N.Y.C.R.R. New York Codes, Rules and Regulations

N.Y. Cr. R. New York Criminal Reports

N.Y. Cr. Rep. New York Criminal Reports

N.Y. Ct. App. New York Court of Appeals

N.Y. Daily L. Gaz. New York Daily Law Gazette

N.Y. Daily L. Reg. New York Daily Law Register

N.Y. Daily Reg. New York Daily Register

N.Y. Daily Tr. New York Daily Transcript, Old and New Series

N.Y. Dept. R. New York Department Reports

N.Y. Dep't R. New York Department Reports

N.Y.D.L.W.C. Dec. New York State Department of Labor. Court Decisions of Workmen's Compensation

N.Y.D.R. New York Department Reports

Nye Nye's Reports (18-21 Utah)

N.Y. El. Cas. New York Election Cases

N.Y. Elec. Cas. New York Election Cases

N.Y. Elect. Cas. New York Election Cases

N.Y.E.T.R. New York Estate Tax Reports (P-H)

N.Y.F. New York Law Forum

N.Y.I.L. Netherlands Yearbook of International Law

N.Y. Int'l L. Rev. New York International Law Review

N.Y. Jud. Rep. New York Judicial Repository

N.Y. Jud. Repos. New York Judicial Repository

N.Y. Jur.
- New York Jurisprudence
- New York Jurist

N.Y.J. Intl & Comp. L. New York Law School Journal of International and Comparative Law

N.Y.L. New York University Law Review

N.Y. Law Bul. New York Monthly Law Bulletin (N.Y.)

N.Y. Law (Consol.) New York Consolidated Law Services

N.Y. Law Gaz. New York Law Gazette

N.Y. Law New York Law Journal

N.Y. Law (McKinney) McKinney's Consolidated Laws of New York

N.Y. Law Forum New York Law Forum

N.Y. Law Rev. New York Law Review

N.Y. Laws Laws of New York

N.Y.L.C. Ann. New York Leading Cases Annotated

N.Y.L. Cas. New York Leading Cases

N.Y. Legal Observer New York Legal Observer (N.Y.)

N.Y. Leg. N. New York Legal News 1880-82

N.Y. Leg. Obs. New York Legal Observer (Owen's).

N.Y. Leg. Reg. New York Legal Register

N.Y.L.F. New York Law Forum

N.Y.L. Gaz. New York Law Gazette, N.Y.

N.Y.L.J. New York Law Journal

N.Y.L.O. New York Legal Observer (N.Y.)

Ny. L.R. Nyasaland Law Reports (S. Africa)

N.Y.L.R.B. New York State Labor Relations Board and Decisions

N.Y.L.R.B. Dec. New York State Labor Relations Board Decisions and orders

N.Y.L. Rec. New York Law Record

N.Y.L. Rev. New York Law Review

N.Y.L. Sch. Int'l. L. Soc'y. J. New York Law School International Law Society Journal

N.Y.L. Sch. J. Hum. Rts. New York Law School Journal of Human Rights

N.Y.L. Sch. J. Intl. & Comp. L. New York Law School Journal of International and Comparative Law

N.Y.L. Sch. J. Int'l. & Comp. L. New York Law School Journal of International and Comparative Law

N.Y.L. Sch. L. Rev. New York Law School Law Review

N.Y.L. School Rev. New York Law School Law Review

N.Y.L.S. Rev. New York Law School Review

N.Y. St. Ba. A. New York State Bar Association Bulletin

N.Y. St. B.A. Antitrust L. Symp. New York State Bar Association Antitrust Law Symposium

N.Y.L.S. Stud. L. Rev. New York Law School Student Law Review

N.Y. Misc. New York Miscellaenous Reports

N.Y. Misc.2d. New York Miscellaneous Reports, Second Series

N.Y. Mo. Law Bul. New York Monthly Law Bulletin (New York City)

N.Y. Mo. L. Bul. New York Monthly Law Bulletin

N.Y. Mo. L.R. New York Monthly Law Reports

N.Y. Mo. L. Rec. New York Monthly Law Record

N.Y. Month. L. Bull. New York Monthly Law Bulletin

N.Y. Month. L. But. New York Monthly Law Bulletin

N.Y. Month. L.R. New York Monthly Law Reports

N.Y. Month. L. Rep. New York Monthly Law Reports

N.Y. Monthly Law Bul. New York Monthly Law Bulletin (N.Y.)

N.Y. Monthly Law Record New York Monthly Law Record (N.Y.)

N.Y. Mun. Gaz. New York Municipal Gazette

N.Y. Off. Dept. R. New York Official Department Reports

N.Y. Op. Att. Gen. Opinions of the Attorneys-General of New York

N.Y. Ops. Atty. Gen. Opinions of the Attorney-General of New York

N.Y.P.R. New York Practice Reports

N.Y. Pr. New York Practice Reports

N.Y.Pr. Rep. New York Practice Reports

N.Y.P.S.C.(1st D.) New York Public Service Commission, First District

N.Y.P.S.C.(2d D.). New York Public Service Commission, Second District

N.Y.R. New York Court of Appeals Reports (N.Y.)

N.Y.R.C. New York Railroad Commission Reports

N.Y. Rec. New York Record

N.Y. Reg. New York Daily Register (1872-89)

N.Y. Rep. New York Court of Appeals Reports

N.Y. Reps New York Court of Appeals Reports (N.Y.)

N.Y. Reptr. New York Reporter

N.Y.R.L. New York Revised Laws

N.Y.R.S. New York Revised Statutes

N.Y.S.
- New York State
- New York State Reporter
- New York Supplement

N.Y.S.2d New York Supplement Second Series

NYSBA New York State Bar Association

N.Y.S.B.A. Bull. New York State Bar Association Bulletin

N.Y.S.B.J. New York State Bar Journal

N.Y.S.C. Thompson and Cook's New York Supreme Court Reports (N.Y.)

N.Y.S. Ct. New York Superior Court Reports (N.Y.)

N.Y.S.D.R. New York State Department Reports

N.Y.S.E. New York Stock Exchange

N.Y.S.E. New York Stock Exchange Guide (CCH)

N.Y. Sea Grant L. & Pol'y J. New York Sea Grant Law and Policy Journal

N.Y.S.E. Guide (CCH) New York Stock Exchange Guide (Commerce Clearing House)

N.Y. Sen. J. New York Senate Journal

N.Y. SLRB Official reporter of New York State Labor Relations Board decisions

N.Y. Spec. Term R. Howard's Practice Reports

N.Y. Spec. Term. Rep. Howard's Practice Reports

N.Y.S.R. New York State Reporter

N.Y. St. New York State Reporter

N.Y. St. B.A. Antitrust L. Symp. New York State Bar Association Antitrust Law Symposium

N.Y. St. B.J. New York State Bar Journal

N.Y. State Bar J. New York State Bar Journal

N.Y. State R. New York State Reporter (N.Y.)

N.Y. St. Reg. New York State Register

N.Y. State Rep. New York State Reporter (N.Y.)

N.Y. St. B.J. New York State Bar Journal

N.Y. St. Dept. Rep. New York State Department Reports

N.Y. St. R. New York State Reporter (1886-96)

N.Y. St. Rep. New York State Reporter (1886-96)

N.Y. St. Repr. New York State Reporter (N.Y.)

N.Y. Sup. Ct. New York Supreme Court Reports

N.Y. Sup. Ct. Rep. Thompson and Cook's New York Supreme Court Reports (N.Y.)

N.Y. Sup. Ct. (T. & C.) Thompson and Cook's New York Supreme Court Reports (N.Y.)

N.Y. Super New York Superior Court Reports

N.Y. Super. Ct. New York Superior Court Reports

N.Y. Super. Ct. R. New York Superior Court Reports (N.Y.)

N.Y. Super. Ct. Rep. New York Superior Court Reports (N.Y.)

N.Y. Supl. New York Supplement (N.Y.)

N.Y. Supp. New York Supplement

N.Y. Supp.2d New York Supplement, Second Series

N.Y. Suppl. New York Supplement (N.Y.)

N.Y. Supplement 2d Series New York Supplement, Second Series (N.Y.)

N.Y. Supr. New York Superior Court Reports (N.Y.)

N.Y. Supr. Ct. New York Superior Court Reports (N.Y.)

N.Y. Supr. Ct. R. New York Superior Court Reports (N.Y.)

N.Y. Supr. Ct. Rep. New York Superior Court Reports

N.Y. Supr. Ct. Repts. (T. & C.) New York Supreme Court Reports by Thompson and Cook

N.Y. Suprm. Ct. New York Supreme Court Reports

N.Y. Tax Cas. New York Tax Cases, (CCH)

N.Y. Them. New York Themis (N.Y. City)

N.Y. Times New York Times

N.Y.T.R. New York Term Reports (Caines' Reports)

N.Y. Trans. New York Transcript (Nos. 1-11, 1861) (New York city)

N.Y. Trans. App. New York Transcript Appeal

N.Y. Trans. N.S. New York Transcript, New Series (New York city)

N.Y. Trans. Rep. New York Transcript Reports

N.Y.T. Rep. Caines'Reports(N.Y.) NYU New York University School of Law

N.Y.U. Conf. Charitable New York University Conference on Charitable Foundations Proceedings

N.Y.U. Conf. Lab. New York University Conference on Labor

N.Y.U. Conf. on Char. Lab. New York University Conference on Labor

N.Y.U. Conf. on Char. Found. Proc. Conference on Charitable Foundations Proceedings, New York University

N.Y.U. Inst. Fed. Tax. New York University Institute on Federal Taxation

N.Y.U. Inst. Fed. Taxation New York University Institute of Federal Taxation

N.Y.U. Inst. on Fed. Tax. New York University Institute on Federal Taxation

N.Y.U. Intra. L. Rev. New York Intramural Law Review

N.Y.U. Intramur. L. Rev. New York University Intramural Law Review

N.Y.U.J. Int. Law & Pol. New York University Journal of International Law and Politics

N.Y.U.J. Intl L. & Pol. New York University Journal of International Law and Politics

N.Y.U.J. Intl Law & Pol. New York University Journal of International Law and Politics

N.Y.U.L. Center Bull. New York University Law Center Bulletin

N.Y.U. L. Q. Rev. New York University Law Quarterly Review

N.Y.U. L. Qu. Rev. New York University Law Quarterly Review

N.Y.U. L.R. New York University Law Review

N.Y.U. L. Rev. New York University Law Review

NYU LT New York University School of Continuing Education, Continuing Education in Law and Taxation

N.Y. Unconsol. Laws New York Unconsolidated Laws (McKinney)

N.Y. Univ. J of Internat. L. and Polit. New York University Journal of International Law and Politics

N.Y. Univ. L. Rev. New York University of Law Review

N.Y.U. Rev. L. & Soc. New York University Review of Law and Social Change

N.Y.U. Rev. L. & Soc. Change New York University Review of Law & Social Change

N.Y.U. Rev. Law & Soc. New York University Review of Law and Social Change

N.Y.U. Rev. Law & Soc.C. New York University Review of Law and Social Change

N.Y.U. T.I. New York University Tax Institute

N.Y. Week. Dig. New York Weekly Digest

N.Y. Weekly Dig. New York Weekly Digest (N.Y.)

N.Y. Wkly. Dig. New York Weekly Digest

NYWT Finger, New York Wills and Trusts, Third Edition

N.Z.
- New Zealand
- New Zealand Reports

N.Z. App. Rep. New Zealand Appeal Reports

N.Z. Awards. New Zealand Awards, Recommendations, Agreements, etc.

N.Z.C.C.L.R.C. New Zealand Contracts and Commercial Law Reform Committee

N.Z.C.L.R.C. New Zealand Criminal Law Reform Committee

N.Z. Col. L.J. New Zealand Colonial Law Journal

N.Z. Ct. App. New Zealand Court of Appeals

N.Z. Ct. Arb. New Zealand Court of Arbitration

N.Z. Foreign Aff. Rev. New-Zealand Foreign Affairs Review. Wellington, New Zealand

N.Z. Gaz. L.R. New Zealand Gazette Law Reports

N.Z.G.L.R. New Zealand Gazette Law Reports

N.Z. Ind. Arb. New Zealand Industrial Arbitration Awards

N.Z.J.P. New Zealand Justice of the Peace (1876-77)

N.Z.J. Pub. Admin. New Zealand Journal of Public Administration

N.Z.J. Pubi. Adm. New Zealand Journal of Public Administration

N.Z. Jur. New Zealand Jurist (1873-78)

N.Z. Jur. S. New Zealand Jurist, New Series

N.Z. Jur. Mining Law Jurist Reports, New Series, Cases in Mining Law (1875-9) (N.Z.)

N.Z. Jur. N.S. New Zealand Jurist, New Series

N.Z. Law Soc. N. New Zealand Law Society Newsletter

N.Z.L.G.R. Local Government Reports (New Zealand)

NZLJ New Zealand Law Journal

N.Z.L.J. New Zealand Law Journal

N.Z.L.J.M.C. New Zealand Law Journal, Magistrates' Court Decisions

N.Z.L.R. New Zealand Law Reports

N.Z.L.R.C. New Zealand Law Revision Commission

N.Z.L.R.C.A. New Zealand Law Reports, Court of Appeal

N.Z.L.R.F. New Zealand Legal Research Foundation

N.Z. Ords. Ordinances of the Legislative Council of New Zealand

N.Z.P.A.L.R.C. New Zealand Public and Administrative Law Reform Committee

N.Z.P.C.C. New Zealand Privy Council Cases

N.Z.P.C. Cas. New Zealand Privy Council Cases

N.Z.P.L.E.R.C. New Zealand Property Law and Equity Reform Committee

N.Z. Recent L. Rev. New Zealand Recent Law Review

N.Z. Rep. New Zealand Reports, Court of Appeals

N.Z. Repr. Stat. Reprint of the Statutes of New Zealand

N.Z.R., Regs. & B. Rules, Regulations and By-Laws under New Zealand Statutes

N.Z.S.C. New Zealand Supreme Court

N.Z. Stat. Statutes of New Zealand

N.Z. Stat. Regs. New Zealand Statutory Regulations

N.Z.T.B.R. New Zealand Taxation Board of Review Decisions

N.Z.T.G.L.R.C. New Zealand Torts and General Law Reform Committee

N.Z.T.S. New Zealand Treaty Series

N.Z.U.L.R. New Zealand Universities Law Review

N.Z.U.L. Rev. New Zealand Universities Law Review

N.Z. Univ. L.R. New Zealand Universities Law Review.

N.Z. Univ. L. Rev. New Zealand Universities Law Review, Wellington, New Zealand

O

o
- Order
- Overruled; ruling in cited case expressly overruled (Used in Shepard's Citations)

O.
- Law Opinions
- Ohio
- Ohio Reports
- Oklahoma
- Ontario
- Ontario Reports
- Oregon
- Oregon Reports
- Otto, United States Supreme Court Reports (91-107 U.S. Reports)
- South African Law Reports, Orange Free State Provincial Division (1910-46)
- orders
- ordinance
- overruled
- Solicitor's Law Opinion (U.S. Internal Revenue Service)

O.A.
- Ohio Appellate Reports
- Oudh Appeals (India)

O.A. 2d Ohio Appellate Reports, Second Series

OAA Old-Age Assistance

O.A. & C. Ohio Circuit Court Decisions (Ohio)

OAG Opinions of the Attorneys General of the United States

O.A.G.Massachusetts Massachusetts Attorney General Reports (Mass.)

O.A.G. West Virginia West Virginia Attorney General Reports (W. Va.)
- O. & T. Oyer and Terminer
- O. & W.Dig. Oldham and White's Digest of Laws, Texas

OAP Office of Alien Property

OAPEC Organization of Arab Petroleum Exporting Countries

O. App. Ohio Appellate Reports

O. App. 2d Ohio Appellate Reports, Second Series

O.A.R.
- Ontario Appeal Reports
- Ohio Appellate Reports

OAS Organization of American States (UN)

OASDI Old Age, Survivors, and Disability Benefits

OASI Old Age and Survivors Insurance, Trust Fund

OAU Organization of African Unity

O.B.
- Official Bulletin, International Commission for Air Navigation
- Old Bailey
- Old Benloe
- Orlando Bridgman

O.B. & F. Ollivier, Bell, & Fitzgerald's Court of Appeal Reports (1878-80) (New Zealand)

O.B. & F. (C.A.) Ollivier, Bell & Fitzgerald's Reports, Court of Appeal (New Zealand)

O.B. & F.N.Z. Ollivier, Bell & Fitzgerald's New Zealand Reports

O.B. & F. (S.C.) Ollivier, Bell & Fitzgerald's Reports, Supreme Court (New Zealand)

O. Bar Ohio State Bar Assn. Reports

O.B.E. Officer of the Order of the British Empire

O.Ben. Old Benloe's Reports, English Common Pleas

O.Benl. Old Benloe's Reports, English Common Pleas (1486-1580)

O.B.J. The Journal, Oklahoma Bar Association Journal

OBRA '90 Omnibus Budget Reconciliation Act of 1990

O.Bridg. Orlando Bridgman's Common Pleas Reports (Eng.) (124 ER)

O.Bridg. (Eng.) Orlando Bridgman's Common Pleas Reports, England (124 ER)

O.Bridgm. Orlando Bridgman's Common Pleas Reports (Eng.)

O'Brien O'Brien's Upper Canada Reports

O'Bri. Lawy. O'Brien's Lawyer's Rule of Holy Life

O'Bri. M. L. O'Brien's Military Law

Obs. The Observer

O.B.S. Old Bailey's Sessions Papers

Observ. Observations

O.B.S.P. Old Bailey, Sessions Papers

Obst. Jus. Obstructing Justice

O.C.
- Official Circular (Poor Law Board, etc.)
- Old Code (Louisiana Code of 1808)

O.C.
- Ope consilio (by aid and counsel, Orphan's Court)
- Order in Council
- Orphans' Court
- Oudh Cases, India

O.C.A. Ohio Courts of Appeal Reports

O'Callaghan, New Neth. O'Callaghan's History of New Netherland

OCAS Organization of Central American States

O.C.B. Office of Collective Bargaining (New York City)

O.C.C. Ohio Circuit Reports or Decisions

Occ. Occupation

OCC Office of the Comptroller of the Currency

Occ. & Prof. Occupations and Professions

Occ. N. Occasional Notes, Canada Law Times

O.C.C.N.S. Ohio Circuit Court Reports, New Series

Occup. Occupations, trades and professions

O.C.D.
- Office of Child Development
- Ohio Circuit Court Decisions

Ocean Dev. & Int. L. Ocean Development and International Law

Ocean Dev. & Intl. L.J. Ocean Development and International Law Journal

OCF Office, Chief of Finance, Army (U.S.)

O.C.G.A. Official Code of Georgia Annotated (Michie Co.)

OCLC Online Computer Library Center; formerly, Ohio College Library Center (Bibliographic Utility Network)

OCLE Continuing Legal Education, University of Oklahoma Law Center

O.C.R.
- Department of Interior, Office of Coal Research
- Organized Crime and Racketeering Section of the Department of Justice

O. Cr. Oklahoma Criminal Reports

O. Cr. C. Oudh Criminal Cases (India)

O.C.S.
- Office of Contract Settlement Decisions (U.S.)
- Outer Continental Shelf

OCSE Office of Child Support Enforcement

OCT Overseas Countries and Territories

Oct. Octaro

Oct. Str. Octavo Strange, Select Cases on Evidence

O.D.
- Obiter Dicta
- Office Decision (U.S. Internal Revenue Bureau)
- Ohio Decisions
- Overdose of narcotics

O'D. & Br. Eq. Dig. O'Donnell & Brady, Equity Digest (Ir.)

ODAP Office of Drug Abuse Policy

ODC Office of Domestic Commerce (U.S.)

O.D.C.C. Ohio Decisions, Circuit Court (properly cited Ohio Circuit Decisions)

O'Dea Med. Exp. O'Dea's Medical Experts

O.D.E.C.A. Organization of Central American States

O.Dec. Rep. Ohio Decisions Reprint

Odeneal Odeneal's Reports (9-11 Oregon)

O.Dep. Rep. Ohio Department Reports

Odgers Odgers on Libel and Slander, 6 editions, (1881-1929)

Odg. Lib. Odger on Libel and Slander

Odg. Pl. Odgers, Principles of Pleading. 20ed. 1975

ODM Office of Defense Mobilization (U.S.)

O.D.N.P. Ohio Decisions

O'Dowd Sh. O'Dowd's Merchant Shipping Act

O'D. Pr. & Acc. O'Dedy, Principal and Accessory. 1812

O.D. Re. Ohio Decisions Reprint (Ohio)

O.D. Rep. Ohio Decisions Reprint (Ohio)

O.D. Reprint Ohio Decisions Reprint (Ohio)

OE Office of Education

OEA Overseas Education Association

O.E.C. Ontario Election Decisions

OECD
- Organization for Economic Co-operation and Development
- Organization for European Co-operation and Development

OEDP Office of Employment Development Programs

OEEC Organization of European Economic Cooperation

OEIA Office of Energy Information and Analysis

OEM Office for Emergency Management (U.S.)

OEO Office of Economic Opportunity

OEOPR Office of Economic Opportunity Procurement Regulations

OEP
- Office of Emergency Preparedness
- Office of Energy Research and Development Policy (NSF)

O.F.C. High Court Reports of Orange Free State (1879-83) (S. Afr.)

OFCC Office of Federal Contract Compliance

OFCCP Fed. Cont. Compl. Man. (CCH) OFCCP Federal Contract Compliance Manual

Of. Cl. Pac. Officium Clerici Pacis

O. F. D. Ohio Federal Decisions

OFDI Office of Foreign Direct Investments

off.
- Office
- Official

Off. Br. Officina Brevium, 1679

Off. Brev. Officina Brevium (1679)

Offend. Rehab. Offender Rehabilitation

Off. Ex. Wentworth's Office of Executors

Off. Exec. Wentworth's Office of Executors

Off. Gaz. Official Gazette, U.S. Patent Office

Off. Gaz. Pat. Off. Official Gazette, United States Patent Office (Washington, D.C.)

Off. Gaz. Pat. Office Official Gazette, US Patent Office

Officer Officer's Reports (1-9 Minnesota)

Official Gazette, U.S.P.O. U.S. Patent Office Official Gazette

Official J. Ind. Comm. Prop. Official Journal of Industrial and Commercial Property (Eire)

Official Rep. Ill. Courts Commission Official Reports:Illinois Courts Commission

Off. Jl. Pat. Official Journal of Patents (Eng.)

Off. Rep. Official Reports of the High Court of the Transvaal

Off. Thrift Supervision J. Office of Thrift Supervision Journal

OFPP Office of Federal Procurement Policy

OFR Office of the Federal Register

O.F.S. Orange Free State Reports, High Court (1879-83) (South Africa)

O.G. Official Gazette, U.S. Patent Office

O.G.B.G. Official Gazette Reports (British Guiana)

OGC Office of General Counsel

Ogd. Ogden's Reports (12-15 Louisiana)

Ogden Ogden's Reports (12-15 Louisiana)

Ogilvie, Dict. Ogilvie's Imperial Dictionary of the English Language

O.G. Pat. Off. Official Gazette, U.S. Patent Office

OGSM Office of the General Sales Manager

Ogs. Med. Jur. Ogston, Medical Jurisprudence. 1878

O.G.TM Official Gazette of the U.S. Patent and Trademark Office:Trademarks

Oh.
- Ohio
- Ohio Court of Appeals

Oh. A. Ohio Appellate Reports

Oh. A. 2d Ohio Appellate Reports, Second Series

OHA L. J. OHA Law Journal

Oh. Ap. Ohio Appellate Reports (Ohio)

O'Hara Wills O'Hara on Wills

Oh. Cir. Ct. Ohio Circuit Court Reports

Oh. Cir. Ct. N.S. Ohio Circuit Court Reports, New Series

Oh. Cir. Dec. Ohio Circuit Decisions

OHD Office of Human Development

Oh.Dec. Ohio Decisions

Oh. Dec. Rep. Ohio Decisions Reprint (Ohio)

Oh. Dec. (Reprint) Ohio Decisions (Reprint)

Oh. F. Dec. Ohio Federal Decisions

OHI Office for Handicapped Individuals

Ohio
- Ohio
- Ohio Reports
- Ohio Supreme Court Reports (1821-51)

Ohio Abs. Ohio Law Abstract

Ohio Abstract Ohio Law Abstract (Ohio)

Ohio Admin. Code Ohio Administrative Code (official compilation published by Banks-Baldwin)

Ohio App. Ohio Appellate Reports

Ohio App. 2d Ohio Appellate Reports, Second Series

Ohio Appellate Reports Ohio Appellate Reports (Ohio)

Ohio Apps. Ohio Appellate Reports (Ohio)

Ohio Bar Ohio State Bar Association Report

Ohio B.T.A. Ohio Board of Tax Appeals Reports

Ohio C.A. Ohio Courts of Appeals Reports

Ohio C.C. Ohio Circuit Court Reports

Ohio C.C.Dec. Ohio Circuit Court Decisions

Ohio C.C.N.S. Ohio Circuit Court Reports, New Series

Ohio C.C. (n.s.) Ohio Circuit Court Reports, new series

Ohio C.C.R. Ohio Circuit Court Reports

Ohio C.C.R.N.S. Ohio Circuit Court Reports, New Series

Ohio C.D. Ohio Circuit Decisions

Ohio C.Dec. Ohio Circuit Decisions

Ohio Circ. Dec. Ohio Circuit Decisions (Ohio)

Ohio Cir. Ct. Ohio Circuit Court Decisions

Ohio Cir. Ct. (N.S.) Ohio Circuit Court Reports, New Series

Ohio Cir. Ct. R. Ohio Circuit Court Reports

Ohio Cir. Ct. R. N.S. Ohio Circuit Court Reports, New Series

Ohio Circuits Ohio Circuit Court Decisions (Ohio)

Ohio Cir. Dec. Ohio Circuit Decisions

Ohio C. of R. & T. Ohio Commissioners of Railroads and Telegraphs (1867-1905)

Ohio Cond. Wilcox's Condensed Reports (Ohio)

Ohio Cond. R. Wilcox Condensed Reports (Ohio)

Ohio Const. Ohio Constitution

Ohio Ct. App. Ohio Courts of Appeals Reports

Ohio Dec. Ohio Decisions

Ohio Dec. N.P. Ohio Decisions Nisi Prius

Ohio Dec. R. Ohio Decisions Reprint (Ohio)

Ohio Dec. Re. Ohio Decisions Reprint (Ohio)

Ohio Dec. Rep. Ohio Decisions Reprint (Ohio)

Ohio Dec. Repr. Ohio Decisions Reprint

Ohio Dec. Reprint Ohio Decisions, Reprint (1840-93)

Ohio Dep't. Ohio Department Reports

Ohio F. D. Ohio Federal Decisions (Ohio)

Ohio F. Dec. Ohio Federal Decisions

Ohio Fed. Dec. Ohio Federal Decisions

Ohio Gov't. Ohio Government Reports

Ohio Jur. Ohio Jurisprudence

Ohio Jur. 2d Ohio Jurisprudence, Second Series

Ohio L. Abs. Ohio Law Abstract

Ohio Law Abs. Ohio Law Abstracts

Ohio Law Abst. Ohio Law Abstract

Ohio Law Abstract Ohio Law Abstract (Ohio)

Ohio Law Bull. Weekly Law Bulletin (Ohio)

Ohio Law J. Ohio Law Journal

Ohio Law R. Ohio Law Reporter

Ohio Law Rep. Ohio Law Reporter

Ohio Law Repr. Ohio Law Reporter (Ohio)

Ohio Laws State of Ohio: Legislative Acts Passed and Joint Resolutions Adopted

Ohio L. B. Weekly Law Bulletin (Ohio)

Ohio L. Bull. Ohio Law Bulletin

Ohio Legal N. Ohio Legal News

Ohio Legis. Bull. Ohio Legislative Bulletin (Anderson)

Ohio Legis. Serv. Ohio Legislative Service

Ohio Leg. N. Ohio Legal News

Ohio Leg. News Ohio Legal News

Ohio L.J. Ohio Law Journal

Ohio Low. Dec. Ohio Lower Court Decisions

Ohio Lower Dec. Ohio Lower Court Decisions

Ohio L.R. Ohio Law Reporter

Ohio L. R. & Wk. Bul. Ohio Law Reporter & Weekly Bulletin

Ohio L. Rep. Ohio Law Reporter

Ohio Misc. Ohio Miscellaneous Reports

Ohio Misc. 2d Ohio Miscellaneous Reports, Second Series

Ohio Misc. 3d Ohio Miscellaneous Reports, Third Series

Ohio Misc. Dec. Ohio Miscellaneous Decisions

Ohio Monthly Rec. Ohio Monthly Record

Ohio (New Series) Ohio State Reports (Ohio)

Ohio Nisi Prius Ohio Nisi Prius Reports (Ohio)

Ohio Nisi Prius (N.S.) Ohio Nisi Prius Reports, New Series (Ohio)

Ohio Northern U. L. Rev. Ohio Northern University Law Review

Ohio North. L. Rev. Ohio Northern University Law Review

Ohio North Univ. L. Rev. Ohio Northern University Law Review

Ohio N.P. Ohio Nisi Prius Reports

Ohio N.P.N.S. Ohio Nisi Prius Reports New Series

Ohio N.S. Ohio State Reports (Ohio)

Ohio N.U.L.Rev. Ohio Northern University Law Review

Ohio O.
- Ohio Opinions
- Ohio Opinions Annotated (Ohio)

Ohio O.2d Ohio Opinions, Second Series

Ohio Op. Ohio Opinions

Ohio Op.2d Ohio Opinions, Second Series

Ohio Op.3d Ohio Opinions, Third Series

Ohio Ops. Ohio Opinions

Ohio Opinions Ohio Opinions Annotated (Ohio)

Ohio Prob. Ohio Probate Reports by Goebel

Ohio Prob.Ct. Goebel's Probate Reports (Ohio)

Ohio P.S.C. Ohio Public Service comm.

Ohio P.U.C. Ohio Public Utilities comm.

Ohio R. Ohio Reports (Ohio)

Ohio R.C. Ohio Railroad Commission

Ohio R.Cond. Ohio Reports Condensed

Ohio Rep. Ohio Reports (Ohio)

Ohio Rev. Code Ann. Ohio Revised Code Annotated

Ohio Rev. Code Ann. (Anderson) Ohio Revised Code Annotated (Anderson)

Ohio Rev. Code Ann. (Baldwin) Ohio Revised Code Annotated (Baldwin)

Ohio Rev. Code Ann. (Page) Ohio Revised Code Annotated (Page)

Ohio S. Ohio State Reports (Ohio)

Ohio S. & C. P. Ohio Superior & Common Pleas Decisions

Ohio S. & C. P. Dec. Ohio Superior and Common Pleas Decisions

Ohio S.B.A. Ohio State Bar Association

Ohio S.B.A. Bull. Ohio State Bar Association Bulletin

Ohio S.L.J. Ohio State Law Journal

Ohio S.R. Ohio State Reports (Ohio)

Ohio S. Rep. Ohio State Reports (Ohio)

Ohio St. Ohio State Reports

Ohio St. 2d. Ohio State Reports 2nd Series

Ohio St. 3d Ohio State Reports, Third Series

Ohio State Ohio State Reports (Ohio)

Ohio St. J. on Disp. Resol. Ohio State Journal on Dispute Resolution

Ohio State L.J. Ohio State Law Journal

Ohio State R. (N.S.) Ohio State Reports (Ohio)

Ohio State Rep. Ohio State Reports (Ohio)

Ohio St. B. A. Rep. Ohio State Bar Association Report

Ohio St. L.J. Ohio State Law Journal

Ohio St. (N.S.) Ohio State Reports, Annotated, New Series

Ohio St. R. Ohio State Reports (Ohio)

Ohio St. Rep. Ohio State Reports (Ohio)

Ohio St. Report Ohio State Reports (Ohio)

Ohio St. R.(N.S.) Ohio State Reports (Ohio)

Ohio S. U. Ohio Supreme Court Decisions (Unreported Cases)

Ohio Sup. & C. P. Dec. Ohio Superior Common Pleas Decisions

Ohio Supp. Ohio Supplement

Ohio Unrep. Ohio Supreme Court Unreported Cases, 1 vol.

Ohio Unrep. Jud. Dec. Pollack's Ohio Unreported Judicial Decisions Prior to 1823

Ohio Unrept. Cas. Ohio Supreme Court Decisions (Unreported Cases)

Oh. Jur. Ohio Jurisprudence

Oh. L. Bul. Ohio Law Bulletin

Oh. L. Bull. Ohio Law Bulletin

Oh. L.Ct. D. Ohio Lower Court Decisions

Oh. Leg. N. Ohio Legal News

Ohlinger, Fed. Practice Ohlinger's Federal Practice

O.H.L.J. Osgoode Hall Law Journal (Can.)

Oh. L.J. Ohio Law Journal

Oh. L. Rep. Ohio Law Reporter

Oh. Misc. Ohio Miscellaneous Reports

OHMO Office of Hazardous Materials Operations

Oh. N.P. Ohio Nisi Prius

Oh. N.P. (N.S.) Ohio Nisi Prius Reports New Series

Oh. N. U. Intra. L. R. Ohio Northern University Intramural Law Review

Oh. N. U. L. R. Ohio Northern University Law Review

OHPA Ohio Public Defenders Association

Oh. Prob. Ohio Probate

Oh.S. & C.P. Ohio Superior & Common Pleas Decisions

Oh. S.C. D. Ohio Supreme Court Decisions (Unreported Cases)

Oh. S. L.J. Ohio State Law Journal

Oh. St. Ohio State Reports

OIC Order-in-Council

Oil & Gas Oil and Gas Reporter

Oil & Gas Compact Bull. Oil and Gas Compact Bulletin

Oil & Gas Inst. Oil and Gas Institute

Oil & Gas J. Oil and Gas Journal

Oil & Gas L. & Tax. Inst. (S.W.Legal Fdn.) Oil & Gas Law & Taxation Institute (Southwestern Legal Foundation)

Oil & Gas. L.R. Oil and Gas Law Review

Oil & Gas.-Nat.Resources (P-H) Oil and Gas Natural Resources (Prentice-Hall)

Oil and Gas Reporter Oil and Gas Reporter

Oil & Gas Reptr. Oil and Gas Reporter

Oil & Gas Rptr. Oil and Gas Reporter

Oil & Gas Tax Q. Oil and Gas Tax Quarterly

O. in C. Order in council

OIT Office of International Trade (U.S.)

O.J. Official Journal of the European Communities

O.J. Act Ontario Judicature Act

O.J. Eur. Comm. Official Journal of the European Communities

O.J. Spec. Ed. Official Journal of the European Communities

O.J.T. On-the-Job Training

O. Jur. Ohio-Jurisprudence

Ok. Oklahoma

O'Keefe Ord. O'Keefe's Order in Chan-cery (Ireland)

Oke Fish.L.   Oke, Fisher Laws. 4ed. 1924.

Oke Game L.   Oke, Game Laws. 5ed. 1912.

Oke Mag. Form.   Oke, Magisterial Formulist. 19ed. 1978

Oke Mag. Syn.   Oke, Magisterial Synopsis. 14ed. 1893

Oke Turn.   Oke, Turnpike Laws. 2ed. 1861

Okl.
- Oklahoma
- Oklahoma Reports (Okla.)

Okla.
- Oklahoma
- Oklahoma Criminal Reports
- Oklahoma Reports
- Oklahoma Supreme Court Reports

Okla. Ap. Ct. Rep.   Oklahoma Appellate Court Reporter

Okla. B. A. J.   The Journal, Oklahoma Bar Assn.

Okla. B. Ass'n. J.   Oklahoma Bar Association Journal

Okla. B. Assn. J.   Oklahoma Bar Association Journal

Okla. B.J.   Oklahoma Bar Journal

Okla.C.C.   Oklahoma Corporation Commission

Okla. City U. L. Rev.   Oklahoma City University Law Review

Okla. Const.   Oklahoma Constitution

Okla. Cr.   Oklahoma Criminal Reports

Okla. Crim.   Oklahoma Criminal Reports

Okla. C. U. L. R.   Oklahoma City University Law Review

Okla. Gaz.   Oklahoma Gazette

Oklahoma   Oklahoma Reports (Okla.)

Oklahoma L. Rev.   Oklahoma Law Review

Oklahoma Reports   Oklahoma Reports (Okla.)

Okla. I. C. R.   Oklahoma Industrial Commission Reports

Okla. Lawy.   Oklahoma Lawyer

Okla. L.J.   Oklahoma Law Journal

Okla. L. Rev.   Oklahoma Law Review

Okl. App.   Oklahoma Court of Appeals

Okla. S. B. A.   The Journal, Oklahoma Bar Association

Okla. S. B. J.   Oklahoma State Bar Journal

Okla. Sess. Laws   Oklahoma Session Laws

Okla. Sess. Law Serv.   Oklahoma Session Law Service (West)

Okla. Stat.   Oklahoma Statutes

Okla. Stat. Ann. (West)   Oklahoma Statutes Annotated

Okl. Car.   Oklahoma Criminal Reports (Okla.)

Okl. City U. L. Rev.   Oklahoma City University Law Review

Okl. Cr.   Oklahoma Criminal Reports

Okl. Cr. R.   Oklahoma Criminal Reports (Okla.)

Okl. Jud.   Oklahoma Court on the Judiciary

Okl. L.J. Oklahoma Law Journal

Ok. L. R. Oklahoma Law Review

Okl. St. Ann. Oklahoma Statutes Annotated

O. L. Ohio Laws

O. L. A. Ohio Law Abstract

O. L. Abs. Ohio Law Abstract

O. L. B. Ohio Law Bulletin

Olc. Olcott's District Reports (Admiralty) (U.S.)

Olc. Adm. Olcott's District Reports (Admiralty) (U.S.)

Olc. Adm. Olcott Olcott's Admiralty Reports (U.S.)

OLCI Ohio Legal Center Institute

Ol. Conv. Oliver's Conveyancing

Olcott Olcott's Admiralty Reports (U.S.)

Olcott Adm. (F.) Olcott, U.S. District Court (Admiralty)

Olcott's Adm. Olcott's Admiralty Reports (U.S.)

O.L.D. Ohio Lower Court Decisions

Old. Oldright's Reports (5, 6 Nova Scotia)

Oldb. Oldbright's Reports, Nova Scotia

Old Bailey Chr. Old Bailey Chronicle

Old Ben. Benloe in Benloe & Dalison's Common Pleas Reports (Eng.)

Old Benloe Benloe in Benloe and Dalison's Common Pleas Reports, 1486-1580

Old Ent. Rastell, Old Entries

Old Nat. Brev. Old Natura Brevium

Oldn. Pr. Oldnall's Sessions Practice

Oldr. Oldright's Reports, Nova Scotia

Oldr. N.S. Oldright's Nova Scotia Reports (5, 6 N.S.) (1860-67)

Old S.C. Old Select Cases (Oudh) (India)

Oleck, Corporations Oleck's Modern Corporation Law

O. Legal News Ohio Legal News

Ol. Horse Oliphant, Law of Horses. 6ed. 1908

Oliph. Hor. Oliphant on the Law of Horses

Oliv. B. & L. Oliver, Beavan & Lefroy (Eng. Ry. & Canal Cases)

Oliv. Conv. Oliver's Conveyancing

Oliv. Prec. Oliver's Precedents

O.L.J.
- Ohio Law Journal
- Oudh Law Journal (India)

O. L. Jour.
- Ohio Law Journal
- Oudh Law Journal (India)

Oll. B. & F. Olliver, Bell & Fitzgerald's Reports (New Zealand)

Olliv. B. & F. Olliver, Bell & Fitzgerald (New Zealand)

Olms. Decisions of the Judicial Committee of the Privy Council re the British North American Act, 1867, and the Canadian Constitution (Canada)

Olmsted Olmsted's Privy Council Decisions (1867-1954)

O.L.N. Ohio Legal News

O. Lower D. Ohio (Lower) Decisions

Ol.Prec. Oliver's Precedents

O.L.R.
- Ohio Law Reporter
- Ontario Law Reporter
- Ontario Law Reports
- Oregon Law Review
- Oudh Law Reports (India)

O.L.R.B. Ontario Labour Relations Board Monthly Report

O. L. Rep. Ohio Law Reporter

Olwine's L.J. (Pa.) Olwine's Law Journal

OM Ohio Miscellaneous

O'Mal. & H. O'Malley and Hardcastel's Election Cases (Eng.)

O'M. & H. O'Malley & Hardcastle's Election Cases (Eng.)

O'M. & H. El. Cas. O'Malley & Hardcastle, Election Cases (Eng.)

OMB Office of Management and Budget

OMBE Office of Minority Business Enterprise

O.M.B.R. Ontario Municipal Board Reports, 1973-

OMGUS Office of Military Gov't., U.S. Zone, Germany

OMI Organization Management, Inc.

O. Misc. Ohio Miscellaneous Reports

Om. Mer. Sh. Omond, Merchant Shipping Acts. 1877

Om. Sea Omond, Law of the Sea. 1916

ONAP Office of Native American Programs

O.N.B. Old Natura Brevium

O'Neal Neg. L. O'Neal's Negro Law of South Carolina

O.N.P. Ohio Nisi Prius Reports (1894-1901)

O.N.P.N.S. Ohio Nisi Prius Reports New Series (1903-13)

O.N.R. Office of Naval Research

Onsl.N.P. Onslow's Nisi Prius

Ont.
- Ontario
- Ontario: Court with Jurisdiction in Ontario
- Ontario Reports (1882-1900) (Canada)

Ont. 2d. Ontario Reports, 2d Series (Can.)

Ont. A. Ontario Appeals

Ont. App. Ontario Appeal Reports

Ontario Cons. Reg. Ontario Consolidated Regulations (Can.)

Ontario L.R.C. Ontario Law Reform Commission

Ont. Dig. Digest of Ontario Case Law

Ont. El. Cas. Ontario Election Cases (1884-1900)

Ont. Elec. Ontario Election Cases (1884-1900)

Ont. Elec. C. Ontario Election Cases

Ont. Elect. Ontario Election Cases (1884-1900)

Ont. L. Ontario Law Reports

Ont. L.J. Ontario Law Journal

Ont. L.J. (N.S.) Ontario Law Journal, New Series

Ont. L. R. Ontario Reports (Can.)

Ont. L.R.C. Ontario Law Reform Commission

Ont. L. Rep. Ontario Law Reports

Ont. P. R. Ontario Practice Reports

Ont. Pr. Ontario Practice

Ont. Pr. Rep. Ontario Practice Reports

Ont. R. Ontario Reports

Ont. R. & W.N. Ontario Reports and Ontario Weekly Notes (Can.)

Ont. Reg. Ontario Regulations (Can.)

Ont. Regs. Ontario Regulations

Ont. Rev. Regs. Ontario Revised Regulations

Ont. Rev. Stat. Ontario Revised Statutes (Can.)

Ont. Ry. & Mun. Bd. Ontario Railway and Municipal Board (Ontario, Can.)

Ont.Stat. Ontario Statutes (Can.)

Ont. Tax Rep. (CCH) Ontario Tax Reporter

Ont. Week N. Ontario Weekly Notes

Ont. Week R. Ontario Weekly Reporter

Ont. Wkly. N. Ontario Weekly Notes (1909-32, 1933)

Ont. Wkly. Rep. Ontario Weekly Reporter

Ont. W.N. Ontario Weekly Notes (Can.)

Ont. W.R. Ontario Weekly Reporter

Ont.W.R.Op. Ontario Weekly Reporter Opinions of Attorneys General (U.S.)

O.N.U. Intra. L. R. Ohio Northern University Intramural Law Review

O.N.U.L.R. Ohio Northern University Law Review

O.O. Ohio Opinions

O.O. 2d Ohio Opinions, Second Series

OOG Office of Oil and Gas

Op. Opinion

OPA Office of Price Administration (U.S.)

Op. A. G. Opinion of the Attorney General

Op. Att. Gen. Opinions of the United States Attorneys-General

Op. Att'y. Gen. Opinions of the Attorney General

Op. Attys. Cen. Opinions of the United States Attorneys General

Op. Cal. Att'y Gen. Opinions of the Attorney General of California

Op. CCCG Opinion, Chief Counsel, U.S. Coast Guard

O.P.D. South African Law Reports, Orange Free State Provincial Division

OPEC Organization of Petroleum Exporting Countries

Op. Ga. Att'y Gen. Opinions of the Attorney General, State of Georgia

Op. GCT   Opinion, General Counsel, U.S. Treasury Department

OPI   Ordinance Procurement Instructions

OPIC   Overseas Private Investment Corporation

Op. Ill. Att'y Gen.   Illinois Attorney General's Opinion

Opin.   Opinions of Attorneys General (U.S.)

Op. JAGAF.   Opinion, Judge Advocate General, U.S. Air Force

Op. JAGN.   Opinion, Judge Advocate General, U.S. Navy

Op. Kan. Att'y Gen.   Opinions of the Attorney General, State of Kansas

Op. Ky. Att'y Gen.   Kentucky Opinion of Attorney General, State of Kentucky

Op. La. Att'y Gen.   Opinions of the Attorney General of the State of Louisiana

Op. Let.   Opinion letter

OPM   Office of Personnel Management

Op. Minn. Att'y Gen.   Opinions of the Attorney General, State of Minnesota

Op. N.D. Att'y Gen.   Opinions of the Attorney General, State of North Dakota

Op. Nev. Att'y Gen.   Official Opinions of the Attorney General of Nevada

Op. N.Y. Atty. Gen.   Opinions of Attorneys-General of New York

Op. Off. Legal Counsel   Opinions of the Office of Legal Counsel

Op. Ohio Att'y Gen.   Opinions of the Attorney General of Ohio

Op. Okla. Att'y Gen.   Opinions of the Attorney General of Oklahoma

Op. Or. Att'y Gen.   Opinions of the Attorney General of Oregon

Op. Pa. Att'y Gen.   Opinions of the Attorney General of Pennsylvania

Opp. Int. L.   Oppenheim, International Law. vol. 1, 8ed. 1955; vol. 2, 7ed. 1952

Opp'n   Opposition

O.P.R.   Ontario Practice Reports

OPS   Office of Price Stabilization (U.S.)

O.P.S.   Official Public Service Reports (N.Y.)

Ops
- Operations
- Opinions

Ops. A.A.G., P.O.D.   U.S. Post Office Department. Official Opinions of the Solicitor

Ops. A.G.   Opinions, Attorney General

Ops. Atty. Gen.   Opinions of Attorney General

Ops. Atty. Gen. Wisc.   Wisconsin Attorney General Reports (Wis.)

Ops. J.A.C.   Opinions, Judge Advocate General, U.S. Army

OPSO   Office of Pipeline Safety Operations

Op. Sol. Dept.   Opinions of the Solicitor, U.S. Department of Labor

Op. Sol. Dept. Labor   Opinions of the Solicitor for the Department of Labor dealing with Workmen's Compensation

Op. Solic. P.O. Dep't. Official Opinions of the Solicitor for the Post Office Department

Op. Sol. P.O.D. Opinions of the Solicitor for the Post Office Department (U.S.)

Opt.County Gov't. Optional County Government

Op. Tenn. Att'y Gen. Opinions of the Attorney General of Tennessee

Op. Tex. Att'y Gen. Opinions of the Attorney General of Texas

Op. Va. Att'y Gen. Opinions of the Attorney General and Report to the Governor of Virginia

Op. Wash. Att'y Gen. Office of the Attorney General (State of Washington) Opinions

Op. Wis. Att'y Gen. Opinions of the Attorney General of the State of Wisconsin

Op. Wyo. Att'y Gen. Opinions of the Attorney General of Wyoming

O.R.
- Official Receiver
- Official Referee
- Official Reports, South Africa
- Oklahoma Law Review
- Ontario Reports

Or.
- Oregon
- Oregon Reports
- Oregon Supreme Court Reports
- Indian Law Reports, Orissa Series

Or. A. Oregon Court of Appeals Reports

Or. Admin. R. Oregon Administrative Rules

Or. Admin. R. Bull. Oregon Administrative Rules Bulletin.

Or. Ad. Sh. Supreme Court of the State of Oregon Advance Sheets

Orange County B. J. Orange County Bar Association Journal

Or. App. Oregon Reports, Court of Appeal

Or. Bar Bull. Oregon Bar Bulletin

O.R.C. Reports of the High Court of the Orange River Colony (South Africa)

Or. Const. Oregon Constitution

ORD Office of Rural Development

Ord.
- Order
- Ordinance

Ord. Amst. Ordinance of Amsterdam

Ord. Antw. Ordinance of Antwerp

Ord. Austl. Cap. Terr. Ordinances of the Australian Capital Territory

Ord. Bilb. Ordinance of Bilboa

Ord. Ch. Orders in Chancery

Ord. Cla. Orders, Lord Clarendon's

Ord. Copen. Ordinance of Copenhagen

Ord. Ct. Orders of Court

Ord. Flor. Ordinance of Florence

Ord. Gen. Ordinance of Genoa

Ord. Hamb. Ordinance of Hamburgh

Ord. Konigs. Ordinance of Konigsberg

Ord. Leg. Ordinance of Leghorn

Ord. Med. Jur. Ordronaux's Medical Jurisprudence

Ord. Port. Ordinance of Portugal

Ord. Prus. Ordinance of Prussia

Ordr. Jud. Ins. Ordronaux on Judicial Aspects of Insanity

Ordr. Med. Jur. Ordronaux's Medical Jurisprudence

Ord. Rott. Ordinance of Rotterdam

Ords. N.Z. Ordinances of the Legislative Council of New Zealand

Ord.Swe. Ordinance of Sweden

Ord.Us. Ord on Usury

Ore Oregon Supreme Court Reports

Ore. Oregon

Ore Ap Oregon Appellate Reports

Ore. App. Oregon Court of Appeals Reports

Oreg.
- Oregon
- Oregon Reports

Oreg. L. Rev. Oregon Law Review

Oregon Oregon Reports (Ore.)

Oreg. Rev. Stat. Oregon Revised Statutes

Oreg. S.B. Bull. Oregon State Bar Bulletin

Ore. L. Rev. Oregon Law Review

O. Rep. Ohio Reports (Ohio)

Ore. Rev. Stat. Oregon Revised Statutes

Ore. St. B. Bull. Oregon State Bar Bulletin

Ore. Tax Ct. Oregon Tax Court Reports

Orf. M. L. Orfila's Medicene Legale

org. organiz[ation, ing]

Oris. All India Reporter, Orissa

Orissa All India Reporter, Orissa

Or. Laws Oregon Laws and Resolutions

Or. Laws Adv. Sh. Oregon Laws Advance Sheets

Or. Laws Spec. Sess. Oregon Laws and Resolutions

Orl. Bridg. Orlando Bridgman's English Common Pleas Reports

Orl. Bridgman Orlando Bridgman's English Common Pleas Reports

Orleans App. Orleans Court of Appeals (La.)

Orleans T.R. Orleans Term Reports (vols. 1, 2 Martin) (La.)

Or. L. R. Oregon Law Review

Or. L. Rev. Oregon Law Review

Or. L. S. J. Oregon Law School Journal. 1902-03

Orl. T. R. Orleans Term Reports (vols. 1, 2 Martin) (La.)

Ormond Ormond's Reports (19-107 Alabama)

Orphans' Ct. Orphans' Court

Or. P.S.C. Oregon Public Service Commission Reports

Or. P.U.C. Ops. Oregon Office of Public Utilities Commissioner. Opinions & Decisions

Or. R. C. Oregon Railraod Commission

Or. Rep. Oregon Reports (Ore.)

Or. Rev. Stat. Oregon Revised Statutes

ORS Office of Rent Stabilization (U.S.)

O.R.S.A.R. Official Reports, South African Republic

Or. St. B. Bull. Oregon State Bar Bulletin

Ort. Hist. Ortolan's History of the Roman Law

Ort. Inst. Ortolan's Institute de Justinian

Or. T. R. Oregon Tax Reporter

Or. T. Rep. Orleans Term Reports (1, 2 Martin, Louisiana)

Ort. Rom. Law Ortolan's History of Roman Law

O.S.
- Ohio State Reports
- Old Style; Old Series
- Upper Canada Queen's Bench Reports, Old Series

O.S. 2d Ohio State Reports, Second Series

O.S.A. Oklahoma Statutes Annotated

OSAHRC Occupational Safety and Health Review Commission

Osaka Pref. Bull. University of Osaka Prefecture Bulletin

Osaka U. L. R. Osaka University Law Review

Osaka U. L. Rev. Osaka University Law Review

Osaka Univ. L. Rev. Osaka University Law Review, Osaka, Japan

O.S. & C.P. Dec. Ohio Superior and Common Pleas Decisions

OSB Oregon State Bar

OSBA Ohio State Bar Association

OSBA Bull. Ohio State Bar Association Bulletin.

O.S.C.D. Ohio Supreme Court Decisions, Unreported Cases

Osgoode Hall L.J. Osgood Hall Law Journal

Osgoode Hall L.S.J. Osgoode Hall Law School Journal

OSHA Occupational Safety and Health Administration

O.S.H. Cas. (BNA) Occupational Safety & Health Cases

OSHA Compl. Guide (CCH) OSHA Compliance Guide

O.S.H.D. Occupational Safety and Health Decisions

O.S.H. Dec. (CCH) Occupational Safety and Health Decisions (CCH)

OSHR Occupational Safety & Health Reports (CCH)

OSHRC Occupational Safety and Health Review Commission

O.S.H. Rep. (BNA) Occupational Safety and Health Reporter (Bureau of National Affairs)

O.S.L.J. Law Journal of Student Bar Assn., Ohio State University

OSOB Old Senate Office Building

O.S.R. Ohio State Reports (Ohio)

O.S. Rep. Ohio State Reports (Ohio)

OSS Office of Strategic Services (U.S.)

O.S. Supp. Oklahoma Statutes Supplement

O. St. Ohio State Reports

O. State Ohio State Reports (Ohio)

O. St. R. Ohio State Reports (Ohio)

O. St. Rep. Ohio State Reports (Ohio)

OSu Ohio Supplement Court Reports

O.S.U. Ohio Supreme Court Decisions, Unreported Cases

O. Su. Ohio Supplement

O. Supp. Ohio Supplement

OT Office of Telecommunications

Ot. Otto's United States Supreme Court Reports (91-107 U.S.)

OTA Office of Technology Assessment

Otago L. R. Otago Law Review (N.Z.)

Otago L. Rev. Otago Law Review

Otago Pol. Gaz. Otago Police Gazette (1861-64) (N.Z.)

OTB Offtrack betting

O.T.C. Organization for Trade Cooperation of Gatt

OTP Office of Telecommunications Policy

O.T.R. Oregon Tax Reports (Ore.)

Ott. Otto's United States Supreme Court Reports (91-107 U.S.)

Ottawa L. R. Ottawa Law Review

Ottawa L. Rev. Ottawa Law Review

Otto Otto's United States Supreme Court Reports (91-107 U.S.)

Ott's. U.S. Sup. Ct. R. Otto, United States Supreme Court Reports (vols. 91-107 U.S.)

Oud.C. Oudh Code, India

Oudh.C. Oudh Code (India)

Oudh L.J. Oudh Law Journal (1914-26) (India)

Oudh L. R. Oudh Law Reports (India)

Oudh Rev. Sel. Cas. Revised Collection of Selected Cases issued by Chief Commissioner and Financial Commissioner of Oudh

Oudh Wkly. N. Oudh Weekly Notes (India)

Oudh W.N. Oudh Weekly Notes (1924-48) (India)

Ought. Oughton's Ordo Judiciorum

Oult. Ind. Oulton, Index to Irish Statutes

Oult. Laws Ir. Oulton, Laws of Ireland

Out. Outerbridge's Reports (97, 98 Pennsylvinia State)

Outerbridge Outerbridge (Pa.)

Outer House Outer House of the Court of Session (Sc.)

O.U.U.I. Decisions given by the Office of the Umpire (Unemployment Insurance) respecting Claims to Out-of-work Donation (Eng.)

O.U.U.I.B.D. Benefit Decisions of the British Umpire

O.U.U.I.D. Umpire Decisions, Benefit Claims (Eng.)

O.U.U.I.S.D. Benefit & Donation Claims, Selected Decisions of Umpire (Eng.)

Over. Overton's Reports (1-2 Tenn.)

overr.
- overruled in
- overruling

Overt. Overton's Tennessee Supreme Court Reports (1791-1816)

Overt.Pr. Overton's Iowa and Wisconsin Practice

Ow.
- New South Wales Reports, v. 1-3 (Aus.)
- Owen's King's Bench Reports (1556-1615) (Eng.)
- Owen's Common Pleas Reports (Eng.)

Owen Owen's English King's Bench Reports (1556-1615)

Owen Bankr. Owen on Bankruptcy

OWM Office of War Mobilization (U.S.)

O.W.N.
- Ontario Weekly Notes
- Oudh Weekly Notes (India)

O.W.R. Ontario Weekly Reporter

OWRT Office of Water Research and Technology

Oxf. Lawy. Oxford Lawyer (1958-61)

Oxford J. Legal Stud. Oxford Journal of Legal Studies

Oxford Law Oxford Lawyer

Oxley
- Young's Vice-Admiralty Decisions, ed. Oxley (Nova Scotia)
- Oxley's Railway Cases (1897-1903)

OYD Office of Youth Development

P

P Plaintiff(s)

P.
- part
- page
- placitum
- particlas
- Court of Probate (Eng.)
- All India Reporter, Patna
- Easter (Paschal) Term
- Indian Law Reports, Panta
- Law Reports, Probate, Divorce, & Admiralty, since 1890 (Eng.)
- Pacific Reporter
- Pennsylvania
- Persian
- Peter's (26-41 U.S. Reports)
- Pickering (18-41 Massachusetts)
- Private trust (includes testamentary, investment, life insurance, holding title, etc.)

P.2d Pacific Reporter, Second Series

PA
- Paying agent
- Pension agency
- Power of Attorney
- Private agency trust (agency accounts)
- Publishers' Association

P/ A Power of attorney

Pa.
- Paine's Circuit Court Reports (U.S.)
- Pennsylvania

- Pennsylvania State Reports
- Pennsylvania Supreme Court Reports (1845-date)

PA Professional Administrator (Official journal of the Australian Division of the Institute of Chartered Secretaries and Administrators) 1949-

P.A. Professional Association

Pa. Admin. Bull. Pennsylvania Bulletin

Pa. Admin. Code Pennsylvania Administrative Code

Pa. B.A. Pennsylvania Bar Association Reports

Pa. B.A.Q. Pennsylvania Bar Association Quarterly

Pa. Bar Asso. Q. Pennsylvania Bar Association Quarterly

Pa. B. Assn. Q. Pennsylvania Bar Association Quarterly

Pa. B. Ass'n. Q. Pennsylvania Bar Association Quarterly

Pa. B. Brief Pennsylvania Bar Brief

Pa. Bk. Cas. Pennsylvania Bank Cases

P. Abr. Pulton's Abridgment of the Statutes

P.A. Browne (Pa.) Browne's Reports (Pa.)

P.A. Browne R. Browne's Reports (Pa.)

Pa C. Pennsylvania Commonwealth Court Reports

Pac
- Pacific
- Pacific Reporter

Pac.2d Pacific Reporter 2d Series

Pa. Cas. Pennsylvania Supreme
Court Cases, Sadler

Pa. C.C. Pennsylvania County
Court Reports

Pac. Coast L.J. Pacific Coast Law
Journal

Pa. C.C.R. Pennsylvania County
Court Reports (Pa.)

Pa. C.C. Reps. Pennsylvania
County Court Reports (Pa.)

Pa. C. Dec. W.C.C. Pennsylvania
Courts, Decisions in Workmen's
Compensation Cases

Pace Envt'l L. Rev. Pace Environmental Law Review

Pace L. Rev. Pace Law Review

Pace Y.B. Int'l L. Pace Yearbook
of International Law

Pacific C.L.J. Pacific Coast Law
Journal, San Francisco

Pacific Law Mag. Pacific Law
Magazine

Pacific L.J. Pacific Law Journal

Pacific Rep. Pacific Reporter

Pacif. Rep. Pacific Reporter

Pac. Law Mag. Pacific Law Magazine

Pac. Law Reptr. Pacific Law Reporter, San Francisco

Pac. Leg. N. Pacific Legal News

Pac. L.J. Pacific Law Journal

Pa. Cmwlth. Pennsylvania Commonwealth Court Reports

Pa. Co. Pennsylvania County
Courts

Pa. Co. Ct. Pennsylvania County
Court Reports

Pa. Co. Ct. R. Pennsylvania
County Court Reports

Pa. Commw. Pennsylvania Commonwealth Court Reports

Pa. Commw. Ct. Pennsylvania
Commonwealth Court Reports

Pa. Com. Pl. Pennsylvania Common Pleas Reporter

Pa. Cons. Stat. Pennsylvania Consolidated Statutes

Pa. Cons. Stat. Ann. Pennsylvania Consolidated Statutes Annotated

Pa. Cons. Stat. Ann. (Purdon)
Pennsylvania Consolidated Statutes Annotated (Purdon)

Pa. Const. Pennsylvania Constitution

Pa. Corp. Pennsylvania Corporation Reporter

Pa. Corp. R. Pennsylvania Corporation Reporter

Pa. Corp. Rep. Pennsylvania Corporation Reporter

Pa. County Ct. Pennsylvania
County Court Reports

Pa. C.P. Pennsylvania Common
Pleas Reporter

Pa. C.Pl. Penn. Common Pleas

Pa. C.R. Pennsylvania County
Court Reports (Pa.)

Pac.R. Pacific Reporter

Pac. Rep. Pacific Reporter

Pac. Repr. Pacific Reporter

Pa. C.S.A. Pennsylvania Consolidated Statutes Annotated

P.A.D. Peters. Admiralty Decisions, United States

Pa. D. & C. Pennsylvania District & County Reports

Pa. D. & C.2d Pennsylvania District and County Reports, second series

Pa. D. & C.3d Pennsylvania District and County Reports, third series

Pa. D. & C. Rep. Pennsylvania District and County Reports (Pa.)

Pa. Dep. L. & I. Dec. Pennsylvania Department of Labor and Industry Decisions

Pa. Dep. Rep. Pennsylvania Department Reports

Pa. Dist. Pennsylvania District Reporter

Pa. Dist. & Co. Pennsylvania District and County

Pa. Dist. & Co.2d Pennsylvania District and County Reports, Second Series

Pa. Dist. & Co. R. Pennsylvania District and County Reports (Pa.)

Pa. Dist. & Co. Repts. Pennsylvania District and County Reports (Pa.)

Pa. Dist. & C. Rep. Pennsylvania District and County Reports

Pa. Dist. R. Pennsylvania District Reporter

Pa. Dist. Rep. Pennsylvania District Reports (Pa.)

Pa. D.R. Pennsylvania District Reports (Pa.)

PADUD Program of Advanced Professional Development, University of Denver College of Law

Pa. Fid. Pennsylvania Fiduciary Reporter

Pa. Fid. Reporter Pennsylvania Fiduciary Reporter

Pa. Fiduc. Pennsylvania Fiduciary Reporter

Page Page's Three Early Assize Rolls, County of Northumberland (Surtees Society Publications, v. 88)

Page Contr. Page on Contracts

Page Div. Page on Divorce

Page, Wills Page on Wills

Pag. Jud. Puz. Paget's Judicial Puzzles

PAHO Pan American Health Organization

Pai.
- Paige's New York Chancery Reports
- Paine's Circuit Court Reports (U.S.)

Pai. Ch. Paige's New York Chancery Reports

Paige. Paige's New York Chancery Reports

Paige Ch. Paige's New York Chancery Reports (1828-45)

Paige Ch. Rep. Paige's Chancery Reports (N.Y.)

Paige's Ch. Paige's Chancery Reports (N.Y.)

Paine. Paine's United States Circuit Court Reports

Paine & D. Pr. Paine & Duer's Practice

Paine C.C. Paine's United States Circuit Court Reports

Paine C.C.R. Paine's U.S. Circuit Court Reports

Paine Cir. Ct. R. Paine's U.S. Circuit Court Reports

Paine, Elect. Paine on Elections

Pak. Pakistan

Pak. Bar J. Pakistan Bar Journal

Pak. Crim. L.J. Pakistan Criminal Law Journal

Pak. L.R. Pakistan Law Reports (India)

Pak. L. Rev. Pakistan Law Review

Pak. Sup. Ct. Q. Pakistan Supreme Court Law Quarterly, Lahore, Pakistan

Pal.
- Palmer's Assizes at Cambridge (Eng.)
- Palmer's King's Bench Reports (1619-29) (Eng.)
- Palmer's Reportrs (53-60 Vermont)

Pa. L. University of Pennsylvania Law Review

PAL Passive Activity Loss

Pal. Ag. Paley, Principal and Agent. 3ed. 1833

Pa. Law. Pennsylvania Lawyer

Pa. Law J. Pennsylvania Law Journal

Pa. Law Jour. Pennsylvania Law Journal (Philadelphia)

Pa. Laws Laws of the General Assembly of the Commonwealth of Pennsylvania

Pa. Law. Ser. Pennsylvania Law Series

Pal. Conv. Paley, Summary Convictions. 10ed. 1953

Pa. Leg. Gaz. Legal Gazette Reports (Campbell) (Pa.)

Pa. Leg. Gaz. Legal Gazette (Pennsylvania) (1869-76)

Pa. Legis. Serv. Pennsylvania Legislative Service (Purdon)

Paley, Ag. Paley on Principal and Agent, or Agency

Paley, Mor. Ph. Wm. Paley's Moral Philosophy (Eng.)

Paley Princ. & Ag. Paley, Principal & Agent. 3ed. 1833

Paley, Prin. & Ag. Paley on Principal and Agent, or Agency

Pa. L.G.
- Legal Gazette (Pennsylvania) (1869-76)
- Legal Gazette Reports (Campbells) Pennsylvania

Palg. Ch. Palgrave's Proceedings in Chancery

Palgrave.
- Palgrave's Proceedings in Chancery
- Palgrave's Rise and Progress of the English Commonwealth

Palg. Rise & Prog. Palgrave, Rise and Progress of the English Commonwealth. 1832

Palg. Rise, etc. Palgrave's Rise and Progress of the English Commonwealth

Pa. L.J.
- Pennsylvania Law Journal
- Pennsylvania Law Journal Reports (1842-52)

Pa. L.J.R. Clark's Pennsylvania Law Journal Reports Palm.

Palm.
- Palmer's Assizes at Cambridge (Eng.)
- Palmer's King's Bench Reports (1619-29) (Eng.)
- Palmer's Reports (53-60 Vermont)

Palm. Comp. L. Palmer, Company Law. 22ed. 1976

Palm. Comp. Prec. Palmer, Company Precedents

Palmer
- Palmer's Assizes at Cambridge (Eng.)
- Palmer's King's Bench Reports (Eng.)
- Palmer's Reports (53-60 Vermont)

Palmer Co. Prec. Palmer's Company Precedents

Palm. Pr. Comp. Palmer, Private Companies. 41 ed. 1950

Palm. Pr. Lords Palmer, Practice in the House of Lords. 1830

Palm. Sh. Palmer, Shareholders. 34ed. 1936

Palm.Wr. Palmer, Law of Wreck. 1843

Pa LR University of Pennsylvania Law Review

Pa. L. Rec. Pennsylvania Law Record

Pa. L. Rev. University of Pennsylvania Law Review

Pa. L.S. Pennsylvania Law Series

Pa. L. Ser. Pennsylvania Law Series

Pa. Misc. Pennsylvania Miscellaneous Reports

Pamph. Pamphlet

Pamph. Laws Pamphlet Laws, Acts

Pamphl. Laws Pamphlet Laws, Acts

Pan. Panama

Pan-Am. T.S. Pan-American Treaty, Series

Pand. The Pandects

P. & A.
- Page and Adams' Code (1912)
- Points and Authorities

P. & B. Pugsley & Burbridge's Reports (New Brunswick)

P. & C. Prideaux & Cole's Reports, English Courts (New Session Cases, Vol. 4)

P.& C.R.
- Planning and Compensation Reports
- Property & Compensation Reports

P. & D.
- Perry, and Davison's Queen's Bench Reports (1834-44) (Eng.)
- Law Reports, Probate & Divorce (1865-75)
- Probate and Divorce

P & F Pike & Fischer

P.& F.
- Pike & Fischer's Administrative Law
- Pike & Fischer's Federal Rules Service
- Pike & Fischer's OPA Price Service

P. & F. Radio Reg. Pike & Fischer's Radio Regulation Reporter

P. & H. Patton (Jr.) & Heath's Reports (Va. Special Court of Appeals)

P. & I. Principal and Interest

P. & K. Perry & Knapp's English Election Cases (1833)

P. & L. Dig. Laws Pepper & Lewis' Digest of Laws, Pa.

P. & L. Laws Private and Local Laws

P. & M.
- Law Reports, Probate & Matrimonial Cases (Eng.)
- Pollock & Maitland's History of English Law

P. & M.H.E.L. Pollock & Maitland's History of English Law

P. & N.G.L.R. Papua and New Guinea Law Reports

P. & R. Pigott and Rodwell, Reports in Common Pleas (1843-45)

P. and R.D. Decisions of the Department of the Interior, Pension and Retirement Claims (U.S.)

P. & T. Pugsley & Trueman's New Brunswick Rep.

P. & W. Penrose & Watts' Reports (Pa. 1829-32)

Panel The Panel, Association of Grand Jurors of New York County Bar

Panj. C. Panjab (or Punjab) Code

Pank. Jur. Pankhurst's Jurisprudence

Pa. N.P. Brightly's Nisi Prius Reports (Pa.)

PANPUB Panel Publishers

Pa. Prac. Standard Pennsylvania Practice

Pa. P.S.C. Pennsylvania Public Service Commission Annual Report

Pa. P.S.C. Dec. Pennsylvania Public Service Comm. Decisions

Papua & N.G. Papua and New Guinea Law Reports

Papua N.G. Papua New Guinea

Papy Papy's Reports (5-8 Florida)

Par.
- Parker's English Exchequer Reports
- Parker's New York Criminal Reports
- Parsons' Reports (65-66 New Hampshire)
- Paragraph

P.A.R. Public Administration Review

Para.
- Paragraph
- Paraguay

Par. Adm. Parsons on the Law of Shipping and Admiralty

Par. Am. Law Parson's Commentaries on American Law

Par. Am. Law Comm. Parson's Commentaries on American Law

Par. & C. Parent and child

Par. & Fonb. Med. Jur. Paris & Fonblanque's Medical Jurisprudence

Par. Ant. Parochial Antiquities

Par. Bills & N. Parsons on Bills and Notes

Par. Cont. Parsons on Contracts

Par. Costs Parsons on Costs

Par. Dec. Parsons' Decisions (from 2-7 Mass.)

Pa. Rec. Pennsylvania Record

Pa. Rep. Pennsylvania Reports

Par. Eq. Cas. Parsons' Select Equity Cases, Pennsylvania (Pa. 1842-51)

Par. Eq. Cases Parsons' Select Equity Cases (Pa.)

Par. Ess. Parsons' Essays on Legal Topics

Paris Topics Paris Topics, France

Parish Ct. Parish Court

Park.
- Parker's Exchequer Reports (1743-67) (Eng.)
- Parker's New York Criminal Cases (1823-68)
- Parker's New Hampshire Reports

Park. Arb. Parker, Arbitration. 1820

Park. Ch. Parker's Chancery Practice

Park. C.R. Parker's Criminal Reports (N.Y.)

Park. Cr. Parker's Criminal Reports (N.Y.)

Park. Cr. Cas. Parker's New York Criminal Cases

Park. Crim. L. Parker's Criminal Reports (N.Y.)

Park. Crim. (N.Y.) Parker's Criminal Cases

Park. Crim. R. Parker's Criminal Reports (N.Y.)

Park. Crim. Rep. Parker's Criminal Reports (N.Y.)

Park. Cr. Rep. Parker's Criminal Reports (N.Y.)

Park. Dig. Parker's California Digest

Park, Dow. Park, Dower. 1819

Parker
- Parker, English Exchequer Reports
- Parker, The Laws of Shipping and Insurance (England)
- Parker, New York Criminal Reports, 6 vols.
- Parker, New Hampshire Reports

Parker, Cr. R. Parker's Criminal Reports, N.Y.

Parker's Crim. R. Parker's Criminal Reports (N.Y.)

Parker's Crim. Rep. (N.Y.) Parker's Criminal Reports (N.Y.)

Parker's Cr. R. Parker's Criminal Reports (N.Y.)

Park. Exch. Parker's English Exchequer Reports (1743-67)

Park. Hist. Ch. Parkes, History of Court of Chancery'. 1828

Park. Ins. Parker's Insurance, Eng. 8 editions (1787-1842)

Park. N.H. Parker's New Hampshire Reports

Park. Pr. Ch. Parker's Practice in Chancery

Park. Rev. Cas. Parker's English Exchequer Reports (Revenue Cases)

Park. R.P. Parke on Real Property

Parks & Rec. Parks & Recreation

Parks & Wild. Parks & Wildlife

Park. Sh. Parker on Shipping and Insurance

Parl. Parliament

Par. L. Parson's Law by Hughes

Par. Laws Bus. Parsons' Laws of Business

Parl. Cas. Parliamentary Cases (House of Lords Reports)

Parl. Deb. Parliamentary Debates (Cobbett, Hansard) 4th Series (1803-1908)

Parl. Hist. Eng. Parliamentary History of England (pre-1803)

Parliam. Aff. Parliamentary Affairs, England

Parl. L. Parliamentary Law

Parl. Reg. Parliamentary Register (Eng.)

Parly. Parliamentary

Par. Mar. Ins. Parsons on Marine Insurance and General Average

Par. Mar. L. Parsons on Maritime Law

Par. Merc. Law Parsons on Mercantile Law

Par. N. & B. Parsons Notes and Bills

Paroch. Ant. Kennett's Parochial Antiquities

Par. Part. Parsons, Partnership. 1889

Par. R. Parsons' Select Equity Cases (Pa.)

Par. Rights Cit. Parsons on the Rights of a Citizen of the United States

Pars. Parsons' Select Equity Cases, Pennsylvania (Pa. 1842-51)

Pars. Ans. Parsons' Answer to the Fifth Part of Coke's Reports

Pars. Bills & N. Parsons on Bills and Notes

Pars. Cont. Parsons on Contracts

Pars. Dec. Parsons' Decisions (2-7 Mass.)

Pars. Eq. Cas. Parsons' Select Equity Cases (Pa. 1842-51)

Par. Sh. & Adm. Parsons on Shipping and Admiralty

Pars. Mar. Ins. Parsons on Marine Insurance

Pars. Mar. Law Parsons on Maritime Law

Pars. Merc. Law Parsons on Mercantile Law

Parsons' Parsons' Select Equity Cases (Pa.)

Pars. Sel. Eq. Cas. (Pa.) Parsons Select Equity Cases

Pars. S. Eq. Cas. Parsons' Select Equity Cases (Pa.)

Pars. Shipp. & Adm. Parsons on Shipping and Admiralty,

Part.
- Participating
- Participation
- Partner

Partic.
- Participation
- Participating

Partidas. Moreau-Lislet and Carleton's Laws of Las Siete Partidas in force in Louisiana

Partit. Partition

Partn. Partnership

Party W. Party Walls

Par. W.C. Parish Will Case

Par. Wills Parsons, Wills. 1854

Pa. S. Pennsylvania Superior Court Reports

Pas.
- Paschal Term
- (Terminus Paschae) Easter Term

Pasc.
- Paschal or Easter Term
- Paschal's Reports (Supp. to 25; 28-31 Texas)

Pasch. Paschal or Easter Term

Paschal. Paschal's Reports, vols. 28-31 Texas and Supplement to vol.25

Paschal's Ann. Const. Paschal's United States Constitution, Annotated

Pasch. Dig. Paschal's Texas Digest of Decisions

PASO Pan-American Sanitary Organization

Pa. S.R.C. Pennsylvania State Railroad Commission

Passp. Passports

Pa. St. Pennsylvania State Reports

Past & Present Past and Present, Oxford, England

Pa. Stat. Ann. Pennsylvania Statutes Annotated

Pa. Stat. Ann. (Purdon) Pennsylvania Statutes Annotated

Pa. State Penn. State Reports

Pa. State R. Pennsylvania State Reports (Pa.)

Pa. St. R. Pennsylvania State Reports (Pa.)

Pa. St. Tr. Pennsylvania State Trials (Hogan)

Pa. Summary Summary of Pennsylvania Jurisprudence

Pa. Super. Pennsylvania Superior Court Reports

Pa. Super. Ct. Pennsylvania Superior Court Reports

Pa. Superior Ct. Pennsylvania Superior Court Reports (Pa.)

PaT Bright, Pennsylvania Taxation

P.A.T. National Patents Appeal Tribunal (Eng.)

Pat.
- Patent
- Paterson's Scotch Appeals, House of Lords
- Paton's Scotch Appeals, House of Lords
- Indian Law Reports, Patna Series
- Indian Rulings, Patna (1929-47) Patent

Pat. Abr. Paterson's Abridgment of Poor Law Cases (1857-63)

Pat. & H. Patton, Jr., & Health's Reports (Va. Special Court of Appeals)

Pat. & Mr. Paterson & Murray's Reports, New South Wales (1870-71)

Pat. & Mur. Paterson & Murray's Supreme Court Reports, New South Wales (Aus.)

Pat. & T.M. Rev. Patent and Trade Mark Review

Pat. & Tr. Mk. Rev. Patent and Trade Mark Review

Pat. App. Craigie, Stewart and Paton's House of Lords Appeals from Scotland (1726-1857)

Pat. App. Cas.
- Paterson's Scotch Appeal Cases
- Paton's Scotch Appeal Cases (Craigie, Stewart & Paton)

Pat. Cas. Reports of Patent, Design and Trade Mark Cases (Eng., Sc., Ire.)

Pat. Comp. Paterson's Compendium of English and Scotch Law

Pat. Copyright & T.M. Cas. Patent, Copyright & Trade Mark Cases (U.S.)

Pat. Dec. Decisions, Commissioner of Patents

Pat. Des. & T.M. Rev. Patent, Design and Trade Mark Review (India)

Pat. Dig. Pattison, Missouri Digest

Pater.
- Paterson's New South Wales Reports
- Paterson's Scotch Appeal Cases

Pater. Ap. Cas. Paterson's Appeal Cases (Sc.)

Pater. App. Paterson's Appeal Cases (Sc.)

Paters. Comp. Paterson's Compendium of English and Scotch Law

Paterson.
- Paterson's Compendium of English and Scotch Law
- Paterson's Law and Usages of the Stock Exchange
- Paterson on the Game Laws
- Paterson on the Liberty of the Subject
- Paterson's Scotch Appeal Cases
- Paterson's Supreme Court Reports, New South Wales (Aus.)

Paterson Sc. App. Cas. Paterson, Scotch Appeal Cases

Pat. Game L. Paterson, Game Laws. 1861

Pat. H.L. Sc. Paton's or Paterson's Scotch Appeals

Patiala Indian Law Reports, Patiala Series

Pat. Ins. Paton, Insurance. 1962

Pat. J. Patent Journal, including Trademarks and Models (S. Afr.)

Pat. L. Ann. Patent Law Annual

Pat. Licens. Paterson, Licensing Acts Annual

Pat. L.J. Patna Law Journal (India)

Pat. L.R.
- Patna Law Reports (India)
- Patent Law Review

Pat. L. Reptr. Patna Law Reporter (India)

Pat. Law Rev. Patent Law Review

Pat. L. Rev. Patent Law Review

Pat. L.T. Patna Law Times (India)

Pat. L.W. Patna Law, Weekly

Pat. Mort. Patch, Mortgages. 1821

Pat. Off. Patent Office

Pat. Off. Gaz. Official Gazette, U.S. Patent Office

Pat. Off. J. Patent Office Journal (India)

Pat. Off. Rep. Patent Office Reports

Pat. Off. Soc. J. Patent Office Society Journal (U.S.)

Paton. Craigie, Stewart, & Paton's Scotch Appeal Cases

Paton App. Cas. Paton's Appeal Cases (Sc.)

Paton Sc. App. Cas. Paton's Appeal Cases (Sc.)

Patr. Elec. CA. Patrick, Contested Elections (Ont.) 1824-1849

Patr. Elect. Cas. Patrick's Election Cases (1824-49) (Upper Canada)

Patrick El. Cas. Patrick's Election Cases (Canada)

Pat. Ser. Indian Law Reports, Patna Series

Pat. St. Tr. Paton, Stoppage in Transitu. 1859

Patt. & H. Patton, Jr., and Heath's Reports (Va.)

Patt. & Heath R. Patton, Jr., and Heath's Reports (Va.)

Patt. & H. (Va.) Patton, Jr., and Heath's Reports (Va.)

Pat. T.M. & Copy. J. Patent, Trademark & Copyright Journal

Pat. T.M. & Copyr. J. of R. & Educ. Patent, Trademark & Copyright Journal of Research and Education

Patton & H. Patton, Jr. & Heath's Reports (Virginia Special Court of Appeals)

Patton & Heath Patton, Jr., and Heath's Reports (Va.)

Patton & H. (Va.) Patton, Jr., & Heath's Reports (Virginia Special Court of Appeals)

Pat. Trademark & Copyright J.(BNA) Patents, Trademark & Copyright Journal

Pat. World Patent World

PAU Pan-American Union

Paulus. Julius Paulus, Sententiae Receptae

Pa. W.C. Bd. Dec. Pennsylvania Workmen's Compensation Board Decisions

Pa. W.C. Bd. Dec. Dig. Digest of Decisions (Workmen's Compensation Board) (Pa.)

Pa. W.C. Bd. (Dep.Rep.Sup.) Workmen's Compensation Supplement to Department Reports of Pennsylvania

Pay. & Iv. Carr. Payne & Ivamy, Carriage by Sea. 10ed. 1976

Paym. Payment

P.B. Parole Board

PBGC Pension Benefit Guaranty Corporation

PBGC Op. No. Pension Benefit Guaranty Corporation Opinion Number

PBI Pennsylvania Bar Institute

P.B.S. Public Buildings Service (U.S.)

P.C.
- All India Reporter, Privy Council (1914-50)
- British & Colonial Prize Cases (1914-22)
- Indian Rulings, Privy Council (1929-47)
- Judicial Committee of the Privy Council
- Parliamentary Cases
- Patent Cases
- Penal Code
- Pleas of the Crown
- Practice Cases
- Precedents in Chancery

- Price Control Cases
- Privy Council
- Prize Court
- Procedure Civile
- Probate Court
- Professional Corporation

P.C.A. Acts of the Privy Council (Eng.)

P.C. Act Probate Court Act

P.C. App. Law Reports, Privy Council Appeals (Eng.)

P. Cas.
- Prize Cases (1914-22 (Eng.)
- Prize Cases (Trehearn, Grant) (Eng.)

P.C.C.
- Peters United States Circuit Court Reports
- Prerogative Court of Canterbury
- Privy Council Cases
- Acts of the Privy Council, Colonial Series

P.C.I. Privy Council Decisions (India)

PCIJ
- Permanent Court of International Justice
- Permanent Court of International Justice Cases

P.C.I.J. Ann. R. Permanent Court of International Justice Annual Reports

P.C. Int. Pacific Coast International

P.C. Judg. Privy Council Judgments (India)

P.L.R. Professional Liability Reporter

P.C.L.J. Pacific Coast Law Journal

P.C.L.L.G. Ollennu, Principles of Customary Land Law in Ghana

P.Cl. R.
- Parker's Criminal Reports, New York
- Privy Council Reports

P. Coast L.J. Pacific Coast Law Journal

PCOB Permanent Central Opium Board (U.N.)

PCR Tang Thanh Trai Le, Protecting Consumer Rights

P.C.R.
- Parker, Criminal Reports, New York
- Pennsylvania Corporation Reporter
- Pennsylvania County Court Reports

P.C. Rep. English Privy Council Reports

P.C.S. Principal Clerk of Session

P.C.T. Patents Cooperation Treaty (Washington)

P. Ct. Probate Court

PD Police Department

P.D.
- Law Reports, Probate Divorce and Admiralty Division (1875-90) (Eng.)
- Parliamentary Debates
- Pension and Bounty (U.S. Department of Interior)

p.d. pro defendente (for on behalf of defendant)

P.D.A. Probate, Divorce, and Admiralty (Eng.)

PDC Price Decontrol Board (U.S.)

P. Div. Law Reports. Probate Division (Eng.)

P.D. Div'l Ct. Probate, Divorce, and Admiralty Division and Divisional Court (Eng.)

PE Weinstock, Planning an Estate

Pea. Peake's Nisi Prius Reports (1790-1812) (Eng.)

Pea.(2) Peake's Additional Cases (1795-1812) (170ER)

Pea. Add. Cas. Peake's Nisi Prius Reports (v. 2 of Peake)

Peab. L. Rev. Peabody, Law & Review

Peake Peake Cases (1790-1812)

Peake Add. Cas. Peake, Additional Cases (1795-1812)

Peake Ev. Peake on the Law of Evidence

Peake N.P. Peake's English Nisi Prius Cases (170 ER)

Peake N.P. Add. Cas. Peake, Additional Cases Nisi Prius (Eng.) (170 ER)

Peake N.P. Add. Cas. (Eng.) Peake, Additional Cases Nisi Prius (Eng.) (170 ER)

Peake N.P. Cas. Peake's Nisi Prius Cases (1790-1812) (170 ER)

Peake N.P. Cas. (Eng.) Peake's English Nisi Prius Cases (170 ER)

PEAL Publishing, Entertainment, Advertising and Allied Fields Law Quarterly

P.E.A.L.Q. Publishing, Entertainment, Advertising & Allied Fields Law Quarterly

Pea. M.S. Peachey, Marriage Settlements. 1860

Pearce C.C. Pearce's Reports in Dearsley's Crown Cases (Eng.)

Pears. Pearson's Reports (Pennsylvania 1850-80)

Pearson Pearson, Common Pleas (Pa.)

Pears. (Pa.) Pearson's Reports (Pennsylvania 1850-80)

Peck.
- Peck's Reports (24-30 Illinois)
- Peck's Reports (7 Tennessee) (1921 -24)
- Peckwell's Election Cases (1802-06) (Eng.)

Peck. El. Cas. Peckwell's Election Cases (Eng.)

Peck. Elec. Cas. Peckwell's Election Cases (1802-06)

Peck (Ill.) Peck's Reports, Illinois Supreme Court Reports (vols. 11-22, 24-30)

Peck (Tenn.) Peck's Tennessee Reports (vol. 7)

Peck Tr. Peck's Trial (Impeachment)

Peckw. Peckwell's English Election Cases

Peeples. Peeples' Reports (vols. 77-97 Georgia)

Peeples & Stevens Peeples & Stevens Reports (vols. 80-97 Georgia)

Peere Williams Peere Williams' Chancery (Eng.)

Peere Wms. Peere Williams' Chancery & King's Bench Cases (1695-1736) (Eng.)

P.E.I.
- Prince Edward Island

- Prince Edward Island Reports (Haviland's)

P.E.I.L.R.C. Prince Edward Island Law Reform Commission

P.E.I. Rep. Prince Edward Island Reports (Haviland's) (1850-1914)

P.E.I. Rev. Stat. Prince Edward Island Revised Statutes (Canada)

P.E.I. Stat. Prince Edward Island Statutes (Canada)

Pelham. Pelham's South Australia Reports (1865-66) (Aus.)

Pelt. Peltier's Orlean's Appeals (1917-23)

Pemb. Judg. Pemberton, Judgments and Orders

Pen Pennypacker's Reports

Pen.
- Pennewill Delaware Reports
- Pennington's Reports (2, 3 New Jersey Law)

Penal Penal

Penal Inst. Penal and correctional institutions

Pen. & W. Penrose & Watts' Reports (Pennsylvania 1829-32)

Pen. C. Penal Code

Pen. Code. Penal Code

Pen. Dec. Pension Decisions, U.S. Interior Department

Pen. Laws Penal Laws

Penn.
- Pennewill's Delaware Reports
- Pennington's New Jersey Reports
- Pennsylvania
- Pennsylvania State Reports

- Pennypacker's Unreported Pennsylvania Cases

Penna. Pennsylvania

Penna. Law Journal Pennsylvania Law Journal (Pa.)

Penna. L.J. Pennsylvania Law Journal (Pa.)

Penna. R. Pennsylvania State Reports (Pa.)

Penna. S.R. Pennsylvania State Reports (Pa.)

Penna. St. Pennsylvania State Reports (Pa.)

Penna. State Rep Pennsylvania State Reports (Pa.)

Penn. B.A. Pennsylvania Bar Association

Penn. B.A.Q. Pennsylvania Bar Association Quarterly

Penn. Co. Ct. Rep. Pennsylvania County Court Reports

Penn. Corp. Rep. Pennsylvania Corporation Reporter

Penn. Del. Pennewill's Delaware Reports

Penn. Dist. & Co. Rep. Pennsylvania District & County Reports

Penn. Dist. Rep. Pennsylvania District Reports

Penne. Pennewill's Delaware Reports (17-23 Del.) (1897-1909)

Pennew. Pennewill's Reports (Delaware)

Pennewill. Pennewill's Delaware Supreme Court Reports (1897-1909)

Penning. Pennington's Reports (2, 3 N.J. Law)

Pen. N.J. Pennington's Reports (2, 3 New Jersey Law)

Penn. Law Jour. Pennsylvania Law Journal

Penn. L.G.
- Pennsylvania Legal Gazette
- Pennsylvania Legal Gazette Reports (Campbell)

Penn. L.J. Pennsylvania Law Journal

Penn. L.J.R. Pennsylvania Law Journal Reports (Clark 1842-52)

Penn. L. Rec. Pennsylvania Law Record, Philadelphia

Penn. L. Rev. Pennsylvania Law Review

Penn. R. Pennsylvania State Reports (Pa.)

Penn. Rep.
- Pennsylvania State Reports
- Penrose & Watts' Pennsylvania Reports

Penn. St. Pennsylvania State Reports

Penn. Stat. Pennsylvania State Reports (Pa.)

Penn. State Rep. Pennsylvania State Reports (Pa.)

Penn. St. Rep. Pennsylyania State Reports (Pa.)

Penn. Super. Pennsylvania Superior Court Reports (Pa.)

Penny.
- Pennypacker's Pennsylvania Colonial Cases
- Pennypacker's Unreported Pennsylvania Cases

Penny. Col. Cas. Pennypacker Colonial Cases (Pa.)

Pennyp. Pennypacker Unreported Pennsylvania Cases

Pennyp. Col. Cas. Pennypacker's Colonial Cases

Pennyp. (Pa.) Pennypacker Unreported Pennsylvania Cases

Penol. Penology

Pen. P. Penault's Prerosti de Quebec

Penr. Anal. Penruddocke, Short Analysis of Criminal Law. 2ed. 1842

Penr. & W. Penrose & Watts' Rep. (Pa. 1829-32)

Pen. Ref. Penal Reformer (1934-39)

Pen. Ref. League M. Rec. Penal Reform League Monthly Record (1909-12)

Pen. Ref. League Q. Rec. Penal Reform League Quarterly Record (1912-20)

Pens. Pensions and retirement funds

Pens. & Profit Sharing (P-H) Pension and Profit Sharing (Prentice-Hall)

Pension Rep. Pension Reporter (BNA)

Pens. Plan Guide (CCH) Pension Plan Guide (CCH)

Pens. Rep. (BNA) Pension Reporter (Bureau of National Affairs)

Pen. St. R. Pennsylvania State Reports (Pa.)

Peo. L. Adv. People's Legal Advisor, Utica, N.Y.

571

P.E.P. Public Employment Program

Pepper & L. Dig. Pepper and Lewis' Digest of Laws (Pa.)

Pepper & L. Dig. Laws Pepper and Lewis' Digest of Laws, Pa.

Pepperdine L.R. Pepperdine Law Review

Pepperdine L. Rev. Pepperdine Law Review

Pepp. L. Rev. Pepperdine Law Review

Pepsu. All India Reporter, Patiala and East Punjab States Union (1950-57)

PEPUSL Pepperdine University School of Law

Pe. R. Pennewill's Reports (Delaware)

Per. Perera's Select Decisions (Ceylon)

Per. & Dav. Perry & Davison's English King's Bench Reports (1838-41)

Per. & Kn. Perry & Knapp's English Election Reports (1838)

P.E.R.B. Public Employment Relations Board (New York State)

Perf. Arts Rev. Performing Arts Review

Performing Arts Rev. Performing Arts Review

Perj. Perjury

Perk.
- Perkins on Conveyancing
- Perkins on Pleading
- Perkins' Profitable Book (Conveyancing)

Perk. Pr. Bk. Perkins' Profitable Book (Conveyancing)

Perm. Permanent

Per. Or. Cas. Perry, Oriental Cases (Bombay)

Per. P. Perrault's Prevoste de Quebec

Perp.
- Perpetual
- Perpetuities and restraints on alienation

Perpet. Perpetual

per pro. per procurationem (Lat.) by proxy

Perrault
- Perrault's Quebec Reports
- Perrault's Prevoste de Quebec

Perry
- Perry's Oriental Cases, Bombay
- Sir Erskine Perry's Reports, in Morley's (East) Indian Digest

Perry & D. Perry & Davison's English King's Bench Reports

Perry & D. (Eng.) Perry & Davison's English King's Bench Reports

Perry & K. Perry & Knapp's Election Cases (Eng.)

Perry & Kn. Perry & Knapp's English Election Cases

Perry Ins. Perry's Insolvency Cases (1831) (Eng.)

Perry O.C. Perry's Oriental Cases (Bombay)

Perry, Trusts Perry on Trusts

Pers.
- Personal
- Personnel Board

Pers. Finance L.Q. Personal Finance Law Quarterly Report

Pershad Privy Council Judgments (1829-69) (India)

Pers. Inj. Ann. Personal Injury Annual

Pers. Inj. Comment. Personal Injury Commentator

Pers. Inj. Comment'r. Personal Injury Commentator

Pers. Inj. Deskbook Personal Injury Deskbook

Pers. Inj. L.J. Personal Injury Law Journal

Personnel Admin. Personnel Administration

Personnel Mgmt. (P-H) Personnel Management

Persp. perspectives

Perspectives: Civ. Rights Q. Perspectives: The Civil Rights Quarterly

Pers. Prop. Personal Property

Per. Tr. Perry on Trusts

Peshawar
- All India Reporter, Peshawar (1933-50)
- Indian Rulings, Peshawar (1933-47)

Pet.
- Peters
- Peters' Admiralty Reports, Dist. Ct. (U.S.)
- Peter's Circuit Court Reports (U.S.)
- Peters' Supreme Court Reports (26-41 U.S.)
- Peters' Prince Edward Island Reports (1850-72) (Can.)

- Petition

Pet. Ab. Petersdorff's Abridgment

Pet. Abr. Petersdorff's Abridgment of Cases (1660-1823)

Pet. Ad. Peters' United States District Court Reports (Admiralty Decisions)

Pet. Ad. Dec. Peters' Admiralty Decisions (U.S.)

Pet. Adm. Peters' United States District Court Reports (Admiralty Decisions)

Pet. Adm. App. Peters' Admiralty Decisions (Appendix) (U.S.)

Pet. Ad. R. Peters' Admiralty Decisions (U.S.)

Pet. Bail Petersdorff, Bail, 1824

Pet. Br.
- Brooke's New Cases (Petit Brooke) (1515-58)
- Bellewe's Cases temp. Hen. VIII (Eng.)

Pet. C.C. Peters' United States Circuit Court Reports

Pet. Cir. C.R. Peters' Condensed U.S. Circuit Reports

Pet. Cond. Peters' Condensed Reports, U.S. Supreme Court

Pet. Cond. Rep. Peters' Condensed U.S. Circuit Reports

Pet. Dig.
- Peters' United States Digest
- Peticolas' Texas Digest

Peter Analysis and Digest of the Decisions of Sir George Jessel aby A.P. Peter (Eng.)

Peters
- Haviland's Prince Edward Island Reports by Peters (1850-72) (Can.)
- Peters' U.S. Supreme Court Reports (26-41 U.S.)

Peters' Ad. Peters' Admiralty Decisions (U.S.)

Peters Adm. Peters' Admiralty Reports, U.S. District Courts

Peters'Adm. Dec. Peters'Admiralty Decisions (U.S.)

Peters' Admiralty Dec. Peters' Admiralty Decisions (U.S.)

Peters' Adm. R. Peters' Admiralty Decisions (U.S.)

Peters Adm. Rep. Peters' Admiralty Decisions (U.S.)

Peters C.C. Peters' United States Circuit Court Reports

Petersd. Ab. Petersdorff's Abridgment

Petg. Pr. & Ag. Petgrave, Principali and Agent. 1857

Peth. Dis. Petheram, Discovery by Interrogations. 1864

Petit Br. Petit Brooke, or Brooke's New Cases, English King's Bench (1515-58)

Pet. L. Nat. Petersdorff, Law of Nations

Pet. M. & S. Petersdorff, Master and Servant. 1876

Petn. Petition

Pet'r petitioner

Petroleum Econ. The Petroleum Economist, London

Petron. Satyric. Petronius'(Titus) Arbiter, Satyricon, etc.

Pet. S.C. Peters' Supreme Court Reports (26-41 U.S.)

Pet. Suppl. Supplement to Petersdorff's Abridgment

PF Peace and Freedom party

Pfd. Preferred

P.F.S. P.F. Smith's Reports, 51-81 Pennsylvania State Reports

P.F. Smith P.F. Smith's Reports (51-81 Pennsylvania State Reports)

Pgh. Leg. Journal Pittsburgh Legal Journal (Pa.)

P-H
- Prentice Hall
- Prentice-Hall, Inc.

Ph.
- Phillimore's English Ecclesiastical Reports
- Phillips' English Chancery Reports (1841-49)
- Phillips' Election Cases (1780-81)

PHA Public Housing Administration (U.S.)

Phal. C.C. Phalen's Criminal Cases

P-H Am. Lab. Arb. Awards American Labor Arbitration Awards (P-H)

P-H Am. Lab. Cas. American Labor Cases (P-H)

Ph. & M. Philip and Mary

Phar. Pharmacy Board

P.H.B. Parliament House Book (Sc.)

P.-H. Cas. American Federal Tax Reports (P-H)

P.H.C.C. Punjab High Court Cases (India)

Ph. Ch. Phillips' English Chancery Reports

P-H Corp. Corporation (P-H)

Phear Wat. Phear, Rights of Water. 1859

Pheney Rep. Pheney's New Term Reports (Eng.)

P-H Est. Plan. Estate Planning (P-H)

Ph. Ev. Phillips, Evidence. 10ed. 1852

P-H Fed. Taxes Federal Taxes (P-H)

P-H Fed. Wage & Hour. Federal Wage and Hour (Prentice-Hall)

Phil.
- Philadelphia Reports
- Phillimore's English Ecclesiastical Reports
- Phillips' Election Cases (1780-81)
- Phillips' English Chancery Reports (1841-49)
- Phillips' Illinois Reports
- Phillips' North Carolina Reports
- Phillips' Treatise on Insurance
- Phillipines
- Philippine Island Reports (1901-46)
- Philosophical
- Philosophy

Phila. Philadelphia, Pa.

Phila. Philadelphia Reports (Pennsylvania 1850-91)

Philad. Philadelphia Reports (Pa.)

Philada. R. Philadelphia Reports (Pa.)

Philada. Rep. Philadelphia Reports (Pa.)

Philadelphia Leg. Int. Philadelphia Legal Intelligencer (Pa.)

Philadelphia Rep. Philadelphia Reports (Pa.)

Phila. Law Lib. Philadelphia Law Library

Phila. Leg. Int. Philadelphia Legal Intelligencer, Pa.

Phila. L.J. Philadelphia Law Journal

Phil. & M. Philip and Mary (as 3 Phil. & M.)

Phil. & Mar. Philip and Mary

Phil. & Phenom. Res. Philosophy and Phenomenlogical Research

Phil. & Publ. Aff. Philosophy and Public Affairs

Philanthrop, The Philanthropist

Phila. (Pa.) Philadelphia Reports (Pennsylvania 1850-91)

Phila. Reports Philadelphia Reports (Pa.)

Phil. Civ. & Can. Law Phillimore's Civil and Canon Law

Phil. Cop. Phillips' Law of Copyright Designs

Phil. Dom. Phillimore's Law of Domicil

Phil. Ecc.
- Phillimore's Ecclesiastical Judgments
- Phillimore's Ecclesiastical Law, 2 editions. (1873, 1895)
- Phillimore's English Ecclesiastical Reports (1809-21)

Phil. Ecc. Judg. Phillimore's Ecclesiastical Judgments in Court of Arches (1867-75)

Phil. Ecc. Law Phillimore's Ecclesiastical Law. 2 editions. (1873, 1895)

Phil. Ecc. R. Phillimore's Ecclesiastical Reports (161 ER) (1809-21)

Phil. El. Cas. Phillips' English Election Cases

Phil. Eq. Phillips' Equity (North Carolina) (1866-68)

Phil. Ev. Phillips on Evidence

Phil. Ev. Cow. & H. & Edw. Notes Phillips' on Evidence, Notes by Cowen, Hill and Edwards

Phil. Fam. Cas. Phillipps' Famous Cases in Circumstantial Evidence

Phil. Grand. Phillip's Grandeur of the Law

Phil. I.L.J. Philippine International Law Journal

Phil. Ins. Phillips on Insurance

Phil. Insan. Phillips, Lunatics. 1858

Phil. Int. Law Phillimore's International Law

Phil. Int. L.J. Philippine International Law Journal

Phil. Int'l L.J. Philippine International Law Journal

Phil. Int. Rom. Law Phillimore's Introduction to the Roman Law

Philippine. Philippine Reports

Philippine Co. Philippine Code

Philippine Internat. L.J. The Philippine International Law Journal, Manila, Philippines

Philippine Int'l. L.J. Philippine International Law Journal

Philippine J. Pub. Admin. Philippine Journal of Public Administration

Philippine L.J. Philippine Law Journal

Philippine L. Rev. Philippine Law Review

Phil. J. Pub. Admin. Philippine Journal of Public Administration

Phil. Jud. Phillimore's Eccles. Judgments (1867-75) (Eng,)

Phil. Judg. Phillimore's Ecclesiastical Judgments (1867-75)

Phill.
- Phillips' Chancery Reports (41 ER)
- Phillips' Election Cases (1780-81)
- Phillips' Equity, North Carolina
- Phillips' Illinois Reports (152-245 Ill.)
- Phillips' Law Reports, North Carolina (61 N.C.) (1866-68)

Phil. Lab. Rel. J. Philippine Labour Relations Journal

Phil. Law Phillips, North Carolina

Phill. Ch. Phillips' Chancery Reports (41 ER) (1841-49)

Phill. Ch. (Eng.) Phillips' Chancery Reports (41 ER)

Phill. Ecc. Judg. Phillimore's Ecclesiastical Judgments (1867-75)

Phill. Eccl. Judg. Phillimore Ecclesiastical Judgments (Eng.)

Phill. Ecc. R. Phillimore's Ecclesiastical Reports (1809-21)

Phill. Eq. (N.C.) Phillips' Equity, North Carolina

Phillim. Phillimore, English Ecclesiastical Reports

Phillim. Dom. Phillimore on the Law of Domicil

Phillim. Eccl.
- Phillimore's Ecclesiastical Judgments (1867-75)
- Phillimore's Ecclesiastical Reports (1809-21) (161 ER)

Phillim. Ecc. Law Phillimore's Ecclesiastical Law

Phillim. Eccl. (Eng.) J. Phillimore Ecclesiastical Reports (161 ER)

Phillim. Int. Law Phillimore's International Law

Phill. Ins. Phillips on Insurance

Phillips.
- Phillips, English Chancery Reports
- Phillips' Election Cases (1780-81)
- Phillips, North Carolina Reports: Law or Equity
- Phillips' Reports (152-245 Illinois)

Phil. L.J. Philippine Law Journal (Manila)

Phill.L. (N.C.) Phillips Law

Phil. L. Rev. Philippine Law Review

Phil. Lun. Phillips on Lunatics

Phil. Mech. Liens. Phillips on Mechanics' Liens

Phil. N.C. Phillips, North Carolina Law Reports

Philos. & Publ. Aff. Philosophy and Public Affairs

Philosophy Philosophy, London, England

Philos. Res. Philosophical Research

Philos. Rev. Philosophical Review

Philos. Today Philosophy Today

Phil. (Pa.) Philadelphia Reports (Pa.)

Phil. Pat. Phillips on Patents

Phil. Q. Philosophical Quarterly

Phil. R. Philadelphia Reports (Pa.)

Phil. Rep. Philadelphia Reports (Pa.)

Phil. Res. Philosophical Research

Phil. Rev. Philosophical Review

Phil. Rom. Law Phillimore's Private Law among the Romans

Phil. St. Leg. R. Phillip's Studii Legalis Ratio

Phil. St. Tr. Phillipps' State Trials (Prior to 1688)

Phil. Stud. Philippine Studies, Manila

Phil. U.S. Pr. Phillips' Practice, United States Supreme Court

Phil. Yb. Int'l. L. Philippine Yearbook of International Law, Manila, Philippines

P-H Ind. Rel., Lab. Arb. Industrial Relations, American Labor Arbitration (P-H)

P-H Ind. Rel., Union Conts. Industrial Relations, Union Contracts and Collective Bargaining (P-H)

Phip.
- Phipson's Digest, Natal Reports (S. Africa)
- Phipson's Reports, Natal Supreme Court (S. Africa)

Phip. Ev. Phipson, Evidence. 12ed. 1976

Phipson. Reports of Cases in the Supreme Court of Natal

Ph. Leg. Gaz. Legal Gazette (Pa.)

P.-H.N.Y.E.T.R. Prentice-Hall New York Estate Tax Reports

Phoenix The Phoenix, Toronto

Photo. reprint photoduplicated reprint

Ph. Rep. Philadelphia Reports (Pa.)

PHS Public Health Service (U.S.)

P.-H Soc. Sec. Taxes Social Security Taxes (P-H)

P-H State & Local Taxes State and Local Taxes (P-H)

Ph. St. Tr. Phillipps' State Trials

P-H Tax. Federal Taxes (Prentice Hall)

P-H Tax Ct. Mem. Tax Court Memorandum Decisions (P-H)

P-H Tax Ct. Rep. & Mem. Dec. Tax Court Reported and Memorandum Decisions (P-H)

P.-H.Unrep. Tr. Cas. Prentice-Hall Unreported Trust Cases

P.H.V. Pro hac vice (for this purpose or occasion)

Phys. & S. Physicians, surgeons and other healers

PI Department of Public Instruction

PIB Public Information Bulletin

P.I.B. Prices and Incomes Board

PIB's Public Information Bulletins 1965-

P.I.C.A.O. Provisional International Civil Aviation Organization (UN)

Pick. Pickering's Massachusetts Supreme Judicial Court Reports (1822-39)

Pickle Pickle's Reports (85-108 Tenn.)

Pick. (Mass.) Pickering's Reports (18-41 Massachusetts)

Pick. Stat. Pickering's English Statutes

Pierce, R.R. Pierce on Railroad Law

Pig. Piggott's Common Recoveries. 3 editions (1739-92)

Pig. & R. Pigott & Rodwell's English Registration Appeal Cases (1843-45)

Pig. Judg. Piggott, Foreign Judgments. 3ed. 1908-09

Pig. Rec. Pigott's Recoveries (Eng.)

Pike. Pike's Reports (1-5 Arkansas)

Pike & F. Adm. Law Pike & Fischer's Administrative Law

Pike & F. Fed. Rules Ser. Pike & Fischer's Federal Rules Service

Pike & F. Fed. Rules Service Pike & Fischer's Federal Rules Service

Pike & Fischer, Admin. Law Pike & Fischer's Administrative Law

Pike. H. of L. Pike's History of the House of Lords

Pim Ten. Pim on Feudal Tenures

Pin. Pinney's Wisconsin Supreme Court Reports (1839-52)

Ping. Chat. Mortg. Pingrey's Treatise of Chattel Mortgages

Pinn. Pinney's Wisconsin Reports

Pinney. Pinney's Wisconsin Reports (Wis.)

Pinney (S.U.) Pinney's Wisconsin Reports (Wis.)

Pin. (Wis.) Pinney's Wisconsin Reports (Wis.)

Pin.Wis. R. Pinney's Wisconsin Reports (Wis.)

Pip. & C. Mil. L. Pipon & Collier, Military Law. 3ed. 1865

Pipe. Pipelines

Pipe Roll Soc'y Publications of the Pipe Roll Society

Pipe Roll Soc'y (N.S.) Publications of the Pipe Roll Society, New Series

P.I.P.S.C.R. Philippine Islands Public Service Commission Reports

P.I.P.U.C.R. Philippine Islands Public Utility Commission Reports

P.I. Rep. Philippine Islands Reports

Pist. Piston's Mauritius Reports

Piston. Piston's Mauritius Reports (1861 -62)

Pitblado Lect, Isaac Pitblado Lectures on Continuing Legal Education

Pitc. Pitcairn's Criminal Trials (1488-1624) (Sc.)

Pitc. Crim. Tr. Pitcairn's Ancient Criminal Trials, Scotland

Pitc. Tr. Pitcairn, Criminal Trials, 3 (Sc.)

Pitisc. Lex. Pitisci's Lexicon

Pit. L. University of Pittsburgh Law Review (Pa.)

Pitm. Prin. & Sur. Pitman on Principal and Surety

Pitm. Sur. Pitman on Suretyship

Pit. Sur. Pitman, Principal and Surety. 1840

Pitt. Pittsburgh

Pitt Bank. Pitt's Bankruptcy Acts

Pitt C.C. Pr. Pitt's County Court Practice

Pitt. L.J. Pittsburgh Legal Journal

Pitts.
- Pittsburgh Reports
- Pittsburgh, Pa.

Pittsb.
- Pittsburg Reports
- Pittsburgh. Pa.

Pittsb. Leg. J.N.S. Pittsburgh Legal Journal New Series (Pa.)

Pittsb. Leg. J. (O.S.) Pittsburgh Legal Journal. Old Series

Pittsb. Leg. J. (Pa.) Pittsburgh Legal Journal (Pa.)

Pittsb. Leg. J. Pittsburgh Legal Journal (Pa.)

Pittsb. L.J. Pittsburgh Legal Journal (Pa.)

Pittsb. L. Rev. Pittsburgh Law Review

Pittsb. R. (Pa.) Pittsburgh Reporter (Pa.)

Pittsburgh Legal Journal Pittsburgh Legal Journal (Pa.)

Pittsburgh Leg. J. Pittsburgh Legal Journal (Pa.)

Pittsburgh Leg. Journal Pittsburgh Legal Journal (Pa.)

Pitts. Leg. J. Pittsburgh Legal Journal (Pa.)

Pitts. Leg. J. (N.S.) Pittsburgh Legal Journal, New Series (Pa.)

Pitts. Leg. Jour. Pittsburgh Legal Journal (Pa.)

Pitts. L.J. Pittsburgh Legal Journal

Pitts. L.J. (N.S.) Pittsburgh Legal Journal, New Series (Pa.)

Pitts. L. Rev. University of Pittsburgh Law Review

Pitts. R. Pittsburgh Reports (Pa.)

Pitts. Rep.
- Pittsburgh Reports
- Pittsburgh, Pa.

Pitts. Rep. (Pa.) Pittsburgh Reports (Pa.)

Pix. Aud. Pixley, Auditors. 8ed. 1901

P.J.
- Presiding Judge
- ICC Practitioners' Journal
- Bombay High Court, Printed Judgments

P.J.J. Provincial Judges Journal (Can.)

P.J.L.B. Lower Burma. Printed Judgments

P. Jr. & H. Patton, Jr., & Heath's Reports (Virginia Special Court of Appeals)

PL Sherman, Products Liability

P.L.
- Pamphlet Laws
- Poor Law
- Public Law

Pl.
- Placitum or Placita (Subdivision)
- plaintiff
- Plowden's Commentarie, (1550-80)

Pla. Placitum or Placita

Plac. Abbrev. Placitorum Abbreviatio

Plac. Angl. Nor. Placita Anglo Normannica (1065-1195)

Plac. Ang. Nor. Bigelow's Placita Anglo-Normanica

Plan. Planning

Plan & Comp. Planning and Compensation Reports (Eng.)

Plan. Can. Plan Canada

Pl. & Pr. Cas. Pleading & Practice Cas. (1837-38) (Eng.)

Pl. Ang.-Norm. Placita Anglo-Normannica Cases (Bigelow)

Plant Sat. Plant and job safety - OSHA and state laws

Plan., Zoning & E.D. Inst. Planning, Zoning & Eminent Domain Institute

Pla. Par. Placita Parliamentaria (Eng.)

Platt.
- Platt on Covenants (1829)
- Platt on Leases

Platt,Cov. Platt on the Law of Covenants

Platt. Leas. Platt, Leases. 1847

Plaxton. Plaxton's Canadian Constitutional Decisions

P.L.B. Poor Law Board

P.L. Boards Public Law Boards

Pl. C. Placita Coronae (Pleas of the Crown)

P.L.C. Professional Legal Corporation

P.L. Com. Poor Law Commissioner

Pl. Com. Plowden's Commentaries (1550-80) (Eng.)

Pl. Cr. Con. Tr. Plowden's Criminal Conversation Trials

PLDM Bass, Products Liability: Design and Manufacturing Defects

P.L.E. Encyclopedia of Pennsylvania Law

Plead. Pleading

Pleb. Plebiscite

P. Leg. J. Pittsburgh Legal Journal (Pa.)

P. Leg. Jour. Pittsburgh Legal Journal (Pa.)

PLF Pacific Legal Foundation

plf. plaintiff

PLI Practicing Law Institute

P.L.J.
- Pennsylvania Law Journal
- Pittsburgh Legal Journal (Pa.)
- Punjab Law Reporter (India)

P.L.J.N.S. Pittsburgh Legal Journal New Series (Pa.)

Pl. L. Platt on Leases

PLM Stern & Felix-Retzke, A Practical Guide to Preventing Legal Malpractice

P.L.M.
- Pacific Law Magazine
- Poor Law Magazine

P.L. Mag. Poor Law Magazine 1858-1930 (Sc.)

P.L.O. Public Land Order (U.S.)

Plow.
- Plowden's English King's Bench Reports
- Plowden's Commentaries and Reports

Plowd. Plowden's English King's Bench Commentaries or Reports

Pl. Par. Placita Parliamentaria

PLPD Vinson/Slaughter, Products Liability: Pharmaceutical Drug Cases

P.L.R.
- Pacific Law Reporter
- Pakistan Law Reports
- Pakistan Law Review
- Patent Law Review
- Patna Law Reporter (India)
- Pennsylvania Law Record, Philadelphia
- University of Pittsburgh Law Review
- Private Legislation Reports (Sc.)
- Punjab Law Reporter (India)

PLRB Pa. Labor Relations Board

P.L.R. Dacca Pakistan Law Reports, Dacca Series

P.L. Rep. Pacific Law Reporter

P.L.R.J. & K. Punjab Law Reporter, Jammu & Kashmir Section (India)

581

P.L.R. Kar. Pakistan Law Reports, Karachi Series (1947-53)

P.L.R. Lah. Pakistan Law Reports, Lahore Series (1947-55)

P.L.R.W.P. Pakistan Law Reports, West Pakistan Series

Pls. plaintiffs

P.L.T.
- Patna Law Times (India)
- Punjab Law Times (India)

Plt. Peltier's Orleans Appeals Decisions (La.)

Pl. U. Plowden on Usury

PLU Korngold, Private Land Use

Plum. Contr. Plumptre, Contracts. 2ed. 1897

P.L.W. Patna Law Weekly (India)

P.M.
- Postmaster
- Post-meridiem (afternoon)
- Prime Minister
- Purchase money

PMA Production & Marketing Admin, (U.S.)

PMDS Property Management and Disposal Service

Pmph. Pamphlet

PMTP Kasner, Post Mortem Tax Planning

P.N.G.L.R. Papua New Guinea Law, Reports

P.N.G.L.R.C. Papua New Guinea Law Reform Commission

P.N.P. Peake's English Nisi Prius Cases (1790-1812)

P.O.
- Patent Office
- Public officer
- Post office
- Province of Ontario

Po Portuguese

P.O.A. Prison Officers' Association

P. of Accountancy Problems of Accountancy

P.O. Cas. Perry's Oriental Cases, Bombay (1843-52)

Poc. Costs Pocock, Costs. 1881

POCS Post Office and Civil Service

Po. Ct. Police Court

PODPR Post Office Department Procurement Regulations

Poe, Pl. Poe on Pleading and Practice

P.O.G. Official Gazette, U.S. Patent Office

P.O.J. Patent Office Journal (India)

Pol.
- Police
- Policy
- Polish
- Political
- Politics
- Pollexfen's English King's Bench Reports (1669-85)
- Poland

Polam. L.J. Polamerican Law Journal

Pol. & Soc'y Politics and Society

Pol. C. Political Code

Pol. Code Political Code

Pol. Cont. Pollock on Contracts

Pol. Dig. Part. Pollock's Digest of the Laws of Partnership

Pol. Fedn. Newsl. Police Federation Newsletter

Police J.   Police Journal

Police J. Ct.   Police Justice's Court

Police L.Q.   Police Law Quarterly

Polish Perspectives   Polish Perspectives, Warsaw, Poland

Polish Soc. Res.   Polish Social Research

Poll.
- Pollack's Ohio Unreported Judicial Decisions (Prior to 1823)
- Pollexfen's English King's Bench Reports

Pollack   Ohio Unreported Judicial Decisions

Pol. Law of Nat.   Polson's Principles of the Law of Nations

Poll. Const.   Pollution control

Poll. Contr. Guide   Pollution Control Guide (CCH)

Pollex.   Pollexfen's Reports, English King's Bench

Pollexf.   Pollexfen, King's Bench (Eng.)

Pollock & Maitl.   Pollock and Maitland's History of English Common Law

Poll. Prod.   Pollock on the Production of Documents

Pol. L.Q.   Police Law Quarterly

Pollution Abs.   Pollution Abstracts

Pollution Cont. Guide (CCH)   Pollution Control Guide

Pol. Mil. Dig.   Poland's Digest of the Military Laws of the United States

Pol.
- Pollexfen's Reports, English King's Bench

- police

Pol. Part.   Pollock's Digest of the Laws of Partnership

Pol. Prod. Doc.   Pollock on the Power of Courts to Compel the Production of Documents

Pol. Q.   Political Quarterly

Pol. Sci. Q.   Political Science Quarterly

Pol. Sci. Rev. (India)   Political Science Review (India), Jaipur

Pols. Nat.   Polson, Law of Nations. 1848

Pol. Studies   Political Studies, London, England

Pol. Theory   Political Theory

Pol. Tr. Mar.   Poland's Law of Trade Marks

Pol'y.   Policy

Pol. Y.B. Int'l L.   Polish Yearbook of International Law

Pol. Yb. of Internal. L.   The Polish Yearbook of International Law. Warsaw, Poland

Poly. L. Rev.   Poly Law Review

Pom. Code Rem.   Pomeroy on Code Remedies

Pom. Const. Law   Pomeroy's Constitutional Law of the United States

Pom. Contr.   Pomeroy on Contracts

Pom. Eq. Jur.   Pomeroy's Equity Jurisprudence

Pom. Eq. Juris.   Pomeroy's Equity Jurisprudence

Pomeroy   Pomeroy's Reports (73-128 California)

Pom. Mun. Law Pomeroy on Municipal Law

Pom. Rem. Pomeroy on Civil Remedies

Pom. Rem. & Rem. Rights Pomeroy on Civil Remedies & Remedial Rights

Pom. Spec. Perf. Pomeroy on Specific Performance of Contracts

Poore Const. Poore's Federal and State Constitution

Poor L. & Local Gov't Poor Law and Local Government Magazine

Pop. Popham's English King's Bench Reports (1592-1627)

Pope Cust. Pope, Customs and Excise. 11ed. 1828

Pope, Lun. Pope on Lunacy

Pop. Govt. Popular Government

Poph. Popham's English King's Bench Reports (1592-1627)

Poph.(2). Cases at the end of Popham's Reports

Popham Popham's King's Bench Reports (1592-1626) (79 ER)

Poph. Insol. Popham's Insolvency Act of Canada

Pop. Mo. L. Tr. Popular Monthly Law Tracts (1877-78)

Pop. Sci. Mo. Popular Science Monthly

P.O.R. Patent Office Reports

Port.
- Porter's Alabama Supreme Court Reports (1834-39)
- Porter's Indiana Reports (3-7 lnd.)
- Portugal

Port. (Ala.) Porter's Alabama Reports

Port. Ala. R. Porter's Reports (Ala.)

Porter
- Porter's Alabama Reports
- Porter's Reports (3-7 Indiana)

Porter (Ala.) Porter's Reports (Ala.)

Porter R. Porter's Reports (Ala.)

Porter's Ala. R. Porter's Reports (Ala.)

Porter's R. Porter's Reports (Ala.)

Porter's Repts. Porter's Reports (Ala.)

Portia L.J. Portia Law Journal

Port. Ins. Porter's Laws of Insurance

Portland U.L. Rev. Portland University Review

Porto Rico Fed. Rep. Porto Rico Federal Reports

Port. U.L. Rev. Portland University Law Rev.

Po S Policy Statements, of the Australian Broadcasting Tribunal

Posey's U.C. Unreported Cases (Tex.)

Posey U.C. Unreported Cases (Tex.)

Posey, Unrep. Cas. Posey's Unreported Cases (Tex.)

Post
- post (after) Used to refer the reader to a subsequent part of the book
- Post's Reports (23-26 Michigan)
- Post's Reports (42-64 Misssouri)

Post. & Reg. Postage and registration

Poste Gai. Poste's Translation of Gaius

Poste's Gaius Inst. Poste's Translation of Gaius

Postl. Dict. Postlethwaite's Dictionary of Trade and Commerce

Post. Off. Post Office

Pot. Dwar. Potter's Dwarris on Statutes

Poth. Cont. Pothier's Contracts

Poth. Contr. Sale Pothier, Treatise on the Contract of Sale

Poth. Cont. Sale Pothier, Treatise on the Contract of Sale

Pothier, Pand. Pothier, Pandectae Justinianeae, etc.

Poth. Mar. Cont. Pothier's Treatise on Maritime Contracts

Poth. Ob. Pothier on the Law of Obligations

Poth. Obl. Pothier on the Law of Obligations

Poth. Oblig. Pothier on the Law of Obligations

Poth. Pand. Pothier's Pandects

Poth. Part. Pothier on Partnership

Pot. L.D. Pott's Law Dictionary

Potomac L. Rev. Potomac Law Review

Pott. Corp. Potter on Corporations

Pott. Dwarris Potter's Edition of Dwarris on Statutes

Potter Potter's Reports (4-7 Wyoming)

Potts L.D. Potts, Law Dictionary. 3ed. 1815

Pov. L. Rep. Poverty Law Reporter (CCH)

Pow. An. Law Powell's Analysis of American Law

Pow. App. Proe. Powell's Law of Appellate Proceedings

Pow. Car. Powell, Inland Carriers. 2ed. 1861

Pow. Cont. Powell on Contracts

Pow. Conv. Powell on Conveyancing

Pow. Dev. Powell, Essay upon the Learning of Devises, etc.

Powers Powers' Reports, New York Surrogate Court

Power's Sur. Powers' Reports, New York Surrogate Court

Pow. Ev. Powell, Evidence. 10ed. 1921

Pow. Inl. Car. Powell on the Law of Inland Carriers

Pow. Mort. Powell, Mortgages. 6ed. 1826

Pow. Mortg. Powell on Mortgages

Pow. Pow. Powell on Powers

Pow. Pr. Powell's Precedents in Conveyancing

Pow. R. & D. Power, Rodwell & Drew's English Election Cases (1847-56)

Pow. Surr. Powers' Reports, New York Surrogate Court

Poynt. M. & D. Poynter, Marriage and Divorce, 2ed. 1824

PP Drake & Morris, Chapter 13 Practice and Procedure

P.P.   Parliamentary Papers

p.p.a.   per power of attorney

P.P.A.P.   Precedents of Private Acts of Parliament

P.P.C.   Pierce's Perpetual Code (1943)

PPE   Shuman, Psychiatric and Psychological Evidence

P.P.I.   Policy proof of interest

PPR
- Price Procedural Regulation (U.S.)
- Probate Practice Reporter

P.P.R.   Principal Probate Registry

P.Q.
- Parliamentary Question
- Province of Quebec

P.Q.   United States Patent Quarterly

p.q.   pro querente (for or on behalf of plaintiff)

P.Q.W.   Placita de Quo Warranto, Record Commission (Eng.)

P.R.

Pacific Reporter
- Parliamentary Reports (Eng.)
- Pennsylvania Reports (Penrose & Watts)
- Philadelphia Reports (Pennsylvania 1850-51)
- Philippine Island Reports
- Pittsburgh Reports (Pennsylvania 1853-73)
- Postal Regulations
- Press Release (U.S. Government Departments)
- Probate Reports
- Puerto Rico

- Puerto Rico Supreme Court Reports
- Punjab Record (India)
- Pyke's Reports (Canada)
- Upper Canada Pratice Reports (1850-1900) (Ontario)

Pr.
- Practice Reports (various jurisdictions)
- Price's Exchequer Reports (1814-24) (Eng.)
- Prior

pr.   private

Prac.
- Practical
- Practice
- Practitioners'

Prac. Act.   Practice Act

Prac. Appr. Pat. T.M. & Copyright   Practical Approach to Patents, Trademarks & Copyrights

Pra. Cas.   Prater's Cases on Conflict of Laws

Prac. Law.   Practical Lawyer

Prac. Litig.   Practical Litigation

Prac. Real Est. Law.   The Practical Real Estate Lawyer

Pract.   Practitioner

Prac. Tax Law.   The Practical Tax Lawyer

Pract. Law.   Practical Lawyer

Pract. Reg.   Practical Register of Common Pleas (Eng.)

Pr. Adm. Dig.   Pritchard, Admiralty Digest. 3ed. 1887

Pra. H. & W.   Prater, Husband and Wife. 2ed. 1836

P.R. & D.   Power, Rodwell and Dew's Election Cases (1847-56)

P.R. & D. El. Cas. Power, Rodwell & Dew's Election Cases (Eng.)

Pr. & Div. Law Reports, Probate & Divorce (Eng.)

Pratt
- Pratt's Contraband of War Cases
- Pratt's Supplement to Bott's Poor Laws (1833)

Pratt B.S. Pratt's Law of Benefit Building Societies

Pratt Cont. Pratt's Contraband-of-War Cases

Pratt Cts. Req. Pratt's Statutes Establishing Courts of Request

Pratt. Fr. Soc. Pratt, Friendly Societies. 15ed. 1931

Pratt. High. Pratt & Mackenzie, Highways. 21ed. 1967

Pratt P.L. Pratt's Edition of Bott on the Poor Laws

Pratt Prop. T. Pratt on the Property Tax Act

Pratt Sav. B. Pratt, Savings Banks. 6ed. 1845

Pratt's Bott Pratt's Edition of Bott's Poor Laws

Pratt S.L. Pratt, Sea Lights. 2ed. 1858

Prax. Brown's Practice (Praxis), or Precedents in Chancery

Prax. Can. Praxis Almae Curiae Cancellariae (Brown)

P.R.B. Pension Review Board Reports

Pr. C. Prize Cases

P.R.C.
- China, People's Republic of
- Postal Rate Commission

Pr. Ca. Great War Prize Cases (Evans) (Eng.)

Pr. Ch. Precedents in Chancery (Finch) (1689-1722) (Eng.)

P.R. Ch. Practical Register in Chancery (Eng.)

Pr. C.K.B. Practice Cases, King's Bench (Eng.)

Pr. Co. Prerogative Court

Pr. Cont. Pratt on Contraband of War (1861)

P.R.C.P. Practical Register in Common Pleas

P.R.D. Puerto Rico, Decisiones

Pr. Dec. Printed Decisions (Sneed's Kentucky Decisions)

Pr. Div. Law Reports, Probate Division (Eng.)

Preb. Dig. Preble Digest, Patent Cases

Preb. Pat. Cas. Preble's Digest of Patent Cases

Prec. Ch. Precedents in Chancery (24 ER)

Pre. Ch. Precedents in Chancery by Finch

Prec. in Ch. Precedents in Chancery (24 ER) (1689-1722)

Prec. in Ch. (Eng.) Precedents in Chancery (24 ER)

Pr. Edw. I. Prince Edward Island Reports (Canada)

Pr. Edw. Isl.
- Prince Edward Island
- Prince Edward Island Reports (Can.)

Pref Preference

Prelim. Preliminary (Incorporated Law Society) (1868-79)

Prem. Premium

Prem. Liab. Premises Liability

Pren. Act. Prentice, Proceedings in an Action. 2ed. 1880

Prep. Preparation

Prer. Prerogative Court

Prerog. Ct. Prerogative Court, New Jersey

Pres. President

Pres. Abs. Preston, Abstracts of Title. 2ed. 1823-24

Pres. Conv. Preston, Conveyancing. 5ed. 1819-29

Pres. Est. Preston, Estates. 3ed. 1829

Pres. Fal.
- Falconer's Decisions Court of Session (1744-51) (Sc.)
- Gilmour & Falconer Reports, Court of Session (1681-86) (Sc.)

Pres. Falc. President Falconer's Scotch Session Cases (Gilmour & Falconer) (1681-86)

Pres. Leg. Preston, Legacies. 1824

Pres. Mer. Preston on Merger

Prest. Conv. Preston on Conveyancing

Prest. Est. Preston on Estates

Prest. Merg. Preston on Merger

Prest. Shep. T. Sheppard's Touchstone, by Preston

Pretrial Conf. Pretrial Conference

Preview Preview of United States Supreme Court Cases

Prev. L. Rep. Preventive Law Reporter

Pr. Exch. Price's Exchequer Reports (1814-24) (Eng.)

PRF Publications Reference File

P.R.F. Puerto Rico Federal Reports

Pr. Falc. President Falconer's Court of Session Cases (1744-51) (Sc.)

P.R. Fed. Puerto Rico Federal Reports

P.R.H. Puerto Rico Federal Reports

Pr.H.C.Ch. Practice of the High Court of Chancery

Pri.
- Price's Exchequer Reports (1814-24) (Eng.)
- Price's Mining Commissioners' Cases (Eng.)

P.R.I.C. Dec. Puerto Rico Industrial Commission Decisions

Price
- Price's Exchequer Reports (Eng.)
- Price's Mining Commissioners' Cases (Eng.)

Price & St. Price & Stewart's Trade Mark Cases

Price Gen. Pr. Price's General Practice

Price Liens Price, Maritime Liens. 1940

Price Min. Cas. Price's Mining Cases

Price Notes P.C. Price's Notes of Practice Cases in Exchequer (Eng.) (1830-31)

Price Notes P.P. Price, Notes of Points of Practice, Exchequer Cases (Eng.)

Price, P.C. Price's Practice Cases (1830-31)

Price Pr. Cas. Price's Practice Cases (Eng.)

Price R. Est. Price on Acts relating to Real Estate

Prickett Prickett's Reports (Idaho)

Prid. & C. Prideaux & Cole's Reports (4 New Session Cases) (1850-51)

Prid. & Co. Prideaux and Cole's Reports (New Sessions Cases, 4) (1850-51)

Prid. Ch. W. Prideaux, Directions to Churchwardens. 10ed. 1835

Prid. Conv.
- Prideaux & Whitcomb's Precedents in Conveyancing
- Prideaux, Forms and Precedents in Conveyancing. 24ed. 1952

Prid. Judg. Prideaux, Judgments and Crown Debts. 4ed. 1854

Prin. Principal

Prince N.M.L. Prince's New Mexico Laws

Prin. Dec. Printed Decisions (Sneed's)(Ky.)

Prin. P.L. Eden's Principles of the Penal Law

Prison L. Rptr. Prison Law Reporter

Prison Serv. J. Prison Service Journal

Pritch. Adm. Dig. Pritchard's English Admiralty Digest

Pritch. M. & D. Pritchard, Divorce & Matrimonial Causes, 3ed. 1874

Pritch. Quar. Sess. Pritchard, Quarter Sessions

Priv. C. App. Privy Council Appeals (Eng.)

Priv. C.D.I. Indian Privy Council Decisions

Priv. Counc. App. Privy Council Appeals (Eng.)

Priv. Counc. D.I. Privy Council Decisions (India)

Priv. Found. Rep. Private Foundations Reporter (CCH)

Priv. Fran. Cont. Private Franchise Contracts

Priv. Hous. Fin. Private Housing Finance

Priv. Inv. Abroad Private Investments Abroad

Priv. J. Privacy Journal

Priv. L. Private Laws

Priv. Laws Private Laws

Priv. Lond. Privilegia Londini (Coustoms of Privileges of London)

Priv. R. Privacy Report

Priv. St. Private Statutes

Prize C.R. Prize Court Reports (S. Afr.)

P.R. Laws Ann. Laws of Puerto Rico Annotated

Pr. L. Private Laws

P.R. Laws Laws of Puerto Rico

Pr. Min. Printed Minutes of Evidence

PRN Practice Notes of the Australian Broadcasting Tribunal

P.R.O. Public Record Office

Prob.
- English Probate and Admiralty Reports for year cited
- Law Reports, Probate Division
- Probate
- Probation
- Problems

Prob. (1891)   Law Reports, Probate Division (1891)

Prob. 1917   Law Reports, Probate Division, Eng.

Prob. & Adm. Div.   Probate and Admiralty Division Law Reports

Prob. & Div.   Probate and Divorce, English Law Reports

Prob. L.J.   Probate Law Journal (National College of Probate Judges and Boston University School of Law)

Prob. & Mat.   Probate and Matrimonial Cases

Prob. & Prop.   Probate and Property

Probat.   Probation

Probation & Parole L. Rep.   Probation and Parole Law Reports

Probation & Parole L. Summ.   Probation and Parole Law Summaries

Prob. C.   Probate Code

Prob. Code.   Probate Court

Prob. Ct. Rep.   Probate Court Reporter, Ohio

Prob. Div.   Probate Division, English Law Reports

Prob. J.   Probation Journal

Prob. Law.   Probate Lawyer

Prob. L.T.   Probyn, Land Tenure. 4ed. 1881

Prob. Pr. Act.   Probate Practice Act

Prob. R.   Probate Reports

Prob. Rep.   Probate Reports

Prob. Rep. Ann.   Probate Reports Annotated

Probs.   Problems

Probs. Communism   Problems of Communism

Proc.
- Procedures
- Proceedings
- Proclamation

Proc. Amer. Soc. of Internat. L.   Proceedings. American Society of International Law

Proc. B. & B.   Proctor's Bench and Bar of New York

Proc. Ch.   Proceedings in Chancery

Proced.   Procedendo (lat.)

Proceed. of the Cambridge Philol. Soc.   Cambridge Philological Society, Cambridge, England, Proceedings

Proc. Indian Soc. of Internat. L.   Proceedings of the Conference, The Indian Society of International Law. New Delhi, India

Proc. Pr.   Proctor's Practice

Proc. Prac.   Proctor's Practice

Prod.
- Product
- Production

Prod. Liab.   Products Liability

Prod. Liab. Int.   Product Liability International

Prod. Liab. Int'l   Product Liability International

Prod. Liab. Rep. (CCH)
- Products Liability Reports
- Products Liability Reporter (CCH)

Prod. Safety & Liab. Rep. (BNA) Product Safety and Liability Reporter (BNA)

Produc.
- produce
- production

Prof.
- Profession
- Professional

Prof Admin
- Professional Administrator
- Professional Administration

Prof. Corp. Proffatt on Private Corporations in California

Prof. Corp. Guide (P-H) Professional Corporation Guide (Prentice-Hall)

(The) Professions (The) Professions (Free quarterly insert with Business Review Weekly) 1986-

Prof. Jur. Proffatt on Trial by Jury

Prof. Not. Proffatt on Notaries

Prof. Wills Proffatt on Wills

Prohib. Prohibition

Pro. L. Province Laws

prolong prolonged

Prom. Promissory

Prop. Property

Prop. & Comp. Property and Compensation Reports

Prop. & Comp. R. Property and Compensation Reports

Prop. Law. Property Lawyer (1826-30)

Prop. Law Bull. Property Law Bulletin

Prop. Law.N.S. Property Lawyer, New Series (Eng.)

PROPRE Property Press

Pro quer. Pro querente (for the plaintiff)

Pros. Atty. Prosecuting Attorney

Pro se For himself; in person (Lat.)

Pros. J. Nat'l Dist. Att'y. A. Prosecutor, Journal of the National District Attorneys Association

prosp. prospectively

Prostit. Prostitution

Prot. Protocol

Prot. C.J. Protocol on the Statute of the European Communities Court of Justice

Prot. P.I. Protocol on Privileges and Immunities

Proud. Dom. Pub. Proudhon's Domaine Public

Proudf. Land Dec. United States Land Decisions (Proudfit)

Prouty Prouty's Reports (61-68 Vermont)

Prov. Province

Prov. Can. Stat. Statutes of the Province of Canada

Prov. Inher. & Gift Tax Rep. (CCH) Provincial Inheritance & Gift Tax Reporter

provns. provisions

Prov. St. Statutes, Laws, of the Province of Massachusetts

P.R.R.
- Puerto Rico Reports
- Puerto Rico Supreme Court Reports

Pr.R.
- Practice Reports (various jurisdictions)
- Practice Reports (Ontario)
- Practice Reports (Quebec)

P.R.R. & Regs. Commonwealth of Puerto Rico Rules and Regulations

Pr. Reg. B.C. Practical Register in the Bail Court

Pr. Reg. Ch. Practical Register in Chancery (1 vol.)

Pr. Reg. C.P. Practical Register in the Common Pleas (1705-42)

Pr. Rep.
- Practice Reports (Eng.)
- Practice Reports (Ontario)

Pr. Rep. B.C. Lowndes, Maxwell, & Pollock's Bail Court Practice Cases (Eng.)

Pr. R. Fed. Porto Rico Federal Reports (Now Puerto Rico)

P.R.S.C.R. Puerto Rico Supreme Court Reports

Pr. Stat. Private Statutes

P.R.T. Petroleum Revenue Tax

P.R.T.C.D. Puerto Rico Tax Court Decisions

prtg. printing

Prt. Rep. Practice Reports

P.R.U.C. Practice Reports (1848-1900) (Upper Canada)

P.S. Parliamentary Secretary

P.S.
- Pension Trust, Profit-Sharing, Stock Bonus, or Annuity Plan Ruling
- Petty Sessions
- Privy Seal
- Public Statutes
- Purdon's Pennsylvania Statutes

P.S.C. Public Service Commission

P.S.C.R. Public Service Commission Reports

P.S.C.U.S. Peters' Reports (26-41 U.S.)

P.S.D. Petty Session Division

P. Shaw Patrick Shaw's Justiciary (1819-31) (Sc.)

P.S.Q. Political Science Quarterly

P.S.R. Pennsylvania State Reports

P.S.S.R.B. Public Service Stops Relations Board

PST
- Preparing for Settlement and Trial
- Profit-sharing trustee

Psych.
- Psychiatry
- Psychology

Psych. & M.L.J. Psychological & Medico-Legal Journal

Psychol.
- Psychological
- Psychology

P.T.
- Pension trustee
- Processing Tax Division, U.S. Internal Revenue Bureau
- Public Trustee
- Purchase Tax

PT   Pennell and Postlewaite, Partnership Taxation

pt.   part

P.T.B.R.   Processing Tax Board of Review Decisions U.S. Internal Revenue Bureau

Ptnr   Partner

PTO
- Desiderio & Taylor, Planning Tax-Exempt Organizations
- Patent and Trademark Office
- Public Trustee Office

P. Tr.   Private trust (includes testamentary, investment, life insurance, holding title, etc.)

pts.   parts

pub., Pub.
- public
- Publication
- publish
- publisher
- publishing
- published

Pub. Acts   Public Acts

Pub. Acts N.S.W.   Public Acts of New South Wales (1824-1957) (Aus.)

Pub. Acts Queensl.   Public Acts of Queensland (Reprint) (1828-1936) (Aus.)

Pub. Admin.   Public Administration, London, England

Pub. Admin. in Israel & Abroad   Public Administration in Israel and Abroad, Jerusalem, Israel

Pub. Admin. Rev.   Public Administration Review

Pub. Adm. Rev.   Public Administration Review

Pub. Ad. Rev.   Public Administration Review

Pub. & Loc. Laws   Public and Local Laws

Pub. Auth.   Public Authorities

Pub. Bargaining Cas.(CCH)   Public Bargaining Cases (CCH)

Pub. Bldgs.   Public Buildings

Pub. Cont. L.J.   Public Contract Law Journal

Pub. Cont. Newsl.   Public Contract Newsletter

Pub. Contract L.J.   Public Contract Law Journal

Pub. Doc.   Public Documents

Pub. Employee Bargaining (CCH)   Public Employee Bargaining

Pub. Employee Bargaining Rep. (CCH)   Public Employee Bargaining Reports (CCH)

Pub. Employee Rel. Rep.   Public Employee Relations Reports

Pub. Ent. Advert. & Allied Fields L.Q.   Publishing, Entertainment, Advertising & Allied Fields Law Quarterly

Pub. Ent. Adv. L.Q.   Publishing, Entertainment, Advertising and Allied Fields Law Quarterly

Pub. F.   Public funds

Pub. Gen. Acts S. Austl.   Public General Acts of South Australia

Pub. Gen. Laws.   Public General Laws

Pub. Health   U.S. Public Health Service, Court Decisions

Pub. Hous.   Public Housing

Pub. Interest Public Interest, The

Pub. Int'l L. Public International Law

publ. publication

Pub. L. Public Law

Publ. Adm. & Dev. Public Administration and Development, London

Pub. Land & Res. L. Dig. Public Land and Resources Law Digest

Pub. Land L. Rev. Public Land Law Review

Pub. Lands Public Lands

Pub. Lands Dec. Department of the Interior, Decisions Relating to Public Lands

Pub. Laws Public Laws

Pub. L.F. Public Law Forum

Publ. Finance Public Finance / Finances Publiques, The Hague

Publ. Finance Q Public Finance Quarterly

Publ. Interest Public Interest

Pub. Loc. Laws Public Local Laws

Publ. Pers. Rev. Public Personnel Review

Publ. Stud. Public Studies

Pub. Manag. Public Management

Pub. Off. Public Officers

Pub. Papers Public Papers of the President

Pub. Rel. Bull. Public Relations Bulletin (A.B.A.)

Pub. Res. Public Resources

Pub. Safety Public Safety

Pub. Sec. Public Securities and Obligations

Pub. Ser. Comm. Public Service Commission

Pub. Serv. Public Service

Pub. St. Public Statutes

Pub. U. Rep. Public Utilities Reports (PUR)

Pub. Util. Public Utilities

Pub. Util. C. Public Utilities Code

Pub. Util. Comm. Public Utilities Commission

Pub. Util. Fort. Public Utilities Fortnightly

Pub. Util. L. Anthol. Public Utilities Law Anthology

Pub. Util. Rep. Public Utilities Reports

Pub. Wks. Public works and contracts

P.U.C. Public Utilities Commission

PUD Planned Unit Development

Puerto Rico Puerto Rico Reports

Puerto Rico F. Puerto Rico Federal Reports

Puerto Rico Fed. Puerto Rico Federal Reports

Puerto Rico Rep. Puerto Rico Supreme Court Reports

Puf. Puffendorf's Law of Nature and Nations

Puffendorf.
- Puffendorf's Law of Nature and Nations
- Puffendorf's Law of Nature

P.U. Fort. Public Utilities Fortnightly

Pug(s). Pugsley's Reports (14-16 New Brunswick)

Pugs. & Bur. Pugsley & Burbidge Reports (17-20 New Brunswick)

Pugs. & Burb. Pugsley & Burbidge Reports (17-20 New Brunswick)

Pugs. & T. Pugsley & Trueman (New Brunswick)

Pugs. & Tru. Pugsley's and Trueman's Reports, New Brunswick (1882-83)

Pull. Acc. Pulling, Mercantile Accounts. 1846

Pull. Accts. Pulling's Law of Mercantile Accounts

Pull. Att. Pulling, Attorneys & Solicitors. 3ed. 1862

Pull. Laws & Cust. Lond. Pulling, Treatise on the Laws, Customs, and Regulations of the City and Port of London

Pull. Port of London Pulling, Treatise on the Laws, Customs, and Regulations of the City and Port of London

Pulsifer (Me.) Pulsifer's Reports (35-68 Maine)

Pult. Pulton de Pace Regis

Pump Ct. Pump Court (London)

Pun.
- All India Reporter, Punjab
- Indian Law Reports, Punjab

Punj. Ind. Punjab, India

Punj. Pak. Punjab, Pakistan

Punj. Rec. Punjab Record (India)

Pur. Purchase

P.U.R. Public Utilities Reports

P.U.R.3d Public Utilities Reports, Third Series

Purd. Dig. Purdon's Digest of Laws, Pennsylvania

Purd. Dig. Laws. Purdon's Digest of Laws (Pa.)

P.U.R. (N.S.) Public Utilities Reports, New Series

Purple's St. Purple's Statutes, Scates' Compilation

Purv. Coll. Purvis' Collection of the Laws of Virginia

Puter Ch. Puterbaugh's Illinois Chancery Pleading

Puter.Pl. Puterbaugh's Common Law (Illinois) Pleading

Putnam. Putnam. Proceedings before the Justices of the Peace

Pv. Par value

Pvt. Private

PW Penrose and Watts' Reports

P.W.
- Peere Williams' English Chancery Reports (1695-1736)
- State Department of Public Welfare
- Public Welfare
- Public Works

PWA Public Works Administration (U.S.)

P.Wms. Peere Williams' English Chancery Reports (1695-1736)

P.Wms. (Eng.) Peere Williams' English Chancery Reports (1695-1736)

Pyke
- Pyke (Lower Can.)
- Pyke's Lower Canada Reports, King's Bench
- Pyke's Reports, King's Bench (Que.)

Py. R. Pyke's Lower Canada Reports, King's Bench

Q

q. questioned; soundness of decision or reasoning in cited case questioned (usedin Shepard's Citations)

Q.
- Quarterly
- Quebec
- Queen
- Queensland
- Quorum
- Year Books, part IV, Quebec

Q. Att. Quoniam Attachiamenta

Q.B.
- Queen's Bench
- Queen's Bench Reports (Adolphus & Ellis, New Series)
- Queen's Bench Reports, Quebec
- Queen's Bench Reports, Upper Canada
- English Law Reports, Queen's Bench

Q.B.D. English Law Reports, Queen's Bench Division

Q.B. Div. Queen's Bench Division (English Law Reports)

Q.B. Div'l Ct. Queen's Bench Divisional Court (Eng.)

Q.B. (Eng.) Queen's Bench

Q.B.L.C. Queen's Bench Reports, Lower Canada

Q.B.R. Queen's Bench Reports, by Adolphus & Ellis (New Series)

Q.B.U.C. Queen's Bench Reports, Upper Canada

Q.C. Queen's Counsel

Q.C.L.L.R. Crown Lands Law Reports, Queensland (Aus.)

Q.C.R. Queensland Criminal Reports (Aus.)

Qd. R. Queensland Reports (Law Book Co.)

Q.E.N. Quare executionem non (wherefore execution should not be issued)

Q. J. Quarterly Journal

Q. Japan Com'l. Arb. Ass'n. Quarterly of the Japan Commercial Arbitration Association

Q.J.P. Queensland Justice of the Peace Reports (Law Book Co.)

Q.J.P. Mag. Cus. Queensland Justice of the Peace, Magisterial Cases (Aus.)

Q.J.P.R. Queensland Justice of the Peace Reports

Q.L.
- Quebec Law
- Queensland Lawyer (Law Book Co.)

Q.Law Soc. J. Queensland Law Society Journal

Q.L. Beor. Beor's Queensland Law Report (Aus.)

Q.L.C.R. Queensland Land Court Reports

Qld. Queensland

Q.L.J.
- Queen's Law Journal
- Queensland Law Journal (1879-1901)

Q.L.J. (N.C.) Queensland Law Journal (Notes of Cases) (1879-1901) (Aus.)

Q.L.R.
- Quebec Law Reports
- Queensland Law Reports

Q.L.R. (Beor). Queensland Law Reports by Beor (Aus.)

Q.L.R.C. Queensland Law Reform Commission

Q.L. Rev. Quarterly Law Review

Qly. Land R. Fitzgibbon's Irish Land Reports (1895-1920)

Q.N. Quarterly Newsletter (ABA)

Q. Newl.-Spec. Comm. Env.L. Quarterly Newsletter-Special Committee on Environmental Law

Q.O.R. Quebec Official Reports

QPL Qualified Products List

Q.P.R. Quebec Practice Reports

Q.R. Quebec Official Reports

Q. Rev. Juris. Quarterly Review of Jurisprudence (1887-88)

Q.R.K.B. Quebec King's (or Queen's) Bench Reports

Q.R.Q.B. Quebec Queen's Bench Reports (Can.)

Q.R.S.C. Quebec Reports, Superior Court

Q.S. Quarter Sessions

Q.S.C.R. Queensland Supreme Court Reports (1860-81)

Q.S.R. Queensland State Reports (Aus.)

Q.t. Qui tam

QTIP Qualified Terminable Interest Property

QTT Kestler, Questioning Techniques and Tactics

Quadr. Quadragesms (Year Books, Part IV)

Quar. Crim. Dig. Quarles' Tennessee Criminal Digest

Quar. Law Journal Quarterly Law Journal, Richmond, Va.

Quar. L. Rev. Quarterly Law Review, Richmond, Va.

Quart. L.J. (Va.) Quarterly Law Journal

Quart. L. Rev. (Va.) Quarterly Law Review

Quart. Newsl. Quarterly Newsletter (ABA)

Que.
- Quebec
- Quebec: Court with jurisdiction in Quebec

Quebec C.C.R.O. Quebec Civil Code Revision Office

Quebec L. (Can.) Quebec Law Reports

Quebec Pr. (Can.) Quebec Practice

Queb. K.B. Quebec Official Reports, King's Bench (Can.)

Queb. Pr. Quebec Practice Reports (1897-1943)

Queens B. Bull. Queens Bar Bulletin (U.S.)

Queens C.B.A. Bull. Queens County Bar Association Bulletin (U.S.)

Queens Intra. L.J. Queens Intramural Law Journal (1968-70) (Can.)

Queen's Intramural L.J. Queen's Intramural Law Journal

Queens J.P. & Loc. Auth. Jo. Queensland Justice of the Peace and Local Authorities' Journal

Queensl.
- Queensland
- Queensland Reports (Aus.)

Queensl. Acts Queensland Acts (1896-1940)

Queensland L. Soc'y J. Queensland Law Society Journal, Brisbane, Australia

Queensl. Cr. Lands L.R. Crown Lands Law Report-Queensland (1859-1973)

Queen's L.J. Queen's Law Journal

Queensl. J.P. (Austr.) Queensland Justice of the Peace

Queensl. J.P.R. Queensland Justice of the Peace Reports (1907-1972)

Queensl. J.P. Rep. Queensland Justice of the Peace Reports

Queensl. L. Queensland Law

Queensl. Land Ct. R. Queensland Land Court Reports (1974-date)

Queensl. Law Queensland Lawyer (1973-date)

Queensl. L.J. & R. Queensland Law Journal and Reports (1879-1901) (Aus.)

Queensl. L.J. & St. R. Queensland Law Journal and State Reports (Aus.)

Queensl. L.J. (Austr.) Queensland Law Journal

Queensl. L.R. Queensland Law Reports (1876-78) (Aus.)

Queensl. L.S.J. Queensland Law Society

Queensl. L. Soc'y J. Queensland Law Society Journal

Queensl. Pub. Acts Public Acts of Queensland (Reprint) (1823-1936)

Queens. L.R. Queensland Law Reports (Aus.)

Queensl. R. Queensland Reports (1958-date)

Queensl. S.C. (Austr.) Queensland Supreme Court Reports

Queensl. S.C.R. Queensland Supreme Court Reports

Queensl. S.Ct. R. Queensland Supreme Court Reports (1860-81) (Aus.)

Queens. L. Soc'y J. Queensland Law Society Journal

Queensl. Stat. Queensland Statutes (Aus.)

Queensl. St. (Austr.) Queensland State Reports

Queensl. St. R. Queensland State Reports (1902-1957)

Queensl. St. Rep. Queensland State Reports

Queensl. W.N. (Aus.) Queensland Law Reporter & Weekly Notes

Queensl. W.N. (Austr.) Queensland Weekly Notes

Queensl. U. Tech. L.J. Queensland University of Technology Law Journal

Queens. St. R. Queensland State Reports

Que. K.B. Quebec Official Reports, King's Bench

Que. L. Quebec Law

Que. L.R. Quebec Law Reports (Can.)

Que. Pr. Quebec Practice

Que. P.R. Quebec Practice Reports

Que. Prac. Quebec Practice Reports

Que. Q.B. Quebec Official Reports, Queen's Bench

Que. Rev. Jud. Quebec Revised Judicial

Que. Rev. Stat. Quebec Revised Statutes (Canada)

Que. S.C. Quebec Official Reports, Superior Court

Que. Stat. Quebec Statutes (Canada)

Que. Super. Quebec Official Reports Superior Court

Que. Tax Rep. (CCH) Quebec Tax Reporter

Quiet T. Quieting title and determination of adverse claims

Quin. Quincy's Massachusetts Reports

Quin Bank. Quin, Banking. 1833

Quincy Quincy's Massachusetts Reports

Quincy (Mass.) Quincy's Massachusetts Reports (Mass.)

Quinti, Quinto Year Book 5 Henry V (Eng.)

Quis Cust. Quis Custodiet

Qu. Jour. Int-Amer. Rel. Quarterly Journal of Inter-American Relations

Qu. L.J. Quarterly Law Journal

Q.U.L.R. Queensland University Law Journal

Qu. L. Rev. Quarterly Law Review

Quo. Attach. Quoniam Attachiamenta

Quon. Attach. Auoniam Attachiamenta

quot.
- quoted in
- quoting
- quotation

Quo War. Quo Warranto

Q.V. Quod vide (to which, refer)

Q.Van Weyt. Q. Van Weytson on Average

Q. Vic. Statutes of Quebec in the reign of Victoria

Q. Vict. Statutes of Province of Quebec (Reign of Victoria)

Q. War. Quo Warranto

Q.W.N. Queensland Weekly Notes, cited by year

R

r.
- repeal
- repealed
- repealing
- rule

R.
- All India Reporter, Rajasthan
- Railway
- Range
- Rawle's Reports (Pennsylvania 1828-35)
- Record
- Abstracted reappraisement Decisions
- Regna (queen)
- Repealed
- The Reports, Coke's King's Bench (Eng.)
- Kentucky Law Reporter (1880-1908)
- King Richard
- Railroad
- Republicana
- Rettie's Court of Session Reports, 4th Series (Scot.)
- Reversed, revoked or rescinded; exisiting order aborgated (used in Shepard's Citations)
- Roscoe's Cape of Good Hope
- Reports
- Rescinded
- Resolved
- Revision
- Revoked
- Rex (King)

- Rolls
- Rule
- Russian

R.A.
- Rating Appeals (U.K.)
- Registration Appeals
- Regulation Appeals
- Rules and Administration
- Rules on Appeal

R.A.C. Ramsay's Appeal Cases (Can.)

Ra. Ca. English Railway and Canal Cases

Race Rel. L. Rep. Race Relations Law Reporter

Rac. Rel. L. Survey Race Relations Law Survey

Radar Radar's Reports (138-163 Missouri)

Rader Rader's Reports (138-163 Mo.)

Rad. Reg. (P & F) Radio Regulation (P & F)

Rad. Reg. 2d (P & F) Radio Regulation Second Series (Pike and Fischer)

Ra. Ent. Lord Raymond's Entries

Raff Pens. Man. Raff's Pension Manual

Rag. Ragland California Superior Court Decisions

Rag. Super. Ct. Dec. (Calif.) Ragland Superior Court Decisions (Cal.)

Rail. & Can. Cas.
- English Railway and Canal Cases
- Railway and Canal Traffic Cases

Rail. Ca. Railway and Canal Cases (1835-54)

Rail (or Railw.) Cas. Railway Cases

Railway & Corp. Law J. Railway & Corporation Law Journal

Railway Cas. Railway Cases

Railw. Cas. Railway Cases

Raith. St.
- Raithby's Statutes at Large, English
- Raithby's Study of the Law

Raj. All India Reporter, Rajasthan

Raj. Rajaratam Revised Reports (Ceylon)

Rajasthan Indian Law Reports, Rajasthan Series

Raj. Ind. Rajasthan. India

Ralw. & Corp. L.J. Railway & Corporation Law Journal

Ram. Ramsey's Quebec Appeal Cases Ramanathan's Reports (Ceylon)

Ramachandrier A. Ramachandrier's Cases on Adoption (India) 1892

Ramachandrier D.G. Ramachandrier's Cases on Dancing Girls (India) 1892

Ramachandrier H.M.L. Ramachandrier's Cases on Hindu Marriage Law (India) 1891

Ram. & Mor. Ramsey & Morin's Montreal Law Reporter

Ram Ass. Ram. Assetts. Debts and Incumbrances. 2ed. 1837

Ram Cas. P. & E. Ram's Cases of Pleading and Evidence

Ram F. Ram on Facts

Ram Leg. J. Ram, Science of Legal Judgment. 2ed. 1834

Ram Leg. Judgm. (Towns.Ed) Ram's Science of Legal Judgment, Notes by Townshend

Rams. App. Ramsey's Appeal Cases (1873-86) (Quebec)

Ramsay, App. Cas. Ramsay, Appeal Cases (Can.)

Ramsay App. Cas. (Can.) Ramsay, Appeal Cases (Can.)

Ram. S.C. Ramanathon, Reports, Supreme Court, Ceylon

Ram. W. Ram, Exposition of Wills of Landed Property. 1827

Rand.
- Randall's Reports (62-71 Ohio State)
- Randolph's Reports (21-56 Kansas)
- Randolph's Reports (7-11 Louisiana)
- Randolph's Reports (22-27 Virginia) (1821-28)

Rand & Fur. Poi. Rand & Furness on Poisons

Rand. Ann. Randolph Annual (La.)

R. & B. Remington & Ballinger's Code (1910)

R. & B. Cas. Redfield & Bigelow's Leading Cases on Bills and Notes

R. & B. Supp. Remington & Ballinger's Code (1913 Supplement)

R. & C. Russell & Chesley's Nova Scotia Reports

R. & Can. Cas. Railway & Canal Cases (Eng.)

R. & Can. Tr. Railway & Canal Traffic Cases, Eng.

R. & Can. Tr. Cas. Railway & Canal Traffic Cases (Eng.)

R. & C.C. Railway & Canal Cases (1835-54)

R. & C.Ca. Railway & Canal Cases (Eng.)

R. & C. Cas. Railway & Canal Cases (Eng.)

R. & C. N. Sc. Russell & Chesley's Reports (Nova Scotia)

Rand. Com. Paper Randolph on Commercial Paper

R. & C. Tr. Cas. Railway & Canal Traffic Cases (Neville) (Eng.)

R. & D. Research and Development

Rand. Em. Dom. Randolph on Eminent Domain

R. & G. Russell & Geldert's Nova Scotia Reports

R. & G. N. Sc. Russell & Geldert's Reports, Novia Scotia

R. & H. Bank. Roche & Hazlitt, Bankruptcy, 2ed. 1873

R. & H. Dig. Robinson & Harrison's Digest (Ontario)

R. & I.T. Rating & Income Tax Reports (Eng.)

R.& J.
- Rabkin & Johnson, Federal, Income, Gift and Estate Taxation
- Rafique & Jackson's Privy Council Decisions (India)

R. & J. Dig. Robinson & Joseph's Digest (Ontario)

RAND J. Econ. RAND Journal of Economics, The

R. & L.L. & T. Redman & Lyon, Landlord and Tenant. 8ed. 1924

R. & M.
- Russell & Mylne's English Chancery Reports
- Ryan & Moody's English Nisi Prius Reports
- Law Reporter, Montreal (Can.)

R. & M.C.C. Ryan & Moody's Crown Cases Reserved (Eng.)

R. & McG. Income Tax Decisions of Australasia, Ratcliffe and M'Grath (1891-1930)

R. & McG. Ct. of Rev. Court of Review Decisions, Ratcliffe and M'Grath, New South Wales (1913-1927)

R. & M.N.P. Ryan & Moody's Nisi Prius Reports (Eng.)

R. & My. Russell & Mylne's Chancery Reports (Eng.)

R. & N. Rhodesia and Nyasaland Law Reports (1956)

R. & N.L.R. Rhodesia and Nyasaland Law Reports (1956-64)

Rand. Peak. Randall's Edition of Peake on Evidence

Rand. Perp. Randall on Perpetuities

R. & R. Russell & Ryan Crown Cases (Eng.)

R. & R.C.C. Russell & Ryan's English Crown Cases, Reserved

R. & Ry.C.C. Russell and Ryan's English Crown Cases

R. & V. R. Rating and Valuation Reports

Raney Raney's Reports (16-20 Florida)

Rang. Cr. L.J. Rangoon Criminal Law Journal

Rang. Dec. Sparks' Rangoon Decisions, British Burmah

Rang. L.R. Rangoon Law Reports (India)

Rank. & S. Comp. L. Ranking & Spicer, Company Law, 11ed. 1970

Rank. P. Rankin, Patents. 1824

Rank. S. & P. Exec. Ranking, Spicer Pegier, Executorship. 21ed. 1971

Rao D.H.L. Rao's Decisions on Hindu Law (India) 1893

RAP Radical Alternatives to Prison

R.A.P. Rules for Admission to Practice

Rapal. & L. Rapalje & Lawrence, American and English Cases

Rapalje & L. Rapalje & Lawrence's Law Dictionary

Rap. & L. Rapalje & Lawrence, American and English Cases

Rap. & Law. Rapalje & Lawrence American and English Cases

Rap. & L. Law. Dict. Rapalje and Lawrence Law Dictionary

Rap.Contempt Rapalje on Contempt

Rap. Fed. Ref. Dig. Rapaije's Federal Reference Digest

Rapid Trans. Rapid Transit

Rap. Lar. Rapalje's on Larceny

Rap. N.Y. Dig. Rapalje New York Digest

Rapp Bount. Rapp on the Bounty Laws

Rap.Wit. Rapalje's Treatise on Witnesses

Rast. Rastoll's Entries & Statutes (Eng.)

Rast. Abr. Rastell's Abridgment of the Statutes

Rast. Ent. Rastell, Entries and Statutes

Ratio Juris Ratio Juris

Rat. Sel. Cas. Rattigan, Select Law Cases in Hindu Law

Rattigan Rattigan's Select Hindu Law Cases (India)

Ratt. L.C. Rattigan's Leading Cases on Hindoo Law

Ratt. R.L. Rattigan's Roman Law of Persons

Rat. Unrep. Cr. Ratanlal's Unreported Criminal Cases (India)

Raw. Rawle's Reports, Pennsylvania, 5 vols.

Raw. Const. Rawle on the United States Constitution

Raw. Cov. Rawle on Covenants for Title

Raw. Eq. Rawle, Equity in Pennsylvania

Rawle Rawle's Pennsylvania Supreme Court Reports (1828-35)

Rawle Const. U.S. Rawle on the Constitution of the United States

Rawle Cov. Rawle on Covenants for Title

Rawle Pen. & W. Rawle, Penrose, & Watts' Reports (Pa. 1828-40)

Rawl. Mun. Corp. Rawlinson, Municipal Corporations. 10ed. 1910

Ray. B. Ex. Raymond's Bill of Exceptions

Rayden Rayden on Divorce

Ray Ins. (or Med.Jur.) Ray's Medical Jurisprudence of Insanity

Raym. Raymond Sir T. Reports, King's Bench (1660-84) (83 ER)

Raym. B. Ex. Raymond on Bills of Exceptions

Raym. Ch. Dig. Raymond's Digested Chancery Cases

Ray, Med. Jur. Ray' Medical Jurisprudence of Insanity

Ray Men. Path. Ray's Mental Pathology

Raym. Ent. Raymond (Lord) Entries

Raym. Ld. Lord Raymond, English King's Bench Reports (3 vols.)

Raymond Raymond's Reports, vols. 81-89 Iowa

Raym. Sir T. Sir Thomas Raymond, English King's Bench Reports

Raym. T. Sir Thomas Raymond (Eng.)

Rayn. Rayner, English Tithe Cases (3 vols.)

Rayn. Lib. Rayner on the Law of Libels

Rayn. Ti. Cas. Rayner's Tithe Cases (1575-1782)

Ray. Sir T. Sir T. Raymond's King's Bench Reports (83 ER) (1660-84)

Ray. Ti. Cas. Rayner's Tithe Cases, Chancery (1575-1782) (Eng.)

RB Renegotiation Board (U.S.)

R.B. Renegotiation Bulletins

R.B.G. British Guiana Reports of Opinions

R.B.R. Renegotiation Board Regulations

R.C.
- Nicholl, Hare & Carrow's Railway Cases (1835-55)
- Railway Cases
- Record Commissioners
- Registration Cases
- Remington's Code
- Revised Code
- Revised Statutes 1855, Missouri
- Rolls of Court
- Ruling Cases

Rc. Rescriptum

R.C. & C.R. Revenue, Civil & Criminal Reporter, Calcutta

RCF Russo, Regulation of the Commodities Futures and Options Markets

R.C.D.I.P. Revue Critique de Droit International Priv

R.C.J. Reports of Certain Judgments of the Supreme Court, Vice-Admiralty Court and Full Court of Appeal, Lagos (1884-92) (Nigeria)

RC(J) Rettie, Crawford & Melville, Session Cases, 4th Series (1873-98) (Sc.)

R.C.I. Ruling Case Law

R.C.L. Ruling Case Law

R.C.M. Revised Code of Montana

R.C.M.P.Q. Royal Canadian Mounted Police Quarterly

R.1 Cro.
- Croke's King's Bench Reports tempore Elizabeth (1582-1603)
- Croke, Elizabeth

R.2 Cro.
- Croke's King's Bench Reports tempore James I (1603-25)
- Croke, James I.

R.3 Cro.
- Croke's King's Bench Reports tempore Charles I (1625-41)

R.C.S. Remington's Compiled Statutes (1922)

R.C.S. Supp. Remington's Compiled Statutes Supplement

R. (Ct. of Sess.) Rettie,Crawford& Melville Session Cases, 4th Series. (1873-98) (Sc.)

R.C.W.A. Revised Code of Washington Annotated

R.D.
- Reappraisement Decisions
- Regio Decreto (Royal Decree)
- Indian Revenue Decisions

R.D.A. Rules for the Discipline of Attorneys

R.D.A.T. Registered Designs Appeal Tribunal

R.D.B. Research & Development Board (U.S.)

R.D. Int'l. & D. Comp. Revue de Droit International et de Droit Compar

R.D.S. Rural Development Service

R.D. Sup. Revenue Decisions, Supplement (India)

R.D.U.S. Revue de Droit (Universit de Sherbrooke)

Re In the matter of; concerning (Lat.)

REA Rural Electrification Administration (U.S.)

R.E.A. Bull. Rurual Electrification Bulletin

Read Dec. (or Pl.) Read's Declarations and Pleadings

Re-af. Re-affirmed

Real Estate L.J. Real Estate Law Journal

Real Estate Time Shar. Real Estate Time Sharing

Real Est. Comm'n. Real Estate Commission

Real Est. L.J. Real Estate Law Journal

Real Est. L. Rep. Real Estate Law Report

Real Est. Rec. Real Estate Record, New York

Real Est. Rev. Real Estate Review

Real Est. Sec. J. Real Estate Securities Journal

Real Pr. Cas. Real Property Cases (Eng.)

Real Prop. Real Property

Real Prop. Acts Real Property Actions and Proceedings

Real Prop.Cas. Real Property Cases (1843-47)

Real Prop.Prob. & Tr. J. Real Property, Probate & Trust Journal

Real Prop.Prob. & Trust J. Real Property, Probate & Trust Journal

Real Prop. Rep. Real Property Reports

Real Prop. Tax Real Property Tax

REAP Rural Environmental Assistance Program

Reap. Dec. United States Customs Court Reports, Reappraisement Decision (U.S.)

Reapp. Dec. United Stated Customs Court Reports. Reappraisement Decision (U.S.)

R.E.B. Real Estate Brokers' Board

Rec.
- Receipt
- American Law Record
- Ceylon Law Recorder
- Record
- Recorder
- Records

Rec. Ass'n. Bar City of N.Y. Record of the Association of the Bar of the City of New York

Rec. Com. Record Commission

Rec. Comm. Record Commission (Eng.)

Recd. Received

Rec. Dec. Vaux' Recorders Dec. (Pa. 1841-45)

Receiv. Receivers

Rec. L. Recent Law

Rec. Laws Recent Laws in Canada

Recons. Reconsideration

Record Record, Association of the Bar, City of New York

Record of N.Y.C.B.A. Record of the Association of the Bar of the City of New York

RECP Rural Environmental Conservation Program

Rec. St. P. Receiving and transporting stolen property

R.E.D. Russell's Eq. Dec., Nova Scotia

R.E.D.
- New South Wales Reserved Equity Decisions
- Ritchie's Equity Decisions (Russell) (Canada)

Red.
- Redfield's New York Surrogates' Reports
- Redington's Reports (31-35 Maine)
- Redwar's Comments on Ordinances of the Gold Coast Colony (1889-1909) (Ghana)

Red. Am. R. Cas. Redfield's American Railway Cases

Red. Am. R.R. Cas. Redfield's Leading American Railway Cases

Red. & Big. Cas. B. & N. Redfield & Bigelow's Leading Cases on Bills and Notes

Red. Bail. Redfield on Carriers and Bailments

Red. Car. Redfield on Carriers and Bailments

Red. Cas. R.R. Redfield's Leading American Railway Cases

Red. Cas. Wills Redfield's Leading Cases on Wills

Redem. Redemption

Redes. Pl. Redesdale's Treatise upon Equity Pleading

Redf. Redfield's New York Surrogate Reports

Redf. (N.Y.) Redfield's New York Surrogate Reports

Redf. Am. Railw. Cas. Redfield's American Railway Cases

Redf. & B. Redfield & Bigelow's Leading Cases, Eng.

Redf. Carr. Redfield on Carriers and Bailments

Redf. Railways Redfield on Railways

Redf. R. Cas. Redfield's Railway Cases, Eng.

Redf. Sur. (N.Y.) Redfield's New York Surrogate Court Reports

Redf. Surr. Redfield's New York Surrogate Reports

Redf. Surr. (N.Y.) Redfield's New York Surrogate Court Report (5 vols.)

Redf. Wills Redfield's Leading Cases on Wills

Redington Redington's Reports (vols. 31-35 Maine)

Red. Int. L. Reddie. Inquiries in International Law. 2ed. 1851

Redman Redman on Landlord and Tenant

Redm. Arb. Redman on Arbitration

Red. Mar. Com. Reddie, Law of Maritime Commerce. 1841

Red. Mar. Int. L. Reddie, Researches in Maritime International Law (1844-45)

Red. Pr. Redfield's Practice, New York

Red. R. L. Reddie's Roman Law

Red. R.R. Redfield on the Law of Railroads

Red. R.R. Cas. Redfield's Leading American Railway Cases

Red. Sc. L. Reddie, Science of Law. 2ed.

Redwar Redwar's Comments on Ordinances of the Gold Coast (1889-1909) (Ghana)

Red. Wilis Redfield on the Law of Wills

Re. Ohio Decisions Reprint (Ohio)

Reed Reed on Bills of Sale

Reed Am. L.S. Reed's American Law Studies

Reed B.S. Reed on Bills of Sale

Reed Car. Reed on Railways as Carriers

Reed Fraud. Reed's Leading Cases on Statute of Frauds

Reed Pa. Black Reed's Pennsylvania Blackstone

Reed Pr. Sug. Reed's Practical Suggestions for the Management of Lawsuits

Rees' Cyclopaedia Abraham Rees' English Cyclopaedia

Reese Reporter, vols. 5, 11 Heiskell's Tennessee Reports

Reeve Des. Reeve on Descents

Reeve Dom. Rel. Reeve on Domestic Relations

Reeve Eng. L. Reeve's English Law

Reeve, Eng. Law Reeve's History of the English Law

Reeve, Hist. Eng. Law Reeve's History of the English Law

Reeve Sh.   Reeves on the Law of Shipping

Reeves H.E.L.   Reeves' History of English Law

Reeves Hist. Eng. Law   Reeves' History of the English Law

Ref.
- Referee
- Referee's
- Reference
- Referred
- Refining
- Reform
- Refunding

Ref. Dec.   Referee's Decision

Ref. J.   Referees' Journal (Journal of National Association of Referees in Bankruptcy) (Eng.)

Ref.n.r.e.   Refused, not reversible error

Reform. Inst.   Reformation of instruments

Ref. Trib.   Referee Tribunal

Ref. w.m.   Refused, want of merit

Reg.   Regina (Queen)

Reg.
- Register
- The Daily Register, New York City
- Registered
- Registrar
- Registration
- Registration Cases. Registry
- Regulation
- Regulatory

Reg. App.   Registration Appeals (Eng.)

Reg. Brev.   Register of Writs

Reg. Cas.   Registration Cases (Eng.)

Regis. L. T.   Registration of land titles

Regd.   Registered

Reg. Deb.   Gales & Seaton's Register of Debates in Congress (1824-37)

Reg. Deb. (Gales)   Register of Debates in Congress (1789-91) (Gales)

Reg. Deb. (G. & S.)   Gales & Seaton's Register of Debates in Congress (1824-37)

Regent U. L. Rev.   Regent University Law Review

Regent Univ. L. Rev.   Regent University Law Review

Reg. Gen.   Regulae Generales

Regional Rail Reorg. Ct.   Special Court Regional Rail Reorganization Act

Reg. Jud.   Registrum Judiciales, Register of Judicial Writs

Reg. Lib.
- Register Book
- Registrar's Book, Chancery

Reg. Maj.   Books of Regiam Majestatem (Sc.)

Reg. Om. Brev.   Registrum Omnium Brevium

Reg. Orig.   Registrum Originale

Reg. Plac.   Regula Plactiandi

Reg. Pl. (or Plac.)   Regula Placitandi

Regs.   Regulations

Reg. T.M.   Registered Trade Mark

Reg.Writ.   Register of Writs

Reh. allowed Rehearing allowed (used in Shepard's Citations)

Reh. den. Rehearing denied (used in Shepard's Citations)

Reh. dis. Rehearing dismissed (used in Shepard's Citations)

Reh'g. Rehearing

Reid P.L. Dig. Reid's Digest of Scotch Poor Law Cases

Reilly Reilly's English Arbitration Cases

Reilly, E.A. Reilly, European Arbitration, Lord Westbury's Decisions

Rein. reinstated; regulation or order reinstated (used in Shepard's Citations)

REIT Real Estate Investment Trust

Rel. Relations

Rel. & Pub. Order Religion and the Public Order

Relig. Corp. Religious Corporations

Relig. Soc. Religious societies

R.E.L.R. Revised and Expurgated Law Reports (India)

Rem.
- Remittance
- Remitted

Rem. Cr. Tr. Remarkable Criminal Trials

Remd., Rem'd Remanded

Rem'g. Remanding

REMIC Real Estate Mortgage Investment Conduit

Remington, Bankruptcy Remington on Bankruptcy

Remitt. Remittance

Rem. Tr. Cummins & Durphy, Remarkable Trials

Rem. Tr. No. Ch. Benson's Remarkable Trials and Notorious Characters

Remy Remys' Reports (145-162 Indiana; 15-33 Indiana Appellate)

Ren. Renner's Reports, Gold Coast Colony

Renaissance Stud. Renaissance Studies

Renn. Renner, Reports, Notes of Cases Gold Coast Colony and Colony of Nigeria (1861- 1914)

Reorg. Reorganizations

Reorg. Plan No. of year Reorganization Plans (U.S.)

Rep.
- Repealed
- Repeal
- Repertoire
- Report
- Reporter
- Reports
- Representative
- Representing
- Reprint
- Republic(an)
- The Reporter, Boston, Mass.
- The Reporter, Washington, & New York
- Wallace's "The Reporters"
- Coke's English King's Bench Reports
- Knapp's Privy Council Reports (Eng.)

Rep.(1,2, & c.) 1, 2, & c., Coke's English King's Bench Reports

Rep. & Ops. Atty. Gen. Ind. Indiana Attorney General Reports (Ind.)

Rep. Ass. Y. Clayton's Reports of Assizes at Yorke

Rep. Atty. Gen. Attorneys General's Reports (U.S.)

Rep. Att'y. Genl. Reports of Attorney General, United States

Rep. Cas. Eq. Gilbert's Chancery Reports (Eng.)

Rep. Cas. Inc. Tax Reports of Cases relating to Income Tax (1875)

Rep. Cas. Madr. Reports of Cases, Dewanny Adawlut, Madras

Rep. Cas. Pr. Cooke's Practice Cases (1706-47)

Rep. Ch. Reports in Chancery (1615-1710) (Eng.)

Rep. Ch. Pr. Reports on Chancery Practice (Eng.)

Rep. Com. Cas. Commercial Cases, Small Cause Court (Bengal, India) (1851-60)

Rep. Com. Cas. Report of Commercial Cases (1895-1941)

Rep. Const. Ct. South Carolina Constitutional Court Reports

Rep. Cr. L. Com. Reports of Criminal Law Commissioners (Eng.)

Rep. Eq. Gilbert's Reports in Equity (Eng.)

Rep. Fam. L. Reports of Family Law

Rep. Hawaii Att'y Gen. Hawaii Attorney General Report

Rep. in C.A. Court of Appeal Reports (N.Z.)

Rep. in Can. Reports in Chancery, English

Rep. in Ch. Reports in Chancery (21ER)

Rep. in Cn. (Eng.) Reports in Chancery (21 ER)

Rep.in Cha. Bittleston's Chamber Cases (1883-84)

Rep.in C. of A. Reports, Courts of Appeal (New Zealand)

Rep. Jur. Repertorium Juridicum (Eng.)

repl. replacement

Replev. Replevin

Rep. Mass. Att'y Gen. Report of the Attorney General, State of Massachusetts

Rep. M.C. Reports of Municipal Corporations

Rep.N.C. Att'y Gen. North Carolina Attorney General Reports

Rep. Neb. Att'y Gen. Report of the Attorney General of the State of Nebraska

Rep. of Sel.Cas. in Ch. Kelynge's Select Cases in Chancery (1730-32)

Reports Coke's King's Bench Reports (76-77 ER) (1572-1616)

Rep. Pat. Cas. Reports of Patents, Designs and Trade-Mark Cases (Eng.)

Rep. Pat. Des & Tr. Cas. Reports of Patents, Designs & Trademark Cases

Rep. Q.A. Reports temp. Queen Anne (11 Modern Reports)

Repr.
- Representing
- Reprint(ed)

Repr. Acts W. Austl. Reprinted Acts of Western Australia

Reprint English Reports, Full Reprint

Reprod. Reproduct[ion, ive]

Repr. Stat. N.Z. Reprint of the Statutes of New Zealand

Rep. Sel. Cas. Ch. Kelynge's (W.) Reports, English Chancery

Rep.t.F. Reports, Court of Chancery tempore Finch (1673-81)

Rep.t.Finch Reports, Court of Chancery tempore Finch (1673-8 1)

Rep.t.Finch (Eng.) Reports, Court of Chancery tempore Finch, (1673-8 1)

Rep.t.Hard. Lee's Reports tempore Hardwicke, King's Bench (1733-38)

Rep.t.Hardw. Lee's Reports tempore Hardwicke, King's Bench (1733-38)

Rep.t.Holt Reports tempore Holt (English Cases of Settlement)

Rep.t.O.Br. Carter's English Common Pleas Reports tempore O. Bridgman

Rep.t.Q.A. Reports tempore Queen Anne, vol. 11 Modern Reports

Reptr. The Reporter (Boston, Los Angeles, New York, Washington)

Rep.t.Talb. Reports tempore Talbot, English Chancery

Rept.t.Finch Cases temp. Finch (Chancery) (Eng.)

Rept.t.Holt Cases temp. Holt (King's Bench) (Eng.)

Rep.t.Wood Manitoba Reports temp. Wood

Repub. Republic(an)

Rep. York Ass. Clayton's Pleas of Assize at York (Eng.)

Req. Request

Res.
- Research
- Reserve
- Residence
- Resigned
- Resolution of a legislative body
- Resolved
- Resources

Res. & Eq. J. A'Beckett's Reserved Judgments, New South Wales (Aus.) 1845

Res. & Eq. J. Reserved and Equity Judgments (New South Wales)

Res. & Eq. Jud. Reserved and Equity Judgments, New South Wales (1845)

Res. & Eq. Judg. A'Beckett's Reserved Judgments, New South Wales (Aus.) 1845

Res. & Eq. Judgm. Reserved & Equity Judgments (N.S. Wales)

Res. Cas. Reserved Cases (Ir.)

Research L. & Econ. Research in Law and Economics

Reserv. Cas. Reserved Cases (1860-64)

Res. Gamma Eta Gamma Rescript of Gamma Eta Gamma

Res Gestae Res Gestae

Res Ipsa Res Ipsa Loquitur

Res. Jud. Res Judicatae (periodical) (Aus.) (University of Melbourne)

Res Judic. Res Judicatae

Res. L. & Econ. Research in Law and Economics

Res. L. & Soc. Research in Law and Sociology

Res. L. Deviance & Soc. Control Research in Law, Deviance & Social Control

Resol. Resolution

Resp. responsibility

resp.
- respectively
- respondent

RESPA Real Estate Settlement Procedures Act

Resp.Merid. Responsa Meridiana (S. Afr.)

Resp't Respondent

Restit. Restitution

restr. restricted

Rest; Rest. 2d Restatement of the Law (American Law Institute)

Restric. Prac. Reports of Restrictive Practices Cases

Ret. Brev. Retorna Brevium

Retire. & Soc. Sec. Retirement & Social Security

retrosp. retrospectively

Rett. Rettie's Court of Session Cases, 4th Series (Sc.)

Rettie
- Rettie, Crawford & Melville's Session Cases (Sc.)

- Rettie's Court of Session Cases, 4th Series (Sc.)

Rev.
- revision
- Revision of the Statutes Revised

rev.
- Review
- Revised

Rev. & Tax. Revenue & Taxation

Rev. C. & C. Rep. Revenue, Civil, & Criminal Reporter, Calcutta (India)

Rev. Cas. Revenue Cases

Rev. Cas. (Ind.) Revised Cases (India)

Rev. Civ. Code Revised Civil Code

Rev. Civ. St. Revised Civil Statutes

Rev. Code Revised Code

Rev. Code Civ.Proc. Revised Code of Civil Procedure

Rev. Code Cr.Proc. Revised Code of Criminal Procedure

Rev. Col. Ab. P.R. Revista del Colegio de Abogados de Puerto Rico

Rev.Contemp.L. Review of Contemporary Law

Rev.Cont.L. Review of Contemporary Law, Bussels, Belgium

Rev.Cr. Code Revised Criminal Code

Rev'd.
- Revised
- Reversed

Rev. D.P. Revista de Derecho Puertorriqueno

Rev.ed. revised edition

Rev. Gn. Revue Generale de Droit

Rev.Gen.Reg. Revised General Regulation, General Accounting Office (U.S.)

Rev. Ghana L. Review of Ghana Law

Rev.Int'l Comm.Jur. Review of the International Commission of Jurists

Rev. Intl Comm. Jurists Review of the International Commission of Jurists, Geneva, Switzerland

Revised R. (Eng.) Revised Reports

Revised Rep. Revised Reports (Eng.)

Rev. J. & P.J. Revenue, Judicial, & Police Journal (Bengal)

Rev., Jud., & Police J. Revenue, Judicial, and Police Journal

Rev. Jur. U.P.R. Revista Jur-dica de la Universidad de Puerto Rico

Rev. L. Revised Laws

Rev. L. & Soc. Change Review of Law and Social Change

Rev. Laws Revised Laws

Rev. Litig. Review of Litigation

Rev. Litigation Review of Litigation

Rev. Mun. Code Revised Municipal Code

Rev. of Ghana L. Review of Ghana Law, Accra, Ghana

Rev. of Polish Law and Econ. Review of Polish Law and Economics, Warsaw, Poland

Rev. Ord. Revised Ordinances

Rev. Ord. N.W.T. Revised Ordinances, Northwest Territories (Canada) (1888)

Rev. Pen. Code Revised Penal Code

Rev. Pol. Code Revised Political Code

Rev. Pol. L. Review of Polish Law

Rev. Proc. Revenue Procedure (U.S. Internal Revenue Service)

Rev. R. Revised Reports (1759-1866) (Eng.)

REVRA '89 Revenue Reconciliation Act of 1989

REVRA '90 Revenue Reconciliation Acto of 1990

Rev. reh. Reversed on rehearing, or reversing on rehearing (used in Shepard's Citations)

Rev. Rep. Revised Reports (Eng.)

Rev. Rul. Revenue Ruling

Rev. Sec. Reg. Review of Securities Regulation, The

Rev. Sel. Code Leg. Review of Selected Code Legislation

Rev. Socialist L. Review of Socialist Law

Rev. Soc. L. Review of Socialist Law (Neth.)

Rev. St. Revised Statutes

Rev. Stat. Revised Statutes (various jurisdictions)

Rev. Sw. Dig. Revision of Swift's Digest of Connecticut Laws

Rev. Tax. Indiv. Review of Taxation of Individuals

Rev. Tax'n Indiv. Review of Taxation of Individuals

Reyn. Reynolds, Reports (40-42 Mississippi)

Reyn. L. Ins. Reynold's Life Insurance

Reynolds Reynolds, Reports (40-42 Mississippi)

Reynolds' Land Laws Reynold's Spanish and Mexican Land Laws

Reyn. Steph. Reynold's Edition of Stephens on Evidence

RFC Reconstruction Finance Corporation (U.S.)

RFD Rural Free Delivery

RFE/RL Res. Rep. RFE/RL Research Report

R.F.L. Reports of Family Law (Can.)

R.F.L. (2d) Reports of Family Law, Second Series

R.F.P. Request for Proposal

R.G. Regula Generalis (general rule or order of court) (Ontario)

R.G.C.R. Renner's Gold Coast Reports (1868-1914) (Ghana)

R.G.L. Review of Ghana Law.

R.H. Rotuli Hundredorum, Record Commission (Eng.)

R.H.C. Road Haulage Cases (1950-55) (Eng.)

Rh. C.A. Rhodesian Court of Appeal Law Reports (1939-46)

Rh.I.
- Rhode Island Reports
- Rhode Island Supreme Court Reports

R.H.L. Rettie, Scotch Sessions Cases, 4th Series (House of Lord's part)

Rh.L.J. Rhodesian Law Journal

RHOB Rayburn House Office Building

Rhode Island Rep. Rhode Island Reports (R.I.)

Rhodesian L.J. Rhodesian Law Journal

Rho. L. Rhodian Law

R.I.
- Rhode Island
- Rhode Island Reports

R.I.A. Research Institute of America

R.I.A.A. United Nations Reports of International Arbitral Awards

R.I.A. Tax. Research Institute of American Tax Coordinator

R.I.Bd. R.C. Rhode Island Board of Railroad Commission Reports

R.I. B.J. Rhode Island Bar Journal

Ric. Richard (King)

RIC Regulated investment company

Ric. & S. Rickards & Saunders' Locus Standi Reports (1890-94)

Rice Rice's South Carolina Law Reports (1838-39)

Rice Ch. Rice's South Carolina Equity Reports

Rice Dig. Rice, Digest of Patent Office Decisions

Rice Eq. Rice's South Carolina Equity Reports (1838-39)

Rice, Ev. Rice's Law of Evidence

Rice L. (S.C.) Rice, South Carolina Law Reports

Rice's Code Rice's Code of Practice (Colo.)

Rich.
- Richard (King)
- Richardson's South Carolina Law Reports
- Richardson's Reports (vols. 2-5 New Hampshire)

Rich. & H. Richardson & Hook's Street Railway Decisions

Rich. & S. Richardson & Sayles' Select Cases of Procedure without Writ (Selden Soc. Pub. 60)

Rich. & W. Richardson & Woodbury's Reports (2 New Hampshire)

Richardson, Law Practice Richardson's Establishing a Law Practice

Richardson's S. Ca. Rep. Richardson (J.S.G.) Law (S.C.)

Rich. Cas. Richardson's South Carolina Cases (1831-32)

Rich. Cas. (S.C.) Richardson, South Carolina Equity Cases

Rich. Ch. Richardson's South Carolina Equity Reports

Rich. Ch. Pr. Richardson, Chancery Practice. 1838

Rich. C.P. Richardson's Practice Common Pleas (Eng.)

Rich. Ct. Cl. Richardson's Court of Claims Reports

Richd. E. Repts. Richardson (J.S.G.) Equity Reports (S.C.)

Rich. Dict. Richardson's New Dictionary of the English Language

Rich'd. Law R. Richardson(J.S.G.) Law (S.C.)

Rich. Eq. Richardson's South Carolina Equity Reports (1844-46, 1850-68)

Rich. Eq. Cas. Richardson's South Carolina Equity Reports

Rich. Eq. Ch. Richardson's South Carolina Equity Reports

Rich. Land A. Richey, Irish Land Act

Rich. Law (S.C.) Richardson's South Carolina Law Reports

Rich. L. (S.C.) Richardson, South Carolina Law Reports

Rich. N.H. Richardson's Reports (3-5 N.H.)

Rich. N.S. Richardson's South Carolina Reports, New Series

Rich. P.R.C.P. Richardson's Practical Register of Common Pleas (Eng.)

Rich. Pr.K.B. Richardson, Attorney's Practice in the Court of King's Bench. 8ed. 1792

Rich. Pr.Reg. Richardson's Practical Register, English Common Pleas

Rich. Wills Richardson's Law of Testaments and Last Wills

Rick. & M. Rickards & Michael's Locus Standi Reports (Eng.)

Rick. & S. Rickards & Saunders' Locus Standi Reports (Eng.)

Rick. Eng. St. Rickard's English Statutes

RICO
- Racketeering Influenced and Corrupt Organizations
- Roddy, RICO in Business & Commercial Litigation

RICO Bus. Disp. Guide (CCH)
RICO Business Disputes Guide
(Commerce Clearing House)

R.I. Comp. of Rules of St. Agencies Rhode Island Compilation
of Rules of State Agencies

R.I. Const. Rhode Island Constitution

R.I. Ct. Rec. Rhode Island Court
Records

R.I.D.C. Revue internationale de
droit compare

Riddle's Lex. Riddle's Lexicon

R.I. Dec. Rhode Island Decisions

Ridg. Ridgeway's Reports temp.
Hardwicke, Chancery & King's
Bench (Eng.)

Ridg. & Hard. Ridgeway's Report
temp. Hardwicke, Chancery and
King's Bench, Eng.

Ridg. Ap. Ridgeway's Appeal
Cases (Ir.)

Ridg. App. Ridgeway's Appeals
Parliament Cases (Ir.)

Ridg. Cas. Ridgeway's Reports
temp. Hardwicke, Chancery &
King's Bench (Eng.)

Ridgew. Ridgeway's Reports tempore Hardwicke, Chancery &
King's Bench (Eng.)

Ridgew. Ir. P.C. Ridgeway's Parliamentary Reports (1784-96) (Ir.)

Ridgew. L. & S. (Ir.) Ridgeway,
Lapp & Schoales Irish Term Reports

Ridgew.t.Hardw. Ridgeway's Reports tempore Hardwicke, Chancery (1744-46) (27 ER)

Ridgew.t.Hardw. (Eng.) Ridgeway tempore Hardwicke (27 ER)

Ridg. L. & S. Ridgeway, Lapp, &
Schoales' Irish Term Reports

Ridg. Parl. Rep. Ridgeway's Parliamentary Reports (1784-96) (Ir.)

Ridg. P.C. Ridgeway's Appeal
Cases (Ir.)

Ridg. Pr. Rep. Ridgeway's Appeal
(or Parliamentary) Cases (Ir.)

Ridg. Rep. Ridgeway's Reports of
State Trials in Ireland

Ridg. St. Tr. Ridgeway's (Individual) Reports of State Trials in Ireland

Ridg. temp. H. Ridgeway's Reports tempore Hardwicke Chancery (1744-46) (27 ER)

Ridg.t.H. Ridgeway's Reports tempore Hardwicke, Chancery (1744-46) (27 ER)

Ridg.t.Hard. Ridgeway's Reports
tempore Hardwicke, Chancery
and King's Bench (27 ER)

Ridg.t.Hardw. Ridgeway's Reports tempore Hardwicke, Chancery and King's Bench (27 ER)

Ridgw. Ir. P.C. Ridgeway Irish
Appeal or Parliamentary Cases

Ridley, Civil & Ecc. Law
Ridley's Civil and Ecclesiastical
Law

Rid. Sup. Proc. Riddle, Supplementary Proceedings, New York

Ried. Riedell's Reports (68, 69
N.H.)

RIF Reduction in Force

R.I. Gen. Laws General Laws of
Rhode Island

Rigg Select Pleas, Starrs, and other Records from the Rolls of the Exchequer of the Jews, ed. J.M. Riggs (Selden Society Publication, v. 15)

Ril.
- Riley, South Carolina Equity Reports
- Riley's South Carolina Chancery Reports (1836-37)

Ril(ey)
- Riley's Reports (Law & Equity)
- Riley's Reports (37-42 West Virginia)

Riley
- Riley's South Carolina Chancery Reports
- Riley's South Carolina Law Reports
- Riley's Reports (37-42 West Virginia)

Riley Ch. Riley, South Carolina Equity Reports

Riley Eq. Riley, South Carolina Equity Reports

Riley Eq. (S.C.) Riley, South Carolina Equity Reports

Riley L. (S.C.) Riley's South Carolina Law Reports

Ril. Harp. Riley's edition of Harper's South Carolina Reports

Rin. Riner's Reports (2 Wyoming)

Riner Riner's Reports (2 Wyoming)

Ring. Bank. Ringwood, Principles of Bankruptcy. 18ed. 1947

R. Int'l Arb. Awards United Nations Reports of International Arbitral Awards

R.I. Pub. Laws Public Laws of Rhode Island

R.I. P.U.C. Rhode Island Public Utilities Commission

R.I.R.C. Rhode Island Railroad Commission

R.I. Rep. Rhode Island Reports (R.I.)

RIS Regulatory Information System

Risk Issues Health & Safety Risk: Issues in Health & Safety

Ritch.
- Ritchie, Cases decided by Francis Bacon (1617-21)
- Ritchie's Equity Reports, Nova Scotia (1872-82)

Ritch. Eq. Dec. Ritchie's Equity Decisions (Nova Scotia)

Ritch. Eq. Rep. Ritchie's Equity Reports (Nova Scotia)

Ritchie Ritchie's Equity (Canada)

Rits. Cts. Leet Ritson's Jurisdiction of Courts - Leet

Rits. Int. Ritso, Introduction to the Science

Riv. Ann. Reg. Rivington's Annual Register

R.J. New South Wales, Port Phillip District Judgments (Aus.)

R.(J.) Justiciary Cases in vols. of Session Cases (1873-98)

R.J. & P.J. Revenue, Judicial & Police Journal, Calcutta (India)

R.J.R. Mathieu's Quebec Revised Reports

R.J.R.Q. Mathieu's Quebec Revised Reports

R.J.T. Revue Juridique Thmis

R.L.
- Revised Laws

- Roman Law

RLA Railway Labor Act

R.L. & S. Robert, Leaming & Wallis County Court (Eng.)

R.L. & S. Ridgeway, Lapp and Schoales' Irish King's Bench Reports (1793-95)

R.L. & W. Robert, Learning and Wallis' County Court Reports (1849-51)

R.L.B. U.S. Railroad Labor Board Decisions

R.L.B. Dec. Railroad Labor Board Decisions

RLIN Research Libraries Information Network (Bibliographic Utility Network)

R.L.J. Rhodesian Law Journal

R.L.Q.B. Revue Legale Reports, Queen's Bench (Canada)

RLR Rutgers Law Review

R.L.S.C. Revue Legale Reports, Supreme Court (Canada)

Rlty Realtor, Realty

R.L.W. Rajasthan Law Weekly (India)

R.M. Rural Municipality

R.M.C. R.M. Charlton Reports (Ga.)

R.M.C.C. Ryan & Moody's Crown Cases (Eng.)

R.M.C.C.R. Ryan & Moody's Crown Cases (Eng.)

R.M. Ch. R.M.Charlton's Reports (Georgia 1811-37)

R.M. Charlt. (Ga.) R.M. Charlton's Reports (Georgia 1811-37)

R.M. Dig. Rapalje & Mack's Digest of Railway Law

Rmdr. Remainder

R.M.L.R. Rocky Mountain Law Review or University of Colorado Law Review

RMMLF Rocky Mountain Mineral Law Foundation

R.M.M.L.R. Rocky Mountain Mineral Law Review

R.M.R. Rocky Mountain Law Review

Rn. Renumbered; existing article renumbered (used in Shepard's Citations)

R.N.C.A. Rhodesia and Nyasaland Court of Appeal Law Reports

R. N. L.J. Rhodesia and Nyasaland Law Journal

R.N.P. Roscoe's Nisi Prius

Ro.
- Rolle's Abridgment
- Romanian

Rob.
- Robard's Reports (12, 13 Missouri)
- Robards' Conscript Cases, (Texas)
- Roberts' Reports (29-31 Louisiana Annual)
- Robertson's Ecclesiastical Reports (Eng.)
- Robertson's Reports (1 Hawaii)
- Robertson's Reports (24-30 New York Superior) (1863-68)
- Robertson's Scotch Appeal Cases (1707-27)
- Robinson's English Admiralty Reports (1799-1809, 1838-1852)

- Robinson's English Ecclesiastical Reports (1844-53)
- Robinson's Louisiana Reports (1-4 Louisiana Annual; Supreme Court Louisiana 1841-46)
- Robinson's Reports (38 California)
- Robinson's Reports (2-9, 17-23 Colorado Appeals)
- Robinson's Reports (1 Nevada)
- Robinson's Reports (1-8 Ontario)
- Robinson's Reports (40, 41 Virginia)
- Robinson's Scotch Appeal Cases (1840-41)
- Chr. Robinson's Upper Canada Reports
- J.L. Robinson's Upper Canada Reports
- Robbery

Rob. A. C. Robinson's Admiralty Reports (1799-1809)

Rob. Adm.
- C. Robinson's Admiralty Reports (Eng.)
- W. Robinson's Admiralty Reports (Eng.)

Rob. Adm. & Pr. Roberts on Admiralty and Prize

Rob. & J. Robards' & Jackson's Reports (26, 27 Texas)

Rob. App. Robinson's Scotch Appeal Cases (1840-41)

Robards
- Robards' Reports (12, 13 Missouri)
- Robards' Conscript Cases (Texas 1862-65)

Robards & Jackson Robards & Jackson's Reports (vols. 26-27 Texas)

Robb.
- Robbins' Reports (67-70 N.J. Equity)
- Robb's United States Patent Cases

Rob. Bank.
- Robertson, Handbook of Bankers' Law
- Robson, Law and Practice in Bankruptcy. 7ed. 1894

Robb. (N.J.) Robbins' New Jersey Equity Reports

Robb Pat. Cas. Robb's United States Patent Cases

Rob. Cal. Robinson's Reports (38 California)

Rob. Car. V. Robertson's History of the Reign of the Emperor Charles V.

Rob. Cas. Robinson's Scotch Appeal Cases (1840-41)

Rob. Chr. Robinson's Reports (2-9, 17-23 Colorado App.)

Rob. Colo. Robinson's Reports (2-9, 17-23 Colo.App.)

Rob. Cons. Cas. (Tex.) Robards' Conscript Cases

Rob. Consc. Cas. Robards' Texas Conscript Cases

Rob. Dig.
- Robert's Digest, Lower Canada
- Robert's Digest of Vermont Reports

Rob. E. Robertson, English Ecclesiastical Reports (2 vols.) (1844-53)

Rob. Ecc. Robertson, English Ecclesiastical Reports (2 vols.) (1844-53)

Rob. Eccl. Robertson, English Ecclesiastical Reports (2 vols.) (1844-53)

Rob. El. Law Robinson's Elementary Law

Rob. Ent. Robinson's Book of Entries

Rob. Eq. Roberts' Principles of Equity

Robert. Robertson's Scotch Appeal Cases (1707-27)

Robert. App. Robertson's House of Lords Appeals (Sc.)

Robert. App. Cas. Robertson's House of Lords Appeals (Sc.)

Roberts Roberts' Reports (vols. 29-31 Louisiana Annual)

Roberts Emp. Liab. Roberts on Federal Liabilities of Carriers

Robertson
- Robertson's Ecclesiastical Reports (Eng.)
- Robertson's Reports (1 Hawaii)
- Robertson's Reports New York Marine Court)
- Robertson's Reports (24-30) New York Superior
- Robertson's Scotch Appeal Cases (1707-27)

Robertson's Rep. Robertson's Reports (24-30 N.Y. Superior Court)

Rob. Forms Robinson's (Virginia) Forms

Rob. Fr. Roberts, Frauds. 1805

Rob. Fr. Conv. Roberts on Fraudulent Conveyances

Rob. Gav. Robinson, Common Law of Kent, or Custom on Gavelkind. 5ed. 1897

Rob. Hawaii Robinson's Reports (1 Hawaii)

Robin. App. Robinson's House of Lords Appeals (Sc.)

Robin. App. Cas. Robinson's Appeal Cases (H.L.), Sc.

Robin. Sc. App. Robinson's Scotch Appeal Cases (1840-41)

Robinson.
- Chr. Robinson's English Admiralty reports
- W. Robinson's English Admiralty Reports
- Robinson's English Ecclesiastical Reports (1844-53)
- Robinson's Reports (1-12 La.)
- Robinson's Reports (38 California)
- Robinson's Reports (17-23 Colorado)
- Robinson's Reports (Louisiana 1841-46)
- Robinson's Reports (1 Nevada)
- Robinson's Reports (Ontario)
- J.L. Robinson's Upper Canada Reports
- Robinson's House of Lords Appeals (Sc.)
- Robinson's Reports (40-41 Virginia)

Robinson Chr.
- Robinson's Admiralty Reports
- W. Robinson's Admiralty Reports, Eng.
- Robinson's Reports (38 Cal.)
- Robinson's Reports (17-23 Colo.)
- Robinson's Reports (La. 1841-46)
- Robinson's Reports (1 Nev.)
- Robinson's Reports (40-41 Va.)
- Chr. Robinson's Reports, Ontario

- J. L. Robinson's Upper Canada Reports

Robinson Sc. App. Cas. Robinson's Scotch Appeal Cases (1840-41)

Rob. Jun. William Robinson's Admiralty Reports (1838-1852) (Eng.)

Rob. Jus. Robinson, Justice of the Peace. 1836

Rob. La. Robinson's Reports (1-4 La. Annual; La. Supreme Court 1841-46)

Rob.(La. Ann.) Robinson's Reports, (Louisiana Annual, vols. 1-4)

Rob. L. & W. Roberts, Leaming, & Wallis' County Court Reports (1849-51)

Rob. Leg. Robertson, Legitimation by Subsequent Marriage. 1829

Rob. Louis. Robinson's Reports (1-12 La.)

Rob. Mar. (N.Y.) Robertson & Jacob's New York Marine Court Reports

Rob. Mo. Robards' Reports (12, 13 Missouri)

Rob. (Mo.) Robard's Missouri Reports

Rob. (Nev.) Robinson's Reports (Nevada Reports, vol. 1)

Rob. Nev. Robinson's Reports (1 Nevada)

Rob. (N.Y.) Robertson's Reports (New York City Superior Court Reports, vols. 24-30)

Rob. Ont. Robinson's Reports (1-8 Ontario)

Rob. Pat. Robinson on Patents

Rob. Per. Suc. Robertson, Law of Personal Succession. 1836

Rob. Pr. Robinson's Practice (Old or New)

Rob. Prior. Robertson's Law of Priority of Incumbrances

Robs. Bank. Robson, Bankruptcy Practice. 7ed. 1894

Robs. Bankr. Robertson's Handbook of Bankers' Law

Rob. Sc. App. Robinson's Scotch Appeal Cases

Rob. S.I. Robertson's Sandwich Island Reports (1 Hawaii)

Robson. Robson on Bankruptcy, 7 editions (1870-94)

Rob. Sr. Ct. Robertson, New York Superior Court Reports, vols. 24-30

Rob. Succ. Roberts on the Law of Personal Succession

Rob. Super. Ct. Robertson's Reports (24-30 New York Superior Court)

Robt.
- Robert
- Robertson

Robt. Eccl. Robertson's Ecclesiastical Reports (1844-53) (163 ER)

Robt. Eccl. (Eng.) Robertson's English Ecclesiastical (163 ER)

Robt. (N.Y.). Robertson's Reports, New York City Superior Court Reports, vols. 24-30

Robt. Sc. App. Cas. Robertson's Scotch Appeal Cases

Rob. U.C. Robinson's Reports (Upper Canada)

Rob. Va. Robinson's Reports (40, 41 Va.)

Rob. Va. Prac. Robinson's Virginia Practice

Rob. W. Roberts on Wills

Rob. Wm. Adm. Wm. Robinson, English Admiralty Reports (3 vols.) (1838-50)

Roc. New Hampshire Reports (N.H.)

Rocc. Roccus' de Navibus et Naulo (Maritime Law)

Rocc. de Nav. et Nau. Roccus de Navibus et Naulo

Roccus. Ins. Roccus on Insurance

Roche & H. Bank. Roche & Hazlitt, Bankruptcy Practice. 2ed. 1873

Roche D. & K. Roche, Dillon, Kehoe, Land Reports (1881-82) (Ir.)

Roc. Ins. Roccus on Insurance

Rock.
- New Hampshire Reports (N.H.)
- Smith's New Hampshire Reports (N.H.)

Rockingham Smith's New Hampshire Reports (N.H.)

Rock. Min. Rockwell on Mines

Rock. Sp. Law Rockwell's Spanish and Mexican Law Relating to Mines

Rocky Mt. L. Rev. Rocky Mountain Law Review

Rocky Mt. Miner. L. Rev. Rocky Mountain Mineral Law Review

Rocky Mt. Min. L. Inst. Rocky Mountain Mineral Law Institute

Rocky Mt. Min. L. Inst. Proc. Rocky Mountain Mineral Law Institute Proceedings

Rocky Mt. Min. L. Newsl. Rocky Mountain Mineral Law Newsletter

Rocky. Mt. M. L. Inst. Rocky Mountain Mineral Law Institute

Rocky Mtn. Rocky Mountain

Rocky Mtn. L. Rev. Rocky Mountain Law Review

Rocky Mtn. Min. L. Inst. Rocky Mountain Mineral Law Institute

Rodm. Rodman's Reports (78-82 Kentucky)

Rodman. Rodman's Reports (78-82 Kentucky)

Roelk. Man. Roelker's Manual for Notaries and Bankers

Roe U.S. Com. Roe's Manual for United States Commissioners

Rog. C.H.R. Rogers' City Hall Recorder (New York 1816-22)

Rog. Ecc. L. Rogers, Ecclesiastical Law. 5ed. 1857

Rog. Ecc. Law Rogers' Ecclesiastical Law

Rog. Elec. Rogers on Elections and Registration

Rogers.
- Rogers on Elections (2 editions) (1812, 1818-19)
- Rogers' Reports (47-51 Louisiana Annual)

Rog. Hov. Roger de Hovenden, Chronica

Rog. Jud. Acts Rogers on the Judicature Acts

Rog. Min. Rogers on Mines and Minerals

Rog. Rec. Rogers' New City Hall Recorder

Rog. Trav. Rogers' Wrongs and Rights of a Traveller

Rol.
- Rolle; Abridgment (2 vols.)
- Rolle, English King's Bench Reports (2 vols.)

Rol. Ab. Rolle's Abridgment

Roll.
- Roll of the Term
- Rolle, Abridgment (2 vols.)
- Rolle, English King's Bench Reports (2 vols.)

Roll. Abr. Rolle's Abridgment

Rolle.
- Rolle, Abridgment
- Rolle, English King's Bench Reports (2 vols.) (1614-25)

Rolle, Abr. Rolle's Abridgment of the Common Law

Rolle R. Rolle's English King's Bench Reports (2 vols.) (1614-25)

Roll. Rep. Rolle's English King's Bench Reports (2 vols.) (1614-25)

Rolls Ct. Rep. Rolls' Court Reports

Rom.
- Romania
- Romilly's Notes of Chancery Cases (1767-87) (Eng.)

Rom. Cas. Romilly's Notes of Chancery Cases (1767-87) (Eng.)

Rom. Cr. Law Romilly, Observations on the Criminal Law. 3ed. 1813

Romilly N.C. (Eng.) Romilly's Notes of Cases

Rom. Law Mackeldy's Handbook of the Roman Law

R.O.N.W.T. Revised Ordinances, North West Territories (Can.)

Root.
- Root's Connecticut Supreme Court Reports (1789-98)
- Root's Reports (Connecticut 1774-89)

Root Bt. Laws Root, Digest of Law and Practice in Bankruptcy. 1818

Root R. Root's Reports (Conn.)

Roots Root's Reports (Conn.)

Root's Rep. Root's Reports (Conn.)

Root's Reports Root's Reports (Conn.)

ROP Gobert & Cohen, Rights of Prisoners

Rop. Roper on Legacies (4 editions) (1799-1847)

Rop. H. & W. Roper, Law of Property between Husband Wife. 2ed. 1826

Rop. Husb. & Wife Roper on Husband and Wife

Rop. Leg. Roper on Legacies

Rop. Prop. Roper, Property between Husband and Wife. 2ed. 1826

Rop. Rev. Roper on Revocation of Wills

Ro. Rep.
- Rolle's King's Bench Reports (Eng.)
- Robards' Conscript Cases (Texas 1862-65)

Rorer, Jud. Sales. Rorer on Void Judicial Sales

Rorer, R.R. Rorer on Railways

Ror. Int. St. L. Rorer on Inter-State Law

Ror. Jud. Sal. Rorer on Void Judicial Sales

Rosc. Roscoe's Reports of the Supreme Court (1861-78) (S. Afr.)

Rosc. Act. Roscoe, Actions. 1825

Rosc. Adm. Roscoe's Admiralty Jurisdiction and Practice

Rosc. Bdg. Cas. Roscoe, Digest of Building Cases. 4ed. 1900

Rosc. Bills Roscoe, Bills of Exchange. 2ed. 1843

Rosc. Civ. Pr. Roscoe, Outlines of Civil Procedure. 2ed. 1880

Rosc. Cr. Roscoe's Law of Evidence in Criminal Cases, 16 Editions (1835-1952)

Rosc. Crim. Ev. Roscoe's Law of Evidence in Criminal Cases, 16 editions (1835-1952)

Rosc. Ev. Roscoe, Nisi Prius Evidence. 20ed. 1934

Rosc. Jur. Roscoe's Jurist (Eng.)

Rosc. Light Roscoe, Law of Light. 4ed. 1904

Rosc. N.P. Roscoe's Law of Evidence at Nisi Prius, 20 editions (1827-1934)

Roscoe. Roscoe's Reports of Supreme Court of Cape of Good Hope (S. Africa)

Roscoe, Bldg. Cas. Roscoe, Digest of Building Cases (Eng.)

Roscoe, Cr. Ev. Roscoe's Law of Evidence in Criminal Cases, 16 Editions (1835-1952)

Roscoe's B.C. Roscoe's Digest of Building Cases (Eng.)

Rosc. P.C. Roscoe's Prize Cases (1745-1859)

Rosc. Pl. Roscoe, Pleading. 1845

Rosc. R.A. Roscoe on Real Actions

Rosc. St.D. Roscoe on Stamp Duties

Rose. Rose's Reports, English Bankruptcy

Rose Bankr. Rose's Bankruptcy Reports (1810-16)

Rose Bankr. (Eng.) Rose's Reports, English Bankruptcy

Rose B.C. Rose's Reports, English Bankruptcy

Rose Dig. Rose's Digest of Arkansas Reports

Rosenberger Street Railway Law (U.S.)

Rosenberger Pock. L.J. Rosenberger's Pocket Law Journal

Rose Notes. Rose's Notes on United States Reports

Rose's Notes (U.S.) Rose's Notes on U.S. Reports

Rose W.C. Rose Will Case, New York

Ross, Cont. Ross on Contracts

Ross, Conv. Ross' Lectures on Conveyancing, etc. (Sc.)

Ross L.C.
- Ross's Leading Cases in Commercial Law (Eng.)

- Ross's Leading Cases in the Law of Scotland (Land Rights) (1638-1840)

Ross Ldg. Cas.
- Ross's Leading Cases on Commercial Law
- Ross's Leading Cases in the Law of Scotland (Land Rights) (1683-1849)

Ross Lead. Cas.
- Ross' Leading Cases (Eng.)
- Ross's Leading Cases in the Law of Scotland (Land Rights) (1638-1840)

Ross V. & P. Ross, Vendors & Purchasers. 2ed. 1826

ROTC Reserve Officers Training Corps

Rot. Chart. Rotulus Chartarum (The Charter Roll)

Rot. Claus. Rotuli Clause (The Close Roll)

Rot. Cur. Reg. Rotuli Curiae Regis 1194-99

Rot. Flor. Rotae Florentine Reports of the Supreme Court, or Rota, of Florence)

Rot. Parl. Rotulae Parliamentariae

Rot. Pat. Rotuli Patenes

Rot. Plac Rotuli Placitorum

Rotuli Curiae Reg. Rotuli Curiae Regis (Eng.)

Roiund Dom. Round, Law of Domicil. 1861

Round L. & A. Round, Right of Light and Air. 1868

Round Lien Round, Law of Lien. 1863

Rouse Conv. Rouse, Practical Conveyancer, 3ed. 1867

Rouse Cop. Rouse, Copyhold Enfranchisement Manual. 3ed. 1866

Rouse Pr. Mort. Rouse, Precedents and Conveyances of Mortgaged Property

Rowe Rowe's Interesting Cases (England and Ireland) (1798-1823)

Rowe. Rowe's Interesting Parliamentary and Military Cases

Rowell. Rowell's Reports (vols. 45-52 Vermont)

Rowell, El. Cas. Rowell's Contested Election Cases

Row. Eng. Const. Rowland, Manual of the English Constitution. 1859

Rowe Rep. Rowe's Reports (Irish)

Rowe Sci. Jur. Rowe's Scintilla Juris

Rowe's Rep. Rowe's Reports, Eng.

Roy. Dig. Royall's Digest Virginia Reports

Royle Stock Sh. Royle on the Law of Stock Shares, & c.

Rp. Revoked or rescinded in part; existing regulation or order abrogated in part (used in Shepard's Citations)

R.P.
- Rent Regulation (Office of Price Stabilization, Economic Stabilization Agency, U.S.)
- Rotuli Parliamentorum (1278-1533) (Eng.)
- Rules of Procedure
- Rules of Procedure of the Court of Justice

R.P. & W. Rawle, Penrose, & Watts' Reports (Pennsylvania 1828-40)

R. Pat. Cas. Reports of Patent, Design and Trade Mark Cases

R.P.B.S.C. Rules Peculiar to the Business of the Supreme Court

R.P.C.
- Real Property Cases (1843-48) (Eng.)
- Real Property Commissioner's Report (1832) (Eng.)
- Reports of Patent Cases (Eng.)
- Reports of Patent, Design & Trade Mark Cases (Eng.)
- Restrictive Practices Court

R.P.C. Rep. Real Property Commissioner's Report (1832) (Eng.)

R.P.D. & T.M. Cas. Reports of Patent, Design & Trade Mark Cases (UK)

RPHP Rothstein, Rights of Physically Handicapped Persons

RP Jud Pan Mult Lit Rules of Procedure, Judicial panel on Multi-district Litigation

RPL Quail, Real Property Practice and Litigation

RPPL Quail, Real Property Practice and Litigation

R.P.P.P. Rules of Pleading, Practice, and Procedure

RPR Rent Procedural Regulation (Office of Rent Stabilization Economic Stabilization Agency) (U.S.)

R.P.R. Real Property Reports (Can.)

R. Prac. Patent Cases Rules of Practice in Patent Cases

R.P.W. Rawle, Penrose & Watts' Reports (Pennsylvania 1828-40)

R. Q. D. I. Revue Qubcoise de Droit International

R.R.
- Pike and Fischer's Radio Regulations
- Railroad
- Rent Regulation (Office of Rent Stabilization, Economic Stabilization Agency (U.S.)
- Revenue Release
- Revised Reports (Eng.)
- Rural Rehabilitation (U.S.)

R.R. 2d Pike and Fischer's Radio Regulations, Second Series

R.R. & Can. Cas. Railway & Canal Cases (Eng.)

R.R. & Cn. Cas. Railway & Canal Cases (1835-54)

R.R.B. Railroad Retirement Board (U.S.)

R.R.B.L.B. U.S. Railroad Retirement Board Law Bulletin

R.R.C. Ryde's Rating Cases

R.R.Cr.R. Revised Reports, Criminal Rulings (1862-75) (India)

R.R.R. Railroad Reports (U.S.)

R.R.Rep. Railroad Reports

R.R.S. Remington's Revised Statutes

R. Rul. Renegotiations Rulings

R.S.
- Revised Statutes (various jurisdictions)
- Rolls Series

R.S.A.
- Rehabilitaton Services Administration

- Revised Statutes Annotated
- Revised Statutes of Alberta (Can.)

R.S.C.
- Revised Statutes of Canada
- Rules of the Supreme Court (Eng.)

R.S. Comp. Statutes of Connecticut, Compilation of 1854

R.S.F.S.R. Russian Soviet Federative Socialist Republic

R.S.L. Reading on Statute Law

R.S.M. Revised Statutes of Manitoba (Can.)

R.S.N. Revised Statutes of Newfoundland (Can.)

R.S.N.B. Revised Statutes of New Brunswick (Can.)

R.S.N.S. Revised Statutes of Nova Scotia (Can.)

R.S.O. Revised Statutes of Ontario (Can.)

RSOB Russell Senate Office Building (also known as OSOB)

R.S.Q. Revised Statutes of Quebec (Can.)

R.S.S. Revised Statutes of Saskatchewan

R.S. Supp. Supplement of Revised Statutes

RSVP Retired Senior Volunteer Program

RT Turner, Revocable Trusts

RT(2) Turner, Revocable Trusts, Second Edition

rt. right

R.T.A. Road Traffic Act

RTB Rural Telephone Bank

R.t.F. Reports tempore Finch, English Chancery

R.t.H.
- Reports tempore Hardwicke (Eng.)
- Ridgway's Chancery & K.B. Reports, tempore Hardwicke (Eng.)
- Reports of Cases Concerning Settlements, tempore, Holt (Eng.)

R.t.Hardw. Reports tempore Hardwicke, English King's Bench

R.t.Holt. Reports tempore Holt, English King's Bench

Rt. Law Rep. Rent Law Reports (India)

R.t.Q.A. Reports tempore Queen Anne (11 Modern) (Eng.)

R.T.R. Road Traffic Reports

Rt(s). Right (s)

R.t.W. Manitoba Reports tempore Wood

Rub. Rubric

Rub. Conv. Rubinstein, Conveyancing. 5ed. 1884

Rucker Rucker's Reports (43-46 West Va.)

Ruegg Emp. L. Ruegg, Employer's Liability. 9ed. 1922

Ruff.
- Statutes at Large, Ruffhead's Edition (Eng.)
- Ruffhead's edition of the Statutes by Serjeant Runnington (1235-1785)
- Ruffin & Hawks' Reports (8 North Carolina)

Ruff. & H. Ruffin & Hawks' Reports (8 North Carolina)

Ruff. (or Ruffh.)St. Ruffhead's English Statutes

Rul. Cas. Campbell's Ruling Cases (Eng.)

Rules Sup.Ct. Rules of the Supreme Court

Runn.
- Runnell's Reports (38-56 Iowa)
- Statutes at Large, Runnington Ed. (Eng.)

Runn. Eject. Runnington, Ejectment. 2ed. 1820

Runnell. Runnell's Reports (38-56 Iowa)

Runn. Stat. Runnington on Statutes

Rural Elec. Coop. Rural Electric Cooperative

Rus.
- Russell's English Chancery Reports
- Russell's Election Cases (1874) (Nova Scotia)

Rus. & C. Eq. Cas. Russell & Chesley's Equity Cases (N.S.)

Rus. E.C.
- Russell's Election Reports (Ir.)
- Russell's Contested Election Cases (Mass.)

Rus. Elec. Rep. Russell's Election Cases (1874) (Nova Scotia)

Rus. Eq. Rep. Russell's Equity Decisions (Nova Scotia)

Rus. E. R. Russell's Election Cases (1874) (Nova Scotia, Can.)

Rushw. Rushworth's Historical Collections

Russ.
- Russell's English Chancery Reports
- Russell's Contested Election Cases (Mass.)
- Russell's Election Cases (1874) (Nova Scotia, Can.)

Russ. & C. Russell & Chesley' Nova Scotia Reports (NSR 10-12) (1875-79)

Russ. & C. Eq. Cas. Russell's & Chesley's Equity Cases (Nova Scotia)

Russ. & Ches. Russell & Chesley's Reports (Nova Scotia)

Russ. & Ches. Eq. Russell & Chesley's Equity Reports (Nova Scotia)

Russ. & Eq. Russell & Chesley, Equity Reports (Nova Scotia)

Russ. & G. Russell & Geldert's Nova Scotia Reports (NSR 13-27) (1879-95) (Can.)

Russ. & Geld. Russell & Geldert's Reports (Nova Scotia)

Russ. & Jap. P.C. Russian and Japanese Prize Cases (London)

Russ. & M. Russell & Mylne chancery (1829-33) (Eng.)

Russ. & My. Russell and Mylne Chancery (1829-33) (Eng.)

Russ. & R. Russell and Ryan's Crown Cases Reserved (1799-1823) (Eng.)

Russ. & R.C.C. Russell & Ryan's Crown Cases Reserved (168 ER) (1799-1823)

Russ. & R.C.C. (Eng.) Russell and Ryan's Crown Cases Reserved (1799-1823) (Eng.)

Russ. & R. Cr. Cas. Russell and Ryan's English Crown Cases Reserved

Russ. & Ry. Russell & Ryan's English Crown Cases Reserved

Russ. Arb. Russell on Arbitrators

Russ. Ch. Russell's English Chancery Reports

Russ. Con. El. (Mass.) Russell's Contested Elections, Massachusetts

Russ. Cr. Russell on Crimes and Misdemeanors

Russ. Crim, Russell on Crime. 12ed. 1964

Russ. Crimes. Russell on Crimes and Misdemeanors

Russ. El. Cas. Russell's Election Cases (Nova Scotia, Can.) 1874

Russ. Elect. Cas.
- Russell's Election Cases, Massachusetts
- Russell's Election Cases (Nova Scotia)

Russell. Russell's Equity Decisions (Nova Scotia)

Russell N.S. Russell's Nova Scotia Equity Decisions

Russ. Eq. Russell's Equity Cases (Nova Scotia)

Russ. Eq. Cas. Russell's Equity Cases (Nova Scotia)

Russ. Eq. Rep. Russell's Equity Decisions (Nova Scotia)

Russ. Fact. Russell on Factors and Brokers

Russian Rev. Russian Review

Russ. Merc. Ag. Russell on Mercantile Agency

Russ. N.Sc. Russell's Equity Cases (Nova Scotia)

Russ.t.Eld. Russell's English Chancery Reports tempore Elden

Rut.-Cam. Rutgers-Camden

Rut.-Cam. L.J. Rutgers-Camden Law Journal

Rutg. Cas. Rutger-Waddington Case, New York City, 1784

Rutgers-Camden L.J. Rutgers-Camden Law Journal

Rutgers Computer & Tech. L. J. Rutgers Computer and Technology Law Journal

Rutgers J. Comp. & L. Rutgers Journal of Computers and Law

Rutgers J. Computers & Law Rutgers Journal of Computers and the Law

Rutgers J. Computer Tech. & L. Rutgers Journal of Computers Technology and the Law

Rutgers L.J. Rutgers Law Journal

Rutgers L. Rev. Rutgers Law Review

Rutgers U. L. Rev. Rutgers University Law Review

Rutg. L. Rev. Rutgers Law Review

Ruth. Inst. Rutherford's Institutes of Natural Law

Rv. Revised; regulation or order revised (used in Shepard's Citations)

RVDA Fitzgerald, Relative Values: Determining Attorneys' Fees

Rwy Railway

Ry. Railway

Ryan. & M. Ryan and Moody's English Nisi Prius Reports (171 ER)

Ryan. & M. (Eng.) Ryan and Moody's English Nisi Prius Reports (171 ER)

Ry. & Can. Cas. Railway and Canal Cases (Eng.)

Ry. & Can. Tr. Cas Reports of Railway and Canal Traffic Cases (1855-1950)

Ry.& Can. Traf. Ca. Railway and Canal Traffic Cases

Ry. & Can. Traffic Cas. Railway & and Canal Traffic Cases (Eng.)

Ry. & C. Cas. (Eng.) Railway & Canal Cases

Ry. & Corp. Law J. Railway and Corporation Law Journal

Ry. & Corp. Law. Jour. Railway and Corporation Law Journal

Rye & C. Traffic Cas. (Eng.) Railway and Canal Traffic Cases (Eng.)

Ry. & M. Ryan & Moody's Nisi Prius Reports (Eng.)

Ry & M. C.C. Ryan and Moody's Crown Cases Reserved (Eng.)

Ry. & M.N P. Ryan & Moody's Nisi Prius Reports (Eng)

Ry. & Moo. Ryan & Moody (1823-26)

Ry.Cas. Reports of Railway Cases(Eng.)

Ry. Corp. Law Jour. Railway & Corporation Law Journal

Ryde. Ryde's Rating Appeals (1871-1904)

Ryde & K. R Konstam's Reports of Rating Appeals (1894-1904)

Ryde & K. Rat. App. Ryde and Konstam's Reports of Rating Appeals (1894-1904)

Ryde Rat. App. Ryde's Rating Appeals (1871-1904)

Ry. Ed. Jur. Ryan's Medical Jurisprudence

Ry. F. Rymer's Fodera, 20 vols. (1704-35)

Ryl. Plac. Parl. Ryley's Placita Parliamentaria (1290-1307) (Eng.)

Ry. M.C.C. Ryan & Moody Crown Cases (Eng.)

Ry. Med. Jur. Ryan's Medical Jurisprudence

Rym. F. Rymer's Foedera

S

S.
- Saskatchewan
- Scotland
- Scottish
- Searle's Cape of Good Hope Reports (S.Africa)
- Searle's Cases in the Supreme Court (1850-67) (S.Afr.)
- Section
- Senate
- Senate Bill
- Shaw, Dunlop, & Bell's Scotch Court of Session Reports (1st Series)
- Shaw's Court of Session Cases (Sc.)
- Shaw's Scotch House of Lords Appeal Cases
- Solicitor's Opinion
- South(ern)
- Southeastern Reporter (properly cited S.E.)
- Southern Reporter
- Southwestern Reporter (properly cited S.W.)
- Spanish
- Statute
- Superseded; new regulation or order substituted for an existing one (used in Shepard's Citations)
- New York Supplement
- Supreme Court Reporter
- Quebec Superior Court Reports

s.
- Same case; same case as case cited (used in Shepard's Citations)
- see
- Scilicet (to wit)
- Section (of Act of Parliament)

S. New York Supplement

S.2d. New York Supplement, second series

S.A. South Africa
- South African Law Reports
- South Australia

S/A Survivorship agreement

S.A.C. Strategic Air Command

SACB Reports of the Subversive Activities Control Board (U.S,)

Sachse N.M. Sachse's Minutes, Norwich Mayoralty Court

S.A.C.L.R.C. South Australian Criminal Law Reform Committee

Sad. Sadler's Cases (Pa.)

S.A.D. Beng. Select Cases, Sudder Dewanny

S.A.D. Bom. Sudder Dewanny Adawlut Reports (Bombay, India)

Sadler Sadler's Cases (Pa.)

Sadler (Pa.) Sadler's Cases

S.A.D.Mad. Madras Sudder Dewanny Adawlut Reports (1805-62) (India)

S.A.D.N.W.F. Sudder Dewanny Adawlut cases, North West Frontier (Pak.)

Sad. Pa. Cas. Sadley's Cases (Pennsylvania 1885-88)

Sad. Pa. Cs. Sadley's Cases (Pennsylvania 1885-88)

S. Afr. South Africa

S. Afr. Bankers J. The South African Bankers, Journal, Cape Town, South Africa

S. Afr. J. Crim. L. South African Journal of Criminal Law and Criminology

S. Afr. L.J. South African Law Journal

S. Afr. L.R. South African Law Reports

S. Afr. L. R. App. South African Law Reports Appellate

S. Afr. L. Rev. South African Law Review

S. Afr. L. T. South African Law Times

S. Afr. Tax South African Tax Cases

S. Afr. Tax Cas. South African Tax Cases

S. Afr.Y.I. L. South African Yearbook of International Law

S/Ag Supervised Agency

S.A.G. Sentencis arbitrales de griefs (Quebec) 1970-

Saint. Saint's Digest of Registration Cases (Eng.)

Saint Louis Univ. L.J. Saint Louis University Law Journal

S.A.I.R. South Australian Industrial Reports

Sal. Salinger's Reports (88-117 Iowa)

S.A. Law Reports, C.P. South African Law Reports, Cape Provincial Division (1910-46)

S.A. Law Reports, C.P.D. South African Law Reports, Cape Provincial Division (1910-46)

S.A. Law Reports, N.P.D. South African Law Reports, Natal Province Division (1910-46)

S.A. L. Reports,O.P.D. South African Law Reports, Orange Free State Provincial Division (1910-46)

S.A. Law Reports, S.W.A. Reports of the High Court of South-West Africa

Sal. Comp. Cr. Salaman, Liquidation and Composition with Creditors. 2ed. 1882

S.A.L.C.R. South Australian Licensing Court Reports (Aus.)

Sales T. Sales and user taxes

S.A. L.J. South African Law Journal

Salk. Salkeld's King's Bench Reports (91 ER)

Salk. (Eng.) Salkeld's King's Bench Reports (91 ER)

Salm. Abr. Salmon's Abridgment of State Trials

Salm. St. R. Salmon's Edition of the State Trials

S.A.L.R.
- South African Law Reports
- South Australian Law Reports

S.A.L.R.C. South Australian Law Reform Committee

S.A.L.R.C.P. South African Law Reports, Cape Provincial Division (1910-46)

S.A.L.R., S.W.A. South African Law Reports, South West African Reports

S.A.L.T.
- South African Law Times
- Strategic Arms Limitation Talks

Salv. Salvage

S. Am. South America

Samoan Pac. L.J. Samoan Pacific Law Journal

Samoan P. L.J. Samoan Pacific Law Journal

San. Sanford's Reports (59 Alabama)

Sanb. & B. Ann. St. Sanborn and Berryman's Annotated Statutes (Wis.)

San. Ch. Sandford's Chancery Reports (N.Y.)

Sand. Sandford, New York Superior Court Reports, 3-7 New York Superior

S. & A. Saunders and Austin's Locus Standi Reports (1895-1904)

Sand. & H. Dig. Sandels and Hill's Digest of Statutes, Ark.

Sandars, Just. Inst. Sandars' Edition of Justinian's Institutes

S. & B.
- Saunders and Bidder's Locus Standi Reports (1905-19)
- Smith and Batty's Irish King's Bench Reports (1824-25)

S. & C.
- Saunders & Cole's English Bail Court Reports

- Swan & Critchfield, Revised Statutes (Ohio)

Sand. Ch. Sandford's Reports (N.Y. Chancery 1843-47)

Sand. Ch. R. Sandford's Chancery Reports (N.Y.)

Sand. Chy. Sandford, New York Chancery Reports, 4

S. & C. Rev. St. Swan and Critchfield's Revised Statutes, Ohio

S. & D.
- Statutes & Court Decisions (FTC) 1914-1975 (vol. 1-9)
- Shaw, Dunlop, & Bell's Scotch Court of Session Reports (1st series) (1821-38)

Sand. Essays Sanders, Essays on Uses and Trusts. 5ed. 1844

Sandf. Sandford's Reports (3-7 New York Superior)

Sandf. Ch. Sandford's New York Chancery Reports

Sandf. Ch. (N.Y.) Sandford's Reports (3-7 New York Superior)

Sandf. Ch. Rep. Sandford's Chancery Reports (N.Y.)

Sandf. (N.Y.)R. Sandford (Lewis H.)(Superior Court Reports (N.Y.)

Sandford Sandford (Lewis H.) Superior Court Reports (N.Y.)

Sanford's Ch. R. Sandford's Chancery Reports (N.Y.)

Sandford's S.C.R. Sandford (Lewis H.) Superior Court Reports (N.Y.)

Sandford's Sup. Ct. R. Sandford (Lewis H.) Superior Court Reports (N.Y.)

Sandf. R. Sandford (Lewis H.) Superior Court Reports (N.Y.)

Sandf. C. Sandford (Lewis H.) Superior Court Reports (N.Y.)

Sandf. S.C.R. Sandford (Lewis H.) Superior Court Reports (N.Y.)

Sandf. Suc. Sandford. Heritable Succession in Scotland

Sandf. Sup. C.R. Sandford (Lewis H.) Superior Court Reports (N.Y.)

Sandf. Sup. Ct. Sandford (Lewis H.) Superior Court Reports (N.Y.)

Sandf. Superior Court R. Sandford (Lewis H.) Superior Court Reports (N.Y.)

S. & G.
- Smale & Giffard's Vice Chancery Reports (Eng.)
- Stone & Graham's Court of Referees Reports (Eng.)
- Stone & Graham's Private Bills Reports (Eng.)

San. Diego L. Rev. San Diego Law Review

Sand. Inst. Just. Introd. Sandars' Edition of Justinian's Institutes

Sand. I. Rep. Sandwich Islands (Hawaiian) Reports

S. & L. Schoales & Lefroy's Irish Chancery Reports (1802-06)

San. D. L.R. San Diego Law Review

Sandl. St. Pap. Sandler's State Papers

S. & M.
- Shaw & Maclean's House of Lords Cases
- Smedes & Marshall's Reports (9-22 Miss.) (1843-50)

- Smedes & Marshall's Chancery Reports

S. & Mar. Smedes & Marshall's Reports (9-22 Miss.)

S. & Mar. Ch. Smedes & Marshall's Chancery (Miss.)

S. & M. Ch. Smedes & Marshall's Mississippi Chancery Reports

S. & M. Ch. R. Smedes & Marshall's Chancery Reports (Miss.)

S. & M. Ch. Rep. Smedes & Marshall's Chancery Reports

S. & M. Chy. Smedes & Marshall's Mississippi Chancery Reports

S. & P. (Ala.) Rep. Stewart and Porter's Reports (Ala.)

Sand. R. Sandford (Lewis H.) Superior Court Reports (N.Y.)

S. & R. Sergeant & Rawles' Reports (Pa. 1824-28)

S. & R. Neg. Shearman & Redfield on the Law of Negligence

S. & R. on Neg. Shearman and Redfield on Negligence

S. & S.
- Sausse and Scully's Irish Rolls Court Reports (1837-40)
- Searle & Smith's Probate & Divorce Reports (1859-60)
- Simons and Stuart's Vice Chancellors' Reports (1822-26)
- Swan and Sayler, Revised Statutes of Ohio

Sand. S.C. Sandford (Lewis H.) Superior Court Reports (N.Y.)

S. & Sc. Sausse & Scully's Rolls Court (Ir.)

Sands. Ch. Sandford's Chancery Reports (N.Y.)

Sand. S.C.R. Sandford (Lewis H.) Superior Court Reports (N.Y.)

S. & Sm. Searle & Smith's Probate & Divorce Reports (Eng.)

Sand. Sup. Ct. Rep. Sandford (Lewis H.) Superior Court Reports (N.Y.)

Sand. Supr. Ct. R. Sandford (Lewis H.) Superior Court Reports (N.Y.)

S. & T. Swabey and Tristram's Probate and Divorce Reports (1858-65)

Sand. Uses and Trusts. Sanders on Uses and Trusts

Sanf. Sanford's Reports, 59 Alabama

San. Fern. V. San Fernando Valley

San. Fern. V. L. Rev. San Fernando Valley Law Review

San. F. L.J. San Francisco Law Journal

Sanf. (N.Y.) Sanford's Reports (3-7 New York Superior)

San Fran. Law Bull. San Francisco Law Bulletin

San Fran. L.J. San Francisco Law Journal

San Fr. L.B. San Francisco Law Bulletin

San Fr. L.J. San Francisco Law Journal

San. Just. Sanders' Edition of Justinian's Institutes

Santa Clara Computer & High Tech. L. J. Santa Clara Computer & High Technology Law Journal

Santa Clara L. Santa Clara Lawyer

Santa Clara Law. Santa Clara Lawyer

Santa Clara Lawyer Santa Clara Lawyer

Santa Clara L. Rev. Santa Clara Law Review

Santerna de Ass. Santerna de Asse curationibus et Sponsionibus Mercatorum

Santo Tomas L. Rev. University of Santo Tomas Law Review

Sanyal Sanyal's Criminal Cases between Natives and Europeans (1796-1895) (India)

S. App. Shaw's Scottish House of Lords Cases (1821-24)

S.A.P.R. South Australian Planning Reports

Sar. Sarswati's P.C. Judgments (India)

S.A.R.
- South African Republic High Court Reports
- South Australian Reports

Sarat. Ch. Sent. Saratoga Chancery Sentinel (New York) (1841-47)

Sarbah Sarbah, Fantti Law Reports (Gold Coast)

Sarbah F.C. Sarbah, Fantti Customary Laws (Gold Coast)

Sar. Ch. Sen. Saratoga Chancery Sentinel (N.Y.)

Sar. F.C.L. Sarbah, Fanti Customary Laws (Ghana) 2ed. 1904

Sar. F.L.R. Sarbah's Fanti Law Cases (1845-1903) (Ghana)

Sar. F.N.C. Sarbah, Fanti National Constitution (Ghana)

Sask.
- Saskatchewan
- Saskatchewan Law Reports (1907-31) (Canada)

Saskatchewan L. Rev. Saskatchewan Law Review

Sask. Bar Rev. Saskatchewan Bar Review

Sask. B.R. Saskatchewan Bar Review (Can.)

Sask. B. Rev. Saskatchewan Bar Review

Sask. Gaz. Saskatchewan Gazette

Sask. L. Saskatchewan Law

Sask. Law Rev. Saskatchewan Law Review

Sask. L.R. Saskatchewan Law Reports (Canada)

Sask. L.R.C. Saskatchewan Law Reform Commission

Sask. L. Rev. Saskatchewan Law Review

Sask. R. Saskatchewan Law Reports (1980-date)

Sask. Rev. Stat. Saskatchewan Revised Statutes (Canada)

Sask. Stat. Saskatchewan Statutes (Canada)

S.A.S.R. South Australian State Reports

S.A. Tax Cas. South African Tax Cases

S.A.T.C. South African Tax Cases

Sau. All India Reporter, Saurashtra (1950-57)

Sau. & Sc. Sausee & Scully, Rolls Court (1837-40) (Ir.)

Sau. L.R. Saurastra Law Reports (India)

Sauls. Reports time of Saulsbury (5-6 Delaware)

Saund. Saunders' King's Bench Reports (1666-73)

Saund. & A. Saunders and Austin's Locus Standi Reports (1895-1904)

Saund. & Aust. Saunders & Austin, Locus Standi Reports (2)

Saund. & B. Saunders & Bidder's Locus Standi Reports (Eng.)

Saund. & B.C. Saunders and Cole's Bail Court Reports (1846-48)

Saund. & C. Saunders and Cole's Bail Court Reports (1846-48)

Saund. & Cole Saunders & Cole, Bail Court (Eng.)

Saund. & M. Saunders & Macrae's County Courts & Insolvency Cases (County Courts Cases & Appeals, II-III) (Eng.)

Saund. & Mac. Saunders & Macrae's English County Court Cases

Saund. Ass. Saunders, Assault and Battery. 1842

Saund. B.C. Saunders & Cole's Bail Court Reports (1846-48) (82 RR)

Saund. Bast. Saunders, Affiliation Sand Bastardy. 11ed. 1915

Saund. Mag. Pr. Saunders, Magistrates' Courts Practice. 6ed. 1902

Saund. Mil. L. Saunders, Militia Law. 4ed. 1855

Saund. Mun. Reg. Saunders, Municipal Registration. 2ed, 1873

Saund. Neg. Saunders, Negligence. 2ed. 1878

Saund. Pl. & Ev. Saunders Pleading and Evidence

Saund. Prec. Saunders, Precedents of Indictments. 3ed. 1904

Saund. War. Saunders, Warranties and Representations. 1874

Sausse & Sc. Sausse & Scully's Irish Rolls Court Reports (1837-40)

S. Aust. South Australia

S. Aust. Indus. R. South Australia Industrial Reports (1916-date)

S. Austl.
- South Australia
- South Australia State Reports

S. Aust. L. South Australia Law

S. Austl. Acts South Australia Acts (1866-1936)

S. Austl. Acts & Ord. Acts & Ordinances of South Australia 1837-1866

S. Austl. L.R. South Australian Law Reports (1866-1920)

S. Austl. Pub. Gen. Acts Public General Acts of South Australia (1837-1936)

S. Aust. L.R. South Australian Law Reports

S. Austl. Sess. Stat. South Australia Statutes (1936-date)

S. Austl. Stat. South Australian Statutes (1837-1975)

S. Austl. St. R. South Australia State Reports

S. Austr. South Australia

S. Austr. L. South Australia Law

Sav.
- Savile's English Common Pleas Reports
- Savings

Sav. Conf. Law Savigny, Conflict of Laws. 2ed. 1880

Savigny, Hist. Rom. Law Savigny's History of the Roman Law

Savile Savile's Common Pleas Reports (1580-94) (123 ER)

Savile (Eng.) Savile's English Common Pleas Reports (123 ER)

Sav. Pos. Savigny, Possessions. 6ed, 1848

Sav. Priv. Trial of the Savannah Privateers

Saw. Sawyer's Circuit Court Reports (U.S.)

Sawy. Sawyer's U.S. Circuit Court Reports

Sawyer Circt. Sawyer's U.S. Circuit Court Reports

Sawyer U.S. Ct. Rep. Sawyer's U.S. Circuit Court Reports

Sax. Saxton's New Jersey Chancery Reports

Saxt. Saxton's New Jersey Chancery Reports

Saxt. Ch. Saxton's Chancery (N.J.)

Say. Sayer's English King's Bench Reports (96 ER)

Sayer Sayer's King's Bench Reports (1751-56) (96 ER)

Sayer (Eng.) Sayer's English King's Bench Reports (96 ER)

Sayles' Ann. Civ. St. Sayles' Annotated Civil Statutes (Tex.)

Sayles' Civ. St. Sayles' Revised Civil Statutes (Tex.)

Sayles' Rev. Civ. St. Sayles'Revised Civil Statutes (Tex.)

Sayles' St. Sayles' Revised Civil Statutes (Tex.)

Sayles' Supp. Supplement to Sayles' Annotated Civil Statutes (Tex.)

Sayre, Adm. Cas. Sayre's Cases on Admiralty

S.B.
- Senate Bill (in state legislation)
- Small Business
- Special Bulletin, N.Y. Dept. of Labor
- Statute Book
- Supreme Bench

SBA Small Business Administration

SBA State Bar of Arizona

S. Bar J. State Bar Journal of California

S.B.C. Statutes of British Columbia

S. Bell. Bell's House of Lords Appeals (1842-50) (Sc.)

SBF Chase, Shields, Lambert, Baker & Shillito, Small Business Financing

SBIC Small Business Investment Companies

S.B.J. Journal of the State Bar of California

SBLI Southeastern Bankruptcy Law Institute

SBLR Conn. State Board of Labor Relations

SBM State Bar of Montana

SBT Professional Development Program, State Bar of Texas

SC Supreme Court Reporter

S.C.
- All India Reporter, Supreme Court Reports
- Cape of Good Hope Reports (S.Afr.)
- Court of Session Cases (Sc.)
- Juta's Supreme Court Reports (1880-1910) (Cape, S.Afr.)
- Quebec, Official Reports, Superior Court (Can.)
- Same Case
- Select Cases, Oudh (India)
- Senior Counsel
- Session Cases (Sc.)
- South Carolina
- South Carolina Reports
- Standing Committee
- Statutory Committee
- Superior Court
- Supreme Court
- Supreme Court Reporter (National Reporter System)
- United Nations Security Council

Sc.
- Scaccaria (Exchequer)
- Scammon, Illinois Reports, 2-5
- Scandinavia(n)
- Scotch or Scotland
- Scots
- Scottish
- Scott's Reports, English Common Pleas

1907 S.C. Court of Session Cases, Sc.

S.Ca. South Carolina Reports (S.C.)

Scac. Scaccaria Curia (Court of Exchequer)

SC (ACT) Supreme Court(Australian Capital Territory)

S.C. Acts Acts and Joint Resolutions of South Carolina

S. Calif. Law Rev. Southern California Law Review

S. Ca.L.R. Southern California Law Review

S.Cal. L. Rev. Southern California Law Review

S. Cal. Rev. L. & Women's Stud. Southern California Review of Law & Women's Studies

S. Cal. Tax Inst. Southern California Tax Institute

Scam. Scammon's Reports (2-5 Illinois)

Sc. & Div. Law Reports, Scotch and Divorce Appeals

Sc. & Div. App. Scotch and Divorce Appeals (English Law Reports)

Scand. Stud. Criminol. Scandinavian Studies in Criminology

Scand. Stud. in L. Scandinavian Studies in Law. Stockholm, Sweden

Scand. Stud. Law Scandinavian Studies in Law

Scan. Mag. Scandalum Magnatum

SCAP Supreme Commander, Allied Powers

S.Car.
- South Carolina
- South Carolina Reports

S.Car. R. South Carolina Law Reports (S.C.)

Scates' Comp. St. Treat, Scates & Blackwell Compiled Statutes (Ill.)

SCB South Carolina Bar

S.C. Bar Assn. South Carolina Bar Association

S.C.C.
- Scottish Consumer Council
- Select Cases in Chancery tempore King, ed. by Macnaghten (Eng.)
- Small Cause Court (India)
- Supreme Court Cases (India)
- Cameron's supreme Court Cases (Canada)
- Supreme Court ol Canada

S.C. Cas. Supreme Court Cases

S.C. Code Code of Law's of South Carolina

S.C. Code Ann. Code of Laws of South Carolina Annotated

S.C. Const. South Carolina Constitution

Sc. Costs Scott, A.B.C. Guide to Costs. 2ed. 1910

Sc. Cts. Scottish Courts

S.C.D.C. Supreme Court Reports, District of Columbia

S.C.D.C.N.S. Supreme Court Reports, District of Columbia, New Series

S.C. Dig. Cassell's Supreme Court Digest (Canada)

S.C.D. (St.V.) Supreme Court Decisions (St. Vincent) (1928-36)

S.C.E. Select Cases Relating to Evidence, Strange

S.C.Eq. South Carolina Equity Reports

Sch. School[s]

Schalk   Schalk's Jamaica Reports

Sch. & Lef.   Schoales & Lefroy's Irish Chancery Reports

Sch. Aq. R.   Schultes, Aquatic Rights. 1811

Sch. Bailm.   Schouler on Bailment

Sch. Dom. Rel.   Schouler on Domestic Relations

Scheif. Pr.   Scheiffer's Practice

Scher.   Scherer, New York Miscellaneous Reports, 22-47

Sch. H. & W.   Schouler on Husband and Wife

S.C.H.L.   Court of Session Cases, House of Lords (Sc.)

Sch. L. Bull.   School Law Bulletin

Sch. Leg. Rec.   Schuylkill Legal Record (Pa.)

Sch. L.R.   Schuylkill Legal Record (Pa.)

Schm. Civil Law   Schmidt's Civil Law of Spain and Mexico

Schmidt,Civ. Law   Schmidt's Civil Law of Spain and Mexico

Schm. L.J.   Schmidt, Law Journal (New Orleans)

Schoales & L.   Schoales and Lefroy's Irish Chancery Reports

Schomberg, Mar. Laws Rhodes   Schomberg,Treatise on the Maritime Laws of Rhodes

School C.   School Code

School L. Rep.(Nat'l Org.on Legal Probs.in Educ.)   School Law Reporter

School of Advanced Studies Rev.   School of Advanced International Studies Review

School of L.R.   School of Law Review, Toronto University (Can.)

Schoul.   Schouler

Schouler, Bailm.   Schouler on Bailments

Schouler, Dom. Rel.   Schouler on Domestic Relations

Schouler, Pers. Prop.   Schouler on Personal Property

Schouler, U.S. Hist.   Schouler's History of the United States under the Constitution

Schouler, Wills   Schouler on Wills

Sch. Per. Prop.   Schouler on the Law of Personal Property

Sch. Reg.   Schuylkill Register (Pa.)

Schuy. Leg. Rec. (Pa.)   Schuylkill Legal Record

Schuyl. Legal Rec.   Schuylkill Legal Record (Pa.)

Schuyl. Leg. Rec.
- Schuylkill Legal Record, Pottsville, Pa.
- Schuylkill Legal Record (Pa.)

Schuyl. L. Rec.   Schuylkill Legal Record (Pa.)

Schuy. Reg. (Pa.)   Schuylkill Register

Schwarz. Int. L.   Schwarzenberger, International Law

Sci.
- Science(s)
- Scientific

Sci. Am.   Scientific American

Sci. Fa.   Scire facias (revival of judgment)

Sci. fa. ad dis. deb.   Scire facias ad disprobandum debitum

Scil. Scilicet (that is to say)

S.C. in Banco Supreme Court in Banco (Can.)

S.C.Is. Selected Judgments of the Supreme Court of Israel

S.C.,J.
- Court of Justiciary Cases (Sc.)
- Nebraska Supreme Court Journal (Neb.)
- Supreme Court Journal (India)

1907 S.C.,J. Court of Justiciary Cases, Sc.

S.C.J.B. Jamaica Supreme Court Judgment Books

Sc. Jur. Scottish Jurist

S.C.L.
- Santa Clara Lawyer
- Select Cases in Chancery, tempore King (1724-33) (25 ER)
- Society for Computers and Law
- Society of Conservative Lawyers
- South Carolina Law Reports (pre-1868)
- Stock Corporation Law

Sc. La. R. Scottish Land Court Reports, being supplementary to the Scottish Law Review

Sc. La. Rep. Report by the Scottish Land Court

Sc. La. Rep. Ap. Appendices to the Report by the Scottish Land Court

Sc. La. Rep. App. Appendices to Scottish Land Court Reports

SCLF Britton, Shepard's California Legal Filing Directory

S.C. L.J. South Carolina Law Journal

Sc. L.J. Scottish Law Journal and Sheriff Court Record

Sc. L. M. Scottish Law Magazine and Sheriff Court Reporter

S.C. L.Q. South Carolina Law Quarterly

S.C. L.R. South Carolina Law Review

Sc. L.R.
- Scottish Law Reporter
- Scottish Law Review Sheriff Court Reports

Sc. L. Rep. Scottish Law Reporter. Edinburgh

S.C. L. Rev. South Carolina Law Review

Sc. L. T. Scots Law Times

S.C.M. Summary Court-Martial

Sc. Mun. App. Rep. Scotch Munitions Appeals Reports (Edinburgh and Glasgow)

S.C. (Nig.) Judgments of the Supreme Court of Nigeria

Sc. N.R. Scott's New Reports (Eng.)

Sco. Scott's Common Pleas Reports (Eng.)

Sco. & J. Tel. Scott and Jarnigan on the Law of Telegraphs

Sco. Costs Scott, Costs in the High Court. 4ed. 1880

S.C. of A.G. Standing Committee of Commonwealth and State Attorneys-General

Sco. Int. Scott's Intestate Laws

SCOLAG Scottish Legal Action Group

SCOLAG Bull. Scottish Legal Action Group Bulletin

Sco. Nat.   Scott on Naturalization of Aliens

Sco. N. R.   Scott's New Reports, Com. Pleas (Eng.)

S. Con. Res.
- Senate Concurrent Resolution
- U.S. Senate Concurrent Resolution

SCOR   Security Council Official Records

SCORE   Service Corps of Retired Executives

Scot.
- Scotland
- Scots
- Scottish

Scot. App. Rep.   Scottish Appeal Reports

Scot. Jur.   Scottish Jurist

Scot. Law. Com.   Scottish Law Commission

Scot. Law J.   Scottish Law Journal (Glasgow)

Scot. L.J.   Scottish Law Journal & Sheriff Court Record

Scot. L. M.   Scottish Law Magazine & Sheriff Court Reporter

Scot. L. Mag.   Scottish Law Magazine, Edinburgh, Scotland

Scot. L.R.
- Scottish Law Reporter
- Scottish Law Review

Scot. L. Rep.   Scottish Law Reporter

Scot. L. Rev.   Scottish Law Review and Sheriff Court Reports

Scot. L.T.   Scots Law Times

Scot. Parl. Acts   The Acts of the Parliaments of Scotland (1124-1707) (1814-1875)

Scots L.T.   Scots Law Times

Scots L.T.R.   Scots Law Times Reports

Scots R.R.   Scots Revised (1707-1873)

Scott
- Scott's Common Pleas Reports (Eng.)
- Scott's Reports (25, 26 N.Y. Civil Procedure)

Scott (Eng.)   Scott's Reports

Scott J.   Reporter, English Common Pleas Reports

Scott N.R.   Scott's New Common Pleas Reports (Eng.)

S.C. Oudh.   Oudh Select Cases (India)

S.C.P.S.C.   South Carolina Public Service Commission Reports

S.C.R.
- Cape Colony Supreme Court Reports
- Law Reports of Supreme Court of Sarawak, North Borneo and Brunei
- South Carolina Reports
- Supreme Court Reports (Can.)
- Supreme Court Reports (India)

S.C.R.
- Canada: Supreme Court Reports (1876-date)
- Juta's Supreme Court Cases (1880-1910) (Cape, S.A.)
- Supreme Court Reports (1862-76) (N.S.W., Aus.)
- Supreme Court Reports (1928-41, 1946-51) (Sarawak)

Scrat. & Bra. Scratchley & Brabook, Building Societies. 2ed. 1882

Scrat. Bdg. Soc. Scratchley, Building Societies. 5ed. 1883

Scrat. Life Ass. Scratchley, Life Assurance. 13ed. 1887

S.C. Rep. Juta's Supreme Court Cases (1880-1910) (Cape, S.A.)

S.C. Res. Senate Concurrent Resolution

Sc. Rev. Rept. Scots Revised Reports

Scrib. Dow. Scribner on the Law of Dower

SCRIBES Scribes, The American Society of Writers on Legal Subjects

Scribes J. Legal Writing Scribes Journal of Legal Writing

Scriv. Cop. Scriven, Copyholds. 7ed. 1896

Scriven Scriven, Law of Copyholds

Scr. L.T. Scranton (Pa.) Law Times

S.C.R. (N.S.) (N.S.W.) Supreme Court Reports (New Series) (1878-79) (N.S.W., Aus.)

S.C.R. (N.S.) (N.S.W.) Eq. Supreme Court Reports, Equity (1862-79) (N.S.W., Aus.)

S.C.R. (N.S.) (N.S.W.) (L.) Supreme Court Reports, Law (1862-79) (N.S.W., Aus.)

S.C.R.N.S.W. New South Wales Supreme Court Reports

S.C.R. (NSW) Eq Supreme Court Reports (New South Wales), Equity

S.C.R. (Q) Queensland Supreme Court Reports (1860-81)(Aus.)

Sc. R.R. Scotch Revised Reports

Scrut.Charter Scrutton, Charterparties. 18ed. 1974

Scrutton Scrutton on Charterparties. 16 editions (1886-1955)

S.C.S. Soil Conservation Service

S.C. (Scot.) Scottish Court of Session Cases, New Series

Sc. Sess. Cas. Scotch Court of Session Cases

S.C.S.S. Scottish Council of Social Service

Sc. St. Crim. Scandinavian Studies in Criminology

Sc. St. L. Scandinavian Studies in Law

Sc. Stud. Criminol. Scandinavian Studies in Criminology. 1965-

Sc. Stud. Law Scandinavian Studies in Law

SCT Le & Murphy, Sales and Credit Transactions Handbook

S.Ct.
- Supreme Court
- Supreme Court Reporter

S.C. (T. & C.) Thompson and Cook's New York Supreme Court Reports (N.Y.)

S. Ct. Bull. (CCH) United States Supreme Court Bulletin (Commerce Clearing House)

S.C.T.I. University of Southern California Tax Institute

S. Ct. Rev. Supreme Court Review

S Ct Rule Revised Rules of the Supreme Court of the United States

S. Ct. Vict. Reports of Cases - Supreme Court of Victoria (1861-69) (Aus.)

S.C.U.C.C.Dec. South Carolina Unemployment Compensation Commission Decisions

S.C.U.C.C.R. South Carolina Unemployment Compensation Commission Reports of Hearings

S.C. (W.A.) Supreme Court (Western Australia)

Sd. Suspended; regulation or order suspended (used in Shepard's Citations)

S.D.
- Sadr Diwani Adalat Court, Bengal (India)
- South Dakota
- South Dakota Compiled Laws Annotated
- South Dakota Reports
- Southern District

S.D.
- Decisions of the Sudder Court (1845-62) (Bengal, India)
- State Department (U.S.)

S.D.A.
- Special Disbursing Agent, Bureau of Indian Affairs (U.S.)
- Sudder Dewanny Adawalut Reports, India

S.D. Admin. R. Administrative Rules of South Dakota

S.D. Admin. Reg. South Dakota Register

S. Dak.
- South Dakota
- South Dakota Reports

S.D. Ala. United States District Court for the Southern District of Alabama

S.D. & B. Shaw, Dunlop, & Bell's Session Reports (1821-38) (Sc.)

S.D. & B. Sup. Shaw, Dunlop, & Bell's Supplement, containing House of Lords Decisions

S.D. & B. Supp. Shaw, Dunlop, & Bell's Supplement, containing House of Lords Decisions (Sc.)

SDB State Bar of South Dakota

S.D. B. Jo. South Dakota Bar Journal

S.D.C. Supreme Court, District of Columbia Reports; New Series

S.D. Cal. United States District court for the Southern District of California

SDCL South Dakota Compiled Laws

S.D. Codified Laws South Dakota Codified Laws

S.D. Codified Laws Ann. South Dakota Codified Laws Annotated

S.D.Compiled Laws Ann. South Dakota Compiled Laws Annotated

S.D. Comp. Laws Ann. South Dakota Compiled Laws Annotated

S.D. Const. South Dakota Constitution

S.D. Fln. United States District Court for the Southern District of Florida

S.D. Ga. United States District Court for the Southern District of Georgia

S.D. Ill. United States District Court for the Southern District of Illinois

S.D. Ind. United States District Court for the Southern District of Indiana

S.D. Iowa United States District Court for the Southern District of Iowa

S.D.K. Si De Ka Quarterly (Ann Arbor, Mich.)

S.D. L. Rev. South Dakota Law Review

S.D. Miss. United States District Court for the Southern District of Mississippi

S.D. N.Y. United States District Court for the Southern District of New York

S.Doc. Senate Document

S.D. Ohio United States District Court for the Southern District of Ohio

Sdp. Suspended in part; regulation or order suspended in part

S.D.P.A. Small Defense Plants Administration (U.S.)

S.D.R. New York State Department Reports

S.D.R.C. South Dakota Railroad Commission

S.D.R.C. Ops. South Dakota Board of Railroad Commissioners Opinions

S.D. Sess. Laws South Dakota Session Laws

S.D. St. B.J. South Dakota State Bar Journal

S.D. Tex. United States District Court for the Southern District of Texas

S.D. Uniform Prob. Code South Dakota Uniform Probate Code

SDWA Safe Drinking Water Act

S.D. W.Va United States District Court for the Southern District of West Virginia

S.E.
- Southeastern Reporter, National Reporter System
- South East

S.E.2d. Southeastern Reporter, Second Series

Sea. & Sm. Searle & Smith's Probate & Divorce Reports (Eng.)

Seab. Vend. Seaborne on Vendors

Seag. Parl. Reg. Seager on Parliamentary Registration

Sea Grant L.J. Sea Grant Law Journal

Sea Grant L. & Pol'y J. Sea Grant Law and Policy Journal

Search & Seizure Bull. (Quinlan) Search & Seizure Bulletin

Search & Seizure L. Rep. Search and Seizure Law Report

Searle Searle's Supreme Court Reports, Cape Colony (1850-67)

Searle & Sm. Searle & Smith's Probate & Divorce Reports (1859-60)

Searle Dig. Searle, Minnesota Digest

Searle Sm. Searle & Smith's English Probate and Divorce Reports

Seat. F. Ch. Seaton's Forms in Chancery

SEATO Southeast Asia Treaty Organization

Sea.Vend. Seaborne, Vendors & Purchasers. 9ed. 1926

Seb. Trade-marks Sebastisan on Trademarks

Seb. Tr. M. Sebastian, Trade Marks. 5ed. 1911

Sec.
- Section
- Secus (otherwise)
- Secundum
- Securities

sec. section(s)

S.E.C. Securities and Exchange Commission Decisions and Reports

SEC Accounting R. (CCH) SEC Accounting Rules

Sec. & Ex. C. Securities & Exchange Commission

Sec. & Fed. Corp. L. Rep. (Clark Boardman) Securities and Federal Corporate Law Report

Sec. Bk. Judg. Second Book of Judgments (Huxley) (Eng.)

SEC Compl. (P-H) Securities and Exchange Commission compliance (Prentice-Hall)

S.E.C. Docket Securities and Exchange Commission Docket

Secd.pt.Edw.III Year Books, Part III (Eng.)

Secd.pt.H.VI Year Books, Part VIII (Eng.)

Sec. Int. Secretary of the Interior (U.S.)

S.E.C. Jud. Dec. Securities & Exchange Commission Judicial Decisions

Sec.leg. Secundum legum (according to law)

Sec. L. Rev. Securities Law Review

Sec. of State Secretary of State

Sec. reg. Secundum regulam (according to rule)

Sec. Reg. & L. Rep. (BNA) Securities Regulation & Law Report(s) (BNA)

Sec. Reg. & Trans. Securities Regulations and Transfer Report

Sec. Reg. Guide (P-H) Securities Regulation Guide (P-H)

Sec. Reg. L.J. Securities Regulation Law Journal

secs. section(s)

Sect. Section

Secur. Reg. Fed. Securities regulation - federal

Secur. Reg. St. Securities regulation - state

Secured Trans. Secured transactions

Secured Transactions Guide (CCH) Secured Transactions Guide

Secy Secretary

Sedg. & W. Tit. Sedgwick and Wait on the Trial of Title to Land

Sedg. & W. Tr. Title Land Sedgwick and Wait on the Trial of Title to Land

Sedg. Dam. Sedgwick on the Measure of Damage

Sedg. L. Cas.
- Sedgwick's Leading Cases on Damages
- Sedgwick's Leading Cases on Real Property

Sedg. St. & Const. Law Sedgwick on Statutory and Constitutional Law

Sedg. Stat. Law Sedgwick on Statutory and Constitutional Law

Sedit. Sedition, subversive activities and treason

Seduc. Seduction

Seign. Rep. Lower Canada Seigniorial Reports

S.E.I.U. Service Employees' International Union (AFL-CIO)

SELA Latin American Economic System

Sel. App. Beng. Selected Appeals, Sudder Dewanny Adawlut (Bengal, India)

Sel. Cas. Select Cases Central Provinces (India)

Sel. Cas. Ch. Select Cases in Chancery (Eng.)

Sel. Cas. Ch. (t.King) Select Cases in Chancery tempore King (1724-33) (25 ER)

Sel. Cas. D.A. Select Cases Sadr Diwani Adalat (India)

Sel. Cas. Ev. Select Cases in Evidence (Strange) (Eng.)

Sel. Cas. K.B. Edw.I. Select Cases in K.B. under Edward I (Sayles) (Eng.)

Sel. Cas. N.F. Select Cases, Newfoundland

Sel. Cas. N.W.P. Select Cases, Northwest Provinces (India)

Sel. Cas. N.Y. Yates' Select Cases (N.Y. 1809)

Sel. Cas. S.D.A. Select Cases Sadr Diwani Adalat (Bengal, Bombay) (India)

Sel. Cas.t.Br. Cooper's Select Cases tempore Brougham

Sel. Cas.t.King Select Cases in Chancery tempore King (Eng.)

Sel. Cas.t.Nap. Select Cases tempore Napier (Ir.)

Sel. Cas. with Opin. Select Cases with Opinions, by a Solicitor

Sel. Ca.t.King Select Cases in Chancery ternpore King (1724-33) (25 ER)

Sel. Ch. Cas. Select Cases in Chancery tempore King, ed. Macnaghten (Eng.)

Sel. Col. Cas. Select Collection of Cases (Eng.)

Sel. Com. Select Committee

Seld. Selden's Reports (5-10 N.Y.)

Sel. Dec. Bomb. Select Cases Sadr Diwani Adalat, Bombay (India)

Sel. Dec. Madr. Select Decrees, Sadr Adalat, Madras (India)

Selden Selden (Henry R.) Court of Appeals Reports (N.Y.)

Selden Notes Selden, New York Court of Appeals Notes of Cases (July 13, 1853, First Edition) (N.Y.)

Seld Fl. Seld's Dissertation, Annexed to Fleta

Seld. J.P. Selden, Judicature in Parliaments. 1681

Seld. Mar. Cl. Seldon's Mare Clausum

Seld. Mare Claus. Selden's Mare Clausum

Seld. Notes Selden's Notes, N.Y. Court of Appeals

Seld. Off. Ch. Selden's Office of Chancellor

Seld. R. Selden (Henry R.) Court of Appeals Reports (N.Y.)

Seld. Soc. Selden Society

Seld. Soc. Yrbk. Selden Society Yearbook (U.S.)

Seld. Tit. Hon. Selden's Titles of Honor

Self. Tr. Selfridge's Trial

Sel. L. Cas. Select Law Cases (Eng.)

Sell. Pr. Sellon's Practice in the King's Bench

Sell. Prac. Sellon's Practice in the King's Bench

Sel. N.P. Selwyn's Law of Nisi Prius

Sel. Off. Ch. Selden, Office of Lord Chancellor, 1671

Sel. Pr. Sellon's Practice

Sel. Serv. L. Rep. Selective Service Law Reporter

Sel. Serv. L. Rptr. Selective Service Law Reporter

Selw. Selwyn's Nisi Prius, Eng.

Selw. & Barn. Barnewall & Alderson's K.B. Reports, 1st part (Eng.)

Selw. N.P. Selwyn Law of Nisi Prius (Eng.)

Sem. (or Semb.) Semble (it seems)

Sen.
- Senegal
- Senator

Sen. Doc. Senate Document

Sen. J. Senate Journal

Sen. Jo. Senate Journal

Sen. Rep.
- Senate Report
- United States Senate Committee Report

Sen. Rept. U.S. Senate Committee Report

Seoul L.J. Seoul Law Journal

SEP Simplified employee pension

Seques. Sequstration

ser. series, serial(s)

Ser. Series

Serg. & Lowb. English Common Law Reports, ed. Sergeant & Lowber

Serg. & Lowb.Rep. English Common Law Reports, American reprints edited by Sergeant & Lowber

Serg. & R. Sergeant & Rawle's Pennsylvania Reports

Serg. & Raw. Sergeant & Rawle's Pennsylvania Reports

Serg. & Rawl. Sergeant and Rawle's Pennsylvania Supreme Court Reports (1814-28)

Serg. Att. Sergeant on Attachment

Serg. Const. L. Sergeant's Constitutional Law

Serg. Land Laws Pa. Sergeant on the Land Laws of Pennsylvania

Serg. L.L. Sergeant's Land Laws of Pennsylvania

Serg. Mech. L. Sergeant on Mechanics' Lien Law

Serv. Service

SESA Social and Economic Statistics Administration

Sess. Session

Sess. Acts Session Acts

Sess. Ca.
- Scotch Court of Session Cases
- Sessions Cases King's Bench (1710-48) (Eng.)

Sess. Cas.
- Scotch Court of Session Cases
- Session Cases, High Court of Justiciary Section (1906-16) (Sc.)
- Sessions Cases, King's Bench (Eng.)
- Session Cases (Sc.)
- S. 1st Series (Shaw) (1821-38)
- D. 2nd Series (Dunlop) (1838-62)
- M 3rd Series (Macpherson) (1862-73)
- R. 4th Series (Rettie) (1873-98)
- F. 5th Series (Fraser) (1898-1906)
- (6 Ser.) 6th Series.

Sess. Cas. K.B. Sessions Settlement Cases, King's Bench (Eng.)

Sess. Cas. Sc. Scotch Court of Session Cases

Sess. Laws Session Laws

Sess. N. Session Notes (Sc.)

Sess. Pap. C.C.C. Central Criminal Court Session Papers (Eng.)

Sess. Pap. O. B. Old Bailey Session Papers

Set. English Settlement and Removal Cases (Burrow's Settlement Cases)

Seton Seton on Decrees, 7editions (1830-1912)

Seton Dec. Seton, Forms of Decrees, Judgments and Orders in Equity. 7ed. 1912

Seton Hall Const. L. J. Seton Hall Constitutional Law Journal

Seton Hall J. Sport Law Seton Hall Journal of Sport Law

Seton Hall Leg. J. Seton Hall Legislative Journal

Seton Hall L. Rev. Seton Hall Law Review

Seton Hall Legis. J. Seton Hall Legislative Journal

Sett. Settlement Cases

Sett. & Rem. Settlement & Removals Cases in Kings Bench (Eng.)

Sett. Cas.
- Settlements & Removals, Cases in Kings Bench (Eng.)
- Burrow's Settlement Cases (Eng.)

Sev. App. Cas. Sevestre's Appeal Cases, High Court (1864-68) (Bengal, India)

Sevestre Calcutta Reports of Cases in Appeal

Sev. H.C. Sevestre's Bengal High Court Reports (India)

Sev. S.D.A. Sevestre's Sadr Diwani Adalat Reports, Bengal (India)

Sew. Cor. Sewell, Coroners. 1843

Sewell, Sheriffs   Sewell on the
Law of Sheriffs

Sew. Sh.   Sewell, Sheriff. 1842

S. Exec. Doc.   Senate Executive
Document

S. Exec. Rep.   Senate Executive
Report

Sex. L. R.   Sexual Law Reporter

Sex. L. Rep.   Sexual Law Reporter

Sex Prob. Ct. Dig.   Sex Problems
Court Digest

Sey.   Seychelles

Seych. L. R.   Seychelles Law Reports

Sey. Merch. Sh.   Seymour, Merchant Shipping Acts. 2ed. 1857

S.F.
- San Francisco
- Sinking Fund
- Standard Form

S.F.A.   Sudder Foujdaree Adawlut
Reports (India)

SFCF   Bromberg & Lowenfels, Securities Fraud and Commodities
Fraud

SFLF   Hill, Shepard's Florida Legal Filing Directory

S.F. L.J.   San Francisco Law Journal

SFLR   University of San Francisco
Law Review

SFO   Defense Solid Fuels Order
(U.S.)

S.F.S.   Sine fraude sua (without
fraud on his part)

S.G.   Solicitor General

Sg.   Supplementing; new matter
added to an existing regulation

or order (used in Shepard's Citations)

S. Georg. & S. Sandwich Is.
South Georgia and the South
Sandwich Islands

Sh.
- Shadforth's Reserved Judgments (Aus.)
- Shand's Reports (11-41 South
  Carolina)
- Shaw's Appeal Cases (Sc.)
- Shaw's Session Cases (Sc.)
- Shaw's Scotch Justiciary Cases
- Shaw's Teind Court Reports
  (Sc.)
- G.B. Shaw's Reports (10, 11 Vermont)
- W.G. Shaw's Reports (30-35 Vermont)
- Sheil's Cape Times Law Reports
  (S. Africa)
- Sheldon's Reports (Buffalo, N.Y.
  Superior Court)
- Shepherd's Alabama Reports
- Shepley's Reports (13-18, 21-30
  Maine)
- Sheriff
- Shipp's Reports (66, 67 North
  Carolina)
- Shirley's Reports (49-55 New
  Hampshire)
- Shower's King's Bench Reports
  (Eng.)
- Shower's Parliamentary Cases
  (Eng.)

S.H.A.   Smith-Hund Illinois Annotated Statutes

Sh. Acc.   Hale's Sheriff's Account

Shad.   Shadforth's Reports (Aus.)

Shale   Decrees & Judgments in
Federal Anti-Trust Cases (U.S.)

Shan. Shannon's Unreported Cases (Tenn.)

Shan. Cas. Shannon's Tennessee Cases

Shand Shand's Reports (11-41 South Carolina)

Sh. & Dunl. Shaw & Dunlop's Scotch Court of Session Reports (1st Series)

Sh. & Macl. Shaw & Maclean's Scotch Appeal Cases

Shand Pr. Shand, Practice, Court of Sessions (Sc.)

Sh. & R. Neg. Shearman & Redfield on Negligence

Shankland's St. Shankland's Public Statutes (Tenn.)

Shannon Cas. (Tenn.) Shannon's Unreported Tennessee Cases

Shannon's Code Shannon's Annotated Code (Tenn.)

SHAPE Supreme Headquarters, Allied Powers in Europe

Sh. App. Shaw's House of Lords Appeal Cases (Sc.)

Shark. Elec. Sharkey, Practice of Election Committees. 2ed. 1866

Sharp. Cong. Ct. Sharp on Congregational Courts

Sharpe Calendar of Coroners Rolls of the City of London

Sharp. Ins. Dig. Sharpstein's Insurance Digest

Shars. & B. Lead. Cas. Real Prop. Sharswood and Budd's Leading Cases of Real Property

Shars. Black. Sharswood's edition of Blackstone's Commentaries

Shars. Bl. Comm. Sharswood's Blackstone's Commentaries

Shars. Comm. L. Sharswood's Commercial Law

Shars. Law Lec. Sharswood's Lectures on the Profession of the Law

Shars. Leg. Eth. Sharswood's Legal Ethics

Shars. Tab. Ca. Sharswood's Table of Cases, Connecticut

Shaw
- Shaw's Scotch Appeal Cases
- Shaw's Court of Session Cases, 1st Series
- Shaw's Justiciary Cases (Sc.)
- Shaw's Teind Court Reports (Sc.)
- G.B. Shaw's Reports (10, 11 Vermont)
- W.G. Shaw's Reports (30-35 Vermont)

Shaw & D. Shaw & Dunlop's Court of Session Reports, 1st Series (Sc.)

Shaw & Dunl. Shaw & Dunlop's Court of Session Reports, 1st Series (Sc.)

Shaw & M. Shaw & Maclean's Scotch Appeal Cases

Shaw & Macl. Shaw & Maclean's Scotch Appeal Cases

Shaw & M. Sc. App. Cas. Shaw & Maclean's Scotch Appeal Cases (1835-38)

Shaw & M. Sc. App. Cas. (Scot.) Shaw & Maclean's Scotch Appeal Cases

Shaw App. Shaw's Appeal Cases, English House of Lords, Appeals from Scotland

Shaw Crim. Cas. Shaw's Criminal Cases, Justiciary Court (Sc.)

Shaw, D. & B. Shaw, Dunlop & Bell's Court of Sessions (1st Series) (Sc.)

Shaw, D. & B. Supp. Shaw, Dunlop, & Bell's Supplement, House of Lords Decisions (Sc.)

Shaw Dec. Shaw's Decisions in Scotch Court of Sessions (1st Series)

Shaw Dig. Shaw's Digest of Decisions (Sc.)

Shaw, Dunl. & B. Shaw, Dunlop and Bell, Session Cases (1821-38) (Sc.)

Shaw Ell. Ins. Shaw's Ellis on Insurance

Shaw (G.B.) G.B. Shaw's Reports (10, 11 Vermont)

Shaw, H.L. Shaw's Scotch Appeal Cases, House of Lords (1821-24)

Shaw, J. John Shaw's Justiciary Cases (1848-52) (Sc.)

Shaw Jus. John Shaw's Justiciary Cases (1848-52) (Sc.)

Shaw, P. Patrick Shaw, Justiciary Cases (1819-31) (Sc.)

Shaw P.L. Shaw's Parish Law

Shaw Sc. App. Cas. Shaw's Scotch Appeal Cases, House of Lords (1821-24)

Shaw Sc. App. Cas. (Scot.) Shaw's Scotch Appeal Cases, House of Lords

Shaw T.C. Shaw, Teind Cases (1821-31) (Sc.)

Shaw T. Cas. Shaw's Scotch Teind Court Reports

Shaw Teind Shaw's Teind Court Decisions (1821-31)

Shaw. (Vt.)
- G.B. Shaw's Vermont Reports (10, 11 vt.)
- W.G. Shaw's Vermont Reports (30, 35 Vt.)

Shaw, W. & C. Shaw, Wilson & Courtenay's Scotch Appeals Reports, House of Lords

Shaw (W.G.) W.G. Shaw's Reports (30-35 Vermont)

Sh. C. Sheriff's Court

Sh. Crim. Cas. Shaw's Justiciary Court, Criminal Cases (Sc.)

Sh. Ct. Sheriff Court District court (Sc.)

Sh. Ct. of Sess. Shaw's Court of Session Cases (Sc.)

Sh. Ct. Rep. Sheriff Court Reports (Sc.)

Sh. Dig. Shaw's Digest of Decisions (Sc.)

Shear. & R. Neg. Shearman and Redfield on Negligence

Shear. Bar Ex. Shearwood's Bar Examinations

Shear. Cont. Shearwood, Contract. 1897

Shearm. & Red. Neg. Shearman & Redfield on Negligence

Shear. Pers. Pr. Shearwood, Personal Property. 1882

Shear. R. Pr. Shearwood, Real Property. 3ed. 1885

Shear. St. G. Shearwood's Student's Guide to the Bar

Sheil. Cape Times Law Reports, edited by Sheil

Sheil Ir. Bar Sheil, Sketches of the Irish Bar

Shel. Sheldon

Shel. Bank. Shelford, Bankrupt and Insolvency Law. 3ed. 1862

Shel. Ca. Shelley's Cases in vol. 1 Coke's Reports

Sheld. Sheldon's Reports, Superior Court of Buffalo, New York

Sheldon Sheldon's Reports, Superior Court of Buffalo, New York

Sheld. Subr. Sheldon on Subrogation

Shelf. Shelford

Shelf. J. St. Cos. Shelford on Joint-Stock Companies

Shelf. Lun. Shelford on Lunacy

Shelf. Mar. & Div. Shelford on Marriage and Divorce

Shel. High. Shelford, Highways. 4ed. 1869

Shel. J. St. Com. Shelford, Joint Stock Companies. 2ed. 1870

Shel. Lun. Shelford, Lunatics. 2ed. 1847

Shel. M. & D. Shelford, Marriage & Divorce. 1841

Shel. Mort. Shelford, Mortmain and Charitable Uses. 1836

Shel. Prob. Shelford, Probate, Legacy etc. 2ed, 1861

Shel. R. Pr. St. Sheldon, Real Property Statutes. 9ed. 1893

Shel. Ry. Shelford, Railways. 4ed. 1869

Shel. Will Shelford, Wills. 1838

Shel. Wills Shelford on Wills

Shep.
- Shepherd's Reports, Alabama
- Select Cases (in 37-39 Ala.)
- Shelpley's Reports (13-18, 21-30 Maine)

Shep. Abr. Sheppard's Abridgment

Shep. Act. Sheppard's Action on the Case

Shep. Cas. Sheppard's Cases of Slander, & c.

Shepherd Shepherd. Reports (19-21, 24-41, 60, 63, 64 Alabama)

Sheph. Sel. Cas. Shepherd's Select Cases (Ala.)

Shepley Shepley, Reports (13-18 and 21-30 Maine)

Shep. Prec. Sheppard, Precedent of Precedents. 9ed. 1825

Shep. Sel. Cas. Shepherd's Select Cases (Ala.)

Shep. Touch. Shepherd's Select Cases (Ala.)

Sher. Ct. Rep. Sheriff Court Reports (Sc.)

Sher. Mar. Ins. Sherman's Marine Insurance

Sher. Pr. Sheridan's Practice, King's Bench

Shiel. Shiel's Reports (Cape Colony)

Shill. W.C. Shillman's Workmen's Compensation Cases (Ir.)

Shingle The Shingle, Phila. Bar Association

Shinn, Repl. Shinn's Treatise on American Law of Replevin

Ship. Shipping

Ship. Gaz. Shipping Gazette, London

Shipp Shipp. Reports (66-67 North Carolina)

Shipping Reg. (P & F) Shipping Regulation

Shir. Cr. L. Shirley, Sketch of the Criminal Law. 2ed. 1889

Shir. D.C. Ca. Shirley's Dartmouth College Case

Shirl. Shirley's Reports (49-55 New Hampshire)

Shirl. L.C. Shirley's Leading Crown Cases (Eng.)

Shirley Shirley, Reports (49-55 New Hampshire)

Shir. Mag. L. Shirley, Magisterial Law. 2ed. 1896

S.H. J.R. Senate-House Joint Reports

Sh. Jus. Shaw's Justiciary Cases (Sc.)

Sh. Just. P. Shaw's Justiciary Decisions (Sc.)

Sh. Lit. Shortt on Works of Literature

Sh. Litt. Shortt, Works of Literature. 2ed. 1884

Shome L. R. Shome's Law Reporter (India)

Shortt Copy. Shortt's Law of Copyright

Shortt. Inf. Shortt, Informations. 1887

Shortt, Inform. Shortt on Informations, Criminal, Quo Warranto, Mandamus, and Prohibition

Shortt Lit. Shortt, Literature and Art. 2ed. 1884

Show.
- Shower's King's Bench Reports (Eng.)
- Shower's Parliamentary Cases

Shower K.B. Shower's King's Bench Reports (1678-95) (89 ER)

Shower K.B. (Eng.) Shower's King's Bench Reports (89 ER)

Shower P.C. (Eng.) Shower's Parliamentary Cases (1 ER)

Show. K.B. Shower's King's Bench Reports (Eng.)

Show. Parl. Cas. Shower's Parliamentary Cases (1 ER)

Show. P.C Shower's Parliamentary Cases (1 ER)

Shrhldr Shareholder

Shr. Sui. Shrady on Suicide and Intemperance in Life Insurance

Sh. Sc. App. Shaw' Scotch Appeals, House of Lords

Sh. Teind Ct. Shaw's Teind Court Decisions (Sc.)

Sh.W. & C. Shaw, Wilson & Courtenay's Scotch Appeals Reports (Wilson & Shaw's Reports)

S.I. Statutory Instruments

Sick. Sickels' Reports (46-85 N.Y.)

Sick. Min. Dec. Sickels' U.S. Mining Laws & Decisions

Sick. Op. Sickels' Opinions of the New York Attorneys-General

Sid. Siderfin's King's Bench Reports (82 ER)

Sid. (Eng.) Siderfin's King's Bench Reports (82 ER)

Sid. Gov. Sidney on Government

SII Givens, Legal Strategies for Industrial Innovation

Sil. Silver Tax Division (I.R. Bull.)

Sil. (Ct. of Ap.) Silvernail's New York Court of Appeals Reports (N.Y.)

Sill Comp. Sill on Composition in Bankruptcy

S. Ill. U. L.J. Southern Illinois University Law Journal

Sil. (Sup.Ct.) Silvernail's Supreme Court Reports (N.Y.)

Silv.
- Silvernails Reports (N.Y. 1886-92)
- Silvernail's Reports (9-14 N.Y. Criminal Reports)
- Silvernail's Supreme (1889-90)

Silv. A. Silvernail's Court of Appeals Reports

Silv. App. Silvernail's Court of Appeals Reports

Silv. Cit. Silvernail's New York Citations

Silv. Ct. App. Silvernail's New York Court of Appeals Reports

Silv. Ct. App. (N.Y.) Silvernail's Court of Appeals Reports

Silvernail's N.Y.Rep. Silvernail's New York Court of Appeals Reports

Silv. Sup. Silvernail's Supreme Court (N.Y.)

Silv. (Sup.Ct.) Silvernail's Supreme Court Reports (N.Y.)

Silv. Unrep. Silvernail's Unreported Cases (N.Y.)

Sim.
- Simmons' Reports (95-97, 99 Wisconsin)
- Simons' Chancery Reports (57-60 ER) (1826-50)

Sim. & C. Simmons & Conover's Reports (99-100 Wis.)

Sim. & S. Simons & Stuart's Chancery Reports (57 ER)

Sim. & St. Simons & Stuart's Chancery Reports (57 ER)

Sim. & Stu. Simon's & Stuart's Vice-Chancery Reports (57 ER)

Sim. & Stu. (Eng.) Simons & Stuart's Chancery Reports (57 ER)

Sim.Ct.M. Simmons on Courts-Martial

Sim. Des. Pat. Simonds' Law of Design Patents

Sim. Dig. Simmons, Wisconsin Digest

Sim. Dig. Pat. Dec. Simonds, Digest of Patent Office Decisions (U.S.)

Sim. Elect. Simeon on Elections

Sim. (Eng.)
- Simons' Reports, vols. 95-97, 99
- Wisconsin Simons' Chancery Reports (57-60 ER)

Simes & S., Future Interests Simes & Smith on the Law of Future Interests

Simia All India Reporter, Simia. 1951

Sim. Int. Simons' Law of Interpleader

Sim. N.S. Simons' English Vice-Chancery Reports, New Series (61 ER)

Sim. N.S. (Eng.) Simons' English Vice-Chancery Reports, New Series (61 ER)

Simon's T.C. Simon's Tax Cases (U.K.)

Sim. Pat. L. Simond's Patent Law

Simp. Inf. Simpson, Infants. 4ed. 1926

Sim. Ry. Acc. Simon, Law relating to Railway Accidents. 1862

Sinclair Sinclair's Manuscript Decisions, Scotch Session Cases

Sind
• All India Reporter, Sind. (1914-50)
• Indian Rulings, Sind (1929-47)

Sind, Pak. Sind, Pakistan

Sing. Singapore

Singapore L. Rev. Singapore Law Review, Singapore

Singer Prob. Cas. (Pa.) Singer's Probate Cases

Singers Singers Probate Court (Pa.)

Sing. L.R. Singapore Law Review

Sir J.S. Sir John Strange's Reports (Eng.)

Sir L. Jenk. Wynne's Life of Sir Leoline Jenkins (1724)

Sir T.J. Sir Thomas Jones, Reports, King's Bench & Common Pleas (Eng.)

Sir T. Ray. T. Raymond's King's Bench Reports (Eng.)

S.I.T.C. Standard International Tariff Classification

S.I.T.E.S. Smithsonian Institution Traveling Exhibition Service

Six Circ. Cases on the Six Circuits (1841-43) (Ir.)

S.J. Scottish Jurist (1829-73) Solicitors' Journal

S.J.D.
• Doctor of the Science of Law
• Doctor of Juristic Science

S.J.L.B. Selected Judgments, Lower Burma

S.J. L. R. St. John's Law Review

S. Jud. Ct. Supreme Judicial Court, Maine, Massachusetts

S.Just. Shaw's Justiciary Cases (Sc.)

S.J.Z. Selected Judgments of Zambia

Skene Sir John Skene's De verborum significatione, 7 editions (1597-1683)

Skene de Verb.Sign. Skene de Verborum Significatione

Skid. Min. Skidmore's Mining Statutes

Skill. Pol. Rep. Skillman's N.Y. Police Reports

Skin. Skinner's King's Bench Reports (Eng.)

Skinker Skinker's Reports (65-79 Missouri)

Skinner Skinner's King's Bench Reports (1681-98) (90 ER)

Skinner (Eng.) Skinner's King's Bench Reports (90 ER)

SL Wehmhoefer, Statistics in Litigation

S.L. Session laws

Sl Slovene

Slade Slade's Reports (15 Vermont)

Slade's St. Slade's Laws, Vt.

SLC Southern Legislative Conference

S.L.C.
- Scottish Land Court Reports
- Scottish Land Courts
- Scottish Law Commission
- Smith's Leading Cases
- Statute Law Committee
- Stuart's Appeals, Lower Canada (1810-35)

S.L.C. App. Stuart's Lower Canada Appeal Cases

S.L.C.R. Scottish Land Court Reports

S.L. Co. Appendices of Proceedings of the Scottish Land Court

S.L. Co. R. Appendices of Proceedings of the Scottish Land Court

SLF The Southwestern Legal Foundation

S.L.F.C. Sierra Leone Full Court Reports

S.L.G. Scottish Law Gazette

S.L.G.B. Society of Local Government Barristers

Slip op. Slip opinions

S.L.J.
- Scottish Law Journal, Edinburgh
- Southwestern Law Journal
- Straits Law Journal (1888-92) (Mal.)

S.L.J.R. Sudan Law Journal and Reports

S.L.L. Society of Labour Lawyers

S.L.L.R. Sierra Leone Law Recorder

Sloan L. & T. Sloan on Landlord and Tenant (New York)

Sloan Leg. Reg. Sloan's Legal Register (N.Y.)

S.L.R.
- Saskatchewan Law Reports
- Scottish Land Court Reports
- Scottish Law Reporter, (Edinburgh)
- Scottish Law Review and Sheriff Court Reports (1885-1963)
- Seychelles Law Reports (1921-23)
- Sind Law Reporter, (India)
- Singapore Law Reports (1946-49, 1953-56)
- Southern Law Review (St. Louis, Mo.)
- Stanford Law Review
- Statute Law Revision

S.L.R.B. State Labor Relations Board

S. L. Rev. Scottish Law Review & Sheriff Court Reports

S.L.R.Leic. Leicester's Straits Law Reports (Mal.)

S.L.R.Leicester Leicester's Straits Law Reports (1827-77) (Mal.)

S.L.R.N.S. Straits Law Reports, New Series (Mal.)

S.L.S. Statute Law Society

SLS Saint Lawrence Seaway Development Corporation

Sl.St. Slade's Compilation of the Statutes of Vermont

S.L.T. Scots Law Times (Scotland)

S.L.T. (Lyon Ct.) Scots Law Times Lyon Court Reports

S.L.T. (notes) Scots Law Times Notes of Recent Decisions

S.L.T. (Sh.Ct.) Scots Law Times Sheriff Court Reports

S.L.T. (Sh.Ct.) Scots Law Times Sheriff Court Reports

S.L.U. L.J. Saint Louis University Law Journal

S.M.
- Senior Magistrate
- Stipendiary Magistrate

S.M. Solicitor's Memorandum, U.S. Internation Revenue Bureau

Sm. Smith

Sma. & Giff. Smale & Giffard's English Vice-Chancellors' Reports

Sm. Act. Smith, Action at Law. 12ed. 1876

Sm. Adm. Pr. Smith, Admiralty Practice. 4ed. 1892

Smale & G. Smale & Giffard's English Vice-Chancellors' Reports

Sm. & Bat. Smith & Batty's K.B. Reports (Ir.)

Sm. & B.R.R. Cas. Smith & Bates' American Railway Cases

Sm. & G.
- Smale & Giffard's Chancery Reports (Eng.)
- Smith & Guthrie's Reports (81-101 Mo. App.)

Sm. & M. Smedes & Marshall's Reports (9-22 Miss.)

Sm. & M. Ch. Smedes & Marshall's Reports (9-22 Miss.)

Sm. & S. Smith & Sager's Drainage Cases (Can.)

Sm. & Sod. L. & T. Smith & Soden, Landlord and Tenant. 2ed. 1878

Sm.C.C.M. Smith's Circuit Courts-Martial Reports, Maine

S.M.C.D. Supreme Military Council Decree (Ghana)

Sm. Ch. Pr. Smith, Chancery Practice. 7ed. 1862

Sm. Com. L. Smith, Manual of Common Law. 12ed. 1905

Sm. Con. Smith, Contracts. 8ed. 1885

Sm. Cond. Ala. Smith's Condensed Alabama Reports

Sm. Const. Cons. Smith on Constitutional and Statutory Construction

Sm. Conv. Smith on Conveyancing

Smeade & Marshall Ch. Smedes & Marshall's Chancery Reports (Miss.)

Sme. & M. Smedes (W.C.) and Marshall (T.A.) (Miss.)

Sm. Ecc. Cts. Smith, Ecclesiastical Courts. 7ed. 1920

Sm.E.D. E.D. Smith's Common Pleas Reports (N.Y.)

Sm.Ed. Smith's Education for the English Bar

Smed. & M. Smedes & Marshall's Mississippi Reports

Smed. & M. Ch. Smedes & Marshall's Mississippi Chancery Reports

Smedes and Marshall's Chy.-Repts. Smedes & Marshall's Chancery Reports (Miss.)

Smedes & M. (Miss.) Smedes & Marshall's Mississippi Reports

Smedes & M. Ch. Smedes & Marshall's Chancery Reports (Miss.)

Smee. Collection of Abstracts of Acts of Parliament

Sm.El. Smith's Elements of Law

Sm.Eng. Smith's King's Bench Reports (Eng.)

Sm.Eq.
- Smith's (J.W.) Manual of Equity
- Smith's Principles of Equity

Smeth.L.S. Smethurst on Locus Standi, 1867

Sm.Ex.Int. Smith on Executory Interest

Sm.For.Med. Smith, Forensic Medicine. 10ed. 1955

Sm. Forms Smith's Forms of Procedure

S.M.H. Sydney Morning Herald (New South Wales)

Sm.Homest. Smyth on Homesteads and Exemptions

Smi. & Bat. Smith & Batty, Irish King's Bench Reports

Sm. Ind. Smith's Reports (In 1-4 Indiana)

Smith
- C.L. Smith's Registration Cases (1895-1914)
- E.B. Smith's Reports (21-47 Illinois Appeals)
- E.D. Smith's New York Common Pleas Reports
- E.H. Smith's Reports (147-162 New York Court of Appeals)
- E.P. Smith's Reports (15-27 New York Court of Appeals)
- J.P. Smith's English King's Bench Reports
- P.F. Smith's Pennsylvania State Reports
- Smith, English Registration
- Smith, Reporter (7, 12 Heiskell's Tennessee Reports)
- Smith's Indiana Reports
- Smith's New Hampshire Reports
- Smith's Reports (54-62 California)
- Smith's Reports (2-4 South Dakota)
- Smith's Reports, (61 -84 Maine)
- Smith's Reports (81-83 Missouri Appeals)
- Smith's Reports (1-11 Wisconsin)

Smith, Act. Smith's Actions at Law

Smith & B.
- Smith & Batty's Irish King's Bench Reports
- Smith & Bates' American Railway Cases

Smith & Bat. Smith & Batty, Irish King's Bench Reports

Smith & B.R.C. Smith & Bates, American Railway Cases

Smith & B.R.R.C. Smith & Bates' American Railway Cases

Smith & G. Smith & Guthrie's Missouri Appeal Reports, vols. 81-101

Smith & H. Smith & Heiskell (Tenn.)

Smith, C.C.M. Smith's Circuit Courts-Martial Reports (Me.)

Smith, Ch. Pr. Smith's Chancery Practice

Smith, Com. Law Smith's Manual of Common Law

Smith Cond. Smith's Condensed Alabama Reports

Smith Cond. Rep. Smith's Condensed Reports (Ala.)

Smith Cong. Election Cases Smith's Election Cases (U.S.)

Smith, Cont. Smith on Contracts

Smith C.P. E.D. Smith's Common Pleas Reports, New York

Smith Ct. App. E.P. Smith's Reports, vols. 15-27 New York Court of Appeals

Smith de Rep. Angl. Smith (Sir Thomas), De Republica Anglica (The Commonwealth of England and the Manner of Government Thereof. 1621)

Smith, Dict. Antiq. Smith's Dictionary of Greek and Roman Antiquities

Smith E.D. E.D. Smith's New York Common Pleas Reports (1850-58)

Smith E.H. Smith's (E.H.) Reports (147-162 New York Court of Appeals)

Smith E.P. E.P. Smith's Reports (15-27 New York Court of Appeals)

Smith, Ext. Int. Smith on Executory Interest

Smith-Hurd Smith-Hurd's Illinois Annotated Statutes

Smith-Hurd Ann.St. Smith-Hurd Illinois Annotated Statutes

Smith Ind. Smith's Indiana Reports

Smith J.P. J.P. Smith's English King's Bench Reports

Smith K.B. Smith's King's Bench (Eng.)

Smith, Laws Pa. Smith's Laws of Pennsylvania

Smith L.C. Smith's Leading Cases

Smith, Lead. Cas. Smith's Leading Cases

Smith, L.J. Smith's Law Journal

Smith, Man. Eq. Jur. Smith's Manual of Equity Jurisprudence

Smith Me. Smith's Reports (vols. 61-84 Maine)

Smith, Merc. Law Smith on Mercantile Law

Smith N.H. Smith's New Hampshire Reports

Smith N.Y. Smith's Reports (vols. 15-27 and 147-162 New York Court of Appeals)

Smith Pa. P.F. Smith's Pennsylvania State Reports

Smith Pat. Smith on the Laws of Patents

Smith P.F. P.F. Smith's Pennsylvania State Reports

Smith Rec. Smith's Law of Receivers

Smith Reg. C.L. Smith's Registration Cases (Eng.)

Smith Reg. Cas. C.L. Smith's Registration Cases (Eng.)

Smith Repar. Smith's Law of Reparation

Smith Rules Smith's Chancery Rules

Smith's (Ind.) R. Smith's Indiana Reports (Ind.)

Smith's Laws Smith's Laws (Pa.)

Smith's Lead. Cas. Smith's Leading Cases

Smith's R. Smith's Indiana Reports (Ind.)

Smith, Wealth Nat. Smith, Inquiry into the Nature and Causes of the Wealth of Nations

Smith Wis. Smith's Reports (1-11 Wisconsin)

Sm. J. St. Comp. Smith on Joint-Stock Companies

Sm. K.B. Smith's King's Bench Reports (Eng.)

Sm. L. & T. Smith's Landlord and Tenant

Sm. Lawy. Smith's Lawyer and his Profession

Sm. L.C. Smith's Leading Cases

Sm.L.Cas.Com.L. Smith's Leading Cases on Commercial Law

Sm. L.J. Law Journal (Smith) (Eng.)

S.M.L.J. St. Mary's Law Journal

Sm. M. & S. Smith, Master and Servant. 8ed. 1931

Sm. Man. Eq. Smith's Manual of Equity

Sm. Me. Smith's Reports (61-84 Maine)

Sm. Merc. L. Smith, Mercantile Law. 13ed. 1931

Sm. Neg. Smith, Negligence. 2ed. 1884

Smoult Notes of Cases in Smoult's Collection of Orders, Calcutta (India)

Sm. Pat. Smith, Patents, 2ed. 1854

Sm. Pl. Somersetshire Pleas Civil & Criminal, ed. Chadwyck-Healey and Landon (Somerset Record Society Publications, v. 11, 36, 41, 44)

Sm. Poor L. Smith's Scotch Poor Law

Sm. Pr. Eq. Smith's Principles of Equity

Sm. Prob. L. Smith's Probate Law and Practice

Sm. R. & P.Prop. Smith on the Law of Real and Personal Property

SMSA Standard Metropolitan Statistical Area

Sm. Stat. Law Smith's Statute Law

SMU Southern Methodist University

SMU L. Rev. Southern Methodist University Law Review

Smy. Smythe's Irish Common Pleas Reports (1839-40)

Smy. & B. Smythe and Bourke's Irish Marriage Cases (1842)

Smy. Home. Smyth on the Law of Homestead and Exemptions

Smythe Smythe's Irish Common Pleas Reports (1839-40)

S.N. Session Notes, Scotland

S.N.A. Sudder Nizamat Adawlut Reports (India)

S.N.A. Beng. Sudder Nizamut Adawlut Reports (1805-50) (Bengal, India)

S.N.A. Beng. (N.S.) Sudder Nizamut Adawlut Reports, New Series (1851-59) (Bengal, India)

Sn. & W. Ch. Snow & Winstanley, Chancery Practice

SNCC The Student Nonviolent Coordinating Committee

SNCLAR University of Santa Clara School of Law

Sneed
- Sneed's Kentucky Decisions (2 Ky.)
- Sneed's Reports (33-37 Tennessee)

Sneed Dec. Sneed's Kentucky Decisions (2 Ky.)

Sneed Tenn. Sneed's Reports (Tenn.)

Sneed (Tenn.) Rep. Sneed's Reports (Tenn.)

Snell, Eq. Snell's Principles in Equity

Snow Snow's Reports (3 Utah)

Snyder, Mines Snyder on Mines and Mining

S.O. Solicitor's Opinion

Sny. Not. Man. Snyder's Notaries' and Commissioners' Manual

Sny. Rel. Corp. Snyder on Religious Corporations

So.
- Southern
- Southern Reporter, National Reporter System

So. 2d Southern Reporter, Second Series

So. African L. South African Law Reports

So. African L.J. South African Law Journal

So. Afr. L.J. South African Law Journal

So. Afr. L. R. South African Law Reports

So. Afr. L.T. South African Law Times

So. Afr. Prize Cas. South African Prize Cases (Juta)

So. Aus. L.R. South Australian Law Reports (1865-92, 1899-1920)

So. Aust. L.R. South Australian Law Reports

So. Austr. L. South Australian Law Reports

So. Austr. St. South Australian State Reports

S.O.C. Standards of Official Conduct

So.C. South Carolina Reports

Soc.
- Social
- Sociological
- Sociology
- Society

Soc. Act. & L. Social Action and the Law

Soc. Action & L. Social Action and the Law

So. Calif. L. Rev. Southern California Law Review

So. Calif. Tax Inst. University of Southern California School of Law Tax Institute

So. Cal. L.R. Southern California Law Review

Soc. & Lab. Bull. Social and Labour Bulletin

So. Car.
- South Carolina
- South Carolina Reports

So. Car. B. A. Rep. South Carolina Bar Association Reports

So. Car. Const. South Carolina Constitutional Reports (by Treadway, by Mill, or by Harper)

So. Car. L.J. South Carolina Law Journal, Columbia

So. Car. L.Q. South Carolina Law Quarterly

So. Car. L. Rev. South Carolina Law Review

So. Car. R. South Carolina Law Reports (S.C.)

Soc. Econ. Social Economist

Soc. Econ. Wetgeving Social Economisch Wetgeving Tijdschrift voor Europees en economisch recht (Netherlands)

Soc. Just. Social Justice

Soc. Resp. Social Responsibility

Soc. Sci. Social Responsibility

Soc. Sec.
- Social Security
- Social security and medicare

Soc. Sec. Bull. Social Security Bulletin

Soc. Ser. Social Services

Soc. Serv. Rev. Social Service Review

Soc'y Society

So. Dak. B. Jo. South Dakota Bar Journal

So. Dak. L. Rev. South Dakota Law Review

So. East. Rep. Southeastern Reporter, commonly cited S.E.

S. of C. Statutes of Canada

Software L. J. Software Law Journal

Soil & Water Conserv. Dist. Soil and Water Conservation Districts

Solic.
- Solicitor(s)

So. Ill. L.J. Southern Illinois University Law Journal

So. Ill. U. L.J. Southern Illinois University Law Journal

So. Jersey L.S. Dictum. South Jersey Law School Dictum

Sol.
- Solicitor
- The Solicitor. 1934-61
- Soloman's Court of Request Appeals (Ceylon)

Solar L. Rep. Solar Law Report

So. Law Southern Lawyer

So. Law T. Southern Law Times

Sol. Cl. Gaz. Solicitors' Clerks' Gazette (1921-40)

Sol. G. Solicitor General

Sol. Gen. Solicitor General

Solic. Solicitor

Solicitor's J. Solicitor's Journal

So. L.J. Southern Law Journal & Reporter

Sol. J. Solicitor's Journal (Eng.)

Sol. J. & R. Solicitors' Journal & Reporter

Sol. Jo. (Eng.) Solicitors' Journal

Sol. Man. Cl. Gaz. Solicitor's Managing Clerks' Gazette (1941-62)

Solom. Solomon Islands

Sol. Op. Solicitors' Opinion (especially of Internal Revenue Bureau) (U.S.)

Sol. Q. Solicitor Quarterly (1962-65)

So. L.Q. Southern Law Quarterly

So. L. R. Southern Law Review (Nashville, Tenn.)

S.O.L. Rev. School of Law Review (Canada)

So. L. Rev.
- Southern Law Review (Nashville, Tn.)
- Southern Law Review (St. Louis)

So. L. Rev. N.S. Southern Law Review New Series (St. Louis, Mo.)

So. L. R. N.S. Southern Law Review, New Series (St. Louis, Mo.)

Solrs. Solicitors

So. L. T. Southern Law Times

Som. Somerset Legal Journal (Pa.)

Somal. Somalia

Somerset Legal Journal Somerset Legal Journal (Pa.)

Somerset L.J. Somerset Legal Journal

Som. Leg. J. (Pa.) Somerset Legal Journal (Pa.)

Som. L.J. Somerset Legal Journal (Pa.)

Som. L. R. Somalia Law Reports

Somn.on Gav. Somner on Gavelkind

Som. Pl. Somersetshire Pleas (Civil and Criminal) edited by Chadwyck Healey and Landon. (Somerset Record Society Publications, vols. 11, 36, 41, 44)

So. Rep. Southern Reporter

So. Repr. Southern Reporter

So. Tex. L.J. South Texas Law Journal

Sou. Aus. L. R. South Australian Law Reports

Soule, Syn. Soule's Dictionary of English Synonymes

So. U. L. Rev. Southern University Law Review

So. Univ. L. Rev. Southern University Law Review

South. Southern Reporter (National Reporter System)

South Afr. L.J. The South African Law Journal. Cape Town, South Africa

Southard Southard, New Jersey Law Reports, vols. 4-5

South Aus. L. R. South Australian Law Reports

South Calif. Rev. Southern California Law Review

South Car.
- South Carolina
- South Carolina Reports

South Carolina L. Rev. South Carolina Law Review

South Dak. L. Rev. South Dakota Law Review

South Dakota L. Rev. South Dakota Law Review

Southeastern Rep. South Eastern Reporter

Southern Southern Reporter

Southern Rep. Southern Reporter

South. Ill. U. L. Southern Illinois University Law

South. Ill. U. L.J. Southern Illinois University Law Journal

South. Law J. Southern Law Journal (Tuscaloosa, Ala.)

South. Law J. & Rep. Southern Law Journal and Reporter

South. Law Rev. Southern Law Review

South. Law Rev. N.S. Southern Law Review, New Series

South. L.J. Southern Law Journal

South. L.J. & Rep. Southern Law Journal & Reporter

South. L. Rev. Southern Law Review

South. L. Rev. N.S. Southern Law Review, New Series

South Texas L.J. South Texas Law Journal

South. U. L. Rev. Southern University Law Review

Southwestern L.J. Southwestern Law Journal

Southwestern U. L. Rev. Southwestern University Law Review

Southwestern Univ. L. Rev. Southwestern University Law Review

Southwest. U. L. Rev. Southwestern University Law Review

Southw. L.J. Southwestern Law Journal & Reporter

Sov. & E. Eur. For. Tr. American Review of Soviet and Eastern European Foreign Trade

Soviet Jewry L. Rev. Soviet Jewry Law Review

Soviet L. & Govt. Soviet Law and Government

Soviet Law & Gov't Soviet Law and Government

Soviet Stat. & Dec. Soviet Statutes and Decisions

Soviet Stud. Soviet Studies, Oxford, England

Soviet Y. B. Int'l L. Soviet Year-Book of International Law

Sov. Stat. & Dec. Soviet Statutes and Decisions

So. West. L.J. Southwestern Law Journal

So.West. Rep. Southwestern Reporter (commonly cited S.W.)

sp. superseded in parl; new matter substituted for part of an existing regulation or order (used in Shepard's Citations)

sp.
- Spear's Reports (S.C. Law 1842-44)
- Spinks' Ecclesiastical & Admiralty Reports (Eng.)
- Spinks' Prize Cases (1854-56) (164ER)

SPA State Planning Agency

Sp.A. Special Appeal

Space L. Space Law

S. Pac. L.R. South Pacific Law Review (Aus.)

S. Pac. L. Rev. South Pacific Law Review

Sp. Acts Special Acts

Spald. Cop. Spalding on Copyright

Sp. & Sel. Cas. Special and Selected Law Cases (1648) (Eng.)

Sparks. Sparks' Reports, British Burmah.

Spaulding. Spaulding's Reports (71-73 Maine)

Sp.C. Special Commissioner

SPC South Pacific Commission (UN)

SPCA Society for the Prevention of Cruelty to Animals

Sp. Ch. Spears' (or Speers') South Carolina Chancery Reports

Sp. CM Special Court-Martial (U.S. Navy)

Sp. Com. Special Committee

Sp. Cr. Ct. Special Criminal Court

Sp. Ct. R.R.R.A. Special Court Regional Railroad Reorganization Act

Spear Ch. Spears' (or Speers') South Carolina Chancery Reports

SPD Baldus & Cole, Statistical Proof of Discrimination

Spear Eq. Spears' (or Speers') South Carolina Equity Reports

Spear Ext. Spear's Law of Extradition

Spear. High. Spearman, Highways. 1881

Spear (or Speer) Spear's (or Speer's) South Carolina Law Reports

Spears Spears' Reports (S.C. Law or Equity)

Spears Eq. Spears' (or Speers') South Carolina Equity Reports

spec.
- special
- specification

Spec. A. Special or local assessments

Sp. Ecc. & Ad. Spinks' Ecclesiastical and Admiralty Reports (1853-55) (164 ER)

Spec. Perf. Specific Performance

Speculum Juris Speculum Juris, Forte Hare, South Africa

Speers. Spears' (or Speers') South Carolina Law Reports

Speers Eq. Spears' (or Speers') South Carolina Equity Reports

Speers Eq. (S.C.) Speers' (or Spears') South Carolina Equity Reports

Speers L. (S.C.) Speers' (or Spears'), South Carolina Law Reports

Spel. Feuds. Spelman on Feuds

Spel. Gl. Spelman's Glossary

Spell. Extr. Rel. Spelling on Extraordinary Relief in Equity and in Law

Spell. Extr. Rem. Spelling's Treatise on Injunctions and Other Extraordinary Remedies

Spel. L.T. Spelman's Law Tracts

Spelm. Spelman's Glossarium Archailogicum. 3 editions (1626-87)

Spelman. Spelman's Glossarium Archailogicum. 3 editions (1626-87)

Spel. Rep Spelman's Reports, Manuscript, English King's Bench

Spenc.
- Spencer's Reports (10-20 Minn.)
- Spencer's Reports (20 New Jersey Law)

Spence, Ch. Spence's Equitable Jurisdiction of the Court of Chancery

Spence Cop. Spence on Copyright of Designs

Spence, Eq. Jur. Spence's Equitable Jurisdiction of the Court of Chancery

Spence Or. L. Spence's Origin of Laws

Spence Pat. Inv. Spence, Patentable Inventions. 1851

Spencer
- Spencer's Reports (10-20 Minn.)
- Spencer's Reports (20 New Jersey Law)

Spen. (N.J.) Spencer's Reports (20 New Jersey Law)

Spens Sel. Cas. Spens' Select Cases, Bombay (India)

SP. Eq. Spears' (or Speers') South Carolina Equity Reports

Sp. Glos. Spelman's Glossary

Spike M. & S. Spike, Master and Servant. 3ed. 1872

Spinks Spinks' English Ecclesiastical and Admiralty Reports (164 ER)

Spinks Eccl. & Adm. (Eng.) Spinks' English Ecclesiastical and Admiralty Reports (164 ER)

Spinks, P.C. Spinks' English Prize Cases

Spinks, Prize Cas. Spinks' Admiralty Prize Cases (164 ER)

Spinks Prize Cas. (Eng.) Spinks' Admiralty Cases (164 ER)

Sp. Laws Spirit of the Laws, Montesquieu

Spoon. Spooner's Reports (12-15 Wisconsin)

Spooner. Spooner's Reports (12-15 Wisconsin)

Spott. Spottiswoode (Sc.)

Spott. C.L. & Eq. Rep. Common Law & Equity Reports published by Spottiswoode

Spott. Eq. Rep. Spottiswoode's English Equity Reports

Spottis. R. Spottiswoode's Court of Session Reports (Sc.)

Spottis. C.L. & Eq. Spottiswoode's Common Law and Eq. Reports, Eng.

Spottis. C.L. & Eq. Rep. Common Law and Equity Reports, published by Spottiswoode

Spottis. Eq. Spottiswoode's Equity (Sc.)

Spottis. Pr. Spottiswoode, Practicles (Sc.)

Spottis. St. Spottiswoode, Styles (Sc.)

Spottisw. Spottiswoode's Equity (Sc.)

Spottisw. Eq. Spottiswoode's Equity (Sc.)

Sp. Pr. Cas. Spinks' Prize Cases (1854-56) (Eng.)

Spr. Sprague's United States District Court (Admiralty) Decisions

S.P.R.
- Puerto Rico Reports, Spanish edition

- Statement of Procedural Rules

Sprague. Sprague's United States District Court (Admiralty) Decisions

Spr. Int. L. Sprague on International Law

Sp. Rul. Special Ruling

Sp. Sess. Special Session

Sp. St. Private and Special Laws

Sp. T. Special Term

Sp. Tax. Rul. Special Tax Ruling (U.S. Internal Revenue Service)

S.P.T.L. Society of Public Teachers of Law

S.Q.R. State Reports (Queensland)

S.Q.T. Queensland State Reports

Squibb Auc. Squibb, Auctioneers. 2ed. 1891

S.R.
- Solicitor's Recommendation, U.S. Internal Revenue Bureau
- Special Regulation, U.S. Army
- New South Wales State Reports
- New York State Reporter
- Supreme Court of Quebec, Reports
- Senate Resolution (USA)
- Southern Rhodesia
- Southern Rhodesia High Court Reports
- Statutes Revised

SRA Service & Regulatory Announcement, Dept. of Agric. (U.S.)

SRA Service & Regulatory Announcement, Dept. of Agric. (U.S.)

S.R. & O. Statutory Rules & Orders (eng.)

S.R. & O. and S.I. Rev. Statutory Rules & Orders and Statutory Instruments Revised

S.R.C. Stuart's Lower Canada Reports

S. Rep.
- Senate Reports
- Southern Reporter

S. Rept. U.S. Senate Committee Report

S. Res. U.S. Senate Resolution

S.R., H.C.R. Southern Rhodesia High Court Reports (1911-55)

SRI Riffer, Sports and Recreational Injuries

SRM Ship Repairs Maintenance Order, Nat'l. Shipping Authority Maritime Adm. (U.S.)

S.R.N.S.W. New South Wales State Reports

S.R. (N.S.W.) B. & P. State Reports, Bankruptcy and Probate (N.S.W., Aus.)

S.R. (N.S.W.) Eq. State Reports, Equity (N.S.W., Aus.)

S.R.O. & S.I. Rev. Statutory Rules and Orders and Statutory Instruments Revised

S.R.Q. State Reports (Queensland)

S.R.R. Scots Revised Reports

SRS
- Statistical Reporting Service
- Social and Rehabilitation Service

S.R. (W.A.) State Reports, Western Australia

ss. sections

s.s. sworn statement

S.S.
- Selden Society
- Silvernail's New York Supreme Court Reports
- Social Security
- Steamship
- Synopsis Series of United States Treasury Decisions

S.S.A.
- Social Security Act
- Social Security Administration (U.S.)

S.S.A.A. Social Security Acts Amendments

SSB
- Salary Stabilization Board (U.S.)
- Social Security Board ruling
- Social Security Board

S.S.C.
- Sanford's Superior Court Reports, New York City
- Sarawak Supreme Court Reports
- Scotch Session Cases

S.S.C.R. Sind Sudder Court Reports (India)

SSIE Smithsonian Science Information Exchange, Inc.

S.S.L.R. Straits Settlements Law Reports

S.S.L.R. Supp. Straits Settlements Law Reports, Supplement (1897-99) (Mal.)

S.S.R. Soviet Socialist Republic

SSR Social Security Ruling on old-age, survivors, and disability insurance benefits (U.S. Internal Revenue Bureau)

SSS Selective Service System (U.S.)

SST Grant, Subchapter S Taxation, Second Edition

S.S.T.
- Social Security Tax Ruling (I.R. Bull.)
- Supersonic Transport

S.T.
- Sales Tax Branch, U.S. Internal Revenue Bureau
- Sales Tax Rulings, U.S. Internal revenue Bureau
- Science and Technology
- State Trials

St.
- Laws or Acts, in some states
- Stair's Decisions, Court of Session (Sc.)
- Stair's Institutes. 5ed. 1832
- State
- Statutes
- Story's Circuit Court Reports (U.S.)
- Street
- Stuart, Milne, & Peddie's Session Cases (Sc.)
- United States Statutes at Large

St. Ab. Statham's Abridgment

Stab. Stabilization

St. Adm. N.S. Stuart's Lower Canada Vice-Admiralty Reports, New Series

Stafford. Stafford's Reports (69-71 Vermont)

Stair. Stair's Decisions of the Lords of Council and Session (1661-81) (Sc.)

Stair I. Stair's Institutes, 5 editions (1681 -1832)

Stair. Inst. Stair's Institutes, 5 editions (1681-1832)

Stair Prin. Stair, Principles of the Laws of Scotland

Stair Rep. Stair's Decisions, Court of Session (Sc.)

Stal. Elect. Stalman, Election and Satisfaction. 1827

Stan. Stanford

Stand. Dict. Standard Dictionary

Stan. Dig. Stanton's Kentucky Digest

Stan. Envtl. L.J. Stanford Environmental Law Journal

Stand. Ex. Prof. Tax. Rep. Standard Excess Profits Tax Reporter (CCH)

Stand. Fed. Tax. Rep. (CCH)
• Standard Federal Tax Reports
• Standard Federal Tax Reporter (CCH)

Stand. Ga. Prac. Standard Georgia Practice

St. & H. Abor. Storer & Heard on Criminal Abortion

Stan. J. Int'l L. Stanford Journal of International Law

Stan. J.L. Gender & Sex Orient. Stanford Journal of Law, Gender & Sexual Orientation

Stan. L. & Pol'y Rev. Stanford Law & Policy Review

Stan. L. Rev. Stanford Law Review

St. John's J. Legal Comment. St. John's Journal of Legal Commentary

St. & Loc. Taxes (BNA) State and Local Taxes (Bureau of National Affairs)

St. & Loc. Tax Serv. (P-H) State and Local Tax Service (Prentice-Hall)

St. & P. Stewart and Porter's Reports (Ala.)

Stand. Pa. Prac. Standard Pennsylvania Practice

St. and Port. Stewart and Porter's Reports (Ala.)

Stan. Env't. Ann. Stanford Environmental Annual

Stan. Envt'l L. Ann. Stanford Environmental Law Annual

Stan. Envt'l L. J. Stanford Environmental Law Journal

Stanford Stanford's Pleas of the Crown (Eng.)

Stanford J. Int'l. Stud. Stanford Journal of International Studies

Stanford L. Rev. Stanford Law Review

Stan. J.Intl. L. Stanford Journal of International Law

Stan. J.Int'l.Stud. Stanford Journal International Studies

Stan. Law. Stanford Lawyer

Stan. L. R. Stanford Law Review

Stan. L. Rev. Stanford Law Review

Stan. Pa. Prac. Standard Pennsylvania Practice

Stanton. Stanton's Reports (11-13 Ohio)

Stanton's Rev. St. Stanton's Revised Statutes (Ky.)

Star. Starkie's English Nisi Prius Reports

Star Ch. Ca. Star Chamber Cases (1477-1648) (Eng.)

Star Ch. Cas. Star Chamber Cases (1477-1648) (Eng.)

Stark. Starkie's Nisi Prius Reports (1815-22) (Eng.)

Stark. C.L. Starkie's Criminal Law

Stark. Cr. Pl. Starkie's Criminal Pleading

Stark. Ev. Starkie on Evidence

Starkie. Starkie's English Nisi Prius Reports

Starkie (Eng.) Starkie's English Nisi Prius Reports (171 ER)

Starkie, Ev. Starkie on Evidence

Starkie's English Nisi Prius Reports (171 ER)

Starkie, Stand. & L. Starkie, on Slander and Libel

Stark. Jury Tr. Starkie on Trial by Jury

Stark. Lib. Starkie on Libel

Stark. N.P. Starkie's English Nisi Prius Reports

Stark. Sl. & L. Starkie on Slander & Libel

Starl. I. Cr. Law Starling's East India Criminal Law and Procedure

St. Arm. Leg. Pow. St. Armand on the Legislative Power of England

Starr & C. Ann. St. Starr and Curtis' Annotated Statutes (Ill.)

Star. S.C. Star Session Cases (1824-25)

Stat.
- Statistic(s)
- Statistical
- Statutes
- Statutes Revised
- U.S. Statutes at Large (Official)

Stat. An. Statistical Annals

Stat. at L. U.S. Statutes at Large

Stat. Def. Statutory Definition(s)

State & Loc. Taxes State and Local Taxes (BNA)

State Court J. State Court Journal

State Dept. Bull. U.S. State Department, Bulletin

State Fin. State Finance

State Gov't State Government

State Locl & Urb. L. Newsl. State, Local and Urban Law Newsletter

State Mot. Carr. Guide State Motor Carrier Guide (CCH)

State Print. State Printing

State R. New York State Reporter (N.Y.)

State Rep. New York State Reporter (N.Y.)

State Reporter New York State Reporter (N.Y.)

State Tax. State and local taxation

State Tax Cas. State Tax Cases (CCH)

State Tax Cas. Rep. State Tax Cases Reporter (CCH)

State Tax Guide (CCH) State Tax Guide

State Tr. State Trials (Howell) (Eng.)

State Tr. N.S. State Trials, New Series, edited by Macdonell (Eng.)

Stat. Glo. Statute of Gloucester

Stath. Abr. Statham's Abridgment

Stat. I.C.J. Statute of the International Court of Justice

Stat. Inst. Statutory Instruments

St.at Large Statutes at Large

Stat. Statute

Stat. F. Statute of Frauds

State. Law. Cttee. Statute Law Committee

Stat. Law Soc. Statute Law Society

Stat. Local Gov'ts Statute of Local Governments

Stat. L.R. Statute Law Review

Stat. Marl. Statute of Marlbridge

Stat. Mer. Statute of Merton

Stat. Merl. Statute of Merton

Stat. Mod. Lev. Fin. Statute Modus Levandi Fines

Stat. N.S.W. Statutes of New South Wales (Aus.)

Stat. N.Z. Statutes of New Zealand

Stat. O. & R. Statutory Orders and Regulations (Canada)

Stat. R. & O. Statutory Rules and Orders (1890-1947) (Eng.)

Stat. R. & O. & Stat. Inst. Rev. Statutory Rules and Orders, Statutory Instruments Revised (Eng.)

Stat. R. & O.N.I. Statutory Rules and Orders of Northern Ireland

Stat. R. & O.N.Ir. Statutory Rules & Orders of Northern Ireland (1922-date)

Stat. Realm Statutes of the Realm (Eng.)

Stat. Reg. N.Z. Statutory Regulations (New Zealand)

Stat. Rev. Statutes Revised

Statute L. Rev. Statute Law Review

Stat. Westm. Statute ofWestminster

Stat. Winch. Statute of Winchester

Staundef. Staundeforde, Exposition of the King's Prerogative

Staundeforde Staundeforde's Pleas of the Crown, Eng.

Staundef. P.C. Staundeforde, Les Plees del Coron

Staundf. Pl. Cor. Staundford's Placita Coronae

Staundf. Prerog. Staundford's Exposition of the King's Prerogative

Staund. Pl Staundford's Pleas of Crown (1557) (Eng.)

Staunf. P.C. Staundeforde's Pleas of the Crown

Staunf. Pr. Staundeforde's King's Prerogative

St. Bar. Rev. State Bar Review

St. Brown Stewart-Brown Cases in the Court of the Star Chamber (1455-1547)

S.T.C.
- State Tax Cases (CCH)
- Sales Tax Cases (India)

St. C. Stephen, Commentaries on the Laws of England. 2led. 1950

St. Cas. Stillingfleet, Ecclesiastical Cases (Eng.)

St. Ch. Cas. Star Chamber Cases (Eng.)

St. Chris.-Nevis St. Christopher (Kitts) - Nevis

St. Clem St. Clement's Church Case (Philadelphia, Pa.)

St. Ct. J. State Court Journal

S.T.D. Synopsis Decisions, U.S. Treasury

St. Dept. State Department Reports

Stearns R.A. Stearns on Real Actions

Stearns, Real Act. Stearn's Real Actions

St. Eccl. Cas. Stillingfleet, Ecclesiastical Cases

Stecher, Agency & Partnership Stecher's Cases on Agency and Partnership

Steer P.L. Steer, Parish Law. 6ed. 1899

S. Teind. Shaw's Teind Cases (Sc.)

STEP Selective Temporary Employment Programme

Steph. Stephens' Supreme Court Decisions (1774-1923) (Jamaica)

Steph. Cl. Stephens, Clergy. 1848

Steph. Com Stephens' Commentaries on the Laws of England

Steph. Comm. Stephens Commentaries on the Laws of England

Steph. Const. Stephens on the English Constitution

Steph. Cr. Stephen's Digest of the Criminal Law

Steph. Crim. Dig. Stephen's Digest of the Criminal Law

Steph. Cr. L. Stephen's General View of the Criminal Law. 9 editions. (1877-1950)

Steph. Cr. Law. Stephen's General View of the Criminal Law

Steph. Dig. Stephen's Digest, New Brunswick Reports

Steph. Dig. Cr. L. Stephens Digest of the Criminal Law

Steph. Dig. Cr. Law Stephen's Digest of the Criminal Law

Steph. Dig. Ev. Stephen's Digest of the Law of Evidence

Steph. Elect. Stephens, Elections. 1840

Stephen, H.C.L. Stephen's History of Criminal Law

Stephens Supreme Court Decisions, by J. E. R. Stephens

Steph. Ev. Stephens Digest of the Law of Evidence

Steph. Gen. View Stephen's General View of the Criminal Law of England

Steph J. St. Comp. Steph's Joint-Stock Companies in Canada

Steph. Lect. Stephen, Lectures on History of France

Steph. N.P. Stephen's Law of Nisi Prius

Steph. Pl. Stephen on Pleading

Steph. Proc. Stephens on Procurations

Steph. Slav. Stephens on Slavery

Stet. L. Rev. Stetson Law Review

Stetson L. Rev. Stetson Law Review

Stev. & Ben. Ins. Stevens & Benecke on Insurance

Stev. & G. Stevens & Graham (Ga.)

Stev. and Porter Stewart and Porter's Reports (Ala.)

Stev. Arb. Stevens, Arbitration. 2ed. 1835

Stev. Av. Stevens, Average. 5ed. 1835

Stev. Dig. Stevens' New Brunswick Digest

Stevens & G. Stevens & Graham's Reports (98-139 Georgia)

Stew.
- Stewart's Reports (Alabama 1827-31)
- Stewart's Reports (28-45 New Jersey Equity)
- Stewart's Nova Scotia Admiralty Reports
- Stewart's Reports (1-10 South Dakota)

Stew. Adm. Stewart's Vice-Admiralty Reports (1803-13) (Nova Scotia)

Stew. Admr.
- Stewart's Admiralty (N.S.)
- Stewart's Nova Scotia Admiralty Reports

Stew. (Ala.) Stewart's Reports (Ala.)

Stew. & P. Stewart and Porter's Alabama Supreme Court Reports (1831-34)

Stew. & P. Rep. Stewart and Porter's Reports (Ala.)

Stew. Ans. Stewart's Answers to Dirleton's Doubts (Sc.) 2 editions (1715, 1762)

Stewart.
- Stewart's Reports (Alabama 1827-31)
- Stewart's Reports (28-45 New Jersey Equity)
- Stewart's Nova Scotia Admiralty Reports
- Stewart's Reports (1-10 South Dakota)

Stewart (Ala.) Stewart's Reports (Ala.)

Stewart-Brown. Stewart-Brown's Lancashire and Cheshire Cases in the Court of Star Chamber

Stewart R. Stewart's Reports (Ala.)

Stew. Dig. Stewart's Digest of Decisions of the Courts of Law and Equity, N.J.

Stewt. Rep. Stewart's Reports (Ala.)

Stewart Vice-Adm. (Nov.Sc.) Stewart's Digest of Decisions of Law and Equity (N.J.)

Stew. Eq. Stewart's Reports (28-45 N.J. Eq.)

Stew. N.Sc. Stewart's Nova Scotia Admiralty Reports

Stew. V.A. Stewart's Vice-Admiralty Reports (Nova Scotia)

S. Texas L.J. South Texas Law Journal

S. Tex. L.J. South Texas Law Journal

S. Tex. L. Rev. South Texas Law Review

St. Ger. D. & S. St. German's Doctor and Student

St. Gloc. Statute of Glocester

Sth. Afr. Rep. South African Reports, High Court

Stil. Stillingfleet's Ecclesiastical Cases (1702-1704)

Stiles. Stiles' Reports (22-29 Iowa)

Stiles (Ia.) Stiles' Reports (22-29 Iowa)

Still. Ecc. Law Stillingfleet's Discourse on Ecclesiastical Law

Still. Eccl. Cas Stillingfleet's Ecclesiastical Cases

Stim. Gloss. Stimson's Law Glossary

Stim. Law Gloss. Stimson's Law Glossary

Stim. L. Gl. Stimson's Law Glossary

Stimson Stimson's Law Glossary

St. Income Taxes (P-H) State Income Taxes (Prentice-Hall)

Stiness. Stiness' Reports (20-34 Rhode Island)

St. Inst. Statutory Instruments (Eng.)

Stip. Stipulation(s)

St.J. Mo. P.U.C. St. Joseph, Missouri, Public Utilities Commission Reports

St. John's J. Legal Comment. St. John's Journal of Legal Commentary

St. John's L. Rev. St. John's Law Review (Brooklyn, N.Y.)

Stk. Stock

St. Law Loughborough's Digest of Statute Law (Ky.)

St. Lim. Statute of Limitations

S. T. L.J. South Texas Law Journal

Stock. Ex. Stock and commodity exchange

St. Louis B.J. St. Louis Bar Journal

St. Louis L. Rev. St. Louis Law Review

St. Louis U. L.J. Saint Louis University Law Journal

St. Louis U. Pub. L. Rev. Saint Louis University Public Law Review

St. Lou. U. L.J. St. Louis University Law Journal

St. L. U.Intra. L. Rev. St. Louis University Intramural Law Review

St.M. & P. Stuart, Milne & Peddie, Scotch

St. Mark. St. Mark's Church Case, Philadelphia

St. Marlb. Statute of Marlbridge

St. Mary's L.J. St. Mary's Law Journal

St. Mary's L. Rev. St. Mary's Law Review

St. Mert. Statute of Merton

St. Mod. Lev. Fin. Statute Modus Levandi Fines

St. Mot. Carr. Guide (CCH) State Motor Carrier Guide (Commerce Clearing House)

Stmt. Statement

Stn. L. Stanford Law Review

677

Sto.
- Storey's Reports (Del.)
- Story's United States Circuit Court Reports

Sto. Abr. Const. Story's Abridgment of the Constitution

Sto. Ag. Story on Agency

Sto. & G. Stone and Graham's Private Bills Decisions (1865)

Sto. & H. Cr. Ab. Storer & Heard on Criminal Abortion

Sto. Att. Lien Stokes, Lien of Attorneys and Solicitors. 1860

Sto. Bailm. Story on Bailment

Sto. Bills Story on Bills

Sto. C.C. Story's United States Circuit Court Reports

Stock.
- Stockton's New Jersey Equity Reports
- Stockton's Vice-Admiralty Reports, New Brunswick (1879-91)

Stock. Adm. Stockton's Admiralty Repts. (New Brunswick)

Stockett Stockett's Reports (27-53 Maryland)

Stock Non Com. Stock on Non Compotes Mentis

Stockt. Stockton's Reports (9-11 N.J. Equity)

Stockt. Ch. Stockton's Reports (9-11 N.J. Equity)

Stockton. Stockton's Vice-Admiralty Reports (New Brunswick)

Stockton Adm. (New Br.) Stockton, Vice-Admiralty Reports, New Brunswick

Stock Transfer Guide (CCH) Stock Transfer Guide

Stockt. Vice-Adm. Stockton's Vice-Admiralty (New Brunswick)

Sto. Comm. Story's Commentaries

Sto. Con. Story on Contracts

Sto. Conf. Law. Story on Conflict of Laws

Sto. Const. Story's Commentaries on the Constitution of the United States

Sto. Const. Cl. B. Story's Constitutional Class Book

Sto. Cont. Story on Contracts

Sto. Eq. Jur. Story on Equity Jurisprudence

Sto. Eq. Pl. Story on Equity Pleadings

Stokes L. of Att. Stokes on Liens of Attorneys

Sto. Laws Story's United States Laws

Sto. Miscel. Writ. Story's Miscellaneous Writings

Stone. Stone's Justices' Manual (Annual)

Stone Ben. Bdg. Soc. Stone, Benefit Building Societies. 1851

Stone Just. Man. Stone, Justices' Manual (Annual)

Stone Just. Pr. Stone's Justices' Practice

Sto. Part. Story on Partnership

Sto. Pl. Story's Civil Pleading

Sto. Pr. Story on Prize Courts (Edited by Platt)

Sto. Pr. Notes Story on Promissory Notes

Stor. & H. Abor. Storer & Heard on Criminal Abortion

Stor. Dict. Stormouth's Dictionary of the English Language

Story.
- Story on Equitable Jurisprudence (1836-1920)
- Story's United States Circuit Court Reports

Story, Ag. Story on Agency

Story, Bailm. Story on Bailments

Story, Bills. Story on Bills

Story, Comm. Const. Story's Commentaries on the Constitution of the United States

Story, Confl. Laws Story on Conflict of Laws

Story, Const. Story's Commentaries on the Constitution of the United States

Story, Cont. Story on Contracts

Story Eq. Jur. Story on Equity Jurisprudence

Story, Eq. Pl. Story's Equity Planning

Story, Laws. Story's Laws of the United States

Story, Merchants Abbott's Merchant Ships and Seamen by Story

Story, Partn. Story on Partnership

Story, Prom. Notes Story on Promissory Notes

Story R. Story's U.S. Circuit Court Reports, First Circuit

Story, Sales Story on Sales of Personal Property

Story's Circuit C.R. Story's Circuit Court Reports (1st Cir.)

Story's Laws Story's United States Laws

Story's Rep. Story's Circuit Court Reports

Story, U.S. Laws Story's Laws of the United States

Sto. Sales Story on Sales of Personal Property

Sto. U.S. Laws Story's United States Laws

Stov. Hors. Stovins' Law Respecting Horses

St. P. State Papers

St. Pl. Cr. Staundford's Pleas of Crown (Eng.)

St. Pr. Staundeforde's King's Prerogative

St. Pr. Reg. Style's Practical Register (Eng.)

St. R. Stuart's Appeal Cases (Quebec)

Str.
- Strange's Cases of Evidence (1698-1732) (Eng.)
- Strange's King's Bench Reports (1716-1749) (Eng.)

Stra. Strange

Strafford Smith's New Hampshire Reports (N.H.)

Strahan Strahan's Reports (19 Oregon)

Strah. Domat Strahan's Domat's Civil Law

Straits L.J. & Rep. Straits Law Journal and Reporter

Stran. Strange

Str. & H.C. Streets and Highways Code

Strange. Strange's Reports, English Courts

Strange (Eng.) Strange's Reports, English Courts (93 ER)

Strange, Madras Strange's Notes of Cases, Madras

Stratton. Stratton's Reports (12-14 Oregon)

Str. Cas. Ev. Strange's Cases of Evidence ("Octavo Strange")

S. Treaty Doc. Senate Treaty Documents

Street Ry. Rep. Street Railway Reports

St. Rep.
- State Reports
- State Reporter

St. Rep. N.S.W. State Reports (New South Wales)

St. Rep. Queensl. (Austr.) Queensland State Reports

Str. Ev. Strange's Cases of Evidence (1698-1732) (Eng.)

Str. H.L. Strange's Hindoo Law

Strick. Ev. Strickland, Evidence. 1830

Stringf. Stringfellow's Reports (9-11 Missouri)

Stringfellow Stringfellow's Reports (9-11 Missouri)

Str. N.C. Sir T. Strange's Notes of Cases, Madras

Strob. Strobhart's South Carolina Law Reports (1846-50)

Strob. Ch. Strobhart's South Carolina Equity Reports

Strob. Eq. Strobhart's South Carolina Equity Reports (1846-50)

Strobh. Eq. (S.C.) Strobhan, South Carolina Equity

Strobh. L. (S.C.) Strobhart, South Carolina Law

Stroud Sl. Stroud on Slavery

St. R. Q. Queensland State Reports (Aus.)

St. R. Qd. Queensland State Reports (Aus.)

St. R. Queensl. State Reports, Queensland (1908-58) (Aus.)

Struve Struve's Reports (Washington Territory 1854-88)

St. Ry. Rep. Street Railway Reports (U.S.)

Sts. & Hy. Streets & Highways

STT Wells, Successful Trial Techniques of Expert Practitioners

St. Tax Cas. (CCH) State Tax Cases

St. Tax Cas. Rep. (CCH)
- State Tax Cases Reports
- State Tax Cases Reporter

St. Tax Guide (CCH) State Tax Guide (Commerce Clearing House)

St. Tax Rep. (CCH)
- State Tax Reports
- State Tax Reporter (Commerce Clearing House)

St. Thomas L. Rev. St. Thomas Law Review

St. Tr. Howell's State Trials (1163-1820)

St. Tri. State Trials

St. Tr. N.S. Macdonell's State Trials (1820-58)

Stu. Adm. Stuart's Lower Canada Vice-Admiralty Reports

Stu. Adm. N.S. Stuart's Lower Canada Vice-Admiralty Reports, New Series

Stu. Adm.V.A. Stuart's Lower Canada Vice-Admiralty Reports

Stu. Ap. Stuart's Lower Canada King's Bench Reports, Appeal Cases

Stuart.
- Stuart, Milne & Peddie's Scotch Session Cases
- Stuart's Lower Canada Reports
- Stuart's Vice-Admiralty Reports

Stuart, Adm. N.S. Stuart's Vice-Admiralty (Lower Canada Cases)

Stuart & Por. Stewart and Porter's Reports (Ala.)

Stuart & Porter Stewart and Porter's Reports (Ala.)

Stuart Beng. Stuart's Select Cases (Bengal, India) 1860

Stuart K.B. Stuart's Kings Bench Reports (Quebec, 1810-25) 1

Stuart K.B. (Quebec) Stuart, Lower Canada King's Bench Reports

Stuart L.C.K.B. Stuart's Lower Canada King's Bench Reports

Stuart L.C.V.A. Stuart's Lower Canada Vice-Admiralty Reports

Stuart M. & P. Stuart, Milne and Peddie, Court of Session Cases (1851-53)(Sc.)

Stuart's Adm. Stuart's Vice-Admiralty Reports (1836-74) (Quebec)

Stuart's R. Stuart's Lower Canada King's Bench Reports. Appeals Cases (Quebec)

Stuart Vice-Adm. Stuart's Vice-Admiralty (Lower Canada)

Stubbs, C. H. Stubb's Constitutional History

Stubbs Sel. Ch. Stubb's Select Charters

S.T.U.C. Scottish Trades Union Congress

Stud. Studies

Stud. & Doc. His. Jur. Studia et Documenta Historiae et Juris, Rome, Italy

Student Law. Student Lawyer

Student Law. J. Student Lawyer Journal

Student L. Rev. Student Law Review

Stud. Hist. Studies in History, Economics and Public Law

Studies Crim. L. Studies in Criminal Law and Procedure

Stud. in Comp. Local Govt. Studies in Comparative Local Government. The Hague, Netherlands

Stud. Int'l Fiscal L. Studies on International Fiscal Law

Stud. L. & Econ. Dev. Studies in Law and Economic Development

Stud. Law Lex. Students' Pocket Law Lexicon

Stu. K.B. Stuart's Lower Canada King's Bench Reports (1810-35)

Stu. L.C. Stuart's Lower Canada King's Bench Reports (1810-35)

Stu. M. & P. Stuart, Milne, & Peddie's Scotch Court of Sessions Reports

Stu. Mil. & Ped. Stuart, Milne & Peddie's Scotch Court of Sessions Reports

Stur. & Porter Stewart and Porter's Reports (Ala.)

Sturg. Ins. D. Sturgeon, Insolvent Debtors Act. 1842

St. Westm. Statute of Westminster

Sty. Style's King's Bench Reports (1646-1655)

Style. Style's English King's Bench Reports

Style, Pr. Reg. Style's Practical Register

Sty. Pr. Reg. Style's Practical Register (1657-1710

Su. Superior Court

Sub.
- Subcommittee
- Subordinated

Subcomm Subcommittee

Subd. Subdivision

sub.nom. under the name

Subpar. Subparagraph

Subrog. Subrogation

Subsc. Subscription

Subsec. Subsection

Subs. Leg. Austl. Cap. Terr. Subsidiary Legislation of the Australian Capital Territory

Suc. Successor

SUCL Stetson University College of Law

Su. Ct. Cir. Supreme Court (Ceylon)

Sudan L.J. & Rep. Sudan Law Journal and Reports, Khartoum, Sudan

Sud. Dew. Ad. Sudder Dewanny Adawlut Reports (India)

Sud. Dew. Rep. Sudder Dewanny Reports, N.W. Province (India)

SuDoc Superintendent of Documents, Government Printing Office

Suffolk Transnat'l L.J. Suffolk Transnational Law Journal

Suffolk U. L. Rev. Suffolk University Law Review

Suffolk Univ. L. Rev. Suffolk University Law Review

Sugd. Sugden

Sugd. Powers. Sugden on Powers

Sugd. Vend. Sugden on Vendors and Purchasers

Sug. Est. Sugden on the Law of Estates

Sug. Hd. Bk. Sugden's Hand-Book of Property Law

Sug. Pow. Sugden on Powers, 8 editions (1808-61)

Sug. Pr. Sugden on the Law of Property

Sug. Prop. Sugden on the Law of Property as administered by the House of Lords

Sug. Pr. St. Sugden on Property Statutes

Sug. V. & P. Sugden on Vendors and Purchasers. 14 editions (1805-62)

Sug. Vend. Sugden on Vendors and Purchasers

Sullivan Smith's New Hampshire Reports (N.H.)

Sull. Ld. Tit. Sullivan's Land Titles in Massachusetts

Sull. Lect. Sullivan's Lectures on Constitution and Laws of England

Su. L.R. Suffolk University Law Review

S.U. L. Rev. Southern University Law Review

Sum.
- Sumner's Circuit Court Reports (U.S.)
- Hale's Summary of Pleas of the Crown (Eng)

Sum. Dec. Summary Decisions, Bengal (India)

Sum. Judg. Summary judgment

Summ. Summary

Summ. Dec. Summary Decisions, Bengal

Summerfield Summerfield's Reports (21 Nevada)

Summerfield, S. Summerfield's (S.) Reports (21 Nevada)

Summers, Oil & Gas Summers on Oil and Gas

Summ. N.P. Summary of the Law of Nisi Prius

Sumn. Sumner's United States Circuit Court Reports

Sumner. Sumner's United States Circuit Court Reports

Sumn. Ves. Sumner's Edition of Vesey's Reports

Sum. Rep. Sumner's U.S. Circuit Court Reports

Sum. U.C.C.R. Sumner's U.S. Circuit Court Reports

Sum. Ves. Sumner's Edition of Vesey's Reports

Sun. & H. Sundays and holidays

Sup Superior

Sup. Supreme

Sup. & C.P. Dec. Ohio Decisions

Sup. Court Rep. Supreme Court Reporter

Sup.Ct.
- Supreme Court
- Supreme Court Reporter (National Reporter System)

Sup. Ct. App. Supreme Court Appeals (India)

Sup. Ct. Err. Supreme Court of Errors

Sup. Ct. Hist. Soc'y Q. Supreme Court Historical Society Quarterly

Sup. Ct. Hist. Soc'y Y.B. Supreme Court Historical Society Yearbook

Sup. Ct. J. Supreme Court Journal (India)

Sup. Ct. L. Rev. Supreme Court Law Review

Sup. Ct. L. Rev. 2d Supreme Court Law Review (Canada) Second Series

Sup. Ct. M.R. Supreme Court Monthly Review (India)

Sup. Ct. Pr. Supreme Court Practice

Sup. Ct. R.
- Supreme Court Reports (India)
- United States Supreme Court Rule

Sup. Ct. Rep. Supreme Court Reporter

Sup. Ct. Repr. Supreme Court Reporter

Sup. Ct. Rev. Supreme Court Review

Sup. Ct. R. (N.Y.) New York Supreme Court Reports (N.Y.)

Super.
- Superior Court
- Superior Court Reports

Super. Ct. Superior Court

Super. Ct. App. Div. Superior Court Appellate Division

Super. Ct. Ch. Div. Superior Court Chancery Division

Super. Ct. Law. Div. Superior Court Law Division

Super. Ct. Rep. Superior Court Reports (New York, Pennsylvania, etc.)

Super. Ct. (R.I.) Rhode Island Superior Court

Sup. Jud. Ct. Supreme Judicial Court, Massachusetts

Supp.
- New York Supplement Reports
- Supplement
- Support

Supp. Code Supplement to Code

Supp. Gen. St. Supplement to the General Statutes

suppl.
- Supplement; supplemented
- supplementary

Support Per. Support of persons

Supp. Rev. Supplement to the Revision

Supp. Rev. Code Supplement to the Revised Code

Supp. Rev. St. Supplement to the Revised Statutes

Supp.Ves. Jun. Supplement to Vesey, Jr.'s, Reports

Supr.
- Superior
- Supreme

supra. above (in same article or treatise)

Supr. Ct. Pennsylvania Superior Court Reports (Pa.)

Supr. Ct. Rep. supreme Court Reporter

Supreme Court Rev. The Supreme Court Review

Sup. Trib. Supremo Tribunal (Supreme Court of Appeal)

Sur. Surety

Sur. Ct. Surrogate's Court

Surety Suretyship

Surin. Suriname

Surr. Surrogate

Surr. Ct. Surrogate's Court

Surr. Ct. Proc. Act Surrogate's Court Procedure Act

surv. survey

Survey Calif. L. Survey of California Law

Sus. Leg. Chron. Susquehanna Legal Chronical (pa.)

susp. suspended

Susq. L. C. Susquehanna Leading Chronicle (Pa.)

Susq. L. Chron Susquehanna Legal Chronicle, Pennsylvania

Susq. Legal Chron. Susquehanna Legal Chronicle (Pa.)

Susq. Leg. Chron. Susquehanna Legal Chronicle, (Pa.)

Susquehanna Leg. Chron. (Pa.) Susquehanna Legal Chronicle (Pa.)

Suth. Sutherland's Calcutta Reports (India)

Suth. App. Sutherland's Appeals Reports, Small Causes Court (1861-65) (Bengal, India)

Suth. Bengal Sutherland's Bengal High Court Reports (India)

Suth. Dam. Sutherland on the Law of Damages

Suth. F.B.R. Sutherland's Bengal Full Bench Reports (India)

Suth. Mis. Indian Weekly Reporter, Miscellaneous Appeals

Suth, P.C.A. Sutherland Privy Council Appeals

Suth. P.C.J. Sutherland Privy Council Judgements (same as above)

Suth. Sp. N.
- Full Bench Rulings (Calcutta)
- Sutherland Special Number of Weekly Reporter

Suth. Stat. Const. Sutherland's Statutory Construction

Suth. St. Const. Sutherland on Statutes and Statutory Construction

Suth. W.R. Sutherland's Weekly Reporter, Calcutta (1864-76)

Suth. W.R. Mis. Sutherland's Weekly Reports, Miscellaneous Appeals (India)

Sutton. Sutton on Personal Actions at Common Law

S.V.A.R. Stuart's Vice-Admiralty Reports (1836-74) (Quebec)

Svensk Jur.-Tidn. Svensk Juristtidnina. Stockholm, Sweden

SvJT Svensk Juristtidning (Sweden)

S.W. South Western Reporter (Nat. Reporter System)

S.W.2d South Western Reporter Second Series

Sw.
- Southwest(ern)
- Swabey Reports, Ecclesiastical (1855-59) (Eng.)
- Swabey's Admiralty Reports (Eng.)
- Swan's Reports (31, 32 Tennessee)
- Swanston's Chancery Reports (England)
- Swedish
- Sweeney's N.Y. Superior Court Reports
- Swinton's Scotch Justiciary Cases

S.W.A. Reports of the High Court of South West Africa (1920-46) South West Africa

Swab. Swabey Reports, Ecclesiastical (1855-59) (Eng.)

Swab. Admr. Swabey's English Admiralty Reports (166 ER)

Swab. & T. Swabey and Tristram's Probate and Divorce Reports (164 ER)

Swab. & Tr. Swabey and Tristram's Probate and Divorce Reports (164 ER)

Swab. Div. Swabey, Divorce and Matrimonial Causes. 3ed. 1859

Swabey Adm. Swabey's Admiralty Reports (1855-59) (166 ER)

Swabey Adm. (Eng.) Swabey's Admiralty (166 ER)

Swabey & T. (Eng.) Swabey & Tristram (164 ER)

Swan
- Swan's Tennessee Supreme Court Reports (1851-53)
- Swanston's Chancery Reports (Eng.)

Swan C. R. St. Swan and Critchfield's Revised Statutes (Ohio)

Swan & S. St. Swan and Sayler's Supplement to the Revised Statutes (Ohio)

Swan. Ch. Swanston's English Chancery Reports

Sw. & Tr. Swabey and Tristram's Probate and Divorce Reports (164 ER)

Swan. Eccl. C. Swan, Ecclesiastical Courts. 1830

Swan Just. Swan's Justice (Ohio)

Swan. Pl. & Pr. Swan, Pleading and Practice (Ohio)

Swan Pr. Swan, Practice (Ohio)

Swans. Swanston's English Chancery Reports

Swan's Swan's Reports (Tenn.)

Swan's R. Swan's Reports (Tenn.)

Swan's St. Swan's Statutes (Ohio)

Swanst. Swanston's English Chancery Reports (36 ER)

Swanst. (Eng.) Swanston's English Chancery Reports (36 ER)

Swan Tr. Swan's Treatise (Ohio)

Swaz Swaziland

SWDA Solid Waste Disposal Act

Swed. Sweden

Swed. & Int'l Arb. Swedish and International Arbitration

Sween. Sweeny's New York Superior Court Reports 31-32 N.Y.S.Ct.) (1869-70)

Sweeney (N.Y.) Sweeney, New York Superior Court Reports, 31-32)

Sweeny. Sweeney, New York Supreme Court Reports, 31-32

Sweet.
- Sweet on the Limited Liability Act
- Sweet on Wills
- Sweet's Law Dictionary
- Sweet's Marriage Settlement Cases
- Sweet's Precedents in Conveyancing

Sweet L.D. Sweet, Dictionary of English Law. 1882

Sweet L.L. Sweet on the Limited Liability Act

Sweet M. Sett. Cas. Sweet's Marriage Settlement Cases (Eng.)

Sweet Pr. Conv. Sweet, Precedents in Conveyancing. 4ed. 1886

Sweet Wills Sweet on Wills

Swen. Sweeney, New York Superior Court Reports, 31-32

Swift, Dig. Swift's Digest, Connecticut

Swift Ev. Swift on Evidence, and Bills and Notes

Swift Sys. Swift's System of the Laws of Connecticut

Swin.
- Swinburne on Wills, 10 editions (1590-1803)

- Swinton's Justiciary Reports (1835-41)

Swinb. Desc. Swinburne, Descents. 1825

Swinb. Mar. Swinburne, Married Women. 1846

Swinb. Spo. Swinburne on Spousals

Swinb. Wills Swinburne on Wills

Swin. Jus. Cas. Swinton's Scotch Justiciary Cases

Swin. Reg. App. Swinton's Scots Registration Appeal Cases (1835-41)

Swint. Swinton's Justiciary Cases (Sc.)

Switz. Switzerland

S.W. Law J. Southwestern Law Journal

Sw. Legal Found. Inst. on Oil & Gas L. & Tax. Southwestern Legal Foundation Institution on Oil & Gas Law & Taxation

Sw. L.J. Southwestern Law Journal

S.W. L.J. Southwestern Law Journal & Reporter

S.W. L. Rev. Southwestern Law Review

S.W. Pol. Sci. Q. Southwestern Political Science Quarterly

S.W. R. South Western Reporter

S.W. Rep. South Western Reporter (commonly cited S.W.)

S. W. Repr. South Western Reporter

Sw. U. L. Rev. Southwestern University Law Review

SWUSL Southwestern University School of Law

Syd. App. Sydney Appeals (Aus.)

Syd. L.R. Sydney Law Review

Sydney L. Rev. Sydney Law Review

Sy. J. Int. L. Syracuse Journal of International Law and Commerce

Syl. The Syllabi

Sy. L.R. Syracuse Law Review

Sym. Code Syms, Code of English Law. 1870

Syme. Syme's Justiciary Reports (1826-30)

Symp. Symposium

Symposum Jun. Bar Symposium l'Association de jeune Barreau de Montreal

Symp. Priv. Invest. Abroad Symposium. Private Investors Abroad

syn.
- synonym
- synopsis

Synop. Snyopsis

Syn. Ser. Synopsis Series of the United States Treasury Decisions

Syracuse J. Int'l L. Syracuse Journal of International Law

Syracuse J. Int'l L. & Com. Syracuse Journal of International Law and Commerce

Syracuse L. Rev. Syracuse Law Review

Syr. J.Int'l L. & Com. Syracuse Journal of International Law & Commerce

SYRUCL Syracuse University College of Law

Sys. System

T

T.
- Tappan's Common Pleas Reports (Ohio)
- Taxes
- Tempore (in the time of)
- Term
- Territory
- Title
- Tobacco Tax Ruling, Internal Revenue Bureau (U.S.)
- Traffic Cases
- Transvaal Provincial Division Reports (S.Africa)
- Trinity
- Turkish

T.A.
- Board of Tax Appeals
- trading as
- Trustee under agreement

TAB. Technical Assistance Board (UN)

T. Ad. The Tax Advisor

TAFO Spragens & Fleming, Tax Aspects of Forming and Operating Closely Held Corporations

Tait.
- Tait's Index to Morison's Dictionary (Sc.)
- Tait's Index to Scottish Session Cases (1823)
- Tait's Manuscript Decisions, Scotch Session Cases

Tait Ev. Tait on Evidence

Tait Ind. Tait's Index to Scotch Session Cases

Tait J.P. Tait's Justice of the Peace

Tal.
- Cases tempore Talbot, English Chancery
- Talbot's Cases in Equity (1734-38)

Talb.
- Cases tempore Talbot, English Chancery
- Talbot's Cases in Equity (1734-38)

Tam. Tamlyn's English Rolls Court Reports (48 ER)

TAM Technical Advice memorandum

Tamb. Tambyah's Reports (Ceylon)

Taml. Tamlyn's English Rolls Court Reports (48 ER)

Taml. Ev. Tamlyn, Evidence in Chancery. 2ed. 1846

Taml. T.Y. Tamlyn, Terms of Years. 1825

Tamlyn. Tamlyn's English Rolls Court Reports (48 ER)

Tamlyn (Eng.) Tamlyn's English Rolls Court Reports (48 ER)

Tamlyn Ch. Tamlyn's English Rolls Court Reports (48 ER)

TAMRA Technical and Miscellaneous Revenue Act of 1988

Tan. Taney's United States Circuit Reports

Tanc. Q.W. Tancred on Quo Warranto

T. & B. Taylor & Bell's Calcutta Supreme Court Reports (India)

T. & C. Thompson & Cooke's New York Supreme Court Reports.

T. & G. Tyrwhitt & Granger, English Exchequer Reports (1835-36)

T. & H. Prac. Troubat and Haly's Pennsylvania Practice

T & M Time and Materials (contract)

T. & M.
- Temple & Mew's Criminal Appeal Cases (Eng.)
- Temple & Mew's Crown Cases (1848-51) (Eng.)

T. & P. Turner & Phillips' Reports, English Chancery

T. & R. Turner & Russell, English Chancery Reports (1822-25)

T. & S. Thomson & Steger's Tennessee Statutes

T. & S. Pr. Tillinghast & Shearman's New York Practice and Pleading

T. & T. Sup. Trinidad & Tobago Supreme Court Judgments

Taney Taney's United States Circuit Court Reports

Taney's C.C. Dec. Taney's U.S. Circuit Court Reports

Taney's Dec. (U.S.C.C.) Taney's U.S. Circuit Court Reports

Tan. L.R. Tanganyika Territory Law Reports

Tann.
- Tanner's Reports (8-14 Indiana)
- Tanner's Reports (13-17 Utah)

Tanner
- Tanner's Reports (8-14 Indiana)
- Tanner's Reports (13-17 Utah)

Tanz. Tanzania

Tap. Tappan's Ohio Common Pleas Reports

Tap. C.M. Tapping's Copyholder's Manual

Tap. Man. Tapping. Writ of Mandamus. 1848

Tapp. Tappan's Ohio Common Pleas Reports

Tappan. Tappan's Ohio Common Pleas Reports

Tappan (Ohio) Tappan's Ohio Common Pleas Reports

Tappan's Ohio Rep. Tappan's Common Pleas Reports (Ohio)

Tappan's R. Tappan's Common Pleas Reports (Ohio)

Tapping Tapping on the Writ of Mandamus

Tapp. M & Ch. Tapp, Maintenance and Champerty. 1861

Tarrif Ind., New. News' Tariff Index

Tarl. Tarleton Term Reports (1881-83) (New South Wales)

Tarl. Term R. Tarleton's Term Reports (New South Wales)

Tas. Tasmania

Tas. Bldg. App. R. Tasmanian Building Appeal Reports

Tasch. Cr. Acts Taschereau's Criminal Law Acts (Canada)

Tas. L.R. Tasmanian Law Reports (Aus.)

Tas. L.R. Tasmanian Law Reports (Law Book Co.)

Tas. L.R.C. Tasmanian Law Reform Commission

Tasm. Tasmanian State Reports

Tasm. Acts Tasmania Acts of Parliament (1901-1959)

Tasmania L.R. University of Tasmania Law

Tasmania U.L. Rev. Tasmania University Law Review

Tasmanian Univ. L. Rev. Tasmanian University Law Review. Hobart, Australia

Tasm. L.R. Tasmania Law Reports (Aus.)

Tasm. Sess. Stat. Tasmania Statutes (1960-date)

Tasm. S.R. Tasmanian State Reports (Law Book Co.) (Tasm.)

Tasm. Stat. Tasmanian Statutes (Aus.)

Tasm. Stat. R. Tasmanian Statutory Rules, with Tables (Aus.)

Tasm. St. R. Tasmania State Reports (Aus.)

Tasm. U.L. Rev. Tasmania University Law Review

Tas. R. Tasmanian State Reports

Tas. S.R. Tasmanian State Reports (Law Book Co.)

Tas.U.L.R. Tasmania University Law Review, Aus.

Tas. Univ. L. Rev. Tasmanian University Law Review

Tasw. Lang. Hist. Tasweil-Langmead, English Constitutional History. 10ed. 1946

Tate Dig. Ind. Tate's Virginia Analytical Digested Index

Tate's Dig. Tate's Digest of Laws (Va.)

Taun. Taunton's English Common Pleas Reports

Taut. Taunton's English Common Pleas Reports

Taunt. (Eng.) Taunton's English Common Pleas Reports (127. 129 ER)

Tax
- Department of Taxation
- Taxation

Tax. Taxation

Tax A.B.C. Canada Tax Appeal Board Cases

Tax. Acct. Taxation for Accountants

Tax. Ad. The Tax Adviser

Tax Adm'rs. News Tax Administrators News

Tax. & Rev. Taxation and Revenue

Tax Cas. Tax Cases

Tax. Conf. Tax Conference

Tax. Coun. Q. Tax Counselor's Quarterly

Tax Counselor's Q. Tax Counselor's Quarterly

Tax Ct. Mem. Dec. (CCH) [or (P-H)] Tax Court Memorandum Decisions (CCH) [or (P-H)]

Tax Ct. Rep. (CCH)
- Tax Court Reports
- Tax Court Reporter (CCH)

Tax Ct. Rep. & Mem. Dec.(P-H) Tax Court Reported and Memorandum Decisions (Prentice-Hall)

Tax Ct. Rep. Dec. (P-H) Tax Court Reported Decisions (P-H)

Taxes Taxes The Tax Magazine

Tax Exec. Tax Executive

Tax-Exempt Org. (P-H) Tax-Exempt Organizations

Tax-Exempt Orgs. Tax-Exempt Organizations (CCH)

Tax. for Law. Taxation for Lawyers

Tax Law. Tax Lawyer

Tax Law Rep. Tax Lax & Reporter

Tax. L.R. Tax Law Reporter

Tax. L.Rep. Tax Law Reporter

Tax L. Rev. Tax Law Review

Tax Mag. Tax Magazine

Tax Magazine Tax Magazine

Tax Man. Tax Management

Tax Management Int'l. Tax Management International Journal

Tax Management Memo Tax Management Memo (Bureau of National Affairs)

Tax Mgmt.(BNA) Tax Management (Bureau of National Affairs)

Tax Mgmt. Int'l J. Tax Management International Journal

Tax Mngm't. Tax Management, (BNA)

Tax'n. Taxation

Tax'n for Acct. Taxation for Accountants

Tax'n for Law. Taxation for Lawyers

Taxp. Act. Taxpayers' actions

Tax Plan. (IPB) Tax Planning (Institute for Business Planning)

Tax Plan. Ideas (IBP) Tax Planning Ideas (Institute for Business Planning)

Tax Pl. Int. Tax Planning International

Tax Pl. Rev. Tax Planning Review

Tax Pract. Forum Tax Practitioners Forum

Tax. R. Taxation Reports (Eng.)

Tax Rev. Tax Review

Tax Treaties (CCH) Tax Treaties

Tay.
- Taylor
- Taylor's King's Bench Reports, Ontario (1823-1827)
- Taylor's Reports (1 North Carolina) (1798-1802)
- Taylor's Supreme Court Reports (1847-48) (Bengal, India)

Tay. & B. Taylor & Bell's Bengal Reports (India)

Tay. Bank. L. Taylor on the Bankruptcy Law

Tay. Bk. R. Taylor, Book of Rights. 1833

Tay. Civ. L. Taylor's Elements of Civil Law

Tay. Eq. Jur. Taylor on Equity Jurisprudence

Tay. Ev. Taylor, Evidence. 12ed. 1931

Tay. Glos. Taylor, Law Glossary. 2ed. 1823

Tay. Gov. Taylor on Government

Tay. J.L. J. L. Taylor's Reports (1 N.C.)

Tay. L. & T. Taylor's Landlord and Tenant

Tayl. Civil Law Taylor on Civil Law

Tayl. Corp. Taylor on Private Corporations

Tayl. Ev. Taylor on Evidence

Tay. L. Gl. Taylor's Law Glossary

Tayl. Gloss. Taylor's Law Glossary

Tayl. Hist. Gav. Taylor (Silas), History of Gavelkind

Tayl. Landl. & Ten. Taylor's Landlord and Tenant

Tayl. Med. Jur. Taylor's Medical Jurisprudence

Tayl. N.C. Taylor's Reports (1 N.C.)

Taylor Taylor's Customary Laws of Rembau (1903-28) (Mal.)

Taylor.
- Taylor's Kings Bench Reports (Canada)
- Taylor's Reports, Bengal (India)
- Taylor's Reports (1 North Carolina)
- Taylor's Term Reports (4 North Carolina)

Taylor K.B. (Can.) Taylor, Upper Canada King's Bench Reports

Taylor (Malaya) Taylor's Customary Laws of Rembau (1903-28) (Mal.)

Taylor U.C. Taylor's Kings' Bench Reports, Ontario

Tayl. Priv. Corp. Taylor on Private Corporations

Tayl. St. Taylor's Revised Statutes (Wis.)

Tay. Med. Jur. Taylor, Medical Jurisprudence, 12ed. 1966

Tay. N.C. Taylor's Reports (1 North Carolina)

Tay. Poi. Taylor, Poisons. 3ed. 1875

Tay. Pr. Tayler's Precedents of Wills

Tay. Rep. Taylor's Reports (1 N.C.)

Tay. Tit. Taylor, Tithe Commutation. 1876

Tay. U.C. Taylor, Upper Canada Reports (K.B. 1823-27) 1 vol.

Tay. Wills Tayler's Precedents of Wills

Tay. Wis. Stat. Taylor's Wisconsin Statutes

TBA Tennessee Bar Association

T.B. & M. Tracewell, Bowers, & Mitchell's U.S. Comptroller's Decisions

T.B.M. Tax Board Memorandum (Internal Revenue Bulletin) (U.S.)

T.B. Mon. T.B. Monroe's Kentucky Supreme Court Reports (1824-28) (17-23 Kentucky)

T.B. Mon. (Ky.) T.B. Monroe's Reports (17-23 Kentucky)

T.B.R. Advisory Tax Board Recommendation (Internal Revenue Bureau) (U.S.)

T.B.R.D. Taxation Board of Review Decisions (New Series) (Aus.)

T.C. All India Reporter, Travancore-Cochin (1950-57)

TC Trusteeship Council (UN)

T.C.
- Tax Court of the United States
- Town Clerk
- Town Council(lor)
- Reports of Tax Cases (Eng.)
- Trade Cases (CCH)
- U.S. Tax Court Cases

T.C.A. Tennessee Code Annotated

TCB Fleming, Tax Aspects of Buying and Selling Corporate Businesses

T.C.B. Title Certificate Book

Tchrs. Teachers

TCL Goff, Federal Income Taxation of Corporate Liquidations

TCLM Canterbury, Texas Construction Law Manual

TCM
- Tax Court Memorandum Decisions (CCH)
- Tax Court Memorandum Decisions (P-H)

T.C.M. (CCH) Tax Court Memorandum Decisions (CCH)

T.C. Memo. Tax Court Memorandum Decisions (CCH) or (P-H)

T.C.M. (P-H) Tax Court Memorandum Decisions (P-H)

TCOR Trusteeship Council

T.C. Pub. U.S. Tariff Commission Publications

T.C.Q. Tax Counselor's Quarterly

T.C.R. Transit Commission Reports (N.Y.)

T.C. Rept. 2d ser. U.S. Tariff Commission Reports of second series

T.C. Res. Trusteeship Council Resolution (UN)

T. Ct. Tax Court of the United States Reports

T.Ct. Mem. Tax Court of the U.S. Memorandum

T Ct Rule Rules of the Tax Court of the United States

T. Cv. Tax Convention

T.D. Treasury Decisions (U.S. Treasury Dept.)

TDB Trade and Development Board (UN)

T.D.B. Total Disability Benefit

TDBOR Trade and Development Board of the Conference on Trade and Development

TDC Treasury Department Circular

TDO Treasury Department Order

TE Rein, Thermographic Evidence of Soft Tissue Injuries

T.E.A. Trade Expansion Act of 1962 (U.S.)

Tech.
- Technical
- Technique
- Technology

Techn. Dict. Crabb's Technological Dictionary

TEFRA Tax Equity and Fiscal Responsibiity Act of 1982

TEI Thorne Ecological Institute

Teiss. Teisser's Court of Appeal, Parish of Orleans Reports (1903-1917)

Teissler Teissler's Court of Appeal, Parish of Orleans, Reports (1903-17)

Tel.
- Telephone
- Telegram
- Telegraph

Tel-Aviv Univ. Stud. L. Tel-Aviv University Studies in Law, Tel-Aviv, Israel

Tel-Aviv U. Stud. L. Tel-Aviv University Studies in Law

Telecom. Telecommunications

Tem.
- Temple
- Temporary
- Tempore (in the time of)
- The Templar (1788-79) (London)

Temp.
- temporary
- Tempore (in the time of)

Temp. & M. Temple and Mew's Crown Cases (1848-51)

Temp. Emer. Ct. App. Temporary Emergency Court of Appeals (U.S.)

Temp. Envtl. L. & Tech. J. Temple Environmental Law & Technology Journal

Temp. Geo. II. Cases in Chancery tempore George II. (Eng.)

Temp. Int'l & Comp. L.J. Temple International & Comparative Law Journal

Temp. L. Rev. Temple Law Review

Temple & M. Temple & Mew Crown Cases (Eng.)

Temple & M. (Eng.) Temple & Mew Crown Cases (Eng.)

Temple L.Q. Temple Law Quarterly

Temple L. Quart. Temple Law Quarterly

Temp. L.Q. Temple Law Quarterly

Temp. Univ. L.Q. Temple University Law Quarterly

Temp. Wood. Manitoba Reports tempore Wood (Canada)

Ten. Tennessee

Ten. App. Tennessee Appeals Reports (Tenn.)

Ten. Cas.
- Shannon's Cases, Tennessee
- Thompson's Unreported Cases, Tennessee

Tenn.
- Tennessee
- Tennessee Reports
- Tennessee Supreme Court Reports

Tenn. Admin. Comp. Official Compilation Rules and Regulations of the State of Tennessee

Tenn. Admin. Reg. Tennessee Administrative Register

Tenn. App.
- Tennessee Appeals
- Tennessee Appellate Bulletin
- Tennessee Civil Appeals Reports

Tenn. App. Bull. Tennessee Appellate Bulletin

Tenn. Appeals Tennessee Appeals Reports (Tenn.)

Tenn. App. R. Tennessee Appeals Reports (Tenn.)

Tenn. B.A. Tennessee Bar Association

Tenn. Bar J. Tennessee Bar Journal

Tenn. B.J. Tennessee Bar Journal

Tenn. Cas.   Shannon's Unreported Cases (Tenn. 1847-1894)

Tenn. Cas. (Shannon)
- R.T. Shannon's Tennessee Cases (Tenn.)
- Thompson's Unreported Cases (Tenn.) (1847-69)

Tenn. C.C.A.   Tennessee Court of Civil Appeals

Tenn. C.C.A. (Higgins)   Higgins' Tennessee Court of Civil Appeals (Tenn.)

Tenn. Ch.   Cooper's Tennessee Chancery Reports (1878)

Tenn. Ch. A.   Tennessee Chancery Appeals

Tenn. Chancery   Tennessee Chancery Reports Cooper (Tenn.)

Tenn. Chancery App.   Tennessee Chancery Appeals Reports - Wright (Tenn.)

Tenn. Ch. App.   Tennessee Chancery Appeals (Wright)

Tenn. Ch. App. Dec.   Tennessee Chancery Appeals Decisions (1895-1907)

Tenn. Ch. Ap. Reps.   Wright's Tennessee Chancery Appeals Reports (Tenn.)

Tenn. Ch. R.   Tennessee Chancery Reports Cooper (Tenn.)

Tenn. Civ. A.   Tennessee Civil Appeals

Tenn. Civ. App.   Tennessee Civil Appeals

Tenn. Civ. App. (Higgins)   Higgins' Tennessee Court of Civil Appeals (Tenn.)

Tenn. Code Ann.   Tennessee Code Annotated

Tenn. Const.   Tennessee Constiution

Tenn. Cr. App.   Tennessee Criminal Appeals

Tenn. Crim. App.   Tennessee Criminal Appeals Reports

Tennessee R.   Tennessee Reports (Tenn.)

Tennessee Rep.   Tennessee Reports (Tenn.)

Tenn. Jur.   Tennessee Jurisprudence

Tenn. Juris.   Tennessee Jurisprudence

Tenn. Law.   Tennessee Lawyer

Tenn. L. Rev.   Tennessee Law Review

Tenn. Legal Reporter   Tennessee Legal Reporter, New Series (Tenn.)

Tenn. Leg. Rep.   Tennessee Legal Reporter

Tenn. L.R.   Tennessee Law Review

Tenn. L.R.C.   Tennessee Law Revision Commission

Tenn. L. Rev.   Tennessee Law Review

Tenn. Priv. Acts.   Private Acts of the State of Tennessee

Tenn. Pub. Acts   Public Acts of the State of Tennessee

Tenn. R.   Tennessee Reports (Tenn.)

Tenn. R. & P.U.C.   Tennessee Railroad & Public Utilities Commission Board

Tenn. R.C. Tennessee Railroad Commission

Tenn. Rep. Tennessee Reports (Tenn.)

Tent. tentative

Ter. Terry's Reports (Delaware)

Ter. Laws. Territorial Laws

Term.
- Term Reports (North Carolina) (1816-18)
- Term Reports, English King's Bench (Durnford & East's Reports)

Term. de la L. Les Termes de la Ley

Termes de la Ley Terms of the Common Laws and Statutes Expounded and Explained by John Rastell (1685)

Term. N.C. Term Reports (Taylor, 4 N.C.)

Term N.C Taylor's North Carolina Term Reports (N.C.)

Term R. Term Reports, English King's Bench (Durnford & East's Reports)

Term. Rep. Term Reports (Durnford & East) (Eng.)

Term. Rep. (N.C) Taylor's Term Reports (4 North Carolina)

Terr.
- Terrell's Reports (38-71 Texas)
- Territories
- Territory

Terr. Sea Journal Territorial Sea Journal

Terr. & Wal. Terrell & Walker

Terr. & Walk. Terrell & Walker's Reports (38-51 Texas)

Terr. L. Territories Law (Northwest Territories)

Terr. L. (Can.) Territories Law Reports (1885-1907) (Can.)

Terr. L.R. Territories Law Reports (1885-1907) (Can.)

Teruv. Teruvenkatachariar's Railway Cases (India)

Test.
- Testamentary
- Testator
- Testimonial
- Testimony

T. Ev. Taylor, Evidence. 12ed. 1931

Tex.
- Texas Reports
- Texas
- Texas Supreme Court Reports

Tex. A. Texas Court of Appeals

Tex. A. Civ. White & Wilson's Texas Civil Appeal Cases

Tex. A. Civ. Cas. White & Wilson's Texas Civil Appeal Cases

Tex. A. Civ. Cas. (Wilson). Texas Court of Appeal Civil Cases

Tex. Admin. Code Texas Administrative Code

Tex. Admin. Reg. Texas Register

Tex. App.
- Texas Civil Appeals Cases
- Texas Court of Appeals Reports (Criminal Cases)

Tex. App. Civ. Cas. (Willson) White & Wilson's Texas Civil Appeal Cases

Texas B.J. Texas Bar Journal

Texas Bus. Rev. Texas Business Review

Texas Civ. Texas Civil Appeals Reports (Tex.)

Texas Civ. App. Texas Civil Appeals Reports (Tex.)

Tex. Cr. Texas Criminal

Texas Cr. App. Texas Court of Appeals Reports (Tex.)

Texas Crim. Texas Criminal Reports (Tex.)

Texas Crim. App. Texas Criminal Appeals Reports (Tex.)

Texas Crim. Rep. Texas Criminal Reports (Tex.)

Texas Cr. Rep. Texas Criminal Reports (Tex.)

Texas Ct. App. Texas Court of Appeals Reports (Tex.)

Texas Ct. App. Civ. Cas. Texas Civil Cases (Tex.)

Texas Ct. of App. Texas Court of Appeals Reports (Tex.)

Texas Ct. Rep. Texas Court Reporter (1900-1908) (Tex.)

Texas Dig. Texas Digest

Texas Internat. L. Forum The Texas International Law Forum

Texas Internat. L.J. Texas International Law Journal

Texas Int'l L.J. Texas International Law Journal

Texas L. Rev. Texas Law Review

Texas R. Texas Reports (Tex.)

Texas Rep. Texas Reports (Tex.)

Texas South. U.L. Rev. Texas Southern University Law Review

Texas Tech L. Rev. Texas Tech Law Review

Tex. B.J. Texas Bar Journal

Tex. Bus. Corp. Act Ann. Texas Business Corporation Act Annotated

Tex. Civ. App. Texas Civil Appeals Reports

Tex. Civ. Cas. Texas Court of Appeals Decisions, Civil Cases (White & Willson) (1876-92)

Tex. Civ. Rep. Texas Civil Appeals Reports

Tex. Code Ann. Texas Codes Annotated

Tex. Code Crim. Proc. Ann. Texas Code of Criminal Procedure Annotated

Tex. Com. App. Texas Commission of Appeals

Tex. Const. Texas Constitution

Tex. Court Reporter Texas Court Reporter (1885-86) (Tex.)

Tex. Cr. App. Texas Criminal Appeals Reports

Tex. Crim. Texas Criminal Reports (Texas Court of Appeals Reports)

Tex. Crim. Rep. Texas Criminal Reports

Tex. Cr. R. Texas Criminal Appeals Reports

Tex. Cr. Rpts. Texas Criminal Reports (Tex.)

Tex. Ct. App. Texas Court of Appeals Reports (Tex.)

Tex. Ct. App. Civ. Texas Civil Cases (Tex.)

Tex. Ct. App. Dec. Civ. Texas Civil Cases (Tex.)

Tex. Ct. App. R. Texas Court of Appeals Reports

Tex. Ct. Rep. Texas Court Reporter

Tex. Dec. Texas Decisions

Tex. Dig. Op. Att'y Gen. Digest of Opinions of the Attorney General of Texas

Tex. Elec. Code Ann. Texas Election Code Annotated

Tex. Gen. Laws General and Special Laws of the State of Texas

Tex. Ins. Code Ann. Texas Insurance Code Annotated

Texas Int'l L.F. Texas International Law Forum

Tex. Int. L. Forum Texas International Law Forum

Tex. Int. L.J. Texas International Law Journal

Tex. Int'l L.J. Texas International Law Journal

Tex. Jur. Texas Jurisprudence

Tex. Jur.2d Texas Jurisprudence, 2d Edition

Tex. Law. Texas Lawman

Tex. Law & Leg. Texas Law and Legislation

Tex. L.J. Texas Law Journal

Texas LR Texas Law Review

Tex. L. Rep. Texas Law Reporter (1882-84)

Tex. L. Rev. Texas Law Review

Tex. Prob. Code Ann. Texas Probate Court Annotated

Tex. R.C. Texas Railroad Commission

Tex. Rev. Civ. Stat. Ann. (Vernon) Texas Revised Civil Statutes Annotated

Tex. S. Texas Supreme Court Reports, Supplement

Tex. S. Ct. Texas Supreme Court Reporter

Tex. Sess. Law Serv. Texas Session Law Service (Vernon)

Tex. So. Intra. L. Rev. Texas Southern Intramural Law Review

Tex. So. U.L. Rev. Texas Southern University Law Review

Tex. Stat. Ann. Texas Statutes Annotated

Tex. S.U.L. Rev. Texas Southern University Law Review

Tex. Supp. Texas Supplement

Tex. Suppl. Texas Supplement

Tex. Tax-Gen. Ann. Texas Tax-General Annotated

Tex. Tech L. Rev. Texas Tech Law Review

Tex. Unrep. Cas. Posey's Unreported Cases (Texas)

TF Baggett, Texas Foreclosure-Law and Practice

T.H. Reports of the Witwatersrand High Court (Transvaal Colony) (South Africa)

Th Thai

Thac. Cr. Cas. Thacher's Criminal Cases (Mass. 1823-42)

Thach. Cr. Thacher's Criminal Cases (Mass.)

Thacher Cr. Thacher's Criminal Cases (Mass.)

Thacher Cr. Cas. Thacher's Criminal Cases (Mass.)

Thacher Crim. Cas. (Mass.) Thacher Criminal Cases (Mass.)

Thail. Thailand

Th. & C. Thompson & Cook's Reports (N.Y. Supreme Court 1873-75)

Thayer Thayer's Reports (18 Oregon)

Thayer, Prelim. Treatise Ev. Thayer's Preliminary Treatise on Evidence

Th. br. Thesaurus Brevium. 2 editions. (1661, 1687)

Th. Ca. Const. Law Thomas' Leading Cases in Constitutional Law

Th. C.C. Thacher's Criminal Cases (Mass. 1823-42)

Th. C. Const. Law. Thomas' Leading Cases in Constitutional Law

Them.
- American Themis (N.Y.)
- La Themis, Montreal, Quebec

Theo. Am. A. Theobald's Act for the Amendment of the Law

Theobald Theobald on Wills, II editions (1876-1954)

Theo. Pr. & S. Theobald, Principal and Surety. 1832

Theo. Pres. Pr. Theory of Presumptive Proof

Theo. Wills Theobald Wills. 13ed. 1971

The Rep.
- The Reporter, Phi Alpha Delta
- The Reports, Coke's Reports (Eng.)

Thes. Thesawaleme (Sri L.)

Thes. Brev. Thesaurus Brevium

Third World Legal Stud. Third World Legal Studies

Tho.
- Thomas
- Thomson
- Thompson

t. Holt Same as Modern Cases (Eng.)

Thom.
- Thomas' Reports (1 Wyoming)
- Thomson, Reports (Nova Scotia)

Thom. & Fr. Thomas & Franklin Reports (1 Maryland Chancery)

Thomas Thomas' Reports (1 Wyoming)

Thomas & Fr. Thomas & Franklin Chancery (Md.)

Thomas M. Cooley L. Rev. Thomas M. Cooley Law Review

Thomas, Mortg. Thomas on Mortgages

Thomas,Negl. Thomas on Negligence

Thom. B. & N. Thomson on Bills and Notes

Thom. B.B.S. Thompson on Benefit Building Societies

Thom. Bills Thomson on Bills

Thom. Co. Lit. Thomas' Edition of Coke upon Littleton

Thom. Co. Litt. Thomas' Edition of Coke upon Littleton

Thom. Const. L. Thomas' Leading Cases on Constitutional Law

Thom. Dec. 1 Thomson, Nova Scotia Reports, 1 (1834-52)

Thom. L.C. Thomas' Leading Cases on Constitutional Law

Thom. Mort. Thomas on Mortgages

700

Thom. N. Sc. Thomson's Nova Scotia Reports (Can.) (1834-51, 1856-59) (Can.)

Thomp. & C. Thompson & Cook's New York Supreme Court Reports

Thomp. & Cook Thompson and Cook's New York Supreme Court Reports (N.Y.)

Thomp. & M. Jur. Thompson & Merriam on Juries

Thomp. & St. Thompson & Steger's Tennessee Code

Thomp. & St. Code. Thompson and Steger's Code (Tenn.)

Thomp. Cal. Thompson's Reports (39, 40 California)

Thomp. Car. Thompson on Carriers

Thomp. Cas. Thompson's Cases, Tenn.

Thomp. Ch. Jur. Thompson on Charging the Jury

Thomp. Cit. Thompson's Citations (Ohio)

Thomp. Corp. Thompson's Commentaries on Law of Private Corporations

Thomp. Dig. Thompson's Digest of Laws (Fla.)

Thomp. Ent. Thompson's Entries

Thomp. Farm Thompson's Law of the Farm

Thomp. H. & Ex. Thompson on Homesteads and Exemptions

Thomp. High. Thompson on the Law of Highways

Thomp. Liab. Off. Thompson on Liability of Officers of Corporations

Thomp. Liab. St. Thompson on Liability of Stockholders

Thomp. Liab. Stockh. Thompson on Liability of Stockholders

Thomp. N.B. Cas. Thompson's National Bank Cases

Thomp. Neg. Thompson's Cases on Negligence

Thomp. Pat. Thompson, Patent Laws of all Countries. 13ed. 1905

Thomp. Prov. Rem. Thompson's Provisional Remedies

Thomps. Cas. Thompson's Cases (Tenn.)

Thompson
- Thompson's Nova Scotia Reports
- Thompson's Reports (39, 40 California)

Thompson & C. Thompson & Cook New York Supreme Court

Thompson's Fla. Dig. Thompson's Digest of Laws, Florida

Thompson Unrep. (Pa.) Thompson's Unreported Cases

Thomp. Tenn. Cas. Thompson's Unreported Tennessee Cases

Thomp. Trials. Thompson on Trials

Thom. Rep. Thomson, Nova Scotia Reports

Thom. Sc. Acts Thomson's Scotch Acts

Thom. Sel. Dec. Thomson, Select Decisions (Nova Scotia)

Thoms Jud. Fac. Thoms' Judicial Factors

Thomson
- Thomson's Nova Scotia Reports

- Thomson's Reports (Nova Scotia)

Thom. St. Sum. Thomas' Leading Statutes Summarized

Thom. Un. Jur. Thomas, Universal Jurisprudence. 2ed. 1829

Thor. Thorington's Reports (107 Alabama)

Thor. Bank. Thorborn on Bankers' Law

Thorn. Thornton, Notes of Ecclesiastical and Maritime Cases (1841-50)

Thorn. Conv. Thornton's Conveyancing

Thornt. & Bl. Bldg. & Loan Ass'ns. Thornton and Blackledge's Law Relating to Building and Loan Associations

Thornton, Gifts. Thornton on Gifts and Advancements

Thorpe. Thorpe's Reports (52 Louisiana Annual)

Thorpe Anc. L. Thorpe's Ancient Laws of England

Thos. Thomas

Thos. Co. Lit. Thomas' Edition of Coke's Littleton

Thr. Hist. Tr. Thrupp's Historical Law Tracts

THR-HR Tydskrif vir Hedendaagse Romeins-Hollandse Reg (Journal of Contemporary Roman-Dutch Law)

Thring J. St. Com. Thring, Joint Stock Companies. 5ed. 1889

Thring. L.D. Thring, Land Drainage Act. 1862

Throop, Pub. Off. Throop's Treatise on Public Officers

Thr. Verb. Agr. Throop on the Validity of Verbal Agreements

Thur. Marsh. L.J. Thurgood Marshall Law Journal

Thur. Mar. L. Rev. Thurgood Marshall Law Review

T.I. Agree. Treaties and Other International Agreements of the United States of America 1776-1949

TIAS United States Treaties and Other International Acts Series

TIC Trust Investment Committee

TICER Temporary International Council for Educational Reconstruction

Tichb. Tr. Report of the Tichborne Trial (London)

T.I.C.M. Trust Investment Committee Memorandum

Tidd.
- Tidd's Costs
- Tidd's Practice

Tidd App. Appendix to Tidd's Practice

Tidd. Co. Tidd's Costs

Tidd Pr. Tidd's Practice

Tidd, Prac. Tidd's Practice

Tidd's Pract. Tidd's Practice

Tiedeman, Real. Prop. Tiedeman on Real Property

Tied. Lim. Police Power. Tiedeman's Treatise on the Limitations of Police Power in the United States

Tied. Mun. Corp. Tiedeman's Treatise on Municipal Corporations

T.I.F. Treaties in Force

Tif. & Bul. Tr. Tiffany & Bullard on Trusts and Trustees

Tif. & Sm. Pr. Tiffany & Smith's New York Practice

Tiff. Tiffany's Reports (28-39 New York Court of Appeals)

Tiffany Tiffany's Reports (28-39 New York Court of Appeals)

Tiffany Landl. & T. Tiffany on Landlord and Tenant

Tiffany, Landlord & Ten. Tiffany on Landlord & Tenant

Tiffany Real Prop. Tiffany on Real Property

Tif. Gov. Tiffany on Government and Constitutional Law

Til. & Sh.Pr. Tillinghast & Shearman, New York Practice

Till. & Yates App. Tillinghast & Yates on Appeals

Tillman. Tillman's Reports (68, 69, 71, 73, 75 Alabama)

Til. Prec. Tillinghast's Precedents

Tils. St. L. Tilsley, Stamp Laws. 3ed. 1871

Timber Tax J. Timber Tax Journal

Times L. (Eng.) Times Law Reports

Times L.R.
- Times Law Reports (Ceylon)
- Times Law Reports (Eng.)

Times L. Rep.
- Times Law Reports (Ceylon)

- Times Law Reports (Eng.)

TIN Taxpayer Identification Number

Tinw. Tinwald's Reports, Court of Session (Sc.)

TIPS Torts and Insurance Practice Section of ABA

T.I.R. Technical Information Release, Internal Revenue Service

T.I.S. Tea Inspection Service (U.S.)

tit. title

tits titles

T.J. Tait's Justice of the Peace

T. Jo. T. Jones' English King's Bench Reports (84 ER)

T. Jones T. Jones English King's Bench Reports (84 ER)

T. Jones (Eng.) T. Jones' English King's Bench Reports (84 ER)

T.L.
- Reports of the Witwatersrand High Court, Transvaal (S. Afr.)
- Termes de la Ley

T.L.J. Tranvancore Law Journal (India)

T.L.Q. Temple Law Quarterly

T.L.R.
- Tanganyika Law Reports (1921 - 52)
- Tanzania Gazette Law Reports
- Tasmanian Law Journal Reports (Aus.)
- Tax Law Review
- Times Law Reports (1884-1952) (Eng.)
- Travancore Law Reports (India)
- Tulane Law Review

T.L.R. (R.) Tanganyika Law Reports (Revised) (1921-52)

T.L.T. Travancore Law Times (India)

T. Lwyr. The Tax Lawyer

TM Technical Memorandum

T.M.
- National Income Tax Magazine
- Tax Magazine
- Tax Management
- Tax Memo
- Technical Manual, U.S. Army
- Trademark

T. Marshall L. Rev. Thurgood Marshall Law Review

T.M. Bull. Trade Mark Bulletin, New Series

T.M.E.P. Trademark Manual of Examining Procedure

TMIJ Tax Management International Journal

T.M.J. Trade Marks Journal

TMLJ Thurgood Marshall Law Journal

T.M.L. Rev. Thurgood Marshall Law Review

T.M.M. Tax Management Memorandum (BNA)

T.M.R. Trade Mark Reporter

T.M. Rec. Trade Mark Record (U.S.)

T.M. Rep. Trade Mark Reporter

T.M.R. Prac. Trademark Rules of Practice

TMT & App. Bd. Trademark Trial and Appeal Board

TN Tennessee

Tn.
- Tennessee
- Tennessee Reports

Tn. A. Tennessee Appeals Reports

Tn. Cr. Tennessee Criminal Appeals Reports

T.N.E.C. Temporary National Economic Committee

Tn. L. Tennessee Law Review

Tn. L.R. Tennessee Law Review

Tob. Tobacco Branch, U.S. Internal Revenue Bureau

Tobey Tobey's Reports (9, 10 Rhode Island)

T.O.C.M. Trust Officers Committee Minutes

TOH Park, Trial Objections Handbook

To. Jo. Sir Thomas Jones' English King's Bench Reports (1667-84)

Tol. Toledo

Toledo L. Rev. University of Toledo Law Review

Toller. Toller on Executors

Toll. Ex. Toller on Executors

Tol. L.R. University of Toledo Law Review

To. L.R. University of Toledo Law Review

Tolst. Div. Tolstoy, Divorce and Matrimonial Causes

Tom. Tomlin

Tom. & J. Comp. Tomkins & Jenckens' Compendium of Modern Roman Law

Tom. & Lem. Gai. Tomkins & Lemon's Translation of Gaius

Tom. Inst. Tomkins' Institutes of Roman Law

Tomkins & J. Mod. Rom. Law.
Tomkins & Jencken, Compendium of the Modern Roman Law

Toml. Tomlins' Election Cases (1689-1795)

Toml. Cas. Tomlins' Election Cases (1689-1795)

Toml. Cr. L. Tomlin's Criminal Law

Tomlins. Tomlins' Law Dictionary

Toml. Law Dict. Tomlins' Law Dictionary

Toml. L.D. Tomlin, Law Dictionary. 4ed. 1835

Toml. Supp. Br. Tomlins' Supplement to Brown's Parliamentary Cases

Toronto U. Faculty L. Rev.
Toronto University Faculty Law Review, Toronto, Canada

Tort & Ins. L.J. Tort & Insurance Law Journal

Tot.
  • Tothill's English Chancery Reports
  • Tothills Transactions in Chancery (21 ER)

Toth. Tothill's Chancery (Eng.)

Tothill (Eng.)
  • Tothills English Chancery Reports
  • Tothill's Transactions in Chancery (21 ER)

Touch. Sheppard's Touchstone

Tourg. Dig. Tourgee, North Carolina Digest

Touro J. Transnat'l L. Touro Journal of Transnational Law

Touro L. Rev. Touro Law Review

Towle Const. Towle's Analysis of the United States Constitution

Town. Co. Townshend's Code

Town. Com. Law Townsend on Commercial Law

Town. Jud. Townsend's Judgment

Town. Pl. Townshend's Pleading

Town. Pr. Townshend's Practice, New York

Town. Pr. Pl. Townshend's Precedents of Pleading

Towns. Townshend

Townsh. Pl. Townshend's Pleading

Townsh. Sland. & L. Townshend on Slander and Libel

Town. Sl. & Lib. Townshend on Slander and Libel

Town. St. & Lib. Townshend on Slander and Libel

Town. St. Tr. Townsend Modern State Trials (1850)

Town. Sum. Proc. Townshend's Summary Landlord and Tenant Process

TP Stone & Liebman, Testimonial Privileges

T.P.
  • Tax Planning
  • Transvaal Supreme Court Reports (S. Africa)

T.P.D. South African Law Reports, Transvaal Provincial Division (S. Africa)

T.P.I. Tax Planning Ideas

T.P.R.S. Trade Practices Reporting Service (Law Book Co.)

TR State Teachers Retirement Board

T.R.
- Taxation Reports (Eng.)
- Term Reports (Durnford & East) (Eng.)
- Caine's Term Reports (N.Y.)

Tr.
- Transaction
- Transcript
- Translated
- Translation
- Treaty
- Trial
- Trinidad
- Tristram's Consistory Judgments (Eng.)
- Trust(s)
- Trustee

TRA '84 Tax Reform Act of 1984

TRA '86 Tax Reform Act of 1986

Trace. & M. Tracewall and Mitchell, United States Comptroller's Decisions

Tracey, Evidence Tracey's Cases on Evidence

Trade Cas. (CCH) Trade Cases (CCH)

Trademark Trademarks and tradenames

Trademark Bull. Bulletin of United States Trademark Association Series

Trademark Bull. (N.S.) Trademark Bulletin (Bulletin of United States Trademark Association), New Series

Trade Mark R. Trade Mark Reporter

Trademark Rep. Trademark Reporter

Trademark Rptr. Trademark Reporter

Trademark World Trademark World

Trade Reg. Rep. (CCH) Trade Regulation Reporter (CCH)

Trade Reg. Rev. Trade Regulation Review

Traff. Cas. Railway, Canal and Road Traffic Cases

Traill Med. Jur. Traill on Medical Jurisprudence

Tr. & Est. Trusts & Estates

Tr. & H. Pr. Troubat & Haly's Practice (Pa.)

Tr. & H. Prec. Ind. Train & Heard's Precedents of Indictment

Tr. & T.T. Trial and Tort Trends

trans.
- transaction
- transcript
- transfer
- transferred
- translation
- translator

Trans. & Wit. Transvaal & Witswatersrand Reports

Trans. Ap. Transcript Appeals (N.Y. 1867-68)

Trans. App. Transcript Appeals; New York

Trans. Appeal R. New York Transcript Appeals Reports (N.Y.)

Transc. A. Transcript Appeals (N.Y.)

Transcr. A. Transcript Appeals (N.Y.)

Transcript Appeals New York Transcript Appeals Reports (N.Y.)

transf.
- transferred from
- transferred to

Trans. I.L.A. Transactions of the International Law Association (1873-1924)

Transit L. Rev. Transit Law Review

transl.
- translated
- translation
- translator

Transnat'l. Transnational

Transnat'l L. & Contemp. Probs. Transnational Law & Contemp. Problems

Transnat'l Law The Transnational Lawyer

Transnat'l. Rep. Transnational Reporter

Transp. Transport[ation]

Transp. Corp. Transportation Corporations

Transp. J. Transportation Journal

Transp. L.J. Transportation Law Journal

Transp. L. Sem. Transportation Law Seminar

Transp. Prac. J. Transportation Practitioners Journal

transtl. transitional

Tr. App. Transcript Appeals (N.Y. 1867-68)

Trav. & Tw. L. of N. Travers & Twiss on Law of Nations

Trav.-Cochin Indian Law Reports, Kerala Series

Trav. Ind. Travancore, India

Trav. L.J. Travancore Law Journal (India)

Trav. L.R. Travancore Law Reports (India)

Trav. L.T. Travancore Law Times (India)

T. Ray. Sir T. Raymond's King's Bench Reports (83 ER) (1660-84)

Tray. Lat. Max. Trayner, Latin Maxims and Phrases, etc.

T. Raym. Sir T. Raymond's King's Bench Reports (83 ER)

T. Raym. (Eng.) Sir T. Raymond's King's Bench Reports (83 ER)

Tr. Ch. Transactions of the High Court of Chancery (Tothill's Reports)

Tr. Consist. J. Tristram's Consistory Judgments (1872-90) (Eng.)

T.R.E. Tempore Regis Edwardi (in the time of King Edward)

Tread.
- Treadway's South Carolina Constitutional Reports
- Treadway's South Carolina Law Reports (1812-16)

Tread. Const. Treadway's South Carolina Constitutional Reports

Treadway Const. (S.C.) Treadway's South Carolina Constitutional Reports

Treas.
- Treasurer
- Treasury

Treas. Dec. Treasury Decisions Under Customs and Other Laws (U.S.)

Treas. Dec. Int. Rev. Treasury Decisions Under Internal Revenue Laws

Treas. Dept. Treasury Department

Treas. Dept. Cir. Treasury Department Circular

Treas. Reg. Treasury Regulations (U.S.)

Treas. Regs. United States Treasury Regulations

Treat. Treaties

Treat. Tro. Treatise on Trover and Conversion

TRED Guerin, Taxation of Real Estate Transactions

Tred. Tredgold's Cape Colony Reports

Trehern British & Colonial Prize Cases

Trem. Tremaine's Pleas of the Crown (Eng.)

Trem. P.C. Tremaine's Pleas of the Crown (Eng.)

T.R. (Eng.) Term Reports (99-101 ER)

Trent L.J. Trent Law Journal

Tr. Eq. Fonblanque's Treatise of Equity

Tresp. Trespass

Trev. Tax. Suc. Trevor, Taxes on Succession. 4ed. 1881

Trf. Transfer

Trial Trial

Trial Advoc. Q. Trial Advocate Quarterly

Trial Diplomacy J. Trial Diplomacy Journal

Trial Law. Forum Trial Lawyers Forum

Trial Law. Guide Trial Lawyer's Guide

Trial Law Q. Trial Lawyers' Quarterly

Trib.
- Tribunal
- Tribune

Tri. Bish. Trial of the Seven Bishops

Tri. E. of Cov. Trial of the Earl of Coventry

Trin. Trinity Term

Trin. & Tobago Trinidad and Tobago

Trinidad L.R. Trinidad Law Reports

Trin. T. Trinity Term (Eng.)

Trint.T. Trinity Term (Eng.)

T.R.O. Temporary Restraining Order

Trip. All India Reporter, Tripura

Tri. per. P. Trials per Pais

Tripp Tripp's Reports (5,6 Dakota)

Tris. Pr. Pr. Tristram, Probate Practice. 25ed. 1978

Trist.
- Tristram's Consistory Judgments (Eng.)
- Supplement to 4 Swabey & Tristram's Probate & Divorce Reports (Eng.)

Tristram
- Tristram's Supplement to 4 Swabey & Tristram
- Tristram's Consistory Judgments (1872-90)
- Tristram's Probate Practice. 25ed. 1978

Tr. Judge J. Trial Judges' Journal

Tr. Law Guide Trial Lawyer's Guide

Tr. Law Q. Trial Lawyer's Quarterly

Tr. L.R. Trinidad Law Reports

T.R.N.S. Term Reports, New Series (East's Reports) 1801-1812

T.R. (N.Y.) Caines' (Term) Reports (New York)

Troub. & H. Pr. Troubat & Haly's Pennsylvania Practice

Troub. & H. Prac. Troubat & Haly's Practice (Pa.)

Troub. Lim. Partn. Troubat on Limited Partnership

Trow. D. & Cr. Trower, Debtor and Creditor. 1860

Trow. Eq. Trower, Manual of the Prevalance of Equity. 1876

T.R.R. Trade Regulation Reporter

Tr. Ser. Treaty Series

Tru. Trueman's Equity Cases (1876-93) (New Brunswick)

True. Trueman's New Brunswick Reports

Trueman Eq. Cas. Trueman's Equity Cases (New Brunswick)

Truem. Eq. Cas. Trueman's Equity Cases (New Brunswick)

Tru. Railw. Rep. Truman's American Railway Rep.

Trust Bull. Trust Bulletin, American Bankers Association

Trust Co. Mag. Trust Companies Magazine (1904-38)

Trusts & Es. Trusts & Estates

Trusts & Est. Trusts & Estates

Trust Terr. Trust Territory Reports

Trye Trye's Jus Filizarii

T.S. Transvaal Supreme Court Reports, South Africa

TS United States Treaty Series

TSCA Toxic Substances Control Act

Ts. L.J. Tulsa Law Journal

TSSD Brown, Tax Strategies for Separation and Divorce

T.S.U.S. Tariff Schedules of the U.S.

T.S.U.S.A. Tariff Schedules of the U.S., Annotated

TT
- Nothstein, Toxic Torts
- Trust Territories

T.T.
- Trinity Term
- Tobacco Tax Ruling Term

T.T.I. Tulane Tax Institute

T.T.L.R. Tanganyika Territory Law Reports (1921-47)

TTPI Trust Territory of the Pacific Islands

T.T.R.
- Tarl Town Reports (New South Wales)

- Trust Territory Reports of Pacific Island

T/U/Ag Trustee under agreement

Tu. & Rus. Turner & Russell Reports, Chancery (1822-24) (Eng.)

T.U.C. Temporary Unemployment Compensation

Tu. Civ. L.F. Tulane Civil Law Forum

Tuck.
- Tucker & Clephan's Reports (21 District of Columbia) (1892-93)
- Tucker's Reports (District of Columbia)
- Tucker's Reports (156-175 Massachusetts)
- Tucker's N.Y. Surrogate Reports
- Tucker's Select Cases (Newfoundland)

Tuck. & C. Tucker & Clephane's Reports (21 D.C.)

Tuck. & Cl. Tucker and Clephane's District of Columbia Reports (1892-93) (21 D.C.)

Tuck. Bl. Com. Tucker's Blackstone's Commentaries

Tuck. Dist. of Col. Tucker's Appeals (D.C.)

Tucker Tucker's New York Surrogate's Court Reports (N.Y.)

Tucker's Blackstone Tucker's Blackstone's Commentaries

Tuck. Lect. Tucker's Lectures

Tuck. Pl. Tucker's Pleadings

Tuck. Sel. Cas. Tucker's Select Cases, Newfoundland (1817-28)

Tuck. Sur. Tucker's Surrogate, Reports (City of New York)

Tuck. Surr. Tucker's Surrogate, Reports, City of New York

Tud. Cas. Merc. Law Tudor's Leading Cases on Mercantile Law 3 editions (1860-84)

Tud. Cas. R.P. Tudor's Leading Cases on Real Property 4 editions (1856-1898)

Tud. Char. Tr. Tudor, Charitable Trusts. 2ed. 1871

Tud. Char. Trusts Tudor's Charitable Trusts 2d edition (1871)

Tudor, Lead. Cas. Real Prop. Tudor's Leading Cases on Real Property

Tudor's L.C.M.L. Tudor's Leading Cases on Mercantile Law

Tudor's L.C.R.P. Tudor's Leading Cases on Real Property

Tul. Tulane

Tu. L. Tulane Law Review (La.)

Tulane L. Rev. Tulane Law Review

Tul. Civ. L.F. Tulane Civil Law Forum

Tul. Envtl. L.J. Tulane Environmental Law Journal

Tul. L. Rev. Tulane Law Review

Tul. Mar. L.J. Tulane Maritime Law Journal

Tu. L.R. Tulane Law Review

Tulsa L.J. Tulsa Law Journal

Tul. Mar. L.J. Tulane Maritime Law Journal

Tul. Tax Inst. Tulane Tax Institute

Tunis. Tunisia

Tup. App. Tupper's Appeal Reports (Ontario)

T.U.P.C. Charlton Reports (Ga.)

T.U.P.Charlt. T. U. P. Charlton's Reports (Ga.)

Tupp.
- Tupper's Reports, Ontario Appeals
- Tupper's Upper Canada Practice Reports

Tupp. App. Tupper's Appeal Reports (Ont.)

Tupper
- Tupper's Reports, Ontario Appeals
- Tupper' Upper Canada Practice Reports

Tur.
- Turkey
- Turner's Reports (35-48 Arkansas)
- Turner's Reports (99-101 Kentucky)
- Turner Select Pleas of the Forest (Selden Society Publication, v. 13)

Tur. & R. Turner & Russell's Chancery Reports (1822-24) (37 ER)

Tur. & Ru. Turner & Russell's Chancery Reports (1822-24) (37 ER)

Tur. & Rus. Turner & Russell's Chancery Reports (1822-24) (37 ER)

Turk. Turkey

Turks & Caicos Is. Turks and Caicos Islands

Turn.
- Turner's Reports (35-48 Arkansas)
- Turner's Reports (99-101 Kentucky)
- Turner Select Pleas of the Forest (Selden Society Publication, v. 13)

Turn. & P. Turner & Phillips' Reports, English Chancery

Turn. & Ph. Turner & Phillips' Reports, English Chancery

Turn. & R. Turner and Russell's Chancery Reports (37 ER)

Turn. & R. (Eng.) Turner and Russell's Chancery Reports (37 ER)

Turn. & Rus. Turner & Russell's English Chancery Reports (37 ER)

Turn. & Russ. Turner & Russell's English Chancery Reports (37 ER)

Turn. Anglo. Sax. Turner, History of the Anglo Saxon

Turn. Ch. Pr. Turner, Practice of the Court of Chancery. 4ed. 1821

Turn. Cop. Turner, Copyright in Designs. 1849

Turner
- Turner's Reports (35-48 Ark.)
- Turner's Reports (99-101 Ky.)

Turn. Pat. Turner, Patents. 1851

Turn. Pr. Turnbull's Practice, New York

Turn. Qui. Tit. Turner on Quieting Titles

Tutt. & C. Tuttle & Carpenter's Reports (52 California)

Tutt. & Carp. Tuttle & Carpenter's Reports (52 California)

Tuttle Tuttle & Carpenter's Reports (52 California)

Tuttle & Carpenter Tuttle & Carpenter's Reports (52 California)

T.U.W. Trustee Under Will

T.V.A.
- Tennessee Valley Authority (U.S.)
- Tax Value Added

Tvl. S.A. Transvaal, South Africa

T.W. Trustee Under Will

Tw. Nat. P. Twiss, Law of Nations in Time of Peace. 2ed. 1884

Tw. Nat. W. Twiss, Law of Nations in Time of War. 2ed. 1875

Twp. Township

Tx.
- Tax
- Texas
- Texas Reports

Tx. Ci. Texas Civil Appeals Reports

Tx. Cr. Texas Criminal Appeals Reports

Tx. L. Texas Law Review

Tx. L.J. Texas Law Journal

Tx. L.R. Texas Law Review

Ty.
- Territory
- Tyler

Tyl. Tyler's Vermont Supreme Court Reports (1800-03)

Tyl. Boun. Tyler on Boundaries, Fences, & c.

Tyl. Eccl. L. Tyler's American Ecclesiastical Law

Tyl. Eject. Tyler on Ejectment and Adverse Enjoyment

Tyler Tyler's Reports (Vermont, 1800-03)

Tyler, Ej. Tyler on Ejectment and Adverse Enjoyment

Tyler, Steph. Pl. Tyler's Edition of Stephen on Principles of Pleading

Tyl. Fix. Tyler on Fixtures

Tyl. Inf. Tyler on Infancy and Coverture

Tyl. Part. Tyler on Partnership

Tyl. St. Pl. Tyler's Edition of Stephen on the Principles of Pleading

Tyl. Us. Tyler on Usury, Pawns and Loans

Tyng Tyng's Reports (2-17 Massachusetts)

Tyr. Tyrwhitt & Granger's English Exchequer Reports (1830-35)

Tyr. & G. Tyrwhitt & Granger, Eng.

Tyr. & Gr. Tyrwhitt and Granger's Exchequer Reports (1830-35)

Tyre, Jus Filiz. Tyre's Jus Filizarii

Tyrw. Tyrwhitt & Granger's English Exchequer Reports (1830-35)

Tyrw. & G. Tyrwhitt and Granger's Exchequer Reports (1835-36)

Tyrw. & G. (Eng.) Tyrwhitt and Granger's Exchequer Reports (1835-36)

Tytler, Mil. Law Tytler on Military Law and Courts-Martial

Tyt. Mil. L. Tytler, Military Law and Courts Martial. 3ed. 1812.

U

U.
- Universities
- University
- Utah
- Utah Reports

U.2d Utah Reports, Second Series

U/A Under agreement

U.A.E. United Arab Emirates

UALR L.J. University of Arkansas at Little Rock Law Journal

U. Ark. Little Rock L.J. University of Arkansas at Little Rock Law Journal

UAW United Auto Workers

U.B. Upper Bench

UB Unemployment Benefit

U. Baltimore L. Rev. University of Baltimore Law Review

U. Balt. J. Envtl. L. University of Baltimore Journal of Environmental Law

U. Balt. L.F. University of Baltimore Law Forum

U. Balt. L.R. University of Baltimore Law Review

U. Balt. L. Rev. University of Baltimore Law Review

U.B.C. Legal N. University of British Columbia Legal Notes

U.B.C. L.N. University of British Columbia Legal News

U.B.C. L. Rev. University of British Columbia Law Review

U.B.C. Notes University of British Columbia Legal Notes

U.B.C. L. Rev. University of British Columbia Law Review (Can.)

U.B.L.R. University of Baltimore Law Review

U.B.L.S. L.J. University of Botswana, Lesotho and Swaziland Law Journal

U.B.Pr. Upper Bench Precedents tempore Car. I

U.B.R. Upper Burma Rulings (India)

U. Bridgeport L. Rev. University of Bridgeport Law Review

U. Brit. Col. L. Rev. University of British Columbia Law Review

U. Brit. Colum. L. Rev. University of British Columbia Law Review

U.C. Upper Canada

UCA Unemployment Compensation Agency

U.C.A. Utah Code Annotated

U.C. App. Upper Canada Appeal Reports

U.C. App. (Can.) Upper Canada Appeal Reports

U.C. App. Rep. Upper Canada Appeal Reports

UCB
- Bureau of Unemployment Compensation

- Unemployment Compensation Board
- Unemployment Compensation Bureau

UCC Unemployment Compensation Commission

U.C.C. Uniform Commercial Code

UCCC Uniform Consumer Credit Code

U.C. Ch. Upper Canada Chancery Reports (1849-82)

U.C. Ch. (Can.) Upper Canada Chancery Reports

U.C. Cham. Upper Canada Chambers Reports

U.C. Cham. (Can.) Upper Canada Chambers Reports (1846-52)

U.C. Chamb. Upper Canada Chambers Reports (1846-52)

U.C. Chamb. Rep. Upper Canada Chamber Reports

U.C. Chan. Upper Canada Chancery Reports

U.C. Ch. Rep. Upper Canada Chancery Reports

U.C.C. Law Letter Uniform Commercial Code Law Letter

U.C.C. L.J. Uniform Commercial Code Law Journal

U.C.C. P. Upper Canada Common Pleas Reports

U.C.C. P. (Can.) Upper Canada Common Pleas Reports

U.C.C.P.D. Upper Canada Common Pleas Division Reports (Ontario)

U.C.C.R. Upper Canada Court Records (Report of Ontario Bureau of Archives)

U.C.C. Rep. Serv. (Callaghan) Uniform Commercial Code Reporting Service

UCD Unemployment Compensation Division

U.C. Davis L. Rev. University of California at Davis Law Review

U.C.D. L. Rev. University of California at Davis Law Review

U.C.E. & A. Upper Canada Error and Appeal Reports (1846-66)

U.C. Err. & App. Upper Canada Error and Appeal Reports (1846-66)

U.C. Err. & App. (Can.) Upper Canada Error and Appeal Reports (1846-66)

U. Ceylon L.R. University of Ceylon Law Review

U. Chicago L. Rev. University of Chicago Law Review

U. Chi. Legal F. University of Chicago Legal Forum

U. Chi. L. Rec. University of Chicago Law School Record

U. Chi. L. Rev. University of Chicago Law Review

UCHILS The University of Chicago Law School

U. Chi. Legal F. University of Chicago Legal Forum

U. Chi. L. Sch. Rec. University of Chicago Law School Record

U. Chi. L.S. Rec. University of Chicago Law School Record

U. Cin. L. Rev. University of Cincinnati Law Review

UCIS Unemployment Compensation Interpretation Service

U.C.I.S.
- Unemployment Compensation Interpretation Service, Benefit Series
- Unemployment Compensation Interpretation Service, Federal Series
- Umemployment Compensation Interpretation Service, State Series

U.C. Jur. Upper Canada Jurist

U.C. Jur. (Can.) Upper Canada Jurist

U.C.K.B. Upper Canada King's Bench Reports, Old Series (1831-44)

U.C.K.B. (Can.) Upper Canada King's Bench Reports, Old Series (1831-44)

UCLA University of California, Los Angeles

U.C.L.A.-Alaska University of California Los Angeles- Alaska

U.C.L.A.-Alaska L. Rev. U.C.L.A.-Alaska Law Review

U.C.L.A. Intra. L. Rev. U.C.L.A. Intramural Law Review

U.C.L.A. J.Envt'l. L. & Pol'y. UCLA Journal of Environmental Law and Policy

U.C.L.A. Law R. University of California Los Angeles Law Review

U.C.L.A. L. Rev. University of California at Los Angeles Law Review

UCLA Pac. Basin L.J. UCLA Pacific Basin Law Journal

U.C.L.A. Pac. Bas. L.J. U.C.L.A. Pacific Basin Law Journal

U.C.L.J. Upper Canada Law Journal (1855-1922)

U.C.L.J. (Can.) Upper Canada Law Journal

U.C.L.J. N.S. Upper Canada Law Journal, New Series

U.C.L.J. N.S. (Can.) Upper Canada Law Journal, New Series

U.C.L.J. O.S. Canada Law Journal, Old Series (10 vols.)

U.C.L.R.
- University of Ceylon Law Review
- University of Chicago Law Review
- University of Cincinnati Law Review
- University of Colorado Law Review

UCMJ Uniform Code of Military Justice (U.S.)

U. Colo. L. Rev. University of Colorado Law Review

U. Color. L. Rev. University of Colorado Law Reviews (formerly Rocky Mountain Law Review)

U.C.O.S. Upper Canada King's Bench Reports, Old Series (1831-44)

UCOSL University of Colorado School of Law

UCPD Unemployment Compensation and Placement Division

U.C.P.R. Upper Canada Practice Reports

U.C. Pr. Upper Canada Practice Reports

U.C. Pract. Upper Canada Practice Reports (1850-1900)

U.C.Pr.(Can.) Upper Canada Practice Reports

U.C. Pr. R. Upper Canada Practice Reports

U.C.Q.B. Upper Canada Queen's Bench Reports

U.C.Q.B. O.S. Upper Canada Queen's (King's) Bench Reports, Old Series

U.C.Q.B. O.S. (Can.) Upper Canada Queen's (King's) Bench Reports, Old Series

U.C.R.
- University of Cincinnati Law Review (Ohio)
- Upper Canada Reports

U.C. Rep. Upper Canada Reports

UDAL Udal's Fiji Law Reports

U. Dayton L. Rev. University of Dayton Law Review

U. Det. J. Urb. L. University of Detroit Journal of Urban Law

U. Det. L.J. University of Detroit Law Journal

U. Det. L. Rev. University of Detroit Law Review

U. Detroit L.J. University of Detroit Law Journal

U. Detroit L. Rev. University of Detroit Law Review

U. Det. Mercy L. Rev. University of Detroit Mercy Law Review

U. Detroit J. Urban L. University of Detroit Journal of Urban Law

U. East L.J. University of the East Law Journal

UE. Law J. University of the East Law Journal, Manila, Philippines

U. Fla. J. L. & Pub. Pol'y University of Florida Journal of Law and Public Policy

U. Fla. L. Rev. University of Florida Law Review

U. Florida L. Rev. University of Florida Law Review

Uganda Leg. Focus Uganda Legal Focus

Uganda L.F. Uganda Law Focus

Uganda L. Foc. Uganda Law Focus

Uganda L.R. Uganda Protectorate Law Reports (1904-51)

U. Ghana L.J. University of Ghana Law Journal

Ug. L.F. Uganda Law Focus

U.G.L.J. University of Ghana Law Journal

Ug. L. R. Uganda Law Reports (Africa)

Ug. Pr. L.R. Uganda Protectorate Law Reports (Africa)

U. Hawaii L. Rev. University of Hawaii Law Review

U. Haw. L. Rev. University of Hawaii Law Review

UIC Unemployment Insurance Commission

U.I.D. Selected Decisions by Umpire for Northern Ireland, respecting Claims to Benefit

UID
- Unemployment Insurance Division
- Division of Placement and Unemployment Insurance

U.Ill. L.B. University of Illinois Law Bulletin

U.Ill. L.Bull. University of Illinois Law Bulletin

U.Ill. L.F. University of Illinois Law Forum

U. Ill. L.Forum University of Illinois Law Forum

U. Ill. L. Rev. University of Illinois Law Review

U.I.L.R. University of IFE Law Reports (Nigeria)

U.Iowa L. Rev. University of Iowa Law Review

UIS Unemployment Insurance Service

U.J. Uganda Journal

U.K. United Kingdom

UKADR United Kingdom NATO Air Defense Region

U. Kan. City L. Rev. University Kansas City Law Review

U. Kan. L.R. University of Kansas Law Review

U. Kan. L. Rev. University of Kansas Law Review

U. Kans. City L. Rev. University of Kansas City Law Review

U. Kansas L. Rev. University of Kansas Law Review

UKIAS United Kingdom Immigrants Advisory Service

U.K.L.R. University of Kansas Law Review

U.L.A. Uniform Laws Annotated

U.L.C.J. University Law College Journal, Rajputana University (India)

Ulm. L. Rec. Ulman's Law Record (New York)

Ulp. Ulpiani Fragmenta

ULR
- Uganda Law Reports
- Utah Law Review
- Utilities Law Reporter

U.L.R.
- Uniform Law Review
- Uganda Protectorate Law Reports (1904-51)
- Uniform Law Review (It.)
- Union Law Review (S. Afr.)
- University Law Review (U.S.)
- Utah Law Review
- Utilities Law Reporter

U. Maine L. Rev. University of Maine Law Review

U. Mary. L. Forum University of Maryland Law Forum

U.Md. L.F. University of Maryland Law Forum

Umfrev. Off. Cor. Umfreville's Office of Coroner

UMI University Microfilms International

U. Miami Ent. & Sports L. Rev. University of Miami Entertainment & Sports Law Review

U. Miami Inter-Am. L. Rev. The University of Miami Inter-American Law Review

U. Miami L. Rev. University of Miami Law Review

U. Mich. J. Law Reform University of Michigan Journal of Law Reform

U. Mich. J. L. Ref. University of Michigan Journal of Law Reform

717

U. Missouri at K.C.L. Rev. University of Missouri at Kansas City Law Review

UMKCLR University of Missouri at Kansas City Law Review

UMKCL Rev. University of Missouri at Kansas City Law Review

UMLC
- Institute of Estate Planning, University of Miami Law Center
- University of Miami Law Center

U.M.L.R.
- University of Miami Law Review
- University of Malaya Law Review

U. Mo. B., Law Ser. University of Misouri Bulletin, Law Series

U. Mo. Bull. L. Ser. University of Missouri Bulletin Law Series

U. Mo.-Kansas City L. Rev. University of Missouri at Kansas City Law Review

U. Mo. K.C. L. Rev. University of Missouri at Kansas City Law Review

U. Mo. L. Bull. University of Missouri Law Bulletin

UMTA Urban Mass Transportation Administration

UN United Nations

UNAC United Nations Appeal for Children

UNAIS United Nations Association International Service (British)

Unauth. Unauthorized

Unauth. Prac. News Unauthorized Practice News

UNBCL University of Nebraska College of Law

U.N.B. Law Journal University of New Brunswick Law Journal (Can.)

U.N.B.L.J. University of New Brunswick Law Journal (Can.)

U.N.B.L.S.J. University of New Brunswick Law School Journal

U.N. Bull. United Nations Bulletin

UNCDF United Nations Capital Development Fund

U.N. Charter Charter of the United Nations

UNCHR United Nations High Commissioner for Refugees

UN Chron. UN Chronicle

UNCIO United Nations Conference on International Organization

UNCIO Doc. United Nations Conference on International Organization Documents

UNCIP United Nations Commission for India and Pakistan

UNCITRAL United Nations Commission on International Trade Law

UNCLOS United Nations Conference on the Law of the Sea

UNCOK United Nations Commission on Korea

U.N. Comm. Int'l Trade L.Y.B. United Nations Commission on International Trade Law Yearbook

Unconsol. Laws Unconsolidated Laws

UNCOPUOS United Nations Committee on the Peaceful Use of Outer Space

UNCRD United Nations Centre for Regional Development

UNCTAD United Nations Conference on Trade and Development

UNCURK United Nations Commission for Relief & Rehabilitation of Korea

Und. Undivided

Und. Art Cop. Underwood on Art Copyright

UNDAT United Nations Development Advisory Team

UNDCC United Nations Development Cooperation Cycle

Und. Ch. Pr. Underhill, Chancery Procedure. 1881

Und. Conv. Underhill, New Conveyancing. 1925

Underhill, Ev. Underhill on Evidence

UNDI United Nations Document Index

UNDoc. United Nations Documents

UNDP United Nations Development Program

Und.Part. Underhill, Partnership. 10ed. 1975.

UNDRO United Nations Disaster Relief Office

Und.Sher. Under Sheriff

Und.Torts Underhill on Torts

Und.Tr. Underhill on Trusts and Trustees

UNECA United Nations Economic Commission for Africa

U.N.ECOSOC United Nations Economic and Social Records

U.N.E.D.A. United Nations Economic Development Administration

UNEF United Nations Emergency Force

Unempl. C. Unemployment compensation

Unemp. Ins. Unemployment Insurance

Unempl. Ins Rep. (CCH) Unemployment Insurance Reports (CCH)

Unempl. Ins. Rep-(CCH) Unemployment Insurance Reports (CCH)

UNEP United Nations Environment Program

UNESCO United Nations Educational, Scientific and Cultural Organization

UNESCOR United Nations Economic and Social Council Official Record

UNESOB United Nations Economic and Social Office at Beirut (Lebanon)

U. Newark L. Rev. University of Newark Law Review

U. New Brunswick L.J. University of New Brunswick Law Journal

U. New South Wales L.J. University of New South Wales Law Journal, Kensington, N.S.W. Australia

U. New So. Wales L.J. University of New South Wales Law Journal

U. News S. Wales L.J. University of New South Wales Law Journal

UNFICYP United Nations Force in Cyprus

UNFPA United Nations Fund for Population Activities

U.N.G.A. United Nations General Assembly

UNGAOR United Nations General Assembly Official Record

UNHCR United Nations High Commission for Refugees

U.N.H.Q. United Nations Headquarters

UNICAP Uniform capitalization rules

UNICEF United Nations International Children's Emergency Fund

UNIDO United Nations Industrial Development Organization

UNIDROIT International Institute for the Unification of Private Law

Unidroit Yb. International Institute for the Unification of Private Law, Yearbook, Rome, Italy

Unif.
- Unified
- Uniform

Unific. L.Y.B. Unification of Law Yearbook

Unif. L. Conf. Proceedings, Uniform Law Conference of Canada

Unif. L. Conf. Can. Uniform Law Conference of Canada

Uniform City Ct. Act. Uniform City Court Act

Uniform Dist. Ct. Act Uniform District Court Act

Uniform L. Rev. Uniform Law Review

Unif. Sys. Citation Uniform System of Citation

Un. Ins. Co. Unemployment Insurance Code

Union Lab. Rep. (BNA) Union Labor Report

Union Pac. L.D.B. Union Pacific Law Department Bulletin

UNITAR United Nations Institute for Training and Research

Univ.
- University
- Universal

Univ. California Los Angeles L. Rev. University of California at Los Angeles Law Review. Los Angeles, California

Univ. Human Rights Universal Human Rights

Univ. Hum. Rts. Universal Human Rights

Univ. Ill. L. Forum University of Illinois Law Forum

Univ. L. Coll. J. University Law College Journal, Rajputana University (India)

Univ. L.R. University Law Review

Univ. L. Rev. University Law Review

Univ. N.S.W.L.J. University of New South Wales Law Journal

Univ. of Brit. Columbia L. Rev. Uni-versity of British Columbia Law Review. Vancouver, British Columbia, Canada

Univ. of Calif., Davis L. Rev.
Univer-sity of California at Davis
Law Review. Davis, California

Univ. of Chicago L. Rev. The
University of Chicago Law Review. Chicago, Illinois

Univ. of Cincinnati L. Rev. University of Cincinnati Law Review. Cincinnati, Ohio

Univ. of Colorado L. Rev. University of Colorado Law Review.
Boulder, Colorado

Univ. of Florida L. Rev. University of Florida Law Review.
Gainesville, Florida

Univ. of Ghana L.J. University of
Ghana Law Journal. London, UK

Univ. of Illinois L. Forum The
University of Illinois Law Forum.
Urbana, Illinois

Univ. of Manila L. Gaz. The University of Manila Law Gazette.
Manila, Philippines

Univ. of Miami L. Rev. University of Miami Law Review. Coral
Gables, Florida

**Univ. of Michigan J. of Law Re-
form** University of Michigan
Journal of Law Reform. Ann Arbor, Michigan

**Univ. of Missouri at Kansas City
L.Rev.** The University of Missouri at Kansas City Law Review. Kansas City, Missouri

Univ. of New Brunswick L.J.
University of New Brunswick
Law Journal. Fredericton, New
Brunswick, Canada

Univ. of Pennsylvania L. Rev.
University of Pennsylvania Law
Review. Philadelphia, Pennsylva-
nia

Univ. of Pittsburgh L. Rev. University of Pittsburgh Law Review. Pittsburgh, Pennsylvania

Univ. of Queensland L.J. University of Queensland Law Journal.
Brisbane, Australia

Univ. of Richmond L. Not. University of Richmond Law Notes.
Richmond, Virginia

Univ. of Richmond L. Rev. University of Richmond Law Reivew.
Richmond, Virginia

**Univ. of San Fernando Valley L.
Rev.** University of San Fernando Valley Law Review. Sepul-
veda, California

Univ. of San Francisco L. Rev.
University of San Francisco Law
Review, San Francisco, California

Univ. of Tasmania L. Rev. University of Tasmania Law Review.
Hobart, Tasmania, Australia

Univ. of Toledo L. Rev. The University of Toledo Law Review.
Toledo, Ohio

Univ. of Toronto L.J. University
of Toronto Law Journal. Toronto,
Ontario, Canada

Univ. of Tulsa L.J. The University of Tulsa Law Journal. Tulsa,
Oklahoma

Univ. of West. Australia L. Rev.
University of Western Australia
Law Review. Perth, Australia

Univ. Pub. Group. University
Publishing Group

Univ. Q. L.J. University of Queens-land Law Journal (Aus.)

Univ. Tas. L.R. University of Tasmania Law Review

Univ. T. L.R. University of Tasmania Law Review

Univ. W.A. Ann. L. Rev. University of Western Australia Annual Law Review

Univ. W.A. L. Rev. University of Western Australia Law Review

U.N. Juridical Y.B. United Nations Juridical Year Book

U.N. Jur. Y.B. United Nations Juridicial Yearbook

UNKRA United Nations Korean Reconstruction Agency

U.N.L.L. United Nations League of Lawyers

UNLOS United Nations Law of the Sea (Conference)

U.N.L.R. United Nations Law Reports

UN Mo.Chron. UN Monthly Chronicle

UNMOGIP United Nations Military Observer Group for India and Pakistan

UN Monthly Chron. UN Monthly Chronicle

U.N.M.T. United Nations Multilateral Treaties

U.N.O. United Nations Organization

Unof. Unofficial Reports

Un. of Gh. L.J. University of Ghana Law Journal

Un. Prac. News. Unauthorized Practice News

Unrep. Cr. C. Bombay Unreported Criminal Cases (India) (1862-98)

Unrep. N.Y. Est. T.C. Unreported New York Estate Tax Cases (P-H)

Unrep.Wills Cas. Unreported Wills Cases (P-H)

U.N. Res., Ser.I. United Nations Resolutions, Series I

U.N. Rev. United Nations Review

UNRIAA United Nations Reports of International Arbitral Awards

UNRISD United Nations Research Institute for Social Development

UNROD United Nations Relief Operation in Dacca

UNRPR United Nations Relief for Palestine Rufugees

UNRRA United Nations Relief and Rehabilitation Administration

UNRWA United Nations Relief and Works Agency

UNRWAPR United Nations Relief & Works Agency for Palestine Refugees in the Near East

UNRWAPRNE United Nations Relief and Works Agency for Palestine Refugees in the Near East

UNSCCUR United Nations Scientific Conference on the Conservation & Utilization of Resources

UNSCOB United Nations Special Committee on the Balkans

UNSCOP United Nations Special Committee on Palestine

U.N. SCOR United Nations Security Council Official Records

UNSDD United Nations Social Development Division

UNSDRI United Nations Social Defense Research Institute

U.N.S.G. United Nations Secretary General

U.N.S.W. L.J. University of New South Wales Law Journal

U.N.T.C. United Nations Trusteeship Council

UNTCOK United Nations Temporary Commission on Korea

UNTCOR United Nations Trusteeship Council Official Record

UNTEA United Nations Temporary Executive Authority

UNTFDPP United Nations Trust for Development Planning and Projections

UNTFDS United Nations Trust Fund for Social Development

Un. Trav. Dec. Unreported Travancore Decisions

UNTS United Nations Treaty Series

UNTSO United Nations Truce Supervision Organization

U.N.T.T. United Nations Trust Territory

UNU The United Nations University

U.N.Y.B.
- United Nations Year Book
- Yearbook of the United Nations

U. of Chi. L. Rev. University of Chicago Law Review

U. of Cin. L. Rev. University of Cincinnati Law Review

U. of Detroit L.J. University of Detroit Law Journal

U. of Fla. L. Rev. University of Florida Law Review

U. of Kans.City L. Rev. University of Kansas City Law Review

U. of Kansas L. Rev. University of Kansas Law Review

U. of Malaya L. Rev. University of Malaya Law Review, Singapore, Malaya

U. of Miami L. Rev. University of Miami Law Review

U. of M.L.B. University of Missouri Law Bulletin

U. of Omaha Bull. Night Law School Bulletin, University of Omaha

U. of Pa. L. Rev. University of Pennsylvania Law Review

U. of Pitt. L. Rev. University of Pittsburgh Law Review

U. of P. L.R. University of Pennsylvania Law Review

U. of P. L. Rev. University of Pennsylvania Law Review

U. of Queensl. L.J. University of Queensland Law Journal, Brisbane, Australia

U. of Toronto L.J. University of Toronto Law Journal. Toronto, Canada

U. of T. School of L.R. School of Law Review, Toronto University (Can.)

U. of West. Aust. L. Rev. University of Western Australia Law Review

UPA Uniform Partnership Act

U. Pa. J. Int'l Bus. L. University of Pennsylvania Journal of International Business Law

U. Pa. L. Rev. University of Pennsylvania Law Review

Up. Ben. Pr. Upper Bench Precedents, temp. Car. I (Eng.)

Up. Ben. Pre. Upper Bench Precedents, tempore Car. I

UPC Uniform Probate Code

Up. Can. Upper Canada

Up. Can. L.J. Upper Canada Law Journal

UPC Practice Manual Uniform Probate Code Practice Manual

Update Update on Law-Related Education

U. Pitt. L. Rev. University of Pittsburgh Law Review

U.P.L.R.
- Uganda Protectorate Law Reports (1904-51)
- United Provinces Law Reports (India)

U.P.L.T. United Provinces Law Times (India)

U.P. News Unauthorized Practice News

UPSSL University of Puget Sound School of Law

Ups. Sto. Upshur's Review of Story on the Constitution

Upt. Mar. W. Upton on Maritime Warfare and Prize

Upt. Tr. Mar. Upton on Trade-Marks

U.P.U. Universal Postal Union

U. Puget Sound L. Rev. University of Puget Sound Law Review

U.Q.L.J. University of Queensland Law Journal (Aus.)

U. Queens. L.J. University of Queensland Law Journal

U. Queensl. L.J. University of Queensland Law Journal

Urb. Urban

Urb. Aff. Rep. Urban Affairs Reporter (CCH)

Urban Affairs Rep. Urban Affairs Reporter (CCH)

Urban L. Ann. Urban Law Annual

Urban Law. Urban Lawyer

Urban Law Ann. Urban Law Annual

Urban Lawyer Urban Lawyer

Urban L.J. University of Detroit, Urban Law Journal

Urban L. Rev. Urban Law Review

Urb. L. & Pol'y Urban Law and Policy

Urb. Law. Urban Lawyer

Urb. Law Pol. Urban Law & Policy (Neth.)

Urb. L. Rev. Urban Law Review

URC Unemployment Reserves Commission

U. Rich. L.N. University of Richmond Law Notes

U. Rich. L. Rev. University of Richmond Law Review

U. Richmond L. Rev. University of Richmond Law Review

Url. Cl. Urling's Legal Guide for the Clergy

Url. For. Pat. Urling on Foreign Patents

Url. Trust. Urling on the Office of a Trustee

UROEA UNESCO Regional Office for Education in Asia and Oceania

Uru. Uruguay

U.S., US
- Supreme Court (federal)
- United States
- United States of America
- United States Supreme Court Reports

USAA United States Arbitration Act

USAAF United States Army Air Force

USAF United States Air Force

USAFR United States Air Force Reserve

U.S.A.M. U.S. Attorney's Manual

U.S. & Can. A.R. United States and Canada Aviation Reports

U.S. & Can. Av. United States and Canadian Aviation Reports

U.S. & C. Av. R. United States and Canadian Aviation Reports

U.S. & C. Avi. Rep. United States and Canadian Aviation Reports

U. San Fernando Valley L. Rev. University of San Fernando Valley Law Review

U. San Fernando V. L. Rev. University of San Fernando Valley Law Review

U. San Francisco L. Rev. University of San Francisco Law Review

U. San. Fran. L. Rev. University of San Francisco Law Review

U.S. Ap. United States Appeals Reports

U.S. App. United States Appeals Reports

U.S. App. D.C. U.S. Court of Appeals for District of Columbia

US Appx. Supreme Court Appendix Case

U.S. Av. United States Aviation Reports

U.S. Aviation Aviation Reports (U.S.)

U.S. Aviation Rep. United States Aviation Reports

U.S. Avi. Rep. U.S. Aviation Reports

U.S. Av. R. United States Aviation Reports

U.S.C. United States Code

U.S.C.A. United States Code Annotated

U.S.C.A. app. United States Code Annotated appendix

U.S. Cal. Sch. L. Tax Inst. University of Southern California School of Law. Tax Institute

USCAPP Advanced Professional Programs, University of Southern California Law Center

U.S.C.App. United States Code Appendix

U.S.C.C.
- United States Circuit Court
- United States Court of Claims

U.S.C.C.A. United States Circuit Court of Appeals Reports

U.S.C.C.P.A. United States Court of Customs and Patent Appeals

U.S. cert. den. Certiorari denied by U.S. Supreme Court

U.S. cert. dis. Certiorari dismissed by U.S. Supreme Court

USCG United States Coast Guard

U.S.C. Govt'l. Rev. University of South Carolina Governmental Review

U.S. Cir. Ct. Rep. D.C. Hayward and Hazleton Circuit Court Reports (D.C.)

USCMA Official Reports, United States Court of Military Appeals

U.S.C.M.A., Adv. Op. United States Court of Military Appeals, Advance Opinions

U.S. Code Cong. & Ad. News United States Code Congressional & Administrative News

U.S. Comp. St. United States Compiled Statutes

U.S. Comp. St. Supp. United States Compiled Statutes Supplement

U.S. Cond. Rep. Peters' Condensed U.S. Reports

U.S. Cong. & Adm. Serv. U.S. Congressional and Administrative Service

U.S. Const. United States Constitution

U.S. Crim. Dig. Waterman's United States Court of Claims

U.S.C.S. United States Code Service

U.S.C.S. app. United States Code Service appendix (Lawyers co-op)

U.S.C. Supp. United States Code Supplement

US Ct App United States Court of Appeals

U.S.Ct.Cl. United States Court of Claims

USDA United States Department of Agriculture

U.S.Daily United States Daily, Washington, D.C.

U.S.D.C.
- United States District Court
- United States District of Columbia

U.S.D.C. Haw.
- U.S. District Court, District of Hawaii (Haw.)
- U.S. District Court, District of Hawaii Reports (Haw.)

U.S.D.C. Hawaii
- U.S. District Court, District of Hawaii (Haw.)
- U.S. District Court, District of Hawaii Reports (Haw.)

U.S. Dept. Int. United States Department of Interior

U.S. Dept. of Commerce, Bureau of Foreign and Domestic Commerce, Gen. Leg. Bull. United States Department of Commerce, Bureau of Foreign and Domestic Commerce, General Legal Bulletin

US Dep't of Justice United States Department of Justice

US Dep't of State United States Department of State

U.S. Dig. United States Digest

U.S. Dig. (L.ed.) Anno. United States Supreme Court Digest Annotated

U.S. Dist. Ct. United States District Court

U.S. Dist. Ct. Haw. United States District Court for Hawaii

U.S. Dist. Ct. Haw. (Estee) Estee (Morris M.), United States District Court for Hawaii

USDk United States Supreme Court Slip Opinion Docket Numbers

U.S.E. Encyclopedia of United States Reports

U.S. Eq. Dig. United States Equity Digest

USES United States Employment Service

U.S.F. L.R. University of San Francisco Law Review

U.S.F. L. Rev. University of San Francisco Law Review

U. S. F. Mar. L. J. University of San Francisco Maritime Law Journal

U.S.F.V. L. Rev. University of San Fernando Valley Law Review

USHA United States Housing Authority

U.S. High Comm. for Germany Inf. Bull. United States High Commissioner for Germany, Information Bulletin

USIA United States Information Agency

U.S.I.C.C. Rep. United States Interstate Commerce Commission Reports

U.S.I.C.C. V.R. U.S. Interstate Commerce Commission Valuation Reports

USIS U.S. Indian Service

U.S.I.T.C.Pub. U.S. International Trade Commission Publication

U.S. Jur. United States Jurist

U.S.L. United States Laws

U.S. Law. Ed. United States Supreme Court Reports, Lawyers' Edition

U.S. Law Int. United States Law Intelligencer and Review (Providence and Philadelphia)

U.S. Law Jour. United States Law Journal

U.S. Law Mag. United States Law Magazine

U.S. L. Ed. Lawyers' Edition, United States Supreme Court Reports

U.S. L. Ed. 2d Lawyers'Edition United States Supreme Court Reports, Second Series

U.S.L.J. United States Law Journal (New Haven and New York)

U.S. L. Mag. United States Law Magazine

U.S. L. Rev. United States Law Review

U.S.L.W. United States Law Week (BNA)

U.S.L. Week United States Law Week

USMC
- United States Marine Corps
- United States Maritime Commission

USMCR United States Marine Corps Reserve

U.S.M.L.Mag. United States Monthly Law Magazine

U.S. Month. Law Mag. United States Monthly Law Magazine

USN United States Navy

U. So. Cal. Tax Inst. University of Southern California Tax Institute

U.S. Pat. Q. U.S. Patent Quarterly

U.S. Pat. Quar. United States Patent Quarterly

U.S. Pat. Quart. United States Patent Quarterly

U.S.P.Q. (BNA) United States Patents Quarterly (BNA)

USPS United States Postal Service

U.S.R. United States Supreme Court Reports

U.S.Reg. United States Register (Philadelphia)

U.S.reh.den. Rehearing denied by U.S. Supreme Court

U.S.reh.dis. Rehearing dismissed by U.S. Supreme Court

U.S.Rep. United States Reports

U.S. Rep. (L. Ed.) United States Reports, Lawyers' Edition

U.S. Reports United States Reports (U.S.)

U.S. Rev. St. United States Revised Statutes

U.S. R.R. Lab. Bd. United States Railroad Labor Board

U.S. R.R. Lab. Bd. Dec. Decisions of the United States Railroad Labor Board

U.S.R.S. United States Revised Statutes

U.S.S.B. United States Shipping Board Decisions

U.S.S.B.B. United States Shipping Board Bureau Decisions

U.S.S.C. Rep. United States Supreme Court Reports

U.S.S.R. Union of Soviet Socialist Republics

U.S. Stat. United States Statutes at Large

U.S. St. at L. United States Statutes at Large

U.S. St. Tr. United States Trials (Wharton)

U.S. Sup. Ct. United States Supreme Court Reporter

U.S. Sup. Ct. (L.Ed.) United States Reports, Lawyers'Edition

U.S. Sup. Ct. R. United States Supreme Court Reporter (West)

U.S. Sup. Ct. Rep. United States Supreme Court Reporter

U.S. Sup. Ct. Reps. Supreme Court Reporter

UST United States Treaties & Other International Agreements

U.S.T. United States Treaties & Other International Agreements

U.S.Tax Cas. (CCH)
- United States Tax Cases (CCH)
- U.S. Tax Cases

USTC U.S. Tax Cases (CCH)

U.S.T.C. United States Tax Cases (CCH)

U.S.T.D. United States Treaty Development

U.S.T.I.T. United States Treaties and Other International Agreements 1950-date

U.S. Treas. Dept. United States Treasury Department

U.S. Treas. Reg. United States Treasury Regulations

U.S. Treaty Ser. United States Treaty Series

USTS United States Travel Service

U.S.V.A.A.D. U.S. Veteran's Administration Administrator's Decisions

U.S.V.B.D.D. U.S. Veterans Bureau Directors Decisions

Ut.
- Utah
- Utah Reports

U/T Under trust

Utah
- Utah
- Utah Reports
- Utah Supreme Court Reports

Utah 2d Utah Reports Second Series

Utah Admin. Bull State of Utah Bulletin

Utah Admin. R. Administrative Rules of the State of Utah

Utah Bar. Bull Utah Bar Bulletin

Utah B. Bull. Utah Bar Bulletin

Utah B.J. Utah Bar Journal

Utah Code Ann. Utah Code Annotated

Utah Const. Utah Constitution

Utah I.C. Bull. Utah Industrial Commission Bulletin

Utah Laws Laws of Utah

Utah L. Rev. Utah Law Review

Utah P.U.C. Utah Public Utilities Commission Report

Utah R. Utah Reports (Utah)

Utah S.B.A. Utah State Bar Association

U. Tas. L.R. University of Tasmania Law Review

U. Tasm. L. Rev. University of Tasmania Law Review

Ut. B.J. Utah Bar Journal

U.T. Fac. L. Rev. University of Toronto Faculty of Law Review

U.T. Faculty L.R. Faculty of Law Review, University of Toronto

Util. Utility; Utilities

Util. L. Rep. (CCH)
- Utilities Law Reports
- Utilities Law Reporter (CCH)

Util. Sect. Newl. Utility Section Newsletter

UTLC University of Tennessee College of Law

U.T.L.J. University of Toronto Law Journal (Can.)

Ut. L.R. Utah Law Review

UTOLCL University of Toledo College of Law

U. Toledo Intra. L.R. University of Toledo Intramural Law Review

U. Toledo L. Rev. University of Toledo Law Review

U. Tol. L. Rev. University of Toledo Law Review

U. Tor. Fac. L.R. University of Toronto Faculty of Law Review

U. Tor. Fac. L. Rev. University of Toronto Faculty of Law Review

U. Tor. L. Rev. University of Toronto School of Law Review

U. Toronto Fac. L. Rev. University of Toronto Faculty of Law Review

U. Toronto L.J. University of Toronto Law Journal

U. Toronto Faculty L. Rev. University of Toronto Faculty of Law Review

U. Toronto Sch. L. Rev. University of Toronto School of Law Review

UTSL University of Texas School of Law

U/W Under will

U. Wash. L. Rev. University of Washington Law Review

U.W. Austl. L. Rev. University of Western Australia Law Review

UWCLA Center for Latin American, University of Wisconsin-Milwaukee

U. West. Aust. Ann. L. Rev. University of Western Australia Annual Law Review

U. Western Aust. L. Rev. University of Western Australia Law Review

U. Western Ont. L. Rev. University of Western Ontario Law Review

U. West. L.A. L. Rev. University of West Los Angeles Law Review

U. West Los Angeles L. Rev. University of West Los Angeles Law Review

U. Windsor L. Rev. University of Windsor Law Review

U.W.L.A. L. Rev.
- University of Western Australia Law Review
- University of West Los Angeles School of Law, Law Review

U.W.L.A. Rev. University of West Los Angeles School of Law, Law Review

U.W.O. L. Rev. University of Western Ontario Law Review

U.W.Ont. L. Rev. University of Western Ontario Law Review

U/wrs Underwriters

U.Y.A. University Year for Action

U. Zambia L.B. University of Zambia Law Bulletin

V

v.   versus

V.
- Abstracted Valuation Decisions
- Vacated; same case vacated (used in Shepard's Citations)
- Verb
- Vermont
- Vermont Reports
- Victoria
- Vide (see)
- Vietnamese
- Virginia
- Virginia Reports
- Voce (word)
- Void; decision or finding held invalid for reasons given (used in Shepard'sCitations)
- Volume

Va.   Virginia

VA
- Veterans Administration/Department of Veterans Affairs
- Veterans' Affairs

V.A.   Vice-AdmiraltyVa.
- Gilmer,Virginia Reports
- Valid; decision or finding held valid for reasons given (used in Shepard'sCitations)
- Virginia
- Virginia Reports
- Virginia Supreme Court Reports

Va. Acts   Acts of the General Assembly of the Commonwealth of Virginia

Va. App.   Virginia Appeals (Va.)

Va. B.A.   Virginia State Bar Association

Va. B.A.J.   Virginia Bar Association Journal

Va. Bar Assn.   Virginia State Bar Association

Va. Bar News   Virginia Bar News

Va. B. Ass'n J.   Virginia Bar Association Journal

Vac'g   Vacating

Va. Cas.
- Virginia Cases (by Brockenbrough & Holmes)
- Virginia Criminal Cases, Virginia Reports, vol. 3-4 (1789-1826)

Va. Ch. Dec.   Wythe's Chancery (1789-99) (Va.)

Va. Cir.   Virginia Ciruit Court Opinions

VACLE   Joint Committee on Continuing Legal Education of the Virginia State Bar andThe Virginia Bar Association

Va. Code   Code of Virginia

Va. Col. Dec.   Virginia Colonial Decisions (Randolph & Barrandall)

Va. Const.   Virginia Constitution

V.A.D.   Veterans' Affairs Decisions, Appealed Pension & Civil Service Retirement Cases(U.S.)

Va. Dec.   Virginia Decisions

Va. Envtl. L.J. Virginia Environmental Law Journal

Vag. Vagrancy

Va. I.C. Ops. Virginia Industrial Commission Opinions

Vaizey Vaizey's Law of Settlements (1887)

Va. J.Int'l. L. Virginia Journal of International Law

Va. J.Nat. Resources L. Virginia Journal of Natural Resources Law

Va. L. Virginia Law Review

Val. Valparaiso

Va. Law J. Virginia Law Journal (Richmond)

Val. Com. Valen's Commentaries

Va. L. Dig. Virginia Law Digest

Va. L.J. Virginia Law Journal

Valparaiso Univ. L. Rev. Valparaiso University Law Review

Va LR Virginia Law Review

Va. L.Reg. Virginia Law Register

Va. L. Reg. N.S. Virginia Law Register, New Series

Val. R. (I.C.C.) Interstate Commerce Commission Valuation Reports

Val. Rep. Valuation Reports, Interstate Commerce Commission

Val. Rep. I.C.C. Valuation Reports, Interstate Commerce Commission

Va. L. Rev. Virginia Law Review

Val.U.L. Rev. Valparaiso University Law Review

Va. L. Wk. Dicta Comp Virginia Law Weekly Dicta Compilation

V.A.M.R. Vernon's Annotated Missouri Rule

V.A.M.S. Vernon's Annotated Missouri Statutes

Vand. Vanderbilt

Vander L. Vanderlinden's Laws of Holland

Vand. J. Transnat'l. L. Vanderbilt Journal of Transnational Law

Vand. Law. Vanderbilt Lawyer, The

Vand. L. Rev. Vanderbilt Law Review

V. & B. Vesey & Beames' English Chancery Reports (1812-14)

Vanderbilt J. Transnat'l L. Vanderbilt Journal of Transnational Law

Vanderbilt L.R. Vanderbilt Law Review

Vanderstr. Vanderstraaten's Reports (1869-71) (Ceylon)

Vanderstraaten Vanderstraaten's Decisions in Appeal, Supreme Court (1869-71) (Sri L.)

Van Diem. L. Acts Acts of Van Dieman's Land (Austl.)

V. & P. Vendor and purchaser

V. & S. Vernon & Scriven's Irish King's Bench Reports (1786-88)

Van Fleet, Coll. Attack Van Fleet on Collateral Attack

Van Hey. Eq. Van Heythuysen's Equity Draftsman

Van Hey. Mar. Ev. Van Heythuysen on Maritime Evidence

Van Hey. Rud. Van Heythuysen's Rudiments of English Law

Van K. Van Koughnet's Reports, vols. 15-21 Upper Canada Common Pleas (1864-71)

Van. K. & H. Upper Canada Common Pleas Reports (1864-71)

Van. L. Vander Linden's Practice (Cape Colony)

Van N. Van Ness' Prize Cases, U.S. District Court, District of New York

Van Ness, Prize Cas. Van Ness' Prize Cases, U.S. District Court, District of New York

Van Sant. Ch. J. Van Santvoord's Lives of the Chief Justices of the United States

Van Sant. Eq. Pr. Van Santvoord's Equity Practice

Van Sant. Pl. Van Santvoord's Pleadings

Van Sant. Prec. Van Santvoord's Precedents

VANUSL Vanderbilt University School of Law

VAPR Veterans Administration Procurement Regulations

Va. R. Gilmer's Virginia Reports

var. various

Va. R. Ann. Virginia Reports, Annotated (Va.)

Va. Rep. Anno. Virginia Reports, Annotated (Va.)

Va. S.B.A. Virginia State Bar Association, Reports

V.A.S.C.A.R. Visual Average Speed Computer and Recorder

Va.S.C.C. Virginia State Corporation Commission

Va. Tax Rev. Virginia Tax Review

Vatican Vatican City State

V.A.T.S. Vernon's Annotated Texas Statutes

Vatt. Vattel's Law of Nations

Vattel Vattel's Law of Nations

Vattel, Law Nat, Vattel's Law of Nations

Vaug. Vaughan's English Common Pleas Reports (124 ER)

Vaugh. Vaughan's English Common Pleas Reports (124 ER)

Vaughan Vaughan's English Common Pleas Reports (124 ER)

Vaughan (Eng.) Vaughan's English Common Pleas Reports (124 ER)

Vaux Vaux's Recorder's Decisions, Philadelphia, Pa. (Pa. 1841-45)

Vaux (Pa.) Vaux's Recorder's Decisions, Philadelphia, Pa. (Pa. 1841-45)

Vaux Rec. Dec. Vaux's Recorder's Decisions, Philadelphia, Pa. (Pa. 1841-45)

V.B. Veterans' Bureau (U.S.)

V.C.
- Vice-Chancellor
- Vice-Chancellor's Courts (Eng.)

V.C. Adm. Victoria Reports, Admiralty

V.C.C. Vice-Chancellor's Court

V.C. Eq. Victoria Reports, Equity

V Chair Vice Chairman, Vice Chairperson, Vice Chairwoman

V.C.J.C. Chief Justices Law Reform Committee, Victoria (Aus.)

V.C. Rep. Vice-Chancellor's Reports (English; Canadian)

V.D. Valuation Decisions

Ve. Vroom's Reports (30-85 New Jersey Law)

Vea. & B. Vesey & Beames' English Chancery Reports

Ve. & B. Vesey & Beames' English Chancery Reports

Veazey Veazey's Reports (36-44 Vermont)

VEBA Voluntary Employees' Beneficiary Association

Veh. Vehicles

Veh. & Traf. Vehicle and Traffic

Veh. C. Vehicle Code

Vend. Ex. Venditioni Exponas

Venez. Venezuela

Vent.
- Ventris' English Common Pleas Reports (86 ER)
- Ventris' English Kings Bench Reports

Vent. (Eng.)
- Ventris' English Common Pleas Reports (86 ER)
- Ventris' English King's Bench Reports

Ventr. Ventris' English Common Pleas Reports (86 ER)

Ven. Venue

Ver. Vermont Reports

Verm. Vermont Reports

Vermont L. Rev. Vermont Law Review

Vermont R. Vermont Reports (Vt.)

Vermont Rep. Vermont Reports (Vt.)

Vermont Reports Vermont Reports (Vt.)

Vermt. Vermont Reports (Vt.)

Vern. Vernons' English Chancery Reports (23 ER)

Vern. & S. Vernon and Scriven's Irish King's Bench Reports (1786-88)

Vern. & Sc. Vernon & Scrive Reports, King's Bench (1786-88) (Ir.)

Vern. & Scr. Vernon and Scriven's Irish King's Bench Reports (1786-88)

Vern. & Scriv. Vernon and Scriven's Irish King's Bench Reports (1786-88)

Vern. & S. (Ir.) Vernon and Scriven's Irish King's Bench Reports (1786-88)

Vern. Ch. Vernon's Chancery (Eng.)

Vern.(Eng.) Vernon's English Chancery Reports (23 ER)

Vernon's Ann. C.C.P. Vernons' Annotated Texas Code of Criminal Procedure

Vernon's Ann. Civ. St. Vernon's Annotated Texas Civil Statutes

Vernon's Ann. P.C. Vernon's Annotated Texas Penal Code

Verpl. Ev. Verplanck on Evidence

Verpl. Cont. Verplanck on Contracts

Ver. Rep. Vermont Reports (Vt.)

Vert. Vermont Reports (Vt.)

Ves. Vesey, Senior's, English Chancery Reports

Ves. & B. Vesey & Beames'English Chancery Reports (35 ER)

Ves. & B. (Eng.) Vesey & Beames' English Chancery Reports (35 ER)

Ves. & Bea. Vesey & Beames' English Chancery Reports (35 ER)

Ves. & Beam. Vesey & Beames' English Chancery Reports (35 ER)

Ves. Jr. Vesey, Junior's, English Chancery Reports (30-34 ER)

Ves. Jr. (Eng.) Vesey, Junior's English Chancery Reports (30-34 ER)

Ves. Jr. suppl. Supplement to Vesey, Junior's English Chancery Reports (34 ER)

Ves. Jun. Vesey, Junior's English Chancery Reports (30-34 ER)

Ves. Jun. Supp. Supplement to Vesey, Junior's, English Chancery Reports, (34 ER)

Ves. Jun. Supp. (Eng.) Supplement to Vesey, Junior's, English Chancery Reports (34 ER)

Ves. Sen. Vesey, Senior's, English Chancery Reports (27, 28 ER)

Ven. Sen. Supp. Supplement to Vesey, Senior's, English Chancery Reports (28 ER)

Ves. Sr. Vesey, Senior's, English Chancery Reports (27, 28 ER)

Ves. Sr. (Eng) Vesey, Senior's English Chancery Reports (27, 28 ER)

Ves. Sr. Supp. Supplement to Vesey Senior's Chancery Reports (1747-56) (28 ER)

Ves. Sr. Supp. (Eng.) Supplement to Vesey, Senior's, English Chancery Reports (28 ER)

Ves. Supp. Supplement to Vesey Junior's Chancery Reports by Hovenden (1789-1817) (34 ER)

Vet. Veterans and veterans laws

Vet. Entr. (or Int.) Veteres Intrationes

Veterinar. Veterinarians

Vet. Na. B. Old Natura Brevium

Vet. N. Br. The Old Natura Brevium

VEVRAA Vietnam Era Veterans' Readjustment and Assistance Act

Vez. Vezey's (Vesey's) English Chancery Reports

V.H. Eq. Dr. Van Heythuysen, Equity Draftsman. 2ed. 1828

V.I.
- Virgin Islands
- Virgin Island Reports

V.I. B.J. Virgin Islands Bar Journal

Vic.
- (Queen) Victoria
- Victoria, Australia

V.I.C. Virgin Islands Code

Vicat Vicat's Vocabularium Juris Utriusque ex Variis Ante Editis

Vicat Voc.Jur. Vicat's Vocabularium Juris Utriusque ex Variis Ante Editis

V.I. Code Ann. Virgin Islands Code Annotated

Vic. L.T. Victorian Law Times

Vict.
- Victoria
- Victorian Reports (Aus.)
- Victoria, Australia

Vict. Acts Victoria Acts of Parliament (1890-date)

Vict. Admr. Victorian Admiralty

Vict. C.S. Victorian Consolidated Statutes

Vict. Eq.   Victorian Equity

Vict. L.   Victorian Law

Vict. J. (Austr.)   Victorian Law Reports (Aus.)

Vict. L.J.   Victorian Law Journal (Aus.)

Vict. L.R.   Victorian Law Reports (Aus.)

Vict. L.R. Min.   Victorian Mining Law Reports (Aus.)

Vict. L.T.   Victorian Law Times (Melbourne) (Aus.)

Vict. R.   Victorian Reports (Austl.)(1857-date)

Vict. Rep.   Victorian Reports (Aus.)

Vict. Rep. (Adm.)   Victorian Reports (Admiralty) (Aus.)

Vict. Rep. (Austr.)   Victorian Reports (Aus.)

Vict. Rep. (Eq.)   Victorian Reports (Equity) (Australia)

Vict. Rep. (Law)   Victorian Reports (Law) (Aus.)

Vict. Rev.   Victorian Review

Vict. S. Ct.   Reports of Cases...Supreme Court of Victoria (1861-1869)

Vict. Stat.   Victorian Statutes; the General Public Acts (Aus.)

Vict. Stat. R. Regs. & B.   Victorian Statutory Rules, Regulations and By-Laws (Aus.)

Vict. St. Tr.   Victorian State Trials (Aus.)

Vict. U. L. Rev.   Victoria University Law Review

Vict. U.of Wellington L. Rev.   Victoria University of Wellington Law Review, Wellington, New Zealand

Vict. U. Wellington L. Rev.   Victoria University of Wellington Law Review

Vict. U. Well. L. Rev.   Victoria University of Wellington Law Review

Vid.   Vidian's Exact Pleader (1684)

Vil. & Br.   Vilas & Bryant's Edition of the Wisconsin Reports

Vilas   Vilas' Reports (1-5 N.Y. Criminal Reports)

Vill.   Villanova

Villanova L. Rev.   Villanova Law Review

Vill. Envtl. L.J.   Villanova Environmental Law Journal

Vill. L. Rev.   Villanova Law Review

Vin. Abr.   Supplement to Vineer's Abridgment of Law and Equity (Eng.)

Vin. Abr. (Eng.)   Viner's Abridgment of Law & Equity (1741-53) (Eng.)

Vinc. Cr.L.   Vincent's Manual of Criminal Law

Vinc. Cr. & Lib.   Vincent on Criticism and Libel

Vin. Comm.   Viner's Abridgment or Commentaries

Viner, Abr.   Viner's Abridgment of Law & Equity (1741-53)

Vinn.   Vinnius

Vinn. ad Inst.   Vinnius' commentary on the Institutes of Justinian

Vin. Supp.   Supplement to Vner's Abridgment of Law and Equity

Vint. Can. Law Vinton's American Canon Law

Vir.
- Virginia
- Virginia Cases (Brockenbrough & Holmes)
- Virgin's Reports (52-60 Maine)

V.I.R. & Regs. Virgin Islands Rules and Regulations

Virch. P.M. Virchow on Post Mortem Examinations

Virg.
- Virginia
- Virginia Cases (by Brockenbrough & Holmes)
- Virgin's Reports (52-60 Maine)

Virg. Cas. Virginia Cases (by Brockenbrough & Holmes)

Virg. J.Int'l. L. Virginia Journal of International Law

Virg. L.J. Virginia Law Journal (Richmond)

Virgin Virgin's Reports (52-60 Maine)

Virginia Rep. Virginia Reports (Va.)

Virgin Is. Virgin Islands

Vir. L.J. Virginia Law Journal

VISTA Volunteers in Service to America

VITA Volunteers in Technical Assistance

Viz. Videlicet (that is to say)

Viz. Pr. Vizard's Practice of the Court in Banc

VJNRL Virginia Journal of Natural Resources Law

V.L.R.
- Vanderbilt Law Review (Tenn.)
- Victorian Law Reports (Australia)

V.L.R. (Adm.) Victorian Law Reports, Admiralty (1875-84) (Aus.)

V.L.R.C. Victorian Law Reform Commissioner (Aus.)

V.L.R. (E.) Victorian Law Reports, Equity (1875-84) (Aus.)

V.L.R. (Eq.) Victorian Law Reports, Equity (1875-84) (Aus.)

V.L.R. (I.P. & M.) Victorian Law Reports, Insolvency, Probate and Matrimonial (1875-84) (Aus.)

V.L.R. (L.) Victorian Law Reports, Law (1875-84) (Aus.)

V.L.R. (M.) Victorian Law Reports, Mining (1875-84) (Aus.)

V.L.R. (P. & M.) Victorian Law Reports, Probate & Matrimonial (1875-84) (Aus.)

V.L.T. Victorian Law Times (1856-57)

V.N. Van Ness' Prize Cases (U.S.)

Vo. Verbo

V.O. De Verborum Obligationibus

V.O.A. Voice of America (U.S.)

vocat. vocational

Voet, Com.ad Pand. Voet, Commentarius ad Pandectas

vol.
- volume
- voluntary
- volunteer

Vol. Fire Ben. Volunteer Firemen's Benefit

Vo. L.R. Villanova Law Review

Von H. Const. Hist. Von Holst's Constitutional History of the United States

Von Ihr. Str. for L. Von Ihring's Struggle for Law

Voorh. Code Voorhies' Code, New York

Voorh. Cr. Jur. Voorhies' Criminal Jurisprudence of Louisiana

Voorh. St. Voorhies' Louisiana Revised Statutes

VP Vice President

V.P. All India Reporter, Vindhya Pradesh (1951-57)

Vp. Void in part; decision or finding held invalid in part for reasons given (usedin Shepard's Citations)

V.P.A. Victorian Planning Appeal Decisions (Law Book Co.)

V.R.
  - Valuation Reports, Interstate Commerce Commission (U.S.)
  - Vermont Reports
  - Victorian Reports, Australia (1870-72)
  - Villanova Law Review (Pa.)
  - Webb, A'Beckett & Williams' Victorian Reports (1870-72) (Aus.)

Vr. Vroom's Reports (30-85 New Jersey Law)

V.R. Adm. Victorian Reports, Admiralty (Aus.)

V.R. (E.) Webb, A'Beckett and Willams' Equity Reports (1870-72) (Victoria, Aus.)

V.R. (Eq.) Victorian Reports (Equity) (Aus.)

V.R. (I.E. & M.) Webb, A'Beckett and Williams' Insolvency, Ecclesiastical and MatrimonialReports (1870-72) (Victoria, Aus.)

V.R.L. Victorian Law Reports (Aus.)

V.R. (Law) Victoria Law Reports (Aus.)

Vroom Vroom's Reports (30-85 New Jersey Law Reports)

Vroom (G.D.W.) G.D.W. Vroom's Reports (36-63 New Jersey Law Reports)

Vroom (N.J.) Vroom's Reports (30-85 New Jersey Law Reports)

Vroom (P.D.) P.D. Vroom's Reports (30-35 New Jersey Law Reports)

Vs. Versus (against)

V.S.
  - Verified Statement
  - Vermont Statutes

V.S.A. Vermont Statutes Annotated

V.S.L.R.C. Victorian Statute Law Revision Committee (Aus.)

Vt.
  - Vermont
  - Vermont Reports

Vt. Acts Laws of Vermont

Vt. Admin. Code Vermont Administrative Code

Vt. Admin. Comp. Vermont Administrative Procedure Compilation

Vt. Admin. Proc. Bull. Vermont Administrative Procedures Bulletin

Vt. B. A. Vermont Bar Association, Reports

Vt. B.J. & L. Dig. Vermont Bar Journal and Law Digest

VTC Voting trust certificate

V.T.C.A. Vernon's Texas Codes Annotated

VTCLE Vermont Bar Association Committee on Continuing Legal Education

Vt. Const. Vermont Constitution

Vt. L. Rev. Vermont Law Review

Vt. P.S.C. Vermont Public Service Commission

Vt. R. Vermont Reports (Vt.)

Vt. R.C. Vermont Railroad Commission

Vt. Rep. Vermont Reports (Vt.)

Vt. Stat. Ann. Vermont Statutes Annotated

V.U.C. L.R. Victoria University College Law Review (1953-57) (N.Z.)

V.U.L.R. Valparaiso University Law Review

V.U.W.L.R. Victoria University of Wellington Law Review (N.Z.)

V.U.W.L. Rev. Victoria University of Wellington Law Review

V.Y. Various years

W

W.
- Wales
- Washington Reports (1890-1939)
- Watermayer's Reports, Supreme Court (Cape of Good Hope)
- Watt's Pennysivania Reports
- Wendell's Reports (New York 1826-41)
- West
- Western
- Westminster
- Wheaton's Reports (14-25 United States)
- William (King of England)
- Wilson's Reports (Texas Civil Cases, Court of Appeals)
- Wisconsin Reports
- Witwatersrand Local Division Reports (S. Afr.)
- Wright's Ohio Reports (1831-34)
- Wyoming Reports

W.2d Washington State Reports, Second Series

W. A.
- West Africa
- Western Australia
- Withholding agent

Wa.
- Washington
- Washington Reports
- Watts' Reports (1890-1939)

Wa. 2d Washington State Reports, Second Series

Wa. A. Washington Appellate Reports

W.A.A. War Assets Administration (U.S.)

W.A.A.R. Western Australian Arbitration Reports

W.A. Arb. R. Western Australia Arbitration Reports

W.A'B. & W. Webb, A'Beckett & Williams Reports (1870-72) (Aus.)

W.A'B. & W. Eq. Webb A'Beckett & Williams' Equity Reports (1870-72) (Victoria, Aus.)

W.A'B. & W.I.E. & M. Webb, A'Beckett & Williams' Insolvency, Ecclesiastical and Matrimonial Reports (1870-72) (Victoria, Aus.)

W.A'B. & W.Min. Webb, A'Beckett & Williams' Mining Cases (1870-72) (Victoria, Aus.)

W.A.C.A. West African Court of Appeal, Selected Judgments

Wad. Dig. Waddilove, Digest of Ecclesiastical Cases. 1849

Wade, Am. Mining Law Wade on American Mining Law

Wade, Attachm. Wade on Attachment and Garnishment

Wade Min. Wade on American Mining Law

Wade Not. Wade on the Law of Notice

Wade Retro. L. Wade on Retroactive Laws

Wad. Mar. & Div. Waddilove, Marriage & Divorce. 1864

W.A.F. Women's Air Force

W.Af. L.R. West African Law Reports

W. Afr. App. West African Court of Appeal Reports

Wage and Hour Cas. (BNA) Wage and Hour Cases (BNA)

Wage & Hour Rep. Wage & Hour Reporter

Wage-Price L. & Econ. Rev. Wage-Price Law and Economics Review

Wage-Pr. L. Wage-Price Law and Economics Review

Wag. St. Wagner's Statutes (Mo.)

Wag. Stat. Wagner's Missouri Statutes

W.A.I.G. Western Australia Industrial Gazette

Wait Act. & Def. Wait's Actions and Defences

Wait Co. Wait's Annotated Code (New York)

Wait Dig. Wait's Digest (New York)

Wait L. & P. Wait's Law and Practice in New York Justices' Courts

Wait Pr. Wait's New York Practice

Waits Prac. Wait's New York Practice

Wait St. Pap. Wait's State Papers of the United States

Wait Tab. Ca. Wait's New York Table of Cases

Wake For. L. Rev. Wake Forest Law Review

Wake Forest Intra. L.Rev. Wake Forest Intramural Law Review

Wake Forest L.Rev. Wake Forest Law Review

Wal. Wallace (usually abbreviated as Wall)

Wal.by L. Wallis' Irish Reports, by Lyne (1766-91)

Wal. Ch. Walker's Michigan Chancery Reports (Mich.)

Walf. Cust. Wallford, Laws of the Customs. 1846

Walf. Part. Walford, Parties to Actions. 1842

Walf. Railw. Walford, Railways. 2ed. 1846

Wal. Jr. J.W. Wallace's United States Circuit Court Reports

Walk.
- Walker's Michigan Chancery Reports
- Walker's Reports (96, 109 Alabama)
- Walker's Reports (1 Mississippi)
- Walker's Reports (Pa. 1855-1885)
- Walker's Reports (22-25, 38-51, 72-88 Texas; 1-10 Civil Appeals Texas)

Walk. Am. Law Walker's American Law

Walk. Bank. L. Walker, Banking Law, 2ed. 1885

Walk. Ch. Walker's Michigan Chancery Reports

Walk. Chanc. Rep. Walker's Michigan Chancery Reports (Mich.)

Walk.Ch. Cas. Walker's Michigan Chancery Reports

Walk. Ch. Mich. Walker's Michigan Chancery Reports

Walk. Com. L. Walker's Theory of the Common Law

Walk. Eq. Pl. Walker's Equity Pleader's Assistant

Walker
- Walker's Michigan Chancery Reports
- Walker's Reports (96, 109 Alabama)
- Walker's Reports (1 Mississippi)
- Walker's Reports (Pa. 1855-1885)
- Walker's Reports (22-25, 38-51, 72-88 Texas; 1-10 Civil Appeals Texas)

Walker's Ch. R. Walker's Michigan Chancery Reports (Mich.)

Walk. Exec. Walker & Elgood, Executors and Administrators. 6ed. 1926

Walk. Int. Walker's Introduction to American Law

Walk. La. Dig. Walker, Louisiana Digest

Walk. (Mic.) Ch. Walker's Michigan Chancery Reports (Mich.)

Walk. Mich. Walker's Michigan Chancery Reports (Mich.)

Walk. Michig. Rep. Walker's Michigan Chancery Reports (Mich.)

Walk. Miss. Walker's Reports (1 Mississippi)

Walk. Pa. Walker's Reports (Pa. 1855-85)

Walk. Pat. Walker on Patents

Walk. Tex. Walker's Reports (22-25, 38-51, 72-88 Texas; 1-10 Civil Appeals Texas)

Walk. Wills Walker on Wills

Wall.
- Wallace
- Wallace's Nova Scotia Reports
- Wallace's Reports (68-90 U.S.)
- Wallace's Circuit Court Reports (U.S.)
- Wallace's Supreme Court Reports (68-90 U.S.) (1863-74)
- Wallis
- Wallis' Irish Chancery Reports
- Wallis Philadelphia Reports (Pa. 1855-85)

Wallace, Jr., Rept. Wallace (J.W.) United States Circuit Court Reports

Wall. By L. Wallis, Irish Chancery (By Lyne)

Wall. C.C. Wallace's Circuit Court Reports (U.S.)

Wallis. Wallis' Irish Chancery Reports

Wallis by L. Wallis' Irish Chancery Reports by Lyne (1776-91)

Wallis by Lyne Wallis' Irish Chancery Reports by Lyne (1766-91)

Wallis (Ir.) Wallis' Irish Chancery Reports

Wall. Jr.
- Wallace, Junior, U.S.
- J.W. Wallace's Circuit Court Reports (U.S.)

Wall. Jr. C.C. J.W. Wallace's Circuit Court Reports (U.S.)

Wall. Lyn. Wallis' Irish Chancery Reports by Lyne (1776-91)

Wall. Pr. Wallace, Principles of the Laws of Scotland

Wall. Rep.
- Wallace, The Reporters (treatise)
- Wallace's Reports (68-90 U.S.)

Wall. S.C. Wallace's Reports (68-90 U.S.)

Wall. Sen. J.B. Wallace's United States Circuit Court Reports

Wall. Sr. Wallace Senior (U.S.)

Wall St. J. Wall Street Journal

Wal. Prin. Wallace, Principles of the Scottish Law

Walp. Rub. Walpole's Rubric of Common Law

Wa. L.R. Washington Law Review

W.A.L.R.
- University of Western Australia Law Review
- West African Law Reports (Gambia, Ghana & Sierra Leone)

W.A.L.R.C. Western Australia Law Reform Commission

Walsh. Walsh, Registry Cases (Ir.)

Wal. Sr. J.B. Wallace's United States Circuit Court Reports

Walter. Waler's Reports (14-16 New Mexico)

Walter C. Walter Code

Walt. H. & W. Walton, Husband and Wife (Sc.)

Walt. Lim. Walter, Statute of Limitations. 4ed.

Wal. U.S. Rep. Wallace U.S. Reports

W. & B. Walferstan and Bristowe, Election Cases (1959-65)

W. & B. Dig. Walter & Bates Digest (Ohio)

W. & C. Wilson & Courtenay's Scotch Appeal Cases

W. & C. Conv. Wolstenholme & Cherry, Conveyancing Statutes. Cherry, 13ed. 1972

W. & D. Wolferstan and Dew, Election Cases (1856-58)

Wandell Wandell's Reports (N.Y.)

Wash. St. B. News Washington State Bar News

W. & H. Wage and Hour Division, U.S. Department of Labor

W. & L. Washington and Lee Law Review (Va.)

W. & L. Dig. Wood & Long's Digest (Illinois)

W. & M.
- William & Mary Law Review
- Woodbury & Minot, United States Circuit Court Reports, 3 vols.

W. & M. L. Rev. William & Mary Law Review

W. & O. Wills Wilgram & O'Hara on Wills

W.& S.
- Watts & Sergeant's Reports (Pa. 1841-1845)
- Wilson & Shaw's Scotch Appeal Case, English House of Lords

W. & S. App. Wilson & Shaw's Scotch Appeals Cases, English House of Lords

W. & T. Eq. Ca. White and Tudor's Leading Cases in Equity. 9 editions (1849-1928)

W. & T. L.C. White and Tudor's Leading Cases in Equity. 9 editions (1849-1928)

W. & W.
- de Witt & Weeresinghe's Appeal Court Reports (Ceylon)
- White & Wilson's Texas Civil Cases, Court of Appeals
- Wyatt & Webb's Victorian Reports (1864-69) (Aus.)

W. & W. C.C. White & Wilson's Texas Civil Cases (Tex.)

W. & W. Cir. Cases, Court of Appeals White & Wilson's Texas Civil Cases (Tex.)

W. & W. Con. Cases White & Wilson's Texas Civil Cases (Tex.)

W. & W. Con. Rep. White & Wilson's Texas Civil Cases (Tex.)

W. & W.(E.) Wyatt & Webb's Reports, Equity (1861-63) (Victoria. Aus.)

W. & W. Eq. Wyatt & Webb's Reports, Equity (1861-63) (Victotoria, Aus.)

W. & W. (I.E. & M.) Wyatt & Webb's Reports, Insolvency, Ecclesiastical & Matrimonial (1861-63) (Victoria, Aus.)

W. & W. (L.) Wyatt & Webb's Reports, Law (1861-63) (Victoria, Aus.)

W. & W. Vict. Wyatt & Webb's Victorian Reports (1864-69) (Aus.)

W. Ap. Washington Appellate Reports

Wap. Pr. R. Waples on Proceedings in Rem

W.A.R. Western Australian Reports

War. Warrants

War. Adv. Att. Warren's Adventures of an Attorney in Search of Practice

War. Bell. Ward on Belligerent and Neutral Powers

War. Cr. L. Warren's Ohio Criminal Law

Ward. Warden's Reports (2,4 Ohio State)

Ward. & Sm. Warden & Smith's Reports (3 Ohio State Reports)

Warden Warden's Reports (2, 4 Ohio Stat Reports)

Warden & Smith Warden & Smith's Reports (3 Ohio State)

Warden's Law & Bk. Bull. Warden's Weekly Law & Bank Bulletin (Ohio)

War Dep. B.C.A. United States War Department, Dec. of Board of Contract Adjustment

War Dept. B.C.A. U.S. War Department, Decisions of Board of Contract Adjustment

Ward Just. Ward's Justice of the Peace

Ward, Leg. Ward on Legacies

Ward Nat. Ward's Law of Nations

Ware. Ware's United States District Court Reports

Wareh. Warehouse

Ware's C.C. Rep. Ware's District Court Reports (U.S.)

Ware's Rep. Ware's District Court Reports (U.S.)

War. L. St. Warren's Law Studies

War. Op. Warwick's Opinions (City Solicitor of Philadelphia, Pa.)

War. Prof. Dut. Warren, Moral, Social and Professional Duties of Attorneys and Solicitors. 2ed. 1851

Warr. Warren

Warth Code. West Virginia Code (1899)

War Trade Reg. War Trade Regulations (U.S.)

Warv. Abst. Warvelle on Abstracts of Title

Warv. El. R. P. Warvelle's Elements of Real Property

Warv. V. & P. Warvelle's Vendors and Purchasers of Real Property

Warwick's Op. Warwick's Opinions (City Solicitor of Philadelphia, Pa.)

Wash Washington Supreme Court Reports

Wash.
- Washburn
- Washington
- Washington Reports
- Washington Territory or State Reports
- Washington's Circuit Court Reports (U.S.)
- Washington's Reports (16-23 Vermont)
- Washington's Reports (1, 2 Virginia)

Wash 2d Washington Supreme Court Reports 2d Series

Wash.2d Washington Reports, Second Series

Wash. Admin. Code Washington Administrative Code

Wash. Admin. Reg. Washington State Register

Wash. & Haz. P.E.I. Washburton & Hazard's Reports (Prince Edward Island, Canada)

Wash. & Lee L. Rev. Washington & Lee Law Review

Wash. App. Washington Appellate Reports

Washb. Easem. Washburn on Easements and Servitudes

Wash. B. News Washington Bar News

Washbourne L.J. Washbourne Law Journal

Washb. Real Prop. Washburn on Real Property

Washburn Washburn's Reports (18-23 Vermont)

Washburn L.J. Washburn Law Journal

Wash. C.C. Washington's United States Circuit Court Reports

Wash. C.C.R. Washington's U.S. Circuit Court Reports

Wash. Co. Washington County Reports, Pennsylvania

Wash. Const. Washington Constitution

Wash. Co. (Pa.) Washington County Reports, Pennsylvania

Wash. Co. R. Washington County Reports (Pa.)

Wash. Co. Repr. Washington County Reports (Pa.)

Wash. Cr. L. Washburn on Criminal Law

Wash. Dec. Washington Decisions

Wash. Dig. Washburn, Vermont Digest

Wash. D.P.W. Washington Department of Public Works

Wash. Ease. Washburn on Easements and Servitudes

Wash. Fin. Rep. (BNA) Washington Financial Reports

Washington and Lee L. Rev. Washington and Lee Law Review

Washington L. Rev. Washington Law Review

Washington Univ. L. Quart. Washington University Law Quarterly

Wash. Jur. Washington Jurist

Wash. Law. Washington Lawyer, The

Wash. Law Rep. Washington Law Reporter (D.C.)

Wash. Laws Laws of Washington

Wash. Legis. Serv. Washington Legislative Service (West)

Wash. L.R. (Dist Col) Washington Law Reporter (D.C.)

Wash. L. Rep. Washington Law Reporter (D.C.)

Wash. L. Rev. Washington Law Review

Wash. Monthly Washington Monthly

Wash. P.S.C. Washington Public Service Commission

Wash. P.U.R. Washington Public Utility Commission Reports

Wash. Rev. Code Revised Code of Washington

Wash. Rev. Code Ann. Washington Revised Code Annotated

Wash. R.P. Washburn on Real Property

Wash. S.B.A. Washington State Bar Association, Proceedings

Wash. St. Washington State Reports

Wash.T.
- Washington Territory Opinions (1854-64)
- Washington Territory Reports (1854-88)

Wash. Ter.
- Washington Territory Opinions (1854-64)
- Washington Territory Reports (1854-88)

Wash. Ter. N.S. Allen's Washington Territory Reports, New Series

Wash. Terr.
- Washington Territory Opinions (1854-64)
- Washington Territory Reports (1854-88)

Wash. Ty.
- Washington Territory Opinions (1854-64)
- Washington Territory Reports (1854-88)

Wash. U. J.Urb. & Contemp. L. Washington University Journal of Urban and Contemporary Law

Wash. U. L.Q. Washington University Law Quarterly

Wash. U. L. Rev. Washington University Law Review

Wash.Va. Washington's Reports (1,2 Va.)

Wat Watts' Reports

Wat. Watermeyer's Supreme Court Reports, Cape of Good Hope (S. Afr.) 1857

Wat. C.G.H. Watermeyer's Cape of Good Hope Reports (S. Africa)

Watch. Board of Examiners in Watchmaking

Wat. Con. Watkins, Conveyancing. 9ed. 1845

Wat. Cop. Watkins, Copholds. 6ed. 1829

Wat. Cr. Dig. Waterman's Criminal Digest (United States)

Wat. Cr. Proc. Waterman's Criminal Procedure

Watermeyer. Watermeyer's Cape of Good Hope Reports (S. Africa)

Wat. Just. Waterman's Justices' Manual

Watk. Con. Watkins on Conveyancing

Watk. Conv. Watkins' Conveyancing

Watk. Cop. Watkins on Copyholds

Watk. Copyh. Watkins' Copyholds

Watk. Des. Watkins on Descents

WATS State Bar of Wisconsin Advanced Training Seminars

Wats. Arb. Watson on Arbitration

Wats. Cler. Law. Watson's Clergyman's Law

Wats. Com. Man. Watson's United States Commissioners' Manual

Wats. Comp. Eq. Watson's Compendium of Equity

Wats. Const. Hist. Watson's Constitutional History of Canada

Wat. Set-Off Waterman on Set-Off

Wats. Med. Jur. Watson's Medical Jurisprudence

Watson. Watson's Compendium of Equity. 2 Editions (1873, 1888)

Watson Eq. Watson's Practical Compendium of Equity

Wats. Part. Watson, Partnership. 2ed. 1807

Wats. Sher. Watson, Office and Duty of Sheriff. 2ed. 1848

Wat. Tres. Waterman on the Law of Trespass

Watts.
- Watts' Reports (Pa. 1832-40)
- Watts' Reports (16-24 West Virginia)

Watts & S. Watts & Sergeant's Reports (Pennsylvania 1841-45)

Watts & Ser. Watts & Sergeant (Pa.)

Watts & Serg. Watts & Sergeant's Reports (Pennsylvania 1841-45)

Watts. & S. (Pa.) Watts & Sergeant's Reports (Pennsylvania 1841-45)

Watts (Pa.) Watts' Reports (Pa. 1832-40)

Wat. wks. Waterworks and water companies

W.A.U. L.R. Western Australia University Law Review

W.Aus. Western Australia

W.Austl.
- West Australia
- Western Australia
- Western Australia Reports

W.Austl. Acts Western Australia Acts

W.Austl. Ind. Gaz. Western Australia Industrial Gazette

W. Austl. J.P. Western Australia Justice of the Peace

W. Austl. L.R. Western Australia Law Reports

W. Austl. R. Western Australia Reports (1960-date)

W. Austl. Stat. Statutes of Western Australia (1918-date) & Western Australia Statutes (1832-1895)

W. Aust. Repr. Acts Reprinted Acts of Western Australia

WAVES Women Accepted for Volunteer Emergency Service

Wayne L.R. Wayne Law Review

Wayne L. Rev. Wayne Law Review

w.b.a. weekly benefit amount

W. Beng. Ind. West Bengal, India

W.Bl. Sir William Blackstone's King's Bench Reports (96 ER) (1746-80)

W.Bla. Sir William Blackstone's English King's Bench Reports (96 ER)

W.Bl. (Eng.) Sir William Blackstone's English King's Bench Reports (96 ER)

Wbl.voor Fiscaal Recht Weekblad voor Fiscaal Recht. Deventer, Netherlands

WBTA Wisconsin Board of Tax Appeals Decisions (Wis.)

WBTA-CCH Tax Reporter Wisconsin Board of Tax Appeals Decisions (CCH) (Wis.)

W.C.A. Workmen's Compensation Act

W.C. & Ins. (Eng.) Workmen's Compensation and Insurance Reports (1912-33) (Eng.)

W.C. & Ins. Rep. Workmen's Compensation and Insurance Reports (1912-33) (Eng.)

W.C. & I.R. Workmen's Compensation and Insurance Reports (1912-33) (Eng.)

W.C. & I.Rep. Workmen's Compensation and Insurance Reports (Eng.)

W.C.B. Workmen's Compensation Bureau

W.C.B.D. (W.A.) Worker's compensation Board Decisions (W. Aus.)

WCC Androphy, White Collar Crime Cases

W.C.C.
- Washington's Circuit Court Reports (U.S.)
- Wisconsin Conservation Commission
- Workmen's Compensation Cases (Minton-Senhouse)

W.C.C. (N.Z.) Worker's Compensation Cases (N.Z.)

W.C.C.R. Washington's U.S. Circuit Court Reports

W.C. Ins. Rep. Workmen's Compensation & Insurance Reports

W.C.L. World Confederation of Labour

W.C.L.J. Workmen's Compensation Law Journal

W.C.L.R. Workmen's Compensation Law Review

W.Coast Rep. West Coast Reporter

W.Con. Rep. Texas Civil Cases (Tex.)

W.C. Ops. Workmen's Compensation Opinions, U.S. Department of Commerce

W.C.R. Workers' Compensation Commission Reports of Cases (N.S.W., Aus.)

W.C. Rep. Workmen's Compensation Reports

W.C.R. (Qn.) Worker's Compensation Reports (Queensland, Aus.)

W.C.R. N.S.W. Workers' Compensation Commission Reports of Cases, New South Wales (Aus.)

W.Ct. S.A. Union of South Africa Water Courts Decisions

W.D.
- Washington Decisions (Wash.)
- Western District

W.D.(2d) Washington Decisions (2d series) (Wash.)

W/D
- Withdrawal
- Withdrawn

W.Dig. New York Weekly Digest (N.Y.)

W.D.Ky. United States District Court for the Western District of Kentucky

W.D.La. United States District Court for the Western District of Louisiana

W.D.Mich. United States District Court for the Western District of Michigan

W.D.Mo. United States District Court for the Western District of Missouri

W.D.N.C. United States District Court for the Western District of North Carolina

W.D.N.Y. United States District Court for the Western District of New York

W.D.Okla. United States District Court for the Western District of Oklahoma

W.D.Pa. United States District Court for the Western District of Pennsylvania

W.D.Tenn. United States District Court for the Western District of Tennessee

W.D.Tex. United States District Court for the Western District of Texas

W.D.Va. United States District Court for the Western District of Virginia

W.D.Wash. United States District Court for the Western District of Washington

W.D.Wis. United States District Court for the Western District of Wisconsin

We.

- West's Chancery Reports (Eng.)
- West's Reports, House of Lords (Eng.)
- Western Tithe Cases (Eng.)

Weap. Weapons and firearms

Webb.

- Webb's Reports (Vols. 6-20 Kansas)
- Webb's Reports (Vols. 11-20 Texas Civil Appeals)

Webb, A'B. & W. Webb, A'Beckett & Williams' Reports (1870-72) (Victoria, Aus.)

Webb, A'B. & W.Eq. Webb, A'Beckett, & Williams' Victorian Equity Reports (Aus.)

Webb, AB. & W.I.E. & M Webb, A'Beckett & Williams' Insolvency Ecclesiastical & Matrimonial Reports (1870-72) (Victoria, Aus.)

Webb, A'B. & W.I.P. & M. Webb, A'Beckett, & Williams' Insolvency, Probate & Matrimonial Reports, (Aus.)

Webb, A'B. & W.Min. Webb, A'Beckett, & Williams Mining Cases (Aus.)

Webb. & D. Webb & Duval's Reports (vols. 1-3 Texas)

Webb & Duval Webb & Duval's Reports (vols. 1-3 Texas)

Webb Cr. Dig. Webb's Digest of Texas Criminal Cases

Webb Jud. Act Webb on the Judicature Act

Webb Pl. & Pr. Webb's Kansas Pleading and Practice

Webb. R.R. Webb's Railroad Laws of Maine

Webb Supr. Ct. Pr. Webb's (English) Supreme Court Practice

Web. Pat. Webster, New Patent Law. 4ed. 1854

Web. Pat. Cas. Webster's Patent Cases (1601-1855)

Web. P.C. Webster's Patent Cases (1601 -1855)

Webs. Webster's Patent Cases (Eng.)

Webs. Pat. Cas. Webster's Patent Cases (Eng.)

Webst. Dict. Webster's Dictionary

Webst. Dict. Unab. Webster's Unabridged Dictionary

Webster Dict. Webster's Dictionary

Webster In Sen. Doc. Webster in Senate Documents

Webster Pat. Cas. Webster's Patent Cases. 1601-1855

Webster Pat. Cas. (Eng.) Webster Patent Cases

Webst. Int. Dict. Webster's International Dictionary

Webst. New Int. D. Webster's New International Dictionary

Web. Tr. The Trial of Professor Webster for Murder

Wedg. & Hom. Wedgwood & Homan's Manual for Notaries and Bankers

Wedg. Gov. & Laws Wedgwood on American Government and Laws

Wedgw. Dict. Eng. Etymology Wedg-wood's Dictionary of English Etymology

Week. Cin. L.B. Weekly Cincinnati Law Bulletin

Week. Dig. New York Weekly Digest (1876-88)

Week. Dig. (N.Y.) New York Weekly Digest (1876-88)

Week. Jur. Weekly Jurist (Bloomington, Ill.)

Week. Law & Bk. Bull. Weekly Law & Bank Bulletin

Week. Law. Bull. Weekly Law Bulletin and Ohio Law Journal

Week. Law Gaz. Weekly Law Gazette (Ohio)

Week. L. Gaz. Weekly Law Gazette

Week. L. Mag. Weekly Law Magazine (1842-43)

Week. L.R. Weekly Law Reports

Week. L. Rec. Weekly Law Record

Week. L. Record Weekly Law Record

Week. L.R. (Eng.) Weekly Law Reports (Eng.)

Week. L. Rev. Weekly Law Review (San Francisco)

Weekly Cin. Law Bull. Cincinnati Weekly Law Bulletin

Weekly Comp. of Pres. Doc. Weekly Compilation of Presidential Documents

Weekly Law B. Weekly Law Bulletin (Ohio)

Weekly L. Bull. Weekly Law Bulletin (Eng.)

Weekly L.R. Weekly Law Reports (Eng.)

Weekly N.C. Weekly Notes of Cases (Pa.)

Weekly Notes Weekly Notes (of Law Reports) (Eng.)

Week. No.
• New South Wales Weekly Notes (Aus.)
• Weekly Notes of Cases (Law Reports) (England)
• Weekly Notes of Cases (Pennsylvania 1874-99)

Week. No. Cas.
• Weekly Notes of Cases (Law Reports) England
• Weekly Notes of Cases (Pennsylvania 1874-99)

Week. Notes Cas. Weekly Notes of Cases (London)

Week. R. Weekly Reporter (1853-1906)

Week. R. (Eng.) Weekly Reporter (Eng.)

Week. Rep. Weekly Reporter (Eng.)

Week. Reptr.
• Weekly Reporter, London
• Weekly Reporter, Bengal

Weeks Att. at Law Weeks on Attorneys at Law

Weeks D.A. Inj. Weeks' Damnum Absque Injuria

Weeks Dep. Weeks on Depositions

Weeks Min. Weeks on Mines and Mineral Law

Weeks Min. Leg. Weeks, The Mining Legislation of Congress

Week. Trans. Rep. Weekly Transcript Reports (N.Y.)

Week. Trans. Repts. Weekly Transcript Reports (N.Y.)

Weer. Weerakoon's Appeal Court Reports (Ceylon)

Weight. M. & L. Weightman, Marriage and Legitimacy. 1871

Weight. Med. Leg. Gaz. Weightman's Medico-Legal Gazette

Weir Weir's Criminal Rulings (India)

Wel. Welsh's Irish Registry Cases

Welf. Welfare

Welf. & Inst. Welfare & Institutions

Welf. & Inst. C. Welfare and Institutions Code

Welfare L. Bull. Welfare Law Bulletin

Welfare L. News Welfare Law News

Welf. Eq. Welford, Equity Pleadings. 1842

Well. High. Wellbeloved, Highways. 1829

Wells Inst. Juries Wells on Instruction to Juries and Bills of Exception

Wells Jur. Wells on the Jurisdiction of Courts

Wells L. & F. Wells Questions of Law and Facts

Wells Mar. Wom. Wells on the Separate Property of Married Women

Wells Rep. Wells on Replevin

Wells, Repl. Wells on Replevin

Wells' Res. Ad. Wells' Res Adjudicata and Stare Decisis

Wellw. Abr. Wellwood's Abridgment of Sea Laws

Welsb. H. & G. Welsby, Hurlstone and Gordon's English Exchequer Reports (1848-56)

Welsb., Hurl. & G. Welsby, Hurlstone and Gordon's English Exchequer Reports (1848-56)

Welsby H. & G. Welsby, Hurlstone & Gordon's Exchequer Reports (1847-56)

Welsby H. & G. (Eng.) Welsby, Hurlstone and Gordon's English Exchequer Reports (1848-56)

Welsh.
- Welsh's Irish Case of James Feighny, 1838
- Welsh's Irish Case at Siligo (1838)
- Welsh's Registry Cases (Ireland)

Welsh Reg. Cas. Welsh's Irish Registry Cases

Wen. Wendell's Reports (N.Y.)

Wend. Wendell's Reports (N.Y. 1826-1841)

Wend. Bl. Wendell's Blackstone

Wendel Wendell's Reports (N.Y.)

Wendell. Wendell's Reports (N.Y. 1826-1841)

Wendell Rep. Wendell's Reports (N.Y.)

Wendell's Rep. Wendell's Reports (N.Y.)

Wend.(N.Y.) Wendell's Reports (N.Y. 1826-1841)

Wend. R. Wendell's Reports (N.Y.)

Wend. Rep. Wendell's Reports (N.Y.)

Wendt. Wendt, Reports of Cases, Ceylon

Wendt. Mar. Leg. Wendt, Maritime Legislation. 3ed. 1888

W.Ent. Winch's Book of Entries

Went. Ex. Wentworth's Executors

Wenz. Wenzell's Reports (60 Minnesota)

Wes. C.L.J. Westmoreland County Law Journal

Weskett, lns. Weskett's Complete Digest of the Theory, Laws and Practice of Insurance

Wesk. Ins. Weskett's Complete Digest of the Theory, Laws and Practice of Insurance

Wes. Res. Law. Jo. Western Reserve Law Journal

Wes. Res. Law Jrl. Western Reserve Law Journal, Ohio

West
- Westbury, European Arbitration (Reilly)
- Western's London Tithe Cases (Eng.)
- Westmoreland County Law Journal (Pa.)
- Weston's Reports (11-14 Vermont)
- West Publishing Company
- West's Chancery Reports (Eng.)
- West's Reports, House of Lords (Eng.)

West A.U.L.R. Western Australia University Law Review

West. Aus. Western Australia

West. Austl. Western Australian Reports

West. Aust. L. Rev. University of Western Australia Law Review

West Austr. L. Western Australian Law Reports

West Ch. West's English Chancery Cases (25 ER)

West Ch. (Eng.) West's English Chancery Cases (25 ER)

West. Chy. West's English Chancery Cases (25 ER)

West Coast Rep. West Coast Reporter

West. Com. Western's Commentaries on the Laws of England

West Co. Rep. West Coast Reporter

Western Law Jour. Western Law Journal (Reprint) (Ohio)

Western Ont. L. Rev. Western Ontario Law Review

Western Res. L. Rev. Western Reserve Law Review

Western Reserve L.N. Western Reserve Law Notes

Western L. Rev. Western Law Review (Can.)

West Ext. West, Extents. 1817

West H.L. West's Reports, English House of Lords

West. Jur. Western Jurist (Des Moines, Iowa)

Westlake Int. Private Law Westlake's Private International Law

West. Law J. Western Law Journal (Cincinnati, Ohio)

West. Law Jour. Western Law Journal (Reprint) (Ohio)

West. Law M. Western Law Monthly (Ohio)

West. Law Mo. Western Law Monthly (Reprint) (Ohio)

West. Law Month. Western Law Monthly (Ohio)

West. Law. Rev. Western Law Review (Can.)

Westl. Confl. Westlake's Conflict of Laws

West Legal Obser. Western Legal Observer

West. Leg. Obs. Western Legal Observer

West. L. Gaz. Western Law Gazette, Cincinnati (Ohio)

West. L.J. Western Law Journal (Ohio)

West. L.J. (Ohio) Western Law Journal (Ohio)

West. L.M. Western Law Monthly (Ohio)

West. L.Mo. Western Law Monthly (Ohio)

West. L.Month. Western Law Monthly (Ohio)

Westl. Priv. Int. Law Westlake's Private International Law

West. L.R. Western Law Reporter (Canada)

West L.R. (Can.) Western Law Reporter (Canada)

West. L. Rev. Western Law Review

West. L.T. Western Law Times (Canada)

Westm. State of Westminster Westmoreland County Law Journal (Pennsylvania)

Westm. Hall. Chron. Westminster Hall Chronicle and Legal Examiner (1835-36)

Westm. L.J. Westmoreland County Law Journal

Westmore Co. L.J. (Pa.) Westmore-land County Law Journal (Pa.)

Westmoreland Westmoreland County Law Journal (Pa.)

Westmoreland Co. L.J. Westmore-land County Law Journal (Pa.)

West. Rev. Westminster Review

West. New Engl. L. Rev. Western New England Law Review

Weston Weston's Reports (11-14 Vermont)

West. Ont. L. Rev. Western Ontario Law Review, Ontario, Canada

West Pat. West on Patents

West. Pr. Int. Law Westlake, Private International Law. 7ed. 1925

West. R. Western Reporter

West. R. Western Reporter

West. Rep. Western Reporter

West. Res. Law Rev. Western Reserve Law Review

West. Res. L. Rev. Western Reserve Law Review

West. School L. Rev. Western School Law Review

West's Op. West's Opinions (City Solicitor of Philadelphia, Pa.)

West's Symb. West's Symboleography. Many editions (1590-1641)

West. State. U. L. Rev. Western State University Law Review

West. St. U. L. Rev. Western State University Law Review

West t. H. West's Chancery Reports tempore Hardwicke (1736-39)

West. t. Hard. West's Chancery Reports tempore Hardwicke (1736-39)

West t. Hardw. West's Chancery Reports tempore Hardwicke (1736-39)

West. Ti. Cas. Western's London Tithe Cases (1535-1822)

West. Tithe Cas. Western's London Tithe Cases (Eng.)

West Va.
- West Virginia
- West Virginia Reports

West Va. B.A. West Virginia Bar Association

West. Va. L. Rev. Western Virginia Law Review

West Va. Rep. West Virginia Reports (W. Va.)

West Virginia L. Rev. West Virginia Law Review.

West Week (Can.) Western Weekly Notes (Canada)

West. Week. N. Western Weekly Notes (Canada)

West Week N. (Can.) Western Weekly Notes (Canada)

West Week N.S. (Can.) Western Weekly New Series (Canada)

West. Week. Rep. Western Weekly Reports (Canada)

West. Wkly. Western Weekly (Can.)

1917 West. Wkly 1917 Western Weekly, Can.

Weth. Wethey's Reports (Canada)

Wethey. Wethey's Reports, Upper Canada Queen's Bench

Weth. U.C. Wethey's Reports, Upper Canada Queen's Bench

Wts. & M. Weights and measures

Welf. L. Welfare Law

W.E.U. Western European Union

WFC World Food Council

W.F.P.D.2d West's Federal Practice Digest, Second Series

W.F.T.U. World Federation of Trade Unions

W.F.U.N.A. World Federation of United Nations Associations

WGLI Warren, Gorham & Lamont Inc.

W. Ger. West Germany

W.H.
- Wage & Hour Cases (BNA)
- Withholding

Wh.
- Warton's Reports (Pa. 1835-41)
- Wheaton's International Law
- Wheaton's Reports (14-25 U.S.)
- Wheeler, New York Criminal Reports, 3 vols.

Whar. Wharves

W.H. & G. Welsby, Hurlstone and Gordon's Exchequer Reports (1848-56)

Wh. & T.L.C. White and Tudor's Leading Cases in Equity. 9 editions (1849-1928)

Wh. & Tud. White & Tudor, Leading Cases in Equity. 9ed. 1928

Whar Wharton's Reports

Whar. Wharton's Reports (Pa. 1835-41)

Whar. Ag. Wharton on Agency

Whar. Am. Cr. L. Wharton's American Criminal Law

Whar. & St. Med. Jur. Wharton & Stille's Medical Jurisprudence

Whar. Confl. Law Wharton's Conflict of Laws

Whar. Con. Law. Wharton's Conflict of Laws

Whar. Conv. Wharton, Principles of Conveyancing. 1851

Whar. Cr. Ev. Wharton on Criminal Evidence

Whar. Cri. Pl. Wharton's Criminal Pleading and Practice

Whar. Cr. Law. Wharton's American Criminal Law

Whar. Cr. Pl. Wharton's Criminal Pleading and Practice

Whar. Dig. Wharton's Digest (Pennsylvania)

Whar. Dom. Wharton on the Law of Domicile

Whar. Ev. Wharton on Evidence in Civil Issues

Whar. Hom. Wharton's Law of Homicide

Whar. Ind. Wharton's Precedents of Indictments

Whar. Innk. Wharton, Innkeepers. 1876

Whar. Law Dic. Wharton, Law Lexicon. 14ed. 1938

Whar. Leg. Max. Wharton, Legal Maxims. 3ed. 1903

Whar. Neg. Wharton's Law of Negligence

Whar. Prec. Ind. Wharton's Precedents of Indictments and Pleas

Whar. St. Tr. Wharton's U.S. State Trials

Whart.
- Legal Maxims with observations by George Frederick Wharton
- Wharton's Pennsylvanis Supreme Court Reports (1835-41)

Whart. Ag. Wharton on Agency

Whart. Am. Cr. Law. Wharton's American Criminal Law

Whart. & S. Med. Jur. Wharton & Stille's Medical Jurisprudence

Whart. Confl. Laws. Wharton's Conflict of Laws

Whart. Cr. Ev. Wharton on Criminal Evidence

Whart. Crim. Law. Wharton's American Criminal Law

Whart. Cr. Law. Wharton's American Criminal Law

Whart. Cr. Pl. & Prac. Wharton's Criminal Pleading & Practice

Whart. Ev. Wharton on Evidence in Civil Issues

Whart. Hom. Wharton's Law of Homicide

Whart. Homicide Wharton's Law of Homicide

Whart. Law Dict. Wharton's Law Dictionary, or Law Lexicon

Whart. Law Lexicon Wharton's Law Dictionary (or Law Lexicon)

Whart. Lex. Wharton's Law Lexicon

Whart. Lex. Wharton's Law Lexicon

Whart. Neg. Wharton on Negligence

Wharton.
- Wharton's American Criminal Law
- Wharton's Law Lexicon
- Wharton's Reports (1835-41) (Pa.)

Wharton, Crim. Evidence. Wharton's Criminal Evidence

Wharton, Crim. Proc. Wharton's Criminal Law & Procedure

Whart. Pa. Wharton's Reports (Pa. (1835-41) (Pa.)

Whart. State Tr. Wharton's State Trials, U.S.

Whart. St. Tr. Wharton's State Trials, U.S.

W.H.C. South African Law Reports, Witwatersrand High Court

W.H.Cas. Wage & Hour Cases (BNA)

WH Cases Wage and Hour Cases (BNA)

W.H. Chron. Westminster Hall Chronicle and Legal Examiner (1835-36)

Wh. Cr. Cas. Wheeler, New York Criminal Cases, 3 vols.

Wh. Crim. Cas. Wheeler's Criminal Cases (N.Y.)

Wheat. Wheaton's Reports (14-25 U.S.)

Wheat. Cap. Wheaton on Maritime Captures and Prizes

Wheat. El. Int. Law. Wheaton's Elements of International Law

Wheat. Int. Law Wheaton, Elements of International Law. 7ed. 1944

Wheat. Hist. Law Nat. Wheaton's History of the Law of Nations

Wheat. Int. Law. Wheaton's International Law

Wheat. Law of Nat. Wheaton's History of the Law of Nations

Wheaton. Wheaton's Reports (14-25 U.S.)

Wheel.
- Wheelock's Reports (32-37 Texas)
- Wheeler's Criminal Cases (N.Y.)

Wheel. Abr. Wheeler's Abridgment of American Common Law

Wheel. Br. Cas. Wheeling Bridge Case

Wheel. Cr. C. Wheeler's New York Criminal Cases

Wheel. Cr. Cas. Wheeler's Criminal Cases (N.Y.)

Wheel. Cr. Rec. Wheeler's Criminal Recorder (1 Wheeler's Criminal Cases) (N.Y.)

Wheel. Cr. Ch. Wheeler's Criminal Cases (N.Y.)

Wheeler Abr. Wheeler's Abridgment

Wheeler, Am. Cr. Law Wheeler's Abridgment of American Common Law Cases

Wheeler C.C. Wheeler's Criminal Cases (N.Y.)

Wheeler, Cr. Cas. Wheeler's Criminal Cases (N.Y.)

Wheeler Cr. Cases Wheeler's Criminal Cases (N.Y.)

Wheeler Crim. Cas. Wheeler's Criminal Cases (N.Y.)

Wheeler's Cr. Cases Wheeler's Criminal Cases (N.Y.)

Wheel. Slav. Wheeler on Slavery

Wheel.(Tex.) Wheelock's Reports (32-37 Texas)

Whishaw. Whishaw's Law Dictionary

Whish L.D. Whishaw, New Law Dictionary. 1829

Whitak. Liens Whitaker on Liens

White.
- White, Justiciary Court Reports (Scotland), 3 vols.
- White, Reports (10-15 West Virginia)
- White's Reports (31-44 Texas Court of Appeals)

White & Civ. Cas. Ct. App. White & Willson's Civil Cases Ct. of Appeals (Texas)

White & T.L. Cas. White & Tudor's Leading Cases in Equity

White & T. Lead Cas. Eq. White & Tudor's Leading Cases in Equity (Eng.)

White & T. Lead Cas. in Eq. (Eng.) White & Tudor, Leading Cases in Equity

White & Tud. L.C. White & Tudor, Leading Cases in Equity, 9ed. 1928

White & Tudor. White & Tudor's Leading Cases in Equity

White & W. White & Willson's Reports (Texas Civil Cases of Court of Appeals)

White & W. Civ. Cas. Ct. App. White & Wilson's Civil Cases Court of Appeals (Tex.)

White & W. Civil Cases Ct. App. Texas Civil Cases (Tex.)

White & Willson Texas Civil Cases (Tex.)

White & W. (Tex.) White & Willson's Reports (Texas Civil Cases of Court of Appeals)

White. Char. Whiteford, Charities. 1878

White, Coll. White's New Collection of the Laws, etc., of Great Britain, France or Spain

White L.L. White's Land Law of California

White New Coll. White, New Collection of the Laws, etc. of Great Britain, France and Spain

Whit. Eq. Pr. Whitworth's Equity Precedents

White's Ann. Pen. Code White's Annotated Penal Code, Tex.

White's Rep.
- White's Reports (31-44 Texas Appeals)
- White's Reports (10-15 West Virginia)

White Suppl. White on Supplement and Revivor

White. W. & M. Whiteley, Weights, Measures and Weighing Machines. 1879

Whit. Lien Whitaker, Rights of Lien and Stoppage in Transitu. 1812

Whitm. Adopt. Whitemore on Adoption of Children

Whitman Pat. Cas. (U.S.) Whitman Patent Cases

Whitman's Patent Cases Whitman's U.S. Patent Cases

Whitm. B.L. Whitmarsh, Bankrupt Law. 2ed. 1817

Whitm. Lib. Cas. Whitman's Massachusetts Libel Cases

Whitm. Pat. Cas. Whitman's Patent Cases (U.S.)

Whitm. Pat. Law. Whitman's Patent Laws

Whitm. Pat. Law Rev. Whitman, Patent Law Review Washington, D.C.

Witn. Witness

Whitney Whitney's Land Laws (Tennessee)

Whit. Pat. Whitman's Patent Laws of all Countries

Whit. Pat. Cas. Whitman's Patent Cases (U.S.)

Whit. St. Tr. Whitaker on Stoppage in Transitu

Whitt. Wittlesey's Reports (32-41 mo.)

Whittier L. Rev. Whittier Law Review

Whittlesey Whittlesey's Reports (32-41 Mo.)

Whitt. L. Rev. Whittier Law Review

Whitt.Pl. Whittaker's Practice and Pleading, New York

W.H.Man. Wages & Hours Manual (BNA)

WHO World Health Organization (UN)

WH Op. Letter Wage and Hour Opinion Letter

W.H.R. Wage & Hour Reporter (BNA)

W.H.R. Man. Wage & Hour Reference Manual (BNA)

WHSUPA Wharton School, University of Pennsylvania

W.I.
- West India(n)
- West Indies

Wi. Wisconsin

W.I.C.A. Judgments of the West Indian Court of Appeal

Wig. Wigram on Loills

Wig. Disc. Wigram, Discovery. 2ed. 1840

Wig. Ev. Wigram on Extrinsic Evidence

Wight.
- Wight's Election Cases, Sc.
- Wight's Section Cases (Sc.)
- Wightwick's Exchequer Reports (Eng.) (145 ER)

Wight El. Cas. Wight, Scottish Election Cases (1784-96)

Wightw. Wightwick's Exchequer Reports (Eng.) (145 ER)

Wightw. (Eng.) Wightwick's Exchequer Reports (Eng.) (145 ER)

Wigm. Ev. Wigmore on Evidence

Wigmore, Evidence Wigmore on Evidence

Wig. Wills Wigmore on Wills

Wil.
- Williams, abbreviated as Will.

- Wilson, abbreviated as Wils.

Wilberforce Wilberforce on Statute Law

Wilb. Stat. Wilberforce, Construction and Operation of Statutes. 1881

Wilc.Cond. Wilcox Condensed Ohio Reports (1-7 Ohio, Reprint)

Wilc. Cond. Rep. Wilcox's Condensed Ohio Reports (1-7 Ohio, Reprint)

Wilc. Mun. Corp. Wilcox on Municipal Corporations, Ohio

Wilcox
- Wilcox's Reports (10 Ohio)
- Wilcox's Lackawanna Reports (Pa.)

Wilcox Cond. Wilcox's Condensed Reports (Ohio)

Wilde Sup. (or Conv.) Wilde's Supplement to Barton's Conveyancing

Wildm. Int. L. Wildman's International Law

Wildm. Int. Law Wildman's International Law

Wildm. Search Wildman on Search, Capture, and Prize

W.I.L.J. West Indian Law Journal (Jamaica)

Wilk.
- Wilkinson, Owen, Paterson & Murray's New South Wales Reports (1862-65)
- Wilkinson's Texas Court of Appeals and Civil Appeals

Wilk. & Mur. Wilkinson, Owen, Paterson & Murray's New South Wales Reports (1862-65)

Wilk. & Ow. Wilkinson, Owen, Paterson & Murray's New South Wales Reports (1862-65)

Wilk. & Pat. Wilkinson, Owen, Paterson & Murray's New South Wales Reports (1862-65)

Wilk. Funds Wilkinson, Public Funds. 1839

Wilk. Leg. Ang. Sax. Wilkins' Leges Anglo-Saxonicae Ecclesiasticae et Civiles

Wilk. Lim. Wilkinson on Limitations of Actions

Wilk.P. & M. Wilkinson, Paterson, & Murray's Reports, New South Wales Reports (1862-65)

Wilk. Prec. Wilkinson, Precedents in Conveyancing. 4ed. 1890

Wilk. Repl. Wilkinson, Replevin. 1825

Wilk. Sh. Wilkinson's Office of Sheriff

Wilk. Ship. Wilkinson, Shipping. 1843

Will.
- Willes' English Common Pleas Reports
- William, as 1 Will. IV
- Williams' Massachusetts Reports (1 Mass.) (1804-05)
- Williams' Vermont Reports (27-29 Vt.)
- Wilson's Reports, vols. 29-30 Texas Appeals, also vols. 1, 2, Texas Civil Appeals

Will. Abr. Williams, Abridgment of Cases (1798-1803)

Willamette L.J. Willamette Law Journal

Willamette L. Rev. Willamette Law Review

Will. & Br. Adm. Jur. Williams & Bruce on Admiralty Practice

Will. & Mar. William and Mary

Will. Ann. Reg. Williams, Annual Register, New York

Will. Auct. Williams, Auctions. 5ed. 1829

Will. Bankt. Williams, Law and Practice of Bankruptcy. 19ed. 1977

Will.-Bund St. Tr. Willis-Bund's Cases from State Trials

Willc. Const. Willcock, The Office of Constable

Willc. Med. Pr. Willcock, Medical Profession. 1830

Willc. Mun. Corp. Willcock's Municipal Corporations

Willcock, Mun. Corp. Willcock's Municipal Corporation

Will. Com. Williams, Rights of Common. 1880

Will. Con. Rep. Texas Civil Cases (Tex.)

Will. Cr. L. Willan's Criminal Law of Canada

Willes Willes English Common Pleas, Reports (125 ER)

Willes (Eng.) Willes English Common Pleas Reports (125 ER)

Will. Eq. Jur. Willard's Equity Jurisprudence

Will. Eq. Pl. Willis. Equity Pleading. 1820

Will. Ex. Williams, Executors. 15ed. 1970

William & Mary L. Rev. William and Mary Law Review

Willamette L.J. Willamette Law Journal

William Mitchell L. Rev. William Mitchell Law Review

Williams
- Peere Williams' Chancery Reports (Eng.)
- Williams' Reports (1 Massachusetts)
- Williams' Reports (10-12 Utah)
- Williams' Reports (27-29 Vermont)

Williams & B. Adm. Jur. Williams and Bruce's Admiralty Practice, 3 editions (1869-1902)

Williams & Bruce Ad. Pr. Williams and Bruce's Admiralty Practice, 3 editions (1869-1902)

Williams B. Pr. Williams' Bankruptcy Practice. 17 editions (1870-1958)

Williams, Common Williams on Rights of Common

Williams, Ex'rs. Williams on Executors

Williams, Ex'rs, R. & T. Ed. Williams on Executors, Randolph and Talcott Edition

Williams P. Peere Williams' English Chancery Reports (1695-1736)

Williams-Peere Peere-Williams' English Chancery Reports

Williams, Pers. Prop. Williams on Personal Property

Williams, Real Prop. Williams on Real Property

Williams, Saund. Williams' Notes to Saunders' Reports

Williams, Seis. Williams on Seisin

William W. Story's Rept. Story's U.S. Circuit Court Reports

Willis Eq. Willis, Equity Pleadings. 1820

Willis Int. Willis on Interrogatories

Willis Trust. Willis on Trustees

Willis, Trustees Willis on Trustees

Williston
- Williston on Contracts
- Williston on Sales

Williston, Contracts Williston on Contracts

Will. Just. Williams' Justice

Will.L.D. Williams' Law Dicitonary

Will. L.J. Willamette Law Journal

Will. Mass. Williams' Reports (1 Massachusetts)

Will. Mass. Cit. Williams' Massachusetts Citations

Willm. W. & D. Willmore, Wollaston, Davison's Queen's Bench Reports (Eng.)

Willm. W. & H. Willmore, Wollaston & Hodges' Queen's Bench Reports (52 RR) (1838-39)

Will.P. Peere-Williams' English Chancery Reports

Will. Per. Pr. Williams, Personal Property. 18ed. 1926

Will. Pet. Ch. Williams, Petitions in Chancery. 1880

Will. Real Ass. Williams, Real Assets. 1861

Will. Real Est. Willard on Real Estate and Conveyancing

Will. Real Pr. Williams on Real Property

Will. Saund. Williams' Notes to Saunders' Reports (1666-73)

Wills, Circ. Ev. Wills on Circumstantial Evidence

Wills, Civ. Ev. Wills on Circumstantial Evidence

Will. Seis. Williams, Seisin of the Freehold. 1878

Wills, Est., Tr. Wills, Estates, Trusts (P-H)

Wills Est. & Tr.(P-H) Wills, Estates & Trust Service

Wills Est. & Tr. Serv. (P-H) Wills, Estates and Trust Service

Will. Sett. Williams on the Settlement of Real Estates

Willson Willson's Reports, 29-30 Texas Appeals, also 1,2 Texas Court of Appeals, Civil Cases

Willson Civ. Cas. Ct. App.
- Willson's Civil Cases Court of Appeals, Tex.
- White & Willson's Civil Cases of Texas Court of Appeals

Willson's C.C. Texas Civil Cases (Tex.)

Willson, Tex. Cr. Law Willson's Revised Penal Code, Code of Criminal Procedure, and Penal Laws of Texas

Will. St. L. Williams on the Study of the Law

Will.Vt. Williams Reports (27-29 Vermont)

Will. Woll. & D. Willmore, Wollaston, Davison's Queen's Bench Reports, 1837 (Eng.)

Will., Woll. & Dav, Willmore, Wollaston, Davison's Queen's Bench Reports, 1837 (Eng.)

Will. Woll. & H. Willmore, Wollaston and Hodges' Queen's Bench Reports (1838)

Will. Woll. & Hodg. Willmore. Wollaston and Hodges' Queen's Bench Reports (1838)

Wilm. Wilmot's Notes and Opinions, King's Bench (97 ER)

Wilm. Burg. Wilmot's Digest of the Law of Burglary

Wilmington, Del. P.U.C. Wilmington, Delaware, Board of Public Utility Commission

Wilm. Judg. Wilmot's Notes and Opinions, King's Bench (97 ER)

Wilm. Mort. Wilmot on Mortgages

Wilm. op. Wilmot's Notes and Opinions, King's Bench (97 ER)

Wilmot's Notes Wilmot's Notes and Opinions, King's Bench (1757-70) (97 ER)

Wilmot's Notes (Eng.) Wilmot's Notes and Opinions, King's Bench (97 ER)

Wilm. W. & D. Willmore, Wollaston & Davison, English Queen's Bench Reports

Wi. L.R. Wisconsin Law Review

Wils.
- Wilson Reports, Chancery (1818-19) (Eng.)
- Wilson, English Common Pleas Reports, 3 (95 ER)

- Wilson's King's Bench Reports (1742-74) (95 ER)

Wils. & Court. Wilson & Courtenay's Scotch Appeal Cases

Wils. & S. Wilson and Shaw's Scottish Appeal Cases (1825-35)

Wils. & S. (Scot.) Wilson and Shaw's Scottish Appeal Cases (1825-35)

Wils. & Sh. Wilson and Shaw's Scottish Appeal Cases (1825-35)

Wils. Arb. Wilson on Arbitrations

Wils. Ch. Wilson's Chancery Reports (37 ER) (1818-19)

Wils. Ch. Wilson's English Chancery Reports (37 ER)

Wils. ch. (Eng.) Wilson's English Chancery, Reports (37 ER)

Wils. C.P. Wilson's Common Pleas (Eng.)

Wils. (Eng.) Wilson, English Common Pleas Reports, 3 (95 ER)

Wils. Ent. Wilson's Entries & Pleading (3 Lord Raymond's King's Bench & Common Pleas Reports) (Eng.)

Wils. Ex. Wilson's Exchequer Reports (159 ER) (1805-17)

Wils. Exch. Wilson's English Exchequer Reports (159 ER)

Wils. Exch. (Eng.) Wilson's English Exchequer Reports (159 ER)

Wils. Fines Wilson on Fines and Recoveries

Wils. Ind. Wilson's Reports, Indiana Superior Court

Wils. Ind. Gloss. Wilson, Glossary of Indian Terms

Wils. Jud. Acts Wilson on the Judicature Acts, & c.

Wils. K.B. Sergeant Wilson's English King's Bench Reports (1724-74)

Wils. K.B. Wilson's King's Bench (Eng.)

Wils. Minn. Wilson's Reports (48-59 Minn.)

Wils. Mod. Eng. Law Wilson's History of Modern English Law

Wilson
- Wilson's Chancery Reports (Eng.)
- Wilson's King's Bench & Common Pleas Reports (Eng.)
- Wilson's Exchequer in Equity Reports (Eng.)
- Wilson's Reports, Indiana Superior Court
- Wilson's Reports (48-59 Minnesota)
- Wilson's Reports (1-3 Oregon)

Wilson & Shaw Wilson and Shaw's Scottish Appeals

Wilson's R. Wilson's Indiana Superior Court Reports (Ind.)

Wilson's Rev. & Ann. St. Wilson's Revised and Annotated Statutes, Oklahoma

Wilson Super. Ct. (Ind.) Wilson's Indiana Superior Court Reports (Ind.)

Wils. Oreg. Wilson's Reports (1-3 Oregon)

Wils. Parl. L. Wilson's Parliamentary Law

Wils. P.C. Wilson's English Privy Council Reports

Wils. Super. (Ind.) Wilson's Reports, Indiana Superior Court

Wils. Uses Wilson on Springing Uses

WILUCL Willamette University College of Law

WIN Work Incentive Program

Win.
- Winch's Common Pleas Reports, England (124 ER)
- Winer's Unreported Opinions (N.Y. Supreme Court, Erie County)
- Winston's North Carolina Reports (1863-64)

Winch Winch's Common Pleas Reports (124 ER)

Winch (Eng.) Winch's Common Pleas Reports (124 ER)

W. Indian L.J. West Indian Law Journal

Windsor Y.B. Access Just. The Windsor Yearbook of Access to Justice

Win. Ent. Winch's Entries

Win. Eq. Winston's Equity Reports, North Carolina

Winfield, Words & Phrases Winfield's Adjudged Words and Phrases, with Notes

Wing. Wingate's Maxims

Wing. Max. Wingate's Maxims

Win. Max. Wingate's Maxims

Wins. Ins. Winslow on the Plea of Insanity in Criminal Cases

Winst. Winston's Law or Equity Reports, North Carolina

Winst. Eq. Winston's Law or Equity Reports, North Carolina

Winst. Eq. (N.C.) Winston's North Carolina Equity Reports

Winst. L. (N.C.) Winston's North Carolina Law Reports

WIP Work Incentive Program

WIPO World Intellectual Property Organization

W.I.R. West Indian Reports

Wis.
- Wisconsin
- Wisconsin Reports

Wis. 2d Wisconsin Reports, Second Series

Wis. Admin. Code Wisconsin Administrative Code

W.I.S.A. Law Rep. Western India States Agency Law Reports

W.I.S.A. Law Reports Western India States Agency Law Reports

W.I.S.A.L.R. Western Indian States Agency Law Reports

Wisb. Laws of Wisbuy

Wis. B.A. Bull. Wisconsin State Bar Association Bulletin

Wis. Bar Assn. Wisconsin State Bar Association

Wis. Bar Bull. Wisconsin State Bar Association Bulletin

Wis. B. Bull. Wisconsin Bar Bulletin

Wis. B.T.A. Wisconsin Board of Tax Appeals Reports

Wisc. Wisconsin Reports (Wis.)

Wisc. Law. Wisconsin Lawyer

Wisconsin L. Rev. Wisconsin Law Review

Wis. Const. Wisconsin Constitution

Wisc. Stud. B.J. Wisconsin Student Bar Journal

Wis. I.C. Wisconsin Industrial Commission (Workmen's Compensation Reports)

Wis. Int'l L.J. Wisconsin International Law Journal

Wis. Law. Wisconsin Lawyer

Wis. Laws Laws of Wisconsin

Wis. Leg. N. Wisconsin Legal News, Milwaukee

Wis. Legis. Serv. Wisconsin Legislative Service (West)

Wis. L.N. Wisconsin Legal News, Milwaukee

Wis. L.R. Bd. Dec. Wisconsin Labor Relations Board Decisions

Wis. L. Rev. Wisconsin Law Review

Wis. P.S.C. Wisconsin Public Service Commission Reports

Wis. P.S.C. Ops. Wisconsin Public Service Commission Opinions & Decisions

Wis. R. Wisconsin Reports (Wis.)

Wis. R.C. Ops. Wisconsin Railroad Commission Opinions and Decisions

Wis. R.C.R. Wisconsin Railroad Commission Reports

Wis. Rep. Wisconsin Reports (Wis.)

Wis. S.B.A. Wisconsin State Bar Association

Wis. S.B.A. Bull. Wisconsin State Bar Association Bulletin

Wis. Stat. Wisconsin Statutes

Wis. Stat. Ann. (West) West's Wisconsin Statutes Annotated

Wis. Tax App. C. Wisconsin Tax Appeals Commission Reports

Wis. Women's L.J. Wisconsin Women's Law Journal

With. Corp. Cas. Withrow, American Corporation Cases

Withrow
- Withrow's American Corporation Cases
- Withrow's Reports (9-21 Iowa)

Witkin, Cal. Summary Witkin's Summary of California Law

Witthaus & Becker's Med. Jur. Witthaus and Becker's Medical Jurisprudence

W.J. Western Jurist (U.S.)

W.Jo. Sir William Jones' King's Bench Reports (82 ER)

W. Jones Sir William Jones' King's Bench Reports (82 ER) (1620-41)

W. Jones (Eng.) Sir William Jones' King's Bench Reports (82 ER)

Wk. Week

W.Kel. William Kelynge's Chancery Reports (25 ER)

W. Kelynge (Eng.) William Kelynge's Chancery Reports (25 ER)

Wkly Weekly

Wkly. Cin. Law Bul. The Weekly Cincinnati Law Bulletin (Ohio)

Wkly. Dig. New York Weekly Digest

Wkly. Law Bul. Weekly Law Bulletin, (Ohio)

Wkly. Law Gaz. Weekly Law Gazette, (Ohio)

Wkly. L. Bul. Weekly Law Bulletin (Ohio)

Wkly. L. Gaz. Weekly Law Gazette (Ohio)

Wkly. N.C. Weekly Notes of Cases (Pa.)

Wkly. Notes Cas. Weekly Notes Cases (Pa.)

Wkly. Notes Cas. (Pa.) Weekly Notes of Cases (Pa.)

Wkly. Rep. Weekly Reporter, London,

Wk. N. Weekly Notes of Cases (Pa.)

W.L.A.C. Western Labour Arbitration Cases, 1966

W. Law Bul.
- Weekly Law Bulletin (Ohio)
- Weekly Law Bulletin (Reprint) (Ohio)

WLB War Labor Board

W.L.B. Weekly Law Bulletin, Ohio

W.L. Bull.
- Weekly Law Bulletin (Ohio)
- Weekly Law Bulletin (Reprint) (Ohio)

W.L. Bull. (Ohio) Weekly Law Bulletin, Ohio

W.L.D. South African Law Reports, Witwatersrand Local Division

W. Legal Hist. Western Legal History

WLF Women's Law Forum

W.L.G. Weekly Law Gazette, Ohio

W.L. Gaz. Weekly Law Gazette (Reprint) (Ohio)

W.L. Gaz. (Ohio) Weekly Law Gazette, Ohio

W.L.J.
- Washburn Law Journal
- Western Law Journal
- Wyoming Law Journal

W. L. Jour.
- Washburn Law Journal
- Western Law Journal
- Willamette Law Journal
- Wyoming Law Journal

W.L.L.R. Washington & Lee Law Review

W.L.M. Western Law Monthly, Cleveland, Ohio

WLN Washington Library Network (Bibliographic Utility Network)

W.L.Q. Washington University Law Quarterly (Missouri)

W.L.R.
- Washington Law Reporter (D.C.)
- Weekly Law Reports (Eng.)
- Washington Law Review (Seattle)
- Western Law Reporter (Canada)
- Wisconsin Law Review
- World Law Review

W.L.T. Western Law Times (1890-95)

W.L.R.P. Wandsworth Legal Resource Project

W.M. Ways and Means

Wm. Williams, as 7 Wm. III

Wm. & M. William and Mary

Wm. & Mary William and Mary

Wm. & Mary L. Rev. William & Mary Law Review

Wm. & Mary Rev. Va. L. William and Mary Review of Virginia Law

Wm. Bl. William Blackstone's English King's Bench Reports (1746-80)

W.M.L. Willamette Law Journal (Or.)

Wm. L.J. Willamette Law Journal

W.M.L.R. William & Mary Law Review

Wm. Mitchell L. Rev. William Mitchell Law Review

W.M.O. World Meterological Organization (UN)

W.M.R. William and Mary Review of Virginia Law (Va.)

Wm. Rob. William Robinson's English Admiralty Reports (1838-52)

Wm. Rob. Adm. William Robinson's English Admiralty Reports

Wms. Williams, commonly abbreviated as Wil.

Wms. & Bruce Williams (R.G.) and Bruce (Sir G.), Admiralty Practice. 3 editions (1869-1902)

Wms. Ann. Reg. Williams' Annual Register, New York

Wms. Bank. Williams (R.V.) on Bankruptcy. 17 editions (1870-1958)

Wms. Ex. Williams, Executors. 15ed. 1970

Wms. Exors. Williams (E.V.) on Executors. 13 editions (1832-1953)

Wms. Ex'rs. Williams (E.V.) on Executors. 13 editions (1832-1953)

Wms. Exs. Williams (E.V.) on Executors. 13 editions (1832-1953)

Wms. Mass. Williams' Reports (1 Mass.)

Wms. Notes Williams' Notes to Saunders' Reports (Eng.)

Wms. P. Peere Williams' Chancery Reports (1695-1736)

Wms. Peere Peere Williams' Chancery Reports (Eng.)

Wms. P.P. Williams (J.) on Personal Property. 18 editions (1848-1926)

Wms. R.P. Williams (J.) on Real Property, 24 editions (1824-1926)

Wms. Saund. Saunders (Sir Edmund Reports, edited by, Williams) N(85 ER)

Wms. Saund. (Eng.) Saunders (Sir Edmund) Reports, edited by Williams (85 ER)

Wms. Vt. Williams' Reports (27-29 Vermont)

W.N.
- Calcutta Weekly Notes
- Weekly Notes of English Law Reports

Wn. Washington Reports

Wn.2d Washington Reports, Second Series

W.N.C. Weekly Notes of Cases (Pa. 1874-99)

W.N. (Calc.) Calcutta Weekly Notes

W.N.Cas. Weekly Notes of Cases (Pa. 1874-99)

W.N.Cas. (Pa.) Weekly Notes of Cases (Pa.)

W.N.C. (Pa.) Weekly Notes of Cases (Pa. 1874-99)

W.N. (Eng.) Weekly Notes of English Law Reports

W. New Eng. L. Rev. Western New England Law Review

Wn.L. Wayne Law Review (Mich.)

W.N.L.N. Western Nigeria Legal Notice.

W.N.L.R. Western Nigeria Law Reports.

Wn.L.R.
- Washington Law Review
- Wayne Law Review

W.N. Misc. Weekly Notes, Miscellaneous

W.N.N.S.W. Weekly Notes, New South Wales

WOAR Women Organized Against Rape

W.O.C. Woods' Oriental Cases (Mal.)

Woerner, Adm'n. Woerner's Treatise on the American Law of Administration

Wol.
- Wolcott's Reports (7 Delaware Chancery)
- Wollaston's Bail Court Reports (Eng.)

Wolf. & B. Wolferstan and Bristow's Election Cases, England (1859-65)

Wolf. & D. Wolferstan and Dew's Election Cases, England (1856-58)

Wolff. Inst. Wolffius, Institutiones Juris Naturae et Gentium

Wolff. Inst. Nat. Wolffius, Institutiones Juris Naturae et Gentium

Wolffius Wolffius, Institutiones Juris Naturae et Gentium

Wolffius, Inst. Wolffius, Institutiones Juris Naturae et Gentium

Woll. Wollaston's English Bail Court Reports, Practice Cases (1840-41)

Woll. B.C. Wollaston's English Bail Court Reports

Woman Offend. Rep. Woman Offender Report

Women & L. Women and Law

Women Law J. Women Lawyers Journal

Women Lawyer's J. Women Lawyers Journal

Women L. Jour.
  • Women Lawyers Journal
  • Women's Law Journal

Women Rights L. Rep. Women's Rights Law Reporter

Women Rts. L. Rep. Women's Rights Law Reporter

Women's L.J. Women's Law Journal

Women's L. Rptr. Women's Law Reporter

Women's Rights L. Rep. Women's Rights Law Reporter

Women's Rights L. Rptr. Women's Rights Law Reporter

Women's Rts. L. Rep. Women's Rights Law Reporter

Wont. Land Reg. Wontner, Land Registry Practice. 12ed. 1975

W. Ont. L. Rev. Western Ontario Law Review

Wood
  • Wood, English Tithe Cases, Exchequer, 4 vols.
  • Wood on Mercantile Agreements

• Woods, United States Circuit Court Reports

Wood. & M. Woodbury & Minot's United States Circuit Court Reports

Wood. & Minot Woodbury & Minot's U.S. Circuit Court Reports

Woodb. & M. Woodbury & Minot's United States Circuit Court Reports

Woodb. & Min. (C.C.) Woodbury & Minot's U.S. Circuit Court Reports (1st Cir.)

Woodbury & Mer. C.C.R. Woodbury & Minot's U.S. Circuit Court Reports (1st Cir.)

Wood Civ. L. Wood's Institutes of the Civil Law

Wood Com. L. Wood's Institutes of the Common Law

Wood Conv. Wood on Conveyancing

Wood Decr. Wood's Tithe Cases (Eng.)

Wooddesson, Lect. Wooddesson's Lecture

Woodd. Lect. Wooddesson's Lectures on the Laws of England

Wood. El.Jur. Wooddeson's Elements of Jurisprudence

Woodf. Woodfall on Landlord and Tenant. 25 editions (1802-1958)

Woodf. Cel. Tr. Woodfall's Celebrated Trials

Wood Fire Ins. Wood on Fire Insurance

Woodf. Landl. & T. Woodfall on Landlord and Tenant. 25 Editions (1802-1958)

Woodf. Landl. & Ten. Woodfall on Landlord and Tenant. 25 editions (1802-1958)

Woodf. L. & T. Woodfall, Landlord and Tenant. 28ed. 1978

Woodf. Parl. Deb. Woodfall's Parliamentary Debates

Wood H. Hutton Wood's Decrees in Tithe Cases (Eng.)

Wood, Inst. Wood's Institutes of English Law

Wood, Inst. Com. Law Wood's Institutes of the Common Law

Wood Inst. Eng. L. Wood's Institutes of English Law

Wood Land. & T. Wood on Landlord and Tenant

Wood. Landl. & Ten. Wood on Landlord and Tenant

Wood. Lect. Wooddeson's Lectures on Laws of England

Wood, Lim. Wood on Limitation of Actions

Wood Man. Wood on Mandamus

Woodm. & T. For. Med. Woodman & Tidy on Forensic Medicine

Wood, Mast. & Serv. Wood on Master and Servant

Woodman Cr. Cas. Woodman's Reports of Thacher's Criminal Cases (Mass.)

Wood Mayne Dam. Wood's Mayne on Damages

Woodm. Cr. Cas. Woodman's Reports of Thacher's Criminal Cases, Massachusetts

Wood, Nuis. Wood on Nuisances

Wood, Ry. Law Wood's Law of Railroads

Woods Woods' United States Circuit Court Reports

Woods C.C. Woods' United States Circuit Court Reports

Wood's Civ. Law Wood's Institutes of the Civil Law of England

Wood's Dig. Wood's Digest of Laws, Cal.

Woods, Ins.
- Wood on Fire Insurance
- Wood's Institutes of English Law

Wood's Inst. Civ. L. Wood's Institutes of the Civil Law

Wood's Inst. Com. L. Wood's Institutes of the (Common) Laws of England

Wood's R. Wood's Manitoba Reports (1875-83)

Woods, St. Frauds Wood's Treatise on the Statutes of Frauds

Wood Ti. Cas. Wood's Tithe Cases (1650-1798)

Wood Tit. Cas. Wood's Tithe Cases (1650-1798)

Wood Tr. M. Wood, Trade Marks. 1876

Woodw. Woodward's Decisions (Pa.)

Woodw. Dec. Woodward's Decisions (Pa. 1861-74)

Woodw. Dec. Pa. Woodward's Decisions (Pa. 1861-74)

Wool. Woolworth's Circuit Court Reports (U.S.)

Wool. C.C Woolworth's Reports, United States Circuit Court (Miller's Decisions)

Woolf. Adult. Woolf, Adultera-
tions. 1874

Wool. Int. Woolsey, Introduction
to International Law. 6ed. 1888

Woolr. Cert. Woolrych, Certifi-
cates. 1826

Woolr. Com. Woolrych, Rights of
Common. 2ed. 1850

Woolr. Cr.L. Woolrych, Criminal
Law. 1862

Woolr. L.W. Woolrych, Law of Waters. 2ed. 1851

Woolr. P.W. Woolrych, Party
Walls. 1845

Woolr. Sew. Woolrych, Sewert.
3ed. 1864

Woolr. Waters Woolrych's Law of
Waters

Woolr. Ways Woolrych, Law of
Ways. 2ed. 1847

Woolr. Wind. L. Woolrych, Window Lights. 2ed. 1864

Woolsey, Polit. Science Woolsey's Political Science

Wools. Int. L. Woolsey, Introduction to Study of International
Law. 6ed. 1888

Wools. Pol. Science Woolsey's Political Science

Woolw.
- Woolworth's Reports (1 Nebraska)
- Woolworth's United States Circuit Court Reports

Woolworth Woolworth's U.S. Circuit Court Reports

Woolworth's Cir. Ct. R. Woolworth's U.S. Circuit Court Reports

Woolw. Rep.
- Woolworth's Reports (1 Nebraska)
- Woolworth's United States Circuit Court Reports

Wor. Bib. Leg. Worrall's Bibliotheca Legum

Worcester Worcester, Dictionary
of the English Language

Worcest. Dict. Worcester's Dictionary

Wor. Dict. Worcester's Dictionary

Words. Elect. Wordsworth, Law
of Elections. 6ed. 1868

Words. Elect. Cas. Wordsworth's
Election Cases (Eng.)

Words. J.S. Wordsworth's Law of
Joint-Stock Companies

Words. Min. Wordsworth's Law of
Mining

Words. Pat. Wordsworth's Law of
Patents

Words. Ry. & C. Wordsworth's
Railway and Canal Companies

Work. Comp. Workmen's Compensation

Workmen's Comp. Div. Workmen's Compensation Division

Workmen's Comp. L Rep. (CCH)
- Workmen's Compensation Law
  Reports
- Workmen's Compensation Law
  Reporter (CCH)

Workmen's Comp. L. Rev. Workmen's Compensation Law Review

Works, Courts Works on Courts
and Their Jurisdiction

Works, Pr. Works' Practice, Pleading, and Forms

World Arb. Rep. World Arbitration Reporter

World Competition & Econ. Rev. World Competition, Law and Economics Review

World L. Rev. World Law Review

World Pol. World Polity

World Today The World Today

World Trade L.J. World Trade Law Journal

Worth. Jur. Worthington, Power of Juries, 1825

Worth. Prec. Wills Worthington, General Precedent for Wills. 5ed. 1852

Wott. Leg. Wal. Wotton, Leges Wallicae

W.P.
- Pakistan Law Reports, West Pakistan Series
- Water Pollution Committee

WPC World Peace Council

W.P.C.
- Webster's Patent Cases (1601-1855)
- Wollaston's English Bail Court Practice Cases

W.P. Cas.
- Webster's Patent Cases (1601-1855)
- Wollaston's English Bail Court Practice Cases

W.P.H.C Western Pacific High Commission

W.P.R.
- Webster's Patent Reports (Eng.)
- Webster's Patent Cases (1601-1855)

WPTLC
- World Peace Through Law Conference
- World Peace Through Law Center

W.R.
- Sutherland's Weekly Reporte (India)
- War Risk Insurance Decisions (U.S.)
- Weekly Reporter, Bengal (India)
- Weekly Reporter (Eng.)
- Weekly Reporter, Cape Provincial Division (S. Africa)
- Wendell's Reports (N.Y. 1826-41)
- Western Region
- West's Chancery Reports (1736-39) (Eng.)
- Willelmus Rex (King William)
- Wisconsin Reports

Wr.
- Wright
- Wright's Reports (vols. 37-50 Pennsylvania State Reports)

W.R. Calc. Sutherland's Weekly Reporter (India)

Wr. Ch. Wright's Reports, Ohio

W.R.C.R. Wisconsin Railroad Commission Reports

W. Rep. West's reports tempore Hardwicke, English Chancery (1736-39)

W. Res. L. Rev. Western Reserve Law Review

Wright
- Wright's Reports (Ohio 1831-34)
- Wright's Reports (37-50 Pa. State)

Wright Ch. Wright's Reports (Ohio 1831-34)

Wright Cr. Cons. Wright, Criminal Conspiracies. 1873

Wright Fr. Soc. Wright on Friendly Societies

Wright N.P. Wright's Nisi Prius Reports (Ohio)

Wright (Ohio C.) Wright's Ohio Reports (Ohio)

Wright R. Wright's Ohio Reports (Ohio)

Wright's Rep. Wright's Ohio Reports (Ohio)

Wright St. L. Wright's Advice on the Study of the Law

Wright, Ten. Wright on Tenures

Writ of error den. Writ of error denied

W.R.I. Western Reserve Law Review (Ohio)

W.R.L.R. Women's Rights Law Reporter

W.R.N.L.R. Western Region of Nigeria Law Reports

W.Rob. W. Robinson's English Admiralty Reports (166 ER)

W.Rob. Adm. W. Robinson's English Admiralty Reports (166 ER)

W.Rob. Adm. (Eng.) W. Robinson's English Admiralty Reports (166 ER)

Wr. Ohio Wright's Reports, Ohio

Wrong. Disch. Wrongful discharge

Wr. Pa. Wright's Reports (37-50 Pennsylvania State Reports)

WS Watts' and Sergeant's Reports

W.S.
- Writer to the Signet
- Wagner's Statutes (Mo.)

W.S.A. Wisconsin Statutes Annotated

W. Samoa Western Samoa

WSB Wage Stabilization Board

Wsb. Washburn Law Journal (Kansas)

WSBA Washington State Bar Association

Wsh. Washington State Reports

Ws.L. Washington Law Review

W. St. U. L. Rev. Western State University Law Review

W.T. Washington Territory Reports

W.T.B.R. War Trade Board Rulings (U.S.)

W.Ten. Wright's Introduction to the Law of Tenures

WTI The World Trade Institute

WTO Warsaw Treaty Organization

W.T.R. Weekly Transcript Reports (N.Y.)

W.Ty.R. Washington Territory Reports (1854-88)

WUSL Washburn University School of Law

W.V. West Virginia Reports

W.Va.
- West Virginia Reports
- West Virginia
- West Virginia Supreme Court Reports

W.Va. Acts Acts of the Legislature of West Virginia

W.Va. Bar. West Virginia Bar

W.Va. Code West Virginia Code

W.Va. Const. West Virginia Constitution

W.Va. Crim. Just. Rev. West Virginia Criminal Justice Review

W.Va. Law Reports West Virginia Reports (W. Va.)

W.Va. L.Q. West Virginia Law Quarterly

W.Va. L. Rev. West Virginia Law Review

W.Va. P.S.C. West Virginia Public Service Commission Decisions

W.Va. P.S.C.R. West Virginia Public Service Commission Reports

W.Va. P.U.R. West Virginia Public Utility Commission Reports

W.Va. Rep. West Virginia Reports (W. Va.)

W.Va. St. B.J. West Virginia State Bar Journal

W.V. Bar West Virginia Bar

WVC West Virginia Code

W.V.L. West Virginia Law Review

W.V.L.Q. West Virginia Law Quarterly

W.V.L.R. West Virginia Law Review

W.V.R. West Virginia Reports (W. Va.)

W.V. Rep. West Virginia Reports (W.Va.)

W.W.
- With warrants
- Wyatt and Webb's Reports (1861-63) (Victoria, Aus.)

W.W. & A'B. Wyatt, Webb & A'Beckett's Reports, Victoria (1864-69)

W.W. & A'B. (E.) Waytt, Webb & A'Beckett's Equity Reports (1864-69) (Victoria, Aus.)

W.W. & A'B.Eq. Wyatt, Webb& A'Beckett's Equity Reports (1864-69) (Vict. Aus.)

W.W. & A'B. (I.E. & M.) Wyatt, Webb & A'Beckett's Reports, Insolvency, Ecclesiastical & Matrimonial (1864-69) (Vict. Aus.)

W.W. & A'B. (M.) Wyatt, Webb & A'Beckett's Reports, Mining (1864-69) (Vict. Aus.)

W.W. & A'B.Min. Wyatt, Webb & A'Beckett's Reports, Mining (1864-69) (Vict. Aus.)

W.W. & D. Willmore, Willaston and Davison's Queen's Bench Reports (1837)

W.W. & H. Willmore, Wollaston and Hodges' Queen's Bench Reports (1838-39)

W.W. & H. (Eng.) Willmore, Wollaston and Hodges' Queen's Bench reports (1838-39)

W.W.D. Western Weekly Digests, 1975

W.W.H. W.W. Harrington's reports (31-39 Delaware)

W.W.Harr. W.W. Harrington's Reports (31-39 Delaware)

W.W.Harr. Del. W.W. Harrington's Reports (31-39 Delaware)

W.W.R. Western Weekly Reports (Canada)

W.W.R. (N.S.) Western Weekly Reports New Series (Canada)

Wy.
- Wyoming
- Wyoming Reports
- Wythe's Chancery Reports (Va. 1788-99)

Wy. & W.
- Wyatt & Webb, Vict.
- Wyatt & Webb's Victorian Equity Reports (Victoria, Aus.)

Wyatt & W. Wyatt & Webb's Reports (1861-63) (Victoria, Aus.)

Wyat. & W. Eq. Wyatt & Webb's Victorian Equity Reports (Victoria, Aus.)

Wyatt & Webb Wyatt & Webb's Reports (Victoria, Aus.)

Wyatt & W. Eq. Wyatt & Webb's Equity Reports (Victoria, Aus.)

Wyatt & W.I.E. & M. Wyatt & Webb's Insolvency, Ecclesiastical & Matrimonial Reports (1861-63) (Victoria, Aus.)

Wyatt & W.I.P. & M. Wyatt & Webb's Insolvency, Probate, & Matrimonial Reports (Victoria, Aus.)

Wyatt & W. Min. Wyatt & Webb's Victorian Mining Cases (Victoria, Aus.)

Wyatt, Prac. Reg. Wyatt's Practical Register in Chancery (1800)

Wyatt Pr. R. Wyatt's Practical Register in Chancery (1800)

Wyatt, W & AB. Wyatt, Webb & A'Beckett's Reports (Victoria, Aus.)

Wyatt, W. & A B. Eq. Wyatt, Webb & A'Beckett's Equity Reports (Victoria, Aus.)

Wyatt, W. & A'B. Ew. Wyatt, Webb & A'Beckett's Equity Reports (Victoria, Aus.)

Wyatt, W. & AB.I.E. & M. Wyatt, Webb & A'Beckett's Insolvency, Ecclesiastical & Matrimonial Reports (1864-69) (Victoria, Aus.)

Wyatt, W. & A'B.I.P. & M. Wyatt, Webb, & A'Beckett's Victorian Insolvencey, Probate, & Matrimonial Reports (Victoria, Aus.)

Wyatt, W. & A'B.Min.
- Wyatt, Webb & A'Beckett's Victorian Mining Cases (Victoria, Aus.)
- Wyatt, Webb & A'Beckett's Mining Cases (1864-69) (Victoria, Aus.)

Wy. Dic. Wyatt's Dickens' Chancery Reports

Wy. Dick. Dickens' Chancery Reports, by Wyatt (Eng.)

Wy. L.J. Wyoming Law Journal

Wyman Wyman Reports, India

Wynne Bov. Wynne, Bovill's Patent Cases

Wynne Eun. Wynne's Eunomus

Wyo.
- Wyoming
- Wyoming Reports

Wyo. B.A. Wyoming Bar Association

Wyo. Const. Wyoming Constitution

Wyo. Law. Wyoming Lawyer

Wyo. L.J. Wyoming Law Journal

Wyom. Wyoming Reports (Wyo.)

Wyo. P.S.C. Wyoming Public Service Commission Reports

Wyo. S.B.A. Wyoming State Bar Association, Proceedings

Wyo. Sess. Laws Session Laws of Wyoming

Wyo. Stat. Wyoming Statutes

Wyo. T. Wyoming Territory

Wy. Pr. R. Wyatt's Practical Register in Chancery (Eng.)

Wythe Wythe's Chancery Reports (Va. 1788-1799)

Wythe Ch. (Va.) Wythe's Chancery Reports (Virginia 1788-1799)

Wythes C.C. Wythe's Virginia Chancery reports (2d ed.) (Va.)

Wythe's R. Wythe's Virginia Chancery Reports (2d ed.) (Va.)

Wythe's Rep. Wythe's Virginia Chancery Reports (Second Edition) (Va.)

Wythe (Va.) Wythe's Chancery Reports (Virginia 1788-99)

W.V.L.Q. West Virginia Law Quarterly (West Virginia Law Review)

Wy.W. & A'Beck. Wyatt, Webb & A'Beckett (Vict.)

XYZ

X.1,9,6,4 Book I., Title 9, Chapter 6, Paragraph 4, of the Decretals of Pope Gregory 9.

X.W.
- Ex warrants
- Without warrants

Y. Yeates Reports (Pa. 1791-1808)

y. year

Y.A. York Antwerp Rules

Y.A.D. Young's Admiralty Decisions (Nova Scotia)

Yale J. Int'l L. Yale Journal of International Law

Yale J.L. & Feminism Yale Journal of Law and Feminism

Yale J.L. & Human. Yale Journal of Law and the Humanities

Yale J.L. & Lib. Yale Journal of Law and Liberation

Yale J. on Reg. Yale Journal on Regulation

Yale J. World Pub. Ord. Yale Journal of World Public Order

Yale L. & Pol'y Rev. Yale Law and Policy Review

Yale L.J. Yale Law Journal

Yale Mines Yale on Legal Titles to Mining Claims and Water Rights

Yale Rev. Law & Soc. Act. Yale Review of Law and Social Action

Yale Rev. Law & Soc. Act'n. Yale Review of Law and Social Action

Yale Rev. of L. and Soc. Action Yale Review of Law and Social Action

Yale Stud. World P.O. Yale Studies in World Public Order

Yale Stud. World Pub. Ord. Yale Studies in World Public Order

Yale St. Wld. Pub. Ord. Yale Studies in World Public Order

Y.& C.
- Younge and Collyer's Chancery Reports, England (1841-43)
- Younge and Collyer's Exchequer Equity Reports, England (1834-42)

Y. & C.C.C. Younge & Collyer's Chancery Cases (1841-43) (62-63 ER)

Y. & C.Ch. Younge and Collyer's Chancery Reports, England (1841-43)

Y. & C.Ch.Cas. Younge & Collyer's Chancery Cases (1841-43) (62-63 ER)

Y. & C.Ex. Younge and Collyer's Exchequer Equity Reports, England (1834-42)

Y. & C. Exch. Younge and Collyer's Exchequer Equity Reports, England (1834-42)

Y. & Coll.
- Younge and Collyer's Chancery Reports, England (1841-43)

- Younge and Collyer's Exchequer Equity Reports, England
  (1834-42)

Y. & J. Younge & Jervis' English
Exchequer Reports (1826-30)

Yate-Lee Yates-Lee on Bankruptcy. 3ed. 1887

Yates Sel. Cas. Yates' Select
Cases (N.Y. 1809)

Yates Sel. Cas. (N.Y.) Yates' Select Cases (New York 1809)

Y.B.
- Yearbook (or Year Book)
- Year Books (ed. Dieser) (1388-
  89) (Eng.)
- Year Books (ed. Maynard),
  King's Bench (1307-1537) (Eng.)

Y.B.A.A.A. Yearbook of the Association of Attenders of Alumni of
the Hague Academy of International Law

Y.B. Air & Space L. Yearbook of
Air and Space Law

Y.B. Ames Year Book, Ames Foundation

Y.B.A.S.L. Yearbook of Air and
Space Law

Y.B.C.A. Yearbook, Commercial
Arbitration

Y.B. Com. Arb. Yearbook Commercial Arbitration

Yb. Commercial Arbitration
Yearbook, Commercial Arbitration, Deventer, Netherlands

Y.B.Ed.I. Year Books of Edward I

Y. B. Eur. Conv. on H.R. Yearbook of the European Convention
on Human Rights

**Y.B. Eur. Conv. On Human
Rights** Year Book of the Euro-
pean Convention on Human
Rights

Y.B. Europ. Conv. H.R. Yearbook
of the European Convention on
Human Rights, The Hague, Netherlands

Y.B. Human Rights Yearbook on
Human Rights

Y.B. Hum. Rts. Yearbook on Human Rights

Y.B.I.C.J. Yearbook on the International Court of Justice

Y.B. Int. L. Comm. Yearbook of
the International Law Community

Y.B. Int'l. L. Comm'n. Yearbook
of the International Law Commission

Y.B. Int'l. Org. Yearbook of International Organizations

Y.B. League Yearbook of the
League of Nations

Yb. of Leg. Stud. The Year Book
of Legal Studies Madras, India

**Yb. of the Eur. Conv. on Human
Rights** Yearbook of the Euro-
pean Convention on Human
Rights. The Hague, Netherlands

Y.B.P.1, Edw.II. Year Books, Part
1, Edward II

Y.B. (Rolls Ser.) Year Books,
Rolls Series (1292-1546)

Y.B. (R.S.)
- Year Books, Rolls Series (1292-
  1546)
- Year Books, Rolls Series ed.
  Horwood (1292-1307)

- Year Books, Rolls Series, ed. Horwood & Pike (1337-46)

Y.B.S.C.   Year Books, Selected Cases

Y.B. Sch. L.   Yearbook of School Law

Y.B.(Sel.Soc.)   Year Books (Seldon Society) (Eng.)

Y.B.(S.S.)   Year Books, Selden Society (1307-19)

Y.B.U.N.   Yearbook of the United Nations

Y.B. World Aff.   Yearbook of World Affairs

Y.B. World Pol.   Yearbook of World Polity

Y.C.P.   Youth Challenge Program

Yea.   Yeates' Reports (Pa. 1791-1808)

Yearb.   Year Book, English King's Bench, etc.

Yearb.P.7, Hen.VI.   Year Books, Part 7, Henry VI

Yeates.   Yeates' Reports (Pa. 1791-1808)

Yeates (Pa.)   Yeates' Reports (Pennsylvania 1791-1808)

Yel.   Yelverton's King's Bench Reports (1603-13) (Eng.)

Yelv.   Yelverton's King's Bench Reports (1603-13) (Eng,)

Yelv. (Eng.)   Yelverton's King's Bench reports (1603-13) (Eng.)

Yer.   Yerger's Tennessee Supreme

Yerg.   Yerger's Reports (9-18 Tennessee)

Yerg. (Tenn.)   Yerger's Reports (9-18 Tennessee)

Y.L.J.   Yale Law Journal

Y.L.R.   York Legal Record (Pa,)

Yo.   Younge's Exchequer Equity Reports (Eng.)

Yool Waste   Yool, Waste, Nuisance and Trespass. 1863

York   York Legal Records (Pa.)

York Ass.   Clayton's Reports (York Assizes)

Yorke Ass.   Clayton's Reports, Yorke Assizes

York Leg. Rec.   York Legal Record (Pa.)

York Leg.Record   York Legal Record (Pa.)

York Legal Record   York Legal Record (Pa.)

York Leg. Rec. (Pa.)   York Legal Record (Pa.)

You.   Younge's Exchequer Equity Reports (1830-32) (Eng.)

You. & Coll. Ch.   Younge and Collyer's Chancery Reports (1841-43) (Eng.)

You. & Coll. Ex.   Younge and Collyer's Exchequer Equity Reports (1834-42) (Eng.)

You. & Jerv.   Younge & Jervis' Exchequer Reports (Eng.)

Young   Young's Reports (21-47 Minnesota)

Young Adm.   Young's Nova Socita Admiralty Cases

Young Adm. Dec.   Young's Nova Scotia Vice-Admiralty Decisions

Young Adm. Dec. (Nov.Sc.) Young's Nova Scotia Vice-Admiralty Decisions

Younge. Younge's English Exchequer Equity Reports (159 ER)

Younge & C.Ch. Younge & Collyer's English Chancery Reports (62, 63 ER)

Younge & Ch. Ch. Cas. Younge & Collyer's Chancery Reports (1841-43) (62, 63 ER)

Younge & C. Ch. Cas. (Eng.) Younge & Collyer's English Chancery Reports (62, 63 ER)

Younge & C. Exch. Younge & Coll-yer's English Exchequer Equity Reports (160 ER)

Younge & C. Exch. (Eng.) Younge & Collyer's English Exchequer Equity Reports (160 ER)

Younge & Coll. Ch. Younge & Collyer's English Chancery Reports (62, 63 ER)

Younge & Coll. Ex. Younge & Collyer's English Exchequer Equity Reports (160 ER)

Younge & J. Younge & Jervis' English Exchequer Reports (148 ER)

Younge & J. (Eng.) Younge & Jervis' English Exchequer Reports (148ER)

Younge & Je. Younge & Jervis' English Exchequer Reports (148 ER)

Younge & Jerv. Younge & Jervis' English Exchequer Reports (148 ER)

Younge Exch. Younge's Exchequer in Equity Reports (1830-32) (159 ER)

Younge Exch. (Eng.) Younge's English Exchequer Equity Reports (159 ER)

Younge French Bar Younge's Historical Sketch of the French Bar

Younge M.L. Cas. Younge Maritime Law Cases (Eng.)

Young M.L.Cas. Young's Maritime Law Cases (Eng.)

Young. Naut. Dict. Young, Nautical Dictionary

Young V.A. Dec. Young's Nova Scotia Vice-Admiralty Decisions

Youth Ct. Youth Court

Yr.Bk. Year Book

Y.T.
- Yukon Territory, Canada
- Yukon Territory: Court with jurisdiction in Yukon Territory

Yugo. Yugoslavia

Yugo.L. Yugoslav Law

Yugoslav L. Yugoslav Law (Droit yougoslav, Belgrad, Yugoslavia)

Yuk. Yukon Territory

Yukon Terr. Yukon Territory

Yuk. Ord. Yukon Ordinances (Canada)

Yuk. Rev. Ord. Yukon Revised Ordinances (Can.)

Y.U.N. Yearbook of the United Nations

Za. Zabriskie's Reports (21-24 New Jersey)

Zab. Land Laws Zabriskie on the Public Land Laws of the United States

Zab. (N.J.) Zabriskie's Reports (21-24 New Jersey)

Zambia L.J. Zambia Law Journal

Zam. L.J. Zambia Law Journal, Africa

Zane. Zane's Reports (4-9 Utah)

Zanzib. Prot. L.R. Zanzibar Protectorate Law Reports (Africa)

Zilla C.D. Zilla Court Decisions (Bengal, Madras, North West Provinces) (India)

Zimb. Zimbabwe

Zimbabwe L. J. The Zimbabwe Law Journal,

Zinn. Ca. Tr. Zinn's Select Cases in the Law of Trusts

Z.L.J. Zambia Law Journal

Z.L.R.
- Zanzibar Protectorate Law Reports (1868-1950)
- Zanzibar Law Reports (1919-50)

Zoning & Plan. L. Rep. Zoning and Planning Law Report

Zouch. Adm. Zouche's Admiralty Jurisdiction

Appendix

United States Courts of Appeals

1st Cir.	U.S. Court of Appeals, First Judicial Circuit
2d Cir.	U.S. Court of Appeals, Second Judicial Circuit
3d Cir.	U.S. Court of Appeals, Third Judicial Circuit
4th Cir.	U.S. Court of Appeals, Fourth Judicial Circuit
5th Cir.	U.S. Court of Appeals, Fifth Judicial Circuit
6th Cir.	U.S. Court of Appeals, Sixth Judicial Circuit
7th Cir.	U.S. Court of Appeals, Seventh Judicial Circuit
8th Cir.	U.S. Court of Appeals, Eighth Judicial Circuit
9th Cir.	U.S. Court of Appeals, Ninth Judicial Circuit
10th Cir.	U.S. Court of Appeals, Tenth Judicial Circuit
11th Cir.	U.S. Court of Appeals, Eleventh Judicial Circuit
D.C. Cir.	U.S. Court of Appeals, District of Columbia Circuit

United States District Courts

Alabama
M.D.Ala.	U.S. District Court for the Middle District of Alabama
N.D.Ala.	U.S. District Court for the Northern District of Alabama
S.D.Ala.	U.S. District Court for the Southern District of Alabama

Alaska
D.Alaska	U.S. District Court for the District of Alaska

Arizona
D.Ariz.	U.S. District Court for the District of Arizona

Arkansas
E.D.Ark.	U.S. District Court for the Eastern District of Arkansas
W.D.Ark.	U.S. District Court for the Western District of Arkansas

California
C.D.Cal.	U.S. District Court for the Central District of California
E.D.Cal.	U.S. District Court for the Eastern District of California
N.D.Cal.	U.S. District Court for the Northern District of California
S.D.Cal.	U. S. District Court for the Southern District of California

Colorado
D.Colo.	U.S. District Court for the District of Colorado

Connecticut
D.Conn.	U.S. District Court for the District of Connecticut

Delaware
D.Del.	U.S. District Court for the District of Delaware

District of Columbia
D.D.C.	U.S. District Court for the District of Columbia

Florida
M.D.Fla.	U.S. District Court for the Middle District of Florida
N.D.Fla.	U.S. District Court for the Northern District of Florida
S.D.Fla.	U.S. District Court for the Southern District of Florida

Georgia

M.D.Ga.	U.S. District Court for the Middle District of Florida
N.D.Ga.	U.S. District Court for the Northern District of Florida
S.D.Ga.	U.S. District Court for the Southern District of Florida

Guam

D.Guam	U.S. District Court for the District of Guam

Hawaii

D.Haw.	U.S. District Court for the Middle District of Hawaii

Idaho

D.Idaho	U.S. District Court for the District of Idaho

Illinois

C.D.Ill.	U.S. District Court for the Central District of Illinois
N.D.Ill.	U.S. District Court for the Northern District of Illinois
S.D.Ill.	U.S. District Court for the Southern District of Illinois

Indiana

N.D.Ind.	U.S. District Court for the Northern District of Indiana
S.D.Ind.	U.S. District Court for the Southern District of Indiana

Iowa

N.D.Iowa	U.S. District Court for the Northern District of Iowa
S.D.Iowa	U.S. District Court for the Southern District of Iowa

Kansas

D.Kan.	U.S. District Court for the District of Kansas

Kentucky

E.D.Ky.	U.S. District Court for the Eastern District of Kentucky
W.D.Ky.	U.S. District Court for the Western District of Kentucky

Louisiana

E.D.La.	U.S. District Court for the Eastern District of Louisiana
M.D.La.	U.S. District Court for the Middle District of Louisiana
W.D.La.	U.S. District Court for the Western District of Louisiana

Maine
D.Me.   U.S. District Court for the District of Maine

Maryland
D.Md.   U.S. District Court for the District of Maryland

Massachusetts
D.Mass.   U.S. District Court for the District of Massachusetts

Michigan
E.D.Mich.   U.S. District Court for the Eastern District of Michigan

W.D.Mich.   U.S. District Court for the Western District of Michigan

Minnesota
D.Minn.   U.S. District Court for the District of Minnesota

Mississippi
N.D.Miss.   U.S. District Court for the Northern District of Mississippi

S.D.Miss.   U.S. District Court for the Southern District of Mississippi

Missouri
E.D.Mo.   U.S. District Court for the Eastern District of Missouri

W.D.Mo.   U.S. District Court for the Western District of Missouri

Montana
D.Mont.   U.S. District Court for the District of Montana

Nebraska
D.Neb.   U.S. District Court for the District of Nebraska

Nevada
D.Nev.   U.S. District Court for the District of Nevada

New Hampshire
D.N.H.   U.S. District Court for the District of New Hampshire

New Jersey
D.N.J.   U.S. District Court for the District of New Jersey

New Mexico
D.N.M.   U.S. District Court for the District of New Mexico

New York
E.D.N.Y.   U.S. District Court for the Eastern District of New York
N.D.N.Y.   U.S. District Court for the Northern District of New York
S.D.N.Y.   U.S. District Court for the Southern District of New York
W.D.N.Y.   U.S. District Court for the Western District of New York

North Carolina
E.D.N.C.   U.S. District Court for the Eastern District of North Carolina
M.D.N.C.   U.S. District Court for the Middle District of North Carolina
W.D.N.C.   U.S. District Court for the Western District of North Carolina

North Dakota
D.N.D.   U.S. District Court for the District of North Dakota

Ohio
N.D.Ohio   U.S. District Court for the Northern District of Ohio
S.D.Ohio   U.S. District Court for the Southern District of Ohio

Oklahoma
E.D.Okla.   U.S. District Court for the Eastern District of Oklahoma
N.D.Okla.   U.S. District Court for the Northern District of Oklahoma
W.D.Okla.   U.S. District Court for the Western District of Oklahoma

Oregon
D.Or.   U.S. District Court for the District of Oregon

Pennsylvania
E.D.Pa.   U.S. District Court for the Eastern District of Pennsylvania
M.D.Pa.   U.S. District Court for the Middle District of Pennsylvania
W.D.Pa.   U.S. District Court for the Western District of Pennsylvania

Puerto Rico
D.P.R.   U.S. District Court for the District of Puerto Rico

Rhode Island
D.R.I.   U.S. District Court for the District of Rhode Island

South Carolina
D.S.C.   U.S. District Court for the District of South Carolina

South Dakota
D.S.D.   U.S. District Court for the District of South Dakota

Tennessee
E.D.Tenn.   U.S. District Court for the Eastern District of Tennessee

M.D.Tenn.   U.S. District Court for the Middle District of Tennessee

W.D.Tenn.   U.S. District Court for the Western District of Tennessee

Texas
E.D.Tex.   U.S. District Court for the Eastern District of Texas

N.D.Tex.   U.S. District Court for the Northern District of Texas

S.D.Tex.   U.S. District Court for the Southern District of Texas

W.D.Tex.   U.S. District Court for the Western District of Texas

Utah
D.Utah   U.S. District Court for the District of Utah

Vermont
D.Vt.   U.S. District Court for the District of Vermont

Virgin Islands
D.V.I.   U.S. District Court for the District of the Virgin Islands

Virginia
E.D.Va.   U.S. District Court for the Eastern District of Virginia

W.D.Va.   U.S. District Court for the Western District of Virginia

Washington
E.D.Wash.   U.S. District Court for the Eastern District of Washington

W.D.Wash.   U.S. District Court for the Western District of Washington

West Virginia
N.D.W.Va.   U.S. District Court for the Northern District of West Virginia

S.D.W.Va.   U.S. District Court for the Southern District of West Virginia

Wisconsin
E.D.Wis.   U.S. District Court for the Eastern District of Wisconsin

W.D.Wis.   U.S. District Court for the Western District of Wisconsin

Wyoming

D.Wyo.   U.S. District Court for the District of Wyoming